JDBC 4.2, Servlet 3.1, and JSP 2.3

(Includes JSF 2.2 and Design Patterns)

Second Edition

Black Book™

Santosh Kumar K.
and
DT Editorial Services

Published by:

dreamtech PRESS

ISBN: 978-93-5119-908-3

Reprint: 2024

Printed at: Srk Graphics

Dedication

Dedicated affectionately to my father (Sri Koona Vijay Kumar),
mother (K Narmada) and all my students

Acknowledgements

I'd like to start by thanking everyone at Dreamtech Press. In particular, I want to thank Ms. Arti Pandey (Publisher – Dreamtech Press) for giving me the opportunity to write this book, and Mr. Mansoor Baig for introducing me to her for initiating this project.

My special thanks for Mr. Rudraksh Batra and his team for their cooperation in organizing the technical content into Black Book format and also for providing the content for Chapters 20 (JSF) and 21 (Design Patterns).

My special appreciation is to appreciate my brother (Sai Kumar), sister (Phani Sree), and friend (Subash Chandra) for encouraging me to take up this project.

My apologies are to my parents, family members and friends whom I neglected for months during the course of developing the content of this book.

Some errors may have accidentally crept in this book despite my best efforts to keep them out. Readers are therefore encouraged to point out the errors so that they are not repeated in the next edition.

About the Author

Santosh Kumar K is an experienced corporate trainer and an independent J2EE consultant. He has conducted numerous corporate/non-corporate result-oriented training sessions in Java and related technologies. His areas of expertise include frameworks (Spring, Struts, JSF, AJAX, Hibernate) and Java Enterprise Components (Servlet, JSP, EJB 2.0 & 3.0). The seminars and workshops of the author are well-known for quality content supplemented by his appealing, influential, and unique style of delivery. As an independent consultant, he has designed and developed various software applications for leading IT conglomerates. The contributions of the author in the IT industry are highly commended and appreciated by the crème of corporate professionals.

The author has founded SANTOSH TECHNOLOGIES, which is one of the prestigious and popular training centers at Hyderabad, India, serving the IT students and professionals. He has been associated with the profession of knowledge sharing for over 16 years starting from the very first year of his bachelor degree. He is currently working as a Technical Architect.

Contents at a Contents

Table of Contents

Chapter 7: Understanding Request Processing and HTTP 191

Introduction

Thanks for buying the *JDBC, Servlet, and JSP Black Book 2nd Edition.* Designed with comprehensive content on the various concepts of Web application development using Servlet and JSP technology, this book provides Web developers with simple and consistent mechanism for extending functionality of a Web server and for accessing existing business systems. Nowadays, Servlets have become a popular choice for building interactive Web applications. They provide a component-based and platform-independent method of building Web-based applications. JSP technology is an extension of the Servlet technology created to support HTML and XML pages.

About this Book

In JDBC, Servlet, and JSP Black Book 2nd Edition, you will find as much Servlet and JSP as can fit between the covers. There are hundreds of topics discussed theoretically as well as practically in different chapters of the book. Each chapter also provides running Web applications to have a better understanding of multiple concepts.

This book is divided into separate, easily accessible topics with each addressing different programming issues in Servlet and JSP, such as:

- Web Applications in Java
- Understanding JDBC
- JDBC Statements and ResultSets
- Advanced JDBC Concepts
- Understanding Servlets
- Sessions in Servlets
- Applet-Servlet Communication
- Interservlet Communication
- New Features in Servlet 3.1
- Java Server Pages
- JSP Basic Tags and Implicit Objects
- JavaBeans and Action Tags in JSP
- JSP Tags Support
- JSP Expression Language
- Internationalization
- Web Design Patterns

That is just a partial list—there is a great deal more. This book gives a special coverage to the latest versions of Servlets, JSP, and JDBC— more than any other book dedicated to the subject.

How to Use This Book

In this book, we are using Java SE 8 (JDK 1.8) to compile all .java files created in the different applications. So, install JDK 1.8 on your system to build applications developed in this book. All applications discussed in this book are Web-based applications and the Web server used throughout the book is Apache Tomcat.

Conventions

There are a few conventions in this book that you should take notice of. For example, all the codes explained in this book are in the form of code listings. The code with listing number and caption will appear like this:

Listing 13.2: FirstServlet.java

```
import java.io.*;
import javax.servlet.*;
import javax.servlet.http.*;
import java.util.Date;
public class FirstServlet extends HttpServlet {
        public void doGet(HttpServletRequest request, HttpServletResponse response)
                throws ServletException, IOException {
                        response.setContentType("text/html");
                        PrintWriter out = response.getWriter();
                        out.write("<html>");
                        out.write("<head>");
                        out.write("<title>First JSP Page</title>");
                        out.write("</head>");
                        out.write("<body>");
                        out.write(new Date().toString());
                        out.write("<hr/>");
                        out.write("<br/>Hello World!<br/>");
                        out.write("</body>");
                        out.write("</html>");
                        out.close();
                }
}
```

The JDBC, Servlet, and JSP Black Book also provides notes, which are designed to give you some additional information:

NOTE

This object does not provide any protocol-specific data like HTTP data. However, it defines generic methods that allow us to get the request data sent by using any protocol.

Every figure contains a descriptive caption to maintain clarity:

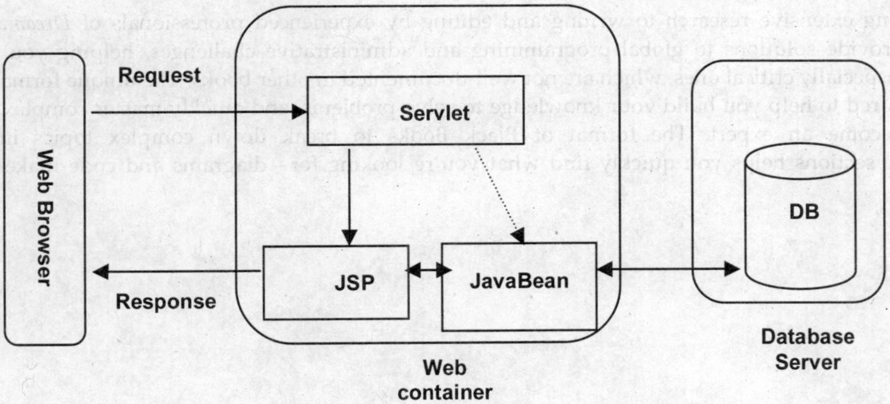

Figure 13.2: JSP Model II Architecture

The tables are placed just below their reference in the chapters like this:

Table 2.1: Attributes of SELECT Annotation		
Name	**Type**	**Description**
Sql	`String`	Specifies a simple SQL SELECT query
`Value`	`String`	Represents the value specified for the sql attribute
`Table name`	`String`	Specifies the name of the database table
`Readonly, connected, scrollable`	`Boolean`	Indicates whether the `DataSet` is ReadOnly or Updatable, whether or not it is connected to a back-end database, and if it is scrollable when the query is used in a connection
`allColumnsMapped`	`Boolean`	Indicates whether or not the column names used in the annotations are mapped to the corresponding fields in the DataSet

Other Resources

Here are some other useful HTML links where you can find text related to JDBC, Servlet, and JSP with some helpful tutorials:

- http://java.sun.com/products/servlet/
- http://www.roseindia.net/jsp/jsp.htm
- http://java.sun.com/javase/technologies/database/index.jsp

There is also much help available on JDBC, Servlet, and JSP technologies, but we hope you will not have to turn to any of it.

The Black Book Philosophy

From conducting extensive research to writing and editing by experienced professionals of *Dreamtech Press*, Black Books provide solutions to global programming and administrative challenges, helping you complete specific tasks, especially critical ones, which are not well-documented in other books. The unique format of Black Books is structured to help you build your knowledge to solve problems, and quickly master complex technical concepts to become an expert. The format of Black Books to break down complex topics into easily understandable sections helps you quickly find what you're looking for—diagrams and code make it all the more simpler!

1

Getting Started with Web Applications in Java

You may have worked on different types of applications while performing your day to day activities on your computer. These applications can be grouped into different categories according to the technologies and platforms they use. However, at a broader level, the applications can be categorized into two categories, Windows applications and Web applications. Windows applications are standalone applications that function on separate computers individually, and Web applications are applications that run on a Web server and are accessed by multiple clients. With the advent of new Internet technologies, the number of users interacting with different Web applications has increased. As a result, the number of Web applications being developed for various purposes, for example, online shopping or banking, is also increasing. These Web applications can be developed by using different technologies, such as ASP.NET or Java Servlet.

In this book, you learn about different Java technologies used to develop Web applications. Any reference to Web applications in this book, therefore, is to be understood as a reference to Web applications developed by using Java technologies.

Before describing various Java technologies used to develop the different components of a Web application, you need to know about various aspects of a Web application in detail. This chapter acquaints you with Web applications, their benefits, and the different Java technologies used to develop them. You also learn about the different Web architecture models, such as Model-1 and Model-2. In addition, the chapter describes the MVC architecture, and its various components, Model, View, and Controller.

Let's begin by providing a detailed introduction to Web applications.

Introduction to Web Applications

A Web application is defined as an application that can be accessed through the Internet by using a Web protocol, such as HyperText Transfer Protocol (HTTP), by a client application, such as a Web browser. You must have interacted with Web applications that process input data and provide the required information. For example, the official Web sites of different banks provide information about clients and their accounts, in addition to allowing different transactions online.

After knowing what a Web application is, let's discuss the various types of architectures used to develop Web applications. At present a modified Web architecture, Web 2.0, is used, which is similar to the traditional 3-tier architecture. We therefore begin with the 2-tier architecture to understand the history of Web applications.

2-tier applications divide a system into two tiers (i.e., into two major components), generally known as a client and a server, respectively. This arrangement is also known as client-server architecture, as shown in Figure 1.1:

2-Tier Architecture

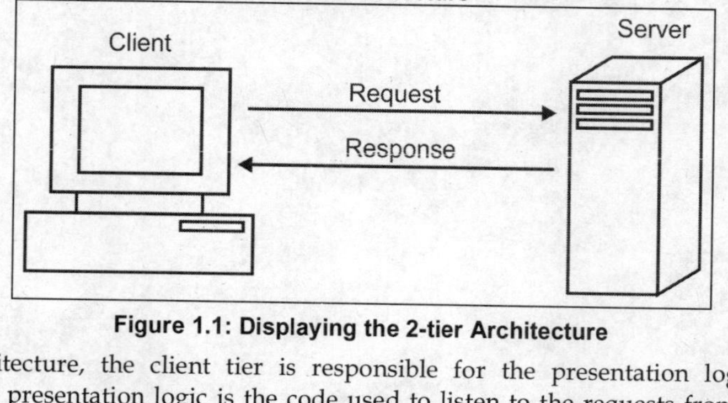

Figure 1.1: Displaying the 2-tier Architecture

In client-server architecture, the client tier is responsible for the presentation logic, business logic, and persistence logic. The presentation logic is the code used to listen to the requests from an end user, render an appropriate response, and present it. The business logic is the code that implements the business rules of a system, and the persistence logic is the code that persists the application data. The data that outlives the process in which it is created is known as persistent data. In general, most applications persist their data by storing the data into a database. The server tier is generally responsible for maintaining business data. In some cases, the server tier also performs simple business logic operations, such as calculations. In such cases, the client is commonly a custom application developed by using Visual Basic (VB), Java, or other programming languages to communicate with a database server, such as Oracle or SQL Server.

Let's now understand 2-tier architecture better through an example. Suppose you want to create software that can be used by the employees of a bank to find out the total transactions of a day as well as other details. In this case, the data (i.e., the account and transaction details) is maintained in a database server (i.e., the server in the architecture shown in Figure 1.1), and the front-end application, which resides on the client machine (the computer the employee is physically interacting with). The following are the two tiers in this system:

- **Front-end application (client)**—Uses the application data and presents it in a format that a user can understand
- **Database (server)**—Maintains the data and makes it available based on Structured Query Language (SQL) queries submitted by the front-end application

The bank employee manipulates the front-end application by clicking buttons, menu options, etc. to retrieve transaction details. The front-end application (client) generates a query for all the transactions in the database, uses the data to calculate the total transaction amount, and displays the amount for the user (employee). This application, though quite simple to understand, presents the following problems:

- Increasing complexity of the client application as the presentation logic is combined with the business logic.
- Difficulty in modifying the presentation logic as it is combined with the business logic.
- Providing services for different types of clients, i.e., different type of presentation layers increase the time and cost of developing the application as the business logic for each type of client needs to be rewritten. However, you can solve this problem by using good design patterns, which allow you to logically separate the business logic and presentation logic.
- Installing the business logic to execute the client environment causes security problems, as it becomes difficult to provide security for various types of clients.

Executing the business logic along with the presentation logic in the client environment causes the following problems:

- Installs the resources that are required to execute the business logic into the client environment, making the client heavy weight.
- Increases the cost of the application.
- Limits the usage of the application as the resources required to run the business logic may not be available in all the client environments.
- Makes it difficult to maintain data integrity.
- Increases the load on the database server with the increase in the number of clients. Let's take an example of bank employees, if the number of employees using this application is a few hundred, then the application works fine; however, if the number of employees is in thousands, then you may have a problem because every time an employee uses the client application, the client application has to query the database, which requires transferring huge amounts of data between the database server and the client. These problems can be solved by using 3-tier architecture.

However, most of these problems will arise if the application has the following requirements:

- Variable number of clients, such as in business to customer applications, where the client application is used by customers
- Different types of clients (i.e., different presentation formats)
- Accessibility to shared data
- Sensitive business logic

If an application lacks the preceding requirements, the application can be designed by using 2-tier architecture as this architecture is less complex compared to other types of architectures, such as 3-tier or n-tier architecture. However, looking into the requirements of the modern enterprise application, you must understand that these are the most common requirements. For this reason, most enterprise applications are designed by using 3-tier and n-tier architecture.

3-tier architecture consists of three tiers, namely, client, middleware server, and back-end server, or simply server. It is an extension of 2-tier architecture with a new tier named middleware server added between the client and server, as shown in Figure 1.2:

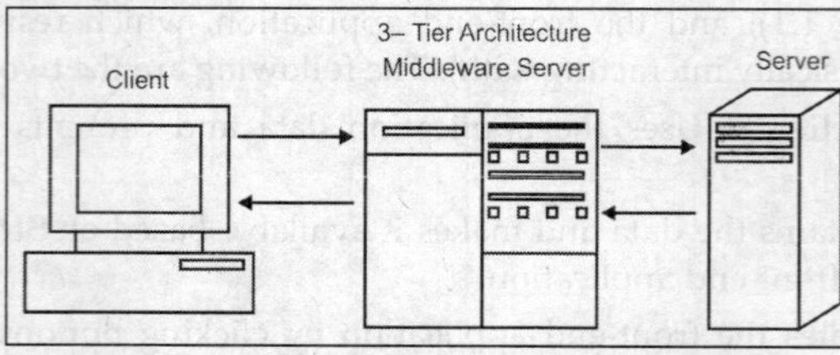

Figure 1.2: Displaying the 3-tier Architecture

In Figure 1.2, the client tier is responsible for the presentation logic and for accessing the middleware server. The middleware server is responsible for implementing business logic. The back-end server maintains business data.

As shown in Figure 1.2, the client and middleware server applications are physically separate, i.e., they run in different processes, possibly on different machines. Communication between these two tiers is maintained through network calls. In this case, the client should be able to make and resolve the network calls according to the middleware server. Therefore, the client should understand the middleware server specific protocol. The following are the advantages of 3-tier architecture over 2-tier architecture:

- Reuse of business logic with different types of clients
- Better management of shared business data
- Fewer resources required in the client environment
- Better performance and availability of the application by managing the access of back-end resources in the middleware server

As already stated, 3-tier architecture solves various problems identified with 2-tier architecture applications. However, 3-tier architecture requires the installation of a client application in the client tier, which can interact with the specific middleware server to service a user request and render the response. This limits the use of 3-tier architecture applications and presents the following problems:

- Inability of the client application to be installed in the specified client environment. For example, if you use VB to develop a front-end client application, then you cannot host it on a non-Windows platform.
- Inability of the client network to support the protocol used to communicate between the client server and middleware server

The preceding problems are solved by using generic client software that is able to communicate with different middleware servers and present their respective services, instead of individual client applications. To meet this requirement the following elements are designed to use with Web architecture:

- General purpose client applications, such as Web browsers, also known as Web clients
- Common protocols such as HyperText Transfer Protocol (HTTP), known as web protocols, for Web communication
- Servers known as Web servers, to serve Web clients

NOTE

The architecture implementing the preceding elements is referred to as a Web architecture, as this architecture is also implemented in three tiers as shown in Figure 1.2. In this case, we use a general purpose client specific to access our middleware application, referred to as the traditional 3-tier architecture.

The traditional 3-tier application had its own client programs. A client program serves as a user interface to an end user and is required to be installed on every client computer. However, with the advent of Web applications, 3-tier applications have changed a lot. A Web application provides a series of Web pages to a client, and these Web pages can be accessed by all types of clients using any browser of their choice. Usually, a Web page is delivered to the client as a static document, but a sequence of Web pages, one after another, (in 3-tier applications) provides an interactive environment to the client. In addition, you do not need to install separate client programs on all client computers as the Web browser being used interprets and displays all the Web pages and works as a common client for a Web application. This reduces the time to develop Web applications as you do not need to create separate client programs in different platforms.

Today, Web applications are in demand in different organizations and enterprises for both personal and commercial use and are preferred over Windows applications. There are various reasons for this. Therefore, in the next section, we discuss the advantages or benefits of Web applications over Windows applications (also known as desktop applications).

Benefits of Web Applications

The numerous issues concerning Windows applications have encouraged the use of Web applications. We look at these issues in this section. A Web application has the following advantages over a Windows application:

- Web applications do not require the installation of any software on client computers. However, in case of Windows 3-tier applications, you have to install the required software, such as Word, Excel, or PowerPoint, to use these applications.
- If new versions of the applications are available in the case of Windows applications, you have to update the installed applications accordingly. In case of Web applications, the latest versions of these applications are available from the Internet. Instead of providing upgrades to individual users, as in case of Windows applications, the upgrades are applied to the server and each Web application user accesses the updated versions of the Web applications.
- Unlike traditional 3-tier applications, Web applications are easily accessible anytime and anywhere through the Web.
- Web applications are platform-independent. On the other hand, Windows applications, such as Microsoft Office, are installed on the Windows operating system (OS) only. However, a Web browser, which is available with every OS, serves as a platform for Web applications.

Now, let's briefly discuss the technologies used to create Web applications in Java. A detailed information on these technologies has been provided in the other chapters of this book.

Technologies used in Web Applications

Java Servlet and JavaServer Pages (JSPs) are also referred to as Java Web technologies. They can be combined to design efficient content-publishing systems that support separation of the presentation and the business logic of Java Web applications.

While building server-side Web applications, the presentation and business logic are kept separate. This allows less-experienced Web designers to generate Web pages with dynamic content easily and quickly. This separation is beneficial where content changes are frequent, and helps to present new information in a Web site faster.

Earlier, Web applications faced maintenance problems. However, using the Model/View/Controller (MVC) paradigm to build user interfaces has solved this problem. In MVC, the back-end system is the Model (in which templates are used to create the look), feel of the response is the View, and the code that combines them all together is the Controller. Sun Microsystems introduced two solid technologies to implement MVC architecture, Java Servlets and JSP. JSP technology provides a way to create a dynamic response or View. Servlets contain the logic to manage requests and act as the Controller, while the existing business rules act as the Model. Since the introduction of Java Servlet and JSP technology, additional Java technologies and frameworks to build interactive Web applications have been developed. In this section, we briefly introduce some Java-based Web technologies, that is Servlets and JSP. Let us first discuss Java Servlet.

Describing Java Servlet

Let's understand the evolution of Java Servlet. The advent of Web architecture introduced Web servers that manage simple, static Hypertext Markup Language (HTML) pages. A client accesses these pages and sends a request to a Web server. The Web server sends back the requested Web page stored on the server by using HTTP. These Web pages are static, which means they exist in a constant state, for example, a text file that does not change.

However, with changing technologies and requirements, you now need to design the Web server such that it processes the data sent by the client and displays dynamic content to the client. To add dynamic behavior, you need to develop applications that can integrated with and run on a Web server run, process client requests, and generate the response content dynamically.

These requirements can be taken care of initially by Web server providers, who offer APIs that provide proprietary solutions, thereby allowing us to build programs that can run with Web servers. However, this approach to build server-side applications results in the following problems:

- Makes the application vendor-dependent
- Migrating the application from one server to another is difficult
- Deciding on the server on which the application is to be deployed while developing the application. Consequently, you have to learn about the vendor-specific API to develop the application.

Common Gateway Interface (CGI) came up as a solution for the preceding problems. CGI is an open standard abstraction between the HTTP adapter (Web server) and an external application written by using any programming language such as C or C++. This external application is known as a CGI application and is responsible for processing client requests and generating dynamic content.

Some of the benefits of CGI are as follows:

- **Simplicity**—Allows you to understand and implement it easily.
- **Open standards**—Allows you to deploy CGI applications on different Web servers.
- **Architecture Independent**—Implies that CGI is not dependent on any particular Web server architecture.
- **Language Independent**—Implies that CGI applications can be written in any language.
- **Process Isolation**—Implies that CGI applications can run on a separate process, that is, outside the Web server process. Consequently, if there is any bug in the CGI application, it will not crash the Web server process.

In the CGI approach, the server creates and destroys the process for every request, which increases the workload on the server and the time taken to process the requests. This, in turn, reduces the availability of the Web applications. This approach works well when there are only a few clients, but with the increase in the number of clients, the Web server using CGI applications is not able to serve the clients. Consequently, CGI too had a few problems, including:

- Low performance
- Poor efficiency
- Inability to maintain a client's state

Java Servlet came as an alternate to CGI. It provides high level component-based, platform-independent, and server-independent standards to develop Web applications in Java. The Java Servlet technology provides a simple, vendor-independent mechanism to extend the functionality of Web servers.

Now, let's discuss the advantages of Java Servlets.

Advantages of Java Servlets

The advantages of Java Servlets over other server-side extension abstractions, such as CGI, are as follows:

- Processes request quicker compared to CGI.
- Uses a standard vendor-independent API, which is supported by many Web servers.
- Provides a high level API to create Web applications in Java.
- Provides support for declarative security management that allows you to easily build and modify the security logic for server-side extensions.
- Extends the functionality of a Web server. Servlets function as applets that run on the server. They are portable platforms and Web server-independent (that is, they deliver dynamic content). A browser-based application that calls a Servlet need not support a Java programming language as the output of a Servlet may be of the HTML, Extensible Markup Language (XML), or any other content type.

- Functions on any platform that has a JVM and a Web server that supports Java Servlets, as a Java Servlet is written in the Java programming language. It can communicate directly with existing enterprise resources by using generic APIs, such as JDBC. Consequently, application development becomes simple and easy.
- Allows developers to extend the functionalities of a Web application similar to any Java application. For example, a Controller Servlet is extended to become a secure Controller. The functionalities of the original Controller are also retained along with the addition of new security features.
- Performs better than a CGI script. For example, after a Servlet is loaded into memory (a Servlet can be loaded into memory once and then called as many times as needed without requiring additional hardware), it can run on a single lightweight thread; On the other hand, CGI scripts must be loaded in a different process for every request. Another benefit of Servlets is that they can maintain and/or pool connections to databases or other necessary Java objects; this saves time in processing requests.
- Eliminates the complexity of retrieving parameters from an HTTP request; Web components have direct access to the parameters because the parameters are presented as objects. Initially, in CGI-based applications, the parameters are submitted by a form. These parameters are then converted to environment properties, which must then read into a program.
- Provides uniform APIs to maintain the data of a session throughout a Web application as well as interacts with user requests. HTTP is a stateless protocol, which means it does not maintain the state of user requests. To overcome the limitations of Web applications due to the stateless nature of HTTP, session data is used to maintain the state of user requests.
- Provides accessibility with a wide range of service APIs available under the Java platform.

However, Java Servlet has also some limitations. Now, let's discuss the limitations of Java Servlets.

Limitations of Java Servlet

- Strong knowledge of Java is required to Design a Web application in Servlet.
- Servlet is a time taking process because any modification in code will need redeployment in servlet.
- It is required to configure Web application configuration file when any application is developed in Servlet.
- There are no provisions for Custom Tags Development in Servlet.
- There is no facility for global or implicit exception handling in Servlet.
- The concept of automatic page compilation is not available in Servlet.

After discussing about Servlets, let's now discuss the other server-side technology, JSP.

Describing JSP

Java Servlets are used to develop server-side extensions to present dynamic content to clients. Using Java Servlet technology to create dynamic views also uses numerous `out.println` statements. These statements make Java Servlet code very complex and difficult to understand. Most code lines in a Servlet contain static content presentation statements (in the form of `out.println` statements), containing very little Java logic. This leads to the following problems:

- Integrated Development Environments (IDEs) cannot be used to design HTML views, thereby increasing the cost and time to develop an application.
- HTML designers cannot provide the presentation view; instead, you have to depend on Java programmers to prepare the views. In other words, the presentation views have to be built by the programmers.

To solve the preceding problems, you need to include additional instructions to process dynamic content in HTML pages. The page containing additional instructions has to be parsed and resolved into a standard server-side extension (or Servlet) that is understood by the Web container. These additional instructions can be provide in the form of tags in a JSP page.

Tag-based additional instructions to process dynamic content provide the following advantages:

- Easily used by the Web designers
- Uses an easily understood format, which IDEs use to design HTML views

The need for tag-based instructions has necessitated the introduction of JSP, a technology that clearly differentiates the application logic and content of application. As a result, content providers are not required to have knowledge of Java technology to update or maintain the content. Instead, they can design interfaces by using JavaBeans components and custom tags provided by Web application developers. Similarly, these developers do not need to be experts in user interface design to build Web applications. The use of JSP pages and Servlet differ, depending on the composition of the development team, time constraints, and application architecture. In addition to the feature of separating the presentation content from the application content, the JSP technology provides all the benefits offered by Java Servlets.

Now, let's find out the process by which a JSP page is processed to handle a request.

Request Processing of a JSP Page

Figure 1.3 shows how a Web container processes a JSP page to handle an incoming user request:

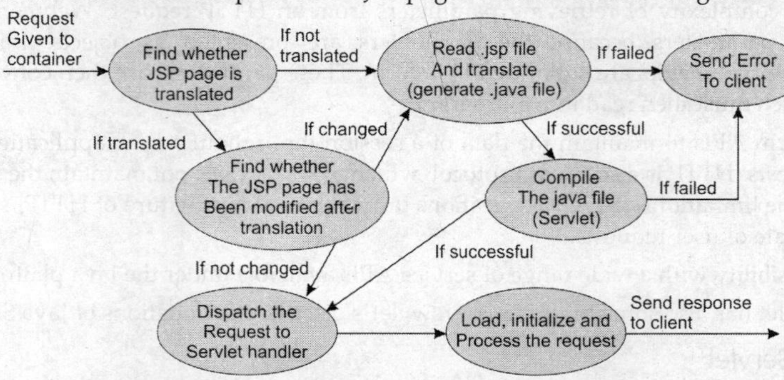

Figure 1.3: Displaying the Request Processing Procedure by a JSP Page

Figure 1.3 shows how the request sent by the client is processed and finally the response is delivered to the client.

Now, let's discuss the advantages of JSP

Advantages of JSP

- Writing code in JSP does not need the knowledge of Java.
- JSP is easy to learn and deploy.
- JSP has the provisions for Custom Tags Development
- JSP provides the facility for global or implicit exception handling
- The concept of automatic page compilation is available in JSP environment.

However. JSP has also some limitations. Now, let's discuss the limitations of JSP.

Limitations of JSP

- JSP page requires huge disk space to hold the JSP pages.
- JSP pages are required to translate to servlet for compilation and thus errors in JSP page are difficult to trace.
- JSP pages are required to be compiled on the server and thus JSP pages need more time.

Describing ODBC and JDBC

Open Database Connectivity (ODBC) is a standard database access method developed by Microsoft in the early 1990s. It is an open standard API which is based on X/OPEN Call Level Interface (CLI) for accessing database. Before the advent of JDBC, if an application is needed to interact with a database, the interaction was carried out by using Native Libraries provided by database vendors and the ODBC API. However, there are many disadvantages of using these approaches to interact with a database.

The following are the disadvantages of Native Libraries provided by database vendors:

- Applications using Native Libraries are vendor-dependent.
- Requires Java Naming and Directive Interface (JNDI) to interact with Native Libraries, which may cause serious problems for platform independency in Web applications.
- Problems in the Native Library may destroy the Java Virtual Machine (JVM); that is, bugs in Native Libraries used can crash the JVM.

The following are the disadvantages of using the ODBC API:

- Solves the problems raised by Native Libraries as it provides a common API to interact with any database that has an ODBC service provider's implementation written in the Native API. However, the ODBC API requires a Data Source Name (DSN) to be configured on each computer that interacts with the database.
- Passes data and SQL call statements through the ODBC layer, which may slow down data transfer speed. Therefore, the implementation of the ODBC API is slower than the Native Libraries.

To solve the preceding problems, a generic Java abstraction is required that allows a Java application to communicate with different databases. To meet this requirement, Sun Microsystems has come up with a common specification API, called JDBC.

JDBC™ is a specification from Sun Microsystems and provides a standard abstraction in the form of APIs or protocols for Java applications to communicate with different relational databases.

JDBC has many advantage over ODBC, such as:

- JDBC is easier and simpler to learn than ODBC.
- Like ODBC, JDBC does not require software on client system.
- JDBC is both platform independent and database independent. This means that if a software is developed on Linux platform, it can be used on Windows platform with a very minor changes.
- JDBC hides the complexity of the many data access tasks.

Till now the chapter has focused on Web application technologies. Let's now discuss the architecture of the Web applications.

Introduction to Web Architecture Models

Different programmers may design an application, each providing the same functionality, in different ways. Designing an application depends on how the programmers recognize the problem and apply their respective approach to solve it. This has made it difficult for other programmers to understand the flow of a program.

Development models solve the problem of flow control and help other programmers understand the flow of a program. They provide a standard way of flow control in an application and describe the technologies used in different parts of the application. A development model facilitates the design process by separating the code according to the functions performed by different parts of the application.

Two types of development models are used in Java for Web applications. These models are classified based on the different approaches used to develop Web applications. These models are:

- Model-1 architecture
- Model-2 architecture

Let's learn about these models in detail.

Describing the Model-1 Architecture

The Model-1 architecture (Figure 1.4) was the first development model used to develop Web applications. Perhaps this was the reason for it being so named. This model uses JSP to design applications, which is responsible for all the activities and functionalities provided by the application. Applications using the Model-1 architecture contain a number of JSP pages, with each page providing different functionality and view to different users.

Figure 1.4 shows the Model-1 architecture:

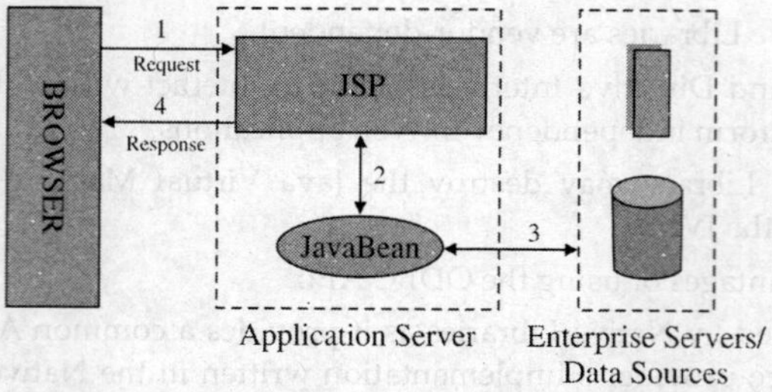

Figure 1.4: Displaying the Model-1 Architecture

In the Model-1 architecture (Figure 1.4), Web applications are developed by mixing the business and presentation logic. In this model, JSP pages receive HTTP requests, which are then transferred to the data layer by JavaBeans. After the requests are serviced, JSPs send HTTP responses back to the client. A JSP page not only contains display elements, but also retrieves HTTP parameters, calls the business logic, and handles the HTTP session.

The Model-1 architecture is page-centric and only suitable for small Web applications. Web applications implementing this type of architecture have a series of JSP pages, where a user navigates from one page to another. The Model 1 architecture is not suitable for large Web applications because of some limitations, as mentioned in the following section.

Limitations of the Model-1 Architecture

Despite its simple structure and easy to learn features, the Model-1 architecture was not successful for designing large projects because of the following limitations:

- Applications are inflexible and difficult to maintain. A single change in one page may cause changes in other pages, leading to unpredictable results.
- Involves the developer at both the page development and the business logic implementation stages. There is no provision for the division of labor between the page designer and the business logic developer.
- Increases the complexity of a program with the increase in the size of the JSP page; therefore, it is difficult to trace the flow of control and debug the program.
- Requires the responsibility of each page to handle the Web application, verify the input, and ensure security.
- Increases the maintenance effort required per page as a series of JSP pages are included in this type of architecture

Let's now understand the second type of architecture, that is, Model-2.

Describing the Model-2 Architecture

The drawbacks in the Model-1 architecture led to the introduction of a new model, called Model-2.

The Model-2 architecture was targeted at overcoming the drawbacks of Model-1 and helping developers to design more powerful Web applications. As it came after the advent of Model-1, it was named Model-2 to recognize it as a part of the Model-1 series. Figure 1.5 shows the Model-2 architecture:

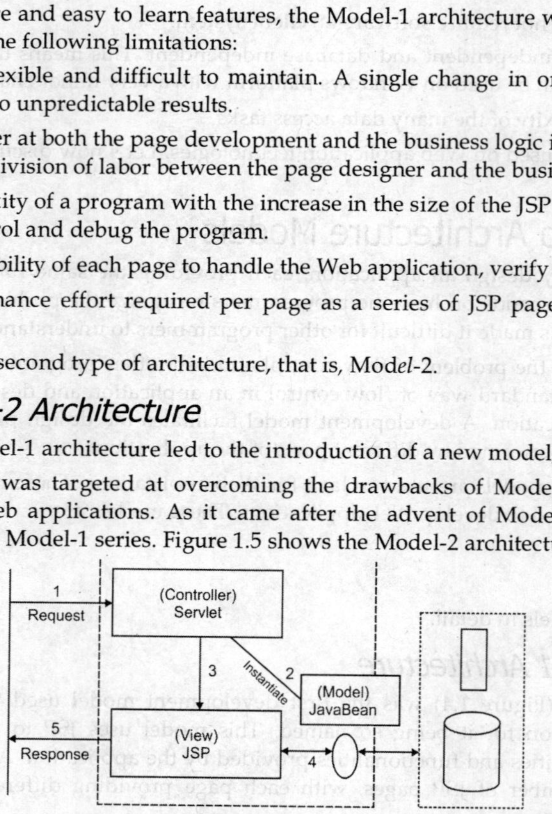

Figure 1.5: Displaying the Model-2 Architecture

Originally, JSPs were introduced as an alternative to Servlets, as JSP is more powerful than the Servlet. Developers soon realized that JSPs and Servlets can be used together to develop a Web application. Servlets handle the control flow while JSPs handle HTML page creation. In due course, the approach of using JSPs and Servlets together evolved as the Model-2 architecture. In this type of design model, the presentation logic is separated from the business logic.

Model-2 architecture is based on the MVC design model. As you can see from Figure 1.5, the Model 2 architecture (or MVC) contains the following components:

- **Model**—Represents enterprise data and business rules that specify how data is accessed and updated. Model is generally implemented by using JavaBeans.
- **View**—Renders the contents of a model. The View component accesses enterprise data through the Model component and specifies how that data should be presented. The View component is designed by using JSP.
- **Controller**—Receives HTTP requests. The Controller component receives requests from a client, determines the business logic to be performed, and delegates the responsibility for producing the next phase of the user interface to an appropriate View component. The Controller has complete control over each View, implying that any change in the Model component is immediately reflected in all the Views of an application. The Controller component is implemented by Servlets.

Advantages of the Model-2 Architecture

So far, Model-2 is the most successful development model used to develop Web applications. It not only overcomes the limitations of the Model-1 architecture, but also provides new features that have their own advantages, such as:

- Allows use of reusable software components to design the business logic. Therefore, these components can be used in the business logic of other applications.
- Offers great flexibility to the presentation logic, which can be modified without affecting the business logic.
- Allows each software component to perform a different task, making it easy to design an application by simply embedding these components in the application.

We learned earlier that the Model-2 architecture resembles the classical MVC architecture. Let's now describe the MVC architecture in the next section.

Introduction to the MVC Architecture

Today, a Web application may need to interact with different types of clients having different types of user interfaces. A Web application may need to represent an HTML view to a client, a Wireless Markup Language (WML) view to a wireless client, a Java Foundation Classes (JFC)/Swing view to the administrator, and an XML view to some other type of client.

When a Web application needs to support only one type of client with one type of interface, it is a good idea to combine client-specific data and business logic with the interface-specific logic. However, if this type of approach is used for Web applications that require interaction with multiple types of clients, it would require different applications to support each type of client. This leads to the repetition of non-interface specific code in the interface-specific code, which further leads to increased effort in designing, debugging, and maintaining Web applications.

The solution to this problem is to use the MVC architecture while designing Web applications. The idea behind the MVC architecture is to separate the core business model functionality of the Web application from the presentation and control logic of the interface-specific application. With this arrangement, it is possible to have multiple views of the same data model of the Web application. Under MVC architecture, data (Model) and user interface (View) are separated from each other so that any change in the user interfaces does not affect the data in the database, and vice versa. The three components of MVC-- Model, View, and Controller--must communicate with each other if the Web application is to ensure a coherent interaction with the user. The communication between the View and Controller components is straightforward because these two components are specifically designed to work together. However, the Model component communicates in a more subtle manner.

Figure 1.6 shows the interaction among the various MVC components:

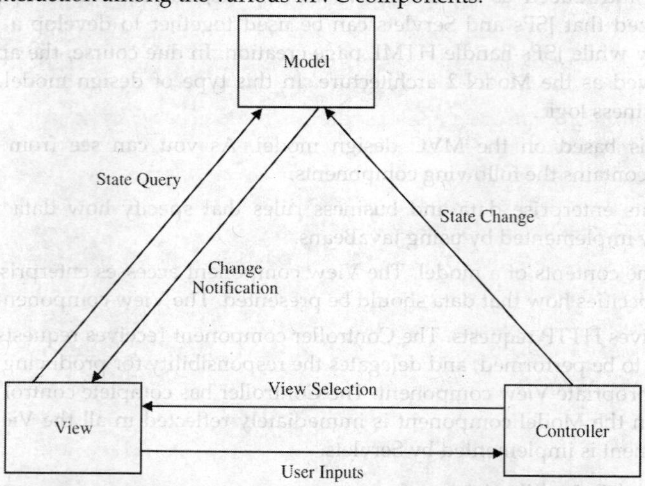

Figure 1.6: Displaying the Interaction among the MVC Architecture Components

Figure 1.6 shows that View uses the query methods of the Model to retrieve content. In addition, whenever a user sends a request, it passes through the Controller. Then, the controller intercepts the request from the View and passes it to the Model for appropriate action. MVC architecture allows separation of the business logic, data, and the presentation logic. In addition, Controller, which is a Servlet, stores all the business logic. A View, normally a JSP page, contains all the code for presentation. A Model is implemented by using a pure Java or bean class. The different components in the application, such as Controller, Model, and View, are reusable and make applications highly scalable.

Let's learn more about each of the components of the MVC architecture next.

Describing the Model Component

The Model component displays the data on which an application is based. In a Web application, JavaBeans hold the data needed by a Web application to process user queries. Events sent to Web Controller serves the basis for all modifications to the data. The Model component represents the data and the business logic of the application and has no concern with the presentation logic of the application. The MVC component does not provide the specification for data access logic. It performs its interfacing with other components by using a set of public methods.

An application may have many states that need to be stored somewhere. These states are encapsulated by the Model component of the application. All the functionalities and features of the application are provided by the Model component. The application behaves according to the business logic of the application, implemented by the Model component. Any change in the state of the Model component state is notified immediately and this change is reflected in all Views.

Describing the View Component

The View component presents the data represented by the Model component in a way that is targeted at a specific type of client. Most Web applications support a number of different views. The same Model can have a Swing view or a Web view. The View for a Web application consists of JSP files, which have the sole responsibility to display Model data.

A View provides the Graphical User Interface (GUI) for Model. A user interacts with the application through View, which represents the information based on Model, and allows the user to alter data. A Model can have multiple Views. The information provided by a Model has different meanings for different users and is interpreted by them in different ways. A View is responsible for representing the information to users in a form that is understandable to them.

Model manages the database, the content of which can be changed and updated frequently. Any change in the database must be reflected to the user as soon as possible. Therefore, a View communicates with a Model to get information if any change takes place in the database. Users who want to modify the content of a Model do not communicate with it directly. Instead, they communicate with the Model through a View, which communicates with the Controller regarding the user input. The Controller then makes the required changes in the Model and also notifies the other associated Views.

Let's now describe the Controller component.

Describing the Controller Component

The Controller component controls all the Views associated with a Model. When a user interacts with the View component and tries to update the Model, the Controller component invokes various methods to update the Model. The Controller of an application also controls the data flow and transfers the requests between Model and View.

The behavior of a Web application is determined by the behavior of its various MVC components. The interaction among the various components is managed by the Controller, which, by controlling the flow among these components, determines the way the application performs the intended tasks.

Let's understand how the Controller performs its role when a user needs to change the data stored in a Model. If the user wishes to change this data, the user sends a request to the Controller, which consults the Model to update all the Views. The following steps are followed to change the data:

1. The user sends a request through an interface provided by the View, which passes the request to the Controller.
2. The Controller receives the input request.
3. The Controller processes the request according to the Controller logic, and if access to the Model is not required, the process moves to step 5.
4. The Model is accessed and modified, if required. It then needs to notify all the associated Views regarding the modification.
5. The View presents a user interface according to the modified or original Model, as the case may be.
6. The View remains idle after the current interaction and waits for the next interaction to begin.

This process is repeated again for every new request.

Summary

In this chapter, you have learned how to make Web applications flexible and easy to maintain by using Java-based Web technologies such as Servlet and JSP, which are used to generate dynamic content that is both portable and scalable. You have also learned about Web architecture and Web models.

In addition, the chapter has explained the importance of using modular components, such as Servlet, JSP pages, and JavaBeans to develop Web applications. The use of JSP pages and Servlet differ, depending on the composition of the development team, time constraints, and the architecture of the application.

The chapter has also described MVC architecture in detail. The process of communication among View, Model, and Controller in a Web application is also explained in the chapter.

In the next chapter, you learn about the JDBC technology and the architecture of JDBC drivers.

Exercise

Q. 1.1 What is a Web application?

Q. 1.2 What does CGI stand for?

Q. 1.3 What is CGI?

Q. 1.4 State one benefit of CGI.

Q. 1.5 What led to the introduction of Java Servlets?

Q. 1.6 Why was JSP introduced?

Q. 1.7 What is MVC?

Q. 1.8 What are Model-1 and Model-2 architectures?

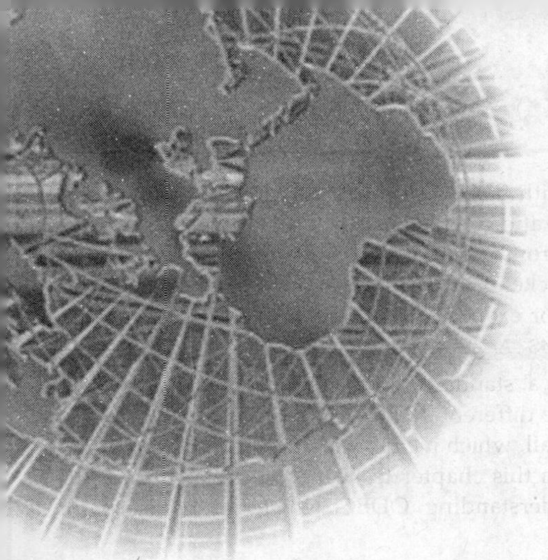

2

Getting Started with JDBC

Nowadays, many enterprise level applications need to interact with databases for storing application specific information. For example, Human Resource Portal is an organization, which needs a database to store the Human Resource department information that can be extracted from various Web pages. Now, you must be thinking how to interact with the database, which acts as the backend of an application. The answer to this question is that you need a protocol to interact with databases. For example, the Open Database Connectivity (ODBC) driver is used to interact with databases, such as `Oracle`, `MS Access`, and `SQL Server`.

A Java application uses Java Database Connectivity (JDBC) as a standard protocol to communicate with databases. JDBC works with different database drivers to connect to different databases. In this chapter, you first learn about the ODBC driver and then you learn about JDBC in detail, which includes features, components, and different types of JDBC architecture. JDBC 4.2 is also discussed in this chapter to keep you updated with the recent technology changes in the IT industry. Let's start understanding ODBC which is the basis for introducing JDBC.

Introducing ODBC

Open Database Connectivity (ODBC) provides a standard abstraction to communicate with different databases. The most common approach to persist the application data is to write it to a database. This allows the enterprise applications to communicate with a database. To communicate with a database, applications can use the database vendor given Application Programming Interface (API) / protocol as shown in Figure 2.1:

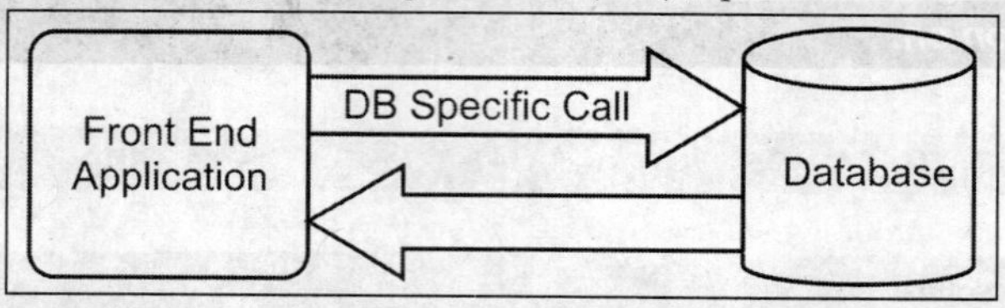

Figure 2.1: Displaying the Process of Accessing Database through an Application

This approach of accessing a database causes the following problems:

- Application becomes vendor dependent.
- The application may not be able to collaborate with the database as the vendor specific API / protocol may not be available for the programming language used to develop the application.
- Migrating applications using one database to other is difficult.
- While developing an application for personal computers you need to write data access routines for each different database that you want to support, which increases the development time and cost, in addition it is difficult to maintain such applications.
- As the application is database vendor specific, the applications are sold not on their quality but on whether they could access the data from a given database and this decreases the clients for the application / product.
- While developing applications for mainframes, this approach forces you to write one version of application for each database that you want to support.

These problems can be solved by using generic API/protocol to communicate with different databases. You can use ODBC to solve these problems as ODBC provides standard abstraction for accessing different databases.

Let's learn about ODBC in detail.

Defining ODBC

ODBC is an open standard API used to access databases. It is developed by Microsoft in collaboration with IBM and other database vendors. This API is implemented by third party DBMS-specific driver vendors for database communications. In general, ODBC is an interface that allows the applications to access databases. The Independent Software Vendors (ISVs) products or applications use ODBC functions to communicate with different databases in a database independent manner, which means that ODBC provides a uniform method to access different Database Management Systems (DBMSs). In addition, one of the major factors that led to the development of ODBC was the need to develop generic and interoperable applications.

ODBC is based on X/OPEN Call Level Interface (CLI) for accessing a database and uses Structured Query Language (SQL) as its database access language. The ODBC interface provides maximum interpretability; that is, an application can access data from various DBMSs through a single interface. Application users can use software components called drivers, which are used as an interface between an application and a specific DBMS, to execute the ODBC application by using these drivers.

ODBC consists of the `DriverManager` (DM) and ODBC drivers. DM determines the specific driver and integrates it with the ODBC application to make calls to a database. An application interacts with DM by specifying a logical name for the database driver. The DM locates the name of the driver and then loads the specific driver for the database. The ODBC driver is a sharable object used to implement the ODBC interface on a database. The driver links the application to the database and also helps to make ODBC calls to the database.

The ODBC interface performs the following tasks:

- Providing a library of functions that allows an application to connect to DBMS, executing the SQL commands, and retrieving the result sets.
- Defining a standard way to connect and log on to DBMS.
- Defining a standardized representation for different data types.
- Allowing you to create an application to use the same object code to access multiple DBMS products.
- Allowing you to create an application to connect to multiple instances of DBMS products.
- Allowing you to create an application to send and receive data in a format recognized by the application. The driver converts data values into the format recognized by a specific DBMS product.

Listing Features of ODBC

The features of ODBC are generally based upon the level of conformance. There are three basic levels—core, level 1, and level 2. Level 2 is the most commonly used conformance level in the ODBC platform. The main features of ODBC are as follows:

- **Standard SQL Syntax**—Implements the SQL syntax for easy understanding of database users. When an application passes an SQL statement to the ODBC driver, the driver passes the SQL statement as an SQL-92 statement and then writes the statement to match with the actual SQL syntax accepted by the database being used. If the ODBC driver fails to pass the SQL statement, the original statement is passed to the database.
- **Standard Error Codes**—Provides an error code mechanism to determine the error produced while processing an SQL query. ODBC provides the SQLSTATE error indicator to indicate the occurrence of the error. The error code is independent of the database being used in an application. The error code varies according to the versions of ODBC. For example, ODBC 2.x returns the S0011 error code when the CREATE statement fails to execute, whereas the ODBC 3.x driver returns 42S11 for the same.
- **Rich Metadata**—Provides a large range of metadata support for both the functions and the data types available in a particular database. It also provides support for the data present in the database. The special types of functions supported by ODBC are tables, columns, special columns, statistics, primary keys, foreign keys, and `getTypeInfo()`.
- **Many Attributes and Options**—Provides a feature to specify the details of the ODBC driver to the datasource to which the driver is connected. The information for the driver can be retrieved by calling the `getInfo()` method. ODBC provides various methods, such as `Get/SetConnectOption()` and `Get/SetStmtOption()`, to retrieve the details of the attributes and functions used in the drivers.

These features provide the following advantages:

- Using single API / protocol to interact with different databases.
- Switching from one database to another easily.
- Migrating an application from one database to another without modifying the application.

Now, let's move further to understand the components of ODBC.

Describing the ODBC Components

ODBC contains the following four main components:

- Application
- DriverManager
- Driver
- DataSource

These components are described in detail, in the next section.

The Application Component

The application component processes application specific operations, such as making calls to a database. The database is then able to process the requests made by the application and return the results. ODBC is used from the calling application in one of the following three ways:

- **Generic Application**—Allows you to work with multiple DBMSs as well as spreadsheets, which are used to import data to the DBMSs for future use. These applications are referred as shrink-wrapped applications.
- **Vertical Application**—Performs a single type of task, such as order entry or tracking manufacturing data and works with a database schema that is controlled by the developer of an application. For a particular customer, an application works with a single DBMS. For example, a small business might use the application with dBase, while a large business might use it with Oracle.

  The vertical application uses ODBC in such a manner that the application is not tied to one DBMS, although it may be tied to a limited number of DBMSs that provide the same functionality. Therefore, the application developer can sell the application independently from the DBMS. Vertical applications are interoperable when they are developed but are sometimes modified to include non-interoperable code once the customer has chosen a specific DBMS.
- **Custom Application**—Performs a specific task in a specific organization.

All these applications perform the following operations:

- Selecting a data source and connecting it to the application
- Executing the SQL statements made by a user
- Retrieving results of the user requests
- Processing the generated errors for the requested statements
- Closing the connection after processing the user requests

The DriverManager Component

`DriverManager` is one of the main components of the ODBC architecture. The `DriverManager` component provides a standard approach to load and unload drivers. It solves a number of problems common to all the applications, such as determining which driver to load, loading and unloading drivers, and calling functions in the drivers. These are considered as problems because if the application directly calls the functions in a driver, it has to link directly with the specific driver. The application also has to build a table of pointers to the functions in that driver and call those functions by using pointers. Moreover, if the same application code has to use more than one driver at a time, it further increases the complexity of the application. The `DriverManager` component solves these problems by providing a single abstraction and calling the required ODBC functions directly.

The Driver Component

The `Driver` component performs application specific ODBC function calls and is loaded in the application by `DriverManager`. A driver processes the function calls made by the application that wants to communicate with a database. It receives the SQL requests, submits the requests to a specific data source, and returns the results to the application. The driver loaded by `DriverManager` can interact with the database in the following two ways:

- **File Based Architecture**—Allows a driver to directly access the physical data. In this case, the driver acts as both the driver and the data source. This implies that the driver makes ODBC calls and executes SQL statements.
- **DBMS-based Architecture**—Allows a driver to access the physical data through a separate database engine. In this case, the database engine processes the ODBC calls. This implies that the SQL statements requested by users are passed to the database engine for processing.

The DataSource Component

The `DataSource` component stores the data that a user wants to access. It also contains the information about the associated operating system, DBMS, and the network platform used to access the database. `Data sources` are of two types, which are as follows:

- **Machine Data Sources**—Refer to data sources that are stored in the system with a user defined name. This data source name is checked by `DriverManager` and the driver that need to connect to the data source.
- **File Data Sources**—Refer to data sources that are stored in a file and the information stored in the file can be shared among several users. When a file Database Source Name (DSN) is used, `DriverManager` makes a connection to the file data source by using the information in the `.dsn` file. This file can be manipulated similar to other files. A file data source does not have a data source name.

Let's now discuss the architecture of ODBC.

Describing the ODBC Architecture

In the ODBC architecture, you can have multiple drivers and data sources, which allow an application to access the data from multiple sources simultaneously. ODBC API is used as an interface between the application and the drivers. Figure 2.2 shows the arrangement of the ODBC components in the ODBC architecture:

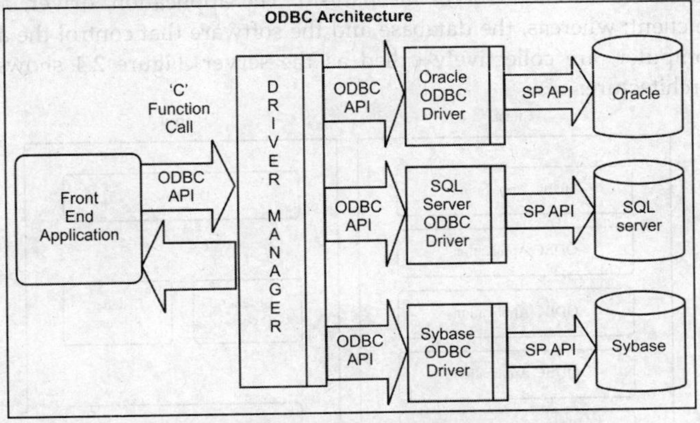

Figure 2.2: Showing the ODBC Architecture

In Figure 2.2, the application component (or the front end application) receives user requests and connects with `DriverManager` to process these requests. `DriverManager` connects to the database and also loads the driver to process the user requests. A driver is used to work upon the database by using the data source name provided by the data source. The database is accessed by the application to process the SQL statements from the user and the subsequent results are displayed to the user.

There are basically two types of ODBC architectures—single-tier architecture and multiple-tier architecture. Let's learn about these in detail.

The Single-tier ODBC Architecture

In case of the single-tier architecture, the driver directly interacts with the database. The driver receives the SQL statements made by a user and retrieves the results according to these SQL statements. An example of the single-tier architecture is the desktop database system, such as DBASE and paradox. Figure 2.3 shows the functionality of the single-tier ODBC architecture:

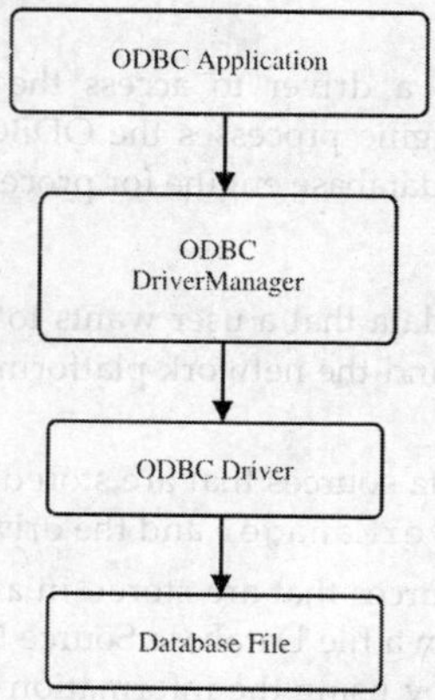

Figure 2.3: Showing the Functionality of the Single-Tier ODBC Architecture

In Figure 2.3, you can see that the ODBC driver interacts directly with the database file. It does not require any database server or support layer to access the data from a database. Therefore, it is referred as the single-tier ODBC architecture.

The Multiple-tier ODBC Architecture

In case of the multiple-tier architecture, the driver sends the SQL requests to the server. Therefore, the multiple-tier architecture is based on the client-server mechanism. The application, driver, and `DriverManager`, are collectively called the client; whereas, the database and the software that control the access to the database and reside on another computer, are collectively called as the server. Figure 2.4 shows the functionality of the multiple-tier ODBC architecture:

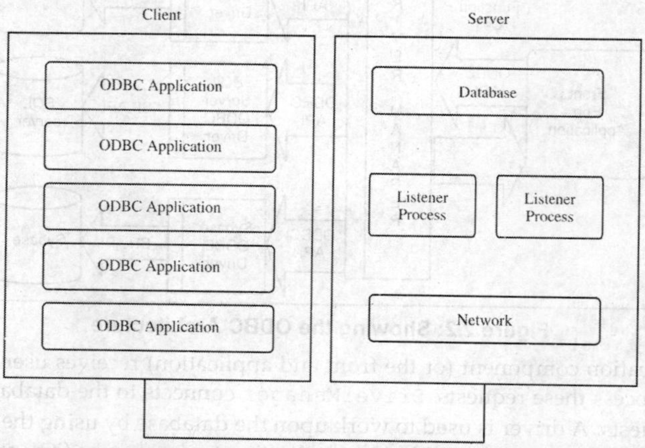

Figure 2.4: Showing the Functionality of the Multiple-Tier ODBC Architecture

The multiple-tier architecture is typically used with database servers, such as Oracle and SQL Server. The SQL Server processes the ODBC calls made by an application and passes the actual SQL statement to DBMS.

Now, let's learn about JDBC in detail.

Introducing JDBC

ODBC has an open API implementation written in Native API and is known as ODBC driver. This ODBC driver is used in an application to interact with a database.

Now, it can be understood that an application can interact with the database by using the following two procedures:

- **Native Libraries**—Refer to the set of APIs that help an application, such as C++ or Java-based applications, to interact with any database. These APIs are vendor specific and are provided by database vendors.
- **ODBC API**—Helps an application to interact with any database. If you use ODBC APIs to connect to a database, you need to create `DSN` for a specific database, such as Oracle. This DSN is used by an application for interaction with the specific database. ODBC API is not vendor-specific as Native Libraries.

The preceding procedures proved to be disadvantageous for Java applications because of the following reasons:

- Native Libraries are given by database vendors. Consequently, this implies that the applications using Native Libraries become vendor dependent. In addition, the applications have to use Java Native Interface (JNI) to interact with Native Libraries, which may cause serious platform independency problems. Moreover, problems in the Native Libraries may destroy Java Virtual Machine (JVM).
- The second option given was using ODBC API that can solve the vendor dependency problems as it provides a common API to interact with any database that has an ODBC Service Provider's implementation, written in Native API. Nevertheless, ODBC API is also a Native API, so you have to use JNI in your Java applications that lead to preceding described problems.

You need a generic Java abstraction that allows Java applications to communicate with different data stores to solve these problems. Sun has introduced a common specification API called JDBC to meet this requirement. In general, the term JDBC is referred as Java Database Connectivity. JDBC™ is a specification from Sun Microsystems that provides a standard abstraction (API / Protocol) for Java applications to communicate with different tabular data stores. It is based on CLI and uses Structured Query Language (SQL) as its data store access language.

The JDBC specification has to be implemented by third party vendors, which is known as JDBC Driver. This means that JDBC Driver is a set of classes that implements JDBC specifications. The JDBC Driver provides the mechanics to JDBC API allowing Java applications to access tabular data stores. It is responsible for transferring the request of a Java application to a database. JDBC, along with the database driver, is capable of accessing databases, spreadsheets, and flat files. This implies that JDBC is used to write Java programs that need to access databases.

JDBC Driver works behind the screen but it has the support to access and work on databases. JDBC is a vendor and platform independent interface between a relational database and the Java application. Therefore, you can say that JDBC is a standard API for Java applications to access the enterprise data from a relational database.

JDBC API allows Java programs to issue SQL statements and retrieve the results according to the statements. JDBC also provides methods to return an error message while accessing a database. JDBC provides classes and interfaces that allow a Java application to send requests made by users to the specified DBMS. While working with ODBC, the users may not specify any DBMS specific details for the requested data; rather they can use the drivers to target a specific database for the user request. JDBC provides the following features, which makes it more efficient for accessing a database:

- Providing JDBC API for Java applications to make JDBC calls. The JDBC call from a Java application can submit SQL statements to the JDBC Driver. These statements are responsible for accessing the data from a database.
- Allowing you to request any type of SQL queries from a database. The JDBC drivers query the database for the SQL queries and retrieve the results.
- Supporting a wide level of portability.
- Providing Java interfaces that are compatible with Java applications and are responsible for representing the JDBC driver services.
- Using a higher level API for the application programmer that is simple and easy to use. The JDBC API specification is used as an interface for the Java application and DBMS.

Let's learn about the components of JDBC.

Describing Components of JDBC

JDBC specification has four main components through which it communicates effectively with a database. These components are as follows:

- **The JDBC API**—Provides methods and interfaces for an easy and effective communication with databases. It provides a standard for connecting a database to an application. The application processes the SQL commands and sends back the result to the user. JDBC API provides two main packages, `java.sql` and `javax.sql`, to interact with the databases. Both the packages are part of the Java platform, including Java SE and Java EE platforms, which conform to the write once run anywhere (WORA) capabilities of Java.
- **The JDBC `DriverManager`**—Manages different types of database drivers used for a Java application. The main objective of `DriverManager` is to load database specific drivers in the application. It is also used to select the most appropriate database specific driver from the previously loaded drivers when a new connection to a database is established. It is also used to make database specific calls to the database to process the user requests. It is important to note that `DriverManager` of JDBC 4.0 automatically loads any JDBC 4.0 drivers found within the CLASSPATH (any drivers that are pre-JDBC 4.0 must be explicitly loaded by the application).
- **The JDBC Test Suite**—Ensures proper functioning of the JDBC driver. The test suite tests the JDBC driver based on the JDBC technology. It also ensures the compliance of the JDBC driver with the Java application.
- **The JDBC-ODBC Bridge**—Represents a reference implementation for JDBC, used to connect the database drivers to the specific databases. This bridge translates JDBC method calls to ODBC function calls. This bridge is used to implement JDBC for any database that uses an ODBC driver. You can import the `sun.jdbc.odbc` package to use JDBC-ODBC Bridge. This package contains a native library for accessing the ODBC features.

After learning about the components of JDBC, let's learn about features of JDBC.

Listing Features of JDBC

The JDBC 4.0 specification provides several features and procedures that can be used by Java database programmers. JDBC 4.0 is introduced to enhance the functionalities of JDBC 3.0. Some important features introduced in JDBC 4.0 are as follows:

- **Named Parameters**—In JDBC 4.0, the `CallableStatement` is updated to support named parameters so that you can access the parameters by using the names rather than by using the index. In the previous version of JDBC 3.0, we used and accessed the parameters with the help of the indexes assigned to them.
- **Auto loading of the JDBC driver class**—Loads the JDBC drivers implicitly. When the `getConnection()` method is called in an application, `DriverManager` automatically loads a driver in the database.
- **Connection management enhancement**—Allows you to establish a new connection by specifying the host name and the available port number. This can be done by using a set of parameters to maintain a standard connection. The enhancement also adds some methods to the pre-existing interfaces, such as `Connection` and `Statement`.
- **Support for `ROWID`**—Supports the `ROWID` data type, which is useful in tables where multiple columns do not have a unique identifier.
- **Dataset implementation of SQL using annotations**—Allows you to use annotations. The use of annotations requires fewer lines of code. The annotations are used along with the queries. The query results can be bound to the Java classes to speed up the processing of the query output. The JDBC 4.0 specification provides two main annotations, which are as follows:
  - **`SELECT`**—Allows you to retrieve query specific data from a database. You can use the `SELECT` annotation in a `SELECT` query within a Java class. The attributes of the `SELECT` annotation are described in Table 2.1:

Table 2.1: Attributes of the SELECT Annotation		
Name	**Type**	**Description**
`Sql`	`String`	Specifies a simple SQL SELECT query
`Value`	`String`	Represents the value specified for the SQL attribute
`Table name`	`String`	Specifies the name of the database table
`Readonly, connected, scrollable`	`Boolean`	Indicates whether the `DataSet` is ReadOnly or Updatable, whether or not it is connected to a back end database, and it is scrollable when the query is used in a connection
`allColumnsMapped`	`Boolean`	Indicates whether or not the column names used in the annotations are mapped to the corresponding fields of `DataSet`

- **`UPDATE`**—Allows you to update the queries used in database tables. The `UPDATE` annotation must include the SQL annotation type to update the fields of a table.

❑ **SQL exception handling enhancements**—Introduces the enhancements in exception handling, which is one of the most important features of all the programming languages. JDBC 4.0 has introduced certain enhancements in the `SQLException` class, which are as follows:

- **New exception sub classes**—Provides new classes as enhancement to `SQLException`. The new classes added to the `SQLException` are SQL non-transient exception and SQL transient exception. The SQL non-transient exception class is called when a retry of the same JDBC operation fails to run again unless the cause of `SQLException` is corrected. On the other hand, the SQL transient exception class is called when a previously failed JDBC operation succeeds after retry.
- **Casual Relationship**—Supports the Java SE chained exception mechanism (also known as Casual facility), which gives an ability to handle multiple SQL Exceptions thrown in a JDBC operation.
- **Support for the `for-each` loop**—Uses the `for-each` loop to iterate on the chain of groups.
- **SQL XML support**—Introduces the concept of `XML` support in SQL `DataStore`.

Apart from the above features, JDBC has the following features:

❑ **The JDBC Metadata API**—The `ParameterMetaData` are included in JDBC `MetaData` to describe the parameter properties and their types that are used with `PreparedStatement`.

❑ **Data Types**—JDBC includes several data types, such as large objects (`BLOB`, `CLOB`, and `REF`), `java.sql.Types.DATALINK` and `java.sql.Types.BOOLEAN`. The `DATALINK` data type is capable of accessing the external resources whereas the BOOLEAN data type is equivalent to the BIT type. The value of the `DATALINK` data type is accessed by using the `getURL()` method and the respective value of the Boolean data type is accessed by using the `getBoolean()` method. Both these methods take an instance of `ResultSet` associated with the application.

❑ **Connector Relationship**—It maintains the connection between JDBC and Java EE. The connector architecture provides a set of connectors through which the enterprise applications connect to JDBC. This connection provides a resource adapter, which is used to connect JDBC to remote systems. JDBC API provides three main service providers to define the connector architecture, which are as follows:

- **`ConnectionPoolDataSource`**—Refers to an interface provided by JDBC API. It is used to connect applications to JDBC `Datasource` and back-end systems.
- **`XADataSource`**—Allows the transactional access to the resources.
- **Security Management**—Provides security to enterprise applications. A driver vendor is specified to map the JDBC driver to the connector system. Then, the JDBC connector deploys its driver as a resource adapter.

❑ **`ResultSet` Functionality**—Supports the functionality of cursor holdability, to ensure that the `Connection` and `ResultSet` objects are closed, when the data is retrieved. To maintain the `ResultSet` holdability within an application, you need to maintain the following two constants:

- **HOLD_CURSOR_OVER_COMMIT**—Ensures that ResultSet objects are opened even after a commit operation is performed.
- **CLOSE_CURSOR_AT_COMMIT**—Ensures that ResultSet objects are closed after a commit operation is performed.

❐ **Returning Multiple Results**—Provides a statement interface to access multiple results simultaneously. The statement interface includes a new method in JDBC API to access multiple results. This method is an overloaded form of the getMoreResults () method. It includes an integer flag, which is used to specify the behavior of the ResultSets. The flags included in JDBC API are as follows:

- **CLOSE_ALL_RESULTS**—Closes all the previously opened ResultSet by calling the getMoreResults() method.
- **CLOSE_CURRENT_RESULT**—Closes the current ResultSet object by calling the getMoreResults() method.
- **KEEP_CURRENT_RESULT**—Retains the current ResultSet object by using the getMoreResults() method.

❐ **Connection Pooling**—Provides the connection pool properties, which allow you to maximize the performance of enterprise applications. These properties are listed in Table 2.2:

Table 2.2: Properties of Connection Pooling

Property Name	Description
maxStatements	Specifies the maximum number of statements that should be kept open by the connection pool
initialPoolSize	Specifies the number of physical connections that should be kept open by the pool while initializing the statements
minPoolSize	Specifies the minimum number of physical connections that the pool should contain during its initialization
maxPoolSize	Specifies the maximum number of physical connections that the pool should contain during its initialization
maxIdelTime	Specifies the time duration during which an unused pool should remain open before the connection is closed
propertyCycle	Specifies the time interval, in seconds, that a pool should wait for the property policy

❐ **PreparedStatement Pooling**—Increases the life time of a PreparedStatement object. A PreparedStatement allows you to compile the commonly used SQL statements for improving the performance of the statement.

❐ **Savepoint**—Represents a point within a transaction to which a transaction may be rolled back. Savepoints are one of the most exciting features which was added to JDBC 3.0 specifications. Transactions in a database ensure that the persisted data remains in a consistent state. However, sometimes the data of a current transaction might be rolled back. A savepoint is a point within a transaction that marks an intermediate point to which a transaction may be rolled back. In a transaction with no savepoints, calling the rollback method rolls back the entire transaction. However if a savepoint is set, an application can control whether the entire transaction is rolled back or if only a part of the transaction is rolled back to the named point.

Along with the preceding discussed features of JDBC, there are some new features added to JDBC 4.2. Let's learn about these features.

Listing New Features in JDBC 4.2

JDBC 4.2 enhanced the functionalities of JDBC 4.0. Some of the important new features introduced in JDBC 4.2 are as follows:

❐ **Addition of REF_CURSOR support**—The data type of REF_CURSOR is supported by various databases. In case if we want to return a REF_CURSOR from a stored process, the method CallableStatement.registerOutParameter() can be used. We can also specify Types.REF_CURSOR as the data type to be returned. If we want to retrieve the ResultSet instance which represents the REF_CURSOR, we invoke the method CallableStatement.getObject(). The data type is specified by ResultSet to which we need to convert the returned object.

Suppose if we want to invoke the method of registerOutParameter() and we specify the datatype Types.REF_CURSOR to be returned and if this data type is not supported by the JDBC driver, an exception SQLFeatureNotSupportedException is thrown.

In the example discussed below is a ResultSet instance, having a class CallableStatement from a REF_CURSOR:

```
CallableStatement cstmt = conn.prepareCall("{callmySproc(?)}");
cstmt.registerOutParameter(1, Types.REF_CURSOR);
cstmt.executeQuery();
ResultSet rs = cstmt.getObject(1, ResultSet.class);
while(rs.next()){
System.out.println("Name="+ rs.getString(1));
}
```

If we want to find out whether JDBC Driver supports REF_CURSOR or not, we need to invoke the method DatabaseMetaData.supportsRefCursors().

- **Addition of java.sql.DriverAction Interface**—It is a type of an interface that can be implemented by any class that implements the java.sql.Driver if it wants to be notified by the Driver class. The static initialization block of JDBC driver should invoke the method DriverManager.registerDriver (java.sql.Driver, java.sql.DriverAction). By initiating this, the information is send to DriverManager class so that DriverAction implementation process is invoked if a request of deregistration of JDBC driver is processed.
- **Addition of the java.sql.SQLType Interface**—This interface is used for creation of an object which identifies a common SQL type, called JDBC type. It is also called vendor specific type. It assists in dealing with the data types that do not appear in ANSI/ISO SQL Standard.
- **Addition of the java.sql.JDBCType Enum**—This interface refers to a common SQL Types, called JDBC Types and is used in place of constants which are defined in Types.java. For each identifier in java.sql.type, an enum is provided by java.sql.JDBCType.
- **Add support for large update counts**—For the update count, JDBC method returns only int type of value. But as the datasets continues to grow, it causes a problem. To solve this problem we have added methods to the Statement class which returns a long value for the update count. We can only use these methods when returned row surpasses the constant Integer.MAX_VALUE.
- **Changes to the existing interfaces**—Several methods are added in JDBC 4.2 for enhancing the existing interfaces. The list of enhanced interfaces are as follows:

```
java.sql.Driver
java.sql.DriverManager
java.sql.DatabaseMetaData
java.sql.Date
java.sql.Time
java.sql.TimeStamp
java.sql.Statement
java.sql.CallableStatement
java.sql.PreparedStatement
java.sql.ResultSet
java.sql.SQLInput
java.sql.SQLOutput
java.sql.Types
javax.sql.DataSource
javax.sql.XADataSource
java.sql.SQLXML
```

Apart from the above interface JDBC 4.2 has also enhanced RowSet1.2 which as listed as follows:

```
javax.sql.rowset.CachedRowSet
javax.sql.rowset.BaseRowSet
javax.sql.rowset.Predicate
javax.sql.rowset.JdbcRowSet
javax.sql.rowset.RowSetMetaDataImpl
javax.sql.rowset.spi.SyncFactory
javax.sql.rowset.serial.SerialArray
javax.sql.rowset.serial.SerialBlob
javax.sql.rowset.serial.SerialClob
javax.sql.rowset.serial.SerialDatalink
javax.sql.rowset.serial.SerialJavaObject
javax.sql.rowset.serial.SerialRef
javax.sql.rowset.serial.SerialStruct
```

Exploring the JDBC Architecture

The JDBC API supports both 2-tier and 3-tier applications. First, let's discuss 2-tier architecture, which is shown in Figure 2.5:

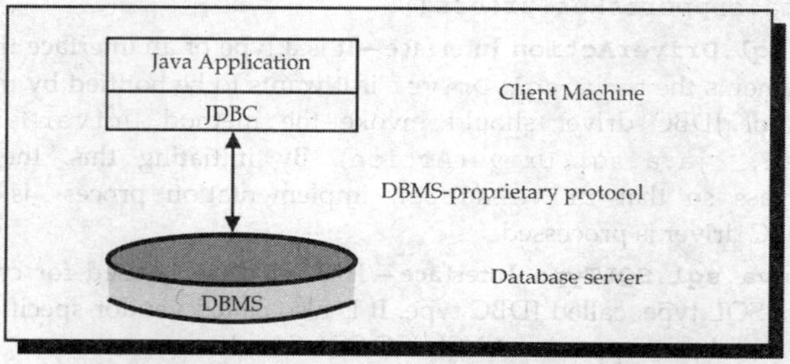

Figure 2.5: Diagram of the JDBC 2-tier Architecture

In 2-tier architecture, a Java application directly communicates with the database server by using JDBC APIs (Figure 2.5). This communication requires a JDBC driver to access the particular database. The client computer (on which the Java application runs) delivers the commands to the database or to another data source and the results are sent back to the client computer by the database server (or server computer). The database or data source may be located on the client computer or on another computer connected through a network. This is referred to as the client-server configuration.

Now, let's consider JDBC 3-tier architecture, shown in Figure 2.6:

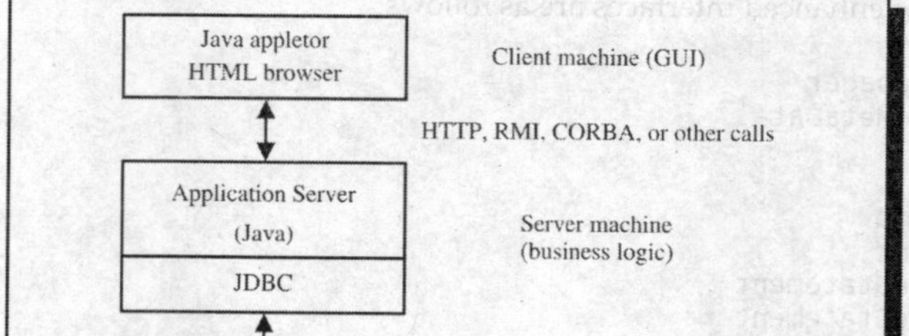

Figure 2.6: Diagram of the JDBC 3-tier Architecture

In JDBC 3-tier architecture (Figure 2.6), the client delivers the command to a middle tier, which sends the command to a database or another data source. The data source then processes the commands and the results are sent back to the middle tier, which sends the results back to the client. The middle tier implements the JDBC driver to interact with the particular database.

Therefore, if we want to communicate with any database through JDBC, we need a JDBC driver, which communicates with the respective database. Currently, more than 220 JDBC drivers are available in the market and they have been designed to communicate with different data stores. All these drivers are categorized into four types, based on their implementation (that is, the approach to communicate with the data store). These categories are popularly known as JDBC Type-1, Type-2, Type-3, Type-4 and Type-5 Driver.

The main function of JDBC is to provide a standard abstraction for Java applications to communicate with databases. A JDBC driver is required to process the SQL requests and generate the results. JDBC API provides classes and interfaces to handle database specific calls from users. Some of the important classes and interfaces are as follows:

- Connection
- DatabaseMetaData
- PreparedStatement
- Statement
- Driver
- CallableStatement
- ResultSet
- DriverManager
- ResultSetMetaData
- SqlData
- Blob
- Clob

`DriverManager` in the JDBC API plays an important role in the JDBC architecture. It uses some database specific drivers to effectively connect enterprise applications to databases. Figure 2.7 shows the JDBC architecture:

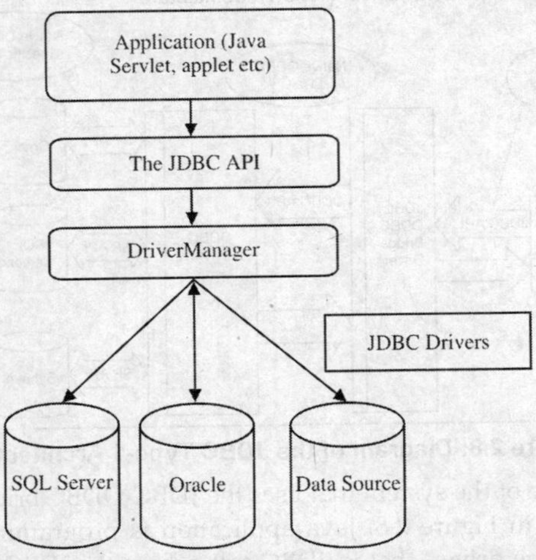

Figure 2.7: Diagram of the JDBC Architecture

As shown in Figure 2.7, the Java application that wants to communicate with a database has to be programmed using JDBC API. A JDBC driver (third party vendor implementation) has to be plugged in, to drive the request to database with which you want to communicate, which can be done dynamically at runtime. This ensures that the Java application is database independent. Therefore, if you want to communicate with any data store through JDBC, you need a JDBC driver, which communicates with the respective data store.

Exploring JDBC Drivers

Currently, more than 220 JDBC drivers are available in the market, which are designed to communicate with different data stores. All these drivers are categorized into five types based on their implementation, i.e., the approach to communicate with the data store. These drivers are JDBC Type-1, Type-2, Type-3, Type-4 and Type-5 drivers.

Some of these drivers are pure Java drivers and are portable for all the environments; whereas, others are partly Java drivers and require some libraries to communicate with the database. The different types of drivers available in JDBC are listed in Table 2.3:

Table 2.3: Types of JDBC drivers

JDBC Driver Types	Description
`Type-1 Driver`	Refers to the Bridge Driver (JDBC-ODBC bridge driver)
`Type-2 Driver`	Refers to the Partly Java and Partly Native code driver
`Type-3 Driver`	Refers to the Pure Java driver that uses a middleware driver to connect to a database
`Type-4 Driver`	Refers to the Pure Java driver and is directly connected to a database
`Type-5 Driver`	Refers to the highly functional drivers that have higher performance

Let's now learn about each of these types of drivers in detail.

The Type-1 Driver

The Type-1 driver acts as a bridge between JDBC and other database connectivity mechanisms, such as ODBC. An example of this type of driver is the Sun JDBC-ODBC bridge driver. The JDBC-ODBC Bridge allows you to access databases using the ODBC drivers. This driver helps the Java programmers to use JDBC and program Java applications to communicate with existing data stores that support ODBC. It converts JDBC calls into ODBC calls and redirects the request to the ODBC driver. The architecture of the Type-1 driver is shown in Figure 2.8:

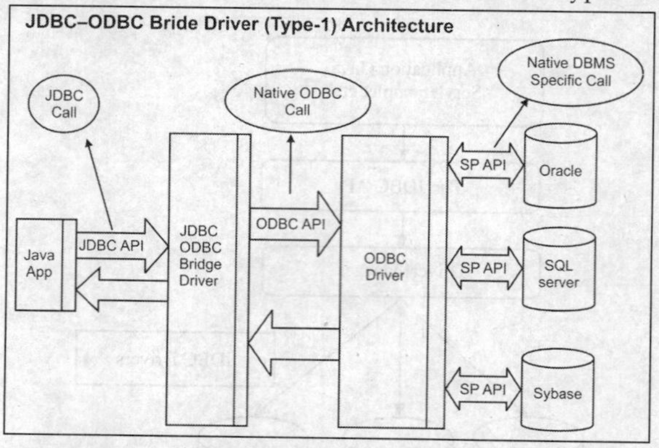

Figure 2.8: Diagram of the JDBC Type-1 Architecture

Figure 2.8 shows the architecture of the system that uses the JDBC-ODBC bridge driver to communicate with the respective database. As shown in Figure 2.8, Java application is programmed to JDBC API and will make a request to the JDBC-ODBC bridge driver, that is, JDBC call, where the JDBC-ODBC bridge driver is responsible to resolve the JDBC call and make an equivalent ODBC calls to the ODBC driver. To do this JDBC-ODBC bridge driver uses ODBC API. Later, the ODBC driver completes the request and sends the response to the JDBC-ODBC bridge driver. Now, the JDBC-ODBC bridge driver converts the response and sends it to the requesting Java application in JDBC standards. The Type-1 driver is generally used in the development and testing phases of Java applications.

Advantages of the Type-1 Driver

Some advantages of the Type-1 driver are as follows:

- Serves as a single driver that can be used to interact with different data stores
- Allows you to communicate with all the databases supported by the ODBC driver
- Represents as a vendor independent driver and is available along with (built-in) JDK

Disadvantages of the Type-1 Driver

Some disadvantages of the Type-1 driver are as follows:

- Decreases the execution speed due to a more number of translations (includes JDBC → ODBC → DB Native calls)
- Depends on the ODBC driver due to which Java applications indirectly become dependent on ODBC drivers
- Requires ODBC binary code (or ODBC client library) that must be installed on every client to access data from the database.
- Uses `JNI` to make ODBC calls.

Example of the Type-1 Driver

JDK1.2 has JDBC-ODBC Bridge which is an example of Type-1 driver.

Situations to Use the Type-1 Driver

In case a database does not have any other JDBC driver implementations, you need to use this driver even in the production environment. However, due to its disadvantages, preferably this driver should not be used.

NOTE

The Type-1 driver is not recommended for use when Java applications are required with auto-installation applications, such as applets.

Let's now learn about the Type-2 driver.

The Type-2 Driver (Java to native API)

The Type-2 driver converts JDBC calls into DB vendor specific native calls in a client machine. This type of driver makes `JNI` calls on database specific native client APIs. These database specific native client APIs are usually written in C or C++. The Type-2 drivers are named as *native-API partly Java technology-enabled driver* or simply *native-API part Java driver*.

The Type-2 driver follows a 2-tier architecture model, as shown in Figure 2.9:

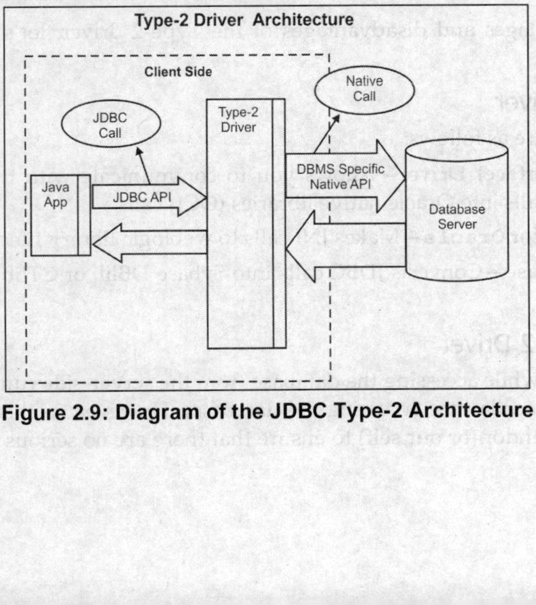

Figure 2.9: Diagram of the JDBC Type-2 Architecture

As shown in Figure 2.9, the Java application that wants to communicate with the database is programmed using JDBC API, making JDBC calls. These JDBC calls are converted into database specific native calls in the client machine and the request is then dispatched to the database specific native libraries. These native libraries are present in the client and these libraries send the request to the database server by using native protocol.

The Type-2 driver is implemented for a specific database and is usually delivered by a DBMS vendor. However, it is not mandatory that Type-2 drivers have to be implemented by DBMS vendors only. An example of the Type-2 driver is the Weblogic OCI driver implemented by BEA Weblogic.

Type-2 drivers are suitable to use with server-side applications. It is not recommended to use Type-2 drivers with client-side applications, since the database specific native libraries for the client platform should be installed on the client machines.

Advantages of the Type-2 Driver

Some advantages of the Type-2 driver are as follows:

- Serves as the fastest driver compared to other type of drivers
- Allows you to use the additional features provided by the specific database vendor to access the database, which are even supported by the JDBC specification

Disadvantages of the Type-2 Driver

Some disadvantages of the Type-2 driver are as follows:

- Requires native libraries, which must be installed on client machines since the conversion from JDBC calls to database specific native calls is done on the client machine
- Allows the database specific native functions to be executed on the client JMV process and any bug in this driver can crash JVM
- Increases the cost of the application if the application needs to run on different platforms.
- Causes the problem of platform independency of the Java application as this type of driver converts the JDBC calls into DBMS specific native calls, and there is a possibility that the database vendor may not support the native libraries for all platforms.

NOTE

The Type-2 driver is vendor (database) specific. This implies that the Type-2 driver implementation is created to communicate with a particular database. This can be considered as one of the disadvantages with the Type-2 driver, compared to the Type-1 driver, which allows you to access multiple databases.

However, this problem needs to be considered only while creating a desktop (client side running) application accessing the database. It will be difficult to update the native libraries in the client place when we want to migrate the application to use another DB.

After discussing the advantages and disadvantages of the Type-2 driver, let's discuss some examples of this driver.

Examples of the Type-2 Driver

Some of the type-2 drivers are as follows:

- **OCI (Oracle Call Interface) Driver**—Allows you to communicate with the Oracle database server. This driver converts JDBC calls into Oracle native libraries (OCI) calls.
- **Weblogic OCI Driver for `Oracle`**—Makes JNI calls to weblogic library functions.
- **Type-2 Driver for Sybase**—Converts JDBC calls into Sybase DBlib or CTlib calls, which are native libraries to connect to Sybase.

Situations to Use the Type-2 Driver

The Type-2 driver is useful while accessing the database from the server-side running applications (For example, Servlet or EJB running in middleware accessing the database). However, in this case you need to get a perfect test report from a trusted vendor (or our self) to ensure that there are no serious bugs in the native libraries that can destroy JVM. The only strong reason to use this driver in the above specified context taking such risk is the speed of operation that it supports, which is highest compared to any other driver.

The Type-3 Driver (Java to Network Protocol/All Java Driver)

The Type-3 driver translates JDBC calls into database server independent and middleware server specific net protocol calls (network calls), which are then translated into database server specific calls by the middleware server. Type-3 drivers follow the 3-tier architecture model, as shown in Figure 2.10:

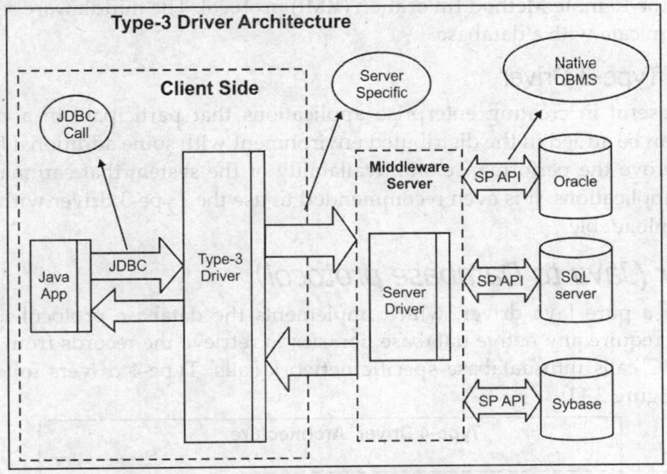

Figure 2.10: Diagram of the JDBC Type-3 Driver

As shown in Figure 2.10, the JDBC Type-3 driver listens for JDBC calls from the Java application and translates them into middleware server specific calls. Then, the driver communicates with the middleware server over a socket. The middleware server converts these calls into database specific calls. The Type-3 drivers are named as net-protocol fully Java technology-enabled drivers, or simply net-protocol drivers.

The middleware server can be added with some additional functionality, such as pool management to improve the performance and availability of connection, which can make this architecture more useful in enterprise applications. The Type-3 driver is recommended to use with applets since this type of drivers are auto downloadable. The Type-3 drivers are named as *net-protocol fully Java technology-enabled drivers* or simply *net-protocol drivers*.

Advantages of the Type-3 Driver

Some advantages of the Type-3 driver are as follows:

- Serves as pure Java drivers and are auto downloadable
- Does not require native libraries on the client machine
- Allows a single driver to access multiple databases, implying that this driver is database independent
- Configures the database details in the middleware server; instead of providing these details to the client
- Allows to switch from one database to another without changing the client-side driver classes
- Follows the 3-tier model; thereby, allows you to access the database between the networks and manage the database resources accurately

Disadvantages of the Type-3 Driver

Some disadvantages of the Type-3 driver are as follows:

- Provides slow communication due to the increased number of network calls
- Are costlier as compared to the other drivers

Examples of the Type-3 Driver

Some examples of the Type-3 driver are as follows:

- **IDS Driver**—Listens for JDBC calls and converts them into the Intrusion Detection System (IDS) Server specific understandable network calls. The Type-3 driver communicates over a socket to IDS Server, which acts as a middleware server.
- **Weblogic RMI Driver**—Listens for JDBC calls and sends the request from the client to the middleware server by using the Remote Method Invocation (RMI) protocol. The middleware server uses a suitable JDBC driver to communicate with a database.

Situations to Use the Type-3 Driver

Type-3 drivers are useful in creating enterprise applications that participate in a distributed transaction. A middleware server can be added in the distributed environment with some additional functionality, such as pool management, to improve the performance and availability of the system that can make this architecture more useful in enterprise applications. It is even recommended to use the Type-3 driver with applets since this type of drivers are auto downloadable.

The Type-4 Driver (Java to Database protocol)

The Type-4 driver is a pure Java driver, which implements the database protocol to interact directly with a database. It does not require any native database libraries to retrieve the records from the database. The Type-4 driver translates JDBC calls into database specific network calls. Type-4 drivers follow the 2-tier architecture model, as shown in Figure 2.11:

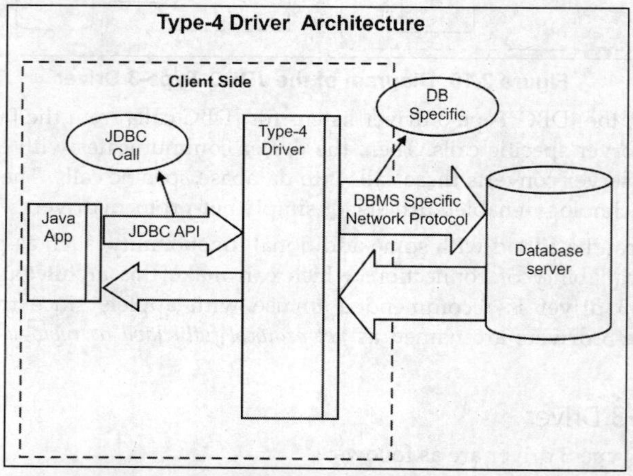

Figure 2.11: Diagram of the JDBC Type-4 Driver

As shown in Figure 2.11, the Type-4 driver prepares a DBMS specific network message and then communicates with a database server over a socket. This type of driver is lightweight and is generally known as a thin driver. The Type-4 driver uses database specific proprietary protocols for communication. Generally, Type-4 drivers are implemented by DBMS vendors, since the protocol used in these drivers are proprietary.

You can use Type-4 drivers when you want an auto downloadable option for the client-side applications. It is also recommended to be used with server-side applications.

Advantages of the Type-4 Driver

Some advantages of the Type-4 driver are as follows:

- Serves as a pure Java driver and are auto downloadable
- Does not require native libraries to be installed on the client machine
- Uses the database server specific protocol and thereby it is secure to use this driver
- Does not require a middleware server

Disadvantage of the Type-4 Driver

The main disadvantage of the Type-4 driver is that it uses database specific proprietary protocol and is DBMS vendor dependent.

Examples of the Type-4 Driver

Some examples of the Type-4 driver are as follows:

- Thin Driver for `Oracle` from `Oracle` Corporation
- Weblogic, MSSQLSERVER4 for MS SQL Server from BEA Systems

The Type-5 Driver (Java to Database protocol)

Type-5 JDBC driver permit modern data-driven java application. Type-5 JDBC driver offers latest functionality with faster performance over other driver types. We can now add features and functionalities without changing application code with the help of Type-5 driver. Type-5 JDBC drivers have overcome the limitation of Type-4 drivers by delivering more benefits to any data-driven java application.

Advantages of the Type-5 Driver

- It has faster performance for any data-driven java application even if it adds more users.
- We can add number of features and functionalities without changing application code.
- With Type-5 driver, there is a significant improvement in resource efficiency. The CPU usage and the memory resources are minimized when an application is switched to Type-5 JDBC drivers.
- Simplified deployment of applications can be achieved with Type-5 JDBC driver.
- Reduced QA is achieved as these applications can be implemented without the need for data source codes.

Examples of the Type-5 Driver

The example of Type-5 driver is DataDirect Connect for JDBC driver.

Summary

In this chapter, you have learned about the basic concepts of ODBC. This chapter has introduced the architecture of ODBC and JDBC. The chapter has helped you to explore Type-1, Type-2, Type-3, Type-4 and Type-5 drivers. You have studied about the advantages and disadvantages of each driver. In addition, you have studied the situations in which these drivers can be used and their examples are also discussed in the chapter. Let's recall the following important points to summarize the chapter:

- ODBC provides a standard abstraction to communicate with different databases vendor independently.
- ODBC is created by Microsoft in collaboration with other DB vendors.
- ODBC abstraction is defined as native C functions. Therefore, the ODBC calls are C function calls. This implies that if Java application has to use ODBC to access DB it needs to invoke C functions through Java Native Interface (JNI).
- JDBC generally referred as Java Database Connectivity is one of the Service APIs of Java platforms that include Java Standard and Enterprise Editions.
- JDBC defines a standard protocol for Java applications to access tabular data stores.
- JDBC API needs to be supported by JDBC driver to communicate with the respective database.
- JDBC driver is a set of classes that implement the JDBC specification; it can be from different vendors, such as DB vendors, middleware server providers and any other Independent Software Vendors (ISV's). Based on the approach followed by JDBC driver to reach the database, it falls in any one of the four types of JDBC drivers described under the JDBC specification.
- JDBC driver is responsible to drive the queries prepared by Java applications to DBMS (or any other data store manager, if supported).

- JDBC Type-1 Driver converts JDBC calls into vendor (database) independent API calls. It acts as an intermediate between the Java application and an existing vendor independent API for accessing DB, such as ODBC.
- JDBC Type-2 Driver converts JDBC calls into the database specific native calls in the client environment (client refers to the Java application that is accessing the Type-2 driver).
- JDBC Type-3 Driver converts the JDBC call into the database independent and middleware specific network call, where the middleware takes the responsibility to drive the request to database using server driver (may be another JDBC driver). The Type-3 architecture is the only driver architecture (among the 4 JDBC architectures) following 3-tier model. Type-1, 2, and 4 follows the 2-tier model.
- JDBC Type-4 Driver converts JDBC Calls into database specific network calls.
- JDBC Type-5 Driver is highly-functional drivers that have higher performance

In the next chapter, we discuss how to implement JDBC APIs.

Exercise

Q. 2.1 What is ODBC?

Q. 2.2 What is JDBC?

Q. 2.3 Write down the different types of JDBC drivers? Give an example of the JDBC Type-1 driver.

Q. 2.4 When can we use the JDBC Type-1 driver?

Q. 2.5 Which type of JDBC driver implementations are categorized as JDBC Type-2 driver?

Q. 2.6 Write a short note on JDBC Type-3 drivers.

Q. 2.7 Which type of JDBC driver is suitable for accessing database over the Internet?

Q. 2.8 Give an example of JDBC Type-5 driver.

3

Working with JDBC APIs

A relational database is usually the primary data source in an enterprise application. The Java Database Connectivity (JDBC) Application Programming Interface (API) provides programmers with classes and interfaces to connect to relational data by using Java code. Using the JDBC API, programmers can create a client that can connect to a database, execute Structured Query Language (SQL) statements, and process the result of those statements.

If you are familiar with SQL and relational databases, the structure of the JDBC API is simple to understand and use. API provides connectivity and data access across the range of relational databases. API provides a set of database access methods for SQL-compliant relational databases. JDBC generalizes the most common database access functions by abstracting the vendor-specific details of a particular database. Therefore, the `java.sql` package provides a set of classes and interfaces, which can be used with any database that has an appropriate JDBC driver.

The chapter discusses the JDBC APIs comprising core as well as extension APIs, new APIs added to JDBC 4.2, and the major classes along with interfaces used to create JDBC applications. Then, the chapter explains how to establish connection with databases by using JDBC APIs. At the end, the various types of JDBC drivers are explored.

Introducing JDBC API

JDBC API is a part of the JDBC specification. This provides a standard abstraction for Java application to access JDBC driver, which is implemented by 3rd party vendor, such as database, middleware server providers, and any other Independent Software Vendors (ISVs). The JDBC driver is a process that is used to drive the queries to Database Management System (DBMS) (or any other data store manager it supports). The queries here are generally a SQL Statements. The SQL standards are used to build statements to be executed by DBMS in its environment. These statements are referred as SQL statements. The SQL statements are used to describe the data access operations to be performed by DBMS, such as inserting the given data into the specified structure (table) and querying the data from the specified tables. The JDBC API acts as a standard abstraction between the Java application and the 3rd party implemented JDBC driver, which makes the Java application use JDBC driver vendor independently. In other words, JDBC API defines a standard protocol between Java application and JDBC driver. The JDBC API includes classes and interfaces that are used by Java applications to communicate with databases. The JDBC driver communicates with a relational database for any requests made by a Java application by using the JDBC API. Therefore, we do not need to write different programs to access the data from different databases. JDBC API satisfies the write once and run anywhere nature of Java.

The JDBC API is based upon the X/open CLI specification and SQL standard statements. This is also the basic standard for Open Database Connectivity (ODBC). The JDBC API is a part of the Java Platform's Standard Edition (Java SE) and is available to Java Platform Enterprise Edition (Java EE). JDBC API is mainly divided into two packages, `java.sql` and `javax.sql`.

The following are the important goals of JDBC API:

- Provides a standard abstraction for submitting the SQL statements to access the data in database to be consistent with SQL 2003. JDBC 3.0 supports SQL-99 features and JDBC 4.2 support SQL 2003 features, which is likely to be widely supported by the industry.
- Provides vendor independent access to common features.
- Maintains focus on SQL.
- Provides a foundation for high-level API, and keep it simple.
- Supports the compatibility with connectors.

Before creating an application, you first need to explore the classes and interfaces available in JDBC API. These classes and interfaces are used in Java applications to establish database connection and generate database queries. In this section, let's explore the following topics to have better understanding of the JDBC APIs:

- Types of JDBC APIs
- New APIs added to JDBC 4.2
- Describing the Major Classes and Interfaces

Explaining the Types of JDBC APIs

JDBC API is a part of JDBC specification, which provides a standard abstraction to use JDBC drivers (which we have learned in the previous chapter). JDBC API is divided into the following two parts:

- JDBC core API
- JDBC extension API

Let's discuss these in the following sections:

The JDBC Core API

It provides a standard abstraction to perform basic operations, such as connecting to a data store, executing SQL queries, executing procedures and functions, retrieving the record set content, getting data store details, getting driver details, and maintaining local transactions. The classes and interfaces of this part of the JDBC API are packed into the `java.sql` package. Table 3.1 lists the interfaces available in JDBC 4.0 Core API:

Table 3.1: Describing the Interfaces of JDBC 4.0 Core API

Interfaces	Description
`Array`	Provides methods for mapping in Java programming language for the SQL type Array.
`Blob`	Represents the Binary Large Objects (BLOB) values in Java. BLOB is a built-in data type used to store the values of binary large objects.
`CallableStatement`	Executes SQL stored procedures. A Java application uses this interface to return a single or multiple result sets, depending on the procedure or function it represents.
`Clob`	Represents the Character Large Objects (CLOB) values in Java. CLOB is a built-in data type used to store the values of character large objects.
`Connection`	Connects a Java application to the required data source. An instance of the Connection interface is created to access user specific data from the database. A user can access the database within the context of the connection.
`DatabaseMetaData`	Provides information about the database management system.
`Driver`	Establishes the connectivity with a database.
`DriverAction`	Used when a JDBC driver selects to create its implementation in a private class.
`NClob`	Provides the mapping of Java objects with the SQL `NClob` type. Generally, the `NClob` type (built-in SQL data type) is used to store the SQL character types.
`PreparedStatement`	Represents an object of a pre-compiled SQL statement. It is used to execute one SQL statement multiple times.
`ParameterMetaData`	Retrieves the types and the properties of the parameters used in the `PreparedStatement` interface.
`Ref`	Indicates the reference of an SQL structured value in a database. This interface is used to provide a mapping of the SQL REF value with a Java application.
`ResultSet`	Represents a set of data in the form of a table, which is generated by executing certain specific SQL statements.
`ResultSetMetaData`	Retrieves the information about the types and properties of the columns used in a `ResultSet` object.
`RowID`	A built-in data type, which is used as the identification key of a row in the database table.
`SavePoint`	Represents a point up to which a transaction can be rolled back. Any transactions made by a database can be undone by rolling back the transaction up to the save point. Save points can be named or unnamed according to the user. The unnamed save points can be identified by an ID generated by the data source.
`SQLData`	Provides a custom mapping of the SQL user defined data to a Java class.
`SQLInput`	Provides an input stream of values representing an instance of the SQL structured data types.

Table 3.1: Describing the Interfaces of JDBC 4.0 Core API	
Interfaces	**Description**
`SQLOutput`	Facilitates custom mapping, which is only performed by JDBC drivers. The `SQLOutput` data type is never invoked by any external user.
`Statement`	Executes static SQL statements and returns the results generated by the statements.
`Struct`	Holds the values of the SQL structured type. The instance of the `Struct` is valid till the scope of the application is valid.
`SQLXML`	Maps Java objects with the XML types. XML is a built-in type and is used to store the XML values as a column value in a row of database table.
`Wrapper`	Wraps all the pre-defined data types available in a database. This interface describes a standard mechanism to access the wrapped resources represented by their proxy, to permit direct access to the resource delegate.

The JDBC specification also provides some classes to interact with databases. Table 3.2 lists the classes wrapped into the JDBC core API:

Table 3.2: Describing the Classes of JDBC 4.0 Core API	
Classes	**Description**
`Date`	Represents a wrapper class for time values and the SQL DATE value.
`DriverManager`	Manages the JDBC drivers used in an application.
`DriverPropertyInfo`	Provides information about the specific drivers present in an application. The driver properties are used to make a connection with the specified database.
`SQLPermission`	Provides permission for which the `SecurityManager` will check when code that is running in an applet calls `Drivermanager.setLogWriter()` method or the `DriverManager.setLogStream()` method.
`Time`	Represents a wrapper class for time values used in SQL types. All the time values are present in the `java.util.Date` package.
`Timestamp`	Represents a wrapper class around the `TIMESTAMP` values of the SQL structured types.
`Types`	Provides methods to define the constants for identifying the SQL types, named as JDBC types.

Let's now discuss the enhancements in the JDBC extension API.

The JDBC Extension API

It provides an abstraction to use extension services, such as Connection pooling services and using XA enabled connections for distributed transactions. The classes and interfaces of this part of JDBC API are packed into the `javax.sql` package. Table 3.3 shows the interfaces of the JDBC extension API, available in the `javax.sql` package:

Table 3.3: Describing the Interfaces of the JDBC 4.0 Extension API	
Interfaces	**Description**
`CommonDataSource`	Determines the common features between the `DataSource`, `XADataSource`, and `ConnectionPooledDataSource`.
`ConnectionEventListener`	Notifies the occurrence of an event. This interface is implemented by the `Connection` pooling component.
`ConnectionPoolDataSource`	Implements the named objects by the Java naming and directory services. It is a factory for the `PooledConnection` objects.
`DataSource`	Makes a connection with a database. An object that implements the `DataSource` object must also satisfy the Java naming and directory interface. It is same as the `DriverManager` class.

Table 3.3: Describing the Interfaces of the JDBC 4.0 Extension API

Interfaces	Description
`PooledConnection`	Provides facilities for handling connections to a database, which are pooled. The Connection Pool object generally represents a physical connection with the `DataSource`.
`RowSet`	Provides a set of JavaBeans properties that allow a `RowSet` instance to be configured to connect to a JDBC data source and read some data from the data source.
`RowSetInternal`	Contains methods that allow the reader or writer to access and modify the internal state of the `RowSet` interface.
`RowSetListener`	Implemented by a component that wants to be notified when a significant event occurs in the lifecycle of a `RowSet` object.
`RowSetMetaData`	Provides information about all the columns in a `RowSet` object.
`RowSetReader`	Populates the `RowSet` objects with the data rows.
`RowSetWriter`	Writes data to a `RowSet` by using a `RowSet` object.
`StatementEventListener`	Notifies for an event that is going to happen. All the events that occur in the `PreparedStatement` object are in the `Statement` pool.
`XAConnection`	Provides support for the distributed transactions. A programmer cannot use this interface by a transaction manager working in a middle-tier server.
`XADataSource`	Provides a factory for `XAConnection` objects registered with a naming service by using Java Naming and Directory Interface (JNDI).

In addition to the interfaces, the `javax.sql` package also contains the following two classes for the JDBC extension API:

- **`ConnectionEvent`**—Provides the source of a connection related object. This object is generated when a connection is closed or an error occurs. The `ConnectionEvent` object provides information about:
  - The pooled connection closed by an application
  - The `SQLException` that is to be thrown when an error occurs
- **`RowSetEvent`**—Extends the `EventObject` class and is raised when an error occurs in a `RowSet`. The `RowSetEvent` object is implemented when a row in a `RowSet` is modified or the cursor of the `RowSet` is moved from its original position.

After becoming familiar with the JDBC APIs, let's now move on to understand the new API and features added in JDBC 4.2 version.

Listing the New APIs and Features Added to JDBC 4.2

JDBC 4.2 extends the functionalities and includes the enhancements over JDBC 4.0. The new APIs and features introduced in JDBC 4.2 are:

- Supporting `JDBCType` enum
- Supporting `SQLType` interface
- Supporting REF_CURSOR
- Supporting `DriverAction` interface
- Supporting security check on `deregisterDriver()` method in `DriverManager` class
- Supporting large update counts

Let's now move further to understand the major classes and interfaces in detail, which are required to establish connections with databases.

Describing the Major Classes and Interfaces

We learned about the classes and interfaces of the JDBC core and extension APIs earlier. Let's look at some of these major classes and interfaces in detail. We specifically learn about tne following classes and interfaces:

- The `DriverManager` class
- The `Driver` interface
- The `Connection` interface
- The `Statement` interface

The DriverManager Class

`DriverManager` is a non-abstract class in the JDBC API. It contains only one constructor that is declared private, which implies that this class cannot be inherited or initialized directly. All the methods and properties of this class are declared as static. The main responsibilities of the `DriverManager` class are as follows:

- Maintains a list of the `DriverInfo` objects, where each `DriverInfo` object holds one Driver implementation class object and its name
- Prepares a connection by using the Driver implementation that accepts the given JDBC URL

The methods of `DriverManager` class have been discussed along with their description in Table 3.4:

Table 3.4: Explaining the Methods of the DriverManager Class

Methods	Description
`static void deregisterDriver(Driver driver)`	Drops a driver from the list of drivers maintained by the `DriverManager` class.
`static Connection getConnection(String url)`	Establishes a connection of a driver with a database. The `DriverManager` class selects a driver from the list of drivers and creates the connection.
`static Connection getConnection(String url, Properties info)`	Establishes a connection of a driver with a database. The `DriverManager` class selects a driver from the list of drivers and creates the connection. This method takes two parameters, URL and info. URL is used to load the selected driver for a database. The info parameter provides information about the string/value tags used in the connection.
`static Connection getConnection(String url, String user, String password)`	Establishes a connection of a driver with a database. The `DriverManager` class selects a driver from the list of drivers and creates the connection. Along with URL, it takes two more parameters, user and password. The user parameter specifies the user for which the connection is being made, and the password parameter represents the password of the user.
`static Driver getDriver(String url)`	Locates the requested driver in the `DriverManager` class. The URL parameter specifies the URL of the requested driver.
`static Enumeration<Driver> getDrivers()`	Accesses a list of drivers present in a database.
`static int getLoginTimeout()`	Specifies the maximum time a driver needs to wait to log on to a database.
`static PrintStream getLogStream()`	Returns logging or tracing `PrintStream` object (`Deprecated`).
`public static getLogWriter()`	Returns the log writer.
`static void println(String message)`	Prints a message used in a log stream.
`static void registerDriver(Driver driver)`	Registers a requested driver with the `DriverManager` class.
`static void setLoginTimeout(int seconds)`	Sets the maximum time that a driver needs to wait while attempting to connect to a database.

Table 3.4: Explaining the Methods of the DriverManager Class

Methods	Description
`static void setLogStream(PrintStream out)`	Sets logging or tracing the `PrintStream` object, which is used by the `DriverManager`.
`static void setLogWriter(PrintWriter out)`	Sets logging or tracing the `PrintWriter` object.

The Driver Interface

`Driver` is the basic interface that every JDBC driver provider has to implement. Generally, we use the term driver class to refer to the implementation class of this interface. The `Driver` interface provides an entry point for database connectivity in response to connection requests. The `Driver` is an interface defined under JDBC API to describe an object (implemented by 3rd party vendor) that is responsible to establish connection to database. All the driver classes implement this interface to connect to a database. The driver interface provides an abstraction to perform various operations implemented by a third party vendor, such as establish a session to the database, get the major and minor versions of the Driver, and find the JDBC driver compliance.

Table 3.5 lists all the enclosed methods in the `Driver` interface:

Table 3.5: Explaining the Methods of the Driver Interface

Methods	Description
`boolean acceptsURL(String url)`	Checks whether or not the format of the given URL is according to the driver. It checks the sub protocol and extra information of the URL.
`Connection connect(String url, Properties info)`	Establishes connectivity with a database. The URL parameter specifies the JDBC URL that describes the database details to which the driver is to be connected. The info parameter specifies the information of the tag/value pair used in the driver.
`int getMajorVersion()`	Accesses the major version number of the driver.
`int getMinorVersion()`	Retrieves the minor version number of the driver.
`DriverPropertyInfo[] getPropertyInfo(String url, Properties info)`	Retrieves the properties of the driver included in a database.
`boolean jdbcCompliant()`	Determines whether or not the driver is JDBC compliant. The true value of the Boolean data type represents that the driver is JDBC complaint; else, this method returns false.

The Connection Interface

The `Connection` interface is a standard type that defines an abstraction to access the session established with a database server. JDBC driver provider must implement the `Connection` interface. Connection type of object (that is, an instance of the class that implements the `Connection` interface) represents the session established with the data store. The `java.sql.Connection` interface, part of JDBC API, is designed to describe an object representing the session established to server (DB server). Such an object is generally termed as JDBC connection/connection object. The JDBC connection helps to perform following operations:

a. Set the session level properties
b. Create JDBC statement objects
c. Control local transaction
d. Create SQL 99 Types object, such as BLOB and CLOB. Note this ability of JDBC Connection is new in JDBC 4.0.

The `Connection` interface provides methods for handling a connection object listed in Table 3.6:

Table 3.6: Describing the Methods of the Connection Interface

Methods	Description
`void clearWarnings()`	Clears all the warnings for a connection object. This method throws a

Table 3.6: Describing the Methods of the Connection Interface

Methods	Description
	`SQLException` when an error occurs.
`void close()`	Closes a connection and releases the connection object associated with the connected database. It also releases the JDBC resources associated with the connection.
`void commit()`	Commits the changes made in the previous commit/rollback and releases any database locks held by the current `Connection` object.
`Statement createStatement()`	Create a `Statement` object to send SQL statements to the specified database. This method takes no argument; therefore, it can be executed by using the `Statement` object.
`Statement createStatement(int resultSetType, int resultSetConcurrency)`	Creates a `Statement` object, which is used to load the SQL statements to the specified database. The `ResultSet` object generated by this `Statement` object is of mentioned type and concurrency.
`Statement createStatement(int resultSetType, int resultSetConcurrency, int resultSetHoldability)`	Creates an object with the mentioned type, concurrency, and holdability.
`boolean getAutoCommit()`	Retrieves the auto-commit mode for the current `Connection` object.
`String getCatalog()`	Retrieves the current catalog name used in the current `Connection` object.
`int getHoldability()`	Retrieves the current holdability of the `ResultSet` object created by using a `Connection` object.
`DatabaseMetaData getMetaData()`	Retrieves the `DatabaseMetadata` object, which contains the `MetaData` about a database. The database must be connected with a `connection` object. The metadata provides the information about the tables, and stored procedures of the current `Connection` object.
`int getTransactionIsolation()`	Returns the transaction isolation level of the `Connection` object associated with a database.
`Map getTypeMap()`	Retrieves a map object associated with a `Connection` object.
`SQLwarning getWarnings()`	Retrieves any warning associated with a `Connection` object.
`boolean isClosed()`	Specifies whether a database `Connection` object is still valid or closed.
`boolean isReadOnly()`	Specifies whether or not a `Connection` object is read-only.
`String nativeSQL(String sql)`	Converts the SQL statements passed to the `Connection` object into the systems native SQL grammar.
`CallableStatement prepareCall(String sql)`	Creates a `CallableStatement` object for calling database stored procedures.
`CallableStatement prepareCall(String sql, int resultSetType, int resultSetConcurrency)`	Creates a `CallableStatement` object, which generates the `ResultSet` object of the given type and concurrency.
`CallableStatement prepareCall(String sql, int resultSetType, int resultSetConcurrency, int resultSetHoldability)`	Creates a `CallableStatement` object, which generates the `ResultSet` object of the given type, concurrency, and holdability.
`PreparedStatement prepareStatement(String sql)`	Creates a `PreparedStatement` object for sending SQL statements over a connection.

Table 3.6: Describing the Methods of the Connection Interface

Methods	Description
PreparedStatement prepareStatement(String sql, int autoGeneratedKeys)	Creates a PreparedStatement object that retrieves auto-generated keys.
PreparedStatement prepareStatement(String sql, int[] columnIndexes)	Creates a PreparedStatement object that retrieves auto-generated keys by using a given array.
PreparedStatement prepareStatement(String sql, int resultSetType, int resultSetConcurrency)	Generates a PreparedStatement object that generates the ResultSet object with the given type and concurrency.
PreparedStatement prepareStatement(String sql, int resultSetType, int resultSetConcurrency, int resultSetHoldability)	Generates a PreparedStatement object that generates the ResultSet object with the given type, concurrency, and holdability.
PreparedStatement prepareStatement(String sql, String[] columnNames) Creates a default	Creates a PreparedStatement object that retrieves the auto-generated keys. The columnNames parameter of PreparedStatement is an array containing the names of the columns that contain the auto-generated keys in the target table.
void releaseSavepoint(Savepoint savepoi nt)	Releases the save point associated with the connection object of the current transaction.
void rollback ()	Rolls back all transactions and releases any database locks that are currently done by the connection object.
void rollback(Savepoint savepoint)	Undo all the changes made by the connection object after a save point object is created.
void setAutoCommit(boolean autoCommit)	Sets the current transaction to the connections auto-commit mode.
void setCatalog(String catalog)	Sets the given catalog name for current Connection object's database.
void setHoldability(int holdability)	Changes the holdability of the current Connection object.
void setReadOnly(boolean readOnly)	Sets the connection to the read-only mode to optimize the specified database.
Savepoint setSavepoint() Creates an unnamed savepoint in	Creates an unnamed Savepoint in the current transaction and returns the save point associated with the previous transactions.
Savepoint setSavepoint(String name)	Creates a save point with the name specified in the current transaction. It returns the new Savepoint object.
void setTransactionIsolation(int level)	Checks the transaction isolation level of the specified connection object.
void setTypeMap(Map map)	Installs the TypeMap object as the current type map for the current connection.

The Connection interface also provides certain constants, which can be used for handling connection transactions. Table 3.7 lists the constants available in the Connection interface:

Table 3.7: Explaining the Constants of the Connection Interface

Constants	Description
static int TRANSACTION_NONE	Indicates that connection transactions are not supported in the current transaction object.
static int TRANSACTION_READ_COMMITTED	Prevents transaction from reading a row with uncommitted changes.

Table 3.7: Explaining the Constants of the Connection Interface	
Constants	**Description**
	It is only used to read non repeatable rows in a table.
`static int TRANSACTION_READ_UNCOMMITTED`	Indicates that non-repeatable and phantom reads are allowed in a transaction. It allows a row to be changed during a transaction. The changed row can be read by other transactions before the changes in the row are committed.
`static int TRANSACTION_REPEATABLE_READ`	Prevents non-repeatable reads and simultaneous transactions in a single row.
`static int TRANSACTION_SERIALIZABLE`	Prevents reading non-repeatable rows in a table.

Let's now learn about the `Statement` interface.

The Statement Interface

The `java.sql.Statement` interface is a part of JDBC API that abstracts an object (implemented as a part of JDBC driver) responsible to drive the SQL statement to DB, execute it (in DB), and return the result. We use Statement in Java application to execute simple SQL statements and collect the result. A Statement object can open a single `ResultSet` object at a time. Therefore, if the reading of one `ResultSet` object is interleaved with the reading of the other, each must have been generated by different `Statement` objects. All the `execute()` methods of the Statement interface implicitly close a statement's current `ResultSet` object if it is open. The `Statement` interface provides specific methods to execute and retrieve the results from a database. The `PreparedStatement` interface provides the methods for dealing with the `IN` parameters whereas the `CallableStatement` interface provides methods to deal with the `IN` and `OUT` parameters.

The `Statement` interface also provides certain methods that are used with a database, as listed in Table 3.8:

Table 3.8: Describing the Methods of the Statement Interface	
Methods	**Description**
`void addBatch(String sql)`	Adds the SQL commands to the existing list of commands for the statement object. These commands are executed in a batch by calling the `executeBatch ()` method.
`void cancel()`	Cancels the statement, if the data sources do not support the statement.
`void clearBatch()`	Clears all the commands listed in the batch of the `Statement` interface.
`void clearWarnings()`	Clears all the warnings that are reported on the statement object. After the execution of this method, the `getWarnings()` method will return null until a new warning is reported for this statement.
`void close()`	Closes the `Statement` object. Therefore, it releases its control from the database and also from the connection.
`boolean execute(String sql)`	Executes the SQL commands, which may return multiple result sets and one or more update counts.
`boolean execute(String sql, int autoGeneratedKeys)`	Executes the SQL commands, which may return multiple result sets and one or more update counts. It also indicates whether a driver or the auto-generated keys are available for the retrieval.
`boolean execute(String sql, int[] columnIndexes)`	Executes the SQL commands, which may return multiple result sets and one or more update counts. It also indicates the driver about the availability of the auto-generated keys in an array. The array contains the list of the indexes and the tables containing the auto-generated keys.
`boolean execute(String sql, String[] columnNames)`	Executes the SQL commands, which may return multiple result sets and one or more update counts. It also indicates the driver about the availability of the auto-generated keys in an array. The array contains the name of the columns in the target table, which contains the auto-generated keys.

Table 3.8: Describing the Methods of the Statement Interface

Methods	Description
`int[] executeBatch()`	Executes the SQL commands in a batch. On successful execution of the batch statements, the method will return the update count as an integer greater or equal to 0. The integer array is used to represent the array of the SQL commands listed in the batch.
`ResultSet executeQuery(String sql)`	Executes a SQL command and returns a single result set.
`int executeUpdate(String sql)`	Executes the `INSERT`, `UPDATE`, and `DELETE` statements or the SQL DDL statements.
`int executeUpdate(String sql, int autoGeneratedKeys)`	Executes the SQL statements and notifies the driver for the availability of the auto-generated keys. The auto-generated keys are responsible for the data retrieval from the database.
`int executeUpdate(String sql, int[] columnIndexes)`	Executes the SQL statements and notifies the driver for the availability of the auto-generated keys in the `columnIndexes` array. The array index of the auto-generated keys indicates the indexes and the tables, which contain the auto-generated keys.
`int executeUpdate(String sql, String[] columnNames)`	Executes the SQL statements and notifies the driver for the availability of the auto-generated keys in the `columnNames` array. The array index of the auto-generated keys indicates the columns of the target table, which contains the auto-generated keys.
`Connection getConnection()`	Accepts the connection object made to the database.
`int getFetchDirection()`	Fetches the direction of the rows from the database tables that are generated from the result set. The fetch direction for a statement object is set by using the `setFetchDirection()` method. If the fetch direction is not set, then the fetch direction is implementation specific.
`int getFetchSize()`	Retrieves the number of rows of default fetch size from the `ResultSet` object generated from the `statement` object.
`ResultSet getGeneratedKeys()`	Retrieves the auto-generated keys created by executing the `statement` object.
`int getMaxFieldSize()`	Retrieves the maximum number of bytes that can be returned for the column values. These column values are obtained by executing the `ResultSet` object that is returned by the `Statement` object.
`int getMaxRows()`	Returns the maximum number of rows in a `ResultSet` produced by the statement object.
`boolean getMoreResults()`	Moves to the next result in the statement's object. It is also used to close the currently opened result set.
`int getMoreResults(int current)`	Moves to the next result in the statement's object. It deals with the result set object by using the instructions specified in the given flag.
`int getQueryTimeout()`	Retrieves the number of seconds that the driver has to wait to execute the statements.
`ResultSet getResultSet()`	Retrieves the current `ResultSet` object generated by the `statement` object.
`int getResultSetConcurrency()`	Retrieves the concurrency of the `Resultset` object generated by the `statement` object.
`int getResultSetHoldability()`	Retrieves the holdability of the `Resultset` object generated by the `statement` object.
`int getResultSetType()`	Retrieves the result set type for the `Resultset` object generated by the `statement` object.

Table 3.8: Describing the Methods of the Statement Interface	
Methods	**Description**
`int getUpdateCount()`	Retrieves the current result set as an update count. This method usually returns a positive value; however, if a negative value is returned, it indicates that there are no results available in the `Resultset`.
`SQLWarning getWarnings()`	Retrieves the warnings reported on the statements object.
`void setCursorName(String name)`	Sets the cursor name to the given string. The cursor name is used by the statement objects to execute the method.
`void setEscapeProcessing(boolean enable)`	Sets the escape processing on or off.
`void setFetchDirection(int direction)`	Sets the direction for the driver for processing the rows in the `ResultSet` object.
`void setFetchSize(int rows)`	Indicates the driver about the number of rows that should be fetched from the database.
`void setMaxFieldSize(int max)`	Sets the maximum number of bytes for the `ResultSet` to store the binary values.
`void setMaxRows(int max)`	Sets the maximum number of rows that a `ResultSet` can contain.
`void setQueryTimeout(int seconds)`	Sets the number of seconds that a driver has to wait for a statement object to execute.

The `Statement` interface also comprises few constants, which are listed in Table 3.9:

Table 3.9: Explaining the Constants of the Statement Interface	
Constants	**Description**
`static int CLOSE_ALL_RESULTS`	Closes all the open `ResultSet` objects. All the `ResultSets` should be closed before calling the `getMoreResults ()` method.
`static int CLOSE_CURRENT_RESULT`	Indicates that the current `ResultSet` connected with the specified database must be closed before calling the `getMoreResults()` method.
`static int EXECUTE_FAILED`	Indicates the occurrence of error while executing a batch statement.
`static int KEEP_CURRENT_RESULT`	Indicates that the current `Resultset` should not be closed before calling the `getMoreResults()` method.
`static int NO_GENERATED_KEYS`	Indicates that the generated keys should not be made available for retrieval.
`static int RETURN_GENERATED_KEYS`	Indicates that the generated keys should be made available for retrieval.
`static int SUCCESS_NO_INFO`	Indicates that a batch statement has been executed successfully.

After understanding the methods of the `Statement` interface, you must know how to create the `Statement` object and invoke the `createStatement()` method.

Creating a Statement Object

A `Statement` object is created after the connection to the specified database is made. It is created by using the `createStatement()` method of the `Connection` interface, as shown in the following code snippet:

```
Connection con = DriverManager.getConnection (url, username, password);
Statement stmt = con.createStatement ();
```

In the preceding code snippet, the `Connection` object is created to establish a connection with the help of the `getConnection()` method of the `DriverManager` class, and the resultant is stored in the con reference of `Connection` interface type. Then, the `con` object is used to invoke the `createStatement()` method, and the resultant is stored in the `stmt` reference of the `Statement` interface.

Communicating with Databases by using JDBC APIs

You must have understood that JDBC API allows to access JDBC driver to drive the SQL statements to execute in DB. Moreover, to execute SQL statement, you need to establish a session within which all the queries can be executed. After understanding that JDBC driver is a process for communicating with database by using JDBC APIs, you must be thinking that how you can access JDBC driver to establish session to database. In addition, you must also be having the question that which JDBC type can be used to represent the opened session.

We use the `Driver` object to access the JDBC driver for establishing a session to database. In addition, the `Connection` is a JDBC object that represents the session opened to the database. Therefore, we understand that as a first step to communicate with database using JDBC API, we want to obtain a connection. While writing the database programming in a Java application, you need to perform various steps to establish a connection with a database. Figure 3.1 shows the basic steps involved in writing database programming in Java using JDBC:

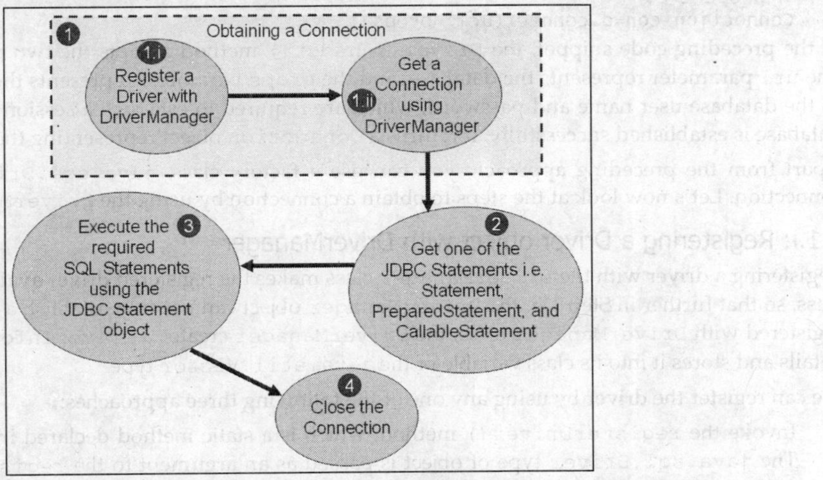

Figure 3.1: Showing the Basic Steps to Use JDBC

Let's discuss the basic steps, shown in Figure 3.1, to implement JDBC in Java applications in detail.

Step 1: Obtaining a Connection

In this step, we want to instantiate a `Connection` object, which establishes a session to the database server. There are the following three approaches to obtain a connection.

- Using a `Driver` object
- Using a `DriverManager` class
- Using `DataSource` object

In this section, let's learn how to obtain connection by using the first two approaches, and the third approach is discussed later in Chapter 5 under the Connection Pool section. In the following section, let's explore the first two approaches of obtaining the connection.

Obtaining a Connection

The following steps are involved in creating a connection:

- You can use the `java.lang.Class.newInstance()` method to create a `Driver` object, which can avoid the preceding problems, as shown in the following code snippet:

```
Class c=Class.forName("oracle.jdbc.driver.OracleDrive");
Driver d= (Driver)c.newInstance();
```

- In the preceding code snippet, we access the Java core API, the `forName()` method of the `Class` class. The `Class.forName()` method loads the `OracleDrive` class into the JVM if it is not loaded earlier. This returns the `java.lang.Class` object representing the given class loaded into this JVM. The `Class` object includes a support to instantiate the class that it is representing. The `Class.newInstance()` method is used to instantiate an object by using a no-argument constructor. The `Class.newInstance()` method in the preceding code snippet creates an instance of `oracle.jdbc.driver.OracleDrive`, which is a subtype of `java.sql.Driver` interface of JDBC API.

- Since this approach overcomes the problems of the preceding approach; thereby, this approach is better to create a `Driver` object.

Establish a connection

After creating the Driver object, we can establish a connection to database by using the `Driver.connect()` method, as shown in the following code snippet:

```
Driver d= (Driver) (Class.forName("oracle.jdbc.driver.OracleDrive")).newInstance();
//Prepare java.util.Properties object encapsulating the database / driver specific
  properties
Connection con=d.connect(url, props);
```

In the preceding code snippet, the `Driver.connect()` method accepts the two parameters, `url` and `props`. The `url` parameter represents the database, and the `props` parameter represents the connection properties, such as the database user name and password, which are required to establish a session to database. If the session to database is established successfully, it returns a `Connection` object representing the session established.

Apart from the preceding approach, you can use a factory class, `java.sql.DriverManager` to establish a connection. Let's now look at the steps to obtain a connection by using the `DriverManager` class.

Step 1.i: Registering a Driver object with DriverManager

Registering a driver with the `DriverManager` class makes the registered driver available to the `DriverManager` class, so that further in Step 1.ii, the `DriverManager` object can use it to establish a connection. When a driver is registered with `DriverManager` class, the `DriverManager` creates a `DriverInfo` object to maintain the driver details and stores it into its class variable of the `java.util.Vector` type.

We can register the driver by using any one of the following three approaches:

a. Invoke the `registerDriver()` method, which is a static method declared in the `DriverManager` class. The `java.sql.Driver` type of object is passed as an argument to the `registerDriver()` method. The following snippet shows how to register the `Driver` object with `DriverManager`:

```
DriverManager.registerDriver (new oracle.jdbc.driver.OracleDrive());
```

b. Invoke the `Class.forName (<driver class name>)` method, which is used to explicitly load the driver class. According to the JDBC specifications, every JDBC driver implementation class should contain a static block, which should invoke a `registerDriver()` method passing an object of the driver implementation class as an argument.

NOTE

It is recommended to call the `newInstance()` method on the Class object, which is returned by the `Class.forName()` method as some of the JVMs do not call the static initializers until an instance of the class is created.

c. Set the `System` property, where the name of the property is `jdbc.drivers`. The value of the System property can be mapped to one or more driver implementation class names, where ':' character is used as a delimiter. The following snippet shows how to register the driver with the `DriverManager` class:

```
System.setProperty ("jdbc.drivers", "oracle.jdbc.driver.OracleDrive");
```

Use the above method in the application, or while executing the application using a Java command, we can set system properties using the –D option of java command, for example:

```
java -Djdbc.drivers=oracle.jdbc.driver.OracleDrive MyJdbcEx1
```

Note that in JDBC 4.2 specification, the `DriverManager.getConnection()` method has been enhanced to support the Java Standard Edition Service Provider mechanism. With this feature, the `DriverManager` can locate and load the `Driver` object described into the `META-INF/services/java.sql.Driver` file. Therefore, while working with JDBC 4.2 driver, we do not need to perform this step; that is, explicitly registering a Driver with `DriverManager`.

Step 1.ii: Establishing a Connection using DriverManager

After registering the driver with `DriverManager`, we can now create or establish the connection with a database. To create a connection using `DriverManager`, invoke any one of the following methods of the `DriverManager` class:

- `getConnection (String url)`
- `getConnection (String url, String username, String password)`
- `getConnection (String url, Properties info)`

Where `<url>` is a JDBC URL, which represents a unique name used to identify the driver and obtain the connection. The JDBC URL even contains additional information, such as username and password, required to establish the connection. The syntax of the JDBC URL is as follows:

```
jdbc: <sub protocol> : <info>
```

In the preceding syntax:

- **`jdbc`**—Represents the protocol in a JDBC URL
- **`<sub protocol>`**—Specifies the vendor-specific name of the driver used to create the connection
- **`<info>`**—Takes additional information required to establish the connection, such as the database name and port number, which varies from one driver to another

The following code snippet shows JDBC URL:

- For Oracle Type-2 driver:

```
String dbName = "sandb";
String oracleURL = "jdbc:oracle:oci8:@" + dbName;
//oracleURL = "jdbc:oracle:oci8:@sandb"
```

- For Oracle Type-4 driver

```
String host = "localhost";
String dbName = "sandb";
int port = 1521;

String oracleURL = "jdbc:oracle:thin:@" + host + ":" + port + ":" + dbName;
//oracleURL = "jdbc:oracle:thin:@localhost:1521:sandb" ;
```

When the `getConnection()` method is invoked, it checks if any one of the drivers registered with the `DriverManager` class (refer to Step 1.i discussed earlier) recognizes the given JDBC URL. If a driver accepts the URL, the driver is used by `DriverManager` to establish the connection with the DBMS located by the given JDBC URL. Moreover, if no driver accepts the URL, `DriverManager` class throws a `SQLException` to the application.

NOTE

The following are possible exceptions raised while executing this step:

a. *Class Not Found Exception — The specified `Driver` class is not available in the JVMs class loaders scope*

b. *SQLException — This exception can be thrown for the following reasons:*

   i. *Driver objects failed to understand given JDBC URL (i.e., it may not be in Driver understandable format)*

   ii. *Driver failed to locate DB Server*

   iii. *User Authentication failed at the DB server*

   iv. *DB Sessions are not available (i.e., possibly the max sessions are opened and all are busy)*

Step 2: Creating a JDBC Statement Object

After the connection is made, we need to create the JDBC `Statement` object to execute the SQL statements. The utility objects available to execute SQL statements are `Statement`, `PreparedStatement`, and `CallableStatement`.

NOTE

In this chapter, we only learn how to get a `Statement` object and use it to execute SQL statements. The next chapter discusses about `PreparedStatement` and `CallableStatement`.

To create a `Statement` object, invoke the `createStatement()` method on the current `Connection` object, "connection". The following code snippet shows how to create a `Statement` object by using the `createStatement()` method:

```
Statement stmt = connection.createStatement();
```

Step 3: Executing SQL Statements

After the `Statement` object is created, it is used to execute the SQL statements. The `Statement.execute()`, `Statement.executeUpdate()`, or `Statement.executeQuery()` methods can be used to execute the SQL Statement. For the database operations, such as INSERT, UPDATE, and DELETE, the `executeUpdate()` method is used to execute the statements. The `executeQuery()` method is only used to execute the SELECT statement. Whereas the `execute()` method is generic, which can be used to execute any SQL statement. The following code snippet shows how to execute an SQL statement:

```
//Using executeQuery()
String query = "SELECT col1, col2, col3 FROM table_name";
ResultSet results = stmt.executeQuery(query);
//Using executeUpdate()
String query= "INSERT into table_name values (value1, value2…value n)";
int count = stmt.executeUpdate(query);
```

If the statement produces a `ResultSet` object after executing the SQL statements, the `ResultSet` instance is used to retrieve the result. The `next ()` method of the `ResultSet` is used to navigate through a row at a time. The following snippet shows the use of the `ResultSet` within a connection:

```
while(resultSet.next()) {
   System.out.println(results.getString(1) + " " +
   results.getString(2) + " " +
   results.getString(3));
}
```

In the preceding code snippet, the `ResultSet` is used to retrieve and read the data from the database. Then, the resultant data is displayed.

Step 4: Closing the Connection

Now, after executing all the required SQL statements and obtaining the results, we need to close the connection and release the session. This can be done by calling the `close()` method of the Connection interface. The following code snippet shows how to close a connection:

```
connection.close();
```

Now, let's understand the various JDBC drivers.

Understanding Various JDBC Drivers

The following types of JDBC drivers are commonly used to communicate with Oracle database:

- OCI8 Driver (Type-2)
- IDS Driver (Type-3)
- Oracle Thin Driver (Type-4)

Let's now discuss these drivers.

The OCI8 Driver for Oracle

The Oracle Call Interface (OCI) driver is a JDBC implementation from Oracle Corporation for communicating with Oracle database. This is implemented by using Type-2 driver architecture; it uses the Oracle's call interface that is written in C language. That means this is not a pure Java driver; therefore, it is not platform independent. The `driver` class name and the JDBC URL to use this JDBC driver implementation are:

- **driverClassName**—`oracle.jdbc.driver.OracleDriver`

- **JDBC URL**—`jdbc:oracle:oci8:@<service name>`

To use OCI8 driver, we perform the following configurations:

- Set path to `<oracle home>\ora81\bin`
- Set classpath to `<oracle home>\ora81\jdbc\lib\classes12.zip (or ojdbc14.jar)`

The IDS Driver

The IDS driver is implemented by using Type-3 driver architecture. This is the most preferred driver to work with Java Applets. The IDS driver is also called the pure Java driver. It does not require any client-side configuration for database communication. The IDS driver is compatible with all the features of JDBC 4.2. To use the IDS driver, you need to download and install the IDS Server. The IDS Server provides a JDBC specific IDS driver for Java and Java EE specific applications. The IDS Server can be downloaded from *http://www.idssoftware.com*.

Oracle Thin Driver

The thin driver for Oracle is implemented on the basis of the Type-4 pure Java driver. Nowadays, the Type-4 driver is widely used because of its simplicity and high performance. As the Type-4 driver is entirely written in Java, it is platform independent and does not require any additional software to be installed on the client side. It can be used on the client side as well as on the server side. The application server is used to access the driver on the client side, whereas the database instance is used to access the driver on the server side. The following configurations need to be performed to access the Type-4 thin driver:

- **driverClassName**—`oracle.jdbc.driver.OracleDriver`
- **url**—`jdbc:oracle:thin:@<host name>:<port>:<database name>` Where
  - `<host name>` is the ip address or host name of the machine, where Oracle data base server is running.
  - `<port>` takes the port number on which Oracle `tns` server is started. The default port number is 1521.
  - `<database name>` takes the Oracle database (i.e., Global Data Base (GDB)) name. For example, `jdbc:oracle:thin:@mysys:1521:sandb`

To use this driver with the configuration, you need to:

- Set classpath to `<oracle home>\ora81\jdbc\lib\classes12.zip`

Summary

In this chapter, we discussed the JDBC APIs comprising core as well as extension APIs, new features added to JDBC 4.2, and the major classes along with interfaces used to create JDBC applications. Then, you studied how to establish connection with databases by using JDBC APIs. At the end, you explored various types of JDBC drivers.

Let's recall the following important points to summarize the chapter:

- JDBC API acts as a standard abstraction between the Java application and the 3rd party implemented JDBC drivers, which makes the Java application to use JDBC driver vendor (JDBC driver provider) independently.
- JDBC API is mainly divided into two packages, `java.sql` and `javax.sql`.
- The new APIs and features introduced in JDBC 4.2 are `JDBCType` enum and `SQLType` interface. It also supports REF_CURSOR.
- The `java.sql.Driver` is an interface defined under JDBC API to describe an object (implemented by 3rd party vendor) that is responsible to establish connection to database.
- The `Connection` interface, part of JDBC API, is designed to describe an object representing the session established to server (DB server). Such an object is generally termed as JDBC connection or `Connection` object.
- The `Statement` interface is a part of JDBC API that abstracts an object (implemented as a part of JDBC driver) that is responsible to drive the SQL statement to DB, execute it (in DB), and return the result.

In the next chapter, we learn about the JDBC ResultSets and Statements.

Exercise

Q. 3.1 Name two parts of JDBC APIs.

Q. 3.2 Mention two new features added in JDBC 4.2.

Q. 3.3 What is `java.sql.Connection`?

Q. 3.4 What is `java.sql.Statement`?

Q. 3.5 Write the syntax of a JDBC URL.

Q. 3.6 Give one sample of JDBC URL to connect to Oracle database by using JDBC Type-4 driver.

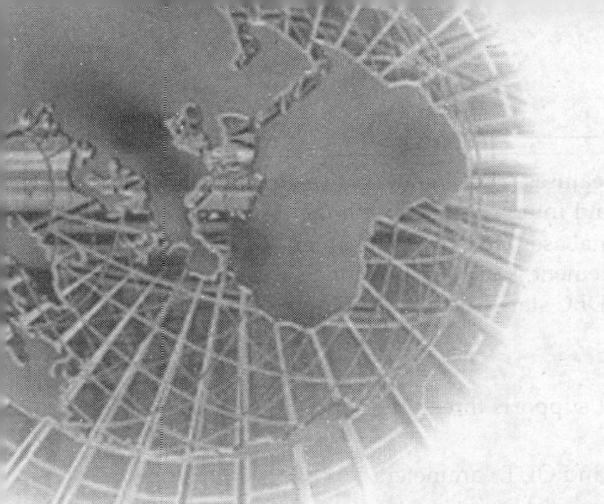

4

Implementing JDBC Statements and ResultSets

In the previous chapter, we introduced you to JDBC API, its features, and the additional features included in JDBC 4.2 API. We also discussed about the JDBC API classes and interfaces used with the `Java` application to access the JDBC driver, and understood how to connect to Database (DB). In this chapter, we focus on JDBC objects, such as JDBC statements and `ResultSet`. A JDBC statement is used to execute SQL statements, while `ResultSet` is used to retrieve results. Let's first discuss about JDBC statements in detail.

Describing JDBC Statements

JDBC statements are used to execute SQL statements. JDBC API supports three types of JDBC statement objects to work with SQL statements, which are as follows:

- **`Statement`**—Executes normal SQL statements with no IN and OUT parameters
- **`PreparedStatement`**—Executes parameterized SQL statement that supports IN parameters
- **`CallableStatement`**—Executes parameterized SQL statement that invokes DB procedure or function and supports IN and OUT parameters

Let's now discuss these three types of JDBC statement objects in detail.

Working with the Statement Interface

The `Statement` object executes a normal SQL statement to update or query the database. The `java.sql.Statement` interface is a part of JDBC API that describes a standard abstraction for the `Statement` object, which is implemented as a part of JDBC driver. A `Statement` object sends the required SQL statement as a query and then returns a set of results, if needed, in response to that query. In addition, the `Statement` object supports two main types of SQL statements: `Update` statements, which are normally used for operations that do not generate a response data, and `Query` statements, which return some response data. We can use the `createStatement()` method of the `Connection` object to obtain a `Statement` object. The `Statement` object is associated with a `Connection` object.

In this section, let's explore the methods that can be invoked with the `Statement` object and then create an application to demonstrate the implementation of Statement.

Exploring the Methods of Statement

You can create multiple `Statement` objects by using a single `Connection` object. The following methods of the `Connection` object are used to retrieve a `Statement` object:

- **`createStatement()`**—Retrieves a statement that can produce a `ResultSet` of the forward-only type and read-only concurrency
- **`createStatement (int ResultSetType, int ResultSetConcurrency)`**—Retrieves a statement that can produce a `ResultSet` of the given type and concurrency
- **`createStatement (int ResultSetType, int ResultSetConcurrency, int ResultSetHoldability)`**—Retrieves a statement that can produce a ResultSet of the given type, concurrency, and holdability

Note that the previously mentioned methods set the `ResultSet` type, concurrency, and holdability of the `Statement` object. We learn about the `ResultSet` and its types later in this chapter.

After discussing how to get a `Statement` object, let's now discuss about some of the methods of the `Statement` object. The following are some of the methods supported by the `Statement` object:

- executeUpdate(String sqlStatement)
- executeQuery(String query)
- execute(String sqlStatement)
- getResultSet()
- getUpdateCount()
- executeUpdate(String sqlStatement)

Let's explore each of these methods of the `Statement` object in detail.

The executeUpdate(String sqlStatement) Method

The `executeUpdate(String)` method executes the SQL statement that creates, inserts, updates, and deletes the database. The SQL statement that updates the database does not return a request set; instead, it specifies the number of records affected by executing this SQL statement. The `executeUpdate()` method returns the `int` value that specifies the number of records affected by the executed SQL statement. Alternatively, the `executeUpdate()` method returns the statement SUCCESS_NO_INFO value, which indicates that the given SQL statement has been successfully executed but the number of records affected is not known. This method may throw `SQLException` in the following cases:

a. The connection to which the `Statement` object was associated is closed.

b. There are network problems to reach DB.

c. There are grammar errors in the given SQL statement.

d. There are problems in executing the SQL statement in DB.

e. The given SQL statement is producing a result table (the input SQL statement is `SELECT` statement).

The following code snippet describes how to use the `executeUpdate()` method:

```
Statement st = con.createStatement();
String sqlStatement = "insert into dept values(50, 'newDept', 'hyderabad')";
try {
//Execute the Query
int count = st.executeUpdate (sqlStatement);
} catch(SQLException e) {
  //Handle exception
}
```

In the preceding code snippet, the `String` variable passed to the `executeUpdate()` method is the SQL statement that has to be executed. The `executeUpdate()` method executes the given SQL statement and returns the integer value as the result. The integer value represents the number of rows affected by the SQL statement.

The executeQuery(String query) Method

The `executeQuery(String)` method is used to execute the SQL statement to query the database. For example, you can execute the `SELECT` statement to retrieve the records from the database. This method returns the query results in the form of a `ResultSet` object. The `ResultSet` object contains the group of results generated after executing the specified SQL query. The following code snippet shows how you can use the `executeQuery()` method to access the data in a table:

```
Statement st = con.createStatement();
String query = "SELECT * from table_name";
ResultSet res = st.executeQuery(query);
while (res.next()) {
//get the data from ResultSet object referred by res, and process the data
}
con.close();
```

The execute(String sqlStatement) Method

The `execute()` method is a generic method that executes any SQL statement used to update or query the database. This method returns a boolean value indicating whether or not the given SQL statement has generated a `ResultSet`. If the boolean value evaluates to true, the `ResultSet` is generated, otherwise it implies that the SQL statement has not generated a `ResultSet`. You can use the `execute()` method to execute Data Definition Language (DDL) or dynamic SQL statements that are dynamically assigned as inputs to the application. Dynamic SQL statements are generated and assigned at runtime and are not specified at the development time. The `execute()` method is not restricted to return a single result; therefore, it can return multiple results. In addition, it is independent of the type of SQL statement on which it is called. The method throws `SQLException` in case of an error. The syntax of this method is as follows:

```
public boolean execute(String sql)
   throws SQLException
```

The execute() method is supported by the Statement.getResultSet() and Statement.getUpdateCount() methods to read the result of the executed SQL statement.

The getResultSet() Method

The getResultSet() method returns the current ResultSet associated with a Statement object. This method is used along with the execute() method, explained earlier. The ResultSet is generated by executing the SQL query and using the execute() method. If the execute() method returns true, we can use the getResultSet() method to obtain the ResultSet. The following code snippet shows how to use the getResultSet() method to access the current ResultSet associated with a Statement object:

```
Statement st = con.createStatement();
String query = "SELECT * from table_name";
if( st.execute (query)) {
   ResultSet rs = st.getResultSet( )
   //get the data from ResultSet and process it
}
con.close();
```

The getUpdateCount() Method

The getUpdateCount() method returns the number of records affected after executing an SQL statement using the execute() method. However, if the execute() method returns false, you can use the getUpdateCount() method to obtain the update count value. The getUpdateCount() method returns an integer value that represents the number of rows affected by executing the SQL statement or alternatively returns the Statement.SUCCESS_NO_INFO value, which indicates that the given SQL statement has been executed successfully but the number of records affected is not known.

After understanding the methods of the Statement interface, let's create an application to implement the Statement interface.

Using Statement

You can create a table by using the CREATE statement. Most of the times, the database administrator creates a table through the interactive editor provided by Database Management System (DBMS). However, at times, we may want to create the database table dynamically. For example, you may want to develop a generic application that stores or retrieves data from a database table. In this application, you can provide an added feature that automatically creates a table based on the descriptions in the application-specific configuration file.

Let's create an application to create a table by using a JDBC statement. You must note that in this application, you create a table, called mytable, that contains three columns, which are as follows:

- **COL1** – Holds string values
- **COL2** – Holds integer values
- **COL3** – Holds floating-point numbers

Now, let's create the mytable table by using the CREATE statement.

Creating a Table

In this subsection, let's learn how to create a table by using the SQL CREATE statement through JDBC. In Listing 4.1, we use the CREATE statement to create a table through JDBC APIs. Listing 4.1 provides the code to create a mytable table dynamically (you can find the CreateTable.java file online in the code/Chapter4 folder):

Listing 4.1: Showing the code for the CreateTable.java File

```
package com.santosh.jdbc;

import java.sql.*;
/**
* @author Santosh
*/
public class CreateTable {
   public static void main(String args[])
         throws SQLException, ClassNotFoundException {
```

```
        //Get Connection
        Connection con=prepareConnection ();

        // obtain a Statement
        Statement st=con.createStatement ();

        String query = "create table mytable (COL1 varchar2 (20),
        COL2 number, COL3 number (10, 2))";

        //Execute the Query
        st.executeUpdate (query);

        System.out.println ("Table created successfully");
        con.close();
    }// End of main

    public static Connection prepareConnection()
        throws SQLException, ClassNotFoundException {

        String driverClassName="oracle.jdbc.driver.OracleDriver";
        String url="jdbc:oracle:thin:@mysys:1521:sandb";
        String username="scott";
        String password="tiger";

        //Load driver class
        Class.forName (driverClassName);

        // obtain a connection
        Connection con= DriverManager.getConnection (url,
        username, password);
        return con;
    }//prepareConnection
}//class
```

In Listing 4.1, we are creating a table, named mytable, with three columns. This application uses the Oracle Thin driver to connect with the database; therefore, does not need to create Data Source Name (DSN) for the application. The user name and password of the database are provided to access the database. This application is using a `java.sql.Statement` object to execute the `CREATE TABLE` statement on the database. When we compile and execute the code shown in Listing 4.1, it raises the `ClassNotFoundException` exception, which is shown in Figure 4.1:

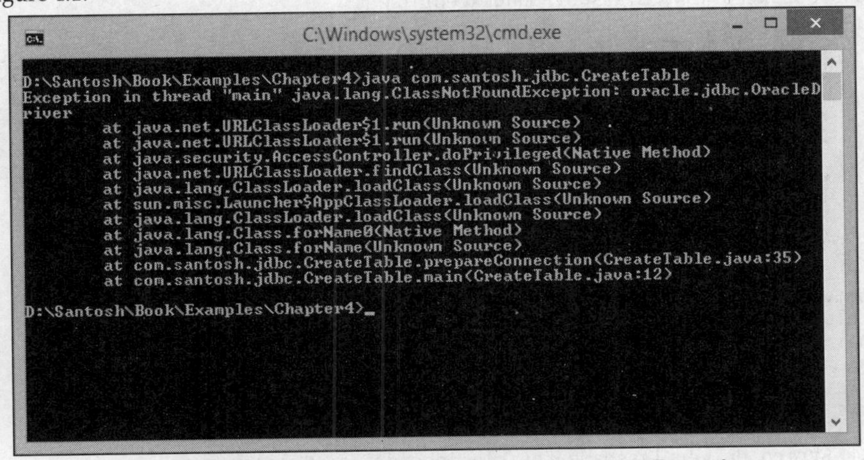

Figure 4.1: Displaying the ClassNotFoundException Exception

We need to add the `classes12.zip` or `ojdbc6.jar` file into the `classpath` variable to ensure that `ClassNotFoundException` is not raised. Figure 4.2 shows how to set the `classpath` by using the `ojdbc6.jar` file:

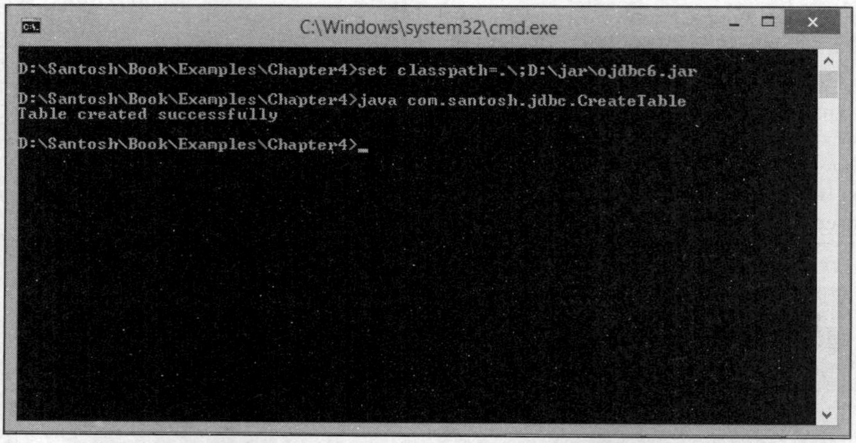

Figure 4.2: Setting the classpath Variable

After creating a table in the database, you need to insert the data in the table. Let's understand how to insert a row in a table dynamically.

Inserting a Row

You can insert a row into a database by using the `INSERT` statement of SQL. In most of the applications, we need to use JDBC to insert rows into a table. For example, we can develop an application that takes the user details as input and performs a registration process, which requires inserting a row into a database. Listing 4.2 provides the code to insert a row into the database (you can find the InsertNewRow.java file online in the code/Chapter4 folder):

Listing 4.2: Showing the code for the InsertNewRow.java File

```
package com.santosh.jdbc;
import java.sql.*;
/**
  * @author Santosh
  */
public class InsertNewRow
{
  public static void main(String args[])
  throws SQLException, ClassNotFoundException {

        //Get Connection
        Connection con=prepareConnection();

        // Obtain a Statement
        Statement st=con.createStatement();

        String query = "insert into mytable values ('Santosh', 36, 158.5)";

        //Execute the Query
        int count=st.executeUpdate (query);

  System.out.println ("Number of Rows Effected by this query = "+count);
  con.close();
  }//main

  public static Connection prepareConnection()
  throws SQLException, ClassNotFoundException   {

        String driverClassName="oracle.jdbc.driver.OracleDriver";
        String url="jdbc:oracle:thin:@mysys:1521:sandb";
        String username="scott";
        String password="tiger";
        //Load driver class
```

```
        Class.forName (driverClassName);

        // obtain a connection
        return DriverManager.getConnection (url, username, password);
    }//prepareConnection
}//class
```

Listing 4.2 shows how you can insert a row containing a string, integer, and floating-point number into the mytable table. It also uses the Oracle Thin driver to connect to the database. You need to compile and run the program to insert a new row into the database table, as shown in Figure 4.3:

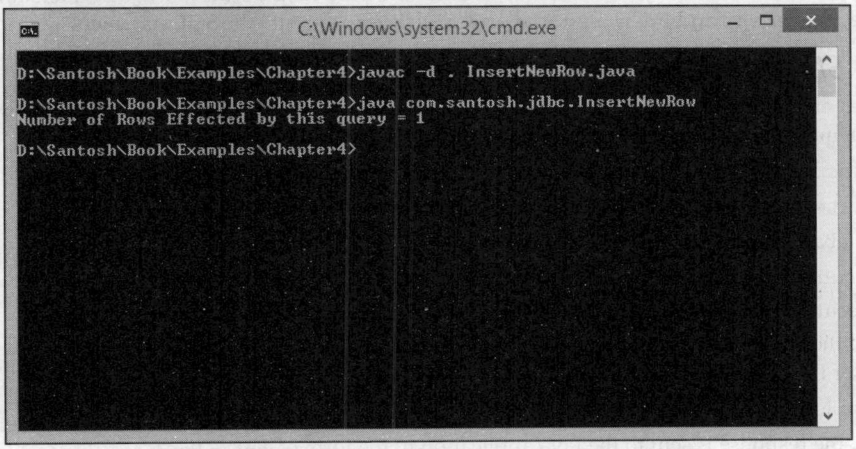

Figure 4.3: Executing the InsertNewRow.java File

After compiling and executing the code shown in Listing 4.2, the output is displayed on the database console, as shown in Figure 4.4:

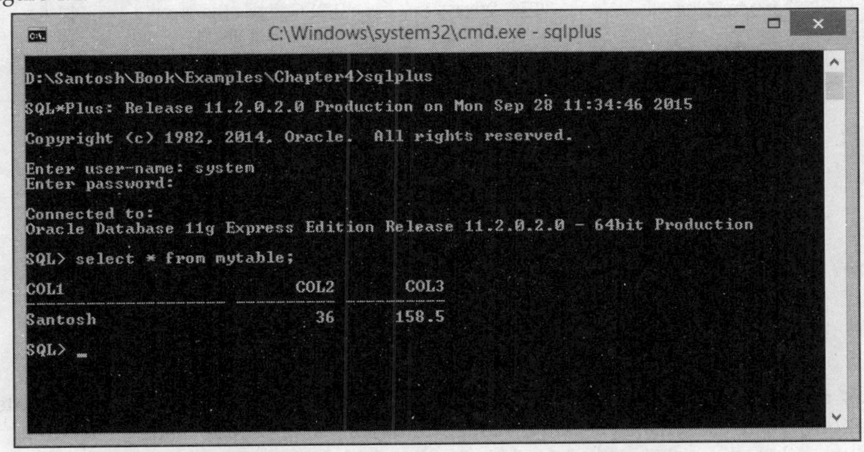

Figure 4.4: Displaying the Output of the InsertNewRow.java File

Similar to inserting data, we can even update and delete the data in a table. We have learned how to use the `Statement` object to execute the queries and obtain the results. Now, we look at some drawbacks of the `Statement` object and introduce the `PreparedStatement` interface.

It is necessary to close the `Statement` object to release the resource it is using. This can be done by simply calling `close()` method. When this `close()` method is called, its `ResultSet` objects are closed.

Working with the PreparedStatement Interface

The `PreparedStatement` object is used to execute the parameterized SQL statement. It is important to note that when the parameterized SQL statement is used with the `PreparedStatement` object, it supports zero or more IN parameters. The `PreparedStatement` object represents a precompiled query that can be executed multiple times without compiling it again and again.

The `java.sql.PreparedStatement` interface is a part of JDBC API that describes the `PreparedStatement` object, which is implemented by a third party vendor as a part of JDBC driver. Let's understand the difference between the `Statement` and `PreparedStatement` objects to execute the SQL statement.

Comparing Statement and PreparedStatement Objects

When a `Statement` object is used to execute an SQL statement (that is, calling any one of the execute methods), the SQL statement is processed by the following steps:

1. The `executeXXX()` method is called on `Statement` object with SQL statement.
2. The `Statement` object submits the SQL statement to database.
3. The database compiles the given SQL statement.
4. An execution plan is prepared by the database to execute the SQL statement.
5. The execution plan for the compiled SQL statement is then executed.
6. Now, if the SQL statement is a Data Retrieval Statement, such as `SELECT` statement, the database caches the results of the SQL statement into buffer.
7. The results are sent to the `Statement` object.
8. Finally, the response is sent to the Java application in the form of `ResultSet`.

Figure 4.5 explains the entire process flow:

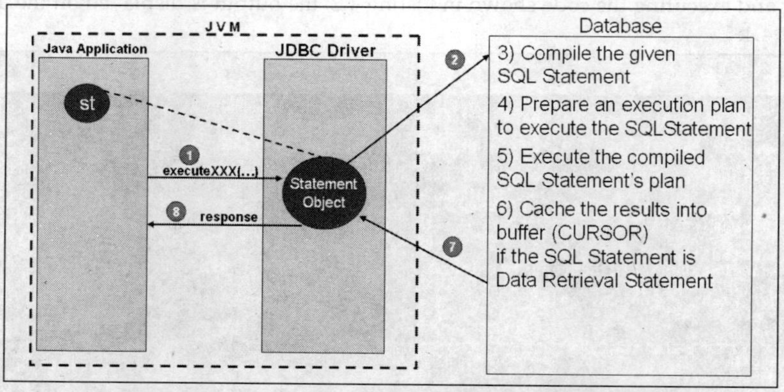

Figure 4.5: Displaying the Process Flow of the Statement Object

In Figure 4.5, `st` represents the `Statement` object reference. The compilation of an SQL statement includes costly operations, such as syntax checking, name validation, and pseudo code generation. After the SQL statement is compiled, the query optimizer evaluates some of the different and feasible plans to execute SQL statement and then returns what it considers the best alternative. Thereafter, the execution plan needs to be executed to get the result.

It is not necessary to compile the SQL statement and prepare an execution plan to execute a statement multiple times. DBMSs are designed to store execution plans and execute them multiple times if required. Consequently, the processing time of the DBMS is optimized. These stored execution plans of SQL statements are known as pre-compiled SQL statements that can be invoked multiple times. DBMSs maintain the compiled statements and provide a unique identity for the prepared execution plan that the client uses to execute the same statement next time. JDBC specifications support the use of this feature provided by DBMS. The `PreparedStatement` interface is designed specifically to support this feature.

The PreparedStatement object represents a pre-compiled SQL statement so that the execution of the SQL statement is much faster as compared to the Statement object. The java.sql.PreparedStatement is a subtype of the java.sql.Statement interface; therefore, it inherits all the properties of the Statement interface. Some of the important points with respect to PreparedStatement are as follows:

- A PreparedStatement object is associated with a Connection object.
- A PreparedStatement object represents the execution plan of an SQL statement saved in the database that is passed as a parameter while creating the PreparedStatement object.
- The SQL statement used with PreparedStatement can be a parameterized SQL statement, that is, it can take parameters whose values can be set while executing.
- A PreparedStatement is implicitly closed after the Connection object on which the PreparedStatement object was created is closed.

The following operations are performed to create and execute the PreparedStatement object:

1. The prepareStatement() method of the Connection object is used to get the object of PreparedStatement.
2. The Connection object submits the given SQL statement to database.
3. The database compiles the given SQL statement.
4. An execution plan is prepared by the database to execute the SQL statement.
5. Database stores the execution plan with a unique ID.
6. Returns the identity to the Connection object.
7. The Connection object prepares a PreparedStatement object, initializes it with the execution plan identity.
8. Returns the reference of the PreparedStatement object to the Java application.
9. The setXXX() methods of the PreparedStatement object are used to set the parameters of the SQL statement it is representing.
10. Then, the executeXXX() method of PreparedStatement object is invoked to execute the SQL statement with the parameters set for the PreparedStatement object.
11. The PreparedStatement object delegates the request to database.
12. The database locates the execution plan.
13. Executes the execution plan with the given parameters.
14. Returns the result to the PreparedStatement object.
15. Finally, the result of the SQL statement is sent to the Java application in the form of ResultSet.

Figure 4.6 explains the flow of execution when PreparedStatement is used to execute the SQL statement:

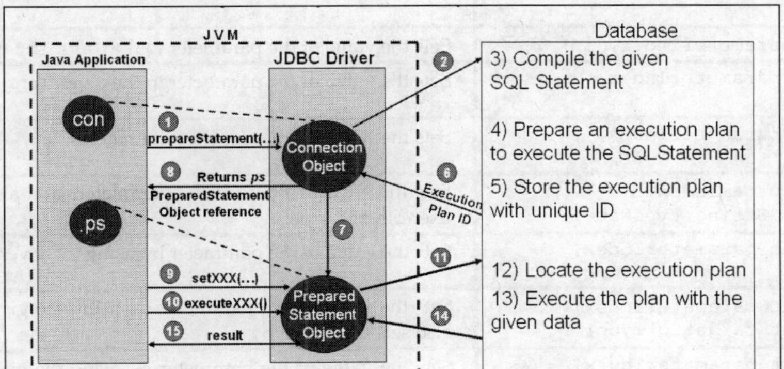

Figure 4.6: Showing Steps of Using PreparedStatement

In Figure 4.6, the `con` and `ps` represent the `Connection` and `PreparedStatement` object references respectively. After comparing the `Statement` and `PreparedStatement` interfaces, let's explore the methods of the `PreparedStatement` interface.

Describing setXXX()methods of PreparedStatement

The value of each placeholder ('?') parameter used inside the query string must be set before executing a `PreparedStatement` object. The values for these placeholder parameters are provided at runtime to the SQL statement. You can set the values of placeholder parameters by using the `setXXX()` methods. Table 4.1 shows the `setXXX()` methods supported by the `PreparedStatement` object:

Table 4.1: Methods Available in PreparedStatement

Method	Description
`setArray(int i, Array x)`	Sets the values of parameters to the given array object.
`setAsciiStream(int parameterIndex, InputStream x, int length)`	Sets the value of the `PreparedStatement` parameter according to the given input stream, specified in the method.
`setBigDecimal(int parameterIndex, BigDecimal x)`	Sets the value of the parameter by using the values specified in the `java.math.BigDecimal` value.
`setBinaryStream(int parameterIndex , InputStream x, int length)`	Sets the binary values for the parameters used in the `PreparedStatement` object.
`setBlob(int i, Blob x)`	Sets the values of the parameters to the given `blob` object.
`setBoolean(int parameterIndex, boolean x)`	Sets the Boolean values for the parameters used in `PreparedStatements.`
`setByte(int parameterIndex, byte x)`	Sets the byte values for the parameters used in `PreparedStatements.`
`setBytes(int parameterIndex, byte[] x)`	Sets the byte values in an array for the parameters used in `PreparedStatements.`
`setCharacterStream(int parameterIndex, Reader reader, int length)`	Sets the character values for the `PreparedStatement` parameters and also specifies the length of the character stream.
`setClob(int i, Clob x)`	Sets the values of the parameters to the given clob object.
`setDate(int parameterIndex, Date x)`	Sets the `PreparedStatement` parameter with a `java.sql.Date` value.
`setDate(int parameterIndex, Date x, Calendar cal)`	Sets the `PreparedStatement` parameter with a `java.sql.Date` value and also uses the calendar object to set the value of the parameter.
`setDouble(int parameterIndex, double x)`	Sets the value of the parameter to the `Java double` value.
`setFloat(int parameterIndex, float x)`	Sets the value of the parameter to the `Java float` value.
`setInt(int parameterIndex, int x)`	Sets the value of the parameter to the `Java Int` value.
`setLong(int parameterIndex, long x)`	Sets the value of the parameter to the `Java long` value.
`setNull(int parameterIndex, int sqlType)`	Sets the NULL values for the parameters.
`setNull(int paramIndex, int sqlType, String typeName)`	Sets the NULL values for the parameters and also specifies the SQL user-defined type.
`setObject(int parameterIndex, Object x)`	Sets the value of the parameter by using the given object value.
`setObject(int parameterIndex, Object x, int targetSqlType)`	Sets the value of the parameter by using the given object value and also sets the SQL type.
`setObject(int parameterIndex, Object x, int targetSqlType, int scale)`	Sets the value of the parameter by using the given object value, the SQL type, and the number of digits after the decimal point.

Table 4.1: Methods Available in PreparedStatement

Method	Description
`setRef(int i, Ref x)`	Sets the values of the parameters to the `REF (<structured-type>)` value.
`setShort(int parameterIndex, short x)`	Sets the value of the parameter to the Java `short` value.
`setString(int parameterIndex, String x)`	Sets the value of the parameter to the Java `String` value.
`setTime(int parameterIndex, Time x)`	Sets the value of the parameter to the `java.sql.Time` value.
`setTime(int parameterIndex, Time x, Calendar cal)`	Sets the value of the parameter to the `java.sql.Time` value using the calendar object.
`setTimestamp(int parameterIndex, Timestamp x)`	Sets the value of the parameter to the `java.sql.TimeStamp` value.
`setTimestamp(int parameterIndex, Timestamp x, Calendar cal)`	Sets the value of the parameter to the `java.sql.TimeStamp` value using the calendar object.
`setURL(int parameterIndex, URL x)`	Sets the value of the parameter to the `java.net.URL` value.

Using PreparedStatement

The prepared statements are used to increase the efficiency and reduce the execution time of an SQL statement. An instance of `PreparedStatement` must be created to execute a precompiled SQL statement. You need to perform the following broad-level steps to use `PreparedStatement`:

1. Create a `PreparedStatement` object.
2. Set the values for the parameters.
3. Execute the `PreparedStatement`.

Let's discuss each of these steps in detail.

Creating a PreparedStatement Object

The `PreparedStatement` object is created by using the `prepareStatement (String sqlStatement)` method of the `Connection` object. At this stage, the `Connection` object submits the given SQL statement to the database to compile and save it. As a result of this, the database returns an identity of the execution plan prepared for the given SQL statement, if it is compiled successfully. The database query compiler does not require values to compile the statement. Therefore, the `sqlStatement` argument of the `prepareStatement()` method used with the `Connection.prepareStatement(String)` method can contain zero or more question marks ('?', known as parameters). The values for these parameters can be set after the SQL statement is compiled, that is, after creating the `PreparedStatement` object, and before executing the statement. The following code snippet shows how to create the `PreparedStatement` object:

```
Connection con= DriverManager.getConnection (url, user, password);
String  sqlSt="insert into mytable values (?,?,?)";
//Step1: Get PreparedStatement object
PreparedStatement ps=con.prepareStatement (sqlSt);
```

In the preceding code snippet, the `Connection` object is used to call the `prepareStatement()` method to create a `PreparedStatement` object. The `ps` in this code snippet refers to the `PreparedStatement` object created by using the `Connection` object. Here, the SQL statement described by the `sqlSt` string contains three parameters.

NOTE

The SQL statement used with PreparedStatement can have zero or more parameters describing dynamic input values, which can be set later after compiling the SQL statement that is after creating the PreparedStatement object. However, the positional parameter cannot describe an SQL keyword, and a table or column name.

Let's now learn how to set values for the parameters.

Setting the Values for Parameters

After creating a `PreparedStatement` object, we need to set the values for the parameters described for this object. The values of the parameters can be set by using the `setXXX()` methods of the `PreparedStatement` object. In addition, the `PreparedStatement` object supports setter methods for all the data types supported by Java. For example, the `PreparedStatement.setInt(int index, int value)` method helps in setting an integer type of parameter value and the `PreparedStatement.setString(int index, String value)` method sets the `String` type parameter value. These setter methods take two arguments: the first argument indicates the parameter index and the second argument indicates the value of the parameter. The following code snippet shows how to set the values of the question mark parameter:

```
//Step2: setting values for the parameters
ps.setString(1,"abc1");
ps.setInt(2,38);
ps.setDouble(3,158.75);
```

NOTE

The parameters in the SQL statement used with **`PreparedStatement`** *are identified by an index assigned to it based on its position in the statement. The parameter index starts from 1, from left to right of the statement. This implies the first identified '?' reading the statement from left is identified with an index 1, next with 2, and so on.*

Now, let's explore the process of executing `PreparedStatement`.

Executing PreparedStatement

After preparing and initializing (includes setting values for parameters) the `PreparedStatement` object, we can execute the SQL statement with the configured parameters. The `execute()`, `executeUpdate()`, or `executeQuery()` methods of the `PreparedStatement` object are used to execute the SQL statement. The result of these methods is same as that of the respective methods supported by the `Statement` object. The following code snippet shows how to execute the SQL statements:

```
//Step3: Executing the SQL statements
int n = ps.executeUpdate(); // n is the number of rows or tables that are being updated
```

As we have discussed how to use `PreparedStatement` to execute the SQL statement, to shed more light on this topic, let's understand more about `PreparedStatement` with the help of an example.

Using PreparedStatement with Parameters

In this subsection, we demonstrate the basic steps involved in using the `PreparedStatement` object to execute an SQL statement with parameters. Let's create the PreparedStatementEx1.java file to demonstrate the use of `PreparedStatement`. Listing 4.3 provides the code to use the `PreparedStatement` object to execute the `INSERT` statement (you can find the PreparedStatementEx1.java file online in the code/Chapter4 folder):

Listing 4.3: Showing the code for the PreparedStatementEx1.java File

```
package com.santosh.jdbc;

import java.sql.*;
/**
 * @author Santosh
 */
public class PreparedStatementEx1 {

  public static void main(String s[]) throws Exception {

      Class.forName("oracle.jdbc.driver.OracleDriver").newInstance();
      Connection con= DriverManager.getConnection (
      "jdbc:oracle:thin:@mysys:1521:sandb","scott","tiger");

      String query="insert into mytable values (?,?,?)";

      //Step1: Get PreparedStatement
      PreparedStatement ps=con.prepareStatement (query);
```

```
        //Step2: set parameters
        ps.setString(1,"abc1");
        ps.setInt(2,38);
        ps.setDouble(3,158.75);

        //Step3: execute the query
        int i=ps.executeUpdate();

        System.out.println("record inserted count:"+i);

        //To execute the query once again
        ps.setString(1,"abc2");
        ps.setInt(2,39);
        ps.setDouble(3,158.75);

        i=ps.executeUpdate();
        System.out.println("query executed for the second time count: "+i);
        con.close();
    }//main
}//class
```

Listing 4.3 uses the `PreparedStatement` object, along with the `Connection` object. The `setXXX()` methods of the `PreparedStatement` object are used to set the values of the parameters. Listing 4.3 sets the values of the integer, String, and Double data types. The `executeUpdate()` method used in Listing 4.3 executes the SQL statement and returns the number of rows affected by executing the SQL statement. The output of Listing 4.3 is shown in Figure 4.7:

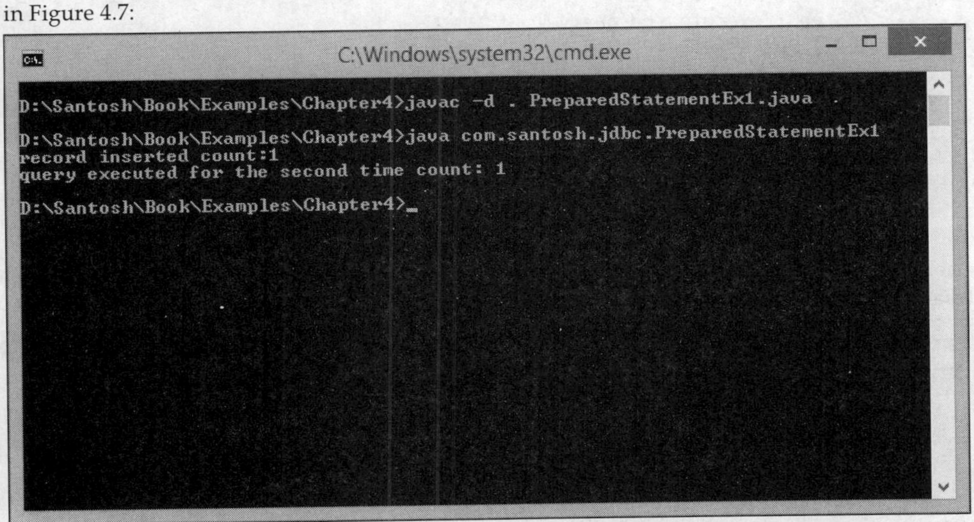

Figure 4.7: Displaying the Output of the PreparedStatementEx1.java File

In Listing 4.3, we have used `PreparedStatement` to execute an SQL `INSERT` statement with simple types such as `int`, `String`, and `double`. Let's look at an example of using `PreparedStatement` to set the date type, as shown in Listing 4.4. Listing 4.4 uses the `setInt ()` and `setString ()` methods to pass the values of the `integer` and `String` data types (you can find the PreparedStatementEx2.java file online in the code/Chapter4 folder):

Listing 4.4: Showing the code for the PreparedStatementEx2.java File

```
package com.santosh.jdbc;

import java.text.*;
import java.sql.*;
/**
 * @author Santosh
 */
public class PreparedStatementEx2 {
```

```
    public static void main(String s[]) throws Exception {

        Class.forName("oracle.jdbc.driver.OracleDriver").newInstance();
        Connection con=DriverManager.getConnection(
"jdbc:oracle:thin:@mysys:1521:sandb","scott","tiger");

        String query="update emp set HIREDATE=?, ENAME=? where empno=?";

        //Step1: Get PreparedStatement
        PreparedStatement ps=con.prepareStatement (query);

        //Prepare java.sql.Date object
        /*
        This logic shows how to convert simple String that is in
        dd-MM-yyyy format into Date object
        */
        SimpleDateFormat sdf=new SimpleDateFormat ("dd-MM-yyyy");
        java.util.Date d=sdf.parse ("26-12-2001");
        java.sql.Date newdate=new java.sql.Date (d.getTime());

        //Step2: set parameters
        ps.setDate (1, newdate);
        ps.setString (2, "Santosh");
        ps.setInt (3, 7839);

        //Step3: execute the query
        int i=ps.executeUpdate ();

        System.out.println ("record updated count: "+i);
        con.close();
    }//main
}//class
```

Listing 4.4 describes a class that has a date in the form of `String` in the `dd-mm-yyyy` format. The class uses the `java.text.SimpleDateFormat` object to convert the `String` into a `Date` object. Thereafter, the date value is set to the `PreparedStatement` object using its `setDate()` method. Then, the `PreparedStatement.executeUpdate()` method is used to execute the SQL statement and display the number of rows affected as a result of execution. The output of Listing 4.4 is shown in Figure 4.8:

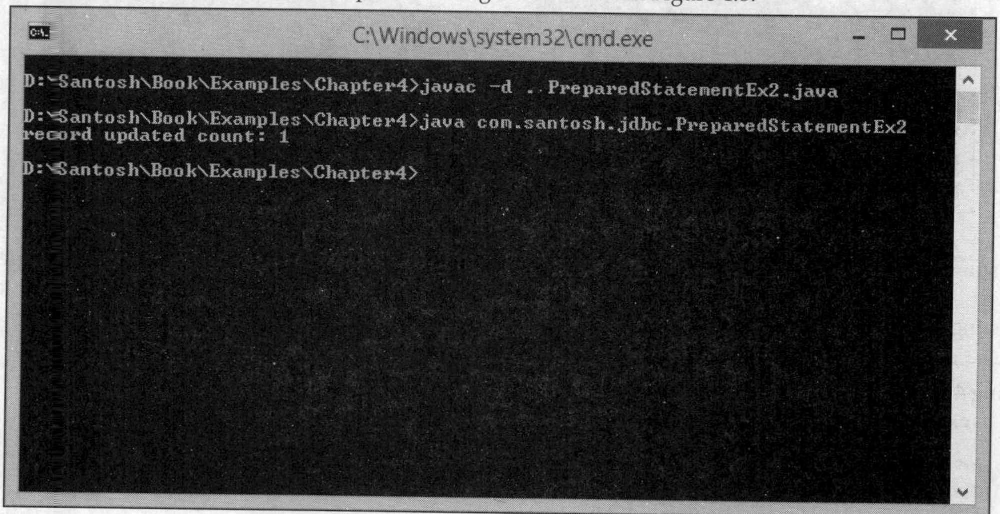

Figure 4.8: Displaying the Output of the PreparedStatementEx2.java File

Closing PreparedStatement Objects

A `PreparedStatement` object should be closed in the same way as in the case of `Statement` objects.

We can close a `PreparedStatement` object by calling a method `close()`. Ideally, if we close a `Connection` object, it will automatically close the `PreparedStatement` object. However, explicitly closing the `PreparedStatement` object will make sure that a proper cleanup of objects has been done.

Let's now explore the use of `PreparedStatement` object.

Exploring the Usage of the PreparedStatement Object

You should use `PreparedStatement` in the following situations:

- When a single SQL statement is being executed multiple times
- When an SQL statement consists of multiple number of parameters and complex types (SQL 99 types)

After understanding the `PreparedStatement` interface, let's list its advantages and disadvantages.

Listing the Advantages and Disadvantages of PreparedStatement

The advantages of using `PreparedStatement` are as follows:

- It improves the performance of an application, in comparison to the `Statement` object, where the same query is required to be executed multiple times; therefore, `PreparedStatement` performs faster by avoiding compilation of multiple queries and preparing them.
- It is easier to insert or update the SQL 99 data type columns, such as `BLOB`, `CLOB`, or `OBJECT`, with the help of `setXXX()` methods.
- It provides a programmatic approach to set the values of parameters in a more descriptive way as compared to the `Statement` object.
- We can write parameterized SQL queries using `PreparedStatement`. With these SQL queries, we can pass a variety of parameters having the same SQL queries. Every time creating a new query is better than passing the same SQL statement with different parameters.
- `PreparedStatements` are known for their faster execution as they get precompiled. If we use parameterized query, it will help us to depict better performance of the SQL query.
- We can prevent SQL injection attacks by using `PreparedStatement`. By passing parametric queries, we can prevent many forms of attacks.
- `PreparedStatements` are more understandable and reliable than string-concatenated queries.

The main disadvantages of `PreparedStatement` are as follows:

- It can represent only one SQL statement. Therefore, we cannot execute more than one statement by a single `PreparedStatement`.
- It supports to add only a single SQL statement to be executed for multiple times with different sets of values in a batch.

After learning about `PreparedStatement`, let's now proceed to learn about `CallableStatement`.

Working with the CallableStatement Interface

The `CallableStatement` object executes an SQL statement to invoke the database procedure or function. The `java.sql.CallableStatement` interface is a part of JDBC API that describes a standard abstraction for the `CallableStatement` object, implemented by a third party vendor as a part of JDBC driver. The `java.sql.CallableStatement` interface extends the `java.sql.PreparedStatement` interface. The `CallableStatement` object provides support for both input and output parameters. `CallableStatement` provides a standard abstraction for the data stores to call stored procedures and functions in a vendor-independent way. The `CallableStatement` interface provides an abstraction for an object that is used to access, invoke, and retrieve the results of SQL-stored procedures and functions. Stored procedures let you write queries that are quick to run and easy to invoke. It is often easier to update an application by making a few changes in the stored procedures. Although functions are similar to procedures in many ways, but there is one major difference between them, that is, a function always returns a scalar value.

Let's explore the use of `CallableStatement` in detail next. We start by providing a brief description of stored procedures and differences between procedures and functions. Then, we demonstrate the use of `CallableStatement` with stored procedures, functions, and cursors.

Describing Stored Procedures

A stored procedure is a subroutine in a database available to all applications accessing the database. As discussed in case of `PreparedStatement`, the pre-compiled statements can improve the performance of the system by avoiding repeated compilation of the SQL statement. However, the pre-compiled SQL statement represented by `PreparedStatement` is session scoped, which means that such statements are cleared when their session is closed. Moreover, if the same SQL statement is reused into multiple sessions, it requires multiple compilations. The stored procedure allows a pre-compiled statement, which can be accessed from multiple sessions, to be defined. The properties of a stored procedure are listed in the following points:

- A stored procedure contains input, output, or both input and output parameters.
- A stored procedure returns a value through the OUT parameter after executing the SQL statements.
- A stored procedure can return multiple `ResultSets`.

Stored procedures are generally a group of SQL statements that allow you to make a single call to a database. The SQL statements in a stored procedure are executed statically for better performance. A stored procedure encapsulates the values of the following types of parameters:

- **IN**—Refers to the parameter that can be referenced by the stored procedure. The value of this parameter cannot be overwritten by the procedure.
- **OUT**—Refers to the parameter that cannot be referenced by the stored procedure, but the value of the parameter can be overwritten by the procedure
- **IN OUT**—Refers to the parameter that can be referenced by the stored procedure. The value of the parameter can be overwritten by the procedure.

The following is the syntax of creating a stored procedure:

```
CREATE or [REPLACE] PROCEDURE procedure_name
  [(parameter [, parameter])]
  IS
  [Declarations]
  BEGIN
        executables
        [EXCEPTION exceptions]
  END [Procedure_name]
```

In the preceding syntax, `procedure_name` represents the name of the procedure, and the executable statements are provided within BEGIN and END statements. Let's now look at the benefits of using `PreparedStatement` with a stored procedure.

Listing the Benefits of Working with a Stored Procedure

The following are the key benefits of using a stored procedure:

- Avoids repeated compilation of an SQL query that is accessed from multiple sessions because pre-compiled statements are accessible among multiple database sessions as compared to prepared statements.
- Helps us in loose coupling between the application and database model; therefore, any changes in the database model do not directly affect the application. For example, consider we are managing the employee details into a single table that requires an insert statement to enter the details of a new employee. If we need to change the database model to save the employee details into two tables, such as general and personal details, we require two insert statements. In this case, we need not change the application as the employee details are not changed, and change in the procedure can do the job.

- Provides a proper responsibility division between developers and database administrators. Instead of forcing application developers to create SQL statements, the database administrator can create efficient SQL statements to access the database model.

Let's understand the implementation of the `CallableStatement` interface with the help of applications.

Using CallableStatement

In Java, `CallableStatement` is used to call the stored procedures and functions by using an object of the `CallableStatement` interface. The broad-level steps to use `CallableStatement` in an application are as follows:

1. Creating the `CallableStatement` object
2. Setting the values of the parameters
3. Registering the OUT parameter type
4. Executing the stored procedure or function
5. Retrieving the parameter values

Let's discuss these steps in detail.

Creating the CallableStatement Object

The first step to use `CallableStatement` is to create the `CallableStatement` object. The `CallableStatement` object can be created by invoking the `prepareCall(String)` method of the `Connection` object. The syntax to call the `prepareCall()` method in an application is as follows:

```
{call procedure_name(?, ?, ...)} //calling the procedure method with parameters.

{call procedure_name}  //with no parameter
```

Setting the Values of Parameters

After creating the `CallableStatement` object, you need to set the values for the IN and IN OUT type parameters of the stored procedure. The values of these parameters can be set by calling the `setXXX ()` methods of the `CallableStatement` object. These methods are used to pass the values to the IN and IN OUT parameters. The values for the parameter can be set by using the following syntax:

```
setXXX(int index, XXX value)
```

Registering the OUT Parameter Type

The OUT or IN OUT parameters, which are used in a procedure and represented by `CallableStatement`, must be registered to collect the values of the parameters after the stored procedure is executed. You can register the parameters by invoking the `registerOutParameter()` method of the `CallableStatement` object. This method defines the type of parameter used in `CallableStatement`. The parameters can be registered by using the following syntax:

```
registerOutParameter (int index, int type)
```

Executing the Stored Procedure or Function

After registering the OUT parameter type, you need to execute the procedure by using the `execute()` method of the `CallableStatement` object. The `execute()` method of `CallableStatement` does not take any argument.

Retrieving Parameter Values

After executing the stored procedure, you can retrieve its OUT or IN OUT type parameter values. You can use the getter methods of the `CallableStatement` object to retrieve the parameter values of the procedure. You can repeat all the preceding steps if you want to execute the same procedure again with a different set of parameter values. After using the `CallableStatement`, it is a good practice to invoke the `close()` method on the `CallableStatement` object to release the resources it holds.

You must have learned how to work with `CallableStatement`. Let's now demonstrate the implementation of `CallableStatement` with parameters.

Using CallableStatement with Parameters

Let's look at some examples of using `CallableStatement` that include executing a stored procedure with the following parameters:

- The IN parameter
- The OUT parameter

The following explanations explain these points in detail.

Executing a Stored Procedure with IN Parameters

In this subsection, we demonstrate how `CallableStatement` is used to execute a stored procedure with IN parameters. Let's create an application in which we execute a stored procedure with IN parameters.

In this application, we demonstrate the process to insert a record into two tables, such as bank and personal_details, as a part of creating a new account. First you need to create two tables called bank and personal_details by using the following SQL queries:

```
Create table bank (
   Accno number,
   Name varchar2(20),
   Bal number(10,2),
   Acctype number
);
Create table personal_details (
   Accno number,
   address varchar2(20),
   phno number
);
```

Now, after creating the tables, we want to create the `createAccount` procedure; that can insert a record into both the tables. The code snippet of the `createAccount` procedure is as follows:

```
create or replace procedure createAccount (accnumber number, actype number,
acname varchar2, amt number, addr varchar2, phno number) is
begin
insert into bank values (accnumber, acname, amt, actype);

insert into personal_details values ( accnumber, addr, phno);
end;
/
```

Figure 4.9 shows the output of the preceding code snippet in the Oracle SQL (SQL* Plus) editor:

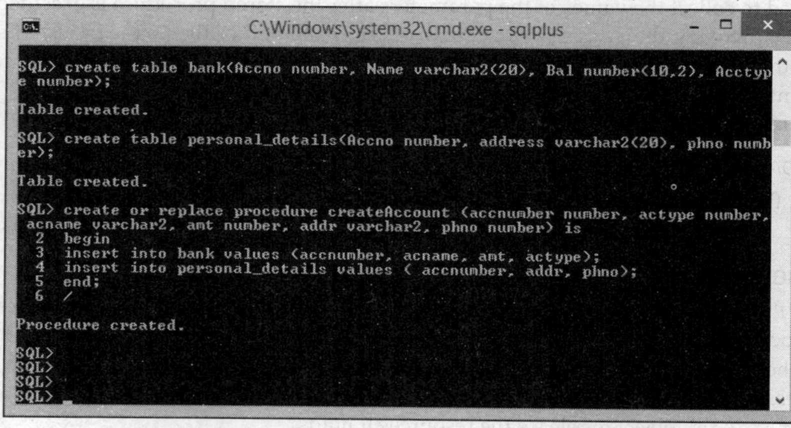

Figure 4.9: Showing the Creation of Tables and a Procedure

The tables and procedures created in the preceding code snippets are used in Listing 4.5 to create a new account by calling the `createAccount` stored procedure and using the `CallableStatement` object. The commented line (//Step2: set IN parameters) in Listing 4.5 shows the use of IN parameters to work with

`CallableStatement`. You can see the use of IN parameter in Listing 4.5 (you can find the CallableStatementEx1.java file online in the code/Chapter4 folder):

Listing 4.5: Showing the code for the CallableStatementEx1.java File

```
package com.santosh.jdbc;

import java.sql.*;
/**
 * @author Santosh
 */
public class CallableStatementEx1 {

  public static void main(String s[]) throws Exception {

        Class.forName("oracle.jdbc.driver.OracleDriver").newInstance();
        Connection con=DriverManager.getConnection(

        "jdbc:oracle:thin:@mysys:1521:sandb","scott","tiger");

        //Step1: Get CallableStatement
        CallableStatement cs= con.prepareCall ("{call
        createAccount (?,?,?,?,?,?)}");

        //Step2: set IN parameters
        cs.setInt(1, 101);
        cs.setInt(2, 10);
        cs.setString(3, "Santosh");
        cs.setDouble(4, 10000);
        cs.setString(5, "Hyderabad");
        cs.setInt(6, 123456789);

        //Step3 : register OUT parameters
        //In this procedure example we don't have OUT parameters
        //Step4
        cs.execute();
        System.out.println("Account Created");

        con.close();
  }//main
}//class
```

The output of Listing 4.5 is shown in Figure 4.10:

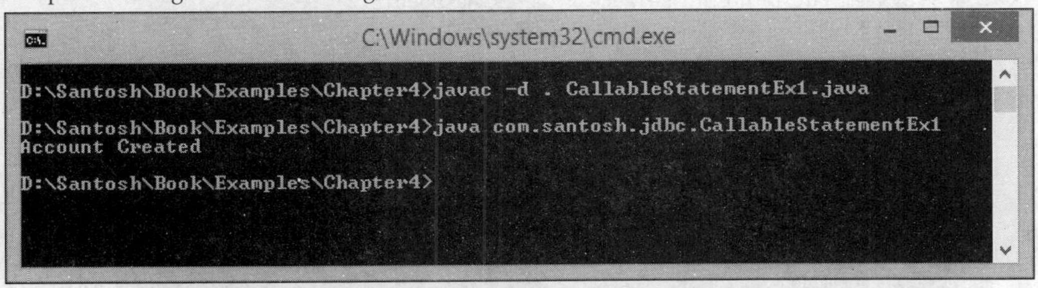

Figure 4.10: Showing the Output of the CallableStatementEx1.java File

If `CallableStatement` uses OUT parameters to deal with the stored procedure, we need to register the OUT parameters by using the `registerOutParameter()` method of the `CallableStatement` interface.

Executing a Stored Procedure with OUT Parameters

In this subsection, we create an application that calls a stored procedure named `getBalance()` by using `CallableStatement`. First create a procedure named `getBalance()`, as shown in the following code snippet:

```
create or replace procedure getBalance (acno number, amt OUT number) is
begin
```

```
select bal into amt from bank where accno=acno;
end;
/
```

Figure 4.11 shows the `getBalance` procedure created by using the SQL* Plus editor:

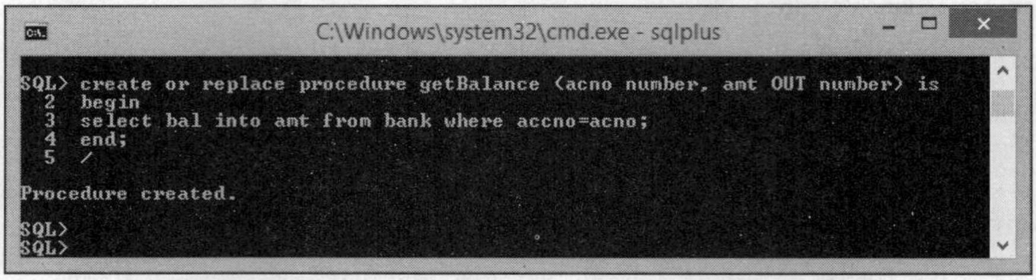

Figure 4.11: Creating a Procedure by Using OUT Parameter

Let's now see how to execute the `getBalance` stored procedure with the OUT parameter of `CallableStatement`. Listing 4.6 shows the use of the OUT parameter with the stored procedure (you can find the CallableStatementEx2.java file online in the code/Chapter4 folder):

Listing 4.6: Showing the code for the CallableStatementEx2.Java File

```
package com.santosh.jdbc;

import java.sql.*;
/**
 * @author Santosh
 */
public class CallableStatementEx2 {
public static void main(String s[]) throws Exception {

        Class.forName("oracle.jdbc.driver.OracleDriver").newInstance();
        Connection con=DriverManager.getConnection(
        "jdbc:oracle:thin:@mysys:1521:sandb","scott","tiger");

        CallableStatement cs= con.prepareCall("{call getBalance(?,?)}");

        cs.setInt(1, Integer.parseInt(s[0]));
        cs.registerOutParameter(2, Types.DOUBLE);
        cs.execute();

        System.out.println("Balance : "+ cs.getDouble(2));
        con.close();
   }//main
}//class
```

Figure 4.12 displays the output of Listing 4.6:

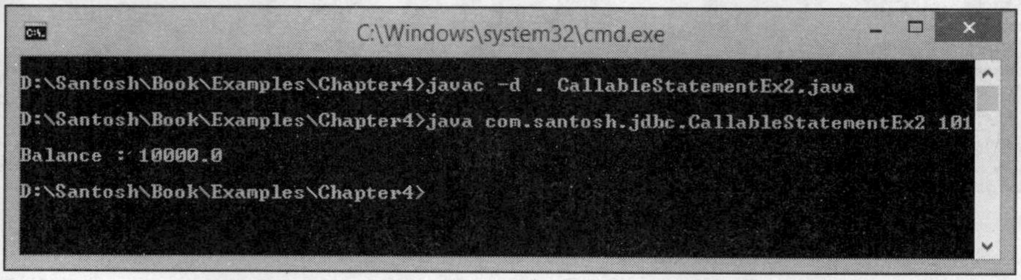

Figure 4.12: Showing the Output of CallableStatementEx2.java by using OUT Parameter

In the next section, we discuss how to call functions using `CallableStatement`.

Calling Functions by Using CallableStatement

Most of the databases provide support for various types of built-in functions, such as numeric, string, time, date, system, and conversion. These functions are used in SQL statements and return scalar values that are stored in a database. The functions returning the scalar values that are supported by a DBMS must also be supported by the database drivers used in the application. The user should access these functions by calling the metadata methods.

Table 4.2 describes the scalar function types supported by Oracle:

Table 4.2: Function Types and their Uses

Function Type	Use
Numeric functions	Operate on numeric data types, such as `greatest()`, `least()`, `round()`, `trunc()`, `length()`, and `lower()`.
String functions	Operate on String data types. The String functions include `Char()`, `concat()`, `insert()`, and `length()`.
Time & Date functions	Access all the time- and date-related information from a database.
System functions	Retrieve information about the database management systems used in an application.
Conversion functions	Convert the data type of a given value into the required type.

In addition to these pre-defined functions, DBMS provides the feature to create user-defined functions that can be used within the DML queries. However, it is not recommended to use DML queries within a function. The user-defined functions can be used in the following situations:

- In the column names of the `SELECT` statement
- As a condition in the `WHERE` clause
- In the value clause of an `INSERT` statement
- In the `SET` clause of an `UPDATE` statement

The following syntax shows how to create a user-defined function:

```
CREATE [OR REPLACE] FUNCTION function_name [(parameter [, parameter])]
RETURN return_datatype
IS/AS
[Declaration_section]
BEGIN
        executable_section
        [EXCEPTION exception_section]
END [function_name];
```

The procedure to call a function in an application is same as it is in the case of stored procedures. The syntax to invoke a function in JDBC (String argument of the `prepareCall()` method) is as follows:

```
    {call ?:=function_name(?, ?, ...)} // with string parameters

    {call ?:=function_name}// with no parameter
```

Listing 4.7 shows the use of a user-defined function in an application by using `CallableStatement` (you can find the CallableStatementEx3.java file online in the code/Chapter4 folder):

Listing 4.7: Showing the code for the CallableStatementEx3.java File

```
package com.santosh.jdbc;

import java.sql.*;
import java.util.*;
/**
 * @author Santosh
 */
public class CallableStatementEx3 {
public static void main(String s[]) throws Exception {
        Properties p=new Properties();
        p.put("user","scott");
        p.put("password","tiger");

        oracle.jdbc.driver.OracleDriver
        od=new oracle.jdbc.driver.OracleDriver ();
        Connection con=od.connect ("jdbc:oracle:thin:@mysys:1521:sandb",p);
```

```
            CallableStatement cs=con.prepareCall ("{call ?:=getBalanceF(?)}");

            cs.registerOutParameter (1, Types.DOUBLE);
            cs.setInt(2,Integer.parseInt(s[0]));

            cs.execute();
            System.out.println(cs.getDouble(1));
            con.close();
    }//main
}//class
```

Listing 4.7 executes a user-defined function by using `CallableStatement` that is required to access the function from the `sandb` database, and the desired output of the function is displayed to the user. Listing 4.7 uses a user-defined function `getBalanceF()`. Figure 4.13 shows the creation of the user-defined function in our application:

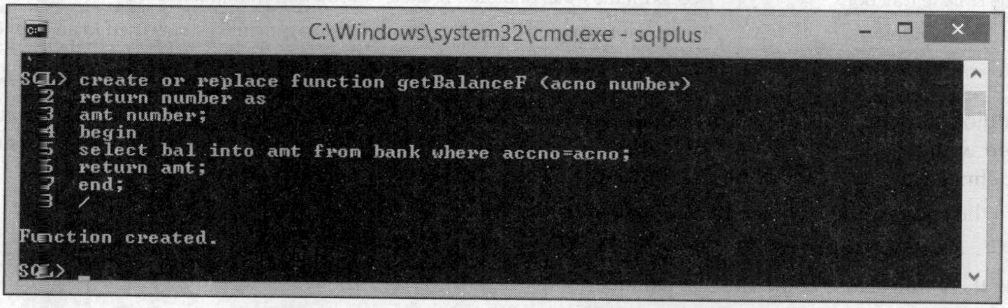

Figure 4.13: Creating a User-Defined Function

Figure 4.14 displays the output of Listing 4.7:

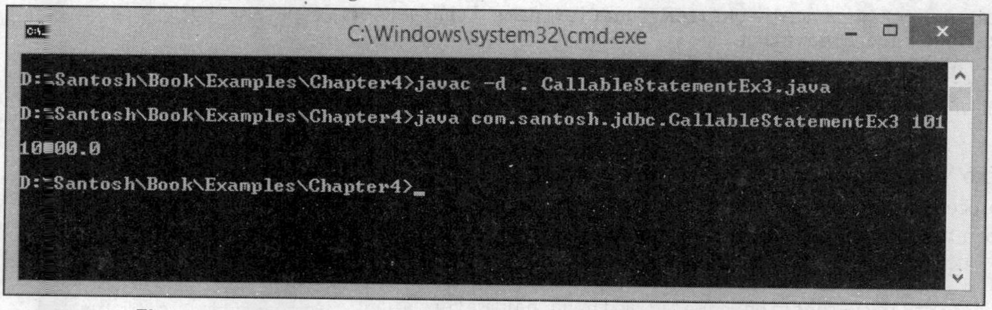

Figure 4.14: Showing the Output of the CallableStatementEx3.java File

All the features discussed so far are used to retrieve a single record from the database. We can use a cursor to retrieve a `ResultSet` from the database.

Let's discuss about the use of cursor in `CallableStatements` to retrieve the `ResultSet` object.

Using Cursors in CallableStatement

A cursor defines the runtime execution environment for a query when the result of the query execution can be captured. That is, we can open the cursor and execute the queries in that environment and read the output of the query from the cursor. The syntax used to create a cursor is as follows:

```
CREATE or REPLACE package package_name as
TYPE type_name IS REF CURSOR;
END;
```

The cursors are used to retrieve the `ResultSet` object from a database through `CallableStatement`. Listing 4.8 shows the use of cursors to get the `ResultSet` object to access multiple records from a database (you can find the CallableStatementEx4.java file online in the code/Chapter4 folder):

Listing 4.8: Showing the code for the CallableStatementEx4.java File

```
package com.santosh.jdbc;

import java.sql.*;
import java.util.*;

public class CallableStatementEx4 {
public static void main(String s[]) throws Exception {

        Properties p=new Properties();
        p.put("user","scott");
        p.put("password","tiger");
        oracle.jdbc.driver.OracleDriver
        od=new oracle.jdbc.driver.OracleDriver();
        Connection con=od.connect("jdbc:oracle:thin:@mysys:1521:sandb",p);

        CallableStatement cs=
        con.prepareCall("{call ?:=getAccountDetails(?)}");
        cs.registerOutParameter(1, oracle.jdbc.driver.OracleTypes.CURSOR);
        cs.setInt(2,Integer.parseInt(s[0]));
        cs.execute();
        ResultSet rs=(ResultSet) cs.getObject(1);

        while (rs.next()){
                System.out.print(rs.getInt(1)+"\t");
                System.out.print(rs.getString(2)+"\t");
                System.out.println(rs.getDouble(3));
        }//while
        con.close();

  }//main

}//class
```

Listing 4.8 uses the cursors and functions in the database to access the `ResultSet` object representing all the accounts of the given account_type. Figure 4.15 displays the creation of the cursor and the functions associated with Listing 4.8:

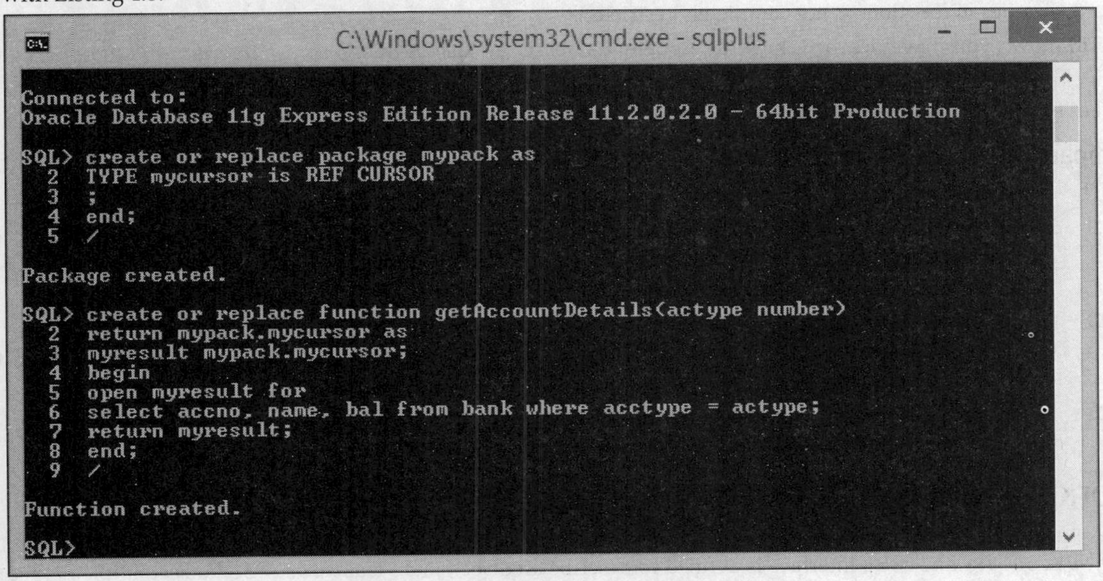

Figure 4.15: Creating a Cursor and Function

Figure 4.16 shows the output of Listing 4.8:

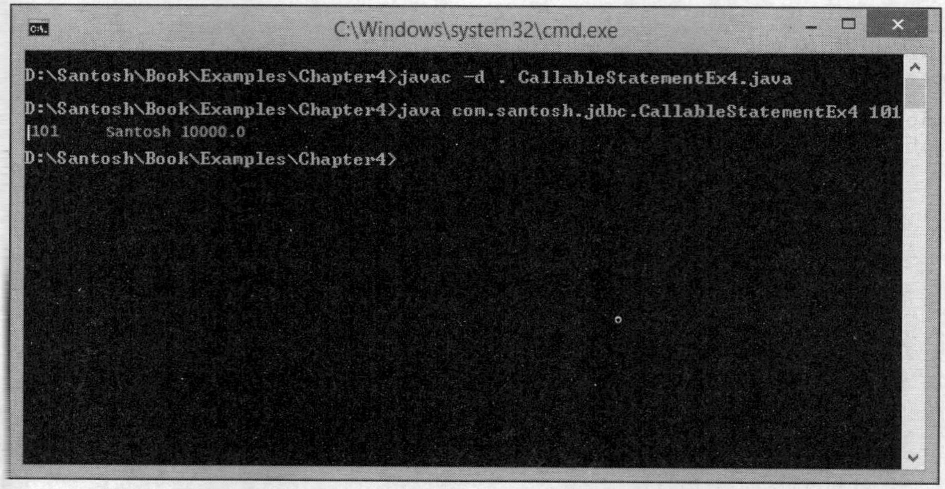

Figure 4.16: Showing the Output of the CallableStatementEx4.java File

Now, let's explore the difference between a procedure and a function.

Comparing Procedure and Function

The points of difference between a procedure and a function are as follows:

- A function has a return type, while a procedure does not have any return type. However, if needed, data can be made available to the client through one or more OUT parameters.
- A function can be used with SQL DML queries, but not procedures.
- A function is not suitable to use DML queries, but can be used in procedures. Note that the use of DML queries in functions is not completely restricted.

Till now, you have learned how to update database by using `Statement`, `PreparedStatement`, and `CallableStatement`.

Let's now learn how to retrieve (query) the data from a database by using the `ResultSet` interface.

Comparing PreparedStatement and CallableStatement

The different between the `PreparedStatement` and `CallableStatement` are:

- In `PreparedStatement`, we use SQL statements a number of times, and these statements accept parameters at run time, whereas in `CallableStatement`, queries uses database stored procedures, and these queres can also accept parameters at run time.
- In `PreparedStatement`, queries in SQL statements are partially compiled, whereas in `CallableStatement`, SQL statements are fully compiled, and objects call stored procedures from the database to execute the query.
- `PreparedStatements` are faster in terms of performance as they can execute multiple statements in less time as compared to `CallableStatements`.

Working with the ResultSet Interface

A `ResultSet` is an interface packaged in the `java.sql` package and provided under the JDBC core API. The `java.sql.ResultSet` interface is defined to describe an object, known as `ResultSet` object, implemented by a third party vendor as a part of JDBC driver. The `ResultSet` object represents the data in a tabular form that is retrieved by executing an SQL query. It implies that a `ResultSet` object represents a table of data that is CURSOR returned by executing an SQL query. The DB CURSOR is a buffer (cache) where the query result can be saved (it means DB CURSOR is a place in the DB). A `ResultSet` object encapsulates the resultant tabular data obtained when a query is executed. A `ResultSet` object holds zero or more objects, where each of the objects represents one row that may span over one or more table columns. We can obtain a `ResultSet` object by using the `executeQuery()` or `getResultSet()` method of a JDBC `Statement` object. Some of the important points related to a `ResultSet` are as follows:

- A `ResultSet` follows the iterate pattern.
- A `ResultSet` object is associated with a statement within a connection.
- A single `ResultSet` object can be opened at a time; however, you can obtain multiple `ResultSets` by using one statement. When we try to open a `ResultSet` using a statement that is already associated with an opened `ResultSet`, the existing `ResultSet` is implicitly closed.
- A `ResultSet` is automatically closed when a JDBC Statement, which is used to generate it, is closed.

The following subsection deals with the methods of the `ResultSet` interface.

Describing the Methods of ResultSet

The `java.sql.ResultSet` interface provides certain methods to work with the `ResultSet` object. The `ResultSet` object supports various methods that include moving the cursor through the rows represented by this object and read the data. Table 4.3 shows some of the most commonly used methods in `ResultSet`:

Table 4.3: Methods of the java.sql.ResultSet Interface

Method	Description
`absolute(int row)`	Moves the cursor to the given number of rows in a `ResultSet` object.
`afterLast()`	Moves the cursor just after the last row in a `ResultSet` object.
`beforeFirst()`	Moves the cursor before the first row in a `ResultSet` object.
`cancelRowUpdates()`	Cancels all the changes made to the rows in a `ResultSet` object.
`clearWarnings()`	Clears all warning messages on a `ResultSet` object.
`close()`	Closes a `ResultSet` object and releases all the JDBC resources connected to it.
`deleteRow()`	Deletes the specified row from a `ResultSet` object, as well as from the database.
`first()`	Moves the cursor to the first row in a `ResultSet` object.
`getArray()`	Retrieves the value of the specified column from the `ResultSet` object.
`getAsciiStream()`	Retrieves a specified column in the current row as a stream of ASCII characters.
`getXXX()`	Retrieves the column values of the specified types from the current row. The type can be any of the Java pre-defined data types, such as `int`, `long`, `Byte`, `character`, `String`, `double`, or large object types.
`getDate()`	Retrieves the specified column from the current row in `ResultSet`. The object retrieved is of the `java.sql.Date` type in the `Java` programming language.
`getDate(String columnName, Calendar cal)`	Retrieves the specified column from the current row in `ResultSet` and uses the given calendar to construct the time in milliseconds. The object retrieved is of the `java.sql.Date` type in the Java programming language.
`getFetchDirection()`	Retrieves the direction (forward or reverse) in which the `ResultSet` retrieves the row from a database.
`getFetchSize()`	Retrieves the size of the associated `ResultSet` object.
`getMetaData()`	Retrieves the number, type, and properties of the `ResultSet` object.
`getObject(int columnIndex)`	Retrieves a specified column in the current row as an object in the Java programming language.

Table 4.3: Methods of the java.sql.ResultSet Interface

Method	Description
`getObject(int i, Map map)`	Retrieves a specified column in the current row as an object in the Java programming language and also uses the `Map` object that contains mapping of the SQL structured or distinct type.
`getObject(String columnName)`	Retrieves a specified column on the basis of the given column name in the current row as an object.
`getObject(String colName, Map map)`	Retrieves a specified column on the basis of the given column name as an object in the Java programming language and also uses the `Map` object that contains mapping of the SQL structured or distinct type.
`getRow()`	Retrieves the current row number associated with the `ResultSet` object.
`getStatement()`	Retrieves the Statement object associated with the `ResultSet` object.
`getTime(int columnIndex)`	Retrieves the column values as a `java.sql.Time` object.
`getTime(int columnIndex, Calendar cal)`	Retrieves the column values as a `java.sql.Time` object and uses the given calendar to construct the time in milliseconds.
`getTime(String columnName)`	Retrieves the column values as a `java.sql.Time` object on the basis of the specified column name.
`getTime(String columnName, Calendar cal)`	Retrieves the column values as a `java.sql.Time` object on the basis of the specified column name and uses the given calendar to construct the time in milliseconds.
`getTimestamp(int columnIndex)`	Retrieves the column values as a `java.sql.Timestamp` object.
`getTimestamp(int columnIndex, Calendar cal)`	Retrieves the column values as a `java.sql.Timestamp` object and uses the given calendar to construct the time in milliseconds.
`getTimestamp(String columnName)`	Retrieves the column values as a `java.sql.Timestamp` object on the basis of the specified column name.
`getTimestamp(String columnName, Calendar cal)`	Retrieves the column values as a `java.sql.Timestamp` object on the basis of the specified column name and uses the given calendar to construct the time in milliseconds.
`getType()`	Retrieves the type of the `ResultSet` object used in a connection.
`getWarnings()`	Retrieves the warning reported on the `ResultSet` object.
`insertRow()`	Inserts the specified row and the contents into the `ResultSet` object as well as into the database.
`isAfterLast()`	Moves the cursor of the `ResultSet` object to the end of the last row.
`isBeforeFirst()`	Retrieves whether the cursor is before the first row in the `ResultSet` or not.
`isFirst()`	Retrieves whether the cursor is on the first row or not.
`isLast()`	Detects whether the cursor is on the last row of the `ResultSet` object or not.
`last()`	Moves the cursor to the first row in the `ResultSet` object. It returns true if the cursor is positioned on first row, and false if the `ResultSet` object does not contain any rows.
`moveToCurrentRow()`	Moves the cursor to the current row in the `ResultSet` object.
`moveToInsertRow()`	Moves the cursor to the inserted row in the `ResultSet` object.
`next()`	Moves the cursor forward one row. It returns true if the cursor is now positioned on a row, and false if the cursor is positioned after the last row.
`previous()`	Moves the cursor backward one row. It returns true if the cursor is now positioned on a row, and false if the cursor is positioned before the first row.
`refreshRow()`	Refreshes the current row associated with the `ResultSet` object with the recent updates.

Table 4.3: Methods of the java.sql.ResultSet Interface

Method	Description
`relative(int rows)`	Moves the cursor to a relative number of rows or columns specified in the method.
`rowDeleted()`	Retrieves whether the row has already been deleted or not.
`rowInserted()`	Determines whether the current row has an insertion or not.
`rowUpdated()`	Retrieves whether the current row has been updated or not.
`setFetchDirection(int direction)`	Sets the direction of the `ResultSet` object.
`setFetchSize(int rows)`	Sets the size of the `ResultSet` object.
`updateArray()`	Updates the column in the `ResultSet` object with a `java.sql.Array` value.
`updateXXX()`	Updates the column values of the current row of the specified types. The type can be any of the Java predefined data types, such as `int`, `long`, `Byte`, `character`, `String`, `double`, and the large object types.
`updateRow()`	Updates the current row with the new contents.
`wasNull()`	Reports whether the last column has an SQL `NULL` value or not.
`updateNull(String columnName)`	Updates a specific column with a `NULL` value.
`updateObject(int columnIndex, Object x)`	Updates the specific column with an `Object` value.
`updateTime(int columnIndex, Time x)`	Updates the time value with a `java.sql.Time` value.
`updateTimestamp(int columnIndex, Timestamp x)`	Updates the time value with a `java.sql.Timestamp` value.
`getConcurrency()`	Retrieves the concurrency mode of the `ResultSet` object.
`getCursorName()`	Retrieves the SQL cursor name used by the `ResultSet` object.

After having the theoretical knowledge about the methods of the `ResultSet` interface, let's now understand the process of retrieving data from a database with the help of `ResultSet`.

Using ResultSet

After obtaining a `ResultSet` object, you can use it to read the data encapsulated in it, that is, the data stored in the `ResultSet`.

Figure 4.17 shows the process flow involved in getting `ResultSet` from the `Statement` object and reading the data from the `ResultSet` object. In Figure 4.17, you can have a look at the `ResultSet` operations:

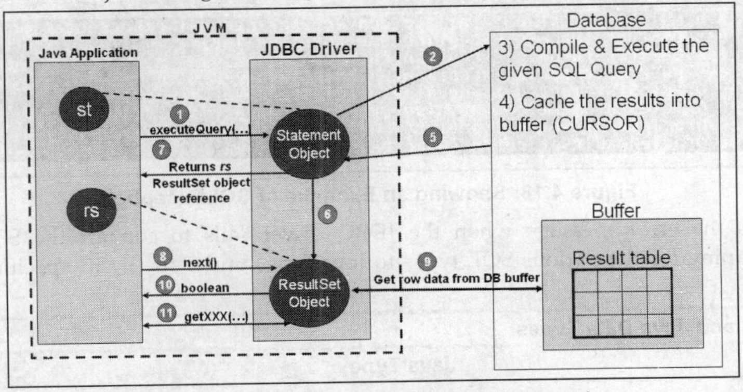

Figure 4.17: Explaining the ResultSet Operations

In Figure 4.17, the **st** and **rs** parameters represent the `Statement` and `ResultSet` object references respectively.

NOTE

*For every `ResultSet.next()` method invoked, the JDBC driver may not necessarily get the data (row) from the database buffer (that is, after Step 8 shown in Figure 4.17, there may not always be a Step 9). Instead, it can get multiple rows of data at a time and buffer it on the client side, and this depends on the fetch size set to the **`ResultSet`** object. The fetch size for the `ResultSet` object can be set using the `setFetchSize(int)` method.*

You can retrieve data from a `ResultSet` in two simple steps:

1. Move the cursor position to the required row.
2. Read the column data using the `getXXX()` methods.

Let's discuss these steps in detail.

Moving the Cursor Position

When you obtain a `ResultSet`, the cursor is positioned before the first row initially. You can use the `next()` method of `ResultSet` to move the cursor position to the next record in `ResultSet`. When the cursor is moved to the next record, it returns a Boolean value that indicates whether or not the cursor has moved after the last record. The `next()` method returns true if it successfully positions the cursor on the next row. However, if the cursor is positioned after the last row, the `next()` method returns false.

Reading the Column Values

After moving the cursor to the respective row, you can use the getter methods of `ResultSet` to retrieve the data from the row where the cursor is positioned. The getter methods of `ResultSet` are overloaded to support the navigation of the column by using its index or name. The `ResultSet` object supports two versions of getter methods for each of the JDBC type. One of these two methods takes column index of type `int` as input, where column index starts with 1, and other method takes column name of type `java.lang.String`. Column names passed into getter methods are not case sensitive. If a select list contains the same column more than once, the first instance of the column returns.

For example, suppose a student's table contains two columns, *stdid* and *stdName*. Now, if we obtain a `ResultSet` for the query `select stdName, stdid from students`, the column index 1 locates *stdName*, whereas index 2 locates *stdid*. The `ResultSet` interface has `getXXX()` method for all the basic and predefined complex types. Some of the `getXXX()` methods are listed in Table 4.3.

When the getter methods of `ResultSet` are invoked, the JDBC driver attempts to convert the requested column value into the respective Java type and returns the Java value. However, if it fails to convert the column value into its respective Java type, it throws `SQLException` and describes it as a conversion error. Figure 4.18 shows the exceptions thrown for the Oracle Thin driver:

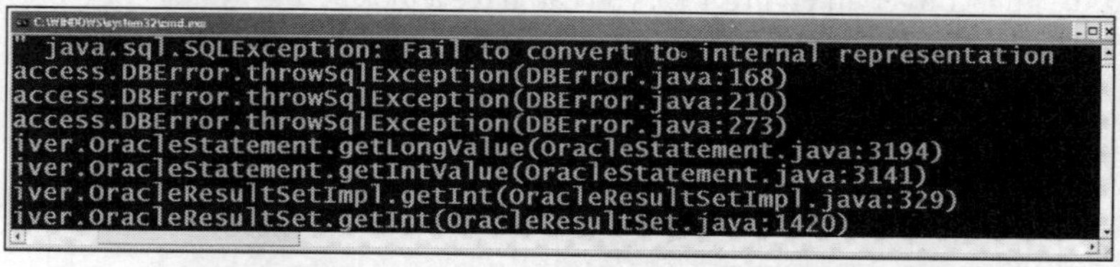

Figure 4.18: Showing an Example of SQLException

Figure 4.18 shows the error message when the JDBC driver fails to convert the SQL type to Java type. The allowable mapping for the various SQL types to Java types under the JDBC specification are described in Table 4.4:

Table 4.4: JDBC and Java Data Types

JDBC Type	Java Type
`CHAR`	`String`
`VARCHAR`	`String`

Table 4.4: JDBC and Java Data Types

JDBC Type	Java Type
LONGVARCHAR	String
NUMERIC	java.math.BigDecimal
DECIMAL	java.math.BigDecimal
BIT	boolean
BOOLEAN	boolean
TINYINT	byte
SMALLINT	Short
INTEGER	int

The `getObject()` method of the `ResultSet` object retrieves the value of the designated column in the current row of `ResultSet` as an object in the Java programming language. The `getObject()` method of the `ResultSet` object uses the conversions as described in Table 4.5:

Table 4.5: Showing the Conversion of JDBC into Java Type

JDBC Type	Java Object Type
CHAR	java.lang.String
VARCHAR	java.lang.String
LONGVARCHAR	java.lang.String
NUMERIC	java.math.BigDecimal
DECIMAL	java.math.BigDecimal
BIT	java.lang.Boolean
BOOLEAN	java.lang.Boolean
TINYINT	java.lang.Integer
SMALLINT	java.lang.Integer
INTEGER	java.lang.Integer
BIGINT	java.lang.Long
REAL	java.lang.Float
FLOAT	Double
DOUBLE	Double
BINARY	byte[]
VARBINARY	byte[]
LONGVARBINARY	byte[]
DATE	java.sql.Date
TIME	java.sql.Time
TIMESTAMP	java.sql.Timestamp
DISTINCT	Object type of underlying Type
CLOB	java.sql.Clob
BLOB	java.sql.Blob
ARRAY	java.sql.Array
STRUCT	java.sql.Struct or java.sql.SQLData
REF	java.sql.Ref
DATALINK	java.net.URL
JAVA_OBJECT	Underlying Java class
ROWID	java.sql.RowId
NCHAR	java.lang.String

Table 4.5: Showing the Conversion of JDBC into Java Type	
JDBC Type	**Java Object Type**
NVARCHAR	java.lang.String
LONGNVARCHAR	java.lang.String

You learned about ResultSet and the steps involved in using it to access data in a database. Let's now look at some examples of using ResultSet.

Retrieving All the Rows from a Table

You can retrieve rows from a table by using the ResultSet object. Let's now understand how you can retrieve all the rows of a table, the mytable table in our case. A row in mytable can store data of different types, such as a String, integer, and floating-point number. Let's create the GetAllRows.java file to retrieve all the rows of the mytable table. Listing 4.9 provides the code of the GetAllRows.java file (you can find this file online in the code/Chapter4 folder):

Listing 4.9: Showing the code for the GetAllRows.java File

```
package com.santosh.jdbc;
import java.sql.*;
/**
 * @author Santosh
 */
public class GetAllRows {

  public static void main(String args[])throws
  SQLException, ClassNotFoundException {

        //Get Connection
        Connection con=prepareConnection ();

        // Obtain a Statement
        Statement st=con.createStatement ();
        String query = "select * from mytable";

        //Execute the Query
        ResultSet rs=st.executeQuery (query);

        System.out.println ("COL1\tCOL2\tCOL3");
/*
Now the ResultSet rs cursor is placed before the first record. So, before using the getXXX
  methods to get the selected column value, move the cursor to the valid record (current
  record).
*/
  while (rs.next ()){
        System.out.print (rs.getString ("COL1") + "\t");
        System.out.print (rs.getInt ("COL2") + "\t");
        System.out.println (rs.getDouble ("COL3"));
        }//while
        con.close();
  }//main

  public static Connection prepareConnection()
        throws SQLException,
        ClassNotFoundException  {

        String driverClassName="oracle.jdbc.driver.OracleDriver";
        String url="jdbc:oracle:thin:@mysys:1521:sandb";
        String username="scott";
        String password="tiger";

        //Load driver class
        Class.forName (driverClassName);
```

```
        // Obtain a connection
        return DriverManager. getConnection (url, username, password);
    }//prepareConnection
}//class
```

In Listing 4.9, we executed the `SELECT` statement to retrieve all the rows of the mytable table. The `SELECT` statement is executed by invoking the `executeQuery()` method of the `ResultSet object (rs)`.

In Listing 4.9, the `next()` method is used to move the cursor position in the forward direction. The GetAllRows.java file throws an exception if the user tries to move the cursor in the backward direction from the relative position of the cursor.

NOTE

*The column names used with the **`getXXX()`** methods of **`ResultSet`** are not the actual table column names; instead, they are the resulted table column names. For an instance, if we use a query select col1 as c1, col2 as c2, col3 as c3 from mytable, the column names that we need to use in these **`getXXX()`** methods are c1, c2, and c3 and not col1, col2, and col3.*

In Listing 4.9, we have obtained data by using column names. However, we can obtain data by using column numbers also. Use the following code snippet in place of the code snippet with column names to obtain the data using column numbers:

```
while (rs.next()) {
    System.out.print (rs.getString (1) + "\t");
    System.out.print (rs.getInt (2) + "\t");
    System.out.println (rs.getDouble (3));
}//while
```

NOTE

*Using the column index form of **`getXXX()`** methods is more efficient than the column name form, because the driver does not have to deal with the extra steps of parsing the column name, finding it in the select list, and then turning it into a number. The **`getXXX(String name)`** methods of **`ResultSet`** locate the first found column with the given name and access the column value with that index.*

Compiling and running the code shown in Listing 4.9 give the output displayed in Figure 4.19:

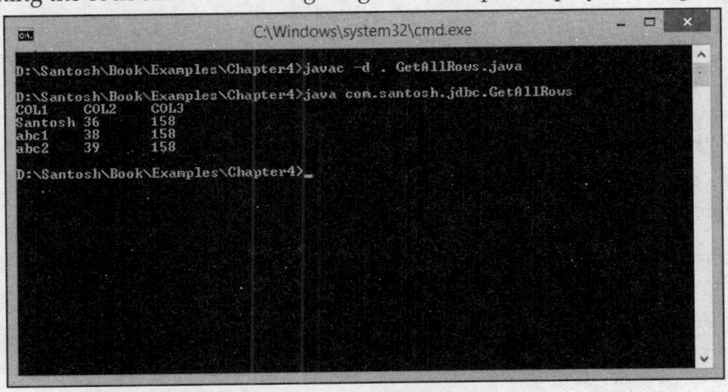

Figure 4.19: Showing the Output of the GetAllRows.java File

If we try to read the column values obtained after executing the query, without calling the `next()` method on `ResultSet`, an exception is raised. This exception is shown in Figure 4.20:

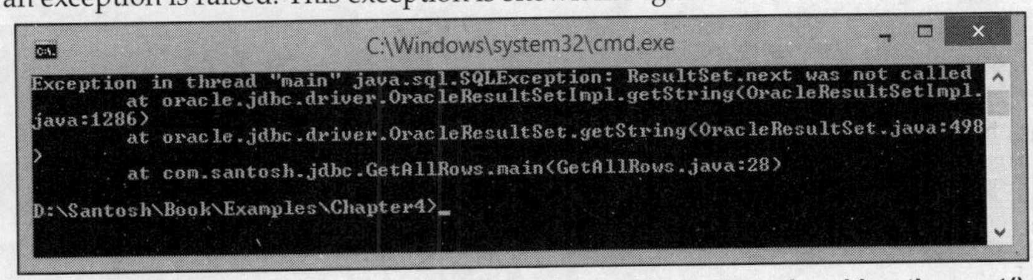

Figure 4.20: Showing the Output of the GetAllRows.java File without Invoking the next() Method

Note that even if we retrieve only one record (that is, one row), we still need to call the `ResultSet.next()` method before reading column values.

If we attempt to retrieve/read the row values even after the last record (in Listing 4.9, for example, if we try to call `getXXX()` methods after the while loop), an exception is raised, as shown in Figure 4.21:

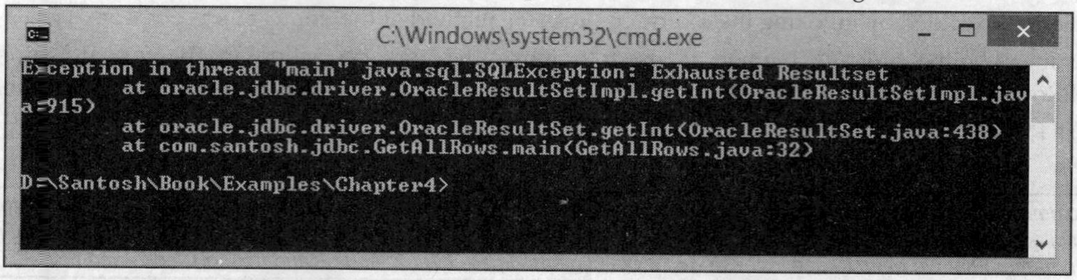

Figure 4.21: Showing the Output of GetAllRows.java by Accessing ResultSet after Last Record

Therefore, if an `SQLException` is raised (Figure 4.21), you must check the control of your application to ensure that it does not read the data when the `ResultSet` cursor position is at `afterLast` and the `ResultSet` type is forward only.

Let's now learn how to retrieve data of a particular column from a table by using `ResultSet`.

Retrieving a Particular Column Using ResultSet

In addition to retrieving all the rows from a table, you can also retrieve data of a particular column from `ResultSet`. Listing 4.10 provides the code of the GetData.java file to retrieve data of the col1 and col2 columns from the mytable table (you can find this file online in the code/Chapter4 folder):

Listing 4.10: Showing the code for the GetData.java File

```
package com.santosh.jdbc;

import java.sql.*;
/**
  * @author Santosh
  */
public class GetData {

   public static void main(String args[])throws SQLException,
   ClassNotFoundException {
   //try{
         //Get Connection
         Connection con=prepareConnection();

         // Obtain a Statement
         Statement st=con.createStatement();

         String query = "select col3, col1 from mytable";

         //Execute the Query
         ResultSet rs=st.executeQuery(query);

         // System.out.println ("COL1\tCOL3");
         while (rs.next()){
                System.out.print (rs.getString(2)+ "\t");
                System.out.println (rs.getDouble(1));
         }//while
                System.out.print (rs.getString(2)+ "\t");
   //}catch(SQLException e){System.out.println(e.getErrorCode());}
   }//main
   public static Connection prepareConnection()throws
```

```
    SQLException, ClassNotFoundException  {
  String driverClassName="oracle.jdbc.driver.OracleDriver";
    String url="jdbc:oracle:thin:@mysys:1521:sandb";
  /*
  String driverClassName="sun.jdbc.odbc.JdbcOdbcDriver";
         String url="jdbc:odbc:santoshDSN";
  */     String username="scott";
         String password="tiger";

         //Load driver class
         Class.forName(driverClassName);

         // Obtain a connection
         return DriverManager.getConnection(url,username,password);
    }//prepareConnection
  }//class
```

In Listing 4.10, the `SELECT` statement is used to retrieve the data of the *col1* and *col2* columns from mytable, and the `next()` method is used to move the cursor position in the forward direction.

The output of Listing 4.10 in respect to the `next()` method is given in Figure 4.22:

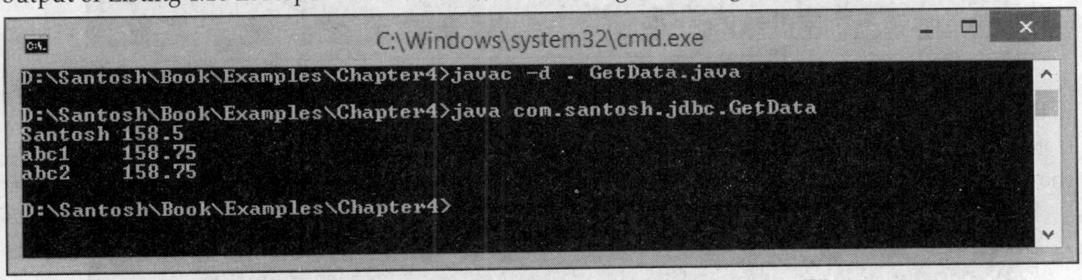

Figure 4.22: Showing the Output of the GetData.java File

If we change the select query (that is, `select col1, col3 from mytable`) of Listing 4.10 with the following select query, then in the `getXXX()` methods of `ResultSet`, we should pass `c1` and `c3` instead of `COL1` and `COL3` respectively:

```
query = "select col1 as c1, col3 as c3 from mytable";
```

In other words, if you use the preceding select query in Listing 4.10, you also need to make the following changes in Listing 4.10:

```
System.out.print (rs.getString ("c1") + "\t");
System.out.println (rs.getDouble ("c3"));
```

The internal implementation of column name version of the `getXXX()` method in a `ResultSet` is shown in the following code snippet:

```
public String getString(String s){
   int index=findColumn(s);
   return getString(index);
}
```

In the preceding code snippet, the `findColumn(String column_name)` of `ResultSet` returns the index number of the first found column, where the column name matches the given string column name.

The following are the possible exceptions that might be raised while executing this application:

a. `ClassNotFoundException` may be raised, as explained in the *Creating a Table* subsection of the *Using Statement* section to create a table through JDBC.

b. If the column names used in the SQL query are not correct, the exception is raised as shown in Figure 4.23:

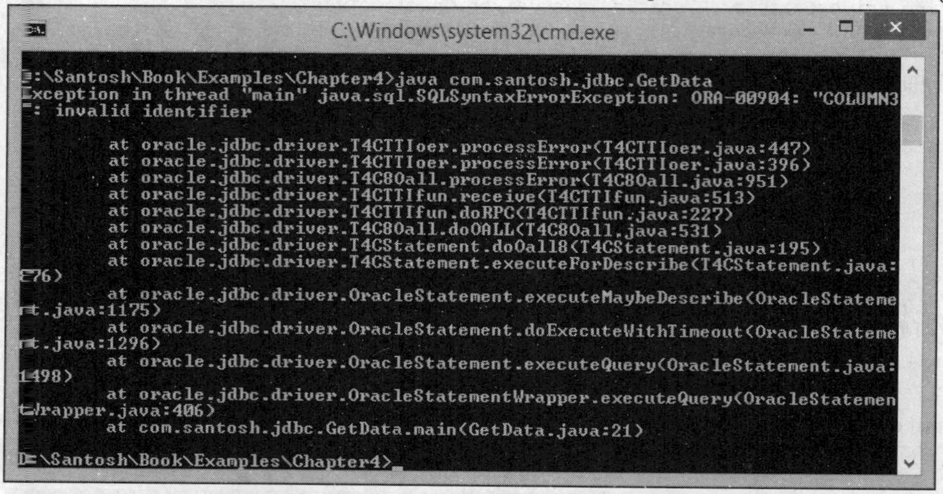

Figure 4.23: Showing an Example of SQLException when Column Name is Incorrect

In this case, verify that the column names used in the query are correct.

c. If the column names used with the `getXXX()` methods of `ResultSet` are wrong, the exception is raised as shown in Figure 4.24:

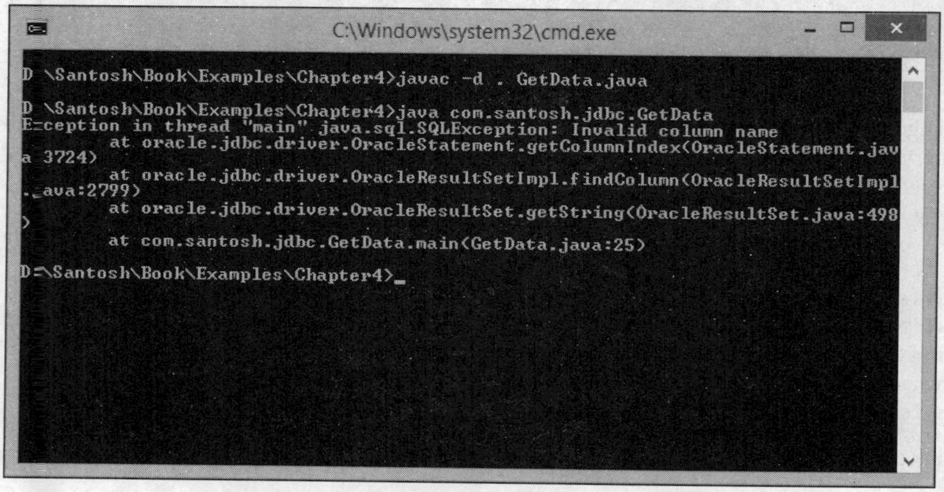

Figure 4.24: Showing the SQLException Exception when Column Name is Wrong in the getXXX() Method

You must note that the column names are not case-sensitive in Oracle.

If the exception is raised, as shown in Figure 4.24, you should check the column names used with the `getXXX()` methods of `ResultSet`. Note that the preceding two exceptions are different, and to programmatically differentiate these exceptions and write supplementary codes, we need to depend on SQL State and Error Code that are vendor-dependent. For example, if we observe the exception message shown in Figure 4.23, we find the exception message as ORA-00904. In this exception message, the 00904 number represents the error code. We use the `getErrorCode()` method of `SQLException` to obtain only the exception error code in an application.

d. Instead of using column names with the `getXXX()` methods of `ResultSet`, we can use column index. However, if improper column index is used, the exception shown in Figure 4.25 is raised:

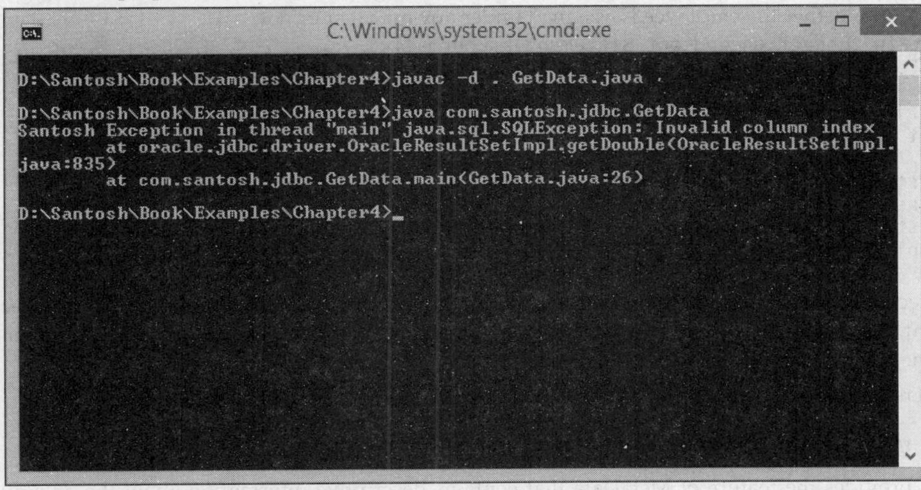

Figure 4.25: Showing an Example of SQLException when Improper Column Index is Used

In this case, verify that the column indexes used with the `getXXX()` methods are correct.

NOTE

You must remember that a column index starts with 1. In addition, the **`ResultSet`** *columns within each row should be read in the left-to-right order, and each column should be read only once for maximum portability. This is done because some of the JDBC drivers with forward-only* `ResultSet` *allow you to neither read the column values in a row multiple times nor move back. For example, after reading column values with index 2, you are not allowed to read column values with index 1 of the same row.*

We can also use the preceding example to query for particular rows. However, for this, you need to change the query as shown in the following code snippet:

```
String query= "select * from mytable where COL1='Santosh'";
  Or
String query= "select * from mytable where COL2=36";
  Or
String query= "select * from mytable where COL2>=36";
```

While retrieving column or row values from a database, you may come across a `NULL` value. In other words, it is possible that due to non-availability of data either for a column or for a row in a table, the `NULL` value is inserted in the column or row. In such a situation, you should know how to work with (retrieve) `NULL` values, which is discussed in the following section.

Handling NULL Values

In a database, when a column contains a `NULL` value, it means that the column's value is unknown (unassigned/unavailable/inapplicable). In Java, `NULL` means that an object type variable has not been initialized with reference to an instance. Moreover, Java primitive types cannot hold `NULL` values. For example, consider a table with a column name col1 of type number. Suppose the col1 value of one row is `NULL` and of the other row is 0. In this case, if we try to get the values of these columns by using the `getInt()` method in Java, the value retuned in both cases would be 0 for both the rows; however, 0 and `NULL` both are different. In this context, 0 is a value and `NULL` indicates that the value is unknown.

Similarly, when we use the `getString()` method in the previous example, it returns a `NULL` value, and when we use the `getDouble()` method, it returns 0. In addition, we can use the `ResultSet.wasNull()` method to realize whether the value retrieved using the `ResultSet` object is `NULL`. The `ResultSet.wasNull()` method returns a Boolean value; if it is true, the last returned value by this `ResultSet` is `NULL`, and if it is false, the value is not `NULL`. To understand this, let's take an example of the standard demo table *emp* in the Oracle database. In this table, the *mgr* column holds the manager ID of the employees, and the *mgr* column shows NULL for the employees who are not under the control of any manager. Now, we can use the following sample code snippet to find whether the employee is assigned under any manager or not:

```
//Obtain Connection and get Statement as normally
ResultSet rs= st.executeQuery ("select ename, mgr from emp");
while (rs.next()){
   String ename=rs.getString(1);
   int mgr=rs.getInt(2);
   if (rs.wasNull())
   System.out.println("Employee, "+ename+" is not under any manager");
   else
   System.out.println("Employee, "+ename+" is working under the manager with an
   employee ID "+mgr);
}
```

In the preceding code snippet, the `wasNull()` method is invoked on the `ResultSet` object after the `rs.getInt(2)` method is called, and therefore, invoking the `ResultSet.wasNull()` method returns whether the *mgr* value returned was `NULL` or not.

After understanding `NULL` values, let's learn how to use the `ResultSetMetaData` interface.

Working with the ResultSetMetaData Interface

JDBC API provides the feature of MetaData that contains descriptive information about the data available in a database. JDBC MetaData provides information about tables, views, column names, column data types, stored procedures, and databases. In short, we can say that MetaData offers information about the data available in a database, as well as all the query results in the database.

JDBC API provides two interfaces, `ResultSetMetaData` and `DatabaseMetaData`, to provide the metadata information of a database. The `ResultSetMetaData` interface offers information about the columns in a `ResultSet`, such as the column name, column data type, and length of the columns. The `DatabaseMetaData` interface provides information about the database structure, table names, views, constraints used in the database, and data types.

Describing ResultSetMetaData

The `java.sql.ResultSetMetaData` interface is used to describe a JDBC Driver object that encapsulates the metadata of the cursor. The `ResultSetMetaData` object is used to retrieve information about the columns in a `ResultSet`. It can also be used to get the information, such as column names, column data types, and column length, related to a particular result. This object does not provide any information about the database or the number of rows present in the result. The `ResultSetMetaData` object is obtained by using the `ResultSet` object, that is, by invoking the `getMetaData()` method on the `ResultSet` object. The `ResultSetMetaData` object obtained by using a `ResultSet` object encapsulates the information about the types and properties of the columns in that `ResultSet`.

Table 4.6 shows some of the most commonly used methods of the `ResultSetMetaData` interface:

Table 4.6: Methods of the ResultSetMetaData Interface

Method	Description
`getColumnCount()`	Returns an integer value and retrieves the number of columns in the `ResultSet` object.
`getColumnName(int index)`	Takes the column index and returns the column name.
`getColumnTypeName(int index)`	Takes the column index and returns the database specific type name.
`getColumnType(int index)`	Takes the column index and returns the integer value that indicates the columns of SQL type. It also compares this value with the `java.sql.Types` constants.
`isAutoIncrement(int index)`	Returns the Boolean value indicating whether the column at the given index is auto-incremented or not.
`isNullable(int index)`	Indicates whether the column at the given index accepts NULL value or not.

Table 4.6: Methods of the ResultSetMetaData Interface

Method	Description
`getCatalogName(int index)`	Accesses the catalog name of the column of a table associated with the `ResultSet` object.
`getColumnClassName(int index)`	Retrieves the `java` class name associated with the `ResultSet` object.
`getColumnDisplaySize(int index)`	Retrieves the width of the columns associated with the `ResultSet` object.
`getColumnLabel(int index)`	Retrieves the title of the specified column in the `ResultSet` object.
`getPrecision(int column)`	Retrieves the precision value (number of digits after the decimal point) of the decimal digits of the particular column in the `ResultSet` object.
`getScale(int column)`	Retrieves the number of decimal digits present to the right of the decimal point for a designated column in the `ResultSet` object.
`getSchemaName(int column)`	Retrieves the schema name of the specified column in the `ResultSet` object.
`getTableName(int column)`	Retrieves the table name of the specified column in the `ResultSet` object.
`isCaseSensitive(int column)`	Indicates whether the case of a column matters in context with the associated `ResultSet` object or not.
`isCurrency(int column)`	Indicates whether the specified column indicates a cash value or not.
`isDefinitelyWritable(int column)`	Indicates that a column is writable.
`isReadOnly(int column)`	Indicates that the specified column is read only, and write operations cannot be performed in the column values.
`isSearchable(int column)`	Indicates whether a column value can be used as a condition in the WHERE clause or not.
`isSigned(int column)`	Indicates whether the column values in a particular column are signed or not.
`isWritable(int column)`	Indicates whether a write operation is possible on a column value or not.

After having the theoretical knowledge about the `ResultSetMetaData` interface, let's create an application to demonstrate the implementation of this interface.

Using ResultSetMetaData

We learned earlier that the `java.sql.ResultSetMetaData` interface provides various methods to retrieve information about the `ResultSet` object. The information for the `ResultSet` object can be retrieved by using the `ResultSetMetaData` object. The following code snippet shows how to create an object of `ResultSetMetaData`:

```
Statement stmt = conn.createStatement();    // Creating a Statement object.
ResultSet rs = stmt.executeQuery();        // creating a ResultSet object.
ResultSetMetaData rsmd = rs.getMetaData(); // Creating  a ResultSetMetaData object.
```

The `ResultSetMetaData` object is used to access the metadata for a `ResultSet`. Listing 4.11 shows the implementation of the `ResultSetMetaData` interface (you can find the ResultSetMDEx.java file online in the code/Chapter4 folder):

Listing 4.11: Showing the code for the ResultSetMDEx.java File

```
package com.santosh.jdbc;

import java.sql.*;
import java.util.*;
/**
  * @author Santosh
  */

public class ResultSetMDEx {
```

```
public static void main(String s[]) throws Exception {

      Driver d=(Driver)
      Class.forName("oracle.jdbc.driver.OracleDriver").newInstance();

      Properties p= new Properties ();
      p.put ("user", "scott");
      p.put ("password", "tiger");

      Connection con=d.connect ("jdbc:oracle:thin:@mysys:1521:sandb",p);
      // Creating a Statement object
      Statement st = con.createStatement ();

      ResultSet rs=st.executeQuery ("select * from "+s [0]);
      //Table name is taken as a command line argument

      // Creating the ResultSetMetaData object
      ResultSetMetaData rsmd=rs.getMetaData();

      System.out.println("Table Name : "+s[0]);

      int colcount=rsmd.getColumnCount();

      for (int i=1; i<=colcount; i++) {
            System.out.print (rsmd.getColumnName(i)+"\t");
            System.out.println (rsmd.getColumnTypeName(i));
      }//for
      con.close();
  }//main
}//class
```

Listing 4.11 is used to access the properties of the `ResultSet` object by using the object of `ResultSetMetaData`. The `ResultSet` object invokes the `getMetaData()` method, which returns the `ResultSetMetaData` object that is further used to retrieve the column names, types, and length for a specific `ResultSet`. In Listing 4.11, the table for the `ResultSet` object is given as an argument in the command line. The `ResultSetMDEx.java` application retrieves the columns of the designated table, along with the column types, and displays it to the user. The user can then put any of the existing tables as a command line argument to retrieve the MetaData information about that table. The output of Listing 4.11 is shown in Figure 4.26, which displays various tables, such as mytable and emp, used as arguments:

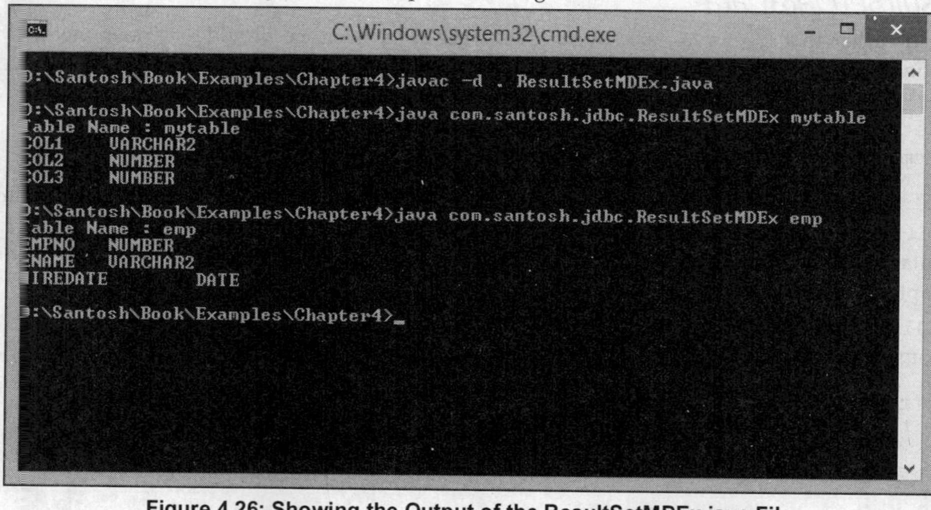

Figure 4.26: Showing the Output of the ResultSetMDEx.java File

Note that the tables for which the metadata is to be displayed must be present in the database to generate a `ResultSet` object. The following exception, as shown in Figure 4.27, is raised if the table or view (for which the user accesses the metadata) does not exist in the database:

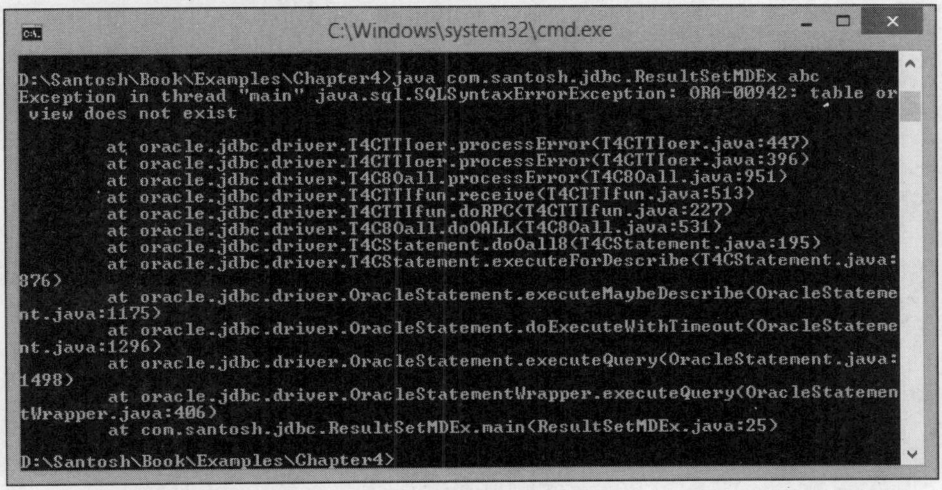

Figure 4.27: Showing Exception while Accessing Table that is not Available in a Database

Figure 4.27 shows the output while accessing a table not present in the database. Let's now understand how to create the SQLEditor in Java.

Creating SQLEditor in Java

The SQLEditor is a Java application created by using JDBC to view and edit the SQL data in the tables of a database. You can create a command-based or Windows-based editor to view the SQL data. We learn to create both these editors next.

Creating the Command-Based SQLEditor

Let's first create the command-based SQLEditor by using the `execute()`, `getUpdateCount()`, and `getResultSet()` methods of the `Statement` object. You can also use `ResultSetMetaData` methods, such as `getColumnCount()` and `getColumnName()`, to create a command-based SQLEditor.

Perform the following steps to create the command-based SQLEditor:

1. Create the MySQLEditor.java file, as shown in Listing 4.12 (you can find this file online in the code/Chapter4 folder):

Listing 4.12: Showing the code of the MySQLEditor.java File

```
package com.santosh.jdbc;

import java.sql.*;
import java.util.*;
import java.io.*;
/**
  * @author Santosh
  */
public class MySQLEditor {

  public static void main(String s[]) throws Exception {

        Properties p= new Properties();
        FileInputStream
```

```
        fis=new FileInputStream("MyDriverDetails.properties");
        p.load(fis);
        Driver d= (Driver) Class.forName
        ((String) p.get("driverClassName")).newInstance();
        Connection con=d.connect ((String)p.get("url"),p);
        Statement st=con.createStatement();
        DataInputStream dis=new DataInputStream(System.in);
        System.out.println("Editor Started, Connected to DB");

        while (true){
                System.out.print ("\nSQL>");
                String query=dis.readLine();

                boolean flag=st.execute(query);

                if (flag) {
                        ResultSet rs=st.getResultSet();
                        ResultSetMetaData rsmd=rs.getMetaData();
                        for (int i=1;i<=rsmd.getColumnCount();i++){
                                System.out.print (rsmd.getColumnName(i)+"\t");
                        }
                        System.out.println ();
                        System.out.println("------------------------------------------------
                        --------");
                        while (rs.next()) {
                                for (int i=1;i<=rsmd.getColumnCount();i++){
                                System.out.print (rs.getString(i)+"\t");
                                }//for
                                System.out.println ();
                        }//while
                }//if
                else {
                        int count=st.getUpdateCount();
                        System.out.println (count+" no(s) of records has
                        been effected by this query");
                }//else
        }//while
    }//main
}//class
```

The Java class in the Listing 4.12 uses the MyDriverDetails.properties file to get the driver and URL details.

2. Create the MyDriverDetails.properties file that allows you to specify the JDBC driver details to locate the required database. The code to create the properties file is shown in Listing 4.13 (you can find the MyDriverDetails.properties file online in the code/Chapter4 folder):

Listing 4.13: Showing the code of the MyDriverDetails.properties File

```
#MyDriverDetails.properties

driverClassName =oracle.jdbc.driver.OracleDriver
url=jdbc:oracle:thin:@mysys:1521:sandb
user=scott
password=tiger
```

3. Compile the Java source code to generate the class file and then execute the class using the following command at the command prompt, as shown in the following code snippet:

```
java com.santosh.jdbc.MySQLEditor
```

4. Connect the MySQLEditor program to the database, and a message, Editor Started, connected to DB is displayed after executing the command in the preceding step. An SQL prompt (`SQL>`) also appears at the command prompt, as shown at the top of Figure 4.28:

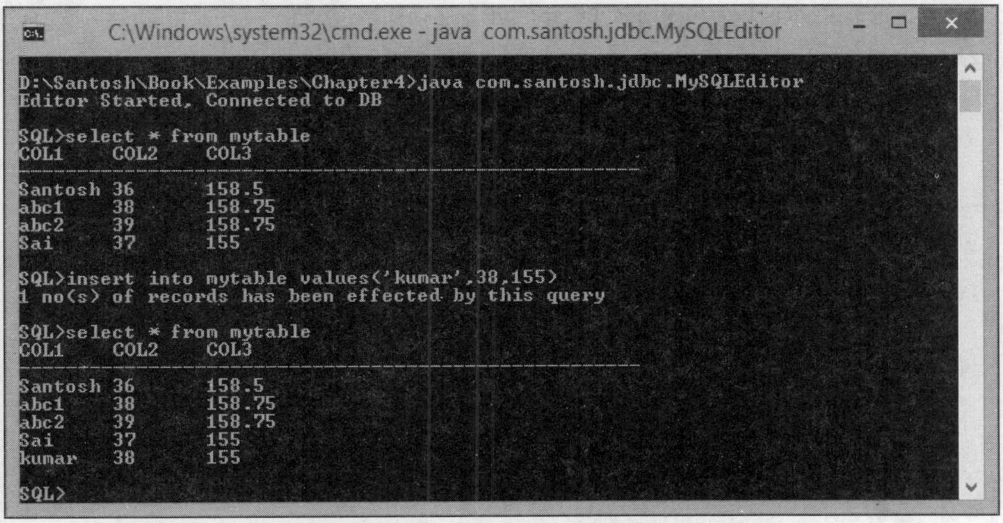

Figure 4.28: Executing Queries in Command-Based SQLEditor

5. Type any valid SQL statement at the `SQL>` prompt and view the results of the queries. Note that you do not end the query with ';'.

Figure 4.28 shows the output of the query executed at the `SQL>` prompt of MySQLEditor created in the preceding example.

In the next section, we add some Graphical User Interface (GUI) elements to our command-based SQLEditor.

Creating the Windows-Based SQLEditor

Let's now create a Windows-based SQL Editor that is required when you want to work with databases using GUI-based applications. First you need to create a `Java` file containing the code to create a Windows-based SQL Editor. You can find the code for SQLEditorWin.java file in Listing 4.14 (you can find the SQLEditorWin.java file online in the code/Chapter4 folder):

Listing 4.14: Showing the code of the SQLEditorWin.java File

```
/*SQLEditorWin.java*/

package com.santosh.jdbc;

import java.sql.*;
import java.awt.*;
import java.awt.event.*;
import java.util.*;
/**
 * @author  Santosh
 */
public class SQLEditorWin extends Frame {

    /** Creates new form SQLEditorWin */
    public SQLEditorWin() {
  try{
        prepareConnection();
        initComponents();
  }catch(Exception e)
  {
        System.out.println("Problem while getting connection");
        System.exit(0);
        }//catch
  }
```

```
void prepareConnection()throws Exception

Driver d=(Driver) Class.forName("oracle.jdbc.driver.OracleDriver").newInstance();

      Properties p= new Properties();
      p.put("user", "scott");
      p.put("password", "tiger");

      Connection con=d.connect("jdbc:oracle:thin:@mysys:1521:sandb",p);
      st=con.createStatement();
}//prepareConnection

private void initComponents() {
      label1 = new Label();
      input = new TextField();
      label2 = new Label();
      output = new TextArea();
      setLayout(null);
      setTitle("SQL Editor");

      addWindowListener(new WindowAdapter() {
              public void windowClosing(WindowEvent evt) {
                      exitForm(evt);
      }
});

    label1.setAlignment(Label.CENTER);
    label1.setFont(new Font("Arial", 1, 14));
    label1.setText("SQL Editor");
    add(label1);
    label1.setBounds(0, 40, 640, 40);
    input.addActionListener(new ActionListener() {
       public void actionPerformed(ActionEvent evt) {
              inputActionPerformed(evt);
       }
});

add(input);
input.setBounds(70, 100, 590, 30);

label2.setAlignment(Label.RIGHT);
label2.setText("SQL>");
add(label2);
label2.setBounds(0, 100, 70, 30);

output.setBackground(new Color(255, 255, 255));
output.setEditable(false);
add(output);
output.setBounds(10, 140, 660, 290);

pack();
Dimension screenSize = Toolkit.getDefaultToolkit().getScreenSize();
setSize(new Dimension(670, 432));
setLocation((screenSize.width-670)/2,(screenSize.height-432)/2);
      setResizable(false);
}
private void inputActionPerformed(ActionEvent evt) {
      try {
      if (input.getText().equals(""))
      throw new Exception("Invalid Query");
      boolean flag=st.execute(input.getText());
      if (flag)
      {
              displayResults();
      }//if
```

```
        else
        {
                output.setText(st.getUpdateCount()+" rows have been effected");
        }//else
}//try
catch(Exception e)
{
        output.setText("");
        output.setText("Invalid Query");
        output.setText(e.getMessage());
        e.printStackTrace();
}//catch
}

private void displayResults()throws SQLException
{
        StringBuffer sb=new StringBuffer();
        rs=st.getResultSet();
        ResultSetMetaData rmd=rs.getMetaData();
        int count=rmd.getColumnCount();
        for (int i=1;i<=count;i++)
        {
                System.out.println(rmd.getColumnDisplaySize(i));

        sb.append(getString(rmd.getColumnName(i),rmd.getColumnDisplaySize(i)));
}
sb.append("\n");
for (int i=1;i<=count;i++)
{
        sb.append(getLines(rmd.getColumnDisplaySize(i)));
}
sb.append("\n");

while (rs.next())
{
for (int i=1;i<=count;i++)
{
sb.append(getString(rs.getString(i),rmd.getColumnDisplaySize(i)));

}
sb.append("\n");
}//while

sb.append(count+" rows selected");
output.setText(sb.toString());
}//displayresults

private String getString(String s,int len)
{
        if (s==null)
        {
                s="";
        }
for(int i=s.length();i<=(len+5);i++)
{
        s+=" ";
}//for
return s;
}//getString

private String getLines(int len)
{
        String s="";
        for(int i=s.length();i<=(len);i++)
        {
                s+="-";
```

```
        }//for
        return s+"      ";
    }//getLines

    /** Exit the Application */
    private void exitForm(WindowEvent evt) {
        System.exit(0);
    }

    public static void main(String args[]) {
        new SQLEditorWin().show();
    }//main

    // Variables declaration
    private TextField input;
    private TextArea output;
    private Label label2,label1;

    private Connection con;
    private Statement st;
    private ResultSet rs;
    // End of variables declaration
}//class
```

Listing 4.14 provides GUI to the SQL Editor by adding the text field and text area to the editor. After compiling and executing the SQLEditorWin.java file, the output is displayed, as shown in Figure 4.29:

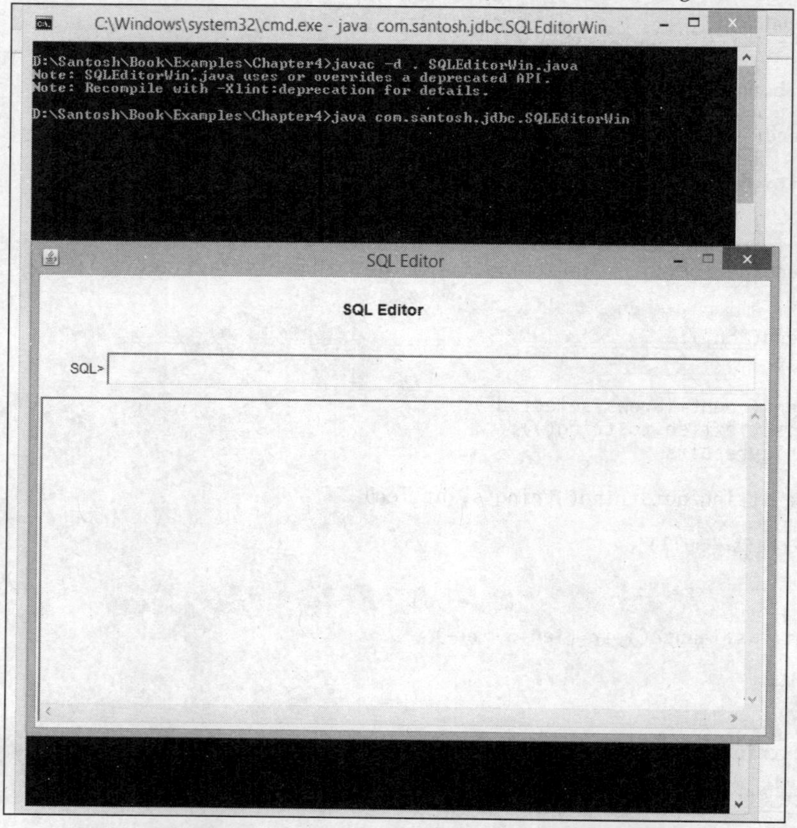

Figure 4.29: Showing the Output of the SQLEditorWin.java File

Now that you are familiar with `ResultSets` and `ResultSetMetaData`, let's understand some advanced concepts related to `ResultSet`.

Using Advanced Concepts of ResultSet

The `ResultSet` allows us to navigate from one record to another in the forward direction only, starting from beforeFirst to afterLast. Therefore, it allows forward-only fetching option. There can be situations when you want to fetch data in different directions or move to the specified record and scroll multiple times to see a record. The `ResultSet` interface addresses all these requirements by providing methods to retrieve the results by scrolling in forward as well as reverse direction and manipulating the results of the executed query. The following section explains the types of `ResultSet` objects that are available as per JDBC 2.0 specifications or higher versions.

Exploring Characteristics of the ResultSet Object

The `ResultSet` object in JDBC 2.0 or higher versions has different characteristics. For example, the `ResultSet` object can move the cursor in different directions or update the result of an executed query. These characteristics of `ResultSet` objects are determined based on the following parameters:

- ResultSet type
- `ResultSet` concurrency
- `ResultSet` holdability

Let's look at the detailed description of these parameters next.

ResultSet Types

The types of `ResultSet` determine the level of functionality of the `ResultSet` object in two ways:

- First is the direction in which its cursor can be moved, either in forward only or in both the directions.
- Second is how the concurrent changes done to the underlying data source are reflected in the `ResultSet` object while fetching the data.

There are three types of `ResultSet` objects, which are as follows:

- **TYPE_FORWARD_ONLY**—Refers to the type of `ResultSet` that is not scrollable. In this type of `ResultSet` object, the cursor moves only in forward direction, from beforeFirst to afterLast, by using the `next()` method. (The examples demonstrated so far in this book were of TYPE_FORWARD_ONLY type.)
- **TYPE_SCROLL_INSENSITIVE**—Refers to the type of `ResultSet` that is scrollable. In this type of `ResultSet` object, the cursor moves in the forward and backward directions, relative to the current or absolute position. The `ResultSet` is insensitive to changes made to the underlying data source while it is open. Therefore, if the selected data in the underlying data source is modified while reading the values from the `ResultSet`, the changes are not reflected in `ResultSet`.
- **TYPE_SCROLL_SENSITIVE**—Refers to the type of ResultSet that is scrollable and sensitive to the changes made to the underlying data source while it is open. The cursor moves in the forward and backward directions, relative to the current and absolute position.

By default, the type of `ResultSet` is TYPE_FORWARD_ONLY. The `ResultSet` type can be found by calling the `getType()` method on the `ResultSet` object. To find whether or not a `ResultSet` type is supported by the driver, an application can use the `supportsResultSetType(int)` method of `DatabaseMetaData` object. The `DatabaseMetaData.supportsResultSetType(int)` method takes `ResultSet` type as an argument and returns true if the specified type is supported, otherwise it returns false.

Let's discuss the methods available in the `ResultSet` interface to handle navigation in `ResultSet`.

Methods to Navigate a ResultSet

The methods declared in the `ResultSet` interface that are used to move the cursor in `ResultSet` are described as follows:

- **`next()`**—Moves the cursor forward one row; returns *true* if the cursor is now positioned in a row, and *false* if the cursor is positioned after the last row
- **`previous()`**—Moves the cursor backward one row; returns *true* if the cursor is now positioned in a row, and *false* if the cursor is positioned before the first row

- **first()** – Moves the cursor to the first row in `ResultSet`; returns *true* if the cursor is now positioned in the first row, and *false* if the `ResultSet` object does not contain any row
- **last()** – Moves the cursor to the last row in `ResultSet`; returns *true* if the cursor is now positioned in the last row, and *false* if the `ResultSet` object does not contain any row
- **relative (int rows)** – Moves relative to the current row where *rows* (the argument of relative method) can be 0 or a positive integer or negative integer value. Different argument values indicate different cursor positions, which are as follows:
  a. **Zero** – Indicates that the cursor position is not changed
  b. **Positive integer value** – Indicates that the cursor position is moved forward by the given number of rows from the current position. In this case, if the given value plus the current cursor position value is greater than the total number of rows, the cursor is positioned after the last row. For example, consider if the current position of the cursor is at 5 and the total number of rows in the `ResultSet` object is 10. Now, if this method is invoked passing a value of greater than 5, the cursor is placed at after the last row.
  c. **Negative integer value** – Indicates that the cursor position is moved backward by the given number of rows from the current position. If the given value plus the current cursor position row number is less than zero, the cursor is placed before the first row. For example, consider that the current position of the cursor is at 5 and the total number of rows in the `ResultSet` object is 10. Now, if this method is invoked passing a value of less than -5 (such as -6 or -7 or -8…), the cursor is placed before the first row.

The relative (`int` rows) method returns true if the cursor is positioned in a valid row, and false if it is positioned before the first or after the last row.

- **absolute (int row_number)** – Moves the cursor to the given position. The cursor position varies on the basis of the following values of the `row_number` parameter:
  a. If the given number is positive, the cursor position is moved forward by the given number of rows from the first row irrespective of the current cursor position, where the first row is given as the position number 1, second as 2 and so on. In this case, if the given value exceeds the number of rows available, the cursor will be positioned after the last row.
  b. If the given value is negative, the cursor position is moved backward by the given number of rows from the last row. Where the last row is given with the position number as -1, last but one as -2 and so on. If the given value is less than the – (minus) (number of rows), the cursor is positioned before the first row.
  c. If the given value is zero, the cursor position is moved before the first row.

The absolute (`int row_number`) method returns *true* if the cursor is positioned in a valid row, and *false* if it is positioned before the first or after the last row.

- **beforeFirst()** – Moves the cursor of the `ResultSet` object before the first row
- **afterLast()** – Moves the cursor of the `ResultSet` object after the last row

NOTE

A `ResultSet` object of type FORWARD_ONLY can use only `next()` method, using any of the other cursor movement methods throws `SQLException`.

ResultSet Concurrency

`ResultSet` concurrency determines the level of update functionality of the `ResultSet` object. Update functionality determines whether the `ResultSet` can be updated or not. The `ResultSet` concurrency defines the following two types:

- **CONCUR_READ_ONLY** – Does not allow manipulation of the results of the executed query. It is the default concurrency of the ResultSet object.
- **CONCUR_UPDATABLE** – Allows manipulation of the results of the executed query to update, delete, or insert a row

The default ResultSet concurrency is CONCUR_READ_ONLY, and to find the ResultSet concurrency of a ResultSet object, an application can call the getConcurrency() method on that object. To find whether a ResultSet concurrency is supported or not by the driver, an application can use supportsResultSetConcurrency(int) method of DatabaseMetaData. The supportsResultSetConcurrency(int) method takes ResultSet concurrency as an argument and returns true if the specified concurrency is supported, otherwise it returns false.

ResultSet Holdability

The ResultSet holdability determines whether the ResultSet object has to be closed when a commit operation is implicitly or explicitly performed or not. The ResultSet holdability defines the following two properties:

- **HOLD_CURSORS_OVER_COMMIT**—Holds the ResultSet objects in the open state when a commit operation is implicitly or explicitly performed. In other words, the ResultSet objects of this property are not closed when a commit operation is performed implicitly or explicitly.
- **CLOSE_CURSORS_AT_COMMIT**—Closes the ResultSet objects when a commit operation is performed implicitly or explicitly. Note that, in general, it is recommended to close ResultSet objects (cursors) at commit. This results in better memory utilization because the information currently in the associated private area of the cursors is removed and its memory is de-allocated.

The default holdability of the ResultSet is specific to the driver implementation, that is, JDBC specification has not described any one of the holdability as default. To determine the default holdability of ResultSets returned by the underlying data source, an application can use the getResultSetHoldability() method of DatabaseMetaData.

Let's now understand how to set type and concurrency of ResultSet objects.

Setting the ResultSet Type and ResultSet Concurrency

We need to set the ResultSet type and concurrency to the Statement object that produces the ResultSet object to work with the ResultSet object of the required type. This is done while creating a statement using the createStatement(), prepareStatement(), and prepareCall() methods of the Connection object. The following code snippet shows the setting to create Statement and PreparedStatement objects that can produce a ResultSet of the scrollable and read-only type:

```
createStatement(ResultSet.TYPE_SCROLL_SENSITIVE, ResultSet.CONCUR_READ_ONLY);
prepareStatement(query, ResultSet.TYPE_SCROLL_SENSITIVE, ResultSet.CONCUR_READ_ONLY);
```

In the preceding code snippet, we have specified the ResultSet type and concurrency while creating the JDBC statement. Now that we have learned about the various types of ResultSet objects, let's look at some examples that demonstrate the working of the types of ResultSet objects by putting the theoretical discussion into action. The example in Listing 4.15 demonstrates the working of various ResultSet navigation methods by using the scrollable ResultSet (you can find the ScrollableRSEx1.java file online in the code/Chapter4 folder):

Listing 4.15: Showing the code of the ScrollableRSEx1.java File

```
package com.santosh.jdbc;

import java.sql.*;
import java.util.*;
import java.io.*;
/**
  * @author Santosh
  */
public class ScrollableRSEx1 {
  public static void main(String s[]) throws Exception {

        Driver d= (Driver)
        (Class.forName("oracle.jdbc.driver.OracleDriver").newInstance());
        Properties p=new Properties ();
        p.put("user","system");
        p.put("password","security");
```

```
        Connection con=d.connect("jdbc:oracle:thin:@localhost:1521:XE",p);
        Statement st= con.createStatement (
        ResultSet.TYPE_SCROLL_INSENSITIVE, ResultSet.CONCUR_READ_ONLY);

        String query="select * from emp where deptno=10";
        ResultSet rs= st.executeQuery(query);
        //Now the cursor of ResultSet will at beforeFirst & the result set produced is
        scrollable

        System.out.println("EmpNo\tName");

        while (rs.next()) {
                System.out.print(rs.getInt(1)+"\t");
                System.out.println(rs.getString(2));
        }//while
        //Now the cursor of ResultSet will at afterLast

        System.out.println("Reading Data, moving the cursor in backward direction\n");
        while (rs.previous()){
                System.out.print(rs.getInt(1)+"\t");
                System.out.println(rs.getString(2));
        }//while
        con.close();
    }//main
}//class
```

In Listing 4.15, the `Connection.createStatement(int, int)` method is used to create a `Statement` object that can produce a scrollable `ResultSet`. Here, we have used `ResultSet.TYPE_SCROLL_INSENSITIVE` to specify the `ResultSet` type, which indicates that `ResultSet` is only scrollable and insensitive to any changes made to the data in the associated database. In addition, we have used `ResultSet.CONCUR_READ_ONLY` to specify the concurrency type, which describes that the `ResultSet` object does not allow you to make changes. It also uses the cursor movement methods, such as `ResultSet.next()` and `ResultSet.previous()`. The `ResultSet.next()` method is used to move the `ResultSet` cursor to the next record in the forward direction, whereas the `ResultSet.previous()` method is used to move the `ResultSet` cursor to the previous record in the backward direction from the current cursor position. The output of Listing 4.15 is shown in Figure 4.30:

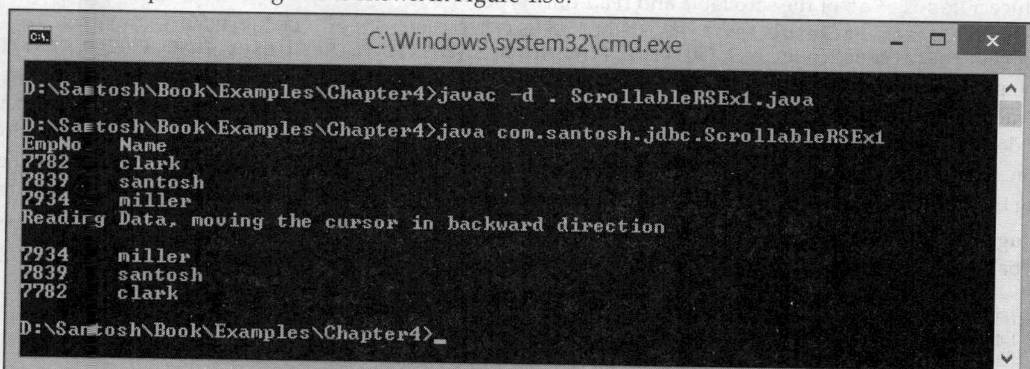

Figure 4.30: Showing the Output of ScrollableRSEx1.java by using ResultSet

Listing 4.15 shows how to create a `Statement` object that can produce the `TYPE_SCROLL_INSENSITIVE` type of the `ResultSet` object. We can also use the `PreparedStatement` object to create `ResultSet` objects. Listing 4.16 shows the use of various cursor movement methods as well as `PreparedStatement` to retrieve the scrollable type of the `ResultSet` object (you can find the ScrollableRSEx2.java file online in the code/Chapter4 folder):

Listing 4.16: Showing the code of the ScrollableRSEx2.java File

```
package com.santosh.jdbc;
```

```
import java.util.*;
import java.io.*;
import java.sql.*;
/**
  * @author Santosh
  */
public class ScrollableRSEx2 {

  public static void main(String s[]) throws Exception {

        Driver d= (Driver)(Class.forName(
        "oracle.jdbc.driver.OracleDriver").newInstance());

        Properties p=new Properties ();
        p.put("user","scott");
        p.put("password","tiger");

        Connection con=d.connect ("jdbc:oracle:thin:@mysys:1521:sandb",p);

        PreparedStatement ps= con.prepareStatement ("select * from emp",
                ResultSet.TYPE_SCROLL_SENSITIVE,
                ResultSet.CONCUR_READ_ONLY);
        ResultSet rs=ps.executeQuery();

        System.out.println ("Index\tEmpNo\tName");
        int i=1;
        while (rs.next()){
                System.out.print ((i++)+"\t");
                System.out.print (rs.getInt(1)+"\t");
                System.out.println (rs.getString(2));
        }//while
        System.out.println ();

 //Now the cursor will be at afterLast
 //From this point to move the cursor to 3rd record

        rs.absolute(3);

        System.out.println ("3rd record EmpNo : "+rs.getInt(1));

 /*
 To move the cursor to first record we can use
 rs.first(); or with reference to the current row we can use
 */
        rs.relative(-2);

        System.out.println ("1st record EmpNo: "+rs.getInt(1));


 /*
 To move the cursor to last record use rs.last () or with reference to the
 current row we can use
 */
        rs.afterLast ();     //this moves the cursor to afterLast
        rs.previous ();
 //moves the cursor backward by one row (which in this case moves the
 cursor last row

        System.out.println ("last record EmpNo: "+ rs.getInt (1));


        con.close ();
   }//main
 }//class
```

In Listing 4.16, we used the PreparedStatement object to retrieve the ResultSet. We have used the Connection.prepareStatement(String, int, int) method that specifies the query as select * from emp, ResultSet type as ResultSet.TYPE_SCROLL_SENSITIVE, and ResultSet concurrency as ResultSet.CONCUR_READ_ONLY.

This example also shows the use of the next(), previous(), afterLast(), and absolute() methods to move the cursor throughout the ResultSet. The ResultSet object works according to these methods and retrieves the output according to the specified query. The output of Listing 4.16 is shown in Figure 4.31:

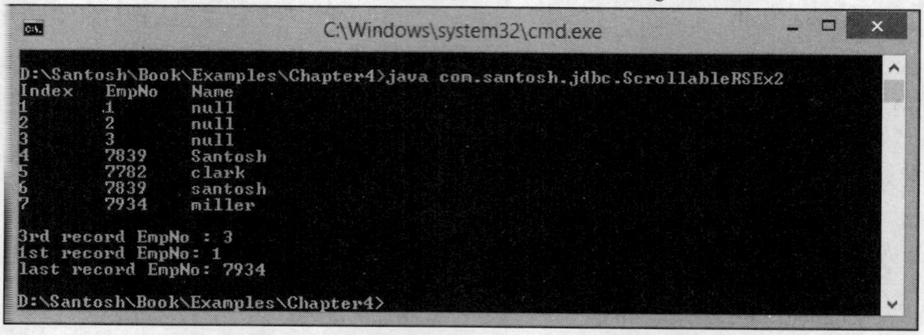

Figure 4.31: Showing the Output of the ScrollableRSEx2.java File

Figure 4.31 shows the output of the application given under Listing 4.16. In this example, we used the `PreparedStatement` object to get the `ResultSet` object of scrollable type. The cursor movement methods are also used to navigate throughout the `ResultSet` object. The `next()` method is used to retrieve the `ResultSet` data in the forward direction, whose output is shown in Figure 4.31, displaying the records in index 1 to 14. The third record of the `ResultSet` object was retrieved by using the `ResultSet.absolute()` method. The integer argument passed to the method specifies the record position to which the cursor is to be moved. The `ResultSet.relative(int n)` method is used to jump to n rows forward or backward within the `ResultSet`, depending on the sign of n. The negative values allow the cursor to move backward from the current position; however, the positive values move the cursor forward from the current position. If the new position is located before the first row or after the last row of the data, false is returned, otherwise true is returned. In this example, we use `ResultSet.relative(-2)`, where the current cursor position is in the third row; thus, the cursor has moved to the first row. We can use the `ResultSet.last()` method to move the cursor to the last row. However, in this example, we used the `ResultSet.afterLast()` method to move the cursor to a position after the last record and then move the cursor one position backward that is to the last record using the `ResultSet.previous()` method.

So far we have discussed examples about how to work with different types of `ResultSets` created by using different Statement objects and cursor movement methods. Let's now take an example that shows the difference between using various `ResultSet` types, such as TYPE_SCROLL_SENSITIVE and TYPE_SCROLL_INSENSITIVE. We learned earlier that the TYPE_SCROLL_SENSITIVE type is scrollable as well as sensitive to all the changes, whereas the TYPE_SCROLL_INSENSITIVE type is only scrollable. Listing 4.17 shows the difference in using both the scroll types (you can find the ScrollableRSEx3.java file online in the code/Chapter4 folder):

Listing 4.17: Showing the code of the ScrollableRSEx3.java File

```
package com.santosh.jdbc;

import java.sql.*;
import java.util.*;
import java.io.*;
/**
  * @author Santosh
  */
public class ScrollableRSEx3 {
  public static void main(String s[]) throws Exception {
        Driver d= (Driver) (
        Class.forName("oracle.jdbc.driver.OracleDriver").newInstance());
        Properties p=new Properties ();
        p.put("user","scott");
        p.put("password","tiger");
```

```
        Connection con1=d.connect("jdbc:oracle:thin:@mysys:1521:sandb",p);
        Connection con2=d.connect("jdbc:oracle:thin:@mysys:1521:sandb",p);

        Statement st1= con1.createStatement(
                                ResultSet.TYPE_SCROLL_INSENSITIVE,
                                ResultSet.CONCUR_READ_ONLY);
        Statement st2= con2.createStatement();

        String query="select * from emp where deptno=10";

        ResultSet rs= st1.executeQuery(query);
        System.out.println("EmpNo\tName");
        System.out.println("-----------------------------------");
        while (rs.next()) {
                System.out.print(rs.getInt(1)+"\t");
                System.out.println(rs.getString(2));
        }//while

        st2.executeUpdate ("update emp set ename=\'kumar\'
                where empno=7934");

        System.out.println("\nData Modified: \nName of the employee
                with empno - 7934 is modified from \'MILLER\'
                to \'kumar\'\n");

        System.out.println("Now reading the data once again from
                the same ResultSet\n");

        rs.beforeFirst();
        while (rs.next()){
                System.out.print(rs.getInt(1)+"\t");
                System.out.println(rs.getString(2));
        }//while
        con1.close();
        con2.close();
    }//main
}//class
```

Listing 4.17 shows an application that uses the TYPE_SCROLL_INSENSITIVE type of the `ResultSet` object, which indicates that the changes made to the data in the database after obtaining `ResultSet` do not update the `ResultSet` object (Figure 4.31). Figure 4.32 shows that modifying the name of the employee having empno 7934 from miller to kumar does not modify the records in the `ResultSet`:

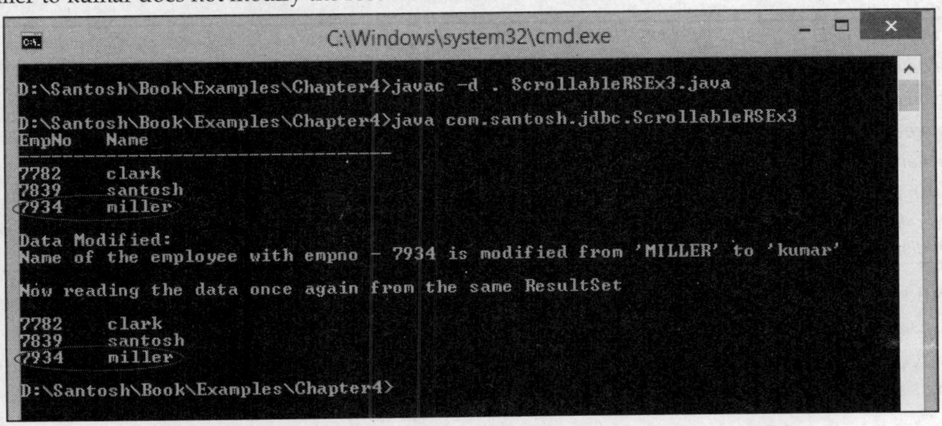

Figure 4.32: Showing the Output of the ScrollableRSEx3.java File

Note that in Figure 4.32, even after the data is modified in the underlying data store, it is not reflected in the `ResultSet` because in the preceding example, we have configured the `ResultSet` type to TYPE_SCROLL_INSENSITIVE.

Now, change the ResultSet type in the preceding example to TYPE_SCROLL_SENSITIVE by replacing the code snippet shown in boldface in Listing 4.17 with the following code snippet:

```
Statement st1= con1.createStatement (
ResultSet.TYPE_SCROLL_SENSITIVE,
ResultSet.CONCUR_READ_ONLY);
```

After applying the preceding code snippet, the ResultSet object is updated with any changes made to the data store. The output of Listing 4.17 now appears, as shown in Figure 4.33:

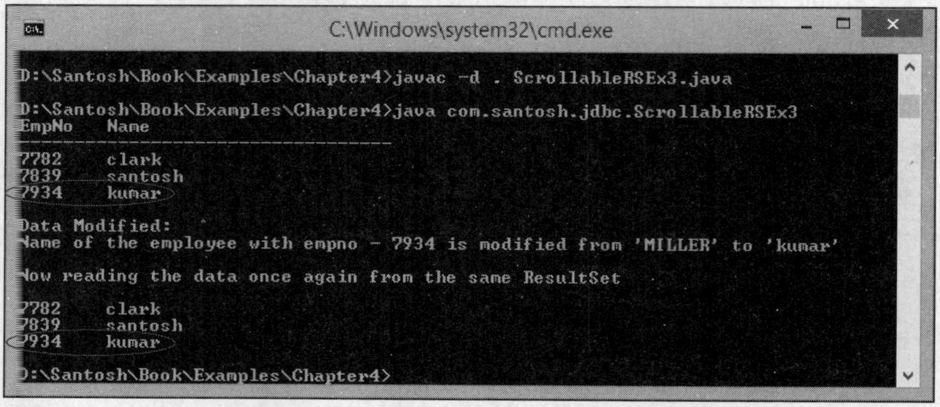

Figure 4.33: Showing the Output of ScrollableRSEx3.java using TYPE_SCROLL_INSENSITIVE

Figure 4.33 shows that the UPDATE statement changes the existing data in the data store, and the changes are reflected in the ResultSet. The changes are reflected in the ResultSet object because the ResultSet type TYPE_SCROLL_SENSITIVE is used with the application.

Figure 4.32 and Figure 4.33 show that the only difference between the ResultSet of TYPE_SCROLL_SENSITIVE and TYPE_SCROLL_INSENSITIVE types is that while reading the values from a ResultSet, if the selected data in the underlying data source is modified through some other session, the TYPE_SCROLL_SENSITIVE type ResultSet reflects the changes, whereas the TYPE_SCROLL_INSENSITIVE type does not. Note that if we want the changes to be reflected at any instant with the TYPE_SCROLL_INSENSITIVE type of ResultSet, we need to explicitly invoke the refreshRow() method of ResultSet before reading the data in the current row.

NOTE

You can use the TYPE_SCROLL_INSENSITIVE type in the following situations:

- *If the data read in a transaction environment is locked until the transaction is ended*
- *If the data being read is not shared*
- *If we are reading the data that is not required with the latest modifications in an application*
- *If we want to process the data that is available at the time of executing the query*

You can use the TYPE_SCROLL_SENSITIVE type in the following situations:

- *If you need the most recent updated data to execute an application, such as a stock ticker (a stock ticker displays the stock market index of different companies listed in a stock exchange.)*

You should remember that selecting an improper ResultSet type may result into performance issues, and in some cases the data may get corrupted.

Till now, you have learned about the types of ResultSets based on cursor movement and concurrency. The following section explains the ability of ResultSets to manipulate results.

Using ResultSet Objects to Manipulate Data

An updatable ResultSet is used to update the database using the ResultSet object. Updating database may include updating, deleting, and inserting a new record. In addition, updating the database allows you to make changes in it without using any additional SQL Statements explicitly. The following section explains how to update, delete, and insert data by using a ResultSet object.

Using the ResultSet Object to Update Data

As discussed earlier, the JDBC 2.0 and the higher version ResultSet object supports data manipulation, such as update, delete, and insert. We need to get the ResultSet object with a concurrence type as ResultSet.CONCUR_UPDATABLE to perform data manipulation. To get an updatable ResultSet object, you can create a JDBC statement setting the ResultSet.CONCUR_UPDATABLE as discussed earlier in the chapter while understanding scrollable ResultSets. The following three steps are involved in using the ResultSet object to update the database:

1. Move the cursor to the row where you need to update the data. You can move the cursor by using the ResultSet navigation method as applicable to the ResultSet object.
2. Use ResultSet.updateXXX() methods to change the data. There are two versions of update methods declared in the ResultSet interface. Both these versions of updateXXX() methods take two arguments. The first argument is int (specifies the column index number) for one version and java.lang.String (specifies the column name) for the other. The second argument for both the versions is their respective data types that specify a new value, which replaces the old value at the specified column using number or name.
3. Invoke the updateRow() method of the ResultSet object. After replacing the data in the row, we need to invoke the ResultSet.updateRow() method to reflect the changes in the database.

NOTE

You must note the following points while updating the data by using ResultSet:

- *The changes are not updated in the underlying data source until the ResultSet.updateRow() method is invoked.*
- *The ResultSet.cancelRowUpdate() method can be invoked to roll back the changes made to the row. If the ResultSet.updateRow() method has already been called or no updates have been made to this row, this method has no effect.*
- *The ResultSet.updateRow() method must be invoked without moving the cursor position from the current row.*

While accessing data from ResultSet or iterating through ResultSet for multiple times, you may want to identify whether the current row was updated using the ResultSet object. An application can use the ResultSet.rowUpdated() method to find whether the current data is updated or not.

NOTE

*The value returned by the ResultSet.rowUpdated() method depends on whether the **ResultSet** can detect updates or not.*

As we have understood how to use the ResultSet object to update the database, let's create an example that can put this discussion into action. Listing 4.18 shows how to update the data using the ResultSet object. To understand this, let's display all the employee details and increase the salary of the specific employees, who draw more than Rs 2000, by 10%. The code for this example is shown in Listing 4.18 (you can find the IncrementSalary.java file online in the code/Chapter4 folder):

Listing 4.18: Showing the code of the IncrementSalary.java File

```
package com.santosh.jdbc;

import java.sql.*;
import java.util.*;
/**
   * @author Santosh
   */
public class IncrementSalary  {
```

```
public static void main(String s[]) throws Exception {

    Driver d= (Driver) ( Class.forName(
    "oracle.jdbc.driver.OracleDriver").newInstance());

    Properties p=new Properties ();
    p.put("user","scott");
    p.put("password","tiger");

    Connection con=d.connect("jdbc:oracle:thin:@mysys:1521:sandb",p);

    Statement st=con.createStatement(
                ResultSet.TYPE_SCROLL_SENSITIVE,
                ResultSet.CONCUR_UPDATABLE);
    ResultSet rs=st.executeQuery("select empno, ename, sal, deptno
          from emp");

    System.out.println("Empno\tName\tSalary\tDeptno");
    System.out.println("-------------------------------");

    while (rs.next()) {
          System.out.print(rs.getInt(1)+"\t");
          System.out.print(rs.getString(2)+"\t");
          System.out.print(rs.getDouble(3)+"\t");
          System.out.print(rs.getInt(4)+"\t");

          if (rs.getDouble(3)>2000) {
                double amt=rs.getDouble(3)*1.1;
                rs.updateDouble(3,amt);
                rs.updateRow();
                System.out.print("Salary Incremented");
          }//if
          System.out.println ();
    }//while
    con.close();
  }//main
}//class
```

Listing 4.13 shows how to update the emp table in the database by using the `ResultSet` object. The listing uses the `ResultSet.CONCUR_UPDATEABLE` concurrency to create a `Statement` object so that the queried data can be updated by using the `ResultSet` object, produced by the `Statement` object. Here, we have selected all the rows of the emp table; while iterating through the `ResultSet`, the application identifies whether the salary of the employee is greater than 2000. If so, it uses the `updateDouble()` method. The `updateRow()` method is used to commit the changes made to the database by using the `ResultSet` object. The output of Listing 4.18 is shown in Figure 4.34:

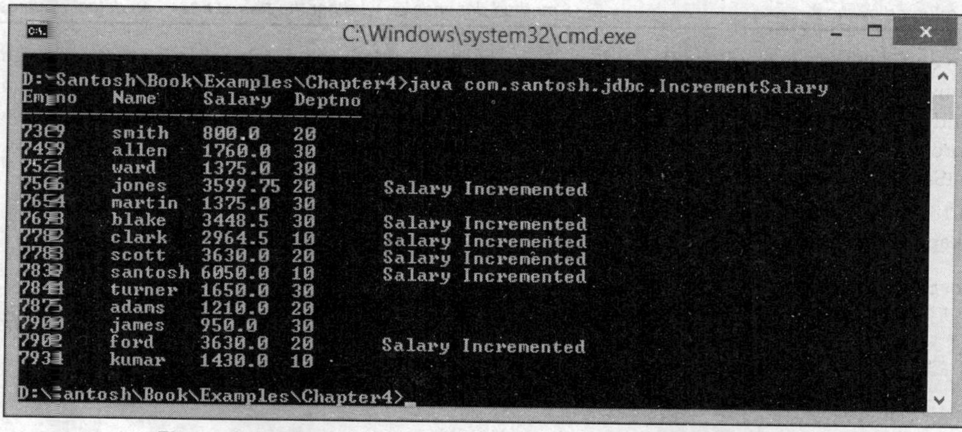

Figure 4.34: Showing the Output of the IncrementSalary.java File

In Figure 4.34, you can see that the changes made to the employee's salary are indicated as 'salary incremented'. The user can view these changes by accessing the database.

Using the ResultSet Object to Delete a Row

You can also delete a row from a database by using the `ResultSet` object. The deletion of a row from the database indicates that the requested row is completely removed from the database. The following steps must be followed to delete a row by using the `ResultSet` object:

1. Move the cursor by using any of the cursor movement methods to the row that has to be deleted. Note that the availability of the cursor movement methods depends on the type of `ResultSet`.
2. Invoke the `deleteRow()` method on the `ResultSet` object after moving the cursor to the row that has to be deleted.

After the row is deleted in the underlying data source, the deletion may or may not be visible in the open `ResultSet` object, depending on the driver implementation. An application can use the `ownDeletesAreVisible(int type)` method of `DatabaseMetaData` to find whether the deletion is visible as a change or not. The `ownDeletesAreVisible()` method returns true if the deleted row is removed or replaced with an empty row in the `ResultSet` object of the given type. It returns false if the `ResultSet` object still contains the deleted row, that is, if the deletion is not visible as a change to the `ResultSet` object of the given type. An application can use the `ResultSet.rowDeleted()` method to find whether the current row has been deleted or not. Note that the `ResultSet.rowDeleted()` method of the `ResultSet` object returns true only if the current row was deleted, otherwise the method returns false.

The example in Listing 4.19 shows how to delete a row by using the `deleteRow()` method of the `ResultSet` object (you can find the RemoveEmployee.java file online in the code/Chapter4 folder):

Listing 4.19: Showing the code of the RemoveEmployee.java File

```
package com.santosh.jdbc;

import java.sql.*;
import java.util.*;
/**
  * @author Santosh
  */
public class RemoveEmployee  {

   public static void main(String s[]) throws Exception {

         Driver d= (Driver) ( Class.forName(
         "oracle.jdbc.driver.OracleDriver").newInstance());

         Properties p=new Properties ();
         p.put("user","scott");
         p.put("password","tiger");

         Connection con=d.connect("jdbc:oracle:thin:@mysys:1521:sandb",p);

         Statement st=con.createStatement(
                                   ResultSet.TYPE_SCROLL_SENSITIVE,
                                   ResultSet.CONCUR_UPDATABLE);

         ResultSet rs= st.executeQuery(
         "select empno, ename, sal, deptno from emp");

         DatabaseMetaData dbmd=con.getMetaData();

         if(dbmd.ownDeletesAreVisible (ResultSet.TYPE_SCROLL_SENSITIVE))
                 System.out.println(
                 "Deletions are visible as a change for this
                 ResultSet object");
         else
                 System.out.println(
```

```
                "Deletions are not visible as a change for this ResultSet object");

        System.out.println();
        System.out.println("RowNo\tEmpno\tName\tSalary\tDeptno");
        System.out.println("-------------------------------");

        while (rs.next()) {
                System.out.print(rs.getRow()+"\t");
                System.out.print(rs.getInt(1)+"\t");
                System.out.print(rs.getString(2)+"\t");
                System.out.print(rs.getDouble(3)+"\t");
                System.out.print(rs.getInt(4)+"\t");

                if (rs.getInt(1)==Integer.parseInt(s[0])) {
                        rs.deleteRow();
                        System.out.print("Employee Removed");
                }//if
                System.out.println();
        }//while
        con.close();
    }//main
}//class
```

The application shown in Listing 4.19 removes a record from the database using the `ResultSet` object. It uses the `ResultSet.deleteRow()` method to delete a specific row using the `ResultSet` object. Here, we have even used the `DatabaseMetaData` object to find whether the deletions are visible to `ResultSet` or not. Figure 4.35 shows the output of Listing 4.19, which deletes a record from the database:

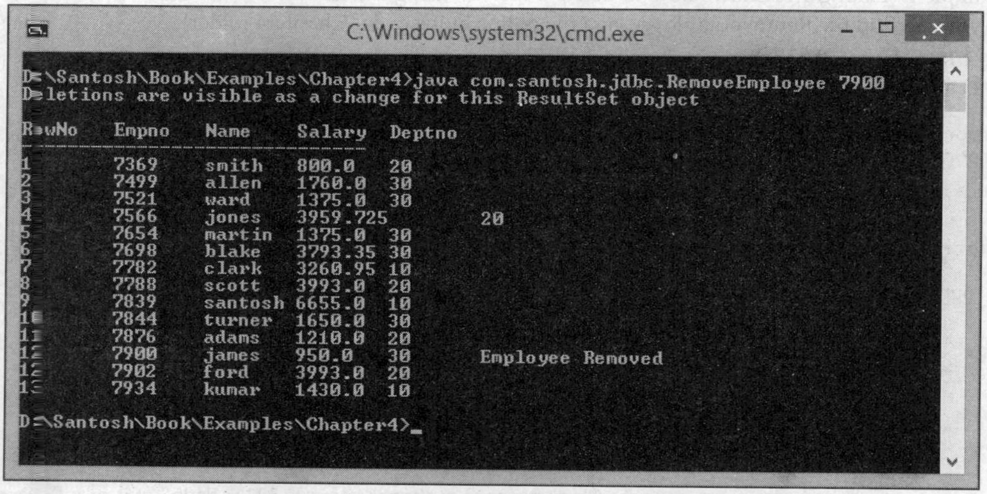

Figure 4.35: Deleting a Row Using a ResultSet

In Figure 4.35, we can observe a message, **Employee Removed,** for the deleted row, invoking the `ResultSet.deleteRow()` method of the `ResultSet` object. The `DatabaseMetaData.onDeletesAreVisible()` method specifies whether the row that is deleted using the `ResultSet` object is visible or not. In this example, the `DatabaseMetaData.onDeletesAreVisible()` method has returned true, which means that the deletions are visible for `ResultSet`. When we observe the number of rows in Figure 4.35, it shows that the row number of both the empno's 7900 and 7934 is 12. This is due to the deletion of the row with empno 7900. After the row with empno 7900 is removed from the `ResultSet`, the row number of the next row is shifted by one number forward, as the row describing 7900 employee is removed from the `ResultSet`. Therefore, both the records shown in Figure 4.35 have the same row number.

Using a ResultSet Object to Insert a Row

Similar to updating and deleting a row, you can insert a row into a database by using a `ResultSet` object. The following steps are performed to insert a new row by using the `ResultSet` object:

1. Move the cursor to the place where you want to insert a row. To do this, you need to invoke the `moveToInsertRow()` method of the `ResultSet` object.
2. Set the column value for the new row by using the `updateXXX()` method.
3. Invoke the `insertRow()` method of the `ResultSet` object, which inserts a record into the database after setting all the values.

After inserting a row, you can use the `moveToCurrentRow()` method to navigate to the previous cursor position.

NOTE

A record is not inserted into the underlying data source until the `ResultSet.insertRow()` method is invoked.

The `ResultSet.insertRow()` method must be invoked without moving the cursor position from the current row.

As we have learned how to insert a row using a `ResultSet` object, let's create an example that can demonstrate this. Listing 4.20 shows how to insert a new row into a database by using the `ResultSet` object (you can find the AddEmployee.java file online in the code/Chapter4 folder):

Listing 4.20: Showing the code of the AddEmployee.java File

```
package com.santosh.jdbc;

import java.sql.*;
import java.util.*;
/**
 * @author Santosh
 */
public class AddEmployee {

  public static void main(String s[]) throws Exception {

        Driver d= (Driver)(Class.forName(
              "oracle.jdbc.driver.OracleDriver").newInstance());

        Properties p=new Properties ();
        p.put("user","scott");
        p.put("password","tiger");

        Connection con=d.connect("jdbc:oracle:thin:@mysys:1521:sandb",p);

        Statement st=con.createStatement(
              ResultSet.TYPE_SCROLL_SENSITIVE,
              ResultSet.CONCUR_UPDATABLE);

        ResultSet rs=st.executeQuery("select empno, ename, sal,
        deptno from emp");

        rs.moveToInsertRow();
        rs.updateInt(1,7900);
        rs.updateString(2,"JAMES");
        rs.updateDouble(3,950);
        rs.updateInt(1,20);
        rs.insertRow();
        System.out.print("Employee Inserted");
        con.close();
  }//main
 }//class
```

Listing 4.20 inserts an employee record into the database by using the `ResultSet` object. The `moveToInsertRow()` method is used to specify the cursor position to insert a new empty row. The `updateXXX()` methods are used to insert the column values for the record to be inserted and then the `insertRow()` method is called by using the `ResultSet` object to insert the row into the database. Figure 4.36 shows the output of Listing 4.20:

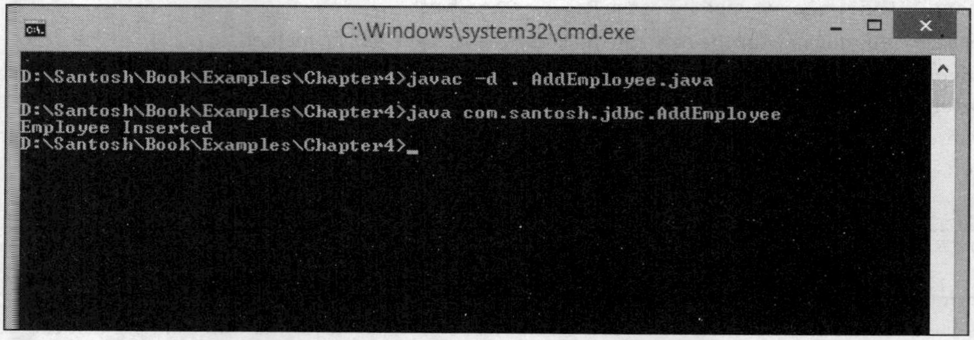

Figure 4.36: Inserting a Row Using a ResultSet

You can also notice that the new record is inserted in the database table. The user can retrieve the database explicitly to view the changes made by the `ResultSet` object.

Let's now learn how to close the connection made to a database.

Closing the Connection

You know that the `Connection` object represents a session established with the server. When a connection is established, some native and network data store resources are allocated for the connection. A user needs to close the connection after completing the required operations to release the allocated resources. JDBC API supports the `Connection.close()` method to close the session represented by the connection. The `close()` method of the `Connection` object allows us to explicitly release the resources blocked by the connection so that they can be assigned to some other clients, thereby increasing the availability of resources.

The database automatically cleans unused sessions; however, it may take a long time to clear the session. Therefore, using the `Connection.close()` method at a proper location in our application is necessary to close the unused session, otherwise the session represented by the connection would remain open (active) for a long time without any use.

The database sessions that are identified as unused are automatically closed by database. The database uses the session timeout to identify the unused sessions. An unused session is the one that is not getting a request for a long time (> session timeout period). Moreover, databases have their own strategies to decide when to find for the unused sessions, such as at regular intervals, or when the number of active sessions reaches the configured load factor. Therefore, it can be understood that leaving the responsibility of closing the database session to DBMS would block the resources for a long time, which will affect the availability of resources and increase the cost of using the system.

NOTE

Opening and closing the database session is a costlier job. Therefore, we need to look for a good design of our application that can utilize the opened connection to the maximum. We will discuss this design under the Exploring Connection Pooling section of Chapter 5.

The `Connection.close()` method closes the database session associated with a connection that results to close the Statements and `ResultSet` (CURSORs) built on this connection. However, with few drivers, the Statements and `ResultSets` would remain open even after closing the connection. In such a situation, although `ResultSet` would not be used to read the data, we need to explicitly close the statement and `ResultSet`. The following section describes closing Statement and `ResultSet`.

Closing the Statement and ResultSet

The JDBC `Statement` object supports the `close()` method to close the statement. The `Statement.close()` method is required to clean the resources of the session allocated for the statement. As described, the closing connection would close the statements built on the `Connection` object; however, due to the following reasons, you need to explicitly close the `Statement`:

As you can create only a limited number of `Statements` on a `Connection` object, to create a new `Statement`, you need to close the unused statements explicitly without closing the underlying connection.

- As you know that the statements are closed as soon as their underlying connection is closed, this is not properly implemented by all the drivers. Therefore, for maximum portability, we may want to explicitly close the statement.

Similarly, the JDBC `ResultSet` object also supports the `close()` method to close the DB CURSOR that it represents. Calling a `close()` method on the `ResultSet` object releases all the resources associated with that object. `ResultSet` used in an application is implicitly closed on the occurrence of the following conditions:

- When all of the rows of a `ResultSet` have been retrieved (if the `ResultSet` type is TYPE_FORWARD_ONLY)
- If the associated `Statement` object is used to execute any query (calls `execute()` / `executeUpdate()` / `executeQuery()` methods)
- The Statement used to create the `ResultSet` object is closed.

However, we know that the DB CURSORs are limited; therefore, it is required to close the unused CURSOR to allow the new clients to access the CURSORs. Therefore, apart from waiting for implicit closing of `ResultSet`, we may want to explicitly close it using the `ResultSet.close()` method in some cases.

NOTE

Closing `Connection`, `Statement`, or `ResultSet` does not make them nullify, which means that these objects still exist in the Java Virtual Machine (JVM). However, such objects cannot service any database operations.

Therefore, to create a reliable code, we may want to identify a `Connection` object in JVM that represents an active database session. We can use the `Connection.isClosed()` method to find whether the `Connection` object represents a valid database session or not. This method returns true if the `Connection` object is currently not representing a session to the server, meaning the session it was representing is closed. Otherwise it returns false. The following code snippet helps to determine when to create a new connection:

```
if (con!=null || !con.isClosed())
  //continue using the Connection represented by a reference variable con
```

Now, after understanding how to work with JDBC `Connection`, `Statement`, and `ResultSet`, let's understand the `DatabaseMetaData` interface.

Working with the DatabaseMetaData Interface

The `java.sql.DatabaseMetaData` is an interface implemented by the JDBC driver provider. The `DatabaseMetaData` object encapsulates all the information related to the database and driver. As we know that different DBMSs often support different features and data types and implement those features in different ways, the `DatabaseMetaData` object is useful for the following operations while creating a generic application, such as Hibernate, with maximum portability and frameworks:

- To use the functionalities of DBMS in combination with JDBC driver. For example, the `DatabaseMetaData.supportsCorrelatedSubqueries()` method is used to find whether it is possible to use a correlated subquery or not.
- To get the database details, such as the DB vendor name, product name, and version.
- To find support for optional JDBC features from a JDBC driver. For example, the `DatabaseMetaData.supportsBatchUpdates()` method is used to find whether it is possible to use batch updates or not.
- To find the approach used with JDBC driver to implement the advanced JDBC options.

We use the `Connection.getMetaData()` method to get the `DatabaseMetaData` object. The various methods declared in the `java.sql.DatabaseMetaData` interface are described in Table 4.7:

Table 4.7: Methods of the java.sql.DatabaseMetaData Interface

Method	Description
`int getDatabaseMajorVersion()`	Helps to retrieve the major version number of the database in use.
`int getDatabaseMinorVersion()`	Helps to retrieve the minor version number of the database in use.
`int getDefaultTransactionIsolation()`	Helps to retrieve the default transaction isolation level.
`int getDriverMajorVersion()`	Helps to retrieve the major version number of the JDBC driver.
`int getDriverMinorVersion()`	Helps to retrieve the minor version number of the JDBC driver.
`int getJDBCMajorVersion()`	Helps to retrieve the major version number of the JDBC for the specified driver.
`int getJDBCMinorVersion()`	Helps to retrieve the minor version number of the JDBC for the specified driver.
`int getMaxBinaryLiteralLength()`	Helps to retrieve the maximum number of hex characters a database allows in an inline binary literal.
`int getMaxCatalogNameLength()`	Helps to retrieve the maximum number of characters that a database allows in a catalog name.
`int getMaxCharLiteralLength()`	Helps to retrieve the maximum number of characters a database allows for a character literal.
`int getMaxColumnNameLength()`	Helps to retrieve the maximum number of characters a database allows for a column name.
`int getMaxColumnsInGroupBy()`	Helps to retrieve the maximum number of columns a database allows in a `GROUP BY` clause.
`int getMaxColumnsInIndex()`	Helps to retrieve the maximum number of columns a database allows in an index.
`int getMaxColumnsInOrderBy()`	Helps to retrieve the maximum number of columns a database allows in an `ORDER BY` clause.
`int getMaxColumnsInSelect()`	Helps to retrieve the maximum number of columns a database allows in a `SELECT` list.
`int getMaxColumnsInTable()`	Helps to retrieve the maximum number of columns a database allows in a table.
`int getMaxConnections()`	Helps to retrieve the maximum number of concurrent connections to a database that are possible.
`int getMaxCursorNameLength()`	Helps to retrieve the maximum number of characters that a database allows in a cursor name.
`int getMaxIndexLength()`	Helps to retrieve the maximum number of bytes a database allows for an index, including all the parts of the index.
`int getMaxProcedureNameLength()`	Helps to retrieve the maximum number of characters that a database allows in a procedure name.
`int getMaxRowSize()`	Helps to retrieve the maximum number of bytes a database allows in a single row.
`int getMaxSchemaNameLength()`	Helps to retrieve the maximum number of characters that a database allows in a schema name.
`int getMaxStatementLength()`	Helps to retrieve the maximum number of characters a database allows in an SQL statement.
`int getMaxStatements()`	Helps to retrieve the maximum number of active statements to a database that can be opened at the same time.

Table 4.7: Methods of the java.sql.DatabaseMetaData Interface

Method	Description
`int getMaxTableNameLength()`	Helps to retrieve the maximum number of characters a database allows in a table name.
`int getMaxTablesInSelect()`	Helps to retrieve the maximum number of tables a database allows in a `SELECT` statement.
`int getMaxUserNameLength()`	Helps to retrieve the maximum number of characters a database allows in a user name.
`int getResultSetHoldability()`	Helps to retrieve the default holdability of the `ResultSet` object.
`int getSQLStateType()`	Helps to indicate whether the SQLSTATE returned by `SQLException.getSQLState()` is X/Open (now known as Open Group) SQL CLI or SQL99.

In the next section, let's look at some examples to retrieve information by using `DatabaseMetaData`. We specifically look at few examples to retrieve database and driver details, table descriptions, column details, and data from a Microsoft Excel sheet.

Retrieving Database and Driver Details

Let's now look at an example to retrieve the `DatabaseMetaData` object and use it to get database and driver details, such as the name and version of the database and the driver. Listing 4.21 shows the code to retrieve database details using `DatabaseMetaData` (you can also find the DBMDEx1.java file online in the code/Chapter4 folder):

Listing 4.21: Showing the code of the DBMDEx1.java File

```
package com.santosh.jdbc;

import java.sql.*;
import java.util.*;
import java.io.*;
/**
  * @author Santosh
  */
public class DBMDEx1 {
public static void main(String s[]) throws Exception {

Properties p= new Properties();
  p.load(new FileInputStream("MyDBDetails.properties"));

  Driver d= (Driver) (Class.forName((String)p.get("driver")).newInstance());

  Connection con=d.connect((String)p.get("url"), p);

  DatabaseMetaData db= con.getMetaData();

  System.out.println("Database name : "+db.getDatabaseProductName());
  System.out.println("Database version : "+db.getDatabaseProductVersion());
  System.out.println("\nDriver Name : "+ db.getDriverName());
  System.out.println("Driver Version : "+ db.getDriverVersion());
  con.close();
  }//main
}//class
```

Notice that Listing 4.21 references a properties file, `MyDBDetails.properties`, which contains the details of the database and driver. Listing 4.22 provides the code for the `MyDBDetails.properties` file (you can find the MyDBDetails.properties file online in the code/Chapter4 folder):

Listing 4.22: Showing the code of the MyDBDetails.properties File

```
driver=sun.jdbc.odbc.JdbcOdbcDriver
url=jdbc:odbc:santoshDSN
user=scott
password=tiger
```

Listing 4.22 uses `DatabaseMetaData` to get the database and driver details, and displays details of the JDBC-ODBC bridge driver. Figure 4.37 shows the output of Listing 4.22:

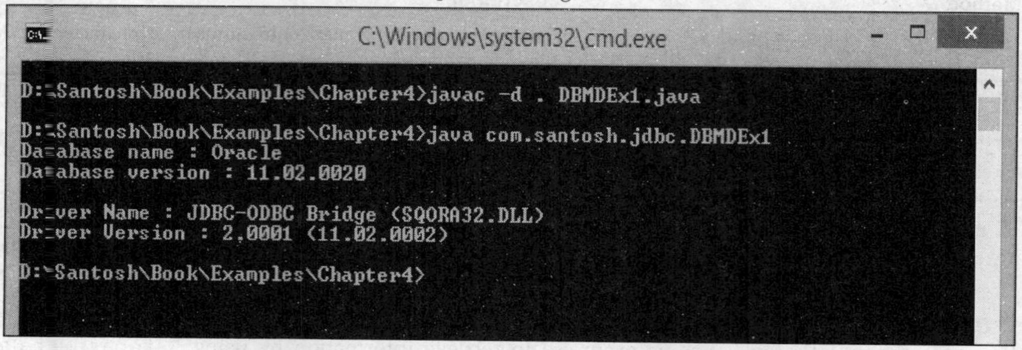

Figure 4.37: Showing the Output of the DBMDEx1.java File

Now, run DBMDEx1 (Listing 4.21) by changing the properties file shown in Listing 4.22. In this case, we can change the driver details, as shown in Listing 4.23:

Listing 4.23: Showing the code of the Modified MyDBDetails.properties File

```
driver=oracle.jdbc.driver.OracleDriver
url=jdbc:oracle:thin:@mysys:1521:sandb
user=scott
password=tiger
```

Figure 4.38 shows the output of Listing 4.23 that uses `DatabaseMetaData` to get the database and driver details, by referencing the modified MyDBDetails.properties file:

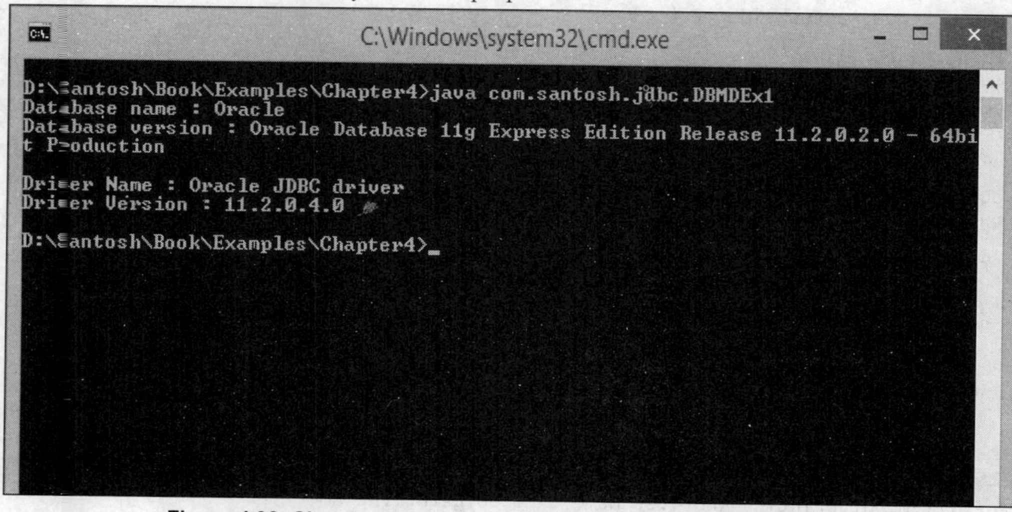

Figure 4.38: Showing the Output of the Modified DBMDEx1.java File

Summary

In this chapter, you learned about JDBC statements, such as `Statement`, `PreparedStatement`, and `CallableStatement`, and `ResultSets`. You also learned about the procedures, functions, database cursors, and metadata in JDBC. Let's recall the following important points to summarize the chapter:

- The JDBC `Statement` object is used to execute the SQL statement. JDBC API supports three types of JDBC statement objects to work with SQL statements to execute on the database.

- The `Statement` object is used to execute the normal SQL statements without IN and OUT parameters. The `Connection.createStatement()` method is used to create the `Statement` object. The `java.sql.Statement` interface is used to describe the `Statement` object implemented by the JDBC driver.
- The `Statement.executeUpdate(String sql_st)` method is used to execute the DB `UPDATE` statements, such as update, delete, and insert SQL statements. This method returns integer value, which describes the number of rows affected by executing a given SQL statement. In addition, a Statement.SUCCESS_NO_INFO describes that a given SQL statement is executed successfully in DB; however, the status describing the number of rows affected is not available.
- The `Statement.executeQuery(String query)` method is used to execute the SQL statements to query the database and returns the `ResultSet` object.
- The `ResultSet` object is used to represent the DB CURSOR to Java application, using JDBC to read the database. The `java.sql.ResultSet` interface of JDBC API is used to describe the `ResultSet` object implemented by the JDBC driver.
- The CURSOR is a buffer (cache) where the query result can be saved.
- The `ResultSet` object follows the iterate pattern. We can obtain any number of `ResultSets` by using a JDBC statement; however, at a time, only one `ResultSet` can be opened. When we try to open a `ResultSet` by using a statement that is already associated with an opened `ResultSet`, the existing `ResultSet` is implicitly closed.
- When the `ResultSet` object is opened, it is not loaded with all the data in CURSOR. In other words, the `ResultSet` object acts as a pointer to DB CURSOR, representing it in the Java environment. Loading the CURSOR rows into the `ResultSet` object depends on the fetch size configured to the `ResultSet` object.
- When a `ResultSet.next()` method is invoked for the first time, it fetches the number of rows as specified by the fetch size, so that during the next fetch size of `ResultSet.next()` method invocation, the `ResultSet` object does not need to go to DB.
- The JDBC 2.0 and the higher version `ResultSet` object supports the SCROLLABLE type `ResultSet` that allows us to navigate the rows in any direction. In support of this feature, the `ResultSet` object supports navigation methods, such as `first()`, `last()`, `previous()`, `absolute(int)`, and `relative(int)`. The JDBC 2.0 and the higher version `ResultSet` also helps to update the database.
- The `PreparedStatement` object is used to execute SQL statements with IN parameters. This supports positional parameters, represented using '?'.
- The `CallableStatement` object is used to execute the DB stored procedure that supports IN and OUT parameters.
- The `DatabaseMetaData` object is used to get the database and JDBC driver details.

In the next chapter, we describe advanced JDBC concepts such as SQL 99 types, batch updates, auto-generated keys, connection pool, and transactions.

Exercise

Q. 4.1 Which method of the `Connection` interface is used to get a basic JDBC `Statement` object?

Q. 4.2 What is the return type of the `executeUpdate()` method and what does it describe?

Q. 4.3 Which method of the `Statement` interface is used to execute data retrieval SQL statements?

Q. 4.4 What is `java.sql.PreparedStatement`?

Q. 4.5 Give a disadvantage of `PreparedStatement`.

Q. 4.6 What is `java.sql.CallableStatement`?

Q. 4.7 Which package provides the `ResultSet` interface?

Q. 4.8 Which version of the `getXXX()` method of `ResultSet` is preferred to get results and why?

Q. 4.9 Which method of `ResultSet` is used to find whether a column contains the `NULL` value in a database or not?

Q. 4.10 What is `ResultSetMetaData`?

Q. 4.11 What is `ResultSet` holdability?

5

Describing Advanced JDBC Concepts

In a distributed environment, multiple users access a single database to perform their daily operations, which often leads to network congestion and slow retrieval of data from the database. To overcome these problems, various advanced concepts and features have been introduced in Java Database Connectivity (JDBC) Application Programming Interface (API). These advanced features of JDBC API help to reduce the time consumed in performing various functions, such as creating a connection pool, opening and closing a connection, executing multiple Structured Query Language (SQL) statements individually, implementing scrollable result sets, and using SQL-99 data types as well as batch updates. JDBC also allows you to use the `PreparedStatement` and `CallableStatement` statements to retrieve data from a database in the form of result sets. In addition, the implementation of batches facilitates to execute multiple SQL statements at a single point of time. This reduces the time consumed in the execution of individual SQL queries. JDBC API also provides transaction management to implement data integrity and security to a database.

In the previous chapter, you learned about JDBC statements and `ResultSet`. In this chapter, you learn about advanced JDBC concepts, such as how to use JDBC to handle large objects and user-defined data types. These concepts are helpful in case you want to store the values of Binary Large Objects (BLOBs) and Character Large Objects (CLOBs) in a database. The chapter also explains batch updates, which are used to implement multiple SQL statements, and about how to work with auto-generated keys using the `Statement` and `PreparedStatement` objects. The chapter then describes JDBC `RowSet object`, connection pooling, transaction mechanisms associated with a data source, Wrapper methods, and `SQLException`. Let's discuss in detail about these advanced concepts.

Exploring SQL-99 Data Types

The SQL-99 alias SQL3 is a standard database language that includes the syntax and semantics for accessing the database. SQL-99 incorporates most of the features of SQL-92 and has an added support for non-scalar types, and some object-oriented features. SQL-99 also includes support for User Defined Types (UDTs). This allows you to define an internal structure, such as an address that might have street, state, and postal code attributes as part of its structure. These types can be used as the data types for columns, SQL variables, fields of a row type, or as attributes of another UDT. In addition to UDT, SQL3 supports few useful data types to store large objects, which can be even used to store Java objects in a serialized byte stream as SQL `BLOB`.

The data types available in SQL-99 types are:

- `BLOB` data type
- `CLOB` and `NCLOB` data type
- `Struct` data type
- `Array` data type
- `REF` data type

JDBC 4.2 includes support to work with all the preceding SQL data types. It also includes specific data types for the SQL-99 types, which are packaged in the `java.sql` package.

Let's describe these data types available in SQL-99 types in detail.

The BLOB Data Type

A `BLOB` is a built-in data type supported by the database implementing SQL-99 standards. As the name implies, this is used to store large binary data, such as bit images, audios, and multimedia clips, as the column values in a database table. The `java.sql.Blob` interface is a part of JDBC API, defined to describe an object (implemented by the JDBC Driver) that represents the database `BLOB` type. The `BLOB` object is implemented using an SQL Locator, which indicates that a `BLOB` contains a pointer to point SQL `BLOB` value in a database. The `BLOB` object represents a logical pointer to the binary large object rather than a copy of the object. Most of the databases process only one data page into memory at a time. It means that you need not process and store the entire `BLOB` in the memory just to access its first few bytes. The `ResultSet.getBlob()` method can be used to get the `BLOB` object. The `BLOB` objects have a lifetime strictly limited by the lifetime of the transaction and database they depend on.

NOTE

The implementation of the `BLOB` object varies from one database to another and depends upon the strategy used by the JDBC Driver, i.e., type of JDBC Driver. The JDBC 4.0 includes a support to release the `BLOB` object resources using the `Blob.free()` method.

The BLOB object supports various methods to store and retrieve BLOB values.

Table 5.1 describes the methods provided by the Blob interface:

Table 5.1: Methods of the Blob Interface

Method	Description
`public InputStream getBinaryStream()`	Retrieves the BLOB value, stored by the BLOB object, as a stream.
`public byte[] getBytes(long pos, int length)`	Retrieves all or some portion of the BLOB values stored by the BLOB object.
`public long length()`	Returns the number of bytes of the BLOB values taken by a BLOB object.
`public long position(Blob pattern, long start)`	Returns the byte position of the BLOB value designated by the BLOB object.
`public long position(byte[] pattern, long start)`	Returns the position of the BLOB value in an array of bytes designated by the BLOB object.
`public OutputStream setBinaryStream(long pos)`	Retrieves the stream used to write the BLOB value.
`public int setBytes(long pos, byte[] bytes)`	Writes the BLOB value in an array of bytes designated by the BLOB object, starting at position pos, and returns the number of bytes written. The position and the number of bytes to be written must be specified in this method.
`public int setBytes(long pos, byte[] bytes, int offset, int len)`	Writes all or part of the given byte array to the BLOB value that this BLOB object represents and returns the number of bytes written to the BLOB value.
`public void truncate(long len)`	Truncates the BLOB value represented by the BLOB object.

Now, let's learn to use the methods described in Table 5.1 to store and query a BLOB value into and from the database under the following heads:

- Store BLOB values into the database
- Read BLOB values

Storing BLOB Values

You can store the BLOB values into a database by using either the `PreparedStatement` or `CallableStatement` objects. The user-defined functions or functions based on the database vendor are used by the `Statement` object to store the BLOB values. The `PreparedStatement` and `CallableStatement` objects support the following two methods to store the BLOB value:

- `setBlob(int index, Blob b)`
- `setBinaryStream (int index, InputStream source, int length)`

The `setBlob(Blob)` method takes a `java.sql.Blob` object as an argument, which describes the BLOB data to be saved into database. This means that to use this method, a Java application needs to instantiate and initialize a `java.sql.Blob` object, which is implemented by the JDBC Driver. Although JDBC API includes a standard abstraction in the form of the `java.sql.Blob` interface for understanding JDBC `Blob` objects, JDBC 3.0 does not include a support for creating the `Blob` object. That means JDBC 3.0 does not provide any database-independent mechanism for constructing a `java,sql.Blob` instance; and therefore, you need to either write your own implementation or depend on the JDBC Driver vendor's implementation for instantiating a `java.sql.Blob` object. If you are working with a previous version of JDBC 4.0, you can use the setBinaryStream(...) method of the PreparedStatement and CallableStatement objects for storing the BLOB data into database. In this case, the constructed BLOB data is described as an InputStream.

Let's now create an application to insert a BLOB value into the database through JDBC using the setBinaryStream() method of the PreparedStatement object. This application is used to store BLOB values, as shown in Listing 5.1 (you can find the InsertBlobEx.java file online in the code/Chapter5 folder):

Listing 5.1: Showing the code of the InsertBlobEx.java File

```
package com.santosh.jdbc;

import java.sql.*;
import java.util.*;
import java.io.*;
/**
* @author Santosh
*/
public class InsertBlobEx {
   public static void main(String s[]) throws Exception {
         Driver d= (Driver) ( Class.forName(
         "oracle.jdbc.driver.OracleDriver").newInstance());
         Properties p=new Properties ();
         p.put("user","scott");
         p.put("password","tiger");
         Connection con=d.connect("jdbc:oracle:thin:@mysys:1521:sandb",p);
         PreparedStatement ps= con.prepareStatement(
         "insert into personaldetails(empno,photo) values(?,?)");
         ps.setInt(1,Integer.parseInt(s[0]));
         File f=new File("MyImage.gif");
         FileInputStream fis= new FileInputStream(f);
         ps.setBinaryStream(2,fis, (int)f.length());
         int i=ps.executeUpdate();
         System.out.println("Record inserted successfully , count : "+i);
         con.close();
   }//main
}//class
```

Before executing the code shown in Listing 5.1, create the personaldetails table in the sandb database by using the following code snippet:

```
Create table personaldetails(empno number, photo BLOB);
```

When you execute the code given in Listing 5.1, an image is inserted into the sandb database. This example is using the PreparedStatement.setBinaryStream() method to save image value into the database. As discussed earlier, we can use the java.sql.Blob object to represent the BLOB value. This provides an opportunity to manage the large binary data in a fine grained manner, using various methods (Table 5.1) supported by the java.sql.Blob object. As the JDBC 3.0 API does not support an abstraction, you need to use the vendor (JDBC Driver) specific API for creating a java.sql.Blob object. The JDBC 4.2 addresses this problem by including the Connection.createBlob() factory method for creating an empty java.sql.Blob object. This method is implemented by the Connection object. The Connection.createBlob() method creates a BLOB object to which the bytes can be set using the Blob.setBytes() method. The java.sql.Blob object is passed as a parameter into the setBlob() method of the PreparedStatement and CallableStatement objects to save in the database. The following code snippet is used to create a java.sql.Blob object using JDBC 4.2 API:

```
Connection con= ... //obtain the connection
Blob b = con.createBlob(); //creates an empty Blob (Blob object with no bytes)
b.setBytes(1, data); //here data is a byte[]
Now, the above created Blob object can be used with setBlob() method
```

The preceding code snippet provides a vendor-independent approach to create a Blob object. After learning how to store the BLOB value in a database using the setBinaryStream() and setBlob() methods of the PreparedStatement object, let's now learn how to retrieve the BLOB value from a database.

Reading BLOB Values

You can read a BLOB value from a database by using the JDBC Blob object. The java.sql.Blob object represents a logical pointer to the BLOB value in a database, and the Blob.getBinaryStream() and Blob.getBytes() methods are used to get the BLOB data. We use the ResultSet.getBlob() method to get the java.sql.Blob object representing the DB BLOB value. Otherwise, you can even use the ResultSet.getBinarySteam() method to directly get an InputStream that points to the DB BLOB value.

Let's now create an application that reads the BLOB value from database using JDBC with the ResultSet.getBinaryStream() method.

Listing 5.2 shows the code of the ReadBlobEx.java file (you can find the ReadBlobEx.java file online in the code/Chapter5 folder):

Listing 5.2: Showing the code of the ReadBlobEx.java File

```
package com.santosh.jdbc;
import java.sql.*;
import java.util.*;
import java.io.*;
/**
 * @author Santosh
 */
public class ReadBlobEx {
  public static void main(String s[]) throws Exception {

        Driver d= (Driver) ( Class.forName(
        "oracle.jdbc.driver.OracleDriver").newInstance());

        Properties p=new Properties ();
        p.put("user","scott");
        p.put("password","tiger");

        Connection con=d.connect(
        "jdbc:oracle:thin:@mysys:1521:sandb",p);

        Statement st=con.createStatement();
        ResultSet rs=st.executeQuery( "select * from personaldetails");

        while (rs.next()) {

                int empno=rs.getInt(1);
                InputStream is=rs.getBinaryStream(2);

                FileOutputStream fos=new FileOutputStream("MyImg"+empno+".gif");

                int i=is.read();

                while (i!=-1){
                        fos.write(i);
                        i=is.read();
                }//while
        }//while
        System.out.println("Image's retrived");
        con.close();
  }//main
}//class
```

Listing 5.2 uses the ResultSet.getBinaryStream() method to get the InputStream for reading the BLOB value from database. The ResultSet.getBlob() method is used along with the ResultSet.getBinaryStream() method to get the BLOB value. The following code snippet shows the use of the ResultSet.getBlob() method to read the BLOB value:

```
ResultSet rs=statement.executeQuery("select * from personaldetails");
rs.next();
Blob b=rs.getBlob(2);
byte[] data=b.getBytes(5, 50);
```

The preceding code snippet reads a part of the BLOB value, which is at the 2nd column of the personaldetails table. As described in Table 5.1, the `Blob.getBytes (long startIndex, int length)` method reads the *length* number of bytes starting from the *startIndex* byte. The `getBytes()` method is used to read 50 bytes starting from the 5th byte into the *data* array.

The CLOB and NCLOB Data Types

A CLOB is a built-in data type supported by the database that implements the SQL-99 standards. As the name implies, it is used to store large amount of textual data. The CLOB is a collection of data stored as a single entity in a Database Management System (DBMS). The `java.sql.Clob` interface is a part of JDBC API, defined to describe an object (implemented by the JDBC Driver) that represents the database CLOB type. The `java.sql.Clob` object is implemented using an SQL Locator, which indicates that a `java.sql.Clob` object contains a pointer to point SQL CLOB value in a database. The `java.sql.Clob` object represents a logical pointer to the character large object rather than a copy of the object. Most of the databases process only one data page into the memory at a time, that is, the whole CLOB does not need to be processed and stored in memory just to access the first few characters of the CLOB value. We use the `ResultSet.getClob()` method to get the `java.sql.Clob` object. The CLOB objects have a lifetime strictly limited by the lifetime of the transaction and database they depend on.

NOTE

The `java.sql.Clob` object implementation varies from one database to another depending upon the strategy used by the JDBC Driver, that is, Type-1, 2, 3, 4, or 5. However, JDBC 4.0 includes a support to release the `java.sq.Clob` object resources using the `Clob.free()` method.

The `java.sql.Clob` object supports various methods to store and retrieve CLOB values. Table 5.2 describes the methods provided by the Clob interface:

Table 5.2: Methods of the Clob Interface

Method	Description
`public InputStream getAsciiStream()`	Retrieves a character large object value designated by the CLOB object.
`public Reader getCharacterStream()`	Returns the `java.io.Reader` object, which is used to read the CLOB value.
`public String getSubString(long pos, int length)`	Retrieves a copy of the substring specified in the method. The CLOB value must be designated by the CLOB object.
`public long length()`	Retrieves the specified number of characters from the CLOB value designated by the CLOB object.
`public long position(Clob searchstr, long start)`	Retrieves the position of the character to be retrieved from the CLOB value designated by the CLOB object.
`public long position(String searchstr, long start)`	Retrieves the character position in the CLOB value where the String "searchstr" appears. The "searchstr" represents the String to be searched in the CLOB value.
`public OutputStream setAsciiStream(long pos)`	Retrieves the stream to be written into the CLOB value. The starting position of the stream must be specified by the "pos" parameter of the method. The CLOB value must be designated by the CLOB object.
`public Writer setCharacterStream(long pos)`	Retrieves the stream used to write the CLOB value, starting from the position specified by the "pos" parameter of the method.
`public int setString(long pos, String str)`	Writes the specified string into the CLOB value. The CLOB value must be designated by the CLOB object.
`public int setString(long pos, String str, int offset, int len)`	Writes the specified length character into the CLOB value, starting from a specified position.
`public void truncate(long len)`	Truncates the CLOB value associated with the CLOB object.

Now, let's use the methods listed in Table 5.2 to perform the following tasks:

- Store CLOB value into database
- Read CLOB values

Storing CLOB Values

You can store the CLOB values in a database by using either the `PreparedStatement` or `CallableStatement` objects. The user-defined functions or functions based on the database vendor are used by the `Statement` object to store the CLOB values. The `PreparedStatement` and `CallableStatement` objects support the following two methods to store the CLOB value:

- `setClob(int index, Clob b)`
- `setCharacterStream(int index, Reader source, int length)`

The `setClob(Clob)` method takes a `java.sql.Clob` object as an argument, which describes the CLOB data to be saved in database. This means that to use this method, Java application needs to instantiate and initialize a `java.sql.Clob` object, which is implemented by the JDBC Driver. Although JDBC API includes a standard abstraction for understanding the `java.sql.Clob` objects in form of the `java.sql.Clob` interface, JDBC 3.0 does not include a support for creating the `java.sql.Clob` object. That means JDBC 3.0 does not provide any database-independent mechanism for constructing a `java.sql.Clob` instance, and therefore, you need to either write your own implementation or depend on the JDBC Driver vendor's implementation for instantiating a `java.sql.Clob` object. If you are working with a previous version of JDBC 4.0, you can use the `setCharacterStream()` method of `PreparedStatement` and `CallableStatement` for storing CLOB data in the database. In this case, the constructed CLOB data is described as a `java.io.Reader` object.

Let's now create an application to insert a CLOB value into the database through JDBC using the `setCharacterStream()` method of the `PreparedStatement` object. This application is used to store the CLOB value and stores the employee details in the database table (empprofiles), which contains employees' names and profiles. The employee profile column is of the CLOB type, as it can save a document describing the profile. Listing 5.3 shows the code of the InsertEmployeeProfile.java file (you can find the InsertEmployeeProfile.java file online in the code/Chapter5 folder):

Listing 5.3: Showing the code of the InsertEmployeeProfile.java File

```
package com.santosh.jdbc;

import java.sql.*;
import java.util.*;
import java.io.*;
/**
 * @author Santosh
 */
public class InsertEmployeeProfile {
  public static void main(String s[]) throws Exception {
        Driver d= (Driver) ( Class.forName(
        "oracle.jdbc.driver.OracleDriver").newInstance());
        Properties p=new Properties ();
        p.put("user","scott");
        p.put("password","tiger");

        Connection con=d.connect("jdbc:oracle:thin:@mysys:1521:sandb",p);

        PreparedStatement ps= con.prepareStatement(
        "insert into empprofiles values(?,?)");

        ps.setInt(1,Integer.parseInt(s[0]));
        File f=new File(s[1]);
        FileReader fr= new FileReader(f);
        ps.setCharacterStream(2,fr, (int)f.length());
        int i=ps.executeUpdate();
        System.out.println("Record inserted successfully , count : "+i);
        con.close();
```

```
    }//main
}//class

To execute this example create the following table
create table empprofiles (
empno number,
profile CLOB );
```

Listing 5.3 shows how to store a CLOB value in the database by using the setCharacterStream() method supported by the PreparedStatement object. In this case, we are storing a word document into the profile column, which is of the sandb CLOB type. The document contains all the details of a particular employee.

As discussed earlier in this section, the java.sql.Clob object can be used to represent the CLOB value. This provides an opportunity to manage the large character data in a fine grained manner, using the various methods supported by the java.sql.Clob object, which are described in Table 5.2. As the JDBC 3.0 API does not support an abstraction, you need to use the vendor (JDBC Driver) specific API for creating a java.sql.Clob object. The JDBC 4.0 addresses this problem by including the factory method, createClob(), for creating an empty java.sql.Clob object. This method is implemented by the Connection object. The Connection.createClob() method creates a CLOB object to which the characters can be set using the Clob.setString() or Clob.setCharacterStream() method. The java.sql.Clob object is passed as a parameter into the setClob() method of the PreparedStatement and CallableStatement objects to save in database. The following code snippet is used to create a java.sql.Clob object using JDBC 4.2 API:

```
Connection con= ... //obtain the connection
Clob b=con.createClob(); //creates an empty Clob (Clob object with no bytes)
b.setString(1, data); //where data is a String
Now, the above created Clob object can be used with setClob() method
```

After learning how to store CLOB values in a database by using the setCharacterStream() or setClob() method, let's learn how to read CLOB values from the database.

Reading CLOB Values

You can read a CLOB value from a database by using the JDBC Clob object. As described earlier, the java.sql.Clob object represents a logical pointer to the CLOB value in database, and the Clob.getCharacterStream() and Clob.getSubString() methods are used to get the CLOB data. The ResultSet.getClob() method is used to get the java.sql.Clob object representing the DB CLOB value. You can even use the ResultSet.getCharacterSteam() method to directly get a java.io.Reader object that points to the DB CLOB value.

Let's create an application that reads the CLOB value from database using the ResultSet.getCharacterStream() method.

Listing 5-4 shows the code of the GetEmployeeProfile.java file (you can find the GetEmployeeProfile.java file online in the code/Chapter5 folder):

Listing 5-4: Showing the code of the GetEmployeeProfile.java File

```
package com.santosh.jdbc;
import java.sql.*;
import java.util.*;
import java.io.*;
/**
 * @author Santosh
 */
public class GetEmployeeProfile {
  public static void main(String s[]) throws Exception {
        Driver d= (Driver) ( Class.forName(
        "oracle.jdbc.driver.OracleDriver").newInstance());
        Properties p=new Properties ();
        p.put("user","scott");
        p.put("password","tiger");
        Connection con=d.connect("jdbc:oracle:thin:@mysys:1521:sandb",p);
        Statement st=con.createStatement();
        ResultSet rs=st.executeQuery(
        "select profile from empprofiles where empno="+s[0]);
```

```
            while (rs.next()) {
                        Reader r=rs.getCharacterStream(1);
                        FileWriter fw=new FileWriter("ProfileOf"+s[0]+".doc");
                        int i=r.read();
                        while (i!=-1){
                                    fw.write(i);
                                    i=r.read();
                        }//while
            }//while
            System.out.println("Profile retrived");
            con.close();
    }//main
}//class
```

Listing 5.4 is used to access the details of the employee by using the `ResultSet.getCharacterStream()` method, which returns the `java.io.Reader` object that is used to read the `CLOB` value from database. The `ResultSet.getClob()` method is used along with the `ResultSet.getCharacterStream()` method to get the `CLOB` value.

The following code snippet shows how to use the `ResultSet.getClob()` method to read a `BLOB` value:

```
ResultSet rs=statement.executeQuery("select * from empprofiles");
rs.next();
Clob c=rs.getClob(2);
String data=c.getSubString(2, 100);
```

The preceding code snippet reads a part of the `CLOB` value, which is at the 2nd column of the empprofiles table. As described in Table 5.2, the `Clob.getSubString(long startIndex, int length)` method reads the *length* number of characters starting from the *startIndex* character. The `getSubString()` method reads 100 characters starting from the 2nd character into the data string.

NOTE

The `BLOB` and `CLOB` objects can persist even after the transaction in which they are created is complete. Moreover, these objects may persist for a long time in case of lengthy transactions. This results in the shortage of resources for the application using these objects. To overcome this problem, JDBC 4.0 provides the `free()` method of the `java.sql.Blob` and `java.sql.Clob` types, which you can use to release the `BLOB` and `CLOB` objects when they are not required by the application.

The NCLOB Data Type

`NCLOB` (National Character Large Object) data type is used to store Unicode data. It can hold up to 4 GB of character data. It is similar to `CLOB` data type. An `NCLOB` data type fully supports and participates in a transaction. If the DBMS_LOB package makes any changes in the `NCLOB` value, PL/SQL or OCI can be committed or rolled back. With `NCLOB` attributes, it is not possible to create an object type, but for an object type, you can specify `NCLOB` parameters in a method.

`NCLOB` data types extend the `Clob` interface. Just like `Clob` objects, `NClob` objects also remain valid for the duration of the transaction in which it was created. Methods like `getNClob()` and `setNClob()` in the interfaces `ResultSet` and `CallableStatement` allow a programmer to access SQL `NCLOB` value. Apart from this, there are methods in `ResultSet` and `CallableStatement` interfaces that allow updating an `NCLOB` value.

The Struct (Object) Data Type

Most of the databases enable you to create structured types, used to define complex data types. This is required in case you want to create a user-defined type in a database. For example, you might need to create a user-defined type to represent the address of an employee in a single column. The following code snippet shows the syntax for creating a structured type in a database:

```
create type <name> as OBJECT (<variable name> <type>, ...);
```

After you have created a structured type, you can reference it to create the required user-defined data type value. The following code snippet shows the example of creating a user-defined type:

```
create type empaddress as OBJECT (
    flatno number,
    street varchar2(20),
    city varchar2(15),
    state varchar2(10),
    pincode number
);

create table employeeDetails (
    empno number,
    addr empaddress
);
```

The preceding code snippet creates a structured type named empaddress that can store the values of the flatno and pincode fields of type `NUMBER`, and the street, city, and state fields of type `VARCHAR2`. It also shows how to create a table with the empaddress type column and insert record into that table.

After learning how to create a structured type, let's now learn how to store and retrieve the values of structured types. JDBC provides two approaches to store and retrieve the values of structured types:

- Use a user-defined type in Java to represent the database object type.
- Use the `java.sql.Struct` interface to access the JDBC Driver-implemented `Struct` object.

Let's learn about these in detail.

Using User-Defined Object Types in Java to Represent Database Object Types

JDBC supports UDT by providing various methods in the `PreparedStatement`, `CallableStatement`, and `ResultSet` interfaces of JDBC API.

The following methods are available in the `java.sql.PreparedStatement` interface for supporting UDT:

- `setObject (int parameterindex, Object o)`
- `setObject (int parameterindex, Object o, int targetSqltype)`
- `setObject (int parameterindex, Object o, int targetSqltype, int scale)`

The following methods are available in the `java.sql.ResultSet` interface for supporting UDT:

- `Object getObject (int columnindex)`
- `Object getObject (int columnindex, java.util.Map m)`
- `Object getObject (String columnName)`
- `Object getObject (String columnName, java.util.Map m)`

The following methods are available in the `java.sql.CallableStatement` interface for supporting UDT:

- `Object getObject (int parameterindex)`
- `Object getObject (int parameterindex, java.util.Map m)`
- `Object getObject (String parameterName)`
- `Object getObject (String parameterName, java.util.Map m)`

Now, let's proceed to learn to create a UDT and map it to the Database (DB) object type.

Creating a JDBC UDT

Creating a JDBC UDT means that you need to create a Java custom object type for the JDBC Driver. The JDBC Driver maps the custom Java object to the DB object type value. The `java.sql.SQLData` is the interface of JDBC API designed to describe the Java Custom Object type to the JDBC Driver. The Java Custom Object type that has to be mapped to database type for JDBC must conform to the following rules:

- It should be declared as public non-abstract classes.

- It should be the subtype of the `java.sql.SQLData` interface. The `java.sql.SQLData` interface declares the following methods:
  - **`String getSQLTypeName ()`** — Returns the fully qualified name of the SQL UDT represented by this Java Custom object type. This method is called by the JDBC driver to retrieve the name of the UDT instance, which is mapped to this Java object of the `java.sql.SQLData` interface.
  - **`void readSQL (SQLInput stream, String typeName)`** — Populates this Java Custom object with data read from a database. This method generally reads each property of the SQL type from the given input stream. This is done by calling a method of the given `SQLInput` object to read each data in the order they appear in the SQL definition of the type. It then assigns the data to the appropriate fields of this object. The JDBC driver initializes the input stream with a type map before calling this method, which is used by the appropriate `SQLInput` reader method on the stream.
  - **`void writeSQL (SQLOutput stream)`** — Writes this object to the given `SQLOutput` stream that converts it back into its SQL value in the data source. The implementation of this method generally writes each element of the SQL type to the given output stream. This is done by calling a method of the given `SQLOutput` object to write each property in the order it appears in the SQL definition of the type.
- It should have a 'no argument' constructor.

Mapping the JDBC UDT

The JDBC Driver (`ResultSet`) represents the DB object type value as a Java Custom Object type; for example, empaddress of DB type to `com.santosh.jdbc.EmployeeAddress` Java type. Moreover, to make JDBC Driver understand the Java custom object type, you need to create the Java custom object type the subtype of `java.sql.SQLData`.

However, the question is how JDBC Driver would know that the database object type has to be mapped to a particular Java custom object type, i.e., how the driver knows that the `com.santosh.jdbc.EmployeeAddress` object is interested to represent DB empaddress type value. To do this, you need to create the `java.util.Map` object with an entry to map the DB type to Java type, as follows:

```
HashMap hm=new HashMap();
hm.put("EMPADDRESS", com.santosh.jdbc.EmployeeAddress.class);
```

The preceding code snippet creates a HashMap object with one entry mapping the DB type named 'EMPADDRESS' to Java type '`com.santosh.jdbc.EmployeeAddress`'. This means that when JDBC Driver (given with this `HashMap`) object encounters the EMPADDRESS type of value from the database, it wants to create the Java `com.santosh.jdbc.EmployeeAddress` object and present it to the client. Note that JDBC Driver uses `SQLData` abstraction to understand the `Java com.santosh.jdbc.EmployeeAddress` object. Now, after understanding how to create and map JDBC UDT, let's proceed to implement it in practical.

Implementing the JDBC UDT

To implement JDBC UDT, create the `EmployeeAddress` object that can represent the EMPADDRESS type of DB. The following steps are implemented to demonstrate working with UDT:

Create an object type named empaddress and a database table named persondetails in the `sandb` database

- Create a Java custom object type, `EmployeeAddress`, to represent the DB object type empaddress.
- Create the `InsertPersonalDetails` class, which inserts the `EmployeeAddress` object into the personaldetails table.
- Create the `GetPersonalDetails` class, which demonstrates to read the empaddress DB object into the `EmployeeAddress` Java Object.

Let's now create object type and database table. Figure 5.1 shows the SQL commands for creating the `empaddress` object type and the `personaldetails` table in the `sandb` database using SQL* Plus editor of Oracle:

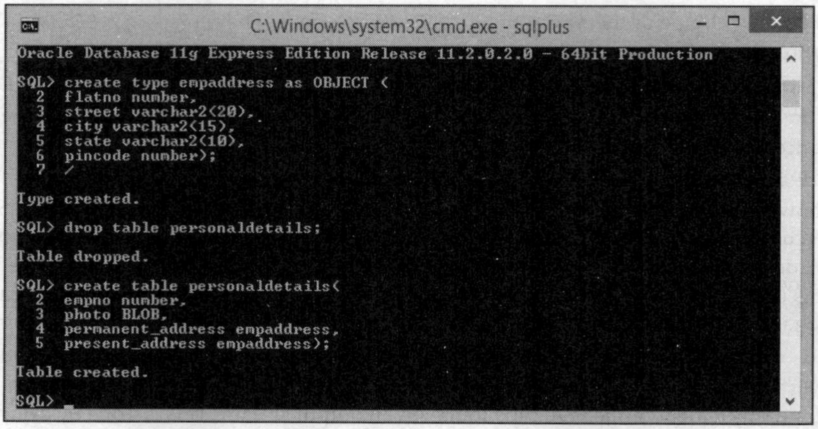

Figure 5.1: Creating Tables Using SQL* Plus Editor of Oracle

After creating the object type and table, let's create the `EmployeeAddress` object, i.e,. a JDBC UDT, which implements the `java.sql.SQLData` interface to represent the empaddress type created in the database. Listing 5.5 shows the code for the EmployeeAddess.java file (you can also find this file online in the code/Chapter5 folder):

Listing 5.5: Showing the code of the EmployeeAddress.java File

```
package com.santosh.jdbc;

import java.sql.*;
/**
 * @author Santosh
 */
public class EmployeeAddress implements SQLData {
    public EmployeeAddress(){}
    public void writeSQL(SQLOutput so) throws SQLException {
          so.writeInt(fno);
          so.writeString(street);
          so.writeString(city);
          so.writeString(state);
          so.writeInt(pin);
    }//writeSQL
    public void readSQL(SQLInput si, String name) throws SQLException{
          fno=si.readInt();
          street=si.readString();
          city=si.readString();
          state=si.readString();
          pin=si.readInt();
          typename=name;
    }//readSQL
    public String getSQLTypeName() {return typename;}
    public void setFlatno(int i){fno=i;}
    public void setStreet(String s){street=s;}
    public void setCity(String s){city=s;}
    public void setState(String s){state=s;}
    public void setPin(int i){pin=i;}
    public void setTypeName(String s){typename=s;}
    public int getFlatno(){return fno;}
    public String getStreet(){return street;}
    public String getCity(){return city;}
    public String getState(){return state;}
    public int getPin(){return pin;}
    String street,city,state, typename;
    int fno,pin;
}//class
```

Listing 5.5 shows the JDBC UDT to represent the empaddress type that holds the values of the flatno, street, city, state, and pin fields. Now, after creating the JDBC UDT Java custom object type, create an `InsertPersonalDetails.java`, which demonstrates to insert the `EmployeeAddress` object into the permanent_address column of the personaldetails table in the database `sandb`.

Listing 5.6 shows the code of the `InsertPersonalDetails.java` file (you can find the `InsertPersonalDetails.java` file online in the code/Chapter5 folder):

Listing 5.6: Showing the code of the InsertPersonalDetails.java File

```
package com.santosh.jdbc;

import java.sql.*;
import java.util.*;
import java.io.*;
/**
 * @author Santosh
 */
public class InsertPersonalDetails {

  public static void main(String s[]) throws Exception {

        Driver d= (Driver) ( Class.forName(
        "oracle.jdbc.driver.OracleDriver").newInstance());

        Properties p=new Properties ();
        p.put("user","scott");
        p.put("password","tiger");
        Connection con=d.connect("jdbc:oracle:thin:@mysys:1521:sandb",p);
        PreparedStatement ps= con.prepareStatement(
        "insert into personaldetails(empno,photo,permanent_address) values(?,?,?)");
        /*
        Here we consider Present Address is same as Permanent Address, so we want to
        insert null in place of Present Address
        */
        ps.setInt(1,7934);
        File f=new File("MyImage.gif");
        FileInputStream fis= new FileInputStream(f);
        ps.setBinaryStream(2,fis, (int)f.length());

        EmployeeAddress addr=new EmployeeAddress ();
        addr.setFlatno(106);
        addr.setCity("Hyd");
        addr.setStreet("SRN");
        addr.setPin(5000049);
        addr.setState("AP");
        addr.setTypeName("EMPADDRESS");
        ps.setObject(3,addr);
        int i=ps.executeUpdate();
        System.out.println("Personal Details of employee 7934 inserted successfully");
        con.close();
   }//main
}//class
```

Listing 5.6 uses the `setObject()` method of the `PreparedStatement` object to store the `EmployeeAddress` object into the `sandb` database.

After creating all the files required for the application to demonstrate the insertion of the EmployeeAddress object into database through JDBC, let's execute the `InsertPersonalDetails.java` file, as shown in Figure 5.2:

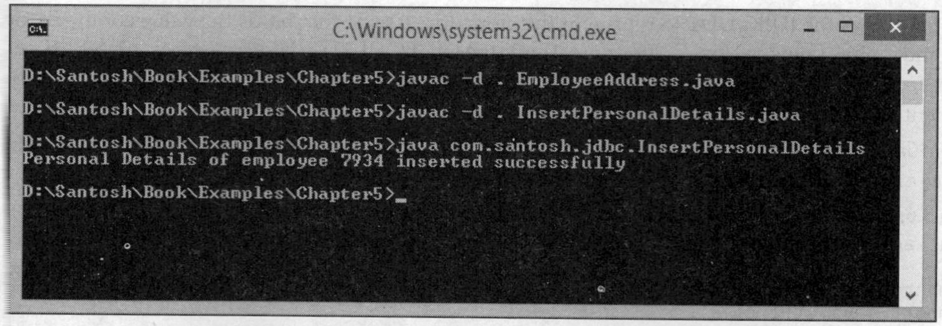

Figure 5.2: Showing the Output of the InsertPersonalDetails.java File

Figure 5.2 shows the output of Listing 5.6, which inserts a record into the personaldetails table. Now, let's see how to retrieve the DB object type value into JDBC UDT Java custom object.

NOTE

To update the Object type, use the same `setObject()` method as used in Listing 5.6.

Let's now learn how to retrieve the object type value. To do this, create the `GetEmployeeAddress.java` file, which uses the JDBC API to access the DB object type value into the EmployeeAddress object.

Listing 5.7 shows the code of the GetEmployeeAddress.java file (you can find this file online in the code/Chapter5 folder):

Listing 5.7: Showing the code of the GetEmployeeAddress.java File

```
package com.santosh.jdbc;

import java.sql.*;
import java.util.*;
import java.io.*;
/**
 * @author Santosh
 */
public class GetEmployeeAddress {
  public static void main(String s[]) throws Exception {
        Driver d= (Driver) ( Class.forName(
        "oracle.jdbc.driver.OracleDriver").newInstance());
        Properties p=new Properties ();
        p.put("user","scott");
        p.put("password","tiger");
        Connection con=d.connect("jdbc:oracle:thin:@mysys:1521:sandb",p);
        Statement st=con.createStatement();
        ResultSet rs=st.executeQuery(
        "select permanent_address from personaldetails where empno="+s[0]);
        if (rs.next()){
              HashMap map=new HashMap();
              map.put("EMPADDRESS", EmployeeAddress.class);
              EmployeeAddress addr=(EmployeeAddress)rs.getObject(1,map);
              System.out.println("Employee Found Address:");
              System.out.println("Flatno : "+addr.getFlatno());
              System.out.println("Street : "+ addr.getStreet());
              System.out.println("Pin    : "+addr.getPin());
        }//if
        con.close();
  }//main
}//class
```

Listing 5.7 shows the code to retrieve the object type value from the `sandb` database and represent it as the EmployeeAddress type of object in Java.

Figure 5.3 shows the output of Listing 5.7:

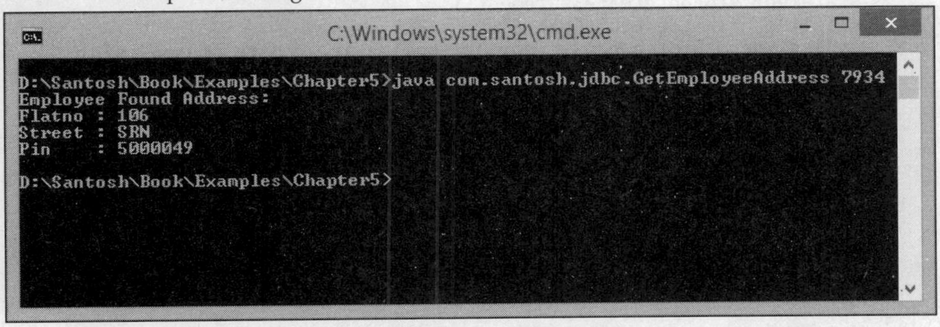

Figure 5.3: Showing the Output of the GetEmployeeAddress.java File

Figure 5.3 shows the output of Listing 5.7 that retrieves the object type value from the `sandb` database by using the EmployeeAddress type. In this section, you learned how to create a JDBC UDT to represent the DB Object type. However, like other DB types, JDBC includes a built-in type to represent the database object type, which is discussed in the following section:

Using the java.sql.Struct Interface

The JDBC API includes a built-in type to represent the database struct/object type. The `java.sql.Struct` interface is designed to describe a JDBC Driver object that represents the SQL structured type. A `Struct` object contains values for each attribute associated with the `Struct` data type. By default, an instance of `Struct` is valid as long as the application has a reference of its instance. The `Struct` interface provides certain methods to work with the `Struct` objects. Table 5.3 describes the methods of the `Struct` interface:

Table 5.3: Methods of the `Struct` Interface

Method	Description
`public Object[] getAttributes()`	Retrieves the structured type attributes and ordered values. `Struct` values are represented by the `Struct` object.
`public Object[] getAttributes(Map map)`	Retrieves the structured type attributes and ordered values in an array. `Struct` values are represented by the `Struct` object.
`public String getSQLTypeName()`	Retrieves the SQL type name and SQL type of the SQL Structured type associated with the `Struct` object.

The `Struct` object of JDBC allows you to access the database object/structured type. Listing 5.8 shows how to use the `Struct` object to read the database object type (you can find the GetEmployeeAddressUsingStruct.java file online in the code/Chapter5 file):

Listing 5.8: Showing the code of the GetEmployeeAddressUsingStruct.java File

```
package com.santosh.jdbc;

import java.sql.*;
import java.util.*;
import java.io.*;
/**
 * @author Santosh
 */
public class GetEmployeeAddressUsingStruct {

  public static void main(String s[]) throws Exception {

        Driver d= (Driver) ( Class.forName(
        "oracle.jdbc.driver.OracleDriver").newInstance());
        Properties p=new Properties ();
        p.put("user","scott");
        p.put("password","tiger");
```

```
            Connection con=d.connect("jdbc:oracle:thin:@mysys:1521:sandb",p);
            Statement st=con.createStatement();
            ResultSet rs=st.executeQuery(
            "select permanent_address from personaldetails where empno="+s[0]);

            if (rs.next()){
                System.out.println("Employee Found: Address");
                Struct struct=(Struct)rs.getObject(1);
                Object addr[]=struct.getAttributes();
                System.out.println("Flatno : "+addr[0]);
                System.out.println("Street : "+ addr[1]);
                System.out.println("Pin    : "+addr[4]);
            }//if
            con.close();
        }//main
    }//class
```

The output of Listing 5.8, in which the `Struct` object is used to read the database object type, is shown in Figure 5.4:

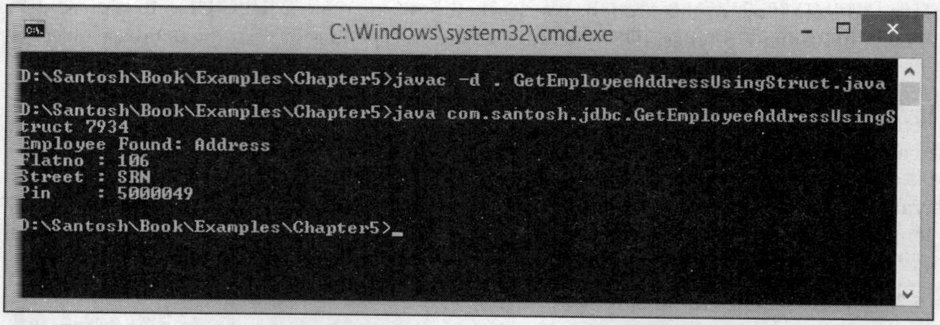

Figure 5.4: Showing the Output of the GetEmployeeAddressUsingStruct.java File

The Array Data Type

Array, one of the SQL-99 data types, allows you to include an ordered list of values within a column. The `java.sql.Array` interface of JDBC API provides an abstraction to understand the JDBC Driver object that represents a database array type. The `Array` object is implemented by using an SQL locator, which indicates that the `array` object contains a logical pointer to locate the array value in a database. The `Array` object supports methods to access the database array value. Table 5.4 describes the methods declared in the `java.sql.Array` interface:

Table 5.4: Methods of the Array Interface

Method	Description
`public Object getArray()`	Retrieves the contents of the `array` object. Array values must be designated by the array objects.
`public Object getArray(long index, int count)`	Retrieves a portion of the array value specified by the index. Array values must be designated by the `array` object.
`public Object getArray(long index, int count, Map map)`	Retrieves a portion of the array value specified by the index. It also specifies the number of elements that you can access. The array value must be designated by the `array` object.
`public Object getArray(Map map)`	Retrieves the contents of the SQL array value. The array value is designated by the `array` object.
`public int getBaseType()`	Retrieves the JDBC elements present in an array. The array value must be designated by the `array` object.
`public String getBaseTypeName()`	Retrieves the name of the SQL elements in an array. The array value must be designated by the `array` object.

Table 5.4: Methods of the Array Interface

Method	Description
`public ResultSet getResultSet()`	Retrieves the SQL `ResultSet` elements present in an array. The array value must be designated by the `array` object.
`public ResultSet getResultSet(long index, int count)`	Retrieves the sub array elements, starting at the index `'index'` of the array. The array value must be designated by the `array` object.
`public ResultSet getResultSet(long index, int count, Map map)`	Retrieves the sub array elements, starting at the index `'index'` of the array. The sub array also contains a count of the elements. The array value must be designated by the `array` object.
`public ResultSet getResultSet(Map map)`	Retrieves the SQL array elements stored in an array. The array value must be designated by the `array` object.

The `Array` type contains more than one value of the same data type. The syntax to create an `array` type in the database is as follows:

```
create Type <type name> as VARRAY(<length>) of <type>
```

For example, you can create an array describing VISA numbers of an employee. This type allows five `VARCHAR2` type values into an array as:

```
create Type VISA_NOS as VARRAY(5) of varchar2;
```

You can create a table with a column of type VISA_NOS. The code for emppassportDetails table is provided as:

```
create table emppassportDetails (
empno number, passportno varchar2(10),
visas_taken visa_nos);
```

The array type can be created in SQL editor and then can be used by the user to insert data into the emppassportDetails table.

Figure 5.5 shows the output of the `Array` type in an SQL* Plus editor:

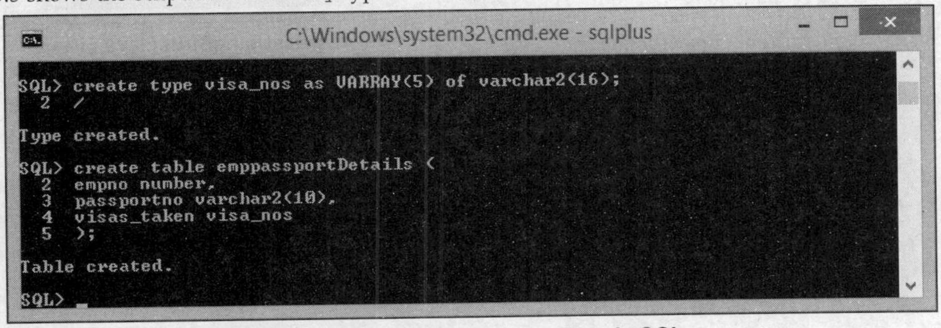

Figure 5.5: Creating an Array Type in SQL

Figure 5.5 shows the `Array` type created in the database. This type is used by the emppassportDetails table to store multiple data of the same type in a column, i.e., the `visas_taken` column.

To insert a record by using the `Statement` object, you do not need to use the `java.sql.Array` interface. Instead, you can execute the following query by using the `executeUpdate()` method:

```
insert into emppassportDetails values(7934, '12345A123',
  visa_nos('v1','v2','v3','v4','v5'));
```

The following code snippet shows how to use the `Statement` object for inserting a record into the emppassportDetails table that has an array type column:

```
Connection con= ... //Get the JDBC Connection
Statement st= con.createStatement();
int count= st.executeUpdate("insert into emppassportDetails values(7934, '12345A123',
  visa_nos('v1','v2','v3','v4','v5'))");
```

You can use the `Array` object to save the `array` type values by using the `PreparedStatement` or `CallabaleStatement` object. The `setArray()` method of the `PreparedStatement` object is used to bind array object as a parameter to a statement. The `PreparedStatement.setArray()` method takes the parameter index of type `int` and the value of type `Array` as arguments. Therefore, Java application using the `setArray()` method needs to instantiate and initialize an `Array` object, which is implemented by the JDBC Driver. Although JDBC API includes a standard abstraction for understanding `Array` objects, in the form of `java.sql.Array` interface, JDBC 3.0 specification does not include a support for creating the `Array` object. This means that JDBC 3.0 does not provide any database-independent mechanism for constructing an Array instance, and therefore, you need to either write your own implementation or depend on the JDBC Driver vendor's implementation for instantiating an `Array` object.

Now, let's create an application that can show saving an `Array` object into the database using Oracle JDBC Driver implementation.

Listing 5.9 shows how to use the SQL array types with the `PreparedStatement` object (you can find the InsertEmpPassportDetails.java file online in the code/Chapter5 folder):

Listing 5.9: Showing the code of the InsertEmpPassportDetails.java File

```
package com.santosh.jdbc;

import java.sql.*;
import java.util.*;
import oracle.sql.*;
/**
 * @author Santosh
 */
public class InsertEmpPassportDetails {
   public static void main(String s[]) throws Exception {
          Driver d= (Driver) ( Class.forName(
          "oracle.jdbc.driver.OracleDriver").newInstance());

          Properties p=new Properties ();
          p.put("user","scott");
          p.put("password","tiger");

          Connection con=d.connect(
          "jdbc:oracle:thin:@mysys:1521:sandb",p);

          PreparedStatement ps=con.prepareStatement(
          "insert into emppassportDetails values(?,?,?)");

          ps.setInt(1,7934);
          ps.setString(2,"12345A134");

          String s1[]={"v1","v2","v3","v4","v5"};

          ArrayDescriptor ad=ArrayDescriptor.createDescriptor("VISA_NOS",con);

          ARRAY a=new ARRAY(ad,con,s1);

          ps.setArray(3,a);

          int i=ps.executeUpdate();
          System.out.println("Row Inserted, count : "+i);
          con.close();
   }//main
}//class
```

Listing 5.9 uses the Oracle JDBC Driver implementation of `Array` to save the value into SQL `Array` type. The `oracle.sql.ArrayDescriptor` object encapsulates the array type created in database, such as the base type for the array and the length of the array. A static factory method, `ArrayDescriptor.createDescriptor()`, is used to create the `ArrayDescriptor` object. This factory method takes the DB array name and the JDBC `Connection` as arguments to access the database for retrieving the description of DB array.

NOTE

The array name specified in the `ArrayDescriptor.createDescriptor()` method is required to be in upper case irrespective to the case used in database while creating the array.

The JDBC `Connection` used with this method should be of `OracleConnection` that means we want to use `OracleDriver` to create the JDBC Connection.

The `oracle.sql.ARRAY` class is an implementation of the `java.sql.Array` interface from Oracle JDBC Driver. The constructor of the `ARRAY` object is used to instantiate an `Array` object. The constructor of the `ARRAY` object takes the `ArrayDescriptor`, the JDBC `Connection`, and a Java object that describes array value. After creating the `Array` object, the `PreparedStatement.setArray()` method is used to set the `Array` object to `PreparedStatement`. The column values inserted through Listing 5.9 are stored in one of the columns in the emppassportdetails table.

Figure 5.6 shows the output of Listing 5.9:

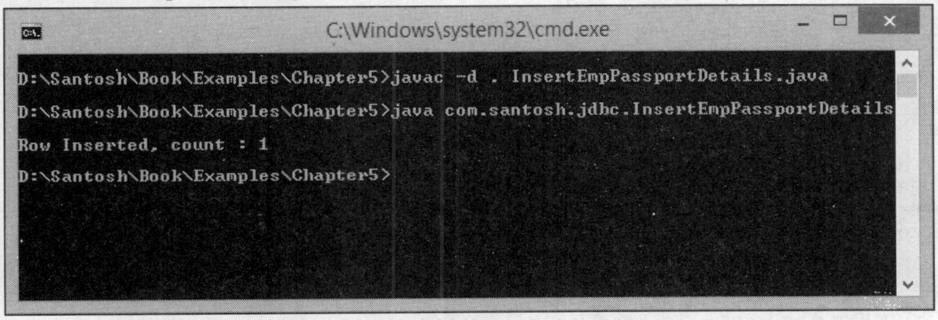

Figure 5.6: Showing the Output of the InsertEmpPassportDetails.java File

Listing 5.9 uses the implementation given by Oracle for `Array` and it works only with Oracle JDBC Driver and it therefore makes our application a vendor-dependent application. In JDBC 4.0 API, a factory method, `createArrayOf()`, is introduced in `java.sql.Connection` interface so that the JDBC Driver can implement the `Connection.createArrayOf()` method providing a vendor-independent approach to create a JDBC `Array` object. The `Connection.createArrayOf()` method allows you to create a vendor-independent `java.sql.Array` type of object with the given element type and value, as shown in the following code snippet:

```
PreparedStatement ps=con.prepareStatement("insert into emppassportDetails values(?,?,?)");
  ps.setInt(1,7934);
  ps.setString(2,"12345A134");
  String s1[]={"v1","v2","v3","v4","v5"};
  Array a=con.createArrayOf("VARCHAR", s1);
  ps.setArray(3,a);
```

In the preceding code snippet, you learned to save an Array value into database through JDBC using the `Statement` and `PreparedStatement` objects. Working with the `CallableStatement` object to save Array is same as working with the `PreparedStatement` object. We can also retrieve the Array type value from a database using JDBC.

Listing 5.10 shows how to read the `Array` type value from the database using JDBC (you can find the GetEmpPassportDetails.java file online in the code/Chapter5 folder):

Listing 5.10: Showing the code of the GetEmpPassportDetails.java File

```
package com.santosh.jdbc;

import java.sql.*;
import java.util.*;
/**
 * @author Santosh
 */
public class GetEmpPassportDetails {
  public static void main(String s[]) throws Exception {
       Driver d= (Driver) ( Class.forName(
```

```
            "oracle.jdbc.driver.OracleDriver").newInstance());

            Properties p=new Properties ();
            p.put("user","scott");
            p.put("password","tiger");

            Connection con=d.connect(
            "jdbc:oracle:thin:@mysys:1521:sandb",p);

            Statement st=con.createStatement();

            ResultSet rs=st.executeQuery("select passportno, visas_taken from
            emppassportDetails where empno="+s[0]);

            if (rs.next())
            {
                  System.out.println(
                  "\nEmployee Found, His Passport Details are:\n");
                  System.out.println("PassportNo:"+rs.getString(1)+"\n");
                  System.out.print("Visa's Taken are :\n\t");

                  Array a=rs.getArray(2);
                  ResultSet rs1=a.getResultSet();
      /*
      The ResultSet produced here to represent Array value has 2 columns
      where 1st column represents the element index
      2nd column represents the values
      */
                  boolean flag=rs1.next();
                  while(flag) {
                        System.out.print(rs1.getString(2));
                        flag=rs1.next();
                        if (flag)
                        System.out.print(",");
                  }//while
            }//if
            else
                  System.out.println("Employee not Found");
            System.out.println();
            con.close();
      }//main
}//class
```

The code, shown in Listing 5.10, reads the `Array` type value from the emppassportDetails table of the `sandb` database

Figure 5.7 shows the output of Listing 5.10:

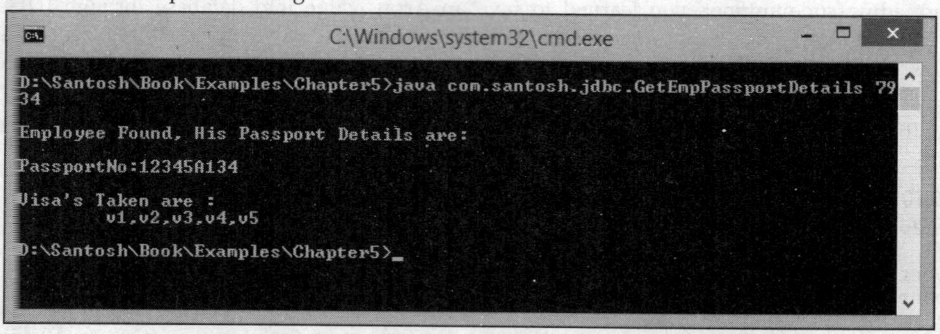

Figure 5.7: Showing the Output of the GetEmpPassportDetails.java File

In the output shown in Figure 5.7, data is selected from the `sandb` database. In Listing 5.10, the data is searched based on the specified employee number. In case the specified employee number is not found in the `sandb` database, the message "`Employee not Found`" is displayed.

NOTE

The `Array` objects remain valid for at least the duration of the transaction in which they are created. This results in the shortage of resources in case of lengthy transactions. We can use the `Array.free()` method introduced in JDBC 4.0 to release the array resources.

The JDBC API includes a support for creating the Java custom object type to represent a DB array value. To use this option, you need to create a custom mapping between the `Class` object for the class implementing the `SQLData` interface and the database array type. Creating and using the UDT is same as discussed with the JDBC UDT in the preceding sections.

The Ref Data Type

The `java.sql.Ref` interface represents the `Ref` type values that are instances of the structured type. Each `Ref` value contains a unique identifier that points to the `Ref` object. The values are stored either as a column value in a table or as an attribute value in the structured type. Since the `Ref` value is a logical pointer to an SQL structured type, a `Ref` object is also used as a logical pointer to the `Ref` values. `Ref` objects are stored in the database by using the `PreparedStatement.setRef()` method. The `Ref` interface provides the following methods to interact with a database.

Table 5.5 describes the methods of the `Ref` interface:

Table 5.5: Methods of the Ref Interface

Method	Description
`public String getBaseTypeName()`	Returns the name of the SQL structured type referenced by the SQL ref object.
`public Object getObject()`	Retrieves the SQL `Ref` object, which references the SQL structured type.
`public Object getObject(Map map)`	Retrieves the SQL structured type and maps the Java type given by the map specified as an argument.
`public void setObject(Object value)`	Sets the values of the SQL structured type, which the `Ref` object references.

Methods for Using Advanced Data Types

The above-described data types are the advanced data types provided by JDBC 4.2 API. These data types can be stored, retrieved, and updated in the same way we handle normal data types. In order to store advanced data types, we use the `PreparedStatement.setDataType` method. To retrieve them, we use either the `ResultSet.getDataType` method or `CallableStatement.getDataType` method. When we need to update them, we can use the method `ResultSet.updateDataType()`.

The methods that are mostly used to perform operations on advanced data types are:

- `getDataType()`
- `setDataType()`
- `updateDataType()`

Table 5.6 describes the methods for using advanced data types:

Table 5.6: Methods for using Advanced Data Types

Advanced Data Types	`getDataType()` Method	`setDataType()` Method	`updateDataType()` Method
`BLOB`	`getBlob()`	`setBlob()`	`updateBlob()`
`CLOB`	`getClob()`	`setClob()`	`updateClob()`
`NCLOB`	`getNClob()`	`setNClob()`	`updateNClob()`
`Array`	`getArray()`	`setArray()`	`updateArray()`
`Struct`	`getObject()`	`setObject()`	`updateObject()`
`Ref`	`getRef()`	`setRef()`	`updateRef()`

Working with the ROWID Type

A ROWID refers to a number that provides a unique identification to each row in a table. It serves as a virtual column, containing the address of the corresponding row. It is useful in identifying cases of duplicate records and identical rows in a database. It is supported by most of the databases, such as Oracle and IBM DB2. As each row has a unique identification, you can easily retrieve the data from the rows by executing the search queries. Versions prior to JDBC 4.0 did not provide any database-independent mechanism to use the ROWID type. So in such cases, you need to depend on the driver vendor's implementation; for example, the oracle.sql.ROWID class supplied by Oracle JDBC driver to use the ROWID type. Consequently, most applications avoided the use of ROWID to achieve portability. JDBC 4.0 and 4.2 provide a built-in type, java.sql.RowId, which can be used to avail the benefits associated with ROWID.

You should consider the following points with respect to ROWID before you use their types:

- ROWIDs are unique only for a table not for the entire database.
- ROWID of a row may not change as long as the row in the database table is not deleted.
- ROWIDs are not supported by all databases and are therefore not portable across all databases.
- A new ROWID is assigned if a row is deleted or reinserted.

In JDBC 4.0, the following interfaces provide support for the ROWID type:

- **java.sql.ResultSet** and **java.sql.CallableStatement**—Provide the getRowId() method to retrieve the java.sql.RowId type object. The following are the two getRowId() methods:
  - The first method takes the index (column index in case of the ResultSet interface and parameter index in case of the CallableStatement interface) as its first parameter.
  - The second method takes the label (column label in case of the ResultSet interface and parameter name in case of the CallableStatement interface) as its first parameter.
- **java.sql.ResultSet**—Contains the updateRowId() method, which is used with the ResultSet interface to update a column with a specific ROWID.
- **java.sql.PreparedStatement**—Contains the setRowId() method, which takes two arguments:
  - The parameter index
  - The java.sql.RowId object

Using the ROWID Object

In a database table, the address of a row is represented by a ROWID object. The ROWID type is generally not a standard SQL type. The values of ROWID are very useful as they can be accessed at a faster rate and are unique identifier for rows in a table. However, it should be noted that ROWID values should not be used as the primary key of a table. This is because in case we delete a row from a table, the database may reassign its ROWID value to a row inserted later.

A ROWID object value is specific to the data source while using it with the set() method of the PreparedStatement interface. It is therefore not recommended to get a ROWID from a ResultSet object with one connection and then attempt to use it with another connection.

ROWID object may be valid as long as the identified row is not deleted and the lifetime of the RowId, specified by the database, is not complete. To know the lifetime of the RowId obtained from a database, you can use the getRowIdLifetime() method of the java.sql.DatabaseMetaData interface. The getRowIdLifetime() method returns a value of the java.sql.RowIdLifetime.

The Lifetime of ROWID Validity

As long as the identified row is not deleted from the database, the ROWID object remains valid. However, the lifetime of the ROWID object remains within the bounds of the lifetime as specified by that data source for the ROWID.

The `DatabaseMetaData.getRowIdLifetime()` method should be called in order to determine the lifetime of `ROWID` objects.

The `getRowIdLifetime()` method may return the following values:

- **ROWID_UNSUPPORTED**—Specifies that the corresponding data source does not support the `ROWID` type.
- **ROWID_VALID_OTHER**—Specifies that the lifetime of a `ROWID` is dependent on database vendor implementation.
- **ROWID_VALID_TRANSACTION**—Specifies that the lifetime of a `ROWID` is valid at least till the time the corresponding transaction persists.
- **ROWID_VALID_SESSION**—Specifies that the lifetime of a `ROWID` is valid at least till the time session persists.
- **ROWID_VALID_FOREVER**—Specifies that the lifetime of the `ROWID` is unlimited and valid as long as the identified row is not deleted.

Working with Batch Updates

The batch update option allows you to submit multiple Data Manipulation Language (DML) operations to a database as a single unit. Submitting multiple DML statements together, rather than submitting them individually, improves the performance of the system by reducing the time consumption in executing the statements and the number of hits to database.

Enterprise applications use the batch update to reduce the interactions to database and, thereby, improve the performance and availability of the system. Now, let's try to understand the concept of batch updates better with the help of the following scenarios:

- **Scenario 1**—The enterprise application is divided into three major tiers, namely presentation, business, and integration (or data access). The presentation tier of the system collects the data from the end user through one or more forms and retrieves it in the presentation or business tier by managing user session. This data is finally submitted to the data access layer of the system for storage. This layer is responsible for updating the data in the database. In this case, the data access layer needs to execute multiple SQL statements to update the database with the given data. The data in the database is distributed into multiple tables, e.g., the employee details are saved into the emp and personalDetails tables. As you know that the SQL DML statement allows operating only on one table, implying that an SQL statement can update or delete or insert a record or records of a single table only. Therefore, an individual SQL statement is required to update each table with the application data. In this context, the data access layer of the system is responsible to decompose the data submitted by the user to build multiple SQL statements and store them in database.

  For example, consider a case where the user is requested to submit all personal and general details to create a new account in a banking system. The user account details are managed into the tables such as accountDetails, personalDetails, and transactionDetails. In this case, creating a new account will include inserting a record into the accountDetails, transactionDetails, and personalDetails tables. Now, instead of submitting these three SQL statements individually to the database, it is better to submit all the statements together. This reduces the number of hits to the database and the attention of the database towards the application, which can improve the speed of operation, performance, and availability of the system.

- **Scenario 2**—The enterprise application separates the data access operations from the business layer and implements them onto the data access layer. The data access layer of the system needs to support a session as well as context-level cache. This helps perform various database update operations (insert, update, and delete) and store the request from the business layer. During transaction commit, session closing, or explicit request to flush the database, the transaction needs to be synchronized with the cache. The data access layer needs to update the cache objects into the database by executing multiple SQL statements. In this scenario, instead of submitting individual SQL statements, it is better to submit multiple SQL statements as a single batch.

JDBC 4.2 API supports working with the batch updates feature of database. As the name implies, submission of multiple SQL statements to database is supported only for database update operations, i.e., DML statement, and not for querying the database. This is because SQL facilitates to create a single complex `SELECT` query with JOINs and subqueries to query the data from multiple tables of a database.

The `Statement` and `PreparedStatement` objects can be used for submitting batch updates. It implies that the `Statement` and `PreparedStatement` objects are capable to keep track of the batches to be processed so that all the batches can be submitted together for processing.

NOTE

The batch update feature is introduced in JDBC 2.0 specification. A JDBC `Statement` object can manage only one batch at a time. Moreover, a batch cannot be spanned over multiple `Statement` objects.

Using Batch Updates with the Statement Object

Using the batch updates option with the `Statement` object allows you to submit a set of heterogeneous DML/DDL commands as a single unit (batch) to the underlying data source. A `Statement` object is initially associated with an empty batch. An application can use the `Statement.addBatch (String SQLStatement)` method to add an `SQLStatement` to the batch. In case the batch needs to be submitted for processing, the application can invoke the `Statement.executeBatch()` method after all `SQLStatement` have been added to the batch. However, if the application decides not to submit the batch, it can invoke the `Statement.clearBatch()` method on the `Statement` object to remove all the `SQLStatement` and render the batch empty.

Batch Update Methods

The following methods have been added to the `Statement` interface to support batch update:

- **`addBatch(String SQLStatement)`** – Adds the given SQL statement to the current batch, i.e., the batch that is managed by this `Statement` object.

NOTE

The batch update supports the database update statements; however, it does not support the statements used to query the database

- **`clearBatch ()`** – Clears the batch currently associated with this `Statement` object.
- **`int [] executeBatch()`** – Submits the current batch of this `Statement` object to the underlying `datasource`. Once the batch is submitted to the data source, the statements in a batch are executed in the sequence in which they have been added to the batch. The following are the outcomes of this method:
  - If the batch executes successfully, `this` method returns an array of integer values whose length is equal to the number of statements in the batch.
  - If the value of any element in this array is equal to `Statement.SUCCESS_NO_INFO`, it indicates that the statement has been executed successfully but the number of rows affected is unknown.
  - In case a statement in a batch fails to be executed or produces a result set, further processing of the batch execution depends on the database that is in use. The database may continue to execute the batch or terminate it. However, in most cases, the database terminates the batch processing. Irrespective of the database behavior, the `Statement.executeBatch()` method throws the `BatchUpdateException` exception in case of any failure in batch execution. After this method is executed, the JDBC driver resets the batch, that is, it renders the batch empty.

Now, let's discuss about the `BatchUpdateException` exception.

The BatchUpdateException Exception

The `java.sql.BatchUpdateException` object describes the error that may occur while executing the batch. If the batch fails to execute in the database, the JDBC Driver throws the `BatchUpdateException` exception. It is a subtype of the `java.sql.SQLException` class. In addition to the description supported by the `SQLException`, such as SQL errorCode, state, and the message, this exception object provides an update count of the SQL statements that have executed successfully before this error occurred. The `BatchUpdateException.getUpdateCounts()` method returns an array of Integer values, which represent the following:

- **Length of the array is less than the size of the batch** – Denotes that the database has terminated the batch after the first failure, i.e., if the length of an array is 'n,' it means the first 'n' statements in the batch have been executed successfully, and each element of the array shows the respective statements' update counts.
- **Length of the array is equal to the size of the batch** – Denotes that the database has continued the batch execution process even after the batch has failed to execute. In this case, the value of each element in the array specifies the update count of the respective SQL statements in the batch. If the array value pertains to the statement that has failed to execute, the array value is equal to `Statement.EXECUTE_FAILED`.

Let's now create an application that demonstrates the use of batch update methods of the `Statement` object and `BatchUpdateException` exception. This application is used to perform batch updates. Listing 5.11 shows the code for the `BatchUpdateEx1.java` file (you can find this file online in the code/Chapter5 folder):

Listing 5.11: Showing the code of the BatchUpdateEx1.java File

```
package com.santosh.jdbc;
import java.sql.*;
import java.util.*;
import java.io.*;
/**
 * @author Santosh
 */
public class BatchUpdateEx1 {
  public static void main(String s[]) throws Exception {
Driver d= (Driver) ( Class.forName("oracle.jdbc.driver.OracleDriver").newInstance());
        Properties p=new Properties ();
        p.put("user","scott");
        p.put("password","tiger");
        Connection con=d.connect("jdbc:oracle:thin:@mysys:1521:sandb",p);
        Statement st=con.createStatement();
        //statement1
        st.addBatch("insert into emp(empno,sal,deptno) values("+s[0]+",1000,10)");
        //statement2
        st.addBatch("update emp set sal=2000 where empno="+s[0]);
        //statement3
        st.addBatch("insert into emp(empno,sal,deptno) values(202,1000,10)");
        //statement4
        st.addBatch("insert into emp(empno,sal,deptno) values(203,1000,10)");
        try {
                int[] counts=st.executeBatch();
                System.out.println("Batch Executed Successfully");
                for (int i=0;i<counts.length;i++){
                System.out.println("Number of records effected by statement"+(i+1)+":
                "+counts[i]);
                }//for
        }//try
        catch(BatchUpdateException e){
        System.out.println("Batch terminated with an abnormal condition");
                int[] counts=e.getUpdateCounts();
                System.out.println("Batch terminated at statement"+ (counts.length+1));
                for (int i=0;i<counts.length;i++) {
                System.out.println("Number of records effected by the statement"+
                (i+1)+": "+counts[i]);
                }//for
        }//catch
        con.close();
  }//main
 }//class
```

Listing 5.11 demonstrates how to perform batch updates using the `Statement` object. It also shows that the SQL statements added to the batch are executed in the order in which they have been added to the batch. In addition, it shows how to get update counts by using the `BatchUpdateException` exception in case of any failure of the batch execution. Figure 5.8 shows the output of Listing 5.11:

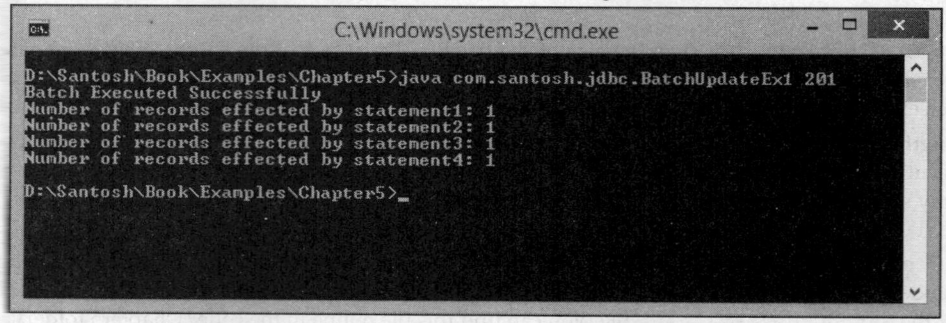

Figure 5.8: Showing the Output of the BatchUpdateEx1.java File

In the example shown in Listing 5.11, the batch was executed successfully. To understand how the `BatchUpdateException` exception functions, run this example once again with argument value 205, as shown in Figure 5.9:

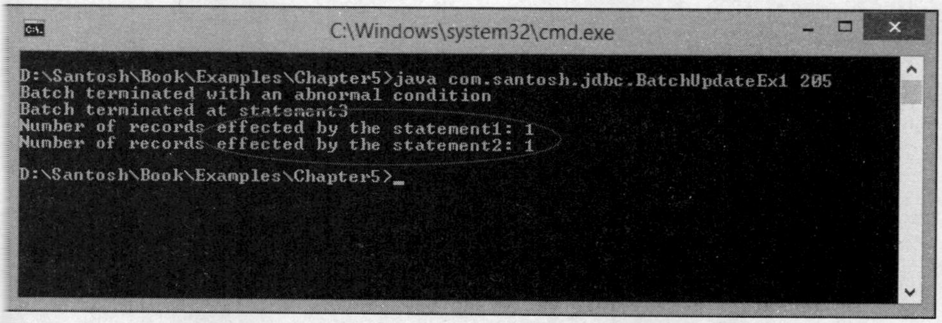

Figure 5.9: Showing the Output of the BatchUpdateEx1.java File with a Different Parameter

Figure 5.9 shows an exception that has occurred at statement3 since statement3 tries to insert a record with empno 205, which already exists in the database and empno column of emp table is set with primary key constraint.

After learning how to use batch updates with the `Statement` object, let's now learn how to implement batch updates using the `PreparedStatement` object.

Using Batch Updates with the PreparedStatement Object

You can perform similar database batch update operations with different sets of values by using the `PreparedStatement` or `Statement` object. However, the batch update implementation with the `PreparedStatement` object is different from the implementation of the `Statement` object. For example, to insert 10 employee details into the database table named emp, you can use multiple sets of input parameter values in a single SQL statement with the `PreparedStatement` object. The following methods are used by the `PreparedStatement` object to support batch updates:

- **`addBatch()`** – Adds a set of input parameter values to the batch managed by the `PreparedStatement` object.
- **`int [] executeBatch()`** – Submits the current batch to the underlying data source. The outcome of this method is similar to the `Statement.executeUpdate()` method.
- **`clearBatch()`** – Clears the batch currently associated with the `PreparedStatement` object.

To understand the concept better, let's create an application that can demonstrate the use of the `PreparedStatement` object to submit batch of SQL statements to database. This application is used to perform batch updates by using the `PreparedStatement` object. The code for BatchUpdateEx2.java file is shown in Listing 5.12 (you can find this file online in the code/Chapter5 folder):

Listing 5.12: Showing the code of the BatchUpdateEx2.java File

```
package com.santosh.jdbc;
import java.sql.*;
import java.util.*;
import java.io.*;
/**
 * @author Santosh
 */
public class BatchUpdateEx2 {
  public static void main(String s[]) throws Exception {
Driver d= (Driver) ( Class.forName("oracle.jdbc.driver.OracleDriver").newInstance());
        Properties p=new Properties ();
        p.put("user","scott");
        p.put("password","tiger");
        Connection con=d.connect("jdbc:oracle:thin:@mysys:1521:sandb",p);
        PreparedStatement ps= con.prepareStatement("insert into emp(empno,sal,deptno)
        values(?,?,?)");
        ps.setInt(1,301);
        ps.setDouble(2,1000);
        ps.setInt(3,10);
        ps.addBatch();

        ps.setInt(1,302);
        ps.setDouble(2,2000);
        ps.setInt(3,10);
        ps.addBatch();

        try {
                int counts[]= ps.executeBatch();
                System.out.println("Batch Executed Successfully");
                for (int i=0;i<counts.length;i++){
                System.out.println("Number of records effected by statement"+(i+1)+":
                "+counts[i]);
                }//for
        }//try
        catch(BatchUpdateException e){
        System.out.println("Batch terminated with an abnormal condition");
                int[] counts=e.getUpdateCounts();
                System.out.println("Batch terminated at statement"+ (counts.length+1));
                for (int i=0;i<counts.length;i++) {
                System.out.println("Number of records effected by the statement"+
                (i+1)+":"+counts[i]);
                }//for
        }//catch
        con.close();
  }//main
}//class
```

Listing 5.12 demonstrates how to perform batch updates using the `PreparedStatement` interface. It also shows that the SQL statements added to the batch are executed in the order in which they are added as well as how to get update counts from the `BatchUpdateException` exception. Figure 5.10 shows the output of Listing 5.12:

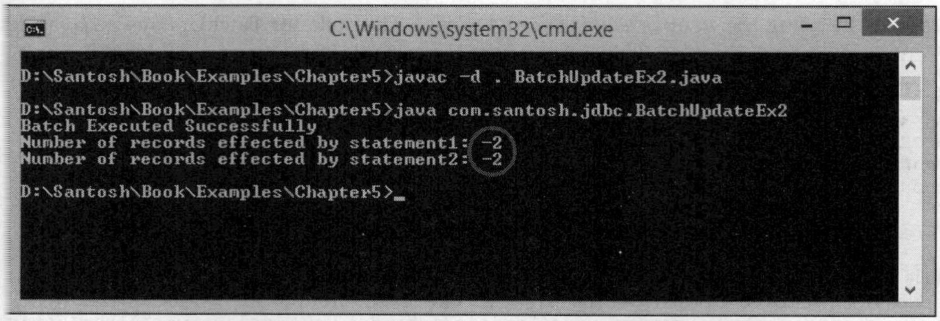

Figure 5.10: Showing the Output of the BatchUpdateEx2.java File

When you execute Listing 5.12, SQL statements specified in the batch are executed and the emp table is modified. Figure 5.11 shows the content of the table emp after the batch updates have been performed:

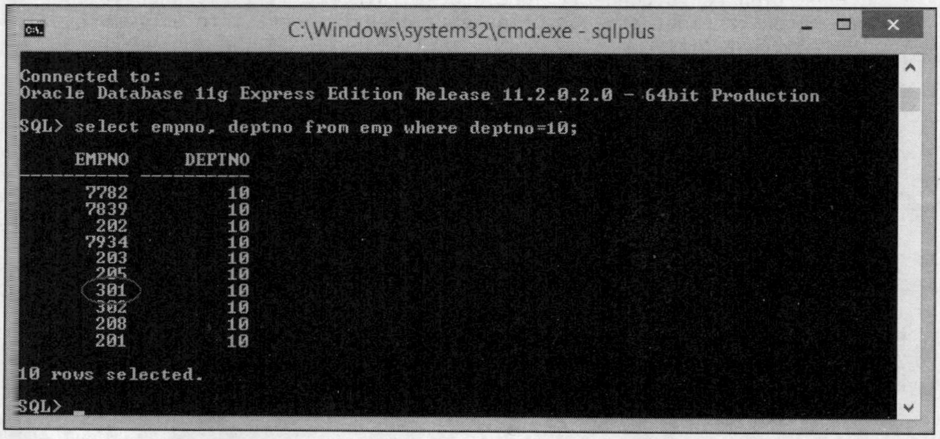

Figure 5.11: Showing the Contents of the emp Table Using SQL* Plus Editor

NOTE

In Figure 5.10, update counts are shown as -2, whereas the records, 301 and 302, have been inserted successfully into the database. The update count value is equal to `Statement.SUCCESS_NO_INFO`, which indicates that the statement has been executed successfully but the number of rows affected is unknown.

Let's now compare the `Statement` and `PreparedStatement` objects to execute batch updates. The `Statement` object supports to prepare a batch with different SQL statements, such as one SQL statement can be used to insert a record into the accountDetails table and one to insert into the personalDetails table. On the other hand, the `PreparedStatement` object allows having only one SQL statement into a batch, which can be executed with multiple sets of values. This means one SQL statement cannot be used to insert data into both the accountDetails and personalDetails tables in a single batch managed by the `PreparedStatement` object.

Describing SQL/XML and XML Support

Most of the enterprise applications maintain a large amount of data in the Extensible Markup Language (XML) format. Moreover, the enterprise using the application can store the XML format content in the database by defining the column type as `CLOB`. Considering the fact that the enterprises may want to store the organizational data in XML format, SQL 2003 specification has defined a new data type for the XML data type by defining a standard XML type. Most database vendors have an implementation of the XML data type in their new releases. With this support, now an XML dataset or document could be one of the column values in a row of a database table. Prior to JDBC 4.0, the way to manipulate such data using JDBC was to use proprietary extensions from the driver vendors or access it as a `CLOB` type.

In JDBC 4.0 and 4.2, SQLXML is provided as the Java data type that maps with the SQL XML type. The SQLXML object supports processing the XML data as a string or as a StAX (Streaming API for XML) stream.

Creating the SQLXML Object

To create an SQLXML object, the createSQLXML() method of java.sql.Connection is used. The object created in such a way is empty, and the data can be added using any one of the following methods as per the user's convenience:

- setString(String)
- java.io.OutputStream setBinaryStream()
- java.io.Writer setCharacterStream()
- javax.xml.transform.Result setResult(Class)

The following code snippet shows the sample code for creating the SQLXML object:

```
Connection con = DriverManager.getConnection(url, uname, pass);
SQLXML sx = con.createSQLXML();
sx.setString(xmldata);
```

The SQLXML object can be used with the setSQLXML() method of the PreparedStatement and CallableStatement interfaces to bind SQLXML as a parameter to the statement.

Retrieving SQLXML Values

To retrieve SQLXML data type value, the getSQLXML() method of ResultSet or CallableStatement is used. The getSQLXML() method of ResultSet and CallableStatement returns an SQLXML object. The following methods of the java.sql.SQLXML interface can be used to retrieve the data from the SQLXML object:

- String getString()
- java.io.InputStream getBinaryStream()
- java.io.Reader getCharacterStream()
- javax.xml.transform.Source getSource(Class)

The following snippet shows the sample code for retrieving data using the SQLXML object:

```
ResultSet rs=ps.executeQuery();
rs.next();
SQLXML sx = rs.getSQLXML(column);
String xmldata=sx.getString();
```

The SQLXML object remains valid for at least the duration of the transaction in which it is created. This results in an application running out of resources during a long running transaction. Applications can release SQLXML resources by invoking the free() method. The getTypeInfo() method of the java.sql.DatabaseMetaData interface can be called to check if the database supports the SQLXML data type.

Retrieving Auto-Generated Keys

In some cases, you may want the database server to generate some column values while inserting a record. For example, while creating a new account in the database server, you want an account number to be generated in the database server automatically. Moreover, for fulfilling this requirement, many databases support a mechanism that automatically generates a unique key field value while inserting a record into the database.

The following code snippet shows how to create a table in MySQL with an auto-increment column:

```
create table bank(
accno int AUTO_INCREMENT PRIMARY KEY,
name char(20),
bal double);
```

The following code snippet shows how to create a table in Oracle database with an auto-increment column:

```
create table bank(
accno number,
name varchar2(20),
bal number(10,2));
create sequence myseq start with 1 increment by 1;
```

```
create trigger mytrigger
on insert of bank
begin
select myseq.nextVal into :new.accno from dual;
end;
```

Note that Oracle does not support the AUTO_INCREMENT keyword.

To overcome the AUTO_INCREMENT flaw in Oracle, you need to create a Sequence myseq that will be triggered using the trigger mytrigger. While inserting a row into a bank table, the mytrigger is invoked for using the myseq sequence, for incrementing the accno column value.

In JDBC 2.0, the following code snippet is used to retrieve the values of automatically generated keys:

```
Connection con= ... //Create Connection
Statement st= con.createStatement();
int count=st.executeUpdate("insert into bank(name, bal) values('abc',1000)");
int accno=0;
if (count==1 || count== st. SUCCESS_NO_INFO){
   ResultSet rs= st.executeQuery("select max(accno) from bank");
   rs.next();
   accno= rs.getInt(1);
}
```

After executing the preceding code snippet, it is possible that you may not retrieve the key generated for the SQL statement executed for a request. This may be because other insert operation is performed after our insert statement and before the select statement. To avoid this problem, you can lock the table till the max value of the accno is retrieved. However, this can reduce the availability and performance of the system.

JDBC 3.0 and the higher version of JDBC provide support for accessing auto-generated keys by introducing some methods in the `Connection` and `Statement` interfaces. The JDBC Statement (`Statement` or `PreparedStatement`) object can be informed about the auto-generated keys in the given insert operation. This helps the `Statement` object to collect the values of the generated keys after executing the given SQL insert statement.

The new methods added in the `java.sql.Statement` interface that support the auto-generated key feature are:

- **`executeUpdate(String,int)`, `execute(String, int)`** – Accepts the SQL statement that needs to be executed as the first argument and `Statement.RETURN_GENERATED_KEYS` or `Statement.NO_GENERATED_KEYS` as the second argument. The second argument indicates whether the values of generated keys have to be returned or not.
- **`executeUpdate(String, int[])`, `execute(String, int[])`** – Accepts the SQL statement that needs to be executed as the first argument and indexes of the columns whose auto-generated key values should be returned as the second argument.
- **`executeUpdate(String, String[])`, `execute(String, String[])`** – Accepts the SQL statement that needs to be executed as the first argument and names of the columns whose auto-generated key values should be returned as the second argument.
- **`ResultSet getGeneratedKeys()`** – Returns a `ResultSet` object with a column for each automatically generated key.

The new methods added in the `java.sql.Connection` class in support of this feature are:

- **`prepareStatement(String, int)`** – Accepts the SQL statement to be prepared as the first argument and `Statement.RETURN_GENERATED_KEYS` or `Statement.NO_GENERATED_KEYS` as the second argument, indicating whether the value of the generated keys has to be returned or not.
- **`prepareStatement(String, int[])`** – Accepts the SQL statement that needs to be prepared as the first argument and indexes of the columns whose auto-generated key values should be returned as the second argument.
- **`prepareStatement(String, String[])`** – Accepts the SQL statement that needs to be prepared as the first argument and names of the columns whose auto-generated key values should be returned as the second argument.

The following code snippet shows using the `Statement` object to execute an SQL statement and access the auto-generated key value:

```
Connection con= ... //Create connection
Statement st= con.createStatement();
int count= st.executeUpdate("insert into bank(name,bal) values('user1', 10000)",
                    Statement.RETURN_GENERATED_KEYS);
ResultSet rs= st.getGeneratedKeys();
rs.next();
int accno= rs.getInt(1);
```

In the preceding code snippet, the `st.executeUpdate()` method executes the SQL statement to insert a new record into the bank table, which results in generating the accno for the new record in the database. The `st.getGeneratedKeys()` method returns the `ResultSet` object to read the generated key values. This example uses the Statement object to read all the generated values for the given SQL statement. However, you can also specify the column index or name for which you want to read the generated values. The `Statement.executeUpdate(String sql, int[] indexs)` method allows you to specify the index of the columns in the table, whose generated values are required to return. For example, you have a table named mytable with 20 columns – col1, col2... – and within these columns, 5 columns – col3, col5, col6, col8, and col20 – are configured to have auto-generated values. Now while inserting a record, if you want to collect only the keys generated for col5 and col8, you can use the `executeUpdate()` method, as shown in the following code snippet:

```
Connection con= ... //Create connection
Statement st= con.createStatement();
int count= st.executeUpdate(
        "insert into mytable(col1,col2) values('col1Value', 'col2Value')",
        new int[]{5,8});
ResultSet rs= st.getGeneratedKeys();
rs.next();
int col5Value= rs.getInt(1);
int col8Value= rs.getInt(2);
```

In the preceding code snippet, a new record is inserted into the mytable table, which generates the values for col3, col5, col6, col8, and col20. However, we have described the `Statement` object to collect the generated values for columns 5 and 8. To do this, we specified the column indexes as `int[]` to the `executeUpdate()` method. Similarly, we can use the `Statement.executeUpdate(String sql, String[] colNames)` method to use column names instead of indexes. The following code snippet shows the code for using this method:

```
Connection con= ... //Create connection
Statement st= con.createStatement();
int count= st.executeUpdate(
        "insert into mytable(col1,col2) values('col1Value', 'col2Value')",
        new String[]{"col5","col8"});
ResultSet rs= st.getGeneratedKeys();
rs.next();
int col5Value= rs.getInt(1);
int col8Value= rs.getInt(2);
```

The preceding code snippet described how to get the generated values from the database using the `Statement` object. The JDBC 3.0 and the higher version of JDBC API allow getting the generated values through the `PreparedStatement` object. The following code shows how to use this option:

```
Connection con= ... //Create connection
PreparedStatement ps= con.prepareStatement(
                    "insert into bank(name,bal) values('user1', 10000)",
                    Statement.RETURN_GENERATED_KEYS);
int count= ps.executeUpdate();
ResultSet rs= ps.getGeneratedKeys();
rs.next();
int accno= rs.getInt(1);
```

The preceding code snippet inserts a new record into the bank table, where the database generates the accno for the new record. Thereafter, it gets the generated keys in the form of `ResultSet` to read the generated key values. In this example, we have described the `PreparedStatement` object to read all the generated values for this SQL statement. However, similar to the Statement object, we can even specify the column index or name for which we want to read the generated values. The Connection.prepareStatement (String sql, int[] index) and Connection.prepareStatement (String sql, String[] colNames) methods allow us to specify the index and names of the columns respectively, whose generated values are returned. In this section, we have learned how to read auto-generated values from a database.

Now let us learn how to work with RowSet object in JDBC.

Working with RowSet in JDBC

A RowSet is an interface provided by JDBC API to work with bean components. It can be used as a JavaBean component and can also be created and configured in a database. An object of the RowSet interface can be configured and connected to a data source by using data from the data source. The RowSet contains some setter methods in order to set the values for the bean's command properties. The command properties in a RowSet are the SQL queries related to the relational database. The RowSet interface also contains the Java bean events. These bean events notify the occurrence of any event on the RowSet. The JDBC rowsets are always connected with the JDBC driver connections. Rowsets are of two types: connected RowSet and disconnected RowSet. Let's discuss each of them in detail.

Connected RowSet

The connected RowSet always need a driver in order to stay connected with the database. The driver connection lets the user distribute data over multiple environments. This RowSet is capable of creating a connection with the data source, maintaining the connection throughout the life cycle and working under multiple environments.

Disconnected RowSet

The disconnected RowSet do not need a driver connection with the database. The data is independent of the connection. JDBC API provides a container for sending the data over the network. Any client working on the same network can also work with the shared data, can read and update the data, and again send it back to the application server. The disconnected RowSet use a reader in order to make a connection and write back to it.

The JDBC API provides three specific classes - JDBCRowSet, CachedRowSet, and WebRowSets - for implementing the RowSet in an application. These classes are categorized according to their implementations, as follows:

- **JDBCRowSets**—Implement the javax.sql.RowSet interface. The RowSet object is capable of turning the ResultSet object into the JavaBean component and also abstracts the details of the ResultSet object. The JDBCRowSets object requires the presence of the JDBC driver in order to implement the interfaces.
- **CachedRowSets**—Implement the same functionality as that of the JDBC RowSets; however, the CachedRowSets class can also work in disconnected networks.
- **WebRowSets**—Extend the CachedRowSets class to use its properties. So, a WebRowSet can be used in a disconnected network. WebRowSets are also capable of generating XML documents that are used to create the copies of the objects of the WebRowSets class, which is used to share information over a network.

All the preceding classes are subtypes of the RowSet interface. A RowSet object is used to perform the following features in a JDBC application:

- Populates with the objects in a network
- Updates the data in disconnected network environments
- Handles the JavaBean components. So, a RowSet can be used to configure the bean properties and also to generate the events
- Generates the self-contained XML documents

An instance of RowSet can be created and configured at the design time, and the methods of the RowSet can be executed at the runtime by using the instances.

Using RowSet at Design Time

The `RowSet` object is created and configured during the design time of the bean components. There are certain procedures in order to configure the `RowSet` objects at the design time. You configure them in a connection using the following steps:

- Setting the properties
- `RowSet` events

Setting the Properties of the RowSet Instance

The JavaBeans-based setter methods present in the `RowSet` interface are used to define properties for the `RowSet` instances. These properties allow the objects to be configured and also to get connected with the underlying data sources. The following code snippet shows the configuration of the `RowSet` objects in a connection:

```
rset.setDataSourceName("jdbc/DataSourceName");
rset.setTransactionIsolation(Connection.TRANSACTION_READ_COMMITTED);
rset.setCommand("SELECT eName, deptno from emp");
```

The data source name specified in the preceding code snippet is used by the `RowSet` object in order to access the data and also to share the data over the network. The transaction isolation property, as shown in the code snippet, specifies that the data produced by the current transaction by the `RowSet` object is committed. The `setCommand()` method specifies the SQL query that is to be executed to retrieve the data using the `RowSet` object.

Working with RowSet Events

You have learned earlier that `RowSet` components are JavaBean components that are used in a connection. These components notify the occurrence of any event to the `RowSet` object available in the connection. The events are to be handled by implementing the `RowSetListener` interface. The components must have to implement the `RowSetListener` interface in order to register the listeners. You can register as many listeners as you wish to a `RowSet`. The following code snippet shows the process of registering the event in the `RegisterSetListener` interface:

```
RowSetListener listener = ...;
rset.addRowSetListener(listener);
```

All the `RowSet` objects generate three different types of events over a connection. These events are as follows:

- **Cursor movement events**—Indicates that the `RowSet`'s cursor has moved.
- **Row change events**—Indicates that a particular row has been inserted, updated, or deleted in a connection.
- **`RowSet` change events**—Indicates that the contents of the `RowSets` have already been changed.

When these events occur, the event handler methods are to be called. The event handler methods are used to handle events. They may also implement some methods on a particular event that performs no action.

Using RowSets at Runtime

At runtime, the `RowSet` objects need to specify different commands used in the `RowSets`. The user needs to specify the commands that are to be executed by the `RowSet` objects. For setting the values for the commands in a `RowSet` object and also to execute them in a connection, you need to perform the following tasks:

- Set `Rowset` object parameters
- Execute the `RowSet`
- Traverse the `RowSet`

Setting Parameter Values of a RowSet Object

The `RowSet` object provides a set of setter methods in order to set the values for the object. The command property specified in a `RowSet` object is an SQL command with the input parameter. The following snippet shows the setting of values for `RowSet` objects:

```
rset.setCommand("SELECT ENAME,Deptno FROM emp WHERE ENAME = ?");
rset.setString(1, "santosh");
```

The setCommand() method is used to set the SQL query that is to be executed by the RowSet object. The setString() method is used to specify the parameter values for the parameters in the RowSet object.

Executing the RowSet

A RowSet is to be executed after providing values for the parameters. The RowSets can be executed by using the execute() method provided by the RowSet interface. This method is used to connect to data source as well as retrieve the data from the data source. The execute() method throws an exception if the necessary properties for the RowSet are not set.

Traversing the RowSet

The RowSet interface extends the java.sql.ResultSet interface. A RowSet is just an enhancement to the ResultSet interface. The ResultSet components can be used as the RowSet components. The RowSet components are also called the ResultSet components that provide the functionality of the bean components. The following snippet shows how a RowSet in a connection traverses:

```
// iterate forward through the rowset rset.beforeFirst();
while (rset.next()) {
    System.out.println(rset.getString(1) + " " + rset.getFloat(2));
}
```

Since rowsets are the same as resultsets, the traversing of a RowSet also includes various cursor movement methods included in a ResultSet.

Exploring Connection Pooling

To connect an application to a data store, you need to perform some initializations in the data store environment. It is identified that performing initializations, establishing a connection and closing it is a time-consuming process. The time taken to open and close the connection to data store depends on various factors such as the network, load on the data store, and data store implementation. The connection to be established is data store-dependent; therefore, the time to be consumed while opening or closing a connection differs in different databases, such as Oracle, MySQL, and SQL Server.

Opening or closing a data store session increases load on the database, which affects the availability and performance of the application. In addition, opening and closing a session (connection) to data store is a resource-consuming process.

To solve all these problems, the pooling mechanism is used to establish connections before the client makes a request. In other words, the Connection objects created to represent the session established to the data store are pooled and recycled for further use. This mechanism is known as Connection Pooling, in which a connection is retrieved from the pool, used by an application, and then returned to the pool. The pool contains the objects of the physical connections. In connection pooling, the connection objects are reused instead of being created each time, when required. The important advantage of the connection pooling mechanism is that it increases the performance and availability of the resource. In connection pooling, the application makes a request to the connection pool manager for the connection. The pool manager picks one of the connections from the pool, creates a logical connection, and returns the logical connection to the application. The application then uses the logical connection to communicate with the data store through the physical connection. Once the application has completed using the connection, it closes the logical connection that releases its physical connection. Now, the physical connection is placed back into the pool so that it can be used by other clients. Note that only one logical connection can be established on one physical connection at a time. To connect to the connection pool manager for getting the connection, you need to a use a standard abstraction, javax.sql.DataSource, given under the JDBC 2.0 extension API.

The JDBC extension API provides support for connection pooling and for the data sources used by the applications. The javax.sql.DataSource interface includes some methods that help get connection from connection pool. Note that the data store is required to be implemented by the third party vendor. One of the implementations of this interface is oracle.jdbc.pool.OracleConnectionPoolDataSource, which is given by the Oracle corporation. Let's discuss about some classes and interfaces given under the javax.sql package for connection pooling. The javax.sql package provides the following interfaces that are to be used with the connection pool. These interfaces are described as follows:

- **javax.sql.ConnectionPoolDataSource**—Retrieves the connection objects represented by the javax.sql.PooledConnection interface. This indicates that the data source is a factory for the pooled connection objects. This interface provides some methods in order to deal with the pooled connection objects.

  Table 5.7 describes the methods provided by the javax.sql.ConnectionPoolDataSource interface:

Table 5.7: Methods of the javax.sql.ConnectionPoolDataSource Interface

Method	Description
getLoginTimeout()	Returns the maximum time to wait for getting a connection.
getLogWriter()	Retrieves the log writer for the connection pool data source.
getPooledConnection()	Creates a connection with the database.
getPooledConnection(String user, String password)	Creates a connection with the database. This connection can be used as a pooled connection.
setLoginTimeout(int seconds)	Sets the maximum time that the user has to wait to log in to the data source.
setLogWriter(PrintWriter out)	Sets the log writer for the connection pool data sources.

- **javax.sql.PooledConnection**—Holds the enabled connection pooling objects. It is used to hold the javax.sql.Connection objects. The methods provided by this interface return the objects of javax.sql.Connection objects.

  Table 5.8 describes the methods provided by the javax.sql.PooledConnection interface:

Table 5.8: Methods of the javax.sql.PooledConnection Interface

Method	Description
addConnectionEventListener (ConnectionEventListener listener)	Notifies the occurrence of an event on the PooledConnection object.
close()	Closes the physical connection represented by the PooledConnection object.
getConnection()	Establishes the connection as well as returns the connection object held by the physical connection.
removeConnectionEventListener(ConnectionEventListener listener)	Removes the event from the list of event listeners and also notifies the occurrence of any event on the PooledConnection object.

- **javax.sql.ConnectionEventListener**—Handles all the events that appear on the PooledConnection objects. This interface provides two methods in order to handle generated events.

  Table 5.9 describes the methods provided by the javax.sql.ConnectionEventListener interface:

Table 5.9: Methods of the javax.sql.ConnectionEventListener Interface

Method	Description
connectionClosed(ConnectionEvent event)	Notifies the connectionEventListener interface that the connection has already called the close() method on the PooledConnection object.
connectionErrorOccured(ConnectionEvent event)	Notifies the connectionEventListener interface that an error has occurred on the PooledConnection object.

The connection objects are stored for future use in the connection pool. After the connection is closed by calling the Connection.close() method, the connection objects are recycled and stored in the connection pool. The pooled connection manager must implement the ConnectionEventListener interface in order to notify the occurrence of any event on the connection pool object. The ConnectionEventListener provides the following two methods that notify the types of events occurring in the connection pool object:

- **connectionClosed**—Notifies that the logical connection on which the object is associated is closed. So all the applications call the `Connection.close()` method on the connection object.
- **connectionErrorOccured**—Notifies the occurrence of any error on the connection object. The error includes any server failure or loss of connection in a data source.

The driver in a connection is used to invoke the `connectionEventListener` method for the preceding methods. Both the methods take `ConnectionEvent` as a parameter, which is used to determine whether the connection is closed or an error has occurred on the connection object. After understanding the connection pooling concept, its importance, and the support from JDBC API to manage and access connection pool, let's learn how to implement connection pooling.

Working with Connection Pool

In this section, you create a simple program to show the time difference in accessing the JDBC connections with and without connection pool. First, create a program to find the time taken to create 16 database connections without using connection pool and then create 10001 connections (logical) with connection pool.

Listing 5.13 shows how to create the database connections with or without connection pool (you can find the ConnectionPoolTest.java file online in the code/Chapter5 folder):

Listing 5.13: Showing the code of the ConnectionPoolTest.java File

```
package com.santosh.jdbc;

import java.sql.*;
import org.apache.commons.dbcp.*;
/**
 * @author Santosh
 */
public class ConnectionPoolTest {
  public static void main(String[] args) throws Exception {

        Class.forName("oracle.jdbc.driver.OracleDriver");
        long beforeTime=System.currentTimeMillis();
        for (int i=0;i<=15;i++) {
               Connection con= DriverManager.getConnection(
                      "jdbc:oracle:thin:@mysys:1521:sandb",
                      "scott", "tiger");
               con.close();
        }
        long afterTime=System.currentTimeMillis();

        System.out.println("Time taken to create 16 database connections;\n
        without using connection pool: "+ (afterTime-beforeTime)+" milli seconds\n\n");
        //Now get connections using connection pool
        BasicDataSource dataSource=new BasicDataSource();
        dataSource.setUrl("jdbc:oracle:thin:@mysys:1521:XE");
        dataSource.setUsername("system");
        dataSource.setPassword("oracle");
        dataSource.setDriverClassName("oracle.jdbc.driver.OracleDriver");

        beforeTime=System.currentTimeMillis();
        for (int i=0;i<=10000;i++) {
               Connection con= dataSource.getConnection();
               con.close();
        }
        afterTime=System.currentTimeMillis();
        System.out.println("Time taken to create 10001 database connections;\n with using
        connection pool: "+ (afterTime-beforeTime)+" milli seconds");
  }
}
```

In Listing 5.13, the OracleDriver (a Type-4) driver is used to access the Oracle database on the local machine and `BasicDataSource` is used as a connection pool implementation. The DBCP connection pool is one of the efficient open source implementations to create a connection pool. In Listing 5.13, we first provide the code to calculate the time consumed in opening and closing 16 JDBC connections. Then, we initialize the apache DBCP connection pool implementation and use `BasicDataSource` to open as well as close 10000 connections. This helps calculate the time consumed in opening and closing a connection in the connection pool. Figure 5.12 shows the output of Listing 5.13:

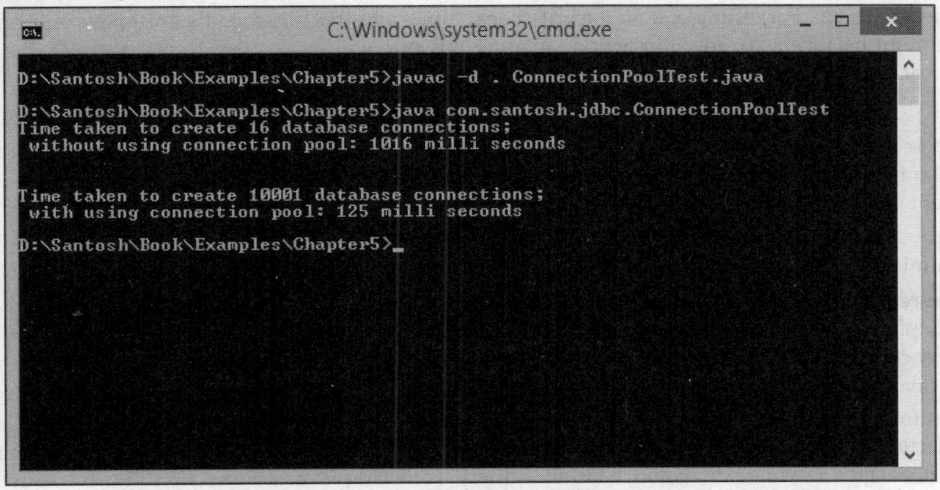

Figure 5.12: Showing the Output of the ConnectionPoolTest.java File

Figure 5.12 shows the output of the ConnectionPoolTest.java file, which clearly describes the difference in the time consumed for accessing database connections without and with connection pool. It shows that 547 milliseconds are consumed for creating 16 database connections without connection pool, whereas it takes only 109 milliseconds to access 10001 connections (logical) with connection pool.

Working with Transactions

Transaction is a set of statements executed on a resource or resources applying ACID (Atomicity, Consistency, Isolation, and Durability) properties. In multiple environments, various users work on databases, and there may be chances of data loss. Therefore, to avoid data loss, DBMS is used to maintain data integrity within databases. Transactions are used to provide the data integrity over multiple users. The database transaction includes the interaction between the databases and users. Transactions are required to provide data integrity, correct application semantics, and a consistent view of data during concurrent access. In general, DBMS provides the feature of atomicity, consistency, isolation, and durability for each transaction in a database. These properties are collectively called ACID properties. Let's now discuss about these properties.

Describing ACID Properties

The ACID properties describe the functionalities that provide support to execute a set of statements, known as a transaction. The ACID properties are maintained by the database management system (transaction manager) in order to maintain the integrity of the data over the database. Let's describe the ACID properties for the transaction mechanism.

Atomicity

Atomicity describes the ability of a transaction to hold the decision of saving the statement (executed in a TX) until the end of the set of statements, i.e., transaction. This property enables you to look at the set of statements executed in the form of a transaction as a single unit. The property provides an ability to save (Commit) or cancel (Rollback) the transaction at any point (which is the end of the transaction) and controls all the statements of the transaction.

Consistency

Consistency guarantees that the data remains in a legal state when the transaction begins and ends. This implies that if the data used in the transaction is consistent before starting the transaction, it will be consistent even after the end of the transaction. If the data satisfies the integrity constraints of that type, it is known as consistent data or data in legal state. For example, if an integrity constraint states that all accounts must have a positive balance, i.e., minimum balance as 0, any transaction violating this rule will be aborted. In other words, the transaction will roll back.

Isolation

Isolation is the ability of a transaction to isolate or hide the data from other transactions until it ends. This is done by preparing locks on the data. The following set of problems may occur when the user performs concurrent operation on the data. These problems are as follows:

- **Dirty Read**—Occurs when a transaction reads data from a row that has been modified but not yet committed by another transaction.
- **Non-repeatable Read**—Occurs when read lock is not acquired while performing the SELECT operation. For example, if we have selected data under transaction T1, and meanwhile, if the same is updated by some other transaction, say T2, the transaction T1 reads 2 versions of data. This type of data read is considered non-repeatable read. It can be avoided by preparing a read lock by transaction T1 on the data that is selected.
- **Phantom Read**—Occurs when, in the course of a transaction, two identical queries are executed and the collection of rows returned by the second query is different from the first. This can occur when range locks are not acquired while performing a SELECT query. For example, in a transaction T1, we executed query Q1 and got some results (say 10 rows), and within the same transaction, if we execute the query Q1 and if it results with a different number of rows (say 11 rows), this problem is referred to as phantom read problem. This happens if some other transaction inserts a new record that satisfies query Q1.

Durability

Durability guarantees that once the user has been notified of the successful transaction, i.e., if a transaction is committed, it will persist all the statements or leave the complete transaction unsaved. It implies that if a transaction succeeds, the system guarantees that its updates will persist even if the computer crashes immediately after the commit. Specialized logging allows the system's restart procedure to complete unfinished operations, making the transaction durable.

Types of Transactions

The database transaction is used to provide data integrity and security to the database. All the JDBC-specific drivers are required to provide transaction support for all database operations. The database operations may include the concurrent access of data from a data source. These transaction mechanisms are used to provide a secure way of accessing data over multiple environments. The transaction mechanism is categorized into three different types. These transactions are described as follows:

- **Local transaction**—Refers to a transaction whose statements are executed on a single transactional resource through one resource object, i.e., through one session. This type of transaction is only based upon the local networks connected to the data source object. The local transactions are easier to use in a local network. These transactions are not supported for the transactions in multiple networks on a distributed system.
- **Distributed transaction**—Refers to a transaction whose statements are executed on one or more transactional resources through multiple resource objects. In the case of distributed transaction, the transaction manager is responsible for all the database-specific operations. It must support all the ACID properties of the transaction mechanism. The distributed transaction must be synchronized and also be available at different locations.
- **Nested transaction**—Refers to a transaction that occurs within the reference of another transaction in its database. It must also satisfy the ACID properties. The changes made by the nested transaction are not visible to the existing transaction or to the host transaction. The changes occurred in the transaction will be notified to the host transaction after they have been committed. This satisfies the isolation property of the transaction mechanism.

Performing Transaction Management

Transaction management in a database operation is necessary to maintain the integrity and security of data from an unauthorized access. The Resource Manager in a transaction management system can manage local transactions because all the statements in it are associated with a single session. To manage distributed transactions, we need a Transaction Manager, which uses the transactional resource objects used in the transaction. The JDBC API provides support for transactions. It includes support for transaction semantics associated with single connection (local transaction) and for participating in transactions involving multiple resource objects (distributed transaction). JDBC API allows you to use connection (which is a resource object in this case) to perform the following operations:

- **Setting the auto commit attribute**—Allows you to specify when to end the transaction. Starting a new transaction is a decision made implicitly by either the JDBC driver or the underlying data source. JDBC API does not have any method to start the transaction explicitly. If no transaction is associated with a connection, you can start a new transaction by executing an SQL statement. The auto commit attribute of connection can be set by using the `setAutoCommit` (boolean) method of the connection object. When you invoke the `setAutoCommit(boolean)` method with an argument true, auto commit is enabled. However, if the false parameter is passed, auto commit is disabled. Moreover, the JDBC driver provider decides the default argument for the auto commit, but in general, it is true. If auto commit is enabled, JDBC driver commits the transaction after each individual SQL statement as soon as it is complete. The point at which a statement is considered complete depends on the type of SQL statement as well as what the application does after executing it. For DML (`Insert`, `Update`, `Delete`) and DDL statements, the statement is complete as soon as it has finished executing. For Select statements, the statement is complete when the associated `ResultSet` is closed. For `CallableStatement` objects, the statement is complete when all of the associated `Resultsets` are closed. The following code snippet is used to set the auto commit mode before creating a new transaction:

```
// Assume con is a Connection object
con.setAutoCommit(false);
```

  If auto commit is disabled, the transaction must explicitly end using the commit or rollback method. The invoking `commit()` method successfully ends the transaction, that is, all the statements in the transaction are successfully saved, whereas invoking the `rollback()` method makes the transaction unsuccessful, implying that none of the statements in the transaction is saved. If you want to group multiple statements in a single transaction, you need to disable the auto commit option. Then, you also need to decide whether or not statements should be saved at the end of the transaction.

- **Setting the isolation levels**—Refers to the transaction isolation levels that need to be set in order to notify the visible data within a transaction. The following are the four isolation levels used in the transaction management:
  - **READ UNCOMMITED**—Refers to a level where dirty reads, non-repeatable reads, and phantom reads can occur.
  - **READ COMMITED**—Refers to a level where dirty reads are not allowed to occur; however, non-repeatable reads and phantom reads can occur.
  - **REPEATABLE READ**—Refers to a level where only phantom reads can occur. Dirty reads and non-repeatable reads are not allowed to occur at this level.
  - **SERIALIZABLE**—Refers to a level where all transactions occur in a completely isolated fashion. At this isolation level, dirty reads, non-repeatable reads, and phantom reads cannot occur.

  The isolation level in a transaction can be specified by using the connection object supplied by the connection. The default isolation level is always specified by the underlying data source. Sometimes, the user needs to specify the isolation level explicitly. The JDBC API provides the `setTransactionIsolation(int)`method in order to set the transaction isolation for a transaction. Similarly, the `getTransactionIsolaion()` method is used by the user in order to retrieve the transaction isolation associated with a connection. If a driver used in a connection does not support the isolation level, the method throws the `SQLException` exception.

- **Savepoint**—Allows you to set points within a transaction. The save point specifies a mark-up to which the user can roll back without affecting the changes. The `DatabaseMetaData` interface available in the JDBC API provides the methods to support the save point within a transaction. You can set or roll back a transaction at a Savepoint as follows:
  - **Setting and rolling back to a Savepoint**—Implies that the Savepoint is to be set by the user explicitly in order to roll back the transaction. The JDBC API provides the `setSavepoint(String)` method of the Connection interface in order to set a Savepoint in a transaction. The transaction can be rolled backed up to the Savepoint by using the `rollback(SavePoint)` method of the Connection interface in the JDBC API. The following code snippet shows the setting of a Savepoint as well as the rollback mechanism in a database:

```
Statement s = conn.createStatement();
int rows = s.executeUpdate("INSERT INTO TABLE1 (COLUMN1) VALUES " + "('FIRST')");
// set Savepoint
Savepoint sp = conn.setSavepoint("SAVEPOINT_1");
rows = s.executeUpdate("INSERT INTO TABLE1 (COLUMN1) " +
"VALUES ('SECOND')");
...
conn.rollback(sp);
...
conn.commit();
```

    The preceding code snippet shows how to insert a record into a table within a database and set a `Savepoint sp` in the database. Therefore, data is successfully updated in the database. However, in the case of the second insertion operation, the transaction is rolled back to the Savepoints. So, this transaction is cancelled, and the changes made to the database are undone due to the calling of the rollback.
  - **Releasing a Savepoint**—Implies that the Savepoints created during a transaction need to be released after the completion of the database transaction. The `releaseSavepoint()` method of the Connection interface can be called in order to release the Savepoints.

The role of the `Connection.releaseSavepoint()` method is to take a Savepoint object as a parameter and then remove it from the current transaction. If you try to reference a Savepoint in a rollback operation, the `SQLException` exception is thrown, after the Savepoint has been released.

To understand the concept better, let's create an application called TransferAmount.java, which is used for performing transaction management. The code for the TransferAmount.java is shown in Listing 5.14 (you can find this file online in the code/Chapter5 folder):

Listing 5.14: Showing the code of the TransferAmount.java File

```
package com.santosh.jdbc;
import java.sql.*;
import java.util.*;
import java.io.*;
/**
 * @author Santosh
 */
public class TransferAmount {
  public static void main(String s[]) throws Exception {
        Driver d= (Driver) ( Class.forName(
        "oracle.jdbc.driver.OracleDriver").newInstance());
        Properties p=new Properties ();
        p.put("user","scott");
        p.put("password","tiger");
        Connection con=d.connect("jdbc:oracle:thin:@mysys:1521:sandb",p);
        con.setAutoCommit(false);
        String srcaccno=s[0];
        String destaccno=s[1];
        PreparedStatement ps= con.prepareStatement(
        "update bank set bal=bal+? where accno=?");
        ps.setDouble(1,500);
        ps.setString(2,destaccno);
```

```
            int i=ps.executeUpdate();
            ps.setDouble(1,-500);
            ps.setString(2,srcaccno);
            int j=ps.executeUpdate();
            if (i==1&&j==1){
                  con.commit();
                  System.out.println("Amount transfered");
                  con.close();
                  return;
            }
            con.rollback();
            System.out.println("Cannot transfer the amount");
            con.close();
      }//main
}//class
```

The application shown in Listing 5.14 is used to transfer some amount from one account to another in a transaction. The following code snippet shows the table that needs to be created before executing Listing 5.14:

```
Create table bank (accno number, bal number (10, 2));
Insert into bank values (101, 10000);
Insert into bank values (102, 10000);
```

As shown in the preceding code snippet, the bank table is to be created in the SQL editor in order to execute the TransferAmount.java application. The data of this table is used by the application in order to transfer the account, and the output of this table in the SQL editor can be represented as shown in Figure 5.13:

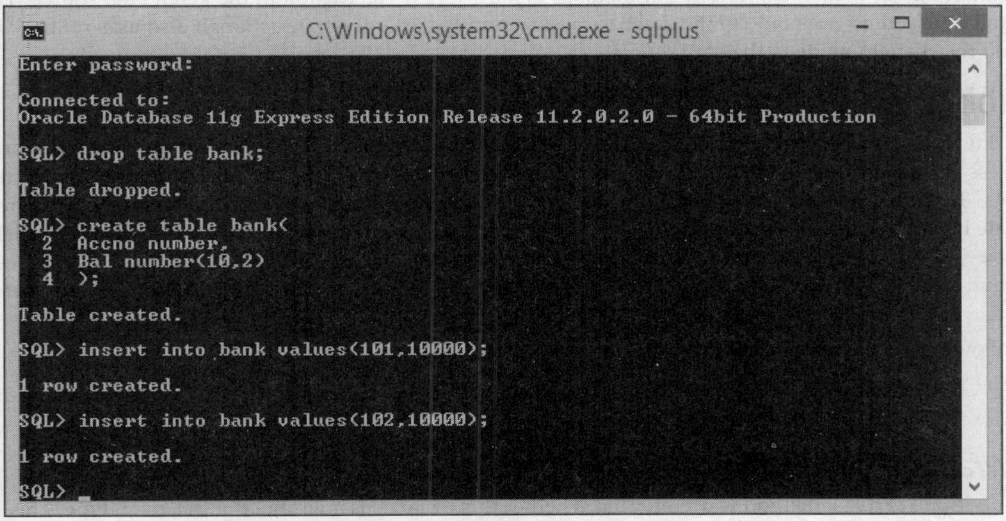

Figure 5.13: Creating a Table

Figure 5.13 shows the creation of the required table (Bank) for the application shown in Listing 5.14. The application uses the contents of the table and performs the transaction. It uses the common SQL queries in order to update the database and also shows the transaction management by using the Savepoints and rollbacks. Figure 5.14 shows the output of the TransferAmount.java file:

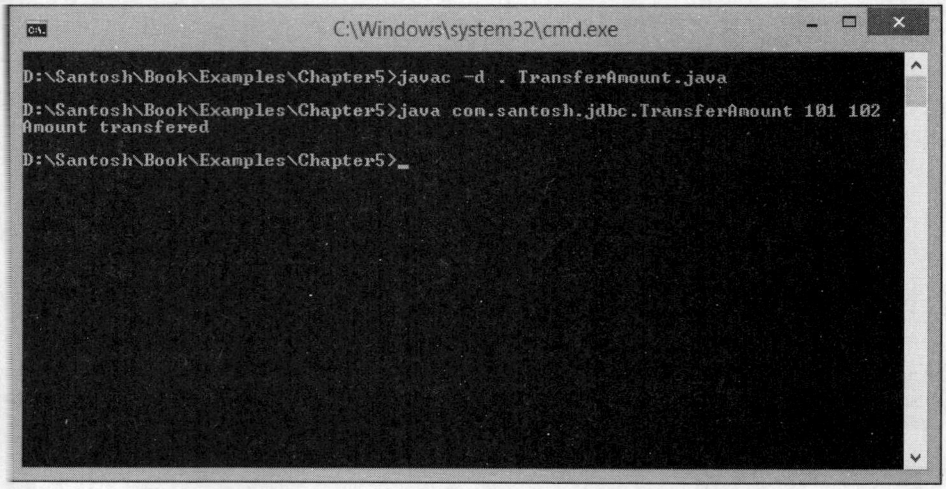

Figure 5.14: Showing the Output of the TransferAmount.java File

Figure 5.14 shows the output of the application, shown in Listing 5.14, by using transaction properties. The application initially sets the auto commit mode as it starts a new transaction in the given data source. Then, the required transactions are made to the database and committed after the transaction. It also uses rollback in order to undo the changes made to the data source.

Describing the Wrapper Interface

JDBC 4.0 introduces the `java.sql.Wrapper` interface that provides a mechanism for applications using JDBC to access an instance of a resource, such as Connection, Statement, etc., that are wrapped for architectural reasons. This interface provides the ability to access data source vendor specific resources by retrieving the delegate instance using the corresponding wrapped proxy instance. The main interface of JDBC API is defined as subtype of `java.sql.Wrapper`. Interfaces included in JDBC API are `java.sql.Connection`, `java.sql.DataSource`, `java.sql.Statement`, `java.sql.ResultSet`, `java.sql.DatabaseMetaData`, `java.sql.ResultSetMetaData`, and `java.sql.ParameterMetaData`.

The following are the methods of the `java.sql.Wrapper` interface:

- The `isWrapperFor()` method
- The `java.lang.Object unwrap()` method

The isWrapperFor() Method

The `isWrapperFor()` method is used to find whether this instance is a wrapper of the given type. This method returns 'true' if this instance class implements the given interface, or it is directly or indirectly a wrapper for this instance. The following snippet shows the sample code, showing the use of the `isWrapperFor()` method:

```
    Connection con=
DriverManager.getConection("jdbc:oracle:thin:@mysys:1521:sandb","scott","tiger");
    Statement st=con.createStatement();
    boolean flag=st.isWrapperFor(oracle.jdbc.driver.OracleStatement.class);
    //Here the flag value is true since the Statement type of object reference 'st' is
       referring an object of OracleStatement
```

The unwrap() Method

The `unwrap()` method is used to get the object that implements the given interface to allow access to vendor-specific methods. The following snippet shows the sample code, showing the use of the `unwrap()` method:

```
    Connection con= DriverManager.getConection(
       "jdbc:oracle:thin:@mysys:1521:sandb","scott","tiger");
    Statement st=con.createStatement();
    Class o_class=oracle.jdbc.driver.OracleStatement.class;
```

```
if (st.isWrapperFor(o_class)){
   OracleStatement os=(OracleStatement)st.unwrap(o_class);
   //use 'os' to access the OracleStatement specific methods
}
```

Describing SQLException

The exceptions defined and used with JDBC API are limited and inconvenient to handle because `java.sql.SQLException` is the only exception thrown for all types of errors while using JDBC API. There is no classification of exceptions, and also no hierarchy is defined for them. The only way to find error is through `SQLState` value, which can be obtained using the `getSQLState()` method of `SQLException`. However, the most `SQLState` values are vendor specific, i.e., they change from one database to another, making the task of finding errors and handling exceptions difficult.

The JDBC 4.0 specification provides a solution for this problem by introducing the new `SQLException` subclasses, each of which describes a specific error allowing the JDBC programmers to write portable exception-handling code. The `SQLException` subclasses are classified into transient, non-transient, and recoverable exception types. Figure 5.15 shows the `SQLException` hierarchy:

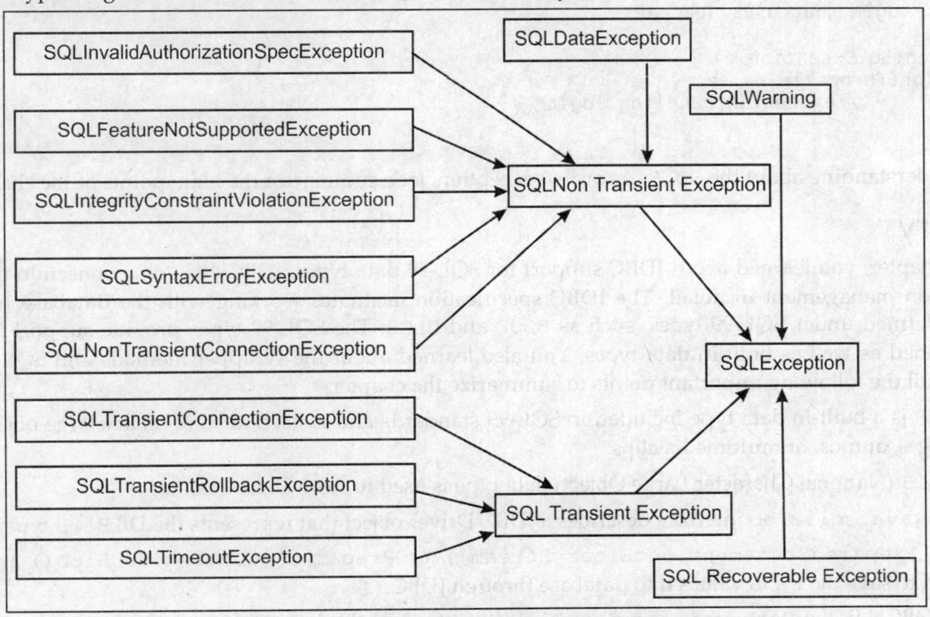

Figure 5.15: Showing the SQLException Hierarchy

The `SQLTransientException` is thrown to let the user know that a previously failed operation may succeed, if retried. The `SQLNonTransientException` is thrown where retrial will not lead to a successful operation unless the cause of the `SQLException` is corrected.

The `SQLException` is a chained exception. It is possible that during the execution of the SQL statement, one or more exceptions could occur, so all the exceptions are added to a single `SQLException` object and thrown to the application. Hence, the `SQLException` cached by the application may possibly include additional `SQLExceptions`. To access these chained `SQLExceptions`, the application can use the `getNextException()` method in a loop until it returns null. The following snippet shows the sample code showing the use of the `getNextException()` method:

```
try{
   //logic that uses JDBC API
}

catch (SQLException e){
```

```
    while (e != null){

          String s=e.getSQLState();
          Throwable t=e.getCause();
          while (t!=null) {
                //exception handling logic
                t=t.getCause();

          }
          e= e.getNextException();

    }
```

SQLException in JDBC 4.0 includes new constructors to add extra parameters to find possible causes for the exception. The getCause() method is additionally included in SQLException to determine the exception's possible cause. In addition, the SQLException class now implements the Iterable interface and supports the Java SE 5.0 and the above version, and it enhanced for loop for easier iteration of chained exceptions.

The following code snippet shows the sample code:

```
try{
   //logic that uses JDBC API
}
catch(SQLException e) {
   for(Throwable t : e) {
         //exception handling logic
   }
}
```

After understanding about the SQLException exception, let's summarize the main points of the chapter.

Summary

In this chapter, you learned about JDBC support for SQL-99 data types, JDBC RowSet, connection pooling, and transaction management in detail. The JDBC specification facilitates working with the database having large objects defined under SQL-99 types, such as BLOB and CLOB. The SQL-99 types provide support for both the user-defined as well as built-in data types. You also learned about the Wrapper methods and SQL exceptions. Let's recall the following important points to summarize the chapter:

- BLOB is a built-in data type included in SQL-99 standards and is used to store binary large objects, such as images, audios, or multimedia clips.
- NCLOB (National Character Large Object) data type is used to store Unicode data.
- The java.sql.Blob interface describes a JDBC Driver object that represents the DB BLOB type.
- The PreparedStatement.setBinaryStream() or PreparedStatement.setBlob() methods are used to save the BLOB values into database through JDBC.
- In JDBC 4.0, the Connection.createBlob() factory method was introduced to create an empty BLOB object vendor independently.
- CLOB is a built-in data type of the SQL-99 standards and is used to store large amount of text data.
- The BLOB and CLOB objects can persist even after the transaction, in which they are created, is complete. This results in the shortage of resources for the application using these objects. To overcome this problem, JDBC 4.0 provides the free() method of the java.sql.Blob and java.sql.Clob interfaces, which you can use to release the BLOB and CLOB objects when they are not required by the application.
- The java.sql.SQLData interface of JDBC API is designed to describe the Java custom object type to the JDBC Driver.
- Apart from creating the Java custom object type to access the database object or structured type, the JDBC 2.0 API includes the java.sql.Struct interface to describe a JDBC Driver object that represents the SQL structured type.

- The Array is an SQL-99 data type that offers you the facility to include an ordered list of values within a column. The java.sql.Array interface of JDBC API provides an abstraction to understand the JDBC Driver object that represents a database array type.
- The Array objects remain valid for at least the duration of the transaction in which they are created. This results in the shortage of resources in case of lengthy transactions. In JDBC 4.0, the Array.free() method is introduced to release the array resources.
- A ROWID is a unique identification for each row in a table. It is a virtual column that contains the address of the corresponding row. ROWID is useful in identifying the instances of duplicate records and identical rows in a database.
- The values of ROWID are very useful as they can be accessed at a faster rate and are unique identifier for rows in a table.
- The batch update option allows you to submit multiple DML operations to a data source for simultaneous processing. The JDBC Statement object can manage only one batch at a time. Moreover, a batch cannot be spanned over multiple Statement objects.
- The Statement object supports to prepare a batch with different SQL statements. On the other hand, the PreparedStatement object allows having only one SQL statement into a batch, which can be executed with multiple sets of values.
- JDBC 4.0 defines SQLXML as the Java data type that maps the database SQL XML type. The SQLXML object supports processing the XML data as a string or as a StAX (Streaming API for XML) stream.
- The JDBC 3.0 provides support for accessing auto-generated keys. You can inform the JDBC statement (Statement or PreparedStatement) object about the auto-generated keys in the given insert operation. This helps the Statement object to collect the values of auto-generated keys after executing the SQL insert statement.
- The JDBC API has the concept of RowSet in order to work with bean components. A RowSet is an interface provided by the JDBC API. A RowSet object is capable of handling JavaBean components. So a RowSet can be used to configure bean properties and generate events.
- Opening or closing a data store session increases load on q database and is a resource-consuming process. Due to increased load on the database, the availability as well as performance of the application is affected. To solve these problems, you should establish the connections before the client makes a request and make it available when the application requires accessing the data store. You can use pooling mechanism to establish the connection. In other words, the Connection objects that represent the session established to the data store are pooled and recycled for further use.
- The javax.sql.PooledConnection interface describes the connection that is managed by the pool. Each PooledConnection object wraps one DB connection. The PooledConnection interface can have logical connection (described using the java.sql.Connection interface) to access its services. A PooledConnection can have only one logical connection at a time. If you try to create a second logical connection on a PooledConnection, its first logical connection is implicitly closed.
- The implementation of ConnectionPool reduces the time consumed in processing the requests made to the database.
- Transaction is a set of statements executed on a resource or resources by applying ACID properties. The ACID properties describe the functionalities for executing or managing a set of statements referred to as transaction.

In the next chapter, we will describe the Java Servlet.

Exercise

Q. 5.1 What do the BLOB type of objects store?

Q. 5.2 Name the method added to the Connection interface for creating a BLOB object.

Q. 5.3 What do the CLOB type of objects store?

Q. 5.4 Write the syntax for creating an array type in a database.

Q. 5.5 What is the necessity of batch update?

Q. 5.6 Why do we use transactions?

Q. 5.7 What does atomicity mean in ACID transaction properties?

Q. 5.8 What are Savepoints?

Q. 5.9 Which method of the Connection interface is used to set the auto commit attribute of the current connection?

Q. 5.10 Define the term 'isolation'.

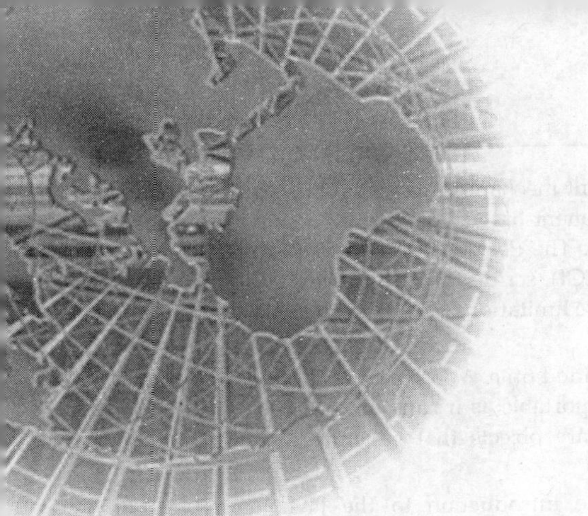

6

Understanding Java Servlet

Java Servlet technology provides a simple, vendor independent mechanism for extending the functionality of a Web server. This technology provides high level, component-based, platform-independent, and server-independent standards to develop Web applications in Java. The Servlet technology is similar to other Web server extensions, such as Common Gateway Interface (CGI) scripts and Hypertext Preprocessor (PHP). However, Java Servlets are more acceptable since they solve the limitations of CGI, such as low performance and low degree scalability.

A Java Servlet is a simple Java class, which is dynamically loaded on a Web server and therefore, enhances the functionality of the Web server. A Java Servlet is secure and portable as it runs on the Web server and cannot operate outside its domain. In other words, Java Servlets are objects that generate dynamic content after processing the requests originating from a Web browser.

This chapter introduces CGI script and proceeds with the introduction to the Java Servlet technology, requirement of Java Servlets, features of the Servlet 3.1, Application Programming Interface (API), and various types of containers used to manage and execute Servlet applications. Further, you create simple applications by using the Servlet API. Finally, you explore the request processing workflow and learn about the `GenericServlet` class.

Understanding the Need for Server-Side Extensions

The advantages of dynamic Web pages have imposed the design of server-side extensions. These server-side extensions are technologies to create dynamic Web pages. Web pages need a container or Web server to host dynamic Web pages. To meet this requirement, independent Web server providers offer some proprietary solutions in the form of APIs. These APIs allow us to build programs that can run with a Web server. However, this solution results in the following problems:

- The application using server-side extension becomes vendor dependent
- Migrating the application from one server to another is difficult
- While developing the application, we have to decide the server on which the application has to be deployed

We need some Web technologies that help to develop both vendor and server-independent Web applications to solve the preceding problems. One of these technologies is CGI. The following section explains CGI and its importance.

NOTE

It is recommended to read Chapter 1, Getting Started with Web Applications in Java, which introduces the Web architecture before reading this chapter.

After learning about the need for server-side extensions, let's learn about CGI.

Introducing CGI

CGI is an open standard abstraction between HyperText Transfer Protocol (HTTP) adapter (Web server) and an external application, which is written by using any of the programming languages, such as C or C++. This external application is known as a CGI application and is responsible for processing client requests and generating dynamic content. Some of the benefits of CGI are as follows:

- **Simplicity**—Provides easy understanding and simple implementation.
- **Open Standards**—Allows us to run our CGI application on different Web servers.
- **Architecture Independent**—Allows you to deploy CGI applications on any Web server without being concerned about the implementation of CGI applications on specific Web servers.
- **Language Independent**—Allows to write programs in any language.
- **Process Isolation**—Allows programs to run in a process outside the Web server process. As a result, if there is any bug in the application, it will not crash the Web server process.

In a CGI application, when a client makes a request to access dynamic Web pages, the Web server performs the following operations:

- Locates the requested Web page (CGI application) using the request Uniform Resource Locator (URL).

- Creates a new process to service the client's request.
- Invokes the CGI application within that process and passes the request information to the server, such as HTTP headers, and the data that the client has sent as input.
- Collects the response from the CGI application along with appropriate headers.
- Destroys the process, prepares the HTTP response message, and sends it to the client.

Operations performed by a Web server are shown in Figure 6.1:

Figure 6.1: Processing a Client Request

We have learned that in CGI-based applications, the server has to create and destroy the process for every request. This approach works well with a few clients, but as the number of client increases, the workload on the server and the time taken to process the requests increases.

Therefore, certain problems with CGI are as follows:

- CGI applications exhibit low performance. This is because every time a request is received, CGI has to create a new process.
- Multiple client requests lead to a heavy workload on the server. Therefore, the server has to create and destroy multiple requests, which lead to poor efficiency.
- Stateless nature, which means that a CGI application cannot maintain and store the state of data between multiple requests.

In response to the preceding problems of CGI, many vendors have developed their own APIs for the server-side, such as NSAPI from Netscape and Internet Server Application Program Interface (ISAPI) from Microsoft Corporation. Applications written using these APIs are faster than CGI applications and almost solve the preceding problems. However, these APIs have the following problems:

- Language dependency
- No process isolation
- Vendor dependency
- Tied to the server specific architecture

FastCGI has been introduced to solve these problems. It is an extension for CGI, and is more scalable, language independent, and acts as an open extension for CGI to enhance the performance of CGI applications, irrespective of the server specific APIs. Instead of creating a new process for each request, FastCGI uses a single process, to process multiple client requests. Moreover, in FastCGI, Web servers can maintain and reuse a pool of processes to service multiple requests one after the other.

However, FastCGI also entails certain problems, some of which are as follows:

- It is process based
- It cannot be used to process large number of clients
- It is difficult to maintain the client state
- It provides a low level approach for both reading the request data and submitting the response content

The features of the Java programming language, such as robustness, security, portability, easy to use, reusability, and crash protection facilities motivate using Java to develop server-side Web applications. You can use CGI or FastCGI standards to create Web applications by using the Java language. However, while using CGI or FastCGI, you may experience few problems, such as heavy-weight as it is process based and it is difficult to maintain client state. The Java Servlet is introduced by Sun - Java Community Process (JCP) to solve these problems by providing a common, vendor independent, and simple abstraction to develop Web server extensions in Java. Let's now explore Java Servlets in detail.

Introducing Java Servlet

Java Servlet is one of the component APIs of Java Platform Enterprise Edition. It sets standards for creating dynamic Web applications in Java. Java Servlet application can run on any Web server integrated with a Servlet container. Java Servlet is usually designed to process HTTP requests, such as GET and POST. Figure 6.2 shows how a Servlet works at higher level:

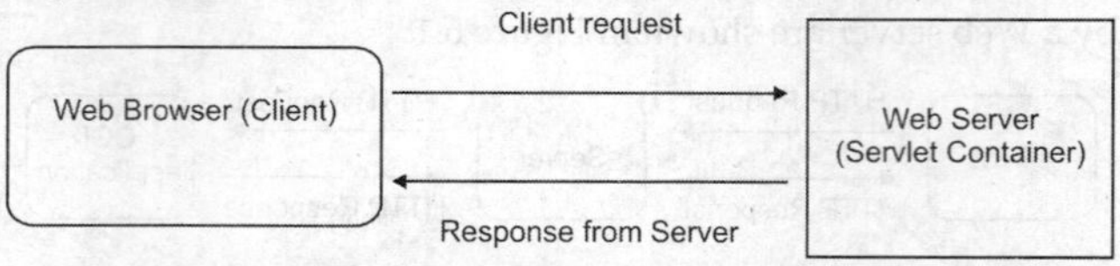

Figure 6.2: Working of a Servlet

Figure 6.2 shows how a Servlet processes user requests.

The process can be summarized as follows:

- A client sends a request to a Servlet container, which acts as the Web server, through a Web browser
- The Web server searches for the required Servlet and initiates it
- The Servlet then processes the client request and sends the response back to the server, which is then forwarded to the client

Advantages of a Servlet

The advantages of Servlets over other server-side extension abstractions, such as CGI, FastCGI, ISAPI, and NSAPI are as follows:

- Servlet is faster than CGI.
- Servlets are platform independent, as Servlets are written in Java. Servlet can run on any platform.
- Use a standard vendor independent API supported by many Web servers. The API designed for Java Servlet automatically acquires the advantages of a Java platform, such as platform independence and portability. In addition, it is easy to use the wide range of APIs created on Java platform, such as JDBC to access the database.
- Removes the overhead of creating a new process for each request, as Servlet does not run in a separate process. There is only a single instance, which handles all requests concurrently. This saves the memory and allows a Servlet to easily manage client state.
- Provides declarative security management support that allows us to build and modify the security logic for our server-side extensions easily.
- It is a server-side component, so Servlet inherits the security provided by the Web server. Servlets are also benefited with Java Security Manager.

You do not need to execute shell commands with user data, since Java Servlet can use the JavaMail API for reading and sending mails, JDBC APIs for accessing resources, and RMI and EJB APIs for accessing legacy systems. There is a separate API available in Java EE platform, which improves security. Security is also improved using Core Java exceptional handling mechanism.

Let's now move on to the new features added in Servlet 3.1.

New Features of Servlet 3.1

Servlet 3.1 is the latest version of Servlet API. It was released on May 2013 and it runs on the platform Java EE 7. Two important changes were introduced in Servlet 3.1.

They are Non-Blocking I/O mechanism and HTTP protocol upgrade mechanism.

- **Non-Blocking I/O Mechanism**—In Servlet 3.0, it was possible to do asynchronous request processing but Servlet 3.0 only allowed the traditional I/O. In Servlet 3.0 scalability of the application was not possible. This means that if a program is designed for a small set of records, it cannot work well on large set of records. But in Servlet 3.1, non building I/O was introduced and it allowed building scalable application.

In Servlet 3.0, the server thread used to wait for the data when the incoming data is blocked or streamed slower than the server can read. The same problem used to occur when the data is written to `ServletOutputStream`. But this problem was resolved in Servlet 3.1. Servlet 3.1 has added event listeners. There are two event listeners interfaces in Servlet 3.1 - `ReadListener` interface and `WriteListener` interface. These two interfaces are registered using `ServletInputStream.setReadListener()` and `ServletOutputStream.setWriteListener()` methods.

`ReadListener` and `WriteListener` also have `callback()` method. Whenever there are contents to be read or to be written without blocking, the `callback()` methods are invoked.

- **HTTP Protocol Upgrade Mechanism**—In Servlet 3.1, HTTP protocol was upgraded and HTTP 1.1 was introduced. An example of this protocol upgrade is Web Socket. `javax.servlet.http.HttpUpgradeHandler` was introduced in Servlet 3.1 in order to allow the protocol upgrade processing.

After reviewing the new features of the Servlet 3.1 specification, let's explore the Servlet container.

Exploring the Servlet Container

Servlet container, sometimes also known as Servlet engine, is an integrated set of objects that provide runtime environment for Java Servlet components. In other words, it is a system that manages Java Servlet components on top of a Web server to handle the Web client request. The third party vendors known as container providers define the behavior of these objects.

The services provided by the Servlet container are as follows:

- **Network services**—Loads a Servlet class. The loading may be from a local file system, a remote file system, or other network services. The Servlet container provides the network services over which the request and response are sent.
- **Decode and encode MIME based messages**—Provides the service of decoding and encoding MIME-based messages. The Servlet container decodes MIME-based requests.
- **Manage Servlet life-cycle**—Manages the lifecycle of a Servlet.
- **Resource management**—Manages the static and dynamic resource, such as HTML files, Servlets, JSP pages.
- **Security service**—Handles authorization and authentication of resource access.
- **Session management**—Maintains a session by appending a session ID to the URL path.

All the Servlet containers must support HTTP as the protocol for sending request and response; however, additional request/response based protocols, such as HTTPS (HTTP over SSL) may be supported based on the vendor. HTTP 1.1 is the new version of HTTP specification, but the minimum required version of the HTTP specification that a Servlet container must implement is HTTP/1.0. It is recommended that Servlet containers implement the HTTP/1.1 specification so that all features of HTTP are available.

Describing the Request Processing Mechanism

The following are the sequence of events in request processing, when a client, such as a Web browser makes a request to a Web server with the Servlet container:

- The Web server (or the HTTP adapter) receives a request and dispatches it to the Servlet container.
- The Servlet container determines which Servlet to invoke on the basis of the request URL. It calls the Servlet whose request URL pattern matches with the pattern provided in the web.xml configuration file. The navigation process implemented by the Servlet container locates the Web resource, which is described in detail later in this chapter.
- The Servlet uses the request object to determine the remote user and retrieves the parameters values sent as part of this request. The Servlet then generates the data to send response back to the client. It sends this data to the Web server through the response object.
- After the Servlet has finished processing the request, the Servlet container ensures that the response is properly flushed, and returns the control back to the host Web server.
- The Web server packs the response content into the response message and sends it back to the client.

Describing the Types of Servlet Container Configurations

A Servlet container implemented by third party vendor can be placed within a Web server or can be installed as an add-on component of the Web server by using the native extension API of that Web server. Moreover, the Servlet container can be configured with the Web server to manage Servlets in three different ways:

- As a standalone container
- As an in-process container
- As an out-process container

Let's describe these in detail.

The Standalone Container

In a standalone Servlet container configuration, the Servlet container is strongly coupled with the Web server functionality. That is, the Servlet container takes the responsibility of the Web server functionality. Figure 6.3 shows the standalone Servlet container configuration:

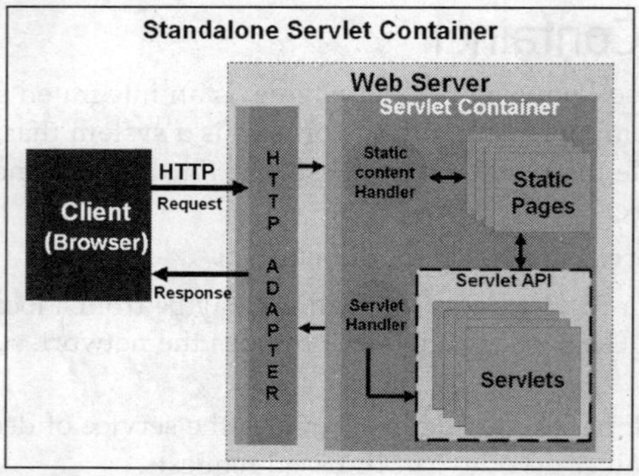

Figure 6.3: Showing the Standalone Servlet Container

You can see in Figure 6.3 that the HTTP adapter receives the request from the client and passes it to the Servlet container. The Servlet container sends the requested data to the HTTP adapter, which further passes the data to the client. In this way, the standalone container performs the working of both Servlet container and Web server.

The In-Process Container

In some cases, we might want to use some already in use Web servers to manage Servlets and service client requests. However, if these servers are not included with the Servlet container, we need to configure a Servlet container with the required Web server. In this situation, we can configure a Servlet container to run within the Web server process. This type of Servlet container configuration is known as an in-process container configuration, since the container runs within the Web server process.

Figure 6.4 shows the in-process container configuration:

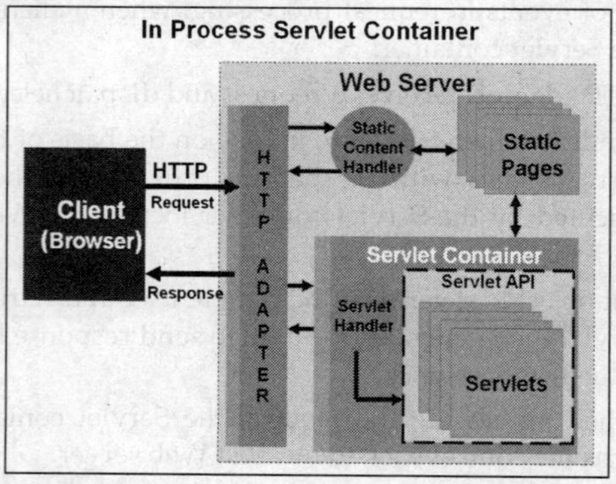

Figure 6.4: Showing the In-Process Container

In Figure 6.4, you can see a separate container included in the Web server. Both work in coordination to process a request and send the required output to the client. The HTTP adapter works as a bridge for receiving the request from and sending the response back to the user. For example, if you use Microsoft Internet Information Services (IIS) Web server for Web server functionalities and want the server-side extensions to be developed in the form of Servlets, you can configure the Tomcat Servlet container to run inside the IIS Web server. In this case, the Tomcat Servlet container runs inside the IIS Web server process and the IIS Web server passes the Servlet-specific requests to the Tomcat Servlet container by using Java Native Interface (JNI) calls.

NOTE

Running the Servlet container in the process of Web server is not always safe, since it causes stability and reliability problems.

Let's learn about the out-process containers.

The Out-Process Containers

The out-process containers are used in the following cases:

- Non-availability of the Servlet container that supports a specific Web server.
- Web server does not provide any support for integrating a Servlet container.
- Need to run both Servlet container and Servlets in a different process or on different systems.
- In all these cases, we need to configure the Servlet container to run outside the Web server process. In this case, the Web server uses the Interprocess Communication (IPC) mechanism, such as TCP/IP, to communicate with the Servlet container.

This configuration even allows us to distribute the load between different processes. For example, all static page requests can be processed by one process (Web server process) and dynamic page requests by another process (Servlet container process), as shown in Figure 6.5:

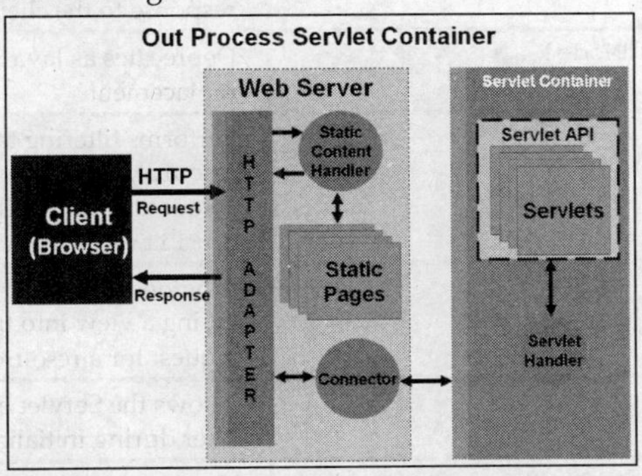

Figure 6.5: Displaying the Out-Process Container

Figure 6.5 shows a separate Web server and a separate Servlet container connected with the help of a connector (the HTTP protocol). The interaction between the Servlet container and the client request is similar to the in-process container configuration.

The next section describes the Servlet API.

Introducing the Servlet API

The Servlet API is a part of the Java Servlet specification designed by Sun - JCP. This API is supported by all Servlet containers, such as Tomcat and Weblogic. This API contains classes and interfaces that define a standard contract between the Servlet class and Servlet container (or Servlet engine). These classes and interfaces are packaged in the following two packages of the Servlet API:

- `javax.servlet`
- `javax.servlet.http`

Let's learn these two packages in detail.

Describing the javax.servlet Package

The javax.servlet package contains some interfaces and classes that allow the Servlet to access the basic services provided by the Servlet container.

The Servlet container provides the implementation of the classes and interfaces packaged under the javax.servlet package. Table 6.1 lists the classes and interfaces packaged under the javax.servlet package.

Table 6.1: Interfaces and Classes of the javax.servlet Package

Type	Name	Description
Interface	Servlet	Defines methods that a Servlet class must implement
Interface	RequestDispatcher	Defines an object that represents the Servlet container that implements delegation logic to send the request to another resource, such as Servlet or JSP file on the Web server
Interface	ServletConfig	Allows the Servlet container, to pass information to a Servlet, during initialization
Interface	ServletContext	Defines a set of methods that a Servlet uses to communicate with its Servlet container
Interface	ServletContextListener	Notifies the changes made to the Servlet context of the Web application
Interface	ServletRequest	Defines an object to provide the client request information to a Servlet
Interface	ServletResponse	Defines an object to assist a Servlet in sending a response to the client
Interface	SingleThreadModel	Deprecates as Java Servlet API 2.4, with no direct replacement
Interface	Filter	Performs filtering tasks on either the request to a resource, such as Servlet or on the response from the resource or both. Filter performs filtering in the doFilter() method
Interface	FilterChain	Provided by the Servlet container to the developer giving a view into the invocation chain of a filtered request for a resource
Interface	FilterConfig	Allows the Servlet container to pass information to a filter during initialization
Interface	ServletContextAttributeListener	Notifies the changes made to the attribute list on the Servlet context of a Web application
Interface	ServletRequestAttributeListener	Receives notification of changes in request attribute
Interface	ServletRequestListener	Receives notification of requests coming in and out of the scope in a Web component
Class	ServletContextEvent	Defines an event class for notifications about changes to the Servlet context of a Web application
Class	ServletInputStream	Provides an input stream for reading binary data from a client request, including readLine() method for reading data one line at a time
Class	ServletOutputStream	Provides an output stream for sending binary data to the client
Class	ServletRequestWrapper	Provides implementation of the ServletRequest interface to receive request from a Servlet
Class	ServletResponseWrapper	Provides implementation of the ServletResponse

Table 6.1: Interfaces and Classes of the javax.servlet Package		
Type	**Name**	**Description**
		interface to send response to a Servlet
Class	`GenericServlet`	Defines a generic, protocol-independent Servlet
Class	`ServletContextAttributeEvent`	Defines an event class for notifications about changes to the attributes of a Servlet context of a Web application
Class	`ServletRequestAttributeEvent`	Defines an event class for notifications of changes to the attributes of `ServletRequest` in a Web application
Class	`ServletRequestEvent`	Indicates lifecycle events for a `ServletRequest`
Class	`ServletException`	Defines a general exception that a Servlet can throw when it encounters difficulty
Class	`UnavailableException`	Defines an exception that a Servlet or filter throws to indicate that it is permanently or temporarily available

Now, let's discuss the classes and interfaces available in the `javax.servlet.http` package.

Describing the javax.servlet.http Package

The `javax.servlet.http` package supports the development of Servlets that use the HTTP protocol. The classes in this package extend the basic Servlet functionality to support HTTP specific features, including request and response headers, different request methods, and cookies. Table 6.2 lists the classes and interfaces defined in the `javax.servlet.http` package:

Table 6.2: Interfaces and Classes of the javax.servlet Package		
Type	**Name**	**Description**
Interface	`HttpServletRequest`	Extends the `ServletRequest` interface to provide request information for HTTP Servlets
Interface	`HttpServletResponse`	Extends the `ServletResponse` interface to provide HTTP –specific functionality while sending a response
Interface	`HttpSession`	Provides a way to identify users across more than one page request or visit to a Website and store the information about that user
Interface	`HttpSessionBindingListener`	Causes an object to be notified when it is bound to or unbound from a session
Class	`Cookie`	Creates a cookie, a small amount of information sent by a Servlet to a Web browser, saved by the browser, and later sent back to the server
Class	`HttpServlet`	Provides an abstract class to be sub classed to create an HTTP Servlet suitable for a Website
Class	`HttpSessionBindingEvent`	Implements `HttpSessionBindingListener` when the object is bound to or unbound from the session
Class	`HttpUtils`	Provides a collection of methods that are useful in writing HTTP Servlets

Let's learn about implementing a Servlet object.

Implementing a Servlet Object

The Servlet object is a Java object that is instantiated and managed by the Servlet container. However, the Java object needs to be implemented that is descriptive to the Servlet container. The following rules are specified by the Java Servlet specification for implementing the Servlet object:

- Should be a public non-abstract class

- Should be a subtype of the `javax.servlet.Servlet` interface, as the Servlet container understands the Servlet object by using this interface
- Should support a no-argument constructor, as Servlet container instantiates the Servlet object by using no-argument constructor only
- Recommended not to declare the methods of the `javax.servlet.Servlet` interface implemented by the Servlet object as final

As we understood the rules for implementing Servlet object, let's learn about the `javax.servlet.Servlet` and `javax.servlet.ServletConfig` interfaces, which are the basic and important elements of Java Servlet API to understand the Servlet life cycle.

The javax.servlet.Servlet Interface

The `javax.servlet.Servlet` interface is the basic interface of the Java Servlet API. This provides a standard abstraction for the Servlet container to understand the Servlet object created by the user. That means this interface is designed to describe the user defined Java object to the Servlet container, which encapsulates the application logic to plug into the Servlet container for processing the client request. The Servlet object must be a subtype of this interface to be managed by the Servlet container. The following are the five methods declared in this interface:

- `void init(ServletConfig)`
- `void service(ServletRequest, ServletResponse)`
- `void destroy()`
- `ServletConfig getServletConfig()`
- `String getServletInfo()`

NOTE

These methods are explained in detail in the later part of this chapter.

Let's learn about the `javax.servlet.ServletConfig` interface.

The javax.servlet.ServletConfig Interface

The `javax.servlet.ServletConfig` interface of Java Servlet API is designed to describe a container object that represents environment details of the Servlet object. This means that the `javax servlet.ServletConfig` interface provides a standard abstraction for the Servlet object to get the environment details from the Servlet container. The container implementing the `ServletConfig` object supports the following operations:

- Gets the initialization parameters configured in a Web application's configuration document; i.e., web.xml
- Gets the `ServletContext` object that describes the Web application's runtime environment
- Gets the Servlet name as configured in the Web application's configuration file; i.e., `web.xml`, for which the Servlet object is created

NOTE

The Servlet container creates a `ServletConfig` object for each Servlet configured to the `web.xml` file.

After having a brief understanding about the `javax.servlet.Servlet` and `javax.servlet.ServletConfig` objects, let's discuss the lifecycle of Servlet object.

Understanding the Servlet LifeCycle

A Servlet object is initialized and managed by the Servlet container. The Servlet container uses the `javax.servlet.Servlet` interface to understand the Servlet object and manage it. Therefore, before we start creating a Servlet object, let's understand the lifecycle of the Servlet object, which describes how the Servlet container manages the Servlet object. The lifecycle of a Servlet object involves creating an instance of the Servlet, associating the Servlet with initialization information, dispatching requests to the Servlet instance, and finally destroying the Servlet instance.

Describing the Stages of the Servlet LifeCycle

The Servlet lifecycle mainly goes through four stages. The fourth stage does not happen immediately after the third stage; instead the Servlet is destroyed after the completion of the request mechanism. These four stages are:

- Loading a Servlet
- Initializing the Servlet
- Request handling
- Destroying the Servlet

Figure 6.6 shows the process diagram of the Servlet lifecycle:

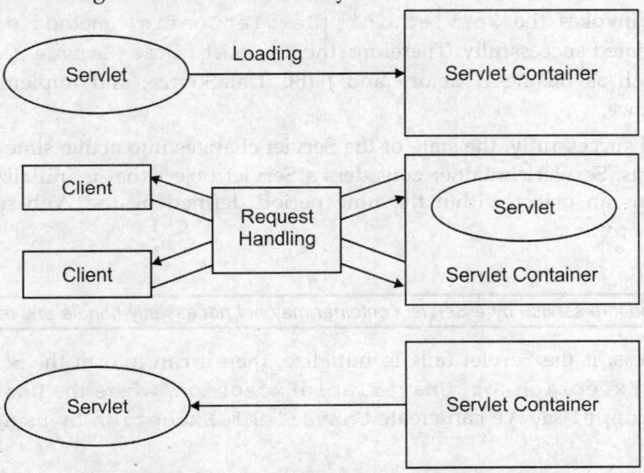

Figure 6.6: Showing the Lifecycle of a Servlet

In this figure, all the stages of the Servlet lifecycle have been described diagrammatically.

Loading a Servlet

The first stage of the Servlet lifecycle involves loading and initializing the Servlet by the Servlet container. The Web container can load the Servlet at either of the following two stages:

- Initializing the context, on configuring the Servlet with a zero or positive integer value to load-on-startup property
- If the Servlet is not loaded in the preceding stage, it may delay the loading process until the Web container determines that this Servlet is needed to service a request.

The Servlet container performs the following operations as a part of the loading process:

- **Loading**—Loads the Servlet class by using the normal Java class loading option. Moreover, the Servlet class may be loaded from a local file system, a remote file system, or other network services. If the Servlet container fails to load the class, it terminates this process.
- **Instantiation**—Creates an instance of the Servlet. To create a new instance of the Servlet, the container uses the no-argument constructor.

The number of instances for a Servlet instance is as follows:

- If the Servlet is not hosted in a distributed environment, and it does not implement the `SingleThreadModel` interface, the container creates only one instance of the Servlet declared in the Deployment Descriptor. A Web application configuration file is also known as Deployment Descriptor.

- If the Servlet is hosted in a distributed environment, the Servlet container creates one Servlet instance per Java Virtual Machine (JVM).
- If the Servlet implements the `SingleThreadModel`, the Servlet container may create multiple instances for the Servlet. If, in this case, the Servlet is hosted as distributable, the Servlet container may create multiple instances per JVM as well.

Initializing a Servlet

After the Servlet is instantiated successfully, the Servlet container initializes the instantiated Servlet object. The container initializes the object by invoking the `Servlet.init(ServletConfig)` method, which accepts the `ServletConfig` object reference as a parameter. The `ServletConfig` object allows the Servlet instance to access name-value configured initialization parameters and other container specific details. The Servlet container creates one `ServletConfig` object per Servlet declared in the deployment descriptor.

The Servlet container invokes the `Servlet.init(ServletConfig)` method once, immediately after the Servlet object is instantiated successfully. Therefore, the `Servlet.init(ServletConfig)` method is used to initialize resources, such as Business Factory and JDBC DataSource, and implement a code that has to be executed once per instance.

If this stage is executed successfully, the state of the Servlet changes into active state and makes it available and ready to handle requests. Servlet container considers a Servlet object that is initialized successfully only if the `init()` method returns an object within the time period defined by the Web server, successfully without throwing `ServletException`.

NOTE

The Servlet instance placed into service by a Servlet container may not necessarily handle any request in its lifetime.

Moreover, in this process, if the Servlet fails to initialize, then it can inform the Servlet container about it by throwing the `ServletException` or `UnavailableException`, where the `UnavailableException` is a subtype of `ServletException`. We can create `UnavailableException` by using any of the following two constructors:

- **`UnavailableException(String msg)`** – Instantiates a permanently unavailable exception with the given message
- **`UnavailableException(String msg, int seconds)`** – Instantiates a temporarily unavailable exception with the given message and estimated time period; i.e., how long it will be unavailable

If the `Servlet.init(ServletConfig)` method throws an exception, the Servlet container does not put Servlet instance into the active state, which means it removes (or destroys) the instance. If an exception is thrown by the `Servlet.init()` method, the Servlet container performs the following operations:

- If it throws temporarily `UnavailableException`, it implies that the Servlet initialization has failed, and will not be available for the specified time period. The Servlet container does not accept any request till the time the Servlet is available. If any request is made, `UnavailableExceptionk` returns the `Service Unavailable (503)` response. However, when there is another request after the given time period, container can try to instantiate and initialize the Servlet.
- If it throws permanently `UnavailableException`, it implies that the Servlet initialization has failed, and will not be available until the context is redeployed.

NOTE

In case of any failure in initialization of Servlet, container does not call the `destroy()` method.

Let's learn how a Servlet container performs request handling.

Handling Request

After initialization, the Servlet instance is ready to serve client requests. The Servlet container performs the following operations when the Servlet instance is located to service a request:

- It creates the `ServletRequest` and `ServletResponse` objects. In case, if this is a HTTP request, the Web container creates the `HttpServletRequest` and `HttpServletResponse` objects, which are subtypes of `ServletRequest` and `ServletResponse`, respectively. The `ServletRequest` object encapsulates the request data that includes request headers and content from the client. The `ServletResponse` object can be used by Servlet to write the response content to client.
- After creating the request and response objects, it invokes the `Servlet.service(ServletRequest, ServletResponse)` method by passing the request and response objects. As described earlier, a Servlet instance can process multiple requests in its life time, now whether the Servlet container uses a single instance of Servlet to process multiple requests at a time or not, depends on whether the Servlet implements SingleThreadModel or not and the service method implementation. The following cases occur while dealing with multiple requests:
  - If the Servlet does not implement the `SingleThreadModel` interface, the Servlet container uses a single instance of the Servlet to process multiple requests at a time. The Servlet container sends concurrent requests to the service method of the Servlet. In this case, you must implement the service method to handle concurrent requests.
  - If the Servlet implements the `SingleThreadModel` interface, the Servlet container uses the Servlet instance to process only one request at a time. The service method is invoked in a thread safe environment. In this case, the container can place all other requests in queue by serializing the requests, or maintaining a pool of Servlet instances to process the requests simultaneously. If the Servlet is marked as distributable, then the container may maintain a separate pool of Servlet instances in each Virtual Machine (VM) that the application is distributed across.
  - If the Servlet does not implement the `SingleThreadModel` interface and the `service` method is defined with the `synchronized` keyword, the Servlet container cannot process multiple requests using a single instance. Therefore, the container cannot use instance pooling; instead, it can only place the requests into queue by serializing the requests.

NOTE

It is strongly recommended not to use this approach (synchronizing the service method) since this reduces the performance of the Servlet container. This means that the processing capabilities of the Servlet container are reduced.

The `SingleThreadModel` is depreciated in Java Servlet 2.4 API, with no replacement.

The `service()` method, while processing the request, may throw the `ServletException`, `UnavailableException`, or `IOException`. If an exception is thrown by service method, the Servlet container performs the following operations:

- If `ServletException` is thrown, it indicates that an error has occurred in the request processing stage, and therefore, the container has to clean up the request and send the error response to the client.
- If `UnavailableException` is thrown, it indicates that the Servlet is currently unavailable to process the request either temporarily or permanently.
- If the Servlet is temporarily unavailable, the Servlet container chooses not to route any request till the time the Servlet is available. Till this time, if any request is made, the Unavailable Exception returns the `Service Unavailable (503)` response.
- If the Servlet is permanently unavailable, the Servlet container calls the `destroy()` method on the Servlet instance and removes the Servlet instance from service. This Servlet is marked unavailable until the context is reloaded.

NOTE

Some Servlet containers ignore the distinction between the permanent and temporary `UnavailableException` and simply remove the Servlet instance from service.

- After the request is processed by the service() method, the Servlet container sends the response to the Web browser.

Destroying a Servlet (End of service)

When a Servlet container decides to destroy the Servlet, it performs the following operations:

- It allows all the threads currently running in the service method of the Servlet instance to complete their jobs and get released. Meanwhile, it makes this instance unavailable to service new requests.
- After the currently running threads have completed their jobs, the Servlet container calls the destroy() method on the Servlet instance.

After the destroy() method is executed, the Servlet container releases all the references of this Servlet instance so that it becomes eligible for garbage collection. The following are the conditions in which container decides to destroy the Servlet:

- When the context is unloaded (shut down)
- When the Servlet.service() method throws UnavailableException marked permanently unavailable

Exploring the Servlet Life Cycle Methods

In the preceding discussion, we have learned the lifecycle of a Servlet object that contains only three methods:

- init()
- service()
- destroy()

Let's describe these in detail.

The init () method

The Servlet.init() method is called by the Servlet container to indicate that this Servlet instance is instantiated successfully and is about to put into service. The following points should be kept in mind for implementing this method:

- This method is invoked by the Servlet container immediately after a Servlet object is created.
- This method is called by the Servlet container to indicate that a Servlet is being placed into service.
- This method can throw ServletException to intimate the container that the initialization process has failed; therefore, it is not eligible to get into service.

The following code snippet explains the use of the init () method:

```
public class MyServlet implements Servlet{
   public void init(ServletConfig config) throws ServletException {
// initialization code;
}
//rest of the code
}
```

Therefore, the Servlet.init(ServletConfig) method is used to initialize resources, such as Business Factory and JDBC DataSource. Moreover, this method implements the code that has to be executed once per instance.

NOTE

We can implement the initialization code into the class constructor of the Servlet object. However, as per the Java Servlet Specification, the Servlet container instantiates the Servlet object by using a no-argument constructor. Therefore, we can perform initializations in no-argument constructor. The difference between the initialization code in the constructor and the init() method is that the init() method can use ServletConfig and can throw UnavailableException as described in the lifecycle while a Servlet class constructor cannot do.

Let's learn how the service() method works.

The service( ) Method

The `service()` method of the Servlet is invoked to inform the Servlet about the client request. The points that we need to consider while implementing this method are as follows:

- This method is invoked only on a Servlet instance that is initialized successfully.
- The Servlet container invokes this method when a client's request is mapped to the Servlet.
- If the Servlet object implements `SingleThreadModel`, this method is invoked in a thread safe environment. Alternatively, multiple threads may invoke this method on the same Servlet instance simultaneously (provided if we even do not define this method as synchronized).
- This method is called by the Servlet container to allow a Servlet to respond to a request.
- This method is available with the client requested data and the service method can collect this data by using the `ServletRequest` object provided as an argument value.
- This method can use the `ServletResponse` object to generate the output content.
- This method can throw the `ServletException` to intimate the container that the request processing has generated an error.

The following code snippet explains the syntax of the `service()` method:

```
public class MyServlet implements Servlet{
public void service (ServletRequest res, ServletResponse res)
throws ServletException, IOException{
        // request handling code;
}
//rest of the code
}
```

Let's learn about the destroy method.

The destroy () Method

The `destroy ()` method runs only once during the lifetime of a Servlet, and signals the end of the Servlet instance. The Servlet container holds a Servlet instance till a Servlet is active or its `destroy()` method is not called. The following code snippet shows the method signature of the destroy method:

```
public void destroy ()
```

As soon as the `destroy()` method is activated, the Servlet container releases the Servlet instance.

NOTE

It is not recommended to implement the `finalize()` method in the Servlet object, instead perform the finalizations in the `destroy()` method.

After learning about Servlet lifecycle, let's learn how to develop a Servlet application.

Developing the First Servlet Application

In this section, we develop a simple Servlet application, **LifeCycle** application, that can demonstrate the lifecycle of Servlet. This example also demonstrates the implementation of the `init()`, `service()`, and `destroy()` methods.

Follow these broad-level steps to develop the application:

- Creating the home.html page
- Creating the LifeCycleServlet
- Creating deployment descriptor
- Deploying the application
- Running the application

Creating the home.html Page

The home.html page is the home page of this application and contains a button labeled, `Invoke Life Cycle Servlet`. When you click this button, it calls the `myFirstServlet` action, which is mapped to `LifeCycleServlet` in `web.xml`. Listing 6.1 shows the home.html page (you can find this file online in the code/Chapter6/LifeCycle folder):

Listing 6.1: Creating the **Home.html** File

```
<html>
<head>
        <title> Servlet Examples (Example to
show Servlet
Lifecycle)</title>
  </head>
  <body>
<form action=" myFirstServlet "><br/><br/><br/>
<center>
<input type="submit" value="Invoke Life Cycle Servlet"/>
</center>
</form>
</body>
</html>
```

Now, let's learn how to create a Servlet.

Creating the LifeCycleServlet

We create the `LifeCycleServlet` Servlet, which implements `init(),service()`, and `destroy()` methods to demonstrate the lifecycle of a Servlet. The `LifeCycleServlet`, Servlet, is created within the package `com.santosh.servlets`. Listing 6.2 shows the code of the LifecycleServlet.java file (you can find this file online in the code/Chapter6/LifeCycle folder):

Listing 6.2: Creating the LifeCycleServlet.java File

```
package com.santosh.servlets;
import javax.servlet.*;
public class LifeCycleServlet implements Servlet {
  public void init(ServletConfig sc)     { config=sc;
System.out.println("in Init");
}//init
  public void service(ServletRequest req,ServletResponse res)
throws ServletException, java.io.IOException        {
java.io.PrintWriter out=res.getWriter();
out.println("Hello from LifeCycleServlet");
System.out.println("in service");
}//service
  public void destroy() {
System.out.println("in destroy");
}//destroy
  public String getServletInfo() { return "LifeCycleServlet";
}//getSI
  public ServletConfig getServletConfig()        {
return config;
}//getServletConfig
private ServletConfig config;
}//class
```

The following methods are used in the preceding listing:

- **`init ()`** – Prints the message "`in Init`" on server's console to ensure the user that `LifeCycleServlet` object is being initialized.
- **`service ()`** – Gets the instance of the `PrintWriter` object to generate the response. The `println ()` method is used to print the message, "`Hello from LifeCycleServlet`" on the browser.

The service() method prints the message, "in service" on the server console to convey that the Servlet is now processing the request.

- **destroy ()** – Destroys the Servlet. It prints the message "in destroy" on the server console.

Creating the Deployment Descriptor

The deployment descriptor is an XML document, used to describe the container customizations of the services supported by it. According to Java Servlet specification, each Web application should have a web.xml file.

The web.xml file for the Servlet application is shown in Listing 6.3 (you can find this file online in the code/Chapter6/LifeCycle/WEB-INF folder):

Listing 6.3: Creating the web.xml File

```
<?xml version="1.0"?>
<web-app>
<servlet>
<servlet-name>LCServlet</servlet-name>
<servlet-class>com.santosh.servlets.LifeCycleServlet</servlet-class>
</servlet>
   <servlet-mapping>
<servlet-name>LCServlet</servlet-name>
<url-pattern>/myFirstServlet</url-pattern>
</servlet-mapping>
</web-app>
```

In the preceding file, the <servlet-name> tag describes a unique name, which is LCServlet in this case. The <servlet-class> tag describes a qualified name of a Servlet class, which in our case is com.santosh.servlets.LifeCycleServlet. The <url-pattern> nested tag in <servlet-mapping> tag takes a string starting with / or *. This string is used to locate Servlet. We have specified <url-pattern> /myFirstServlet, which is same as value specified in action attribute of home.html page.

Deploying Web Application

The steps to package and deploy the LifeCycle application are explained as follows:

- Compile the LifeCycleServlet.java file. To compile the LifeCycleServlet.java file, we need to set the classpath so that the javax.servlet package is available in the classpath. For Tomcat Web server, this package comes inside the servlet-api.jar file and for Weblogic, this package is present inside weblogic.jar file. See the following examples to set classpath:
  - If we are using Tomcat Web server, set the classpath to servlet-api.jar (for tomcat 4.x servlet.jar) which is in the <Tomcat home>/common/lib folder. For example, set classpath=d:\tomcat5.0\ common\lib\servlet-api.jar. In this case, we have assumed that Tomcat is installed in the D: drive in the tomcat5.0 folder.
  - If we are using Weblogic 8.1, set the classpath to weblogic.jar in the <weblogic home>/server/lib folder. For example, set classpath=d:\bea\weblogic81\server\lib\ weblogic.jar. In this case, we have assumed that the Weblogic server is installed in the D:\bea folder.
- After compiling the Servlet, arrange the files as per the following directory structure:

```
   <work_folder>\*.html
\WEB-INF\web.xml
\WEB-INF\lib\*.jar & *.zip (files if any)
\WEB-INF\classes[\<package_name>]\ *.class
```

As shown in this path, the <work folder> can contain publicly available files, such as .jsp, .html, .jpg, and .gif files. The classes directory contains compiled Java classes, including the Servlet used by the Web application. The lib directory contains .jar files used by the Web application. For example, if the E:\Santosh\Book\Examples\Chapter6\LifeCycle folder represents the work folder, then arrange the files as shown in Figure 6.7:

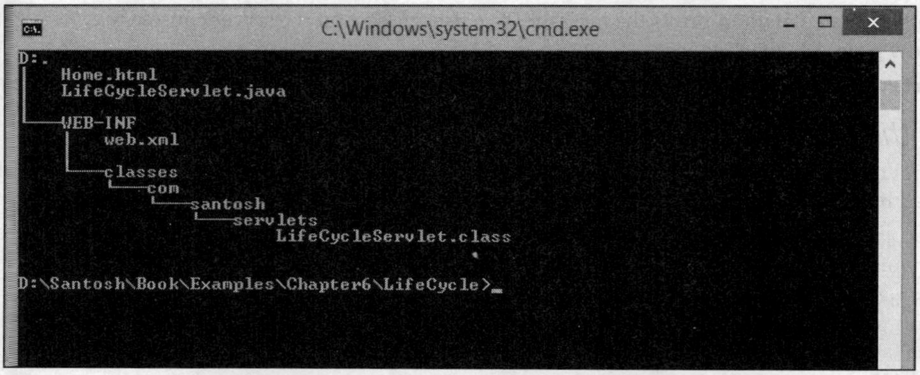

Figure 6.7: Showing the Directory Structure

Next, prepare a war file using the `jar` tool. To use the `jar` tool, open the command prompt and navigate to the work folder of your application (In our case, it is the **LifeCycle** folder) and type `jar -cvf <war file name>.war *`.

For example, we type the following in our example: `E:\Santosh\Book\Examples\ Chapter6\ LifeCycle> run jar -cvf LifeCycle.war *` or `jar -cvf LifeCycle.war Home.html WEB-INF`.

NOTE

It is optional to create a WAR file, as generally, we create a WAR file after completing the development phase of an application and moving towards the production phase.

Now, the application is ready to be deployed on a specific server. Perform the following steps to deploy this application:

- To deploy the application on the Tomcat Web server, copy the `LifeCycle.war` file into the `<Tomcat home>\webapps` folder.
- To deploy the application on the Weblogic application server, copy the `LifeCycle.war` file into the `<weblogic domain root>\applications` folder.

NOTE

We can even copy the `<work folder>` (LifeCycle folder).

Let's now run the application.

Running the LifeCycle Application

Perform the following steps to invoke and run the **LifeCycle** application:

- Before running the application, start the server on which the application has been deployed, by executing the appropriate file:
  - To start the Tomcat server, run the `startup.bat` file in the `<Tomcat_home>\bin` folder.
  - To start the Weblogic server, execute the `<weblogic server domain root>\startWeblogic.cmd` command at the command prompt.
- To run the application, open the browser and invoke the `Home.html` file by using the appropriate URL for the respective server:
  - If you are using Tomcat, use `http://localhost:9090/LifeCycle/Home.html` to invoke the Home.html file.
  - If you are using Weblogic server, use `http://localhost:7001/LifeCycle/Home.html` to invoke the Home.html file.

In these URLs, `localhost` represents the computer name (you can also use the IP address), `9090` or `7001` is the port number of the server, and LifeCycle is the context root of the **LifeCycle** application.

As we are using the Tomcat server, we run the application by using the `http://localhost:9090/LifeCycle/Home.html` URL. This URL displays the home page of the **LifeCycle** application, as shown in Figure 6.8:

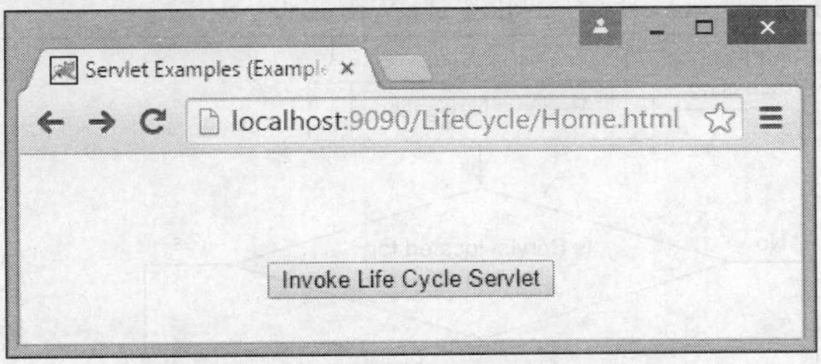

Figure 6.8: Invoking the Home.html File

When we click the Invoke Life Cycle Servlet button, as shown in Figure 6.8, the response generated by the LifeCycleServlet Servlet is displayed, as shown in Figure 6.9:

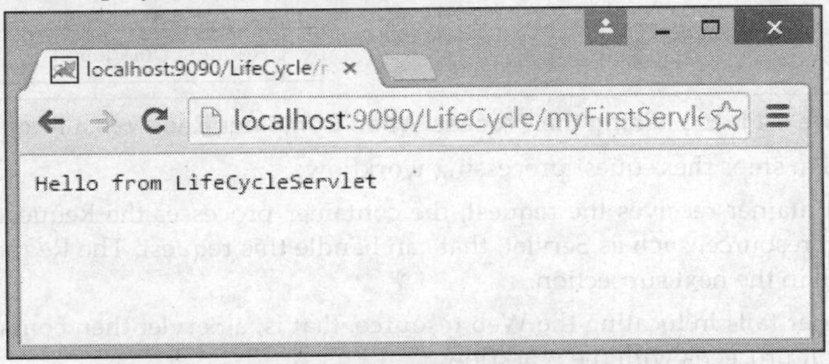

Figure 6.9: Invoking the Servlet

Figure 6.9 displays the message "`Hello from LifeCycleServlet`". You can see "`in Init`" and "`in service`" messages on the Tomcat server console, as shown in Figure 6.10:

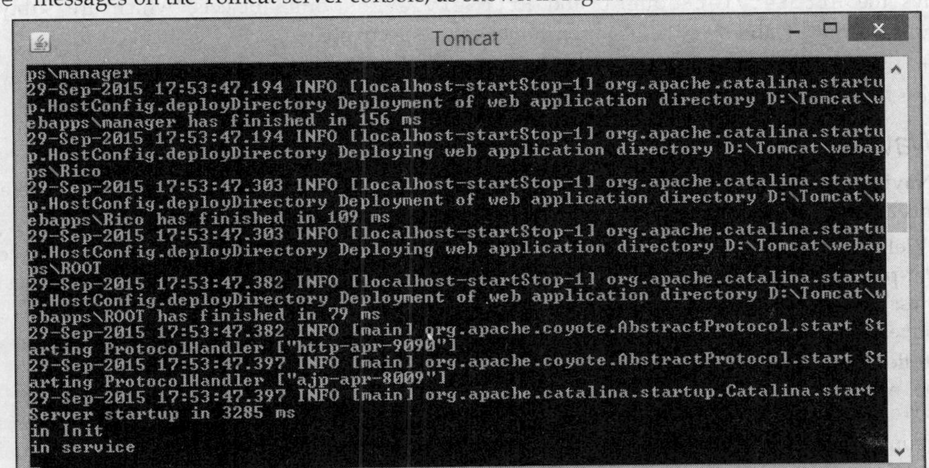

Figure 6.10: Displaying the Output of the init() and service() Methods

We can also invoke the `myFirstServlet` Servlet directly, using the following URLs:

- In case of Tomcat server, use `http://localhost:9090/LifeCycle/myFirstServlet`.
- In case of Bea Weblogic server, use `http://localhost:7001/LifeCycle/myFirstServlet`.

Understanding the Request Processing Workflow

The Web container performs various operations to process the web client, such as a Web browser request. Figure 6.11 shows the request processing workflow of a Web container:

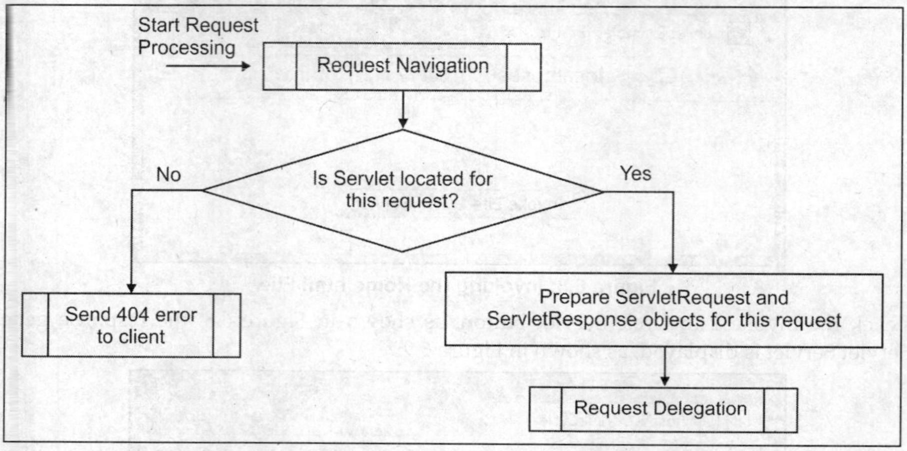

Figure 6.11: Explaining the Process When Container Receives a Request

Now, let's understand in steps the request processing workflow:

- When the Web container receives the request, the container processes the Request Navigation, in which it identifies the web resource, such as Servlet, that can handle this request. The Request Navigation process is described in detail in the next subsection.
- If the Web container fails in locating the Web resource, that is, a Servlet then container sends a 404 error to client. Otherwise, it proceeds with the workflow.
- After successfully locating the Servlet for this request, container now prepares the `ServletRequest` and `ServletResponse` objects describing the request and response. If the request is a HTTP request, container creates the `HttpServletRequest` and `HttpServletResponse` objects, which are subtypes of the `ServletRequest` and `ServletResponse` objects, respectively.
- After creating the request and response objects, the workflow proceeds to execute the Request Delegation process. It is described in detail in the following subsections.

Request Navigation

Request Navigation is a process of identifying the Web resource that can handle the request. The Web container implements a URL based navigation process. The following steps explain this process in detail:

- The Web container resolves the requested URI to get the path. The request-path includes the context-path, servlet-path, and an optional path-info, separated by a / character. The syntax of the request-path is as follows:

```
/<context-path>/<servlet-path>/<path-info>
```

The following snippet shows the example of the request-path:

```
Example 1: /myctxt/login
Example 2: /myctxt/myservlets/loginController
```

The context-path element of the request-path is used to map the request to the context; i.e., a Web application deployed on the Web server. If this context is the default context rooted at the base of the Web server's URL name space, this path will be an empty string. Otherwise, the path starts with a / character but does not end with a / character. The servlet-path element is the part of request path that directly matches to the mapping, which maps to this request. This path starts with a / character except in the case where the request is matched with the /* pattern, in such a case, it is an empty string. The path-info of request-path is request URI minus context-path and the servlet-path. It is either null if there is no extra path, or is a string starting with /.

- The path used by the Web container to locate the Servlet is the request URI minus the context-path, we further refer this as request-path, the following code snippet shows the request URL:

```
http://localhost:9090/myctxt/myFirstServlet
```

In this URL, the `/myctxt/myFirstServlet` is the request URI, `/myctxt` is the context-path, and `/myFirstServlet` is the servlet-path. The container attempts to match the request-path with the url-pattern configured in the Web application, in the following order:

- Find the exact match of the request path with the url-pattern as specified in the `web.xml` file
- Recursively try to match the request path by stepping down the path tree one directory at a time

For example, if the request path is `/abc/xyz/myser`, the Web container first tries to match `/abc/xyz/myser`. If not, it tries to match `/abc/xyz/*`. If not, it tries to match `/abc/*`. Otherwise, it tries to match with `/*`. Table 6.3 lists the specified URL patterns for Servlets, such as Servlet1, Servlet2, and Servlet3:

Table 6.3: Various Mappings Defined in the web.xml File

URL Pattern	Servlet
`/abc/xyz/myser`	Servlet1
`/abc/xyz/*`	Servlet2
`/abc/*`	Servlet3

Table 6.4 shows how the Web container matches the request-paths entered by the user to execute different Servlets:

Table 6.4: Various Request Paths Defined in the web.xml File

Request Path	Servlet
`/abc/xyz/myser`	Servlet1
`/abc/xyz/myser1`	Servlet2
`/abc/xyz1/myser`	Servlet3
`/abc/xyz1`	Servlet3

- If the request path contains an extension, such as `.do`, the container tries to match the request-path pattern with the pattern specified for a Servlet in web.xml. The matched Servlet handles the requests, that is, if the URL pattern for a Servlet, `s1` is given as `*.do` in `web.xml`, the Web container matches the request-path `/abc/xyz/test.do` with the Servlet, '`s1`'.

NOTE

Wildcard character (*) in the URL pattern matches any character and any number of characters.

The URL pattern matched by the Web container is case sensitive.

The Web container uses the first successful match in the preceding specified order with no further attempts to match the URL.

In addition to the mappings defined in the `web.xml`, the Web container includes default mappings, such as `*.jsp` and `/servlet/*`.

Let's learn about request delegation.

Request Delegation

After successfully locating the Web resource, the Web container wants to delegate the request to the located Web resource so that the request can be further handled accordingly. Figure 6.12 shows the Request Delegation process implemented by the Web container to delegate the request to the located Web resource:

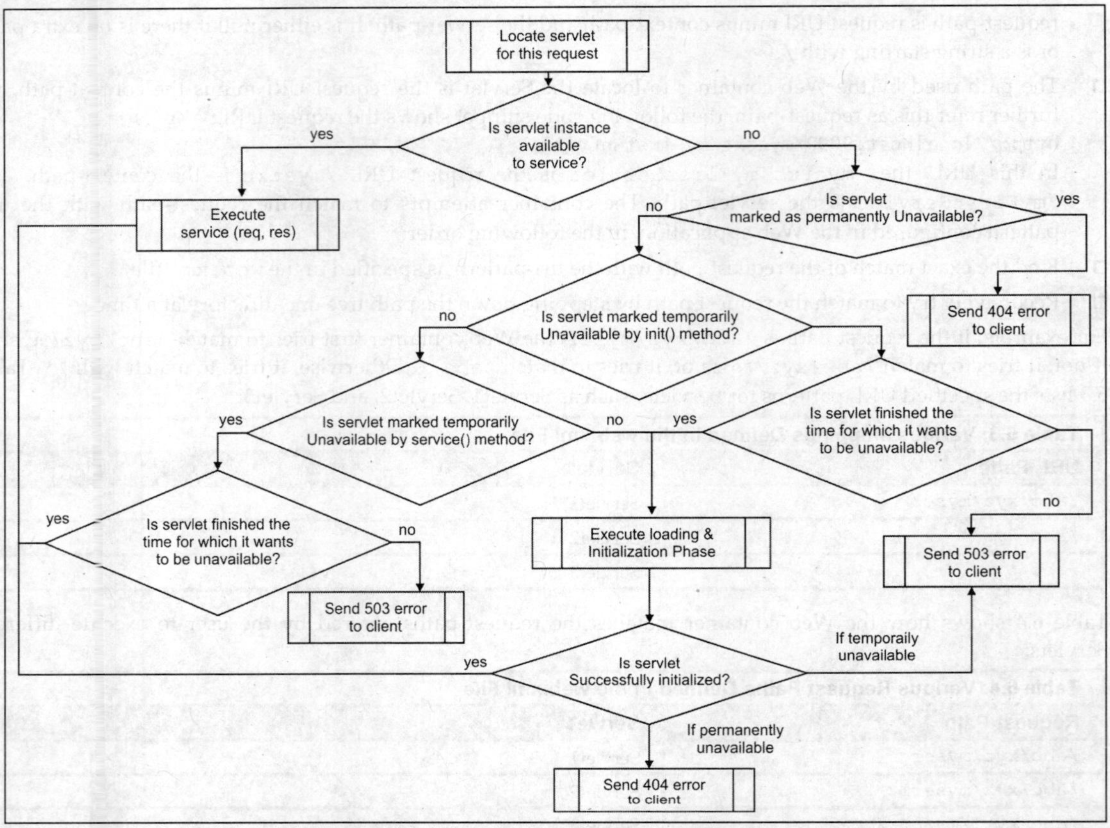

Figure 6.12: Describing the Request Delegation Process

The following steps describe this process in detail:

- As shown in Figure 6.12, in the process of delegating the request to the located Servlet, first the Web container finds whether or not the Servlet object is available to service. If the Servlet object is available to service the request, the Web container delegates the request invoking the `Servlet.service (ServletRequest, ServletResponse)` method on this Servlet object.

NOTE

If the request-path maps to any filters configured in the application then the filters are executed accordingly before the request is delegated to the `Servlet.service()` method.

- If the located Servlet instance is not available to service, container finds whether or not this Servlet is marked as permanently unavailable. If yes, it sends 404 Error to client, which describes the client that the requested resource is not available.
- If this Servlet is not marked permanently unavailable, container checks whether or not this Servlet is marked temporarily unavailable by the `init()` method. If yes, it identifies whether the unavailable time period is finished. In case, if the time period is finished, the container tries to initialize the Servlet executing the Loading and Initialization phases. After a successful initialization of the Servlet instance, container uses that instance to execute the `service()` method to complete the request. If initialization fails and throws the `UnavailableException`, it marks the Servlet as unavailable until the context is reloaded and sends 404 error message to client. If initialization fails describing temporarily unavailable, it marks the Servlet unavailable until the specified time period and sends 503 error message to client.

- If this Servlet is not even marked temporarily unavailable by the `init()` method, it means the Servlet would be marked unavailable by the `service()` method; i.e., while servicing the previous requests. In such a case, if the time period in which it is marked unavailable is completed, container executes the `service()` method to complete the request. Otherwise, it sends 503 error message to the client, describing that the requested resource is currently unavailable to service.
- If the Servlet is not marked temporarily unavailable by the `service()` method, it means that the Servlet is not initialized till now or it is destroyed for some reason (but not marked permanently unavailable). Therefore, the Servlet will be initialized by executing the Loading and Initialization phases. Thereafter, it proceeds the request processing as per the output.

NOTE

Before executing the `service()` method, the Web container prepares the `ServletRequest` and `ServletResponse` objects. If the request is of HTTP type, then the Web container creates the `HttpServletRequest` and `HttpServletResponse` type of objects.

The request and response objects created are of the request scope. The Web container can create new request and response objects for each of the request and destroy them after the request processing is completed. Alternatively, it can recycle these objects instead of destroying them to avoid the performance overhead of object creation.

- After understanding the request processing workflow of Servlet container, now let's learn about the `GenericServlet` class.

Working with the GenericServlet Class

The Servlet object must be a subtype of the `javax.servlet.Servlet` interface and should not be an abstract class. Therefore, the implementation class needs to implement all the (five) methods declared in the `javax.servlet.Servlet` interface. However, most of the Servlet objects do not need the initializing and destroying operations, but still we need to implement all the methods declared in the `javax.servlet.Servlet` interface. To solve this problem, the Servlet API provides an adapter class, `javax.servlet.GenericServlet`, which implements the `javax.servlet.Servlet` interface and provides the basic implementation for the methods in this interface (except the service method).

`GenericServlet` is an abstract class provided in the Servlet API. It provides a simplified approach to implement Servlet objects by giving a simple version of the Servlet lifecycle methods. `GenericServlet` is a subtype of Servlet interface and it even implements the `ServletConfig` interface. This class implements the adapter pattern.

Exploring Methods of the GenericServlet Class

The `GenericServlet` class provides an implementation for all the methods in the Servlet and `ServletConfig` interfaces except the `service()` method. Apart from the methods of the Servlet and `ServletConfig` interfaces, this class defines three additional methods, two `log()` methods and one `init()` with no argument method.

The methods implemented in the `GenericServlet` class are as follows:

- **`init(ServletConfig)`** – Indicates that this Servlet instance is being placed into service. This method performs the following operations:
  - Stores the given `ServletConfig` object reference into instance variable. The `ServletConfig` object reference is used in the `ServletConfig` interface methods implemented in the `GenericServlet` class
  - Invokes `init()` method with no-argument on the reference

  The following code snippet shows the predefined implementation of the `init ()` method in the `GenericServlet` class:

```
public class GenericServlet implements Servlet, ServletConfig {
private transient ServletConfig config;
public void init(ServletConfig sc) throws ServletException{
config=sc
```

```
    init();
    }
    … //rest of the code
    }
```

- **init()** – The init() method is invoked by init(ServletConfig) method of GenericServlet.

NOTE

Servlet container does not call this method.

The init() method is a utility method given for the convenience of the subclass of GenericServlet to provide custom initializations without disturbing the initializations performed by GenericServlet in the init(ServletConfig) method.

That is, as we know that Servlet container invokes init method passing ServletConfig object reference as an argument on the Servlet object immediately after the Servlet object is instantiated. This is done for the following reasons:

- To inject the ServletConfig object into the newly instantiated Servlet object so that Servlet can hold it and use it further to get runtime information and initialize parameters from container.

NOTE

The Servlet container injects ServletConfig object into a Servlet object only once in the life time of Servlet object, i.e., in initialization process so the Servlet object needs to take the responsibility to hold this reference if it has to use config object further in its lifetime.

- To allow Servlet to perform initializations.

The GenericServlet is also a subtype of ServletConfig interface, it uses the ServletConfig object that is injected by container through init(ServletConfig) method. Therefore, GenericServlet's init(ServletConfig) method takes the ServletConfig object into its instance variable. Therefore, if we want to use ServletConfig's methods implemented in GenericServlet, then we need to allow GenericServlet to implement the init(ServletConfig) method that is executed in the initialization process. If we override the init(ServletConfig) method of GenericServlet in our Servlet class and even require to use ServletConfig object then we need to perform any of the following steps:

- Call super.init(config) in it to let the GenericServlet store the given config object into its instance variable. This allows us to use ServletConfig methods implemented by GenericServlet
- Take the ServletConfig object into our own instance variable and use it to get the details further.

NOTE

In this case invoking ServletConfig methods implemented in GenericServlet results with NullPointerException.

- **destroy()** – Indicates that the Servlet instance is being taken out of service.
- **getServletInfo()** – Returns the information about the respective Servlet. The implementation of this method given by GenericServlet returns an empty string.
- **getServletConfig()** – Returns the ServletConfig interface reference.
- **service(ServletRequest, ServletResponse)** – Refers to an abstract method that is called by the Servlet container to intimate the Servlet about the client request.
- **getInitParameter(String)** – Returns the Servlet initialization parameter of the given name and if the requested named parameter is not available, then it returns null.
- See the default implementation of this method in the following code snippet:

```
public class GenericServlet implements Servlet, ServletConfig {
    private transient ServletConfig config;
    public String getInitParameter(String name){
        return config.getInitParameter(name); }
    … //rest of the code }
```

- **`getInitParameterNames()`** — Returns the names of the Servlet initialization parameters as an enumeration of String objects. This method returns an empty enumeration if the Servlet does not contain any initialization parameters.
- **`getServletName()`** — Returns the Servlet instance name as defined in the Deployment Descriptor (web.xml).
- **`getServletContext()`** — Returns the `ServletContext` object reference.

NOTE

The preceding four methods are declared in `ServletConfig` interface and `GenericServlet` implementation of these methods depend on the `ServletConfig` object injected by the container through `init()` method. If we do not allow the `init(ServletConfig)` method of `GenericServlet` to execute, then these methods throw `NullPointerException`.

- **`log(String)`** — Writes the given message to a Servlet log file, prefixed by the Servlet instance name, as specified in the Deployment Descriptor.
- **`log(String, Throwable)`** — Writes the given message to a Servlet log file, prefixed by the Servlet instance name, as specified in the Deployment Descriptor, and traces the stack of the given `Throwable` object.

Using the GenericServlet Class

In this section, we create a Web application that displays Home.html as a home page of the application. Then this home page passes the control to `HelloServlet`, a Java Servlet, which extends the `GenericServlet` class. This Servlet class displays a welcome message.

The broad level steps to create this application are:

- Creating the Home.html page
- Creating the HelloServlet.java Servlet
- Deploying and running the application

Creating the Home.html Page

The application displays `Home.html` as the home page, which contains a submit button. When a user clicks the Submit button, the control is sent to the `HelloServlet` servlet, which further processes the client's request. Listing 6.4 shows the source code for the Home.html page (you can also find this file online in the code/Chapter6/GSExample folder):

Listing 6.4: Adding code to the Home.html Page

```
<html> <head>
        <title> Servlet Example </title>
   </head>
   <body>
        <form action="myFirstServlet">
               <input type="submit" value="Invoke Hello Servlet">
        </form>
   </body>
</html>
```

Let's learn how to develop the HelloServlet.java Servlet.

Developing the HelloServlet.java Servlet

The HelloServlet Servlet extends the `javax.servlet.GenericServlet` class. Therefore, this class overrides the service method of the `GenericServlet` class. The HelloServlet Servlet class displays the Hello message to the users. Listing 6.5 shows the HelloServlet.java file (you can find this file online in the code/Chapter6/GSExample folder):

Listing 6.5: Showing the HelloServlet.java File

```
package com.santosh.servlets;
import javax.servlet.*;
/**
 * @author Santosh
 */
```

```
public class HelloServlet extends GenericServlet {
   public void service(ServletRequest req,ServletResponse res)
   throws java.io.IOException,ServletException {
         System.out.println("In service");
         res.setContentType("text/html");
         java.io.PrintWriter out=res.getWriter();
         out.println("Hello from HelloServlet (subclass of GenericServlet)");
   }//service
}//class
```

Let's learn how to deploy and run the application.

Deploying and Running the Application

The web.xml file for HelloServlet consists of the <servlet> and <servlet-mapping> tags. These tags map the URL specified in the action attribute of the Hello.html page to the compiled HelloServlet class. The web.xml file is shown in Listing 6.6 (you can find this file online in the code/Chapter 6/GSExample /WEB-INF folder):

Listing 6.6: Creating the web.xml File

```
<?xml version="1.0"?>
<web-app>
   <servlet>
         <servlet-name>hs</servlet-name>
         <servlet-class>com.santosh.servlets.HelloServlet</servlet-class>
         <load-on-startup>0</load-on-startup>
   </servlet>
   <servlet-mapping>
         <servlet-name>hs</servlet-name>
         <url-pattern>/myFirstServlet</url-pattern>
   </servlet-mapping>
</web-app>
```

Perform the following steps to deploy and run the application:

- Create a directory structure and arrange all the preceding files accordingly, as shown in Figure 6.13:

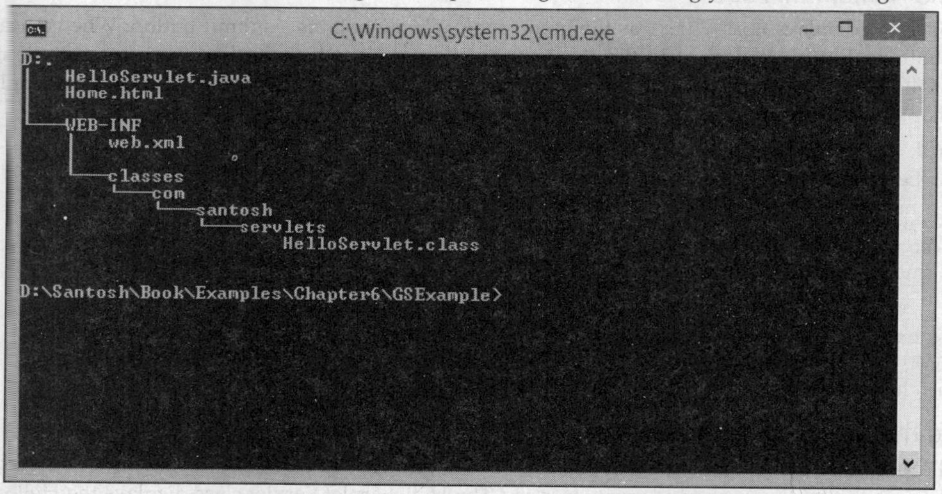

Figure 6.13: Displaying the Directory Structure of the GSExample Application

- Copy the **GSExample** folder into the <Tomcat home>\webapps folder. Now, start the server by running the startup.bat file. To run the application, open the Web browser and invoke the Home.html page using the http://localhost:9090/GSExample/Home.html URL. Figure 6.14 shows the home page of the GSExample application:

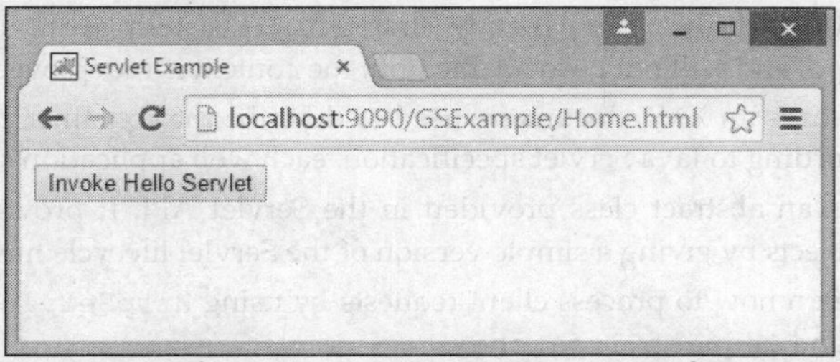

Figure 6.14: Invoking the Home.html File of the GSExample Application

- Click the `Invoke Hello Servlet` button shown in Figure 6.14 to send a request to `HelloServlet`. This action displays the response of `HelloServlet`, as shown in Figure 6.15:

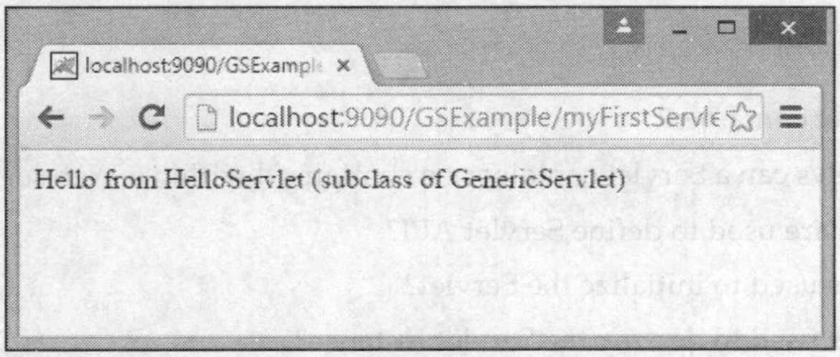

Figure 6.15: Invoking the HelloServlet

Now, let's have a glance on the topics we have covered in this chapter.

Summary

This chapter discussed the need for server-side extensions, such as CGI, and their benefits and limitations. It introduced Java Servlet, Servlet container, and various Servlet container configurations. This chapter also described the commonly used classes and interfaces of the Servlet API. You also learned about the details of the Servlet lifecycle and the lifecycle methods, such as `init ( )`, `service( )`, and `destroy ( )`. Finally, you created two applications—the first described the lifecycle process of a Servlet and the second used the `GenericServlet` class to implement a Servlet.

Let's recall the following important points to summarize the chapter:

- Java Servlet is one of the component APIs of Java Platform Enterprise Edition standards for creating dynamic Web applications in Java.
- Servlet container, sometimes also known as Servlet engine, is an integrated set of objects that provides runtime environment for Java Servlet components.
- The Servlet API is a part of the Java Servlet specification designed by Sun - JCP. All Servlet containers, such as Tomcat and Weblogic, support this API.
- The Servlet lifecycle mainly goes through four stages, such as loading a Servlet, initializing the Servlet, request handling, and destroying the Servlet.
- A Servlet object is initialized and managed by the Servlet container. The Servlet container uses the `javax.servlet.Servlet` interface to understand the Servlet object.
- The Servlet instance placed into service by a Servlet container may not necessarily handle any request in its lifetime.
- In case of any failure in initialization of Servlet, container does not call the `destroy()` method.
- If the Servlet is temporarily unavailable, the Servlet container do not receive any request till the time the Servlet is available. Within this time, if any request is made, the Unavailable Exception returns the `Service Unavailable (503)` response.

- If the `init()` method throws permanently `UnavailableException`, it indicates that the Servlet initialization has failed, and will not be available until the context is redeployed.
- Deployment descriptor is an XML document, used to describe the container customizations of the services supported by it. According to Java Servlet specification, each web application should have a `web.xml` file.
- `GenericServlet` is an abstract class provided in the Servlet API. It provides a simplified approach to implement Servlet objects by giving a simple version of the Servlet lifecycle methods.

In the next chapter, we learn how to process client requests by using `HttpServlet`. The chapter also discusses about Request attributes and `RequestDispatcher`.

Exercise

Q.6.1 What is CGI?

Q.6.2 What is a Servlet?

Q.6.3 Define the Servlet container?

Q.6.4 In how many ways can a Servlet container be configured within a Web server?

Q.6.5 Which packages are used to define Servlet API?

Q.6.6 Which method is used to initialize the Servlet?

Q.6.7 Which method is used to destroy the Servlet instance?

Q.6.8 Name the Servlet lifecycle methods.

Q.6.9 What is a `GenericServlet`?

Q.6.10 Which design pattern is used to implement a `GenericServlet`?

7

Understanding Request Processing and HTTP

In the client-server programming, the request message is used by the client to send a request to the server. The request message contains data, such as headers and message content. The server processes the client's request and generates a result and sends it back as a response to the client. The HyperText Transfer Protocol (HTTP) is used to exchange the request and response between a Web server and clients.

In this chapter, you learn about the HTTP protocol in detail. You also learn about Servlets to process requests and responses. The chapter also discusses a Servlet initialization and context initialization parameters in detail. You also learn how to use the `RequestDispatcher` object to forward requests to other Servlet or Internet Service Provider (ISP) pages.

As a Servlet is a server-side extension, we use it to read the data requested by the client, process the request, and send a response. The Servlet API provides the `javax.servlet.ServletRequest` interface through which the Servlet can access the requested data. Let's start by discussing the `ServletRequest` interface.

Implementing the ServletRequest Interface

The `javax.servlet.ServletRequest` interface of Servlet API defines a container object, known as the `ServletRequest` object, which represents the client request and its data. The `ServletRequest` object encapsulates the requested data that includes the request parameters and headers. The Servlet container creates this object, sets the request information into it, and passes it to a Servlet as an argument of the `service()` method. The `ServletRequest` object is active within the request scope. The Servlet container can manage the `ServletRequest` object in the following two ways:

- As a throwaway object
- As the `ServletRequest` object pool

Let's discuss these two ways.

Managing the ServletRequest Object as a Throwaway Object

The Servlet container manages the `ServletRequest` object as a throwaway object on receiving the request by performing the following steps:

- Creating a new `ServletRequest` object
- Setting all the information submitted in the request to the newly created `ServletRequest` object
- Invoking the `Servlet.service()` method passing the `ServletRequest` object as an argument. However, if any filters are configured to intercept the request, those filters are executed accordingly along with the Servlet.
- Destroying the `ServletRequest` object when the requested `Servlet.service()` method returns to the container after the request processing. In other words, it finalizes the object so that the garbage collector can garbage this object.

In this process, the number of objects that are created and destructed are very high; therefore, this process increases the load on Java Virtual Machine (JVM) and affects the performance of server and application. Most of the containers implement pooling to improve the performance.

Managing the ServletRequest Object Pool

In this case, the Servlet container manages a pool of `ServletRequest` objects, which can be reused for handling multiple requests. The Servlet container on receiving the request performs the following operations on the `ServletRequest` object:

- Finds whether the `ServletRequest` object is available in the request object pool. If the `ServletRequest` object is found, it picks one of the objects from the pool, and marks the located object as in use. Otherwise, it creates a new instance of `ServletRequest`, puts it into the pool, and picks it to mark as in use.
- Sets the information requested by the client in the request to the `ServletRequest` object.
- Invokes the `Servlet.service()` method and passes the `ServletRequest` object as an argument. However, if any filters are configured to intercept the request, those filters are executed accordingly along with the Servlet.

- Once the request processing is completed and the requested `Servlet.service()` method returns to the container, the Servlet container refreshes the `ServletRequest` object, marking the object as free in the pool so that the `ServletRequest` object can be used to describe another request.

In this case, the Web container recycles `ServletRequest` objects to avoid the performance overhead of request objects creation. However, it does not use the same request object to serve more than one request at a time. This implies that `ServletRequest` is thread-safe, irrespective of the approach used by the Servlet container to manage these objects.

The `javax.servlet.ServletRequest` interface is used to abstract a container object (`ServletRequest`) that describes client request data. Therefore, the `javax.servlet.ServletRequest` interface supports methods for reading the client request data which includes request parameters and headers.

NOTE

The `ServletRequest` object does not provide any protocol-specific data, such as the HTTP data. However, it defines generic methods that allow us to get the request data sent by using any protocol.

The `ServletRequest` interface provides the following methods to access the client request data:

- **`String getProtocol()`** – Returns the name and version of the protocol when a request is made. For example, if you make a request by using HTTP 1.1, this method returns HTTP/1.1.
- **`String getScheme()`** – Returns the name of the scheme used to handle a request, such as HTTP, HTTPS, or File Transfer Protocol (FTP).
- **`String getRemoteAddr()`** – Returns the IP address of the client.
- **`String getRemoteHost()`** – Returns the fully qualified name of the client sending the request.
- **`String getServerName()`** – Returns the name of the server receiving the request.
- **`int getServerPort()`** – Returns the port number on which the server is running and receiving the request.
- **`void setAttribute(String name, Object obj)`** – Stores an attribute for a specific client request.
- **`Object getAttribute(String name)`** – Returns the value of the named attribute as an object form, or returns null if the attributes do not exist.
- **`void removeAttribute(String name)`** – Removes an attribute associated with a specific client request.

Let's now learn about request parameters and methods available in the `ServletRequest` object to read the request parameters.

Working with Request Parameters

The name-value pairs submitted by the client as a request to process are known as request parameters. The Servlet object implements the `service()` method to handle the client request, which processes the data (or a form) submitted by the client. For example, a client requesting to login into your application wants to submit the login details, such as user id and password. The Servlet object that you create to handle this request should read and process the login details submitted by the client and respond to the client accordingly. These details are submitted to the server as name-value pairs, known as request parameters. A request parameter is a query string in the Uniform Resource Locator (URL) or in the body of the request message. The query string is separated from the URL path with a question mark (?) character and each parameter has a name and value that are separated with a (=) character. A request can have multiple parameters separated by the (&) character. For example, the URL, **http://www.hostname.com?param1=val1&param2=val2**, contains two request parameters, **param1** and **param2**, with their corresponding values, **val1** and **val2**. These parameters are taken from the request when a user enters data and clicks the Submit button in the form. The `ServletRequest` interface provides the following methods to get request parameters:

`String getParameter(String name)` – Returns the value of a request parameter with the given name as a `String` format, or returns null value if the parameter does not exist.

- **String[] getParameterValues(String name)** — Returns an array of String objects containing all the values in a request parameter or returns null value if the parameter does not exist.
- **Enumeration getParameterNames()** — Returns an enumeration of String objects containing the names of the parameters in a request.

Now, after understanding the concepts of the ServletRequest interface and request parameters, let's use them in an example.

The following **login** Web application demonstrates the handling of request parameters of a client. In this Web application, you need to develop a form, which in our case is the Login form (Login.html) and a Servlet (LoginServlet.java) that uses request parameters' names and their corresponding values to display the resultant view page (You can find this Web application online in the code/Chapter7 folder).

Perform the following broad-level steps to create the Web application:

- Create the Login form (Login.html)
- Create the LoginServlet Servlet
- Create the deployment descriptor file
- Run the application

Creating the Login Form

Let's create the Login.html page, which contains two input text fields, one to enter the user name and the other to enter the password. It also contains a submit button. Listing 7.1 provides the code of the Login.html file (you can find this file online in the code/Chapter7/login folder):

Listing 7.1: Creating the Login Form

```
<html> <body>
<center><h1>XYZ Company Ltd.</h1><br><br>
<form action="login">
  <table>
  <tr>
        <td>User Name</td>
        <td><input type="text" name="uname"/></td>
  </tr>
  <tr>
        <td>Password</td>
        <td><input type="password" name="pass"/></td>
  </tr>
  <tr>
        <td> </td>
        <td> </td>
  </tr>
  <tr>
        <td colspan="2" align="center">
        <input type="submit" value="LogIN"/>
        </td>
  </tr>
  </table>
</form> </center></body> </html>
```

In Listing 7.1, the LogIN button is created to submit the user name and password in the textboxes. When a user clicks the LogIN button, the values of the uname and pass fields are attached to the URL as request parameters. The LoginServlet Servlet is invoked by finding the url-pattern defined in the web.xml file with its corresponding action (login). Let's create the LoginServlet Servlet to handle the request forwarded by the Login.html page.

Creating the LoginServlet Servlet

The LoginServlet Servlet gets the request parameter values from the Login.html form and inserts them into the user details table. The source code of the LoginServlet.java file is given in Listing 7.2 (You can also find this file online in the code/Chapter7/login folder):

Listing 7.2: Creating a Servlet

```
package com.santosh.servlets;

import javax.servlet.*;
import java.io.*;
import java.sql.*;

/**
* @author Santosh
*/
public class LoginServlet extends GenericServlet {

  private Connection con;
  private PreparedStatement ps=null;

  public void init() throws ServletException {
        System.out.println("In init");
        /*Getting the connection in init method and using it to
         *handle the request is not a better practice in all the cases
         */
        try {
               Class.forName("oracle.jdbc.driver.OracleDriver");
               con=DriverManager.getConnection(
               "jdbc:oracle:thin:@localhost:1521:sandb", "scott", "tiger");
               ps=con.prepareStatement(
               "select * from userdetails where uname=? and pass=?");
        }//try
        catch(Exception e){
               e.printStackTrace();
               throw new ServletException(
               "Initialization failed, Unable to get DB connection");
        }//catch
  }//init

  public void service (ServletRequest req, ServletResponse res)
  throws ServletException, IOException {

        System.out.println("In service");

        res.setContentType("text/html");
        PrintWriter out=res.getWriter();
        try {

               String uname=req.getParameter("uname");
               String pass= req.getParameter("pass");

               if(uname==null||uname.equals("")||pass==null||pass.equals("")) {

                      out.println("<html><body><center>");
                      out.println("<li><i>User Name and Password cannot be
                      empty</i></li><br/>");
                      out.println("<li><i>We cannot log you into your account at this
                      time. Please try again later</i>");
                      out.println("</center></body></html>");
                      return;
               }//if

               ps.setString(1,uname);
               ps.setString(2,pass);
               ResultSet rs=ps.executeQuery();

               out.println("<html><body>");
               if (rs.next()){
                      out.println("<h3>Welcome, "+uname+"</h3><br/>");
                      out.println("<h2>Enjoy browsing the Site</h2>");
               }
               else
```

```
                out.println("<h2>We cannot log you into your account at this time. Please
                try again later</h2>");
                out.println("</body></html>");
        }//try
        catch(Exception e){
        out.println("<h2>Unable to the process the request try after some time</h2>");
        }//catch
    }//service

    public void destroy () {
        System.out.println("In destroy");
        try {con.close();}
        catch(Exception e){}
    }//destroy
}//class
```

Listing 7.2 retrieves the user details (user name and password) from the user details table. If the user name and password entered by a user match with the details provided in the user details table then the welcome message is displayed to the users. Otherwise, the message to try again is displayed. As you know that the login action is provided in the Login.html file, which passes the request to the `LoginServlet` Servlet; therefore, you need to map the login action in the web.xml file. Let's now create the `web.xml` file.

Creating the Deployment Descriptor File

The final step in completing an application is to create a deployment descriptor file. The deployment descriptor file is used to map the `LoginServlet` Servlet so that the client is able to access it by providing `/login` in the `<url-pattern>` tag of the `web.xml` file. Listing 7.3 provides the code of the `web.xml` file (you can also find this file online in the code/Chapter7/login/WEB-INF folder):

Listing 7.3: Creating a Deployment Descriptor File

```
<?xml version="1.0"?>
<web-app>
  <servlet>
        <servlet-name>ls</servlet-name>
        <servlet-class>com.santosh.servlets.LoginServlet</servlet-class>
  </servlet>

  <servlet-mapping>
        <servlet-name>ls</servlet-name>
        <url-pattern>/login</url-pattern>
  </servlet-mapping>
</web-app>
```

Figure 7.1 shows the directory structure in which all the files of this example are arranged:

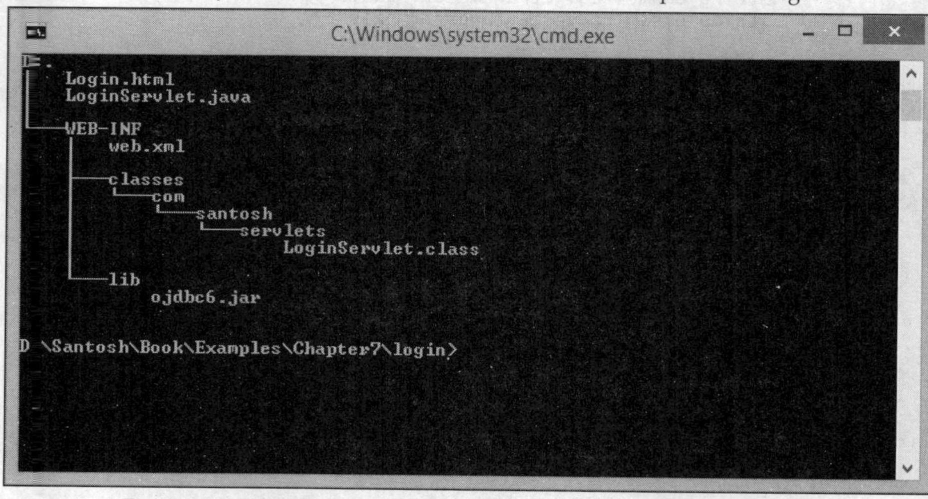

Figure 7.1: Showing the Directory Structure for the login Application

After placing all the files of the **login** application, as shown in Figure 7.1, let's run the application to display its output.

Running the Application

You need to create a table, which is used by your login form, to run this application. In our case, we create the userdetails table in the Oracle database since this table is used by the LoginServlet.java file. The userdetails table is created by typing the following command in the SQL prompt:

```
create table userdetails(
uname varchar2(20),
pass varchar2(15),
address varchar2(20),
phno number,
email varchar2(25));
```

Insert a row in the userdetails table by typing the following command in the SQL prompt:

```
insert into userdetails values(
'Santosh','kumar','Hyd', 9704309999,'to_santoshk@yahoo.com');
```

After arranging all the files in a directory structure, shown in Figure 7.1, copy the **login** folder into the `<Tomcat home>\webapps` folder.

Now, start the Tomcat server. If it is already started, you need not restart it. We are using port number 9090 since Tomcat is running on this port in our computer. Run the application using the following URL:

```
http://localhost:9090/login/Login.html
```

The Login form appears on your screen, as shown in Figure 7.2:

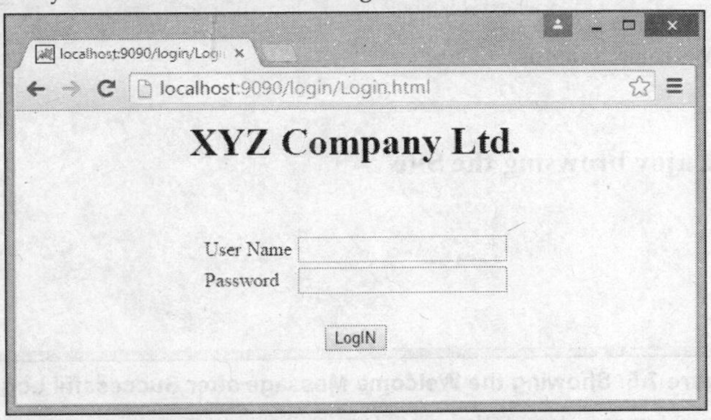

Figure 7.2: Showing the Login Form

If you click the LogIN button without entering the user name and password, the validation messages appear on your screen, as shown in Figure 7.3:

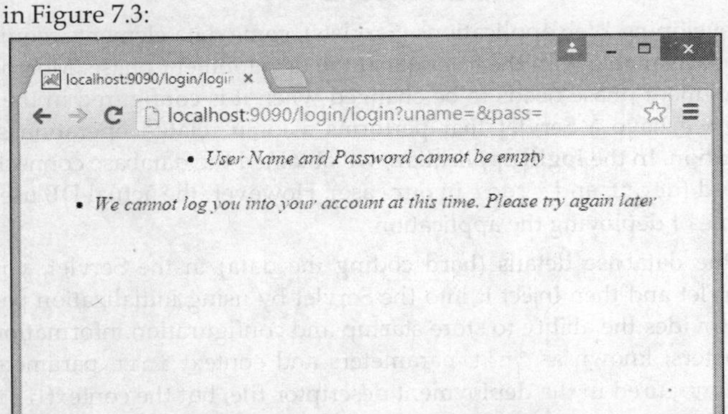

Figure 7.3: Showing Validation Messages

Now, enter the values in the User Name and Password fields and click the LogIN button, as shown in Figure 7.4:

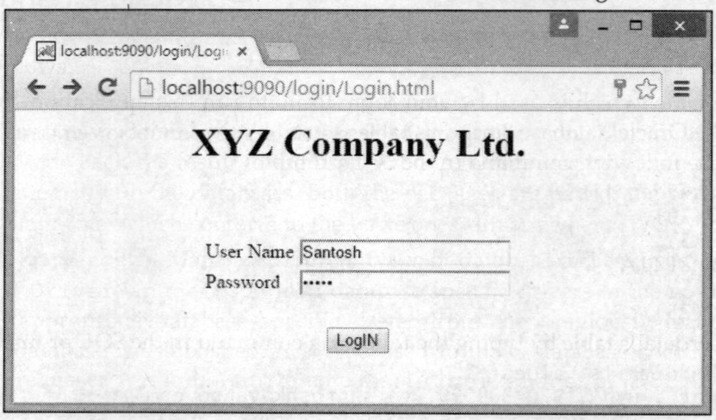

Figure 7.4: Showing the Login Page with User Name and Password Fields

After entering the user name and password, these values are added in the URL as a request parameter and the `LoginServlet` Servlet is invoked to generate the resultant page, as shown in Figure 7.5:

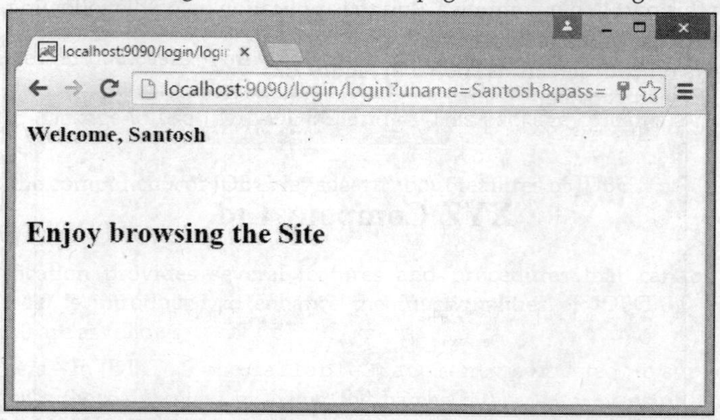

Figure 7.5: Showing the Welcome Message after Successful Login

After learning about request parameters, let's learn about initialization parameters, in the next section.

Working with Initialization Parameters

In most cases, while developing Web applications (Servlets), some data elements required to process the request are not known or may be available with the test data at the development phase. Moreover, the test data coded in the Servlet at the deployment phase needs to be changed when it is configured in the production environment. For example, suppose we have a Servlet that performs a login related operation similar to the one in our preceding **login** application. In the **login** application, we obtained the database connection by using the database user name and password (`scott` and `tiger` in our case). However, the actual DB user name and password are available only at the time of deploying the application.

Instead of providing the database details (hard coding the data) in the Servlet, you can configure the data externally from the Servlet and then inject it into the Servlet by using initialization parameters. In other words, the Servlet container provides the ability to store startup and configuration information for a Servlet in the form of initialization parameters, known as `init` parameters and context `init` parameters. `Init` parameters are specific to the Servlet configured in the deployment descriptor file, but the context `init` parameters are specific to all or multiple Servlet's configured in the deployment descriptor file. In the following sections, you learn about `init` parameters and context `init` parameters.

Exploring the Need for Initialization Parameters

You need to minimize the complexity of the server-side programming and reduce the maintenance of your Web application to build a successful Web application in Java. For example, suppose you configure an administrator email address of a company in your Servlet by writing the following code in the Servlet:

```
PrintWriter out = response.getWriter();
out.println("XYZ@yourcompany.com");
```

In this code, you have to recompile the Servlet every time the administrator's email address changes. Rather than hard-coding the email value directly into your Servlet's source code, you should always maintain these data values in the deployment descriptor file, so that any change in the email address does not affect the Web application. In other words, you can pass the value of the administrator's email address through the `init` parameter in the `web.xml` file. You can write the following code snippet to provide the initialization parameters in the `web.xml` file:

```
<servlet>
   <servlet-name> - - - -  </servlet-name>
   <servlet-class> - - - -  </servlet-class>
   <init-param>
         <param-name>adminEmail </param-name>
         <param-value>XYZ@yourcompany.com</param-value>
   </init-param>
</servlet>
```

You can access the initialization parameters, defined in `web.xml`, by using the following code snippet:

```
out.println(getServletConfig().getInitParameter("adminEmail"));
```

Let's now learn how to retrieve and use these parameters in the context of the Servlet.

Retrieving Initialization Parameters

The Servlet initialization parameters are retrieved by using the `ServletConfig` object. The following methods of the `ServletConfig` interface provides the functionality to retrieve the values of the initialization parameters:

- **`String getInitParameter(String)`** – Returns a string containing the value of the named initialization parameter, or null if the requested parameter does not exist in the `web.xml` file.
- **`Enumeration getInitParameterNames()`** – Returns the names of the Servlet's initialization parameters as an `Enumeration` of `String` objects, or an empty `Enumeration` if the Servlet has no initialization parameters specified in the `web.xml` file.

`init` parameters are specified in the deployment descriptor file (`web.xml`). Each of these parameters consists of a name and value, where the name should be unique. You can specify any number of parameters for a Servlet configured in `web.xml`.

You can configure `init` parameters for a Servlet by using the following tag under the `<servlet>` tag after the `<servlet-class>` tag in the `web.xml` file:

```
<init-param>
   <param-name>  parameter name </param-name>
   <param-value>  parameter value </param-value>
</init-param>
```

Initialization parameters are available to the Servlet during initialization, client servicing, and destruction of the Servlet.

Handling Servlet Initialization Parameters

Let's create an application called **initParams** to learn how to access the `init` parameters from the deployment descriptor file. You can also find this application online in the code/Chapter7 folder. You need to perform the following broad-level steps to create this application:

- Create the Home.html file
- Create the `InitParamsServlet` Servlet

- ❑ Create the deployment descriptor file
- ❑ Run the application

Let's start by creating the entry point for the application, which is the Home.html page.

Creating the Home.html File

The application starts with a home page displaying a button with the label, "Get Init Parameters Configured in DD file". Listing 7.4 provides the code for the Home.html file (you can also find this file online in the code/Chapter7/initParams folder):

Listing 7.4: Creating a Home Page

```
<HTML>
    <HEAD>
            <TITLE> Servlet Examples (Init Parameters Example) </TITLE>
    </HEAD>
    <BODY>
            <FORM ACTION="initParamsSer">
                    <INPUT TYPE="submit"
                            value="Get Init Parameters Configured in DD file"/>
            </FORM><br/>
    </BODY>
</HTML>
```

In Listing 7.4, we have created a button and when you click that button, the request is forwarded to the `InitParamsServlet` Servlet. Let's now create the `InitParamsServlet` Servlet.

Creating the InitParamsServlet Servlet

The `InitParamsServlet` Servlet handles the request sent from the Home.html page. The Servlet retrieves the `init` parameters defined in the deployment descriptor file. The source code for the InitParamsServlet.java file is given in Listing 7.5 (you can also find this file online in the code/Chapter7/initParams folder):

Listing 7.5: Creating the `InitParamsServlet` Servlet

```
package com.santosh.servlets;

import javax.servlet.*;
import java.util.*;
/**
* @author Santosh
*/
public class InitParamsServlet extends GenericServlet {

  public void init()throws ServletException {

          //Test Code to demonstrate hot to get init parameters
          //Here to demonstrate this we will print the name & values

          //Getting the parameter value of the given name
          String value=getInitParameter("param1");
          System.out.println("param1 value is : "+value);

          //To get all the parameter values
          System.out.println("Getting all the parameters");
          System.out.println("----------------------");
          System.out.println("Name \t Value");
          System.out.println("----------------------");

          Enumeration enum=getInitParameterNames();
          while (enum.hasMoreElements()){

                  String name=(String)enum.nextElement();
                  value=getInitParameter(name);
                  System.out.println(name+"\t"+value);
          }//while
  }
```

```
public void service(ServletRequest req,ServletResponse res)
throws java.io.IOException,ServletException    {

        res.setContentType("text/html");
        java.io.PrintWriter out=res.getWriter();

        out.println("<html><body>");
        /*
        As described like Initialization parameters are available to the servlet at any
        time i.e. in initialization, servicing the client and destroying.
        */

        //Getting the parameter value of the given name
        String value=getInitParameter("param1");
        out.println("param1 value is : <b>"+value+"</b><br/>");

        //To get all the parameter values
        out.println("Getting all the parameters<br/>");
        out.println("<table border='1'>");
        out.println("<tr><th>Name</th>");
        out.println("<th>Value</th></tr>");

        Enumeration enum=getInitParameterNames();
        while (enum.hasMoreElements()){

                String name=(String)enum.nextElement();
                value=getInitParameter(name);
                out.println("<tr><td>"+name+"</td>");
                out.println("<td>"+value+"</tr>");
        }//while

        out.println("</table>");
        out.println("</body></html>");
    }//service
}//class
```

After creating the `InitParamsServlet` Servlet, let's provide the Servlet mapping in the deployment descriptor file.

Creating the Deployment Descriptor File

The final step in completing the application requires creating the deployment descriptor file (`web.xml`). This file defines the three `init` parameters in name-value pairs under the three `<init-param>` tags, as shown in Listing 7.6 (You can find this file online in the code/Chapter7/initParams folder as well):

Listing 7.6: Creating the `web.xml` File

```
<?xml version="1.0"?>
<web-app>
  <servlet>
        <servlet-name>myser</servlet-name>
        <servlet-class>
                com.santosh.servlets.InitParamsServlet
        </servlet-class>
        <init-param>
                <param-name>param1</param-name>
                <param-value>Value1</param-value>
        </init-param>
        <init-param>
                <param-name>param2</param-name>
                <param-value>Value2</param-value>
        </init-param>
        <init-param>
                <param-name>param3</param-name>
                <param-value>Value3</param-value>
        </init-param>
  </servlet>
```

```
<servlet-mapping>
    <servlet-name>myser</servlet-name>
    <url-pattern>/initParamsSer</url-pattern>
</servlet-mapping>
<welcome-file-list>
<welcome-file>Home.html</welcome-file>
</welcome-file-list>
</web-app>
```

After creating all the files, arrange them in a directory structure, as shown in Figure 7.6:

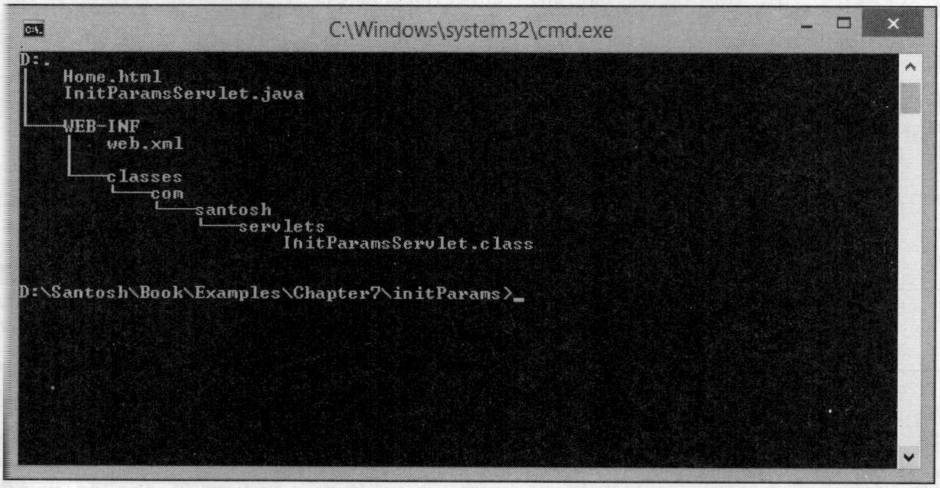

Figure 7.6: Showing the Directory Structure for the initParams Application

After placing all the files of the `initParams` application, as shown in Figure 7.6, let's run the application to display its output.

Running the Application

After arranging the files, copy the `initParams` folder and paste it into the `<Tomcat home>\webapps` folder and start the Tomcat server. If it is already started, you need not to restart it. We are using port number 9090 because Tomcat is running on this port at our computer. You can run this application by using the following URL:

```
http://localhost:9090/initParams/Home.html
```

After running the application, the home page appears, as shown in Figure 7.7:

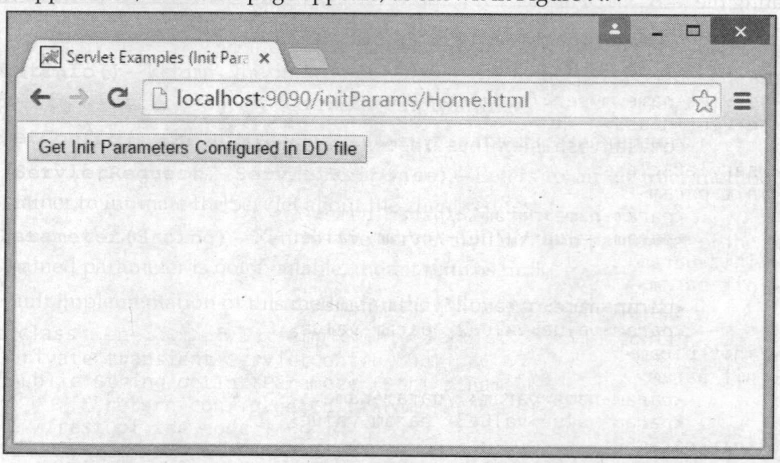

Figure 7.7: Showing the Home Page of the initParams Application

Now, click the Get Init Parameters Configured in DD file button to retrieve the init parameters with their values from the deployment descriptor file. The response from the Servlet is shown in Figure 7.8:

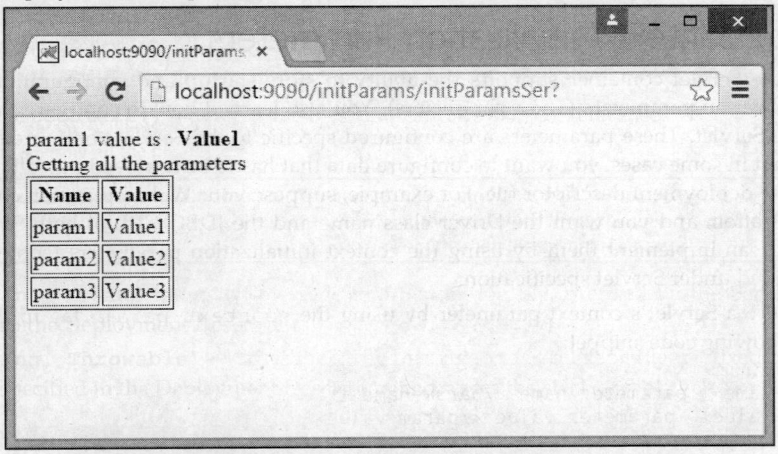

Figure 7.8: Showing the Retrieved Parameters with Values

In this example, we have overridden the `init()` method with the no-argument method of `GenericServlet` and used the `getInitParameter()` and `getInitParameterNames()` methods implemented in `GenericServlet`. Besides this, you can override the `init()` method with the `ServletConfig` argument, that is, `init(ServletConfig)`. The following two approaches can be used to override the `init()` method of `GenericServlet`:

- Invoking the `super.init(config)` method with the `ServletConfig` argument. If this is not done, the `getInitParameter()` and `getInitParameterNames()` methods are invoked on the `ServletConfig` reference (that is, implemented by `GenericServlet`) and throws the `NullPointerException` exception. Listing 7.7 provides the implementation of the `super.init(config)` method:

Listing 7.7: Using the `super.init(config)` Method

```
public class InitParamsServlet extends GenericServlet{
  public void init(ServletConfig config) throws ServletException {
        super.init(config);
        //rest of the code is same as shown in the above example
}
```

In the preceding code snippet, the `super.init(config)` method to override the `init()` method.

- Invoking the `getInitParameter()` and `getInitParameterNames()` methods on the `ServletConfig` reference. Listing 7.8 shows the implementation of the `getInitParameter()` and `getInitParameterNames()` methods:

Listing 7.8: Using the `getInitParameterNames()` Method

```
public class InitParamsServlet extends GenericServlet{

  ServletConfig config;

  public void init(ServletConfig config) throws ServletException {

        this.config=config;
        /*
        Rest of the code is same as shown in the above example but invoke
        getInitParameter() and getInitParameterNames() methods on config reference
        e.g.
        String value=config.getInitParameter("param1");
        */
}
```

After understanding the concepts of request parameters and Servlet initialization parameters, let's move on to context parameters.

Working with Context Initialization Parameters

As discussed, the Servlet container supports the ability to store startup and configuration information for a Servlet as initialization parameters (`init` parameters). You also learned how to configure these parameters and use them in the Servlet. These parameters are configured specific to the Servlet configured in the deployment descriptor file but in some cases, you want to configure data that has to be retrieved into all or multiple Servlet's configured in the deployment descriptor file. For example, suppose your Web application contains two Servlets, login and registration, and you want the Driver class name and the JDBC URL of both Servlets to establish a connection. You can implement them by using the context initialization parameters (context init parameters), which are provided under Servlet specification.

You can configure a Servlet's context parameter by using the `<context-param>` tag in the `web.xml` file, as shown in the following code snippet:

```
<context-param>
  <param-name>  parameter name </param-name>
  <param-value>  parameter value </param-value>
</context-param>
```

For a Web application, you can configure one or more context parameters, where the parameter's name should be unique.

Retrieving Context Initialization Parameters

The `ServletContext` object is used to retrieve the context `init` parameters. The following methods are declared in the `ServletContext` interface in support of this requirement:

- **`String getInitParameter(String)`** — Returns a string containing the value of the named initialization parameter, or null if the requested parameter does not exist in the `web.xml` file.
- **`Enumeration getInitParameterNames()`** — Returns the names of the context initialization parameters as an `Enumeration` of `String` objects, or an empty `Enumeration` if initialization parameters are not specified in the `web.xml` file.

Using Context Initialization Parameters

Let's create the **mysite** application, which shows how to configure and access Servlet and context initialization parameters. You can also find this application online in the code/Chapter7 folder. You need to perform the following broad-level steps to create this application:

- Create the Home.html file
- Create the Login.html file
- Create the Register.html file
- Create the `RegistrationServlet` Servlet
- Create the `LoginServlet` Servlet
- Create the deployment descriptor file
- Run the application

Let's start by creating the entry point for the application, which is the Home.html page.

Creating the Home.html File

The application starts with the Home page. This page displays a user interface with links, Login and Register (you can also find the Home.html file online in the code/Chapter7/mysite folder):

Listing 7.9: Creating the Home.html File

```
<html><body>
   <center><h1>XYZ Company Ltd.</h1></center>
   <table border="1" width="100%" height="100%">
```

```
        <tr>
                <td width="15%" valign="top" align="center">
                        <br/><a href="Login.html">Login</a><br/>
                        <br/><a href="Register.html">Register</a><br/>
                </td>
                <td valign="top" align="center"><br/>
                        Welcome to xyz.com
                </td>
        </tr>
    </table>
</body></html>
```

Listing 7.9 provides the Login and Register hyperlinks. When a user clicks the Login hyperlink, the Login page is displayed and the Register page is displayed on clicking the Register hyperlink. Let's first create the Login.html file.

Creating the Login.html File

The Login page prompts a user to enter the user name and password for login. The source code for this page is given in Listing 7.10 (you can also find the Login.html file online in the code/Chapter7/mysite folder):

Listing 7.10: Creating the Login.html File

```
<html> <body>
<center><h1>XYZ Company Ltd.</h1></center>
<table border="1" width="100%" height="100%">
<tr>
   <td width="15%" valign="top" align="center">
        <br/><a href="Login.html">Login</a><br/>
        <br/><a href="Register.html">Register</a><br/>
   </td>
   <td valign="top" align="center"><br/>
        <form action="login"><table>
        <tr>
                <td colspan="2" align="center"><b>Login Page</b></td>
        </tr>
        <tr>
                <td colspan="2" align="center"><b> </td>
        </tr>
        <tr>
                <td>User Name</td>
                <td><input type="text" name="uname"/></td>
        </tr>
        <tr>
                <td>Password</td>
                <td><input type="password" name="pass"/></td>
        </tr>
        <tr>
                <td> </td>
                <td> </td>
        </tr>
        <tr>
                <td colspan="2" align="center">
                        <input type="submit" value="LogIN"/>
                </td>
        </tr>
        </table></form>
   </td>
</tr>
</table>
</body></html>
```

After creating the Login.html file for the Login hyperlink, let's create the Register.html file for the Register hyperlink.

Creating the Register.html File

The Register.html page prompts a new user to enter his or her user name, password, email, phone number, and address for registration. The source code for the Register.html page is given in Listing 7.11 (you can also find the Register.html file online in the code/Chapter7/mysite folder):

Listing 7.11: Creating the Register.html File

```
<html> <body>
<center><h1>XYZ Company Ltd.</h1></center>
<table border="1" width="100%" height="100%">
<tr>
  <td width="15%" valign="top" align="center">
        <br/><a href="Login.html">Login</a><br/>
        <br/><a href="Register.html">Register</a><br/>
  </td>
  <td valign="top" align="center"><br/>
        <form action="register"><table>
        <tr>
                <td colspan="2" align="center"><b>Registration Page</b></td>
        </tr>
        <tr>
                <td colspan="2" align="center"><b> </td>
        </tr>
        <tr>
                <td>User Name</td>
                <td><input type="text" name="uname"/></td>
        </tr>
        <tr>
                <td>Password</td>
                <td><input type="password" name="pass"/></td>
        </tr>
        <tr>
                <td>Re-Password</td>
                <td><input type="password" name="repass"/></td>
        </tr>
        <tr>
                <td>Address</td>
                <td><input type="text" name="addr"/></td>
        </tr>
        <tr>
                <td>Phone Number</td>
                <td><input type="text" name="phno"/></td>
        </tr>
        <tr>
                <td>Email ID</td>
                <td><input type="text" name="email"/></td>
        </tr>
        <tr>
                <td> </td>
                <td> </td>
        </tr>
        <tr>
                <td colspan="2" align="center">
                        <input type="submit" value="Register"/>
                </td>
        </tr>
        </table></form>
  </td>
</tr>
</table>
</body></html>
```

When the new user submits his or her information, the `RegistrationServlet` Servlet will be called to process the request. Now, let's create the `RegistrationServlet` Servlet.

Creating the RegistrationServlet Servlet

The `RegistrationServlet` Servlet retrieves the values of the request parameters (the new user's information) and inserts it into the database. The Servlet gets the database connection from the context initialization parameters defined in the `web.xml` file. The source code for the RegistrationServlet.java file is given in Listing 7.12 (you can also find this file online in the code/Chapter7/mysite folder):

Listing 7.12: Creating the `RegistrationServlet` Servlet

```
package com.santosh.servlets;

import javax.servlet.*;
import java.io.*;
import java.sql.*;
/**
* @author Santosh
*/
public class RegistrationServlet extends GenericServlet {

   private Connection con;
   private PreparedStatement ps=null;

   public void init() throws ServletException {
         System.out.println("In init");
         try {
                   ServletContext ctxt=getServletContext();
                   //Getting the Driver class name from context parameter
                   String driverClassName=
                   ctxt.getInitParameter("driverClassName");
                   Class.forName(driverClassName);

                   //Getting the JDBC URL from context parameter
                   String url=ctxt.getInitParameter("url");

                   /*Getting the DB Username, password & sqlstatement from servlet init
                   parameter */

                   String dbuser=getInitParameter("dbuser");
                   String dbpass=getInitParameter("dbpass");
                   String sqlst=getInitParameter("sqlstatement");

                   con=DriverManager.getConnection(url, dbuser, dbpass);
                   ps=con.prepareStatement(sqlst);
         }//try
         catch(Exception e){
                   e.printStackTrace();
                   throw new ServletException(
                   "Initialization failed, Unable to get DB connection");
         }//catch
   }//init

   public void service (ServletRequest req, ServletResponse res)
   throws ServletException, IOException {

         System.out.println("In service");

         res.setContentType("text/html");
         PrintWriter out=res.getWriter();
         try {

                   String uname=req.getParameter("uname");
                   String pass= req.getParameter("pass");
                   String repass= req.getParameter("repass");

                   if (uname==null||uname.equals("")
                          ||pass==null||pass.equals("")
```

```
                    ||!pass.equals(repass)) {

                    out.println("<html><body><center>");
                    out.println("<li><i>");
                    out.println(
                    "Given details are not valid to register</i></li><br/>");
                    out.println("<li><i>Please try again later</i>");
                    out.println("</center></body></html>");
                    return;
                }//if

                String addr=req.getParameter("addr");
                String phno=req.getParameter("phno");
                String email=req.getParameter("email");

                ps.setString(1,uname);
                ps.setString(2,pass);
                ps.setString(3,addr);
                ps.setString(4,phno);
                ps.setString(5,email);

                int count=ps.executeUpdate();

                if (count==1||count==Statement.SUCCESS_NO_INFO){
                out.println("<html><body>");
                out.println("<center><h1>XYZ Company Ltd.</h1></center>");
                out.println("<table border='1' width='100%' height='100%'>");
                out.println("<tr>");
                out.println("<td width='15%' valign='top' align='center'>");
                out.println("<br/><a href='Login.html'>Login</a><br/>");
                out.println("<br/><a href='Register.html'>Register</a>");
                out.println("</td>");
                out.println("<td valign=\"top\" align=\"center\"><br/>");
                out.println("<h3>Welcome, "+uname+"</h3><br/>");
                out.println("<h2>Enjoy browsing the Site</h2>");
                out.println("</td></tr></table>");
                out.println("</body></html>");
                }
                else{
                    out.println("<html><body><center>");
                    out.println("Given details are incorrect<br/>");
                    out.println("<li><i>Please try again later</i>");
                    out.println("</center></body></html>");
                }
        }//try
        catch(Exception e){
                out.println("<html><body><center>");
                out.println("<h2>Unable to the process the request try after some
                time</h2>");
                out.println("</center></body></html>");
        }//catch
    }//service

    public void destroy () {
        System.out.println("In destroy");
        try {con.close();}
        catch(Exception e){}
    }//destroy
}//class
```

When the new user submits his or her user name and password from the login page, the `LoginServlet` will be called to process the request. Let's now create the `LoginServlet` Servlet.

Creating the LoginServlet Servlet

The `LoginServlet` Servlet retrieves the values of the request parameters (the new user's information) and checks the database to see whether the user is registered or not. The Servlet gets the database connection from the context initialization parameters defined in the `web.xml` file. The source code for the LoginServlet.java file is given in Listing 7.13 (you can also find this file online in the code/Chapter7/mysite folder):

Listing 7.13: Creating the `LoginServlet` Servlet

```
package com.santosh.servlets;

import javax.servlet.*;
import java.io.*;
import java.sql.*;

/**
* @author Santosh
*/
public class LoginServlet extends GenericServlet {

   private Connection con;
   private PreparedStatement ps=null;

   public void init() throws ServletException {
         System.out.println("In init");
         try {
                 ServletContext ctxt=getServletContext();
                 //Getting the Driver class name from context parameter
                 String driverClassName=
                 ctxt.getInitParameter("driverClassName");
                 Class.forName(driverClassName);
                 //Getting the JDBC URL from context parameter
                 String url=ctxt.getInitParameter("url");
                 /*Getting the DB Username, password &
                 sqlstatement from servlet init parameter */
                 String dbuser=getInitParameter("dbuser");
                 String dbpass=getInitParameter("dbpass");
                 String sqlst=getInitParameter("sqlstatement");
                 con=DriverManager.getConnection(url, dbuser, dbpass);
                 ps=con.prepareStatement(sqlst);
         }//try
         catch(Exception e){
                 e.printStackTrace();
                 throw new ServletException(
                 "Initialization failed, Unable to get DB connection");
         }//catch
   }//init

   public void service (ServletRequest req, ServletResponse res)
   throws ServletException, IOException {

         System.out.println("In service");

         res.setContentType("text/html");
         PrintWriter out=res.getWriter();
         try {

                 String uname=req.getParameter("uname");
                 String pass= req.getParameter("pass");

                 if (uname==null||uname.equals("")
                 ||pass==null||pass.equals("")) {

                 out.println("<html><body><center>");
                 out.println("<li><i>");
                 out.println(
```

```
                    "User Name and Password cannot be empty</i></li><br/>");
                    out.println("<li><i>We cannot log you into your account at this time.
                    Please try again later</i>");
                    out.println("</center></body></html>");
                    return;
                    }//if

                    ps.setString(1,uname);
                    ps.setString(2,pass);
                    ResultSet rs=ps.executeQuery();

                    if (rs.next()){
                    out.println("<html><body>");
                    out.println("<center><h1>XYZ Company Ltd</h1></center>");
                    out.println("<table border='1' width='100%' height='100%'>");
                    out.println("<tr>");
                    out.println("<td width='15%' valign='top' align='center'>");
                    out.println("<br/><a href='Login.html'>Login</a><br/>");
                    out.println("<br/><a href='Register.html'>Register</a>");
                    out.println("</td>");
                    out.println("<td valign='top' align='center'><br/>");
                    out.println("<h3>Welcome, "+uname+"</h3><br/>");
                    out.println("<h2>Enjoy browsing the Site</h2>");
                    out.println("</td></tr></table>");
                    out.println("</body></html>");
                    }
                    else{
                            out.println("<html><body><center>");
                            out.println("Given username and password are incorrect<br/>");
                            out.println("<li><i>We cannot log you into your account at this
                            time. Please try again later</i>");
                            out.println("</center></body></html>");
                    }
            }//try
            catch(Exception e){
                    out.println("<html><body><center>");
                    out.println("<h2>Unable to the process the request try after some
                    time</h2>");
                    out.println("</center></body></html>");
            }//catch
    }//service

    public void destroy () {
            System.out.println("In destroy");
            try {con.close();}
            catch(Exception e){}
    }//destroy
  }//class
```

After creating the required Servlets, let's map the Servlets and context parameters in the `web.xml` file.

Creating the Deployment Descriptor File

The final step in completing the application requires creating the deployment descriptor (`web.xml`) file. The deployment descriptor file defines the two context parameters in name-value pairs under two `<context-param>` tags. The first context parameter, `driverClassName`, specifies the class name of the driver you are using, which is `oracle.jdbc.driver.OracleDriver` in our case. The second context parameter specifies the URL for connecting to the Oracle database, which is `jdbc:oracle:thin:@santosh:1521:sandb` in our case. The URL can be changed for different drivers if you are using different databases. In our case, santosh is the Oracle server machine name and `sandb` is the database name. Listing 7.14 provides the code for the `web.xml` (you can find this file online in the code/Chapter7/mysite/WEB-INF folder):

Listing 7.14: Creating a Deployment Descriptor File

```
<?xml version="1.0"?>
<web-app>
```

```
<context-param>
       <param-name>driverClassName</param-name>
       <param-value>oracle.jdbc.driver.OracleDriver</param-value>
</context-param>
<context-param>
       <param-name>url</param-name>
       <param-value>
               jdbc:oracle:thin:@santosh:1521:sandb
       </param-value>
</context-param>
<servlet>
       <servlet-name>ls</servlet-name>
       <servlet-class>com.santosh.servlets.LoginServlet</servlet-class>
       <init-param>
               <param-name>dbuser</param-name>
               <param-value>scott</param-value>
       </init-param>
       <init-param>
               <param-name>dbpass</param-name>
               <param-value>tiger</param-value>
       </init-param>
       <init-param>
               <param-name>sqlstatement</param-name>
               <param-value>
                       select * from userdetails where uname=? and pass=?
               </param-value>
       </init-param>
</servlet>
<servlet>
       <servlet-name>rs</servlet-name>
       <servlet-class>
               com.santosh.servlets.RegistrationServlet
       </servlet-class>
       <init-param>
               <param-name>dbuser</param-name>
               <param-value>scott</param-value>
       </init-param>
       <init-param>
               <param-name>dbpass</param-name>
               <param-value>tiger</param-value>
       </init-param>
       <init-param>
               <param-name>sqlstatement</param-name>
               <param-value>
                               insert into userdetails values(?,?,?,?,?)
               </param-value>
       </init-param>
</servlet>
<servlet-mapping>
       <servlet-name>ls</servlet-name>
       <url-pattern>/login</url-pattern>
</servlet-mapping>
<servlet-mapping>
       <servlet-name>rs</servlet-name>
       <url-pattern>/register</url-pattern>
</servlet-mapping>
       <welcome-file-list>
<welcome-file>Home.html</welcome-file>
</welcome-file-list>

</web-app>
```

Now, arrange all the files in a directory structure, as shown in Figure 7.9:

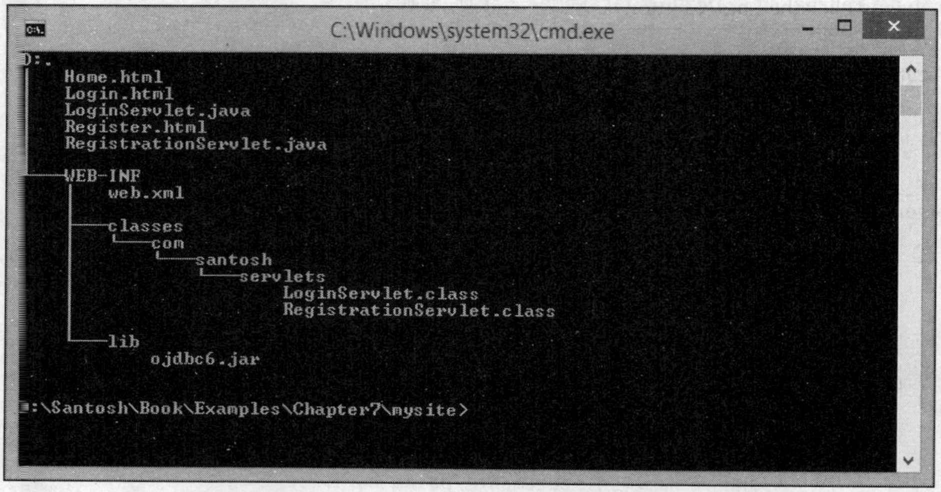

Figure 7.9: Showing the Directory Structure for the mysite Application

After arranging the files, copy the **mysite** folder into the `<Tomcat home>\webapps` folder. Ensure that the user details table is created in the database. If the table is not there, you can create it in Oracle by using the following SQL command:

```
create table userdetails(uname varchar2(20) , pass varchar2(15) , address varchar2(20) ,
   phno number(15) , email varchar2(25));
```

Next, insert a row in the user details table by using the following SQL command:

```
insert into userdetails values('Santosh','kumar','hyderabad',
9704309999,'to_santoshk@yahoo.com');
```

Let's now run the application.

Running the Application

Now, start the Tomcat server. If it is already started, you need not to restart it. We are using port number 9090 because Tomcat is running on this port at our computer. To run this example, use the following URL: http://localhost:9090/mysite/.

The home page of this application appears, as shown in Figure 7.10:

Figure 7.10: Showing the Home.html Page

Click the Login link to display the login page. Enter the user name and password as **Santosh** and **kumar**, respectively and click the **LogIN** button, as shown in Figure 7.11:

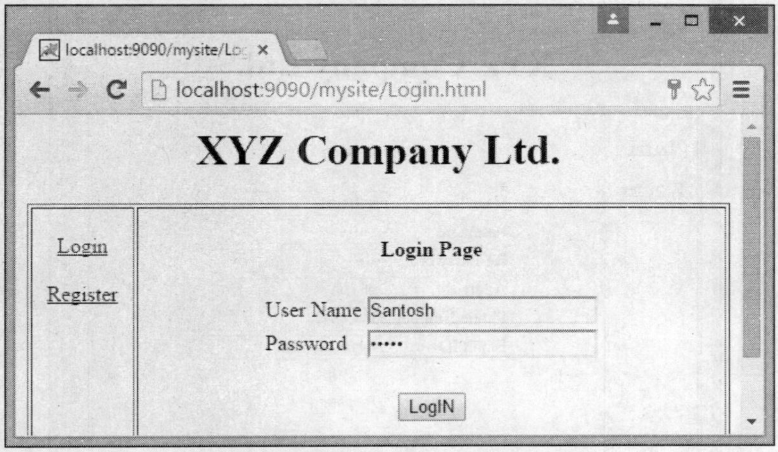

Figure 7.11: Showing Login.html.

A successful login displays the welcome page, as shown in Figure 7.12:

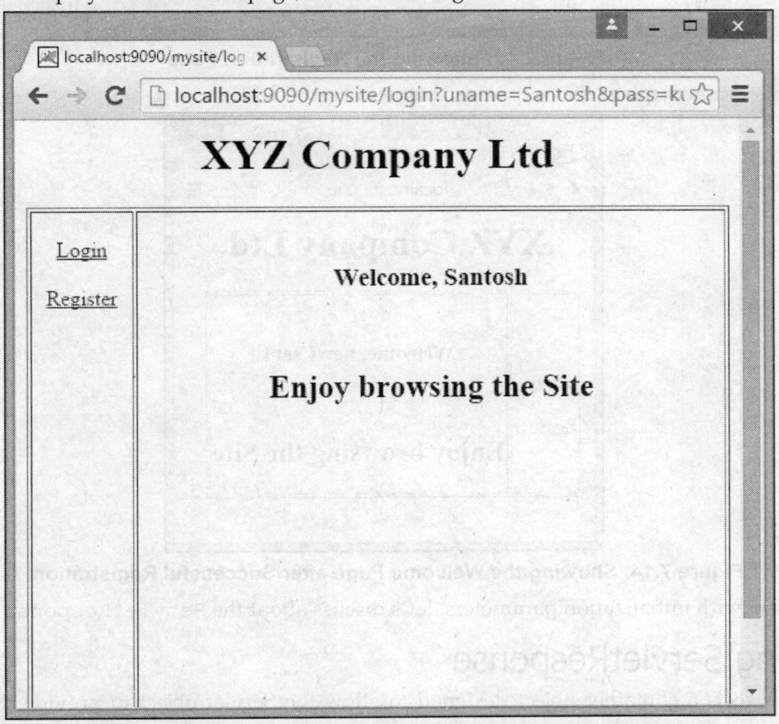

Figure 7.12: Showing the Welcome Page after Successful Login

If you are a new user then you have to click the Register link to display the registration page. Now, enter your details in the registration page and click the Register button, as shown in Figure 7.13:

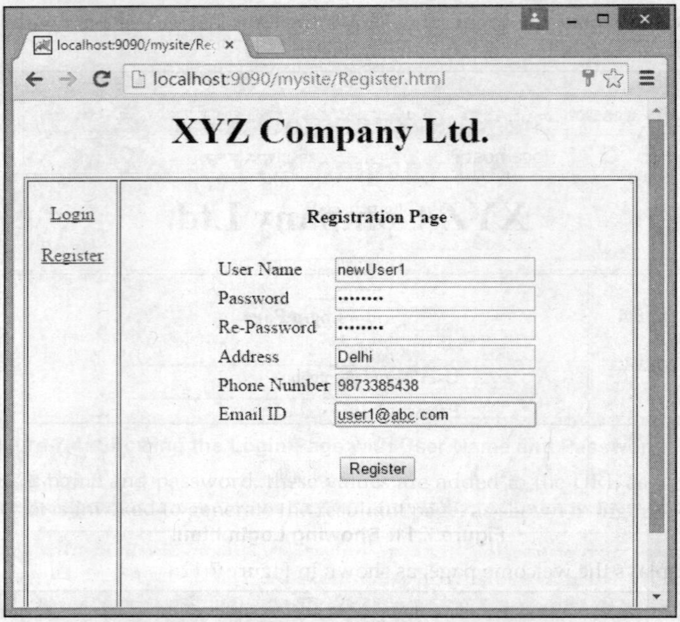

Figure 7.13: Showing the Registration Page

A successful registration displays the output, as shown in Figure 7.14:

Figure 7.14: Showing the Welcome Page after Successful Registration

After familiarizing with initialization parameters, let's discuss about the `ServletResponse` object.

Understanding ServletResponse

`ServletResponse` is a container object designed to allow the Servlet object to provide the details about the response to the client. This implies that the `ServletResponse` object (a part of Servlet container) is designed to listen events from the Servlet object with respect to response to be sent to a client. The `ServletResponse` interface of Java Servlet API is designed to describe the `ServletResponse` object.

The `ServletResponse` object is managed by Servlet containers as a throwaway object or is maintained into a pool, similar to the `ServletRequest` object.

The following methods are supported by the `ServletResponse` object:

- **`void setContentType(String mime)`** — Sets the content type, optionally with encoding style of the response content. For example, `setContentType("text/html")` describes that the response content is a text content and of the .html extension.

NOTE

Invoking the `ServletResponse.setContentType()` method after starting the response content generation is not effective. This implies that you need to use the `ServletResponse.setContentType()` method before accessing `ServletResponse.getWriter()` or `ServletResponse.getOutputStream()` and generate response content.

- **`PrintWriter getWriter()`** — Returns a `PrintWriter` object that allows the Servlet object to write the response content to a client.
- **`ServletOutputStream getOutputStream()`** — Returns a `ServletOutputStream` object that allows the Servlet object to write binary content as a response to a client.

NOTE

You can invoke either the `getWriter()` or `getOutputStream()` method on the `ServletResponse` object (i.e., in a request). In addition, the response stream will be closed in the following situations:

- *Calling the `close()` method explicitly using the response stream object (i.e., `ServletOutputStream`, or `PrintWriter` obtained using `ServletResponse.getWriter()`)*
- *Executing the `RequestDispatcher.forward()` method successfully*
- *Executing the `HttpServletResponse.sendError()` method successfully*
- *Executing the `HttpServletResponse.sendRedirect()` method successfully*

- **`void setBufferSize(int)`** — Sets the specified buffer size for the response content. The servlet container uses a buffer at least as large as the size requested. You can use the `ServletResponse.getBufferSize()` method to find the actual buffer size. Increasing the buffer size allows more response content to be written before it is actually sent to a client. Therefore, provides more time the Servlet object to set appropriate status codes and headers. However, a smaller buffer decreases server memory load and allows the client to start receiving data more quickly.

NOTE

The `void setBufferSize(int)` method must be used before writing any response body content; if content has been written or the response object has been committed, this method throws an `IllegalStateException`.

- **`int getBufferSize()`** — Returns the actual buffer size used for the response. If no buffering is used, this method returns 0.
- **`void flushBuffer()`** — Writes any content in the buffer to the client. A call to this method automatically commits the response, meaning the status code and headers will be written.

NOTE

The response status code and headers are written to the client when the response buffer is committed (flushed) for the first time.

- **`void resetBuffer()`** — Clears the content of the buffer in the response without clearing headers or status code. If the response has been committed, this method throws an `IllegalStateException`.
- **`void reset()`** — Clears the content of the buffer in the response as well as the headers or status code. If the response has been committed, this method throws an `IllegalStateException`.
- **`boolean isCommited()`** — Specifies whether or not the response has been committed, true specifies that the response has been committed.

You have learned about the `ServletRequest` and `ServletResponse` objects that helps the Servlet object in processing the incoming request and generating the response content. However, for various reasons, such as reusability, you want to distribute the request processing and response generation to multiple Servlet objects.

In this context, you need to dispatch the request from one Servlet to another. The next section explains you the concept of request dispatching.

Understanding Request Dispatching

While developing complex web applications, you generally need to distribute the request processing and response generation to multiple Servlet objects. In this case, you need to dispatch requests from one component to another. This is required in the following cases:

- If you want to reuse any part of the request processing or response generation logic. For example, in our **mysite** application, we have created `LoginServlet` and `RegistrationServlet` Servlets for the successful login and registration process. Instead of rewriting the code for both the Servlets, you can create a new Servlet and include it in both the Servlets during the response time.
- If you want to separate the responsibilities of request processing and response generation.
- If your request comes out with multiple outcomes after processing, such as in case of a login request a user can be valid or invalid. After a user is identified as valid, you may want to present different views based on the user type (such as admin). However, defining all the logic into a single component increases the complexity of the component. Therefore, to reduce this complexity, you can divide the functionalities and implement them in parts (that is, into multiple components) and then integrate them so that they work together. This requires interaction or dispatching functionality among the components.

To meet these requirements, the Servlet container provides support to dispatch requests from one Servlet to another Servlet within the context. The Servlet container implements the navigation and delegation logic for request dispatching, as shown in Figure 7.15:

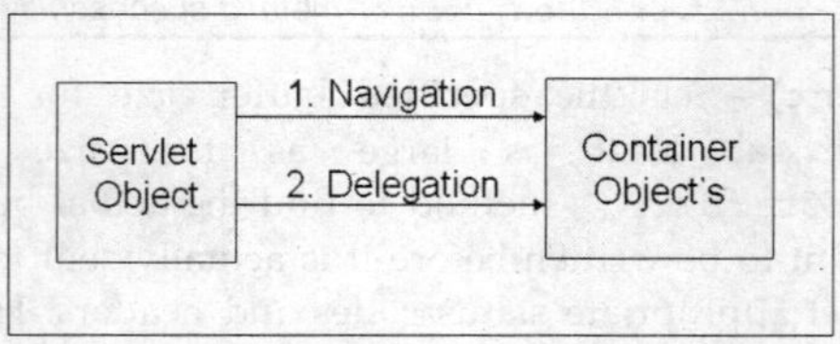

Figure 7.15: Showing the Servlet Object Accessing Container for Request Dispatching

In Figure 7.15, the Servlet object uses the container objects for accessing the navigation and delegation logics implemented by the Servlet container to dispatch the request. The navigation logic includes locating the web resource to which you want to delegate the request. The delegation logic includes passing on the request to the resource located in the navigation process. Let's understand these two processes in details.

Navigation

The Servlet container supports two approaches for navigating to the web resource to dispatch the request. The first approach is the URL Path and the other is the Servlet name, as shown in Figure 7.16:

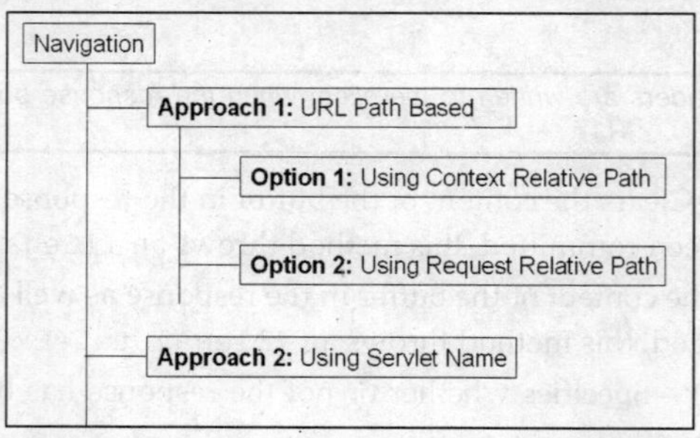

Figure 7.16: Showing the Navigation Approaches

The Java Servlet API includes standard abstraction for accessing both the approaches of navigation supported by the Servlet container. The `ServletContext.getRequestDispatcher()` and `ServletRequest.get`

RequestDispatcher() methods access Approach 1, and ServletContext.getNamedDispatcher() method accesses Approach 2 of the navigation process implemented by the container. In case of navigating to the Web resource using URL Path, you have an option to specify the path relative to context or request URI. The ServletContext.getRequestDispatcher(String) method supports the context relative path option. The ServletRequest.getRequestDispatcher(String) method supports both context and request relative path options. In other words, if the input path starts with the / character then it is considered as context relative path; otherwise, it is considered as request relative path, to navigate to the web resource. A successful execution of this process results to produce a RequestDispatcher object, which is implemented to delegate the request to the navigated resource.

Delegation

The Servlet container supports two styles of delegation, include and forward, as shown in Figure 7.17:

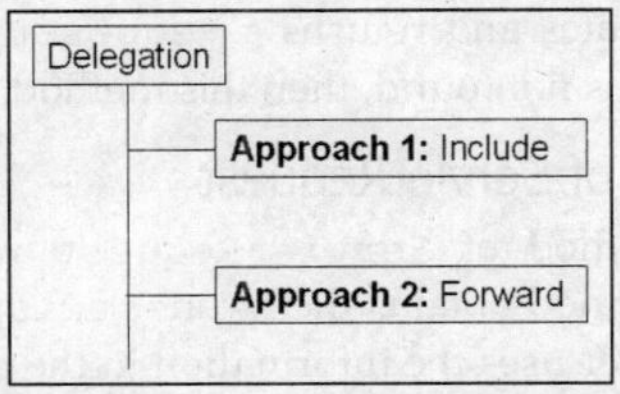

Figure 7.17: Showing Two Approaches of Request Delegation

The javax.servlet.RequestDispatcher interface of Java Servlet API provides an abstraction to access the delegation logic implemented by the Servlet container to dispatch the request from a Web component to other Web resource in the context. You can use the RequestDispatcher.include() or RequestDispatcher.forward() methods to delegate the request from a Servlet to Web resource navigated to get the RequestDispatcher object. The signatures of these methods are as follows:

- void include(ServletRequest, ServletResponse)
- void forward(ServletRequest, ServletResponse)

After understanding the request dispatching, let's learn how to use RequestDispatcher to dispatch the request.

Dispatching the Request

You can dispatch the request from Servlet or Java Server Pages (JSP) to a Web resource in the context using RequestDispatcher by performing the following tasks:

- Getting a RequestDispatcher object
- Using the include() or forward() method of RequestDispatcher

Getting a RequestDispatcher object

As discussed, a RequestDispatcher object is implemented by a Servlet container to delegate the request to a Web resource, such as a Servlet, HTML page, and JSP page. The RequestDispatcher object can be obtained by using the following methods:

- The getRequestDispatcher() method of ServletContext
- The getNamedDispatcher() method of ServletContext
- The getRequestDispatcher() method of ServletRequest

The getRequestDispatcher() Method of ServletContext

The getRequestDispatcher() method of ServletContext takes a String argument describing the path to locate the resource to which the request is to be dispatched. When this method is called, the container locates the resource with the given path (where the path should start with the / character). If the given path does not start with the / character, the ServletContext.getRequestDispatcher() method throws IllegalArgument Exception.

If the `getRequestDispatcher()` method locates a dynamic Web resource, such as Servlet or JSP, it creates and returns a `RequestDispatcher` object that wraps the resource object, that is, the Servlet object. If the `getRequestDispatcher()` method locates a static Web resource, such as Hyper Text Markup Language (HTML) page or Joint Photographic Experts Group (JPEG) image, it creates and returns a `RequestDispatcher` object that encapsulates the path locating the resource. If the resource cannot be located by using the path, it creates a `RequestDispatcher` object to add the message. If the requested resource (<path>) is not available, in the output, and returns the resultant object.

The getNamedDispatcher() Method of ServletContext

The `getNamedDispatcher()` method of `ServletContext` takes a `String` argument describing the Servlet name used to locate the Servlet to which the request is to be dispatched. When this method is called, the container locates the Servlet with the given name in the context.

If the specified Servlet is found, it creates and returns a `RequestDispatcher` object that wraps the located `Servlet` object. If the required Servlet is not found, then this method returns null.

The getRequestDispatcher() Method of ServletRequest

The `getRequestDispatcher()` method of `ServletRequest` works as the `getRequestDispatcher()` method of `ServletContext`. This method obtains the `RequestDispatcher` object using the paths relative to the current request. The Servlet container uses the information in the request object to build a complete path and locates the resource using the path, as provided in the `getRequestDispatcher()` method of `ServletContext`. The path to this method can also be relative to the context. For example, if the given path starts with the / character, then, the path is considered as the context relative path; else the request relative path.

Let's consider an example to demonstrate the use of the `getRequestDispatcher()` method in different cases. Consider Table 7.1 for configurations under the context path, `/myctxt` and URL for accessing the Servlet:

Table 7.1: Configurations of Servlets

Servlet Name	URL	URL Pattern
Ser1	http://localhost:9090/myctxt/myser	/myser1
Ser2	http://localhost:9090/myctxt/myser12	/myser2
Ser3	http://localhost:9090/myctxt/myservlets/myser3	/myservlets/myser3
Ser4	http://localhost:9090/myctxt/myservlets/myser4	/myservlets/myser4

Now, to forward the request from the `Ser1` Servlet to the `Ser4` Servlet, you can call the `getRequestDispatcher()` method using the following commands:

```
ctxt.getRequestDispatcher("/myservlets/myser4");
```

or

```
request.getRequestDispatcher("myservlets/myser4");
```

NOTE

Using the `ServletRequest.getRequestDispatcher()` method, the resource can be located even if the path starts with the / character.

You can forward a request from the `Ser4` Servlet to the `Ser1` Servlet, for the same paths by calling the `getRequestDispatcher()` method using one of the following commands:

```
ctxt.getRequestDispatcher("/myser1");
```

or

```
request.getRequestDispatcher("/myser1")
```

However, `request.getRequestDispatcher("myser1")` will not locate the `Ser1` Servlet because the original path used to invoke `Ser4` is `/myctxt/myservlets/myser4`.

Moreover, when you use the `getRequestDispatcher()` method of `ServletRequest` and the path specified in the method does not start with the / character, then the relative path is considered as the current path request. In such a case, the path is resolved to:

```
/myctxt/myservlets/myser1
```

This path does not locate `Ser1` as `Ser1` is configured to support the request with a URL path `/myser1`, and not with a URL path `/myservlets/myser1`.

Let's now compare the `getRequestDispatcher()` methods of `ServletContext` and `ServletRequest`.

Comparing the getRequestDispatcher() Methods of ServletContext and ServletRequest

The only difference between the `getRequestDispatcher()` methods of `ServletContext` and `ServletRequest` is that in case of the `getRequestDispatcher()` method of `ServletContext`, you can locate the resource relative to the context path; whereas, in case of the `getRequestDispatcher()` method of `ServletRequest`, you can also locate the resource by using the path relative to current request path.

Comparing the getRequestDispatcher() and getNamedDispatcher() Methods

The differences between the `getRequestDispatcher()` and `getNamedDispatcher()` methods of `ServletContext` are as follows:

- **With respect to navigation**—Allows you to use the `getRequestDispatcher()` method to navigate to any Web resource in the context, static or dynamic; whereas, the `getNamedDispatcher()` method can navigate only to dynamic Web pages configured in a Web deployment descriptor file. The `getNamedDispatcher()` method navigates the resource by using the component name instead of path.
- **With respect to delegation**—Does not manipulate the path elements while delegating the request in case of using `getNamedDispatcher()` for navigating to the resource to dispatch the request. This implies while delegating the request by using the `include()` method, then the included path elements are set to the request attributes, without changing the path elements in this request object. When forwarding the request, the request path elements are changed to forward path details, and with the evolution of Servlet 2.4, the request adds the original request path elements to the request attributes. This operation is performed at delegation time if the `RequestDispatcher` object is obtained using `getRequestDispatcher()`, but not if it is obtained using the `getNamedDispatcher()` method.

Understanding the include() and forward() Methods of RequestDispatcher

The `RequestDispatcher` object can be used to include the response of another Servlet by calling the `include()` method, or forward the request to another Servlet by calling the `forward()` method. Let's briefly discuss these methods.

Describing the include() Method

The `include()` method of the `RequestDispatcher` object includes the response of another Servlet into the calling Servlet. You can invoke this method any time from the calling Servlet while servicing the request.

The include() method of RequestDispatcher performs the following tasks:

1. Sets the request attributes, such as `javax.servlet.include.request_uri`, `javax.servlet.include.context_path`, `javax.servlet.include.servlet_path`, `javax.servlet.include.path_info`, `javax.servlet.include.query_string`, to make the included Servlet accessible with its path information. The path element methods, such as `ServletRequest.getRequestURI()`, `ServletRequest.getServletPath()`, and `ServletRequest.getPathInfo()` of this request object describe the original request path elements. Therefore, the included servlet can access the original path elements from the request objects path element methods, and the included resource path elements (i.e., itself) from the request attributes.

NOTE

This task is not performed if the `RequestDispatcher` object used is obtained through the `getNamedDispatcher()` method.

2. If the navigated resource represented by the `RequestDispatcher` object is a dynamic Web page, i.e., Servlet or JSP, it invokes the `service()` method of the target Servlet by passing the request and response objects as arguments to this method. If the navigated resource is a static Web page, it reads the content of the file and writes it to the current request's response stream.
3. Return to the including servlet.

Figure 7.18 explains various operations performed while using the include() method:

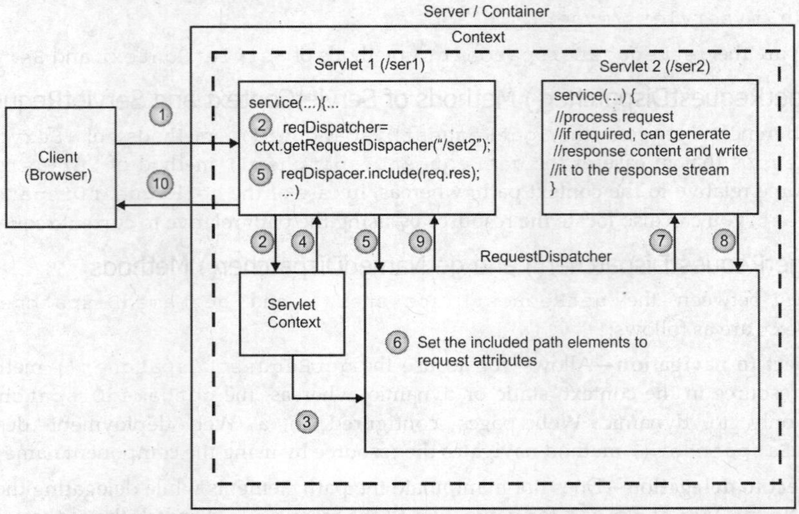

Figure 7.18: Displaying the Flow of Control Using the include() Method

The numbers, shown in Figure 7.18, represent the following operations:

1. Client requesting for Servlet 1 resources
2. Servlet 1 requesting `ServletContext` for navigating to the resource to dispatch the request. This can be done using `getRequestDispatcher()` or `getNamedDispatcher()` methods. This results in getting the `RequestDispatcher` object, which is further used to delegate the request. In Figure 7.18, the request to context is done to navigate to Servlet 2 (`/ser2`); `ctxt.getRequestDispatcher("/ser2")`.
3. `ServletContext` using the container objects navigates to the specified Web resource. In this case, it is Servlet2 which is located using the `/ser2` path. If it navigates to the resource successfully, it creates a RequestDispatcher object that wraps located resource.
4. `ServletContext` returns the `RequestDispatcher` object to Servlet 1.
5. Servlet 1 invokes the `include()` method on the `RequestDispatcher` object.
6. The `RequestDispatcher` object sets the included path elements to the request attributes, so that the included servlet can access the included path elements. Note that the request object describing the original path elements are not modified.
7. `RequestDispatcher` invokes the `service()` method of Servlet 2 passing the request and response objects that are sent as arguments for this method.
8. The Servlet 2 `service()` method returns to `RequestDispatcher`, after it completes processing the request.
9. The `RequestDispatcher include()` method returns to Servlet 1.
10. The Servlet 1 `service()` method returns the response and completes the request processing.

Limitations of the include() Method

The `include()` method has the following limitations with respect to the response object:

- The included servlet can write the response content but it should write the response data to the response stream earlier accessed by the including servlet, that is, either `ServletOutputStream` or `PrintWriter`. You can use the response object to access either the binary or character stream to write the response content. Moreover, the response content written by the included resource is added to the end of the existing content in the response buffer.
- The included resource cannot set the response headers. If it tries to do this, then those invocations are ignored.

Describing the forward() Method

The `forward()` method of `RequestDispatcher` forwards requests to the navigated resource, such as Servlet (the target Servlet) and this method can be invoked by the Servlet while servicing the request when no output has been committed.

The `forward()` method of `RequestDispatcher` performs the following tasks:

- Checks whether the source servlet has obtained the response stream and output data exists in the response buffer. If the response buffer is not committed, the content is cleared. However, if the response buffer is already committed, it throws `IllegalStateException`. In other words, after committing the response data, you cannot forward the request.
- Changes the path elements of the request object to the forward path elements, that is, the path used to navigate to the target resource (obtain the `RequestDispatcher` object); therefore, making the target Servlet accessible with the forward path information.

NOTE

This task is not performed if the `RequestDispatcher` object is obtained through the `getNamedDispatcher()` method. In such a case, the target Servlet can get only the original request path information.

In Servlet 2.4, this method adds the original request path information to the request attributes, such as `javax.servlet.forward.request_uri`, `javax.servlet.forward.context_path`, `javax.servlet.forward.servlet_path`, `javax.servlet.forward.path_info`, `javax.servlet.forward.query_string`, to make the forwarded Servlet accessible with original path information.

- Invokes the `service()` method, if the navigated resource represented by the `RequestDispatcher` object is a dynamic Web page , that is, Servlet or JSP. The `service()` method of the target Servlet is invoked by passing the request and response objects as arguments to this method. If the navigated resource is a static Web page, it reads the content of the file and writes it to the current response stream.
- Commits the response content. It implies that after invoking the `forward()` method, the source Servlet cannot add any response content.
- Returns the control of an application to the source Servlet.

Figure 7.19 explains the various operations performed while using the `RequestDispatcher forward()` method:

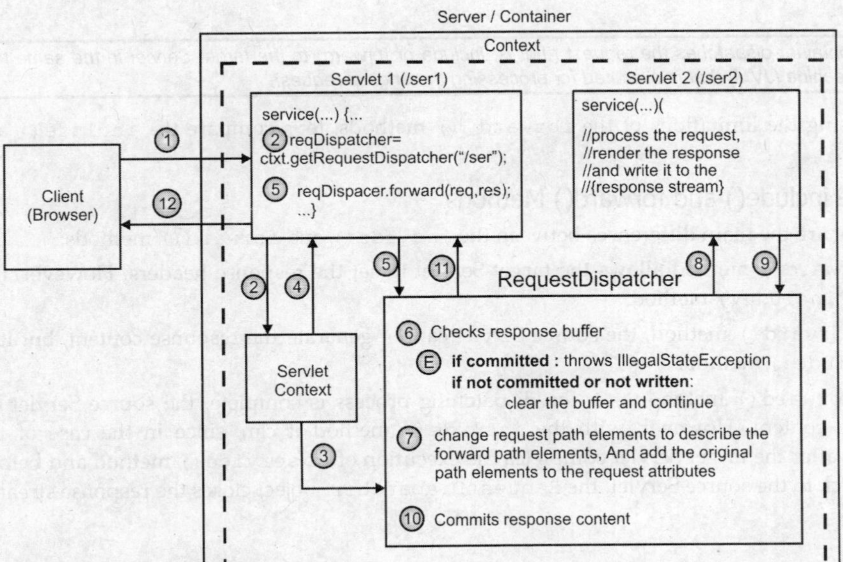

Figure 7.19: Showing Flow of Control Using the forward() Method

The numbers specified in Figure 7.19 represent the operations, which are as follows:

1. Client requesting for Servlet 1 resources.
2. Servlet 1 requesting `ServletContext` for navigating to the resource to dispatch the request. This can be done using `getRequestDispatcher()` or `getNamedDispatcher()` methods. This results in getting the RequestDispatcher object, which is used further to delegate the request. In Figure 7.19 the request to context is done to navigate to Servlet 2 (`/ser2`); `ctxt.getRequestDispatcher` ("`/ser2`").
3. `ServletContext` creates a `RequestDispatcher` object that wraps Servlet 2 instance.
4. `ServletContext` returns `RequestDispatcher` object to Servlet 1.
5. Servlet 1 invoking `forward()` method on `RequestDispatcher` object.
6. Checks whether the output data exist in the response buffer.
   a. If the data exist in the response buffer and if it is committed then throw `IllegalStateException`. That is, once the response data is committed we cannot forward the request to another Servlet.
   b. If the data exist in the response buffer that is not committed then the content is cleared.
7. `RequestDispatcher` object changes the request path elements to describe the forward path elements. And adds the original path elements to the request attributes.
8. Thereafter the `RequestDispatcher` object invokes the `service()` method of Servlet 2 passing the request and response objects that are sent as an arguments for this method.
9. After processing the request includes rendering the response the Servlet 2 `service()` method returns to `RequestDispatcher`.
10. `RequestDispatcher` commits the response and closes the response stream, so that further we cannot add any content to response.
11. `RequestDispatcher forward()` method returns to Servlet 1.
12. Servlet 1 `service()` method returns the response which completes the request processing.

Limitations of the forward() Method

When you use the `forward ()` method, the target Servlet has access to all parts of the request and response objects. However, the source Servlet is limited with respect to the response object in which it cannot generate any response before forwarding the request and after completing the forward operation.

NOTE

The Servlet container dispatches the request (that is, include or forward) to the target Servlet in the same thread of the same Java Virtual Machine (JVM) that is allocated for processing the original request.

After discussing the limitations of the `forward ()` methods, let's compare the `include()` and `forward()` methods.

Comparing the include() and forward() Methods

The following are the main differences between the `include()` and `forward()` methods:

- The `forward()` method allows the target Servlet to set the response headers. However, it cannot do this with the `include()` method.
- In the `forward()` method, the source Servlet cannot generate the response content, but it can do so with the `include()` method.
- In the `forward()` method, after the dispatching process is complete, the source Servlet cannot add any response content. However, with the `include()` method it can, since in the case of the `forward()` method, after the target Servlet completes the execution of its `service()` method and before the control is given back to the source Servlet, the `RequestDispatcher` object closes the response stream.

NOTE

With both the `include()` and `forward()` methods, the control comes back to the source Servlet after the target Servlet's service method execution has been completed. However, in the case of the forward method, before the control comes to the source Servlet, the response is already committed and ended (that is, you cannot add any more content into the response).

After understanding the difference between the `include()` and `forward()` methods, let's now discuss the conditions in which you can use the `include()` and `forward()` methods.

Considering the Situations to use the include() and forward() Methods

You can use the `include()` and `forward()` methods in the following conditions:

- If you want the target Servlet to be responsible for generating the response completely, then you should use the `forward()` method.
- If you want to partially generate the response in the source Servlet, then you should use the `include()` method.

Let's now consider an example that can demonstrate how to use `RequestDispatcher` to access the navigation and delegation logics of the Servlet container.

Working with RequestDispatcher

Let's create the **reqdisp** application to demonstrate the basic steps to dispatch a request. The application also demonstrates the difference between the `getRequestDispatcher()` methods of `ServletContext` and `ServletRequest` (You can also find this application online in the code/Chapter7 folder). You need to perform the following broad-level steps to create this application:

- Create the Home.html file
- Create the `TestServlet1` Servlet
- Create the `TestServlet2` Servlet
- Create the deployment descriptor file
- Run the application

Let's start by creating the entry point for the application, which is the Home.html page.

Creating the Home.html File

The Home.html page is the home page of the application. The page displays a text box with a button. The text box prompts a user to enter a path to which the request would be forwarded. The source code for the Home.html file is given in Listing 7.15 (you can find this file online in the code/Chapter7/reqdisp folder):

Listing 7.15: Creating the Home.html File

```
<html><body><center><br><br>
<b>This is an example to demonstrate the difference between <br/>
the various methods of getting RequestDispatcher object</b>
   <form action="test/ser1"><br><br>
          <table>
                 <tr>
                        <th>Path : </th>
                        <td><input type="text" name="path"/></td>
                 </tr>
                 <tr><td colspan="2"> </td></tr>
                 <tr>
                        <td colspan="2" align="center">
                        <input type="submit" value="Invoke TestServlet1"/>
                        </td>
                 </tr>
          </table>
   </form>
</center></body></html>
```

After creating the home page of the `reqdisp` application, let's create the `TestServlet1` Servlet to which the request of the user would be forwarded.

Creating the TestServlet1 Servlet

When a user enters the path in the Path text field and clicks the Invoke TestServlet1 button from Home.html, the `TestServlet1` Servlet is invoked and the value of the path is used to forward the request to `TestServlet2` through the `RequestDispatcher` object. The source code of the TestServlet1.java file is shown in Listing 7.16 (you can also find this file online in the code/Chapter7/reqdisp folder):

Listing 7.16: Creating the TestServlet1.java File

```
package com.santosh.servlets;
import javax.servlet.*;
import java.io.*;
import java.sql.*;

/**
* @author Santosh
*/
public class TestServlet1 extends GenericServlet {

   public void service(ServletRequest req, ServletResponse res)
   throws ServletException, IOException {

         String path=req.getParameter("path");

         res.setContentType("text/html");
         PrintWriter out=res.getWriter();

         out.println("<html><body>");
         out.println(
         "<b>Output Results for the path : <i>"+path+"</i></b>");
         out.println("<br/><br/>");
         out.println("<table border='1' width='100%'><tr>");
         out.println(
         "<th>Method used to get RequestDispatcher object</th>");
         out.println("<th>Result of invoking the respective method using the given
         path</th></tr>");
         out.println("<tr>");

         try {
                out.println("<td>servletcontext.getRequestDispatcher
                (\"<b>"+path+"</b>\")</td>");

                RequestDispatcher rd=
                getServletContext().getRequestDispatcher(path);

                out.println("<td>");
                rd.include(req,res);
                out.println("</td>");
         }//try
         catch(Exception e){
                e.printStackTrace();
                out.println("<td><b>Exception :</b><br/>    ");
                out.println("The given path is invalid, since it does not start with
                <b>/</b>");
                out.println("</td>");
         }//catch

         out.println("</tr>");
         out.println("<td>servletrequest.getRequestDispatcher
         (\"<b>"+path+"</b>\")</td>");

         RequestDispatcher rd=req.getRequestDispatcher(path);
         out.println("<td>");
         rd.include(req,res);
         out.println("</td></tr>");
```

```
        RequestDispatcher rd1=
        getServletContext().getNamedDispatcher(path);

        out.println("<td>servletcontext.getNamedDispatcher
        (\"<b>"+path+"</b>\")</td>");

        if (rd1==null)
        out.println("<td>Cannot locate the resource, returned <i>null</i></td>");
        else{
        out.println("<td><b>Located the resource, response
        :</b><br/>    ");
                rd.include(req,res);
                out.println("</td>");
        }//else

        out.println("</table><br/><br/><br/>");
        out.println("<a href='../Home.html'>Go back to test with different path</a>");
        out.println("</body></html>");
   }//service
}//class
```

After creating the `TestServlet1` Servlet, let's create the `TestServlet2` Servlet to which the value is passed with the help of the `RequestDispatcher` object.

Creating the TestServlet2 Servlet

The `TestServlet2` Servlet accepts requests from the `TestServlet1` Servlet, and also includes the additional text, response from `TestServlet2`, into the result. The source code of the TestServlet2.java file is shown in Listing 7.17 (you can also find this file online in the code/Chapter7/reqdisp folder):

Listing 7.17: Creating the TestServlet2.java File

```
package com.santosh.servlets;

import javax.servlet.*;
import java.io.*;
import java.sql.*;

/**
* @author Santosh
*/
public class TestServlet2 extends GenericServlet {

  public void service(ServletRequest req, ServletResponse res)
  throws ServletException, IOException {

        PrintWriter out=res.getWriter();
        out.println("Response from TestServlet2");
  }//service
}//class
```

After creating the required Servlets, let's create the web.xml file to map these Servlets.

Creating the Deployment Descriptor File

The final step in completing our application requires the creation of the deployment descriptor file (`web.xml`), as shown in Listing 7.18 (you can also find this file online in the code/Chapter7/ reqdisp/WEB-INF folder):

Listing 7.18: Creating the `web.xml` File

```
<?xml version="1.0"?>
<web-app>
  <servlet>
        <servlet-name>ts1</servlet-name>
        <servlet-class>com.santosh.servlets.TestServlet1</servlet-class>
  </servlet>
  <servlet>
        <servlet-name>ts2</servlet-name>
        <servlet-class>com.santosh.servlets.TestServlet2</servlet-class>
  </servlet>
```

```
    <servlet-mapping>
          <servlet-name>ts1</servlet-name>
          <url-pattern>/test/ser1</url-pattern>
    </servlet-mapping>
    <servlet-mapping>
          <servlet-name>ts2</servlet-name>
          <url-pattern>/ser2</url-pattern>
    </servlet-mapping>

    <welcome-file-list>
    <welcome-file>Home.html</welcome-file>
    </welcome-file-list>
  </web-app>
```

After creating all the files, arrange them in a directory structure, as shown in Figure 7.20:

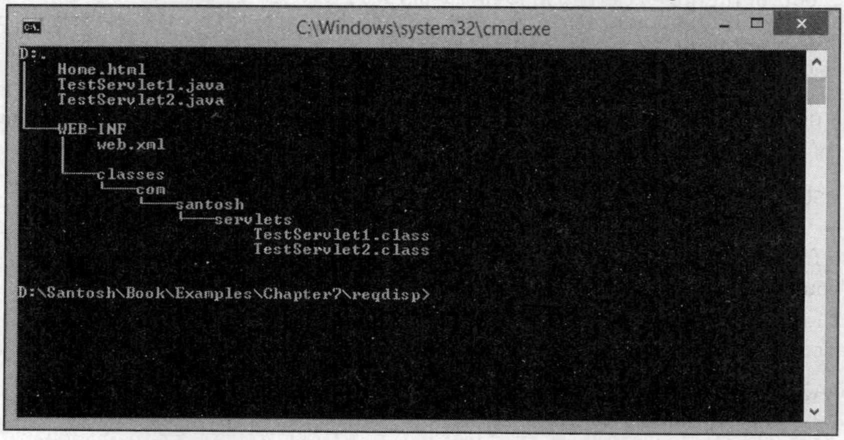

Figure 7.20: Showing the Directory Structure for the reqdisp Application

After arranging the files, copy the reqdisp folder into the `<Tomcat home>\webapps` folder.

Running the Application

Now, start the Tomcat server. We are using port number 9090 because Tomcat is running on this port in our computer. To run the `reqdisp` application, type the following URL:

```
http://localhost:9090/reqdisp
```

The home page of the **reqdisp** application appears, as shown in Figure 7.21:

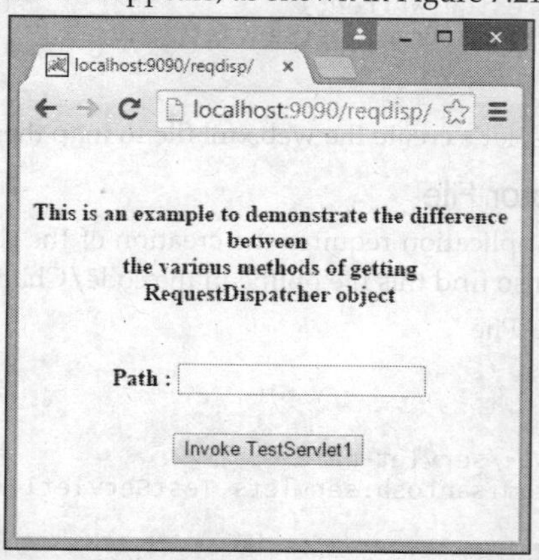

Figure 7.21: Showing the output of Home.html

When a user enters `/ser2` in the Path text field and clicks the Invoke TestServlet1 button, `TestServlet2` is invoked and the result is displayed, including the content of the `TestServlet1` Servlet, as shown in Figure 7.22:

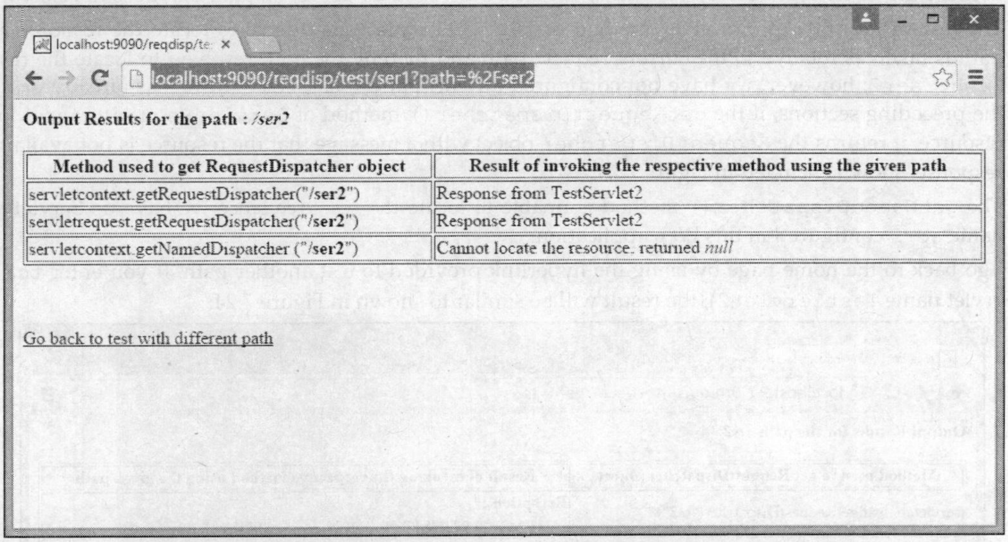

Figure 7.22: Showing the Result after Getting the Response from /ser2

The `getRequestDispatcher()` methods of `ServletContext` and `ServletRequest` locate `TestServlet2` (we have configured the url-pattern as `/ser2` in `web.xml`), but the `getNamedDispatcher()` method is unable to locate `TestServlet2` and returns null since we have no Servlet with the `/ser2` name configured in this Web application.

To go back to the home page, click the hyperlink provided to test a different path; if `ser2` (observe that in the previous case, we had started the path with /) is entered in the Path text field, the result will be similar to the one shown in Figure 7.23:

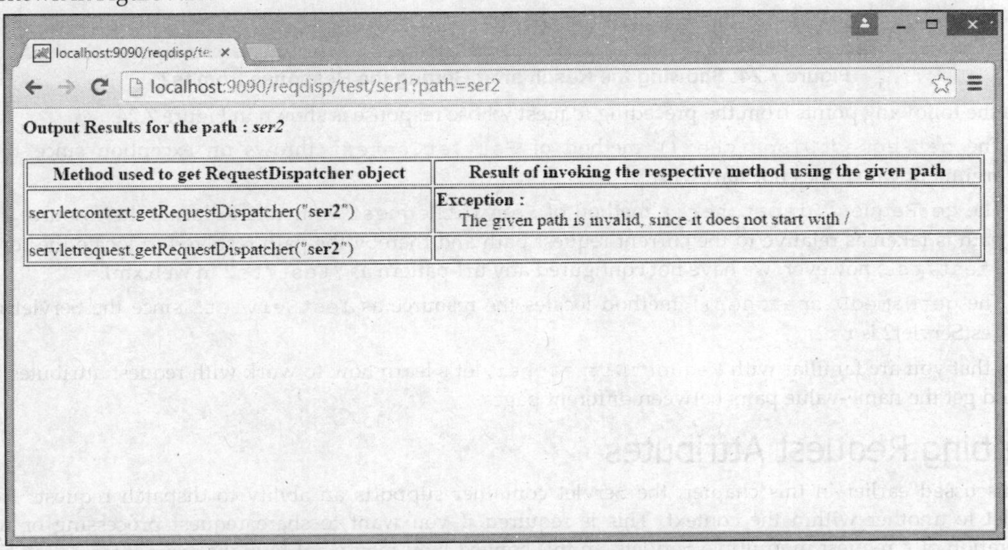

Figure 7.23: Showing the Result after Getting the Response from ser2

Note the following points from the preceding request whose response is shown in Figure 7.23:

- The `getRequestDispatcher()` method of `ServletContext` throws `IllegalArgumentException` because the `getRequestDispatcher()` method is invoked by passing a path that does not start with /.
- The `getRequestDispatcher()` method of `ServletRequest` is unable to locate the resource since the path is taken as relative to the current request path and thereby the path resolved to locate the resource is `/test/ser2`; however, we have not configured any url-pattern as `/test/ser2`. As already described in the preceding sections, if the `getRequestDispatcher()` method of `ServletRequest` cannot locate the resource, it returns the `RequestDispatcher` object with a message that the resource is not available to the response, shown encircled in Figure 7.23.
- The `getNamedDispatcher()` method is unable to locate the resource since we have no Servlet with the name `ser2` configured in this Web application.

Now, go back to the home page by using the hyperlink provided to test another path. If you enter **`ts2`** (that is, the Servlet name `TestServlet2`), the result will be similar to shown in Figure 7.24:

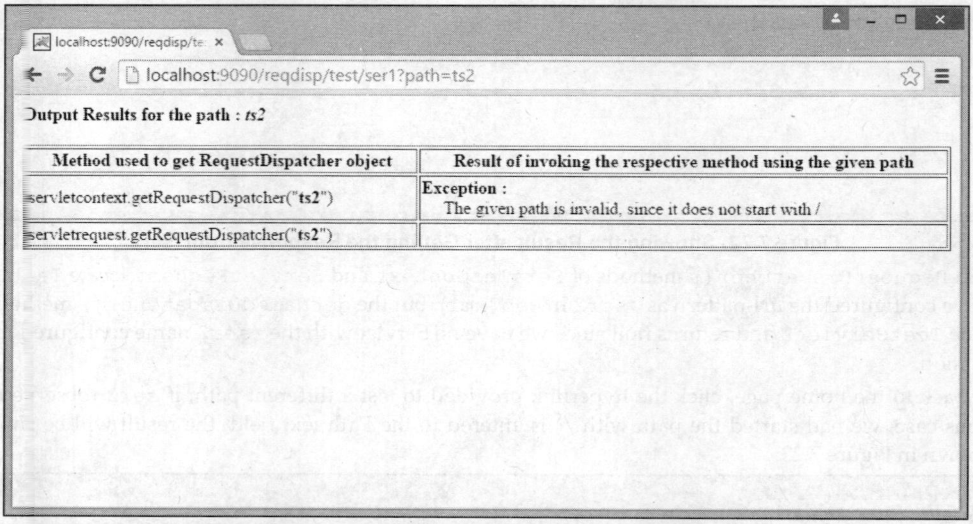

Figure 7.24: Showing the Result after Getting the Response from ts2

Note the following points from the preceding request whose response is shown in Figure 7.24:

- The `getRequestDispatcher()` method of `ServletContext` throws an exception since the given argument value does not start with /.
- The `getRequestDispatcher()` method of `ServletRequest` is unable to locate the resource since the path is taken as relative to the current request path and thereby the path resolved to locate the resource is `/test/ts2`; however, we have not configured any url-pattern as `/test/ts2` in web.xml.
- The `getNamedDispatcher()` method locates the resource as `TestServlet2` since the Servlet name of TestServlet2 is `ts2`.

Now, that you are familiar with `RequestDispatcher`, let's learn how to work with request attributes, used to set and get the name-value pairs between different pages.

Describing Request Attributes

As discussed earlier in this chapter, the Servlet container supports an ability to dispatch requests from one Servlet to another within the context. This is required if you want to share request processing or response generation of a request in multiple Servlets. In this context, you may want to make some information available from the source Servlet to the target Servlet or vice-versa. The `ServletRequest` object manages the data within the request scope to meet this requirement. The `javax.servlet.ServletRequest` interface that provides an abstraction to access the `ServletRequest` object implemented by the Servlet container includes methods to set and get name-value pairs into the request scope. Such name-value pairs are known as request attributes.

Request attributes consist of name-value pair, where the value can be any object and the name is a `String` representing the object and it should be unique. Request attributes are used by Servlet when communicating with other Servlets or JSP by using the `RequestDispatcher` object.

Attributes can be set and accessed by using the following methods of the `ServletRequest` interface:

- **`void setAttribute(String, Object)`** – Sets an attribute with the current request. If the given String name is already bonded with an object, it is replaced by the new object. If the given value is null, this method performs the same function as that performed by the `removeAttribute()` method.
- **`Object getAttribute(String)`** – Returns the value of an attribute located with the given name or returns null value if an attribute with the given name is not found.
- **`Enumeration getAttributeNames()`** – Returns all the attribute names in the current request as an `Enumeration` of String or returns empty `Enumeration`, if there are no attributes in the request.
- **`void removeAttribute(String)`** – Removes an attribute identified by the given name from the request.

NOTE

Request attributes are thread-safe since the scope of these attributes is request scope. Also, remember that one request is processed completely using only one thread.

Let's create an application in the next section to explain request attributes and illustrate how they are used.

Working with Request Attributes

As discussed, request attributes consist of the name and value used to communicate information from one Servlet to another. Let's create an application named **reqAttributes** to understand how to use request attributes. In this application, you learn how to set and get request attributes by using the `RequestDispatcher` `include()` and `forward()` methods and perform multiple actions by using one form. In addition, the application also helps you to understand how to implement the business logic of each of these actions into different Servlets

NOTE

This application is made simple by using simple business operations, such as addition and subtraction so that we can concentrate on the point this application is demonstrating. Apart from addition and subtraction, you may have different requirements, such as if you want a single employee form to perform various operations (insert and update), then you can use request attributes.

You need to perform the following steps to create this application:

- Create the `Home.html` file
- Create the `ValidationServlet` Servlet
- Create the `AddServlet` Servlet
- Create the `SubServlet` Servlet
- Create the deployment descriptor file
- Run the application

Let's start by creating the entry point for the application, which is the Home.html file.

Creating the Home.html File

The Home page contains two text fields used to add and subtract a number entered into these fields. The source code of the Home.html file is shown in Listing 7.19 (you can also find this file online in the code/Chapter7/reqAttributes folder):

Listing 7.19: Creating the Home.html File

```
<html><body>
```

```
    <form action="entry"><pre>
    <b>
        Operand 1 : <input type="text" name="op1"/>

        Operand 2 : <input type="text" name="op2"/>

        <input type="submit" name="action" value="Add"/> <input type="submit"
        name="action"
        value="Substract"/>
    </b></pre></form>
  </body></html>
```

After creating the Home.html file, let's create the `ValidationServlet` Servlet, which retrieves the values from the textboxes shown in the Home page.

Creating the ValidationServlet Servlet

The `ValidationServlet` Servlet gets the data from the text fields and if the data is not in a numeral format, it is sent back to Home.html. If the data is in a numeral format, it is stored through the `setAttribute()` method and the request is forwarded to the other Servlet where the computing is done based on the values entered in the text fields. The source code of the ValidationServlet.java file is shown in Listing 7.20 (you can also find this file online in the code/Chapter7/reqAttributes folder):

Listing 7.20: Creating the ValidationServlet.java File

```
package com.santosh.servlets;
import javax.servlet.*;
import java.io.*;
/**
* @author Santosh
*/
public class ValidationServlet extends GenericServlet {

   public void service (ServletRequest req, ServletResponse resp) throws ServletException,
   IOException {

        try {
                req.setAttribute("operand1",new Integer(req.getParameter("op1")));
                req.setAttribute("operand2",new Integer(req.getParameter("op2")));
        }//try
        catch(Exception e){
                resp.setContentType("text/html");
                PrintWriter out=resp.getWriter();
                out.println("Operand1 and Operand2 value should be numbers<br/>");
                RequestDispatcher rd=req.getRequestDispatcher("/Home.html");
                rd.include(req,resp);
                return;
        }//catch

        String action=req.getParameter("action");
        RequestDispatcher rd=null;

        if (action.equals("Add"))
                rd=req.getRequestDispatcher("/add");
        else
                rd=req.getRequestDispatcher("/sub");

        rd.forward(req,resp);
   }//service
}//class
```

After handling the request forwarded by the Home page, the addition or subtraction operation is performed. Therefore, let's create the `AddServlet` Servlet to add the values entered in the Home page.

Creating the AddServlet Servlet

The `AddServlet` Servlet receives two numbers from `ValidationServlet`, performs addition on the numbers, and forwards the request to the `ResponseServlet` Servlet based on the URL specified in the url-pattern of the `web.xml` file. The source code of the AddServlet.java file is shown in Listing 7.21 (you can also find this file online in the code/Chapter7/reqAttributes folder):

Listing 7.21: Creating the AddServlet.java File

```
package com.santosh.servlets;

import javax.servlet.*;
import java.io.*;
/**
* @author Santosh
*/
public class AddServlet extends GenericServlet {

   public void service (ServletRequest req, ServletResponse res)
   throws ServletException, IOException {

         int op1=((Integer)req.getAttribute("operand1")).intValue();
         int op2=((Integer)req.getAttribute("operand2")).intValue();

         int result=op1+op2;

         req.setAttribute("operation", "Addition");
         req.setAttribute("result", new Integer(result));

         RequestDispatcher rd=req.getRequestDispatcher("/resp");
         rd.forward(req,res);
   }//service
}//class
```

After performing the addition operation in the `AddServlet` Servlet, let's create the `SubServlet` Servlet for subtraction operation.

Creating the SubServlet Servlet

The `SubServlet` Servlet gets the numbers from `ValidationServlet`, performs the subtract function, and forwards the request to the `ResponseServlet` Servlet based on the URL specified in the url-pattern of the `web.xml` file. The source code of the AddServlet.java file is shown in Listing 7.22 (you can also find this file online in the code/Chapter7/reqAttributes folder):

Listing 7.22: Creating the SubServlet.java File

```
package com.santosh.servlets;

import javax.servlet.*;
import java.io.*;
/**
* @author Santosh
*/
public class SubServlet extends GenericServlet {

   public void service (ServletRequest req, ServletResponse res) throws ServletException,
   IOException {

         int op1=((Integer)req.getAttribute("operand1")).intValue();
         int op2=((Integer)req.getAttribute("operand2")).intValue();

         int result=op1-op2;

         req.setAttribute("operation", "Subtraction");
         req.setAttribute("result", new Integer(result));

         RequestDispatcher rd=req.getRequestDispatcher("/resp");
         rd.forward(req,res);
   }//service
}//class
```

As discussed previously, you need to create the `ResponseServlet` Servlet to display the output of the addition or subtraction operation.

Creating the ResponseServlet Servlet

The `ResponseServlet` Servlet gets the value to be added or subtracted from the AddServlet.java or the SebServlet.java file, respectively, and prints the result. After printing the result, it forwards the request to the Home.html file. The source code of the ResponseServlet.java file is shown in Listing 7.23 (you can also find this file online in the code/Chapter7/reqAttributes folder):

Listing 7.23: Creating the ResponseServlet.java File

```
package com.santosh.servlets;
import javax.servlet.*;
import java.io.*;
/**
* @author Santosh
*/
public class ResponseServlet extends GenericServlet {
   public void service (ServletRequest req, ServletResponse res)
   throws ServletException, IOException {

        Integer result=(Integer) req.getAttribute("result");

        RequestDispatcher rd=req.getRequestDispatcher("/Home.html");

        if (result==null){
                rd.forward(req,res);
                return;
                /*
                Here return is required since we know that after forward the control
                comes back to the source servlet, and here we do not want to execute the
                remaining part of this service if our request is forwarded
                */
        }//if

        res.setContentType("text/html");
        PrintWriter out=res.getWriter();

        String op=(String) req.getAttribute("operation");
        out.println(op+" Result : <b>"+result.intValue()+"</b><br/>");

        rd.include(req,res);
   }//service
}//class
```

After creating the required Servlets, let's create the `web.xml` file to map these Servlets.

Creating the Deployment Descriptor File

After developing all Servlets and HTML files, it's time to configure the **reqAttributes** application by using the deployment descriptor (the `web.xml` file). The source code of the `web.xml` file is shown in Listing 7.24 (you can also find this file online in the code/Chapter7/reqAttributes/WEB-INF folder):

Listing 7.24: Creating the `web.xml` File

```
<?xml version="1.0"?>
<web-app>
   <servlet>
        <servlet-name>es</servlet-name>
        <servlet-class>com.santosh.servlets.ValidationServlet</servlet-class>
   </servlet>
   <servlet>
        <servlet-name>as</servlet-name>
        <servlet-class>com.santosh.servlets.AddServlet</servlet-class>
   </servlet>
   <servlet>
```

```
        <servlet-name>ss</servlet-name>
        <servlet-class>com.santosh.servlets.SubServlet</servlet-class>
    </servlet>
    <servlet>
        <servlet-name>rs</servlet-name>
        <servlet-class>com.santosh.servlets.ResponseServlet</servlet-class>
    </servlet>

    <servlet-mapping>
        <servlet-name>es</servlet-name>
        <url-pattern>/entry</url-pattern>
    </servlet-mapping>
    <servlet-mapping>
        <servlet-name>as</servlet-name>
        <url-pattern>/add</url-pattern>
    </servlet-mapping>
    <servlet-mapping>
        <servlet-name>ss</servlet-name>
        <url-pattern>/sub</url-pattern>
    </servlet-mapping>
    <servlet-mapping>
        <servlet-name>rs</servlet-name>
        <url-pattern>/resp</url-pattern>
    </servlet-mapping>
</web-app>
```

Arrange the files in a directory structure, as shown in Figure 7.25:

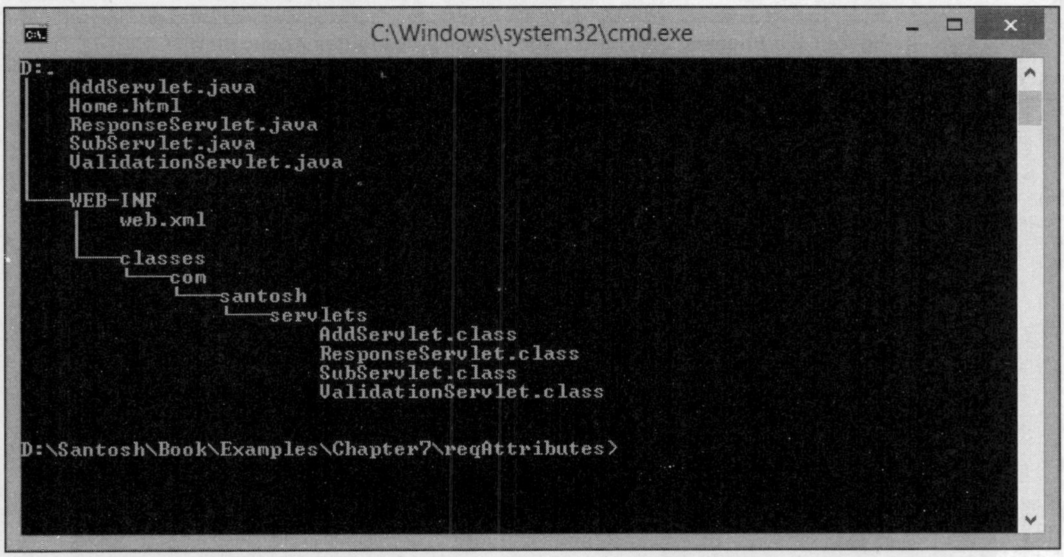

Figure 7.25: Showing the Directory Structure for the reqAttributes Application

After arranging the files, copy the **reqAttributes** folder into the `<Tomcat home>\webapps` folder.

After creating and arranging the files, let's run the application.

Running the Application

Now start the Tomcat server. If it is already started, you need not restart it. To run this example, type the following URL:

```
http://localhost:9090/reqAttributes/Home.html
```

The home page of this application appears. After you get this screen, enter some numbers (20 and 10 in our case) and click the Add or Subtract button, as shown in Figure 7.26:

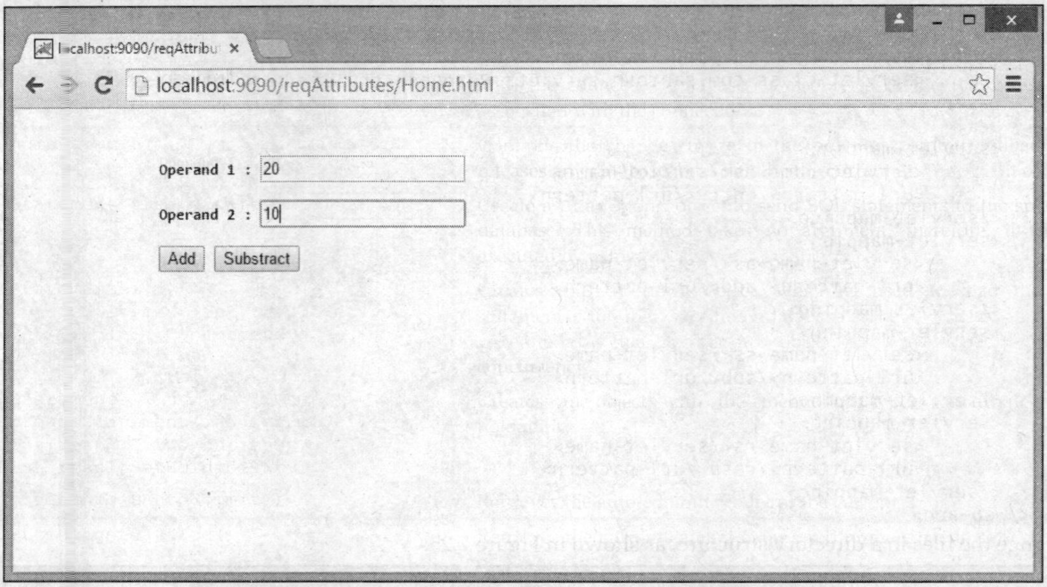

Figure 7.26: Showing the Home Page of the reqAttributes Application

If you click the Add button, you get the result, as shown in Figure 7.27:

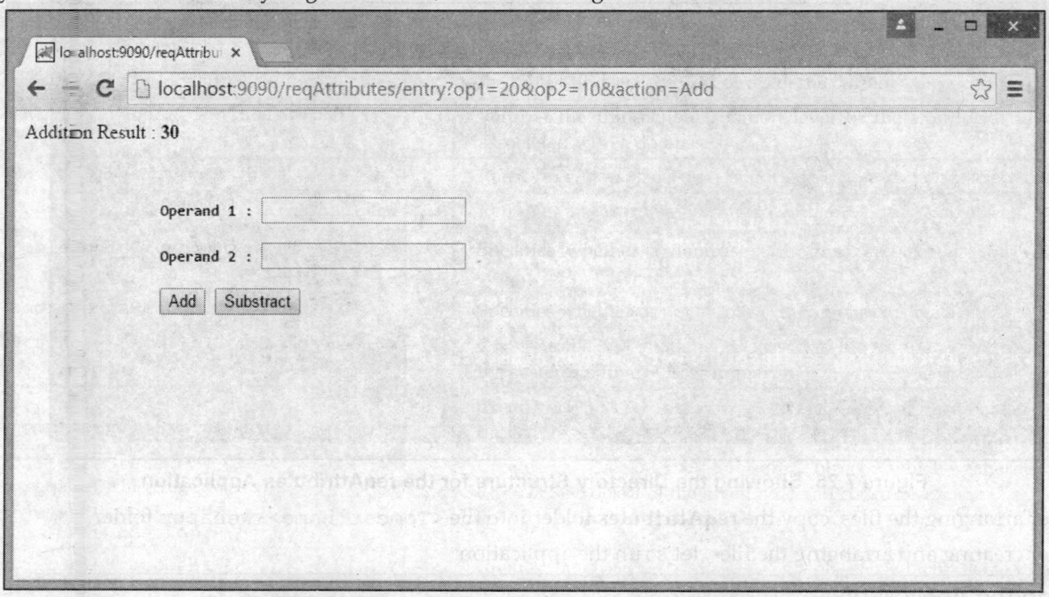

Figure 7.27: Showing the Result after Addition of Two Operands

If you enter numbers and click the Subtract button, you get the result, as shown in Figure 7.28:

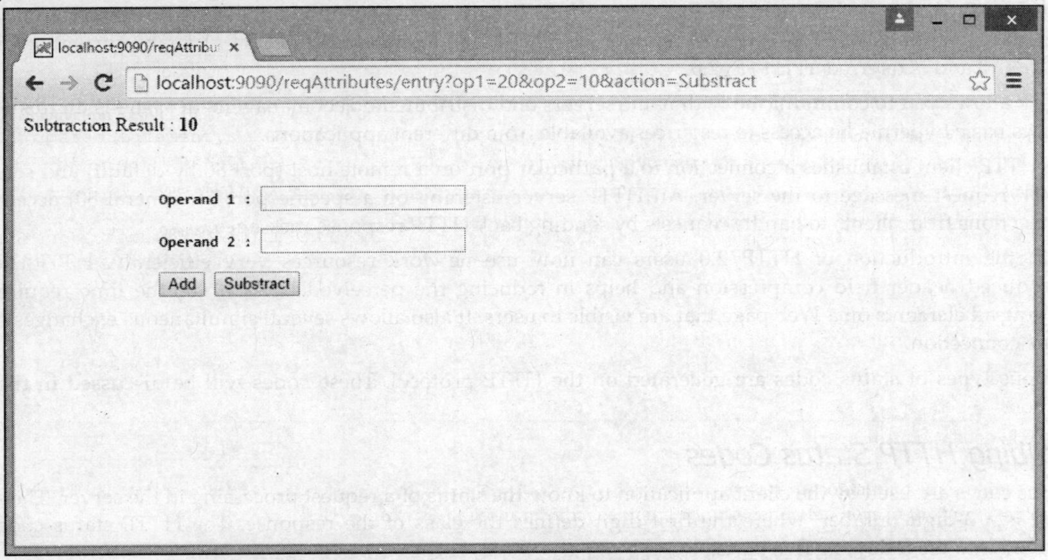

Figure 7.28: Showing the Result after Subtraction of Two Operands

If the given values are not numbers, the validation check message appears, as shown in Figure 7.29:

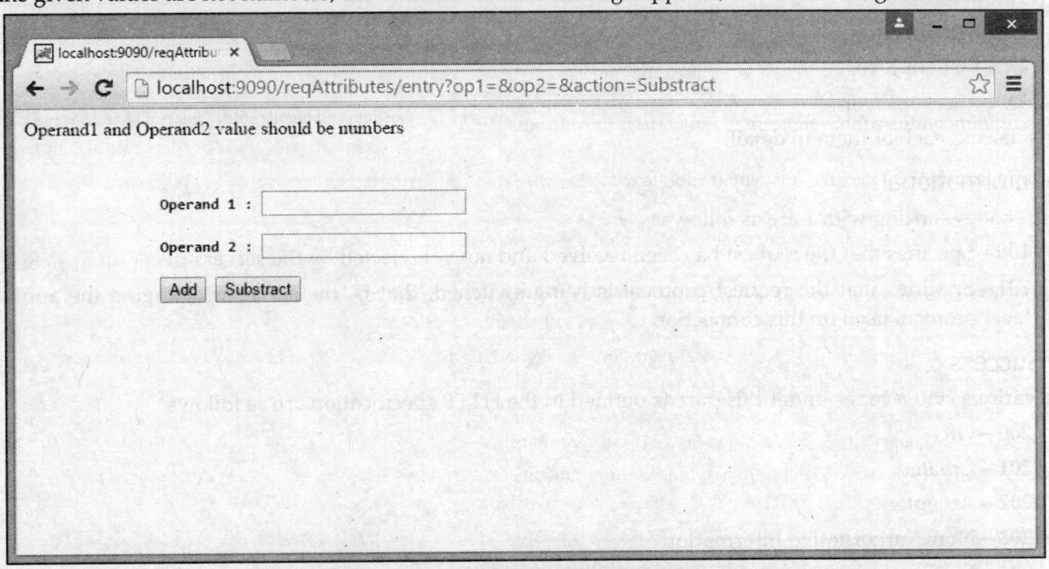

Figure 7.29: Showing a Validation Message

Now that you are familiar with request attributes, let's move on to a new topic and learn something about the HTTP protocol used to handle HTTP requests and responses.

Describing HTTP Basic

Hypertext Transfer Protocol (HTTP) is an application-level protocol for common hypermedia information systems. HTTP is a request/response protocol between clients and servers. It is a generic stateless protocol, used to transfer hypertext.

The first version of HTTP, 0.9, was designed to transfer simple raw data. The next version, 1.0, was designed to transfer Multipurpose Internet Mail Extensions (MIME) type messages and contains META information about the data being transferred. The next version of HTTP is 1.1 and is referred as HTTP/1.1. The current version of HTTP is 2 and is referred as HTTP/2.0.

HTTP allows you to communicate with name servers and distributed object management systems. In this way, it allows basic hypermedia access to resources available from different applications.

An HTTP client establishes a connection to a particular port on a remote host (port 80 by default) and sends an HTTP request message to the server. An HTTP server listening on a specific port (in general 80) accepts the connections from clients to handle requests by sending back HTTP response messages.

With the introduction of HTTP/2.0 users can now use network resources very efficiently. HTTP/2.0 has introduced header field compression and helps in reducing the perceived latency, i.e., the time required for loading all elements on a Web page that are visible to users. It also allows several simultaneous exchanges on the same connection.

Various types of status codes are generated on the HTTP protocol. These codes will be discussed in the next section.

Describing HTTP Status Codes

Status codes are used by the client application to know the status of a request processing in the server. The status code is a 3-digit number, where the first digit defines the class of the response. The HTTP status codes are divided into the following five parts:

- 1XX—Informational
- 2XX—Success
- 3XX—Redirection
- 4XX—Client Error
- 5XX—Server Error

Let's discuss each of them in detail.

1XX – Informational

Status codes starting with 1 are as follows:

- **100**—Specifies that the request has been received and not yet rejected by the server.
- **101**—Specifies that the request protocol is being switched, that is, the server is changing the application level protocol used on this connection.

2XX – Success

The various status codes under this part as defined in the HTTP specification are as follows:

- **200**—OK
- **201**—Created
- **202**—Accepted
- **203**—Non-Authoritative Information
- **204**—No Content
- **205**—Reset Content
- **206**—Partial Content

3XX – Redirection

The various status codes under this part as defined in the HTTP specification are as follows:

- **300**—Multiple Choices
- **301**—Moved Permanently
- **302**—Found

- 303 – See Other
- 304 – Not Modified
- 305 – Use Proxy
- 307 – Temporary Redirect

4XX – Client Error

The various status codes under this part as defined in the HTTP specification are as follows:

- 400 – Bad Request
- 401 – Unauthorized
- 402 – Payment Required
- 403 – Forbidden
- 404 – Not Found
- 405 – Method Not Allowed
- 406 – Not Acceptable
- 407 – Proxy Authentication Required
- 408 – Request Time-out
- 409 – Conflict
- 410 – Gone
- 411 – Length Required
- 412 – Precondition Failed
- 413 – Request Entity Too Large
- 414 – Request-URI Too Large
- 415 – Unsupported Media Type
- 416 – Requested range not satisfy able
- 417 – Expectation Failed

5XX – Server Error

The various status codes under this part as defined in the HTTP specification are as follows:

- 500 – Internal Server Error
- 501 – Not Implemented
- 502 – Bad Gateway
- 503 – Service Unavailable
- 504 – Gateway Time-out
- 505 – HTTP Version not supported

All these status codes are given for HTTP 1.1 protocol specifications. Now, after getting familiar with the HTTP protocol and HTTP status codes, let's discuss how to create the Servlet object, which uses the HTTP protocol for request processing.

Describing the HttpServletRequest and HttpServletResponse Interfaces

The Java Servlet API includes support to create the Servlet object accessing the HTTP request and response specific details. The `javax.servlet.http.HttpServletRequest` and `javax.servlet.http.HttpServletResponse` interface of Java Servlet API provides a standard abstraction for accessing HTTP-specific request and response information from the Servlet container. We discussed the importance of HTTP as well as various HTTP message formats. Now, let's suppose that you want to design the server-side extension in Java (that is, Servlet) taking all the advantages of HTTP. You also want to get HTTP-specific request content and set some HTTP-specific response headers and response content. To do this, you want a Servlet container that can understand the HTTP standards and expose HTTP-specific requests and responses to the Servlet through API. To meet this requirement, the Servlet specification has included an instruction that all Servlet containers must support HTTP as a protocol for requests and responses. In other words, all Servlet containers can make and resolve HTTP messages. Moreover, the Servlet API includes the `javax.servlet.http` package containing classes and interfaces that describe and define the abstraction between Servlets and the Servlet container to use HTTP protocol data. The `HttpServletRequest` and `HttpServletResponse` interfaces have been included into the `javax.servlet.http` package to provide an abstraction to get HTTP-based request data and set HTTP-based response content. When a client uses the HTTP protocol to request information from the server, the Servlet container uses the `HttpServletRequest` and `HttpServletResponse` objects (the instances of `HttpServletRequest` and `HttpServletResponse`), calls the `service()` method, and passes these request and response objects to access Web pages.

Working with HttpServletRequest

`HttpServletRequest` is an interface and a subtype of the `ServletRequest` interface. The Web container provider implements this interface to encapsulate all HTTP-based request information, including headers and request methods.

All properties, such as request parameters and attributes, of the `ServletRequest` interface are also accessible through the `HttpServletRequest` interface.

Servlet can access request header information of an HTTP request by using the following methods:

- **`String getHeader(String)`** — Returns the value of a request header for the given header name. If there are multiple headers with the same name, this method returns the first header value in the request.
- **`Enumeration getHeaders(String)`** — Returns all header values associated with the given name in the form of Enumeration of String objects.
- **`Enumeration getHeaderNames()`** — Returns all header names.

Servlet can access request path elements. Request paths are paths that allow a container to locate a Servlet. Request paths are composed of three parts, Context Path, Servlet Path, and Path Info. `HttpServletRequest` contains various methods to access the request path/URI, which are as follows:

- **`String getContextPath()`** — Returns an empty String if the context is the default context, that is, the context rooted at the base of the Web server. If not, this path starts with the / character but does not ends with /. The context path is the first part of the request Uniform Resource Identifier (URI) and is a path associated with the `ServletContext` of which this Servlet is a part.
- **`String getServletPath()`** — Returns an empty string, if the Servlet path starts with the / character except when the pattern is /*. The Servlet path of the request URI is a path that matches the mapping that activated this request.
- **`String getPathInfo()`** — Accesses the path of the request URI that is not a part of the Context path or the Servlet path.
- **`String getRequestURI()`** — Returns the complete path, in the form of a combination of the Context path, the Servlet path, and the Path info, as shown in the following code snippet:

```
Request URI = Context Path + Servlet Path + Path Info
```

Let's now discuss the `HttpServletResponse` interface, which handles the response related to the HTTP protocol.

Working with HttpServletResponse

`HttpServletResponse` is an interface, which is a subtype of the `ServletResponse` interface. The container provider implements this interface to encapsulate all HTTP protocol-based information, including headers, to be returned from the server to the client. The following are the situations in which response is closed:

- When the `service()` method of the Servlet invoked by the container for the original request is terminated.
- When the `service()` method of the Servlet, invoked as a part of forwarding a request (that is, using the `RequestDispatcher's forward()` method), is terminated.

- When the amount of content specified in content length is written to the response. You can use the `setContentLength()` method of `ServletResponse` to specify content length for a response.
- When the `sendError()` method is called.
- When the `sendRedirect()` method is called.

Let's now look at the various methods available in `HttpServletResponse` to abstract HTTP response messages.

Exploring the Methods for Response Headers

HTTP response headers are helpful for clients to get information on content, such as the type of content being sent back, the amount of content being sent, and the type of server sending the content. The following are the methods available in the `HttpServletResponse` object to manipulate HTTP response headers:

- **`addHeader(String name, String value)`**—Adds a response header with the given name and value. This method allows response headers to have multiple values.
- **`containsHeader(String name)`**—Returns a Boolean, indicating that the named response header has already been set.
- **`setHeader(String name, String value)`**—Sets a response header with the given name and value. The new value overwrites the previous one. This method can be used to test for the presence of a header before setting its value.
- **`setIntHeader(java.lang.String name, int value)`**—Sets a response header with the given name and integer value. The new value overwrites the previous one. This method can be used to test for the presence of a header before setting its value.
- **`setDateHeader(String name, long date)`**—Sets a response header with the given name and date value. The date is specified in terms of milliseconds. The new value overwrites the previous one. This method can be used to test for the presence of a header before setting its value.
- **`addIntHeader(String name, int value)`**—Adds a response header with the given name and integer value. This method allows response headers to have multiple values.
- **`addDateHeader(String name, long date)`**—Adds a response header with the given name and date value. The date is specified in terms of milliseconds. This method does not override the previous response headers and allows response headers to have multiple values.

Table 7.2 describes HTTP headers that can be set by `HttpServletResponse` objects:

Table 7.2: HTTP Headers and their Values

Header field	Header value
Age	Represents a positive integer representing the estimated time since the response was generated from the server.
Content-Length	Indicates the size of the message body, in decimal number of octets (8-bit bytes), which is sent to the recipient.
Content-Type	Represents the MIME type corresponding to the content of the HTTP response. A browser to determine if the content should be rendered internally or launched for rendering by an external application often uses this value.
Date	Represents the date and time at which the message originated.
Location	Specifies the location of a resource, as the absolute URL some HTTP response codes redirect a client to a new resource.
Pragma	Includes implementation-specific directives that may apply to any recipient along the request–response chain. The most commonly used value is no-cache, indicating a resource that should not be cached.

Table 7.2: HTTP Headers and their Values

Header field	Header value
Retry After	Indicates how long the service is expected to be unavailable to the requesting client, if it is used with a 503 (Service Unavailable). The value of this field can be a date or an integer number of seconds (in decimals) after the time of the response.
Server	Represents a `String` for the information about the server generating a response.

It is important to note that you need to set the Content-Type header to text/html when a Servlet is sending back HTML content. For other formats, the appropriate MIME type should be set.

Exploring the Methods for Buffering

The `ServletResponse` interface allows a Servlet to access and set buffering parameters. Servlet containers may or may not support buffering of the output going to the client, but most containers support it to improve their performance.

The following methods of the `ServletResponse` interface are used to access and set buffering information:

- **`setBufferSize(int)`** — Sets the required buffer size. This method must be called before any content is written by using `ServletOutputStream` or `Writer`. Invoking this method after writing the content throws `IllegalStateException`. It is recommended to set a large buffer size.
- **`int getBufferSize()`** — Gets the buffer size of the underlying buffer being used. If the container does not support buffering or if it is disabled, this method returns zero.
- **`flushBuffer()`** — Forces the content in the buffer to be written to the client.

NOTE

The container immediately flushes the buffer filled for the client.

- **`boolean isCommited()`** — Returns true if the response bytes have been sent to client; otherwise, it returns false.
- **`reset()`** — Clears the data in the buffer, including the status codes and headers set, if the response is not committed. However, if the response is committed, it throws `IllegalStateException`.
- **`resetBuffer()`** — Clears the data in the buffer if the response is not committed; however, if the response is committed, it throws `IllegalStateException`.

Other methods commonly used with `HttpServletResponse` are as follows:

- **`sendError(int), sendError(int, String)`** — Sets the appropriate header and body content for sending error messages to the client. The following types of arguments are used in this method:
  - If an optional String argument is provided to this method, it sets the body content to the given value.
  - If the data is written to the response after this method is called, the data is ignored. In other words, after this method is invoked, you cannot send any output content to the client.
  - Before invoking this method, if the data was written to the response buffer but not committed, the data in the response buffer is cleared and replaced with the data set by this method. If the response is committed, this method throws `IllegalStateException`.
- **`sendRedirect(String)`** — Sets the appropriate header to redirect the client to a different URL. This method takes an absolute URL path. If a relative path is given, the container transforms it to a fully qualified URL. In this case, if for any reason, the container fails to transform, it throws `IllegalStateException`.

Now, you should know the difference between the implementation of the `forward()` and `sendRedirect()` methods, which is discussed in the following sections.

Comparing `RequestDispatcher forward()` and `sendRedirect()`

Both the `forward()` and `sendRedirect()` methods redirect you to a new resource, such as a Servlet or JSP. Let's compare these two methods:

- The `redirect(sendRedirect)` instruction is executed in the client side; whereas, the forward `(RequestDispatcher)` instruction is executed in the server, i.e., in the container.
- The redirect option is provided under HTTP and hence it can be used only with HTTP clients; whereas, the `RequestDispatcher's forward()` method does not depend on the client's request protocol since the `forward()` method is provided by the Servlet container.
- With the `forward()` method, the request object is shared by the target resource; whereas, with the `sendRedirect()` method a new request is created for the destination resource (if the destination resource is a Servlet).
- With the `sendRedirect()` method, two request and response calls are consumed; whereas, only one call is consumed in the case of the `forward()` method.

Now that you are familiar with the `HttpServletRequest` and `HttpServletResponse` interfaces, let's take an example to explain how these interfaces are used.

Handling the HttpServletRequest and HttpServletResponse Interfaces

We are going to create an application by the name of **httpRequestEx** that will show you how to handle the `HttpServletRequest` and `HttpServletResponse` interfaces. The application uses different Request URIs for sending requests. You can find this application online in the code/Chapter7/httpRequestEx folder. You need to perform the following steps to create this application:

- Create the Home.html file
- Create the `HttpServletRequestEx` Servlet
- Create the deployment descriptor file
- Run the application

Let's start by creating the entry point for the application, which is the Home.html page.

Creating the Home.html File

The **httpRequestEx** application starts with the home page, Home.html. This page creates a user interface for sending requests. The home page displays three buttons with Send Request labels on them and each button points to a different request URI. The source code for the home page is given in Listing 7.25 (you can also find the Home.html file online in the code/Chapter7/httpRequestEx folder):

Listing 7.25: Creating the Home.html File

```
<html>
  <body>
        <form method=post action="/httpRequestEx/myser">
        Click on this button to make a request using Request URI as
        <b>/httpRequestEx/myser</b>
              <br> <input type="submit" value="Send Request"/>
        </form> <br> <br>
        <form method=post action="/httpRequestEx/myservlets1/Test">
        Click on this button to make a request using Request URI as
        <b>/httpRequestEx/myservlets1/Test</b>
              <br> <input type="submit" value="Send Request"/>
        </form> <br> <br>
              <form method=post action="/httpRequestEx/Test.do">
              Click on this button to make a request using Request URI as
              <b>/httpRequestEx/Test.do</b>
              <br> <input type="submit" value="Send Request"/>
        </form>
  </body>
</html>
```

Let's now create the `HttpServletRequestEx` Servlet to handle the request sent by the Home page.

Creating the `HttpServletRequestEx` Servlet

The name of a Servlet is `HttpServletRequest`. The methods used in this Servlet have been explained earlier in the chapter. The source code for this Servlet is shown in Listing 7.26 (you can also find the HttpServletRequestEx.java file online in the code/Chapter7/httpRequestEx folder):

Listing 7.26: Creating the HttpServletRequestEx.java File

```
package com.santosh.servlets;
import javax.servlet.*;
import javax.servlet.http.*;
import java.io.*;
import java.util.*;
/**
 * @author Santosh
 */
public class HttpServletRequestEx extends GenericServlet {
   public void service(ServletRequest req, ServletResponse res)
   throws ServletException, IOException {
         res.setContentType("text/html");
         PrintWriter     out = res.getWriter();
         HttpServletRequest httpreq=null;
         try {
                httpreq=(HttpServletRequest)req;
         }
         catch (ClassCastException cce){
         out.println("Request protocol is not a HTTP, it is "+ req.getProtocol());
         }
         out.println("<html><body>");
         out.println("<b>Requested URL:  </b>");
         out.println(httpreq.getRequestURL()+"<br/>");
         out.println("<br/><h4>Request Path information:</h4>");
         out.println("<table border='1'><tr><th>");
         out.println("Name</th><th>Value</th></tr>");
         print(out, "HTTP Request method", httpreq.getMethod());
         print(out, "Request URI", httpreq.getRequestURI());
         print(out, "Context Path", httpreq.getContextPath());
         print(out, "Servlet path", httpreq.getServletPath());
         print(out, "Path info", httpreq.getPathInfo());
         print(out, "Path translated", httpreq.getPathTranslated());
         out.println("</table><br/>");
         out.println("<br/><h4>Request Headers:</h4>");
         out.println("<table border='1'><tr><th>");
         out.println("Name</th><th>Value</th></tr>");
         Enumeration e = httpreq.getHeaderNames();
         while (e.hasMoreElements()) {
                String name = (String)e.nextElement();
                print(out, name, httpreq.getHeader(name));
         }

         out.println("</table><br/>");
         out.println("</body></html>");
   }
   private void print(PrintWriter out, String name, String value) {
         out.print("<tr><td>"+name+"</td><td>"+value+"</td></tr>");
   }
}
```

After creating the required Servlet, let's map the Servlet in the `web.xml` file.

Creating the Deployment Descriptor File

The final step in completing the application is to create the deployment descriptor file. This file maps the Servlet at different URLs. The source code for deployment descriptor file (the `web.xml` file) is shown in Listing 7.27 (you can find this file online in the code/Chapter7/httpRequestEx/WEB-INF folder):

Listing 7.27: Creating the `web.xml` File

```
<?xml version="1.0" encoding="UTF-8"?>
<web-app>
  <servlet>
        <servlet-name>hrs</servlet-name>
        <servlet-class>com.santosh.servlets.HttpServletRequestEx</servlet-class>
  </servlet>
  <servlet-mapping>
        <servlet-name>hrs</servlet-name>
        <url-pattern>/myser</url-pattern>
  </servlet-mapping>
  <servlet-mapping>
        <servlet-name>hrs</servlet-name>
        <url-pattern>/myservlets1/*</url-pattern>
  </servlet-mapping>
  <servlet-mapping>
        <servlet-name>hrs</servlet-name>
        <url-pattern>*.do</url-pattern>
  </servlet-mapping>

  <welcome-file-list>
        <welcome-file>home.html</welcome-file>
  </welcome-file-list>
</web-app>
```

Arrange all these files in a directory structure, as shown in Figure 7.30:

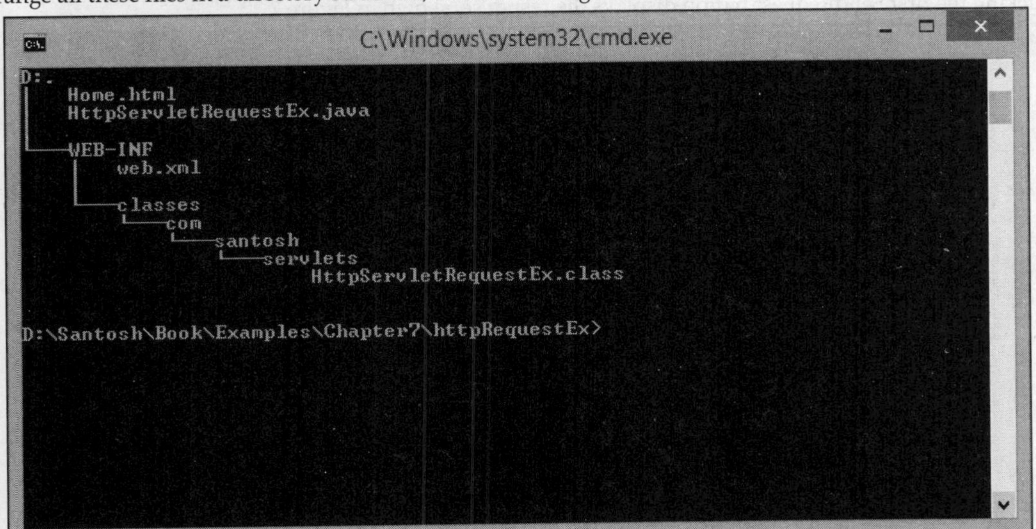

Figure 7.30: Showing the Directory Structure for the httpRequestEx Application

Copy the **httpRequestEx** folder into the `<Tomcat home>\webapps` folder.

Running the Application

Now start the Tomcat server. If it is already started, you need not restart it. We are using port number 9090 because Tomcat is running on this port at our computer. To run this application, use the following URL:

```
http://localhost:9090/httpRequestEx/Home.html
```

The home page of this application is displayed in Figure 7.31. After you get this screen, click the three SendRequest buttons (any one) and observe the outputs.

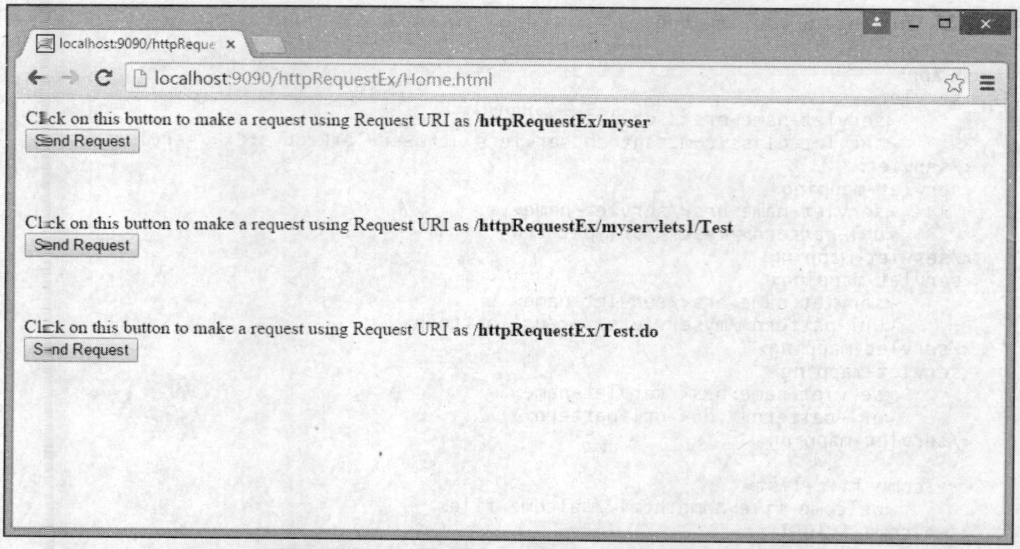

Figure 7.31: Showing the Home Page of the httpRequestEx Application

Clicking the first SendRequest button displays the response, shown in Figure 7.32:

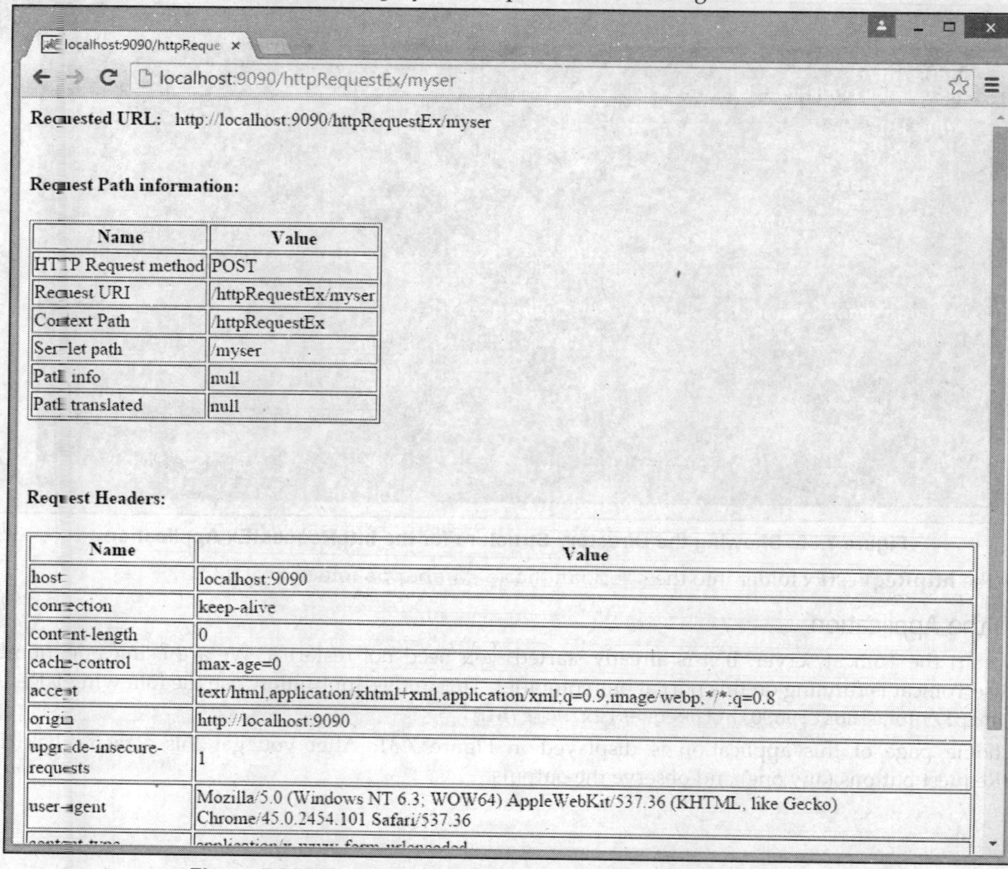

Figure 7.32: Showing the Response for the Servlet Path /myser

Clicking the second Send Request button displays the response shown in Figure 7.33:

NOTE

When you make a request with a request URI / httpRequestEx/myservelts1/Test, the output will be displayed, as shown in Figure 7.33:

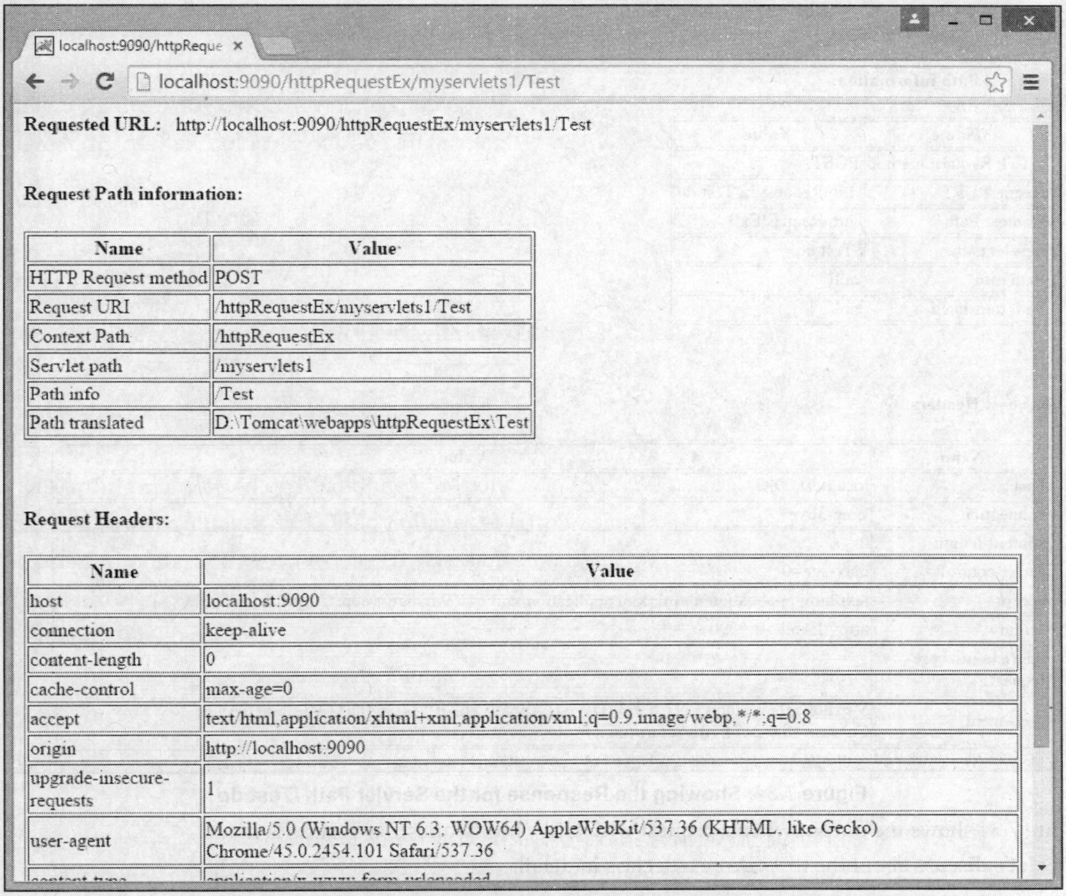

Requested URL: http://localhost:9090/httpRequestEx/myservlets1/Test

Request Path information:

Name	Value
HTTP Request method	POST
Request URI	/httpRequestEx/myservlets1/Test
Context Path	/httpRequestEx
Servlet path	/myservlets1
Path info	/Test
Path translated	D:\Tomcat\webapps\httpRequestEx\Test

Request Headers:

Name	Value
host	localhost:9090
connection	keep-alive
content-length	0
cache-control	max-age=0
accept	text/html,application/xhtml+xml,application/xml;q=0.9,image/webp,*/*;q=0.8
origin	http://localhost:9090
upgrade-insecure-requests	1
user-agent	Mozilla/5.0 (Windows NT 6.3; WOW64) AppleWebKit/537.36 (KHTML, like Gecko) Chrome/45.0.2454.101 Safari/537.36

Figure 7.33: Showing the Response for the Servlet Path /myservlets1

In the output shown in Figure 7.33, note the following:

1. Request URI: /httpRequestEx/myservelts1/Test
2. Context Path: /httpRequestEx
3. Servlet Path: /myservlets1
4. Path Info: /Test

You can see the following relation:

Request URI = Context Path + Servlet Path + Path Info

Clicking the third Send Request button displays the response shown in Figure 7.34:

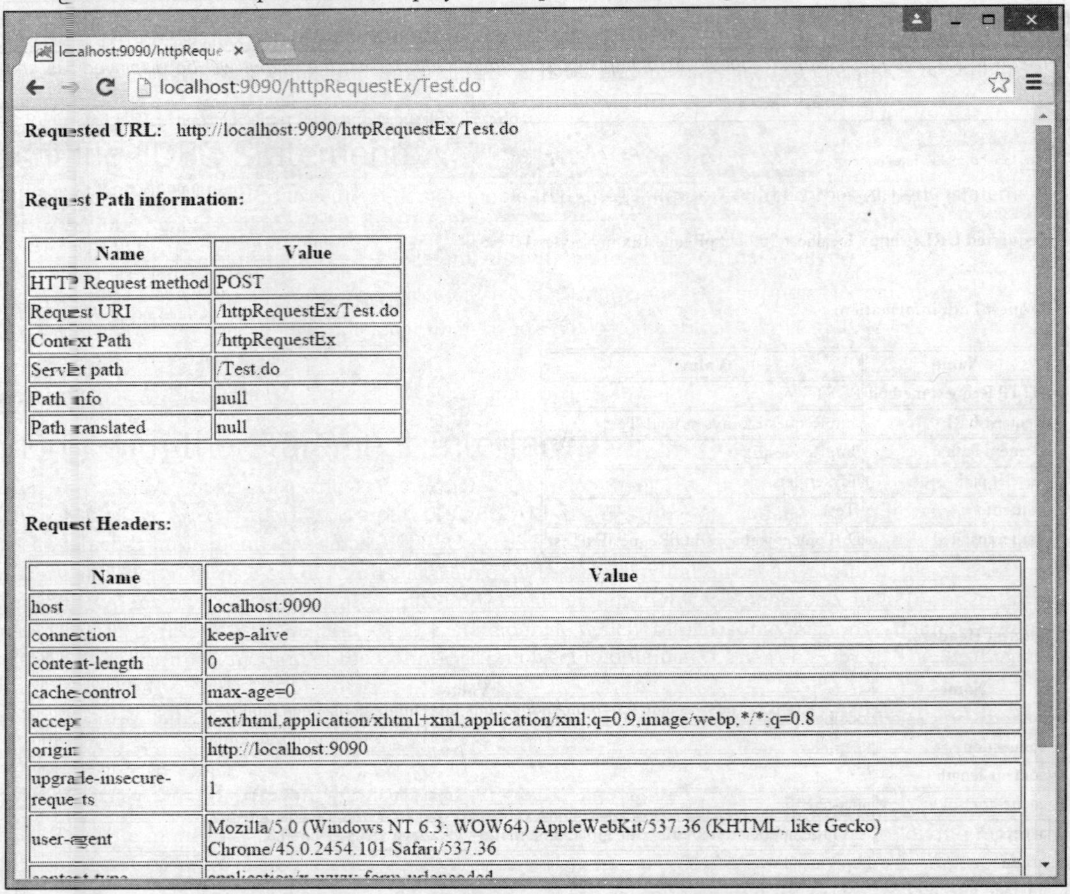

Figure 7.34: Showing the Response for the Servlet Path /Test.do

Figure 7.34 shows the output when a request with URI /httpRequestEx/Test.do is made.

Now let's discuss about the `HttpServlet` class in detail.

Describing HttpServlet

As you know, the Servlet container provides support for the HTTP protocol. It creates `HttpServletRequest` and `HttpServletResponse` objects if the HTTP protocol is used for sending a request. The `HttpServletRequest` object encapsulates all HTTP protocol based request information, including headers and request methods and the `HttpServletResponse` object encapsulates all HTTP protocol based information, including headers to be returned from the server to the client.

If you want to use the services provided by these objects, you need to typecast the `ServletRequest` and `ServletResponse` type references into `HttpServletRequest` and `HttpServletResponse`, respectively. Moreover, if you want to process the client request differently for each of the HTTP request methods, you need to write the *`if`* and *`else`* conditions in the service methods comparing the result of the `getMethod()` method of `HttpServletRequest` with different `Http` request methods.

Instead of performing these operations in every Servlet that wants to use HTTP-based information, you want a simple adapter class that can perform these operations for your Servlet. To meet this need, the Servlet specification provides `HttpServlet`.

`HttpServlet` is a utility class given under the Servlet API's `javax.servlet.http` package. It is an abstract class with no abstract methods. `HttpServlet` provides convenient methods for handling HTTP request.

`HttpServlet` is a subtype of `GenericServlet` and does not override `init()`, `destroy()`, and other methods. However, it implements the `service()` method, which is an abstract method in `GenericServlet`.

The other methods in the `HttpServlet` class are as follows:

- `protected void service(HttpServletRequest, HttpServletResponse)`
- `protected void doPost(HttpServletRequest, HttpServletResponse)`
- `protected void doPut(HttpServletRequest, HttpServletResponse)`
- `protected void doHead(HttpServletRequest, HttpServletResponse)`
- `protected void doTrace(HttpServletRequest, HttpServletResponse)`
- `protected void doOptions(HttpServletRequest, HttpServletResponse)`
- `protected void doDelete(HttpServletRequest, HttpServletResponse)`

Each of these methods allows you to handle the respective HTTP request method. For example, `doGet()` handles the HTTP GET method request.

The HttpServlet Lifecycle

As you know, when client uses the HTTP protocol to request, container prepares `HttpServletRequest` and `HttpServletResponse` objects, i.e., the instances of `HttpServletRequest` and `HttpServletResponse` implementation classes. You know that Servlet container calls the `service()` method by passing the request and response objects. The Servlet container invokes the `service()` method on our Servlet instance, which is taken into the reference of `javax.servlet.Servlet` interface type. This results in invoking public `service()` method (i.e., service method taking arguments of `ServletRequest` and `ServletResponse`). It is because when a subclass instance is taken into, super type reference and if the methods in super type are overloaded in subclass then Java uses early binding to locate the method.

The following are the implementations of the methods of `HttpServlet`:

- **public service() method, i.e., service() method taking `ServletRequest` and `ServletResponse` as arguments**—The default implementation provided for this method in `HttpServlet` is that it casts the given request and response references into `HttpServletRequest` and `HttpServletResponse`, respectively, and calls the protected service method passing the request and response references of HTTP type.
- **protected service() method, i.e., service() method taking `HttpServletRequest` and `HttpServletResponse` as arguments**—The default implementation provided for this method in `HttpServlet` is that it gets the HTTP request method used by the client to make a request and depending upon the request method it calls the respective `doXXX()` method, such as for GET method the `doGet()` is invoked, and for HTTP POST method request the `doPost()` method is invoked.
- **`doXXX()` methods, i.e., `doGet()`, `doPost()`, etc.**—The default implementation provided for all the `doXXX()` methods in `HttpServlet` class is to generate a response describing the client that the respective method is not supported by the requested URI.

With this, we come to the end of the chapter. Let's now summarize the main topics learned in this chapter.

Summary

In this chapter, we discussed the `ServletRequest` and `ServletResponse` objects and their various methods with examples. The chapter explained how request parameters are handled as well as the working and purpose of Servlet initialization and context initialization parameters. The chapter also covered the `RequestDispatcher` object, which dispatches request in two ways: using `include()` and `forward()` methods. The differences between `RequestDispatcher's forward()` and `include()` methods, and the situations to use these methods, have been explained. The chapter covered `HttpServlet` and explained its lifecycle and also discussed the `HttpServletRequest` and `HttpServletResponse` interfaces along with their various methods, with examples. Let's recall the following important points to summarize the chapter:

- The `ServletRequest` object encapsulates the request data and includes the request parameters and headers.
- Most of the Web container recycles `ServletRequest` objects to avoid the performance overhead of request objects creation.
- The `javax.servlet.ServletRequest` interface is used to abstract a container object (ServletRequest) that describes client request data.
- The data from the client is submitted to the server in the form of the request as name-value pairs, known as request parameters.
- The request parameters are described as query string into the URL or are described into the body of the request message.
- The Servlet container supports the ability to store startup and configuration information for a Servlet as initialization parameters.
- The `ServletResponse` is a container object designed to allow the Servlet object to describe about the response, to the container.
- The `javax.servlet.ServletResponse` interface of Java Servlet API is designed to describe this object (i.e., ServletResponse object, a part of Servlet container).
- The Servlet container supports an ability to dispatch requests from one Servlet to another within the context. The `ServletContext.getRequestDispatcher()` and `ServletRequest.getRequestDispatcher()` methods support to access URL Path Based, and `ServletContext.getNamedDispatcher()` method support to access the Servlet Name approach of the navigation process implemented by the Servlet container.
- The Servlet container supports two styles of delegation include and forward. The major difference between these two styles of delegating the request is with the response stream management. In case of forward, the response stream is closed immediately after the forward operation.
- Request attributes are thread-safe since the scope of these attributes is request scope. Also, remember that one request is processed completely using only one thread.
- The differences between `RequestDispatcher.forward()` and `ServletResponse.sendRedirect()`.
- `HttpServlet` is a utility class given under the Servlet API's `javax.servlet.http` package. It is an abstract class with no abstract methods. `HttpServlet` provides convenient methods for handling HTTP request.

In the next chapter, we discuss how to handle Sessions in Servlet.

Exercise

Q. 7.1 Name the methods provided by the `ServletRequest` interface for retrieving the parameters send by client.

Q. 7.2 Distinguish between the Servlet context initialization parameters and Servlet initialization parameters.

Q. 7.3 Which object of the Servlet API is used to retrieve the Servlet initialization parameters?

Q. 7.4 Write down the syntax to declare Servlet initialization parameters in the `web.xml` file.

Q. 7.5 What is the difference between the `getRequestDispatcher()` method of `ServletContext` and `ServletRequest`?

Q. 7.6 Name the method of `ServletRequest` that is used to add a request attribute.

Q. 7.7 What is the use of HTTP status codes?

8

Handling Sessions in Servlet

Session tracking helps a Servlet to keep track of the activities of a user and the origin of HyperText Transfer Protocol (HTTP) requests. This is required so that a group of requests from a single user can be managed in a stateful manner. Servlet session tracking is similar to other session tracking techniques used in previous technologies, such as Common Gateway Interface (CGI).

Servlets provide convenient ways to synchronize multiple sessions between a client and a server. As a result, stateful Servlets are able to maintain the session state on the server until clients complete their browsing sessions.

Some common and widely used techniques to maintain HTTP sessions over the Internet include persistent cookies, Uniform Resource Locator (URL) rewriting, hidden form fields, and user authorization. Few proprietary session tracking strategies, which are vendor dependent and persist the state to a disk or a database, also exist.

It is a cumbersome task to manually identify and use the most suited of these session tracking techniques in Web applications, as all these techniques have pros and cons associated with them. Alternatively, you can use an Application Programming Interface (API) to identify and select the most appropriate HTTP session technique based on the capabilities of the client and server. Therefore, the Servlet Session Tracking API is introduced to provide abstraction to developers, wherever possible, from the details such as whether the browser has cookies enabled or the server supports URL rewriting.

The chapter describes various mechanisms of session handling, such as URL rewriting, hidden form fields, cookies, and HTTP session. In addition, the chapter provides applications to implement the URL rewriting and hidden form field mechanisms. Further, the chapter helps to create applications to implement cookies. Then, you are explained about the `HttpSession` and ServletContext attributes. The chapter also discusses the scopes of the Web application objects and single thread model. Towards the end, you learn about the `ServletOutputStream` class.

Introducing Session Tracking

A session is a collection of HTTP requests over a period of time between a client and a Web server. The lifetime of a session specifies the period of time till the session is active. When a session expires, the session is destroyed, and its resources are returned to the Servlet engine.

Session tracking, also known as session handling, is a mechanism used to maintain the state of a user within a series of requests across some period, i.e., the lifetime of a session. In other words, session tracking is a means to keep track of session data, which represents the data being transferred into a session. Session data needs to be managed in the Web application or by the Web container as the protocol, i.e., HTTP, used in this communication is a stateless protocol. As HTTP is stateless, each time a client requests for a Web page, the HTTP adapter at client opens a separate connection to the Web server. The server does not automatically maintain appropriate information about a client, such as the client IPAddress and the port number. Even with servers that support persistent (keep-alive) HTTP connections and keep a socket open for multiple client requests that occur close together in time, there is no built-in support for maintaining client information.

Session tracking is used when session data from one session may be required by a Web server to complete specific operations in the same or different sessions. For example, suppose you are shopping on an online book store. You access the online book store's Web site and add items to your shopping cart. When you proceed for checkout and payment, the Web server must have the information about the books or items you added to the shopping cart. Without this information, the Web server will not be able to generate the required invoice, and the online shopping process will not be completed. The information required by the Web server, in this example, is session data.

The preceding example shows how session data of a single session is used to complete online shopping processes. Consider another similar example wherein you add books to the shopping cart and decide to make the payment later. You may log out of the online book store and log on again at a later point of time. When you log on to the online book store again, you expect to simply make the payment of the books added to the shopping cart. In such a situation, the Web server must have the required session data generated in the previous session (when you had first logged in and added books to the shopping cart). This information is also provided to the Web server through session tracking. This exemplifies a situation where you may need to use the session data of one session in another session.

After identifying the need of session tracking, let's discuss the different mechanisms for session tracking. These include the following:

- URL rewriting
- Hidden form fields
- Cookies
- HTTP session

Let's discuss each of these mechanisms one by one, beginning with URL rewriting.

Describing URL Rewriting

URL rewriting implies adding session data to the URL path, which is then interpreted by a Web container to associate the request with a session. That is, in this mechanism, the session data required in the next request is appended to the URL path used by the client to make the next request. Consequently, the required session data is retrieved by the Web server as request parameters. This process is abstracted from the users making requests to the Web server.

An HTTP request consists of the location of the server resource (URL), followed optionally by a query string containing pairs of parameters and values. The following is an example of a URL:

```
http://www.myserver.com/servlet/getSchedule;uid=user1?begPeriod=3&endPeriod=6
```

In the preceding example, the server is www.myserver.com, the resource path is /servlet/getSchedule; uid=user1, and the query string is begPeriod=3&endPeriod=6.

You also know that HTTP GET method request is used to retrieve session data from the resource that is located by the given URL. However, the HTTP GET method allows you to send a small amount of data from the client to the server (recommended size up to 255 characters).

In the URL rewriting mechanism, a client's session data can be appended to the request path as a query string or as a part of path info. Let's first discuss how to use a query string for URL rewriting.

Using Query String for URL Rewriting

A query string is a string appended after the requested Uniform Resource Identifier (URI), with the '?' character as a separator. The requested URI is context path plus Servlet path plus path info.

Generally, a query string is divided into different parameters, separated by the '&' character. Each of these parameters consists of name and value pairs separated by the '=' character.

Consider the following URL:

```
http://localhost:9090/myctxt/login?uname=abc&pass=xyz
```

In the preceding URL, /myctxt/login is the request URI and `uname=abc&pass=xyz` is a query string. A Servlet can retrieve the uname and pass parameters by using the `getParameter(String)`, `getParameterNames()`, and `getParameterValues(String)` methods of the `ServletRequest` object.

Using Path Info for URL Rewriting

Path info is a part of the request URI, which is not a part of context path or Servlet path. You can add session data to the path info part of the request URI.

Consider the following URL:

```
http://localhost:9090/myctxt/myservlets/login;uname=abc&pass=xyz
```

In the preceding URL, `/login; uname=abc&pass=xyz` is path info. In this case, you first need to set the url-patterns for the Servlets with extension mapping and then use the `getPathInfo()` method of the `HttpServletRequest` interface to get the data.

Using URL rewriting with a query string is the simplest way of session tracking, as Servlet containers can decode the query string and present the parameters to the Servlet with the methods of `ServletRequest`, such as `getParameter(String)` and `getParameterNames()`.

Listing the Disadvantages of URL Rewriting

URL rewriting works well for navigation purposes; for example, a view may have multiple links to select and identify which link is selected by a user. In such a situation, URL rewriting mechanism is a better choice as compared to other session handling mechanisms. However, URL rewriting has a few disadvantages as well. These include the following:

- If you append data by using a query string, only the HTTP GET method is allowed to append the data in the request URI. If you want to use the POST method, you need to use some special url-patterns, as this method does not support query strings.
- The appended data, along with the request URI, is restricted to a maximum of 255 characters. That is, this approach can be used only if you want to maintain a small amount of data. For large data, URL rewriting proves to be an invalid mechanism. Therefore, the new mechanisms of session tracking, such as cookies, were introduced.
- As data flows between the client and server through a network, the heavy data transfer increases the network traffic.
- URL rewriting is not secure, as data is transferred across the network multiple times; moreover, confidential data may be displayed in the address bar.
- All the views, till the data is required, should be dynamic views, since the data has to be added to the request path. In other words, URL rewriting works only if every page in a session is dynamically generated.
- URL rewriting increases the dependency on URI, as the views in a session need to use session data, irrespective of whether or not they require it. For example, if some data in the login page needs to be maintained for the last request, i.e., logout, all the views between the login and logout pages have to read this data and write it to the URLs of the next views.
- URL rewriting is not suitable for form-based requests (form view); if you want to use URL rewriting, you need to use JavaScript or path info.

Considering Situations to Use URL Rewriting

URL rewriting is recommended for use in the following conditions:

- When you need to maintain a small amount of data for a short period of time, such as between two or three consecutive requests
- When you need to navigate a specific resource, then the query strings can be used. That is, in a view, you may have multiple links to the same resource, but different URLs are generated based on the link selected. For instance, in a Web site providing mailing services (such as Yahoo!), when a user clicks the Inbox option, the request is sent to the Web server, which gets all the mails in the Inbox folder from the mail server and displays them to the user. Now, a particular user may have sent multiple mails. However, when the user clicks one of the mails, the request is sent to the Web server. The Web server is required to identify the specific mail requested by the user. When the user clicks the other mail sent by the same sender, further request is sent to the Web server. In this case, each of the mail's request paths is added with extra information, such as message id. Based on this message id, the particular mail is displayed.

Let's now discuss another session tracking mechanism, that is, the hidden form field.

Exploring Hidden Form Fields

A hidden form field is a type of HTML form field but remains hidden in the view. Similar to other fields, a hidden form field can also be enclosed within a form. Hidden fields in a form are also included in the request while submitting the form along with the other type of form fields. The following is the syntax for using a hidden form field:

```
<input type="hidden" name="uname" value="user1"/>
```

Listing the Advantages and Disadvantages of Hidden Form Fields

The hidden form field mechanism is similar to the URL rewriting mechanism but works even with the HTTP POST method. This mechanism is not restricted to the GET method only; you can also use the POST method without using path info.

However, the hidden form field mechanism also has some disadvantages. For example, it only works when every page is dynamically generated by a form submission. Therefore, general session tracking is not supported by hidden form fields.

Considering the Situations to Use Hidden Form Fields

You can use hidden form fields with form-based requests; however, if you go for hyperlinks, use the URL rewriting mechanism. The hidden form field approach can be used when you need to hide user data from other users. If you use the URL rewriting mechanism, the user can reveal the information passed through the URL. In that case, the hidden form field mechanism is useful for session tracking.

Working with URL Rewriting and Hidden Form Fields

After discussing URL rewriting and hidden form fields, let's create an application, **sessionex1**, which demonstrates the use of the URL rewriting and hidden form field mechanisms to maintain a client state. You can find the **sessionex1** application online in the code/Chapter8 folder. The **sessionex1** application contains the following files:

- SiteHome.html
- Login.html
- Send.html
- DriverConnection.java
- UserDAO.java
- LoginServlet.java
- Mail.java
- MailsDAO.java
- InboxServlet.java
- ViewMailServlet.java
- SendReplyServlet.java
- web.xml

Let's learn to create these files one by one in the following sections.

Creating the SiteHome.html Page

The SiteHome.html page is the home page of the **sessionex1** application. This page simply displays a user interface that provides link to the Login.html page. The code of the SiteHome.html file is shown in Listing 8.1 (you can find this file online in the code/Chapter8/sessionex1 folder):

Listing 8.1: Displaying the Code of the SiteHome.html Page

```
<html>
   <head>
        <title>URL Rewriting and Hidden fields Example</title>
   </head>
   <body>
        This is the Home page for the example to demonstrate how to use <BR>
        URL Rewriting and Hidden form fields to maintain the client state. <BR><BR>
        <a href="Login.html">Login</a>
   </body>
</html>
```

In Listing 8.1, the link for the Login.html page is created. Now, let's create the Login.html page, which would be displayed when the user clicks the link.

Creating the Login.html Page

When a user clicks the Login hyperlink on the SiteHome.html page, the control is passed to the Login.html page, which prompts the user to enter the user name and password. Listing 8.2 shows the code of the Login.html file (you can also find this file online in the code/Chapter8/sessionex1 folder):

Listing 8.2: Displaying the Code of the Login.html Page

```
<html>
   <head>
         <title>URL Rewriting Example</title>
   </head>
   <body>
         <form name="loginform" action="login" method="post">
               <table border="0">
                     <tr>
                           <td>UserName:</td>
                           <td><input type="text" name="uname"></td>
                     </tr>
                     <tr>
                     <td>Password:</td>
                     <td><input type="password" name="password"></td>
                     </tr>
                     <tr>
                           <td colspan="2" align="center">
                           <input type="submit" value="Login"></td>
                     </tr>
               </table>
         </form>
   </body>
</html>
```

In Listing 8.2, the two textboxes are created to enter the user name and password. When the user clicks the Login button, the login action is generated and the LoginServlet is called.

Creating the Send.html Page

The Send.html page simply displays the Page under construction message, when the user tries to send a mail. Listing 8.3 displays the code of the Send.html file (you can also find this file online in the code/Chapter8/sessionex1 folder):

Listing 8.3: Creating the Send.html Page

```
<html><body>
   Page under construction
</body></html>
```

After creating the Send.html page, you need to create the `DriverConnection` class so that the required connection to the database is established to maintain the database communication with the application. Let's create the DriverConnection.java file.

Creating the DriverConnection.java File

The DriverConnection.java file is used to connect to the `sandb` Oracle database to verify the entered data (that is, the user name and password). The source code for this file is shown in Listing 8.4 (you can find this file online in the code/Chapter8/sessionex1 folder):

Listing 8.4: Creating the DriverConnection.java File

```
package com.santosh.servlets;
/**
* @author Santosh
```

```
*/
import java.sql.*;
public class DriverConnection {

   public static Connection getConnection() throws Exception{
         Class.forName("oracle.jdbc.driver.OracleDriver");
         return DriverManager.getConnection(
         "jdbc:oracle:thin:@localhost:1521:sandb","scott","tiger");
   }
}
```

In Listing 8.4, the `OracleDriver` driver is loaded and the connection string is created by providing the database name, user name, and password. After creating the `DriverConnection` class, you need to create the Java class to verify the user details. Let's create the UserDAO.java file, which handles the task of verifying user credentials.

Creating the UserDAO.java File

The UserDAO.java file is used to validate user credentials entered in the Login.html page. In other words, this file checks whether or not the specified user exists in the **sandb** database. Listing 8.5 shows the UserDAO.java file (you can find this file online in the code/Chapter8/sessionex1 folder):

Listing 8.5: Creating the UserDAO.java File

```
package com.santosh.servlets;
/**
 * @author Santosh
 */
import java.sql.*;
public class UserDAO {
   public boolean validate(String uname, String pass){

         try {
                Connection con=DriverConnection.getConnection();
                Statement st=con.createStatement();
                ResultSet rs=st.executeQuery(
                "select count(*) from userdetails where uname=\'"+uname+"\' and
                pass=\'"+pass+"\'");
                return rs.next();
         }//try
         catch(Exception e){
                e.printStackTrace();
         }
         return false;
   }
}
```

In Listing 8.5, the `getConnection()` method of the `DriverConnection` class is invoked and then the `st` instance of the `Statement` interface is created. Finally, the select query is executed on the basis of the user details entered in the Login.html page. As you know that the request from the Login page is forwarded to the LoginServlet, let's now create the `LoginServlet` Servlet.

Creating the LoginServlet.java Servlet

The `LoginServlet` Servlet handles the request sent from the Login page. It checks whether the specified fields are filled or not. If any of the fields is empty, it displays an error message stating that the user name or password cannot be empty. If these fields are not empty, an instance of the `UserDAO` class is created to invoke the `validate()` method of the `UserDAO` class. Listing 8.6 shows the source code of the LoginServlet.java file (you can find this file online in the code/Chapter8/sessionex1 folder):

Listing 8.6: Creating the LoginServlet.java File

```
package com.santosh.servlets;
/**
* @author Santosh
*/
import java.io.IOException;
import java.io.PrintWriter;

import javax.servlet.*;
import javax.servlet.http.*;

public class LoginServlet extends HttpServlet {

   public void doPost(HttpServletRequest request, HttpServletResponse response)
   throws ServletException, IOException {

         String uname=request.getParameter("uname");
         String pass=request.getParameter("password");

         response.setContentType("text/html");
         PrintWriter out = response.getWriter();
         out.println("<HTML>");
         out.println("  <HEAD><TITLE>A Servlet</TITLE></HEAD>");
         out.println("  <BODY>");

         if (uname==null||uname.equals("")){
                 out.println("<b><i>Username Cannot be empty</i></b>");
                 RequestDispatcher rd=request.getRequestDispatcher("/Login.html");
                 rd.include(request, response);
                 return;
         }
         if (pass==null||pass.equals("")){
                 out.println("<b><i>Password Cannot be empty</i></b>");
                 RequestDispatcher rd=request.getRequestDispatcher("/Login.html");
                 rd.include(request, response);
                 return;
         }

         UserDAO ud=new UserDAO();

         if(ud.validate(uname,pass)){
                 out.println("<table width=98% height=95% border=1><tr>");
                 out.println("<td height=45 colspan=2 align=center>");
                 out.println("<font size=5>My Email Site</font></td>");
                 out.println("</tr><tr>");
                 out.println("<td width=12% height=545 align=center valign=top>");
                 out.println("<p> </p><p><font size=4>");
                 out.println("<a href='inbox?uname="+uname+"'>InBox</a>");
                 out.println("</font></p>");
                 out.println("<p><font size=4>Bulk Mail</font></p>");
                 out.println("<p><font size=4>Sent Items</font></p>");
                 out.println("<p><font size=4>Write Mail</font></p>");
                 out.println("<p><font size=4>");
                 out.println("<a href='Login.html'>Logout</a></font></p>");
                 out.println("<p> </p></td>");
                 out.println("<td width=88% align=left valign=top>");
                 out.println("<p> </p>");
                 out.println("<p><font size=4>Welcome, "+uname+"</font></p></td>");
```

```
                out.println("</tr><tr align=center>");
                out.println("<td colspan=2><div align=center>@Copyrights 2015-16
                </div></td>");
                out.println("</tr></table>");
        }//if

        else{
                out.println("<b><i>Username or Password given are not valid</i></b>");
                RequestDispatcher rd=request.getRequestDispatcher("/Login.html");
                rd.include(request, response);
                return;
        }
        out.println("  </BODY>");
        out.println("</HTML>");
        out.flush();
        out.close();
    }
}
```

In Listing 8.6, various links, such as InBox, Bulk Mail, Sent Items, Write Mail, and Logout, are displayed for the user. You need to create various Java classes to handle the mailing activities, such as sending and receiving mails in inbox. Let's now create the Mail.java file.

Creating the Mail.java File

When a user clicks the InBox hyperlink from the view, the `InboxServlet` object along with the `MailsDAO` object uses the `Mail` Java Bean class, which holds the properties related to e-mails, including `mailid`, `fromid`, `subject`, `sentDate`, and `content`. The Mail.java file contains the get and set methods used to set and retrieve these properties. Listing 8.7 shows the Mail.java file (you can find this file online in the code/Chapter8/sessionex1 folder):

Listing 8.7: Creating the Mail.java File

```
package com.santosh.servlets;
/**
* @author Santosh
*/
public class Mail {
  private String mailid, fromid, subject, sentDate, content;

  public String getFromid() {
        return fromid;
  }

  public void setFromid(String fromid) {
        this.fromid = fromid;
  }

  public String getMailid() {
        return mailid;
  }

  public void setMailid(String mailid) {
        this.mailid = mailid;
  }

  public String getSentDate() {
        return sentDate;
  }

  public void setSentDate(String sentDate) {
```

```
            this.sentDate = sentDate;
      }

      public String getSubject() {
            return subject;
      }

      public void setSubject(String subject) {
            this.subject = subject;
      }

      public String getContent() {
            return content;
      }

      public void setContent(String content) {
            this.content = content;
      }
}
```

Creating the MailsDAO.java File

The MailsDAO.java file is used to connect to the sandb database and get all the mails for the given user name. Listing 8.8 provides the source code for this file (you can find this file online in the code/Chapter8/sessionex1 folder):

Listing 8.8: Creating the MailsDAO.java File

```
package com.santosh.servlets;
/**
* @author Santosh
*/
import java.util.*;
import java.sql.*;

public class MailsDAO {

   public Collection getMails(String uname){
         /*
          * Connect to Mail server and get all
          * the mails of the given username
          * This can be done using Java Mail API
          * Java Mail API concept is out of scope of this book
          * and thus for this example we will get the mails from DB
          * instead of getting diverted towards Java Mail API
          */
         try {
                Connection con=DriverConnection.getConnection();
                Statement st=con.createStatement();
                ResultSet rs=st.executeQuery(
                "select fromid, subject, sentdate from mails where uname='"+uname+"'");
                ArrayList al=new ArrayList();
                int count=1;
                while (rs.next()){
                        Mail m=new Mail();
                        m.setMailid(count+"");
                        m.setFromid(rs.getString(1));
                        m.setSubject(rs.getString(2));
                        m.setSentDate(rs.getString(3));
                        al.add(m);
                        count++;
```

```
                }
                return al;
            }
            catch(Exception e){e.printStackTrace();}
            return null;
    }

    public Mail getMail(String uname, String id){
            try {
                Connection con=DriverConnection.getConnection();
                Statement st=con.createStatement();
                ResultSet rs=st.executeQuery(
                "select fromid, subject, sentdate, content from mails where
                uname='"+uname+"' and mid="+id);
                if (rs.next()){
                        Mail m=new Mail();
                        m.setFromid(rs.getString(1));
                        m.setSubject(rs.getString(2));
                        m.setSentDate(rs.getString(3));
                        m.setContent(rs.getString(4));
                        return m;
                }
            }
            catch(Exception e){e.printStackTrace();}
            return null;
    }
}
```

NOTE

Although the MailsDAO.java file can also be created by using the Java Mail API, but if you need to retrieve the mails from the sandb database, the Java Mail API is not used.

Creating the InboxServlet Servlet

The `InboxServlet` Servlet displays all the mails retrieved by the previous page of a given user name. The inbox shows all the mails received by a specified user name, along with other details such as sender id, sent date, and subject. Listing 8.9 shows the code for the InboxServlet.java file (you can find this file online in the code/Chapter8/sessionex1 folder):

Listing 8.9: Creating the InboxServlet.java File

```
package com.santosh.servlets;
/**
* @author Santosh
*/
import java.io.IOException;
import java.io.PrintWriter;
import java.util.*;

import javax.servlet.ServletException;
import javax.servlet.http.HttpServlet;
import javax.servlet.http.HttpServletRequest;
import javax.servlet.http.HttpServletResponse;

public class InboxServlet extends HttpServlet
{

   public void doGet(
   HttpServletRequest request,
   HttpServletResponse response)
```

```
	throws ServletException, IOException
	{
		response.setContentType("text/html");
		PrintWriter out = response.getWriter();

		String uname=request.getParameter("uname");

		out.println("<html><head>");
		out.println("<title>InBox Page</title>");
		out.println("</head><body>");
		out.println("<table width=98% height=95% border=1><tr>");
		out.println("<td height=45 colspan=2 align=center><font size=5>My Email
		Site</font></td>");
		out.println("</tr><tr>");
		out.println("<td width=12% height=545 align=center valign=top>");
		out.println("<p> </p><p><font size=4>");
		out.println("<a href='inbox?uname="+uname+"'>InBox</a>");
		out.println("</font></p>");
		out.println("<p><font size=4>Bulk Mail</font></p>");
		out.println("<p><font size=4>Sent Items</font></p>");
		out.println("<p><font size=4>Write Mail</font></p>");
		out.println("<p><font size=4><a href='Login.html'>Logout</a></font></p>");
		out.println("<p> </p></td>");
		out.println("<td width=88% align=left valign=top><p><font size=4>Welcome,
		"+uname+"</font></p>");
		out.println("<table width=100% height=82 border=0 cellpadding=0
		cellspacing=0>");
		out.println("<tr bgcolor=#CCCCCC>");
		out.println("<th width=8%>  </th>");
		out.println("<th width=26% align=center>From</th>");
		out.println("<th width=41%>Subject</th>");
		out.println("<th width=25%>Sent Date</th>");
		out.println("</tr>");

		MailsDAO md=new MailsDAO();
		Collection c=md.getMails(uname);
		Iterator i=c.iterator();
		while (i.hasNext()){
			Mail m=(Mail)i.next();
			out.println("<tr>");
			out.println("<td align=center><input type=checkbox
			name=checkbox></td>");
			out.println("<td align=left>"+m.getFromid()+"</td>");
			out.println("<td><a href='viewMail?id="+m.
			getMailid()+"&uname="+uname+"'>"+m.getSubject()+"</a></td>");
			out.println("<td>"+m.getSentDate()+"</td>");
			out.println("</tr>");
		}
		out.println("</table>");
		out.println("<p><font size=4></font></p>");
		out.println("</td></tr><tr align=center>");
		out.println("<td colspan=2><div align=center>@Copyrights
		2015-16</div></td>");
		out.println("</tr></table>");
		out.println("</body></html>");
	}
}
```

Creating the ViewMailServlet Servlet

The `ViewMailServlet` Servlet displays all the information related to a particular mail in the inbox of a given user name, such as sender id, sent date, subject, and message. This Servlet displays the information when a user clicks a hyperlink of a specific mail to read the mail. Listing 8.10 provides the source code for ViewMailServlet.java file (you can find this file online in the code/Chapter8/sessionex1 folder):

Listing 8.10: Creating the ViewMailServlet.java File

```
package com.santosh.servlets;
/**
 * @author Santosh
 */
import java.io.IOException;
import java.io.PrintWriter;

import javax.servlet.ServletException;
import javax.servlet.http.HttpServlet;
import javax.servlet.http.HttpServletRequest;
import javax.servlet.http.HttpServletResponse;

public class ViewMailServlet extends HttpServlet {

  public void doGet(
  HttpServletRequest request,
  HttpServletResponse response)
  throws ServletException, IOException {

        response.setContentType("text/html");
        PrintWriter out = response.getWriter();

        String uname=request.getParameter("uname");
        String mail_no=request.getParameter("id");

        MailsDAO md=new MailsDAO();
        Mail m=md.getMail(uname, mail_no);
        out.println("<html><head>");
        out.println("<title>View Mail Page</title>");
        out.println("</head><body>");
        out.println("<table width=98% height=95% border=1><tr> ");
        out.println("<td height=45 colspan=2 align=center><font size=5>My Email
        Site</font></td>");
        out.println("</tr><tr> ");
        out.println("<td width=12% height=545 align=center valign=top> ");
        out.println("<p> </p><p><font size=4>");
        out.println("<a href='inbox?uname="+uname+"'>InBox</a>");
        out.println("</font></p>");
        out.println("<p><font size=4>Bulk Mail</font></p>");
        out.println("<p><font size=4>Sent Items</font></p>");
        out.println("<p><font size=4>Write Mail</font></p>");
        out.println("<p><font size=4><a href='Login.html'>Logout</a></font></p>");
        out.println("<p> </p></td>");
        out.println("<td width=88% align=left valign=top><p><font size=4>Welcome,
        "+uname+"</font></p>");
        out.println("<table width=100% height=100% border=0 cellpadding=0
        cellspacing=0>");
        out.println("<tr bgcolor=#CCCCCC> ");
        out.println("<th height=34 colspan=2 bgcolor=#CCCCCC>Read Mail</th>");
        out.println("</tr><tr bgcolor=#CCCCCC> ");
        out.println("<td width=37% height=54 bgcolor=#FFFFFF>From ID :
        <strong>"+m.getFromid()+"</strong></td>");
```

```
            out.println("<td width=63% bgcolor=#FFFFFF>Subject :
            <strong>"+m.getSubject()+"</strong></td>");
            out.println("</tr><tr bgcolor=#FFFFFF> ");
            out.println("<td height=36 colspan=2><form method=post action=sendReply>");
            out.println("<input type=submit name=Submit value=Reply>");
            out.println("<input name=uname type=hidden value='"+uname+"'>");
            out.println("<input name=fromid type=hidden value='"+m.getFromid()+"'>");
            out.println("<input name=subject type=hidden value='"+m.getSubject()+"'>");
            out.println("<input name=content type=hidden value='"+m.getContent()+"'>");
            out.println("</form></td></tr>");
            out.println("<tr valign=top bgcolor=#CCCCCC> ");
            out.println("<td height=375 colspan=2
            bgcolor=#FFFFFF><p><strong>Message</strong>:</p>");
            out.println("<blockquote> ");
            out.println("<p>"+m.getContent()+"</p>");
            out.println("</blockquote></td>");
            out.println("</tr></table>");
            out.println("</td></tr>");
            out.println("<tr align=center> ");
            out.println("<td colspan=2><div align=center>@Copyrights
            2015-16</div></td>");
            out.println("</tr></table>");
            out.println("</body></html>");
    }
}
```

Creating the SendReplyServlet Servlet

The `SendReplyServlet` Servlet is used to send replies of a mail. Listing 8.11 shows the code of the SendReplyServlet.java file (you can find this file online in the code/Chapter8/sessionex1 folder):

Listing 8.11: Creating the SendReplyServlet.java File

```
package com.santosh.servlets;
/**
 * @author Santosh
 */
import java.io.IOException;
import java.io.PrintWriter;

import javax.servlet.ServletException;
import javax.servlet.http.HttpServlet;
import javax.servlet.http.HttpServletRequest;
import javax.servlet.http.HttpServletResponse;

public class SendReplyServlet extends HttpServlet {

   public void doPost(HttpServletRequest request, HttpServletResponse response)
   throws ServletException, IOException {

         response.setContentType("text/html");
         PrintWriter out = response.getWriter();

         String uname=request.getParameter("uname");
         String fromid=request.getParameter("fromid");
         String subject=request.getParameter("subject");
         String content=request.getParameter("content");

         out.println("<html><head>");
         out.println("<title>Reply Page</title>");
         out.println("</head><body>");
```

```
            out.println("<table width=98% height=95% border=1><tr>");
            out.println("<td height=45 colspan=2 align=center><font size=5>My Email
            Site</font></td>");
            out.println("</tr><tr>");
            out.println("<td width=12% height=545 align=center valign=top>");
            out.println("<p> </p><p><font size=4>");
            out.println("<a href='inbox?uname="+uname+"'>InBox</a>");
            out.println("</font></p>");
            out.println("<p><font size=4>Bulk Mail</font></p>");
            out.println("<p><font size=4>Sent Items</font></p>");
            out.println("<p><font size=4>Write Mail</font></p>");
            out.println("<p><font size=4><a href='Login.html'>Logout </a></font></p>");
            out.println("<p> </p></td>");
            out.println("<td width=88% align=left valign=top><p><font size=4>Welcome,
            "+uname+"</font></p>");
            out.println("<form name=form1 method=post action=Send.html>");
            out.println("<table width=100% height=100% border=0 cellpadding=0
            cellspacing=0>");
            out.println("<tr bgcolor=#CCCCCC> ");
            out.println("<th height=34 colspan=2 bgcolor=#CCCCCC>Read Mail</th>");
            out.println("</tr>");
            out.println("<tr bgcolor=#CCCCCC> ");
            out.println("<td width=15% height=38 bgcolor=#FFFFFF>To : </td>");
            out.println("<td width=85% bgcolor=#FFFFFF><input name=to type=text id=to
            value="+fromid+"></td>");
            out.println("</tr>");
            out.println("<tr bgcolor=#CCCCCC> ");
            out.println("<td height=35 bgcolor=#FFFFFF>Subject : </td>");
            out.println("<td bgcolor=#FFFFFF><strong>");
            out.println("<input name=subject type=text id=subject value='Re:
            "+subject+"'>");
            out.println("</strong></td></tr>");
            out.println("<tr bgcolor=#CCCCCC> ");
            out.println("<td height=35 bgcolor=#FFFFFF><strong>Message:</strong></td>");
            out.println("<td bgcolor=#FFFFFF> </td>");
            out.println("</tr>");
            out.println("<tr align=left valign=top bgcolor=#CCCCCC> ");
            out.println("<td colspan=2 bgcolor=#FFFFFF><textarea name=content cols=100
            rows=20 id=content>"+content+"</textarea></td>");
            out.println("</tr>");
            out.println("<tr bgcolor=#CCCCCC> ");
            out.println("<td height=35 bgcolor=#FFFFFF> </td>");
            out.println("<td bgcolor=#FFFFFF><input type=submit value=Send></td>");
            out.println("</tr></table>");
            out.println("</form></td></tr>");
            out.println("<tr align=center> ");
            out.println("<td colspan=2><div align=center>@Copyrights
            2015-16</div></td>");
            out.println("</tr></table>");
            out.println("</body></html>");
    }
}
```

Creating the Deployment Descriptor File

Now, the final step in completing the application is to create the deployment descriptor file (`web.xml`). This file maps all the Servlets used in this application with their respective URLs. Listing 8.12 shows the `web.xml` file (you can find this file online in the code/Chapter8/sessionex1/WEB-INF folder):

Listing 8.12: Creating the `web.xml` File

```
<?xml version="1.0" encoding="UTF-8"?>
<web-app>
  <servlet>
        <servlet-name>LoginServlet</servlet-name>
        <servlet-class>com.santosh.servlets.LoginServlet</servlet-class>
  </servlet>
  <servlet>
        <servlet-name>InboxServlet</servlet-name>
        <servlet-class>com.santosh.servlets.InboxServlet</servlet-class>
  </servlet>
  <servlet>
        <servlet-name>ViewMailServlet</servlet-name>
        <servlet-class> com.santosh.servlets.ViewMailServlet</servlet-class>
  </servlet>
  <servlet>
        <servlet-name>SendReplyServlet</servlet-name>
        <servlet-class> com.santosh.servlets.SendReplyServlet </servlet-class>
  </servlet>
  <servlet-mapping>
        <servlet-name>LoginServlet</servlet-name>
        <url-pattern>/login</url-pattern>
  </servlet-mapping>
  <servlet-mapping>
        <servlet-name>InboxServlet</servlet-name>
        <url-pattern>/inbox</url-pattern>
  </servlet-mapping>
  <servlet-mapping>
        <servlet-name>ViewMailServlet</servlet-name>
        <url-pattern>/viewMail</url-pattern>
  </servlet-mapping>
  <servlet-mapping>
        <servlet-name>SendReplyServlet</servlet-name>
        <url-pattern>/sendReply</url-pattern>
  </servlet-mapping>
  <welcome-file-list>
        <welcome-file>SiteHome.html</welcome-file>
  </welcome-file-list>
</web-app>
```

Creating Database Tables

After creating all the preceding files, you need to create two tables, `userdetails` and `mails`, in the `sandb` database. The `userdetails` table stores user details and the `mails` table stores the mails of a user.

Perform the following steps to create the two tables and insert rows into them:

1. Create the `userdetails` table in the `sandb` database by using the following SQL command:

```
create table userdetails(uname varchar2(20), pass varchar2(15), address varchar2(20),
phno number(15), email varchar2(25));
```

2. Insert a row into the `userdetails` table by using the following SQL command:

```
insert into userdetails values ('to_santoshk','123456','Hyderabad',
9704309999,'to_santosh@yahoo.com');
```

3. Create the `mails` table by using the following SQL command:

```
create table mails(mid number(4), uname varchar2(15), fromid varchar2(15), subject
varchar2(25), sentdate date, content varchar2(30));
```

4. Insert rows into the `mails` table by using the following SQL commands:

```
insert into mails values(1,'to_santoshk','user1@xyz.com','Test Mail1 Subject',
 '10-jan-02','Test Mail1 Content');
```

```
insert into mails values(2,'to_santoshk','user2@xyz.com','Test Mail2 Subject',
   '10-jan-02','Test Mail2 Content');
insert into mails values(3,'to_santoshk','user3@xyz.com','Test Mail3 Subject',
   '10-jan-02','Test Mail3 Content');

insert into mails values(4,'to_santoshk','user4@xyz.com','Test Mail4 Subject',
   '10-jan-02','Test Mail4 Content');
```

After creating the required tables, let's discuss the directory structure of the application, which will help to understand where to place the appropriate files.

Creating Directory Structure

Now, create a directory structure and arrange all the files created in the preceding sections accordingly, as shown in Figure 8.1:

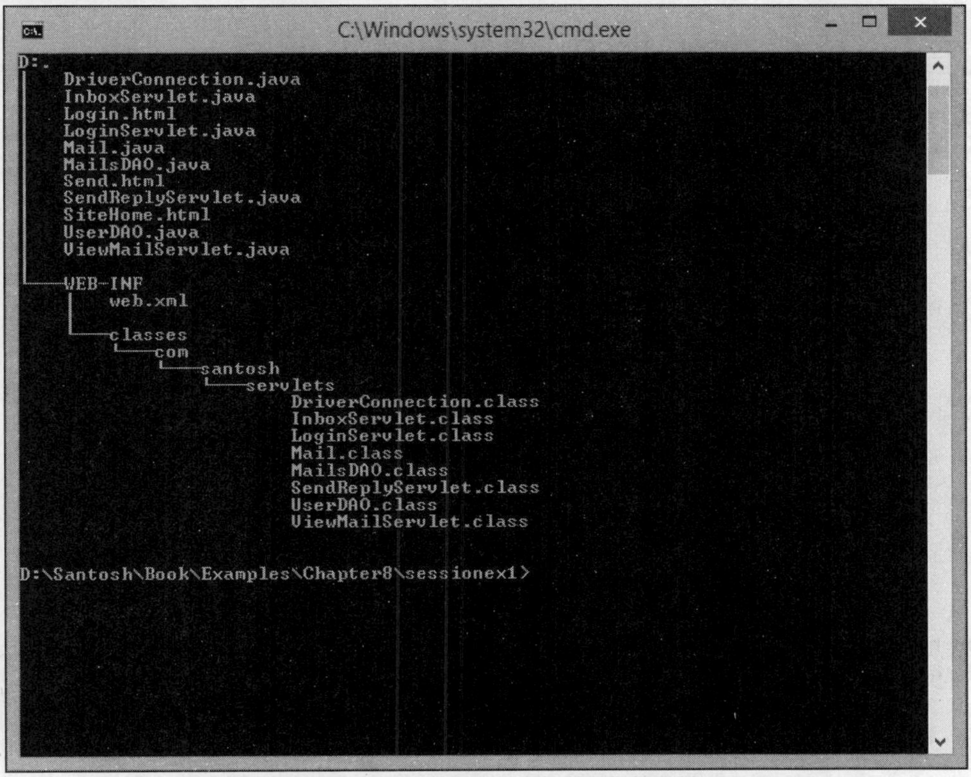

Figure 8.1: Displaying the Directory Structure of the sessionex1 Application

After arranging all the files in the directory structure, copy the **sessionex1** folder to the `<tomcat home>\webapps` folder.

After creating all required files for the application, let's run the application.

Running the Application

To run the **sessionex1** application, perform the following tasks:

1. Start the Tomcat server and use the http://localhost:9090/sessionex1/ URL to run the application. In our case, we use port number 9090 because at our computer, Tomcat is running on this port.

The home page of the application appears, as shown in Figure 8.2:

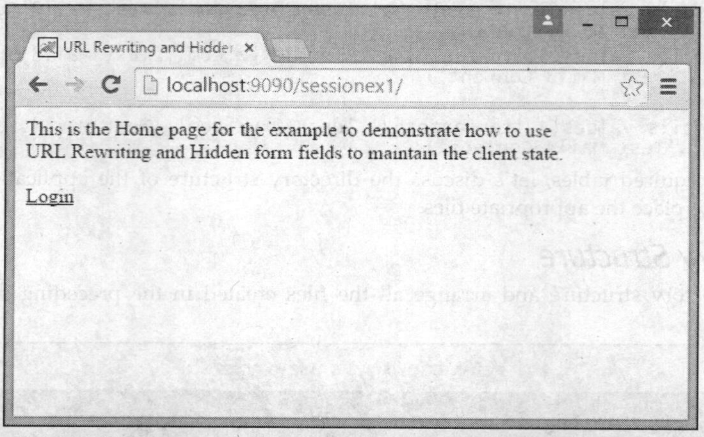

Figure 8.2: Showing the Home Page of the sessionex1 Application

2. Click the Login hyperlink to display the Login.html page, as shown in Figure 8.3:

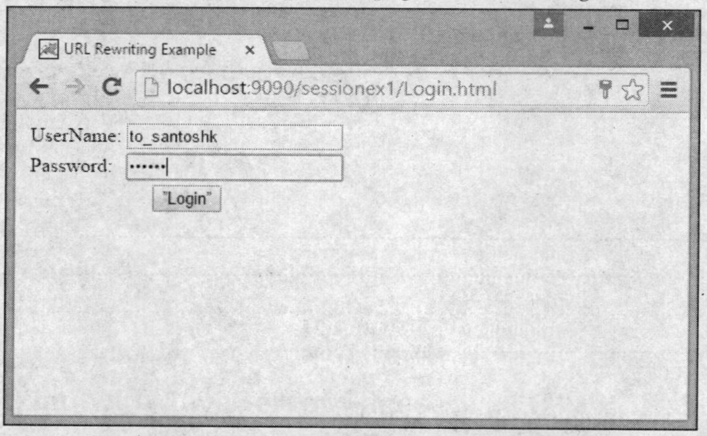

Figure 8.3: Showing the Login Page of the sessionex1 Application

3. Enter the user name and password as `to_santoshk` and `123456`, respectively, and click the Login button. The next view appears, as shown in Figure 8.4:

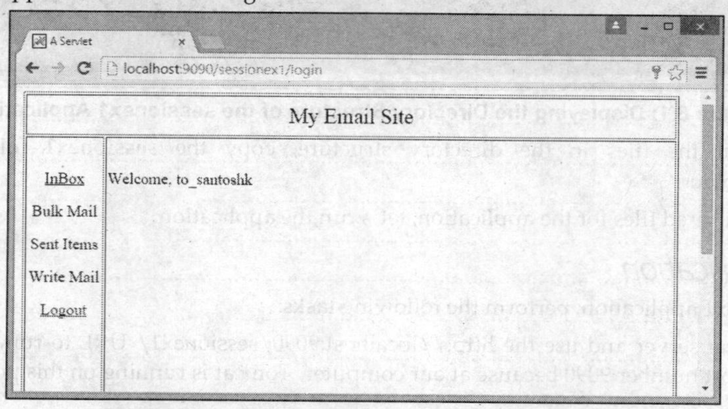

Figure 8.4: Showing the Mail Box of to_santoshk

4. Click the InBox hyperlink to display the inbox for the `to_santoshk` user, as shown in Figure 8.5:

Figure 8.5: Displaying the Mails Received by to_santoshk

Figure 8.5 shows the mails received by the `to_santoshk` user.

5. Click the subject of a particular mail to display information related to the mail, as shown in Figure 8.6:

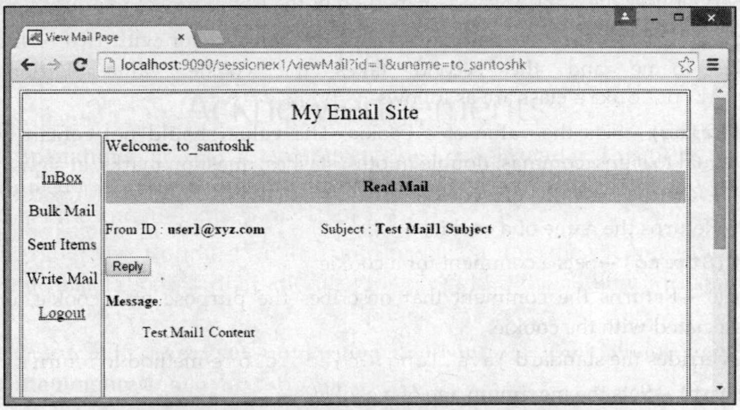

Figure 8.6: Showing the Details of the Selected Mail.

6. Click the Reply button on this page. The next screen appears, as shown in Figure 8.7:

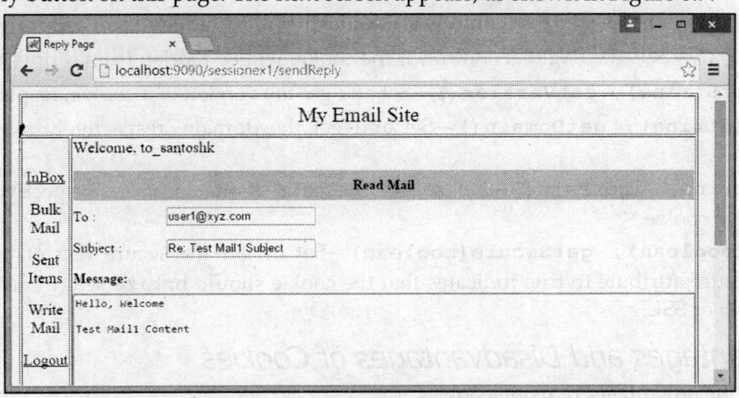

Figure 8.7: Sending Reply of the Mail

After understanding how to perform session tracking by using the URL rewriting and hidden form field mechanisms and creating the application to implement these mechanisms, let's discuss another session tracking mechanism – cookies.

Describing Cookies

A cookie is a file containing the information that is sent by a Web server to a client. Cookies are transmitted to clients through the HTTP response header from the server. They are saved at the client side for the given domain and path. The cookie file persists on the client machine, and the client browser returns the cookies to the original server Whenever the browser requests a resource, the cookie matching the domain and path of the request URL is sent to the Web server as a request header. Cookies are transmitted to the server through HTTP headers when the request is sent to the server. A cookie consists of various attributes, such as name, value, maxage, domain, path, comment, and version number. Cookies should be used only to store non-sensitive information or information that can be retrieved from an authorized source.

The Servlet API provides a class named `Cookie` under the `javax.servlet.http` package. The `javax.servlet.http.Cookie` object is designed to represent an HTTP cookie, which provides a convenient way to exchange data of a cookie between the container and the Servlet. To send cookies to a client, a Servlet can use the `addCookie(Cookie)` method of the `HttpServletResponse` object. This method adds fields to HTTP response headers to send cookies on the client browser. To retrieve the cookies in a request returned by the browser, the Servlet uses the `getCookies()` method of the `HttpServletRequest` interface.

The `javax.servlet.http.Cookie` class consists of one constructor with two String arguments: the first takes the cookie name and the second takes the cookie value. Various methods in the `javax.servlet.http.Cookie` class are as follows:

- **`setValue(String)`** – Sets the value of a cookie. The value should not contain white space, brackets, parentheses, equal to signs, commas, double quotes, slashes, question marks, at signs, colons, or semicolons.
- **`getValue()`** – Returns the value of a cookie.
- **`getName()`** – Returns the name of a cookie.
- **`setComment(String)`** – Sets a comment for a cookie.
- **`getComment()`** – Returns the comment that describes the purpose of a cookie, or null if there are no comments associated with the cookie.
- **`clone()`** – Overrides the standard `java.lang.Object.clone` method to return a copy of the cookie.
- **`setMaxAge(int)`** – Sets the maximum age of a cookie.
- **`getSecure()`** – Returns true when the browser sends a cookie over a secure protocol and returns false otherwise.
- **`isHttpOnly()`** – Gets the flag that controls if the cookie will be hidden from scripts on the client side.
- **`setHttpOnly()`** – Sets the flag that controls if the cookie will be hidden from scripts on the client side.
- **`setVersion(String), getVersion()`** – Set and get the version of a cookie, respectively.
- **`setDomain(String), getDomain()`** – Set and get the domain, respectively, with which a cookie is associated.
- **`setPath(String), getPath()`** – Set or get the path of the location, respectively, where the client should return a cookie.
- **`setSecure(boolean), getSecure(boolean)`** – Set or get the secure flag of a cookie, respectively. Setting the secure attribute to true indicates that the cookie should only be sent by using a secure protocol, such as HTTPS or SSL.

Listing the Advantages and Disadvantages of Cookies

The following are the advantages of using cookies:

- Cookies reduce network traffic compared to URL rewriting.
- Cookies maintain client data.

- Cookies help reduce the complexity of application logic, as you do not need to read and write the query string or path info in all the views.

The following are the disadvantages of using cookies:

- Cookies are not secure; they can be viewed and modified and so personal information can be exposed.
- Cookies are HTTP-specific and so can be used for HTTP requests only.
- Cookie size allocated for a client is limited and varies from one client application to another. Most browsers support 20 cookies for each domain, a total of 300 cookies, and 4 KB as the maximum size of each cookie. Due to this limited size, cookies cannot store large user data.
- Clients can disable cookies, i.e., a client may not allow you to save a cookie in its system.

Considering the Situations to Use Cookies

You can use the cookie mechanism under the following situations:

- When we want to reduce the network traffic
- Cookies are stored at the client side so that we can use static pages between the requests to maintain user data.

Now, let's create an application, named **cookiesEx**, to understand the implementation of cookies.

Using Cookies

In the **cookiesEx** application, you learn how to add and retrieve cookies to maintain client data. The application requires following files:

- Home.html
- AddCookieServlet.java
- GetCookieServlet.java
- web.xml

Now, let's create these files one by one in the following sections.

Creating the Home.html File

The Home.html page of the **cookiesEx** application prompts the user to enter the name of the cookie with its values. Listing 8.13 provides the source code for the Home.html file (you can find this file online in the code/Chapter8/cookiesEx folder):

Listing 8.13: Creating the Home.html File

```
<html><body>
<form action="addcookie"> <pre>
  Name : <input type="text" name="cname"/>
  Value : <input type="text" name="cvalue"/>
  <input type="submit" value="Add Cookie"/>
</pre></form></body></html>
```

Creating the AddCookieServlet.java File

The `AddCookieServlet` Servlet is called when a user adds a cookie. The Servlet uses the `addCookie()` method, which adds fields to HTTP response headers, to send cookies to the Web browser. Listing 8.14 shows the code of the AddCookieServlet.java file (you can also find this file online in the code/Chapter8/cookiesEx folder):

Listing 8.14: Creating the AddCookieServlet.java File

```
package com.santosh.servlet;

import javax.servlet.http.*;
import javax.servlet.*;
import java.io.*;
public class AddCookieServlet extends HttpServlet {
```

```
    public void service (HttpServletRequest req, HttpServletResponse res)
    throws ServletException, IOException {
            String name=req.getParameter("cname");
            String value=req.getParameter("cvalue");
            Cookie c=new Cookie(name,value);

            res.addCookie(c);

            res.setContentType("text/html");
            PrintWriter out=res.getWriter();

            String output="<html><body>";
            output+="Cookie Added Successfully <br/>";
            output+="<a href='Home.html'>Add One More</a><br/>";
            output+="<a href='viewcookies'>View Cookies</a>";
            output+="</body></html>";

            out.println(output);
    }//service
}//class
```

Creating the GetCookieServlet.java File

The `GetCookieServlet` Servlet retrieves the requested cookie. This Servlet uses the `getCookies()` method of the `HttpServletRequest` object to retrieve the cookies returned by the browser. Listing 8.15 provides the source code for the GetCookieServlet.java file (you can also find this file online in the code/Chapter8/cookiesEx folder):

Listing 8.15: Creating the GetCookieServlet.java File

```
package com.santosh.servlet;
import javax.servlet.http.*;
import javax.servlet.*;
import java.io.*;
public class GetCookieServlet extends HttpServlet {
    public void service (HttpServletRequest req, HttpServletResponse res)
    throws ServletException, IOException {
            res.setContentType("text/html");
            PrintWriter out=res.getWriter();
            out.println("<html><body><table border=1>");
            out.println("<tr><th>Name</th><th>Value</th></tr>");
            Cookie[] c=req.getCookies();
            if (c!=null){
                    for (int i=0;i<c.length;i++){
                            out.println("<tr><td>"+c[i].getName()+"</td>");
                            out.println("<td>"+c[i].getValue()+"</td></tr>");
                    }//for
            }//if
            out.println("</table><br/><br/>");
            out.println("<a href='index.jsp'>Add One More</a><br/>");
            out.println("</body></html>");
    }//service
}//class
```

Creating the web.xml File

The final step in creating the application is creating the deployment descriptor file (`web.xml`). This file maps the Servlets with their URLs. Listing 8.16 shows the deployment descriptor file (you can find this file online in the code/Chapter8/cookiesEx/WEB-INF folder):

Listing 8.16: Displaying the Code for the `web.xml` File

```
<?xml version="1.0" encoding="UTF-8"?>
  <web-app>
        <servlet>
        <servlet-name>ts1</servlet-name>
        <servlet-class>
               com.santosh.servlet.AddCookieServlet
        </servlet-class>
  </servlet>
  <servlet>
        <servlet-name>ts2</servlet-name>
        <servlet-class>
               com.santosh.servlet.GetCookieServlet
        </servlet-class>
  </servlet>
  <servlet-mapping>
        <servlet-name>ts1</servlet-name>
        <url-pattern>/addcookie</url-pattern>
  </servlet-mapping>
  <servlet-mapping>
        <servlet-name>ts2</servlet-name>
        <url-pattern>/viewcookies</url-pattern>
  </servlet-mapping>
        <welcome-file-list>
        <welcome-file>Home.html</welcome-file>
  </welcome-file-list>
</web-app>
```

After creating all the files, you have to create a directory structure, as shown in Figure 8.8:

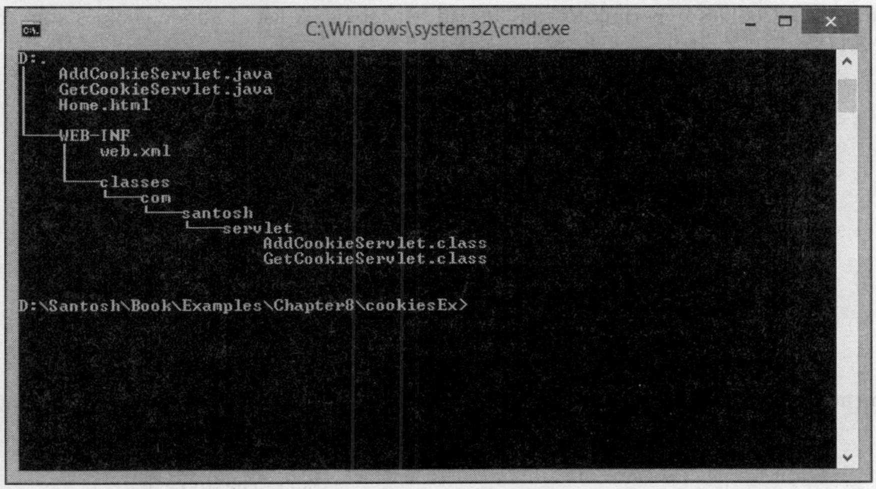

Figure 8.8: Displaying the Directory Structure of the cookiesEx Application

Running the Application

After arranging all the files in a directory structure (Figure 8.8), copy the cookiesEx folder to the `<tomcat home>\webapps` folder. Perform the following steps to run the application:

1. Start the server, if it is not already started. Use the following URL to run the `cookiesEx` application: http://localhost:9090/cookiesEx/

The home page of this application appears, as shown in Figure 8.9:

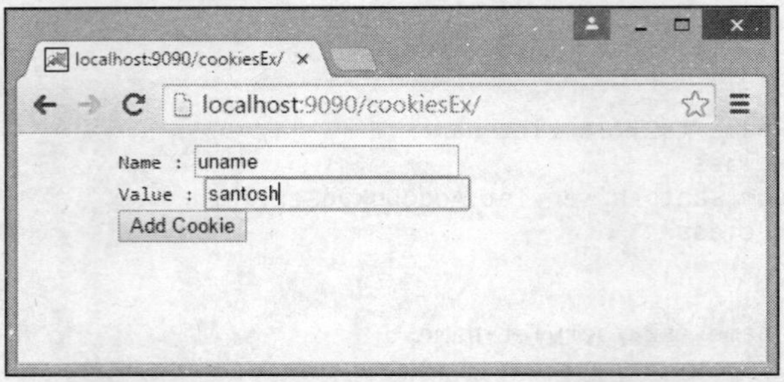

Figure 8.9: Showing the Home Page of the cookiesEx Application

2. Enter `uname` and `santosh` in the Name and Value textboxes, respectively, and click the Add Cookie button. The message `Cookie Added Successfully` is displayed, as shown in Figure 8.10:

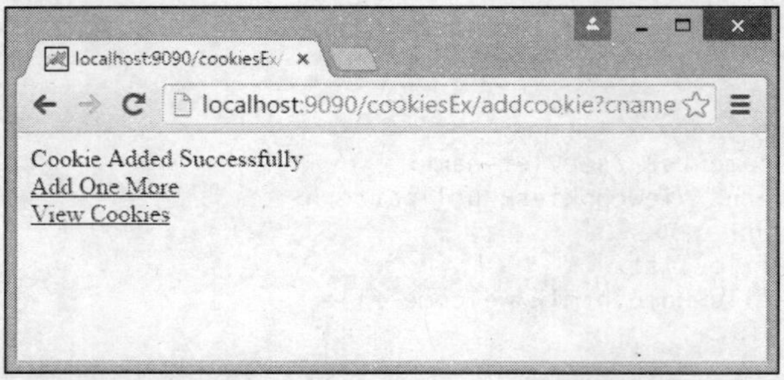

Figure 8.10: Displaying the 'Cookie Added Successfully' Message

3. Click the View Cookies hyperlink to view the added cookie. A list of added cookies appears, as shown in Figure 8.11:

Figure 8.11: Displaying the Page for Viewing Cookies

You can add more cookies by following the preceding steps. The added cookies are shown in Figure 8.12:

Figure 8.12: Showing the Cookies Added

After creating the application with the implementation of the cookies mechanism for session handling, let's now discuss the `HttpSession` mechanism.

Exploring HttpSession

You know that there are many problems associated with URL rewriting, hidden form fields, and cookies; therefore, to associate a user's state with sessions, the Servlet container provides a session management service that is implemented through the `HttpSession` object.

In the `HttpSession` mechanism, the Web container maintains the user's data and tracks the user's session by using URL rewriting or cookies. This mechanism helps maintain a unique identity for each session without using URL rewriting or cookies. The Servlet API defines a simple `HttpSession` interface that allows Servlets to use the session management service provided by the Servlet container.

Using `HttpSession` in Servlets involves the following tasks:

- Creating a new session object when necessary
- Locating the session object associated with the current request
- Storing information in a session
- Attaching the session identity to the URLs
- Looking up information in a session
- Discarding completed or abandoned sessions

Now, let's describe each of these one by one in the following sections.

Creating a Session Object

A session is considered new if the client request does not carry the session identity or the client has not yet selected to join the session. The `isNew()` method of the `HttpSession` interface returns true if the session is created in the current request and returns false if it is a pre-existing session.

When you want to create and associate a new session with a client, you call the `getSession()` or `getSession(boolean)` method of the `HttpServletRequest` interface.

Locating a Session Object Associated with the Current Request

When a Servlet needs to locate a session associated with the current request and use it to retrieve or store data, it calls the `getSession()` method of the `HttpServletRequest` object. The `getSession()` method requests the Servlet container for the `HttpSession` object. This method takes an optional parameter, boolean, i.e., you have two versions of this method: `getSession()` and `getSession(boolean)`.

The `getSession()` method is used to create or locate a session. This method performs the following operations:

- Finds whether or not the current request holds the session id in cookies or requests the URI's path info. This method also determines whether or not it can locate a session. If a session is located, it considers the request as a part of an existing session; if not, it implies that the client has not yet joined the session. If the session is located, it returns the located `HttpSession` object. However, if the session cannot be located, it implies that the user has not joined the session.
- Returns null value if false Boolean argument is passed through the `getSession()` method.
- Performs the following operations if it is invoked either with no argument or by passing true as the argument:
  - Creates a new session
  - Prepares a unique identity for the new session
  - Sets this identity into a cookie with the name `jsessionid`
  - Returns a session object

Difference between getSession() and getSession(Boolean) Methods

The only difference between the `getSession()` and `getSession(Boolean)` methods is that when the `getSession(false)` method is used, the Web container tries to locate and return the session, but if the Web container is not able to locate the session, it returns null. On the other hand, if the `getSession()` or `getSession(true)` method is called, the Web container tries to locate the session and returns it. If the `getSession()` method is not able to locate the session, it creates a new session and associates it with the client request.

Storing Information in a Session

Session objects have a built-in data structure that allows you to store any number of key value (or name value) pairs. The `HttpSession` interface defines two methods to associate a value with a key (or name):

- **`putValue(String key, Object value)`** — Stores a value, with a name, in the session object. The `putValue()` method is deprecated in Servlet 2.2 and has been replaced with the `setAttribute()` method. Therefore, `putValue()` method is recommended to be used only with Servlet 2.1.
- **`setAttribute(String key, Object value)`** — Stores a value, with a name, in the session object.

NOTE

The `putValue()` or `setAttribute()` method replaces the attribute value if the attribute already exists in the session, that is, if the given name is already mapped to a value. In this case, if the given value is null, these methods act similar to the `removeAttribute()` method.

Attaching Session Identity to URLs

You learned earlier that the `getSession()` method can be used to create a new session. When the Servlet container creates a session object, it creates a unique identity and sets it into the cookie with the name `jsessionid`. However, in some situations, a browser may not accept cookies, which means that session tracking with cookies is not possible. In such cases, you need to append the session identity to URLs by using URL rewriting. You can use the `getId()` method of the `HttpSession` interface to get the session identity and add it to the path info of all the URLs returned to the clients. However, adding session ids to the URLs is not necessary if the client supports cookies, and therefore, you want to find out whether the requested session id is from the cookie or not, before setting the session identifier to the URLs. You can use the `isRequestedSessionIdFromCookie()` method of the `HttpServletRequest` object to find out whether the requested session identity is from a cookie or not.

The `isRequestedSessionIdFromCookie()` method returns true if the session to which the current request is associated is located by using the session identity obtained from the cookie, and false if it is located from the request URI. The following code snippet shows the implementation of the `isRequestedSessionIdFromCookie()` method:

```
public void service(HttpServletRequest req, HttpServletResponse res)
{
   HttpSession hs=req.getSession();
   if (hs.isNew()){
         String sid= hs.getId();
         out.println("<a href='nextPage;jsessionid="+sid+"'>");
         out.println("Go to Next Page</a>");
   }
   else{
         if (req.isRequestedSessionIdFromCookie()){
                out.println("<a href='nextPage'>");
                out.println("Go to Next Page</a>");
         }
         else {

                String sid= hs.getId();
                out.println("<a href='nextPage;jsessionid="+sid+"'>");
```

```
            out.println("Go to Next Page</a>");
        }
    }
}
```

As shown in the preceding code snippet, for each URL, you need to write a huge logic. This unnecessarily increases code complexity and affects its understandability. To avoid this problem, a utility method, `encodeURL(String)`, is defined in the `HttpServletResponse`.

The `encodeURL()` method determines whether or not the URL needs to be rewritten and, if necessary, includes the session ID in the URL.

Most Servlet containers use URL rewriting when a session is new, even if the browser accepts cookies, because the server cannot determine during the first visit of a session whether the browser accepts cookies or not.

The `encodeURL()` method takes the URL as absolute or relative. This method determines whether the session is new or not. If the session is new, this method adds the session id to the given URL as path info and returns it. However, if the session is not new, the method determines if the session to which the current request is associated is available by using the session id obtained from cookie. If this is the case, the `encodeURL()` method returns the URL given as an argument without changing it. If the session identity is not from the cookie, the session id is added to the given URL as path info and is returned, as shown in the following code snippet:

```
public void service(HttpServletRequest req, HttpServletResponse res) …{
  …
  HttpSession hs=req.getSession();
  out.println("<a href='"+res.encodeURL("nextPage")+"'>");
  out.println("Go to Next Page</a>");
}
```

To understand the preceding code snippet, consider the following example:

`String s=res.encodeURL("nextPage");`

In the preceding example, the `encodeURL()` method is invoked by providing the URL as path info..

If the client accepts cookies, the preceding method returns a string with the value, `nextPage`, and if the client does not accept cookies or if the session is new, the method returns a string with the value `nextPage;jsessionid=<sessionid>`, where `<sessionid>` is the session identity of the session.

Looking Up Information in a Session

The `HttpSession` interface defines the following methods to look up information in a session:

- **`Object getValue(String key)`** – Looks up a previously stored value with the given name in the session object. This method returns *null* if no value has been set during the current session.
- **`Object getAttribute(String key)`** – Looks up a previously stored attribute with the given name in the session object. This method returns *null* if no attribute has been set during the current session.
- **`Enumeration getAttributeNames()`** – Returns all the attribute names in the current session. The return value is an enumeration of String.
- **`void removeValue(String attribute)` or `void removeAttribute(String attribute)`** – Removes the attribute from the session. You can use the `removeValue()` or `removeAttribute()` method for removing any values or attributes set during the current session. These two methods take `String` arguments, i.e., the name attribute that has to be removed.
- **`long getCreationTime()`** – Returns the time in milliseconds since midnight, January 1, 1970 (GMT), the exact time at which this session was created.
- **`long getLastAccessedTime()`** – Returns the time in milliseconds since midnight, January 1, 1970 (GMT), the time at which this session was last accessed by the client.
- **`String getId()`** – Returns the unique identifier generated for this session. This identity can be used as the key name when information about sessions is being logged.
- **`void setMaxInactiveInterval(int interval)`** – Returns the time in sec between the client requests before the time servlet container invalidates the session.

- **int getMaxInactiveInternal()** — Returns the maximum time interval in sec that the servlet container will keep the session open between the client accesses.

Discarding Completed or Abandoned Sessions

A session can be invalidated by explicitly calling the `invalidate()` method on the session object. The session can also be invalidated automatically if it is not accessed within a specified time interval, i.e., at timeout. The following methods are helpful while invalidating a session:

- **invalidate()** — Invalidates a session and unbinds all the objects associated with it.
- **setMaxInactiveInterval(int seconds)** — Sets the amount of time, in seconds, that a session can be idle before being automatically invalidated. A negative value indicates that the session will never time out. Note that timeout is maintained on the server and is not the same as the cookie expiration date, which is sent to a client. This timeout period can also be set declaratively in the `web.xml` file by using the `<session-timeout>` tag, as shown in the following code snippet:

```
<session-config>
  <session-timeout>10</session-timeout>
</session-config>
```

In the preceding code snippet, the timeout period is expressed in minutes, but the `setMaxInactiveInterval()` method that allows you to programmatically set this period takes the time period in seconds.

- **int getMaxInactiveInterval()** — Returns the amount of time, in seconds, that a session should be idle before being automatically invalidated.

Listing the Advantages and Disadvantages of HttpSession

The advantages of using `HttpSession` are as follows:

- It is secure and fast as the session is maintained on the server side.
- There is no limit on the size of the session data kept; therefore, you do not have to worry about the size of the session data.

The disadvantages of using `HttpSession` are:

The `HttpSession` mechanism requires huge memory in the Web server, as client data is saved on the server.

You cannot share the data in `HttpSession` among multiple Web applications, which can be done by using cookies.

Considering the Situations to Use HttpSession

`HttpSession` is used when you do not want to expose sensitive and private data to other users. It is also used when you want fast accessing of user data in comparison to other approaches because it is stored at the server side.

Threading Issues of a Session

A single session may get multiple requests at a time. In other words, multiple Servlets executing multiple request threads may access a single session object simultaneously. You need to synchronize the access to session resources as appropriate such that a single request accesses a single session instance at a time.

Sessions in a Clustered Environment

If you configure your application to work in a clustered environment, you must store `Serializable` type objects in the sessions. The `HttpSession` object may need to be transferred from one server instance to another in a cluster.

The servlet container may throw an `IllegalArgumentException` exception if an object is placed in the session that is not serializable while migrating a session.

After understanding the concept of `HttpSession`, let's discuss how to create an application implementing the `HttpSession` mechanism.

Working with HttpSession

In this section, you create a shopping cart application, **httpsessionex**, to demonstrate the use of the `HttpSession` object for session tracking. This application allows you to add and view products in the shopping cart. The application uses the following files:

- Login.html
- DriverConnection.java
- UserDAO.java
- Product. java
- ProductsDAO.java
- LoginServlet.java
- UserHomeServlet.java
- GetProductsServlet.java
- AddProductServlet.java
- GetCartDetailsServlet.java
- LogoutServlet.java
- web.xml

Let's learn to create these files one by one in the following sections.

Creating the Login.html File

The Login page is the starting page of the application, which prompts the user to enter the user name and password for logging in. Listing 8.17 provides you the source code for the Login.html file (you can also find this file online in the code/Chapter8/httpsessionex folder):

Listing 8.17: Creating the Login.html File

```
<html>
  <head> <title>Shopping Cart Example</title> </head>
  <body>
  <table width="95%" height="82%" border="0">
        <tr align="center">
              <td height="39" colspan="2"><strong>
              <font size="5"> MyShopping Site</font></strong>
              </td>
        </tr>
        <tr>
              <td width="21%" height="478" valign="top"><p> </p>
              <blockquote>
                    <p> </p>
              </blockquote></td>
              <td width="70%" align="center" valign="middle">
              <p><font size="6">Login</font></p>
              <form name="form1" method="post" action="login">
              <table width="36%" border="0">
              <tr>
                    <td width="45%"><strong>User Name</strong></td>
                    <td width="55%"><input type="text" name="uname"></td>
              </tr>
              <tr>
                    <td><strong>Password</strong></td>
                    <td><input type="password" name="pass"></td>
              </tr>
              <tr>
                    <td> </td>
                    <td> </td>
```

```
                </tr>
                <tr align="right">
                <td><div align="center">
                <input type="submit" name="Submit" value="LogIN">
                </div></td>
                <td align="center">
                <input type="reset" name="Submit2" value="Reset"></td>
                </tr>
                </table>
                </form></td>
        </tr>
        <tr align="center">
                <td colspan="2"><em>&copy; Copyrights 2015-16</em></td>
        </tr>
    </table>
    </body>
</html>
```

Creating the DriverConnection.java File

The DriverConnection.java file is used to connect to the Oracle database. Listing 8.18 provides the source code for this file (you can find this file online in the code/Chapter8/httpsessionex folder):

Listing 8.18: Creating the DriverConnection.java File

```
package com.santosh.servlets;

import java.sql.*;

public class DriverConnection {

   public static Connection getConnection()
   throws Exception{
         Class.forName("oracle.jdbc.driver.OracleDriver");
         return DriverManager.getConnection(
         "jdbc:oracle:thin:@localhost:1521:sandb","scott","tiger");
   }
}
```

Creating the UserDAO.java File

The UserDAO.java file is used to validate whether the specified user exists in the database or not. Listing 8.19 provides the source code for this file (you can also find this file online in the code/Chapter8/httpsessionex folder):

Listing 8.19: Creating the UserDAO.java File

```
package com.santosh.servlets;
import java.sql.*;
public class UserDAO {
   public boolean validate(String uname, String pass){

        try {
                Connection con=DriverConnection.getConnection();
                Statement st=con.createStatement();
                ResultSet rs=st.executeQuery(
                "select * from userdetails where uname=\'"+uname+"\' and
                pass=\'"+pass+"\'");
                return rs.next();
        }//try
        catch(Exception e){
                e.printStackTrace();
        }
```

```
            return false;
    }
}
```

Creating the Product.java File

The Product.java file is a simple JavaBean that holds the properties related to products. It contains properties such as the product's code, name, and quantity. The `Product` class defines the getter and setter methods for these properties. Listing 8.20 provides the source code for the Product.java file (you can also find this file online in the code/Chapter8/httpsessionex folder):

Listing 8.20: Creating the Product.java File

```
package com.santosh.servlets;

public class Product {
   String code, name;
   double qty;
   public String getCode() {
         return code;
   }
   public void setCode(String code) {
         this.code = code;
   }
   public String getName() {
         return name;
   }
   public void setName(String name) {
         this.name = name;
   }
   public double getQty() {
         return qty;
   }
   public void setQty(double qty) {
         this.qty = qty;
   }
   public boolean equals(Object o){
         if (o instanceof Product)
         return ((Product)o).code.equals(code);
         return false;
   }
}
```

Creating the ProductsDAO.java File

The ProductsDAO.java is a simple Java Data Access Object, and it connects with the database and accesses all the information about a product. Listing 8.21 provides the source code for the ProductsDAO.java file (you can also find this file online in the code/Chapter8/httpsessionex folder):

Listing 8.21: Creating the ProductsDAO.java File

```
package com.santosh.servlets;
import java.sql.*;
import java.util.*;
public class ProductsDAO {

   public Collection getProducts(){
         try {
                Connection con=DriverConnection.getConnection();
                Statement st=con.createStatement();
                ResultSet rs=st.executeQuery("select * from products");
```

```
                ArrayList products=new ArrayList();
                while (rs.next()){
                    Product p=new Product();
                    p.code=rs.getString(1);
                    p.name=rs.getString(2);
                    p.qty=rs.getDouble(3);
                    products.add(p);
                }
                return products;
            }//try
            catch(Exception e){
                e.printStackTrace();
            }
            return null;
    }
}
```

Creating the LoginServlet.java File

The `LoginServlet` Servlet handles the request sent from the Login page. It checks whether the specified username-password pair exists in the database or not. Listing 8.22 provides the source code for the LoginServlet.java file (you can also find this file online in the code/Chapter8/httpsessionex folder):

Listing 8.22: Creating the LoginServlet.java File

```
package com.santosh.servlets;

import java.io.*;
import javax.servlet.*;
import javax.servlet.http.*;
public class LoginServlet extends HttpServlet {

    public void init(){ ud=new UserDAO(); }

    public void doPost(HttpServletRequest request,
    HttpServletResponse response)
    throws ServletException, IOException {

        String uname=request.getParameter("uname");
        String pass=request.getParameter("pass");

        ud=new UserDAO();
        if (ud.validate(uname,pass)){
            //start a session
            HttpSession hs=request.getSession();
            hs.setAttribute("UserName",uname);
            RequestDispatcher rd=request.getRequestDispatcher("home");
            rd.forward(request,response);
        }
        else{
            RequestDispatcher rd=
            request.getRequestDispatcher("Login.html");
            rd.forward(request, response);
        }
    }
    UserDAO ud;
}
```

Creating the UserHomeServlet.java File

The UserHomeServlet Servlet displays a welcome screen with some links. These links allow you to view information about the products and details of the cart, and log out of the application. Listing 8.23 provides the source code for the UserHomeServlet.java file (you can also find this file online in the code/Chapter8/httpsessionex folder):

Listing 8.23: Creating the UserHomeServlet.java File

```
package com.santosh.servlets;

import java.io.*;
import javax.servlet.*;
import javax.servlet.http.*;

public class UserHomeServlet extends HttpServlet {

  public void doPost(HttpServletRequest request,
  HttpServletResponse response)
  throws ServletException, IOException {
        HttpSession hs=request.getSession(false);
        if (hs==null){
               RequestDispatcher rd=
               request.getRequestDispatcher("Login.html");
               rd.forward(request, response);
               return;
        }
        String uname=(String)hs.getAttribute("UserName");

        response.setContentType("text/html");
        PrintWriter out = response.getWriter();
        out.println("<html> <head>");
        out.println("<title>Shopping Cart Example</title>");
        out.println("</head> <body>");
        out.println("<table width='100%' height='90%' border='1'>");
        out.println("<tr align='center'> ");
        out.println("<td height='39' colspan='2'>");
        out.println("<strong><font size='5'>MyShopping Site</font>");
        out.println("</strong></td>");
        out.println("</tr>");
        out.println("<tr> ");
        out.println("<td width='18%' height='500' valign='top'>");
        out.println("<p> </p>");
        out.println("<blockquote><p>");
        out.println("<a href='"+response.encodeURL("getProducts")+"'>");
        out.println("View Products</a></p>");
        out.println("<p><a href='"+response.encodeURL("getCart")+"'>");
        out.println("View Cart Details</a></p>");
        out.println("<p><a href='"+response.encodeURL("logout")+"'>");
        out.println("Logout</a></p>");
        out.println("</blockquote></td>");
        out.println("<td width='82%' align='left' valign='top'>");
        out.println("<font size='6'>Welcome , "+uname+"</font></td>");
        out.println("</tr>");
        out.println("<tr align='center'> ");
        out.println("<td colspan=2>");
        out.println("<em>&copy;Copyrights 2015-16</em></td>");
        out.println("</tr>");
        out.println("</table>");
        out.println("</body> </html>");
```

```
            out.flush();
            out.close();

    }
```

Creating the GetProductsServlet.java File

The GetProductsServlet Servlet is called when the user clicks the View Products link from the UserHomeServlet page. This Servlet displays information of all the products. It also displays a checkbox for every product so that you can select the products and add them to your cart. It displays a textbox where you can enter the quantity of the products to be added to the cart. Listing 8.24 provides the source code for the GetProductsServlet.java file (you can find this file online in the code/Chapter8/httpsessionex folder):

Listing 8.24: Creating the GetProductsServlet.java File

```
package com.santosh.servlets;

import java.io.*;
import javax.servlet.*;
import javax.servlet.http.*;
import java.util.*;

public class GetProductsServlet extends HttpServlet {

   public void init() throws ServletException {
         productsdao=new ProductsDAO();
   }
   public void doGet(HttpServletRequest request,
   HttpServletResponse response)
   throws ServletException, IOException {

         HttpSession hs=request.getSession(false);
         if (hs==null){
                RequestDispatcher rd=
                request.getRequestDispatcher("Login.html");
                rd.forward(request, response);
                return;
         }
         String uname=(String)hs.getAttribute("UserName");


         response.setContentType("text/html");
         PrintWriter out = response.getWriter();

         out.println("<html> <head>");
         out.println("<title>Shopping Cart Example</title>");
         out.println("</head> <body>");
         out.println("<table width='100%' height='90%' border='1'>");
         out.println("<tr align='center'> ");
         out.println("<td height='39' colspan='2'><strong><font size='5'>MyShopping
         Site</font></strong></td>");
         out.println("</tr>");
         out.println("<tr> ");
         out.println("<td width='18%' height='500' valign='top'><p> </p>");
         out.println("<blockquote><p>");
         out.println("<a href='"+response.encodeURL("getProducts")+"'>");
         out.println("View Products</a></p><p>");
         out.println("<a href='"+response.encodeURL("getCart")+"'>");
         out.println("View Cart Details</a></p><p>");
         out.println("<a href='"+response.encodeURL("logout")+"'>");
```

```
        out.println("Logout</a></p>");
        out.println("</blockquote></td>");
        out.println("<td width='82%' align='left' valign='top'><p>");
        out.println("<font size='6'>Welcome , "+uname+"</font></p>");
        out.println("<form method='post'
        action='"+response.encodeURL("addProducts")+"'>");
        out.println("<table width='100%' border='1'>");
        out.println("<tr> ");
        out.println("<th width='8%'>Check</th>");
        out.println("<th width='24%'>Product Code</th>");
        out.println("<th width='28%'>Product Name</th>");
        out.println("<th width='20%'>Available Quantity</th>");
        out.println("<th width='20%'>Required Quantity</th>");
        out.println("</tr>");

        Collection products=productsdao.getProducts();
        if (products==null){
                out.println("<tr><td colspan=5 align=center>");
                out.println("No Products Available");
                out.println("</td></tr>");
        }
        else{
                Iterator i=products.iterator();
                while(i.hasNext()){
                Product p=(Product)i.next();
                out.println("<tr>");
                out.println("<td align='center'>");
                out.println("<input type='checkbox' name='products'
                value='"+p.getCode()+"'/>");
                out.println("<input type='hidden' name='"+p.getCode()+"Name'
                value='"+p.getName()+"'/></td>");
                out.println("<td>"+p.getCode()+"</td>");
                out.println("<td>"+p.getName()+"</td>");
                out.println("<td>"+p.getQty()+"</td>");
                out.println("<td>");
                out.println("<input type='text' name='"+p.getCode()+"'/>");
                out.println("</td></tr>");
                }
        }
        out.println("</table>");
        out.println("<br/><center>");
        out.println("<input type=submit value='Add Products to Cart'/>");
        out.println("</center>");
        out.println("</form>");
        out.println("</td></tr>");
        out.println("<tr align='center'> ");
        out.println("<td colspan='2'>");
        out.println("<em>&copy;Copyrights 2015-16</em></td>");
        out.println("</tr>");
        out.println("</table>");
        out.println("</body> </html>");

        out.flush();
        out.close();
    }
    ProductsDAO productsdao;
}
```

Creating the AddProductServlet.java File

The `AddProductServlet` Servlet is used to add the selected product to the cart. Listing 8.25 provides the source code for the AddProductServlet.java file (you can find this file online in the code/Chapter8/httpsessionex folder):

Listing 8.25: Creating the AddProductsServlet.java File

```
package com.santosh.servlets;

import java.io.*;
import javax.servlet.*;
import javax.servlet.http.*;
import java.util.*;

public class AddProductsServlet extends HttpServlet {

  public void doPost(HttpServletRequest request, HttpServletResponse response)
  throws ServletException, IOException {

        HttpSession hs=request.getSession(false);
        if (hs==null){
               RequestDispatcher rd=request.getRequestDispatcher("Login.html");
               rd.forward(request, response);
               return;
        }
        String uname=(String)hs.getAttribute("UserName");
        ArrayList products=(ArrayList)hs.getAttribute("products");
        if (products==null){
               products=new ArrayList();
               hs.setAttribute("products",products);
        }
        String[] pcodes=request.getParameterValues("products");

        for (int i=0;i<pcodes.length;i++){
               if (request.getParameter(pcodes[i]).equals(""))
               continue;
               Product p=new Product();
               p.code=pcodes[i];
               int j=products.indexOf(p);
               if (j!=-1){
               p=(Product)products.get(j);
               p.qty+=Double.parseDouble(request.getParameter(pcodes[i]));
               }
               else{
               p.name=request.getParameter(pcodes[i]+"Name");
               p.qty=Double.parseDouble(request.getParameter(pcodes[i]));
               products.add(p);
               }
        }//for

        response.setContentType("text/html");
        PrintWriter out = response.getWriter();
        out.println("<html> <head>");
        out.println("<title>Shopping Cart Example</title>");
        out.println("</head> <body>");
        out.println("<table width='100%' height='90%' border='1'>");
        out.println("<tr align='center'> ");
        out.println("<td height='39' colspan='2'><strong><font size='5'>MyShopping
        Site</font></strong></td>");
```

```
        out.println("</tr>");
        out.println("<tr> ");
        out.println("<td width='18%' height='500' valign='top'><p> </p>");
        out.println("<blockquote>");
        out.println("<p><a href='"+response.encodeURL("getProducts")+"'>View
        Products</a></p>");
        out.println("<p><a href='"+response.encodeURL("getCart")+"'>View Cart
        Details</a></p>");
        out.println("<p><a href='"+response.encodeURL("logout")+"'>Logout</a></p>");
        out.println("</blockquote></td>");
        out.println("<td width='82%' align='left' valign='top'><p><font
        size='6'>Welcome , "+uname+"</font></p>" );
        out.println("Products Added successfully to your cart</td>");
        out.println("</tr>");
        out.println("<tr align='center'> ");
        out.println("<td colspan='2'><em>&copy;Copyrights
        2015-16</em></td>");
        out.println("</tr>");
        out.println("</table>");
        out.println("</body> </html>");
        out.flush();
        out.close();
    }
}
```

Creating the GetCartDetailsServlet.java File

The `GetCartDetailsServlet` Servlet shows the details of the cart. It displays the products you have added, with their quantities, product codes, and names. Listing 8.26 provides the source code for the GetCartDetailsServlet.java file (you can find this file online in the code/Chapter8/httpsessionex folder):

Listing 8.26: Creating the GetCartDetailsServlet.java File

```
package com.santosh.servlets;

import java.io.IOException;
import java.io.PrintWriter;
import java.util.Collection;
import java.util.Iterator;

import javax.servlet.RequestDispatcher;
import javax.servlet.ServletException;
import javax.servlet.http.HttpServlet;
import javax.servlet.http.HttpServletRequest;
import javax.servlet.http.HttpServletResponse;
import javax.servlet.http.HttpSession;

public class GetCartDetailsServlet extends HttpServlet {

  public void doGet(HttpServletRequest request, HttpServletResponse response)
  throws ServletException, IOException {
        HttpSession hs=request.getSession(false);
        if (hs==null){
              RequestDispatcher rd=request.getRequestDispatcher("Login.html");
              rd.forward(request, response);
              return;
        }
        String uname=(String)hs.getAttribute("UserName");

        response.setContentType("text/html");
        PrintWriter out = response.getWriter();
```

```
        out.println("<html> <head>");
        out.println("<title>Shopping Cart Example</title>");
        out.println("</head> <body>");
        out.println("<table width='100%' height='90%' border='1'>");
        out.println("<tr align='center'> ");
        out.println("<td height='39' colspan='2'><strong><font size='5'>MyShopping
        Site</font></strong></td>");
        out.println("</tr>");
        out.println("<tr> ");
        out.println("<td width='18%' height='500' valign='top'><p> </p>");
        out.println("<blockquote>");
        out.println("<p><a href='"+response.encodeURL("getProducts")+"'>View
        Products</a></p>");
        out.println("<p><a href='"+response.encodeURL("getCart")+"'>View Cart
        Details</a></p>");
        out.println("<p><a href='"+response.encodeURL("logout")+"'>Logout</a></p>");
        out.println("</blockquote></td>");
        out.println("<td width='82%' align='left' valign='top'><p><font
        size='6'>Welcome , "+uname+"</font></p>");
        out.println("<center>Your cart contains the following products");
        out.println("<table width='80%' border='1'>");
        out.println("<tr>");
        out.println("<th width='24%'>Product Code</th>");
        out.println("<th width='28%'>Product Name</th>");
        out.println("<th width='20%'>Quantity</th>");
        out.println("</tr>");

        Collection products=(Collection)hs.getAttribute("products");
        if (products==null){
                out.println("<tr><td colspan=3 align=center>");
                out.println("You have not added any products into cart");
                out.println("</td></tr>");
        }
        else {
                Iterator i=products.iterator();
                while(i.hasNext()){
                        Product p=(Product)i.next();
                        out.println("<tr>");
                        out.println("<td>"+p.getCode()+"</td>");
                        out.println("<td>"+p.getName()+"</td>");
                        out.println("<td>"+p.getQty()+"</td>");
                        out.println("</tr>");
                }
        }
        out.println("</table></center>");
        out.println("</td></tr>");
        out.println("<tr align='center'> ");
        out.println("<td colspan='2'><em>&copy;Copyrights
        2015-16</em></td>");
        out.println("</tr>");
        out.println("</table>");
        out.println("</body> </html>");

        out.flush();
        out.close();

}
```

Creating the LogoutServlet.java File

The `LogoutServlet` Servlet is called when the user clicks the Logout link from the home page. This Servlet invalidates the session by invoking the `invalidate()` method of the `HttpSession`. Listing 8.27 provides the source code for the LogoutServlet.java file (you can also find this file online in the code/Chapter8/httpsessionex folder):

Listing 8.27: Creating the LogoutServlet.java File

```
package com.santosh.servlets;
import java.io.*;
import javax.servlet.*;
import javax.servlet.http.*;
public class LogoutServlet extends HttpServlet {

   public void doGet(HttpServletRequest request,
   HttpServletResponse response)
   throws ServletException, IOException {
         HttpSession hs=request.getSession(false);
         if (hs!=null)
         hs.invalidate();
         RequestDispatcher rd=request.getRequestDispatcher("Login.html");
         rd.forward(request, response);
   }
}
```

Creating the web.xml File

The final step in completing the application is creating the deployment descriptor file (`web.xml`). This file maps all the Servlets with their URLs. Listing 8.28 provides the `web.xml` file (you can find this file online in the code/Chapter8/httpsessionex folder):

Listing 8.28: Creating the `web.xml` File

```
<?xml version="1.0" encoding="UTF-8"?>
<web-app>
   <servlet>
         <servlet-name>LoginServlet</servlet-name>
         <servlet-class>com.santosh.servlets.LoginServlet</servlet-class>

   </servlet>
   <servlet>
         <servlet-name>UserHomeServlet</servlet-name>
         <servlet-class>com.santosh.servlets.UserHomeServlet</servlet-class>
   </servlet>
   <servlet>
         <servlet-name>GetProductsServlet</servlet-name>
         <servlet-class>com.santosh.servlets.GetProductsServlet</servlet-class>
   </servlet>
   <servlet>
         <servlet-name>AddProductsServlet</servlet-name>
         <servlet-class>com.santosh.servlets.AddProductsServlet</servlet-class>
   </servlet>
   <servlet>
         <servlet-name>GetCartDetailsServlet</servlet-name>
         <servlet-class>com.santosh.servlets.GetCartDetailsServlet</servlet-class>
   </servlet>
   <servlet>
         <servlet-name>LogoutServlet</servlet-name>
         <servlet-class>com.santosh.servlets.LogoutServlet</servlet-class>
   </servlet>
   <servlet-mapping>
```

```
        <servlet-name>LoginServlet</servlet-name>
        <url-pattern>/login</url-pattern>
    </servlet-mapping>
    <servlet-mapping>
        <servlet-name>UserHomeServlet</servlet-name>
        <url-pattern>/home</url-pattern>
    </servlet-mapping>
    <servlet-mapping>
        <servlet-name>GetProductsServlet</servlet-name>
        <url-pattern>/getProducts</url-pattern>
    </servlet-mapping>
    <servlet-mapping>
        <servlet-name>AddProductsServlet</servlet-name>
        <url-pattern>/addProducts</url-pattern>
    </servlet-mapping>
    <servlet-mapping>
        <servlet-name>GetCartDetailsServlet</servlet-name>
        <url-pattern>/getCart</url-pattern>
    </servlet-mapping>
    <servlet-mapping>
        <servlet-name>LogoutServlet</servlet-name>
        <url-pattern>/logout</url-pattern>
    </servlet-mapping>

    <welcome-file-list>
        <welcome-file>Login.html</welcome-file>
    </welcome-file-list>
</web-app>
```

After creating all the preceding files, make sure that the `userdetails` table is created in the `sandb` database (discussed in the Creating Database Tables section). Perform the following steps to create and insert data into the `products` table:

1. Create the `products` table by using the following SQL command:

```
create table products(
pcode varchar2(5),
pname varchar2(20),
avlqty number(10,2));
```

2. Insert data into the `products` table by using the following SQL command:

```
insert into products values('p101','Mouse',250);
insert into products values('p102','Keyboard',500);
insert into products values('p103','Printer',36);
insert into products values('p104','Monitor',80);
insert into products values('p105','Laptop',25);
insert into products values('p106','CD Writer',100);
```

After creating the preceding table in the database, create a directory structure and arrange all the files accordingly, as shown in Figure 8.13:

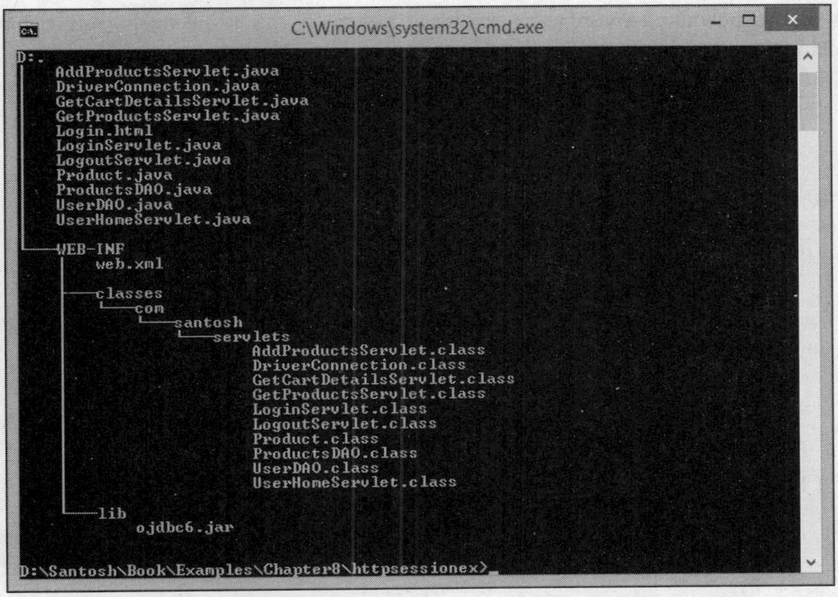

Figure 8.13: Showing the Directory Structure for the httpsessionex Application

After arranging all the files, copy the **httpsessionex** folder to the `<tomcat home>\webapps` folder. Perform the following steps to run the application:

1. Start the Tomcat application server. If it is already in the start mode, you need not restart it. We use the port number 9090 because Tomcat is running on this port in our machine.
2 Use the following URL to run the **httpsessionex** application:

   http://localhost:9090/httpsessionex/

   Figure 8.14 shows the Login page of this application:

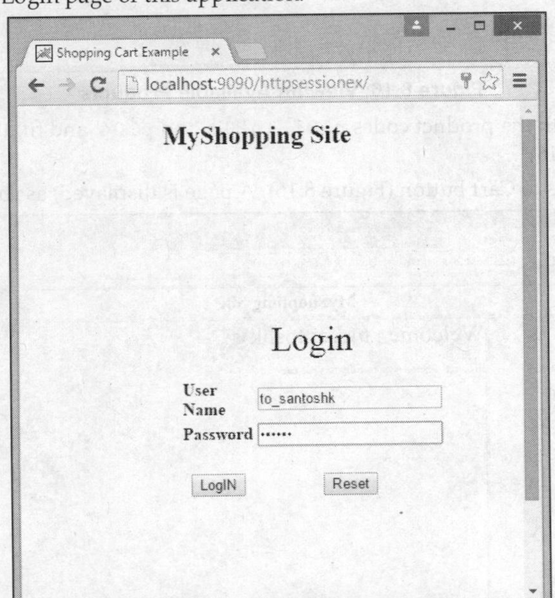

Figure 8.14: Displaying the Login Page

3. Enter the user name and password as `to_santoshk` and `123456`, respectively, and click the Login button. After clicking the Login button the welcome page appears, as shown in Figure 8.15:

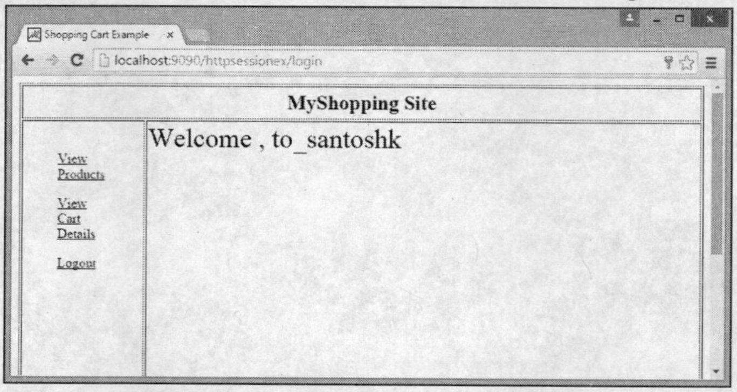

Figure 8.15: Displaying the Welcome Page

4. Click the View Products link. A list of all available products is displayed, as shown in Figure 8.16:

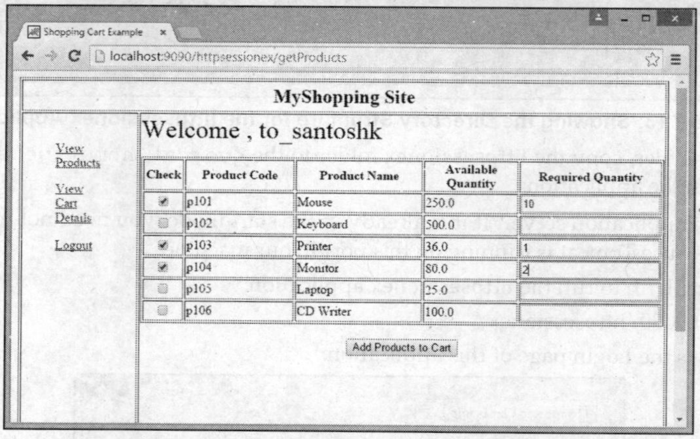

Figure 8.16: Viewing Available Products

5. Select the products with the product codes `p101`, `p103`, and `p104`, and fill their quantities as `10`, `1`, and `2`, respectively (Figure 8.16).
6. Click the Add Products to Cart button (Figure 8.16). A page is displayed, as shown in Figure 8.17:

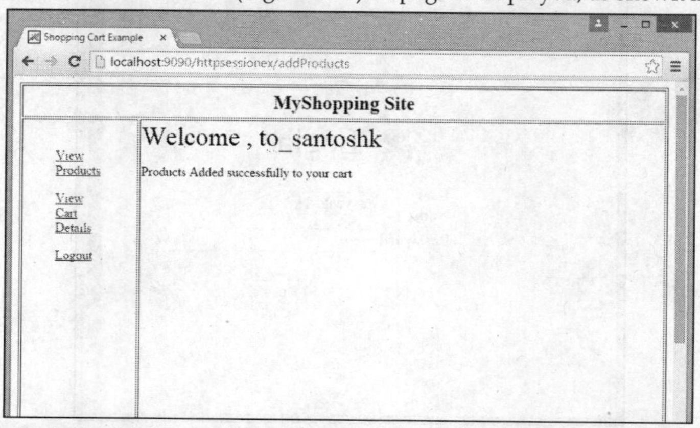

Figure 8.17: Showing the 'Products Added successfully to your cart' Message

7. Click the View Cart Details link (Figure 8.16). A page displaying the selected products with their quantities appears, as shown in Figure 8.18:

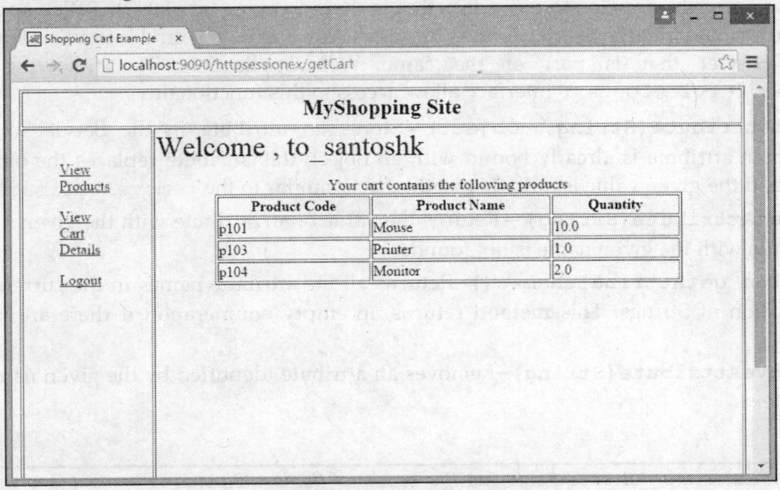

Figure 8.18: Viewing Cart Details

If you do not add any product to the cart, the Cart Details page will display 'You have not added any products into cart' message.

8. Click the View Products link again to view all the products. You can add more products in your cart if you wish. In case the selected product is already available in the cart, the entered product is added to the already selected quantity. For example, you have already selected products `p101`, `p103`, and `p104`, and entered their quantities as `10`, `1`, and `2`, respectively. Now, if you select `p103` and `p106` (Figure 8.16) and enter their quantities as `3` and `5`, respectively, (Figure 8.16) and click the Add Products to Cart button, then in the case of product `p103`, `3` more quantities are added to the existing `1` (taking the total as `4`), and in the case of product `p106`, a new entry is added to the cart (Figure 8.19).

9. Click the View Cart Details link to view the products added to your cart (Figure 8.19).

Figure 8.19 shows the newly added product `p106` and the increased quantity of `p103`:

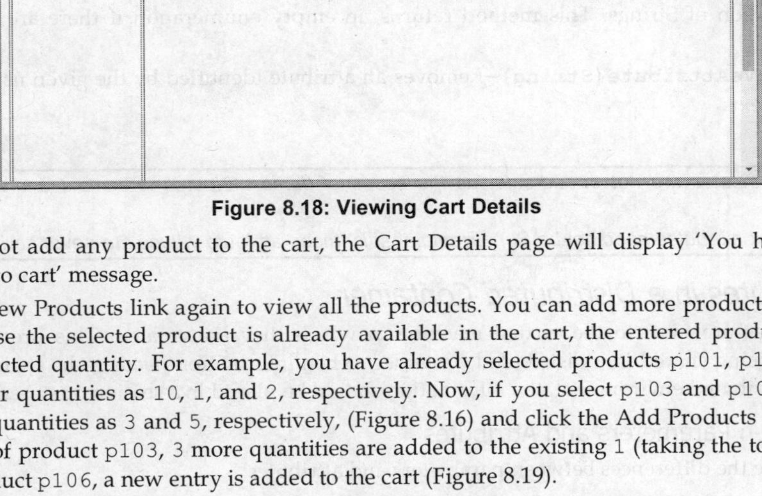

Figure 8.19: Showing Cart Details

After learning how to use the `HttpSession` object, let's discuss about the `ServletContext` attributes.

Describing ServletContext Attributes

In this section, we describe how to store the data that is shared among Servlets in a Web application. For this, a Servlet binds an attribute into the ServletContext by name. Any attribute bound into a ServletContext is available to any other Servlet that is part of the same Web application. The following methods of the `javax.servlet.ServletContext` interface allow access to this functionality:

- **`void setAttribute(String, Object)`**—Stores an attribute in the ServletContext. If the name specified to an attribute is already bound with an object, this attribute replaces the old attribute with the given object. If the given value is null, this method acts similar to the `removeAttribute()` method.
- **`Object getAttribute(String)`**—Returns the value of an attribute with the given name. It returns null if the attribute with the given name is not found.
- **`Enumeration getAttributeNames()`**—Returns all the attribute names in the current ServletContext as an enumeration of Strings. This method returns an empty enumeration if there are no attributes in the context.
- **`void removeAttribute(String)`**—Removes an attribute identified by the given name from the current ServletContext.

NOTE

ServletContext attributes are not thread-safe, as the scope of these attributes is context and multiple requests can process at a time.

In addition context attributes need not be Serializable, that is, these attribute values are never serialized.

Context Attributes in a Distributed Container

Context attributes are local to the virtual machine in which they are created. This prevents ServletContext attributes from being shared in a distributed container. When information needs to be shared between Servlets running in a distributed environment, the information should be placed in a session or stored in a database.

Difference between Parameters and Attributes

The following are the differences between parameters and attributes:

- Parameters are set by the Web container based on the request data or data configured in the deployment descriptor file, that is, request parameters or initialization parameters respectively. Servlets can access parameters by using the `get()` method, but the value of the attributes can also be set by the using `set()` method.
- Parameters provide an abstraction to retrieve the required data from the Web container, which are obtained through request or configuration, whereas attributes provide an abstraction to share data between the Servlets, depending on the scope of the Servlets.

Describing Scopes of Web Application Objects

Scope describes the lifetime and availability of Web application objects. The following is a brief description of the various scopes available in a Web application:

- **Page**—Starts when a request enters the service method of a Servlet and ends as the request leaves the service method. Page scope objects can be maintained in the service method as local variables.
- **Request**—Starts when a request object comes into the scope of a Web component and ends when the request object goes out of the Web component scope. A request is said to be coming into scope when it is about to enter the first filter or Servlet in a Web application and going out of scope when it exits the last Servlet or the first filter in the filter chain. That is, objects of the request scope are available to all the filters and Servlets, which are invoked under a particular request. We can maintain application objects in this scope as request attributes.

NOTE

You learn about filters in Chapter 9 – Implementing Filters, Listeners, and Wrappers.

- **Session**—Starts when a client request enters the session and ends when the client leaves the session. Session scope objects are available to all the requests in a session. As Web application developers, you can maintain application-specific objects in this scope by using `HttpSession` as session attributes.
- **Context (or) application**—Starts when a Web application is started and ends when the Web application is destroyed. Context scope objects are available for all the components in a Web application, irrespective of the session to which a request is associated.

The preceding scopes help us in the following situations:

- The request scope is used when you want to put an object in the `javax.servlet.ServletRequest` object. This object is used to share data with any Servlet. The shared data can be used by the other Servlet to handle the request of a client.
- The session scope is used if you want to put an object in the `javax.servlet.http.HttpSession` object. This object is accessed by any Servlet to use session data under two conditions: first, while the Servlet is servicing a request for the same client that put the object into the session, and second, while the current session is valid.
- The application scope is used if you want to put an object in the `java.servlet.ServletContext` object. This object is accessed by any Servlet of the same Web application.

Exploring the Single Thread Model

In general, the Servlet container considers that a Servlet object implements the thread-safe code. If you cannot implement the Servlet object thread-safe for any reason, you can request the container to make it thread-safe. To make the Servlet instance execute thread-safe, the container makes sure that the Servlet instance is to be used by only one thread at a time. The `javax.servlet.SingleThreadModel` interface is used to describe about this to the Servlet container. The single thread model is explained in Figure 8.20:

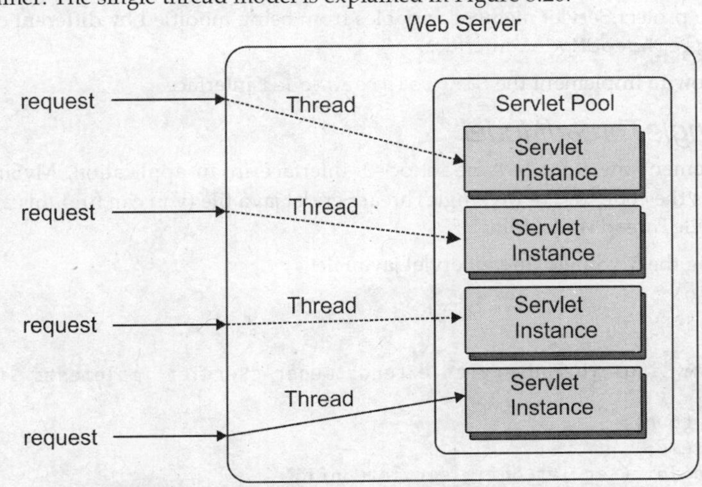

Figure 8.20: Displaying the Single Thread Model of Servlets

The `javax.servlet.SingleThreadModel` interface is a marker interface that marks the Servlet instance to be thread-safe. That is, implementing the `SingleThreadModel` interface guarantees that only one thread is executed at a time in a given Servlet instance's service method. It is important to note that this guarantee only applies to each Servlet instance, as the container may choose to pool such objects to process multiple clients requesting for the same Servlet simultaneously. Objects that are accessible to more than one Servlet instance at a time, such as instances of `HttpSession`, may be available at any particular time to multiple Servlets, including those that implement the `SingleThreadModel`.

Explaining the Need of Synchronization in Servlets

You know that a single Servlet's instance can handle multiple requests at the same time. This means that the Servlet instance is generated possibly when it is invoked for the first time. The same instance may be used by other client requests, and when a new request arises, the Servlet instance generates a thread to handle the request. That is called a multithread model, which means that multiple clients can access the same Servlet's instance. Therefore, if two threads are running, it is possible that both are using the same Servlet's instance at the same time, as shown in Figure 8.21:

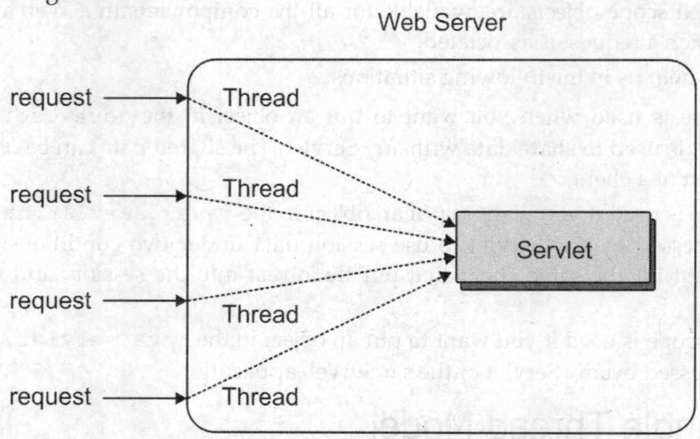

Figure 8.21: Displaying the Servlet Model

Interaction between Servlets does not matter in case Servlets only read the request, write the response, and save information in local variables (member variables). However, if you define a variable in a class outside a method, each thread has the ability to manipulate the variable. This means that you have to deal with concurrency issues, such as data consistency and data corruption. This concurrency control is called Servlet synchronization. In such cases, if you want to protect Servlet member variables from being modified by different clients, the Servlet must implement the `SingleThreadModel` interface.

Let's now discuss how to implement the `SingleThreadModel` interface.

Implementing SingleThreadModel

Let's learn to implement the `SingleThreadModel` interface in an application, MySingleThreadServlet.java. Listing 8.29 provides the code for the MySingleThreadServlet.java file (you can find this application online in the code/Chapter8/SingleThreadModel folder):

Listing 8.29: Creating the MySingleThreadServlet.java File

```
import java.io.*;
import javax.servlet.*;

public class MySingleThreadServlet extends GenericServlet implements SingleThreadModel
{
  static int count;
  int instanceId;
  public void init(ServletConfig servletConfig)
  throws ServletException
  {
        count++;
        instanceId = count;
  System.out.println("Servlet Initialized with InstanceId : " + instanceId);
  }
  public void service(ServletRequest servletRequest, ServletResponse servletResponse)
  throws ServletException, IOException
  {
```

```
            System.out.println("In service InstanceId : " + instanceId);
            servletResponse.setContentType("text/html");
            try
            {
                    Thread.sleep(10000L);
            }
            catch(Exception exception) { }
            PrintWriter printWriter = servletResponse.getWriter();
            printWriter.println("Response from service : InstanceId : " + instanceId);
            System.out.println("Service ended InstanceId : " + instanceId);
        }
        public void destroy()
        {
            System.out.println("In destroy InstanceId : " + instanceId);
        }
    }
```

In Listing 8.29, `MySingleThreadServlet` implements the `SingleThreadModel` interface. The `MySingleThreadServlet` Servlet prevents handling multiple requests at a single time.

NOTE

The SingleThreadModel interface is deprecated in the Servlet 2.4 specification. It is recommended that a developer avoid the use of an instance variable or synchronize the block of code accessing resources, such as HTML pages or Servlets, instead of implementing the SingleThreadModel interface.

Describing the ServletOutputStream Class

`ServletOutputStream` is an abstract class in the `javax.servlet` package and is a subtype of `java.io.OutputStream`. The `ServletOutputStream` class is used in Servlets to write the response to a client. The `getWriter()` and `getOutputStream()` methods of the `ServletResponse` interface allow Servlets to get the `Writer` and `ServletOutputStream` objects, respectively, to which a Servlet can write content. The `getWriter()` method returns a `java.io.PrintWriter` type of object, and the `getOutputStream()` method returns a `javax.servlet.ServletOutputStream` type of object.

The `javax.servlet.ServletOuputStream` class includes the print() and `println()` methods, where these two methods are overloaded to take the most general types, such as `Boolean`, `char`, `byte`, and `String`.

NOTE

It is recommended to use a Writer for writing general content, whereas ServletOutputStream is preferred for writing binary content.

Using ServletOutputStream

Let's take an example to understand how the `ServletOutputStream` class is used to write the response on a client browser. This example helps you learn another approach to deploy a Web application on the Tomcat server, and configure and use connection pooling.

In this example, we create an application that contains a home page, Home.html. The home page contains a textbox and the Get Employee Photo button. The textbox is used to enter the employee number and get the photograph of the corresponding employee by clicking the Get Employee Photo button. The application also contains the GetEmpImage.java file, which connects to the `myds` data source to retrieve the required information. Let's start by creating the Home.html page first.

Listing 8.30 provides the code for the Home.html file (you can find this file online in the code/Chapter8/sos folder):

Listing 8.30: Creating the Home.html File

```
<html>
  <body>
    <form method=post action="myser">
```

```
            Employee Number : <input type="text" name="empno"><br><br>
            <input type="submit" value="Get Employee Photo"/>
      </form>
    </body>
  </html>
```

When the user clicks the Get Employee Photo button, the request is forwarded to the `GetEmpImage` Servlet (declared in the GetEmpImage.java file). Listing 8.31 provides the code for the GetEmpImage.java file (you can find the GetEmpImage.java file online in the code/Chapter8/sos folder):

Listing 8.31: Creating the GetEmpImage.java File

```
package com.santosh.servlets;
import javax.servlet.*;
import java.io.*;
import javax.naming.*;
import java.sql.*;
import javax.sql.*;

public class GetEmpImage extends GenericServlet {

   public void service (ServletRequest req, ServletResponse res)
   throws ServletException, IOException {
         Connection con=null;
         try {
                 InitialContext ic=new InitialContext();
                 DataSource ds=(DataSource) ic.lookup("java:comp/env/myds");
                 con=ds.getConnection();

                 PreparedStatement ps=con.prepareStatement(
                 "select photo from personaldetails where empno=?");
                 ps.setString(1,req.getParameter("empno"));

                 ResultSet rs=ps.executeQuery();
                 if (rs.next()) {
                         res.setContentType("image/gif");
                         ServletOutputStream sos=res.getOutputStream();

                         InputStream is=rs.getBinaryStream(1);
                         int i=is.read();
                         while (i!=-1){
                                 sos.print(i); i=is.read();
                         }//while
                         return;
                 }//if
         }//try
         catch(Exception e){e.printStackTrace();}
         finally{
                 try{con.close();}catch(Exception e){}
         }//finally
         res.setContentType("text/html");
         res.getWriter().println("Emp not found");
   }//service
}//class
```

In Listing 8.31, the `GetEmpImage` Servlet class establishes the connection with the `myds` data source, retrieves the employee's photograph from the data source, and displays it on the client browser. The `GetEmpImage` Servlet class uses the `getOutputStream()` method of the `ServletResponse` object to write the response.

The final step is to configure this Servlet class in the `web.xml` file. Listing 8.32 shows the `web.xml` file (you can find the `web.xml` file online in the code/Chapter8/sos/WEB-INF folder):

Listing 8.32: Creating the `web.xml` File

```
<?xml version="1.0" encoding="UTF-8"?>
<web-app>
   <servlet>
         <servlet-name>hs</servlet-name>
         <servlet-class>com.santosh.servlets.GetEmpImage</servlet-class>
   </servlet>
   <servlet-mapping>
         <servlet-name>hs</servlet-name>
         <url-pattern>/myser</url-pattern>
   </servlet-mapping>
</web-app>
```

You also need to configure the `myds` data source, which enables the Servlet class to establish a connection. Listing 8.33 provides the code for configuring the data source (you can find the `myctxt.xml` file online in the code/Chapter8/sos folder):

Listing 8.33: Creating the **myctxt.xml** File

```
<Context path="/myctxt"
 docBase="E:\Santosh\Book\Examples\Chapter8\sos">
 <Resource name="myds" type="javax.sql.DataSource"
 auth="container"
 driverClassName="oracle.jdbc.driver.OracleDriver"
 url="jdbc:oracle:thin:@localhost:1521:sandb"
 username="scott"
 password="tiger"/>
</Context>
```

Arrange all the created files according to the directory structure, as shown in Figure 8.22:

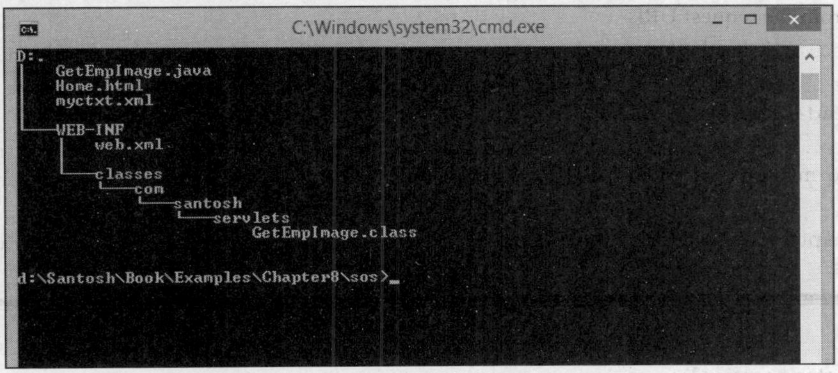

Figure 8.22: Showing the Directory Structure

Copy the `myctxt.xml` file to the `<Tomcat home>\conf\Catalina\localhost` folder and then start the Tomcat server to see the output.

NOTE

If you are using Tomcat 5.5 or a upper version, use myctxt.xml. If you are using Tomcat 5.0, use myctxt_For_Tomcat5.0.xml. You must also note that in a request, Servlets are allowed to get either `ServletOutputStream` *or* `Writer`.

Summary

This chapter discussed the need for session tracking, various approaches of session tracking, their advantages and disadvantages, and when to use these approaches. The chapter also discussed the use of hidden form fields and URL rewriting for session tracking. Then, you learned about the cookie approach for session tracking.

Further, you learned about the `HttpSession` and Servlet Context attributes. Next, the chapter discussed various scopes of objects and when to use these scopes. We also discussed the `SingleThreadModel`, which is used for Servlet synchronization. Finally, you were explained about the `ServletOutputStream` class. Let's recall the following important points to summarize the chapter:

- A session is a collection of HTTP requests, over a period of time, between a client and a Web server.
- Session tracking, also known as session handling, is a mechanism used to maintain the state of a user within a series of requests across some period, i.e., the lifetime of a session.
- Session tracking is used when session data from one session may be required by a Web server to complete specific operations in the same or different sessions.
- A cookie is a file containing the information that is sent by a Web server to a client.
- Cookies are transmitted to clients through the HTTP response header from the server.
- The Servlet API provides a class named Cookie under the `javax.servlet.http` package.
- The `javax.servlet.http.Cookie` class consists of one constructor with two String arguments: the first argument takes the cookie name and the second takes the cookie value.
- In the `HttpSession` mechanism, the Web container maintains the user's data and tracks the user's session by using URL rewriting or cookies.
- A session is considered new if the client request does not carry the session identity or the client has not yet selected to join the session.
- The `isNew()` method of the `HttpSession` interface returns true if the session is created in the current request and returns false if it is a pre-existing session.
- When a Servlet needs to locate a session associated with the current request and use it to retrieve or store data, it calls the `getSession()` method of the `HttpServletRequest` object.
- The `isRequestedSessionIdFromCookie()` method returns true if the session to which the current request is associated is located by using the session identity obtained from the cookie, and false if it is located from the request URI.
- `HttpSession` is used when you do not want to expose sensitive and private data to other users.
- The `javax.servlet.SingleThreadModel` interface is a marker interface that marks the Servlet instance to be thread-safe.
- The `javax.servlet.ServletOuputStream` class includes the print() and `println()` methods, where these two methods are overloaded to take the most general types, such as `Boolean`, `char`, `byte`, and `String`.

In the next chapter, you will learn about some advance concepts of Servlets, such as Filters, Events, Listeners, and Wrappers.

Exercise

Q. 8.1 What is a session?

Q. 8.2 What is session tracking?

Q. 8.3 List different mechanisms for session tracking.

Q. 8.4 What is Query String?

Q. 8.5 What is the use of `encodeURL()` method?

Q. 8.6 What is the disadvantage of `HttpSession`?

Q. 8.7 What is the difference between parameters and attributes?

Q. 8.8 What are the different scopes available in a Web application?

Q. 8.9 What is the `javax.servlet.SingleThreadModel` interface?

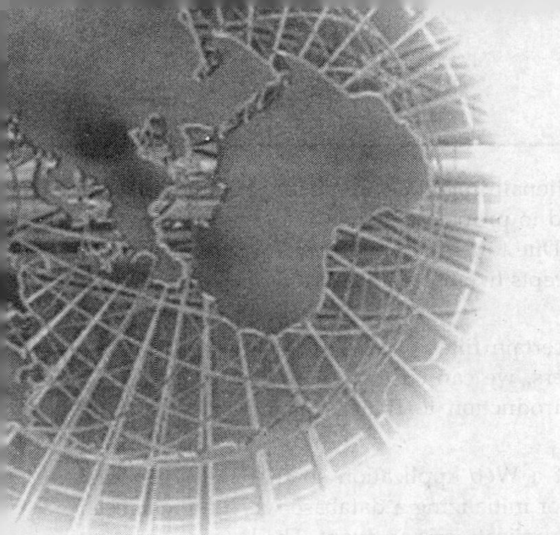

9

Implementing Filters, Listeners, and Wrappers

Most of the Web applications have some common functionalities, such as user authentication and internationalization. Therefore, Web application developers need to provide the code of these functionalities in seperate classes apart from main Servlets of a Web application. Due to this reason, filters have been introduced in Servlet 2.3 by Sun Microsystems. In addition, some other concepts like listeners and wrappers have also been introduced.

We can use filters to configure the Web container to invoke certain filter objects during the HTTP request-response process. In this manner, as Web application developers, we can customize how HTTP requests are handled within a Web container. This chapter presents an introduction to filter API and provide the Web application to illustrate the power of filters in Web containers.

Listeners allow developers to recognize the lifecycle events of a Web application so that they can perform common tasks. For example, a developer can execute the code for initializing a database when an instance of a Web application is created. Here, creating an instance of a Web application is an event. The listener Application Programming Interface (API) has predefined methods to listen to such events. Before the Servlet 2.3 specification was introduced, overriding of methods, such as the `getParameter()` method of the `HttpServletRequest` interface, was not possible. Now, developers can override these methods and define their own functionality.

The wrapper classes in Servlet API implement all the methods needed for resources you want to wrap, delegating all calls to the underlying request or response object.

This chapter introduces you to filters, listeners, and wrappers. It also describes how they are used to filter requests and responses, listen and handle various types of events, and wrap requests and responses.

Exploring Filters

Filters are reusable code that can transform the content of requests, responses, and header information from one format into another. Take an example of a Web application that formats the data before it is presented to the client. However, different clients might require different formats such as Wireless Markup Language (WML), spreadsheet, or Portable Document Format (PDF). To serve this requirement, there is a need of transformation or filtering in a Web application.

The filter classes encapsulate the logic that has to be executed before or after the actual request processing, which is done by the requested resource. The filter class is declared in the deployment descriptor. In addition, filters provide the ability to encapsulate recurring tasks in reusable units, which allows us to modularize the code. Modular code is more manageable, documentable, easier to debug, and can be reused in other settings.

Many Servlet containers have introduced proprietary filter mechanisms to enable transformation of requests and responses; however, these filter mechanisms are specific to Servlet containers. As a result, the reusability of these filters is reduced. With the introduction of filters as part of the Java Servlet specification, developers now have the opportunity to write reusable transformation components that are portable across different types of Servlet containers.

Numerous other tasks can be implemented in a Web application using filters, such as security verification, session validation, internationalization, resource access events triggering, data compression, MIME type changing, caching, and XSL transformations of XML response from a Servlet or JSP page. Unlike other methods of introducing interception points, filters allow you to introduce interception points at the time of deploying your Web applications. Let's learn about the filter interception design pattern next.

Filter Interception Design Pattern

All tasks such as authentication and changing the format of data require filters to have special permissions, such as the permission to intercept requests before they are processed. The filter interception design pattern tells us about various instances where we can use a filter to intercept a request. In other words, this pattern provides various permissions to filter Servlet requests. For example, a filter can:

- Process the request for a resource before it is invoked
- Modify the request headers and data by wrapping the request in customized versions of the request object
- Modify the response headers and response data by providing customized versions of the response object
- Intercept the invocation of a resource after its call

- Perform actions, such as session validation and security verification, on a Servlet, a group of Servlets, or on a static content.

Let's learn how the Servlet container invokes filters.

How the Servlet Container Invokes Filter

We know that a Servlet is a java object that extends from the `javax.servlet.http.HttpServlet`. A Servlet container is a part of a Web server. It interacts with Java Servlet and generates the Web page on the server. There are many Servlet containers in the market, such as Apache Tomcat, JBoss, Glassfish, WebLogic, etc.

When a method is called by a Servlet container, by default, the HTTP request is passed to the Servlet. The Servlet generates the text of the Web page and delivers it to the Servlet container. Then, the response generated by the Servlet passes directly to the client.

Filters are not Servlets as the methods of the `HttpServlet` class can not be implemented or overridden by filters. Filters implement the methods of `javax.servlet.Filter` interface, which are `init()`, `destroy()`, and `doFilter()`.

Let us see how a Servlet container can invoke filters.

Figure 9.1 shows the process of invocation of a Servlet with and without filters. Figure 9.1 (a) shows the situation in which no filters are configured for the Servlets that are being called. Figure 9.1 (b) shows the situation in which several filters like filter1, filter2, ..., filterN are configured that are to be invoked by the container before the Servlet is called and after the Servlet responds.

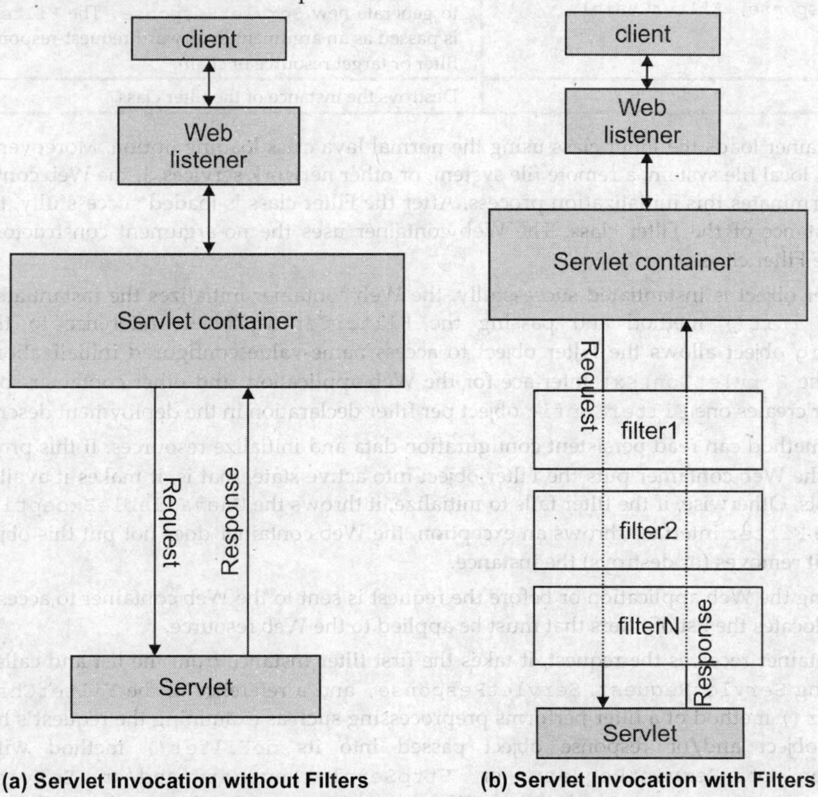

Figure 9.1: Servlet Invocation with and without Filters

In the case of Servlet invocation with filters, the `web.xml` file specifies which Servlets cause the container to invoke filters. The filters are invoked in the order in which they are configured in the `web.xml` file. In general, during the request, the first filter in `web.xml` will be invoked first, and during the response, the last filter in web.xml will be invoked first. Thus, the order of invocation of filters during response is just the reverse of request.

Let's learn about the filter API next.

Filter API

Filter API comprises three interfaces – Filter, FilterChain, and FilterConfig – which are present in the javax.servlet package. The filter implementation class uses the FilterConfig interface to pass configuration information to a filter during initialization and needs to implement the Filter interface. The FilterChain interface is used when more than one filter is implemented in your Web application. Let's discuss these interfaces and their methods in detail.

The Filter Interface

The javax.servlet.Filter interface is the basic interface that provides a standard abstraction for Servlet container to understand and interact with the filter component (Filter class). All Filter classes must implement this interface directly or indirectly. Methods declared in this interface are listed in Table 9.1.

Table 9.1: Methods of the Filter Interface

Method	Description
init(FilterConfig)	Initializes a Filter and makes it ready for providing service.
doFilter(ServletRequest, ServletResponse, FilterChain)	Encapsulates service logic to be implemented on ServletRequest to generate new ServletResponse. The FilterChain reference is passed as an argument to forward request-response pair to the next filter or target resource of chain.
destroy()	Destroys the instance of the filter class.

The Web container loads the Filter class using the normal Java class loading option. Moreover, the class may be loaded from a local file system, a remote file system, or other network services. If the Web container fails to load the class, it terminates this initialization process. After the Filter class is loaded successfully, the Web container creates an instance of the Filter class. The Web container uses the no-argument constructor to create a new instance of the Filter class.

After the Filter object is instantiated successfully, the Web container initializes the instantiated Filter object by invoking the init() method and passing the FilterConfig object reference to this method. The FilterConfig object allows the Filter object to access name-value configured initialization parameters, the reference to the ServletContext interface for the Web application, and other container-specific details. The Web container creates one FilterConfig object per filter declaration in the deployment descriptor.

The init() method can read persistent configuration data and initialize resources. If this process is performed successfully, the Web container puts the Filter object into active state, that is, it makes it available and ready to handle requests. Otherwise, if the filter fails to initialize, it throws the UnavailableException. If the init() method of the Filter interface throws an exception, the Web container does not put this object into the active state. That is, it removes (or destroys) the instance.

After deploying the Web application or before the request is sent to the Web container to access a Web resource, the container locates the list of filters that must be applied to the Web resource.

When the container receives the request, it takes the first filter instance from the list and calls its doFilter() method passing ServletRequest, ServletResponse, and a reference of the FilterChain object it uses. The doFilter() method of a filter performs preprocessing such as examining the request's headers, wrapping the request object and/or response object passed into its doFilter() method with a customized implementation of ServletRequest or HttpServletRequest and/or ServletResponse or HttpServletResponse, respectively, to modify request/response headers or data. After performing all its preprocessing operations, if any, the filter may call the doFilter() method on the FilterChain object passing in the request and response objects. The doFilter() method of FilterChain is responsible to invoke the next entity in the chain. The next entity may be another filter, or if the filter making the invocation is the last filter configured for this chain, the next entity is the target Web resource. Otherwise, filter can block the request by not making the call to invoke the next entity, that is, by not calling the `doFilter()` method on the `FilterChain` object. After the `doFilter()` method invocation on the `FilterChain` object, filter can perform post-processing operations.

The `destroy()` method is called either after all threads have completed their functionality or when the thread's timeout period elapses. This method detaches all resources, such as memory and threads, from filter instance.

The FilterConfig Interface

The object of `FilterConfig` interface is used during the initialization of filter. This object is used to fetch configuration information about the filter specified in the deployment descriptor. The methods of the `FilterConfig` interface are listed in Table 9.2.

Table 9.2: Methods of the FilterConfig Interface

Method	Description
`getFilterName()`	Returns the name of the filter specified in Deployment Descriptor.
`getInitParamter(String)`	Returns the specified initialization parameter's value from Deployment Descriptor.
`getInitParamterNames()`	Returns enumeration of all initialization parameters of the filter.
`getServletContext()`	Returns the `ServletContext` object, which represents the context of Web application.

The FilterChain Interface

The object of this interface stores information about a chain of filters. All filters in this chain should be applied on request before the processing of a request. Any filter can use this interface to invoke the next filter on changed request/response pair. In case the filter is the last one in the chain, the target resource is invoked. This interface has one `doFilter(ServletRequest, ServletResponse)` method, which invokes the next filter or targeted resource.

Working With Filters

In this section, we create two filters, MyFilter1 and MyFilter2, to intercept the request going to the `TestServlet` Servlet. We also explain mapping of these filters to `TestServlet` using `<url-pattern>` and `<servlet-name>` tags.

Perform the following broad-level steps to create the application:

- Create the Home.html page
- Create the TestServlet.java file
- Create the MyFilter1.java file
- Create the MyFilter2.java file
- Configure the application
- Run the application

Creating the Home.html Page

The Home.html page consists of a form having two submit buttons. The user submits page by choosing the appropriate button. The request is processed either through both filters or only through one filter before reaching `TestServlet`. Listing 9.1 shows the code of Home.html file of the **filters** application (you can find this file online in the code/Chapter9/filters folder):

Listing 9.1: The Home.html Page

```
<html>
<body>
   <form method=post action="ser1">
   <input type="submit" value="Invoke TestServlet using path /ser1"/>
   </form><br><br>
   <form method=post action="ser2">
   <input type="submit" value="Invoke TestServlet using path /ser2"/>
```

```
</form>
</body>
</html>
```

Creating the TestServlet.java File

The TestServlet Servlet is used to test the filters created in the application. When the TestServlet class is initialized, the Filter1 is invoked implicitly. The TestServlet class extends the GenericServlet class to override its service() method. In the service() method, a simple message "In TestServlet, processing request" is built by using the println() function of the PrintWriter object, and when this message is displayed on the browser, it gives an indication to the user that now TestServlet is handling the request. Listing 9.2 shows the code of the TestServlet.java file (you can find this file online in the code/Chapter9/filters folder):

Listing 9.2: The TestServlet.java File

```
package com.santosh.servlets;
import javax.servlet.*;
import java.io.*;
public class TestServlet extends GenericServlet {

   public void service (ServletRequest req, ServletResponse res)
   throws ServletException, IOException {

         PrintWriter out=res.getWriter();
         out.println("In TestServlet, processing request<br/>");
   }//service
}//class
```

Creating the MyFilter1.java File

The MyFilter1 class implements the Filter interface to override its doFilter() method to filter request and response. The MyFilter1 class displays two messages on the browser one by one. The first message "In MyFilter1, filtering Request..." ensures the user that MyFilter1 begins filtering the request. The second message "In MyFilter1, filtering Response..." ensures the user that now the response is being filtered. Listing 9.3 shows the code of the MyFilter1.java file (you can find this file online in the code/Chapter9/filters folder):

Listing 9.3: The MyFilter1.java File

```
package com.santosh.servlets;

import javax.servlet.*;
import java.io.*;

public class MyFilter1 implements Filter {

   public void init(FilterConfig fc){}

   public void doFilter( ServletRequest req, ServletResponse res,
   FilterChain fc)throws ServletException, IOException
   {
         res.setContentType("text/html");
         PrintWriter out=res.getWriter();
         out.println("In MyFilter1, filtering Request...<br/>");
         fc.doFilter(req,res);
         //Post Processing can be performed here if any
         out.println("In MyFilter1, filtering Response...<br/>");
   }//doFilter

   public void destroy() {}
}//class
```

Creating the MyFilter2.java File

The MyFilter2 class also implements the Filter interface to have permission to filter request by using the doFilter() method. The MyFilter2 class also displays two messages on the browser one by one. The first message "In MyFilter2, filtering Request..." ensures the user that MyFilter2 begins filtering the same request. The second message "In MyFilter2, filtering Response..." ensures the user that now the response is being filtered. Listing 9.4 shows the code of the MyFilter2.java file (you can find this file online in the code/Chapter9/filters folder):

Listing 9.4: The MyFilter2.java File

```
package com.santosh.servlets;

import javax.servlet.*;
import java.io.*;
public class MyFilter2 implements Filter {

   public void init(FilterConfig fc){}

public void doFilter(ServletRequest req, ServletResponse res,
FilterChain fc)throws ServletException, IOException {
        PrintWriter out=res.getWriter();
        out.println("In MyFilter2, filtering Request...<br/>");

        fc.doFilter(req,res);

        //Post Processing can be performed here if any
        out.println("In MyFilter2, filtering Response...<br/>");
   }//doFilter

   public void destroy() {}
}//class
```

Configuring the filters Application

A filter is declared in the Deployment Descriptor using the <filter> element. In the <filter> element, we can declare the following:

- **filter-name**—It is used to map the filter to a servlet or URL.
- **filter-class**—It is used by the container to identify the filter type.
- **zero or more init-param**—These are initialization parameters for a filter.

Here is an example of declaring a filter:

```
<filter>
   <filter-name>myFilter1<filter-name>
   <filter-class>com.santosh.servlets.TestFilter<filter-class>
</filter>
```

Once a filter has been declared in the Deployment Descriptor, the <filter-mapping> element is used to define servlets and static resources in the Web application to which the filter is to be applied. Filters can be associated with a servlet by using the <servlet-name> element. For example, the following element maps the myFilter1 filter to the myser servlet:

```
<filter-mapping>
   <filter-name>myFilter1</filter-name>
   <servlet-name>myser</servlet-name>
</filter-mapping>
```

Filters can be associated with groups of Servlets and static resources by using the <url-pattern> of the filter-mapping element. For example, the following element maps the SecurityFilter filter to all the Servlets and static pages:

```
<filter-mapping>
   <filter-name>SecurityFilter</filter-name>
   <url-pattern>/*</ url-pattern >
</filter-mapping>
```

When the container builds the chain of filters to be applied for a particular request, it first selects filters by the <url-pattern> matching filter mappings in the same order that these elements appear in the Deployment Descriptor. Next, it selects filters by the <servlet-name> matching filter mappings in the same order that these elements appear in the Deployment Descriptor.

Creating the web.xml Deployment Descriptor

Now we are creating `web.xml` after learning how to configure and map filters to Servlets. The `web.xml` file first declares two filters with names `filter1` and `filter2` by using `<filter>` tags. Then, it maps `filter1` using `<url-pattern>` such as `/ser1` and then maps `filter2` by using a `<servlet-name>` tag such as `ts1`. It also contains mapping of servlet `TestServlet`. The same servlet is mapped on two URIs: `/ser1` and `/ser2`. Listing 9.5 shows the code of the `web.xml` file (you can find this file online in the code/Chapter9/filters/WEB-INF folder):

Listing 9.5: The `web.xml` File

```
<?xml version="1.0" encoding="UTF-8"?>
<web-app>
  <filter>
        <filter-name>filter1</filter-name>
        <filter-class>com.santosh.servlets.MyFilter1</filter-class>
  </filter>
  <filter>
        <filter-name>filter2</filter-name>
        <filter-class>com.santosh.servlets.MyFilter2</filter-class>

  </filter>
  <filter-mapping>

        <filter-name>filter1</filter-name>
        <url-pattern>/ser1</url-pattern>

  </filter-mapping>
  <filter-mapping>

        <filter-name>filter2</filter-name>
        <servlet-name>ts1</servlet-name>

  </filter-mapping>
  <servlet>

        <servlet-name>ts1</servlet-name>
        <servlet-class>com.santosh.servlets.TestServlet</servlet-class>
  </servlet>

  <servlet-mapping>
        <servlet-name>ts1</servlet-name>
        <url-pattern>/ser1</url-pattern>

  </servlet-mapping>
  <servlet-mapping>

        <servlet-name>ts1</servlet-name>
        <url-pattern>/ser2</url-pattern>
  </servlet-mapping>
</web-app>
```

Running the Application

To run the application, perform the following steps:

1. Arrange all the files according to the standard directory structure of the Web application. Figure 9.2 shows the directory structure of the **filters** application:

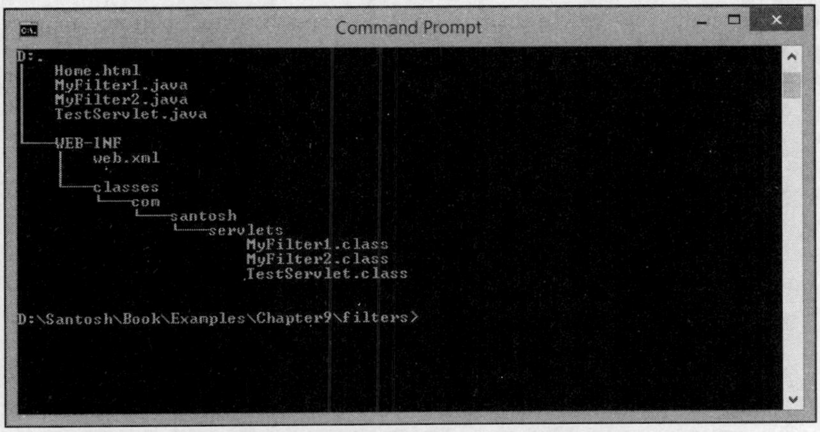

Figure 9.2: Showing the Directory Structure of the filters Application

2. Copy the `filters` folder in the `<Tomcat home>/webapps` directory. Start the Tomcat server and browse the application by using the URL `http://localhost:9090/filters/Home.html`. The home page of the **filters** application will appear, as shown in Figure 9.3:

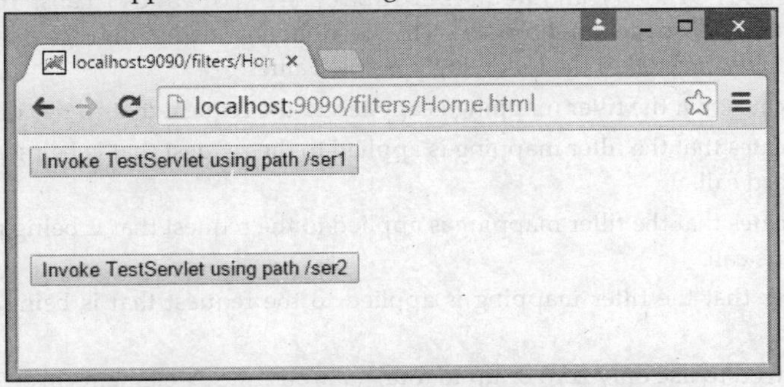

Figure 9.3: Home Page of the filters Application

The home page has two buttons: `Invoke TestServlet using path /ser1` and `Invoke TestServlet using path /ser2`.

3. When the user clicks on the `Invoke TestServlet using path /ser1` button, a request is made using the URI `/ser1` (specified in the `action` attribute of first form in the Home.html page), which invokes `MyFilter1` according to the first filter mapping in `web.xml`. The second filter mapping enforces the Web container to invoke `MyFilter2` before sending request to the `TestServlet`. The output is shown in Figure 9.4:

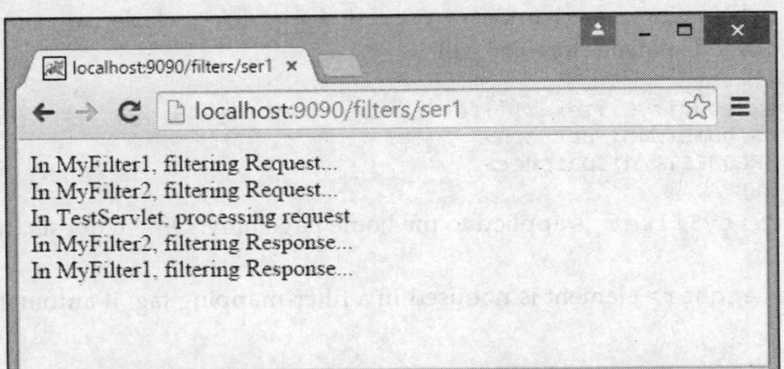

Figure 9.4: Filtering a Request Using Two Filters

4. If the user clicks on the Invoke TestServlet using path /ser2 button, a request is made using the URL /ser2 (specified in the action attribute of second form in the Home.html page), which invokes only MyFilter2 to intercept the request. The output is shown in Figure 9.5:

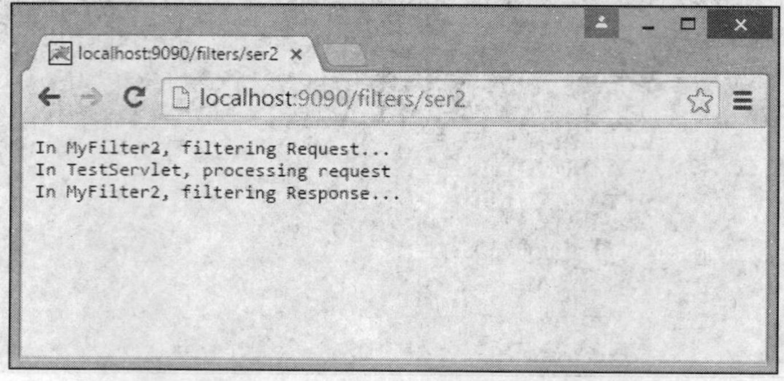

Figure 9.5: Filtering of Request Using a Filter

Using Filters with forward() and include() Methods in Java Servlet

The Java Servlet 2.4 specification provides the ability to configure filters to be invoked before or after the RequestDispatcher.include() and RequestDispatcher.forward() calls. You can also invoke a filter before displaying the error page on browser. This is done by using the <dispatcher> element in the Deployment Descriptor, which takes the following possible values:

- **REQUEST** – Indicates that the filter mapping is applied to the request that comes directly from client.
- **FORWARD** – Indicates that the filter mapping is applied to the request that is being processed under a request dispatcher forward call.
- **INCLUDE** – Indicates that the filter mapping is applied to the request that is being processed under a request dispatcher include call.
- **ERROR** – Indicates that the filter mapping is applied to the request that is being processed with the error page mechanism.

Note that we are allowed to use only zero or up to four <dispatcher> elements in a filter-mapping.

Following are some examples of filter configurations using the <dispatcher> element:

```
<filter-mapping>
   <filter-name>LoggingFilter</filter-name>
   <url-pattern>/home</url-pattern>
   <dispatcher>REQUEST</dispatcher>
   <dispatcher>INCLUDE</dispatcher>
   <dispatcher>FORWARD</dispatcher>
</filter-mapping>
```

In this example, LoggingFilter is applied to the home page when the request comes directly from the client, or the request that is being processed under a request dispatcher include call, or the request that is being processed under a request dispatcher forward call.

```
<filter-mapping>
   <filter-name>SecurityFilter</filter-name>
   <url-pattern>/home</url-pattern>
   <dispatcher>REQUEST</dispatcher>
</filter-mapping>
```

In this example, SecurityFilter is applied to the home page only. Only requests that come directly from the client are filtered.

Note that if the <dispatcher> element is not used in a filter-mapping tag, it automatically takes default value REQUEST

Describing Event Handling in Servlet

The occurance of something that causes change in the state of an object is called an event. The events that can occur with Servlets are as follows:

- Initializing and destroying servlets
- Adding, removing, and replacing attributes in servlet context
- Creating, activating, validating, and invalidating a session
- When an HTTP request comes or goes out of Servlet scope

Event Classes

Following are the event classes available in `javax.servlet` and `javax.servlet.http` packages:

- `ServletRequestEvent`
- `ServletContextEvent`
- `ServletRequestAttributeEvent`
- `HttpSessionEvent`
- `HttpSessionBindingEvent`

Event Interfaces

Following are the event interfaces available in `javax.servlet` and `javax.servlet.http` packages:

- `ServletRequestListener`
- `ServletRequestAttributeListener`
- `ServletContextListener`
- `HttpSessionListener`
- `ServletContextAttributeListener`
- `HttpSessionAttributeListener`
- `HttpSessionBindingListener`
- `HttpSessionActivationListener`

Describing Listeners

Sometimes, you may like to initialize a database during server start-up and save its state, if the server is being shut down, to manage the number of concurrent users, to track session of a particular user of a Web application, and to know when the Servlet's life cycle events occur. All these jobs can be performed by using listeners. For example, listeners listen to event of beginning a session by new client and track a number of users.

Listeners may recognize application events, which help Web developers in controlling the life cycle of `ServletContext`, `ServletRequest`, and `HttpSession` objects. Therefore, developers can efficiently manage the resources of Web applications. These listeners are implementation classes of event listener interfaces. Instances of these classes are created and registered in Web container during the deployment of a Web application.

Need of Event Programming and Importance of Listeners

If we try to understand the programming of the most commonly used software, such as operating system or any command line interface (or MS-DOS), we find that these software are also programmed in event driven manner. Operating systems use interrupt handlers as event handlers for hardware events generated by the CPU. In most of the programming languages, event-driven programming is done to control the flow of programs according to user actions, such as clicking the mouse button or pressing a key. An event-driven program is made up of functions that listen and handle events. The best example of an event-driven program is a Graphical User Interface (GUI) program. In Java Enterprise Edition, Web container transfers the control to event handlers (which are also called event listeners) to listen events related to the entire Web application and its components, such as Servlets, JSPs.

Java EE Web developers use various methods, such as `init()` and `jspInit()`, to control the life cycle of a Servlet or JSP page. Request processing is done using `service()` and `jspService()` methods. The `destroy()` and `jspDestroy()` methods destroy the instances of Servlets and JSPs. All these methods help developers to handle the life cycle of a Servlet or JSP page. Before listeners came into use, we could set shared resources using the `<context-param>` tag of `web.xml` and access them using the `getInitParameter()` method of the `ServletContext` object. However, we do not know the order in which various Servlets of an application are accessed. Therefore, the code to access the resources can be repeated in many Servlets. A solution to this problem is to give major control to only one servlet. To implement this solution, listeners are required to listen to application life cycle events and so there is no need to repeat the code in many Servlets.

Types of Listeners

Listeners are classified on the basis of event types. Events can be of the request, session, or application level scope. The request, session, and application level scope are represented by `ServletRequest`, `HttpSession`, and `ServletContext`, respectively. Table 9.3 lists the event types and the listener interfaces associated with these events.

Table 9.3: Event Types and Corresponding Listener Interfaces

Scope Level Events	Event Type	Description	Listener Interface
Application level events	Lifecycle events	Occur when a servlet context is either initialized or destroyed.	`javax.servlet.ServletContextListener`
	Changes to `ServletContext` attributes	Occur when a new attribute of the `ServletContext` interface is added or an existing attribute is removed or replaced by another attribute.	`javax.servlet.ServletContextAttributeListener`
Session level events	Lifecycle events	Occur when an instance of `HttpSession` is created, invalidated, or destroyed.	`javax.servlet.http.HttpSessionListener`
	Binding events	Occur when an object is bound or unbound from an instance of `HttpSession`.	`javax.servlet.HttpSessionBindingListener`
	Session passivation or activation events	Occur when an instance of `HttpSession` is passivated or activated.	`javax.servlet.HttpSessionActivationListener`
Request level events	Lifecycle events	Occur when a servlet processes a `ServletRequest` instance.	`javax.servlet.ServletRequestListener`
	Changes to `ServletRequest` attributes	Ocur when any addition of new attribute, removal of attribute, or replacement of existing attributes of `ServletRequest` instance is performed.	`javax.servlet.ServletRequestAttributeListener`

Describing Listener Interfaces

`Listener` interfaces are defined under the `javax.servlet` package. These listener interfaces are of request, session and application level interfaces. The following is the broad-level category of listener interfaces:

- `ServletContextListener`
- `ServletContextAttributeListener`
- `HttpSessionListener`
- `HttpSessionAttributeListener`
- `HttpSessionBindingListener`
- `HttpSessionActivationListener`

- `ServletRequestListener`
- `ServletRequestAttributeListener`

The ServletContextListener Interface

We know that a `ServletContext` object is created and associated with a Web application when it is deployed. All the resources in the Web application, such as Servlets and JSPs, can retrieve any information stored in the servlet context.

As a Web application programmer, you need to initialize and place objects in the `servlet context`, which are finally removed when the servlet context is destroyed. For example, we may decide to create a database connection when the servlet context is created and close the connection when the servlet context is destroyed. This introduces the need of `ServletContextListener` that allows us to monitor the life cycle events of a `ServletContext` object.

The `ServletContextListener` notifies about the following two events:

- The servlet context has just been created and is available to service its first request.
- The servlet context is about to be shut down.

Methods of the javax.ServletContextListener Interface

To write a `ServletContext` life cycle event listener that is executed when the servlet context is created and destroyed, write a Java class that implements the `javax.Servlet.ServletContextListener` interface. This interface has two methods:

- **`void contextInitialized (ServletContextEvent)`**—This method indicates that the `Servlet Context` interface is initialized and the Web application is ready to process the requests.
- **`void contextDestroyed (ServletContextEvent)`**—This method indicates that the `Servlet Context` interface is about to be shut down.

The javax.servlet.ServletContextEvent Class

The object of `javax.servlet.ServletContextEvent` class is passed as an argument to the methods of the `ServletContextListener` interface. The object of the `ServletContextEvent` class gives the details of the life cycle events of the `ServletContext` object. The `javax.servlet.ServletContextEvent` class has only one method, `ServletContext getServletContext()`. This method returns the `ServletContext` object for which an event is generated.

Working with the ServletContextListener Interface

Let's create an application, **listenersex1**, which uses simple `ServletContext` life cycle event listener to write a message to the console of the server when a Web application is ready to accept requests and when servlet context is going to be destroyed.

Let's create the files required for this application, such as Home.html page shown in Listing 9.6 (you can find this file online in the code/Chapter9/listenersex1 folder):

Listing 9.6: The Home.html Page

```
<html>
   <body>
   <a href="/manager/html">Click</a> here to go to tomcat manager console.<br>
Tomcat Manager Console can be used to start or stop the application <br>and reload the
application, that destroys the ServletContext object and once again initializes<br> so that
we can test the ServletContextListener.
   </body>
</html>
```

The `MyContextListener` class implements `ServletContextListener` interface. It implements two methods of this interface, which are `contextInitialized()` and `contextDestroyed()`. They accept `ServletContextEvent` as an argument for the notifications of the `ServletContext` life cycle events. The `ServletContextEvent` gives the details of life cycle events. Listing 9.7 shows the code for the MyContextListener.java file (you can find this file online in the code/Chapter9/listenersex1 folder):

Listing 9.7: The MyContextListener.java File

```
package com.santosh.servlets;

import javax.servlet.*;

public class MyContextListener implements ServletContextListener {

   public MyContextListener() {}

   /*
   */
   public void contextInitialized(ServletContextEvent sce) {
         //to get the Context object for which this event is generated
         ServletContext context = sce.getServletContext();
         System.out.println("ServletContext is initialized");
   }


   public void contextDestroyed(ServletContextEvent sce) {
         System.out.println("ServletContext is about to be destroyed");
   }
}//class
```

The `contextInitialized()` method is invoked to indicate that the `ServletContext` is just now initialized and the Web application is ready to process the requests. The `contextInitialized()` method has one `println()` method, which displays "`ServletContext is initialized`" message on Tomcat server console. The `contextDestroyed()` method is invoked to indicate that the `ServletContext` is about to be shut down. The `contextDestroyed()` method has one `println()` method, which displays "`ServletContext is about to be destroyed`" message on Tomcat server console.

The `web.xml` registers the preceding `MyContextListener` class in the `<listener>` element of the `web.xml` file using its fully qualified class name, as shown in Listing 9.8 (you can find this file online in the code/Chapter9/listenersex1/WEB-INF folder):

Listing 9.8: The `web.xml` File

```
<?xml version="1.0" encoding="UTF-8"?>
<web-app>
   <listener>
         <listener-class>
                  com.santosh.servlets.MyContextListener
         </listener-class>
   </listener>
</web-app>
```

Arrange all the files according to the standard directory structure of Web application. We are also showing you the directory structure of the **listenersex1** application in Figure 9.6:

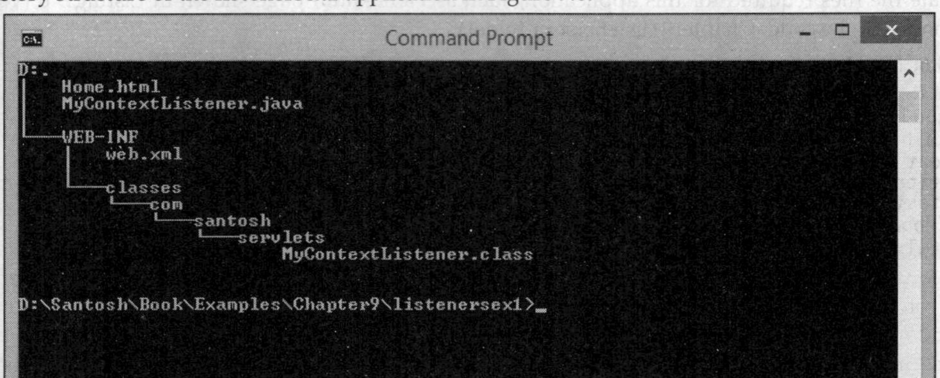

Figure 9.6: Showing the Directory Structure of the listenersex1 Application

Copy the `listenersex1` folder to the `<Tomcat home>/webapps` directory and start the server. The `contextInitialized()` method of `MyContextListener` is invoked. While starting the server, since it initializes all the available Web applications, you will find the output printed in the `contextInitialized()` method in the server console, as shown in Figure 9.7:

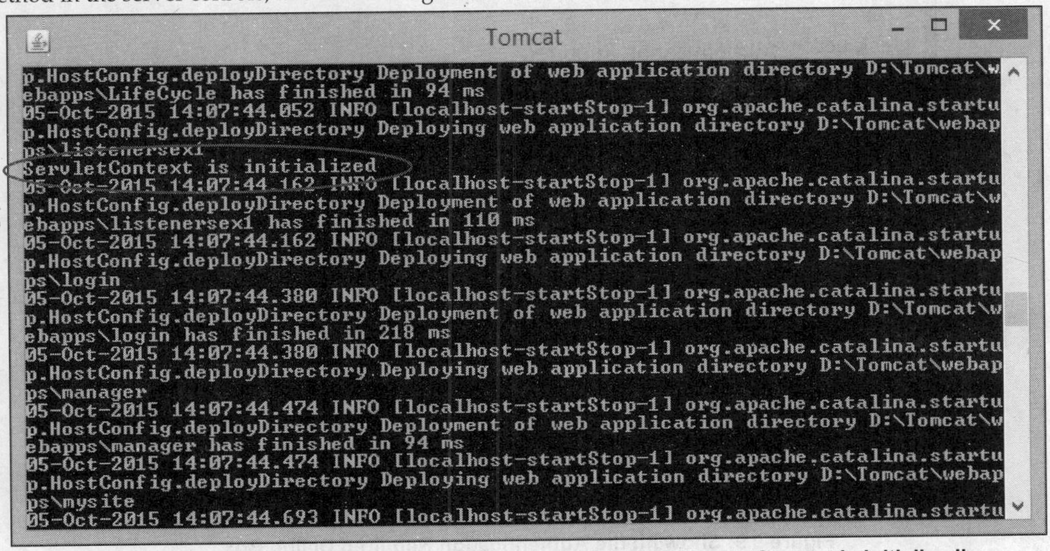

Figure 9.7: Tomcat Server Console Showing the Message 'ServletContext is initialized'

Now, browse the application using the URL `http://localhost:9090/listenersex1/Home.html`.

You will find the home page, as shown in Figure 9.8:

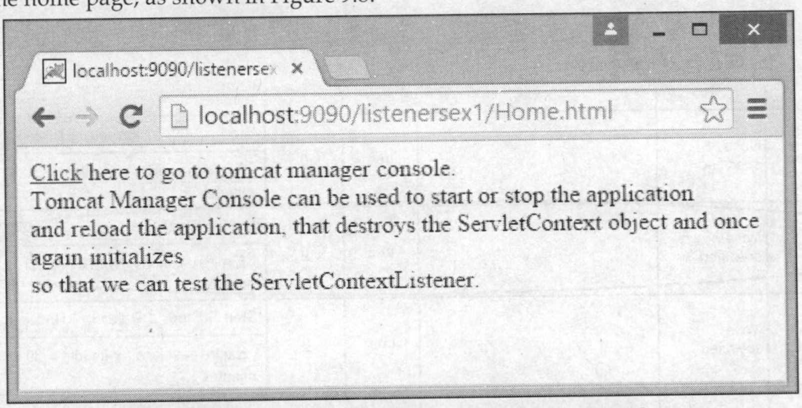

Figure 9.8: Home Page of the listenersex1 Application

Now, click the hyperlink "`Click`" in Figure 9.8. You will get the `Authentication Required` dialog box (Figure 9.9) to proceed to the main task of testing the context destruction and re-initialization. But the Tomcat manager console is accessible only for users with admin and manager roles. So, enter the respective user name and password (you can find the user name and password in <tomcat home>/conf/tomcat-users.xml file), as shown in Figure 9.9:

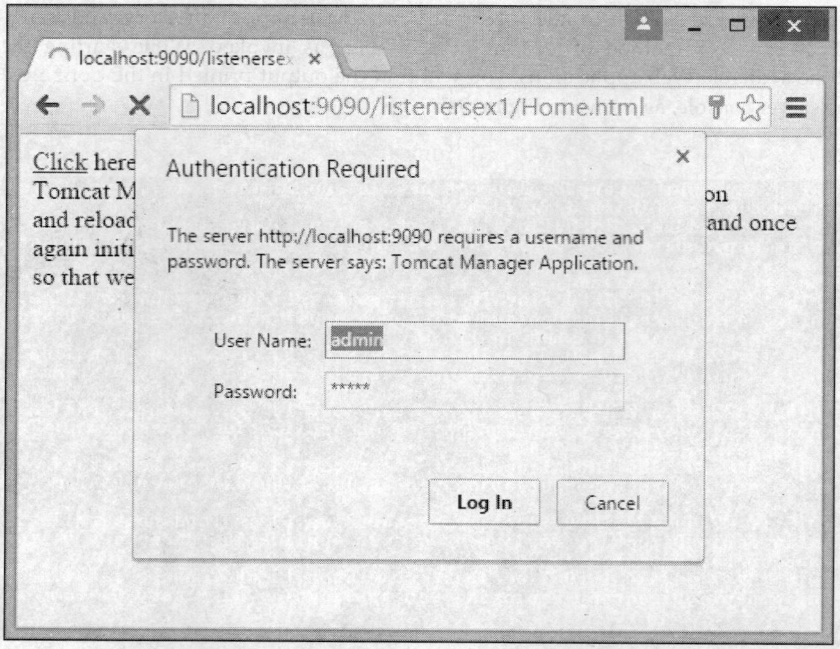

Figure 9.9: Showing the Authentication Required Dialog Box

When the user enters a valid username and password in Figure 9.9 and clicks the Log In button, Tomcat manager console will appear, as shown in Figure 9.10:

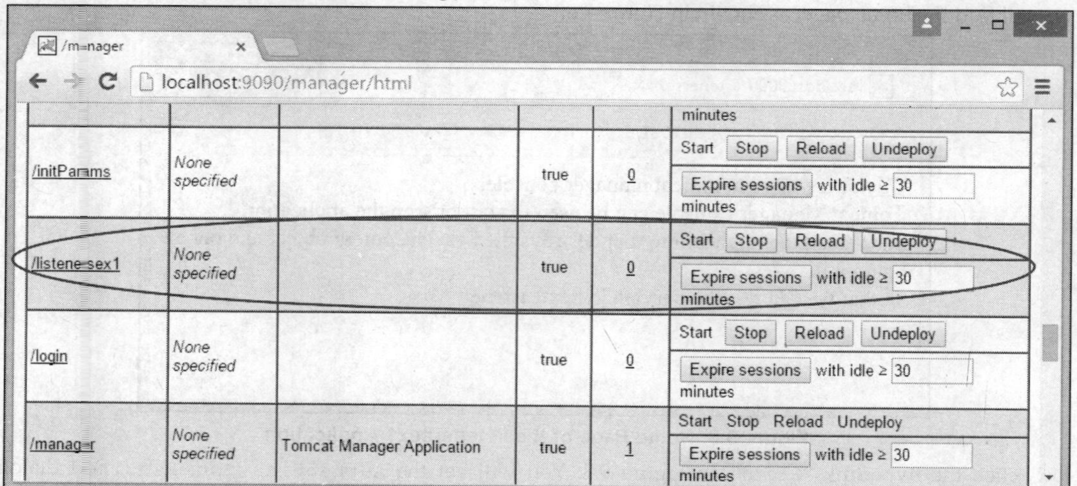

Figure 9.10: Tomcat Manager Console

This view allows the user to start/stop/reload/undeploy Web applications. To test this example, first stop this Web application from the `Stop` button highlighted in an ellipse (Figure 9.10). This action will destroy the Web application and thus its `ServletContext` object, which results to call the `contextDestroyed()` method of `MyContextListener`. You can find the output in the Tomcat server console, as shown in Figure 9.11:

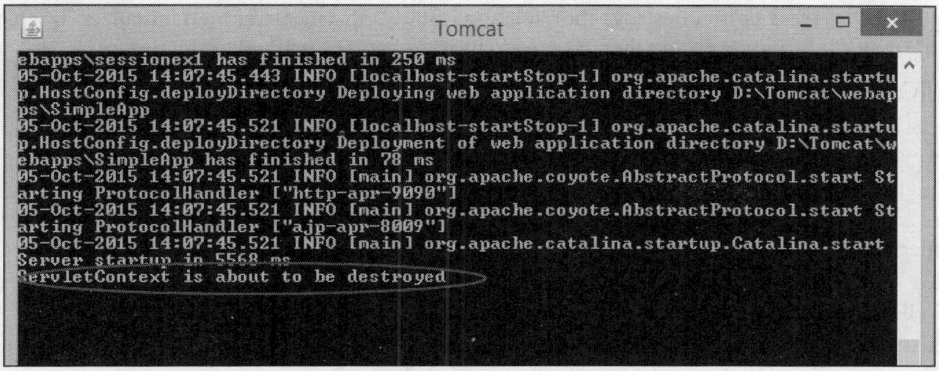

Figure 9.11: Tomcat Server Console Showing the Message 'ServletContext is about to be destroyed'

Now, start this Web application by clicking the `Start` button (Figure 9.10). This action will initialize the Web application and thus its `ServletContext` object, which results to call the `contextInitialized()` method of `MyContextListener`. You can find the output in the Tomcat server console, as shown in Figure 9.12:

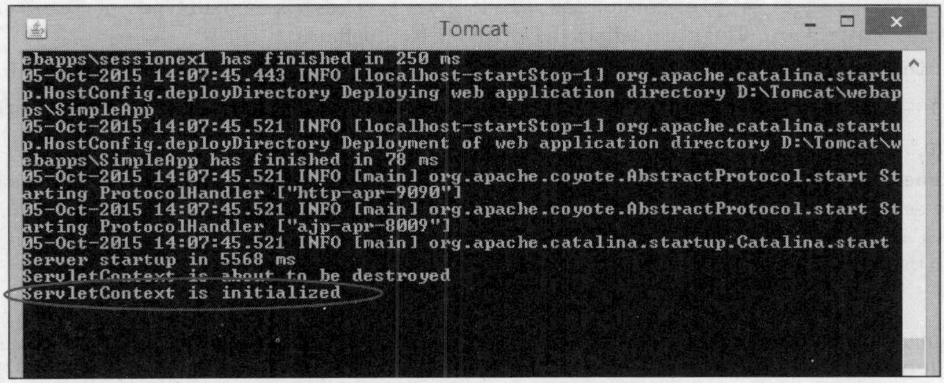

Figure 9.12: Tomcat Server Console Showing the Message 'ServletContext is initialized'

Reload this Web application by clicking the `Reload` button (Figure 9.10). You can find the output in the Tomcat server console, as shown in Figure 9.13:

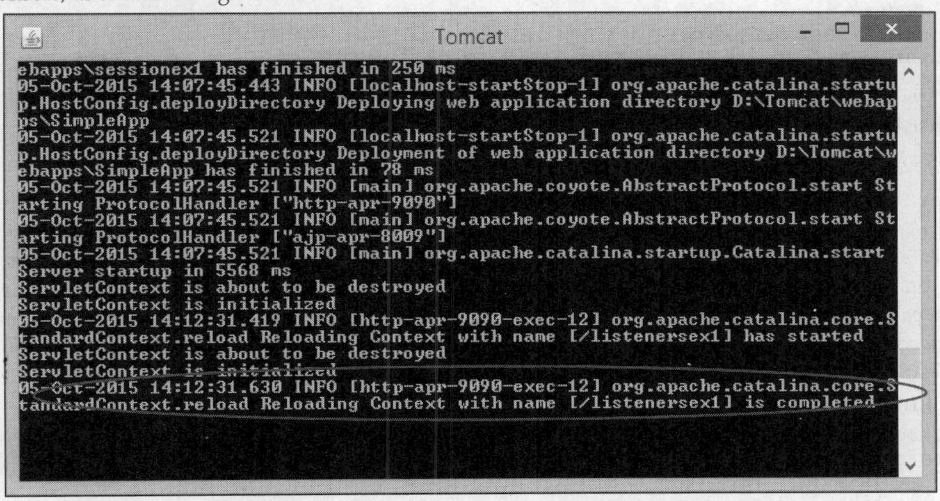

Figure 9.13: Tomcat Server Console Showing Two Messages Highlighted In Ellipse

Clicking on the Reload button destroys the Web application's instance and then initializes it, which results to call the contextDestroyed() and then contextInitialized() method of MyContextListener.

The ServletContextAttributeListener Interface

The ServletContextAtrributeListener interface allows us to monitor changes to the ServletContext attribute events. These three events are adding, replacing, and removing an attribute.

To write a ServletContext attribute events listener, write a class implementing javax.servlet.ServletContextAttributeListener interface, where we need to implement the following three methods of this interface:

- **void attributeAdded(ServletContextAttributeEvent)**– Servlet container invokes this method to indicate that a new attribute is added into the context.
- **void attributeReplaced(ServletContextAttributeEvent)**–Servlet container invokes this method to indicate that a context attribute is replaced, that is, an attribute is added with the name that already exists in the context.
- **void attributeRemoved(ServletContextAttributeEvent)**–Servlet container invokes this method to indicate that an attribute is removed from the context.

The javax.servlet.ServletContextAttributeEvent class is a subtype of javax.servlet.ServletContextEvent. This class defines the following two methods:

- **String getName()**– This method returns the attribute name for which the event is generated.
- **Object getValue()**–This method returns the value of the attribute for which the event is generated.

Working with ServletContextAttributeListener

The **listenersex2** application demonstrates the usage of ServletContextAttributeListener interface. The example sets context attributes, updates the values of existing context attributes, and finally removes context attributes. Now, we are creating the required files to perform these operations. You can find this application online in the code/Chapter9 folder.

Home.html

The Home.html page, as shown in Listing 9.9, has one submit button. When the user submits this page, the control forwards to TestServlet Servlet. You can find this file online in the code/Chapter9/listenersex2 folder.

Listing 9.9: The Home.html Page

```
<html>
   <body>
         <form method=post action="test">
<input type="submit" value="Invoke TestServlet to test ServletContextAttributeListener"/>
         </form>
   </body>
</html>
```

TestServlet.java

The TestServlet class extends GenericServlet and overrides its service() method. Then, instance sc of the ServletContext class is created, and setAttribute() methods are invoked on this instance to set attributes att1 and att2 to values "att1value", "att2value" respectively. Invoking the setAttribute() method on the same attribute att1 replaces its old value by a new value specified in its second argument. An attribute can be removed either by setting its value to null or by using the removeAtrribute() method. Both ways are coded in this class. This Servlet also displays one message on the browser. Listing 9.10 shows the code of the TestServlet.java file (you can find this file online in the code/Chapter9/listenersex2 folder):

Listing 9.10: The TestServlet.java File

```
package com.santosh.servlets;
import javax.servlet.*;
import java.io.*;
public class TestServlet extends GenericServlet {
```

```
    public void service ( ServletRequest req, ServletResponse res)
    throws ServletException, IOException {
        //test logic
        ServletContext sc=getServletContext();

        System.out.println("setting a context Attribute with name: att1");
        sc.setAttribute("att1","att1value");
        System.out.println("\nsetting a context Attribute with name: att2");
        sc.setAttribute("att2","att2value");

        System.out.println("\nsetting a context Attribute with name: att1");
        System.out.println("Here already an attribute with a name att1 exist in context
        so now it replaced");
        sc.setAttribute("att1","newvalue");

        System.out.println("\nremoving an Attribute with name: att1");
        sc.removeAttribute("att1");

        System.out.println("\nremoving an Attribute with name: att2 using setAttrbute
        method");
        sc.setAttribute("att2",null);

        res.getWriter().println("Hello, to find the output of this"+
        " example<br/>look into the tomcat server console");
    }//service
}//class
```

MyContextAttributeListener.java

The `MyContextAttributeListener` class implements the `ServletContextAttributeListener` interface. Therefore, it defines `attributeAdded()`, `attributeReplaced()`, and `attributeRemoved()` methods. All these methods accept `ServletContextAtributeEvent`, which listens to `ServletContextAttributeEvents`. The `getName()` and `getValue()` methods of `ServletContextAtributeEvent` are used to get names and values of the new attribute, the replaced attribute, and the currently removed attribute. Listing 9.11 shows the code of the MyContextAttributeListener.java file (you can find this file online in the code/Chapter9/listenersex2 folder):

Listing 9.11: The MyContextAttributeListener.java File

```
package com.santosh.servlets;
import javax.servlet.*;
public class MyContextAttributeListener implements ServletContextAttributeListener {

    public void attributeAdded( ServletContextAttributeEvent sce){
        System.out.println("Context attribute Added");

        System.out.println("Name : "+ sce.getName());
        System.out.println("Value : "+ sce.getValue());
    }//attributeAdded

    public void attributeReplaced( ServletContextAttributeEvent sce){
        System.out.println("Context attribute Replaced");

        System.out.println("Name : "+ sce.getName());
        System.out.println("Old Value : "+ sce.getValue());

        ServletContext sc=sce.getServletContext();
        System.out.println("New Value : "+ sc.getAttribute(sce.getName()));
    }//attributeReplaced

    public void attributeRemoved( ServletContextAttributeEvent sce){
        System.out.println("Context attribute removed");
        System.out.println("Name : "+ sce.getName());
        System.out.println("Value : "+ sce.getValue());
    }//attributeRemoved
}//class
```

web.xml

The web.xml file registers MyContextAttributeListener using its fully qualified class name and maps TestServlet to the URI specified in action attribute of Home.html page. You can find this file online in the code/Chapter9/listenersex2/WEB-INF folder.

Listing 9.12: The web.xml File

```
<?xml version="1.0" encoding="UTF-8"?>
<web-app>
   <listener>
        <listener-class>
               com.santosh.servlets.MyContextAttributeListener
        </listener-class>
   </listener>
   <servlet>
        <servlet-name>ts</servlet-name>
        <servlet-class>com.santosh.servlets.TestServlet</servlet-class>

   </servlet>
   <servlet-mapping>
        <servlet-name>ts</servlet-name>
        <url-pattern>/test</url-pattern>
   </servlet-mapping>
</web-app>
```

Arrange all the files according to the standard directory structure of Web application. Figure 9.14 shows the directory structure of the **listenersex2** application:

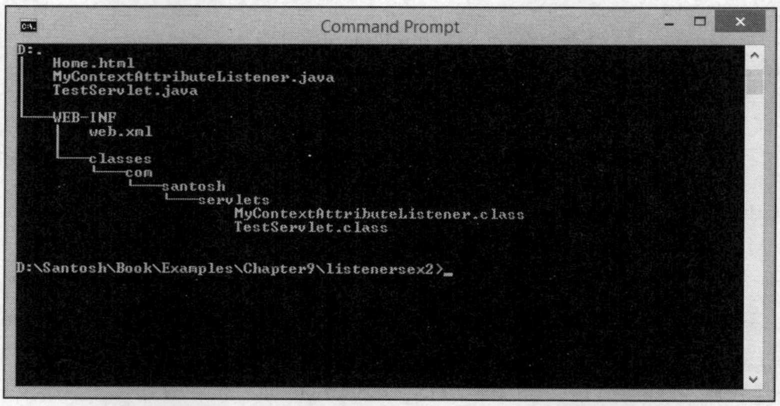

Figure 9.14: Showing the Directory Structure of the listenersex2 Web Application

Copy the listenersex2 folder to the <Tomcat home>/webapps directory and start the server. Open the Internet Explorer and type the URL http://localhost:9090/listenersex2/Home.html. The home page of the Web application appears, as shown in Figure 9.15:

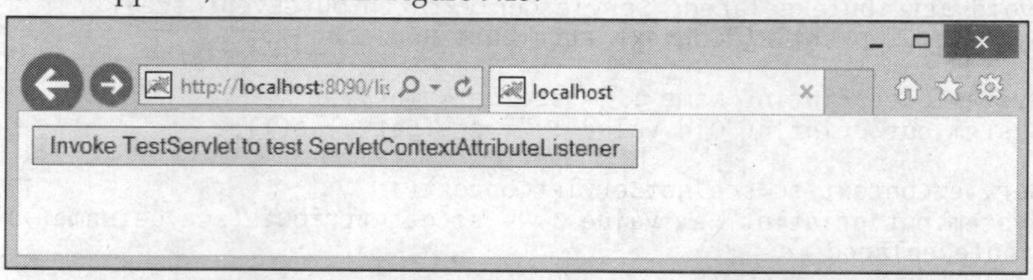

Figure 9.15: Home Page of the listenersex2 Web Application

Now, click the Invoke TestServlet to test ServletContextAttributeListener button (Figure 9.15) to invoke the TestServlet Servlet where we have added, replaced, and removed the context attributes.

The output appears, as shown in Figure 9.16:

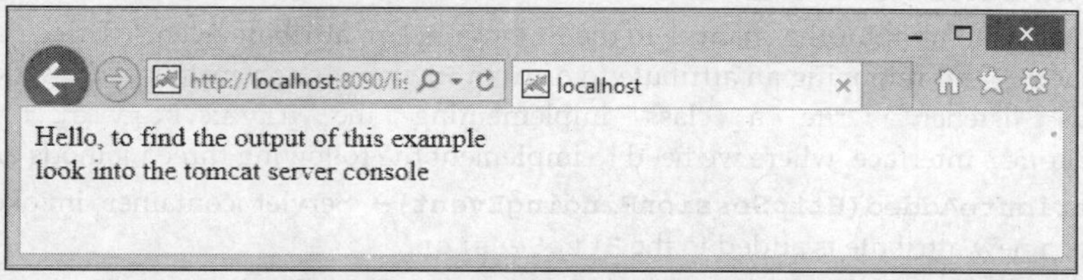

Figure 9.16: Showing a Message, indicating TestServlet is Successfully Executed

Now, switch to the Tomcat server console where you can find the outputs generated by `MyContextAttributeListener` for adding, replacing, and removing the context attributes. The output appears, as shown in Figure 9.17:

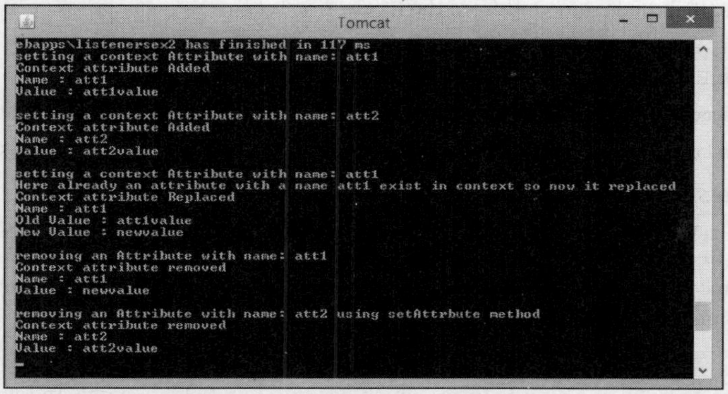

Figure 9.17: Tomcat Server Console Showing which Attributes are Added, Replaced, or Removed from ServletContext

The HttpSessionListener Interface

During session handling in Web applications, we create `HttpSession` objects and place them in the `HttpSession` when it is created and remove the objects when the `HttpSession` is invalidated or timed out, so that these objects can be used for the client throughout the session. The `HttpSessionListener` allows us to monitor the life cycle events of the `HttpSession` object, where it notifies about the following two events:

- The `HttpSession` has just been created.
- The `HttpSession` is invalidated or timed out.

Methods for Writing a Listener to Monitor HttpSession Life Cycle

To monitor an `HttpSession` life cycle, write a Java class that implements the `javax.servlet.http.HttpSessionListener` interface. This interface has the following two methods:

- **`void sessionCreated (HttpSessionEvent)`** – This method indicates that the `HttpSession` is just now created.
- **`void sessionDestroyed (HttpSessionEvent)`** – This method indicates that the `HttpSession` is invalidated or timed out and is about to be destroyed.

The javax.servlet.http.HttpSessionEvent Class

The `javax.servlet.http.HttpSessionEvent` object that is passed in as an argument for the notifications of `HttpSession` life cycle events gives the details of the event. The `javax.servlet.http.HttpSessionEvent` has only one method, which is as follows:

- **`HttpSession getSession()`** – This method returns the `HttpSession` object for which the event is generated.

The HttpSessionAttributeListener Interface

This listener allows us to monitor the changes to the HttpSession attribute events. These three attribute events are adding, replacing, and removing an attribute to or from HttpSession instance. To write an HttpSession attribute events listener, write a class implementing the javax.servlet.http.HttpSession AttributeListener interface, where we need to implement the following three methods of this interface:

- **void attributeAdded(HttpSessionBindingEvent)** – Servlet container invokes this method to indicate that a new attribute is added to the HttpSession.
- **void attributeReplaced(HttpSessionBindingEvent)** – Servlet container invokes this method to indicate that a session attribute is replaced, that is, an attribute is added with the name that is already existing in the session.
- **void attributeRemoved(HttpSessionBindingEvent)** – Servlet container invokes this method to indicate that an attribute is removed from the HttpSession.

The javax.servlet.http.HttpSessionBindingEvent class is a subtype of javax.servlet.http.HttpSessionEvent. This class defines following two methods:

- **String getName ()** – This method returns the attribute name for which the event is generated.
- **Object getValue()** – This method returns the value of the attribute for which this event is generated.

Working with the HttpSessionListener and HttpSessionAttributeListener Interfaces

Here, we create a Web application named **listenersex3**, which demonstrates the usage of HttpSessionListener and HttpSessionAttributeListener interfaces. This example shows when HttpSession instance is created, it sets session attributes, updates the values of existing session attributes, and finally removes session attributes. Now, we are creating the required files to perform these operations.

Home.html

The Home.html page consists of a simple form, which has two text fields - name and value. The user will enter attribute name and its value in these fields. The form also has two submit buttons - Add and Remove. Clicking on either button forwards the control to TestServlet. Listing 9.13 shows the code of the Home.html file (you can find this file online in the code/Chapter9/listenersex3 folder):

Listing 9.13: The Home.html Page

```
<html><body><pre>
<form action="test">
<b>Attribute Name  :</b> <input type="text" name="name"/>
<b>Attribute Value :</b> <input type="text" name="value"/>
    <input type="submit" name="submit" value="Add"/> <input type="submit" name="submit"
value="Remove"/>
</form>
</pre></body></html>
```

MySessionListener.java

The MySessionListener class implements HttpSessionListener and HttpSessionAttribute Listener interfaces. Therefore, it needs to define sessionCreated() and sessionDestroyed() methods of the HttpSessionListener interface and attributeAdded(), attributeReplaced(), and attributeRemoved() methods of the HttpSessionAttributeListener interface. The sessionCreated() and sessionDestroyed() methods accept HttpSessionEvent, which listens to session creation or destruction events, and the other three methods accept HttpSessionBindingEvent, which listens to session attribute change events. The getName() and getValue() methods of HttpSession BindingEvent are used to get names and values of new attribute, replaced attribute, and currently removed attribute Listing 9.14 shows the code of the MySessionListener.java file (you can find this file online in the code/Chapter9/listenersex3 folder):

Listing 9.14: The MySessionListener.java File

```
package com.santosh.servlets;
import javax.servlet.http.*;
public class MySessionListener implements
```

```
    HttpSessionListener, HttpSessionAttributeListener {
      public void sessionCreated( HttpSessionEvent hse) {
            System.out.println("New Session Created");
      }
      public void sessionDestroyed( HttpSessionEvent hse) {
            System.out.println("Session destroyed");
      }

      public void attributeAdded( HttpSessionBindingEvent hb) {
            System.out.println("New Attribute is added into session : ");

            System.out.println("\tName : "+hb.getName());
            System.out.println("\tValue: "+hb.getValue());
      }//attributeAdded

      public void attributeReplaced( HttpSessionBindingEvent hb) {
    System.out.println("Attribute with a name "+hb.getName()+" is replaced");
            System.out.println("\tOld Value : "+hb.getValue());

            HttpSession hs=hb.getSession();
            System.out.println("\tNew Value : "+hs.getAttribute(hb.getName()));
      }//attributeReplaced

      public void attributeRemoved( HttpSessionBindingEvent hbe) {
            System.out.println("attribute removed from session");
            System.out.println("\tName : "+hbe.getName());
            System.out.println("\tValue : "+hbe.getValue());
      }//attributeRemoved
    }//class
```

TestServlet.java

The `TestServlet` class extends the `HttpServlet` class and defines the `service()` method, which contains all requests processing logic. After creating instance of the `HttpSession` class, `getParameter()` and `equals()` methods are used to determine which button the user has clicked. In case, the user has clicked the `Add` button, both attribute name and value are fetched and set as attribute key value pair in `HttpSession` instance; otherwise, the removal operation is performed. Note that the `removeAttribute()` method takes the only name of the attribute to be removed. Finally, the Servlet forwards control to the home page, Home.html. Listing 9.15 shows the code of the TestServlet.java file (you can find this file online in the code/Chapter9/listenersex3 folder):

Listing 9.15: The TestServlet.java File

```
package com.santosh.servlets;

import javax.servlet.*;
import javax.servlet.http.*;
import java.io.*;

public class TestServlet extends HttpServlet {

  public void service(HttpServletRequest req, HttpServletResponse res)
  throws ServletException, IOException {

        HttpSession hs=req.getSession();
        System.out.println("After getting session in TestServlet");

        String submit=req.getParameter("submit");

        res.setContentType("text/html");
        PrintWriter out=res.getWriter();

        if (submit.equals("Add")) {
        hs.setAttribute(req.getParameter("name"), req.getParameter("value"));
              out.println("Attribute Added<br/>");
        }else if (submit.equals("Remove")){
```

```
                hs.removeAttribute(req.getParameter("name"));
                out.println("Attribute Removed<br/>");
            }//else if

            RequestDispatcher rd=req.getRequestDispatcher("Home.html");
            rd.include(req,res);
        }//service
    }//class
```

web.xml

The `web.xml` file registers the `MySessionListener` class with the Web container and also maps `TestServlet` to the URI specified in `action` attribute of Home.html page. Listing 9.16 shows the code of the `web.xml` file (you can find this file online in the code/Chapter9/listenersex3/WEB-INF folder):

Listing 9.16: The `web.xml` File

```
<?xml version="1.0" encoding="UTF-8"?>
<web-app>
   <listener>
         <listener-class>
               com.santosh.servlets.MySessionListener
         </listener-class>
   </listener>
   <servlet>
         <servlet-name>ts</servlet-name>
         <servlet-class>com.santosh.servlets.TestServlet</servlet-class>
   </servlet>
   <servlet-mapping>
         <servlet-name>ts</servlet-name>
         <url-pattern>/test</url-pattern>
   </servlet-mapping>
</web-app>
```

Arrange all the files according to the standard directory structure of Web application. Figure 9.18 shows the directory structure of the **listenersex3** application:

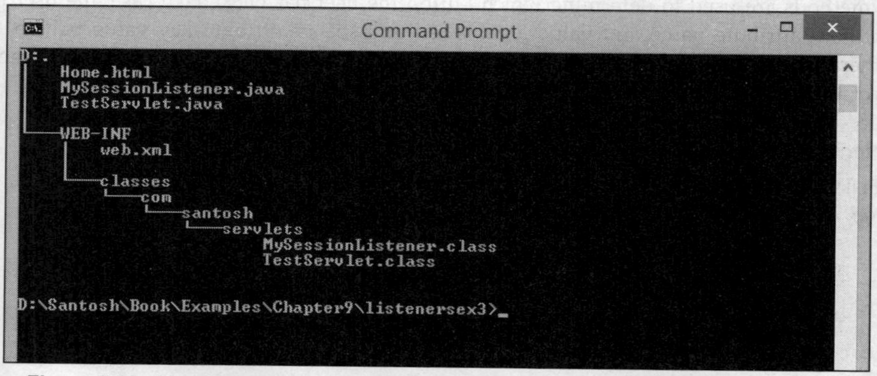

Figure 9.18: Showing the Directory Structure of the listenersex3 Web Application

Copy the `listenersex3` folder to the `<Tomcat home>/webapps` directory and start the server. Browse the application by using the URL `http://localhost:9090/listenersex3/Home.html`. The home page of the Web application appears, as shown in Figure 9.19:

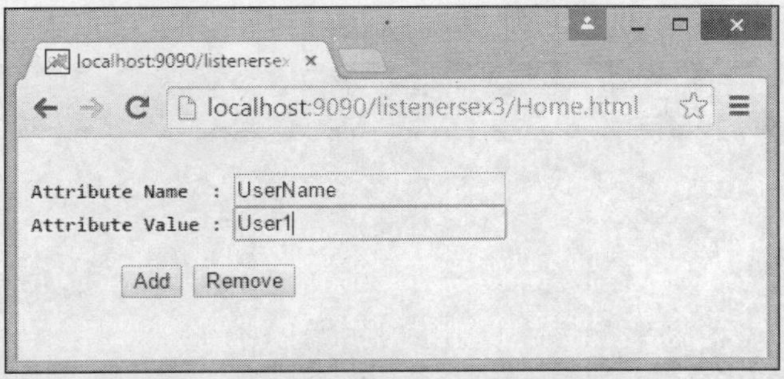

Figure 9.19: Home Page of the listenersex3 Web Application

Enter any name and value, and click the `Add` button (Figure 9.19). Now, observe the outputs printed in the Tomcat server console, as shown in Figure 9.20:

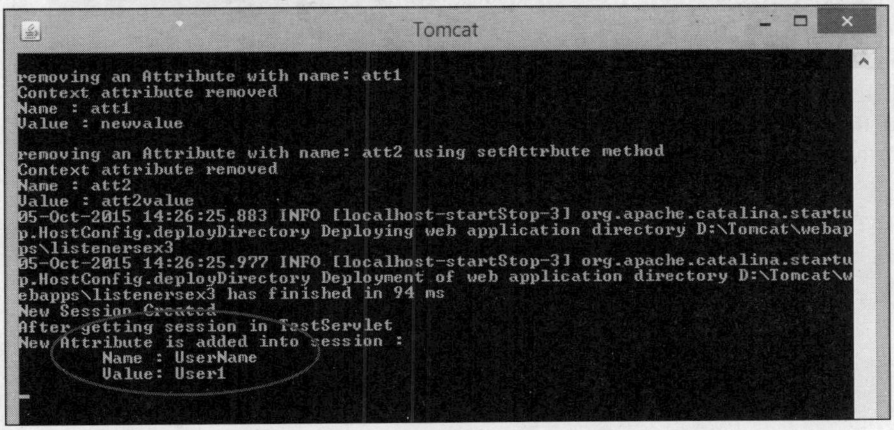

Figure 9.20: Tomcat Server Console Showing Messages Highlighted in Ellipse

You will find that `sessionCreated()` and `attributeAdded()` methods are invoked. Since this is the first request of the session, an `HttpSession` object is created. Now, enter the same name and any other value, as shown in Figure 9.21, and click the `Add` button. This will replace the existing attribute.

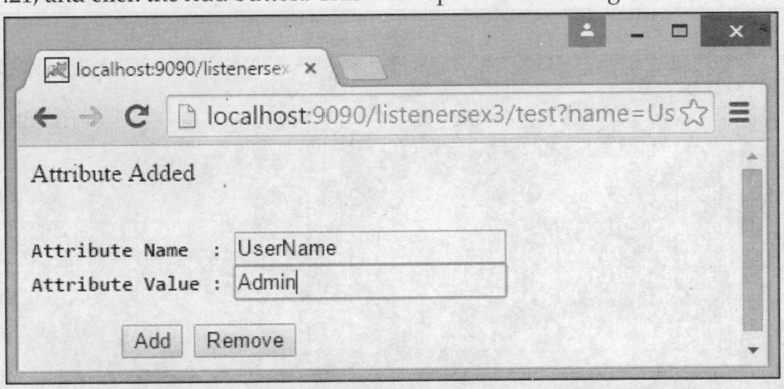

Figure 9.21: Showing the Use of Attribute Value Replacement Operation

Switch to the Tomcat server console to observe the outputs, as shown in Figure 9.22. You will find that the `attributeReplaced()` method is invoked.

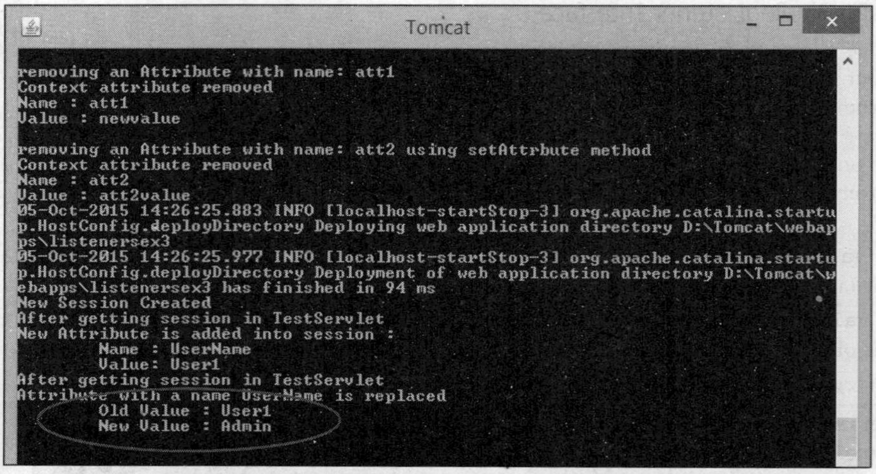

Figure 9.22: Showing the Changed Value of Attribute UserName

Now, enter the same name and a different value, as shown in Figure 9.23, and click the `Remove` button. The existing attribute will be removed.

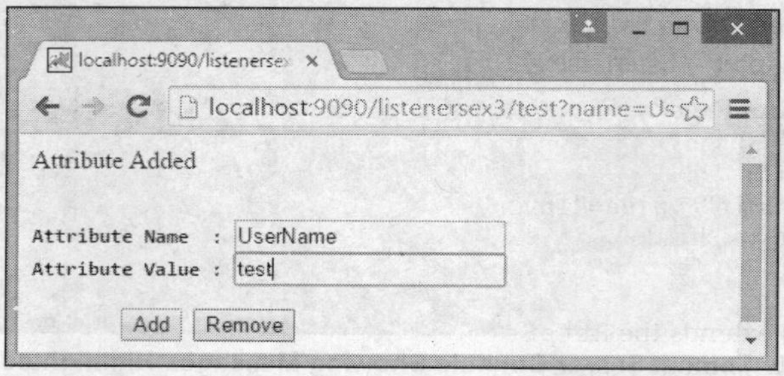

Figure 9.23: Showing the Use of Attribute Removal Operation

Switch to the Tomcat server console to observe the outputs, as shown in Figure 9.24. You will find that the `attributeRemoved()` method is invoked.

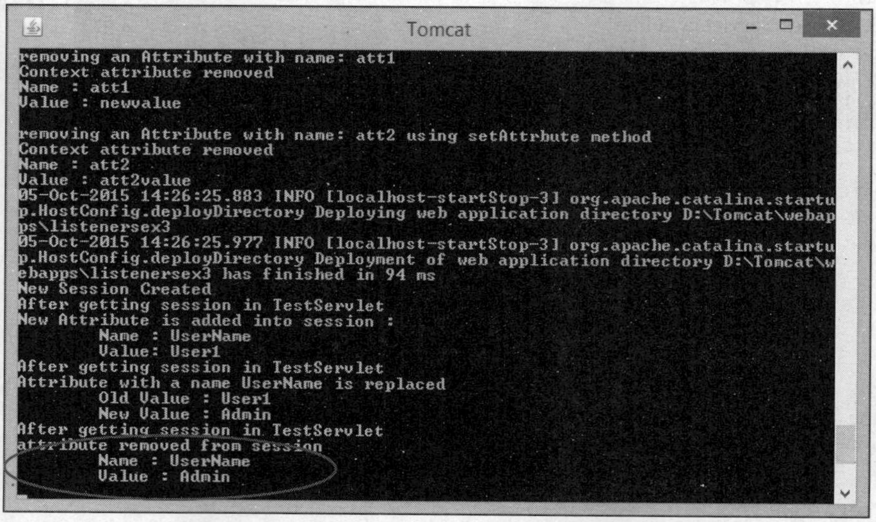

Figure 9.24: Tomcat Server Console Showing the Name and Value of the Removed Attribute

The HttpSessionBindingListener Interface

This interface allows us to monitor an object binding event. The `HttpSessionBindingListener` interface notifies about the events as a Java object has been bound to or unbound from an `HttpSession` object. This is different from `HttpSessionAttributeListener`, such as `HttpSessionAttributeListener` notifies about the events related to the changes to the attributes of `HttpSession`, but `HttpSessionBindingListener` notifies only when the object of its implementation class is added or removed from the `HttpSession`. The `HttpSessionBindingListener` interface has the following two methods:

- **void valueBound(HttpSessionBindingEvent)** – Servlet container invokes this method to indicate that the Java object is added to the HttpSession object.
- **void valueUnbound(HttpSessionBindingEvent)** – Servlet container invokes this method to indicate that the object is removed from the HttpSession object.

Working with the HttpSessionBindingListener Interface

The **listenersex4** application created here illustrates the usage of `HttpSessionBindingListener` interface. This example first binds an object and then unbinds the same object from session by implementing the `HttpSessionBindingListener` interface.

Home.html

The Home.html page consists of one submit button `Invoke TestServlet`. When the user submits this page, the control forwards to `TestServlet`. Listing 9.17 shows the code of the Home.html page (you can find this file online in the code/Chapter9/listenersex4 folder):

Listing 9.17: The Home.html Page

```
<html><body><pre>
<form action="test">
  <input type="submit" value="Invoke TestServlet"/>
</form></pre></body></html>
```

TestServlet.java

The `TestServlet` class extends the `HttpServlet` class and defines the `service()` method. First instance of `HttpSession` class is created and then `att1` and `att2` are set to string "`att1value`" and object of `MyBean` class respectively. When we again set `att2` to string value, the previous bound object of `MyBean` class unbinds from the session. Finally, Servlet prints message on Web browser. Listing 9.18 shows the code of the TestServlet.java file (you can find this file online in the code/Chapter9/listenersex4 folder):

Listing 9.18: The TestServlet.java File

```
package com.santosh.servlets;
import javax.servlet.http.*;
import javax.servlet.*;
import java.io.*;
public class TestServlet extends HttpServlet {

  public void service (HttpServletRequest req, HttpServletResponse res)
  throws ServletException, IOException {

       HttpSession hs=req.getSession();

       hs.setAttribute("att1","att1value");
       hs.setAttribute("att2", new MyBean());

       hs.setAttribute("att1", "new value");
       hs.setAttribute("att2", "new value for att2");

       hs.removeAttribute("att1");
       res.getWriter().println("To find the events of HttpSession binding listener
       observe the server console");
  }//service
}//class
```

MyBean.java

The `MyBean` class implements the `HttpSessionBindingListener` interface. Therefore, it has to define `valueBound()` and `valueUnbound()` methods. These methods accept `HttpSessionBindingEvent` object. The `valueBound()` method notifies the object that is being bound to a session and identifies the session. The `valueUnbound()` method notifies the object that is being unbound from a session and identifies the session. Listing 9.19 shows the code of the MyBean.java file (you can find this file online in the code/Chapter9/listenersex4 folder):

Listing 9.19: The MyBean.java File

```
package com.santosh.servlets;
import javax.servlet.http.*;
public class MyBean implements HttpSessionBindingListener {
    //our required variable and methods
    public void valueBound(HttpSessionBindingEvent hs) {
            System.out.println("In value bound of MyBean");
    }

    public void valueUnbound(HttpSessionBindingEvent hs) {
            System.out.println("In value unbound of MyBean");
    }
}//class
```

Web.xml

The `web.xml` file maps `TestServlet` to the URI specified in `action` attribute of `Home.html` page. Listing 9.20 shows the code of the `web.xml` file (you can find this file online in the code/Chapter9/listenersex4/WEB-INF folder):

Listing 9.20: The `web.xml` File

```
<?xml version="1.0" encoding="UTF-8"?>
<web-app>
   <servlet>
         <servlet-name>ts</servlet-name>
         <servlet-class>com.santosh.servlets.TestServlet</servlet-class>
   </servlet>
   <servlet-mapping>
         <servlet-name>ts</servlet-name>
         <url-pattern>/test</url-pattern>
   </servlet-mapping>
</web-app>
```

Arrange all the files according to the standard directory structure of Web application. Figure 9.25 shows you the directory structure of the **listenersex4** application:

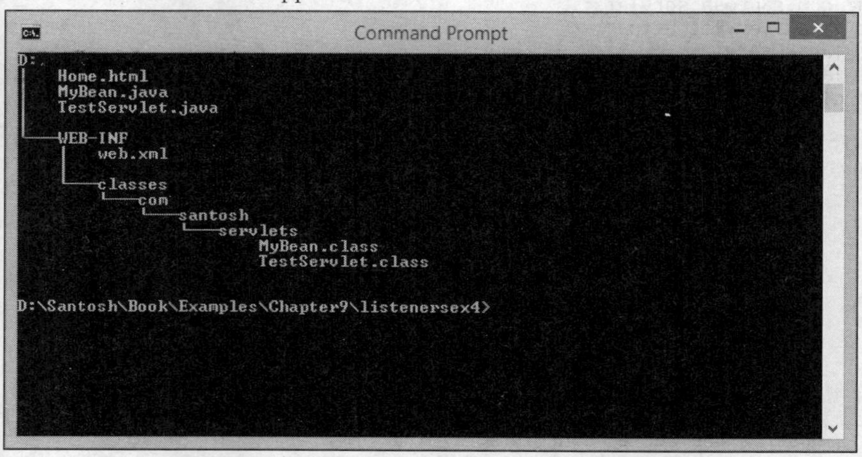

Figure 9.25: Showing the Directory Structure of the listenersex4 Web Application

Copy the listenersex4 folder to the <Tomcat home>/webapps directory and start the server. Browse the application by using the URL http://localhost:9090/listenersex4/Home.html. The home page of the Web application appears, as shown in Figure 9.26:

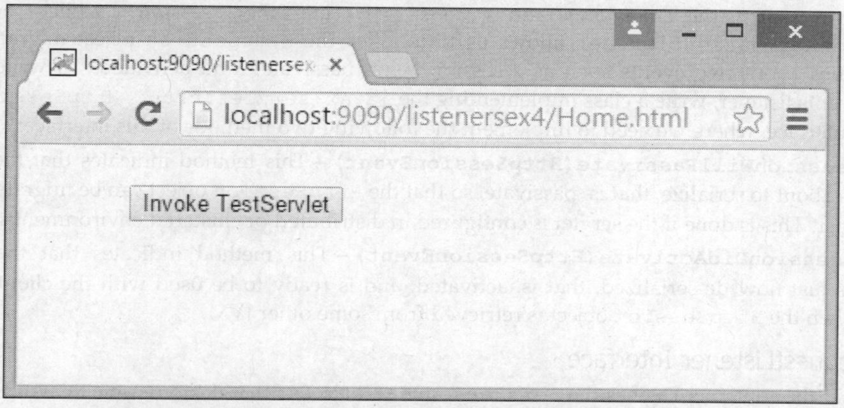

Figure 9.26: Home Page of the listenersex4 Web Application

Click the Invoke TestServlet button and observe the output in the Tomcat server console. You will find messages, as shown in Figure 9.27:

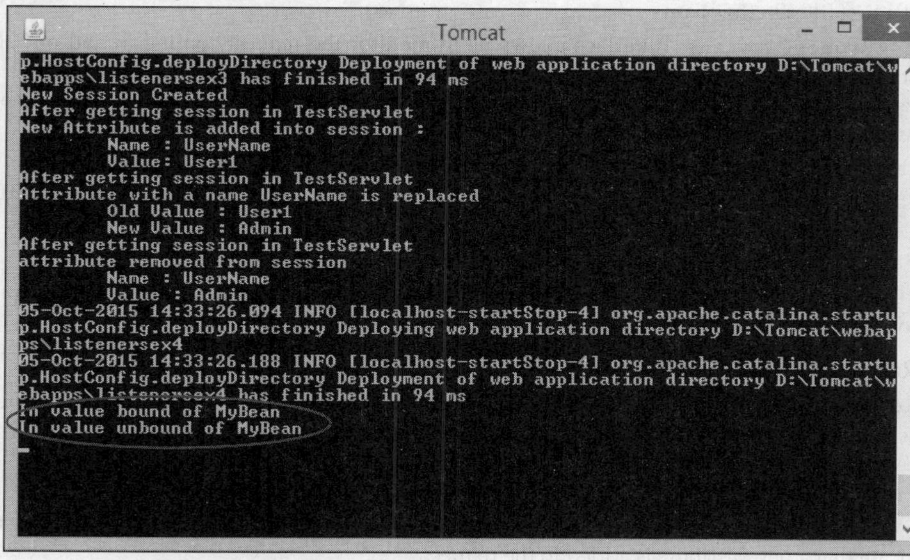

Figure 9.27: Tomcat Server Console Showing Two Messages Highlighted in Ellipse

The message In value bound of MyBean is printed when we add MyBean object to the session object with a name att2.

The message In value unbound of MyBean is printed when we add new value for att2 to the session object with a name att2. This will replace the MyBean object earlier added to the session, which results in the unbinding of the MyBean object.

The HttpSessionActivationListener Interface

We know that the scope of an HttpSession object is visible to the particular JVM servicing the session requests. In distributed or clustered environments, when a client makes a request, that request is dispatched to any one of the JVMs for request handling. In this case, it is required to migrate the HttpSession object created in one JVM to another. To perform HttpSession object migration, we may want to handle some objects stored in HttpSession. For example, suppose we want to store a 3rd party vendor's non-serializable object in a session. We need to extract the values from such an object and store it in another form in the session in the source JVM while passivation. Thereafter in the destination, JVM reconstructs that object using the data stored in another form in the session and stores it in the session while activation. The HttpSessionActivationListener allows us to monitor the HttpSession object migration events. This listener notifies about two events such as a session being passivated and activated. To write HttpSession migration events listener, write a class implementing the javax.servlet.http. HttpSessionActivationListener interface, where we need to implement the following two methods of this interface:

- **void sessionWillPassivate(HttpSessionEvent)** – This method indicates that the HttpSession object is about to serialize, that is, passivate, so that the HttpSession object can be migrated from one JVM to another. This is done if the servlet is configured in distributed or clustered environments.
- **void sessionDidActivate(HttpSessionEvent)** – This method indicates that the HttpSession object is just now de-serialized, that is, activated, and is ready to be used with the client request. This is done when the HttpSession object is retrieved from some other JVM.

The ServletRequestListener Interface

We know that the container catches the ServletRequest object so that it can recycle to avoid the performance overhead of request object creation. The ServletRequestListener allows the developer to monitor the request coming in and out of scope in a Web component. A request is defined as coming into scope when it is about to enter the first filter or servlet in each Web application and going out of scope when it exits the last servlet or the first filter in the chain.

The ServletRequestListener interface allows us to monitor the request coming in and out of scope in a Web component so that we can include objects that initiate tasks when a new request comes into our application and finalize/close them while the request leaves our application. For example, we can count the number of requests by incrementing a static variable.

To write a ServletRequest life cycle events listener, write a class implementing javax.servlet. ServletRequestListener, where we need to implement the following two methods of this interface:

- **void requestInitialized(ServletRequestEvent)** – This method indicates that the request is about to come into the Web component scope.
- **void requestDestroyed(ServletRequestEvent)** – This method indicates that the request is about to go out of scope of the Web component.

The ServletRequestAttributeListener Interface

The ServletRequestAttributeListener interface allows us to monitor changes to ServletRequest attribute events. These events involve addition of an attribute, changing its value, and its removal. To write a request attribute events listener, write a class implementing the javax.servlet.ServletRequestAttribute Listener interface, where we need to implement the following three methods of this interface:

- **void attributeAdded(ServletRequestAttributeEvent)** – Servlet container invokes this method to indicate that a new attribute is added to the request.
- **void attributeReplaced(ServletRequestAttributeEvent)** – Servlet container invokes this method to indicate that a request attribute is replaced.
- **void attributeRemoved(ServletRequestAttributeEvent)** – Servlet container invokes this method to indicate that an attribute is removed from the request.

The javax.servlet.ServletRequestAttributeEvent class is a subtype of javax.servlet.ServletRequestEvent. This class defines two methods:

- **String getName()** – This method returns the attribute name for which the event is generated.
- **Object getValue()** – This method returns the value of the attribute for which the event is generated.

Describing Wrappers

Wrappers are very useful because they can easily handle Servlet environment by wrapping its API. They are sandwiched between Servlets and Servlet container. Servlet API's core objects are `ServletRequest` and `ServletResponse`, and Http-specific objects are `HttpServletRequest` and `HttpServletResponse`. After introducing wrapper API, interaction with Servlets is done by using wrapper classes. Servlets's core objects are not used directly.

Need of Wrappers

Wrappers allow the Web application developer to add additional functionalities to the request and response objects given by Servlet container. You can either change, add more data to request before reaching it at Servlet / JSP, or perform some pre/post operations for the calls made on the request or response object. Wrappers enable the developer to change the functionality of predefined methods on request and response objects with their new API. To override the functionality, wrapper objects passed as arguments to calling Servlet should be the same as request and response objects of the called servlet. Some scenarios where we need wrappers are making response object able to output DOM objects on client, checking the content type when it is being set into the response, caching the output printed to the client, and then flushing it after the entire response is generated.

Filters also can make use of wrappers to wrap a request or response so that it can change the behavior to do some filter-related tasks.

Types of Wrapper Classes

Java Servlet API provides the following four wrapper classes:

- `javax.servlet.ServletRequestWrapper`
- `javax.servlet.ServletResponseWrapper`
- `javax.servlet.http.HttpServletRequestWrapper`
- `javax.servlet.http.HttpServletResponseWrapper`

These classes implement Decorator Pattern. The Decorator Pattern is a core design pattern that is used for providing additional functionality to a particular object.

All these four classes are public non-abstract classes provided with one constructor, which takes an argument of their respective wrapped types, that is, `ServletRequestWrapper` takes `ServletRequest` as an argument and `ServletResponseWrapper` takes `ServletResponse` as an argument.

The ServletRequestWrapper Class

The `ServletRequestWrapper` class implements the `ServletRequest` interface. This class is further extended by Web developers to call their overridden methods. See Table 9.4 for some commonly used methods of this class.

Table 9.4: Methods of the ServletRequestWrapper Class

Method	Default Behavior
`getRequest`	Returns wrapped request object.
`getAttribute`	Calls `getAttribute()` request method on wrapped request object.
`getParameter`	Calls `getParameter()` request method on wrapped request object.
`getParameterValues`	Calls `getParameterValues()` request method on wrapped request object.
`getRequestDispatcher`	Calls `getRequestDispatcher()` request method on wrapped request object.
`removeAtrribute`	Calls `getRequestDispatcher()` request method to remove the wrapped request object.
`setAttribute`	Calls `setAttribute()` request method on wrapped request object.

The ServletResponseWrapper Class

The `ServletResponseWrapper` class implements the `ServletResponse` interface. This class is further extended by Web developers to define their overridden methods. See Table 9.5 for some commonly used methods of this class.

Table 9.5: Methods of the ServletResponseWrapper Class

Method	Default Behavior
getBufferSize	Calls getBufferSize() response method on wrapped response object.
getResponse	Returns wrapped ServletResponse object.
getWriter	Calls getWriter() response method on wrapped response object.
setContentLength	Calls setContentLength() response method on wrapped response object.
setContentType	Calls setContentType() response method on wrapped response object.

The HttpServletRequestWrapper Class

The `HttpServletRequestWrapper` class implements the `HttpServletRequest` interface. This class is further extended by Web developers to define their overridden methods. See Table 9.6 for some commonly used methods of this class.

Table 9.6: Methods of the HttpServletRequestWrapper Class

Method	Default Behavior
getCookies	Calls getCookies() request method on wrapped request object.
getHeaders	Calls getHeaders() request method on wrapped request object.
getMethod	Calls getMethod() request method on wrapped request object.
getPathInfo	Calls getPathInfo() request method on wrapped request object.
getSession	Calls getSession() request method on wrapped request object.
getRequestURI	Calls getRequestURI() request method on wrapped request object.

The HttpServletResponseWrapper Class

The `HttpServletResponseWrapper` class implements the `HttpServletResponse` interface. This class is further extended by Web developers to define their overridden methods. See Table 9.7 for some commonly used methods of this class.

Table 9.7: Methods of the HttpServletResponseWrapper Class

Method	Default Behavior
addCookie	Calls addCookie() response method on wrapped response object.
encodeRedirectURL	Calls encodeRedirectURL() response method on wrapped response object.
encodeURL	Calls encodeURL() response method on wrapped response object.
sendRedirect	Calls sendRedirect() response method on wrapped response object.
setHeader	Calls setHeader() response method on wrapped response object.

Using Wrappers

In this section, we discuss the use of wrappers in a Web application. This application gets parameter from the request. This request parameter is not sent in request URI; therefore, the `getParameter()` method must return null. With the help of wrapper, we customize servlet to return 'None' string, instead of returning null value. This application also checks whether the content type set for the response is supported type or not. Now we are creating the required files to implement wrapper interfaces. You can find this application online in the code/Chapter9 folder.

Creating the Home.html Page

The Home.html page consists of a form that has two submit buttons. The user submits page by choosing the appropriate button. Request is processed either through filter or through `TestServlet`. Listing 9.21 shows the code of the Home.html page (you can find this file online in the code/Chapter9/wrapper folder.):

Listing 9.21: The Home.html Page

```
<html>
  <body>
        <form method=post action="ser1">
                <input type="submit" value="Request through Filter"/>
        </form><br><br>
        <form method=post action="ser2">
                <input type="submit" value="Request without Filter"/>
        </form>
  </body>
</html>
```

Creating the TestServlet.java File

The `TestServlet` class gets request parameter that is not sent by the user and then prints value of this parameter using the `out.println()` method. Listing 9.22 shows the code of the TestServlet.java file (you can find this file online in the code/Chapter9/wrapper folder):

Listing 9.22: The TestServlet.java File

```
package com.santosh.servlets;

import javax.servlet.*;
import java.io.*;
public class TestServlet extends GenericServlet {

  public void service (ServletRequest req, ServletResponse res)
  throws ServletException, IOException {
        String testparam=req.getParameter ("myparam");
        res.setContentType ("text/xml");
        //These methods is invoked just to test
        //whether the wrapper functionality is working or not

        PrintWriter out=res.getWriter ();
        out.println ("<html><body><b>");
        out.println ("Parameter value is "+ testparam);
        out.println ("</b></body></html>");
  }//service
}//class
```

Creating the MyRequestWrapper.java File

The `MyRequestWrapper` class extends the `ServletRequestWrapper` class to have permission to override the methods of `ServletRequestWrapper` class. This class overrides the `getParameter()` method of `ServletRequestWrapper` class. The `getParameter()` method of `MyRequestWrapper` class first calls the `getParameter()` method of `ServletRequestWrapper` super class, which returns the value of `testparam` and assigns it to string `s1`. If request parameter or s1 is found to be null, it sets `s1` to "None" string and returns it. Hence, in this way, the `getParameter()` method of `ServletRequestWrapper` class is overridden;

otherwise, this method will return null value. Listing 9.23 shows the code of the MyRequestWrapper.java file (you can find this file online in the code/Chapter9/wrapper folder:

Listing 9.23: The MyRequestWrapper.java File

```
package com.santosh.servlets;
import javax.servlet.*;
public class MyRequestWrapper extends ServletRequestWrapper {

    public MyRequestWrapper (ServletRequest req) {super(req);}

    public String getParameter(String s) {
        String s1=super.getParameter(s);
        if(s1==null)
            s1="None";
        return s1;
    }//getParameter
}//class
```

Creating the MyResponseWrapper.java File

The `MyResponseWrapper` class extends the `ServletResponseWrapper` class to have permission to override the methods of `ServletResponseWrapper` class. This class overrides the `setContentType()` method of `ServletRequestWrapper` class. The `setContentType()` method of `MyResponseWrapper` class sets the content type of response to "`text/html`" using the `setContentType()` method of `ServletResponseWrapper` super class. Listing 9.24 shows the code of the MyResponseWrapper.java file (you can find this file online in the code/Chapter9/wrapper folder):

Listing 9.24: The MyResponseWrapper.java File

```
package com.santosh.servlets;
import javax.servlet.*;

public class MyResponseWrapper extends ServletResponseWrapper {

    public MyResponseWrapper ( ServletResponse res){super(res);}
    public void setContentType(String s){

        if (!s.equals("text/html"))
                s="text/html";
        /*
Here we consider that our application is designed intelligent to provide only html
response content
If we want different types also to be allowed then we need to check accordingly
        */
        super.setContentType(s);
    }//setContentType
}//class
```

Creating the MyWrapperFilter.java File

The `MyWrapperFilter` class implements filter class and acts as a filter to intercept the request and wrap it into our wrapper types. This class creates instances of `MyRequestWrapper` and `MyResponseWrapper` classes to apply them on `ServletRequest` and `ServletResponse` objects and invokes the `doFilter()` method on wrapper objects. Listing 9.25 shows the code of the MyWrapperFilter.java file (you can find this file online in the code/Chapter9/wrapper folder):

Listing 9.25: The MyWrapperFilter.java File

```
package com.santosh.servlets;
import javax.servlet.*;
import java.io.*;
public class MyWrapperFilter implements Filter {
    public void init(FilterConfig fc){}
    public void destroy(){}
    public void doFilter(
ServletRequest req, ServletResponse res, FilterChain fc)
throws ServletException, IOException {
```

```
            MyRequestWrapper mreq=new MyRequestWrapper(req);
            MyResponseWrapper mres= new MyResponseWrapper(res);
            fc.doFilter(mreq,mres);
        }//doFilter
    }//class
```

Creating the Web.xml File

The web.xml file maps MyWrapperFilter to be invoked before TestServlet is called with the URI /ser1. When TestServlet is called using the URI /ser2, MyWrapperFilter is not invoked before the servlet according to the filter-mapping specified in web.xml. Listing 9.26 shows the code of the web.xml file (you can find this file online in the code/Chapter9/wrapper folder/WEB-INF):

Listing 9.26: The web.xml File

```
<?xml version="1.0" encoding="UTF-8"?>
<web-app>
  <filter>
        <filter-name>f1</filter-name>
        <filter-class>com.santosh.servlets.MyWrapperFilter</filter-class>
  </filter>

  <filter-mapping>
        <filter-name>f1</filter-name>
        <url-pattern>/ser1</url-pattern>
  </filter-mapping>

  <servlet>
        <servlet-name>s1</servlet-name>
        <servlet-class>com.santosh.servlets.TestServlet</servlet-class>
  </servlet>

  <servlet-mapping>
        <servlet-name>s1</servlet-name>
        <url-pattern>/ser1</url-pattern>
  </servlet-mapping>
  <servlet-mapping>
        <servlet-name>s1</servlet-name>
        <url-pattern>/ser2</url-pattern>
  </servlet-mapping>
</web-app>
```

Deploying and Running the Application

Arrange all the files according to the standard directory structure of Web application, as shown in Figure 9.28:

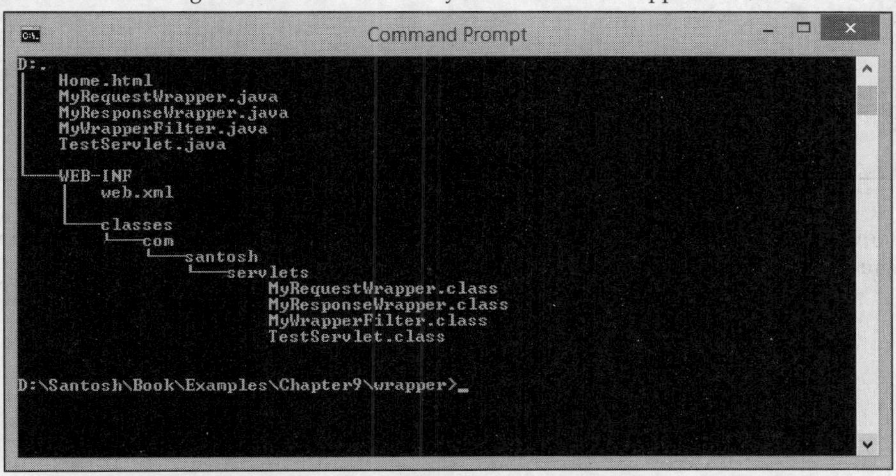

Figure 9.28: Showing the Directory Structure of the wrapper Application

Copy the `wrapper` folder to the `<Tomcat home>/webapps` directory and start the server. Browse the application by using the URL `http://localhost:9090/wrapper/Home.html`. Figure 9.29 shows the home page of this Web application. The home page has two buttons: `Request through Filter` and `Request without Filter`.

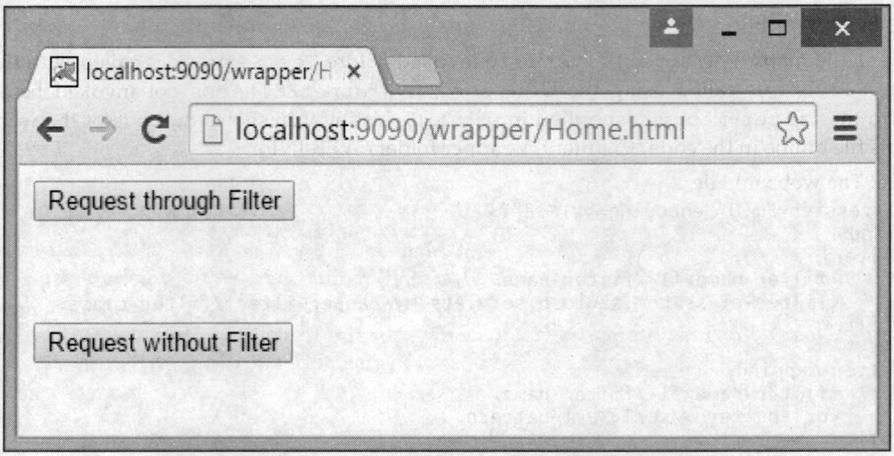

Figure 9.29: Home Page of the wrapper Application

Click the `Request through Filter` button to apply the wrappers to the request and response. This will show the response, as in Figure 9.30:

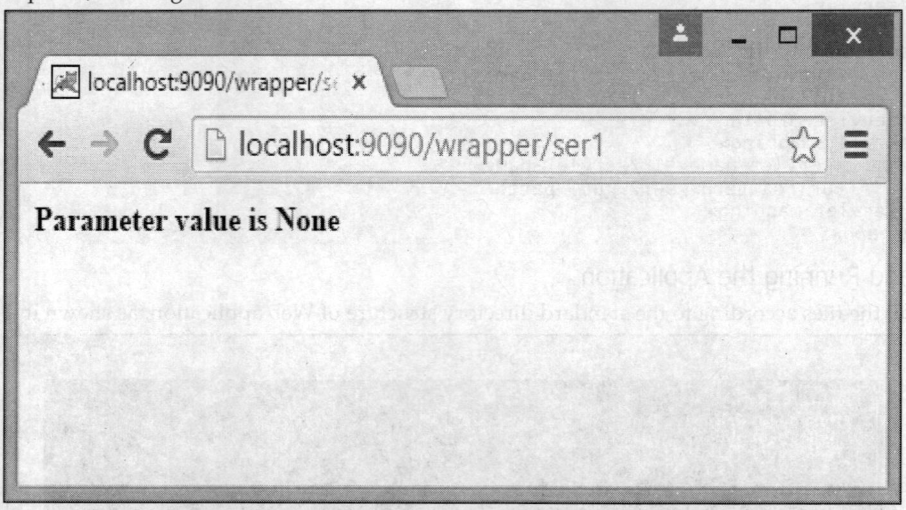

Figure 9.30: Showing the Customized Value of myparam

Click the `Request without Filter` button to invoke the servlet without filter. In this case, wrappers are not applied. Figure 9.31 shows the response:

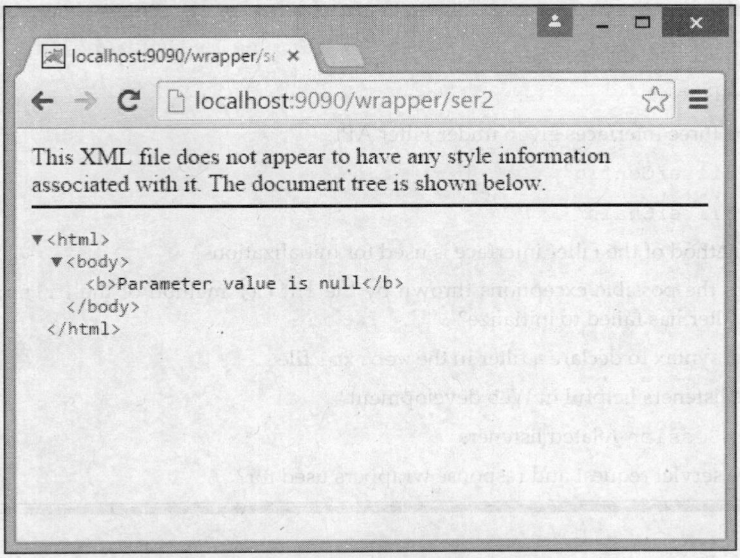

Figure 9.31: Showing XML Response

Response is displayed in an already set response content type, which is "`text/xml`", since no `ResponseWrapper` is applied, and the parameter value returned is null, since no `RequestWrapper` class is applied. Till now, we discussed filters, listeners, and wrappers; let's summarize the main points of the chapter.

Summary

This chapter started with an introduction to filters and discussed their needs in Web applications. Next, the chapter discussed the Filter API, which contains three interfaces: `Filter`, `FilterChain`, and `FilterConfig`. It then explained the working of filters with the help of a simple application that intercepts a request using two filters before the processing of the request starts. It also covered the ways of configuring filters. You also learned about various listener interfaces, such as `ServletContextListener`, `HttpSessionActivationListener` of listener API, which are used to handle request, session, and application level events. Finally, the chapter discussed the Wrapper API, which is used to wrap Servlet requests and responses. Let's recall the following important points to summarize the chapter:

- Filters are reusable code that can transform the content of requests, responses, and header information from one format into another.
- Filter API comprises three interfaces, `Filter`, `FilterChain`, and `FilterConfig`, which are present in the `javax.servlet` package.
- The `javax.servlet.Filter` interface is the basic interface, which provides a standard abstraction for Servlet container to understand and interact with the Filter component (`Filter` class).
- Listeners may recognize application events, which help Web developers in controlling the life cycle of the `ServletContext`, `ServletRequest`, and `HttpSession` objects.
- Java EE Web developers use various methods, such as `init()` and `jspInit()`, to control the life cycle of a Servlet or JSP page.
- The `ServletContextAtrributeListener` interface allows us to monitor changes to `ServletContext` attribute events.
- Wrappers are very useful because they can easily handle Servlet environment by wrapping its API.
- Wrappers allow the Web application developer to provide additional functionalities to the request and response objects given by Servlet container.

In the next chapter, you will learn about Applet Servlet Communication.

Exercise

Q. 9.1 What are Filters?

Q. 9.2 Write the three interfaces given under Filter API.

Q. 9.3 What is `FilterConfig`?

Q. 9.4 What is `FilterChain`?

Q. 9.5 Which method of the Filter interface is used for initializations?

Q. 9.6 What are the possible exceptions thrown by the `init()` method of the `Filter` interface to indicate that the filter has failed to initialize?

Q. 9.7 Write the syntax to declare a filter in the `web.xml` file.

Q. 9.8 How are listeners helpful in Web development?

Q. 9.9 List `HttpSession`-related listeners.

Q. 9.10 What are servlet request and response wrappers used for?

10

Applet-Servlet Communication

Applet is a small Java program that is embedded in a Web page. Java applets are very useful in making Internet-based applications. Java applets can communicate with servlets through various techniques. These techniques are HTTP connection with CGI program, raw socket connection with a non-HTTP server, Java servlets and object serialization, JDBC and RMI. The concept of HTTP connection with CGI program and raw socket connection with a non-HTTP server was used before the introduction of trusted and untrusted applets in JDK 1.1. However, it has some disadvantages due to which trusted and untrusted was introduced in JDK 1.1 and the method of fine-grained access control system was introduced in JDK 1.2. Java servlets and object serialization was newly introduced technique for applet-servlet communication. The concept of JDBC and RMI was introduced in JDK 1.1 and it has a very high impact on servlet-applet communication.

In this chapter, we will discuss the concept of trusted and untrusted applets. Besides, we will explain the techniques of applet-servlet communication. We have also discussed the advantages and disadvantages of those techniques. After that we have discussed how applet to servlet communication takes place with the help of example.

Let's discuss the concept of trusted and untrusted applet.

Concepts of Trusted and Untrusted Applets

A Web browser can easily download the Java applet embedded in a Web page. It can execute the Java applet automatically, which was very unsafe to do as the unauthorized users can easily access the information. So, in order to safeguard the customer, it was assumed in JDK 1.0 that all the applets are untrusted and thus JDK 1.0 introduced a system to run the applet through `SecurityManager`. `SecurityManager` provides security by making sure that no applet can write to the file system of the user and read the properties of the system. It also made sure that incoming socket connections cannot be accepted by the applet or the outgoing socket connections cannot be established to any host by the applet.

JDK 1.1, with its release, introduced the concept of trusted applets. Trusted applets are those applets that operate normally like any other application and have full access to the client machine. They should be digitally signed from the client side in order to maintain its authenticity. This digital signature helps to authenticate the origin of the applet as well as it also assures integrity during the transfer. Also, it will maintain the integrity during the exchange of information. This assures the client that the code for applet was not changed.

JDK 1.2 introduced the method of fine-grained access control system. This method gives the client more control over the security issue. It does not fully trust the digitally signed applets. It does not allow the free reign on the systems, it just give a few ability to access the system. Thus, in this system applets from unknown sources can be accepted. But those applets from the unknown sources are only given small privileges and they are not allowed to wipe the hard drive of the client.

Now, let's learn about the methods used for servlet-applet communication.

HTTP and Raw Socket Connections

The following two methods are used for applet-servlet communication:

- **HTTP connection with a CGI program**—On the server machine, the applet is allowed to establish an HTTP connection with a CGI program. In this case, the applet will be represented as a Web browser which will request a page and parse the response for its own use. Using a query string and POST data, an applet can give information. Apart from that, it can also retrieve information from the page which has been returned.
- **A raw socket connection with a non-HTTP server**—Another method is to allow the applet to establish a raw socket connection with a non-HTTP server that is running on the server machine. By using the specific custom protocol that is already decided, the non-HTTP server can listen to a specific port and can interact with the applet.

Advantages and Disadvantages of HTTP Connection with CGI Program

The following are the advantages of having HTTP connection with CGI programs:

- It is simple to write code of the applet. In order to manage communication channel, the applet can take benefit of the `java.net.URL` and `java.net.URLConnection` classes and writing the CGI program are almost similar to writing other programs.
- It also works perfectly for applets, which are running behind a firewall. In almost all firewalls, HTTP connections are permitted, however the raw socket connections are generally denied.
- Java applet is also allowed to communicate with any given program written in any language. The most advantageous features are that the CGI program is not required to be written in Java. It can be written in any language like Perl, C, C++, or any other language.
- It can work well with all browsers that are Java-enabled, since the applet are written using JDK 1.0.
- In this system, the applet is only allowed to communicate with a safe server. It is done by utilizing the encrypted HTTPS (HTTP + SSL) protocol.
- Both Web browser as well as applet can use the CGI program.

The disadvantages of HTTP connection with a CGI program are as follows:

- The process of HTTP connection with a CGI program is slow as in HTTP request/response model, the interaction cannot be done interactively between the applet and the CGI program. For every request and response, the CGI program needs to reestablish a new communication channel. Apart from that, there occurs a little delay when the CGI program is launched and the CGI programs are initialized in order to handle a request.
- It often requires to form the request as an array of names/value pairs.
- All kinds of response are required to be formatted as per some standard that were already set. In the HTTP connection with a CGI program method, the applet is only allowed to initiate the communication. The CGI programs do not have the permission to initiate the communication rather they have to wait for the applet for any response.

Advantages and Disadvantages of Raw Socket Connection with a Non-HTTP Server

An applet and server can also communicate by allowing the applet to establish a socket connection with a non-HTTP server process. The following are the advantages of raw socket connection with a non-HTTP server:

- A raw socket connection permits bidirectional and continuous communications. In this process, the same socket can be used to communicate interactively and allows to forward or backward the messages. Thus, in order to enforce security, the connection should always be initiated by the applet. The applet can initiate the connection by connecting to a server socket on the server machine. Once the socket connection is established, both applet and servlet can write to the socket at any point of time.
- On the server side, it permits to run more efficient programs. Without launching an external CGI program, the non-HTTP server can be written to handle a request.

The following are the disadvantages of raw socket connection with a non HTTP server:

- It cannot work for applets which are running behind a firewall. Since most of the firewall does not have raw socket connections, this type of applet-servlet communication is not allowed. However, for Intranet applications this mechanism of raw socket connection is possible.
- It is difficult to write the applet code that runs on the server. On the server machine, there should be some procedures for listening to the well–known port.
- In some cases, it is needed to develop a custom protocol.
- A Web browser cannot communicate with a non-HTTP server.

Now, let's learn about servlet and object serialization.

Servlets and Object Serialization

Java servlets and object serialization was newly introduced and it is assumed as a better technique than the traditional applet servlet communication. In the traditional approach of HTTP connection with CGI programs, for every request and response it was required to reestablish a new communication channel. This resulted in a delay when the CGI program is launched and the CGI program is initialized in order to handle a request. But in servlet and object serialization, in order to handle each of its repeated request, the server can launch a CGI program and thus applet are not required to wait like HTTP connection.

In the traditional approach of applet-servlet communication, it was required to be formatted as per some predefined standard. In Java object serialization, this problem has been resolved.

NOTE

Object Serialization generally executes with applets that are running inside browsers that support JDK 1.1 or higher editions.

Advantages and Disadvantages of Servlets and Object Serialization

The following are the advantages of using Servlets and Object Serialization:

1. Object Serialization can be used and customized easily.
2. Complex data can be passed to and from a servlet very easily.
3. It is very secure as serialized stream can be encrypted, authenticated and compressed.

The following are the disadvantages of using Servlets and Object Serialization:

1. The method of object serialization can only be used in JDK 1.1 or the higher version.
2. The fine-grained control over the object access is not offered by the `Serializable` interface.
3. Object serialization is not useful for the applications that need concurrent access.

Now let's learn about JDBC and RMI.

JDBC and RMI

In JDK 1.1, JDBC and RMI were introduced. These have a very high impact on servlet-applet communication. In order to interact with a database that are on a particular server, Java applets can use JDBC. This special type of communication through JDBC is also very useful for an applet to connect to the database straightway. It is also helpful to a servlet that handles the database communication instead of the applet.

RMI stands for Remote Method Invocation. It is a method that allows to create distributed application in Java. The RMI Application Programming Interface (API) permits an applet to invoke the method of executing the Java object which is on server machine.

Advantages and Disadvantages of RMI for Applet-Servlet Communication

RMI is very useful in applet-servlet communication. The following are the advantages of RMI in applet-servlet communication:

1. In applet-servlet communication, high level and object-oriented model is used. Responses are received in the form of serialized objects or references to other remote objects.
2. In RMI, the server objects are allowed to make callback to the methods of applets.
3. RMI can work for applets which are running behind a firewall. The transport layer of RMI generally depends on socket connection. But when an applet is executed behind the firewall, the socket connection fails. In this scenario, the transport layer of RMI can begin to operate automatically within HTTP protocol.

The following are the disadvantages of RMI in applet-servlet communication:

1. RMI uses naming registry for communication. It also uses special stub and skeleton class for all the remote object. So, RMI is bit difficult to use.
2. RMI is supported on a very few browsers. The browser that supports RMI includes Netscape Navigator 4. The previous version of Netscape Navigator or the other browser like Microsoft's Internet Explorer requires special plug for RMI.

3. Java clients can only use RMI. Here the server object cannot be shared or used by a web browser or a C++ client.

Let's learn how applet to servlet communication takes place with the help of an example.

Applet to Servlet Communication

You can choose Java Applet to create the user interface as it provides a rich graphical user interface using Swing and AWT. Java applets are used to make real world Internet applications, which are supported by most of the web browsers. However, an Applet also has some limitations. It does not allow us to access the local resources, and it causes security problems if we try to communicate to the host other than the host from where the applet is loaded. This means that an applet retrieved from, for example `www.seminalminds.com`, will only be able to communicate with the machine `www.seminalminds.com`.

This is not a problem most of the time, but if we want the applet to access a database running on the machine then there is a problem. One of the solutions is to run our database on `www.seminalminds.com`, but running everything on the same machine is not suggested for both security and performance reasons. A better solution is to use a servlet as an intermediary that is proxy. The applet communicates with a servlet, which in turn communicates with the database or any other resources and sends the results back to the applet.

An Example Using Applet in Servlet

In this section, we are creating an application named **apptoster**, which shows how a Servlet communicates with an Applet. The Servlet further does not communicate with database. This example involves a simple Applet with one text field and one button. When user clicks button after entering name, the request goes to servlet which displays Hello message in applet window at specified x, y co-ordinates. You can find this application online in the code/Chapter10/ folder. You need to create the MyApplet.java file for creating an applet. Listing 10.1 provides the code of the MyApplet class (you can find this file online in the code/Chapter10/apptoster folder):

Listing 10.1: Creating the MyApplet.java File

```
package com.santosh.applets;
import java.awt.*;
import java.applet.*;
import java.awt.event.*;
import java.net.*;
import java.io.*;
public class MyApplet extends Applet implements ActionListener {
   public void init() {
         b=new Button("Get Value");
         tf=new TextField(20);
         b.addActionListener(this);
         add (new Label("Name:"));
         add(tf);
         add(b);
   }
   public void actionPerformed(ActionEvent ae) {
         try{
                  String url=getCodeBase().toString()+
                  "/myser?name="+URLEncoder.encode(tf.getText());
                  URL u=new URL(url);
                  URLConnection uc=u.openConnection();
                  uc.setDoInput(true);
                  DataInputStream dis=
                  new DataInputStream(uc.getInputStream());
                  message=dis.readLine();
         }//try
         catch(Exception e){ message=e.getMessage(); }
         repaint();
   }
   public void paint(Graphics g){
         g.drawString(message,50,100);
   }//paint
   String message=" ";
```

```
    Button b;
    TextField tf;
}//class
```

In Listing 10.1, the `MyApplet` applet is created containing a label, a button, and a textfield. When the "`Get Value`" button is clicked, the message is sent from applet to servlet (request) and then the response is sent by servlet in applet. In Listing 10.2, the Home page is designed, which uses the `MyApplet` applet created in Listing 10.2 (you can find this file online in the code/Chapter10/apptoster folder):

Listing 10.2: Creating the Home.html File

```
<html><body>
<applet code="com.santosh.applets.MyApplet"
width="300" height="300"/>
</body></html>
```

In Listing 10.3, the `MyServlet` Servlet is created to communicate with the `MyApplet` applet, which is created in Listing 10.1. The `MyServlet` Servlet sends the response in the `MyApplet` applet(you can find this file online in the code/Chapter10/apptoster folder):

Listing 10.3: Creating the MyServlet.java File

```
package com.santosh.servlets;
import javax.servlet.*;
import java.io.*;
public class MyServlet extends GenericServlet {
   public void service (ServletRequest req, ServletResponse res)
   throws ServletException,IOException {
         String message=req.getParameter("name");
         System.out.println("Message : "+message);
         PrintWriter out=res.getWriter();
         out.println("Response from Servlet Message : "+message);
   }//service
}//class
```

The servlet mapping is done for `MyServlet` in `web.xml`, as shown in Listing 10.4. You can also find this file online in the code/Chapter10/apptoster/WEB-INF folder.

Listing 10.4: Creating the `web.xml` File

```
<?xml version="1.0" encoding="UTF-8"?>
<web-app>
   <servlet>
         <servlet-name>ms</servlet-name>
         <servlet-class>com.santosh.servlets.MyServlet</servlet-class>
   </servlet>

   <servlet-mapping>
         <servlet-name>ms</servlet-name>
         <url-pattern>/myser</url-pattern>
   </servlet-mapping>
</web-app>
```

Figure 10.1 shows the directory structure of the **apptoster** example:

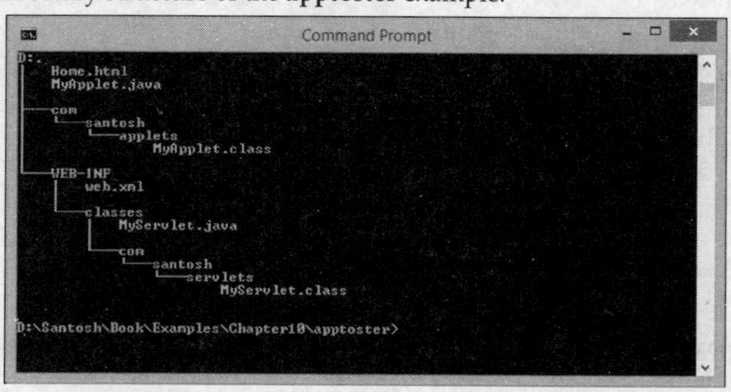

Figure 10.1: Directory Structure of apptoster Application

Copy the **apptoster** folder in the `<Tomcat home>/webapps` directory. Start the Tomcat Server, use `http://localhost:9090/apptoster/Home.html` URL for browsing the `Home.html` of the **apptoster** application, which displays the applet, as shown in Figure 10.2.

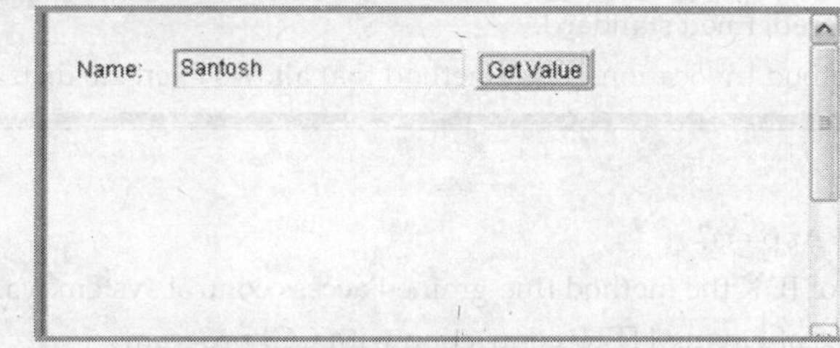

Figure 10.2: Showing the Home.html of the Application

After entering any name in the given text box in Figure 10.2, click the `Get Value` button. This makes a request to servlet, collects the response, and prints on the applet panel, as shown in Figure 10.3.

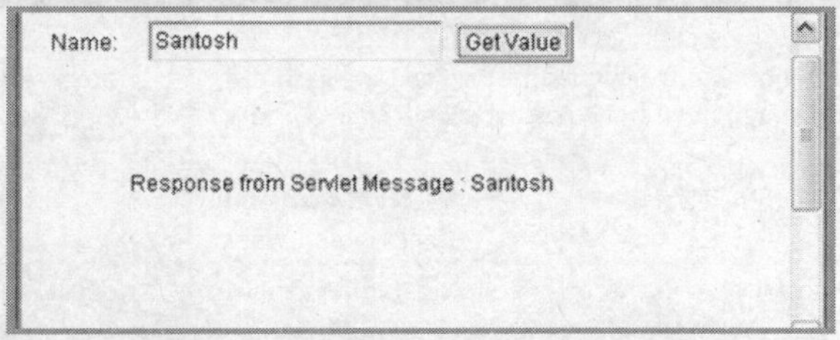

Figure 10.3: Showing the response sent by Servlet to Applet

Now, after understanding the Applet and Servlet communication, let's quickly recall what we learned in the chapter.

Summary

In this chapter, we have learned about the procedures by which applet and servlet will communicate with each other. Further, we have discussed the HTTP and Raw Socket Connections between the applet-servlet communication, Java servlets and object serialization, JDBC and RMI. We have also discussed about their advantages and disadvantages. Lastly, we have discussed the process of Applet to Servlet Communication by taking an example of simple Applet with one text field and one button. Let's recall the following important points discussed in the chapter:

- Applet is a small Java program that is embedded in a Web page.
- Java applets are supported by most of the Web browser and Java applet can communicate with servlets through various techniques.
- A web browser can easily download the Java applet that is embedded in a web page and it can execute the Java applet automatically.
- JDK 1.1 presented the concept of trusted applets. Trusted applets are those applets that operate normally like any other application and have full access to the client machine.
- Trusted applet should be digitally signed from the client side in order to maintain its authenticity.
- JDK 1.2 introduced the method of fine-grained access control system. This method gives the client more control over the security issue.
- The process of HTTP connection with a CGI program is slow as in HTTP request/response model the interaction cannot be place interactively between the applet and the CGI program.
- All kinds of response are required to be formatted as per some standard that were already set.
- An applet and server can also communicate by allowing the applet to establish a socket connection with a non-HTTP server process.

- Java servlets and object serialization was newly introduced and it is assumed as a better technique than the traditional applet servlet communication.
- In the traditional approach of applet-servlet communication in all kinds of response as it was required to be formatted as per some predefined standard.
- RMI means Remote Method Invocation. It is a method that allows to create distributed application in Java.

Exercise

Q. 10.1 What are Trusted Applets?

Q. 10.2 In which version of JDK the method fine-grained access control system was introduced?

Q. 10.3 List one advantage of having HTTP connection with CGI programs.

Q. 10.4 What is the full form of RMI?

Q. 10.5 List one disadvantage of RMI.

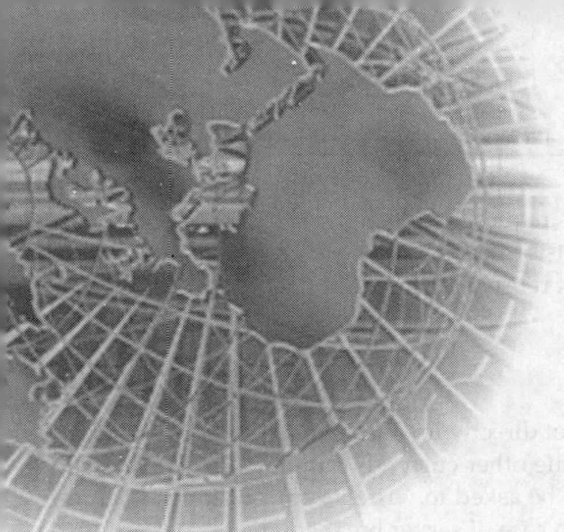

11

Interservlet Communication

If you need information on:	See page:

Interservlet communication means the communications between two servlets by transferring data. The information shared between servlets can be of various types, such as request dispatching, HTTP redirect, servlet chaining, HTTP request, shared session request, or application objects or beans. In this chapter, we discuss three sorts of interservlet communication, i.e., servlet manipulation, servlet reuse, and servlet collaboration.

Types of InterServlet Communication

Following are the three types of interservlet communication:

1. **Direct servlet manipulation** – This is a method where one servlet directly invokes the method of another. In direct servlet manipulation, a servlet can gain access rights to the other currently running servlets and can perform operations on each of them. For example, a servlet can be asked to write its current state at certain intervals to a disk. This is done in order to protect information in case of server breakdown.
2. **Servlet reuse** – This is a method where one servlet uses another's servlet capability for its own purpose.
3. **Servlet collaboration** – This is the most widely used interservlet communication. It includes two or more servlets sharing the state data. The servlet collaboration can be done through the system properties list, shared objects, and inheritance.

Let's discuss these types in detail in the following sections.

Direct Servlet Manipulation

Direct servlet manipulation is a method in which a servlet has the permission to access the loaded servlets on its server and perform operations on one or more servlets. The servlet uses the `ServletContext` object to get information about the other servlets. In order to get a specific servlet, we can use the method `getServlet()` as follows:

```
public Servlet ServletContext.getServlet(String name) throws ServletException
```

If the servlet of the given name is not found, the `getServlet()` method returns the servlet name or null. The specific name of the servlet can be its enrolled name (for example, `"file"`) or its class name (for example, `"com.sun.server.webserver.FileServlet"`). For each name, the server maintains one servlet instance in order to ensure that the `getServlet("file")` method can return an alternate servlet instance than what is returned by the `getServlet("com.sun.server.webserver.FileServlet")` method. If `SingleThreadModel` is implemented by the servlet, any instance of the servlet may be returned from the present pool. The server may load the named servlet and execute its `init()` method. However, it may not be required to load the named server in case it has been already loaded. The Java Web server is not able to perform the operation of loading the specified servlet. Thus, an exception named `ServletException` is thrown in case there is any problem during the loading operation.

The `getServlets()` methods can also be used to get information regarding all of the servlets in the following way:

```
public Enumeration ServletContext.getServlets()
```

The `getServlets()` method returns an `Enumeration` of the `Servlet` objects that are loaded in the current `ServletContext`. In general, for each server, only one servlet context is available, but in case there is a need to provide security, a server may choose to partition its servlets into separate contexts. The `Enumeration` always incorporates calling servlet itself.

However, in the Servlet API 2.0, this method is deprecated and a new method `getServletNames()` was introduced with the release of Servlet 2.0. The `getServletNames()` method can be used as follows:

```
public Enumeration ServletContext.getServletNames()
```

Just like the `getServlets()` method, the `getServletsNames()` method also returns an `Enumeration` of the `Servlet` objects that are loaded in the current `ServletContext`.

As we know `Enumeration` always incorporates the calling servlet itself, when we use the `getServlet()` method, this `getServletsNames()` method can also perform the same function as the `getServlets()` method which was deprecated. Just like the `getServlet()` method, the `getServletsNames()` method can also return the registered name (for example, `"file"`) or a class name (for example, `"com.sun.server.webserver.FileServlet"`). This `getServletsNames()` was introduced in Servlet 2.0 version.

In some circumstances, throwing the `Servlet` object returned by `getServlet()` to its particular subclass can throw a `ClassCastException`. Consider the following example where the code at times works in the same way we want and at times may throw an exception.

```
MyServlet servlet = (MyServlet)getServletContext().getServlet("MyServlet");
```

Now we need to find out how a servlet automatically is reloaded into the server as soon as its class files change.

The reason behind this is that whenever a server reloads a servlet, the server uses a new `ClassLoader` that can automatically reload the servlet into the server as soon as its class files changes. However, in this case a different version of `MyServlet` is actually loaded than the version used by other classes. Thus, despite the fact that the returned class type is `MyServlet`, the cast is different from classes. Thus, it throws an exception as `ClassCastException`.

This exception occurs because the new `ClassLoader` cannot find the `Myservlet` by using the existing class loader and it will load its own copy of servlet. Thus, a mismatch occurs and an exception is thrown.

There are three possible ways to remove the above exception. These are:

- If possible, do not use the method of casting the returned Servlet object and invoke the method by using reflection. A reflection is a procedure whereby a Java class can inspect and manipulate itself at runtime.
- Verify that the servlet that is already casted is never reloaded. We can ensure this by moving the servlet out of the default servlet directory (usually, server_root/servlets) and into the server's standard classpath (usually server_root/classes).
- The returned servlet should be casted to an interface that declares the applicable method, and the interface should be placed in the standard `classpath` of the servlet where it will not be reloaded. Then, each and every class will remain in the servlet directory.

Viewing and Saving the Currently Loaded Servlets

The `getServletNames()` method is used in Listing 11.1 to show the information about the currently loaded servlets.

Listing 11.1: The loadservlet.java File

```
import java.io.*;
import java.util.*;
import javax.servlet.*;
import javax.servlet.http.*;

public class Loadservlet extends HttpServlet {

  public void doGet(HttpServletRequest req1, HttpServletResponse res1)throws
  ServletException, IOException {
    res1.setContentType("text/plain");
    PrintWriter out = res1.getWriter();

    ServletContext context = getServletContext();
    Enumeration names = context.getServletNames();
    while (names.hasMoreElements()) {
      String name = (String)names.nextElement();
      Servlet servlet = context.getServlet(name);
      out.println("Name of Servlet: " + name);
      out.println("Class of Servlet: " + servlet.getClass().getName());
      out.println("Information about Servlet: " + servlet.getServletInfo());
      out.println();
    }
  }
}
```

Saving the State of All the Servlets Currently Loaded

Listing 11.2 shows how to save the state of all the servlets that are currently loaded.

Listing 11.2: The SaveServletState.java File

```
import java.io.*;
import java.lang.reflect.*;
import java.util.*;
import javax.servlet.*;
import javax.servlet.http.*;

public class SaveServletState extends HttpServlet {

  public void doGet(HttpServletRequest req1, HttpServletResponse res1)
                              throws ServletException, IOException {
    res1.setContentType("text/plain");
    PrintWriter out = res1.getWriter();

    ServletContext context = getServletContext();
    Enumeration names = context.getServletNames();
    while (names.hasMoreElements()) {
      String name = (String)names.nextElement();
      Servlet servlet = context.getServlet(name);

      out.println("Saving the state of " + name + "...");
      out.flush();
      try {
        Method save = servlet.getClass().getMethod("saveState", null);
        save.invoke(servlet, null);
        out.println("Saved!");
      }
      catch (NoSuchMethodException e) {
        out.println("Sorry! Could not Save the state as this servlet has no saveState()
         method");
      }
      catch (SecurityException e) {
        out.println("Not saved. SecurityException: " + e.getMessage());
      }
      catch (InvocationTargetException e) {
        out.print("Not saved. The saveState() method threw an exception: ");
        Throwable th = e.getTargetException();
        out.println(th.getClass().getName() + ": " + th.getMessage());
      }
      catch (Exception e) {
        out.println("Not saved. " + e.getClass().getName() + ": " +
                    e.getMessage());
      }
      out.println();
    }
  }
  public String getServletInfo() {
    return "The saveState() method are called for all the " +
           "currently loaded servlets";
  }
}
```

Servlet Reuse

Interservlet communication is also used to allow one servlet to reuse the capabilities of another servlet. However, the major problem that comes in the way is for the "user" servlet to acquire the best possible instance of the "usee" servlet when the usee servlet has not been loaded into the server.

There is no assurance that `getServlet()` will load the named servlet on all servers. It might simply return `null`. If we create a new instance of the usee servlet directly, it will not work either. This is because the recently created servlet does not have access permission to its own `ServletConfig` and `ServletContext` objects.

Furthermore, the server would use an alternate instance to handle customer requests and leave new instances of the servlet without the right state information.

There can be one solution to such types of problems, i.e., first the user servlet should ask the server to load the usee servlet and then the `getServlet()` method should be invoked to get a reference to it. The fact is that Servlet API exactly does not have any techniques whereby a servlet can control the servlet life cycle for itself or for different servlets. Thus, it is considered a security risk and is officially left for future considerations.

Luckily, there is a secondary way we can use today. An HTTP connection can be opened by a servlet with the server in which the servlet is running. It then requests the server to load the unloaded servlet. Then, a call to `getServlet()` gets the accurate instance.

Listing 11.3 shows the coding for an improved `getServlet()` method.

Listing 11.3: Improved `getServlet()` Code

```
public static Servlet getServlet(String name, ServletRequest req1,ServletContext context)
{
  try {
        Servlet servlet = context.getServlet(name);
    if (servlet != null) return servlet;
    Socket socket = new Socket(req.getServerName(), req.getServerPort());
    socket.setSoTimeout(4000);
    PrintWriter out = new PrintWriter(socket.getOutputStream(), true);
    out.println("GET /servlet/" + name + " HTTP/1.0");
    out.println();
    try {
      socket.getInputStream().read();
    }
    catch (InterruptedIOException e) { /* timeout: ignore, hope for the best */ }
    out.close();

    return context.getServlet(name);
  }
  catch (Exception e) {
    return null;
  }
}
```

In Listing 11.3, a raw socket connection is used by the `getServlet()` method in order to perform HTTP GET request. It is necessary to set a timeout to wait for a response. However, `URL` and `URLConnection` classes do not provide this facility. In Listing 11.3, the timeout is set for four seconds and if there is no acknowledgement after the set time, the `read()` method will throw `InterruptedIOException` and the method will continue.

Reusing ChatServlet

Listing 11.4 shows how one servlet, `ChatPage`, is reused by another servlet, `ChatServlet`.

Listing 11.4: The ChatPage.java File

```
import java.io.*;
import java.util.*;
import javax.servlet.*;
import javax.servlet.http.*;

import com.santosh.servlet.ServletUtils;

public class ChatPage extends HttpServlet implements Runnable {

  static final int msg_arv_size = 15;

  ChatServlet chat1 = null;  // It is the servlet to reuse
  String[] messages = new String[msg_arv_size];
  int msgIndex = 0;  // It is the index into the messages array
  Thread update1 = null;  // It is the thread to update new messages

  public void run() {
    while (true) {
```

```
      String message = chat1.getNextMessage();
      synchronized (this) {
        messages[msgIndex] = message;
        msgIndex = (msgIndex + 1) % msg_arv_size;
      }
    }

  // It will print the message archive i.e the latest 15 message and a text
  // field where the reader can input a new message.
  public void doGet(HttpServletRequest req1, HttpServletResponse res1)
                              throws ServletException, IOException {
    res1.setContentType("text/html");
    PrintWriter out = res1.getWriter();

    // It will turn off caching. This is done to always display the latest messages.

    res1.setHeader("Pragma", "no-cache");

  if (chat1 == null) {
      chat1 = (ChatServlet)ServletUtils.getServlet(
                  "ChatServlet", req1, getServletContext());
      if (chat1 != null) {
        update = new Thread(this);
        update.start();
      }
    }

    // Print a pretty header.
    out.println("<HTML><HEAD>");
    out.println("<TITLE>ChatPage</TITLE>");
    out.println("</HEAD><BODY>");
    out.println("<CENTER><H1>You are Welcome to ChatPage!</H1></CENTER>");

    // It will Print the message archive. The oldest message will be printed first.
    // It will be synchronized so it does not change while we are printing it.
    synchronized (this) {
      out.println("<FONT SIZE=11>Recent messages:</FONT><P>");
      int i = msgIndex;
      do {
        String message = messages[i];
        if (message != null) out.println(message + "<P>");
        i = (i + 1) % msg_arv_size;
      } while (i != msgIndex);
    }

    // It will print a button that gets new messages.
    out.println("<FORM METHOD=GET>");
    out.println("<INPUT TYPE=submit VALUE=\"Get New Messages\">");
    out.println("</FORM>");

    // It will print a form where the reader can submit a new message.
    out.println("<HR>");
    out.println("<FORM METHOD=POST>");
    out.println("<FONT SIZE=11>Submit a message:</FONT>");
    out.println("<INPUT TYPE=text NAME=message>");
    out.println("</FORM>");

    // Print a pretty footer.
    out.println("<HR>");
    out.println("<CENTER><FONT SIZE=11><B>");
    out.println(" Thanks to ChatServlet for acting as back-end");
    out.println("</B></FONT></CENTER>");
    out.println("</BODY></HTML>");
  }
```

```
    public void doPost(HttpServletRequest req1, HttpServletResponse res1)
                                 throws ServletException, IOException {

    if (chat1 == null) {
      chat1 = (ChatServlet)ServletUtils.getServlet(
            "ChatServlet", req1, getServletContext());
      if (chat1 != null) {
        update = new Thread(this);
        update.start();
        Thread.currentThread().yield();        }
    }
    String user = req1.getRemoteUser();
    if (user == null) user = "anonymous";

    String message = req1.getParameter("message");
    if (message != null && chat1 != null) {
      chat1.broadcastMessage(user + ": " + message);
      Thread.currentThread().yield();    }
        doGet(req1, res1);
  }
  public void destroy() {
    if (update != null)
      update.stop();
  }
  public String getServletInfo() {
    return "An HTML chat server front end, reusing ChatServlet";
  }
}
```

Servlet Collaboration

At times, servlets have to share some useful information. When this type of communication happens, we call it servlet collaboration. Servlets can share the information with one another through invocations method. The invocation method requires each servlet to know the other servlets with which it is working. However, this is an additional burden to the servlets and so this approach is not useful. There are few better procedures, which are discussed below.

Collaboration through the System Properties List

The easiest way to perform collaboration is using Java system-wide properties list, which can be found in the `java.lang.System` class. Apart from holding the standard system properties, like `java.version` and `path.separator`, this list also holds application-specific properties. Servlets can utilize the list to hold the information that they need to share. A property can be added or changed by calling the following method:

```
    System.getProperties().put("key", "value");
```

However, if it is required to get the value of the property, any servlet running in the same JVM can call the following method:

```
    String value = System.getProperty("key");
```

In order to remove the property call, the following method can be used:

```
    System.getProperties().remove("key");
```

Collaboration through a Shared Object

Information sharing between servlets can be done through shared objects as well. A shared object holds a pool of shared information, and this information can be used by each servlet whenever required. In other words, the system holds the `Properties` list having the information that can be used by any shared objects to solve their specific issue.

Whenever a shared object incorporates a business logic or set of instructions for manipulating the data, the servlets tend to secure the shared object's information by sharing the instructions with well-defined strategies. It can implement data integrity and invoke certain methods to handle certain conditions. If at any moment the object is not referenced by stacked servlet, it can be recovered by the shared object.

Collaboration through Inheritance

Another simplest strategy for servlet collaboration can be through inheritance. The servlets that are interested in collaborating can extend the same class and inherit the same shared information to their appropriate subclasses.

The common superclass can hold a reference to the shared information or can itself hold the information. Any number of references can be held by the common superclass in order to share the objects that can be made available to its subclass.

After understanding the concept of interservlet communication, let's summarize the main points of the chapter.

Summary

In this chapter, you learned about interservlet communication. We then discussed the three most commonly used interservlet communications – direct servlet manipulation, servlet reuse, and servlet collaboration. Let's recall the following important points to summarize the chapter:

- Direct servlet manipulation is a method in which a servlet has the permission to access the loaded servlets on its server and perform operations on one or more servlets.
- The `getServlets()` methods returns an `Enumeration` of the `Servlet` objects that are loaded in the current `ServletContext`.
- In Servlet API 2.0, the `getServlets()` method is deprecated and a new method `getServletNames()` was introduced.
- Another use of Interservlet communication is that it allows one servlet to reuse the capabilities of another servlet.
- There is no assurance that `getServlet()` will load the named servlet on all servers. It might simply return null.
- At times, servlets have to share some useful information. When this type of communication happens, we call it "servlet collaboration".
- The easiest way to perform collaboration is using Java system-wide Properties list, which can be found in the `java.lang.System` class.
- Apart from holding the standard system properties, like `java.version` and `path.separator`, the Java system properties list also holds application-specific properties.
- A shared object holds a pool of shared information, and this information can be used by each servlet whenever required.
- Whenever a shared object incorporates a business logic or set of instructions for the manipulation of data, they tend to secure the shared object's information by sharing it with well-defined strategies.
- The servlets that are interested in collaborating can extend the same class and inherit the same shared information to their appropriate subclasses.
- The common superclass can hold a reference to the shared information or can itself hold the information.

Exercise

Q. 11.1 What is Interservlet communication?

Q. 11.2 List the three types of Interservlet communication.

Q. 11.3 What is direct servlet manipulation?

Q. 11.4 What do you mean by servlet collaboration?

Q. 11.5 List three methods by which servlet collaboration can be performed.

12

New Features in Servlet 3.1

Servlet 3.1 is the latest version of Servlet API. It was released on May 2013 and it runs on the platform Java EE 7. However, some important changes were introduced in this release. One such feature is the non-blocking I/O mechanism. It was introduced to allow low latency and high throughput application. Servlet 3.1 also upgraded HTTP protocol mechanism. In addition, Servlet 3.1 has also enhanced security features.

In this chapter, we will study about all the new features introduced in Servlet 3.1. These features include non-blocking I/O mechanism, HTTP protocol upgrade mechanism, and security enhancement. We will be studying these features in detail.

Before learning about non-blocking I/O, let's learn about the mechanism of asynchronous request processing.

Asynchronous Request Processing

Asynchronous request processing was an important feature added in Servlet 3.0. With the help of asynchronous support Servlet 3.0 does not need to wait for a response from a resource. Rather the thread can continue to process and thus in Servlet 3.0 threads are not blocked. Before the introduction of Servlet 3.0, asynchronous support can be given in Java EE Web container by API that is built on the top of the Servlet 2.5 API.

But nowadays, it becomes necessary that the Web application should handle some part of the request asynchronously to provide fast processing to the users. This becomes essential because in such mechanism the Web container can continue to serve the other requests in a seamless fashion. An example of such mechanism is a chat room application.

In a Java Web based application, if a numerous number of threads will run then it is obvious that they will consume a lot of resources. In this scenario, the dedicated HTTP worker threads will handle the incoming requests. HTTP worker threads will process the request until a response is assembled and sent back to the client. This causes the problem of HTTP thread pool exhaustion.

Asynchronous support has made it possible to enable an application to process an incoming request in an asynchronous fashion. This means that the incoming request will be handled by the specific HTTP worker thread and after that the HTTP worker thread will pass the request to another background thread and that background thread will in turn process the request and sent the request back to the client. As soon as the initial HTTP worker thread will pass the request to the background thread, the initial HTTP worker thread will return the request to the HTTP thread pool. Thus, the initial HTTP worker thread can process another request. In this way the asynchronous support can solve the problem of HTTP thread pool exhaustion.

Though the problem of HTTP thread pool exhaustion was solved in Servlet 3.0, but the problem of system resource consumption was not solved. This is because in asynchronous Servlet mechanism, for processing request another background thread was created. Thus, the number of active thread was not reduced and the system resource consumption was not improved.

In asynchronous Servlet, we should have `@WebServlet` annotation with `asyncSupported` value as true. In asynchronous Servlet the actual work of a thread gets delegated to another thread and so it is necessary to have a thread pool implementation. The thread pool can be created by using framework of executors and in order to initiate the thread pool, we need to use Servlet context listener.

`ServletRequest.startAsync()` method can be used to get an instance of `AsyncContext`. `AsyncContext` are very useful because it provides the method to get `ServletRequest` and `ServletResponse` references. Apart from that the `AsyncContext` also provides the method that is required to forward the request to another resource by using `dispatch()` method.

Non-Blocking I/O Mechanism

Since the inception of Servlet 3.1, traditional input/output was allowed in Servlet during the request processing. With these traditional input/output mechanism Servlet used to face the problem of blocking. But Servlet 3.1 has brought a new revolution in the mechanism of input/output. Servlet 3.1 has made it possible to read or write without facing the problem of blocking of resources.

In Servlet 3.0, asynchronous request processing was allowed for traditional input/output. Thus, in Servlet 3.0 scalability of the application was not possible. Scalability of application means that if a program is designed for a small set of records, it cannot work well on large set of records. But this problem was resolved in Servlet 3.1 with the introduction of two interfaces, `ReadListener` and `WriteListener`.

`ReadListener` interface should be implemented when it is required to perform non-blocking reads whereas `WriteListener` interface should be implemented when it is required to perform non-blocking writes. After that it is required to register the implementation class to a `ServletInputStream` or `ServletOutputStream`. It is very essential to register the implementation class because by registering the implementation class it is possible to perform read or write operation when the listener finds that the Servlet content can be read or written without blocking.

It should be noted that in almost all the cases, the `ReadListener` and `WriteListener` implementation classes can be embedded within the calling Servlet.

The new mechanism of non-blocking I/O API helps to bring the Servlet API into compliance with the new Web standard. With the introduction of the non-blocking I/O API it becomes possible to create Web-based applications that perform well in an asynchronous fashion.

HTTP Protocol Upgrade Mechanism

In Servlet 3.1, HTTP protocol was upgraded and HTTP 1.1 was introduced. An example of this protocol upgrade is Web Socket. `javax.servlet.http.HttpUpgradeHandler` was introduced in Servlet 3.1 in order to allow the protocol upgrade processing.

The general header of the upgraded protocol allows the client to specify the additional communication protocol that it supports. The additional communication protocol can be used in some specific case where the server finds it appropriate to switch the protocol. In such case the server must use the upgrade header field within 101 responses in order to indicate the protocol that is being switched.

The decision to upgrade the protocol is made in `Servlet.service()` method. Then the upgraded protocol can be achieved by adding `HTTPServletRequest.Upgrade` and two new interfaces, namely, `javax.servlet.http.HttpUpgradeHandler` and `javax.servlet.http.WebConnection`.

The nature and ability of the application will depend on the new protocol chosen. A negotiation takes places between the client and the server and for the exchange of message the subsequent request uses the new chosen protocol.

Security Enhancement

In Servlet 3.1, there was an enhancement in the security features of Servlet. Servlet 3.1 applied run-as security roles to both `#init()` and `#destroy()` method. Apart from that Servlet added two new interfaces, `HttpServletRequest.changeSessionId()` and `HttpSessionIdListener`. By adding these two interfaces Servlet 3.1 can provide session fixation attack. This makes it possible to listen for any session id. Apart from these, Servlet 3.1 also provides default security semantics for non-specified HTTP method. It also clarifies the semantics in case the parameter is specified in the URI.

`ServletResponse.reset()` is the method that helps in clearing any data existing in the buffer and header. Servlet 3.1 also clears the state of calling `getServletOutputStream()` or `getWriter()`.

Summary

In this chapter, you learned about the latest version of Servlet 3.1 which runs on the platform Java EE 7. We have also learned about the important changes that were introduced in Servlet 3.1. Two important changes are non-blocking I/O mechanism and HTTP protocol upgrade mechanism.

Let's recall the following important points to summarize the chapter:

- Servlet 3.1 is the latest version of Servlet API.
- With the help of asynchronous support, Servlet 3.0 does not need to wait for a response from a resource. Rather the thread can continue to process and thus in Servlet 3.0 threads are not blocked.

- Asynchronous support has made it possible to enable an application to process an incoming request in an asynchronous fashion.
- In asynchronous Servlet, we should have `@WebServlet` annotation with `asyncSupported` value as true.
- In asynchronous Servlet the actual work of a thread gets delegated to another thread and so it is necessary to have a thread pool implementation.
- The thread pool can be created by using framework of executors and in order to initiate the thread pool, we need to use Servlet context listener.
- `AsyncContext` are very useful because it provides the method to get `ServletRequest` and `ServletResponse` reference.
- Since the inception of Servlet 3.1, traditional input/output was allowed in Servlet during the request processing.
- Servlet 3.1 has made it possible to read or write without facing the problem of blocking.
- In Servlet 3.0, asynchronous request processing was allowed for traditional input/output. Thus, in Servlet 3.0 scalability of the application was not possible.
- Scalability of application means that if a program is designed for a small set of records, it cannot work well on large set of records.
- `ReadListener` interface should be implemented when it is required to perform non-blocking reads whereas `WriteListener` interface should be implemented when it is required to perform non-blocking writes.
- It should be noted that in almost all the cases, the `ReadListener` and `WriteListener` implementation classes can be embedded within the calling Servlet.
- In Servlet 3.1, HTTP protocol was upgraded and HTTP 1.1 was introduced.
- The upgraded protocol can be achieved by adding `HTTPServletRequest.Upgrade` and two new interfaces, namely, `javax.servlet.http.HttpUpgradeHandler` and `javax.servlet.http.WebConnection`.
- The general header of the upgraded protocol allows the client to specify about the additional communication protocol that it supports.
- Servlet 3.1 applied run-as security roles to both `#init()` and `#destroy()` method. Apart from that servlet added two new interfaces, `HttpServletRequest.changeSessionId()` and `HttpSessionIdListener`.
- `ServletResponse.reset()` is the method that helps in clearing any data existing in the buffer and header.

Exercise

Q. 12.1 List the new features introduced in Servlet 3.1.

Q. 12.2 What is the advantage of asynchronous request processing?

Q. 12.3 Which method should be used to get an instance of `AsyncContext`?

Q. 12.4 What do you mean by scalability of an application?

Q. 12.5 When `ReadListener` and `WriteListener` interface should be implemented in non-blocking I/O mechanism?

Q. 12.6 List two interfaces introduced in Servlet 3.1 for security enhancement.

13

Introduction to JSP

In the previous chapters (6 to 12), we have discussed the importance of Servlets in Web programming. However, nowadays, Servlets, which were once a popular means to create Web pages, have been replaced by better technologies such as JavaServer Pages (JSP). Java Servlets have many shortcomings that have contributed to their decline. The major shortcomings are as follows:

- **Inability to use IDEs**—You cannot use Integrated Development Environments (IDEs) to design HTML views. This increases the development time of Web applications.
- **Inability to use HTML Designer**—You cannot use HTML designer services to prepare the presentation view. Instead, you need to depend on the Java programmer to prepare this view.
- **Dependence on Web configuration**—Servlet programs depend on the Web configuration. The `web.xml` file is used to configure your Servlet. When you create several views by using Servlets, you have to ensure that, in the `web.xml` file, each Servlet is mapped to invoke the correct Servlet. This increases the complexity of your web site because you must know which Servlet-mapping (in the `web.xml` file) has been used to invoke which Servlet.
- **Recurring Recompilation**—When you make changes in the code of a Servlet, you need to recompile the Servlet's source file. This is a problem when we create complex views because each time you make a change; you have to compile the modified Servlet program before generating the output.

To solve these problems, we want our HTML page, generated with the help of some IDEs, to include additional instructions wherever dynamic content is required. For example, a page with additional instructions can be parsed and resolved into a standard server-side extension (that is, a Servlet), which is understood by the Web container. If these additional instructions are tag-based, they can be directly used by Web designers to create HTML views. Moreover, tag-based instructions are easily understood by the IDEs used to design HTML views. The requirement of tag-based instruction has impelled the introduction of JSP technology.

In this chapter, we discuss what JSP is and how it is used to create dynamic Web pages. We also discuss why JSP is preferred over Servlets to create views. In addition, we look at the JSP architecture as well as give a detailed description of the various stages of the JSP life cycle. Last but not the least; we create a simple JSP page. Let's start with a brief introduction of JSP.

Understanding JSP

JSP is a standard Java extension used to simplify the creation and management of dynamic Web pages. JSPs allow us to separate the dynamic content of a Web page from its static presentation content. As described earlier, programming in Servlets is very complex and requires additional files, such as web.xml and Java class files, to generate the required Web pages. JSP offers an easier approach to build dynamic Web pages. JSP consists of HTML tags and special tags, known as JSP tags. HTML tags are used to create static page content and JSP tags are used to add dynamic content to Web pages. JSP pages are compiled into a Java Servlet by a JSP translator. This Java Servlet is then compiled and executed to generate an output for the browser (client). Building dynamic Web pages by using JSP offers the following benefits:

- Web pages created by using JSP are portable and can be used easily across multiple platforms and Web servers without making any changes.
- Programming in JSP is easier than in Servlets because of the introduction of tag-based approach in JSP.
- JSP pages are automatically compiled by the Web server, such as Tomcat and WebLogic. Developers need not compile a JSP page when the source code of the JSP page is changed.
- One of the most important benefits of JSP is the separation of business logic from the presentation logic. The tag handler classes or JavaBeans contain business logic, whereas JSP pages contain presentation logic. The separation of business and presentation logic makes an application created in JSP more secure and reusable.

Now that we are familiar with the approach to build dynamic Web pages using JSP, let's learn about the advantages of JSP over Servlets.

Advantages of JSP over Servlets

JSP provides a better server-side scripting support as compared to Servlets. Java developers can create Servlets easily, but for Web page designers, handling Java code is always a tough job. A JSP page can have HTML code, and some Java code embedded with the HTML code. In this way, creating a Web page becomes easy as the basic designing of the page is done by using the HTML code. We can use the Java code to add dynamic content to the page. The Java code is embedded by using different JSP constructs.

The following are the reasons to prefer JSP over Servlets:

- Most of the content of a Web page is static and different components need to be placed on the page in a symmetrical way. These static pages are designed by Web designers by using HTML code. Designing static pages using Servlets requires a good knowledge of Java, but Web designers may not be comfortable with Java programming constructs. In addition, while using Servlets, you have to enclose HTML code in the `out.println()` method, which disables all IDE support for generating HTML content. Therefore, using JSP is always easier than using Servlets for the same HTML output.
- You need to recompile your Servlet for every single change in the source code of the Servlet; whereas in case of JSP, recompilation is not required since JSP are automatically handled by the Web container for any update in their code.
- Servlets cannot be accessed directly and have to be first mapped in the web.xml file, whereas a JSP page can be accessed directly as a simple HTML page.
- Both, Servlets and JSPs are server-side components used to generate dynamic HTML pages; however, JSP is preferred over Servlet as it is developed by using a simple HTML template and automatically handled by the JSP container.

These advantages of JSP make it a popular component to use in the presentation layer of any Web application.

To bring out the advantage of using JSP over Servlets, let's take an example. Let's assume that a user needs a Web page with some dynamic content (for example, current date and time). The required HTML code for this page is shown in Listing 13.1. You can also find this file online in the code/Chapter13/JSPEx folder.

Listing 13.1: Creating the Index.html File

```
<html>
   <head>
          <title>First JSP Page</title>
   </head>
   <body>
          //The current Date and time dynamically inserted.
          <hr/>
          <br/>Hello World!<br/>
   </body>
</html>
```

You can create a simple Servlet for this Web page, similar to other Servlets created in Chapter 6, *Understanding Java Servlet*. The code for this Servlet is shown in Listing 13.2. In this listing, you can see the Servlet named `FirstServlet` and its `doGet()` method, which generates the required output. You can also find this file online in the code/Chapter13/JSPEx/ folder.

Listing 13.2: Creating the FirstServlet.java File

```
import java.io.*;
import javax.servlet.*;
import javax.servlet.http.*;
import java.util.Date;

public class FirstServlet extends HttpServlet {
public void doGet(HttpServletRequest request, HttpServletResponse response)
  throws ServletException, IOException {
         response.setContentType("text/html");
         PrintWriter out = response.getWriter();
         out.write("<html>");
         out.write("<head>");
         out.write("<title>First JSP Page</title>");
         out.write("</head>");
         out.write("<body>");
```

```
            out.write(new Date().toString());
            out.write("<hr/>");
            out.write("<br/>Hello World!<br/>");
            out.write("</body>");
            out.write("</html>");
            out.close();
        }
    }
```

This source code for your Servlet needs to be compiled, and the generated class file needs to be placed in the WEB-INF\classes folder of your Web application. In addition, a Servlet mapping is done in the deployment descriptor (`web.xml`) to access this Servlet.

Alternatively, you can replace this Servlet by a simple JSP page named firstpage.jsp, the code for which is provided in Listing 13.3. You can also find this file online in the code/Chapter13/JSPEx folder.

Listing 13.3: Creating the firstpage.jsp File

```
<%@ page import="java.util.Date;"%>
<html>
    <head>
            <title>First JSP Page</title>
    </head>
    <body>
            <%
                        out.println(new Date().toString());
            %>
            <hr />
            <br>Hello World! </br>
    </body>
</html>
```

You can see some delimiters and objects being used here, such as `<%@ %>`, `<% %>`, and `out`. These JSP elements and implicit objects have been discussed in detail in Chapter 14. This page can be accessed as a simple HTML page and does not need to be compiled and mapped in `web.xml` every time the Web container accesses it. When you compare the views generated by the Servlet and JSP pages, you find that both show the same output.

We have discussed the advantages of JSP over Servlet. Next, we discuss the tag-based approach with respect to JSP.

Introducing the Tag-based Approach

JSP is totally tag-based, which means that each piece of code in JSP is enclosed within a tag. JSP tags reduce the necessity of large amount of Java code in JSP pages by implementing the functionality of the tags into tag implementation classes. These tags help developers build dynamic pages, improve their code by reducing Java code, and separate the presentation logic from the business logic.

JSP tags have the following features:

- Reduce Web development and maintenance costs.
- Help you to reduce Java code in a JSP page.
- Make the task of developing Web applications easier and faster.
- Enable developers to reuse Java code in multiple Web applications.
- Ensure ease of work with Java Beans within JSP tags.

After learning the benefits of the tag-based approach used in JSP, let's discuss the JSP architecture next.

Describing the JSP Architecture

JSP specifications demonstrate two approaches to build Web applications by using JSP. These approaches are known as JSP Model 1 and JSP Model 2 architecture, respectively. Let's discuss these models in detail.

JSP Model I Architecture

In JSP Model I architecture, the Web browser directly accesses the JSP pages of a Web container. The JSP pages interact with the Web container's JavaBeans, which represent the application model. When a client sends a request from a JSP page, the response (that is, the JSP page) is sent back to the client depending on which hyperlinks are selected or which request parameters are invoked by the client request. If the generated response requires accessing a database, the JSP page uses JavaBean, which gets the required data from the database. Figure 13.1 shows the architecture of JSP Model I:

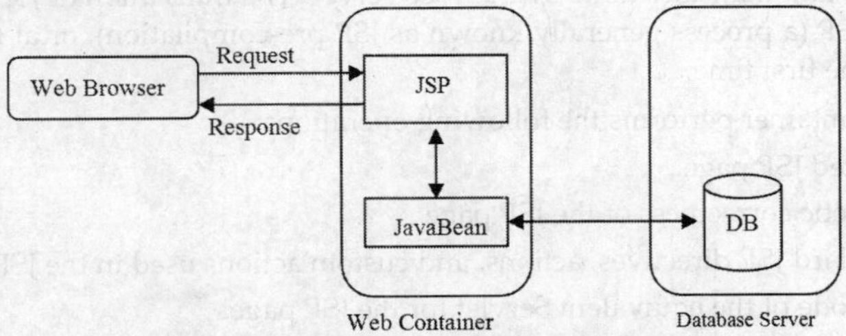

Figure 13.1: JSP Model I Architecture

JSP Model II Architecture

The JSP Model II architecture uses Servlets as well, which are positioned between the Web browser and the JSP pages. The Servlet acts as a controller to dispatch requests to the next JSP view, such as the URL, based on the client request and input parameters. It also creates JavaBean instances, if they are required by the JSP page. The controller also decides which JSP page needs to be forwarded as a response, based on the client request. The JavaBean invokes the database server if data are needed from a database server. Figure 13.2 shows the architecture of JSP Model II:

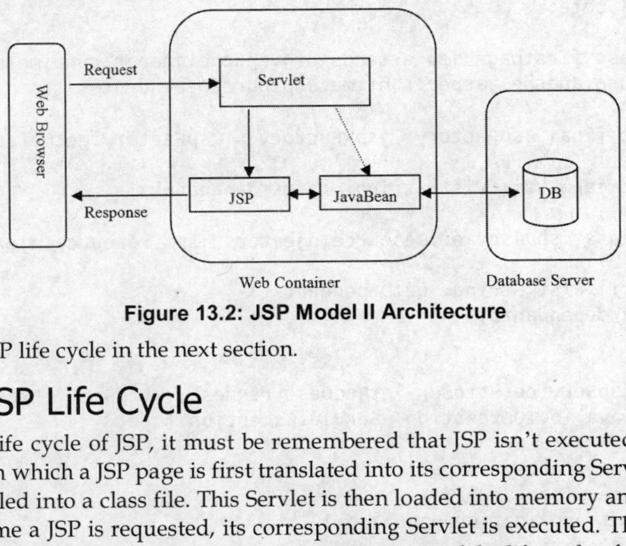

Figure 13.2: JSP Model II Architecture

Let's learn about the JSP life cycle in the next section.

Describing the JSP Life Cycle

Before discussing the life cycle of JSP, it must be remembered that JSP isn't executed directly. The execution of JSP follows a process in which a JSP page is first translated into its corresponding Servlet and then the source file of this Servlet is compiled into a class file. This Servlet is then loaded into memory and initialized, similar to any other Servlet. Every time a JSP is requested, its corresponding Servlet is executed. Therefore, most of the stages of the JSP life cycle are similar to that of a Servlet. The major stages of the life cycle of a JSP are as follows:

- Page Translation
- Compilation
- Loading and Initialization
- Request Handling
- Destroying

Let's now discuss each stage of the JSP life cycle one by one.

The Page Translation Stage

In the page translation stage of the JSP life cycle, the Web container translates the JSP document into an equivalent Java code—that is, a Servlet. Usually, a Servlet contains Java code with some markup language tags, such as HTML or XML. JSPs, on the other hand, consist primarily of markup language with some Java code. The objective of page translation, therefore, is to convert a document chiefly consisting of HTML/XML code, to one that has more of Java code, which can be executed by the Java Virtual Machine (JVM).

The translation of JSP is automatically done by the Web server. The translation of JSP can take place either at the time of deploying the JSP (a process generally known as JSP pre-compilation), or at the time when a request for the JSP is received for the first time.

In this stage, the Web container performs the following operations:

- Locates the requested JSP page.
- Validates the syntactic correctness of the JSP page.
- Interprets the standard JSP directives, actions, and custom actions used in the JSP page.
- Writes the source code of the equivalent Servlet for the JSP page.

All requests for a given JSP page are served by its corresponding Servlet class. This Servlet class works as a simple Servlet, similar to what we designed in Chapter 6.

Let's now look at the source file of the Servlet generated for our JSP (See Listing 13.3), as shown in Listing 13.4:

Listing 13.4: Showing the Code of the firstpage_jsp.java File

```
package org.apache.jsp;

import javax.servlet.*;
import javax.servlet.http.*;
import javax.servlet.jsp.*;
import java.util.Date;;

public final class firstpage_jsp extends org.apache.jasper.runtime.HttpJspBase
    implements org.apache.jasper.runtime.JspSourceDependent {

  private static final JspFactory _jspxFactory = JspFactory.getDefaultFactory();

  private static java.util.List<String> _jspx_dependants;

  private org.glassfish.jsp.api.ResourceInjector _jspx_resourceInjector;

  public java.util.List<String> getDependants() {
    return _jspx_dependants;
  }

  public void _jspService(HttpServletRequest request, HttpServletResponse response)
        throws java.io.IOException, ServletException {

    PageContext pageContext = null;
    HttpSession session = null;
    ServletContext application = null;
    ServletConfig config = null;
    JspWriter out = null;
    Object page = this;
    JspWriter _jspx_out = null;
    PageContext _jspx_page_context = null;

    try {
      response.setContentType("text/html");
      pageContext = _jspxFactory.getPageContext(this, request, response,
                      null, true, 8192, true);
```

```
        _jspx_page_context = pageContext;
        application = pageContext.getServletContext();
        config = pageContext.getServletConfig();
        session = pageContext.getSession();
        out = pageContext.getOut();
        _jspx_out = out;
        _jspx_resourceInjector  =  (org.glassfish.jsp.api.ResourceInjector)  application.get
            Attribute("com.sun.appserv.jsp.resource.injector");

        out.write("\r\n");
        out.write("<html>\r\n");
        out.write("\t<head>\r\n");
        out.write("\t\t<title>First JSP Page</title>\r\n");
        out.write("\t</head>  \r\n");
        out.write("\t<body>\r\n");
        out.write("\t\t");

                    out.println(new Date().toString());

        out.write("\r\n");
        out.write("\t\t<hr />\r\n");
        out.write("\t\t<br>Hello World! </br>\r\n");
        out.write("\t</body>\r\n");
        out.write("</html>\r\n");
      } catch (Throwable t) {
        if (!(t instanceof SkipPageException)){
          out = _jspx_out;
          if (out != null && out.getBufferSize() != 0)
            out.clearBuffer();
          if (_jspx_page_context != null) _jspx_page_context.handlePageException(t);
          else throw new ServletException(t);
        }
      } finally {
        _jspxFactory.releasePageContext(_jspx_page_context);
      }
    }
  }
```

The Servlet created as a result of the translation of JSP has the following special characteristics:

- The name of the Servlet generated for a JSP page is the name of JSP merged with "jsp" and separated by an underscore. Therefore, for the firstpage.jsp page, we have a Servlet class with the name "firstpage_jsp" and its source code, firstpage_jsp.java, as shown in Listing 13.4.
- The generated Servlet class is a subtype of the `javax.servlet.jsp.JspPage` class or the `javax.servlet.jsp.HttpJspPage` interface, depending on the protocols you are using. `HttpJspPage` is most widely used, whereas `JspPage` is used by Web containers that support non-Http protocols.
- The generated Servlet implements the `jspInit()`, `jspDestroy()`, and `_jspService()` methods. You can compare them with the `init ()`, `destroy ()`, and `service ()` methods of a common Servlet class, since they are used in the same manner.

The `jspInit()` and `jspDestroy()` methods are invoked once in the lifetime of JSP, whereas the `_jspService()` method is executed each time a JSP page is requested. All the presentation logic placed in a JSP page is enclosed in the `_jspService()` method. You can see how different objects, such as `pageContext`, application, session, and out, have been obtained and used in the `_jspService()` method. We will study about these implicit objects of JSP in Chapter 14.

The JSP page translation occurs only when necessary, that is, at some point before a JSP page has to serve its first request. This process is also performed when the JSP source code is updated and the page is redeployed. A Web container can decide when the translation should occur. The two possible instances where a translation can occur are:

- When a first-time user requests a JSP page.
- When a JSP is loaded into a Web container. This is also called JSP pre-compilation.

If there is any error in the translation of the JSP life cycle, then the container raises an exception, 500 (internal server error). If any change occurs in the JSP page, all the stages of the JSP life cycle are executed again.

The Compilation Stage

The compilation stage of the JSP life cycle follows the page translation stage. In this stage, the JSP container compiles the Java source code for the corresponding Servlet and converts it into Java byte (class) code. After the class file is generated, the container can decide to either discard the code or retain it for debugging. Generally, most containers discard the generated Java source code by default. After the compilation stage, the Servlet is ready to be loaded and initialized.

The Loading and Initialization Stage

In the loading and initialization stage of the JSP life cycle, the JSP container loads and instantiates the Servlet that has been generated and compiled in the translation and compilation stages, respectively. The Web container, as part of this process, performs the following operations:

- **Loading**—In this stage, the Web container loads the Servlet generated in the translation and compilation stages, using the normal Java class loading option. If the Web container fails to load the class, it terminates the loading process.
- **Instantiation**—After the Servlet class is loaded successfully, the JSP container creates an instance of the Servlet class. To create a new instance of the generated Servlet, the JSP container uses the no-argument constructor. The JSP translator (part of the JSP container) is responsible for including a no-argument constructor in the Servlet generated after the translation of the JSP.
- **Initialization**—After the JSP equivalent Servlet object is instantiated successfully, the JSP container initializes the instantiated object. As per the Servlet's life cycle, the container initializes the object by invoking the `init (ServletConfig)` method. Here, this method is implemented by the container by calling the `jspInit()` method. This indicates that the `jspInit()` method acts as the `init(ServletConfig)` method of the Servlet.

If the loading and initialization stage is performed successfully, the Web container activates the Servlet object and makes it available and ready to handle client requests.

The next stage in the JSP life cycle is request handling.

The Request Handling Stage

In the request handling stage of the JSP life cycle, the Web container uses only those objects of a JSP equivalent Servlet that are initialized successfully, to handle the client request. The container performs the following operations in this stage:

- Creates `ServletRequest` and `ServletResponse` objects. If the client uses HTTP protocol to make the request, the container creates `HttpServletRequest` and `HttpServletResponse` objects. The requested data and client information can be retrieved by the Servlet by using the request object. The response object can be used by the Servlet to generate the response.
- As per the Servlet's life cycle, the Web container invokes the `service ()` method on the Servlet object by passing the request and response objects created in the preceding step. In case of JSP equivalent Servlet, the container invokes the `_jspService ()` method.

Let's now look at the final stage of the JSP life cycle, that is, the destroying stage.

The Destroying Stage

If the Servlet container decides to destroy the JSP page's Servlet instance, that is, if it decides to end the services provided by the Servlet instance, it performs the following operations:

- It lets all the currently running threads in the service method of the Servlet instance complete their operations. Meanwhile, it makes the Servlet instance unavailable for new requests.
- After the current threads have completed their operations on the `service ()` method, the container calls the `destroy ()` method on a Servlet instance, which invokes the `jspDestroy ()` method.
- After the destroy method is processed, the Servlet's life cycle is complete and the Web container releases all the references of the Servlet instance and renders them for garbage collection.

We now learn how to create simple JSP pages next.

Creating Simple JSP Pages

Here, we are creating a simple Web application with two JSP pages. Since we have not yet discussed the various constructs used in JSP, such as scriptlets and directives, we create simple JSP pages to give you an idea of how they can be designed, used, and accessed by a Web application named **SimpleApp**. You can also find this application online in the code/Chapter13 folder.

The first JSP page we will create is user.jsp, which provides an HTML form with two input fields to enter the name and city of a user. The code of the user.jsp page is provided in Listing 13.5. You can also find this file online in the code/Chapter13/SimpleApp folder.

Listing 13.5: Creating the user.jsp File

```
<%@ page import="java.util.*"%>
<!DOCTYPE>
<html>
  <head>
        <title>Welcome</title>
  </head>
  <body>
  <%=new Date().toString()%>
  <hr>
  <h2>Welcome</h2>
        <form action="showuser.jsp">
                <table>
                        <tr>
                                <td colspan="2" align="center">
                                        Enter User Information
                                </td>
                        </tr>
                        <tr>
                                <td>User Name</td>
                                <td><input type="text" name="name"></td>
                        </tr>
                        <tr>
                                <td>City</td>
                                <td><input type="text" name="city"></td>
                        </tr>
                        <tr>
                                <td colspan="2"><input type="submit" value="Enter"></td>
                        </tr>
                </table>
        </form>
  </body>
</html>
```

The second JSP page we create in this application is showuser.jsp, which shows the `name` and `city` that can be entered by the user through the input fields of the user.jsp page. You can view the code of the showuser.jsp page in Listing 13.6. You can also find this file online in the code/Chapter13/SimpleApp folder.

Listing 13.6: Creating the showuser.jsp File

```
<%@ page import="java.util.*" %>
<!DOCTYPE>
<html>
    <head>
            <title>Welcome</title>
    </head>
    <body>
    <%=new Date().toString()%>
    <hr>
    Hello <b><%=request.getParameter("name")%></b><br><br>
    Your City is <b><%=request.getParameter("city")%></b><br><br>

    <a href="user.jsp">Back</a>
    </body>
</html>
```

The directory structure of the Web application, which has been named **SimpleApp**, can be seen in Figure 13.3:

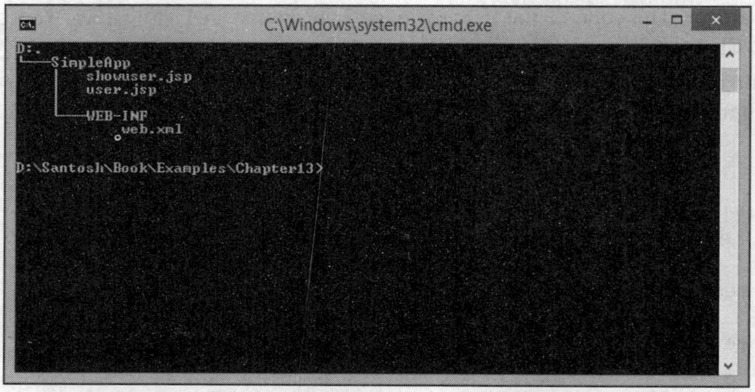

Figure 13.3: Directory Structure of SimpleApp Application

The WEB-INF\classes and WEB-INF\lib folders (see Figure 13.3) are empty as we have not created any class or used any library. However, they are created here as per the standards for developing Web applications.

Since we are using JSPs, you do not need to provide any kind of mapping in the web.xml file. However, the code written in the web.xml file for this application is shown in Listing 13.7. You can also find this file online in the code/Chapter13/SimpleApp/WEB-INF folder.

Listing 13.7: Creating the web.xml File

```
<?xml version="1.0" encoding="UTF-8"?>
<web-app>

</web-app>
```

Copy the `SimpleApp` folder in the `<Tomcat home>/webapps` directory to deploy it on Tomcat server. Now, start your server and access the user.jsp page by entering the URL `http://localhost:9090/SimpleApp/user.jsp` into your browser. The output of the user.jsp page is shown in Figure 13.4:

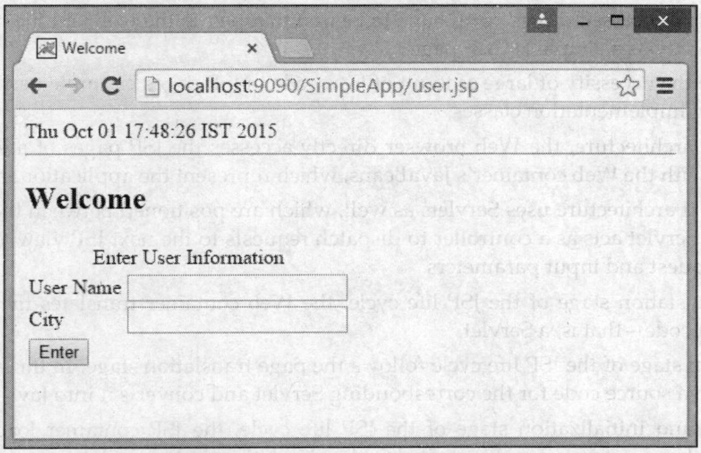

Figure 13.4: Output of user.jsp Page

You can click the Enter button after entering a string into the User Name and City fields. Assuming that the user enters "Santosh" and "Mumbai", respectively, you will see the showuser.jsp page, as shown in Figure 13.5:

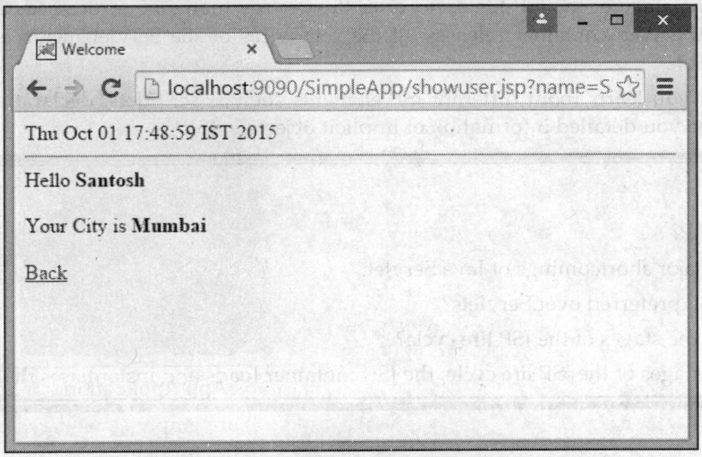

Figure 13.5: Output of showuser.jsp Page

This was a simple application created with two JSP pages. Though the code written in Listing 13.5 and Listing 13.6 is quite simple and mostly contains HTML tags, other JSP constructs have also been used. For example, you can see JSP scriptlets enclosed in `<%= %>` and JSP directives enclosed in `<%@ %>`. These will be discussed in detail in Chapter14.

Summary

This chapter describes JavaServer Pages (JSP), a technology used to create dynamic Web pages. After introducing JSP, the chapter covers the advantages of JSP over Servlets to create complex views. It also describes JSP architecture and then gives a detailed description of the various stages of the JSP life cycle. The chapter ends by explaining how JSP pages are created and accessed in Web applications. Let's recall the following important points to summarize the chapter:

- JSP is a standard Java extension used to simplify the creation and management of dynamic Web pages.
- Web pages created by using JSP are portable and can be used easily across multiple platforms and Web servers without making any changes.

- Servlets cannot be accessed directly and have to be first mapped in the web.xml file, whereas a JSP page can be accessed directly as a simple HTML page.
- JSP tags reduce the necessity of large amount of Java code in JSP pages by implementing the functionality of the tags into tag implementation classes.
- In JSP Model I architecture, the Web browser directly accesses the JSP pages of a Web container. The JSP pages interact with the Web container's JavaBeans, which represent the application model.
- The JSP Model II architecture uses Servlets as well, which are positioned between the Web browser and the JSP pages. The Servlet acts as a controller to dispatch requests to the next JSP view, such as the URL, based on the client request and input parameters.
- In the page translation stage of the JSP life cycle, the Web container translates the JSP document into an equivalent Java code—that is, a Servlet.
- The compilation stage of the JSP life cycle follows the page translation stage. In this stage, the JSP container compiles the Java source code for the corresponding Servlet and converts it into Java byte (class) code.
- In the loading and initialization stage of the JSP life cycle, the JSP container loads and instantiates the Servlet that has been generated and compiled in the translation and compilation stages, respectively.
- In the request handling stage of the JSP life cycle, the Web container uses only those objects of a JSP equivalent Servlet that are initialized successfully, to handle the client request.
- In the destroying stage of the JSP life cycle, after the destroy method is processed, the Servlet's life cycle is complete and the Web container releases all the references of the Servlet instance and renders them for garbage collection.

In the next chapter, you learn about different JSP elements such as scriptlets, declaration and expression. The chapter will also give you detailed information of implicit objects in JSP.

Exercise

Q. 13.1 What is JSP?

Q. 13.2 List the major shortcomings of Java Servlet.

Q. 13.3 Why is JSP preferred over Servlets?

Q. 13.4 What are the stages of the JSP life cycle?

Q. 13.5 In which stages of the JSP life cycle, the JSP container loads and instantiates the Servlet?

14

Working with JSP Basic Tags and Implicit Objects

A JSP document contains elements or tags, such as directives, scripting elements, and implicit objects. Directives are used in a JSP document to include the content of a static or dynamic file within another file. Directives are also used to import Java files within JSP pages. Scripting elements, such as declaration tags, expression tags, and scriptlet tags, help declare variables and object references in a JSP page. Scripting elements also help generate and display dynamic content. Similar to the scripting tags, JSP actions also help to create and manipulate dynamic content; however, JSP actions are similar to regular HTML tags. This chapter primarily focuses on scripting tags; the JSP actions have been discussed in detail in chapter 15.

The Servlet API includes interfaces such as `HttpServletRequest`, `HttpServletResponse`, and `HttpSession`, which provide convenient abstractions to the developers. These abstractions encapsulate the object's implementation; for example, the `HttpServletRequest` interface represents the HTTP request sent from the client along with headers, form parameters, and so on, and provides convenient methods such as `getParameter()` and `getHeader()` that extract relevant data from the request. JSP implicit objects provide a convenient way to access the interfaces and objects of the Servlet API, without writing additional code.

Note that in this chapter, we have used both JSP page and JSP document to denote a JSP file. These terms have been used interchangeably. The JSP page is a term used to refer a JSP file written by using the traditional JSP syntax, whereas the term JSP document is used to refer a JSP file written by using XML syntax of JSP supported by the JSP 1.2 specification.

In this chapter, we learn about scripting and directive tags used in JSP. In addition, we learn to work with implicit objects. Let's start by discussing JSP scripting tags.

Exploring Scripting Tags

JSP scripting tags, also called as JSP scripting elements, allow you to add a script code into the Java code of a JSP page generated by the JSP translator. In most of the cases, Java is the scripting language used to build a JSP page; however, other supported languages can also be used, depending on the Web containers.

You learn how to set the scripting language for a JSP page in the next section. However, before that, let's discuss about the different types of scripting tags.

Types of Scripting Tags

JSP defines three scripting tags, namely scriptlet, declarative, and expression tags. We describe these tags in detail next.

The Scriptlet Tag

Scriptlet tags allow you to write the script code (or the Java code) for implementing the `_jspService()` method functionality. The JSP translator translates the statements of this tag into the `_jspService()` method of the generated servlet. You can use a scriptlet tag to perform the following tasks:

- Declare variables that you can use later in a JSP page. That is, you can declare variables and write valid expressions in the page scripting language, within the scriptlet tags.
- Use any of the JSP implicit objects or any object declared with a `<jsp:useBean>` element.

Note that if the script code is not valid, an exception is thrown at the Compilation stage of the JSP life cycle.

You can include multiple scriptlet tags in a single JSP document. The traditional JSP Syntax to use a scriptlet tag is as follows:

```
<%
   script code (allows multiple statements)
%>
```

The XML based syntax for the scriptlet tag is as follows:

```
<jsp scriptlet>
   script code (allows multiple statements)
</jsp:scriptlet>
```

Let's look at an example to use the scriptlet tag:

```
<html><body>
<%
```

```
    for (int i=1;i<=5;i++) {
            out.println(i);
    }
 %>
 </html></body>
```

In the preceding example, the `for` loop of Java has been used in a JSP page to print numbers 1 to 5 in a single line. The servlet code for this JSP page, generated by the JSP container, is as follows:

```
    public    void    _jspService(HttpServletRequest    request,    HttpServletResponse
    response) throws ServletException, IOException {
    …
    out.write("<html><body>");
    for (int i=1;i<=5;i++) {
            out.println(i);
    }
    out.write("</body></html>");
    …
```

The Declarative Tag

The declarative tag allows you to write the script code that you need to provide in the generated servlet class, outside the `_jspService()` method. This tag allows you to declare instance and class variables and implement class methods, such as `jspInit()` and `jspDestroy()`. The syntax of the declarative tag is as follows:

```
 <%!
    script code (allows multiple statements)
 %>
```

The XML based syntax for the declarative tag is as follows:

```
 <jsp:declaration>
    script code (allows multiple statements)
 </jsp:declaration>
```

Here is an example showing how to use the declarative tag:

```
 <%!
 int a,b;
 int fun(int a)
    {
            return a;
    }%>
 <%a=1;%>
 <%b=fun(a);%>
 <%out.println(b);%>
```

In this example, we declare two integer variables, `a` and `b`; and define a function, `fun()`, by using the declarative tag. Then, we assign `1` as the value to the `a` variable and pass it as an argument to the `fun()` function. The `fun()` function processes the argument and stores the result in the `b` variable. Finally, the value received by the `b` variable is displayed on the browser.

The Expression Tag

The expression tag allows you to write a Java expression, which is then resolved and the resultant value is displayed. The expression tag places the given Java expression in the `out.print()` method during the translation stage of the JSP life cycle. Consequently, the output of the Java expression is displayed with the output of the JSP page.

This tag also provides a simple and convenient way to access the script (i.e. Java) variables. The syntax of the expression tag is as follows:

```
 <%=
    script code (allows only one expression)
 %>
```

The XML based syntax for the expression tag is as follows:

```
<jsp:expression>
  script code (allows only one expression)
</jsp:expression>
```

Let's look at an example to use the expression tag:

```
<%! int count; %>
<html><body>
<% count++; %>
This page is requested by <%=count%> number of users till now.
</body></html>
```

The above code snippet can be embedded on a JSP page to count the number of requests received for the specific JSP page. Each time a new user accesses this Web page on the browser, the value of count is incremented by 1, which is displayed on the browser as well. For example, when a user accesses this page for the first time, the count variable is declared and is initialized at 0 (by default). The expression written in the scriptlet tag (`<%count++%>`) increments the value of the count variable by one and prints this value on the Web page. Now, when the other user accesses this page, the value of count is incremented by 1 and the browser displays the result as 2.

You must consider the following points when using expression tags:

- Don't end an expression with ';' since the expression given in this tag is placed into the `out.print()` method.
- The expression given in this tag can be resolved into any type, such as `int`, `float`, `double`, `Boolean`, `String`, or `Object`; but not to void.

If you write any code violating these rules, a translation stage error is raised. In addition, nested scripting tags are not allowed while using expression tags. It means a scripting tag cannot have another type of scripting tag. For example, in the following code snippet, the expression tag (`<%= %>`) is nested within the scriptlet tag (`<% %>`) which would raise a translation error.

```
<%
for (int i=0;i<5; i++){
<%=i%>    //out.println(+i);
}
%>
```

Working with JSP Scripting Tags

Let's now learn how to use JSP scripting tags, such as declaration, expression, and scriptlets, in an application. Use of scripting tags varies as we go from building simple applications to complex ones. In simple applications, we use Servlet, JSP's scripting tags, with JavaBeans to build Web applications; whereas in complex applications, the scripting tags are used with custom tags and other Model-View-Controller (MVC) frameworks, such as Struts and JSF. Here, we create a simple application by using scripting tags.

The **ScriptingTags.jsp** page, as shown in Listing 14.1, uses page directives to import the `java.util` package and specifies the scripting language as Java. In the declaration tag, we declare three integer variables: `count`, `a`, and `b`. We then define a function, `fun()`, which multiplies the integer value of 'a' variable, passed as an argument, with 10 and returns the result of the multiplication. The count variable is used to keep a track of number of times this Web page is being accessed. You can also find this file online in the code/Chapter14/ScriptingElements folder.

Listing 14.1: Creating the ScriptingTags.jsp File

```
<%@ page import ="java.util.*" language="java" %>

<html><body>

<center><h1>Using Scripting Elements</h1></center>

<%! int count,a,b;
int fun(int a)
```

```
    {
           return 10*a;
    }%>
    <% a=1;
    count++;
    for (int i=0;i<5;i++)

    {
           out.println("Value of i in iteration no."+i+":  <b>"+i+"</b><br/>");
    }

    b=fun(a);
    out.println("Value returned by fun():  <b>"+b+"</b><br/>");
%>

This page is requested by <b><%=count++%></b> number of times on date
<b><%=new Date()%></b>.

</body></html>
```

You do not need to map this JSP page in the `web.xml` file; however, an empty `web.xml` file must exist at the appropriate place in the root directory. An empty `web.xml` configuration file is shown in the following code snippet:

```
<web-app/>
```

Arrange all the files according to the standard directory structure of Web application. Figure 14.1 shows the directory structure of the **ScriptingElements** application:

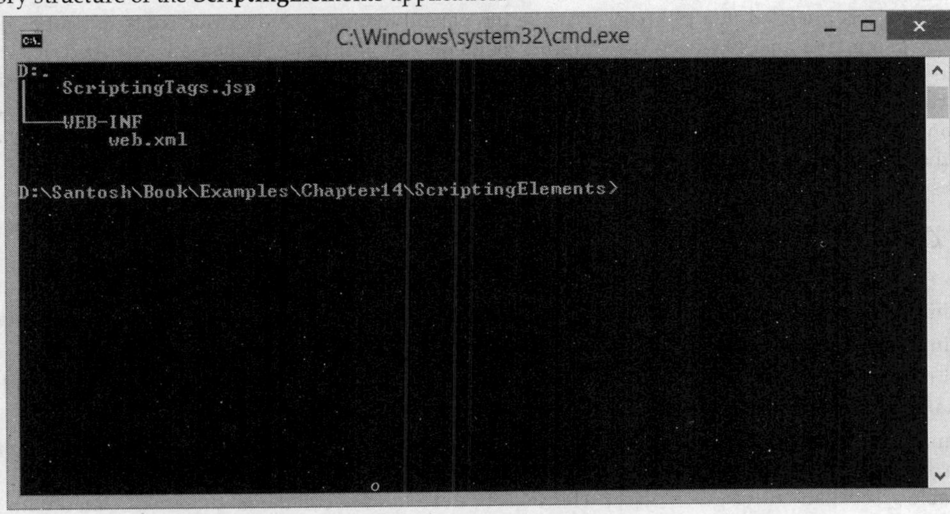

Figure 14.1: Directory Structure of the ScriptingElements Application

Now, copy the **ScriptingElements** folder in the `<Tomcat home>/webapps` folder. Start the Tomcat server and browse the application by using the URL `http://localhost:9090/ScriptingElements/ScriptingTags.jsp`. The output of the application is displayed in the Web browser, as shown in Figure 14.2:

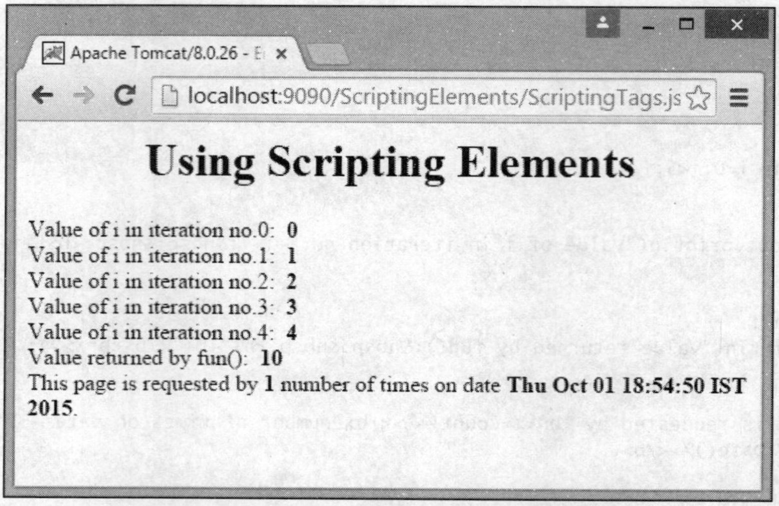

Figure 14.2: Showing the Use of Scripting Elements

Figure 14.2 shows the use of JSP scripting tags in ScriptingTags.jsp page. The scripting tags are used to iterate the values of the counter variables. The figure also shows the number of times a user has requested the specific Web page.

Exploring Implicit Objects

JSP implicit objects are used in a JSP page to make the page dynamic. The dynamic content can be created and accessed by using Java objects within the scripting elements. JSP implicit objects are predefined objects that are accessible to all JSP pages. These objects are called implicit objects because you don't need to instantiate them. The JSP container automatically instantiates these objects while writing the script content in the scriptlet and expression tags. JSP specification standardizes some object reference names, which are available for every JSP page so that any vendor-implemented translators have to take the responsibility of initializing these objects in the `_jspService()` method.

Features of Implicit Objects

The following are the features of JSP implicit objects:

- JSP implicit objects allow developers to access services and resources provided by the Web container.
- JSP implicit objects are used to generate dynamic content of Web pages.
- JSP implicit objects are termed as implicit, so that you do not have to declare these objects explicitly; the JSP container automatically instantiates these objects.
- JSP implicit objects are available to all JSP pages, and you can use these objects without importing them into your JSP page. Since the implicit objects are declared automatically, the user only needs to use a reference variable associated with a given object. This object can be used to call the methods associated with it.
- JSP implicit objects help in handling the HTML parameters, forward a request to a Web component, and include the content of a component, log data through the JSP container, control the output stream, and handle exceptions very easily.

Types of Implicit Objects

During the translation of a JSP page, the JSP engine initiates nine most commonly used JSP implicit objects in the `_jspService()` method. These JSP implicit objects are:

- `request`
- `response`
- `out`

- page
- pagecontext
- application
- session
- config
- exception

Let's learn about these objects in detail.

The request Object

The `request` objects are passed as parameters to the `_jspService()` method when a client request is made. A `request` object is of the `javax.servlet.http.HttpServletRequest` type. You can use the request objects in a JSP page similar to using these in servlets.

The response Object

The `response` object is used to carry the response of a client request after the `_jspService()` method is executed. The `response` object is of the `javax.servlet.http.HttpServletResponse` type.

The out Object

The `out` implicit object provides access to the servlet's output stream. This object is a subtype of `javax.servlet.jsp.JspWriter`. The `out` object can be used directly in JSP scriptlets to display the text data on the browser, since JSP expressions are automatically placed in the output stream. In other words, the `out` object is used to write the text data.

The page Object

The `page` object refers to the servlet of the JSP page processing the current request, and is of the `java.lang.Object` type. It also works as an instance of the generated servlet in a JSP page. Since it is a variable of type `Object`, it is rarely used in a document. It cannot be used directly to call the Servlet methods.

The pageContext Object

The `pageContext` object represents the context of the current JSP page. It provides a single API to manage the various scoped attributes. This object is of the `javax.servlet.jsp.PageContext` type.

The application Object

The `application` object refers to the entire environment of a Web application to which a JSP page belongs. This object is of the `javax.servlet.ServletContext` type.

The session Object

The `session` object helps access session data and is of the `HttpSession` type. It is declared if the value of the session attribute in a page directive is true. By default, the value of the session attribute is always true. If we explicitly specify the session attribute to false, the JSP engine does not declare this object. In such a case, if you try to access the session object, an error is generated.

The config Object

The `config` object specifies the configuration of the parameters passed to a JSP page. This object is of the `javax.servlet.ServletConfig` type. To demonstrate the use of the `config` object within a JSP page, we need to associate a servlet with a JSP file by using the `<jsp-file>` element. After associating a Servlet, all the initialization parameters for the named servlet are made available to the JSP page by the `ServletConfig` object.

The exception Object

The `exception` object is of the `java.lang.Throwable` type and is only available for the JSP pages that act as the error handlers for other pages. This object is only available to the JSP error pages that have the `isErrorPage` attribute set to 'true' with page directive.

All objects discussed here are always available within the scriptlet and expression tags only. These objects are not applicable to use in declaration tag. However, use the `getServletConfig()` method if you want to get the `ServletConfig` type of object reference in a declaration tag while implementing the `jspInit()` or `jspDestroy()` methods. Use the `getServletContext()` method of `ServletConfig` to get the `ServletContext` object.

Working with Implicit Objects

Let's now learn how to use the implicit objects in a JSP page to create a dynamic Web page. Let's develop a simple Web application, **ImplicitObjects**, by using implicit objects, such as `request`, `session`, and `pageContext`. This application performs three tasks — overriding the `jspInit()` method to perform initializations, using initialization parameter to implement the `config` object, and accessing the JSP document placed in a private folder.

This application contains the following Web pages:

- **Home.html**—Represents the index page of the application
- **request.jsp**—Displays the welcome message
- **pageContext.jsp**—Demonstrates the use of the `pageContext` implicit object
- **other.jsp**—Demonstrates the use of other implicit objects such as `page`, `session`, `out`, `application` and `config`

The Home.html page of this application consists of a simple form with a text field, Name, and a button, Invoke JSP. Listing 14.2 shows the code for the Home.html page. You can also find this file online in the code/Chapter14/ImplicitObjects folder.

Listing 14.2: Creating the Home.html File

```
<html>
   <body>
         <form action="request.jsp">
               Name : <input type="text" name="name">
               <input type="submit" value="Invoke JSP"/>
         </form>
   </body>
</html>
```

When a user clicks the Invoke JSP button on the Home.html page, the next page, request.jsp page, is displayed. The request.jsp page displays a greeting message followed by the user name entered on the Home.html page. It then displays request details, such as type of request, its URI, and request protocol, in the tabular form. These request details are retrieved using the request implicit object's methods, such as `getMethod()`, `getRequestURI( )`, `getProtocol( )`, and `getHeader( )`. Listing 14.3 shows the request.jsp page. You can also find this file online in the code/Chapter14/ImplicitObjects folder.

Listing 14.3: Creating the request.jsp File

```
<html>
   <head><title>
         Using Implicit Objects
         </title></head>
   <body>

   Hello, <b><%=request.getParameter("name")%></b><br/><br/>
   Your request details are <br/><br/>
   <table border="1">
   <tr><th>Name</th><th>Value</th></tr>
   <tr><td>request method</td>
   <td><%= request.getMethod() %></td></tr>
   <tr><td>request URI</td>
   <td><%= request.getRequestURI() %></td></tr>
   <tr><td>request protocol</td>
   <td><%= request.getProtocol() %></td></tr>
```

```
    <tr><td>browser</td>
    <td><%= request.getHeader("user-agent") %></td></tr>
    </table>
    <%if (session.getAttribute("sessionVar")==null) {
          session.setAttribute("sessionVar",new Integer(0));
    }%>

    <table>
          <tr><th align=left>Would you like to see use of remaining
                imlplicit objects?</th></tr>
          <tr>
          <form name=form1 action="pageContext.jsp" method="post">
          <td><input type="radio" name="other" value="Yes">Yes</td>
          <td><input type="radio" name="other" value="No" > No</td></tr>
          <tr><td><input type="submit" value="Submit"></td></tr>
          </form>
    </table>
    </body></html>
```

After submitting the form on the request.jsp page, the control is transferred to the pageContext.jsp page. The pageContext.jsp page uses the `pageContext` implicit object to forward a request to another JSP page, other.jsp. Listing 14.4 shows the pageContext.jsp page. You can also find this file online in the code/Chapter14/ImplicitObjects folder.

Listing 14.4: Creating the pageContext.jsp File

```
<html>
    <head>
    <title> Intermediate </title></head>

    <body>
    <%
          if("Yes".equals(request.getParameter("other")))
          {
                pageContext.forward("other");
          }
    %>
    </body>
</html>
```

The other.jsp page shows the use of `page`, `session`, `out`, `config`, and `application` implicit objects. This page first overrides the `jspInit()` function, which retrieves the initialization parameter of the other.jsp page from the `web.xml` file. The same initialization parameter value is fetched by calling the `getInitParmeter()` method of the `config` implicit object `(config.getInitParameter("count"))`. In the other.jsp page, we use the page implicit object's log method to log a message, `anothermessage` `(((HttpServlet)page).log("anothermessage");)`. The session implicit object is used to get the value of the `sessionVar` attribute, which shows the number of active sessions in the request.jsp page (`.getAttribute("sessionVar"`)). The application implicit object is used to retrieve the value of the context parameter, `param1`, set in `web.xml`. We use the `application.getInitParameter("param1")` method to retrieve the value of the `param1` parameter in this JSP page. Listing 14.5 shows the other.jsp page. You can also find this file online in the code/Chapter14/ImplicitObjects /WEB-INF/jsppages folder.

Listing 14.5: Creating the other.jsp File

```
<html><body>
<%!int count;
  public void jspInit() {
  ServletConfig sc=getServletConfig();

  count=Integer.parseInt( sc.getInitParameter("count"));
  System.out.println("In jspInit");
```

```
  }
%>

Count value without using config implicit object: <b> <%=count%></b> <br/>
<%
this.log("log message");
((HttpServlet)page).log("anothermessage");
ServletContext ct = config.getServletContext();
out.println("Value of sessionVar
  is:"+"  <b>"+session.getAttribute("sessionVar")+"</b><br/>");
out.println("Server name and version using config implicit
  object:"+"  <b>"+ct.getServerInfo()+"</b><br/>");
out.println("Value of context parameter param1 get using application implicit
  object:"+"  <b>"+application.getInitParameter
        ("param1")+"</b><br/>");
out.println("Count value retrieved using config implicit
  object:" +"  <b>"+config.getInitParameter("count")+"</b>");
%>
</body> </html>
```

The web.xml file initializes an application level parameter, param1, with the value param1. In the **ImplicitObjects** Web application, we have configured the other.jsp page in web.xml, (although it is not mandatory to declare JSP page in web.xml, as described earlier). However, the other.jsp page has been declared in web.xml in our case due to the following reasons:

- Initialization parameter 'count' for the other.jsp page has been configured in web.xml.
- The other.jsp page has been placed into a private folder (jsppages) to avoid direct access to this JSP page.

The other.jsp page is configured using the <jsp-file> nested tag of the <servlet> tag. The servlet name specified in the <servlet-name> tag is **'myjsp'**, which is mapped to the URI for accessing this page.

The other.jsp document is placed in the WEB-INF/jsppages folder. Listing 14.6 shows web.xml file, which you can also find online in the code/Chapter14/ImplicitObjects/WEB-INF folder.

Listing 14.6: Creating the web.xml File

```
<?xml version="1.0" encoding="UTF-8"?>

<web-app>
  <context-param>
        <param-name>param1</param-name>
        <param-value>param1</param-value>

  </context-param>

  <servlet>

        <servlet-name>myjsp</servlet-name>
        <jsp-file>/WEB-INF/jsppages/other.jsp</jsp-file>
        <init-param>
              <param-name>count</param-name>
              <param-value>10</param-value>
        </init-param>
  </servlet>

  <servlet-mapping>
        <servlet-name>myjsp</servlet-name>
        <url-pattern>/other</url-pattern>

  </servlet-mapping>

</web-app>
```

Arrange all files, such as Home.html, pageContext.jsp, web.xml and so on, under the directory structure of **ImplicitObjects**. The directory structure for **ImplicitObjects** application is shown in Figure 14.3:

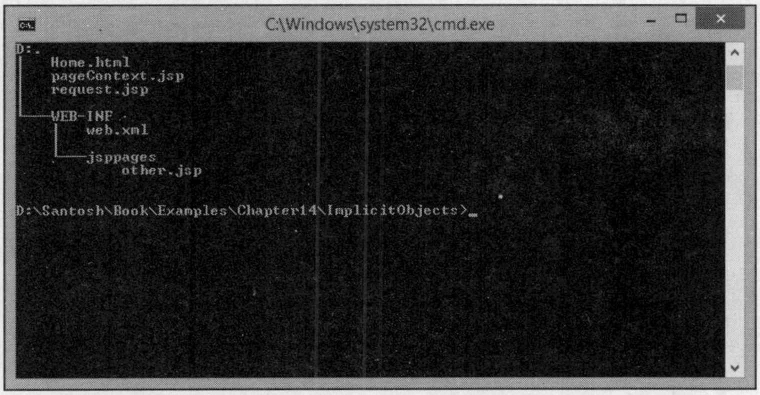

Figure 14.3: Directory Structure for ImplicitObjects Application

Now, copy the **ImplicitObjects** folder in the `<Tomcat home>/webapps` directory. Start the Tomcat server and browse the application using the URL `http://localhost:9090/ImplicitObjects/Home.html`. Figure 14.4 displays the home page of this application:

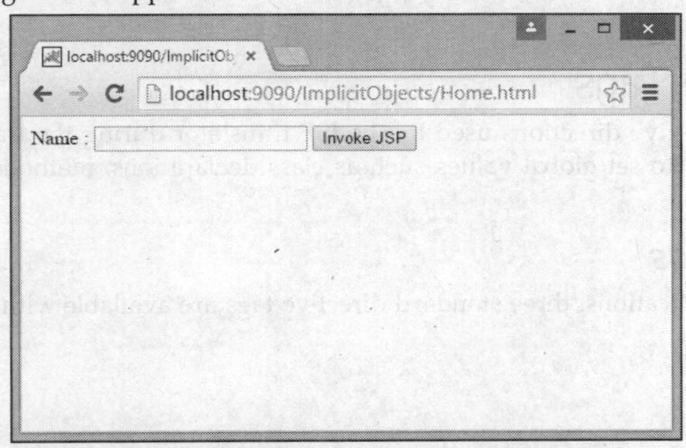

Figure 14.4: Displaying the Output of Home.html

When a user clicks the Invoke JSP button, the request.jsp page is displayed, as shown in Figure 14.5:

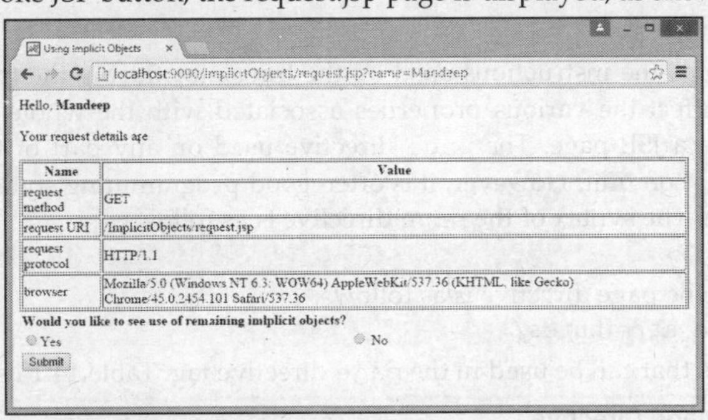

Figure 14.5: Displaying the Result of Processing request.jsp

Figure 14.5 shows all request details, such as request type, request URI, and request protocols, in the form of a table.

When a user selects the Yes radio button and clicks the Submit button, the **other.jsp** page is displayed, as shown in Figure 14.6:

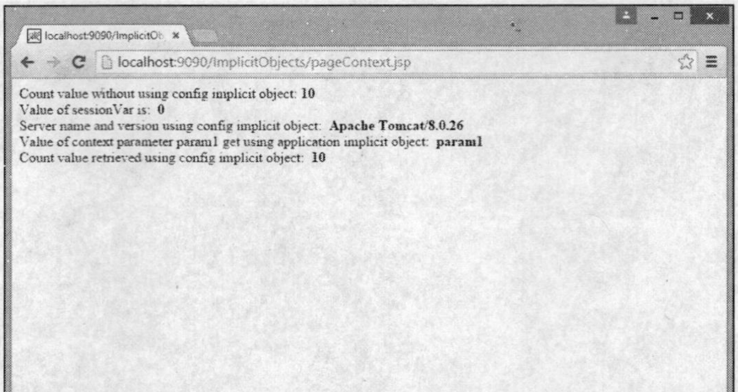

Figure 14.6: Displaying the Use of Implicit Objects

Figure 14.6 shows the use of the implicit objects in an application. It shows the values of the implicit objects that are implicitly being used by the application. When the user selects any of the radio buttons shown in Figure 14.5 and clicks the Submit button, the pageContext.jsp page is invoked to display the values of the implicit objects used in the application.

Exploring Directive Tags

Directive tags are used to give directions used by the JSP translator during the translation stage of the JSP life cycle. These tags are used to set global values such as class declarations, methods to be implemented, output content type, and so on.

Types of Directive Tags

According to the JSP specifications, three standard directive tags are available with all JSP compliant containers. These directive tags are:

- `page`
- `include`
- `taglib`

Let's discuss each of these directives in detail.

The page Directive Tag

The `page` directive tag holds the instructions used by the translator during the translation stage of the JSP life cycle. These instructions affect the various properties associated with the whole JSP page. You can use `page` directive multiple times in a JSP page. The `page` directive used on any part of the JSP page is automatically applied to the entire translation unit. However, it is often good programming style to place the page directive at the starting of the JSP page. The syntax of the `page` directive is as follows:

```
<%@page attributes %>
```

The XML based syntax for the page directive is as follows:

```
<jsp:directive.page attributes/>
```

There are total 11 attributes that can be used in the `page` directive tag. Table 14.1 lists these attributes:

Table 14.1: Attributes of page Directive

Attribute	Value
`language`	Takes the scripting language as the value to be used in scripting tags. The default value is Java
`import`	Specifies a list of packages or classes to be used in JSP

Table 14.1: Attributes of page Directive

Attribute	Value
`extends`	Takes a complete qualified class name extended by the servlet equivalent class written by the translator of the current JSP page
`buffer`	Takes the buffer size in kilobytes, for example none, 8kb, 16kb, 32kb, and 64kb. The default value is 8kb
`autoFlush`	Specifies whether the output has to be flushed automatically when the buffer is full. If this attribute is set to true, it automatically flushes the buffer as soon as the buffer is full. If this attribute is set to false, an exception is raised when buffer overflows. The default value of this attribute is true
`isThreadSafe`	Takes true or false as its value; the default value is true. This attribute specifies whether or not a JSP page is safe for thread. That is, whether or not the instance of the servlet equivalent class of the JSP page is capable of handling simultaneous requests. If this attribute is set to false, only one thread can use the service provided by one object. If the value of this attribute is true, simultaneous requests can be handled by this page
`errorPage`	Takes the URL path of the page to which a request has to be dispatched when an exception is raised in the current page
`isErrorPage`	Takes true or false as its value; the default value is false. This attribute specifies whether or not the current page is an error page. Note that if this attribute is set to true, an additional implicit object, exception, is available for the current JSP page
`contentType`	Takes the response content MIME type, and optionally, character encoding. The default value is text/html
`Session`	Takes true or false, which indicates whether or not the session is required; the default value is *true*. If this attribute is set to *false,* the JSP page cannot use the session implicit object
`Info`	Takes a string, which can be retrieved by using the `getServletInfo( )` method
`pageEncoding`	Specifies the encoding type to be used by the Web container to compile a JSP page. Some of the encoding types are ISO-8859-1 and UTF-8
`isELIgnored`	Specifies whether the EL expression will be ignored or not
`isScriptingEnables`	Specifies whether scripting elements will be allowed to use or not

The JSP page, as described earlier, can contain any number of page directive tags. However, except the import tag, none of the other tags are allowed to be specified more than once.

The include Directive

The `include` directive tag is used to merge the contents of two or more files during the translation stage of the JSP life cycle. The `include` directive adds the text of the included file to the JSP page, without any processing or modification. The included file can be static or dynamic. If the included file is dynamic, its JSP elements are translated and included. In this case, if there are any changes in the included page after the included JSP page is translated, the changes are not applied until the included JSP page is translated once again.

The syntax of the `include` directive is as follows:

```
<%@include file=" file path" %>
```

The XML based syntax for `include` directive is as follows:

```
<jsp:directive.include file=" file path  "/>
```

Here is an example to use the `include` directive for merging the Test.jsp and Test1.html files:

```
<%@include file="/Test.jsp" %>
<%@include file="/Test1.html" %>
```

Note that the behavior of the `include` directive with respect to the recompilation of the included page, if any changes are done to it, depends on the Web container. This means that if the included page is changed, some containers recognize and apply the changes to the JSP page, while others do not.

The taglib Directive

The `taglib` directive tag is used to declare a custom tag library in a JSP page so that the tags related to that custom tag library can be used in the same JSP page. The syntax of `taglib` directive is as follows:

```
<%@taglib uri=" URI" prefix=" unique_prefix " %>
```

We do not have any special XML equivalent element for this tag since this declaration is done by using the XML namespace syntax.

Working with JSP Directive Tags

JSP directives are used in a JSP page to add functionality to the JSP page. Let's create an application using the JSP directives. This application contains the following pages:

- **Login.html** – Accepts user details and redirects the user to the required JSP page.
- **LoginProcess.jsp** – Connects to a database to process the user request.
- **MyError.jsp** – Represents the JSP page that is called when an error or exception is raised.

In this application, we use the Oracle database to access the related tables in the application. Therefore, you need to create the database table to work with the application before creating these JSP pages. The code to create the table is as follows:

```
create table userdetails(
uname varchar2(15),
pass varchar2(10));
insert into userdetails values('to_santoshk','123456');
```

Let's now create these pages.

Listing 14.7 shows the Login.html page, which is the home page of the application. You can also find this file online in the code/Chapter14/directiveTags folder.

Listing 14.7: Creating the `Login.html` File

```
<html> <body><pre>
  <form action="LoginProcess.jsp">
        <b>User Name</b> : <input type="text" name="uname"/>
        <b>Password</b>  : <input type="password" name="pass"/>
        <input type="submit" value="LogIN"/>
  </form> </pre></body></html>
```

The `Login.html` page allows the user to enter a user name and password, which are stored in a database.

After entering the user name and password, the `LoginProcess.jsp` page is called to handle the request. Listing 14.8 shows the `LoginProcess.jsp` page. You can also find this file online in the code/Chapter14/directiveTags folder.

Listing 14.8: Creating the `LoginProcess.jsp` File

```
<%@page import="java.sql.*" errorPage="/MyError.jsp"%>
<html><body>
<%
  Connection con=null;
  String uname=request.getParameter("uname");
  String pass=request.getParameter("pass");
  try {
       Class.forName("oracle.jdbc.driver.OracleDriver");
       con=DriverManager.getConnection(
       "jdbc:oracle:thin:@localhost:1521:sandb","scott","tiger");
       Statement st=con.createStatement();
       ResultSet rs=st.executeQuery(
       "select * from userdetails where uname=\'"+uname+ "\'
             and pass=\'"+ pass +"\'");
       if (!rs.next()){
%>
User details given for uname : <%=request.getParameter("uname")%> are not
```

```
valid <br/> Try again
<%@include file="Login.html"%>
</body></html>
<%
  return;
  }//if
  }//try
  finally {
        try{con.close();}catch(Exception e){}
  }//finally
%>
This is a Home Page <br/>
Welcome, <%=uname%>
</body></html>
```

The `LoginProcess.jsp` page shows the use of the JSP page directive, which imports the `java.sql` package into the `LoginProcess.jsp` page. The `java.sql` package helps the `LoginProcess.jsp` page to access the database that stores user information. After the request is submitted by the user, the `LoginProcess.jsp` page is used to generate the appropriate response for each request made.

The `LoginProcess.jsp` page also includes another page, named `MyErro.jsp`, which is used to handle any exception that may occur in the JSP page. Any exception in the `LoginProcess.jsp` page is forwarded to the `MyError.jsp`. Listing 14.9 shows the `MyError.jsp` page. You can also find this file online in the code/Chapter14/directiveTags folder.

Listing 14.9: Creating the `MyError.jsp` File

```
<%@page isErrorPage="true"%>
<html><body>
  An exception is raised while processing the request: <br/>
  <b>Exception : </b> <br/>
      <%=exception.getMessage()%>
</body> </html>
```

Listing 14.10 shows `web.xml` file, which you can also find online in the code/Chapter14/directivTags/WEB-INF folder.

Listing 14.10: Creating the `web.xml` File

```
<?xml version="1.0"?>
<web-app>
<context-param>
                <param-name>param1</param-name>
                <param-value>param1</param-value>
</context-param>
<servlet>
        <servlet-name>myjsp</servlet-name>
        <jsp-file>/WEB-INF/jsppages/other.jsp</jsp-file>
                <init-param>
                        <param-name>count</param-name>
                        <param-value>10</param-value>
                </init-param>
</servlet>

<servlet-mapping>
                <servlet-name>myjsp</servlet-name>
                <url-pattern>/other</url-pattern>
</servlet-mapping>
</web-app>
```

Since the application imports the java.sql package, you need to include the classes12.jar files in the lib directory of the application. This is an executable jar file used to access a database within a JSP page. In this case, we have included classes12.jar file in the directory since we are using the Oracle database for the application. Figure 14.7 shows the directory structure for **directiveTags**:

Figure 14.7: Directory Structure for directiveTags

Copy the **directiveTags** folder into the <Tomcat home>\webapps folder. Start the Tomcat server and browse the application by using the URL http://localhost:9090/directiveTags/Login.html. Figure 14.8 shows the Login.html page as it appears on the Web browser:

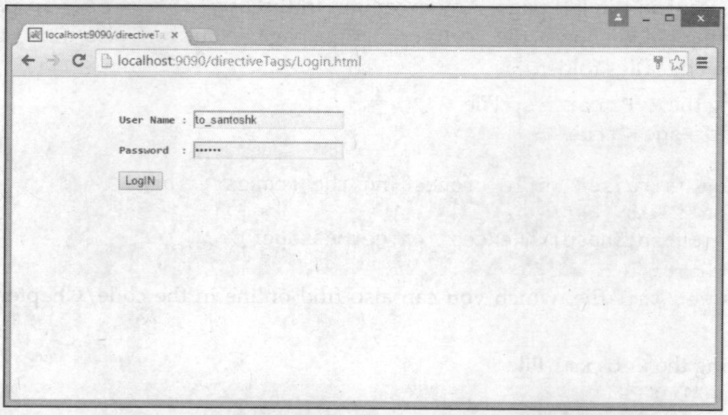

Figure 14.8: Displaying the Output of Login.html

Enter the username and password on the Login.html page. After entering the user name and password, the JSP engine checks for the availability of the user name and the password in the specified database. If the entries are valid, you are directed to the LoginProcess.jsp page, as shown in Figure 14.9:

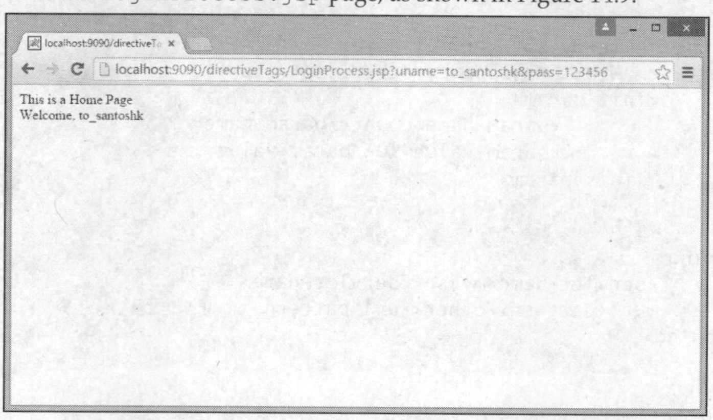

Figure 14.9: Displaying the Output of LoginProcess.jsp

Figure 14.9 shows the output for the successful login in the `Login.html` page. The database is called each time a user enters the values for the user name and password fields. If the entries are not available in the database, the user is redirected to another page, as shown in Figure 14.10:

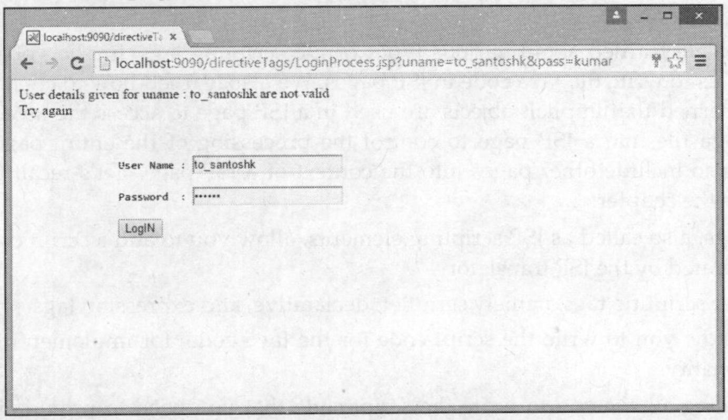

Figure 14.10: Displaying Output of LoginProcess.jsp for an Invalid Login

Now, to test the `errorPage` and `isErrorPage` functionalities, drop the table from the database, as shown in Figure 14.11:

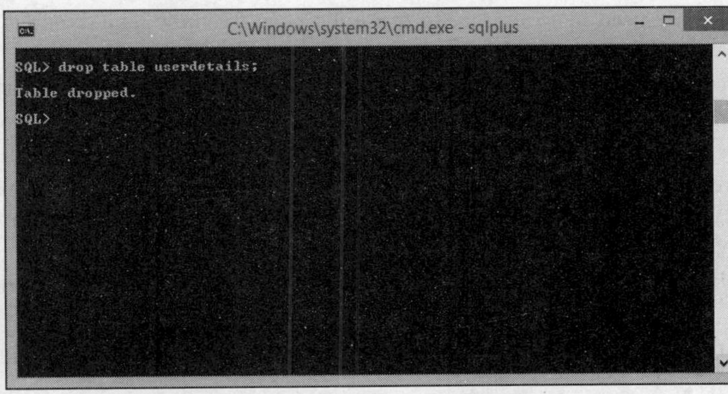

Figure 14.11: Dropping the Table from the Database

If you make a request to the `LoginProcess.jsp` by clicking the Login button, a `SQLException` is raised in the `LoginProcess.jsp` page. The request is then forwarded to the `MyError.jsp` page, as shown in Figure 14.12:

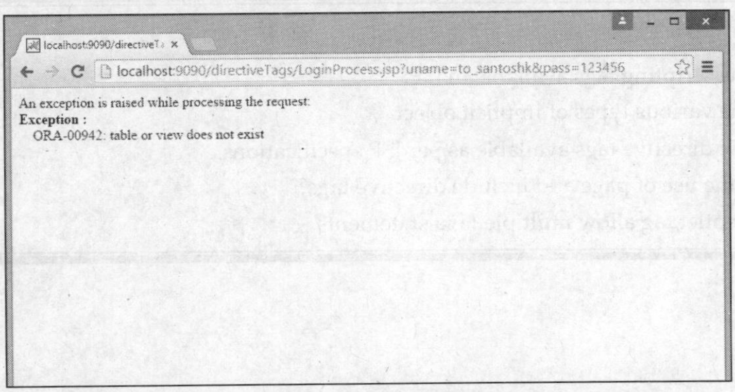

Figure 14.12: Displaying an Invalid Access to the Database

Since the table storing user information has been dropped from the database, the Oracle exception 'ORA-00942' is raised, stating that the table does not exist in the database.

Summary

In this chapter, we have learned about various types of JSP scripting tags, implicit objects, and JSP directives. Scripting tags allow us to write the Java code in JSP pages. We also learned how to create JSP pages by using the scripting tags. We learned that implicit objects are used in a JSP page to access the Java code. JSP directives are used to import a Java file into a JSP page to control the processing of the entire page in an application. JSP directives allow you to include other pages into the context of a JSP page. Let's recall the following important points to summarize the chapter:

- JSP scripting tags, also called as JSP scripting elements, allow you to add a script code into the Java code of a JSP page generated by the JSP translator.
- JSP defines three scripting tags, namely scriptlet, declarative, and expression tags.
- Scriptlet tags allow you to write the script code (or the Java code) for implementing the `_jspService()` method functionality.
- The declarative tag allows you to write the script code that you need to provide in the generated servlet class, outside the `_jspService()` method.
- The expression tag allows you to write a Java expression, which is then resolved and the resultant value is displayed.
- JSP implicit objects are used in a JSP page to make the page dynamic. The dynamic content can be created and accessed by using Java objects within the scripting elements.
- JSP implicit objects allow developers to access services and resources provided by the Web container.
- JSP implicit objects are available to all JSP pages, and you can use these objects without importing them into your JSP page.
- Directive tags are used to give directions used by the JSP translator during the translation stage of the JSP life cycle. These tags are used to set global values such as class declarations, methods to be implemented, output content type, and so on.
- The `page` directive tag holds the instructions used by the translator during the translation stage of the JSP life cycle.
- The `include` directive tag is used to merge the contents of two or more files during the translation stage of the JSP life cycle.
- The `taglib` directive tag is used to declare a custom tag library in a JSP page so that the tags related to that custom tag library can be used in the same JSP page.

In the next chapter, we learn about using Action tags and JavaBeans with JSP pages.

Exercise

Q. 14.1 Name the scripting tags available in JSP.

Q. 14.2 Name the various types of implicit object.

Q. 14.3 Name the directive tags available as per JSP specifications.

Q. 14.4 What is the use of page and include directive tags?

Q. 14.5 Does scriptlet tag allow multiple Java statements

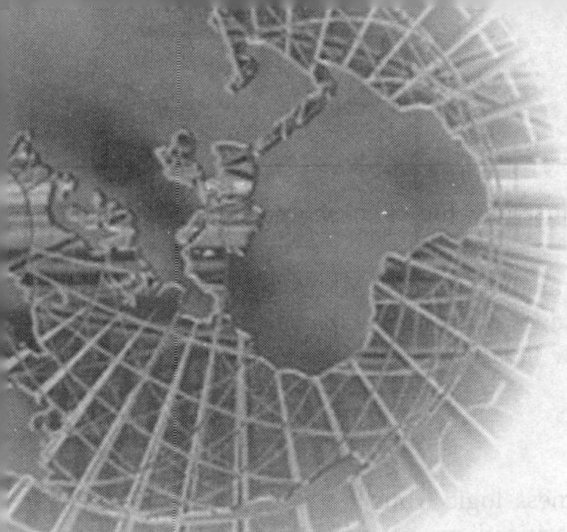

15

Working with JavaBeans and Action Tags in JSP

Use of JavaBeans with JSP has made the work of developers easy because developers do not need to handle long Java syntax within a JSP page.

We start this chapter by introducing JavaBeans. In addition, we try to analyze why JavaBeans are required when we work with JSP. We start the discussion by describing the advantages of using JavaBeans. The components and properties of JavaBeans are described next. We also examine how JavaBeans can be used with JSP. Finally, we learn about JSP Action tags. Let's start discussing about JavaBean.

What is JavaBean?

JavaBeans are reusable software components that separate the business logic from the presentation logic. In general, JavaBeans are simple Java classes that follow certain specifications to develop dynamic content. JavaBeans are required to create effective and dynamic Web pages by providing the benefit of using separate Java classes instead of embedding large amount of Java code directly in a JSP page. These separate JavaBean classes are easier to write, compile, test, debug, and reuse. JavaBean uses `getter` and `setter` methods to invoke various methods explicitly to use their functionality with JSP pages.

You can create reusable and platform-independent JavaBean components with the JavaBeans API. JavaBean components are also known as beans. JavaBeans can be created or manipulated by using JavaBeans-compliant application builder tools such as NetBeans IDE. The JavaBeans-compliant application builder tools automatically discover information about the classes, based on JavaBeans specifications, and can create and manipulate these classes.

Advantages of using JavaBeans

JavaBeans have many advantages over scriptlets and JSP expressions. Some advantages of using JavaBeans are as follows:

- With the use of JavaBeans, users can manage presentation code and business logic separately. This feature of JavaBeans is more advantageous in big organizations that have separate Web and Java development teams. Both the presentation logic and business logic are developed separately, and JavaBeans ensure proper communication between them.
- Using JavaBeans with JSP has made object sharing between multiple Web pages simple.
- Using JavaBeans with JSP has simplified the process of request and response handling.

These are the advantages of using JavaBeans. Now, we learn about using the JavaBeans component with JSP action tags.

NOTE

A JavaBean component refers to any Java class that follows certain design conventions.

Action Tags

Action tags have been introduced in JSP 1.1, and some additional tags have been added in the JSP 1.2 and 2.0 specifications. These set of tags allow us to include some basic actions, such as inserting some other page resources, forwarding the request to another page, creating or locating the JavaBean instances, and setting and retrieving bean properties, in JSP pages.

The action tags are specific to a JSP page. When the JSP container encounters an action tag while converting a JSP page into a servlet, it generates the Java code that corresponds to the required predefined task. For example, when it comes across the 'include' action tag:

```
<jsp:include page="myjsp.jsp" flush="true" />
```

In the preceding code snippet, the `jsp:include` action tag allows to include the myjsp.jsp page.

Some important action tags available in JSP are as follows:

- `<jsp include>`
- `<jsp forward>`
- `<jsp param>`
- `<jsp useBean>`

- <jsp:setProperty>
- <jsp:getProperty>
- <jsp:plugin>
- <jsp:params>
- <jsp:fallback>
- <jsp:attribute>
- <jsp:body>
- <jsp:element>
- <jsp:text>

Let's now describe these action tags in detail.

Describing the Include Tag

The include action tag allows a static or dynamic resource such as HTML or JSP page, specified by a URL, to be included in the current JSP while processing a request. If the included resource is static, its content is included in the calling JSP page. If the resource is dynamic, it acts on a request and sends back a result, which is included in the JSP page. For example, if the resource is another JSP page, the output content generated by the second JSP page is included in the first JSP page. The following code snippet shows the syntax of the include action tag in a JSP page:

```
<jsp:include attributes>
<!-- Zero or more jsp:param tags -->
</jsp:include>
```

NOTE

If the included resource is dynamic, we can use the `jsp:param` tag to pass the name and value of a parameter to the resource, as you can see in the previous code snippet. You learn about `jsp:param` later in this chapter.

The include action tag has certain attributes, which are used to accept values for the specified JSP page. The attributes specific to the include tag are as follows:

- **page**—Takes a relative URL, which locates the resource to be included in the JSP page. This allows us to give an expression that evaluates to a String equivalent to the relative URL that locates the resource. We can specify the relative URL directly or in an expression within a page attribute. The following syntax shows the use of the page attribute in a JSP page:
  - <jsp:include page="/Header.html"/>
  - <jsp:include page="<%=mypath%>"/>

  The relative URL cannot contain a protocol name, port number, or domain name. The relative URL starts with the '/' (forward slash) character, specifying that the URL is taken relative to the context path.
- **flush**—Takes true or false, which indicates whether or not the buffer needs to be flushed before including the resource. If the value is true, the buffer is flushed before including the resource. The default value of this attribute is false. After the include action is completed, the JSP container continues to process the rest of the JSP page.

You might be thinking how is the include action tag different from the include directive tag described in Chapter 14. Now let's discuss the difference between the 'include' directive tag and the 'include' action tag.

Difference Between Include Directive Tag and Include Action Tag

Though both the 'include directive tag' and 'include action tag' are used to include the content into a JSP page, the differences between the two are as follows:

Include Directive Tag

The 'include' directive tag inserts the given page and includes the content in the generated Servlet page during the translation phase of the JSP life cycle. In general, the 'include' directive is used to include files, such as HTML, JSP, XML, or a simple .txt file, into a JSP page statically. The file attribute is the only mandatory attribute available in the include directive tag and is used to refer to the file to be included. The following snippet shows the use of the JSP include directive tag in a JSP file:

```
%@include file="menu.jsp"
```

In the preceding snippet, menu.jsp is the file included in the current JSP page. The content of the menu.jsp page is included in the current JSP page during the translation stage.

The include directive tag does not allow you to use the expression for giving the URL path, for including the resource in the JSP page.

Include Action Tag

The 'include' action tag is used to include the response generated by executing the specified JSP page or Servlet. The response is included during the request processing phase, when the page is requested by the user. The specified JSP page is included in request handling phase of the included JSP page life cycle. The following snippet shows the use of the include action tag in a JSP file:

```
<jsp:include page= "menu.jsp">
```

In the preceding snippet, the output of menu.jsp needs to be included in the current page. The respective logic for include is written into the Servlet equivalent generated for the current JSP page.

Unlike the include directive tag, the include action tag accepts expressions. That is, with the include action tag, we can decide the page to be included at runtime, whereas it is not possible with the include directive tag.

Describing the Forward Tag

The jsp:forward tag forwards a JSP request to another resource, which can be either static or dynamic. If the resource is dynamic, we can use a jsp:param tag to pass the name and value of the parameter to the resource. We use the page directive with the buffer ="none" parameter to specify that the output of the JSP page should not be buffered.

If the output stream is not buffered, and some output has been written to it, a <jsp:forward> action throws a java.IllegalStatexception. The forward action in a JSP page works similar to the forward() method of RequestDisapatcher. The following code snippet shows the use of the jsp:forward action in a JSP page:

```
<jsp:forward attributes>
<!-- Zero or more jsp:param tags -->
</jsp:forward>
```

The jsp:forward action takes a page attribute to specify the page to which the current request is to be forwarded. The page attribute takes the relative URL that locates the resource to which the request has to be forwarded. This allows us to give an expression that evaluates to a String equivalent to the relative URL that locates the resource. We can specify the relative URL directly or by using an expression. The following snippet shows the use of the page attribute in the jsp:forward action:

```
<jsp:forward page="/Header.html"/>
<jsp:forward page="<%=mypath%>"/>
```

The given URL cannot contain a protocol name, port number, or domain name. If the given URL starts with the / character, the URL is taken relative to the context path, if not relative to the JSP page. After the forward action is completed, the JSP container does not continue processing the rest of the JSP page.

Describing the Param Tag

The <jsp:param> tag allows us to pass a name and value pair as parameter to a dynamic resource, while including it in a JSP page or forwarding a request from a JSP page to another JSP page. The <jsp:param> tag can be even used to pass parameters to an applet configured in JSP page by using the <jsp:plugin> tag. The following syntax shows the use of the <jsp:param> tag in a JSP page:

```
<jsp:param attributes />
```

We can use more than one <jsp:param> tags if we want to pass more than one parameter. The <jsp:param> action tag contains two attributes, name and value, which are discussed next.

name

The `name` attribute specifies the parameter name and takes a case-sensitive literal string. The parameter `name` should be unique, that is, it should be different for each parameter.

value

The `value` attribute specifies the parameter value and takes either a case-sensitive literal String or an expression that is evaluated in the request handling stage of the JSP life cycle. The following snippet shows the use of the JSP param and include actions, along with the attributes of `<jsp:param>` action:

```
<jsp:include page="/MyPage2.jsp">
<jsp:param name="uname" value="User1"/>
<jsp:param name="user_type" value="admin"/>
</jsp:include>
```

Let's create an application **actiontags_ex1** to use the functionality of the discussed action tags in a JSP page. The Home.html page, which we created in the previous chapter, is used to create the user interface where the user needs to enter the values for the specified fields. Listing 15.1 shows the Home.html page. You can also find this file online in the code/Chapter15/actiontags_ex1 folder.

Listing 15.1: Creating the Home.html File

```
<html> <body> <pre>
<form action="FrontJSP.jsp">
   <b>Operand 1 :</b> <input type="text" name="field1"/>
   <b>Operand 2 :</b> <input type="text" name="field2"/>
   <input type="submit" name="submit" value="Add"/>
   <input type="submit" name="submit" value="Sub"/>
</form> </pre> </body></html>
```

When you execute Listing 15.1, the Home.html page is displayed, which provides options to enter the values of certain fields. After entering the values for the required fields in the Home.html page, the control is transferred to the FrontJsp.jsp. Let's now create the FrontJsp.jsp page, as shown in Listing 15.2. You can also find this file online in the code/Chapter15/actiontags_ex1 folder.

Listing 15.2: Creating the FrontJSP.jsp File

```
<%@page errorPage="/Home.html"%>
<%
String s1=request.getParameter("field1");
String s2=request.getParameter("field2");
Integer.parseInt(s1); Integer.parseInt(s2);
String submit=request.getParameter("submit");
if (submit.equals("Add")) {
%>
   <jsp:forward page="/AddJsp.jsp"/>
<%
} else if (submit.equals("Sub")){
%>
   <jsp:forward page="/SubJsp.jsp"/>
<%
} else {
%>
   <jsp:forward page="/Home.html"/>
<%}%>
```

The Home.html page provides two buttons, Add and Sub. From the FrontJSP.jsp, the control can be transferred to the AddJsp.jsp or SubJsp.jsp page, depending on the button that a user clicks. The `<jsp:forward>` action is used to forward the action to the respective pages. Listing 15.3 shows the AddJsp.jsp. You can also find this file online in the code/Chapter15/actiontags_ex1 folder.

Listing 15.3: Creating the AddJsp.jsp File

```
<%
   int f1=Integer.parseInt(request.getParameter("field1"));
   int f2=Integer.parseInt(request.getParameter("field2"));
   int result=f1+f2;
%>
<jsp:forward page="/Result.jsp">
<jsp:param name="result" value="<%=result%>"/> </jsp:forward>
```

The AddJsp.jsp is called if the user clicks the Add button. The AddJsp.jsp page is used to add the values entered by the user. This page then transfers the control to the Result.jsp page to view the result of addition.

Similarly, if the user clicks the Sub button, the SubJsp.jsp page is displayed. Listing 15.4 shows the SubJsp.jsp page of the application. You can also find this file online in the code/Chapter15/actiontags_ex1 folder.

Listing 15.4: Creating the SubJsp.jsp File

```
<%
   int f1=Integer.parseInt(request.getParameter("field1"));
   int f2=Integer.parseInt(request.getParameter("field2"));
   int result=f1-f2;
%>
<jsp:forward page="/Result.jsp">
   <jsp:param name="result" value="<%=result%>"/>
</jsp:forward>
```

The SubJsp.jsp page also transfers the control to the Result.jsp page. Listing 15.5 shows the Result.jsp page. You can also find this file online in the code/Chapter15/actiontags_ex1 folder.

Listing 15.5: Creating the Result.jsp File

```
<%
   String result=request.getParameter("result");
   String submit=request.getParameter("submit");
%>
<html><body><center>
   <%
          if (submit.equals("Add")){
   %>
   Result of Add : <%=result%>
   <%
          } else {
   %>
   Result of Sub : <%=result%>
   <%}%>
   </center>
   <jsp:include page="/Home.html"/>
</body></html>
```

The pages designed above must be mapped in the `web.xml` file to access them in the browser. Listing 15.6 shows the `web.xml` file associated with the preceding application. You can also find this file online in the code/Chapter15/actiontags_ex1/WEB-INF folder.

Listing 15.6: Creating the `web.xml` File

```
<?xml version="1.0"?>
<web-app>
   <welcome-files-list>
          <welcome-file>Home.html</welcome-file>
   </welcome-files-list>
</web-app>
```

All the specified files should be placed under a common directory named **actiontags_ex1**. Place this directory in the `<Tomcat home>/webapps` directory and start the Tomcat server. Figure 15.1 shows the directory structure of the **actiontags_ex1** application:

Figure 15.1: Directory Structure of actiontags_ex1

Now, browse the application **actiontags_ex1** using the URL, `http://localhost:9090/actiontags_ex1/Home.html`, as shown in Figure 15.2. Now, you can add or subtract any two numbers. Enter some numbers, as shown in Figure 15.2, and click the **Add** button to get the result, as shown in Figure 15.3:

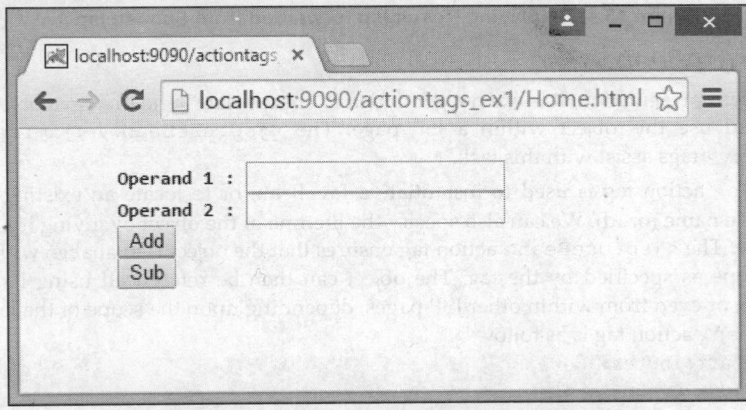

Figure 15.2: Output of the Home.html Page

If the user enters 20 and 30 as the values for the Operand 1 and Operand 2 fields, respectively and clicks the Add button (Figure 15.2), the control is transferred to the AddJsp.jsp page. Figure 15.3 shows the AddJsp.jsp page, as it appears after the user clicks the Add button:

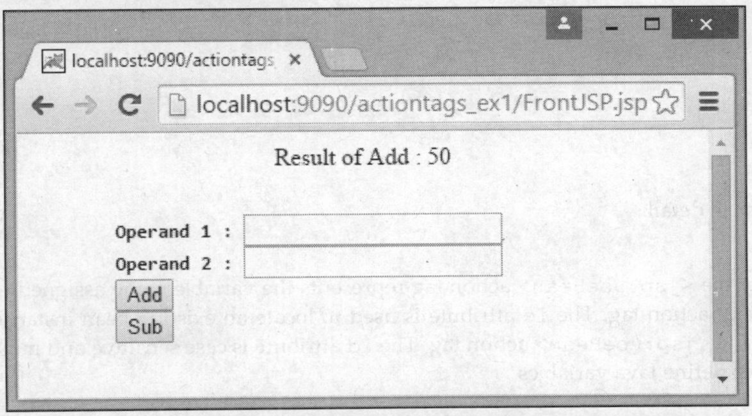

Figure 15.3: Displaying Result.jsp forwarded from AddJsp.jsp

Similarly, if the user clicks the Sub button on the Home.html page after entering 50 and 30 as the values of Operand 1 and Operand 2, the control is transferred to the SubJsp.jsp page. Figure 15.4 shows the result of clicking the **Sub** button:

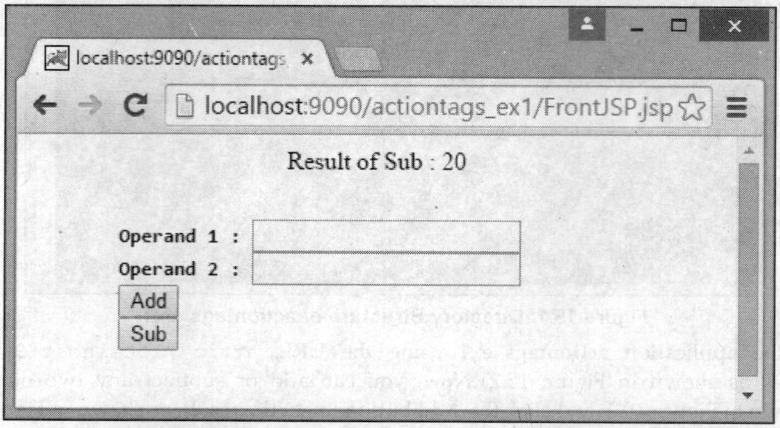

Figure 15.4: Displaying Result.jsp forwarded from SubJsp.jsp

Describing the <useBean> Tag

To separate logic from presentation, it is often a good idea to encapsulate logic in a Java object (a JavaBean), and then instantiate and use this object within a JSP page. The `<jsp:useBean>`, `<jsp:setProperty>`, and `<jsp:getProperty>` tags assist with this task.

The `<jsp:useBean>` action tag is used to instantiate a JavaBean, or to locate an existing bean instance, and assign it to a variable name (or id). We can also specify the lifetime of the object by giving it a specific scope, such as application scope. The `<jsp:useBean>` action tag ensures that the object is available, with the specified id, in the appropriate scope as specified by the tag. The object can then be referenced using its associated id from within the JSP page, or even from within other JSP pages, depending upon the scope of the JavaBean. The syntax of the `<jsp:useBean>` action tag is as follows:

```
<jsp useBean attributes>
<!-optional body content-->
</jsp:useBean>
```

Describing the Attributes of the <jsp:useBean> Tag

The attributes add extra characteristics to a tag, irrespective of its basic functionality. For example, the scope attribute of the `<jsp:useBean>` action tag makes a JavaBean instance available in different scopes. Some attributes specific to the `<jsp:useBean>` tag are:

- `id`
- `scope`
- `class`
- `beanName`
- `type`

Let's describe these in detail.

id

The `id` attribute of the `<jsp:useBean>` action tag represents the variable name assigned to the `id` attribute of the `<jsp:useBean>` action tag. The `id` attribute is used to locate an existing bean instance in the appropriate scope specified in the `<jsp:useBean>` action tag. The `id` attribute is case sensitive and must follow the naming conventions used to define Java variables.

scope

The scope attribute represents the scope in which the bean instance has to be located or created. Scopes can be page, request, session, and application. The default scope is page. All the scopes are defined as follows:

- **page scope**—Indicates that the bean can be used where the <jsp:useBean> action tag is used within the JSP page, until the page sends a response back to the client or forwards a request to another resource.
- **request scope**—Indicates that the bean can be used from any JSP page that is processing the same request, until a JSP page sends a response to the client.
- **session scope**—Indicates that the bean can be used from any JSP page invoked in the same session as the JSP page that created the bean. The bean exists throughout the entire session, and can be accessed by any page that shares the session. Note that the page in which you create the bean must have a page directive with session="true".
- **application Scope**—Indicates that the bean can be used from any JSP page in the same application as the JSP page that created the bean. The bean exists throughout an entire Web application, and can be accessed by any page in the application.

class

The class attribute takes the qualified class name to create a bean instance if the bean instance is not found in the given scope. The class name given in this attribute should have a no-argument constructor and should not be an abstract class. This is because the JSP container uses the new keyword and no-argument constructor to create a bean instance.

NOTE

This attribute doesn't allows expression, i.e. we need to enter the class name while coding the JSP page it cannot be dynamically given

beanName

The beanName attribute takes a qualified class name or an expression that resolves to a qualified class name or serialized template. The JSP container uses instantiate method of the java.beans.Beans class to instantiate the bean. The instantiate method of the java.beans.Beans class instantiates the given bean in the following approach:

First it checks whether the given name represents the serialized template, if found, then it reads the serialized template by using the class loader to instantiates the bean, the serialized form will be located in the file with a name packagename.classname.ser. If the given name does not represent a serialized template, then it creates an instance by using the no-argument constructor.

NOTE

In a <jsp:useBean> tag, you can either use the class or beanName attribute; both the class or beanName attributes cannot be used together in a <jsp:useBean> tag both refers to the same values.

type

The type attribute takes a qualified class or interface name, which can be the class name given in the class or beanName attribute or its super type. This attribute can be used with or without class or beanName. If this attribute is used with the class or beanName attribute, the bean located or created will be taken into the reference variable of the type as given under this attribute. The variable name will be as specified in the id attribute. If this attribute is used without the class or beanName attribute, the JSP container only tries to locate the Bean but does not instantiate the Bean. If the Bean is not found, the JSP container throws InstantiationException.

Using the <jsp:useBean> Tag Attributes

The <jsp:useBean> tag attributes can be used in different combinations, as shown in Listing 15.7:

Listing 15.7: Various ways of using <jsp:useBean> tag

```
<jsp:useBean id="mybean" class="com.santosh.jspex.MyBean" scope="session"/>
<jsp:useBean id="mybean" beanName="com.santosh.jspex.MyBean"/>
```

```
<jsp:useBean    id="mybean"    class="com.santosh.jspex.MyBean"    scope="session" type="com.santosh.jspex.MyBeanIntf"/>
<jsp:useBean    id="mybean"    beanName="com.santosh.jspex.MyBean"    scope="session" type="com.santosh.jspex.MyBeanIntf"/>
<jsp:useBean id="mybean" scope="session" type="com.santosh.jspex.MyBeanIntf"/>
```

If you use the `<jsp:useBean>` action tag in a JSP page, you must include the logic into the Java code generated for the JSP page. The generated logic performs the following operations:

- Declares an object reference variable with the given name (that is, the value of the id attribute) of the type specified in the class or `beanName` attribute. If the type attribute is already specified, the reference variable should be of the type specified in the type attribute.
- Determines whether or not the bean instance is available in the given scope with the given name. If the bean is found in the given scope, the reference of the bean instance is stored in the reference variable, as described in previous step.
- If the bean cannot be located in the given scope, the `<jsp:useBean>` action tag instantiates the class specified in the class or `beanName` attribute and then stores a reference of that class in the new reference variable. Thereafter, the `<jsp:useBean>` action tag executes its body content if it has body content.
- If the bean cannot be located in the given scope, the class or `beanName` attribute is not assigned to the class or bean reference, and only type attribute is used, an `InstantiationException` is thrown.

Generating Servlets with the <jsp:useBean> Tag

Let's try to evaluate how a Servlet is created after a JSP page using some combinations of the `<jsp:useBean>` tag is compiled. For simplicity, we take some combinations of the `<jsp:useBean>` tag specified in Listing 15.7. Suppose your JSP page contains the following `<jsp:useBean>` tag:

```
<jsp:useBean id="regDetails" class="com.santosh.jspex.UserDetails" scope="session"/>
```

Let's look at how this `<jsp:useBean>` tag is processed by the Web container. Listing 15.8 shows the Servlet code generated by the Tomcat Web container:

Listing 15.8: Generated Servlet Code

```
public void_jspService(
HttpServletRequest request,
HttpServletResponse response)
  throws java.io.IOException, ServletException {
  com.santosh.jspex.UserDetails regDetails = null;
      synchronized (session) {
      regDetails = (com.santosh.jspex.UserDetails)
      _jspx_page_context.getAttribute("regDetails",
      PageContext.SESSION_SCOPE);
      if (regDetails == null){
            regDetails = new com.santosh.jspex.UserDetails();
            _jspx_page_context.setAttribute("regDetails", regDetails,
            PageContext.SESSION_SCOPE);
  }//if
  }//synchronized
...
```

The implementation logic to create the Servlet may be different for other servers since most of the servers use built-in utility classes to perform these operations.

Let's look at another example next. Now suppose that your JSP page contains the following `<jsp:useBean>` action tag:

```
<jsp:useBean id="regDetails" type="com.santosh.jspex.UserDetails" scope="session"/
```

Notice that Listing 15.8 generates an exception if the specified instance type is not found. In our second example, the type attribute is specified with the `<jsp:useBean>` tag without using the class attribute. Listing 15.9 shows the Servlet code generated with the second example of the `<jsp:useBean>` tag:

Listing 15.9: Servlet Code Generated in Second Example

```
public void _jspService(
HttpServletRequest request,
HttpServletResponse response)
throws java.io.IOException, ServletException {
    …
    com.santosh.jspex.UserDetails regDetails = null;
    synchronized (session) {
         regDetails = (com.santosh.jspex.UserDetails)
         _jspx_page_context.getAttribute("regDetails",
         PageContext.SESSION_SCOPE);
         if (regDetails == null){
                throw new java.lang.InstantiationException(
                "bean regDetails not found within scope");
         }//if
    }//synchronized
    …
}
```

In Listing 15.8, if the specified class is not found, `UserDetails`, a new instance of the `UserDetails` class, is created and bound to the specified scope. In the Listing 15.9, the type attribute is specified and no class attribute has been provided, so if 'regDetails' does not exist in the "session" scope, then `InstantiationException` is thrown.

In this topic, we learned about using the `<jsp:useBean>` tag. Let's now learn about the `<jsp:setProperty>` tag next.

Describing the `<setProperty>` *Tag*

The `<jsp:setProperty>` action tag sets the value of a property in a bean, using the bean's setter methods. Before using the `<jsp:setProperty>` action tag; the bean must be instantiated. In addition, the `name` attribute of the bean must be the same as the reference variable name of the bean instance. The bean can be instantiated by using the `<jsp:useBean>` action tag as explained earlier. In this case, the attribute name of the `<jsp:setProperty>` action tag must be the same as the attribute `id` of `<jsp:useBean>`. Since both tags work together, these attributes are used to ensure coordination between them. The syntax of the `<jsp:setProperty>` tag is as follows:

```
<jsp:setProperty attributes/>
```

The `<jsp:setProperty>` tag contains various attributes, such as:

- name
- property
- value
- param

Let us now discuss these attributes in detail.

name

The `name` attribute takes the name of the already existing bean as a reference variable to invoke the setter method. This attribute must match with the value of the id attribute of `<jsp:useBean>` to set the properties of a bean. Consequently, the `<jsp:useBean>` tag must be declared before the `<jsp:setProperty>` tag in a JSP page.

property

The `property` attribute of the `<jsp:setProperty>` tag takes property name that has to be set, and specifies the `setter` method that has to be invoked. You can use this attribute in two different ways. The first way is to use '*' with the value of this attribute. Using '*' with the property attribute matches all the properties of a bean with the request parameter names. However, if you want to match any specific property of bean, you need to specify the value of the property attribute with the property name rather than using '*'. See the following syntax to use this attribute with '*' and with a specific property name:

```
// Syntax to use property attribute with '*'

<jsp:setProperty name=" name of reference variable " property="*" />

// Syntax to use property attribute with specific value

<jsp:setProperty name="name of reference variable" property="property name" />
```

Note that when you use '*' with the `property` attribute, the `value` and `param` attributes are not applicable with this tag. If you specify a specific property name for this attribute, the `value` and `param` attributes are applicable.

The values of the request parameters sent from the client to the server are always of type String. These values must be converted into the bean property types when stored in bean properties. If a property has a `PropertyEditor` class, as indicated in the JavaBeans specification, the `setAsText(String)` method is used to convert the value of the request parameter from String to a bean compatible data type. If the `setAsText(String)` method fails to convert the type, it throws an `IllegalArgumentException`.

value

The `value` attribute takes the value that has to be set to the specified bean property. This attribute accepts the value as the String type or as an expression that is evaluated at run time. If the value is not of the String type, the value is converted to a Bean compatible data type.

NOTE

This attribute should not be used if property="", because it refers to all properties and we cannot set all properties using one value.*

The syntax to use the `<jsp:setProperty>` tag with the value attribute is as follows:

```
    <jsp:setProperty name=" name of reference variable " property="property name" value= "
Property value as String "/>

                                    Or

    <jsp:setProperty name=" name of reference variable " property="property name" value= " <%=
Property value as expression %> "/>
```

param

When setting bean properties from request parameters, it is not necessary that the bean has the same property names as the request parameters. The `param` attribute is used to specify the name of the request parameter whose value we want to assign to a bean property. If the `param` value is not specified, it is assumed that the request parameter and the bean property have the same names.

NOTE

This attribute must also not to be used when property="", because it refers to all properties and we cannot set requested parameters for all properties using one value.*

The syntax to use the `param` property is as follows:

```
    <jsp:setProperty name="reference variable name" property="property name" param="request
parameter name"/>
```

Let us see some examples to use the syntax given with attributes of the `<jsp:setProperty>` action tag, as given here:

- To set all properties in the JavaBean while setting bean properties from the request object:

```
<jsp:setProperty name="abcbean" property="*"/>
```

- To set a specific property in the JavaBean while setting bean properties from the request object:

```
<jsp:setProperty name="abcbean" property="uname" param="uname"/>
```

- When setting a bean property to a value, you should specify the value attribute as either a String or an expression that is evaluated at runtime:

```
<jsp:setProperty name="abcbean" property="uname" value="<%=uname%>"/>
```

You learned about the `<jsp:setProperty>` action tag in this section. Let's now learn about the `<jsp:getProperty>` action tag next.

Describing the <getProperty> Tag

The `<jsp:getProperty>` action tag gets the value of a property in a bean by using the bean's `getter` methods and writes the value to the current `JspWriter`. The syntax to use the `<jsp:getProperty>` action tag is as follows:

```
<jsp:getProperty attributes/>
```

The `<jsp:getProperty>` action tag takes two attributes, name and property, which are described next.

The name Attribute

The `name` attribute takes the reference variable name on which you want to invoke the getter method. If a bean is instantiated by using the `<jsp:useBean>` action tag, the value assigned to the name attribute should match with the `id` attribute value of the `<jsp:useBean>` action tag. In this case, the `<jsp:useBean>` action tag must appear before the `<jsp:setProperty>` tag in the JSP page.

The property Attribute

The property attribute of the `<jsp:getProperty>` tag gets the value of a bean property and invokes the getter method of the bean property. This attribute takes the name of the property as an argument. For example, if the `getUname` method needs to be called, the property attribute takes `uname`, as shown in the following snippet:

```
<jsp:getProperty name="mybean" property="uname"/>
```

In the above code snippet, the `<jsp:getProperty>` tag gets the value of the `uname` property, by using the `mybean` instance, and includes this value into the output.

NOTE

`<jsp:getProperty>` is not designed to access Enterprise JavaBeans and indexed properties.

Plugin

The `<jsp:plugin>` action tag provides easy support for including a Java applet or bean in the client Web browser, using a built-in or downloaded Java plug-in. In the request handling stage of the JSP life cycle, the `<jsp:plugin>` action tag is replaced by either the `<object>` or the `<embed>` tag, depending on the browser version. In general, the attributes of the `<jsp:plugin>` action tag perform the following operations:

- Specify whether the component added in the `<object>` tag is a bean or an applet
- Locate the code that needs to be run
- Position the object in the browser window
- Specify a URL from which to download the plug-in software
- Pass parameter names and values to the object

The following syntax shows the use of the JSP `plugin` action tag in a JSP page:

```
<jsp:plugin attributes>
<!-optionally one jsp:params and or one jsp:fallback tag can be used -->
</jsp:plugin>
```

The `plugin` tag takes some predefined attributes, which are:

- **`type`** – Specifies the type of object that needs to be presented to the browser. The object can be an applet or a JavaBean.
- **`code`** – Takes the qualified class name of the object that has to be presented.

- **codebase**—Takes the base URL where the specified class can be located. This attribute is optional.
- **name**—Specifies the name of the instance of the bean or applet, which helps the applets or beans called by the same JSP page to communicate with each other.
- **archive**—Specifies a comma-separated list of pathnames, which locate archive files that are preloaded with a class loader located in the directory named 'codebase'. The archive files are loaded securely, often over a network, and typically improve the applet's performance. This attribute is similar to the archive attribute of the HTML applet tag.
- **width**—Specifies the initial width, in pixels, of the image the applet or bean displays.
- **height**—Specifies the initial height, in pixels, of the image the applet or bean displays.
- **align**—Specifies the position of the applet. The values that the align attribute can take are bottom, top, middle, left, and right. The default value is bottom.
- **hspace**—Specifies the amount of space, in pixels, to the left and right of the applet or bean displayed by the browser. The value must be a nonzero number.
- **vspace**—Specifies the amount of space, in pixels, to the bottom and top of the applet or bean. The value must be a nonzero number.
- **jreversion**—Specifies the version of the Java Runtime Environment (JRE) that the corresponding applet or bean requires. The default value is 1.2.
- **nspluginurl**—Specifies the URL where the client can download the JRE plug-in for Netscape Navigator. The value of this attribute is the full URL specifying a protocol name, port number (this is optional), and domain name.
- **iepluginurl**—Specifies the URL where the client can download the JRE plug-in for Internet Explorer. The value of this attribute is the full URL specifying a protocol name, port number (optional), and domain name.

Params

The `<jsp:params>` action tag sends the parameters that we want to pass to an applet or bean. The following snippet shows the syntax of using the `<jsp:params>` action tag in a JSP page:

Syntax:

```
<jsp:params>
<!- One or more jsp:param tags-->
</jsp:params>
```

To specify more than one parameter value, we can use more than one `<jsp:param>` action tag within a `<jsp:params>` tag.

Fallback

The `<jsp:fallback>` action tag allows us to specify a text message to be displayed if the required plug-in cannot run. This action tag must be used as a child tag with the `<jsp:plugin>` action tag. If the plug-in runs but the applet or bean does not, the plug-in usually displays a popup window explaining the error to the user. The following syntax shows the use of the `<jsp:fallback>` action tag in a JSP page:

```
<jsp fallback>
Text message that has to be displayed if the plugin cannot be started
</jsp:fallback>
```

Attribute

The `<jsp attribute>` action tag can be used to specify the value of a standard or custom action attribute. For example, we can use the `<jsp:attribute>` tag to set the attributes of the `<jsp:setProperty>` attribute, as shown in the following code snippet:

```
<jsp:setProperty name="mybean">
   <jsp:attribute name="property">uname</jsp:attribute>
   <jsp:attribute name="value">
         <jsp:expression>uname</jsp:expression>
```

```
        </jsp:attribute>
    </jsp:setProperty>
```

The <jsp:attribute> tag accepts the name and trim attributes; where name specifies the attribute name that we want to set, as shown in the preceding sample code; and trim takes true or false, indicating whether or not the whitespace appearing at the beginning and at the end of <jsp:attribute> tag should be discarded. By default, the leading and trailing whitespaces are discarded; consequently, the default value of the trim attribute is true.

NOTE

The JSP container performs this operation at transaction time and not at request handling phase. For example, if we use an expression tag in the body part of this action tag, and the expression tag produces a value with leading and trialing whitespaces, then these whitespaces are not discarded by the JSP container. In the preceding code snippet, if the uname variable contains leading and trailing whitespaces then container does not eliminate the whitespaces.

If the body of the <jsp:attribute> tag is empty, you can specify its value by " ".

Body

The <jsp:body> action tag can be used to specify the content (or the body) of a standard or custom action tag. Generally, the body of a standard or custom action invocation is implicitly defined as the body of that tag. However, if one or more <jsp:attribute> tags appear in the body of the tag, the body of a standard or custom action can be defined explicitly by using the <jsp:body> tag. The <jsp:body> tag is required if the standard action or custom tag has multiple <jsp:attribute> tags.

You can use the <jsp:body> tag to specify the content for the body of JSP actions tags, except for some action tags such as <jsp:body>, <jsp:attribute>, <jsp:scriptlet>, <jsp:expression>, and <jsp:declaration>.

If one or more <jsp:attribute> tags appear in the body of a tag invocation but no or empty <jsp:body> tag appears, it is equivalent of the tag having an empty body. The following code snippet shows the usage of the <jsp:body> tag:

```
<jsp:useBean id="mybean">
    <jsp:attribute name="class" trim="true">
          com.santosh.jspex.MyBean
    </jsp:attribute>
    <jsp:attribute name="scope">session</jsp:attribute>
    <jsp:body>
          <jsp:setProperty name="mybean" property="*"/>
    </jsp:body>
</jsp:useBean>
```

Element

The <jsp:element> action tag is used to dynamically define the value of the tag of an XML element. This action tag allows you to create an XML tag with a given name. The content of the <jsp:element> tag is a template for the attributes and child nodes of the XML tag you want to create. This action tag can be used in JSP pages and tag files. The following code snippet shows the syntax of the element tag:

```
<jsp:element name="name">
  jsp:attribute*
  jsp:body?
</jsp:element>
```

The name attribute of the element tag specifies the name of the XML element it has to create. You can also give an expression as the name of the XML element. The <jsp:element> tag can be an empty tag or can contain one <jsp:body> or multiple <jsp:attribute> attributes; with or without the <jsp:body> tag. The code snippet below shows how to use the name attribute with the element action tag:

```
<jsp:element name="mytag"/>
```

The <jsp:element> shown in the above code snippet creates an empty tag with the name, mytag.

The following code snippet shows another example of using the <jsp:element> tag with the <jsp attribute> tag:

```
<jsp:element name="mytag">
  <jsp:attribute name="myatt">Myval</jsp:attribute>
</jsp:element>
```

The <jsp:element> tag shown in the above code snippet, creates an empty element, named mytag, with an attribute myatt="Myval".

The following code snippet shows the use of <jsp:tag> to create an tag with attribute and body content:

```
<jsp:tag name="mytag">
  <jsp:attribute name="myatt">Myval</jsp:attribute>
  <jsp:body>Hello</jsp:body>
</jsp:tag>
```

The preceding snippet creates the tag named mytag with an attribute myatt="Myval" and body text content as Hello.

Text

A <jsp:text> tag is used to enclose the template data in an XML tag. The text tag can be used in a JSP page or Tag file. The content of a <jsp:text> tag is passed to the out implicit object. A <jsp:text> tag has no attributes and can appear at any place where template data appears. The syntax to use the Text tag is:

```
<jsp:text> template data </jsp:text>
```

Note that the template data can also contain expressions.

In this section, you learned about the new JSP standard action tags introduced in JSP 2.0. Let's now learn how to declare a bean in JSP.

Declaring a Bean in a JSP

Before declaring a Bean in a JSP, you must create a Bean. Let's look at an example to create a Bean. In this example, we create a Bean called RegForm, which is used to set and get the attributes (such as user name and email address) of a user. You can find the code file of **useBeanEx** application online in the code/chapter 15/ useBeanEx folder.

Follow these broad-level steps to declare a bean in a JSP:

1. Create a Bean
2. Declare the Bean in a JSP by using the <jsp:useBean> tag
3. Access the Bean properties
4. Generate Dynamic Content
5. Deploy and run the application

Creating a Bean

We start by creating a Bean called RegForm. Listing 15.10 shows how to create the RegForm Bean:

Listing 15.10: Creating the RegForm.java File

```
package com.santosh.jspex;
public class RegForm implements java.io.Serializable {

  private String uname, pass, repass, email, fn, ln, address;

  public void setUserName(String s){uname=s;}
  public void setPassword(String s){pass=s;}
  public void setRePassword(String s){repass=s;}
  public void setEmail(String s){email=s;}
  public void setFirstName(String s){fn=s;}
  public void setLastName(String s){ln=s;}
  public void setAddress(String s){address=s;}
```

```
    public String getUserName(){return uname;}
    public String getPassword(){return pass;}
    public String getRePassword(){return repass;}
    public String getEmail(){return email;}
    public String getFirstName(){return fn;}
    public String getLastName(){return ln;}
    public String getAddress(){return address;}
}//class
```

Declaring the Bean in a JSP

After creating the Bean, you can declare it in a JSP page by using the <jsp:useBean> tag. To declare the Bean in a JSP, you have to create a JSP page. In Listing 15.11, we have created a JSP page with the name RegProcess, in which we declare the bean created in Listing 15.10.

Listing 15.11: Creating the RegProcess.jsp File

```
<%@page errorPage="Registration.html"%>
<html>
<body>
<jsp:useBean id="regform" class="com.santosh.jspex.RegForm" scope="session"/> <%-- This is
the Jsp action tag used to declare bean --%>
<jsp:setProperty name="regform" property="*"/>
<form action="RegProcessFinal.jsp"><pre> <b>
First Name  : <input type="text" name="first_name"/>
Last Name   : <input type="text" name="last_name"/>
Address     : <input type="text" name="address"/>

            <input type="submit" value="Register"/>
</b></pre></form>
</body>
</html>
```

The <jsp:useBean> action tag creates an instance of a bean class according to the attributes specified in the JSP page. The attributes of the <jsp:useBean> tag used here are:

- id—Specifies the name of the bean that you want to declare
- class—Specifies name of the Bean class, which helps the JSP container in searching the Bean class and creating its instance.
- scope—Specifies the scope of the bean

All these attributes help JSP container to create an instance of the Bean class. The <jsp:useBean> action tag has some more attributes along with the attributes used in. You can also specify these attributes to make the Bean more specific.

Accessing the Bean Properties

You can verify the bean properties by using the <jsp:getProperty> action tag. The <jsp:getProperty> action tag uses the name and property tags to read the Bean properties. We have created the ViewRegistrationDetails.jsp page in this application to demonstrate how the <jsp:getProperty> action tag is used to read the Bean property, as shown in Listing 15.12:

Listing 15.12: Creating the ViewRegistrationDetails.jsp File

```
<jsp:useBean id="regform" type="com.santosh.jspex.RegForm" scope="session"/>
<%@page errorPage="Registration.html"%>
<html>
<body>
<pre>

<b>User Name   :</b> <jsp:getProperty name="regform" property="userName"/>

<b>Password    :</b> <jsp:getProperty name="regform" property="password"/>
```

```
<b>Email ID    :</b> <jsp:getProperty name="regform" property="email"/>

<b>First Name  :</b> <jsp:getProperty name="regform" property="firstName"/>

<b>Last Name   :</b> <jsp:getProperty name="regform" property="lastName"/>

<b>Address     :</b> <jsp:getProperty name="regform" property="address"/>

</pre>
<form   method=post   action="javascript:alert('The   remaining   process   is   under
development');">
<input type="submit" value="Register"/>
</form>
</body>
</html>
```

Before reading the Bean properties, the JSP container needs to locate the instance of the Bean class created by you. After the JSP container locates the instance of the Bean class, it starts reading the Bean properties by using the `<jsp:getProperty>` tag. In Listing 15.12, you can see the attributes used with the `<jsp:getProperty>` tag. The name attribute specifies the name of the Bean class to the JSP container and the property attribute specifies the Bean properties that have to be read.

Generating Dynamic Content within a JSP

The next step is to create an HTML page, named Registration.html, to retrieve the required data from users. The Registration.html page contains a button called Register. When a user clicks the Register button after providing all user details, he/she is directed to the RegProcess.jsp page to set the properties of 'RegForm' JavaBean, based on the details entered by the user. In other words, we use the Registration.html page to generate dynamic content in the RegProcess.jsp page. Listing 15.13 shows how to create the Registration.html page:

Listing 15.13: Creating the Registration.html File

```
<html>
<body>
<pre>
<form action="RegProcess.jsp"><pre><b>
UserName   : <input type="text" name="userName"/>
Password   : <input type="password" name="password"/>
RePassword : <input type="password" name="rePassword"/>
EMail ID   : <input type="text" name="email"/>

           <input type="submit" value="Register"/>
</b></pre></form>
</pre>
</body>
</html>
```

In the Registration.html page, the param names such as `userName`, `password`, and `rePassword` are the same as the property names in the RegForm bean. However, the other param names, such as `first_name` and `last_name`, are different from the property names such as `firstName` and `lastName`. Therefore, the RegProcess JSP page is created to set these properties in the RegForm bean.

Using this page, you can declare a bean in JSP. The RegProcessFinal JSP page also collects some more information about the user in the RegForm JavaBean in addition to what we have collected by using the Registration.html page. Here also, a Register button is provided. When you click on that button after entering all user information, you are directed to the RegProcessFinal.jsp page, as shown in Listing 15.14:

Listing 15.14: Creating the RegProcessFinal.jsp File

```
<%@page errorPage="Registration.html"%>

<jsp:useBean    id="regform"
```

```
type="com.santosh.jspex.RegForm" scope="session"/>
<jsp:setProperty name="regform" property="firstName" param="first_name"/>
<jsp:setProperty name="regform" property="lastName" param="last_name"/>
<jsp:setProperty name="regform" property="address"/>

<html>
<body>

<pre>

Your registration details are valid,
<a  href="ViewRegistrationDetails.jsp">Click</a>  to  view  Registration  Details  and
  confirm.
</pre>

</body>

</html>
```

NOTE

Before using the `<jsp:setProperty>` or `<jsp:getProperty>` tag in a JSP page, you must declare a bean in that JSP page by using the `<jsp:useBean>` tag.

Since we are using JSPs, you do not need to provide any kind of mapping in the web.xml file. However, the code written in the web.xml file for this application is shown in Listing 15.15. You can also find this file online in the code/Chapter15/useBeanEx/WEB-INF folder.

Listing 15.15: Creating the web.xml File

```
<?xml version="1.0" encoding="UTF-8"?>
<web-app>

</web-app>
```

Deploying and Running Application

You must place the pages and other resources as per the correct directory structure of the application **useBeanEx**. Figure 15.5 shows the directory structure of this application:

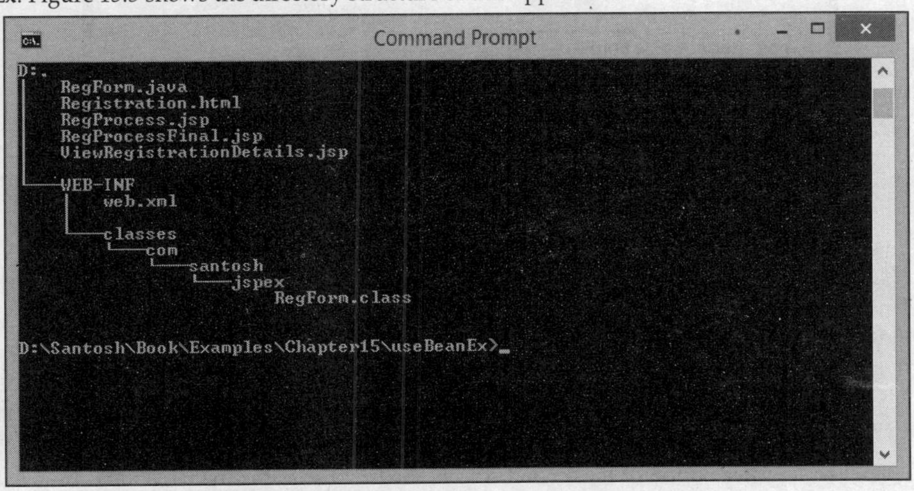

Figure 15.5: Directory Structure of useBeanEx Application

Copy the `userBeanEx` folder in the `<Tomcat home>/webapps` directory to deploy it on Tomcat server. Now, start your server, browse the application by using the URL `http://localhost:9090/userBeanEx/Registration.html` and enter the details as shown in Figure 15.6:

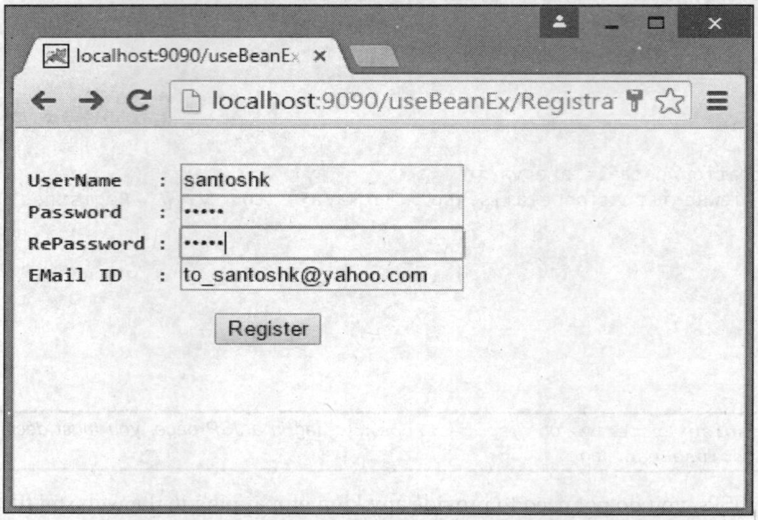

Figure 15.6: Registration Window

Click the Register button to continue with the registration process. In this example, we store the username, password, and email id into the RegBean by using the `<jsp:useBean>` and `<jsp:setProperty>` tags. We also set the RegBean instance in the session scope. After you enter the details and click the Register button in the first screen as shown in Figure 15.6, the next screen displays the information of the user as shown in Figure 15.7:

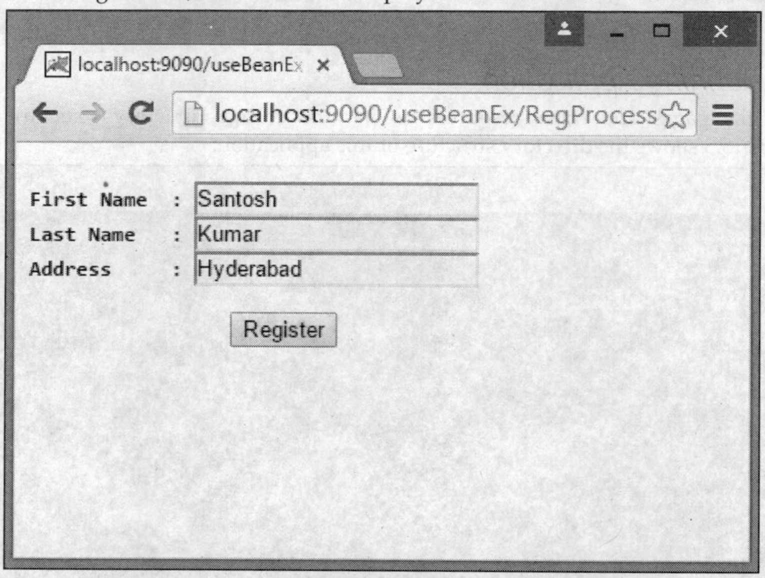

Figure 15.7: Registration Process Window

When you click the Register button of the second screen, the first name, last name, and address values are also stored into the RegBean. The next screen confirms the validity of the registration details, as shown in Figure 15.8:

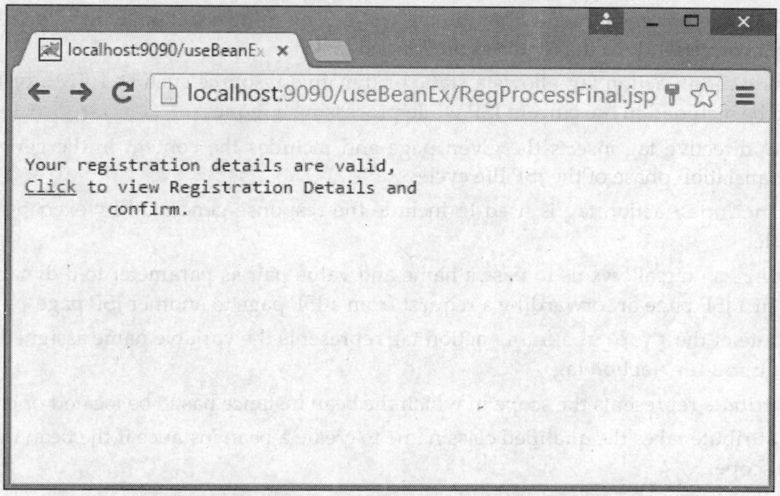

Figure 15.8: Registration Final Process Window

Clicking the hyperlink shown in Figure 15.8 displays all the details entered in the first and second screens, as shown in Figure 15.9:

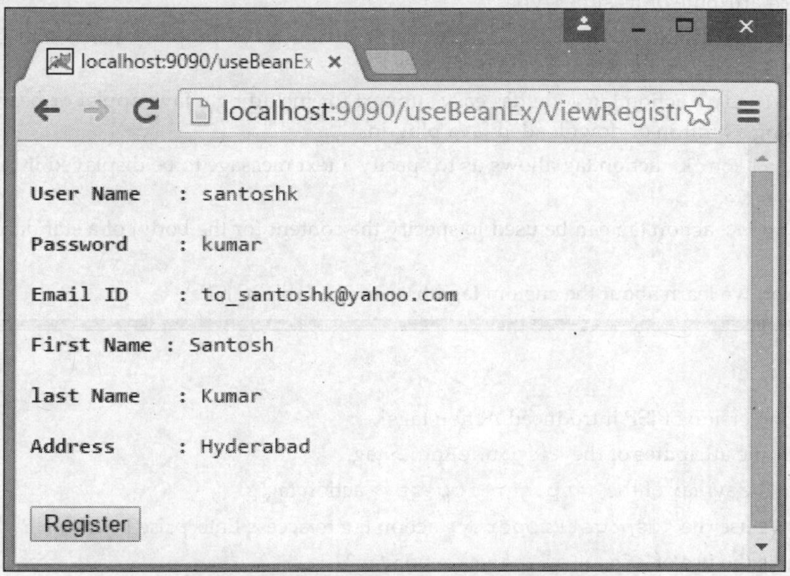

Figure 15.9: Registration Detail Window

This screen confirms that the RegBean has been successfully created and set.

Let's now summarize what we learned in this chapter.

Summary

This chapter describes the JSP action tags and bean components available in a JSP page. In this chapter, action tags such as `<jsp:useBean>`, `<jsp:setProperty>`, `<jsp:getProperty>`, and `<jsp:text>` have been discussed along with the syntax to use them. Then, we created an application that helps in creating, declaring, and reading the properties of a bean. We also deployed and executed the application to see its output. Let's recall the following important points to summarize the chapter:

- JavaBeans are reusable software components that separate the business logic from the presentation logic.

- When the JSP container encounters an action tag while converting a JSP page into a servlet, it generates the Java code that corresponds to the required predefined task.
- The `<jsp:include>` action tag allows a static or dynamic resource such as HTML or JSP page, specified by a URL, to be included in the current JSP while processing a request.
- The 'include' directive tag inserts the given page and includes the content in the generated Servlet page during the translation phase of the JSP life cycle.
- The `<jsp:include>` action tag is used to include the response generated by executing the specified JSP page or Servlet.
- The `<jsp:param>` tag allows us to pass a name and value pair as parameter to a dynamic resource, while including it in a JSP page or forwarding a request from a JSP page to another JSP page.
- The id attribute of the `<jsp:useBean>` action tag represents the variable name assigned to the `id` attribute of the `<jsp:useBean>` action tag.
- The scope attribute represents the scope in which the bean instance has to be located or created.
- The `class` attribute takes the qualified class name to create a bean instance if the bean instance is not found in the given scope.
- The `beanName` attribute takes a qualified class name or an expression that resolves to a qualified class name or serialized template.
- The `type` attribute takes a qualified class or interface name, which can be the class name given in the class or `beanName` attribute or its super type.
- The `property` attribute of the `<jsp:setProperty>` tag takes property name that has to be set, and specifies the `setter` method that has to be invoked.
- The `<jsp:plugin>` action tag provides easy support for including a Java applet or bean in the client Web browser, using a built-in or downloaded Java plug-in.
- The `<jsp:fallback>` action tag allows us to specify a text message to be displayed if the required plug-in cannot run.
- The `<jsp:body>` action tag can be used to specify the content (or the body) of a standard or custom action tag.

In the next chapter, we learn about the custom tag libraries available in JSP.

Exercise

Q. 15.1 Which version of JSP introduced Action tags?

Q. 15.2 Name the attributes of the `<jsp:useBean>` tag.

Q. 15.3 Write the syntax of the `<jsp:getProperty>` action tag.

Q. 15.4 Can we use the `<jsp:getProperty>` action tag to access Enterprise JavaBeans?

Q. 15.5 What is the use of `<jsp:fallback>` action tag?

16

Enhancing the JSP Tags Support

In this chapter, you learn all about the use of the JSP custom tags. After reading this chapter, the user will be able to identify when the custom tags are required to build and how to build different types of custom tags. The JSP syntaxes along with the programming logic increase the amount of Java code in the pages. So the developers use different tag interfaces to increase the performance and productivity of their Web applications. The JSP custom tags are an extension to the JSP languages. The tags are available in different tag libraries which are used within a JSP page. The custom actions are generally referred as the custom tags. All the JSP tags available in the context of a JSP document are available in a library named as JSP tag library. So a JSP tag library is a container for all the tags. From the JSP tag libraries, the tags are available in the JSP page. Along with the custom tags, the tag libraries also provide the feature of using the JSP implicit objects in the JSP pages. The tag libraries are portable between the JSP pages and also within the JSP containers. This enables the JSP code to be used in all the JSP containers. The use of the JSP tag libraries reduces the use of the JSP scripting elements in a page. So the programmers can use Java codes within the JSP pages in order to access the tags. The use of Java codes within a JSP page creates certain shortcomings, which are as follows:

- Accessing the system configuration by using the Java codes provides the mixing of business logic along with the JSP elements. This reduces the potential of the JSP presentation layer.
- Mixing of the Java codes along with the JSP elements are difficult to maintain and also to debug.

The use of the tag libraries along with the JSP elements provides support for all the Java specific codes in a JSP page. So the page will be application specific and also easier to use. This also reduces the use of the JSP scripting elements in the JSP pages. The different types of tags available in the JSP tag libraries are described later in this chapter.

Custom Tags

A custom tag is a user-defined JSP language element. If a JSP page which contains a custom tag is translated into a servlet, then the custom tag is converted to operations on a tag handler. When the JSP page's servlet is executed, the web container invokes those operations.

JSP specification includes a Tag library under the section, Tag Extensions, which provides an ability to develop custom tags to build new and reusable presentation components. The custom tags are user defined sets of the JSP element present in the JSP tag libraries. The custom tags used in the JSP page are translated into a servlet. The tag is also converted to operations on an object named as the tag handler. The tag handler is responsible for the execution of the servlet generated by the translation of the custom tags. The custom tags used in the JSP pages provide the following features in the context of the JSP page.

- The tags are customized to pass the attributes from the current page to the calling page within an application.
- These are able to access all the objects available in a JSP page.
- These are used to modify the response generated by calling the attributes from the main page.
- The custom tags can communicate with each other. The user will be able to initialize a Java bean component and a variable which refers to the bean. This variable can be used in other tags in order to access the bean components in another tag.
- The custom tags can be nested within each other to provide complexity in a JSP page.

Along with the above mentioned features, the tags are also used to perform the following set of tasks within the scope of a JSP page:

- Create new objects that can be referenced and used as scripting variables in a JSP page, such as `<jsp useBean>` tag.
- Iterate over body content of the tags until a certain condition is satisfied.

Need of Custom Tags

So far, you learned about the various standard tags given under the JSP specification that can be used to build JSP pages. All these standard JSP tags are by default understood by all JSP containers. While translating the document, JSP containers know what to write in place of the tag used in the document. However, these tags are not enough to build the view or it may be difficult to build the view using these limited standard tags because the JSP standard tags cannot meet all the requirements for all the views. In such cases, we may require to use the scripting tags and write some Java code to meet the requirements. The problem with using scripting tags in JSP page is that the page developer has to write the Java code inside tags. The preceding problem has motivated to include the custom tags features into JSP specification, which does not require writing Java code inside tags. The basic use of JSP custom tags is described here in detail.

- **Reusability**—Code reusability is one of the most important features in all the programming languages. This prevents the repetition of the same code in a JSP document. The tag libraries provide the support of using custom tags to reuse the codes in a JSP page. The user can use any number of custom tags in a single or many JSP pages throughout the scope of the application.
- **Readability**—The use of the custom tags enhances the readability of the used codes in a JSP page. The readability increases by encapsulating the use of the Java codes in a JSP page. So the encapsulation of the Java codes by replacing these codes makes the page clean, short, and more readable.
- **Maintainability**—This feature enables the user to reduce the duplicity of codes present in a JSP page. The use of the custom tags in a JSP page reduces the use of the same code in a JSP page. Any changes made to the custom tags in an application appear throughout the scope of the application.

Elements of Custom Tags

The custom tags are used in a JSP page in order to increase its performance and productivity. The tags generally refer to the custom actions by the users. The tags are being used in the pages by using certain elements. The Tag Library Descriptor (TLD) and the Tag Handlers are the basic elements of custom tags. Both the elements along with their use in a page are described here in detail.

Tag Library Descriptor

A tag library is a collection of events that encapsulate some functionality to be used from within a JSP page. The tag library definitions are described to the JSP container using a Tag Library Descriptor (TLD) document, where Tag Library Descriptor is an XML document. The tag library directive includes the description of the tag library on the whole and of individual tags in the library also. TLD document describes about the version information, tag library validator class that is used to validate the tag library, individual tag description, where each of the tag description includes a name, its tag handler class, optionally tag extra info class, and the attributes description. Each attribute description includes a name and indication about whether the attribute is mandatory and whether it accepts a runtime expression.

A tag library is made available to a JSP page through a `taglib` directive that identifies the tag library through a URI (Universal Resource Identifier). The URI identifying a tag library may be any valid URI as long as it can be used to uniquely identify the semantics of the tag library. The user needs to specify the TLD within a JSP page. The following syntax is used to specify a TLD in a JSP page:

```
<%@ taglib prefix="p" uri="example.tld" %>
```

The preceding syntax is to be included into JSP page to load the required TLD for the particular page. After loading of the tag library, the user will be able to access the tags by using the given prefix. The preceding snippet shows that the custom tags are located in the example.tld with the prefix 'p'. The tags from the tag library can be accessed by using the prefix 'p' in the JSP page. The user has to specify the location of the TLD in order to use it in the preceding application.

Location of TLD

The location of the TLD is to be specified in order to be accessed by the application. The tags from the specified directory are to be used by the application. The user can specify the TLD file within the directory structure of the application. The position of the TLD can be specified in two ways. In the first case, the TLD file can be positioned into the directory of a Web application. The following syntax shows the placing of the TLD file within the directory structure of the Web application:

```
<docroot>/exampleLib.tld
<docroot>/myLibs/exampleLib.tld
<docroot>/WEB-INF/exampleLib.tld
<docroot>/WEB-INF/myLibs/exampleLib.tld
```

The placing of a TLD in a directory instead of a JAR file increases the testing cycles of the application. The testing cycle includes the designing of new tags, addition of new tag handler classes, and modification of the TLD files. Secondly, the TLD files can be placed in the subdirectory of the WAR file or in the /META-INF/ directory or the subdirectory packaged in JAR file. A TLD must be started with a `taglib` element, which is used to specify the schema and the version of JSP used by the application. The following snippet shows the specification of a TLD file showing the schema and the JSP version used in an application:

```
<taglib xmlns="http://java.sun.com/xml/ns/j2ee"
xmlns:xsi="http://www.w3.org/2001/XMLSchema-instance"
xsi:schemaLocation="http://java.sun.com/xml/ns/j2ee/web-jsptaglibrary_2_0.xsd"
version="2.0">
```

The preceding snippet shows that the XML schema is used in the Web application. XML schema is used to develop the application. It also shows that the application uses the JSP 2.0 to design the web pages for the application.

Elements of a TLD

The TLD file used in a JSP page contains certain elements for building the TLD for a particular Web application. The elements of the TLD file are as follows:

- **description**—This is an optional element associated with the TLD file. This specifies the description for a particular tag used in the application.
- **display-name**—This element is also an optional element. This is used to specify the name that is to be used by the application.
- **icon**—This is also an optional element. This is used by the tools.
- **name**—The tag name is a unique element associated with the tag. The tag name specifies the name of the tag present in the TLD.
- **path**—This is a unique element associated with the tag used in the Web application. The path specifies the path of the TLD used in the Web application. It specifies whether the TLD is present in the directory of the Web application or in the subdirectory of the WAR file or in the/META-INF/ directory or the sub directory packaged in JAR file.
- **example**—This is an optional attribute and is used to show the use of the TLD in an application.
- **tag-extension**—This is an optional element used in the TLD. This provides extra information about the tags available in the tag library.
- **uri**—This is used to uniquely identify the tag library associated in the Web application.
- **tlib-version**—This element is used to specify the version of the tag library used in the application.
- **validator**—This is an optional element associated with the TLD file. It is used to define the tag library validator which is used to validate the JSP page.
- **listener**—A tag library can specify some classes which are used as event listeners for the JSP pages. These listeners are used as the listener elements in a TLD file.

Tag Handler

Tag handler is a Java class that implements one of the subtypes of `JspTag` interface, which defines the run time behavior of the custom tag. The various tag handler interfaces that are included under the JSP specifications are `Tag`, `BodyTag`, `IterationTag`, and `SimpleTag`. The handler object is responsible for the interaction between the JSP page and additional server-side objects.

Tag Handler Life Cycle

The methods inherited from the tag interfaces are implemented by using the methods of the tag handler during the processing of a JSP page. The JSP engine invokes these methods to handle the tags. Figure 16.1 describes the workflow of tag handler, which are explained later.

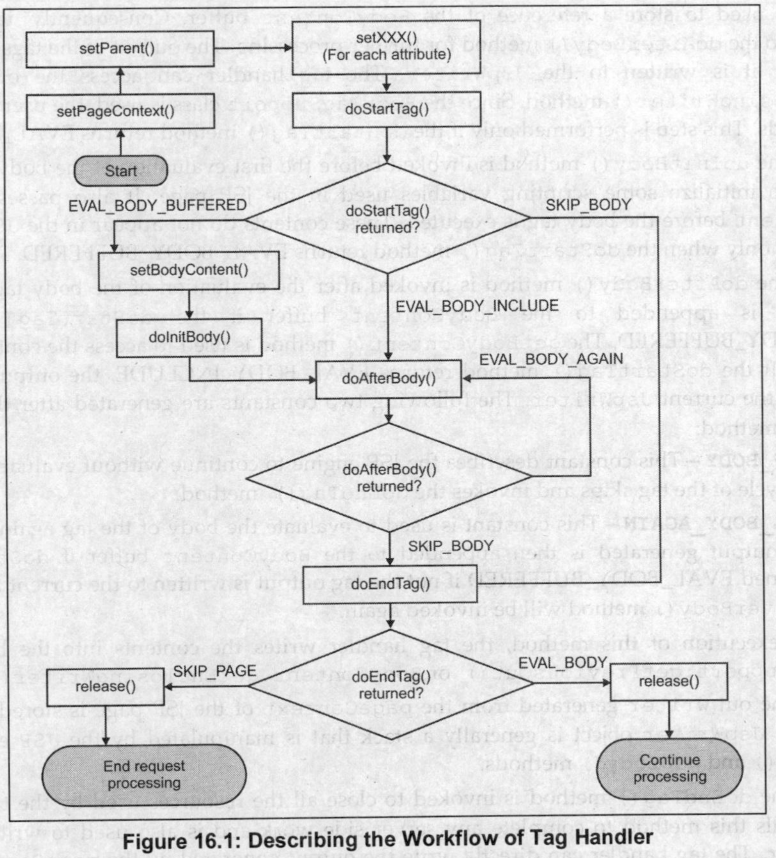

Figure 16.1: Describing the Workflow of Tag Handler

The execution of these methods is called the lifecycle of a tag handler. The methods are executed in the following order:

- **Step 1** – When a JSP engine finds a new tag in the JSP page, it initializes a tag handler to handle the tag. The `javax.servlet.jsp.tagext.Tag` interface is implemented to give access to the `setPageContext()` and `setParent()` methods. These methods are used to inject `PageContext` and parent tag handler in the JSP page.
- **Step 2** – The `setXXX()` methods are invoked to set the values for the attributes used in the tags.
- **Step 3** – The `doStartTag()` method is invoked to initialize the tag handler for the respective tags. This method returns the following constants to determine whether or not the tag body should be evaluated:
  - **`SKIP_BODY`** – This constant instructs the JSP engine to skip the body content of the tag. This value is returned in case of an empty tag. The body of the tag is skipped and the `doEndTag()` method is called to close the tag.
  - **`EVAL_BODY_INCLUDE`** – This constant instructs the JSP engine to evaluate the tag body and include the result into the current `JspWriter`. Then, the `doAfterBody()` method is called.
  - **`EVAL_BODY_BUFFERED`** – This constant describes the JSP engine to evaluate the body content of the tag and write the result to the buffer, the buffer is represented by the `BodyContent` object. The `BodyContent` object is injected into the tag using the `setBodyContent()` method. This constant is generally used if the tag body content needs to be processed by the tag handler; and then, if required, may be written to the output.
- **Step 4** – After the preceding step, the output from all the tags are converted to a `JspWriter`, named as `BodyContent`. The output from the tags is stored in the `BodyContent` buffer. The `setBodyContent()`

method is used to store a reference of the `BodyContent` buffer. Consequently, the stored content is available to the `doAfterBody()` method for further processing. The output of the tags is passed to the JSP page after it is written to the `JspWriter`. The tag handler can access the output by using the `getEnclosingWriter()` method. Since the `BodyTagSupport` class is used, the user need not implement the methods. This step is performed only if the `doStartTag()` method returns EVAL_BODY_BUFFERED.

- **Step 5**—The `doInitBody()` method is invoked before the first evaluation of the body tag. This method is invoked to initialize some scripting variables used in the JSP page. It also passes some content into `BodyContent` before the body tag is executed. These contents do not appear in the JSP page. This step is performed only when the `doStartTag()` method returns EVAL_BODY_BUFFERED.
- **Step 6**—The `doAfterBody()` method is invoked after the evaluation of the body tag. The output of the body tag is appended to the `BodyContent` buffer if the `doStartTag()` method returns EVAL_BODY_BUFFERED. The `getBodyContent()` method is used to access the content of the evaluated body tag. If the `doStartTag()` method returns EVAL_BODY_INCLUDE, the output of the body tag is written to the current `JspWriter`. The following two constants are generated after the evaluation of the preceding method:
  - **`SKIP_BODY`**—This constant describes the JSP engine to continue without evaluating the body. So the life-cycle of the tag skips and invokes the `doEndTag()` method.
  - **`EVAL_BODY_AGAIN`**—This constant is used to evaluate the body of the tag again after the execution. The output generated is then appended to the `BodyContent` buffer if `doStartTag()` method returned EVAL_BODY_BUFFERED if not the tag output is written to the current `JspWriter` and the `doAfterBody()` method will be invoked again.

  After the execution of this method, the tag handler writes the contents into the buffer by using the `BodyTagSupport.getPreviousOut()` or `BodyContent.getEnclosingWriter()` method.
- **Step 7**—The out `writer` generated from the `pageContext` of the JSP page is stored in the `JSPWriter` object. The `JspWriter` object is generally a stack that is manipulated by the JSP engine by using the `pushBody()` and `popBody()` methods.
- **Step 8**—The `doEndTag()` method is invoked to close all the resources used by the tag handler. The tag handler calls this method to complete any server side work and is also used to write the output to the `JspWriter`. The tag handler can directly write the output generated by the `pageContext.getOut()` to the `JspWriter`. The output can also be written to the enclosing `writer` by using the `popBody()` method in the pageContext. The following two constants are retrieved from the method to control the flow of evaluation:
  - **`EVAL_PAGE`**—This constant describes the JSP engine to continue the processing of the remaining JSP page.
  - **`SKIP_PAGE`**—This constant describes to force the JSP engine to skip the evaluation of the page.
- **Step 9**—At the end of the execution, the `release ()` method is invoked to de-reference all the instances made by the tag handler and also to perform garbage collection.

The Tag Extension API

The tag API is the collection of tags and interfaces for handling the tags appearing in a JSP page. So the tag interface works as a protocol between the tag handler and the implementation classes used in the JSP page. The tag extension API provides the `javax.servlet.jsp.tagext` interface to handle all the tags in a JSP page. The tag interfaces specify the methods for the `pageContext` and the parent properties for a tag in the JSP page. All the properties of the tags can be called before the calling of the `doStartTag()` and the `doEndTag()` methods provided by the tag interface. The tag interface provides the following two sub-interfaces:

- **IterationTag Interface**—This interface extends the tag interface and provides a method to support the iteration of the tags used in a JSP page. The `doAfterBody()` method provides the support of evaluating the iteration of the tags used in a JSP page.

- **BodyTag Interface**—The BodyTag Interface extends the IterationTag interface. This interface provides two methods to support the buffered output generated from the JSP page. The methods available in this interface are doInitBody() and the setBodyContent().

Along with these interfaces, the tag interface also supports some classes that are to be extended in a JSP page. The methods from the classes are used to handle the tags that appear in the context of a JSP page. These classes are described as follows:

- **TagSupport**—This class implements the IterationTag interface. This class can be used as a base class for all the simple or custom tags used in a JSP page.
- **BodyTagSupport**—This class implements the BodyTag interface and provides the implementation for all the method of the BodyTag interface. This class can be used as a base class for all the custom tags that are having body content.
- **BodyContent**—This class extends the JspWriter class and is used to write the output to the parent class. This class is only used in the BodyTag interface and in the BodyTagSupport class.

The tag interface is the base interface for all the custom tags used in the JSP page. These methods are used in the tag handler life-cycle and thus generate the respective output after the evaluation of the tags. The methods provided by the tag interface are given as follows:

- **setPageContext()**—This is the initial method that is to be called during the life-cycle of a tag. This is used to pass the implicit objects of the JSP page. The value of the method can be set during the implementation of the doEndTag() method in a JSP page. The method can be represented as follows:

```
public void setPageContext(PageContext);
```

- **setParent()** and **getParent ()**—These methods are invoked in case of nested tags. The outer tag is called as the parent tag whereas the enclosing tag is referred as the child tag. The JSP container calls the setParent() method on a child tag enclosed in a parent tag and the reference of the tag is to be sent to the parent tag. The getparent() method is called by the child tag. The JSP engine passes a reference of the parent tags to each child tag. These methods can be represented as follows:

```
public void setParent(Tag);
public Tag getParent();
```

- **doStartTag()**—The doStartTag() method is used to initialize the actual processing of the tag. This method is used to work after setting all the appropriate reference for the tag in the JSP page. This method can be represented as follows:

```
public int doStartTag() throws JspException;
```

  This method throws the JspException to handle any exception that has occurred during the execution of a tag. This method also decides whether the body of the tag is to be evaluated or not. The evaluation can be done by using the constants provided by the tag interfaces, such as EVAL_BODY_INCLUDE and SKIP_BODY. The EVAL_BODY_INCLUDE constant indicates that the body of the tag must be evaluated during the execution whereas the SKIP_BODY indicates that the evaluation can skip the processing of the body of the tag.

- **doEndTag()**—Depending upon the value of the doStartTag() method, the JSP container calls the doEndTag() method. The doEndTag() method can be represented as follows:

```
public int doEndTag() throws JspException;
```

  This method is called after the execution of the tags available in the JSP page. This method throws the JspException to handle any exception on the JSP page. The method decides whether the JSP engine will continue evaluating the JSP page or not. The tag interface provides two constants which determine the execution of the JSP page. The EVAL_PAGE constant indicates that the rest of the JSP page is to be evaluated after getting the output from the tags whereas the SKIP_PAGE constant is used to indicate that the execution of the rest of the JSP page will be skipped.

- **release()**—This method is called after the execution of all the tags in the JSP page. This method is called whenever the tag handler object is no longer required by the JSP engine. This method is called once after the completion of executing the tags. This method can be represented as follows:

```
Public void release()
```

The tag API is used by all the custom tags used in a JSP page and the respective output is sent as a response to the user. The response generated by the custom tags is stored in the `JspWriter`. Let's discuss the processing of all the tags described earlier by using the methods of the tag API.

Empty Tags

These types of tags can optionally have attributes and no body content, hence they are known as empty tags. The basic type of JSP custom classic tags (empty tags) are designed to perform some operations and insert some content into the response. For example, use this tag to implement a template-based insertion. Empty tags are even used to perform server-side work based on their attributes, and determine whether the rest of the page is processed or not, empty tags can even redirect the request to other page. For example, we can use Empty tags to check whether the user is logged in before accessing a page; if not, redirect them to a login page. In case of Empty tags, the tag handler class should implement `javax.servlet.jsp.tagext.Tag` interface or extend an adapter class, `javax.servlet.jsp.tagext.TagSupport`.

Empty Tag Handler Life Cycle

The tag handler objects of this type are recycled by container to avoid the performance overhead of tag handler objects creation. Web container manages the tag handler objects through a well-defined life-cycle. The life-cycle of an empty tag handler object is defined as follows:

- **Instantiation**—In this phase, a tag handler object is created using a no argument constructor.
- **Initialization**—In this phase, a successfully instantiated object is set with the required properties by invoking a setter method on the tag handler object. The following methods are invoked in a sequence:
  - `setPageContext()`
  - `setParent()`
  - `setXXX()` method for each of the attribute in this tag
- **Processing the Start tag**—The JSP Container uses an initialized tag handler object to perform this operation. In this phase, the `doStartTag ()` method of tag handler is invoked. The `doStartTag ()` method return type is `int` and for empty tags the only legal return value is SKIP_BODY. This method can possible throw a `JspException`.
- **Processing the Closing tag**—After the successful execution of the `doStartTag ()` without a `JspException` in this phase, `doEndTag ()` method is invoked. This method's return type is `int` and the possible values that it can return are SKIP_PAGE and EVAL_PAGE. If SKIP_PAGE is returned, then the rest of the JSP page will not be evaluated. If this method returns EVAL_PAGE, then the rest of the page continues to be evaluated.
- **Releasing the object**—In this phase, `release()` method on the tag handler is called. This process is performed when a tag handler object has finished its job and becomes available for garbage collection.

When JSP container encounters a custom tag in a JSP page, it performs the following operations:

- Finds whether this tag is used already in the JSP page. If the tag is used, then it uses the Tag Handler object created/located for the previous same tag in this JSP page. If the tag is appearing for the first time in this page, then the container tries to locate the Tag Handler object from tag pool. If the container cannot locate the object in the pool, then it performs tag handler instantiation, which is creating a new object.
- Initializes the tag handler object located or created in the first step. If the object is located from the same JSP page, then `setPageContext()` method is not invoked. If the object is located and being reused in the same parent, then the `setParent()` is also not invoked. If the object is located from pool or created newly, then complete initialization is performed.
- If the second step is performed successfully, then the container processes start tag, that is it invokes `doStartTag()` method.
- Processes the end tag, that is it invokes `doEndTag()`
- Invokes `release()` method

Using Empty Tags

The following application demonstrates the use of an empty tag within a JSP page. Listing 16.1 uses the custom tag libraries and the support for using custom tag libraries in the JSP pages. You can also find this file online in the folder code/Chapter16/customtagsex1

Listing 16.1: Creating the HelloTagHandler.java File

```
package com.santosh.jspex.customtags;
import javax.servlet.jsp.*;
import javax.servlet.jsp.tagext.*;
public class HelloTagHandler extends TagSupport {
/*The javax.servlet.jsp.tagext.TagSupport is a subtype of Tag interface*/
  public int doStartTag() {
        /*
All the statements that have to be executed when an opening tag of this custom tag
is found have to be written here.
        */
        try {
                JspWriter out=pageContext.getOut();
                /*
Here pageContext is a object reference variable of type
javax.servlet.jsp.PageContext in TagSupport
                */
                out.println("Hello from TagHandler");
        }//try
        catch(Exception e){}
        return SKIP_BODY;
   }//doStartTag
   public int doEndTag() {
        return EVAL_PAGE;
   }//doEndTag
}//class
```

The preceding file extends the `TagSupport` class to define the behavior for `getMessage` tag, which is an empty tag. Since the `getMessage` tag is an empty tag, the `SKIP_BODY` constant of the tag interface is used to skip the execution of the body of the tag. All the tag libraries must be declared in the .tld file. Listing 16.2 shows the declaration of the `getMessage` tag, which is defined in the MyTags.tld file. You can also find this file online in the folder code/Chapter16/customtagsex1/WEB-INF.

Listing 16.2: Creating the MyTags.tld File

```
<!DOCTYPE taglib
PUBLIC "-//Sun Microsystems, Inc.//DTD JSP Tag Library 1.2//EN"
"http://java.sun.com/dtd/web-jsptaglibrary_1_2.dtd">
<taglib>
   <tlib-version>1.1</tlib-version>
   <jsp-version>1.2</jsp-version>
   <short-name>exampletags</short-name>
   <info>Example Custom Tags</info>
   <uri>http://www.mysite.com/jspexamples/exampletags</uri>
   <tag>
         <name>getMessage</name>
         <tag-class>
                com.santosh.jspex.customtags.HelloTagHandler
         </tag-class>
         <body-content>empty</body-content>
   </tag>
</taglib>
```

The MyTags.tld file is declared in the `web.xml` file in order to access the tags in JSP documents. All the tags used by the application are present here. The `web.xml` file used in the application specifies the location and the URI of the tag library used in the preceding application. The following snippet shows the content of the `web.xml` file used in the preceding application. You can also find this file online in the folder code/Chapter16/customtagsex1/WEB-INF.

Listing 16.3: Creating the `web.xml` File

```
<?xml version="1.0"?>
<web-app>
<!--
To register a TLD with the context and associating a unique URI that can be further used to refer this TLD. This is an optional declaration, you can refer the TLD directly, I will explain you the other options of referring the TLD in JSP page after this example
 -->
<jsp-config>
  <taglib>
        <taglib-uri>mytags</taglib-uri>
        <taglib-location>/WEB-INF/MyTags.tld</taglib-location>
  </taglib>
</jsp-config>
</web-app>
```

The preceding file specifies that the tag library is present in the WEB-INF directory in the application. The JSP container searches for the file in the WEB-INF file and executes the tag according to the user's choice. Listing 16.4 shows the JSP page used in the Web application. Through this page, the JSP container initializes the empty tag used in the application. The tag library is to be imported to the JSP page before the starting of the execution. Listing 16.4 shows the TestPage.jsp used in the application. You can also find this file online in the folder code/Chapter16/customtagsex1

Listing 16.4: Creating the TestPage.jsp File

```
<%@ page language="java"  pageEncoding="ISO-8859-1"%>
<%
String path = request.getContextPath();
String        basePath        =        request.getScheme()+"://"+request.getServerName()+":"+request.getServerPort()+path+"/";
%>
<%@taglib uri="mytags" prefix="exampletags"%>
<html>
<body>
  <b>Response of getMessage tag : </b>
  <i><b> <exampletags:getMessage/>
  </b> </i>
</body>
</html>
```

The preceding JSP file imports the tag library defined in `web.xml` file. It also uses the `<getMessage>` tag in order to access the `HelloTagHandler` service. Figure 16.2 shows the directory structure of the Web application:

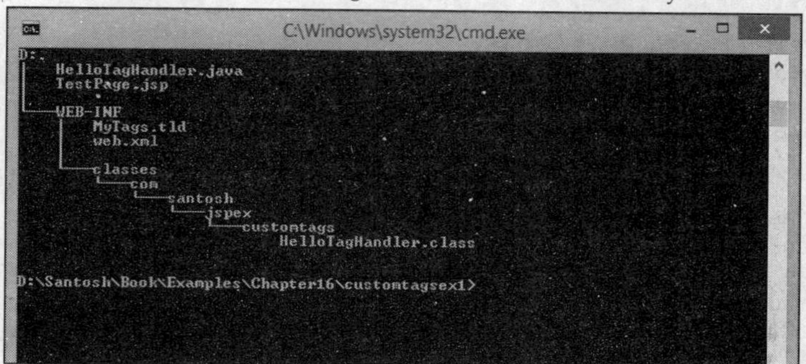

Figure 16.2: Directory structure for customtagsex1.

All the preceding mentioned files are to be present in the **customtagsex1** folder, as shown in the Figure 16.2. The work folder is then copied to the `<Tomcat home>/webapps` folder. Now, browse the application by opening the browser. Type the `http://localhost:9090/customtagsex1/TestPage.jsp` URL in the browser to access the page. This results in invoking the TestPage.jsp page where we have used `<exampletags:getMessage/>`. When the `<exampletags:getMessage/>` tag is encountered in the processing of JSP, then it will invoke the `doStartTag()` method of `HelloTagHandler` class, which displays the message "`Hello from TagHandler`". Figure 16.3 shows the output of the preceding application using the empty tags.

Figure 16.3: Output by using an Empty tag.

Figure 16.3 uses the empty tag in the application. The tag only accesses the message associated with it and the response from the tag is shown to the user. In this example, TestPage.jsp refers the TLD, MyTags.tld by the `URI` declared in `web.xml` file by using the `<taglib>` element. The other approaches to refer TLD file in TestPage.jsp document are as follows:

- Directly referring the TLD document with location path, for example, in TestPage.jsp, we can use the following `taglib` directive to make MyTags.tld available:

```
%@taglib uri="/WEB-INF/MyTags.tld" prefix="exampletags"%
```

- Using the URI declared in TLD document, for example, in TestPage.jsp, we can use the following `taglib` directive to make MyTags.tld available:

```
<%@taglib uri="
http://www.mysite.com/jspexamples/exampletags"prefix="exampletags"%>
```

The preceding application is used to create the custom tag for creating the empty tags without any attributes. We can also create the custom tag having attributes in it. These attributes are injected into the tag handler class during the execution of the tags. If we want to pass some data as input to the tag handler from the JSP page, we can configure attributes for the tag. Configuring attribute for a custom tag requires two things to be done. First is to declare the attribute in TLD document while describing the tag. Second is to implement the setter and getter methods in tag handler class for the attributes declared. The following snippet shows the declaration of the attributes to the tags used in the application:

```
<attribute>
  <name> attribute name </name>
  <required> true </required>
  <rtexprvalue> true </rtexprvalue>
</attribute>
```

Here, element `<name>` takes attribute name that has to be declared while element `<required>` takes `true` or `false`. `True` indicates that this attribute is mandatory to use. Element `<rtexprvalue>` also takes `true` or `false`, where `true` indicates that this attribute takes runtime expression. Now, it is time to implement the setter and getter methods in tag handler class for the attributes declared. Listing 16.5 shows the use of the tags having attributes that are used in the JSP pages. You can also find this file online in the folder code/Chapter16/customtagsex2

Listing 16.5: Creating the AddTagHandler.java File

```
package com.santosh.jspex.customtags;

import javax.servlet.*;
import javax.servlet.jsp.*;
import javax.servlet.jsp.tagext.*;
public class AddTagHandler extends TagSupport {
```

```
    public void setOp1(int i){op1=i;}
    public void setOp2(int i){op2=i;}
    public void setName(String s){name=s;}
    public void setScope(String s){scope=s;}

    public int getOp1(){return op1;}
    public int getOp2(){return op2;}
    public String getName(){return name;}
    public String getScope(){return scope;}

    public int doStartTag() throws JspException {
         int scope_id=-1;
         if (scope==null||scope.equals("") || scope.equals("page"))
                scope_id=PageContext.PAGE_SCOPE;
         else if (scope.equals("request"))
                scope_id=PageContext.REQUEST_SCOPE;
         else if (scope.equals("session"))
                scope_id=PageContext.SESSION_SCOPE;
         else if (scope.equals("application"))
                scope_id=PageContext.APPLICATION_SCOPE;
         else
                throw new JspException("Invalid Scope");

         Integer result=new Integer(op1+op2);
         pageContext.setAttribute(name,result,scope_id);
         return SKIP_BODY;
    }//doStartTag
    public int doEndTag() {
         return EVAL_PAGE;
    }
    int op1,op2;
    String name,scope;
  }//class
```

The preceding application extends the `TagSupport` class to implement the tag handler. In this case, the tag takes some attributes as the input. The `doStartTag()` method is used to initialize the tags used in the application. The `EVAL_PAGE` constant is used to explain the JSP container to evaluate the tags used in the scope of the JSP page and appear after this tag. Listing 16.6 shows the listing to write the output to the `JspWriter` provided by the container. You can also find this file online in the folder code/Chapter16/customtagsex2.

Listing 16.6: Creating the WriteTagHandler.java File

```
  package com.santosh.jspex.customtags;
  import javax.servlet.*;
  import javax.servlet.jsp.*;
  import javax.servlet.jsp.tagext.*;
  public class WriteTagHandler extends TagSupport {
    public void setName(String s){name=s;}
    public void setScope(String s){scope=s;}
    public String getName(){return name;}
    public String getScope(){return scope;}
    public int doStartTag() throws JspException {
         int scope_id=-1;
         if (scope==null||scope.equals(""))
                scope_id=-1;
         else if (scope.equals("page"))
                scope_id=PageContext.PAGE_SCOPE;
         else if (scope.equals("request"))
                scope_id=PageContext.REQUEST_SCOPE;
         else if (scope.equals("session"))
```

```
                scope_id=PageContext.SESSION_SCOPE;
        else if (scope.equals("application"))
                scope_id=PageContext.APPLICATION_SCOPE;
        else
                throw new JspException("Invalid Scope");
        try {
                JspWriter out=pageContext.getOut();
                if (scope_id!=-1)
                        out.print(pageContext.getAttribute(name,scope_id));
                else
                        out.print(pageContext.findAttribute(name));
        }//try
        catch(Exception e){}
        return SKIP_BODY;
    }//dostarttag
    String name,scope;
}//class
```

The preceding snippet writes the output to the `JspWriter`. This listing is also used to specify the name and the scope of the attributes used in the application. Both the preceding specified listings use the custom tag libraries for evaluating the tags used in the JSP page. The MyTags.tld is used here to evaluate the tags in a JSP page. Listing 16.7 shows the use of the MyTags.tld in the application. You can also find this file online in the folder code/Chapter16/customtagsex2/WEB-INF.

Listing 16.7: Creating the MyTags.tld File

```
<!DOCTYPE taglib

PUBLIC "-//Sun Microsystems, Inc.//DTD JSP Tag Library 1.2//EN"
"http://java.sun.com/dtd/web-jsptaglibrary_1_2.dtd">

<taglib>

  <tlib-version>1.1</tlib-version>
  <jsp-version>1.2</jsp-version>
  <short-name>exampletags</short-name>
  <info>Custom tags with attributes</info>
  <uri>http://www.mysite.com/jspexamples/exampletags</uri>

  <tag>
        <name>add</name>
        <tag-class>
                com.santosh.jspex.customtags.AddTagHandler
        </tag-class>
        <body-content>empty</body-content>

        <attribute>
                <name>op1</name>
                <required>true</required>
                <rtexprvalue>true</rtexprvalue>
        </attribute>
        <attribute>
                <name>op2</name>
                <required>true</required>
                <rtexprvalue>true</rtexprvalue>
        </attribute>
        <attribute>
                <name>name</name>
                <required>true</required>
                <rtexprvalue>false</rtexprvalue>
```

```
        </attribute>
        <attribute>
                <name>scope</name>
                <required>false</required>
                <rtexprvalue>false</rtexprvalue>
        </attribute>
</tag>

<tag>

        <name>write</name>
        <tag-class>
                com.santosh.jspex.customtags.WriteTagHandler
        </tag-class>
        <body-content>empty</body-content>
        <attribute>
                <name>name</name>
                <required>true</required>
                <rtexprvalue>false</rtexprvalue>
        </attribute>
        <attribute>
                <name>scope</name>
                <required>false</required>
                <rtexprvalue>false</rtexprvalue>

        </attribute>

</tag>

</taglib>
```

The MyTags.tld file in Listing 16.7 shows the version of tag library and JSP used in the application. The tag library specifies the name and scope attributes used in both the AddTagHandler.java and in WriteTagHandler.java files. The following file shows the index.html file, which is used to enter the values for the attributes. The attributes are named as `op1` and `op2` in the tag library. Listing 16.8 represents the index.html file used in the application. You can also find this file online in the folder code/Chapter16/customtagsex2.

Listing 16.8: Creating the index.html File

```
<html>

<body>

<pre>

<form action="Add.jsp">

<b>Operand 1 :</b> <input type="text" name="op1"/>

<b>Operand 2 :</b> <input type="text" name="op2"/>

<input type="submit" value="Add"/>
</form></pre></body></html>
```

The preceding file is used to enter the respective values for the attributes. The values entered from this file will get evaluated by using the Add.jsp file shown here.

The `web.xml` file used in the application specifies the location and the `URI` of the tag library used in the preceding application. The following snippet shows the content of the web.xml file used in the preceding application. You can also find this file online in the folder code/Chapter16/ customtagsex2/WEB-INF.

Listing 16.9: Creating the `web.xml` File

```
<?xml version="1.0"?>
<web-app>
</web-app>
```

Listing 16.10 shows the Add.jsp file used in the preceding application. You can also find this file online in the folder code/Chapter16/customtagsex2.

Listing 16.10: Creating the Add.jsp File

```
<%@taglib uri="http://www.mysite.com/jspexamples/exampletags"

prefix="exampletags"%>

<%@page errorPage="index.html"%>

<%
   int op1=Integer.parseInt(request.getParameter("op1"));
   int op2=Integer.parseInt(request.getParameter("op2"));
%>

<html><body>

<exampletags:add op1="<%=op1%>" op2="<%=op2%>"

name="addResult" scope="session"/>

Result : <exampletags:write name="addResult"/> <br/>

</body></html>
```

Listing 16.10 imports the custom tag library to use the custom tags in the application. It retrieves the value from the index.html page. The add tag is used to add the values of the attributes. After the evaluation of the tags, the output is to be written to the `JspWriter`. The output from the `JspWriter` is not directly available to the user. So the write tag is used to display the output to the user. Figure 16.4 shows directory structure for the preceding application.

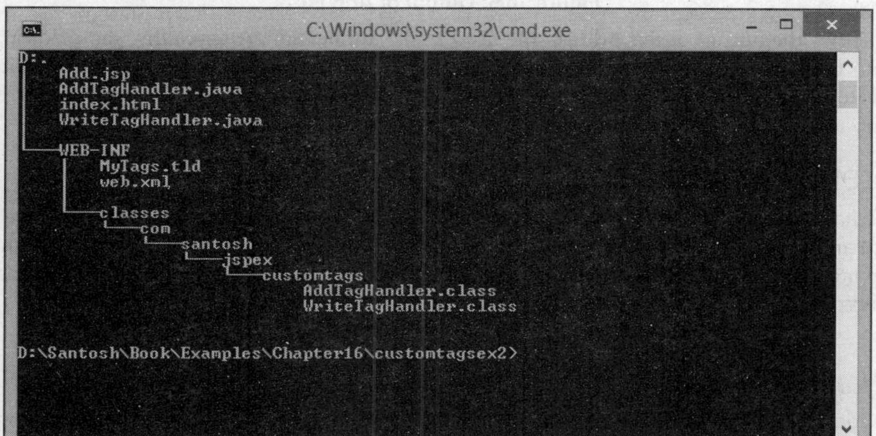

Figure 16.4: Directory Structure for customtagsex2.

All the preceding mentioned files are present in the **customtagsex2** folder, as shown in Figure 16.3. The work folder is then copied to the `<Tomcat home>/webapps` folder. Now browse the application by opening the browser. Type the `http://localhost:9090/customtagsex2/index.html` link in the browser to access the page. The output of the preceding requests is shown in Figure 16.5.

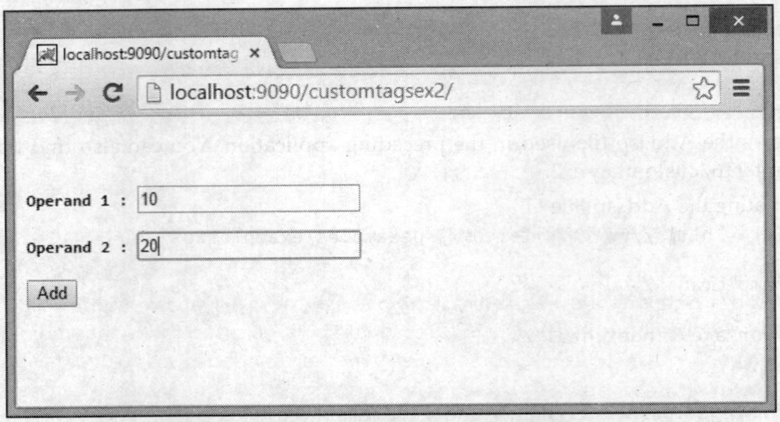

Figure 16.5: Output of index.html.

Figure 16.5 shows the output of index.html file used in the application. The user needs to insert the values for the attributes (`operand 1`, `operand 2`). After entering the values for the attributes, the Add.jsp is called to access the respective tag for the application. Entering non-numbers results in the same index.html page. It is due to the fact that the index.html is referred for an error occurrence. Entering valid values for the attributes results in the following output, as shown in Figure 16.6:

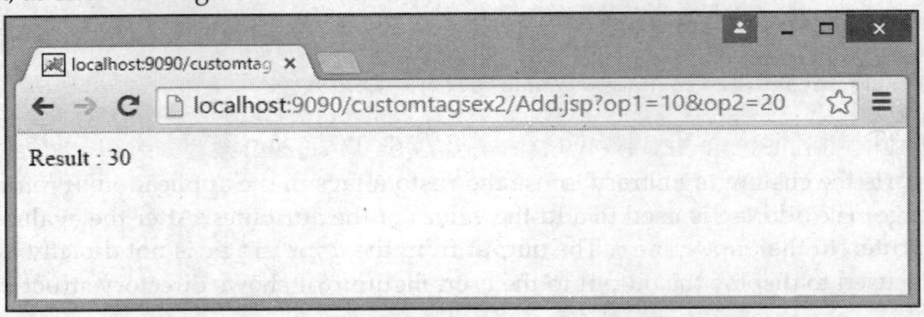

Figure 16.6: Output of Add.jsp.

Figure 16.6 shows the output of the Add.jsp file used in the application. After calling the Add.jsp, the control is transferred to the tags used in the application. The custom tags access the corresponding result from the Tag library used in the application. The custom tags generate the result from the application. The `<write>` tag from the tag library accesses the result and displays it to the user.

Body Content Tag Interface

Till now, we have learned how to write an empty JSP classic custom tag but most of the time, we want to allow body content and process the body content. JSP specification allows us to design a custom tag with body content, and develop tag handler that can process the body content of our tag. The tag handler for this type of tag should be the subtype of `javax.servlet.jsp.tagext.BodyTag` interface. We will use an adapter class `javax.servlet.jsp.tagext.`

Body Tag Handler Life Cycle

When a JSP container encounters this type of custom tag in a JSP page, it performs the following operations:

- The container finds whether this tag is already used in the JSP page or not. If the tag is already used in JSP page, then the container uses the Tag Handler object created/located for the previous same tag in this JSP page. If this tag is appearing for the first time in JSP page then container tries to locate the Tag Handler object from tag pool. If container cannot locate the object from the pool then it performs tag handler instantiation, that is, it creates a new object.

- It initializes the tag handler object located or created in the first step. If the object is located from the same JSP page, then the `setPageContext()` method is not invoked. If the object is located and being reused in the same parent, then `setParent()` is also not invoked. If the object is located from pool or created newly, then the complete initialization is performed.
- If the second step is performed successfully, then container processes start tag, that is, it invokes `doStartTag()` method and collects the response.
  - If `doStartTag()` method returns EVAL_BODY_INCLUDE, then the container evaluates the body content and it adds the outcome into the output.
  - If `doStartTag()` method returns EVAL_BODY_BUFFERED, then the container evaluates the body content, and then instead of including it into the output, it is set into buffer that can be retrieved in tag handler class using `BodyContent` object.
  - If `doStartTag()` method returns `SKIP_BODY`, then the container does not evaluate the body content of this tag and directly invokes `doEndTag()` method.
- It processes the end tag, that is it invokes `doEndTag()` method.
- It invokes `release()` method to release all the resources attached to the page and performs garbage collection.

Using BodyContent Tag

We have already discussed the `BodyContent` tag interface and its life cycle. Let's discuss an example to demonstrate the use of the `Tag` interface. Listing 16.11 is used to demonstrate the use of the `EVAL_BODY_INCLUDE`. In this example, we have developed a simple `TagHandler` for representing IF condition action, like if the given request parameter value is equal to the specified value, then the body content of the tag will be evaluated and included into the output; if not, then it will not be evaluated. You can also find this file online in the folder code/Chapter16/customtagsex3

Listing 16.11: Creating the IFTagHandler.java File

```
package com.santosh.jspex.customtags;

import javax.servlet.*;
import javax.servlet.jsp.*;
import javax.servlet.jsp.tagext.*;
public class IFTagHandler extends BodyTagSupport
{

  public void setParamName(String s)
{
  pname=s;
}
  public String getParamName()
{
  return pname;
}
  public void setValue(String s)
{
  value=s;
}
  public String getValue(){
  return value;
  }

  public int doStartTag()
  {
        ServletRequest req=pageContext.getRequest();

        String pvalue=req.getParameter(pname);
```

```
        System.out.println(pvalue==null||(!pvalue.equals(value)));

        if (pvalue==null||(!pvalue.equals(value)))
                return SKIP_BODY;
        return EVAL_BODY_INCLUDE;
    }//doStartTag

    public int doAfterBody()
    {
        return SKIP_BODY;
    }//doAfterBody

    public int doEndTag()
    {
        return EVAL_PAGE;
    }//doEndTag

    String pname,value;

}//class
```

Listing 16.11 shows the use of `EVAL_BODY_INCLUDE` constant in order to execute the custom tags used in the JSP pages. This is used to generate the response along with the body content of the tag. The `BodyTagSupport` class is used in order to support the body content of the tags used in the application. To execute the custom tags used in the Web application, the following tag library is used. You can also find this file online in the folder code/Chapter16/customtagsex3/WEB-INF

Listing 16.12: Creating the MyTags.tld File

```
<!DOCTYPE taglib

PUBLIC "-//Sun Microsystems, Inc.//DTD JSP Tag Library 1.2//EN"
"http://java.sun.com/dtd/web-jsptaglibrary_1_2.dtd">

<taglib>
  <tlib-version>1.1</tlib-version>
  <jsp-version>1.2</jsp-version>
  <short-name>exampletags</short-name>
  <info>Custom tags with attributes</info>
  <uri>http://www.mysite.com/jspexamples/exampletags</uri>

  <tag>
        <name>if</name>
        <tag-class>
                com.santosh.jspex.customtags.IFTagHandler
        </tag-class>
        <body-content>JSP</body-content>

        <attribute>
                <name>paramName</name>
                <required>true</required>
                <rtexprvalue>false</rtexprvalue>
        </attribute>
        <attribute>
                <name>value</name>
                <required>true</required>
                <rtexprvalue>true</rtexprvalue>
        </attribute>
  </tag>
</taglib>
```

The preceding specified tag library is used in order to declare the tags that have to be used in the JSP pages. The preceding specification also shows the versions of the components used in building the Web application. The JSP and the HTML pages used in the preceding application are shown here. You can also find this file online in the folder code/Chapter16/customtagsex3

Listing 16.13: Creating the Home.html File

```
<html>
   <body> <pre>

         <form action="TestPage.jsp">
                <b>User Name   :</b> <input type="text" name="uname"/>
                <b>Password    :</b> <input type="password" name="pass"/>
                <b>RePassword  :</b> <input type="password" name="repass"/>
                <input type="submit" value="Register"/>

         </form>

         </pre>
   </body>
</html>
```

This Home.html is used to accept the input from the user. From this, the request will be forwarded to the TestPage.jsp.

The `web.xml` file used in the application specifies the location and the URI of the tag library used in the preceding application. The following snippet shows the content of the `web.xml` file used in the preceding application. You can also find this file online in the folder code/Chapter16/customtagsex3/WEB-INF.

Listing 16.14: Creating the `web.xml` File

```
<?xml version="1.0"?>
<web-app>
</web-app>
```

Listing 16.15 shows the TestPage.jsp used in the application. You can also find this file online in the folder code/Chapter16/customtagsex3

Listing 16.15: Creating the TestPage.jsp File

```
<%@taglib uri="http://www.mysite.com/jspexamples/exampletags"
prefix="exampletags"%>

<html>
<body>
This is a test logic to test the IF conditional tag designed to demonstrate how to
   use EVAL_BODY_INCLUDE. <br/><br/><br/>
   <exampletags:if paramName="uname" value="user1">
         <b>User Name is valid</b><br/>
         <exampletags:if paramName="pass"
                value="<%=request.getParameter("repass")%>">
                Even Password and Re-password are same
         </exampletags:if>
   </exampletags:if>
</body>

</html>
```

All the preceding specified listings are used in generating the Web application. Here, we are saving all the files in the **customtagsex3** folder. Copy the folder to the `<Tomcat home>/webapps` directory. Figure 16.7 shows the directory structure for the preceding application.

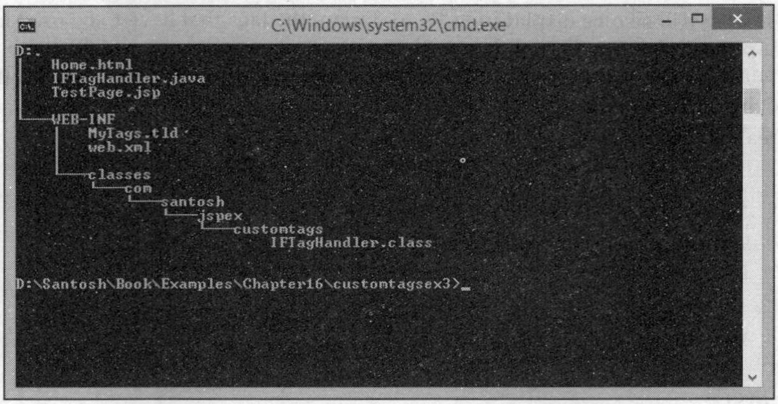

Figure 16.7: Directory structure for customtagsex3.

Then, start the server to run the application. Now, browse the home page of this example using the URL `http://localhost:9090/customtagsex3/Home.html`. The output is shown in Figure 16.8.

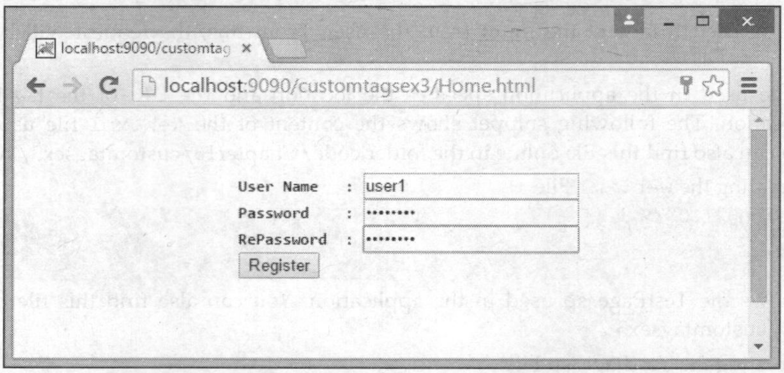

Figure 16.8: Output from Home.html

Figure 16.8 shows the output of the Home.html. The user needs to enter the required User Name, Password and the RePassword must be same as shown in the preceding figure. Figure 16.9 shows the output after clicking the Register button:

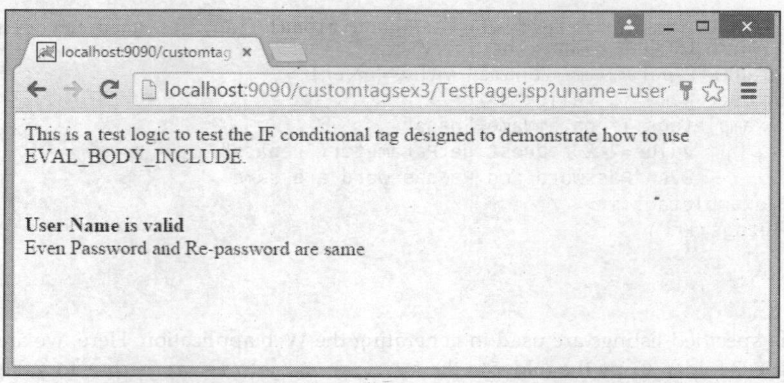

Figure 16.9: Output of TestPage.jsp by using EVAL_BODY_INCLUDE.

Figure 16.9 shows the output of TestPage.jsp used in the preceding application. The application uses the IF condition statement in order to test the application logic. Here, it tests for the equality of the password and the RePassword fields. If the values for both the fields are same then the tag will get executed and the content associated with the tag will also be displayed to the user as shown in the preceding figure. If you enter different password and re-password, then you will find the view as shown in Figure 16.10 where you will find only the message 'User Name is valid' but not the message in the body part of the inner IF because the password and re-password are not same and thus SKIP_BODY will be returned by doStartTag() method.

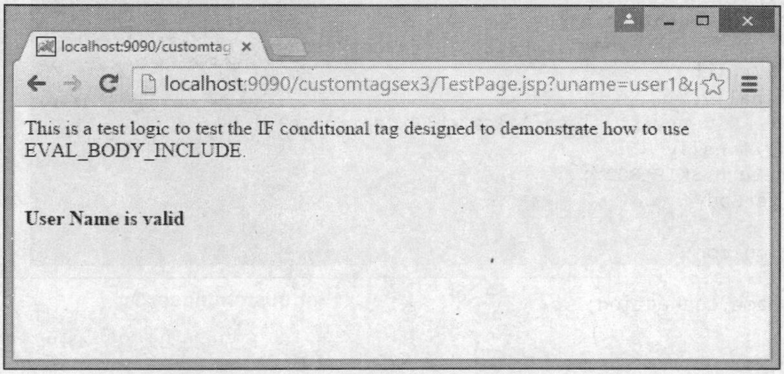

Figure 16.10: Output showing the use of SKIP_BODY

The preceding output is generated when the user enters different passwords in the Home.html. Since the condition is not satisfied in the JSP page, the JSP engine stops the execution of the 'if' tags body content by returning the SKIP_BODY constant. So in this case, only the tag body will get executed and the output is displayed to the user if the password and re-password are same.

The preceding application shows the use of the EVAL_BODY_INCLUDE and the SKIP_BODY constants used with the body content tag interface. Let's here discuss the use of the EVAL_BODY_BUFFERED constant used in the following application. In Listing 16.16, a database tag is used to update a SQL statement. You can also find this file online in the folder code/Chapter16/customtagsex4

Listing 16.16: Creating the UpdateTagHandler.java File

```
package com.santosh.jspex.customtags;

import javax.servlet.jsp.*;
import javax.servlet.jsp.tagext.*;
import java.sql.*;

public class UpdateTagHandler extends BodyTagSupport {

  public void setName(String s){name=s;}
  public void setConnection(String s){connection=s;}
  public String getConnection(){return connection;}
  public String getName(){return name;}

  public int doStartTag() throws JspException {
       con=(Connection)pageContext.getAttribute(connection,
       PageContext.PAGE_SCOPE);

       if (con!=null)
              return EVAL_BODY_BUFFERED;
              throw new JspException();
  }//doStartTag

  public int doAfterBody() throws JspException {

       String query=getBodyContent().getString();
       Statement st=null;
       try {
```

```
                st=con.createStatement();
                int i=st.executeUpdate(query);
                pageContext.setAttribute(name, new Integer(i),
                PageContext.PAGE_SCOPE);
        }//try
        catch(Exception e){
                throw new JspException(e.getMessage());
        }//catch
        finally{
                try{st.close();}catch(Exception e){}
        }//finally
        return SKIP_BODY;
    }//doAfterBody

    Connection con;

    String name,connection;

}//class
```

The preceding listing is used to evaluate the body content if it is able to create a connection successfully. This is done by returning EVAL_BODY_BUFFERED in `doStartTag()` method. The following tag library shown in Listing 16.17 is used to update the database according to the user's choice. You can also find this file online in the folder code/Chapter16/customtagsex4/WEB-INF

Listing 16.17: Creating the MySQLTags.tld File

```
<!DOCTYPE taglib
PUBLIC "-//Sun Microsystems, Inc.//DTD JSP Tag Library 1.2//EN"
"http://java.sun.com/dtd/web-jsptaglibrary_1_2.dtd">

<tag-lib>
  <tlib-version>1.1</tlib-version>
  <jsp-version>1.2</jsp-version>
  <short-name>exampletags</short-name>
  <info>Custom tags with attributes and body</info>
  <uri>http://www.mysite.com/jspexamples/exampletags</uri>
  <tag>
        <name>update</name>
        <tag-class>
                com.santosh.jspex.customtags.UpdateTagHandler
        </tag-class>
        <body-content>JSP</body-content>

        <attribute>
                <name>name</name>
                <required>false</required>
                <rtexprvalue>false</rtexprvalue>
        </attribute>
        <attribute>
                <name>connection</name>
                <required>true</required>
                <rtexprvalue>false</rtexprvalue>
        </attribute>

  </tag>
</tag-lib>
```

The preceding SQL tag library is used in the application in order to handle the user requests made by the user to update the database. The tag library specifies the attributes and their names used in the application. The tag library is to be specified in the web.xml file so that the JSP engine can detect the location of the tag library.

Listing 16.18 shows the `web.xml` file used in the preceding application. You can also find this file online in the folder code/Chapter16/customtagsex4/WEB-INF

Listing 16.18: Creating the web.xml File

```
<?xml version="1.0" encoding="UTF-8"?>

<web-app>
<jsp-config>
  <taglib>
  <taglib-uri>http://www.mysite.com/jspexamples/exampletags</taglib-uri>
  <taglib-location>/WEB-INF/MySQLTags.tld</taglib-location>
  </taglib>
</jsp-config>
  <welcome-file-list>
        <welcome-file>index.html</welcome-file>
  </welcome-file-list>

</web-app>
```

The JSP pages are used in this application to initialize the custom tags used in the application. Initially, the request from the user is passed from the index.html file. From this file, the control is then transferred to the TestPage.jsp, which is used to update the database. Listing 16.19 shows the index.html file used in the application. You can also find this file online in the folder code/Chapter16/customtagsex4

Listing 16.19: Creating the index.html File

```
<html> <body> <pre>

<form action="TestPage.jsp">

<b>Emp No      :</b> <input type="text" name="empno"/>

<b>New Salary :</b> <input type="text" name="sal"/>

  <input type="submit" value="Change Sal"/>

</form> </pre> </body> </html>
```

The preceding snippet is used to enter the request made by the user. An existing empno and salary is to be inserted from this page. Then the control is transferred to the TestPage.jsp. The TestPage.jsp contains the database connection for accessing the database. For this, `classes12.jar` or `ojdbc14.jar` file is to be added in the lib directory of the application. The application uses the Type 4 driver in order to access the database. Listing 16.20 shows the TestPage.jsp used in the preceding application. You can also find this file online in the folder code/Chapter16/customtagsex4

Listing 16.20: Creating the TestPage.jsp File

```
<%@taglib uri="http://www.mysite.com/jspexamples/exampletags"

prefix="exampletags"%>

<html><body>

<%@page import="java.sql.*"%>

<%@page errorPage="Error.jsp"%>

<%!
  public void jspInit() {
        try {
              Class.forName("oracle.jdbc.driver.OracleDriver");
        }//try
```

```
        catch(Exception e){e.printStackTrace();}
    }//jspInit
  %>
  <%

    Connection    con=DriverManager.getConnection    ("jdbc:oracle:thin:@mysys:1521:sandb",
  "scott","tiger");
    pageContext.setAttribute("mycon", con, PageContext.PAGE_SCOPE);

  %>

  <exampletags:update name="updateCount" connection="mycon">
  update emp set sal=<%=request.getParameter("sal")%> where
  empno=<%=request.getParameter("empno")%>
  </exampletags:update>

  Given employee's salary is updated

  <br/> Update Count is :

  <%=pageContext.findAttribute("updateCount")%>

  </body></html>
```

This page accepts the requests made by the user and updates the requests according to the data entered by the user. The data can be accessed by using the Type 4 driver used in the preceding application. All the files specified in the preceding applications are placed under the **customtagsex4** folder. Copy the folder into the `<Tomcat home>webapps` folder. Figure 16.11 shows the directory structure of the application.

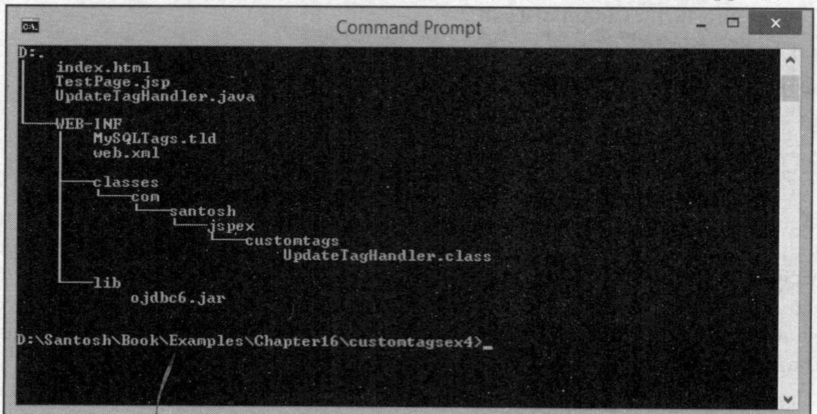

Figure 16.11: Directory structure for customtagsex4.

Then, start the server to run the application. Now, browse the home page of this example using the URL `http://localhost:9090/customtagsex4/`. The output is as shown in Figure 16.12.

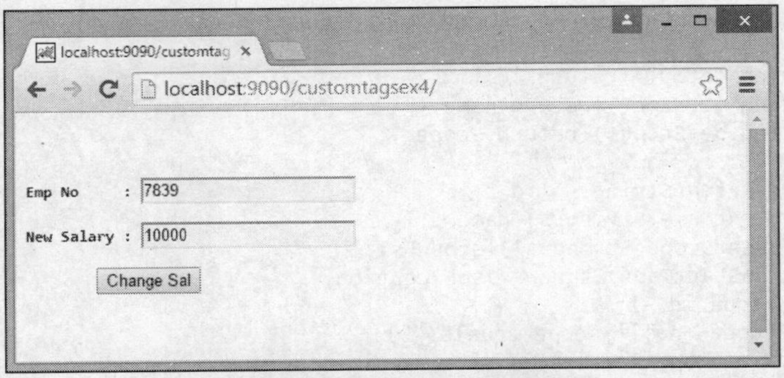

Figure 16.12: Output of Index.html.

Enter the details as shown in Figure 16.12 and click the "**Change Sal**" button. The control is then transferred to the TestPage.jsp and the output is generated as shown in Figure 16.12. The output is generated and is updated in the database. Figure 16.13 shows the output of the preceding application by using the EVAL_BODY_BUFFERED.

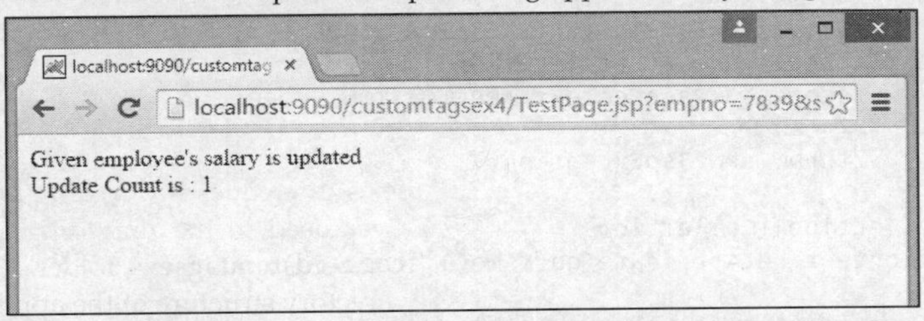

Figure 16.13: Output of TestPage.jsp by using EVAL_BODY_BUFFERED.

The EVAL_BODY_BUFFERED constant is used to evaluate the tag and the output is stored in another instance. Here, the output is updated in the database and only the body of the JSP page is executed to show the output as a response to the user.

Iteration tag Interface

This interface extends the basic tag interface and it provides a method to support the iteration of the tags used in a JSP page. The iteration tag interface is implemented by the body tag interface described earlier. This interface implements the tag interface and can be represented as `javax.servlet.jsp.tagext.IterationTag` interface. The `doAfterBody()` method provides the support of evaluating the iteration of the tags used in a JSP page.

Iteration Tag Handler Life Cycle

The life-cycle of this type of tag is same as discussed in JSP custom classic tag with body. In this case, the output of `doAfterBody()` method is used to determine whether to reevaluate the body or not. If `doAfterBody()` method returns EVAL_BODY_AGAIN, then the body is reevaluated; if not, then it invokes `doEndTag()` method to process the end tag.

The following application shows the use of the iterate tag handler. The EVAL_BODY_AGAIN constant is used to evaluate the body content multiple times throughout the scope of the page. Listing 16.21 shows the use of the EVAL_BODY_AGAIN constant in the application. You can also find this file online in the folder code/Chapter16/customtagsex5

Listing 16.21: Creating the IterateTagHandler.java File

```
package com.santosh.jspex.customtags;

import javax.servlet.jsp.*;
import javax.servlet.jsp.tagext.*;
import java.util.*;
```

```
public class IterateTagHandler extends BodyTagSupport {

    public String getId(){return id;}
    public String getName(){return name;}
    public String getScope(){return scope;}

    public void setId(String s){id=s;}
    public void setName(String s){name=s;}
    public void setScope(String s1){scope=s1;}
    public int doStartTag() throws JspException{
          int scope_id=-1;
          if (scope==null||scope.equals(""))
                  scope_id=-1;
          else if(scope.equals("page"))
                  scope_id=PageContext.PAGE_SCOPE;
          else if(scope.equals("request"))
                  scope_id=PageContext.REQUEST_SCOPE;
          else if(scope.equals("session"))
                  scope_id=PageContext.SESSION_SCOPE;
          else if(scope.equals("application"))
                  scope_id=PageContext.APPLICATION_SCOPE;
          else
                  throw new JspException();

          mycollection=(Collection)
          pageContext.getAttribute(getName(),scope_id);

          if (mycollection==null)
                  return SKIP_BODY;

          myiterator=mycollection.iterator();
          if (myiterator.hasNext()){
                  pageContext.setAttribute( getId(), myiterator.next(),
                  PageContext.PAGE_SCOPE);
                  return EVAL_BODY_INCLUDE;
          }//if
          return SKIP_BODY;
    }//doStartTag

    public int doAfterBody() {
          if (myiterator.hasNext()){
                  pageContext.setAttribute(getId(), myiterator.next(),
                  PageContext.PAGE_SCOPE);
                  return EVAL_BODY_AGAIN;
          }//if
          return SKIP_BODY;
    }//doAfterBody
    public int doEndTag() {
          return EVAL_PAGE;
    }
    Collection mycollection;
    Iterator myiterator;
    String name,id,scope;
}//class
```

The preceding snippet shows the use of the EVAL_BODY_AGAIN tag in the application. It also extends the `BodyTagSupport` class to execute the body content of the tags. The body of the tag will get executed multiple times throughout the scope of the page. The preceding application is used to get the values from the collection located in the given scope and write them to the current `JspWriter`. The attribute for the tags are specified in the tag library used in the application. Listing 16.22 shows the tag library used in the preceding application. You can also find this file online in the folder code/Chapter16/customtagsex5/WEB-INF

Listing 16.22: Creating the MyTags.tld File

```
<!DOCTYPE taglib
PUBLIC "-//Sun Microsystems, Inc.//DTD JSP Tag Library 1.2//EN"
"http://java.sun.com/dtd/web-jsptaglibrary_1_2.dtd">

<taglib>
  <tlib-version>1.1</tlib-version>
  <jsp-version>1.2</jsp-version>
  <short-name>mylogic</short-name>
  <info>Custom tags with attributes</info>
  <uri>http://www.mysite.com/jspexamples/exampletags</uri>

  <tag>
        <name>iterate</name>
        <tag-class>
        com.santosh.jspex.customtags.IterateTagHandler
        </tag-class>
        <body-content>JSP</body-content>

        <attribute>
                <name>name</name>
                <required>true</required>
                <rtexprvalue>false</rtexprvalue>
        </attribute>
        <attribute>
                <name>id</name>
                <required>true</required>
                <rtexprvalue>false</rtexprvalue>
        </attribute>
        <attribute>
                <name>scope</name>
                <required>false</required>
                <rtexprvalue>false</rtexprvalue>
        </attribute>
  </tag>
</taglib>
```

The preceding tag library specifies the attributes specified in the JSP page used by the application. It also specifies the version of the tag library and the JSP pages used in the application. The tag library is to be specified in the `web.xml` file in order to be accessed by the custom tags used in the preceding application. Listing 16.23 shows the use of the `web.xml` file in the application. You can also find this file online in the folder code/Chapter16/customtagsex5/WEB_INF

Listing 16.23: Creating the web.xml File

```
<?xml version="1.0" encoding="UTF-8"?>
<web-app >
<jsp-config>
  <taglib>
  <taglib-uri>http://www.mysite.com/jspexamples/exampletags</taglib-uri>
  <taglib-location>/WEB-INF/MyTags.tld</taglib-location>
  </taglib>
</jsp-config>

  <welcome-file-list>
        <welcome-file>index.jsp</welcome-file>
  </welcome-file-list>
</web-app>
```

The tags from the tag library are used in the JSP pages in order to execute the body multiple times. The tags will be executed after the JSP engine executes the body of the JSP page. Listing 16.24 shows the JSP page used by the preceding application. You can also find this file online in the folder code/Chapter16/customtagsex5

Listing 16.24: Creating the TestPage.jsp File

```
<%@page import="java.util.*"%>
<%
/*creating a simple vector object and setting into request attribute to test the
  iterate tag*/
Vector names=new Vector();
names.add("User1");
names.add("User2");
names.add("User3");
names.add("User4");
names.add("User5");
request.setAttribute("names",names);
%>
<%@taglib       uri="http://www.mysite.com/jspexamples/exampletags"
  prefix="exampletags"%>

<html> <body>

The following are the names available in the given collection, <br>
These values are retrieved using a iterate custom tag

<table border="1">
  <tr><th>Names</th></tr>
  <exampletags:iterate id="ele" name="names" scope="request">
  <tr> <td>
       <%=pageContext.getAttribute("ele")%>
<!--instead of preceding expression tag we can use our write tag which we have
  designed in previous Example -->
  </td> </tr>
  </exampletags:iterate>
</table></body></html>
```

All the files specified earlier are placed in the **customtagsex5** folder. Copy the folder from the root directory to the `<Tomcat home>webapps` directory. Figure 16.14 shows the directory structure of the preceding application.

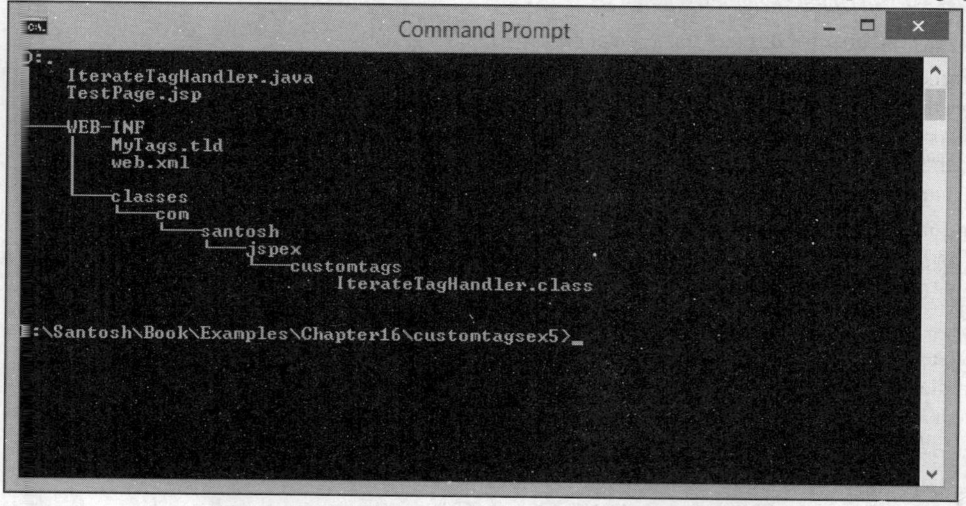

Figure 16.14: Directory structure for customtagsex5.

Now, browse this example using the URL `http://localhost:9090/customtagsex5/TestPage.jsp`. You will find the view, as shown in Figure 16.15. This displays all the elements in the given vector. The elements to the vector will get executed after the execution of the custom tags in the JSP page.

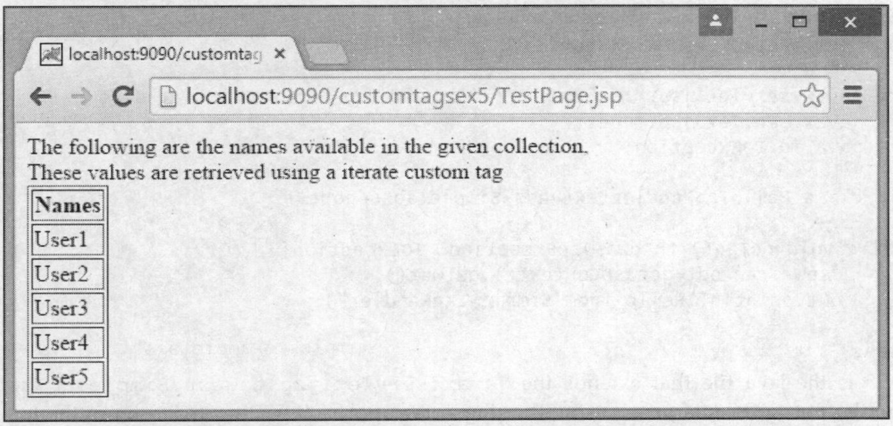

Figure 16.15: Output of TestPage.jsp by using EVAL_BODY_AGAIN

Figure 16.15 shows the output of the TestPage.jsp. The body content of the JSP page is executed and included into the output because of using EVAL_BODY_INCLUDE constant. All the preceding discussion gives an idea of using custom tags in a JSP page. The custom tags need to be defined in the `web.xml` file in order to be used in the application. Now, let's discuss the standard tag libraries available in JSP. The standard libraries are available in the JSP page along with the specification. These provide the functionality for many of the JSP pages used in the Web applications.

Simple Tags

A simple tag handler is a Java class that implements the `SimpleTag` interface and it should have a no-argument constructor. This class is mainly used by the authors to make the use of tags flexible in the tag handlers. The `javax.servlet.jsp.tagext.SimpleTagSupport` class provides a default implementation of all methods in `SimpleTag`.

Life Cycle of Simple Tag Handlers

When a JSP container encounters this type of custom tag in a JSP page, it performs the following operations:

- A new tag handler instance is created using no-argument constructor.

NOTE

Unlike classic tag handlers, simple tag handlers are not cached and reused by the JSP container.

- The `setJspContext()` and `setParent()` methods are called. The `setParent()` method is only called if the element is nested within another tag invocation.
- The setters for each attribute defined for this tag are called.
- If a body exists, the `setJspBody()` method is called by the container to set the body of this tag, as a `JspFragment`. If the action element is empty in the page, this method is not called at all. The container invokes the `setJspBody()` method with a `JspFragment` object encapsulating the body of the tag. The tag handler implementation can call `invoke ()` on that fragment to evaluate the body as many times as it needs.
- The `doTag()` method is called by the container. All the logic and iteration of the tag as well as the evolution of its body occur in this method.
- The `doTag()` method returns and all the variables are synchronized.

Let's here create an example to demonstrate the use of the simple tag in a JSP page. The following application shows the use of the JSP simple tag in a JSP page. Listing 16.25 shows the HelloTagHandler.java file used in the application. You can also find this file online in the folder code/Chapter16/simpleTagex

Listing 16.25: creating the HelloTagHandler.java File

```
package com.santosh.jspex.customtags;

import javax.servlet.jsp.*;
import javax.servlet.jsp.tagext.*;
import java.io.IOException;

public class HelloTagHandler extends SimpleTagSupport {

   public void doTag() throws JspException, IOException{
         JspWriter out=getJspContext().getOut();
         out.println("Hello from Simple TagHandler");
   }
}//class
```

Listing 16.25 is the java file that extends the `javax.servlet.jsp.tagext.SimpleTagSupport` class to create a handler for `getMessage` tag using the simple tag approach. Listing 16.26 shows the tag library that is being used by the application. You can also find this file online in the folder code/Chapter16/simpleTagex/WEB-INF

Listing 16.26: creating the MyTags.tld File

```
<!DOCTYPE taglib
PUBLIC "-//Sun Microsystems, Inc.//DTD JSP Tag Library 1.2//EN"
"http://java.sun.com/dtd/web-jsptaglibrary_1_2.dtd">
<taglib>

   <tlib-version>1.1</tlib-version>
   <jsp-version>1.2</jsp-version>
   <short-name>exampletags</short-name>
   <info>Example Custom Tags</info>
   <uri>http://www.mysite.com/jspexamples/exampletags</uri>

   <tag>
         <name>getMessage</name>
         <tag-class>
               com.santosh.jspex.customtags.HelloTagHandler
         </tag-class>
         <body-content>empty</body-content>
   </tag>
</taglib>
```

The MyTags.tld file is used by the application to use the simple tag support in the application. Listing 16.27 shows the TestPage.jsp used by the application. You can also find this file online in the folder code/Chapter16/simpleTagex

Listing 16.27: Creating the TestPage.jsp File

```
<%@taglib uri="http://www.mysite.com/jspexamples/exampletags"
prefix="exampletags"%>

<html><body>

<b>Response of getMessage tag : </b> <i> <exampletags:getMessage/> </i> <br>
</body></html>
```

All the files in the application are to be placed **simpleTagex** directory. Figure 16.16 shows the directory structure of the application.

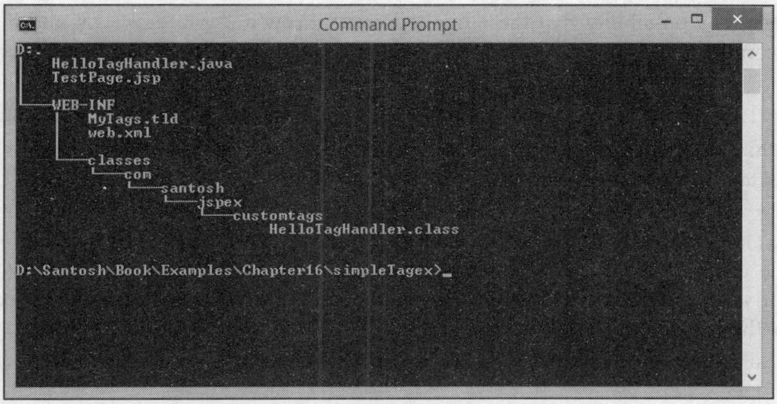

Figure 16.16: Directory structure of simpleTagex.

Copy the **simpleTagex** folder into the <Tomcat home>\webapps folder and start the server. Now, browse this application using the URL by using http://localhost:9090/simpleTagex/TestPage.jsp. You will find the view as shown in Figure 16.17. This displays the message that is written by Simple Tag Handler.

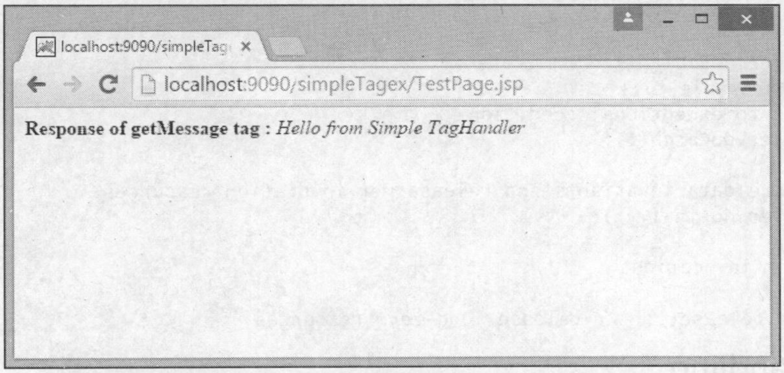

Figure 16.17: Output from Simple Tag handler.

Figure 16.17 shows the output of the TestPage.jsp, which uses the `getMessage` tag whose handler is implemented using Simple Tag approach.

Differences between Simple Tag and Classic Tag Handlers

The following are the differences between classic tag and simple tag handlers:

- The `ClassicTag` interface have `doStartTag()` and `doEndTag()` methods and the `SimpleTag` interface provides a simple `doTag()` method, which is called once and only once for any given tag invocation.
- Simple tag handler can be used for tag with body content and without body content. Thus, simple tag handlers have the equivalent power of `BodyTag`, but with a much simpler lifecycle and interface. All tag logic, iteration, and body evaluations are to be performed in `doTag()` single method.
- When simple tag is used, the tag handler, that is built, must implement `javax.servlet.jsp.tagext.SimpleTag` interface, but when classic tag is used the tag handler must implement `javax.servlet.jsp.tagext.Tag` interface.
- Classic tag handler objects are cached and reused whereas simple tag handler objects are not cached.

The TryCatchFinally Interface

The `TryCatchFinally` is a supporting interface for JSP tag handler that wants additional notifications from container for managing resources. When JSP invokes the tag handler methods, such as `doStartTag()` and doEndTag(), there is a possibility that these methods may throw a JspException and if we want to handle these abnormal conditions or do some finalization within the tag handler class then we need to implement this interface.

The javax.servlet.jsp.tagext.TryCatchFinally interface is declared with two methods:

- **doCatch(Throwable)** – This method is called when there is an exception raised while evaluating the body of this tag or when doStartTag(), doEndTag(), doInitBody(), doAfterBody() methods are invoked.
- **doFinally()** – This method is invoked in all cases after doEndTag(). It is invoked even if an exception occurs while evaluating the body of this tag or when doStartTag(), doEndTag(), doInitBody(), doAfterBody () methods are invoked. This method is not invoked if the exception occurs during one of the setter methods.

The typical invocation of these methods in the servlet equivalent code generated by the JSP container is shown in the following snippet

```
taghandler = get_a_Tag();
// get a tag handler from pool, the method used varies from one JSP container to
  other
// tag invocation protocol
try {
  taghandler.doStartTag();
  ...
  taghandler.doEndTag();
} catch (Throwable t) {
  // react to exceptional condition
  taghandler.doCatch(t);
} finally {
  // restore data invariants and release per-invocation resources
  taghandler.doFinally();
}
... //other invocations
...
taghandler.release();  // release long-term resources
```

Exception Handling

In any programming language, an exception means a situation, which disrupts the general flow of the program. It is generally an object that is thrown at run time. JSP code can have three types of exceptions - checked exception, runtime exception, and errors. Checked exception is generally a user error or problem which is not expected by the programmer at the time of coding the program. These types of errors are checked during the compilation of the program. Runtime exception occurs while running the program. These types of exceptions are ignored at the time of compilation. Errors are not exceptions but they are problems, which arise beyond the control of the user or the programmer.

In JSP, exception handling generally means to handle the run time errors. Generally, there are two ways to handle exceptions in JSP. They are as follows:

1. By errorPage and isErrorPage attributes of page directive
2. By <error-Page> element in web.xml file

The exception object is an instance of a subclass of Throwable class. Table 16.1 lists the methods that are available in Throwable class:

Table 16.1: Methods that are available in Throwable class

Methods	Description
public String getMessage()	Returns message about the exception that occurred
public Throwable getCause()	Returns the cause of exception that are represented by Throwable object

Table 16.1: Methods that are available in Throwable class

Methods	Description
public String toString()	Returns the name of the class that are concatenated with the result of `getMessage()`
public void printStackTrace()	Returns the result of `toString()`
public StackTraceElement [] getStackTrace()	Returns an array containing each element on the stack trace
public Throwable fillInStackTrace()	Fills the stack trace of the `Throwable` object with the current stack trace and adds the previous information in the stack trace

Summary

In this chapter, we learned how to develop JSP custom tags – empty, with body content, iteration tags, and simple tags. This chapter also provides you the details of the JSP tag libraries both classic and simple tags lifecycles. Later for each of the tag, we discussed an example that explains the respective topic. In the next chapter, we learn about the JSP Expression language, its importance, and how to use JSP expression language in a JSP document. Let's recall the following important points to summarize the chapter:

- A custom tag is a user-defined JSP language element. If a JSP page which contains a custom tag is translated into a servlet, then the custom tag is converted to operations on a tag handler.
- JSP specification includes a Tag library under the section, Tag Extensions, which provides an ability to develop custom tags to build new and reusable presentation components.
- The custom tags are used in a JSP page in order to increase its performance and productivity. The tags generally refer to the custom actions by the users.
- A tag library is a collection of events that encapsulate some functionality to be used from within a JSP page.
- A tag library is made available to a JSP page through a `taglib` directive that identifies the tag library through a URI (Universal Resource Identifier).
- The location of the TLD is to be specified in order to be accessed by the application.
- Tag handler is a Java class that implements one of the subtypes of `JspTag` interface, which defines the run time behavior of the custom tag.
- The tag API is the collection of tags and interfaces for handling the tags appearing in a JSP page.
- Empty tags are used to perform server-side work based on their attributes, and determine whether the rest of the page is processed or not, empty tags can even redirect the request to other page.
- The tag handler objects of this type are recycled by container to avoid the performance overhead of tag handler objects creation.
- A simple tag handler is a Java class that implements the `SimpleTag` interface and it should have a no-argument constructor.
- When simple tag is used, the tag handler that is built must implement `javax.servlet.jsp.tagext.SimpleTag` interface but, when classic tag is used, the tag handler must implement `javax.servlet.jsp.tagext.Tag` interface.
- The `TryCatchFinally` is a supporting interface for JSP tag handler that wants additional notifications from container for managing resources.
- JSP code can have three types of exceptions – checked exception, runtime exception, and errors.

Exercise

Q. 16.1 What is a `TagHandler`?

Q. 16.2 Which method of Tag is invoked to set the `BodyContent` object into a `TagHandler` object?

Q. 16.3	Name the valid constants that `doStartTag()` method can return.
Q. 16.4	Which constant does the `doAfterBody()` method return for evaluating body content of the tag once again?
Q. 16.5	Which method of `PageContext` is used to locate an attribute from any scope?
Q. 16.6	Which interface of JSP tag library is used to handle the exceptions and finalizations?
Q. 16.7	What is the main difference between classic tag handler and simple tag handler?
Q. 16.8	Which method of `SimpleTagHandler` is used to process the tag?

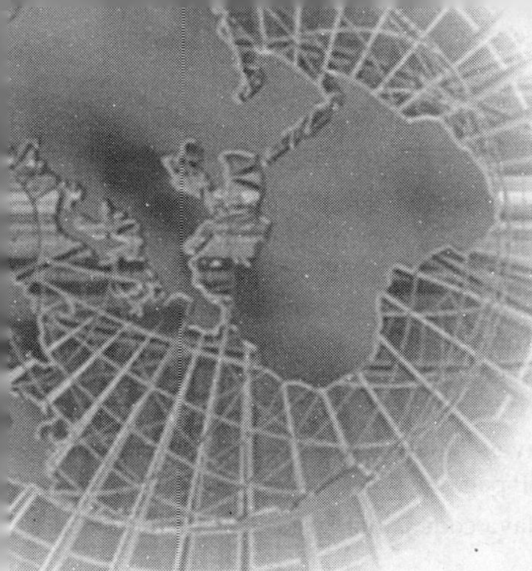

17

Understanding JSP Expression Language

Expression Language (EL) is a language that enables JSP developers to access application data stored in JavaBeans components. EL features were introduced in JSP 2.0. In JSP 2.1, the Expression Languages of JSP 2.0 and JSF 1.1 have been merged into a single unified EL (EL 2.1). Merging is done so that JSP developers do not need to worry about different lifecycles of JSP and JSF and can take advantage of new mechanisms that JSF applications already use. The EL specification was previously defined within the JSP 2.1 specification. It now has its own independent specification document, which states that EL is generally applicable to a variety of technologies and is not dependent on the JSP specification.

The methods to embed Java code or business logic in the presentation layers have been changing continuously. At present, we have the following methods to call the Java code from a JSP page:

- Put the entire Java code in a JSP page. This method is useful when Java code is not large. This method also demands the JSP developers to be familiar with the Java technology.
- Define separate helper classes that hold the entire Java code and call these helper classes in the JSP page. In this case, the `JSP` page simply contains few blocks of code to use these classes.
- Use JavaBeans and JSP page actions, such as `jsp:useBean`, `jsp:getProperty`, and `jsp:setProperty`, to call the Java code.
- Use JSP EL, which uses short notations to access and display object properties.
- Create tag handler classes to embed the Java code. These classes are invoked by using custom tags, which are similar to XML tags.

Till now, we have learned how to access Java bean's properties to show output data in JSP page using standard JSP actions, such as `jsp:useBean` and `jsp:getProperty`. But it becomes a little verbose and complex when we are accessing a bean property, which is a collection or some other Java bean.

The addition of EL to the JSP technology has reduced the use of scriptlets in JSP pages. EL expressions cannot be used in JSP scriptlets, expressions, or declaration elements. On the other hand, it provides short hand notations to retrieve, present, and manipulate Web application data.

Basic Syntax of using EL

EL expressions are enclosed between the "`${`" and "`}`" characters. The most general example of an EL expression is `${object.data}`. The object in this expression can be any Java object representing different scopes, such as request, session. Thus, it reduces the quantity of code written for these operations. This usage pattern can be enforced through the scripting-invalid JSP configuration element. JSP EL has the following features:

- Deferred expressions, which can be evaluated at different stages of the page life-cycle.
- Method expressions, which can invoke the methods that perform event handling, validation, and other functions for the JavaServer Faces technology UI components.
- Value expressions, which can set the data of external objects as well as get that data.
- A flexible mechanism to enable the customization of variable and property resolution for `EL` expression evaluation.
- Expressions that carry out arithmetic calculations

Types of EL Expressions

EL expressions can be categorized into the following types:

- Immediate and deferred expressions
- Value expressions
- Method expressions

Let's learn about these in detail next.

Immediate and Deferred Expressions

There are two constructs to represent the EL expressions—`${expr}` and `#{expr}`. In a JSP Page, `${expr}` is used for expressions that need to be evaluated immediately and `#{expr}` is used for expressions that are evaluated at a later time. Therefore, an EL expression using the `${expr}` syntax is called immediate expression; and the EL expression using the `#{expr}` syntax is called deferred expression.

In immediate expressions, the JSP container assesses the expression and gives results to response immediately during request handling. Deferred expressions have been introduced by the JSF technology. This technology uses deferred expressions because evaluation of the expression needs to defer due to multiple phases in the JSF lifecycle. All operations, such as component data validation and event handling, should be performed in a specific order. Therefore, we need to postpone the evaluation of deferred expressions to an appropriate time.

Immediate expressions may be used in template text or as values of the attributes of a JSP tag that takes a runtime value. The immediate expression can only read, but cannot set, the value of a property. Here is an example of JSP tag which uses an immediate expression:

```
<fmt:formatNumber value="${sessionScope.cart.sum}"/>
```

In the preceding example, the `${ sessionScope.cart.sum }` expression retrieves the value of the sum property from the JavaBean named cart. The sum property specifies the total price of all constituent items in the cart.

In deferred expressions, JSF Controller evaluates the expression in different phases of the JSF lifecycle, based on the component in which the expression is used. Here is an example of a JSF HTML tag which uses a deferred expression:

```
<h:inputText id="name" value="#{employee.name}" />
```

In the above example, when the JSF page containing `<h:inputText>` tag is requested, the JSF implementation evaluates the `#{employee.name}` expression in the Render Response phase of the JSF page lifecycle. After submitting this page, JSF assesses this expression in more than one phase of its lifecycle, during which the operations such as retrieving the value of `#{employee.name}` expression from the previous page, validating it, and setting this value to the name property of the managed bean are performed. This means that deferred expressions are `lvalue` expressions. The `lvalue` expressions can read or write data on a bean. The `#{employee.name}` expression acts as an `rvalue` expression, which only reads data during the initial request and acts as the `lvalue` expression during postback.

Value Expressions

Value Expressions are used to refer to objects such as JavaBeans, Collections, enumerations, and implicit objects, and their properties. Reference to an object is made using the value expression containing the name of the object. Suppose the `${employee}` expression is used in a JSP page, where employee refers to the name of a JavaBean. When the Web container sees this expression, it invokes the `PageContext.findAttribue (String)` method internally, which searches for the employee bean in the request, session, and application scopes. If the employee bean does not exist, a null value is returned.

To refer an `enum` constant using value expression, we use `String` literal. Let's look at an example of the `enum` constant. Let's consider the following `Enumeration` declaration:

```
public enum PlayCardSuite {hearts, spades, diamonds, clubs}
```

Now to access the constant defined by the Enumeration `PlayCardSuite` using expression language, we need to write the expression as shown below:

```
${PlayCardSuite.spades}
```

The above expression is an example of value expression, which is used for referring to the `enum` constant of `PlayCardSuite`.

Now let's discuss the syntax of value expressions for accessing the properties and elements of a collection in a bean. For this, we use the `(.)` and `([ ])` operators. These operators are also used in JavaScript; and are also known as ECMAScript. For example, the name property of the employee bean can be referred using either the `${employee.name}` or `${employee["name"]}` expression. We can use double or single quotes around `String` literal. To access a particular element of a collection, for example, a list or array inside a JavaBean, we use the [ ] notation having an int value. For example, ${employee.phonenos[1]} accesses the second phone number of the phonenos array.

Value expressions are of two types, rvalue and lvalue expressions. An rvalue expression can only read the data only but it cannot write the data while lvalue expression can both read and write the data. Some examples of rvalue expressions are ${"hello"}, ${ employee.age+20}, and ${ false}. EL supports all types of literals in Java, such as Boolean, integer, floating point, and string.

Value expressions may be embedded in static text or as a value of a tag attribute that can take an expression. Here is an example of a value expression embedded in static text.

```
<prefix:tag>
  some text ${expr} some text
</prefix:tag>
```

In the above code snippet, the ${expr} expression is embedded within a text string. If the body of the tag is dependent on the tag then, the embedded expression is not evaluated.

Method Expressions

Method expressions are used to call public methods, which return a value or object. Method expressions are usually deferred expressions. JSF HTML tags represent UI components on a JSF page. These tags use method expressions to call functions that perform operations such as validating a UI component or handling the events generated on a UI component. Let's look at an example of a JSF code snippet to demonstrate the use of method expressions:

```
<h:form>
  <h:inputText
        id="email"
        value="#{employee.email}"
        validator="#{employee.validateEmail}"/>
  <h:commandButton
  id="submit"
  action="#{customer.submit}" />
</h:form>
```

In the preceding code snippet:

- The inputText tag shows the UIInput component in the form of text field on a Web page.
- The validator attribute is used to call the validateEmail method of the employee bean.
- The action attribute of the commandButton tag is used to call the submit method, which performs some processing after submitting the Web page.
- The TLD (Tag Library Descriptor) defines the signatures of methods referenced by the attributes used in the code snippet.
- The validateEmail method is called during the validation phase of the JSP lifecycle.
- The submit method is called during the invoke application phase of the JSP lifecycle.

Let's now learn about tag attributes and resolving EL expressions.

Tag Attribute Types

Resolving the EL expressions depends on the type of tag attribute defined in the TLD. For custom tags, we need to specify the type of expression that the custom tag accepts. There are four categories of attribute types that define how an EL expression is evaluated:

- Static attribute, where rtexprvalue = false (attribute of any type, such as int, String, and com.Example.Order). A static attribute produces a translation error if an expression is passed to it.
- Dynamic attribute, where rtexprvalue = true (attribute of any type, such as int, String, and com.example.Order). Whenever an expression is provided to a dynamic attribute that is not a deferred-value or deferred-method, the expression is parsed with the type equal to the attribute type, and the expression is resolved immediately.

- Deferred-value (attribute of type `javax.el.ValueExpression`).
- Deferred-method (attribute of type `javax.el.MethodExpression`). If an attribute is declared as deferred-value or deferred-method in the TLD, the attribute must be of type `ValueExpression` or `MethodExpression`. The JSP container parses the expression but does not evaluate it. The result of parsing the expression is passed to the Tag handler attribute.

Resolving EL Expressions

Resolving an EL expression involves searching each component of the EL expression separated by dot operators. EL expressions are resolved from left to right. The unified EL API includes some classes and implementations to resolve EL expressions. Table 17.1 lists commonly used classes of this API.

Table 17.1: Most commonly used classes of EL API

Class	Description
`ValueExpression`	Represents a value expression
`MethodExpression`	Represents a method expression
`ELResolver`	Defines object resolution rules to resolve EL expressions
`ELContext`	Stores the state of EL resolution. The object of this class provides access to other objects, such as `JspContext`, to resolve the EL expressions

Several implementations of the `ELResolver` class are available for resolving an EL expression referring to a specific object or its property. The preceding classes are used to build custom EL resolvers.

Let's look at the process of resolving an EL expression:

If the EL expression is a value expression:

1. When a JSP page containing an EL value expression is requested for the first time, this expression is parsed and the `ValueExpression` object is generated.
2. Subsequently, the `getValue()` method of the `ValueExpression` object is called.
3. The `getValue()` method further calls the `getValue()` method of the suitable resolver.
4. On submitting this page, the `setvalue()` method is called if the expression is of `lvalue` type.

If the EL expression is a method expression:

1. First the `BeanELResolver` object is created, which searches the object that has the definition of the method referred in this expression.
2. The `MethodExpression` object is created to represent the method expression.
3. Then, the `getMethodInfo()` method is invoked, which calls the `getValue()` method of the `BeanELResolver` object, which resolves the expression.

After resolving the expression, the `propertyResolved` flag of the `ELContext` object is set to true. This detaches the resolver from the EL expression at the end.

Let's now learn about the EL resolver classes and their implementation next.

Describing the EL Resolver Classes

Many standard implementations of EL resolver classes exist in the EL API. For example, in resolving the `${employee.name}` expression, a standard `BeanELResolver` object is used, which first resolves or searches for the employee bean. Then, it resolves a specific property name. Table 17.2 lists all the standard EL resolver classes.

Table 17.2: Standard EL resolvers

Class	Description
`ArrayELResolver`	Performs property resolution on arrays
`BeanELResolver`	Performs property resolution on `JavaBeans`
`ListELResolver`	Performs property resolution on objects of the List class

Table 17.2: Standard EL resolvers

Class	Description
`MapELResolver`	Performs property resolution on objects of the Map class
`ResourceBundleELResolver`	Performs property resolution on objects of `ResourceBundle` class

Now we discuss examples of few EL expressions that implicitly use the classes specified in Table 17.2. Table 17.3 lists these examples and their functionalities.

Table 17.3: EL expressions examples

EL Expression example	Description
`${arr[2]}`	Returns the value of the element at position 2 of an array named `arr`
`${employee.name}`	Returns the value of the name property of the employee bean
`${list1[4]}`	Returns the value of fourth element of the `list1` list
`${map1.key1}`	Returns the value of the `key1` key in the `map1` map
`${RB1.key1}`	Returns the message corresponding to the `key1` key in the resource bundle named RB1

If you do not have an EL resolver implementation to handle your EL expression, you need to create a custom EL resolver and register it with the corresponding JSP application. A `CompositeELResolver` instance holds references to all standard and custom resolvers. This instance is iterated to check whether or not the current resolver can resolve the specified EL expression.

Since the release of JSP 2.1, JSP has a set of default EL resolvers. These resolvers are `ImplicitObjectResolver`, `MapELResolver`, `ListELResolver`, `ArrayELResolver`, `BeanELResorver`, and `ScopedAttributeResolver`. `ImplicitObjectResolver` and `ScopedAttributeResolver` refers to implicit objects. Consider this expression—`${sessionScope.map}`. When JSP 2.1 container encounters this expression, it resolves the implicit object `sessionScope`. Then, `MapELResolver` is used to resolve map attribute since `map` represents the instance of `Map` class. The `ScopedAttributeResolver` resolves an object stored in one of the scopes. For example, in case of `${employee}` expression, `ScopedAttributeResolver` searches for employee bean in all scopes, such as page, request, session, and application. Otherwise, it will return a null value.

NOTE

Various J2EE expert groups are trying to incorporate EL into the JSP specification.

In JSP 2.1, all classes and interfaces that were in the `javax.Servlet.jsp.el` package have been deprecated and have been introduced in the new unified EL APIs (`javax.el`).

EL Operators

EL operators are introduced in unified EL API so that developers can perform arithmetic calculations. Now, we can create EL expressions performing operations by using operators of EL.

Types of EL Operators

EL provides the support for any type of arithmetic, relational, or logical operations. In general, we look at the following types of EL operators in this section:

- Arithmetic operators
- Relational and logical operators
- The empty operator
- Conditional operators

Arithmetic Operators

All types of arithmetic operators (+,-, /,*, or %) can be used in EL expressions. The % operator is used on two integer values and returns modulus. Div and mod are alternative names of division (/) and modulus (%)

operators. We can use the minus (-) operator as a unary operator to work with negative numbers. EL also supports floating point numbers, which are fractional numbers.

Relational and Logical Operators

EL provides a set of relational and logical operators used in many programming languages. All relational and logical operators can be denoted by either using symbols or using alternate short text form. Table 17.4 lists all relational operators.

Table 17.4: Relational operators in EL

Operator Symbol	Alternate short text form	Description
>	`gt`	Greater than
>=	`ge`	Greater than or equal to
<	`lt`	Less than
<=	`le`	Less than or equal to
==	`eq`	Equal to
!=	`ne`	Not Equal to

In case any operand of these operators is a character, EL changes the character data into numerical value.

Parentheses can override precedence of most of the operators, but they cannot override the precedence of some operators such as [ ] and ;. Following is the list of EL operators with their precedence in decreasing order:

1. [ ] . ;
2. ( )
3. Unary operators such as -, !, and empty
4. * / %
5. + -
6. < > <= >=
7. == !=
8. &&
9. | |
10. ? :

The Empty operator

The empty operator is a prefix operator, which means it takes one operand on its right side. This operator is used to check for empty values, which differ according to the data type of the operand. Table 17.5 lists the empty values for different data types.

Table 17.5: Empty values

Data Type	Empty Value
`String`	" "
`Identifier`	Null
`Array`	No elements
`Map`	No elements
`List`	No elements

The Conditional Operators

Conditional operators are ternary operators. It takes three operands. The first operand is condition based. Depending on the condition, it provides two results. It returns the second operand if the first operand is true otherwise it returns the third operand.

For example, if we have three operands, say `result`, `var1`, and `var2`. `Now`, if the value of `var1` is 5 and `var2` is 10, then the conditional operator will be shown as follows:

```
Result = (var1<var2)? var1:var2
```

It will return 10.

JSP EL Reserve Words

The following are the JSP EL Reserve words. These reserve words should *not* be used as identifiers:

Reserve Words			
and	Or	not	eq
ne	Lt	gt	le
ge	True	false	null
instanceof	Empty	div	mod

Let's now look at an example to use the EL operators.

An Example of Using EL Operators

Now, let's put all these operators in use. Listing 17.1 demonstrates several EL expressions using arithmetic, relational, logical, and empty operators. You can also find this file online in the code/Chapter17/Operators folder.

Listing 17.1: The operators.jsp page

```
<html>
    <head>
    <title>Using EL Operators</title></head>
    <body>
        <h2>Using EL Operators</h2>
        <h3>Arithmetic Expressions</h3>
        <b>You Score in IELTS is ${1 + 2 * 4 - 6 / 2}.</b><br/>
        <b>Today temperature of Delhi is ${-4 - 8} degree celsius.</b><br/>
        <b>Is 3/4 equals to 0.75 ? ${(3/4 == 0.75)? "Yes" : "No"}</b><br/>
        <b>Mathematical Constant PI has value ${22/7} </b><br/>
        <b>GDP of India is  ${20 div 2}.</b><br/>
        <b>I have ${2003 mod 8} mobiles.</b><br/>
        <b>I have ${2003 % 8} mobiles.</b><br/>
        <h3>Logical Operators </h3>
<b>This Logical and EL expression \${(1&lt;2) && (4&lt;3)} is ${(1<2) && (4<3)}</b><br/>
<b>This Logical or EL expression \${(1&lt;2) || (4&lt;3)} is ${(1<2) || (4<3)}
        </b><br/>
<b>This Logical not EL expression \${!(1&lt;2)} is ${!(1<2)} </b><br/>
        <h3>Comparison Operators </h3>
        <b>Is 4 > 3 ?  ${4 > 3}</b><br/>
        <b>Is "a" > "b"? ${"a" > "b"}</b><br/>
        <b>Is 4 >= 3 ${4 >= 3}</b><br/>
        <b>Is 4 <= 3 ${4 < 3}</b><br/>
        <b>Is 4 == 4? ${4 == 4}</b><br/>
        <h3>empty Operator</h3>
        <b>empty "" ${empty ""}</b><br/>
        <b>empty "string" ${empty "string"}</b><br/>
        <b>empty null ${empty null}</b>
    </body>
</html>
```

In Listing 17.1, under the heading "Arithmetic Expressions", we show you the use of addition, subtraction, division, and modulus operators in EL expressions. The Conditional operator (?:) is also used in the line <b> Is 3/4 equals to 0.75? ${(3/4 == 0.75)? "Yes": "No"} </b>
. Under second heading <h3> named "Logical Operators", we form some logical expressions, which show the use of the &&, | |, and ! operators. You must have noticed that if you want to print an EL expression as it is, you need to prefix it with backslash (/), as shown in case of logical operators.

Under third heading <h3> named "Comparison Operators", we perform some comparisons using the <, <=, >, >=, and == relational operators. Finally, we use an empty prefix operator on a blank string and null value.

Arrange all the files in the Operators directory according to the directory structure of Web applications. Copy Operators directory in the <Tomcat-home>/webapps directory and start the Tomcat server. browse the application by using the URL http://localhost:9090/Operators/operators.jsp to view the output of Listing 17.1. Figure 17.1 shows the output of Listing 17.1:

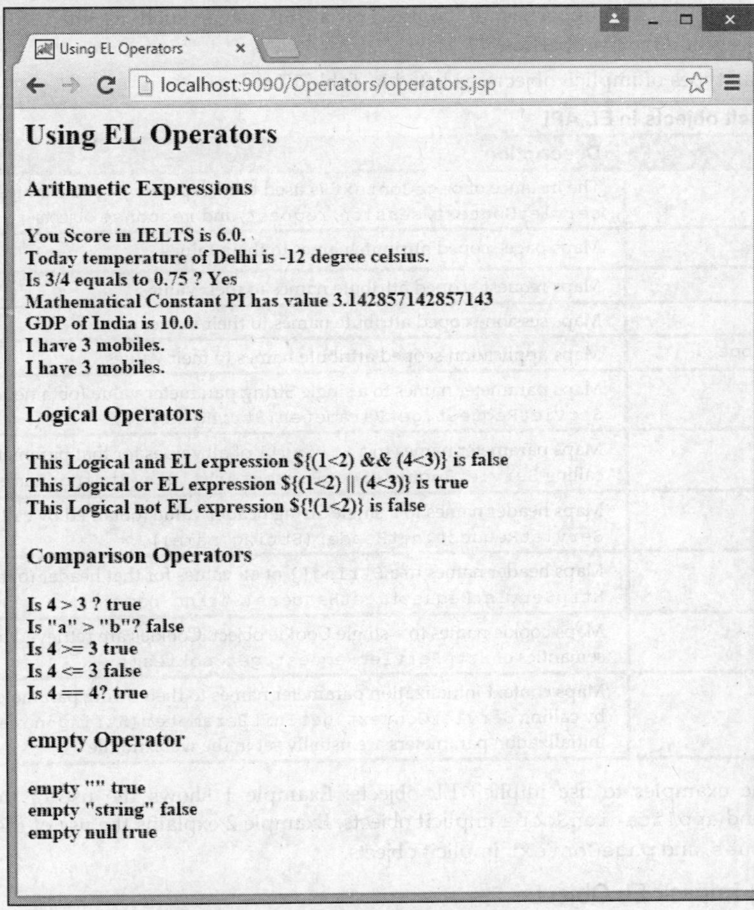

Figure 17.1: Using EL Operators

All arithmetic numbers under the Arithmetic Expressions heading, as shown in Figure 17.1, are displayed using arithmetic EL expressions and all false and true results are displayed using relational and logical operators. You have to scroll down to see the results after using the empty operator on various types of strings.

Implicit EL Objects

JSP developers can directly use implicit objects in an EL expression. They do not need to write extra code for using these objects. Some of these objects allow the access to variables held in the particular JSP scopes. The EL implicit objects are pageScope, requestScope, sessionScope, and applicationScope objects. All these mentioned Scope objects map the respective scope attribute names to their values.

Moreover, it is also possible to access HTTP request parameters by using the param and paramValues implicit objects. The request header information can be retrieved using the header and headerValues implicit objects. The param and header objects map the parameter or header name to a String. The paramValues and headerValues objects map the parameter and header names of all values for that parameter or header to a String[]. Previously in Servlet API, the ServletRequest.getParameter(String name) and ServletRequest.getHeader(String name) methods were used to map the parameter and header names to a String. Moreover, the ServletRequest.getParameterValues(String name) and HttpServletRequest.getHeaders(String) methods were used to map parameter and header names of all values for that parameter or header to a String[]

The role of initParam is to provide access to context initialization parameters. The pageContext implicit object provides access to all properties of context of a JSP page, such as the ServletContext and HttpSession objects and their properties.

Let's now look at all types of implicit objects, as listed in Table 17.6:

Table 17.6 Implicit objects in EL API

Object Name	Description
pageContext	The instance of pageContext is used to manipulate page attributes and access servletContext, session, request, and response objects
pageScope	Maps page-scoped attribute names to their values
requestScope	Maps request-scoped attribute names to their values
sessionScope	Maps session-scoped attribute names to their values
applicationScope	Maps application-scoped attribute names to their values
param	Maps parameter names to a single String parameter value (obtained by calling ServletRequest.getParameter(String name))
paramValues	Maps parameter names to a String[] of all values for that parameter (obtained by calling ServletRequest.getParameterValues(String name))
Header	Maps header names to a single String header value (obtained by calling ServletRequest.getHeader(String name))
headerValues	Maps header names to a String[] of all values for that header (obtained by calling HttpServletRequest.getHeaders(String name))
cookie	Maps cookie names to a single Cookie object. Cookies are retrieved according to the semantics of HttpServletRequest.getCookies()
initParam	Maps context initialization parameter names to their String parameter value (obtained by calling ServletContext.getInitParameter(String name)). The context initialization parameters are usually set in the web.xml file

Let's look at some examples to use implicit EL objects. Example 1 shows the use of the requestScope, sessionScope, and applicationScope implicit objects. Example 2 explains the use of the cookie, header, param, paramValues, and pageContext implicit objects.

Example 1 of Using Implicit EL Objects

This example illustrates how to access scoped variables in JSP EL. The process of accessing scoped variables starts from the Servlet, which is configured in web.xml file for handling the respective request. The Servlet performs the business logic on the data sent with the request and sets the output data in different scopes like request, session, and application. The Servlet sets the output data in request, session or application scopes by invoking setAttribute() method on HttpServletRequest, HttpSession, or ServletContext object, respectively, and then forward the control to JSP page to display output data using RequestDispatcher.forward() method or HttpServletResponse.sendRedirect() method. There is another scope, called `pageContext`, which stores page scoped variables or objects used on a JSP or Servlet page. Thus, this scope is not shared by servlets and JSPs.

Now, let's see how scoped variables are accessed in EL. To access and display a scoped variable on the browser, EL requires expression such as `${name}`, where name is a scoped variable. When an EL supporting container encounters this expression, it searches for the name variable in the specified order: `PageContext`, `HttpServletRequest`, `HttpSession`, and `ServletContext`. If it gets the name variable, it calls the `toString()` method on the variable value and provides the output.

We use the following syntax to access the name variable `<%=pageContext.findAttribute("name") %>`; however, in this case, the search is only limited to the Page scope. If syntax to use is `<jsp:useBean>`, it looks like `<jsp:useBean id="name" type="package.class" scope=""> <%=name%>`. For using this syntax, you should have information about the scope of the servlet and the qualified path of the bean class.

We created one servlet, which sets attributes or variables in different scopes, and one JSP page, which accesses these variables using EL syntax. Listing 17.2 shows SetScopeVariables.java Servlet, which sets the value of the "`attribute1`" attribute. You can also find this file online in the code/Chapter17/ImplicitObjects folder.

Listing 17.2: The SetScopeVariables.java File

```
import java.io.*;
import javax.servlet.*;
import javax.servlet.http.*;
public class SetScopeVariables extends HttpServlet
{
    public void doGet(HttpServletRequest request,
    HttpServletResponse response)
    throws ServletException, IOException {
            request.setAttribute("attribute1", "First Value");
            HttpSession session = request.getSession();
            session.setAttribute("attribute2", "Second Value");
            ServletContext application = getServletContext();
            application.setAttribute("attribute3",new java.util.Date());
            request.setAttribute("repeated", "Request");
            session.setAttribute("repeated", "Session");
            application.setAttribute("repeated", "ServletContext");
            RequestDispatcher dispatcher =
            request.getRequestDispatcher("GetScopeVariables.jsp");
            dispatcher.forward(request, response);
    }
}
```

In Listing 17.2, we set the `attribute1`, `attribute2`, and `attribute3` attributes to the "`First Value`", "`Second Value`" values and current date and time strings, respectively. The `attribute1`, `attribute2`, and `attribute3` attributes are set in the request, session, and application scope, respectively. There is one another attribute, called `repeated`, which sets in all these three scopes. Finally, the Servlet transfers the control to the GetScopeVariables.jsp JSP page.

In Listing 17.3, we use the same syntax for accessing the `attribute1`, `attribute2`, `attribute3` attributes, irrespective of the scopes where they are stored. You can find the syntax in statements such as "Accessing attribute directly". We have also embedded some statements that restrict the search of a particular attribute in a particular scope; such as `sessionScope.attribute1`. Listing 17.3 shows the use of some implicit objects. You can also find this online in the code/Chapter 7/ImplicitObjects folder.

Listing 17.3: The GetScopeVariables.jsp Page

```
<html>
<head><title>Accessing Scoped Variables</title></head>
<body>
    <table border=2 align="center">
    <tr><th>
    Accessing Scoped Variables
```

```
        </table>
        <p>
        <ul>
        <li><b>Accessing attribute1 directly:</b> ${attribute1}
        <li><b>Accessing attribute1 using requestScope implicit object:</b>
        ${requestScope.attribute1}
        <li><b>Checking whether attribute1 is present in session scope using
        sessionScope implict object:</b>${sessionScope.attribute1}
        <li><b>Accessing attribute2 directly:</b> ${attribute2}
        <li><b>Checking whether attribute2 is present in application scope using
        applicationScope implict object:</b> ${applicationScope.attribute2}
        <li><b>Accessing attribute3 directly:</b> ${attribute3}
        <li><b>Accessing repeated attribute directly:</b> ${repeated}
        <li><b>Checking repeated attribute only in application scope using
        applicationScope implicit object:</b> ${applicationScope.repeated}
        </ul>
    </body></html>
```

To execute Listing 17.2 and 17.3, create an empty directory and name it as ImplicitObjects. Properly store Listings 17.2 and 17.3 in the ImplicitObjects directory according to standard directory structure of Web applications. Copy the Operators folder in <Tomcat home>/webapps folder. Start the Tomcat server. Browse the application by using the URL `http://localhost:9090/ImplicitObjects/SetScopeVariables`, as shown in Figure 17.2:

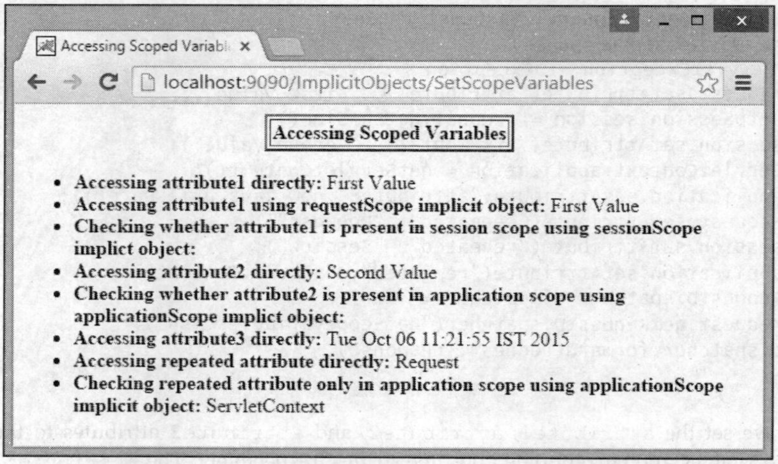

Figure 17.2: Accessing attributes using Scoped Variables

In the third and fifth lines of Figure 17.2, no value is displayed because the JSP container is not able to find `attribute1` in the request scope and `attribute2` in the application scope, respectively. This is another advantage of EL that it does not generate `NullPointerException` or return null value if it is unable to find an attribute in a particular scope. It only displays an empty string as the output.

Example 2 of Using Implicit EL Objects

In the second example, the user is asked to enter some information and then that information is retrieved and displayed along with other information, such as the server name- jsessionid.

The index.html page is a simple HTML form that contains the email text box, three checkboxes, and a Submit button. When the user submits this form, the control is transferred to the impobjects2.jsp page. Listing 17.4 shows the index.html page. You can also find this file online in the code/Chapter 17/ImplicitObjects folder.

Listing 17.4: The index.html page

```
    <html>
        <head><title>Index Page</title></head>
```

```
    <body>
          <form action="impobject2.jsp" method="get">
          <table border=2 align="center">
          <TR><Th>
          Using Implicit Objects</th>
          </TABLE>
          <table>
                   <tr><td colspan=2><h3>Pet Shopping Cart</h3></td></tr>
                   <tr>
                   <td>
                          Your Email Id :<input type="text" name=email
                          size="30" /><td></tr>
                   <tr><td>
                   What type of pets do you have?</td></tr>
                   <tr><td>cat <input type="checkbox" name="pettype"
                   value="cat" /></td></tr>
                   <tr><td>dog <input type="checkbox" name="pettype"
                  value="dog" /></td></tr>
                   <tr><td>rabbit <input type="checkbox" name="pettype"
                   value="rabbit"/></td></tr>
          </table>
                   <tr><td><input type=submit value="Submit"></td></tr>
          </table>
          </form>
    </body>
</html>
```

The impobjects2.jsp page displays the email id of the user by using the `param` implicit object. We have used the `<c:forEach>` tag of the JSTL core library, which iterates over the collection represented by the `paramValues` implicit object; assigns each value to the pet variable, and prints them. Listing 17.5 shows the impobject2.jsp page. You can also find this file online in the code/Chapter17/ImplicitObjects folder.

Listing 17.5: The impobject2.jsp page

```
<%@ taglib prefix="c" uri="http://java.sun.com/jsp/jstl/core" %>
<html>
    <head><title>Using Implicit Objects</title></head>
    <body>
          <table border=2 align="center">
          <tr><th>
          Using Implicit Objects
          </table>
          <p><ul>
                   <li><b>Your Email ID is :</b> ${param.email}
                   <li><b>You have selected pets:</b>
                   <c:forEach var="pet" items="${paramValues.pettype}">
                     ${pet}  
                   </c:forEach>
                   <li><b>User-Agent Header:</b> ${header["User-Agent"]}
                   <li><b>JSESSIONID Cookie Value:</b>
                   ${cookie.JSESSIONID.value}
                   <li><b>Server:</b> ${pageContext.servletContext.serverInfo}
          </ul>
    </body>
</html>
```

In the above listing, we have also included the JSTL core library to use its `<c:forEach>` tag. The `{header["User-Agent"]}` expression displays the browser associated with the user agent header. The cookie implicit object is used to retrieve the value of JSESSIONID, which is a large string consisting of alphabets and numbers. Finally, the `pageContext` object is used to fetch the server name, which processes the index.html page and displays the results.

Arrange all the files in the ImplicitObjects directory according to the standard directory structure of Web applications. Also, you must place the `standard.jar` and `jstl.jar` files in the lib folder under the WEB-INF folder of the ImplicitObjects root directory. You can download the jar files from the `http://jakarta.apache.org/site/downloads/downloads_taglibs.html` hyperlink. Select the Standard Taglib 1.1 option and download the zip file. After extracting this zip file, you can find these jar files in the lib folder of the unzipped directory. Redeploy the ImplicitObjects folder on Tomcat server. Browse the application by using the URL `http://localhost:9090/ImplicitObjects/index.html`, as shown in Figure 17.3:

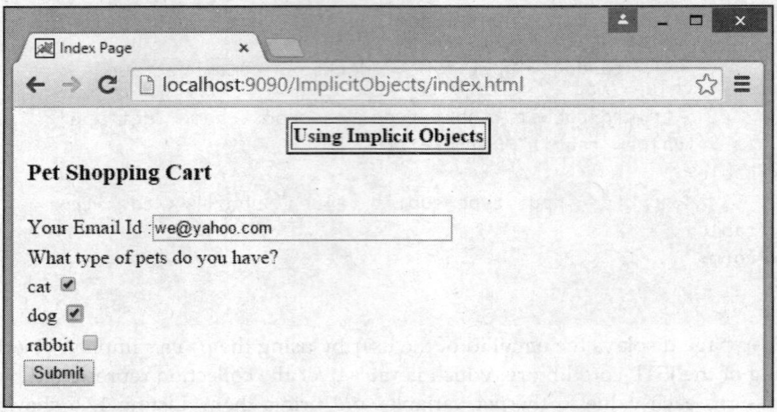

Figure 17.3: Using JSP Implicit Objects

In Figure 17.3, the user enters **we@yahoo.com** as the email id and then selects the check boxes corresponding to cat and dog. After clicking the Submit button, an Internet Explorer window appears, as shown in Figure 17.4.

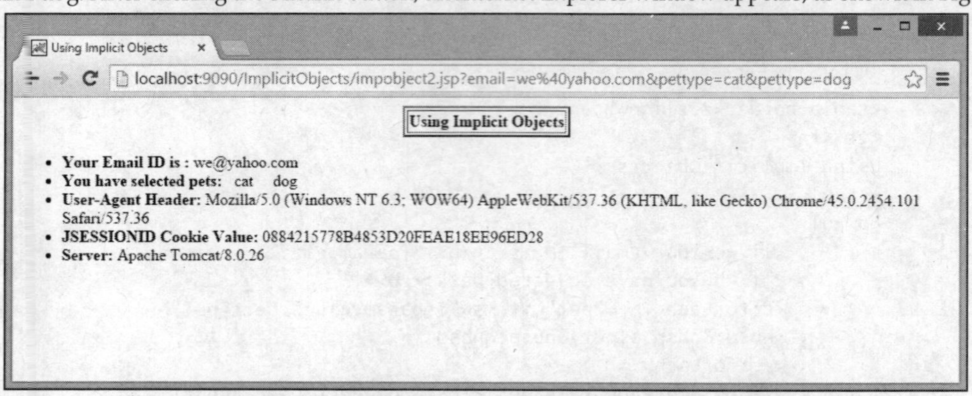

Figure 17.4: Displaying user details using Implicit Objects.

Figure 17.4 displays the email id and the selected check boxes values, the compatible browser type, JSESSIONID, and the server name with version, in the form of a bulleted list.

Introducing Functions with EL

Sometimes, the developer may require changing the format of data or manipulating the data before it gets displayed on a Web page. Custom tag library can easily solve this purpose; however, EL provides no such built-in library. Developers need to define their own methods. The prefix assigned to the function tag library is used to access the EL functions. In other words, the EL has the concept of qualified functions. The EL functions are public static methods in Java classes, which are mapped in the TLD.

As far as the Tag library is concerned, each Tag library might include zero or more static functions that are listed in the TLD. Moreover, the name given to a function in the TLD is exposed to the EL. A public static method in the specified public class implements the functions. You have to be very careful about naming the function in the tag library, since the function name must be unique in the tag library. If the function is not declared correctly, or if there are multiple functions bearing the same name, a translation-time error is generated.

We have already covered method expressions, which appear similar but are not identical to EL functions. The following are the differences between function expressions and method expressions:

- Functions are static methods that return single values but method expressions use non static public methods.
- Functions are recognized during translation time but methods are recognized dynamically at runtime.
- The identification of a particular method is provided in the method expression and that method is invoked in the tag attribute definition by using the method expression. Alternatively, in functions, the function parameters and their invocations are a part of EL expressions.

Using EL Functions

This section explains the use of EL functions with an example, where we use two EL functions. The first one accepts a signed integer value and returns its absolute value; while the second function accepts a floating point value and rounds it into an integer value. The functions.jsp page includes the custom tag library represented by uri http://www.kogentindia.com/el-functions-taglib, and invokes the abs and round functions by using XML namespaces notation, such as f:abs( ). Listing 17.6 invokes two functions inside the EL expressions. You can also find this file online in the code/Chapter 17/ELFunction folder.

Listing 17.6: The functions.jsp page

```
<%@ taglib prefix="f" uri="http://www.dt.com/el-functions-taglib" %>
<html>
<head>
  <title>Using EL Functions</title>
</head>
<body>
  <h1>Using EL Functions </h1>
  The absolute value of \${num} is ${f:abs(-300)}.<br/>
  The rounded value of \${calc} is ${f:round(6.666666666666667)}.<br/>
</body>
</html>
```

The JSP container locates the imported tag library in the web.xml file of this application. The web.xml file consists of the <taglib> tag having two nested tags, <taglib-uri> and <taglib-location>. The <taglib-uri> tag takes the specified uri in the uri attribute of the taglib directive in the functions.jsp page; and the actual location of the TLD file is specified in <taglib-location> tag, which is /WEB-INF/function-taglib.tld. Listing 17.7 shows the web.xml file. You can also find this file online in the code/Chapter17/ELFunction/WEB-INF folder.

Listing 17.7: The web.xml file

```
<?xml version="1.0" encoding="UTF-8"?>
<web-app>
<jsp-config>
  <taglib>
        <taglib-uri>
```

```
                    http://www.dt.com/el-functions-taglib
            </taglib-uri>
            <taglib-location>
                    /WEB-INF/function-taglib.tld
            </taglib-location>
    </taglib>
  </jsp-config>
  </web-app>
```

We have also explained earlier that EL function definitions are contained within another TLD file. The function-taglib.tld file maps the function calls in the functions.jsp page to the `<function>` tags. The Java class implementing the function, which in this case is `java.lang.Math` for both the `abs` and `round` functions, is specified in the `<function-class>` tag. These functions signatures are specified in the `<function-signature >` tag. Listing 17.8 consists of function definitions of the functions used in Listing 17.6. You can also find this file online in the code/Chapter 17/ELFunction/WEB-INF folder.

Listing 17.8: The function-taglib.tld file

```
  <?xml version="1.0" encoding="UTF-8" ?>

  <taglib xmlns="http://java.sun.com/xml/ns/j2ee"

    xmlns:xsi="http://www.w3.org/2001/XMLSchema-instance"
    xsi:schemaLocation="http://java.sun.com/xml/ns/j2ee web-
    jsptaglibrary_2_0.xsd"
    version="2.0">
    <description>A taglib to define some EL accessible functions.</description>
    <tlib-version>1.0</tlib-version>
    <short-name>ELFunctionTaglib</short-name>
    <uri>/ELFunctionTagLibrary</uri>

    <function>

            <name>abs</name>
            <function-class>java.lang.Math</function-class>
            <function-signature>int abs( int )</function-signature>

    </function>

    <function>
            <name>round</name>
            <function-class>java.lang.Math</function-class>
            <function-signature>int round( double )</function-signature>

    </function>

  </taglib>
```

Arrange all the files according to the standard directory structure of Web applications. Copy the ELFunction folder in the `<Tomcat home>/webapps` directory to deploy it on Tomcat server. Now, start your server and browse the application by using the URL `http://localhost:9090/ELFunction/functions.jsp`.

The Internet Explorer window appears, as shown in Figure 17.5:

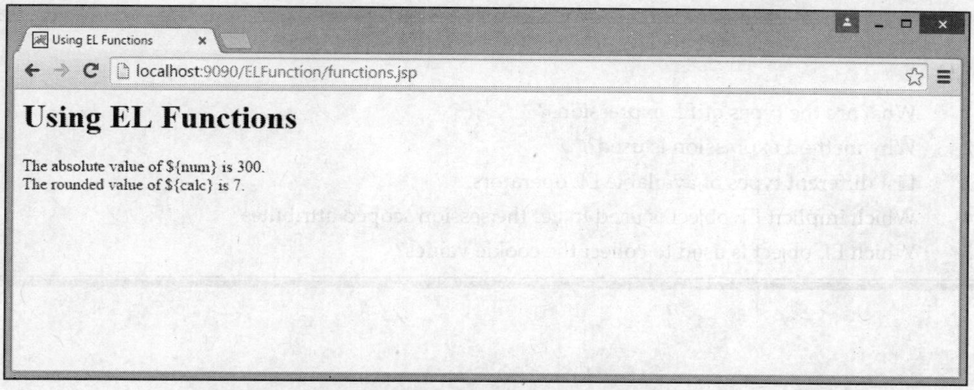

Figure 17.5: Displaying the output of EL Functions

Figure 17.5 displays the absolute value of signed integer 300. The second expression rounds 6.6666666667 to 7. In this application, the absolute value of signed integer, are returned by the method evaluation but a null value is returned if the return type of the Java method is void.

If an exception is thrown during method evaluation, the exception must be wrapped in an `ELException`. This is because the EL uses an `ELException` exception for any exception that may occur during parsing or expression evaluation.

Summary

This chapter discusses the need and features of EL. The various types of EL expressions and EL operators that can be used in EL expressions are also discussed. The implementation of EL operators is also discussed with the help of a simple application. Finally, the chapter describes implicit objects and demonstrates how they are used in JSP pages.

Let's recall the following important points to summarize the chapter:

- Expression Language (EL) is a language that enables JSP developers to access application data stored in JavaBeans components.
- EL expressions are enclosed between the "`${`" and "`}`" characters.
- There are two constructs to represent the EL expressions – `${expr}` and `#{expr}`.
- In immediate expressions, the JSP container assesses the expression and gives results to response immediately during request handling.
- Immediate expressions may be used in template text or as values of the attributes of a JSP tag that takes a runtime value.
- Value Expressions are used to refer to objects such as JavaBeans, Collections, enumerations, and implicit objects, and their properties.
- Method expressions are used to call public methods, which return a value or object. Method expressions are usually deferred expressions.
- Resolving an EL expression involves searching each component of the EL expression separated by dot operators.
- EL operators are introduced in unified EL API so that developers can perform arithmetic calculations.
- All types of arithmetic operators (+,-, /,*, or %) can be used in EL expressions.
- EL provides a set of relational and logical operators used in many programming languages.
- The empty operator is a prefix operator, which means it takes one operand on its right side.
- JSP developers can directly use implicit objects in an EL expression.

In the next chapter, we will learn how internationalization support is implemented in a Web application.

Exercise

Q. 17.1	What are the types of EL expressions?
Q. 17.2	Why method expression is used?
Q. 17.3	List different types of available EL operators.
Q. 17.4	Which implicit EL object is used to get the session scoped attributes?
Q. 17.5	Which EL object is used to collect the cookie values?

18

Implementing Internationalization

Introducing Internationalization

With the advent of globalization, the importance of globalizing or internationalizing Web applications has increased manifold. This is important because Web applications are accessed by users from various regions and countries.

In today's globalized era, business transactions involve customers worldwide. Customers generally expect data to be presented according to their specific culture and locale, especially when it comes to the language and data formats. Therefore, Web applications, which are accessed by users worldwide, must support different languages, text formats, number and date formats, and currency formats being used in different regions of the world. In other words, Web applications must present information in many languages according to different users from different locales.

Globalization of Web applications can be accomplished through the process of Internationalization and Localization. Internationalization can be defined as the process of enabling a Web application to present different country and region specific formats without making any changes in the code or recompiling the application. The term 'Internationalization' is generally abbreviated as i18n; since there are 18 characters between "i" and "n". The process of customizing a software or Web application for a specific region or language, by introducing locale-specific components, is known as localization. It enables Web applications to adapt message, number, and date formats according to a given locale. Localization can be abbreviated as l10n, because this word contains 10 letters between "l" and "n".

Although every application should be internationalized and localized, it is particularly important for the Web applications because of the global nature of the Internet. This chapter provides an overview of Java core Internationalization and Localization APIs and then further explains how to implement Internationalization of Web applications.

Java and Internationalization

Java Standard Edition, (Java SE) provides a rich set of APIs to support Internationalization and Localization of an application. This section gives the reader a brief introduction about how to use the APIs provided with the Core Java platform to implement Internationalization and Localization. The Internationalization APIs provided with Java SE can easily adapt different messages, number, date, and currency formats according to different country and region conventions. Java also provides support for Unicode character sets and a rich set of APIs to manage locale-specific content. The Internationalization and Localization APIs specified under Java SE Platform is based on the Unicode 3.0 character encoding. Java SE provides two common classes to implement Internationalization, `Locale` and `ResourceBundle`. Let's explore these two classes one by one.

Describing the Locale Class

The `java.util.Locale` class is used while creating International Java applications. The `java.util.Locale` class is a non-abstract final class packed into the `java.util` package. A Locale object (an instance of the `Locale` class) encapsulates the language, country, and variant of the specific locale. In other words, Locale is a relatively simple object, which defines the specific language and geographic region. These Locales affect language choice, collation, calendar usage, date and time formats, number and currency formats, and many other cultural sensitive data representations. All other locale-oriented classes use the Locale object to adapt to the specific locale and provide the output accordingly.

The `Locale` class consists of three constructors that allow us to construct a Locale object according to the specific requirements:

- **`Locale (String language)`** – Constructs a Locale object with the given language code.
- **`Locale (String language, String country)`** – Constructs a Locale object with the given language and country code.
- **`Locale (String language, String country, String variant)`** – Constructs a Locale object with the given language, country, and variant.

The Locale object depicts the language and cultural preferences of a specific geographical area. Dates, time, numbers, and currency are the examples of data formatted according to the cultural expectations of the customers.

Parameters of the Locale Object

Let's discuss the three parameters passed in the constructors for creating Locale object:

- Language
- Country
- Variant

The Language Parameter

The language parameter provides the valid language codes that can be used to construct a Locale object, and is specified by the ISO 639 standard. The valid language code must be a two-letter language code in lowercase, such as 'en' for English, 'hi' for Hindi, and 'te' for Telugu. For the complete list of valid language codes, refer to the following URL: `http://www.ics.uci.edu/pub/ietf/http/related/iso639.txt`

The Country Parameter

The country parameter describes valid two-letter codes for a country's name, and is also specified by an ISO standard, ISO 3166. The ISO 3166 standard defines the country codes in uppercase. The Locale constructor allows lowercase letters as it promptly converts the code into uppercase, to create the correct internal representation. Some of the valid country codes are 'IN' for India, 'US' for United States, and 'GB' for United Kingdom. For the complete list of valid country codes, refer to the following URL: `http://userpage.chemie.fu-berlin.de/diverse/doc/ISO_3166.html`

The Variant Parameter

The variant parameter is an optional extension to a Locale class. Variants can be used to add additional context with the Locale and make it more descriptive. For example, the Locale `en_US` represents English (United States), but `en_US_CA` represents more information and might identify a locale for English (California, U.S.A). Therefore, software vendors can use variants to create more descriptive Locales for their specific environments.

Locale-sensitive operations, such as `getDataInstance()`, `getTimeInstance()`, and `getDateTimeInstance()`, use the Locale parameter to retrieve data, time, and date and time instance. These Locale-sensitive operations behave differently depending on the Locale, and they also format the information according to the customs/conventions of the user's native country, region, or culture.

Using the Locale Class

As discussed previously, the `Locale` class has three constructors; the following code snippet describes how to use either of the constructors to create a Locale object:

```
Locale myLocale = new Locale("en","US");
```

In the preceding code snippet, en represents English and US is used for the United States of America. Moreover, the Locale object can also be constructed by using variant. The following code snippet creates a Locale object with the optional variant, which can be used to create a specific Locale, as compared to the Locale created by using just language and country codes:

```
Locale  myLocale = new Locale("en","US","VENTURA");
```

The `Locale` class contains the following access methods:

- `getLanguage()`
- `getCountry()`
- `getVariant()`
- `toString()`

The getLanguage() method returns the ISO language and the getCountry() method returns the country codes, which comprise a Locale object. However, these codes may not be much user-friendly, other methods such as getDisplayLanguage() and getDisplayCountry() return String objects, which are easily understandable by the users.

Listing 18.1 creates the myLocale object, which provides an access to the getDisplayLanguage() and getDisplayCountry() methods. The getDisplayLanguage() and getDisplayCountry() methods are locale-sensitive methods, implying that the Locale parameter can be provided to retrieve the language or country string in the target language, passed as a parameter. As in Listing 18.1, Locale.FRENCH locale gives the reference of the Locale object for FRENCH language. You can also find this file, Locales.java, online in the code/Chapter18/intl folder.

Listing 18.1: Creating the Locales.java File

```
package com.santosh.i18n;
import java.util.Locale;
public class Locales
{
    public static void main(String s[]) throws Exception
    {
        Locale myLocale=null;
        String language=null;
        String country=null;
        myLocale = new Locale("en", "US");
        language = myLocale.getDisplayLanguage();
        System.out.println(language);
        country=myLocale.getDisplayCountry();
        System.out.println(country);
        System.out.println(myLocale.getDisplayLanguage(Locale.FRENCH));
        System.out.println(myLocale.getDisplayCountry(Locale.FRENCH));

}
```

Figure 18.1 displays the output, after compiling Listing 18.1. In Figure 18.1, the language displayed is English and the country is United States. Notice that Figure 18.1 also displays the language and country name in FRENCH.

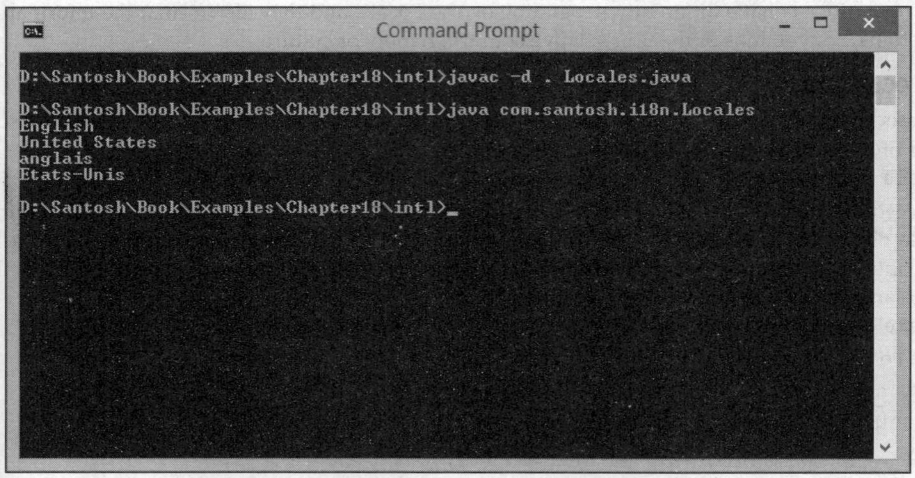

Figure 18.1: Displaying the Output of Locales.java

Now, after understanding the Locale class and learning how to create a Locale object, let's see which class should be used to format numbers and dates for a specific locale.

Formatting Numbers and Dates

We know that it is always hard to make standardization on how to write dates and numbers. Sometimes we use the date format in month, day and year and sometimes we use day, month and year. Besides, we use sometimes numeric value to represent month and sometimes we use the name of the month. We also use different characters to differentiate between the fractional parts of number. These specifications differ from countries to countries. In addition, these specifications are different even in countries that use the same language. For example, if we say that a particular work needs to be completed by 5/3; this may be interpreted by an American as May 3, but a citizen of Sweden may interpret the same as March 5. Therefore, Java introduces `java.text.NumberFormat` and `java.text.DateFormat` classes. These classes are used for formatting dates and numbers for a specific locale. The standard converter of JSF uses `java.text.NumberFormat` and `java.text.DateFormat` classes for converting dates/time and numeric values.

Operating systems use `NumberFormat` class by default to format numbers. Suppose that if we have configured a server to use U.S. English locale, it will format the numbers and date according to American custom. Similarly, if we have configured a server to use Italian locale, it will format the numbers and date according to Italian custom.

NOTE

We can explicitly specify a locale to format number and date on operating system.

In the next chapter, we will specify how JSP Standard Tag Library (JSTL) formatting is used by a locale and we will also identify which formatting action is used on the basis of Accept-Language header. The `DateFormat` class implements in the same way.

The `DateFormat` class is the basis of JSTL `<fmt:formatDate>` action ,which we will be studying in detail in the next chapter.

Now, let's see how to use localized text.

Using Localized Text

The `java.util.ResourceBundle` class is used to deal with the localized resources, such as images, text, and sounds. The `java.util.ResourceBundle` class has two subclasses, `ListResourceBundle` and `PropertyResourceBundle`. `java.util.ResourceBundle` class provides the methods to get the appropriate subclass, hiding the details of localized resources that are provided in the subclass.

`PropertyResourceBundle` is used for a lot of web applications. It is associated with the named set of localized text resources where a key is used to identify each resource.

The following code shows the storing mechanism:

```
company_name=The Reliance Pvt Ltd.
company_logo =/images/logo1_Rellogo.gif
welcome_msg = Welcome to the world of Reliance!
```

In the above code, the logo of Reliance will be stored as `logo1_Rellogo.gif` and the variable `welcome_msg` will show the message `Welcome to the world of Reliance!`

In the above code, we have used three keys: `company_name`, `company_logo` and `welcome_msg`. All of the three keys have been assigned with a value. Here key is a string that does not have any space or any supplementary singular characters and the value assigned to the key is in the form of any text. If we have more than one line for the value, we should use backslash character (\) for line break. For example:

```
Multiple_line_messages = This code value\
is continued .
```

`.properties` extension should be used by file, for example `sitetext.properties`. The file must be placed in the classpath that is used by Java Virtual Machine (JVM). In `WEB-INF/classes` directory, the file of Web applicant can be stored. We create the resource bundles for each locale to localize an application. However, these different resource bundles have the same main name or base name and they have unique suffixes to determine the locale. For example, `sitetext_hi_IND.properties`, where `hi` is language code for Hindi and IND is the country code for India. Here, file can include the text for the Indian Hindi locale.

Let's discuss the `ResourceBundle` class.

Describing the ResourceBundle Class

The ResourceBundles class provides the mechanism to separate user interface (UI) elements and other locale-sensitive data from the application logic. The ResourceBundle class is used to segregate localizable elements such as buttons labels, error messages, and headings from the rest of the application. These localizable elements are bundled into a .properties file, which is known as resource bundle. The resource bundle contains either the resource (UI elements and local-sensitive data) itself or a reference for it. Therefore, with all the resources separated into a bundle, a Java application simply loads the appropriate bundle for the active locale.

The ResourceBundle names have two parts: a base name and a locale suffix. The base name defines the name of the default ResourceBundle and the suffix defines the specific locale. For example, suppose you create a ResourceBundle named myresBundle. Now, imagine you have translated myresBundle for two different locales, en_US and ja_JP. The myresBundle ResourceBundle will be the default ResourceBundle, and you need to create two more bundles, myresBundle_en_US and myresBundle_ja_JP, for the two different locales en_US and ja_JP, respectively. The ResourceBundle.getBundle() method relies on this naming convention to search for the bundle used for the active locale.

The ResourceBundle class is a container used by a program to retrieve an object for a particular Locale. The ResourceBundle class is an abstract class packaged in the java.util package. The ResourceBundle object encapsulates locale-specific resources for an application, where the resource can be stored in a list or a property file. The ResourceBundle class is not intended to be used directly, because it is an abstract class. ResourceBundle has two direct subclasses:

- **PropertyResourceBundle**—Provides a mechanism for using properties files to store resources. The PropertyResourceBundle class is the most commonly used for working with resource bundles in Java.
- **ListResourceBundle**—Provides a mechanism for using lists to store resources.

Let's now discuss these two subclasses next.

The PropertyResourceBundle Class

A PropertyResourceBundle class is a subclass of ResourceBundle that manages resources for a locale using a set of static strings from a properties file. A property file is a plain text file containing editable text. The syntax of the name of the property file is:

```
<basename>_<language>_<country>.properties
```

The getBundle() method of the ResourceBundle class automatically looks for the property file, provided as a parameter. Then a PropertyResourceBundle is created that refers to the specified property file. A call to the ResourceBundle.getBundle("ApplicationResources",new Locale("en", "US")) method attempts to retrieve the object of the PropertyResourceBundle class for the file with the name "ApplicationResources_en_US.properties".

The PropertyResourceBundle class can be used by creating a property file that contains the key/value pairs in the form of <key>=<value>. Each key/value pair is listed on the same line of the .properties file and each pair is separated with the new-line character. Listing 18.2 explains the implementation of the key/value pairs. You can also find this file, Applications_en.properties, online in the code/Chapter18/intl folder.

Listing 18.2: Creating the Applications_en.properties File

```
FILE_NOT_FOUND = The file could not be found
HELLO_MESSAGE = Hello, How are you?
WARNING_MESSAGE = There are 0 warnings in this file.
```

Listing 18.2 can be saved in the Applications_en.properties file and this properties file (or resource bundle) can be loaded by calling the ResourceBundle.getBundle ("Applications") method. After loading the ResourceBundle class, individual elements of the properties file can be loaded by using the getString () method.

The ResourceBundle object can be obtained by using any one of its static getBundle() methods according to the requirements. These methods use the PropertyResourceBundle class as a reference to the specified property class.

The signature of the `getBundle ()` methods are shown here:

- **`getBundle(String baseName)`** — Returns a resource bundle by using the specified base name, the default locale, and the caller's class loader.
- **`getBundle(String baseName, Locale locale)`** — Returns a resource bundle by using the specified base name and locale, and the caller's class loader.
- **`getBundle (String baseName, Locale locale, ClassLoader loader)`** — Returns a resource bundle by using the specified base name, locale, and class loader.

By default, the `getBundle()` method searches for the .class file, but uses the .properties file, if it exists, instead of the .class file. The `PropertyResourceBundle` class has a significant limitation, that all values are limited to string objects because the .properties file contains only text. Therefore, only text strings can be placed in the `PropertyResourceBundle` class. So, for more complex key/value pairs, the `ListResourceBundle` class may be used. `ListResourceBundle` class is used instead of `PropertyResourceBundle` class because of complex data, containing multiple strings, needs to be provided to configure certain `classpath` components.

After understanding the `PropertyResourceBundle`, let us create a simple Java application implementing the `PropertyResourceBundle` class. The following code snippet describes the `PropertyResourceBundle` class for the different locales such as en, en_US:

```
//ApplicationResources_en.properties
welcome.message=Hello English user, Welcome to internationalization
```

In the preceding code snippet, the value specified for the key `welcome.message`, is a welcome message for English users.

```
//ApplicationResources_en_US.properties
Welcome.message = Hello US English user, Welcome to internationalization
```

In the preceding code snippet, the value specified for the key `welcome.message`, is a Welcome message for US English users.

```
//ApplicationResources_it.properties
welcome.message = Hello Italian user, welcome to internationalization
```

In the preceding code snippet, the value specified for the key `welcome.message`, is a Welcome message for Italian users.

Listing 18.3 provides the code for the I18NTest.java file, which loads the `ResourceBundle` class based on the locale provided by the user. The `getString()` method then retrieves the value of the "`welcome.message`" key defined in the `ResourceBundle` class. You can also find this file online in the code/Chapter18/intl folder.

Listing 18.3: Creating the I18NTest.java File

```
package com.santosh.i18n;

import java.util.*;

public class I18NTest {

   public static void main(String s[]) throws Exception {
         Locale l=null;
         if (s.length==3)
         l=new Locale(s[0],s[1],s[2]);
         else if (s.length==2)
         l=new Locale(s[0],s[1]);
         else
         l=new Locale(s[0]);
         ResourceBundle
         rb=ResourceBundle.getBundle("ApplicationResources",l);
         System.out.println(rb.getString("welcome.message"));

   }//end main

}//end class
```

Execute the I18NTest.java file after compiling it. The output is displayed in Figure 18.2:

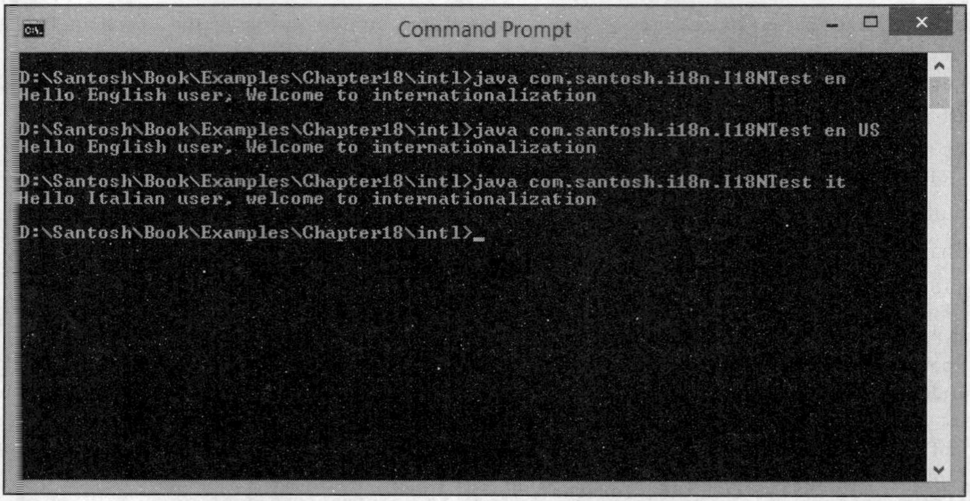

Figure 18.2: Displaying the Output of I18NTest.java

As shown in Figure 18.2, when we execute I18NTest.java file with different arguments, we observe the respective locale-specific messages.

After understanding and implementing `PropertyResourceBundle`, let's now discuss the `ListResourceBundle` class, which is more appropriate for complex key/value pairs.

The ListResourceBundle Class

The `ListResourceBundle` class is a bit complex as compared to the `PropertyResourceBundle` class because it handles complex data. In addition, the `PropertyResourceBundle` class can store only text, whereas the `ListResourceBundle` class can contain any type of Java objects. Since `ListResourceBundle` is an abstract class, you must extend it to create a usable class, as shown in Listing 18.4.

Similar to the `PropertyResourceBundle` class, the `ListResourceBundle` class also contains the list of key/value pairs. However, in `ListResourceBundle`, these key/value pairs are arranged as elements in a two-dimensional array of `java.lang.Object`. Moreover, `ListResourceBundle` class should use the single method `getContents()`, as well as an array of the Object type, which lists the key/value pairs. Listings 18.4, 18.5, and 18.6 provide the key/value pairs for the different locales.

Listing 18.4: Creating the ListBundle_en_CA.java File

```
import java.util.*;
public class ListBundle_en_CA extends ListResourceBundle {
  public Object[][] getContents() {
       return contents;
  }
  private Object[][] contents = {
       { "GDP", new Integer(51300) },
       { "Population", new Integer(125440000) },
       { "Literacy", new Double(0.67) },
  };
}
```

In Listing 18.4, the key/value pairs are arranged as elements in a two-dimensional array of `java.lang.Object`, providing the values for the en_CA locale. You can also find this file online in the code/Chapter 18/intl folder.

Listing 18.5: Creating the ListBundle_fr_FR.java File

```
import java.util.*;
public class ListBundle_fr_FR extends ListResourceBundle {
```

```
    public Object[][] getContents() {
          return contents; }
    private Object[][] contents = {
          { "GDP", new Integer(15300) },
          { "Population", new Integer(125447800) },
          { "Literacy", new Double(0.55) },
    };
}
```

In Listing 18.5, the key/value pairs are arranged as elements in a two-dimensional array of `java.lang.Object`, providing the values for the fr_FR locale. You can also find this file online in the code/Chapter18/intl folder.

Listing 18.6: Creating the ListBundle_ja_JP.java File

```
import java.util.*;
public class ListBundle_ja_JP extends ListResourceBundle {
    public Object[][] getContents() {
          return contents;
    }
    private Object[][] contents = {
          { "GDP", new Integer(21300) },
          { "Population", new Integer(125449703) },
          { "Literacy", new Double(0.99) },
    };
}
```

In Listing 18.6, the key/value pairs are arranged as elements in a two-dimensional array of `java.lang.Object`, providing the values for the ja_JP locale. You can also find this file online in the code/Chapter18/intl folder.

Listing 18.7 demonstrates how to display the values of the `ListResourceBundle` class, depending on the user specified locale. You can also find this file online in the code/Chapter18/intl folder.

Listing 18.7: Creating the ListResBundleDemo.java File

```
import java.util.*;

public class ListResBundleDemo

{
    static public void main(String[] args)

    {
          Locale supportedLocales=null;
          if (args.length==3)
          supportedLocales=new Locale(args[0],args[1],args[2]);
          else if (args.length==2)
          supportedLocales=new Locale(args[0],args[1]);
          else
          supportedLocales=new Locale(args[0]);
ResourceBundle stats=ResourceBundle.getBundle("ListBundle",supportedLocales);
          System.out.println("Locale = " + supportedLocales);
          Integer gdp = (Integer)stats.getObject("GDP");
          System.out.println("GDP = " + gdp.toString());
          Integer pop = (Integer)stats.getObject("Population");
          System.out.println("Population = " + pop.toString());
          Double lit = (Double)stats.getObject("Literacy");
          System.out.println("Literacy = " + lit.toString());

    } // end main

} // end class
```

In the preceding listing, the `ResourceBundle` class is loaded based on the locales specified by the user. The `getObject()` method then retrieves the value of the specified parameter and displays it, as shown in Figure 18.3:

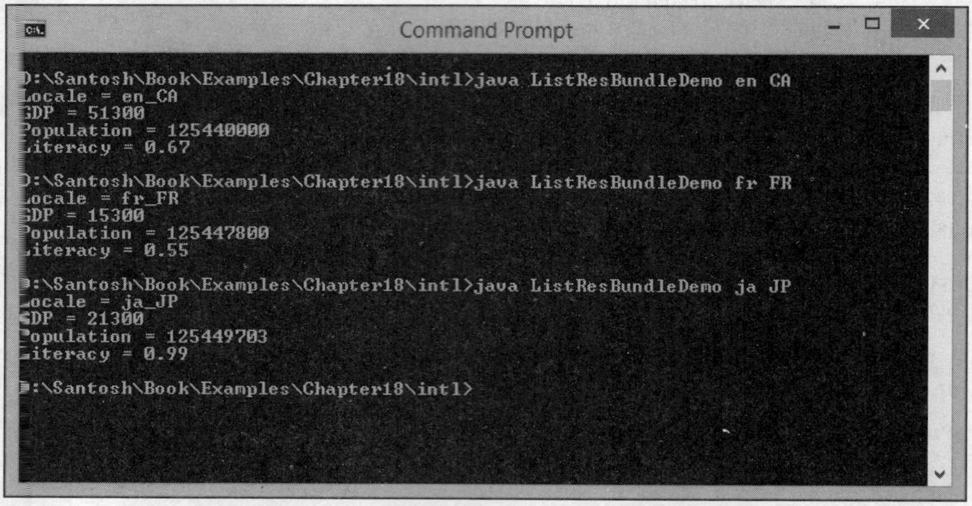

Figure 18.3: Displaying the Output of ListResBundleDemo.java File

In Figure 18.3, the GDP, Population, and Literacy data for the `en_CA`, `fr_FR`, and `ja_JP` locales are displayed. Now, let's learn about internationalizing Web applications.

Internationalizing Web Applications

One to select Java for developing Internationalized Web applications is the power and easy to use Internationalization classes available in Java APIs. In addition, Java handles text internally in Unicode, so it can represent almost all the languages as long as the client browser is capable of displaying the character set.

Internationalization is the process of preparing an application to support more than one language and data format. For internalizing Java web application, we must first decide how to determine the user's language and locale preferences. A web application has two ways to find out the user's language preferences: First, it can use locale preferences that are sent from the client to the server using the HTTP request header field Accept-Language. Browsers usually let the user create a list of languages as part of their preferences. Java servlet API provides a utility method to get this Locale objects using `getLocale()` and `getLocales()` methods of `javax.servlet.ServletRequest`. The second way, it provides a user view letting the user to choose the language from a list of supported languages, and gets it as a request parameter. A good approach is to use the Accept-Language information initially, but give the user an opportunity to choose a language explicitly from the applications view. Now after determining the locale for presenting localized content, we have two approaches. The following are the two approaches to internationalize a Web application:

- The first approach is to provide a version of a JSP page in each of the target locales and have the controller Servlet to dispatch the request to the appropriate page. This approach is beneficial if large amount of data is available on a page or an entire Web application needs to be internationalized because the application contains JSP pages for each locale. The disadvantage of this approach is that you need to create separate JSP pages for each locale.
- The second approach is to isolate the locale-sensitive data on a page into resource bundles (.properties files). The locale-sensitive data can be an error message, string literals, or button labels. The locale-sensitive data can be automatically retrieved from the .properties files and used in the JSP page. This approach does not require specifying the text data into the code; rather the resource bundle can be created, which contains the locale-sensitive data in the form of key/value pairs. This approach may be preferred if the pages contain mainly text, or if the structure of JSP pages is significantly different for different locales.

After discussing both the approaches used to internationalize Web applications, let's create a simple application named **i18nWebex1**, which demonstrates how to internationalize Web applications. The **i18nWebex1** application consists of the following components:

- The index.html view
- The Home.jsp view
- The `I18NServlet` class
- The `ApplicationResource_en.properties`, `ApplicationResource_en_US.properties`, and `ApplicationResource_it.properties` resource bundles

The basic view components designed are index.html and Home.jsp. The request sent by the user through the index.html page invokes the `I18NServlet` class, which sets an attribute and forwards the request to the Home.jsp, which displays the final result.

Creating the JSP Views

The view components are designed by using JSP. In this application, we design two JSP pages:

- **index.html**—The first view (or page) of the application
- **Home.jsp**—The view displaying the output based on the language selected by the user

Now, let's create these JSP views.

Creating the index.html View

Create a folder for the web application **i18nWebex1,** which hold the files of the application. The index.jsp view is the first page that appears when the application is accessed. This page provides the link for the English, English (US), and the Italian users. The source code for the index.html page is shown in Listing 18.8. You can also find this file online in the code/Chapter18/i18nWebex1 folder.

Listing 18.8: Creating the index.html File

```
<html>
<body>
<center>
This is an example to demonstrate the internationalization of web application, click
   on the following links to find the output<pre>
         <a href="testser?language=en">English User </a>
         <a href="testser?language=en&country=US">English (US) User</a>
         <a href="testser?language=it">Italian User</a>
   </pre>
</center>
</body>
</html>
```

The hyperlinks included in Listing 18.8 automatically call the `I18NServlet` class. We can see the relationship between the index.html view and the `I18NServlet` class in the Servlet-mapping provided in the `web.xml` file. In Listing 18.8, two parameters, `language` and `country`, are passed with the request, when the user clicks the reference link.

Creating the Home.jsp View

The Home.jsp view is designed to display the welcome message to the users based on the language preference selected by them in the index.html view. Based on the language and country parameters, the resource bundle is loaded, as shown in Listing 18.10. Listing 18.10 also sets the resource bundle value to the "`resource`" attribute. In Listing 18.9, the value of the "`resource`" attribute is retrieved and the welcome message, saved in the `ResourceBundle`, is displayed by using the key `welcome.message`. You can also find this file online in the code/Chapter18/i18nWebex1 folder.

Listing 18.9: Creating the Home.jsp File

```
<%@page import="java.util.*"%>

<jsp:include page="index.html"/>
```

```
<hr>
<h2>Output</h2><br/>
<%
  ResourceBundle rb= (ResourceBundle) request.getAttribute("resource");
%>
<%=rb.getString("welcome.message")%>
```

After designing the view components, now let us create the I18NServlet class, which loads the ResourceBundle.

Creating the I18NServlet Class

I18NServlet is the HTTPServlet class that loads the ResourceBundle, based on the parameters passed by the index.jsp view. The I18NServlet class retrieves the value of the parameters passed by the index.html page in Listing 18.8. Then, based on these parameters, the new Locale instance, l, is initialized and the ResourceBundle is loaded according to the l Locale instance. Then, the new attribute "resource" is created and the request is forwarded to the Home.jsp view.

See Listing 18.10 for the code of the I18NServlet.java file. Compile the code and put the I18NServlet.class file in the WEB-INF/classes/com/santosh/servlets folder. You can also find this application online in the code/Chapter18/i18nWebex1 folder.

Listing 18.10: Creating the I18NServlet.java File

```
package com.santosh.servlets;

import javax.servlet.*;
import javax.servlet.http.*;
import java.io.*;
import java.util.*;

public class I18NServlet extends HttpServlet
{
  public void service (HttpServletRequest req, HttpServletResponse res)
  throws ServletException, IOException {
        String cc=req.getParameter("country");
        String ln=req.getParameter("language");
        Locale l=null;
        if (cc==null)
        l=new Locale(ln);
        else
        l=new Locale(ln,cc);

ResourceBundle rb= ResourceBundle.getBundle("ApplicationResources",l);
        req.setAttribute("resource",rb);
        RequestDispatcher rd=req.getRequestDispatcher("Home.jsp");
        rd.forward(req,res);
  }//end service

}// end class
```

Now, let us create the various resource bundles for the English, English (US) and Italian users, required in this application.

Creating the Resource Bundles

The PropertyResourceBundle class allows the application to define resources using the key/value syntax. We create three resource bundles (or the .properties files) for three specific locales, which are:

- ApplicationResource_en.properties(for English)

- `ApplicationResource_en_US.properties` (for English (US))
- `ApplicationResource_it.properties` (for Italian)

These files are added to the **i18nWebex1** application, which prepares the resource bundle with the welcome `String` message. Listings 18.11, 18.12, and 18.13 provide the key/value pairs for various Locales such as en, en_US, and it.

Listing 18.11: Creating the ApplicationResources_en.properties File

```
welcome.message=Hello English user, Welcome to internationalization
```

In the preceding listing, the key `welcome.message` is defined for the en Locale.

Listing 18.12: Creating the ApplicationResources_en_US.properties File

```
welcome.message=Hello US English user, Welcome to internationalization
```

In the preceding listing, the key `welcome.message` is defined for the en_US Locale.

Listing 18.13: Creating the ApplicationResources_it.properties File

```
welcome.message=Hello Italian user, Welcome to internationalization
```

In the preceding snippet, the key `welcome.message` is defined for the it Locale.

Configuring the Application

The Deployment Descriptor is used to configure and map Servlets used in the **i18nWebex1** application. The `web.xml` configuration file is used to configure the **i18nWebex1** application.

The `web.xml` file defines the servlet name, the servlet class, and the URL pattern for the `I18NServlet` Servlet. The URL pattern for the `I18NServlet` Servlet is /testser. See Listing 18.14 for the full code of the `web.xml` file. You can also find this file online in the code/Chapter18/i18nWebex1/WEB-INF folder.

Listing 18.14: Creating the `web.xml` File

```
<?xml version="1.0" encoding="UTF-8"?>
<web-app>

   <servlet>

        <servlet-name>i18n</servlet-name>
        <servlet-class>com.santosh.servlets.I18NServlet</servlet-class>

   </servlet>

   <servlet-mapping>

        <servlet-name>i18n</servlet-name>
        <url-pattern>/testser</url-pattern>

   </servlet-mapping>

   <welcome-file-list>

        <welcome-file>index.jsp</welcome-file>

   </welcome-file-list>

</web-app>
```

Now, after creating all the required files, let's understand how to arrange these files in the directory structure.

Designing the Application Directory Structure

The directory structure of the **i18nWebex1** application is shown in Figure 18.4

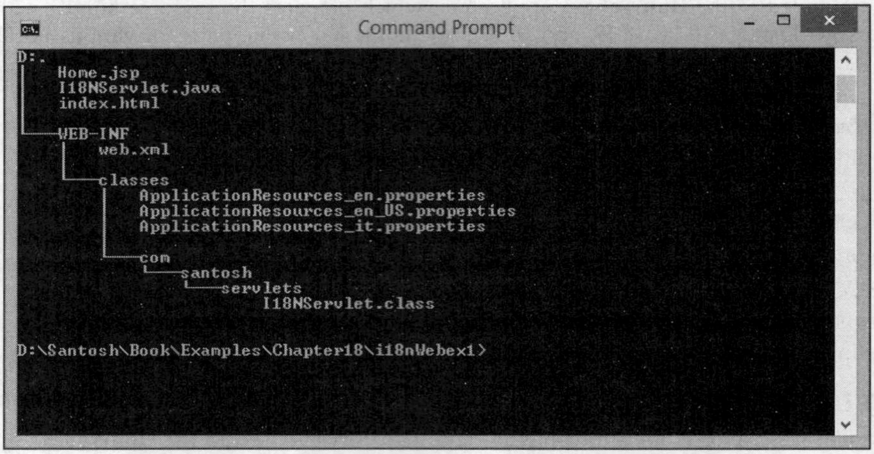

Figure 18.4: Displaying the Root Directory Structure for i18nWebex1 Web Application

Now, let's run the i18nWebex1 application.

Running the Application

After developing and configuring various components, we can now run the application to see the output of various JSP pages and the implementation of Internationalization. Copy the **i18nWebex1** folder in the `<Tomcat-home>/webapps` directory. Start your Tomcat server, open your browser, and access the application using the `http://localhost:9090/i18nWebex1/index.html` URL. The index.html page appears, as shown in Figure 18.5:

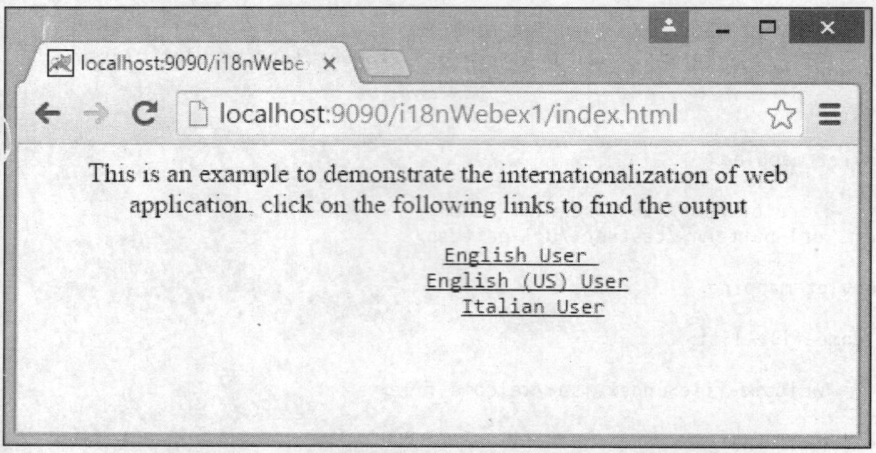

Figure 18.5: Displaying the index.jsp Page

Click any of the three hyperlinks to get the message from the respective locale properties file. For example, we have clicked the **`English User`** hyperlink, which displays the output as shown in Figure 18.6:

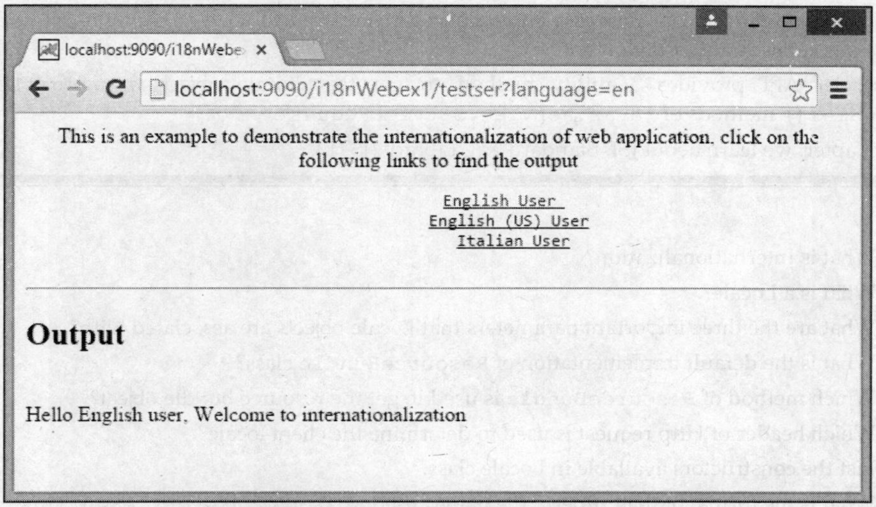

Figure 18.6: Displaying the Home.jsp Page

In this example, we have determined the user's locale by allowing the user to select his required language using the given links. Instead we can get the user's locale directly using `getLocale()` method of `ServletRequest` as well. Let us summarize the chapter to get a quick recall of Internationalization.

Summary

In this chapter, we got a brief overview of Internationalization. Internationalization is mostly required for the non-native environments where a software program is capable of handling all local environments. Internationalization is specifically required for Web applications so that these Web applications can be exposed to the global audience worldwide. We then learned about Locales and `ResourceBundles`. In addition, we also learned how to implement Internationalization in a Web application.

Let's recall the following important points to summarize the chapter:

- Globalization of Web applications can be accomplished through the process of Internationalization and Localization.
- Internationalization can be defined as the process of enabling a Web application to present different country and region specific formats without making any changes in the code or recompiling the application.
- The `java.util.Locale` class is used while creating International Java applications.
- The `java.util.ResourceBundle` class is used to deal with the localized resources, such as images, text, and sounds.
- The `java.util.ResourceBundle` class has two subclasses, `ListResourceBundle` and `Property ResourceBundle`.
- The `ResourceBundles` class provides the mechanism to separate user interface (UI) elements and other locale-sensitive data from the application logic.
- The `Resourcebundle` names have two parts: a base name and a locale suffix. The base name defines the name of the default `Resourcebundle` and the suffix defines the specific locale.
- The `ResourceBundle` class is a container used by a program to retrieve an object for a particular Locale.
- A `PropertyResourceBundle` class is a subclass of `ResourceBundle` that manages resources for a locale using a set of static strings from a properties file.
- The `ResourceBundle` object can be obtained by using any one of its static `getBundle()` methods according to the requirements.

- The ListResourceBundle class is a bit complex as compared to the PropertyResourceBundle class because it handles complex data.
- Java servlet API provides a utility method to get this Locale objects using getLocale() and getLocales() methods of javax.servlet.ServletRequest.

In the next chapter, we learn about JSP Standard Tag Library (JSTL).

Exercise

Q. 18.1 What is Internationalization?

Q. 18.2 What is a Locale?

Q. 18.3 What are the three important parameters that Locale objects are associated with?

Q. 18.4 What is the default implementation of ResourceBundle class?

Q. 18.5 Which method of ResourceBundle is used to get the resource bundle object?

Q. 18.6 Which header of Http request is used to determine the client locale?

Q. 18.7 List the constructors available in Locale class.

Q. 18.8 What is the format of the property file names used in PropertyResourceBundle?

19

Working with JSP Standard Tag Library (JSTL)

The JSP Standard Tag Library (JSTL) is a collection of custom tag libraries, which provide core functionality used for JSP documents. JSTL reduces the use of scriptlets in a JSP page. The use of JSTL tags allows developers to use predefined tags instead of writing the Java code. JSTL provides four types of tag libraries that can be used with JSP pages:

- **The JSTL Core tag library**—Used to process a JSP page in an application.
- **The XML Tag library**—Used for parsing, selecting, and transforming XML data in a JSP page.
- **The Format Tag library**—Used for formatting the data used in a JSP page.
- **The SQL Tag library**—Used to access the relational database used in a JSP page.
- **JSTL Functions** — Used for string manipulation and string length.

These tag libraries are described in detail next.

Describing JSTL Core Tags

The JSTL core tag library provides the JSTL core tags used in the JSP pages. The core tags are used to perform iteration, conditional processing, and also provide support of expression language for the tags in JSP pages. The core tag library can be used in a JSP page by accessing the following tag library:

```
<%@ taglib prefix="c" uri="http://java.sun.com/jsp/jstl/core"%>
```

The core tags in a JSP page can be accessed by using the prefix ‘c’, the preferred prefix for core tag libraries.

The JSTL core tags are divided into three categories as listed here:

- General-purpose Tags
- Conditional and Looping Tags
- Networking Tags

The following section explains all these tags categories in detail. First, we start with general-purpose tags.

General-Purpose Tags

General-purpose tags include tags for writing the values to the output stream, as well as retrieving, setting, and removing attributes and also include tags for catching exceptions. The general-purpose tags contain four tags:

- <c:out>
- <c:set>
- <c:remove>
- <c:catch>

Let's now discuss these tags.

The <c:out> tag

The `<c:out>` tag evaluates an expression that may be given in its `value` attribute or in its tag body and the resulting value is written in the output. The syntax of the `<c:out>` tag is as follows:

```
<c:out attributes> [body content] </c:out>
```

The attributes of the `<c:out>` tag are:

- **`value`**—Specifies the output data to be displayed.
- **`escapeXml`**—Specifies whether or not the tag should ignore the special XML characters. If boolean value of `escapeXML` is *true,* then the tag converts the XML special characters, such as <,>, & to their character entity equivalents, such as < > and &. If the value of `escapeXml` is *false,* then it does not convert the XML special characters. The default value is true.
- **`default`**—Takes the value to be written to output if the given value resolves to null. If the value does not resolve to null, the value specified in the value attribute is displayed. The default attribute can be even specified in the body of the tag.

Using the <c:out> Tag

Let's create an application, **jstlex1**, which shows the use of the `<c:out>` tag. The application prints some request-related data by using the `<c:out>` tag. Listing 19.1 shows the uses of the `<c:out>` tag. You can also find this file online in the code/Chapter19/jstlex1 folder.

Listing 19.1: Creating the GetRequestData.jsp File

```
<%@taglib uri="http://java.sun.com/jsp/jstl/core" prefix="c"%>
<html>
<body>
  <b>Requested URL:  </b><br/>
  <c:out value="${pageContext.request.requestURL}"/><br/>
  <br/><h4>Request Path information:</h4>
  <table border='1'>
        <tr><th>Name</th><th>Value</th></tr>
        <tr><td>HTTP Request method</td>
        <td><c:out value="${pageContext.request.method}"/></td></tr>
        <tr><td>Request URI</td>
        <td><c:out value="${pageContext.request.requestURI}"/></td></tr>
        <tr><td>Context Path</td>
        <td><c:out value="${pageContext.request.contextPath}"/></td></tr>
        <tr><td>Servlet path</td>
        <td><c:out value="${pageContext.request.servletPath}"/></td></tr>
        <tr><td>Path info</td>
        <td><c:out value="${pageContext.request.pathInfo}"/></td></tr>
        <tr><td>Path translated</td>
        <td><c:out value="${pageContext.request.pathTranslated}"/></td></tr>
  </table><br/>
  <h4>Accessing Request Parameter value:</h4>
  Value of parameter <b>uname</b> is:
  <b><c:out value="${param.uname}"/></b>
</body>
</html>
```

Listing 19.2 shows the `web.xml` file used for **jstlex1** application. You can also find this file online in the code/Chapter19/jstlex1/WEB-INF folder.

Listing 19.2: Creating the `web.xml` File

```
<?xml version="1.0"?>
<web-app>
  <welcome-file-list>
  <welcome-file>GetRequestData.jsp</welcome-file>
  </welcome-file-list>
</web-app>
```

Now to run **jstlex1** application, we need two jar files, the first one is the `jstl.jar`, which is used to support the JSTL API classes. The second is the `standard.jar`, which is used to implement classes of libraries. The `jstl.jar` and standard.jar files enable us to access the JSTL tag library. Both `jstl.jar` and `standard.jar` files are present in the Tomcat specification. To provide the support of JSTL in our Web application, copy the `jstl.jar` and `standard.jar` files into the lib directory of your application. Since the libraries are present in the lib directory of our Web application, so we do not have to update the deployment descriptor. The JSP container automatically detects and executes these JAR files.

After creating all the preceding files, arrange them, along with the `jstl.jar` and `standard.jar` files, in the directory structure shown in Figure 19.1:

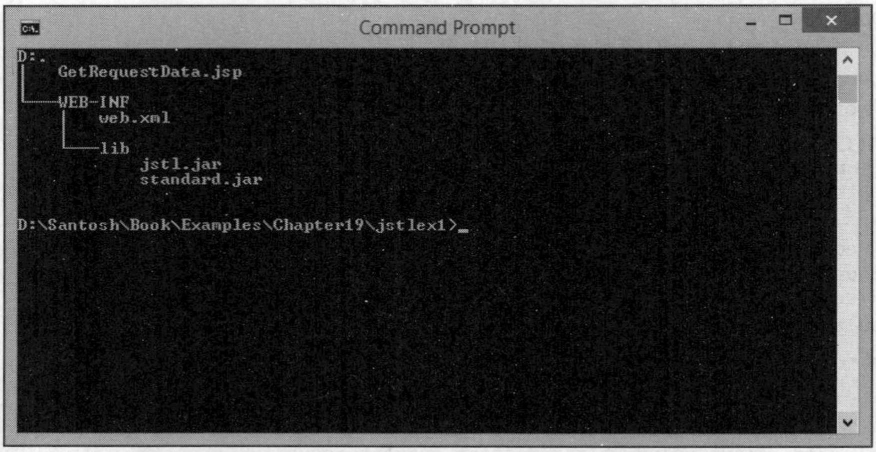

Figure 19.1: Showing Directory Structure of jstlex1 Application

Copy the **jstlex1** folder into the `<Tomcat home>\webapps` folder. Start the server and launch the application by using the `http://localhost:9090/jstlex1/GetRequestData.jsp?uname=santosh` URL. The requested URL page opens, as shown in Figure 19.2:

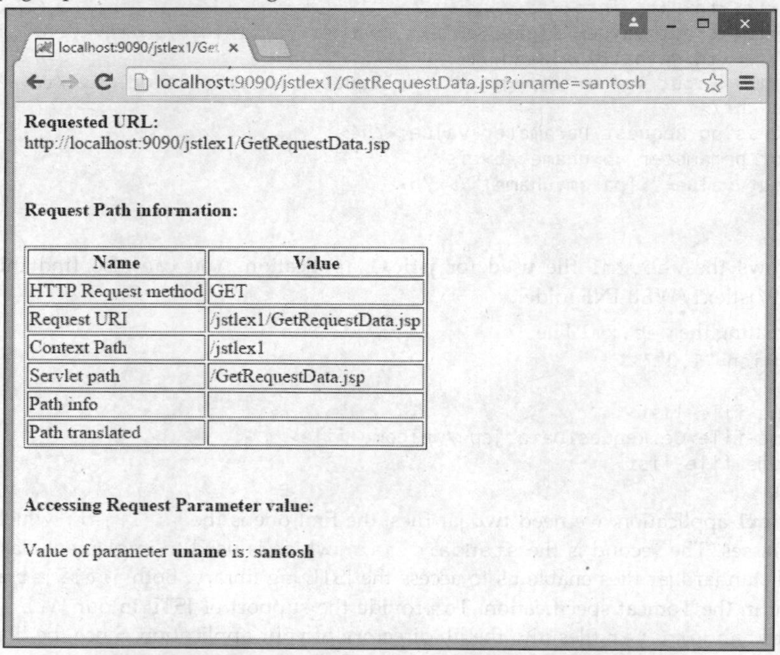

Figure 19.2: Showing the Output of GetRequestData.jsp

Figure 19.2 shows the output of the GetRequestData.jsp file in which we have used the `pageContext` implicit object of Expression Language and retrieved the request data. We have also used the `param` object to get the parameter value.

The <c:set> Tag

The `<c:set>` tag is another general-purpose tag, which allows us to set the value of a variable or property into the given scope. The following code snippet shows the syntax of the `<c:set>` tag:

```
<c:set attribute> [body content] </c:set>
```

The attributes of the <c:set> tag are listed here:

- **value**—Specifies the value being set. The value can also be an expression.
- **var**—Specifies the name of the variable to store.
- **scope**—Specifies the scope of the variable defined in the `var` attribute. Scope can be page, request, session, or application.
- **target**—Specifies the name of the variable whose property is to be set.
- **property**—Specifies the name of the property to be set.

Note that if `target` attribute is specified, the `property` attribute must be specified. In addition, you can use either the `var` or `target` attribute for specifying the name of the variable.

The <c:remove> Tag

The <c:remove> general-purpose core JSTL tag allows us to remove a variable from the specified scope. The syntax of the <c:remove> tag is:

```
<c:remove attributes/>
```

The <c:remove> tag takes two attributes, which are:

- **var**—Name of the variable to be removed.
- **scope**—Scope of the variable, and scope can be page, request, session, or application.

The <c:catch> Tag

The <c:catch> tag is used to allow JSP pages to handle exceptions that might be raised by any of the tag inside the body of the <c:catch> tag. The syntax of the <c:catch> tag is:

```
<c:catch attributes> body content </c:catch>
```

The <c:catch> tag accepts the `var` attribute, which takes the name of the variable that stores the exception thrown.

Let's now describe the conditional and looping tags of JSTL.

Conditional and Looping Tags

The conditional and looping tags include tags for writing `if` conditions, `switch` cases, and loops.

Types of Conditional and Looping Tags

Conditional and looping tags are of six types:

- <c: if>
- <c: choose>
- <c: when>
- <c: otherwise>
- <c: forEach>
- <c: forTokens>

The following sections explain all these tags in detail.

The <c:if> Tag

The <c:if> tag evaluates an expression that is given in its '`test`' attribute. If the resulting value is *true*, the body of the <c:if> tag is evaluated; otherwise not. The following snippet shows the syntax of the <c:if> tag of JSTL:

```
<c:if attributes> body content </c:if>
```

The attributes of <c:if> tag are listed here:

- **test**—The boolean variable or expression resolving to boolean value
- **var**—Name of the variable to store the conditions result
- **scope**—Scope of the variable to store the conditions result

The following code snippet shows the example for <c:if> tag:

```
<c:if test="${param.uname==''}">
  Username cannot be empty
</c:if>
```

In the preceding shown snippet, the <c:if> tag checks whether or not the value of request parameter uname is an empty string. If it is an empty string, the body part of the <c:if> tag is evaluated; if not, the body part is skipped. Note that we do not have a tag that allows us to specify else part for the <c:if> tag. If we want to implement the else part of the <c:if> tag, then use <c:if> once again. The following section explains the <c:choose> tag.

The <c:choose> Tag

The <c:choose> tag acts like a Java switch statement. The <c:choose> tag encloses one or more <c:when> tags and a <c:otherwise> tag. The syntax of the <c:choose> tag is:

```
<c:choose> body content </c:choose>
```

The following section explains about the <c:when> tag.

The <c:when> Tag

The <c:when> tag encloses a single case within the <c:choose> tag. The <c:when> tag must appear inside the <c:choose> element. More than one <c:when> tag can be defined in a single <c:choose> element.

The syntax of the <c:when> tag is:

```
<c:when attribute> body content </c:when>
```

The <c:when> tag accepts only one attribute, named test. The test attribute takes the Boolean variable or an expression resolving to a boolean value. If this boolean value is *true*, the body content of the <c:when> tags is evaluated. If this value is *false*, then the body content of the <c:when> tag is skipped.

The <c:otherwise> Tag

The <c:otherwise> is same as the <c:when> tag, but is unconditional. That is, the <c:otherwise> tag is equivalent to the default case in a Java switch statement. The body content of the <c:otherwise> tag is evaluated if none of the <c:when> conditions in the <c:choose> tag are resolved to *true*.

The syntax of the <c:otherwise> tag is:

```
<c:otherwise> body content </c:otherwise>
```

The <c:forEach> Tag

The <c:forEach> tag is used to iterate over a collection of objects or as a fixed loop over a range of numbers. A common use of the <c:forEach> tag is to produce a HTML table containing data gathered from a SQL query or other data source.

The syntax of the <c:forEach> tag of JSTL is:

```
<c:forEach attributes> body content </c:forEach>
```

The attributes of the <c:forEach> are:

- **items** — Specifies the collection to iterate over. The collection can be ArrayList, Map, or List.
- **var** — Specifies the name of the variable into which the current iteration item has to be set.
- **varStatus** — Specifies the name of the variable that defines the status of the variable given in the var attribute. The varStatus attribute is optional.
- **begin** — Takes the starting index for the loop; this attribute is optional.
- **end** — Takes the ending index for the loop; this attribute is optional.
- **step** — An optional increment for the loop; the default value is 1.

The <c:forTokens> Tag

The <c:forTokens> tag is used for looping over tokenized elements of a string.

The syntax of the <c:forTokens> tag of JSTL is:

```
<c:forTokens attributes> body content </c:forTokens>
```

The attributes of the <c:forTokens> tag are:

- **items**—Specifies the String to be tokenized. This attribute allows an expression
- **var**—Specifies the name of the variable into which the current iteration item has to be set
- **delims**—Specifies the delimiter or delimiters, which are to be tokenized
- **varStatus**—Defines the status of the variable given in var attribute, The varStatus attribute is optional
- **begin**—Takes the starting index for the loop; this attribute is optional
- **end**—Takes the ending index for the loop; this attribute is optional
- **step**—Provides an optional increment for the loop; the default value is 1

Using Conditional and Looping Tags

We demonstrate two examples to use conditional and looping tags. The first example uses the <c:if>, <c:when>, <c:choose>, and <c:otherwise> tags. The second example uses the <c:forEach> tag.

An Example of Using Conditional

Let's create the **jstlex2** application that demonstrates the use of conditional tags. In this application, we create two pages, index.html and ProcessRequest.jsp.

Listing 19.3 shows the code for the index.html page. This page contains two text boxes, to accept two operands from the users, and two buttons named Add and Subtract to demonstrate the add and subtract operations on the operands. You can also find the code for this file online in the code/Chapter19/jstlex2 folder.

Listing 19.3: Creating the index.html File

```
<html>
  <body>
        <form action="ProcessRequest.jsp"><pre>
                Operand 1 <input type="text" name="op1"/>
                Operand 2 <input type="text" name="op2"/>
                <input type="submit" name="submit" value="Add"/>
                <input type="submit" name="submit" value="Subtract"/>
        </form></pre>
  </body>
</html>
```

When the user clicks the Add or Subtract button on the index.html page, the control is transferred to the ProcessRequest.jsp page. Listing 19.4 shows the code for ProcessRequest.jsp. This page takes the operand from the index.html page. The JSP page uses the <c:if> tag to check the condition. The condition is either add or subtract, and depending on the condition, the required operation is performed. The output is displayed by using <c:out>tag. You can also find this file online in the code/Chapter19/jstlex2 folder.

Listing 19.4: Creating the ProcessRequest.jsp File

```
<%@taglib uri="http://java.sun.com/jsp/jstl/core" prefix="c"%>
<html>
<body>
  <c:if test="${param.submit eq 'Add'}">
Sum  of  <c:out  value="${param.op1}"/>  and  <c:out  value="${param.op2}"/>  is  <c:out
value="${param.op1 + param.op2}"/>
  </c:if>
  <c:if test="${param.submit eq 'Subtract'}">
<c:out    value="${param.op1}"/>    -    <c:out    value="${param.op2}"/>    =    <c:out
value="${param.op1 - param.op2}"/>
  </c:if>
</body>
</html>
```

After creating two pages, we need to configure the application by using the web.xml file. Listing 19.5 contains the web.xml file to configure the **jstlex2** application. You can also find this file online in the code/Chapter19/jstlex2/WEB-INF folder.

Listing 19.5: Creating the web.xml File

```
<?xml version="1.0"?>
<web-app>
   <welcome-file-list>
         <welcome-file>index.html</welcome-file>
   </welcome-file-list>
</web-app>
```

After creating all the preceding files, arrange them along with the `jstl.jar` and `standard.jar` files, as shown in Figure 19.3:

Figure 19.3: Showing Directory Structure of jstlex2 Application

Then, copy the **jstlex2** folder into the `<Tomcat home>\webapps` folder and start the Tomcat server. After starting the server, launch the application by using the following URL: `http://localhost:9090/jstlex2/`. The requested URL page opens, as shown in Figure 19.4:

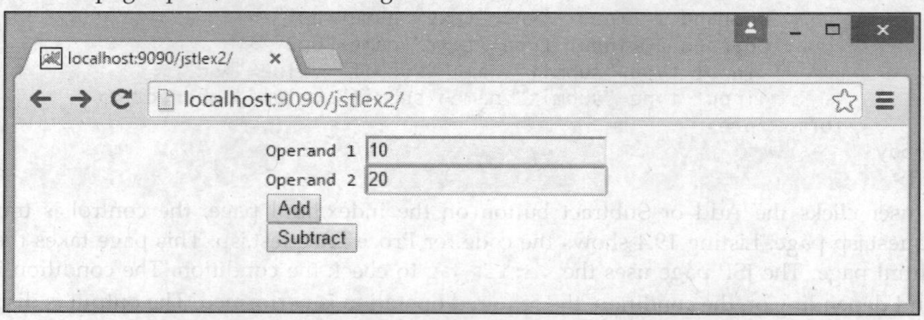

Figure 19.4: Showing index.html to enter the Operands

Enter some numbers into the text fields— Operand 1 and Operand 2—as shown in Figure 19.4 and click the required arithmetic operation, Add or Subtract. After entering the operand, when a user clicks the Add or Subtract button, the control is transferred to the ProcessRequest.jsp page. In our case, we have clicked the Add button, and the ProcessRequest.jsp page demonstrates the output of the add operation, as shown in Figure 19.5:

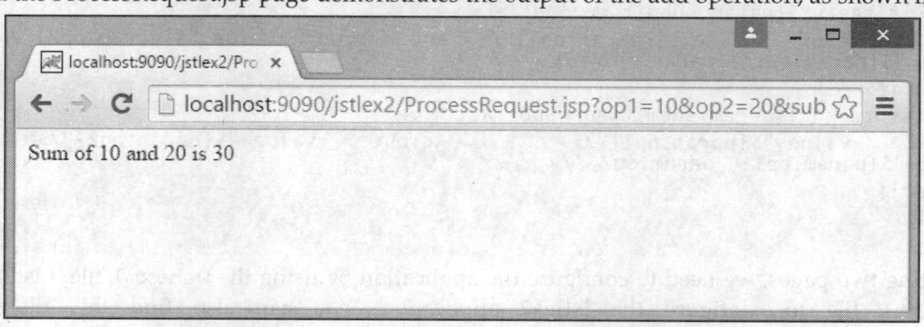

Figure 19.5: Showing Addition of Two Numbers

In the preceding example, we can use the <c:choose> tag instead of using two <c:if> tags, as shown here:

```
<c:choose>
   <c:when test="${param.submit eq 'Add'}">
   Sum of <c:out value="${param.op1}"/> and <c:out value="${param.op2}"/> is
   <c:out value="${param.op1 + param.op2}"/>
   </c:when>
   <c: otherwise>
        <c:out value="${param.op1}"/> - <c:out value="${param.op2}"/> =
        <c:out value="${param.op1 - param.op2}"/>
   </c:otherwise>
</c:choose>
```

Using the <c:forEach> Tag

The **jstlex3** application demonstrates to get an employee information from the database and represents it to the user with a JSP page using the <c:forEach> tag. The <c:forEach> tag is used to display each employee details. Here in the **jstlex3** application, GetEmpDetailsServlet.java is created to retrieve the data from the database using DriverConnection.java. The DriverConnection.java is used to create connection to Oracle data source. The EmpDetailsView.jsp displays the data retrieved by the servlet GetEmpDetailsServlet.java.

To get the data from the database, we use a servlet named GetEmpDetailsServlet.java, a Java bean named EmpDetails.java and a connection class named DriverConnection.java. To represent the Employee's details to the user, we use a JSP page (EmpDetailsView.jsp) in which we use <c:forEach> tag. Listing 19.6 shows the code for EmpDetais.java, where Java bean is used in our application to set and get data from the database. You can also find this file online in the code/Chapter19/jstlex3 folder:

Listing 19.6: Creating the EmpDetails.java File

```
package com.santosh.jstl;
import java.io.*;

public class EmpDetails implements Serializable {

   public EmpDetails (){}
   public EmpDetails (int i, String s, int j, double d){
        empno=i; name=s; deptno=j; sal=d;
   }

   public void setEmpNo(int i){empno=i;}
   public int getEmpNo(){return empno;}

   public void setName(String s){name=s;}
   public String getName(){return name;}

   public void setDeptNo(int i){deptno=i;}
   public int getDeptNo(){return deptno;}

   public void setSal(double d){sal=d;}
   public double getSal(){return sal;}

   String name; double sal;
   int empno,deptno;

}//class
```

Listing 19.7 shows the code for DriverConnection.java, which is used to connect the Oracle database. You can also find this file online in the code/Chapter19/jstlex3 folder:

Listing 19.7: Creating the DriverConnection.java File

```
package com.santosh.jstl;
import java.sql.*;
public class DriverConnection {
```

```
    public static Connection getConnection() throws Exception{
            Class.forName("oracle.jdbc.driver.OracleDriver");
            return DriverManager.getConnection(
                    "jdbc:oracle:thin:@localhost:1521:sandb","scott","tiger");
    }
}
```

Listing 19.8 shows the source code of GetEmpDetailsServlet.java file. The GetEmpDetailsServlet.java file is used to retrieve the employee details from the database table (emp) into a result set, which is then stored in the array list. The retrieved details are then forwarded to the EmpDetailsView.jsp (see Listing 19.9) through `RequestDispatcher`. You can also find this file online in the code/Chapter19/jstlex3 folder:

Listing 19.8: Creating the GetEmpDetailsServlet.java File

```
package com.santosh.jstl;
import java.io.*;
import javax.servlet.*;
import javax.servlet.http.*;
import java.util.*;
import java.sql.*;
public class GetEmpDetailsServlet extends HttpServlet {
    public void service(HttpServletRequest request,HttpServletResponse response)
    throws ServletException, IOException {
            Connection con=null;
            try {
                    con=DriverConnection.getConnection();
                    Statement st=con.createStatement();
                    ResultSet rs=st.executeQuery("select * from emp");
                    ArrayList al=new ArrayList();
                    while (rs.next()){
                            al.add(new EmpDetails(
                            rs.getInt(1),
                            rs.getString("ename"),
                            rs.getInt("deptno"),
                            rs.getDouble("sal")));
                    }//while
                    HttpSession session=request.getSession();
                    session.setAttribute("emps",al);
                    RequestDispatcher rd=
                    request.getRequestDispatcher("EmpDetailsView.jsp");
                    rd.forward(request, response);
                    return;
            }//try
            catch(Exception e){e.printStackTrace();}
            finally{try{con.close();}
            catch(Exception e){e.printStackTrace();}}
    }
}
```

Listing 19.9 shows the source code of EmpDetailsView.jsp page, which is used to display the employee details forwarded through `RequestDispatcher` (see Listing 19.8). You can also find this file online in the code/Chapter19/jstlex3 folder:

Listing 19.9: Creating the EmpDetailsView.jsp File

```
<%@taglib uri="http://java.sun.com/jsp/jstl/core" prefix="c"%>
<html> <body>
    <table border="1">
            <tr><th>Empno</th>
            <th>Name</th><th>DeptNo</th>
            <th>Sal</th></tr>
            <c:forEach items="${sessionScope.emps}" var="emp">
                    <tr> <td>
```

```
                    <c:out value="${emp.empNo}"/>
                    </td> <td>
                    <c:out value="${emp.name}"/>
                    </td> <td>
                    <c:out value="${emp.deptNo}"/>
                    </td> <td>
                    <c:out value="${emp.sal}"/>
                    </td> </tr>
            </c:forEach>
        </table>
    </body> </html>
```

Listing 19.10 describes the servlet mapping in `web.xml` file. You can also find this file online in the code/Chapter19/jstlex3/WEB-INF folder:

Listing 19.10: Creating the `web.xml` File

```
<?xml version="1.0"?>
<web-app>
  <servlet>
        <servlet-name>ser1</servlet-name>
        <servlet-class>com.santosh.jstl.GetEmpDetailsServlet
        </servlet-class>
  </servlet>
  <servlet-mapping>
        <servlet-name>ser1</servlet-name>
        <url-pattern>/GetEmpDetails</url-pattern>
  </servlet-mapping>
</web-app>
```

After creating all the preceding files, arrange them along with `jstl.jar`, `ojdbc14.jar`, and `standard.jar` as the directory structure shown in Figure 19.6:

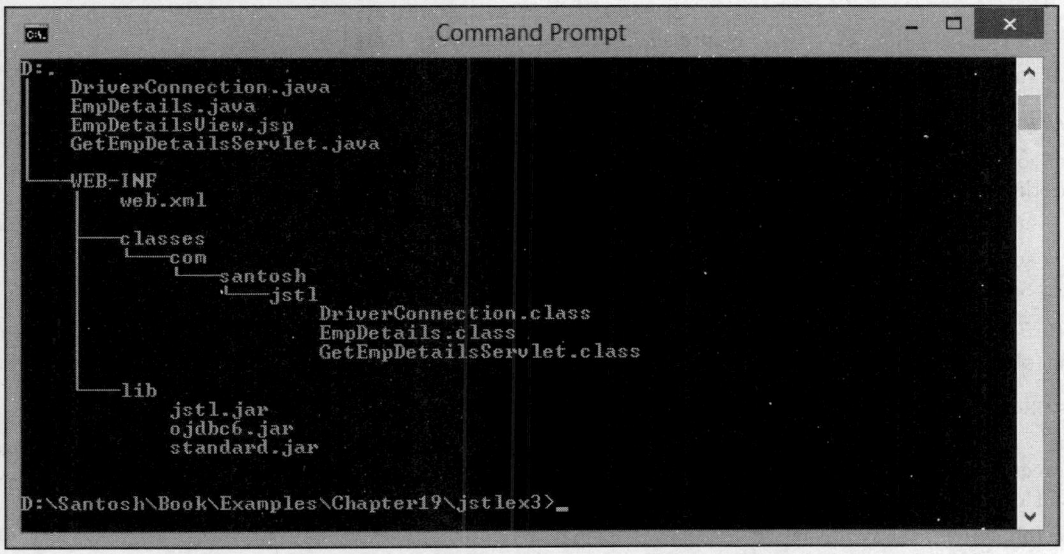

Figure 19.6: Showing Directory Structure of jstlex3 Application

Now, copy **jstlex3** folder into `<Tomcat home>\webapps` folder and start the server. Browse the jstlex3 application by using the URL `http://localhost:9090/jstlex3/GetEmpDetails`, as shown in Figure 19.7:

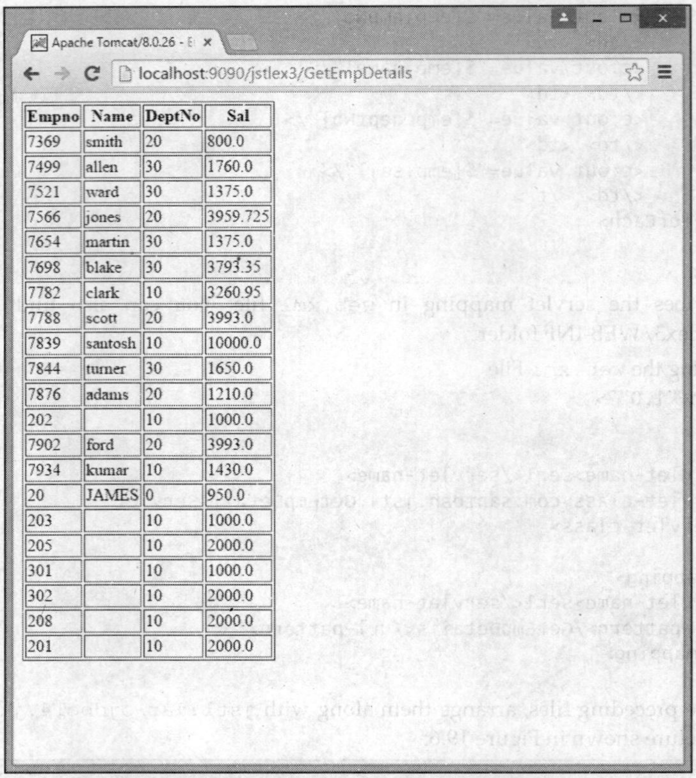

Empno	Name	DeptNo	Sal
7369	smith	20	800.0
7499	allen	30	1760.0
7521	ward	30	1375.0
7566	jones	20	3959.725
7654	martin	30	1375.0
7698	blake	30	3793.35
7782	clark	10	3260.95
7788	scott	20	3993.0
7839	santosh	10	10000.0
7844	turner	30	1650.0
7876	adams	20	1210.0
202		10	1000.0
7902	ford	20	3993.0
7934	kumar	10	1430.0
20	JAMES	0	950.0
203		10	1000.0
205		10	2000.0
301		10	1000.0
302		10	2000.0
208		10	2000.0
201		10	2000.0

Figure 19.7: Showing Employees' Details

In Figure 19.7, the application displays all employees' details.

Networking Tags

Networking tags contain tags that perform certain operations on URLs, such as including some other Web pages, encoding the URL, and redirecting the client request. The networking tags of JSTL tags contain four tags:

- <c:import>
- <c:url>
- <c:redirect>
- <c:param>

The following section explains all these tags in detail.

The <c:import> Tag

The `<c:import>` tag is used to include another resource, such as another JSP or HTML page, in a JSP page. Moreover, the resource can be either static or dynamic. The `<c:import>` tag is similar to the `<jsp:include>` tag. However, the `<c:import>` tag allows you to include the pages in another Web application.

The following is the syntax of the `<c:import>` tag of JSTL:

```
<c:import attributes> </c:import>
```

The attributes of the `<c:import>` tag are:

- **url** – Specifies the URL of the resource to include
- **context** – Specifies the context name in which the page has to be located, this is an optional attribute
- **var** – Specifies the name of the variable into which the result has to be stored, if specified
- **scope** – Specifies the scope into which the variable has to be stored

The <c:url> Tag

The `<c:url>` tag creates a URL and is added with a session ID if the user session needs to be maintained. This tag functions similar to the `encodeURL()` method of the `HttpServletRequest` interface.

The following is the syntax of the `<c:url>` tag of JSTL:

```
<c:url attributes> [zero or more <c:param> tags] </c:url>
```

The attributes of the `<c:url>` tag are:

- **value**—Specifies the URL to be rewritten if required added with session ID
- **context**—Specifies the context name of another Web application, required if the URL refers to the resource in another servlet context
- **var**—Specifies the name of the variable into which the new rewritten URL has to be stored
- **scope**—Specifies the scope of the variable defined in `var` attribute.

The <c:redirect> Tag

The `<c:redirect>` tag is used to redirect a client request. This tag acts similar to the `sendRedirect()` method of the `HttpServletResponse` interface.

The following is the syntax of the `<c:redirect>` tag of JSTL:

```
<c:redirect attributes> [zero or more <c:param> tags] </c:redirect>
```

The attributes of the `<c:redirect>` tag are:

- **value**—Specifies the URL of the resource to which the request has to be redirected
- **context**—Specifies the context name of another Web application, required if the URL refers to the resource in another servlet context

The <c:param> Tag

The `<c:param>` tag is used to add a request parameter to the URL. This tag can be used in `<c:url>` and `<c:redirect>` tags.

The following is the syntax of the `<c:param>` tag of JSTL:

```
<c:param attributes/>
```

The attributes of the `<c:param>` tag are:

- **name**—Specifies the name of the parameter
- **value**—Specifies the parameter value

Describing JSTL SQL Tags

The SQL tag library is used to access the relational database used in the JSP pages. The SQL tags are used for rapid prototyping and developing Web applications. The SQL tag libraries can be accessed in a JSP page by importing the following tag library in the JSP page:

```
<%@ taglib prefix="sql" uri="http://java.sun.com/jsp/jstl/sql" %>
```

Types of JSTL SQL Tags

The SQL tag library provides certain tags that are used in a JSP page to access a database. Table 19.1 shows the different SQL tags available in the JSTL SQL Tag libraries:

Table 19.1: The SQL Tag Library

Tag Name	Description
`query`	Executes a query specified in a JSP page
`update`	Updates an SQL statement used in a JSP page
`param`	Specifies a parameter in the SQL statement
`dateParam`	Sets a parameter in the SQL statement into a `java.util.Date` value
`setDataSource`	Specifies a data source that is to be accessed by executing a query

Table 19.1: The SQL Tag Library	
Tag Name	**Description**
transaction	Provides a connection to all the database operations that are to be executed in a JSP page

Now, we discuss these SQL tags in detail in the next sections.

The <sql:query> Tag

The <sql:query> tag executes the query specified in the sql attribute or in the tag body. Then, the result of the query is set to the variable specified in the var attribute.

The following is the syntax of the <sql:query> tag of JSTL:

```
<sql:query attributes> [body content] </sql:query>
```

The attributes of the <sql:query> tag are:

- **sql** – Specifies the SQL query that has to be executed. This attribute is optional and if not given, the query needs to be specified in the tag body. The SQL query can be parameterized.
- **var** – Specifies the variable name to which the result of the query has to be set
- **scope** – Specifies the scope of the variable
- **dataSource** – Specifies the data source JNDI name or java.sql.DataSource object
- **maxRows** – Specifies the maximum number of rows that has to be included into the result, this value needs to be greater than or equal to -1
- **startRow** – Specifies the starting row number

The body content for the <sql:query> tag accepts an SQL query and <sql:param> tags.

The <sql:update> Tag

The <sql:update> tag executes a SQL statement specified in the sql attribute or in the tag body. Then, the result of the query is set to the variable specified in the var attribute.

The following is the syntax of the <sql:update> tag of JSTL:

```
<sql:update attributes> [body content] </sql:update>
```

The attributes of <sql:update> tag are listed here:

- **sql** – Specifies the update SQL statement that has to be executed. This attribute is optional and if not given, the SQL statement needs to be specified in the tag body. The SQL query can be parameterized
- **var** – Specifies the variable name to which the result has to be set
- **scope** – Specifies the scope of the variable
- **dataSource** – Specifies the data source JNDI name or java.sql.DataSource object

The <sql:param> Tag

The <sql:param> tag is used to set a parameter in the SQL statement.

The following is the syntax of the <sql:param> tag of JSTL:

```
<sql:param attributes>[parameter value]</sql:param>
```

The attribute of <sql:param> tag is value, which is used to specify the parameter value that has to be substituted in the SQL statement.

The <sql:dateParam> Tag

The <sql:dateParam> tag is used to set a Date parameter in the SQL statement.

The following is the syntax of the <sql:dateparam> tag of JSTL:

```
<sql:dateParam attributes/>
```

The attributes of the <sql:dateParam> tag are:

- **value** – Specifies the date parameter value that has to be substituted in the SQL statement
- **type** – Takes either 'date' or 'time' or 'timestamp'

The <sql:setDataSource> Tag

The `<sql:setDataSource>` tag binds a data source to the specified variable.

The following is the syntax of the `<sql:setDataSource>` tag of JSTL:

```
<sql:setDataSource attributes/>
```

The attributes of the `<sql:setDataSource>` tag are:

- **dataSource**—Specifies the data source JNDI name or `java.sql.DataSource` object
- **driver**—Specifies the JDBC driver class name
- **url**—Specifies the JDBC URL referring to database
- **user**—Specifies the database username
- **password**—Specifies the database password
- **var**—Specifies the name of the variable to which the `DataSource` object has to be set
- **scope**—Specifies the scope of the variable

Note that if `dataSource` attribute is used, then `driver`, `url`, `user` and `password` attributes are not applicable.

The <sql:transaction> Tag

JSTL allows you to use transactions through the `<sql:transaction>` tag. You use this tag to specify a data source that you can use with the transaction. The `<sql:transaction>` tag groups `<sql:update>` and `<sql:query>` in its body part into a transaction.

The following is the syntax of the `<sql:transaction>` tag of JSTL:

```
<sql:transaction attributes>
  [<sql:query> |
  <sql:update>]+
</sql:transaction>
```

The attributes of the `<sql:transaction>` tag are:

- **dataSource**—Specifies the data source JNDI name or `java.sql.DataSource` object to be used with this transaction
- **isolation**—Specifies the possible values for isolation attribute are READ_COMMITTED, READ_UNCOMMITTED, REPEATABLE_READ, or SERIALIZABLE

Note that the `<sql:query>` or `<sql:update>` tags are used in `<sql:transaction>` tag.

Using JSTL SQL Tags

The **jstlex4** example demonstrates the use of JSTL SQL tags, which are used to create a connection with the database. We have created data source by using `<sql:setDataSource>` tag and set the data source object in the variable "`myds`". Listing 19.11 is used to create the GetEmpDetails.jsp page to retrieve the employee detail from the database table. To get the data from the database table (`emp`), we use `<sql:query>` tag and execute SQL select statement whose result has been set to the variable "result". Next, the page displays the records stored in the "result" variable using the `<c:forEach>` tag. In corresponding to the each row retrieved from the database, a hyperlink to remove the employee from the database is created. When, you click on that link, a new JSP page RemoveEmp.jsp opens. You can also find this file online in the code/Chapter19/jstlex4 folder.

Listing 19.11: Creating the GetEmpDetails.jsp File

```
<%@taglib uri="http://java.sun.com/jsp/jstl/sql" prefix="sql"%>
<%@taglib uri="http://java.sun.com/jsp/jstl/core" prefix="c"%>
<sql:setDataSource driver="oracle.jdbc.driver.OracleDriver"
url="jdbc:oracle:thin:@localhost:1521:sandb"
user="scott"
password="tiger" var="myds" scope="request"/>
<sql:query  sql="select  empno,deptno,ename,sal  from  emp"  var="result"  scope="page"
  dataSource="${requestScope.myds}"/>
<html> <body>
```

```
    <table border="1">
        <tr>
        <c:forEach items="${pageScope.result.columnNames}" var="colname">
            <th><c:out value="${colname}"/></th>
        </c:forEach>
        <th> </th>
        </tr>

        <c:forEach items="${pageScope.result.rows}" var="row">
            <tr> <td>
            <c:out value="${row.empno}"/>
            </td> <td>
            <c:out value="${row.deptno}"/>
            </td> <td>
            <c:out value="${row.ename}"/>
            </td> <td>
            <c:out value="${row.sal}"/>
            </td> <td>
            <a href= "RemoveEmp.jsp?empno=<c:out value="${row.empno}"/>">
            Remove</a> </td> </tr>
        </c:forEach>
    </table>
</body> </html>
```

Listing 19.12 is used to create the RemoveEmp.jsp page to delete the employee detail from the database table "emp". To delete the employee detail from the database table, we use the `<sql:query>` tag and execute the DELETE SQL statement. The result of the DELETE statement is stored in the variable "`count`". Then, the `<sql:param>` tag has been used to set the "`empno`" in the SQL DELETE statement. Next, the code to check the value of the count has been written. If the value of count is equal to 1, the details corresponding to the "`empno`" are deleted. If the value of count is not equal to 1, the message "`Problem in removing Employee`" is displayed. After removing the details of the employee from the database, a link (View Employees) to navigate to the previous page has been created. You can also find this file online in the code/Chapter19/jstlex4 folder.

Listing 19.12: Creating the RemoveEmp.jsp File

```
<%@taglib uri="http://java.sun.com/jsp/jstl/core" prefix="c"%>
<%@taglib uri="http://java.sun.com/jsp/jstl/sql" prefix="sql"%>
<sql:setDataSource        driver="oracle.jdbc.driver.OracleDriver"
url="jdbc:oracle:thin:@localhost:1521:sandb"
user="scott"
password="tiger" var="myds" scope="request"/>
<sql:update  dataSource="${requestScope.myds}"  sql="delete  from  emp  where  empno=?"
var="count">
<sql:param value="${param.empno}"/>
</sql:update>
<c:if test="${count eq 1}">
  <b>Employee Removed</b>
</c:if>
<c:if test="${count ne 1}">
  <b>Problem in removing Employee</b>
</c:if>
<br/>
<a href="GetEmpDetails.jsp">View Employees</a>
```

Listing 19.13 shows the `web.xml` file in which, we have set the GetEmpDetails.jsp as welcome page (page that will be the starting page). You can also find this file online in the code/Chapter19/jstlex4/WEB-INF folder.

Listing 19.13: Creating the `web.xml` File

```
<?xml version="1.0"?>
<web-app>
  <welcome-file-list>
```

```
        <welcome-file> GetEmpDetails.jsp </welcome-file>
    </welcome-file-list>
</web-app>
```

After creating all the preceding files, arrange them along with `jstl.jar` and `standard.jar` as shown in Figure 19.8:

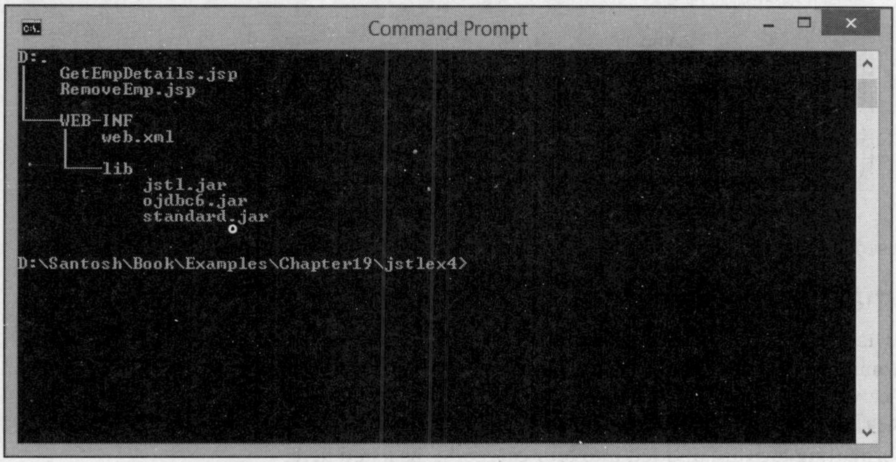

Figure 19.8: Showing Directory Structure of jstlex4 Application

Now, copy the **jstlex4** folder into the `<Tomcat home>\webapps` folder and start the Tomcat server. Enter the URL `http://localhost:9090/jstlex4/GetEmpDetails.jsp` in your browser. It displays all the employees' details as shown in Figure 19.9:

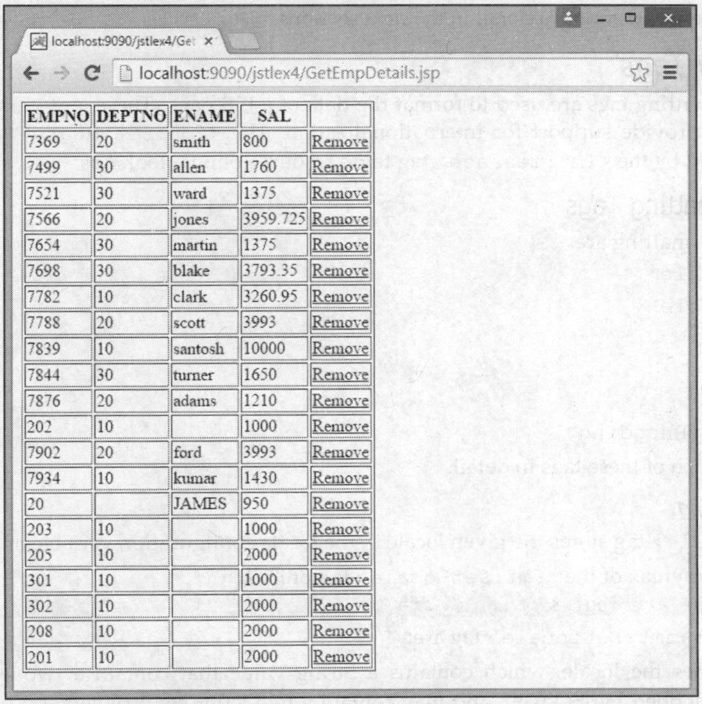

EMPNO	DEPTNO	ENAME	SAL	
7369	20	smith	800	Remove
7499	30	allen	1760	Remove
7521	30	ward	1375	Remove
7566	20	jones	3959.725	Remove
7654	30	martin	1375	Remove
7698	30	blake	3793.35	Remove
7782	10	clark	3260.95	Remove
7788	20	scott	3993	Remove
7839	10	santosh	10000	Remove
7844	30	turner	1650	Remove
7876	20	adams	1210	Remove
202	10		1000	Remove
7902	20	ford	3993	Remove
7934	10	kumar	1430	Remove
20		JAMES	950	Remove
203	10		1000	Remove
205	10		2000	Remove
301	10		1000	Remove
302	10		2000	Remove
208	10		2000	Remove
201	10		2000	Remove

Figure 19.9: Showing Employees' Details with Remove Link

Click on any of the Remove link to remove the respective employee; for example, clicking on the Remove link in the last row will delete the employee record with `empno 201`. This operation presents the view as shown in Figure 19.10:

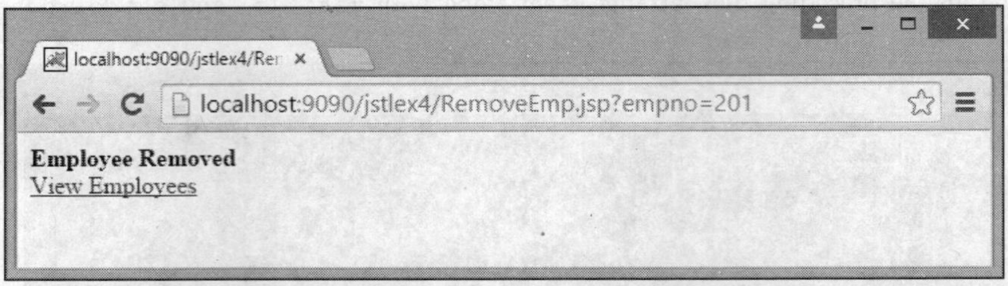

Figure 19.10: Showing Employee Removed Message

In the next section, we discuss about JSTL formatting tags.

JSTL Formatting Tags

The format tag library provides the support for internationalization. This provides the formatting of data in different domains. The data can be dates, numbers, or the time specifications in different domains. The format tag library can be used in a JSP page by using the following specification:

```
<%@ taglib prefix="fmt" uri="http://java.sun.com/jsp/jstl/fmt" %>
```

The JSTL formatting tags are divided into four categories as listed here:

- Basic Formatting Tags
- Number Formatting Tags
- Date Formatting Tags
- Time Zone Formatting Tags

Now, we discuss these categories in detail in the next sections.

Basic Formatting Tags

The JSTL basic formatting tags are used to format the data of a JSP page. These tags parse the data based on the current Locale and provide support for internationalization. The `<fmt:setLocale>` tag sets the localization settings that are used by the `<fmt:message>` tag to do resource bundle look ups.

Types of Basic Formatting Tags

The tags used for formatting are:

- `<fmt:setLocale>`
- `<fmt:setBundle>`
- `<fmt:bundle>`
- `<fmt:message>`
- `<fmt:param>`
- `<fmt:requestEncoding>`

Now let's discuss each of these tags in detail.

The <fmt:setLocale> Tag

The `<fmt:setLocale>` tag stores the given locale in the locale configuration variable of the given scope.

The following is the syntax of the `<fmt:setLocale>` tag of JSTL:

```
<fmt:setLocale attributes/>
```

The attributes of the `<fmt:setLocale>` tag are:

- **value**—Specifies the locale, which contains a String value that contain a two-letter language code (in lower-case as defined by ISO-639), and may contain a two-letter country code (in uppercase as defined by ISO-3166). Language and country codes must be separated by hyphen '-'or underscore '_'.

- **variant**—Specifies the locale variant of the language referenced by value attribute.
- **scope**—The scope into which this object has to be set

The <fmt:setBundle> Tag

The `<fmt:setBundle>` tag creates a `ResourceBundle` object using the `Locale` object in the locale configuration variable and the given `basename`, and stores the `ResourceBundle` object into the given variable and scope.

The following is syntax of the `<fmt:setBundle>` tag of JSTL:

```
<fmt:setBundle attributes/>
```

The attributes of the `<fmt:setBundle>` tag are:

- **basename**—Specifies the resource bundle name
- **var**—Specifies the variable name to which this resource bundle object has to be set
- **scope**—Specifies the scope of the variable defined in "`var`" attribute

The <fmt:bundle> Tag

The `<fmt:bundle>` tag creates a `ResourceBundle` object by using the `Locale` object in the locale configuration variable and the given `basename` and applies it to the formatting actions in its body content.

The following snippet shows the syntax of the `<fmt:Bundle>` tag of JSTL:

```
<fmt:bundle attributes> body content </fmt:bundle>
```

The attributes of `<fmt:bundle>` tag are listed here:

- **basename**—Specifies the resource bundle name
- **prefix**—Specifies prefix that has to be used for the messages used in this elements body content

The <fmt:message> Tag

The `<fmt:message>` tag maps key to localized message and performs parameter replacements using the resource bundle specified in bundle attribute.

The following is the syntax of the `<fmt:message>` tag of JSTL:

```
<fmt:message attributes> body content </fmt:message>
```

The attributes of `<fmt:message>` tag are listed here:

- **key**—Specifies the key that whose value has to be retrieved
- **bundle**—Specifies the resource bundle that has to be used to get the value of the specified key
- **var**—Specifies the variable to which the retrieved message has to be stored
- **scope**—Specifies the scope of the variable defined in "`var`" attribute

The body part of `<fmt:message>` tag allows to use `<fmt:param>` tag to supply parametric values.

The <fmt:param> Tag

The `<fmt:param>` tag is used within the `<fmt:message>` element. This tag supplies the argument for the parametric replacement in a message.

The following is the syntax of the `<fmt:param>` tag of JSTL:

```
<fmt:param attributes/>
```

The `<fmt:param>` tag accepts one attribute, value, which specifies the value of the parameter to be passed.

The <fmt:requestEncoding> Tags

The `<fmt:requestEncoding>` tag allows to set the character encoding of a request. This tag invokes the `setCharacterEncoding()` method of the `ServletRequest` interface to set the character encoding of a request.

The following is the syntax of the `<fmt:requestEncoding>` tag of JSTL:

```
<fmt:requestEncoding attributes/>
```

The `<fmt:requestEncoding>` tag accepts one attribute, value, which represents the character encoding to be set. The character encoding is further used to decode the request parameters.

Using Basic JSTL Formatting Tags

The **jstlex5** example demonstrates the usage of the basic JSTL formatting tags. Listing 19.14 shows the code to implement the concept of internationalization. You can also find this file online in the code/Chapter19/jstlex5 folder.

Listing 19.14: Creating the I18NExample.jsp File

```
<%@taglib uri="http://java.sun.com/jsp/jstl/fmt" prefix="fmt"%>
<%@taglib uri="http://java.sun.com/jsp/jstl/core" prefix="c"%>

This example demonstrates the basic JSTL formatting tags:
<br/><br/>
Locale from client :
<b><c:out value="${pageContext.request.locale}"/></b> <br/>

<fmt:setBundle basename="ApplicationResources" var="mybundle"/>
<fmt:message key="welcome.message" bundle="${mybundle}">
  <fmt:param value="${param.uname}"/>
</fmt:message> <br/></br>

<b>Now testing &lt;fmt:setLocale&gt; tag:</b><br/>
<br/><br/>

Creating a ResourceBundle with client locale and setting it to <i>mybundle1</i>
variable.<br/>

<fmt:setBundle basename="ApplicationResources" var="mybundle1"/>

Setting the locale to <i>it</i> (italian). <br/>

<fmt:setLocale value="it"/>

Creating a ResourceBundle with <i>it</i> (italian) locale and setting it to
<i>mybundle2</i> variable.
<br/><br/>

<fmt:setBundle basename="ApplicationResources" var="mybundle2"/>
<b>Message using <i>mybundle1</i>:</b> <br/>
  <pre>
        <fmt:message bundle="${mybundle1}" key="welcome.message">
               <fmt:param value="${param.uname}"/>
        </fmt:message>
  </pre>
<br/>
<b>Message using <i>mybundle2</i>:</b> <br/>
<pre>
  <fmt:message bundle="${mybundle2}" key="welcome.message">
        <fmt:param value="${param.uname}"/>
  </fmt:message>
</pre>
```

Listing 19.15 shows the web.xml file to set the welcome page. You can also find this file online in the code/Chapter19/jstlex5/WEB-INF folder.

Listing 19.15: Creating the web.xml File

```
<?xml version="1.0"?>
<web-app>
  <welcome-file-list>
        <welcome-file> I18NExample.jsp </welcome-file>
  </welcome-file-list>
</web-app>
```

Listings 19.16, 19.17, and 19.18 show the code to create properties files to set the language according to the locale. These properties files contain a key `welcome.message` and a `value` corresponding to this key. You can also find these files online in the code/Chapter19/jstlex5 folder.

Listing 19.16: Creating the ApplicationResources_en.properties File

```
welcome.message=Welcome to internationalization <b>{0}</b> (English user)
```

Listing 19.17: Creating the ApplicationResources_en_US.properties File

```
welcome.message=Welcome to internationalization <b>{0}</b> (US English user)
```

Listing 19.18: Creating the ApplicationResources_it.properties File

```
welcome.message=Welcome to internationalization <b>{0}</b> (Italian user)
```

Arrange all the files in the directory structure, as shown in Figure 19.11:

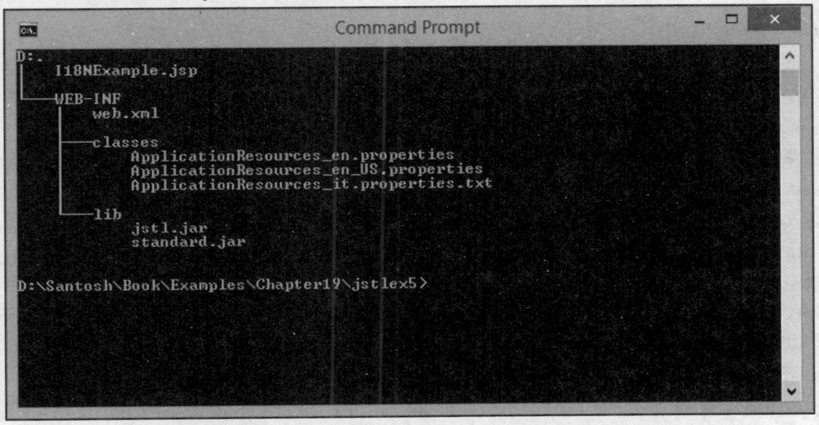

Figure 19.11: Showing Directory Structure of jstlex5 Application

Now, copy the **jstlex5** folder into `<Tomcat home>\webapps` and start the server. Browse the **jstlex5** application by using the URL `http://localhost:9090/jstlex5/I18NExample.jsp?uname=Santosh`, which presents the output as shown in Figure 19.12:

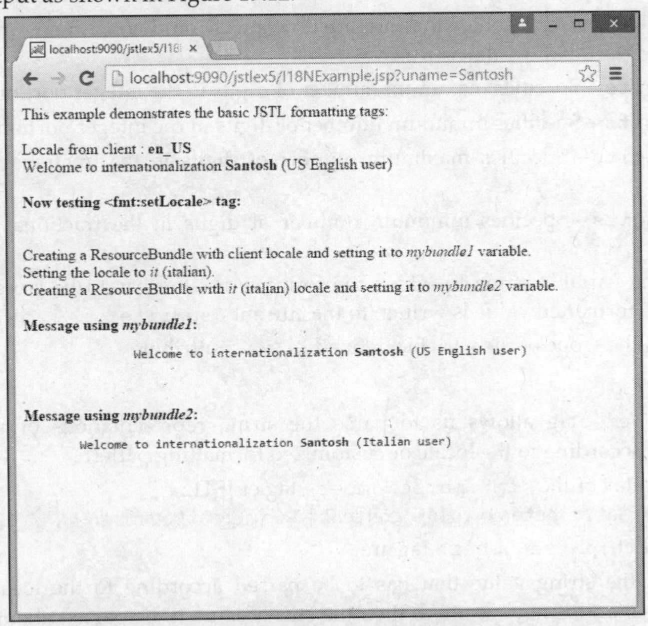

Figure 19.12: Showing Basic JSTL Formatting Tags

Number Formatting Tags

The JSTL number formatting tags are used to format the number data. The formatting aspect of number formatting tags includes the currency-related formatting, number parsing and formatting, and formatting percentages.

Types of Number Formatting Tags

The tags used for number formatting are:

- `<fmt:formatNumber>`
- `<fmt:parseNumber>`

Now let's discuss each of these tags in detail.

The <fmt:formatNumber> Tag

The `<fmt:formatNumber>` tag allows us to format numbers, currencies, and percentages according to the locale or customized formatting pattern.

The following is the syntax of the `<fmt:formatNumber>` tag of JSTL:

```
<fmt:formatNumber attributes> [body content] </fmt:formatNumber>
```

The attributes of the `<fmt:formatNumber>` tag are:

- **value**—Specifies the numeric value that has to be formatted to the locale or given pattern. This attribute is optional and if not specified, then the numeric value to be formatted should be given into the body content of this tag.
- **type**—Specifies the value type, accepted values are number, currency, and percent. If this attribute is not specified, default is taken as number.
- **pattern**—Specifies custom pattern to which the given value has to be formatted.
- **currencyCode**—Specifies the currency code as per ISO 4217 that has to be used in formatting. This is applicable only when the type is currency (i.e. when formatting currency) otherwise this attribute is ignored.
- **currencySymbol**—Specifies the currency symbol that has to be included into the formatted number. This attribute is applicable only if `type=currency` is set otherwise this attribute is ignored.
- **groupingUsed**—Specified whether the formatted output should contain any grouping separators. Takes boolean value and the default value is true.
- **maxIntegerDigits**—Specifies maximum number of digits in the integer portion of the formatted output.
- **minIntegerDigits**—Specifies minimum number of digits in the integer portion of the formatted output.
- **maxFractionDigits**—Specifies maximum number of digits in the fractional portion of the formatted output.
- **minFractionDigits**—Specifies minimum number of digits in the fractional portion of the formatted output.
- **var**—Specifies the variable name to which the formatted value has to be stored. If this attribute is not specified, then the formatted value is written to the current `JspWriter`.
- **scope**—Specifies the scope of the variable defined in "`var`" attribute.

The <fmt:parseNumber> Tag

The `<fmt:parseNumber>` tag allows us to parse the string representations of numbers, currencies, and percentages formatted according to the locale or customized formatting pattern.

The following is the syntax of the `<fmt:parseNumber>` tag of JSTL:

```
<fmt:parseNumber attributes> [body content] </fmt:parseNumber>
```

The attributes of the `<fmt:parseNumber>` tag are:

- **value**—Specifies the string value that has to be parsed according to the locale or given pattern. This attribute is optional and if not specified, then the string value to be parsed should be given into the body content of this tag.

- **type**—Specifies the value type, accepted values are number, currency, and percent. If this attribute is not specified, default is taken as number.
- **pattern**—Specifies the custom formatting pattern that determines how the given value is to be parsed.
- **parseLocale**—Specifies the Locale whose default formatting pattern is to be used during the parse operation, or to which the pattern specified via the pattern attribute (if present) is applied.
- **integerOnly**—Specifies whether just the integer portion of the given value should be parsed. Default is false.
- **var**—Specifies the variable name to which the parsed value has to be stored. If this attribute is not specified, then the formatted value is written to the current `JspWriter`.
- **scope**—Specifies the scope of the variable defined in "`var`" attribute.

Using Number Format Tags

The **jstlex6** example, shown in Listing 19.19, demonstrates you how to use JSTL number format tags. The example uses `<fmt:formatNumber>` and `<fmt:parseNumber>` tag.

Listing 19.19 shows the code to create index.html page to get the number from a user. This listing contains one text box, where user will enter the number and a button. On clicking the button, the control will transfer to the TestApp.jsp (Listing 19.20). You can also find this file online in the code/Chapter19/jstlex6 folder.

Listing 19.19: Creating the index.html File

```
<html> <body>
<form method=post action="TestApp.jsp"> <pre> <b>
  Number : <input type="text" name="mynumber"/>

  <input type="submit" value="Format Number"/>
</b> </pre> </form>
</body> </html>
```

Listing 19.20 shows the code to convert the number retrieved through index.html page into a specific format. You can also find this listing online in the code/Chapter19/jstlex6 folder.

Listing 19.20: Creating the TestApp.jsp File

```
<%@taglib uri="http://java.sun.com/jsp/jstl/fmt" prefix="fmt"%>

<%@taglib uri="http://java.sun.com/jsp/jstl/core" prefix="c"%>

<html> <body>

My Number:
<b><c:out value="${param.mynumber}"/></b> </br>
Formatting My Number: <br/><br/>
<fmt:setLocale value="it"/>
In Italy:
<pre>
  Default pattern:<b>
  <fmt:formatNumber type="currency" value="${param.mynumber}"/></b>
  Using pattern (0,00,00.0000): <b>
<fmt:formatNumber type="currency" value="${param.mynumber}" pattern="00,0,00.0000"/> </b>
</pre>
<br/>
In US:
<fmt:setLocale value="en_US"/>
<pre>

  Default pattern:<b>
  <fmt:formatNumber type="currency" value="${param.mynumber}"/></b>
  Using pattern (0,00,00.0000):<b>
```

```
<fmt:formatNumber    type="currency"    value="${param.mynumber}"    currencySymbol="$"
pattern="0,00,00.0000" var="fmt_mynumber"/>
  <c:out value="${fmt_mynumber}"/></b>
</pre>
<br/>
After  parsing  the  formatted  mynumber:  <fmt:parseNumber  value="${fmt_mynumber}"
  type="currency" pattern="0,00,00.0000"/>
</body></html>
```

Listing 19.21 shows the `web.xml` page to set the welcome page. You can also find this file online in the code/Chapter19/jstlex6/WEB-INF folder.

Listing 19.21: Creating the `web.xml` File

```
<?xml version="1.0"?>
<web-app>
  <welcome-file-list>
       <welcome-file> index.html </welcome-file>
  </welcome-file-list>
</web-app>
```

Arrange all the files as shown in Figure 19.13, copy **jstlex6** folder into `<Tomcat home>\webapps` folder, and start the server.

Figure 19.13: Showing Directory Structure of jstlex6 Application

Browse the example by using the URL: `http://localhost:9090/jstlex6/index.html`, which displays a form as shown in Figure 19.14:

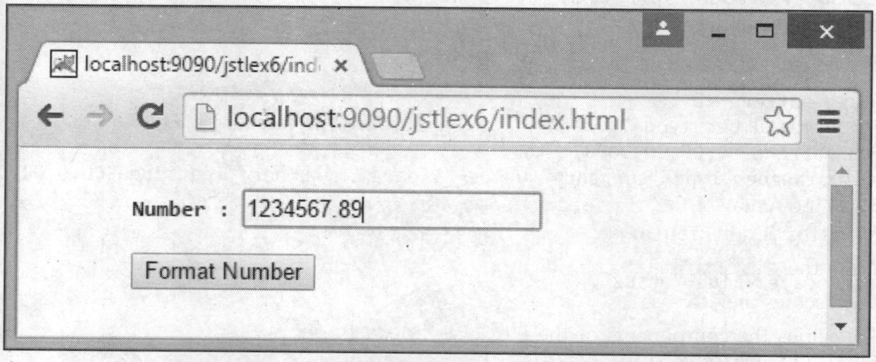

Figure 19.14: Showing index.html to enter the Number

Enter a number as shown in Figure 19.14 and click on Format Number button. This makes a request to TestApp.jsp. The TestApp.jsp formats the given number in Italian and US locale formats with default and given pattern as shown in Figure 19.15:

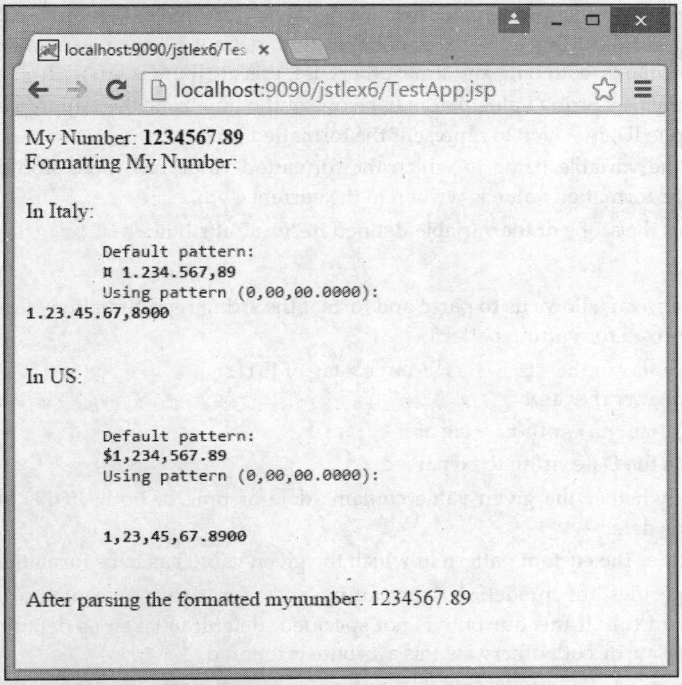

Figure 19.15: Showing JSTL Number Format Tags

Date Formatting Tags

The JSTL date formatting tags are used to format the date type of data. These tags help in formatting and parsing date-time data. The `<fmt:formatDate>` tag formats the date-time data and `<fmt:parseDate>` tag parses the date-time data.

Types of Date Formatting Tags

The tags used for date formatting are:

- ❑ `<fmt:formatDate>`
- ❑ `<fmt:parseDate>`

Now let's discuss each of these tags in detail.

The <fmt:formatDate> Tag

The `<fmt:formatDate>` tag allows us to format dates and times according to the locale or customized formatting pattern.

The following is the syntax of the `<fmt:formatDate>` tag of JSTL:

```
<fmt:formatDate attributes/>
```

The attributes of the `<fmt:formatDate>` tag are:

- ❑ **value**—Specifies the `java.util.Date` object whose Date and/or Time to be formatted.
- ❑ **type**—Specifies the components of the given date object which has to be formatted, accepted values are date, time, and both. If this attribute is not specified, default is taken as date.
- ❑ **pattern**—Specifies the custom pattern to which the given value has to be formatted.

- **dateStyle**—Specifies the predefined formatting style for dates. Accepted values are default, short, medium, long, and full. This is applicable only when the type is date or both date and time; otherwise this attribute is ignored.
- **timeStyle**—Specifies the predefined formatting style for time. Accepted values are default, short, medium, long, and full. If this attribute is not specified, default is taken as default. This is applicable only when the type is time or both date and time; otherwise, this attribute is ignored.
- **timeZone**—Specifies a String value that may be one of the time zone IDs supported by the Java platform or a custom time zone ID, in which to represent the formatted time.
- **var**—Specifies the variable name to which the formatted value has to be stored. If this attribute is not specified, then the formatted value is written to the current `JspWriter`.
- **scope**—Specifies the scope of the variable defined in "`var`" attribute.

The <fmt:parseDate> Tag

The `<fmt:parseDate>` tag allows us to parse and format the string representation of dates and times according to the locale or customized formatting pattern.

The following is the syntax of the `<fmt:parseDate>` tag of JSTL:

```
<fmt:parseDate attributes/>
```

The attributes of the `<fmt:parseDate>` tag are:

- **value**—Specifies the Date string to be parsed.
- **type**—Specifies whether the given value contains date or time or both. If this attribute is not specified, default is taken as date.
- **pattern**—Specifies the custom pattern to which the given value has to be formatted.
- **dateStyle**—Specifies the predefined formatting style for dates. Accepted values are default, short, medium, long, and full. If this attribute is not specified, default is taken as default. This is applicable only when the type is date or both otherwise this attribute is ignored.
- **timeStyle**—Specifies the predefined formatting style for times. Accepted values are default, short, medium, long, and full. If this attribute is not specified default is taken as default. This is applicable only when the type is time or both, otherwise this attribute is ignored.
- **timeZone**—Specifies a String value that may be one of the time zone IDs supported by the Java platform or a custom time zone ID, in which it represents the formatted time.
- **parseLocale**—Specifies the Locale whose default formatting pattern is to be used during the parse operation, or to which the pattern specified via the pattern attribute (if present) is applied.
- **var**—Specifies the variable name to which the formatted value has to be stored. If this attribute is not specified, then the formatted value is written to the current `JspWriter`.
- **scope**—Specifies the scope of the variable defined in "`var`" attribute.

Using Date Formatting Tags

Listing 19.22 of **jstlex7** application demonstrates you how to use JSTL date format tags. The application uses `<fmt:formatDate>` and `<fmt:parseDate>` tag for formatting and parsing of Date information.

Listing 19.22 shows the code to format the date according to the specific locale corresponding to the specific pattern. You can also find this file online in the code/Chapter19/jstlex7 folder.

Listing 19.22: Creating the TestApp.jsp File

```
<%@taglib uri="http://java.sun.com/jsp/jstl/fmt" prefix="fmt"%>
<%@taglib uri="http://java.sun.com/jsp/jstl/core" prefix="c"%>

<html> <body>
<%pageContext.setAttribute("mydate",new java.util.Date(),PageContext.PAGE_SCOPE);%>
Current Date and Time:
<b><c:out value="${mydate}"/></b> </br>
```

```
    Formatting Date: <br/><br/>
    <fmt:setLocale value="it"/>
    In Italy:
    <pre>
      Default pattern:<b>
      <fmt:formatDate type="both" value="${mydate}"/></b>
      Using pattern (dd-MMM-yyyy hh:mm:ss): <b>
    <fmt:formatDate type="both" value="${mydate}" pattern="dd-MMM-yyyy hh:mm:ss"/> </b>
    </pre>
    <br/>

    In US:
    <fmt:setLocale value="en_US"/>
    <pre>
      Default pattern:<b>
      <fmt:formatDate type="both" value="${mydate}"/></b>
      Using pattern (dd-MMM-yyyy hh:mm:ss): <b>
    <fmt:formatDate    type="both"    value="${mydate}"    pattern="dd-MMM-yyyy    hh:mm:ss"
var="fmt_mydate"/> </b>
      <c:out value="${fmt_mydate}"/></b>
    </pre>
    <br/>
    After  parsing  the  formatted  mydate:  <fmt:parseDate  value="${fmt_mydate}"  type="both"
pattern="dd-MMM-yyyy hh:mm:ss"/>

    </body></html>
```

Listing 19.23 shows the `web.xml` page to set the welcome page. You can also find this file online in the code/Chapter19/jstlex7/WEB-INF folder.

Listing 19.23: Creating the web.xml File

```
    <?xml version="1.0"?>
    <web-app>

      <welcome-file-list>
           <welcome-file>TestApp.jsp </welcome-file>
      </welcome-file-list>

    </web-app>
```

Arrange all the files as shown in Figure 19.16, copy **jstlex7** folder into `<Tomcat home>\webapps` folder, and start the server.

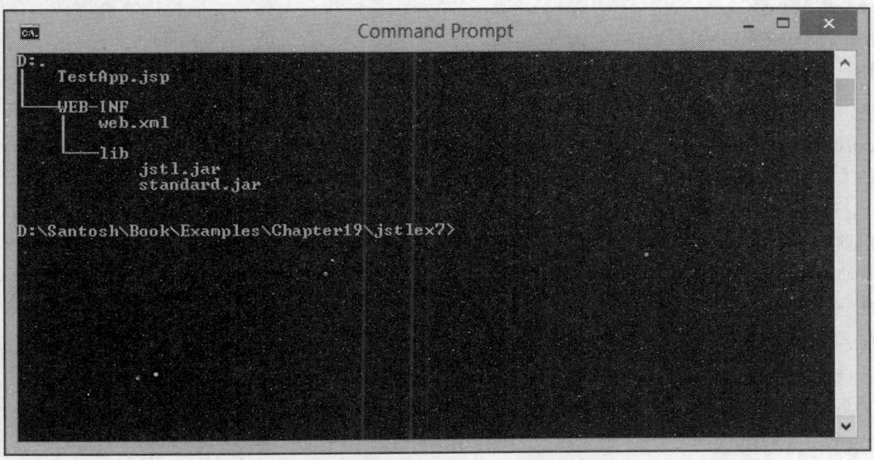

Figure 19.16: Showing Directory Structure of jstlex7 Application

Browse the application using the URL: `http://localhost:9090/jstlex7/TestApp.jsp`, which formats current date into Italian and US locale formats with default and given pattern as shown in Figure 19.17:

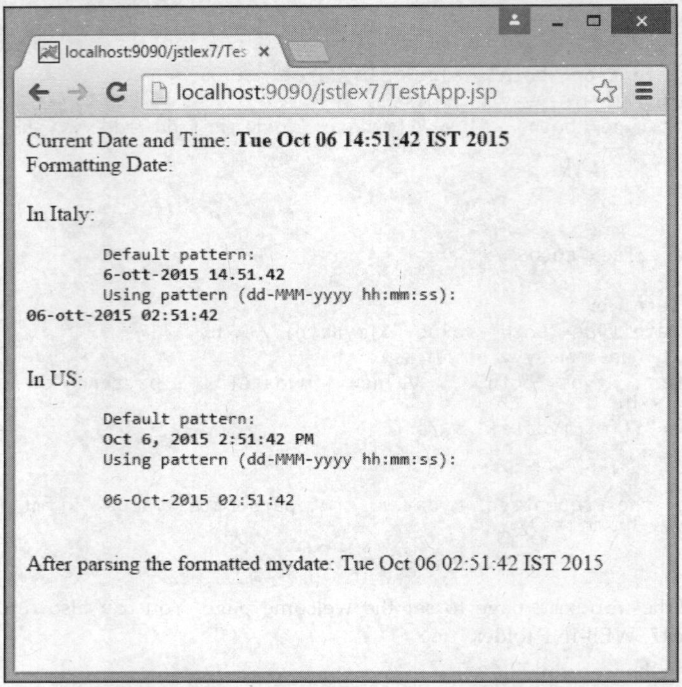

Figure 19.17: Showing JSTL Date Format Tags

Time Zone Formatting Tags

The JSTL time zone formatting tags are used to format the time zone type of data. These tags help in setting the time zone by using `<fmt:setTimeZone>` tag. The `<fmt:timeZone>` tag specifies the time zone to be used by all the tags within this tag.

Types of Time Zone Formatting Tags

The tags used for time zone formatting are:

- `<fmt:timeZone>`
- `<fmt:setTimeZone>`

Now let's discuss each of these tags in detail

The <fmt:timeZone> Tag

The body content of the `<fmt:timeZone>` tag specifies the tags that will be controlled by the time zone specified in `<fmt:timeZone>` tag.

The following is the syntax of the `<fmt:timeZone>` tag of JSTL:

```
<fmt:timeZone attributes> body content </fmt:timeZone>
```

The `<fmt:timeZone>` tag accepts one attribute, value, which specified the `java.util.TimeZone` object or a `String` that represents a time zone ID.

The <fmt:setTimeZone> Tag

The `<fmt:setTimeZone>` tag stores the given time zone in the time zone configuration variable of the given scope.

The following is the syntax of the `<fmt:setTimeZone>` tag of JSTL:

```
<fmt:setTimeZone attributes/>
```

The attributes of the <fmt:setTimeZone> tag are:

- **value**—Specifies a String value that may be one of the time zone IDs supported by the Java platform or a custom time zone ID
- **var**—Specifies the variable name
- **scope**—Specifies the Scope into which this object has to be set

Using TimeZone Formatting Tags

Listing 19.24 of **jstlex8** example demonstrates you how to use JSTL timezone format tags. The following example uses <fmt:timeZone> tag. Listing 19.24 shows the code to specify the time zone corresponding to a specific timezone ID. You can also find this file online in the code/Chapter19/jstlex8 folder.

Listing 19.24: Creating the TestApp.jsp File

```
<%@taglib uri="http://java.sun.com/jsp/jstl/fmt" prefix="fmt"%>
<%@taglib uri="http://java.sun.com/jsp/jstl/core" prefix="c"%>

<html> <body>
<%pageContext.setAttribute("mydate",new java.util.Date(),PageContext.PAGE_SCOPE);%>
Current Date and Time:
<b><c:out value="${mydate}"/></b> </br>

Formatting Date based on Time Zone: <br/><br/>
GMT:
<pre>
  <b><fmt:timeZone value="GMT">
        <fmt:formatDate type="both" value="${mydate}"/>
  </fmt:timeZone></b>
</pre>
<br/>

6 hours 30 minutes ahead of GMT :
<pre>
  <b><fmt:timeZone value="GMT+06:30">
        <fmt:formatDate type="both" value="${mydate}"/>
  </fmt:timeZone></b>
</pre>
<br/>

10 hours 30 minutes behind the GMT :
<pre>
  <b><fmt:timeZone value="GMT-10:30">
        <fmt:formatDate type="both" value="${mydate}"/>
  </fmt:timeZone></b>
</pre>
</body></html>
```

Listing 19.25 shows the web.xml file to set the welcome page. You can also find this file online in the code/Chapter19/jstlex8/WEB-INF folder.

Listing 19.25: Creating the web.xml File

```
<?xml version="1.0"?>
<web-app>

  <welcome-file-list>
        <welcome-file>TestApp.jsp </welcome-file>
  </welcome-file-list>

</web-app>
```

Arrange all the files as shown in Figure 19.18, copy **jstlex8** folder into `<Tomcat home>\webapps` folder, and start the server. Figure 19.18 shows the directory structure of **jstlex8** application:

Figure 19.18: Showing Directory Structure of jstlex8 Application

Browse the example using the URL: `http://localhost:9090/jstlex8/TestApp.jsp`, which converts the current time of IST to GMT, GMT +06:30, and GMT -10:30 as shown in Figure 19.19:

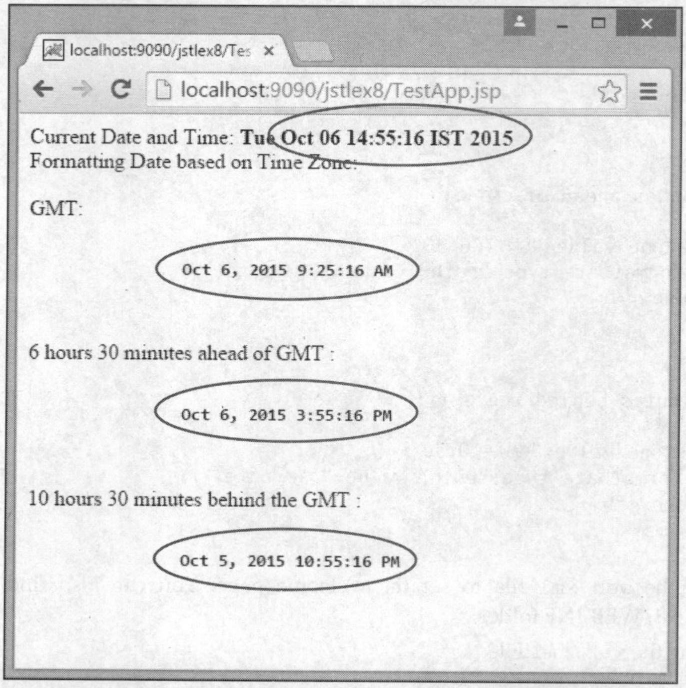

Figure 19.19: Showing Date Formatting based on Time Zone

JSTL XML Tags

The XML tag library is used to work with XML data used in the JSP pages. The XML tag library helps parse and transform the data used in the JSP page. These operations can be done by using the XPath expressions associated with an XML document. An XPath expression includes both the relative and the absolute path of the XML element. The XML tags can be used with the JSP pages after importing the following tag library by using the following code:

```
<%@ taglib prefix="x" uri="http://java.sun.com/jsp/jstl/xml" %>
```

XML tags can be accessed by using the prefix 'x'. It is the predefined prefix used for XML tag libraries.

All the JSTL XML tags can be categorized into following categories:

- XML Core Tags
- XML Flow Control Tags
- XML Transformation Tags

Let's explore all these categories in detail.

XML Core Tags

The JSTL XML Core tags include the tags for parsing XML documents and performing XPath operations. The XML Core tags are of three types:

- `<x:parse>`
- `<x:out>`
- `<x:set>`

The following section explains all these tags in detail.

The <x:parse> Tag

This tag parses the given XML document and stores the resulted XML Document Object Model (DOM) into the specified variable.

The following is the syntax of the `<x:parse>` tag of JSTL:

```
<x:parse attributes> [body content] </x:parse>
```

The attributes of the `<x:parse>` tag are:

- **`doc`**—Accepts an XML document to be parsed in the form of a string or Reader object that locates the XML document to be parsed.
- **`systemId`**—Accepts the system identifier (URI) for parsing the XML document.
- **`filter`**—Accepts an `org.xml.sax.XMLFilter` object to be applied for the XML document.
- **`var`**—Specifies the variable name to which the parsed XML document has to be set.
- **`scope`**—Specifies the scope of the `var` attribute.
- **`varDom`**—Specifies the variable name to which the `org.w3c.dom.Document` object of the parsed XML document has to be set.
- **`scopeDom`**—Specifies the scope of the `varDom` attribute.

The <x:out> Tag

The `<x:out>` tag evaluates an XML XPath expression and writes the result of the evaluation to the current `JspWriter`.

The following is the syntax of the `<x:out>` tag of JSTL:

```
<x:out attributes/>
```

The attributes of the `<x:out>` tag are:

- **`select`**—Accepts an XML XPath expression to be evaluated.
- **`escapeXML`**—Accepts a boolean value that describes whether the characters such as >, <, &, ',' in the result string has to be converted to their corresponding character entity codes. The default value is true.

The <x:set> Tag

The `<x:set>` tag evaluates an XML XPath expression and stores the result of the evaluation in a scoped variable.

The following is the syntax of the <x:set> tag of JSTL:

```
<x:set attributes/>
```

The attributes of the <x:out> tag are:

- **select**—Accepts an XML XPath expression to be evaluated.
- **var**—Specifies the name of the scoped variable to hold the result obtained after evaluating the given XPath expression.
- **scope**—Specifies the scope of the var attribute.

XML Flow Control Tags

The JSTL XML Flow Control tags help perform various operations such as easily parse and access XML data, iterate over elements in an XML document, and conditionally process JSP code fragments depending on the result of the given XPath expression.

The XML Flow Control tags of JSTL tags contain five tags:

- <x:if>
- <x:choose>
- <x:when>
- <x:otherwise>
- <x:forEach>

The following sections explain all these tags in detail.

The <x:if> Tag

The <x:if> tag evaluates an XPath expression that is given in its 'select' attribute. If the resulting value is true, then the body of the <x:if> tag is evaluated; otherwise not.

The following is the syntax of the <x:if> tag of JSTL:

```
<x:if attributes>  body content </x:if>
```

The attributes of the <x:if> tag are:

- **select**—Takes an XPath expression that resolves to a boolean value
- **var**—Takes the name of the scoped variable to store the conditions result
- **scope**—Specifies the scope of a variable

The <x:choose> Tag

The <x:choose> tag acts similar to the Java switch statement. The <x:choose> tag encloses one or more <x:when> tags and a <x:otherwise> tag.

The following is the syntax of the <x:choose> tag of JSTL:

```
<x:choose> body content </x:choose>
```

Body content of <x:choose> tag includes one or more <x:when> tags and zero or one <x:otherwise> tag.

The <x:when> Tag

The <x:when> tag encloses a single case within the <x:choose> tag.

The following is the syntax of the <x:when> tag of JSTL:

```
<x:when attribute> body content </x:when>
```

The <x:when> tag accepts only one attribute **select**, which takes an XPath expression resolving to boolean value. If the boolean value is true, the <c:when> tags body is evaluated.

The <x:otherwise> Tag

This is same as <x:when> tag but is unconditional; this is equivalent to default case in the Java switch statement. The body content of this tag is evaluated if none of the <x:when> conditions in the <x:choose> tag are resolved to true.

The following is the syntax of the <x:otherwise> tag of JSTL:

```
<x:otherwise> body content </x:otherwise>
```

The <x:forEach> tag

The <x:forEach> tag is used for looping over a list of elements obtained after evaluating the given XPath expression.

The following is syntax of the <x:forEach> tag of JSTL:

```
<x:forEach attributes> body content </x:forEach>
```

The attributes of the <x:forEach> are:

- **select**—Takes an XPath expression that results a node list
- **var**—Specifies the name of the variable into which the current iteration item has to be set
- **varStatus**—Specifies the name of the variable that lets us to know the information about where are we in the overall iteration such as getting count, index, knowing isFirst, isLast, etc., this attribute is optional
- **begin**—Takes the starting index for the loop, this attribute is optional
- **end**—Takes the ending index for the loop, this attribute is optional
- **step**—Specifies an optional increment for the loop, default is 1

XML Transformation Tags

The XML Transformation tags of the JSTL XML tags provide support to transform the XML document with the given XSL stylesheet. This part of JSTL tags contain two tags, <x:transform> and <x:param>. The following section explains these tags in detail.

The <x:transform> Tag

The <x:transform> tag transforms an XML document using the given XSL style sheet.

The following is the syntax of the <x:transform> tag of JSTL:

```
<x:transform attributes> [body content] </x:transform>
```

The attributes of the <x:transform> tag are:

- **doc**—Takes an XML document to be parsed in the form of a string or a Reader object. The Reader object locates the XML document, or an org.w3c.dom.Document object or an object that is exported by <x:parse> or <x:set> tag.
- **xslt**—Takes an XSLT stylesheet document for transformation in the form of a string or a Reader object. The Reader object locates the XML document or an org.w3c.dom.Document object or an javax.xml.transform.Source object.
- **docSystemId**—Takes the system identifier (URI) for parsing the XML document.
- **xsltSystemId**—Takes the system identifier (URI) for parsing the XSLT stylesheet document.
- **var**—Takes the variable name to which the transformed XML document has to be set.
- **scope**—Specifies the scope of the var attribute.
- **result**—The javax.xml.transform.Result object that captures or processes the transformation result.

The <x:param> Tag

The <x:param> tag is used to set transformation parameters. The <x:param> tag should be used within the body of the <x:transform> tag.

The following is the syntax of the <x:param> tag of JSTL:

```
<x:param attributes> [body content] </x:param>
```

The attributes of the <x:param> tag are:

- **name**—Takes the name of the transformation parameter.
- **value**—Specifies the value of the transformation parameter. This attribute is optional; you can specify the value of the param tag in the body content if you do not want to use the value attribute.

Implementing JSTL Tags

JSTL can be used with the Web applications in order to access the specified tag libraries. The user needs to specify the tag libraries in the JSP page. The JSP engine is capable of accessing the specified tag library by using the Jar files available in the lib directory of the application. The tags from the specified tag library can be accessed by using the prefix of the tag library. The **jstlex9** application demonstrates the use of JSTL tags in the JSP page. In Listing 19.26, the JSP pages are used to show the use of the JSTL tags in generating a web page. You can also find this file online in the code/Chapter19/jstlex9 folder.

Listing 19.26: Creating the GetEmpDetails.jsp File

```
<%@taglib uri="http://java.sun.com/jsp/jstl/sql" prefix="sql"%>
<%@taglib uri="http://java.sun.com/jsp/jstl/core" prefix="c"%>
<%@taglib uri="http://java.sun.com/jsp/jstl/fmt" prefix="fmt"%>

<c:if test="${!empty param.language}" var="lang_flag">
   <fmt:setLocale value="${param.language}"/>

</c:if>
<c:if test="${!empty param.country && lang_flag}">
   <fmt:setLocale value="${param.language}_${param.country}"/>
</c:if>
<sql:setDataSource driver="oracle.jdbc.driver.OracleDriver"
   url="jdbc:oracle:thin:@localhost:1521:sandb" user="scott" password="tiger"
   var="myds" scope="request"/>
<sql:query sql="select empno,deptno,ename,sal,hiredate from emp" var="result"
   scope="page" dataSource="${requestScope.myds}"/>
<html> <body>
   Display Currency and Date in: <pre>
   <a href="GetEmpDetails.jsp?language=en&country=US">English(US)</a>
<a href="GetEmpDetails.jsp?language=en&country=gb">English(UK)</a>
 <a href="GetEmpDetails.jsp?language=en&country=AU">English(AU)</a>
<a href="GetEmpDetails.jsp?language=it">Italian</a>

   </pre>

   <table border="1">

   <tr>
         <c:forEach items="${pageScope.result.columnNames}" var="colname">
         <th><c:out value="${colname}"/></th>
         </c:forEach>
   </tr>

   <c:forEach items="${pageScope.result.rows}" var="row">
   <tr> <td>
         <c:out value="${row.empno}"/>
   </td> <td>
         <c:out value="${row.deptno}"/>
   </td> <td>
         <c:out value="${row.ename}"/>
   </td> <td>
         <fmt:formatNumber value="${row.sal}" type="currency"/>
   </td> <td>
         <fmt:formatDate value="${row.hiredate}" type="date"/>
   </td> </tr>
   </c:forEach>
   </table>
</body> </html>
```

Listing 19.27 shows the `web.xml` file to set the welcome page. You can also find this file online in the code/Chapter 19/jstlex9/WEB-INF folder.

Listing 19.27: Creating the `web.xml` File

```
<?xml version="1.0"?>
<web-app>
  <welcome-file-list>
        <welcome-file> GetEmpDetails.jsp</welcome-file>
  </welcome-file-list>
</web-app>
```

Figure 19.20 shows the tree structure of **jstlex9** application. Copy **jstlex9** folder into `<Tomcat home>\webapps` folder, and start the server.

Figure 19.20: Showing Directory Structure of jstlex9 Application

Browsing GetEmpDetails.jsp page with the URL `http://localhost:9090/jstlex9/GetEmpDetails.jsp` which presents the employee details as shown in Figure 19.21, considering the browser language which is configured to en-US.

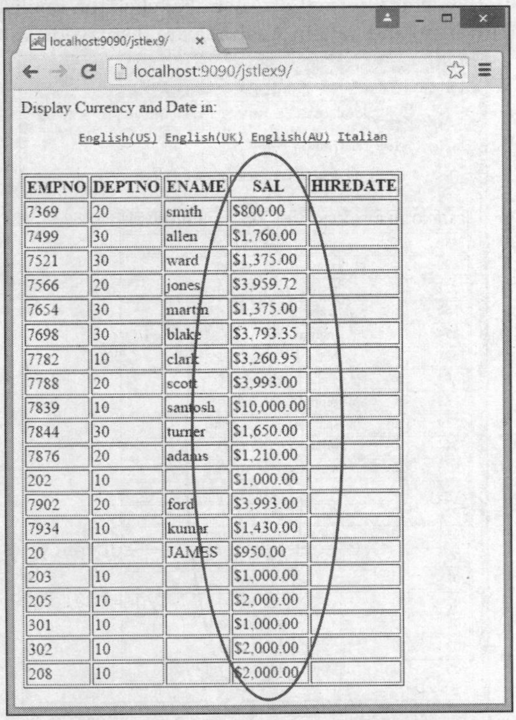

Figure 19.21: Displaying Currency in US English

Now, to view the date and salary in the default format of UK, click the English (UK) hyperlink in Figure 19.21. The default format of salary (currency) and data in UK are displayed as shown in Figure 19.22:

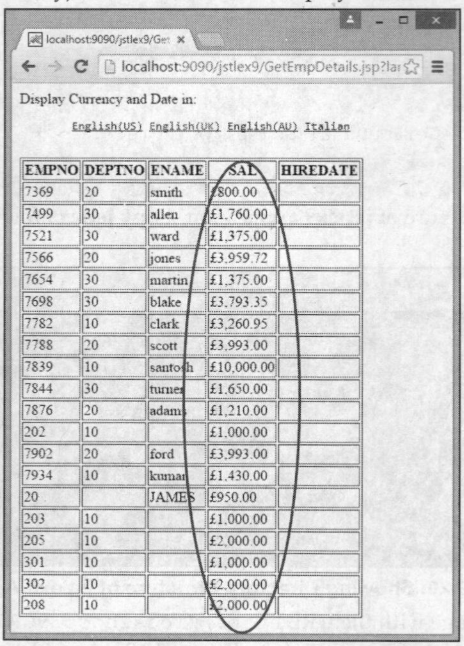

EMPNO	DEPTNO	ENAME	SAL	HIREDATE
7369	20	smith	£800.00	
7499	30	allen	£1,760.00	
7521	30	ward	£1,375.00	
7566	20	jones	£3,959.72	
7654	30	martin	£1,375.00	
7698	30	blake	£3,793.35	
7782	10	clark	£3,260.95	
7788	20	scott	£3,993.00	
7839	10	santosh	£10,000.00	
7844	30	turner	£1,650.00	
7876	20	adams	£1,210.00	
202	10		£1,000.00	
7902	20	ford	£3,993.00	
7934	10	kumar	£1,430.00	
20		JAMES	£950.00	
203	10		£1,000.00	
205	10		£2,000.00	
301	10		£1,000.00	
302	10		£2,000.00	
208	10		£2,000.00	

Figure 19.22: Displaying Currency in UK English

To view the date and salary in the default format of Australia, click the English (AU) hyperlink in Figure 19.22. The default format of salary (currency) and data in Australia are displayed as shown in Figure 19.23:

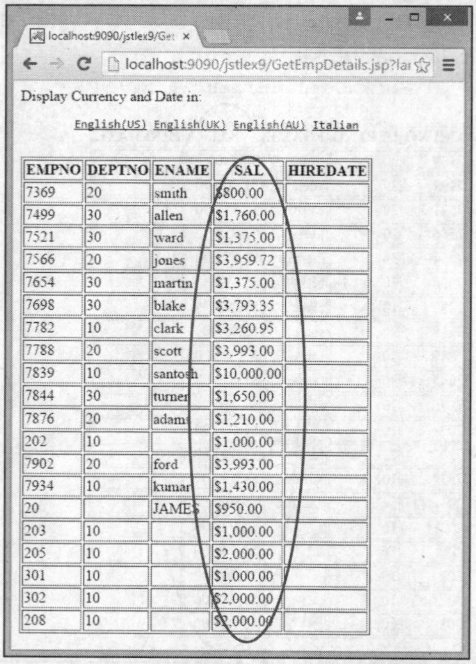

EMPNO	DEPTNO	ENAME	SAL	HIREDATE
7369	20	smith	$800.00	
7499	30	allen	$1,760.00	
7521	30	ward	$1,375.00	
7566	20	jones	$3,959.72	
7654	30	martin	$1,375.00	
7698	30	blake	$3,793.35	
7782	10	clark	$3,260.95	
7788	20	scott	$3,993.00	
7839	10	santosh	$10,000.00	
7844	30	turner	$1,650.00	
7876	20	adams	$1,210.00	
202	10		$1,000.00	
7902	20	ford	$3,993.00	
7934	10	kumar	$1,430.00	
20		JAMES	$950.00	
203	10		$1,000.00	
205	10		$2,000.00	
301	10		$1,000.00	
302	10		$2,000.00	
208	10		$2,000.00	

Figure 19.23: Displaying Currency in English (AU)

To view the date and salary in the default format of Italy, click the Italian hyperlink in Figure 19.23. The default format of salary (currency) and data in Italy are displayed as shown in Figure 19.24:

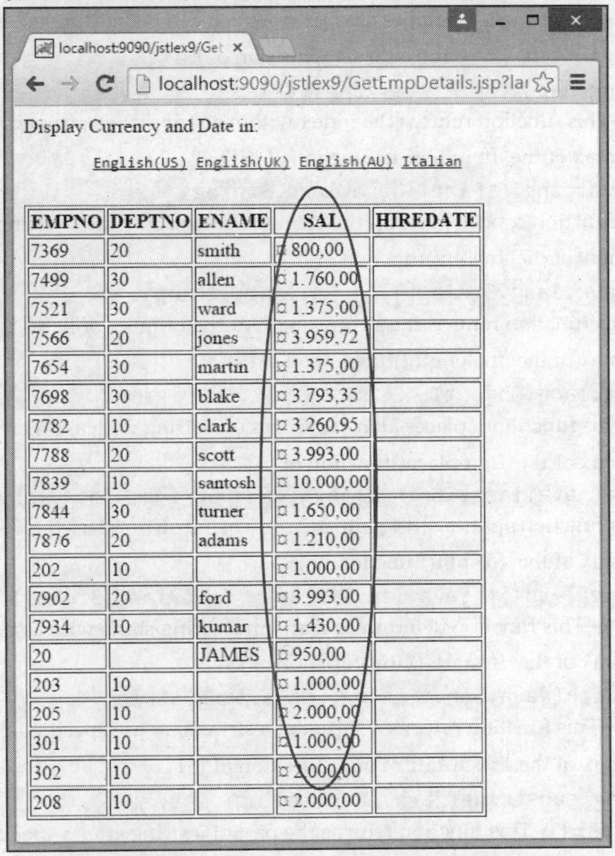

EMPNO	DEPTNO	ENAME	SAL	HIREDATE
7369	20	smith	¤ 800,00	
7499	30	allen	¤ 1.760,00	
7521	30	ward	¤ 1.375,00	
7566	20	jones	¤ 3.959,72	
7654	30	martin	¤ 1.375,00	
7698	30	blake	¤ 3.793,35	
7782	10	clark	¤ 3.260,95	
7788	20	scott	¤ 3.993,00	
7839	10	santosh	¤ 10.000,00	
7844	30	turner	¤ 1.650,00	
7876	20	adams	¤ 1.210,00	
202	10		¤ 1.000,00	
7902	20	ford	¤ 3.993,00	
7934	10	kumar	¤ 1.430,00	
20		JAMES	¤ 950,00	
203	10		¤ 1.000,00	
205	10		¤ 2.000,00	
301	10		¤ 1.000,00	
302	10		¤ 2.000,00	
208	10		¤ 2.000,00	

Figure 19.24: Displaying Currency in Italian

In this application, we have used the core, SQL, and formatting tags to create a connection with database and to format the data to be displayed on JSP page. To implement these JSTL tags, the JSTL tag library is imported in the JSP page.

JSTL Functions

Several standard functions are included in JSTL. Among these standard functions, most of them are string manipulation functions. The following are JSTL functions:

- **`fn:contains()`**—This function determines if an input string contains the specified substring.

The following is the syntax of the `fn:contains()` function of JSTL:

```
boolean contains(java.lang.String, java.lang.String)
```

- **`fn:containsIgnoreCase()`** — This function determines if an input string contains the specified substring but it searches the string ignoring the cases.

The following is the syntax of the `fn:containsIgnoreCase()` function of JSTL:

```
boolean containsIgnoreCase(java.lang.String, java.lang.String)
```

- **`fn:endsWith()`**—This function determines if an input string ends with a suffix that are specified.

The following is the syntax of the `fn:endsWith()` function of JSTL:

```
boolean endsWith(java.lang.String, java.lang.String)
```

- **fn:escapeXml()**—This function escapes characters which can be interpreted as XML markup.

The following is the syntax of the `fn:escapeXml()` function of JSTL:

```
java.lang.String escapeXml(java.lang.String)
```

- **fn:indexOf()**—This function returns the index within a string of a specified substring.

The following is the syntax of the fn:indexOf()function of JSTL:

```
int indexOf(java.lang.String, java.lang.String)
```

- **fn join()**—This function concatenates all the elements of an array into a string with a specified separator.

The following is the syntax of the fn:join()function of JSTL:

```
String join (java.lang.String[], java.lang.String)
```

- **fn length()**—This function returns the string length or the number of items in a collection.

The following is the syntax of the fn: length()function of JSTL:

```
int length(java.lang.Object)
```

- **fn:replace()**—This function replaces all occurrences of a string with another string.

The following is the syntax of the fn:replace()function of JSTL:

```
boolean replace(java.lang.String, java.lang.String, java.lang.String)
```

- **fn:split()**—This function splits a string into an array of substrings based on a delimiter string.

The following is the syntax of the fn:split()function of JSTL:

```
java.lang.String[] split(java.lang.String, java.lang.String)
```

- **fn:startsWith()**—This function determines if an input string starts with a specified substring.

The following is the syntax of the fn:startsWith()function of JSTL:

```
boolean startsWith(java.lang.String, java.lang.String)
```

- **fn:substring()**—This function returns a subset of a string that are specified by start and end indices.

The following is the syntax of the `fn:substring()` function of JSTL:

```
java.lang.String substring(java.lang.String, int, int)
```

- **fn:substringAfter()**—This function returns the part of a string after a specified substring.

The following is the syntax of the `fn:substringAfter()` function of JSTL:

```
java.lang.String substringAfter(java.lang.String, java.lang.String)
```

- **fn:substringBefore()**—This function returns the part of a string before a specified substring.

The following is the syntax of the `fn:substringBefore()` function of JSTL:

```
java.lang.String substringBefore(java.lang.String, java.lang.String)
```

- **fn:toLowerCase()**—This function converts all the characters of a string to lowercase.

The following is the syntax of the `fn:toLowerCase()` function of JSTL:

```
java.lang.String toLowerCase(java.lang.String)
```

- **fn:toUpperCase()**—This function converts all the characters of a string to uppercase.

The following is the syntax of the `fn:toUpperCase()` function of JSTL:

```
java.lang.String toUpperCase(java.lang.String)
```

- **fn:trim()**—This function removes white space from both ends of a string.

The following is the syntax of the `fn:trim()` function of JSTL:

```
java.lang.String trim(java.lang.String)
```

Summary

This chapter has familiarized you with the JSTL core tags, SQL tags, formatting tags, XML tags, and JSTL functions. This chapter has also demonstrated the implementation of JSTL tags with the help of numerous applications. Let's recall the following important points to summarize the chapter:

- The JSP Standard Tag Library (JSTL) is a collection of custom tag libraries, which provide core functionality used for JSP documents.
- General-purpose tags include tags for writing the values to the output stream, as well as retrieving, setting, and removing attributes and also include tags for catching exceptions.
- The `<c:out>` tag evaluates an expression that may be given in its value attribute or in its tag body and the resulting value is written in the output.
- The `<c:set>` tag is another general-purpose tag, which allows us to set the value of a variable or property into the given scope.
- The `<c:remove>` general-purpose core JSTL tag allows us to remove a variable from the specified scope.
- Networking tags contain tags that perform certain operations on URLs, such as including some other Web pages, encoding the URL, and redirecting the client request.
- The `<c:import>` tag is used to include another resource, such as another JSP or HTML page, in a JSP page.
- The `<c:url>` tag creates a URL and is added with a session ID if the user session needs to be maintained.
- The SQL tag library is used to access the relational database used in the JSP pages.
- The format tag library provides the support for internationalization.
- The JSTL basic formatting tags are used to format the data of a JSP page.
- The `<fmt:setLocale>` tag stores the given locale in the locale configuration variable of the given scope.
- The `<fmt:message>` tag maps key to localized message and performs parameter replacements using the resource bundle specified in bundle attribute.
- The JSTL date formatting tags are used to format the date type of data. These tags help in formatting and parsing date-time data.
- The `<fmt:parseDate>` tag allows us to parse and format the string representation of dates and times according to the locale or customized formatting pattern.
- The XML tag library is used to work with XML data used in the JSP pages. The XML tag library helps parse and transform the data used in the JSP page.
- The XML Transformation tags of the JSTL XML tags provide support to transform the XML document with the given XSL stylesheet.
- A number of standard functions are included in JSTL. Among these standard functions, most of them are string manipulation functions.

The next chapter discusses the JSF technology in detail with appropriate examples.

Exercise

Q. 19.1 What is JSTL?

Q. 19.2 How many types of tag libraries are provided by JSTL?

Q. 19.3 What are JSTL core tags used for?

Q. 19.4 Which tag of JSTL is used to output to the `JspWriter` class?

Q. 19.5 What is the function of the `<c:import>` tag?

Q. 19.6 What is the difference between `<c:import>` and `<jsp:include>`?

Q. 19.7	Why are JSTL SQL tags used?
Q. 19.8	How many tags are available in the JSTL SQL tag library?
Q. 19.9	Why are JSTL formatting tags used?
Q. 19.10	Why are JSTL XML tags used?

20

Working with JavaServer Faces

If you need Information on:	See page:

While developing a Web application, the developer designs a User Interface (UI) to interact with the clients, develops business logic to process data, and implements navigation rules to follow when the clients access the application. Prior to the introduction of JavaServer Faces (JSF), the developer had to manually write the code to define the common tasks, such as validating user inputs and converting user input strings into specific Java objects to build Web applications. JSF is a Web application framework, which allows a developer to handle Web-based tasks easily with the help of its Application Programming Interfaces (APIs) and tags and to design rich user interfaces with its components.

JSF can be defined as a framework that makes Web application development easy by supporting different rich, powerful, and ready-to-use UI components. JSF framework is based on Model-View-Controller (MVC), which is one of the most popular design patterns available for implementing separate layers, such as view, model, and controller to provide greater maintainability of an application.

JSF not only provides simple tags to design a UI component, such as label, text box, list box, but also enables you to perform the following tasks:

- Binding of UI components with some model data
- Handling different events on UI components (such as text change in a text box) on server side
- Validating user inputs and conveying all validation error messages to the client
- Defining navigation rules from one view to another according to the output of business process

Creating a Web application using JSF is a simple and easy task from the perspective of a Web developer. The standard and powerful features of JSF, such as UI components and use of annotation make it a preferred choice among all available Java technologies used for developing a Web application.

JSF is a product of Java Community Process (JCP), which provides new suggestions for new Java application programming interfaces and technology enhancements in the form of Java Specification Requests (JSR). The first specification for the initial release of JSF came as JSR 127. This specification was for both JSF 1.0 and JSF 1.1 versions. JSF 2.0 has been specified in JSR 314. The latest version of JSF is JSF 2.2 that has been specified in JSR 344.

You need to download different JARs and TLD files to support the development of JSF-based Web applications for the versions prior to Java EE 5. Later, JSF 1.2 has become a part of Java Platform, Enterprise Edition 5 (Java EE 5); therefore, while using Java EE 5 and the higher version as development platform for your Web application, you can use JSF tags and other APIs, such as `java.util`, `javax.faces` for creating UI components, handling events, input validation, and defining page navigation.

In the chapter you learn about JSF, its features, architecture, and elements. Then, you learn about the JSF request processing life cycle. Next, you learn about JSF tag libraries, UI components, and backing beans. In addition, you also learn about the implementation of input validation and type conversion in JSF application. Moreover, how to handle navigation among various JSF pages and implement internationalization in JSF pages is also described in the chapter. Towards the end, a Web application is created by using the JSF framework. In this application, you can add, edit, update, and delete the records of employees of an organization.

Introducing JSF

JSF technology includes a set of APIs, which represent different UI components and helps in managing their states. These APIs further help in handling events on the UI components and validate user inputs through the UI components. JSF framework provides the flexibility of creating simple as well as complex applications. As this technology uses the most popular Java server technologies (Servlet and JavaServer Page) and does not limit a developer to a specific markup language or client device. The UI component classes bundled with JSF APIs contain logic implementation for various component functionalities and do not have any client-specific presentation logic; therefore, the JSF UI components can be rendered for different client devices. Currently, JSF provides a custom renderer and JavaServer Page (JSP) custom tag library for rendering UI components for an HTML client.

JSF is a robust Web application framework that implements an event programming model to handle different events and actions performed by the client on different UI components. To handle each event, a listener should be registered on server side. While developing a Web application, a developer has to write navigation rules inside source code to navigate from one Web page to another. JSF provides a simple way to define navigation rules in a configuration file, and displays different error messages showing the real cause of errors to clients. These messages are generated while validating user inputs against some validation rule and can be displayed on the same page that contains the UI components.

There are different Web application frameworks that implement one or more forms of MVC design pattern. JSF is based on MVC 2 pattern and this pattern is based on component type development. In this pattern, the developers have to concentrate only on their respective component. This introduces separate layers, such as model, view, and controller and helps the developer to concentrate on a single type of component by making a Web application easy to maintain. The different categories of UI components, such as model, view, and controller are created for different functionalities, such as use of TextField, Dialog, SimpleLabel, and ColorChooser and can be used separately.

NOTE

JSF technology is based on the MVC architecture. It is used for separating presentation logic from business logic; therefore, if you have been practicing MVC, then it is very simple to work with JSF.

Explaining the Features of JSF

We have a number of Java technologies and frameworks available that can be used to develop a Web application. Some of these frameworks, such as Struts, are more popular than JSF, but the rich yet simple features of JSF make it one of the preferred choices for designing and managing UI components in a Web application. Following are the various features of JSF:

- JSF specification provides an easy-to-use IDE for developing Web applications with JSF UI components. It has extensive tool support from the companies, such as Sun, IBM, and Oracle.
- JSF makes creating complex UI components in a Web page easy through its own set of tags, which are provided as JSP custom tag library. Designing a component is easy with JSF as it is based on MVC design pattern, which clearly separates presentation and business logic.
- JSF provides a fine way to manage all UI components in the page. Managing UI components includes validation of user input, state of component, page navigation, and event handling.
- JSF architecture is extensible, which means that we can add other functionalities over JSF and can easily customize and reuse JSF UI components.
- JSF supports multiple types of client devices. We can have different renderers to make same UI component to be rendered or displayed for different client devices. Various component classes can be extended to create custom component tag libraries to support a particular type of client.
- JSF components support internationalization and enable displaying localized messages according to the specified locale.
- JSF can also be defined as a standard Java Rapid Application Development (RAD) Web application framework, which enables fast development of a powerful application with a set of reusable components.
- JSF provides the developer with a way to link visual components to the Controller or Model components without breaking the layering.
- Earlier, the JSP and JSF technologies have their own Expression Language (EL). As JSF pages use JSP tags, it is difficult to embed separate ELs into one page. One of the key concerns of Java EE 5 specification is to keep its different Web tier technologies, such as JSP, JSF, and JSTL aligned. This alignment resulted in the creation of a Unified EL, which integrates JSP 2.0 EL and JSF 1.1 EL. JSP 2.1 and JSF 1.2 support this Unified EL. Now, we can use the JSTL tags with JSF components.
- JavaServer Faces 1.2 helps in building Web 2.0 applications that use AJAX (Asynchronous JavaScript and XML) technology and further reduces the complexities involved in creating UI components.
- JSF 1.2 allows configuration of application wide ResourceBundle to the EL using `<resource-bundle>` element in `faces-config.xml` file.
- JSF 1.2 also fixes some bugs from the previous releases.

In addition to the features mentioned so far, JSF 2.2, the latest version of JSF, has some new features. Now, let's explore the new features of JSF 2.2.

New Features of JSF 2.2

The following are the features of JSF 2.2:

In JSF 2.2, a new tag `<f:viewAction>` is introduced. `<f:viewAction>` tag is an ActionSource2 UI component which can specify an application-specific action. The component `viewAction` is a child of the metadata facet (`<f:metadata>`). `<f:metadata>` allows the `viewAction` component to be incorporated in the lifecycle of JSF for both initial and postback requests. Thus, the process of conditional checks on initial and postback requests are simplified by the new component `viewAction` introduced in JSF 2.2. It also enables implicit and explicit navigation. Apart from that `viewAction` feature has a number of advantages, such as:

1. It is possible to control the timing of `viewAction`
2. Just like the GET request, `viewAction` can also be used in the same context.
3. `viewAction` provides support for both implicit and explicit navigation.
4. It also provides support for both initial and postback requests.

Another improvement introduced in JSF 2.2 is the Faces Flow. It is included in Java EE 7. Faces Flow is useful in business tasks as it can be used to encapsulate a set of steps that can guide a user through the execution of business task. Consider a situation of shopping cart having multiple pages. Suppose the first Web page is designed for selecting the items, in the second page there are options for shipping, in the third page there are options for entering credit card details, and the fourth page is used for final confirmation. In this case, buttons are used to navigate from one page to another. Managed beam is used in capturing the data that are entered by the users and session scope variables pass the information between the pages. But this approach has certain issues, such as the flow of the page cannot be reused as the view or pages cannot be encapsulated as a logical unit. Again in this scenario, as the session scoped variables are used to pass the information between the pages it is not possible to open the same flow in multiple windows. But JSF 2.2 provides the solution to these problems by introducing nodes in Faces Flow. Now, the flow of the application is not restricted to flow between the pages rather the flow of the applications is done between the nodes.

JSF 2.2 has introduced five types of nodes. These nodes are used to define the entry and exit point of a flow. The five types of nodes are as follows:

1. **View Node**—This type of node is very common and it represents a certain view that is the part of the flow.
2. **Method Call Node**—This type of node is used to call a method wherein the called method may decide which is the next mode to be visited.
3. **Switch Node**—It consists of a random number of statements. In switch node, every statement produces a result that is used in case the statement evaluates to Boolean True.
4. **Return Node**—This node forms the exit node that is explicitly defined.
5. **Flow Call Node**—This node is used to call another flow with parameters. Thus, these nodes are used to transit between flows.

Apart from these nodes, JSF 2.2 has introduced two new annotations:

1. **`@FlowScoped`**—It is a CDI scope. It defines the scope of a bean in the specified flow. When the scope is entered or exit, `@FlowScoped` annotation enables the automatic activation or passivation of the bean.
2. **`@FlowDefinition`**—It is a class level annotation. The use of `FlowBuilder` API allows the flow definition.

Now, lets explore the architecture of JSF.

Exploring the JSF Architecture

Similar to most of the popular Web application frameworks, JSF implements MVC design pattern. The implementation of MVC design pattern helps to design different components separately and each of these components implement different types of logic. For example, you can create view component for presentation logic and model component for business logic implementation. A controller is another component, which controls the execution of various model methods and navigates from one view to another in a Web application. In JSF, you have a single front controller, which handles all JSF requests mapped to it. Figure 20.1 shows the MVC design pattern:

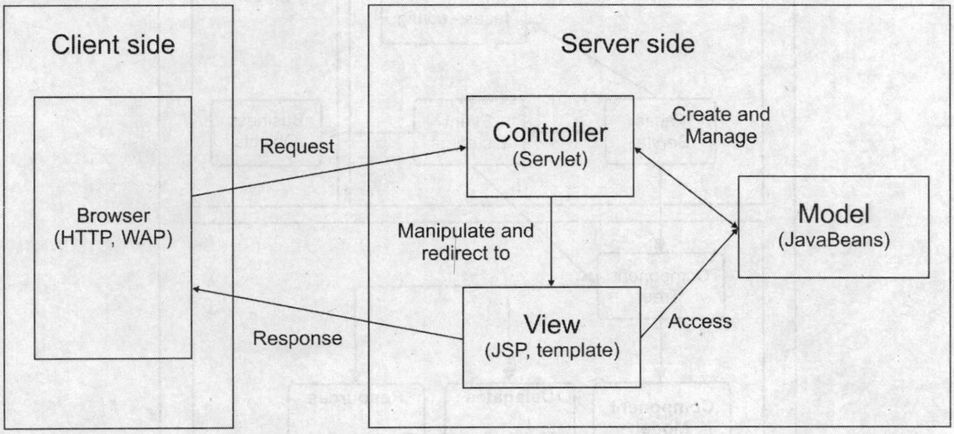

Figure 20.1: Displaying the MVC Design Pattern

In Figure 20.1, the controller part of JSF architecture consists of `FrontController` Servlet, that is, `FacesServlet`, centralized configuration file, `faces-config.xml`, and a set of event handlers for the Web application. The `FrontController` Servlet receives all the requests and manages the request processing life cycle of each request to generate response for the client. In JSF, the `FacesServlet` is a Servlet that is responsible to manage the request processing life cycle of the Web application and it is also used by JSF to design the user interface. Every JSF application contains the `web.xml` file, which specifies a Java Servlet of type `FacesServlet`. The application settings are also configured in `FacesServlet` through which all requests are channeled. On the basis of the results of component events, the flow of an application's pages is also controlled by the `FacesServlet`. This process of handling the flow of pages is represented in the `FrontController` design pattern. The `FacesServlet` also manages client requests by referencing the page mappings provided in the `faces-config.xml` configuration file. This configuration file contains a number of JSF configurations that we discuss in the Configuring JSF Application section later in this chapter. Event listeners respond to component events, which perform some processing and generate an outcome that can be used by `FacesServlet`.

The Model in JSF architecture (Figure 20.2) is a set of server-side JavaBeans that retrieves the values from the model components, such as the database and defines methods on the basis of these values. These JavaBeans may further persist in a database through an underlying persistence layer. This layer may include Java Data Objects, Enterprise JavaBeans, or an Object-Relational Mapping implementation, such as hibernate. The view in JSF architecture comprises stateful UI components.

The UI components are rendered in different ways according to the type of the client. The view delegates this task to separate the renderers, each taking care of one specific output type, such as HTML or Wireless Markup Language (WML). You can also attach various additional delegates such as validators and converters to specific components. Converters are used to validate and convert the values entered by the user. The client always submits strings as values for input fields that may need to be converted to a numerical data type, if the string values have to be used in a calculation. Validators check if the values delivered by the client are syntactically correct or are according to a specified format. The view also features resources, which may be used for localization of the Web application.

Figure 20.2 shows the MVC architecture implemented in JSF:

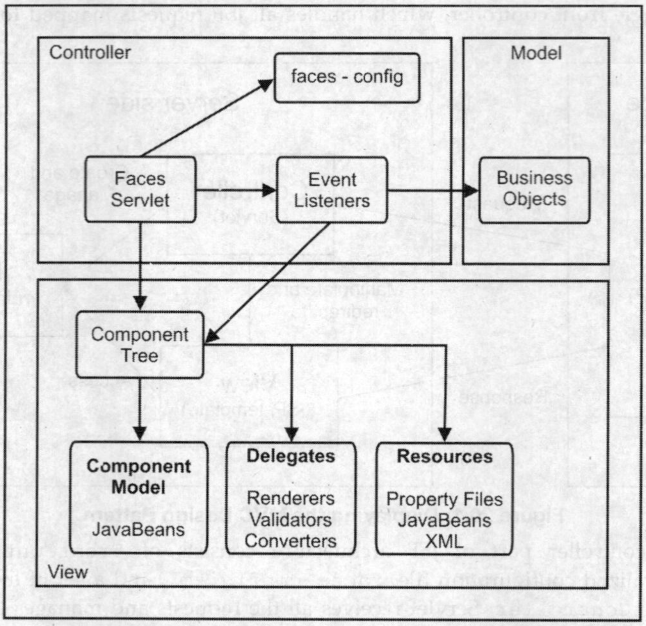

Figure 20.2: Displaying the MVC Architecture of JavaServer Faces

In Figure 20.2, various JSF elements as mapped with MVC architecture. Let's discuss different JSF elements, such as UI components, backing beans, and event listeners in the following section.

Describing JSF Elements

JSF technology has its own set of elements, such as, UI component, renderer, converter, and backing beans, which altogether form the JSF framework. These elements provide the core features of JSF technology. In this section, we are talking about various JSF components (or elements), such as UI components, validators, and renderers. Let's discuss all the JSF components and explain how they all are related to each other. The following are the elements of JSF:

- UI Component
- Renderer
- Validator
- Backing Beans
- Converter
- Events and Listeners
- Message
- Navigation

UI Component

UI components are the basic reusable components for developing UIs using the JSF framework. The developer can define UI components as stateful objects maintained on server side. The server communicates with the client through these UI components. These components are simple JavaBeans containing properties, methods, and events. The JSF UI components are also called the Web application UI components.

In a Web application, every interaction between a client and a server requires a complete HTTP request-response cycle to generate a message on client side to invalid data input or any other server side error. Each interaction between a client and a server needs to redisplay the request page with an additional error message for previously entered data in input fields. In JSF, no separate logic is required to redisplay the request page with past data values since the JSF UI components can remember their values. The JSF UI components are known as stateful UI components. All UI components are organized as a component tree and are usually displayed as a JSF page. The component tree, also known as view, is the internal presentation of a JSF page. The nested components in the component tree are presented as child components for the component that encloses it. Figure 20.3 shows an internal presentation of a component tree designed for a UI:

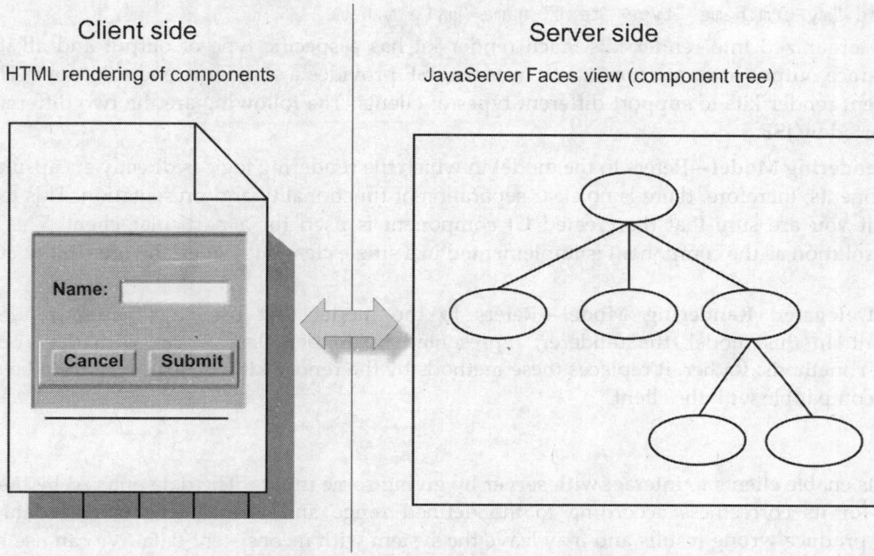

Figure 20.3: Displaying the UI Components that are being Managed as Component Tree

In Figure 20.3, you can see a form with one label, one text field, and a panel with two buttons. The rendering language other than HTML is used to display a form on client side and store the internal representation of the request page. The UI components provide only the functionality and do not involve any presentation logic for displaying the form. The element named renderer is used to ensure how a UI component appears to the user. The separation of UI components from presentation logic provides an easy way to display the responses for different client requests.

Each UI component in a view has its own component identifier to identify it. The component identifier can either be provided by the developer or can be generated automatically by JSF implementation at runtime. UI components can also support accessibility properties.

To use the JSF UI components, instead of writing any code (HTML, JavaScript, and CSS), you just need to assemble and configure them. JSF provides various standard UI components, such as labels, text boxes, check boxes, radio buttons, panels, and data grids. All the UI components are discussed later in the chapter.

Renderer

Usually, Web applications send a response in HTML format to the clients Web browser. However, the client devices, such as mobile phones or PDAs do not provide the HTML based browser. Some of the formats supported by these handheld devices are WML and Extensible HyperText Markup Language (XHTML) basic. Since handheld technology is growing very fast, there arises a need to create a Web application that could respond to other markup languages as well. Earlier, without JSF, we had to incorporate many changes in the Web application to add support for different clients.

JSF introduces renderers, which completely separate the functionality of a component from the presentation logic on the client-side. A Web application does not require many changes in it due to the use of renderers. A JSF UI component is capable of rendering itself, which is known as direct rendering. JSF also supports another type of rendering, called as indirect/delegated rendering, in which a separate class handles the process of rendering. This separate class is known as renderer. A renderer class is responsible for handling the encoding, which is a process of creating the presentation of UI components in some markup language for the given client. The renderers are child components of UI components and used to set and get data from UI components. Let's create a simple HtmlInputText component using the following code snippet:

```
<h:inputText label="Name" id="name" required="true"/>
```

When a component is rendered and the response is created for the HTML client, the following HTML code lines are sent to the client browser, as shown in the following code snippet:

```
<input id="myForm:name" type="text" name="myForm:name" />
```

Renderers are organized into render kits. Each render kit has a specific type of output and all its registered renderers produce output in same format. For instance, JSF provides a standard render kit for HTML 4.0. You can use different render kits to support different types of clients. The following are the two different rendering models supported by JSF:

- **Direct Rendering Model**—Refers to the model in which the rendering logic is directly encapsulated into the UI components; therefore, there is no clear separation of functionality and presentation. This technique can be used if you are sure that the created UI component is used for a particular client. This results in a compact solution as the component is implemented in a single class. However, the reusability of component is poor.
- **Indirect/Delegated Rendering Model**—Refers to the model that uses a separate renderer for the component. In this model, the renderer, represented by render class works with the `encode()` and `decode()` methods. Rather, it replaces these methods by the render kit to get the output to be displayed in a format compatible with the client.

Validators

UI components enable clients to interact with server by giving some inputs. The data entered by the client must be validated for its correctness according to the defined range and format. The invalid data may cause application to produce wrong results and may leave the system with inconsistent data. We can use JavaScript or Java for writing validation logic, either on client side or on server side according to its complexity. While working with JSF components, the Java code is not required to validate the input data; instead, JSF can handle the validation of data in the following three different ways:

- Implementing validation inside the UI component
- Using validator method in backing beans
- Using validator classes

The first way of handling validation is at UI component level where the component itself handles simple validation logic, which is specific to it only; therefore, cannot be used by other components. We can also implement validation logic in validator method of the backing bean that helps in validating one or more fields of a form, but again other components cannot use it. The third way to handle validation is to use validator classes, also known as validators. The validators provide validation for generic cases, such as validating a field for allowed length of string or for an allowed number range.

We can attach validators with the component that needs to be validated for its data; however, more than one validator can be attached with one component. When some validation error is encountered, validators simply add error message in the existing message list. You can see in the following code snippet how a length validator is associated with the `HtmlInputText` component:

```
<h:inputText label="Name" id="name" required="true">
        <f:validateLength minimum="2" maximum="25"/>
</h:inputText>
```

The preceding code snippet shows a text field whose id is name and validates the length of that field. Let's discuss backing beans in next.

Backing Beans

JSF architecture follows MVC design pattern and consequently focuses on separating business logic and data from presentation logic. The model part in backing beans contains business logic and data, while the view consists of presentation logic with UI components.

In a JSF application, there are some JavaBean objects, which handle or store data between the business model and UI component at intermediate stage. These JavaBean objects are known as backing beans. Backing beans also play the role of a Controller by handling the interaction between the view and the Model. In other words, in JSF, the objects that handle the interaction between view and Model are called backing beans.

Generally, a single backing bean is created for a single view, but you can create a number of backing beans for a single view. Backing bean data model is usually a copy of the application model. All changes in the component model are often propagated back to the application model through the backing beans model.

Backing beans are normal JavaBeans that contain properties and event listener methods for storing and manipulating the user's data. The event listener methods can also manipulate the UI or execute the application logic in the backend. We can associate a UI component with a property of backing bean through EL value binding. We can also bind the method of backing beans with some UI action component (such as button) to process the logic. For example, we can enable the execution of backing bean method when a button is clicked to perform some action. The following code snippet shows the code to bind a UI component with a property of a given backing bean:

```
<h:inputText label="Name" id="name" value="#{student.name}" required="true"/>
```

We can also bind a backing bean instance directly with a component instance. This binding is useful when you want to manipulate a component using a Java code. We can bind a backing bean property with the component instance directly by using the binding property of a component's tag, as shown in the following code snippet:

```
<h:inputText label="Name" id="name" value="#{student.name}"
binding="#{student.inputName}" required="true"/>
```

The model objects are not directly bound to UI components and are manipulated by backing beans. In addition, you do not need to write codes for creation or instantiation of backing beans, because in JSF a declarative mechanism is used for the creation of backing beans. That is you can configure a backing bean in `faces-config.xml` file and define the name of the object, the class to be, and the scope of that object. The beans that are configured are also known as managed beans. Therefore, all backing beans are managed beans. The following code snippet shows the code to configure a backing bean:

```
<managed-bean>
    <managed-bean-name>student</managed-bean-name>
    <managed-bean-class>com.dt.Student</managed-bean-class>
    <managed-bean-scope>session</managed-bean-scope>
</managed-bean>
```

The preceding code snippet shows the configuration of a backing bean in the `faces-config.xml` file. Let's now discuss the converters in the next subsection.

Converters

In general, Web applications interact with the client through HTTP request and response. The data from client to server travels as HTTP request parameter, which can be a string only. We can enter only a string through a UI component, whereas in the backing bean or in the model layer the data can be any Java object. This is where we need a converter. A converter is a translator, which can convert a Java object into a string and an input string into some Java object. JSF provides a number of standard converters for common types, such as date and numbers. We can also develop our own custom converters, which further support extendibility from third party.

We can associate a converter with any UI component through simple markup style, as shown in the following code snippet:

```
<h:inputText id="dob" value="#{student.dob}">
    <f:convertDateTime type="date" pattern="dd-MM-yyyy"/>
</h:inputText>
```

The renderers use converters during the process of encoding and decoding. JSF converters also support formatting and localization. For example, we have a DateTime converter to display Date object in different string formats (short and long) according to the client locale.

Events and Listeners

JSF implements an event driven processing, where events generated on different UI components can be mapped to the execution of a method. A user can interact with the Web application by generating different events on different UI components. For example, a user can generate a click event on a command button or the value change event on some input text box. The JSF event model is based on simple JavaBean's event model. It means that JSF uses JavaBeans to handle events with event objects and event listeners. A UI component can generate one or more types of events, and we can register respective event listener with the component to respond to those events. The event listeners further invoke associated backing bean method to process the appropriate logic. Now, the developers do not need to work on stateless request response HTTP model directly.

While writing JSF applications, we just need to assign listeners to the UI components for the generated events on these UI components. JSF supports an interesting way to create a simple method in your backing bean and assigns it as event listener to the UI component, as shown in the following code snippet:

```
<h:inputText id="empid" valueChangeListener="#{employee.valueChanged}"/>
```

In the preceding code snippet, the `valueChanged()` method of employee backing bean has been registered as listener for Value-change event of an HtmlInputText component.

JSF defines four different types of standard events, which are as follows:

- Action events
- Value-change events
- Data model events
- Phase events

In addition to these standard events defined in the JSF framework, this framework's UI components can be customized to support a number of other types of events. Let's discuss the standard JSF events.

Action Events

The UI component, which represents a command, can generate action events. A component that can generate an action event is also known as an action source. For example, `HtmlCommandButton` is an action source and can trigger an action event. For handling action events, you can associate an action listener with the UI component.

There are two types of action listeners, one that affects navigation, and the other does not. The action listener, which does not affect navigation executes the code, modifies backing bean or application model, and redisplays the current page. On the other hand, the action listener, which affects navigation, executes the logic and returns the output to navigation model to select the next page to be displayed to the client.

The action listener, which affects navigation, checks the output of action method configured with the component responsible for firing the action event. An action method is a backing bean method, which is invoked when an action event is fired. The string returned from the action method is dynamic in nature; therefore, can have different values. The following code snippet shows the code to configure an action method with the `HtmlCommandButton` component:

```
<h:commandButton type="submit" value="Add Employee" action="#{employee.addNew}"/>
```

The action listener shown in the preceding code snippet is `addNew()`. The method to be used as action method must return a string according to the logic performed. The `addNew()` method of backing bean, employee is shown in the following code snippet:

```
public class Employee {
    ..
   public String addNew() {
         if(...){
                return "success";
         }
         else{
                return "error";
         }
   }
}
```

In some cases we can directly put some string as action attribute instead of retrieving a string from an action method. The action listener returns the hard coded (or static) outcome string. The following code snippet shows how you can hard code a string instead of invoking a backing bean method:

```
<h:commandButton type="submit" value="Cancel" action="cancel"/>
```

In the preceding code snippet, the submit type command button is created and string type value is provided for the action attribute.

NOTE

The way an output string maps to another view has been discussed later in this chapter.

If you do not want to affect navigation by an action event and just need to process some logic, you need to configure an action listener method instead of action method with the component. The action listener method again is a backing bean method, which returns void and takes an `ActionEvent` object as an argument. The action listener method has the access to action resource component. The following code snippet shows the code to configure an action listener method:

```
<h:commandButton type="submit" value="Update"
actionListener="#{employee.update}"/>
```

The backing bean method, update() must have the structure shown in the following code snippet:

```
public class Employee {
    ...
    public void update(ActionEvent e) {

    }
}
```

Value-change Events

We have different input UI components, such as the text box and text area that are used to take input from the client. Whenever, an end user enters a new value into these components, a value-change event is fired. We have a `valueChangeListener` attribute to store the reference of the method that handles the value-change event. In the same way as configuring backing bean methods as action event listener, we can set backing bean method as a value-change listener. The following code snippet shows how to set a backing bean's method as `valueChangelistener`:

```
<h:inputText id="rollno" name="rollno"
valueChangeListener="#{student.processValueChange}"/>
```

In the preceding code snippet, the `processValueChange()` method of the `student` backing bean takes an object of `javax.faces.event.ValueChangeEvent` class as argument. The structure of the `processValueChange()` method is shown in the following code snippet:

```
public class Student {
    ......
    public void processValueChange(ValueChangeEvent e){
          HtmlInputText comp=(HtmlInputText)e.getComponent();
          ... ...
    }
}
```

When a form is submitted with some value changes in the component, the value-change event is fired only after the associated validators validate the new value entered in the input component. Similar to an action listener, we can also register some event listener classes that implement an interface instead of configuring value-change event method.

Data Model Events

The data model events are associated with data-aware UI components. A data-aware component is a component that gives a list of items to select. The example of data-aware component is `HtmlDataTable`. This component cycles through rows in a data source and exposes individual rows to child components. The data model event is fired when data-aware components process a row. Data model event is different from other two events discussed earlier as we cannot register DataModelListener with the component itself in JSP, rather it is registered in the Java code.

The data model event is not fired by the data-aware component itself, rather it is fired by an object of javax.faces.model.DataModel. DataModel is an abstraction for different data binding technologies that are used to adapt a variety of data sources, such as arrays, lists, and resultsets. The object of DataModel allows the registration of DataModelListener to handle DataModelEvent.

Phase Events

Every request in a JSF application has a life cycle, which is a set of six different stages or phases. These phases include getting request-based view, obtaining component values from request parameters, validate user input, update backing bean and model objects, invoking action listener and returning response back to the client. We have discussed all these life-cycle phases later in this chapter.

Each phase has its start point and end-point and a single event is fired when a phase either begins or ends. Both events, the event at start point and the event at end point, are known as phase events. Phase events are not fired by any UI component; rather, they are generated by JSF. Similar to implementing the data model events, we need to implement a Java interface to register an event listener. However, phase events are used internally and you can use them for implementing some specific logic in your application. The listener for a phase event is registered directly with the instance of javax.faces.lifecycle, which represents the entire life cycle of request processing.

Message

Messages are an integral part of the JSF framework. Generally, a message is used to inform the user about different errors that occur while processing the logic. A message may be associated with some component or it can be an application level message; therefore, we have two categories of messages, application errors (business logic) and user input errors (empty text field, invalid input text). Different validators can add messages to FacesContext and also provide different validations. The converters can convert the messages into application or user input errors. In addition to error messages, we can also have informational messages, such as the messages conveying information to the user about successful addition of a new record in the database.

HtmlMessage and HtmlMessages are two components used to display messages. HtmlMessage is used to display a single message associated with a specific component, as shown in the following code snippet:

```
<h:message for="name" style="color:red"/>
```

All messages associated with FacesContext can be displayed at a single location using HtmlMessages component, as shown in the following code snippet:

```
<h:messages style="color:red"/>
```

JSF supports Internationalization; therefore, all messages can be localized to support client locale. Messages provide an easy way to communicate different errors and other processing details to the user. The standard validators and converter automatically generates an error message if it finds any incorrect data. We can also create messages in our validator method, action method, and action listener methods, as shown in the following code snippet:

```
FacesContext fc=FacesContext.getCurrentInstance();
fc.addMessage(null, new FacesMessage(FacesMessage.SEVERITY_WARN,
"Your Error Message", ""));
```

You can create an object of FacesMessage with its severity level, message summary, and message detail. The created message needs to be added in FacesContext and can be displayed on any page using <h:messages/> tag.

Navigation

A Web application is a collection of Web pages linked together in a particular sequence to solve a particular purpose, such as shopping. The clients need to go through these pages to perform the desired task and the Web developer has to implement this navigation logic. Earlier, the navigation logic was implemented in Servlet or JSP code to dispatch the client's request to an appropriate view. However, if the Web application is small (consisting of two or three pages) it is a simple task to dispatch the client's request to an appropriate view; but it becomes complex to keep track of all the paths when the size of an application (number of Web pages) increases to enterprise level.

JSF provides an efficient yet simple way to configure all navigation rules declaratively in a single location, that is, in `faces-config.xml` file. You can define a set of navigation rules to navigate from one view to another view, which are used by navigation handler. It is the responsibility of navigation handler to load the JSF page according to the outcome (or return value) of action method. For every page, you can define a navigation rule with a number of navigation cases for different outcomes. The example of a navigation rule for a page with two navigation cases is shown in the following code snippet:

```
<navigation-rule>
   <from-view-id>/login.jsp</from-view-id>
   <navigation-case>
         <from-outcome>success</from-outcome>
         <to-view-id>/welcome.jsp</to-view-id>
   </navigation-case>
   <navigation-case>
         <from-outcome>failure</from-outcome>
         <to-view-id>/login.jsp</to-view-id>
   </navigation-case>
</navigation-rule>
```

In the preceding code snippet, a navigation rule is defined for login.jsp page. The two cases are provided for two different outcomes, `success` and `failure`. This approach of defining navigation rules in a centralized configuration file helps you to maintain all logical paths in an application easily.

You have learned about JSF elements, their functionalities, and their integration. All these elements, such as all UI components, management of backing beans, implementation of standard validators and converters, and configuration of navigation rules in a JSF Web application are discussed later in this chapter.

Exploring the JSF Request Processing Life cycle

The JSF framework processes a request in predefined steps similar to other Web application frameworks. You can also develop a Web application in JSF, without knowing the request processing details. This reduces the efforts in the enhancements of the existing JSF application. While discussing about the phases of the JSF request process life cycle, the request processing details are also explored.

The request-processing life cycle starts as soon as a request is submitted to the JSF controller Servlet and ends when the client receives a response for the request. Following are the six different phases of JSF request processing life cycle and are given in the order they are executed by the JSF framework:

- The Restore View Phase
- The Apply Request Values Phase
- The Process Validation Phase
- The Update Model Values Phase
- The Invoke Application Phase
- The Render Response Phase

The execution of all these phases is not required for a given request. The request processing life cycle can be terminated in any phase by executing `FacesContext.responseComplete()` method, which skips the other phases of the life cycle. For example, when any invalid input is found in the Process Validation phase, the current page/view is to be redisplayed and some of the phases, such as Invoke Application phase, may not execute.

These phases altogether make sure that the processing of a request follows a logical path. For example, no application logic is executed before the form is validated for the input data. Further, implementation of these life cycle phases helps a developer in concentrating on business logic instead of form validation and data conversion. The basic idea behind implementing the life cycle is to make sure that before executing any business logic invoked as a consequence of some action, we have a fully populated backing bean with all validated data.

If you want to create custom JSF UI components, you need to concentrate on first and last phases of JSF request life cycle. Figure 20.4 represents the JSF request processing life cycle:

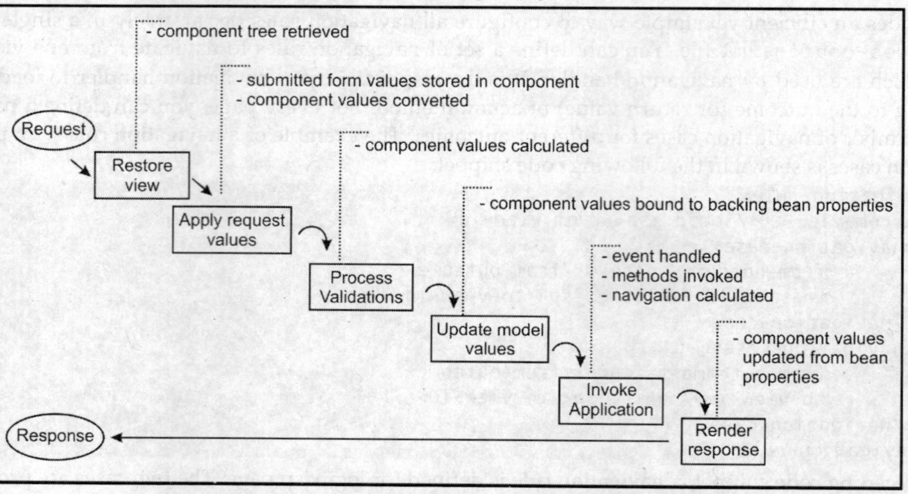

Figure 20.4: Displaying the JSF Request Processing Life Cycle

In a JSF-based application, whenever the controller Servlet receives a request, an instance of the `javax.faces.context.FacesContext` class is created. The `FacesContext` object contains the state information related to the current JSF request. The `FacesContext` object is accessed and modified in almost all of the request life cycle phases. Let's discuss all six phases of the JSF request processing life cycle with the description of all the functions performed by the framework.

The Restore View Phase

A view can be defined as a collection of components in a request page. All the components in a request page or view are grouped together as a tree; therefore, every view is a tree of components having a unique identification, i.e., view ID. The JSF controller Servlet finds the view ID from the request, which can be determined by the requested JSP page name. The controller can load the existing view or can create a new view if it does not exist.

The Restore View phase can handle three different views, new view, initial view, and postback. In case of a new view, this phase creates the view of the request page and associates event handlers and validators to the components in the view. This phase also stores the view as root component using `setViewRoot()` method on `FacesContext` instance. When the JSF page is requested for the first time, the view needs to be loaded for the first time (initial view) and the controller creates an empty view. In case of initial view, the framework directly moves to render the response page.

If the user requests a page accessed earlier (postback), the controller needs to restore the view with the current state of the view. In case of postback, the next phase after Restore View phase is the Apply Request Values phase.

The Apply Request Values Phase

There are a set of JSF UI components that receive the input as request data from the user and then processes it. In the Apply Request Values phase, the JSF implementation iterates the component objects in the component tree and requests every component to decode itself. Decoding is the process in which the framework sets the submitted values for the components based on the request parameters. The component value can be validated in this phase if the immediate property is true for the component. In case of validation error, an error message is added and the render response phase starts. If the immediate property of the component is set to false, then the submitted string values are converted into the desired data type. At the end of this phase, each component stores recent values submitted through current request. After the completion of this phase, the existing events are broadcasted for the associated event listeners.

The action events can fire in this phase but are handled in the invoke application phase. In this phase, they are created and added to the `FacesContext` instance.

The Process Validation Phase

In this phase, the values of all the components are validated against some validation rules. We can associate a given component with some JSF standard validator or can define our own validators. The validators are registered with the components of the JSF page. In case, the value of a given component is found invalid, a validation error message is added in the FacesContext and the render response phase starts to display the current view with the validation message. The following code snippet shows an `HtmlInputText` component created with a validator to validate its value for its length:

```
<h:inputText label="Name" id="name" value="#{student.name}" required="true"
   valueChangeListener="#{student.change}">
   <f:validateLength minimum="2" maximum="25"/>
</h:inputText>
```

All the value change events associated with different components are fired and used by the appropriate listener in this phase. If all the submitted values are found valid, the framework enters into the update model values phase of the life cycle.

The Update Model Values Phase

The Process Validation phase ensures that all component values are valid. After validating component values, all values of the backing beans or model objects are updated with the component values to save the state of components so that these values can be used in subsequent requests. Every component can be associated with some backing bean property and the backing bean is updated with the current value of the component. The following code snippet shows the code to associate the `name` property of `student` backing bean with an `HtmlInputText` component:

```
<h:inputText label="Name" id="name" value="#{student.name}" required="true">
</h:inputText>
```

In the preceding code snippet, backing bean properties are associated with a component through a value binding expression, such as `#{sudent.name}`. When these expressions are evaluated, the `FacesServlet` searches for an appropriate backing bean in request, application, or session scope. By the end of this phase, we have all component values set with all validated user inputs and updated backing beans. Now, we are ready to execute our business logic in the invoke application phase.

The Invoke Application Phase

In the previous phases, we have not executed any business logic. We have just updated component model and backing bean model with the current and valid data. In the Apply Request Values phase, we have added all action events in the `FacesContext` for their handling in invoke application phase. In invoke application phase, the JSF framework broadcasts all the added action events, which are further handled by the registered action event listeners. We can register some backing bean methods as action listeners or action methods. The action method may contain the logic for different operations, such as rendering responses and adding messages. Action methods are also integrated with the navigation model and helps in determining the next view or page to be displayed.

After the completion of all phases and handling of all events by the respective listeners, the framework is ready with the next view for the user.

The Render Response Phase

The Render Response phase is the last phase in the JSF request-processing life cycle. This phase is responsible for sending responses to the client. The state of the view (component tree) is saved in this phase before the response is rendered for the client. The state of the view can be stored on the server side using client session or can be saved on the client side using hidden fields. Saving the state of a view is important, so that it can be restored in the Restore view phase in case of postback. In case of postback, all error messages that are added in Apply

Request Values phase, Process Validation phase, or Update Model Values phase are also displayed along with the current state of the components in the view.

JSF framework is not bound to a particular display technology to render the response to the client. We can have different approaches to render the responses. We can use the output of encoding method with the markup code, which is either stored in some template resource or generated by another application for the client. The JSF implementations use a different approach, that is, it uses the output of decoding methods with some dynamic resources such as JSP page.

During Render Response phase, all component values are converted into a string to be displayed. When this phase completes, the Web container sends the response to the client as a response page in browser.

We have discussed all six phases of the JSF request life cycle that explain how a JSF request (read it Faces request) is changed into JSF response (read it Faces response). A brief explanation of Faces and Non-Faces request and responses are as follows:

- **Faces Response**—Refers to the Servlet response constructed after the execution of Render Response phase of request processing life cycle.
- **Non-Faces Response**—Refers to the Servlet response, which is not constructed by the execution of Render Response phase, for example, a JSP page that does not have JSF components.
- **Faces Request**—Refers to the Servlet request sent from previously generated faces response, for example, a form submitted from a JSF UI component, where request URI recognizes JSF component tree for processing the request.
- **Non-Faces Request**—Refers to the Servlet request sent to an application component, such as Servlet of JSP page, rather than directed to the JSF component tree.

These four request and response types lead to four combinations, which define the request and response scenarios that may occur in a Web application based on JSF. In case of Non-Faces request or Non-Faces response, the JSF request processing life cycle is not followed.

Exploring JSF Tag Libraries

We can design pages in a JSF application by using different JSF UI components. The various UI components can be created easily for the page by using tags defined in the JSF tag library. In addition to laying out different components in the page, designing a page in JSF application includes making provision in the page to use backing beans, validators, converters, and other backend objects associated with the components.

In JSF 1.2 two different tag libraries were provided, JSF HTML tag library and JSF core tag library. These tag libraries provide tags to create pages in JSF application with a rich set of UI components supporting event handling and input validation. You must include the following standard tag libraries to use JSF UI components in a JSP page:

- **JSF HTML tag library**—Defines the tags that represent general HTML UI components. These HTML components include `HtmlInputText`, `HtmlInputTextarea`, `HtmlForm`, and `HtmlCommandButton`.
- **JSF core tag library**—Defines the tags that perform core actions. This tag library does not depend upon specific render kit.

We can use these tag libraries simply by providing a taglib directive in our JSP page with proper uri and prefix, as shown in the following code snippet:

```
<%@taglib uri="http://java.sun.com/jsf/html" prefix="h"%>
<%@taglib uri="http://java.sun.com/jsf/core" prefix="f"%>
```

The code lines in the preceding code snippet must be the first two lines in a JSP page in a JSF based Web application.

Let's discuss all JSF HTML tags and JSF core tags. All these tags have been fully described with their syntax and behavior.

JSF HTML Tags

The JSF HTML tag library provides JSF component tags for all UI components and HTML RenderKit. It means that all the tags discussed for JSF HTML tag library are rendered to some HTML response for the client browser. Each tag in JSF HTML tag library corresponds to a specific class of UI components present in the `javax.faces.component.html` package.

All HTML UI components created using the tags defined in the JSF HTML tag library render to different HTML tags. For example, `<h:form>` tags render to the HTML `<form>` element. All JSF HTML tags support common HTML tag attributes, such as alt, style, tabindex, and width. In addition, Dynamic Hyper Text Markup Language (DHTML) event attributes, such as onclick, ondbclick, onmouseover are also supported by JSF HTML tags. All JSF HTML tags have some common attributes, which are listed in Table 20.1:

Table 20.1: Representing the Basic HTML Tag Attributes

Attribute	Description	Component Type
`id`	Takes a string, which is a component identifier and must be unique within the closest parent component	
`binding`	Binds a component with a backing bean property	
`rendered`	Takes a boolean value. By default, this value is true, which indicates rendering of component. If this value is set to false, it suppresses rendering of component, which means the component is not rendered at all.	UI components
`styleClass`	Refers to the class name of the Cascading Style Sheets (CSS)	
`value`	Sets the value of a component. Typically used for value binding	Input, output, and command type of components
`valueChangeListener`	Binds a method, which can respond to value change events	Input component
`converter`	Sets converter class name	Input and output components
`validator`	Sets validator class or validator method for a component	Input component
`required`	Takes a boolean value. If the value is true, then it requires a value to be entered in the associated field; otherwise, it is not necessary to enter the value in associated field.	Input component

Now, let's discuss various JSF HTML tags and their behavior with examples.

The <h:commandButton> Tag

The `<h:commandButton>` tag is used to create a command button in the JSP page. This represents an `HtmlCommandButton` component. This tag is rendered to HTML `<input>` element with a type attribute, `submit` or `reset`; therefore, this tag can be used to create a submit button which when clicked would send the form data to the server and would fire an action event. The most commonly used attributes of the `<h:commandButton>` tag are shown in Table 20.2:

Table 20.2: Showing the Common Attributes of <h:commandButton > Tag

Attribute	Description
`action`	Accepts a string or a method binding expression as its value. The navigation handler determines the JSF page to be loaded next according to the string or the outcome of the action method.
`actionListener`	Accepts a method binding expression as its value. You should note that the signature of this method must be void `methodName(ActionEvent object)`.

Table 20.2: Showing the Common Attributes of <h:commandButton > Tag

Attribute	Description
`image`	Accepts the context relative path of an image as its value, which would be displayed on the button.
`immediate`	Accepts a boolean value. The default value of this attribute is false, in which the action and action listener methods are invoked at the end of request life cycle.
`type`	Accepts the type of the rendered input element. This can be set as a button, submit or reset. The default type is submit.
`value`	Accepts a string as its value, which would be displayed on the button. We can provide string or value expression for the value attribute.

Let's consider the following code snippet that uses the `<h:commandButton>` tag:

```
<h:commandButton value="Login" action="#{user.login}"/>
<h:commandButton value="Check Availability" actionListener="#{user.check}" />
```

In the preceding code snippet, the first `<h:commandButton>` tag displays the `Login` submit button and binds a `login()` method of the `user` backing bean with the button. The method of backing bean (`user()`) assigned to the `action` attribute in method binding expression returns a string that determines navigation flow. The second `<h:commandButton>` tag displays the Check Availability (a submit) button and registers an action listener method (`check()`) from backing bean (`user`) that performs an operation named Check Availability.

The <h:link> Tag

In JSF 2.0, a new tag `<h:link>` was introduced. It is used to render the HTML anchor element. The most commonly used attributes of the `<h:link>` tag are shown in Table 20.3:

Table 20.3: Showing the Common Attributes of <h:link> Tag

Attribute	Description
`id`	Used as identifier for a component
`Binding`	It is a Used in backing beam
`Rendered`	It is Boolean value. False means to suppress rendering
`styleClass`	Name of Cascading Style Sheets (CSS) class
`Value`	It is a component's value
`valueChange Listener`	A method binding that responds to value change
`converter`	Name of converter class
`validator`	Class name of a validator that is created and attached to a component
`required`	It is a Boolean value. If the value is true, it requires a value to be entered in the associated field
`accessKey`	It is a key that focuses an element
`accept`	It is a comma or space separated list of content for a form
`alt`	It is an alternative text for nontextual elements like images or applets
`border`	It is the pixel value for an element's border width
`charset`	It is a character encoding for a linked resource
`dir`	It gives the direction for the text. There are two valid values, `ltr` and `rtl`. `ltr` value are for left to right and `rtl` values are for right to left.
`lang`	It is the base language of an element's attributes and text
`maxlength`	It refers to maximum number of characters for text field
`readonly`	It is a read-only state of an input field. The text can be selected in a readonly field but it cannot be edited
`size`	Represents the size of input field

Table 20.3: Showing the Common Attributes of <h:link> Tag	
Attribute	**Description**
`style`	Gives the instyle information
`tabindex`	Gives numerical value that specifies a tab index
`onclick`	Represents that the mouse button is clicked over the element
`onchange`	Represents that the value of element changes
`onfocus`	Represents that the element received focus
`onkeydown`	Represents that the key is pressed
`onkeypress`	Represents that the key is pressed and released subsequently
`onkeyup`	Represents that the key is pressed
`onmousedown`	Represents that the mouse button is pressed over the element
`onmousemove`	Represents that the mouse moves on to the element
`onmouseup`	Represents that the mouse button is released
`onselect`	Represents that the text is selected in an input field
`Onreset`	Represents that the form is reset

The <h:commandLink> Tag

Normally, we use a button to submit the data of a form or to invoke an action. However, sometimes we may want to perform the same thing using HTML hyperlink. The `<h:commandLink>` tag renders an HTML hyperlink, which is capable of submitting form data and firing some action. It also supports sending of parameters to an action method or action listener method using UIParameter component. Table 20.4 shows the most commonly used attributes of the `<h:commandLink>` tag:

Table 20.4: Showing the Common Attributes of the <h:commandLink> Tag	
Attribute	**Description**
`action`	Accepts a string or a method binding expression as its value. The navigation handler determines the JSF page to be loaded next according to the string or the outcome of the action method. The signature of the action method should be `String methodName()`.
`actionListener`	Accepts a method binding expression as its value. You should note that the signature of the method must be `void methodName(ActionEvent object)`.
`charset`	Accepts the character encoding of the linked reference as its value.
`immediate`	Accepts a boolean value. If the value is set to false, the action or action listener methods are invoked in the end of request life cycle. The default value of the `immediate` attribute is false.
`type`	Accepts the content type of the linked resource as its value. For example, text/html and image/gif.
`value`	Accepts a string or an expression referencing a value. For example, the label displayed by the link.

Let's consider the following code snippet that uses the `<h:commandLink>` tag:

```
<h:commandLink action="#{student.delete}" value="Delete">
   <f:setPropertyActionListener target="#{student.roll}" value="#{user.roll}"/>
</h:commandLink>
```

In the preceding code snippet, the `roll` property of the backing bean, `student` is set with the value of roll property of user bean before the action invoke phase, that is, before the `delete()` method of student backing bean is executed. You learn about the `<f:setPropertyActionListener>` tag in detail later in the JSF Core Tags section.

The <h:dataTable> Tag

This tag is used to create an `HtmlDataTable` component and helps to create a data grid. The `HtmlDataTable` component automatically populates with data sets. The data grid is a necessary component for any UI framework; therefore, it has been developed as a standard data grid. The `<h:dataTable>` tag renders to an HTML `<table>` element but its rows are automatically created according to the data set stored in the table. The columns of this table can be defined using the UIColumn components. Table 20.5 shows the most commonly used attributes of the `<h:dataTable>` tag:

Table 20.5: Showing the Common Attributes of <h:dataTable> Tag

Attribute	Description
bgcolor	Specifies the background color for the table
border	Accepts an integer value as the width of table border
cellpadding	Accepts an integer value that specifies how much padding can exist around table cells
cellspacing	Specifies spacing between table cells
columnClasses	Accepts comma-separated list of CSS classes for columns of tables
first	Accepts the index of the first row shown in the table
footerClass	Specifies the CSS class for the table footer
frame	Specifies the values of the sides of the frame surrounding the table. The allowed values are none, above, below, hsides, vsides, lhs, rhs, box, and border.
headerClass	Specifies the CSS class for the table header
rowClasses	Accepts comma-separated list of CSS classes for rows
rules	Specifies the lines to be drawn between cells. The allowed values are groups, rows, columns, and all.
summary	Sets the summary of the table depicting the purpose as well as structure of the table. The value of the `summary` attribute is mainly used for non-visual feedback such as speech.
var	Accepts a string value, which is created by the data table and used to represent the current item. This value is associated with the `var` attribute.

The following code snippet shows the use of the `<h:dataTable>` tag:

```
<h:dataTable value="#{applicationScope.students}" var="student" cellspacing="1">
<h:column>
  <f:facet name="header">
      <h:outputText value="Roll No."/>
  </f:facet>
  <h:outputText value="#{student.roll}"/>
  </h:column>
        <h:column>
        <f:facet name="header">
              <h:outputText value="Student Name"/>
        </f:facet>
        <h:outputText value="#{student.name}"/>
  </h:column>
</h:dataTable>
```

In the preceding code snippet, the column component tags represent the UIData and UIColumn components, respectively. We have created columns for standard data grid using the `<h:column>` element, which represents the UIColumn component. The `HtmlDataTable` component supports data binding to a set of data objects represented by the `DataModel` instance. The `DataModel` instance holds the data model of a component and can be instantiated, saved in a separate context from the component definition, and can be used by different components simultaneously. As the UIData component iterates over the rows of the data represented by the `DataModel` instance, it also processes the UIColumn component for each row.

The <h:form> Tag

The `<h:form>` tag is used to create an HTML form element on the JSF page. The `<h:form>` contains other required input fields, such as name, age, address, and zip. You should place all the input UI components within the `<h:form>` tag, because the form is concerned with user input. The HTML form created by this tag behaves as a normal form element, which can be submitted to the server with data to be processed.

We can have more than one `<h:form>` tags in a single page. Only one form, which contains the click command button is submitted to the server.

While using the `<h:form>` tag, you do not need to provide method and action attributes as they are required in an HTML form element. The default method used to provide method and action attributes in an HTML form element is post and action would be the result obtained from the `getActionURL()` method of ViewHandler for the application. Table 20.6 shows the commonly used attributes of the `<h:form>` tag:

Table 20.6: Showing the Common Attributes of the <h:form> Tag

Atrribute	Description
id	Accepts a string that is a component identifier and must be unique within the closest parent component
binding	Accepts a value expression, which binds it with some backing bean property
rendered	Accepts a boolean value indicating that whether the component will be rendered or not
styleClass	Sets the style class to be applied when the component is rendered

Let's consider the following code snippet that uses the `<h:form>` tag:

```
<h:form id="loginForm">
   //Other UI components
</h:form>
```

The `<h:form>` tag in the preceding code snippet is used to encapsulate UI components into a form named loginForm.

The <h:graphicImage> Tag

The `<h:graphicImage>` tag is used to display images on a Web page. In JSF pages, the `HtmlGraphicImage` component is created to handle the images embedded in the designed page. The `<h:graphicImage>` tag creates a simple HTML `<img>` element. The `src` property of `<img>` tag is obtained from the `uri` attribute of the `<h:graphicImage>` tag. Table 20.7 shows the most commonly used attributes of the `<h:graphicImage>` tag:

Table 20.7: Showing the Common Attributes of the <h:graphicImage> Tag

Attribute	Description
id	Accepts a string, which is component identifier and must be unique within the closest parent component.
binding	Accepts a value expression, which binds this attribute with a backing bean property.
rendered	Accepts a boolean value indicating whether or not the component will be rendered.
styleClass	Sets the style class to be applied when the component is rendered
value	Accepts the image file name with full path as its value. This value is rendered as the value for the `src` attribute of the `<img>` element.
alt	Sets some textual description of the image
height	Sets the height of the image
style	Specifies the CSS style to be applied
url	Accepts the context relative path for the resource image. It works as an alias for the `value` attribute.
width	Sets the width of the image

Let's consider the following code snippet that uses the <h:graphicImage> tag:

```
<h:graphicImage value="images/animal.jpg" width="300"/>
```

The <h graphicImage> tag in the preceding code snippet displays a graphic image (animal.jpg) located in images directory.

The <h:inputHidden> Tag

The <h:inputHidden> tag is used to create an input element, which is not displayed to the user of the page. Using this tag a hidden field can be added to the page, which need not be displayed on the page, but required to process logic. The <h:inputHidden> tag corresponds to the HtmlInputHidden component and renders to a simple <input> element with its type set to hidden. Table 20.8 shows the most commonly used attributes of the <h:inputHidden> tag:

Table 20.8: Showing the Common Attributes of the <h:inputHidden> Tag

Attribute	Description
immediate	Accepts a boolean value. If the value of this attribute is set to true the value of the component is validated immediately in the apply request phase instead of waiting for validation phase.
required	Accepts a boolean value. If the value of this attribute is set to true the user is required to enter some value for this input component.
valueChangeListener	Accepts a method expression to define a listener to handle the value change event for this component

Let's consider the following code snippet that uses the <h:inputHidden> tag:

```
<h:inputHidden id="roll" value="#{student.roll}"/>
```

The preceding code snippet shows the use of the <h:inputHidden> tag. When you use this tag inside the <h:form> tag, the value of the roll parameter is sent to the server as a hidden parameter.

The <h:inputSecret> Tag

The <h:inputSecret> tag creates an HtmlInputSecret component and renders an HTML <input> element with type set as password. The text entered into this secret field cannot be read, as the characters are displayed using asterisk or other character. Table 20.9 shows the most commonly used attributes of the <h:inputSecret> tag:

Table 20.9: Showing the Common Attributes of the <h:inputSecret> Tag

Attribute	Description
immediate	Accepts a boolean value. If the value of this attribute is set to true the value of the component is validated immediately in the apply request phase instead of waiting for validation phase.
redisplay	Accepts a boolean value. When the value of the redisplay attribute is set to true, the value of input field is redisplayed on reloading the Web page.
required	Accepts a boolean value and setting this value to true ensures that the user is required to enter some value for this input component.
valueChangeListener	Accepts a method expression to define a listener to handle the value change event for this component.

The following code snippet shows the use of the <h:inputSecret> tag:

```
<h:inputSecret redisplay="false" value="#{user.password}"/>
```

The preceding code snippet converts the password entered by a user into encoded form such as ****.

The <h:inputText> Tag

The <h:inputText> tag is used to create a single line text box, which is the most common component to take input from the user. The <h:inputText> tag corresponds to the HtmlInputText class and renders to simple

<input> element with type, text. As other input UI components, this tag can also be attached with some validator or converter. Table 20.10 shows the most commonly used attributes of the <h:inputText> tag:

Table 20.10: Showing the Common Attributes of the <h:inputText> Tag

Attribute	Description
immediate	Accepts a boolean value. If this value is set to true the value of a component is validated immediately in the apply request phase instead of waiting for validation phase.
required	Accepts a boolean value. If this value is set to true the user is required to enter some value for this input component.
valueChangeListener	Accepts a method expression to define a listener to handle the value change event for this component.

Let's consider the following code snippet that uses the <h:inputText> tag:

```
<h:inputText id="uname" label="User Name" value="#{user.fullName}" required="true"/>
```

In the preceding code snippet, the HtmlInputText component has been bound with the fullName property of the user backing bean with a value expression. Setting all the required attributes to true ensures that the user must enter some string in the text field.

The <h:inputTextarea> Tag

The <h:inputTextarea> tag is used to create a multiline text input control. This tag corresponds to HTML rich text box and renders to HTML <textarea> element. The <h:inputTextarea> tag has the properties to set column (that is width in characters) as well as row (that is height in characters) of text area. Table 20.11 shows the most commonly used attributes of the <h:inputTextarea> tag:

Table 20.11: Showing the Common Attributes of the <h:inputTextarea> Tag

Attribute	Description
cols	Sets the number of characters in the text area.
immediate	Accepts the boolean value. This value is set to true to process validation early in the request processing life cycle.
required	Accepts a boolean value If this value is set to true the user is required to enter some value for this input component.
rows	Sets the number of rows.
valueChangeListener	Accepts a method expression to define a listener to handle the value change event for this component.

Let's consider the following code snippet that uses the <h:inputTextarea> tag:

```
<h:inputTextarea id="address" cols="20" rows="3" value="#{student.address}"/>
```

The HtmlInputTextarea component in the preceding code snippet creates a multiline text box, which has been bound with the address property of the student backing bean.

The <h:message> Tag

The JSF provides a simple way of displaying messages, which have been added to FacesContext by some validator, converter, or some other method for a specific UI component. A message can be displayed using the <h:message> tag. The associated UI component can be referred by setting the for attribute with the id of that particular component. Table 20.12 shows the most commonly used attributes of the <h:message> tag:

Table 20.12: Showing the Common Attributes of the <h:message> Tag

Attribute	Description
for	Specifies the ID of the component whose message is displayed as applicable only to h:message.
errorClass	Applies the specified CSS class to error messages
errorStyle	Applies the provided CSS style to error messages
fatalClass	Applies the specified CSS class to fatal messages

Table 20.12: Showing the Common Attributes of the <h:message> Tag	
Attribute	**Description**
fatalStyle	Applies the provided CSS style to fatal messages
infoClass	Applies the specified CSS class to information based messages
infoStyle	Applies the provided CSS style to information based messages
showDetail	Accepts a boolean value specifying whether or not the message details should be displayed.
showSummary	Accepts a boolean value specifying whether or not the summary part of the message should be displayed. By default, the value of this attribute is false for the `<h:message>` tag.
tooltip	Accepts a boolean value specifying whether or not the summary message should be displayed in tooltip
warnClass	Applies the specified CSS class to warning message
warnStyle	Applies the provided CSS style to warning message

Let's consider the following code snippet that uses the `<h:message>` tag:

```
<h:message for="uname"></h:message>
or
<h:message for="uname" errorClass="error"/>
```

The first `<h:message>` tag displays an error message for the component named, `uname`. The second tag additionally applies the CSS style class (error) to display same error message in a particular format.

The <h:messages> Tag

There may be a number of messages that can be added during the request processing process. In addition, there can be different application level messages, which are not associated with any particular component. The `<h:messages>` tag is used to display all the messages added into `FacesContext` at once.

Table 20.13 shows the most commonly used attributes of the `<h:messages>` tag:

Table 20.13: Showing the Common Attributes of the <h:messages> Tag	
Attribute	**Description**
errorClass	Applies the specified CSS class to the error messages
errorStyle	Applies the provided CSS style to the error messages
fatalClass	Applies the specified CSS class to fatal messages
fatalStyle	Applies the provided CSS style to fatal messages
globalOnly	Accepts a boolean value specifying whether or not to display only global messages. By default, its value is false.
infoClass	Applies the specified CSS class to information based messages
infoStyle	Applies the provided CSS style to information based message
layout	Specifies the layout for a message, which can either be a list or a table. If you do not use this attribute then the layout is displayed in the form of a list.
showDetail	Accepts a boolean value specifying whether the message details should be provided or not. By default, this value is false.
showSummary	Accepts a boolean value specifying whether the message summaries are should be displayed or not. By default, this value is true.
tooltip	Accepts a boolean value specifying whether the message details are rendered in a tooltip or not; if the showDetail and show Summary attributes are true then the tooltip is rendered.
warnClass	Applies the CSS class for warning message
warnStyle	Applies the CSS style for warning message

Let's consider the following code snippet that uses the <h:messages> tag:

```
<h:messages errorClass="error" warnClass="warn"/>
```

The <h:messages> tag in the preceding code snippet displays all error and warning messages in their respective formats.

The <h:outputFormat> Tag

The <h:outputFormat> tag works similar to the <h:outputText> tag but it also formats the compound messages. The <h:outputFormat> tag allows a page author to display the concatenated messages as a message format pattern. This tag is used to display parameterized text. The value attribute of the <h:outputFormat> tag specifies a message format pattern and the substation parameters are specified with the <f:param> tag. The associated parameters should be defined in the same order as they appear in the message format pattern. Table 20.14 shows the most commonly used attribute of the <h:outputFormat> tag:

Table 20.14: Showing the Common Attribute of the <h:outputFormat> Tag

Important Attribute	
escape	Accepts a boolean value. If set to true, escapes <, >, and & characters. The default value of the escape attribute is false.

Let's consider following code snippet to understand the use of the <h:outputFormat> tag.

```
<h:outputFormat id="msg" value="Hello {0}, Your Roll number is {1}.">
   <f:param value="#{student.name}"/>

   <f:param value="#{student.rollno}"/>
</h:outputFormat>
```

The <h:outputFormat> tag in the preceding code snippet displays a command message, which automatically contains the name and roll number of the student.

The <h:outputLabel> Tag

The <h:outputLabel> tag is used to create the HtmlOutputLabel component on a JSF page. The HtmlOutputLabel component is used as a label for a given component. It displays a label for a component, which is associated with the component through the given id. Table 20.15 shows the most commonly used attribute of the <h:outputLabel> tag:

Table 20.15: Showing the Common Attribute of the <h:outputLabel> Tag

Attribute	Description
for	Specifies the ID of the component to be labeled.

Let's consider the following code snippet that uses the <h:outputLabel> tag:

```
<h:outputLabel for="msg">Your Message</h:outputLabel>
<h:inputText id="msg" value="#{user.message}"/>
```

The <h:outputLabel> tag in the preceding code snippet displays the label, Your Message before the text field component named msg.

The <h:outputLink> Tag

The <h:outputLink> tag is used to create an HTML anchor on a Web page that helps you to navigate through the current Web page to other locations. Unlike the HtmlCommandLink component, the HtmlOutputLink component does not generate any action event, as the URL is already specified using the value attribute. The <h:outputLink> tag renders to the HTML <a> element, and the href attribute of this anchor element is set with the value set for value attribute of the <h:outputLink> tag.

Table 20.16 shows the most commonly used attributes of the `<h:outputLink>` tag:

Table 20.16: Showing the Common Attributes of the <h:outputLink> Tag	
Attribute	**Description**
id	Accepts a string, which is component identifier and must be unique within the closest parent component.
binding	Accepts a value expression, which binds this attribute with some backing bean property.
layout	Accepts the type of layout markup used while rendering the component group. If this attribute is set to block, then the HTML <div> element is produced; otherwise, <span> is produced.
rendered	Accepts boolean value indicating whether or not the component will be rendered
style	Applies the specified CSS style when the component is rendered
styleClass	Applies the CSS style class when the component is rendered
value	Accepts the linked resource name with its path. The value set for the value attribute is set as the value for the href attribute of the rendered HTML anchor tag

Let's consider the following code snippet that uses the `<h:outputLink>` tag:

```
<h:outputLink value="login.faces">Login</h:outputLink>
or
<h:outputLink value="login.faces">
   <h:outputText value="Login"/>
</h:outputLink>
```

The `<h:outputLink>` tag in the preceding code snippet displays a hyperlink (named Login) on a Web page. When a user clicks this hyperlink, request goes to the login.faces page.

The <h:outputText> Tag

The `<h:outputText>` tag is used to display the single line output string. The string to be displayed can be defined giving JSF expression for value attributes. The `<h:outputText>` tag corresponds to `HtmlOutputText` component. Table 20.17 shows the most commonly used attributes of the `<h:outputText>` tag:

Table 20.17: Showing the Common Attribute of the <h:outputText> Tag	
Attribute	**Description**
escape	Defines whether or not special characters, such as <,>, and & is to be escaped. For escaping these characters the value should be true but by default the value is false.

Let's consider following code snippet that uses the `<h:outputText>` tag:

```
<h:outputText value="#{user.name}"/>
or
<h:outputText value="Welcome"/>
```

The first `<h:outputText>` tag in the preceding code snippet reads the value of the name property of (user) backing bean and displays it on browser. The second tag displays the Welcome string (specified in its value attribute) on browser.

The <h:panelGrid> Tag

The `<h:panelGrid>` tag corresponds to the `HtmlPanelGrid` component and renders to the HTML `<table>` element. An entire table can be presented using the `<h:panelGrid>` tag. You can also define header and footer using the `<f:facet>` tag, which renders the `<thead>` and `<tfoot>` elements. The number of columns can be set by using the columns property of the `<h:panelGrid>` tag. Table 20.18 shows the most commonly used attributes of the `<h:panelGrid>` tag:

Table 20.18: Showing the Common Attributes of the <h:panelGrid> Tag	
Attribute	**Description**
bgcolor	Specifies the background color of a table
border	Specifies the width of table border

Table 20.18: Showing the Common Attributes of the <h:panelGrid> Tag	
Attribute	**Description**
cellpadding	Specifies the padding space to be provided around the table cells
cellspacing	Specifies the space to be provided between table cells
columnClasses	Specifies the lists of CSS classes (separated by comma) for columns
columns	Specifies the total number of columns in a table
footerClass	Specify the CSS class for the footer of the table
frame	Specifies the frame surrounding the table that needs to be drawn; valid values for this purpose are: none, above, below, hsides, vsides, lhs, rhs, box, and border
headerClass	Specifies the CSS class for the header of the table
rowClasses	Specifies the lists of CSS classes (separated by comma) for rows
rules	Specifies the lines drawn between cells; valid values are: groups, rows, columns, and all
summary	Provides the purpose and structure of the table, that is basically used for non-visual feedback such as speech

The following code snippet shows the use of the `<h:panelGrid>` tag:

```
<h:panelGrid id="panel" columns="2" border="1">
  <h:outputLabel for="uid">User ID</h:outputLabel>
  <h:inputText id="uid" value="#{user.userName}"/>
  <h:outputLabel for="pwd">Password</h:outputLabel>
  <h:inputText id="pwd" value="#{user.password}"/>
</h:panelGrid>
```

In the preceding code snippet, a table with two columns and two rows is created by using the `<h:panelGrid>` tag. The number of rows created depend on the number of other components enclosed in the `<h:panelGrid>` tag.

The <h:panelGroup> Tag

The `<h:panelGroup>` tag can encapsulate a set of other components to make a single entity. This tag creates `HtmlPanelGroup` components that do not render any output, but are used as a place holder. The `<h:panelGroup>` tag is used to create a blank cell inside a table rendered by the `<h:panelGrid>` element. Table 20.19 shows the most commonly used attributes of the `<h:panelGroup>` tag:

Table 20.19: Showing the Common Attributes of the <h:panelGroup> Tag	
Attribute	**Description**
id	Accepts a string, which is a component identifier and must be unique within the closest parent component
binding	Accepts a value expression, which binds this attribute with some backing bean property
layout	Allows you to set the type of layout markup to be used when rendering the component group. If this attribute is set to block, the HTML <div> element is produced; otherwise, <span> is produced
rendered	Accepts a boolean value indicating whether the component should be rendered or not
style	Allows you to set the CSS style to component when the component is rendered
styleClass	Allows you to set the CSS style class to component when the component is rendered

The following code snippet shows the use of the `<h:panelGroup>` tag:

```
<h:panelGroup id="panel1">
  <h:commandButton value="Login" action="#{user.login}"/>
  <h:commandButton value="New User" action="#{user.newUser}"/>
</h:panelGroup>
```

The `<h:panelGroup>` tag in the preceding code snippet displays the Login and New User buttons as one group.

The <h:selectBooleanCheckbox> Tag

The `<h:selectBooleanCheckbox>` tag is used to create a `HtmlSelectBooleanCheckbox` component, which represents single boolean value. The `<h:selectBooleanCheckbox>` tag renders to an HTML `<input>` element with type checkbox. Table 20.20 shows the most commonly used attributes of the `<h:selectBooleanCheckbox>` tag:

Table 20.20: showing the Common Attributes of the <h:selectBooleanCheckbox> Tag

Attribute	Description
binding	Accepts a value expression, which binds the value (entered by user) with some backing bean property.
converter	Allows you to set the converter instance registered with the component.
id	Accepts a string, which is a component identifier and must be unique within the closest parent component.
immediate	Allows you to set the process validation early in the life cycle of JSF, by default it is true.
styleClass	Allows you to set the CSS style class to be applied when the component is rendered.
required	Allows you to set a boolean value to a field and setting it to true ensures that the user is required to enter some value for this input component.
rendered	Accepts a boolean value indicating whether the component should be rendered or not.
validator	Accepts a method expression and represents the validator method to be invoked to validate the current value of the component.
value	Allows you to set the current value of a component. A value expression can be used to bind the current value with a backing bean property.
valueChangeListener	Allows you to set the method expression to define a listener to handle the value change event for this component

The following code snippet shows the use of the `<h:selectBooleanCheckbox>` tag:

```
<h selectBooleanCheckbox value="#{student.status}"/>
```

The preceding code snippet, code is written to display a checkbox, which takes the value of `status` property of `student` backing bean.

The <h:selectManyCheckbox> Tag

As the name suggests, the `<h:selectManyCheckbox>` tag renders a group of checkboxes to be selected. This tag corresponds to `HtmlSelectManyCheckbox` component that renders to the HTML `<table>` element and `<input>` elements of type checkbox. The items to be selected can be encapsulated within the `<h:selectManyCheckbox>` tag by using the `<f:selectItem>` or `<f:selectItems>` tag (discussed later in this chapter). Table 20.21 shows the most commonly used attributes of the `<h:selectManyCheckbox>` tag:

Table 20.21: Showing the Common Attributes of the <h:selectManyCheckbox> Tag

Attribute	Description
binding	Accepts a value expression, which binds the attribute with some backing bean property.
converter	Allows you to set the converter instance registered with the component.
disabledClass	Accepts a CSS style class to be applied on disabled options.
enabledClass	Accepts a CSS style class to be applied on enabled options.
id	Accepts a string, which is a component identifier and must be unique within the closest parent component.
immediate	Allows you to set the value of process validation early in the life cycle of JSF. By default this value is true.
layout	Allows you to set the orientation of components for the Web page that needs to be displayed. The allowed values are pageDirection and lineDirection. The default value is lineDirection and its options are rendered horizontally.

Table 20.21: Showing the Common Attributes of the <h:selectManyCheckbox> Tag	
Attribute	**Description**
styleClass	Allows you to set the CSS style class to be applied when the component is rendered.
required	Allows you to set the boolean value and setting it to true ensures that the user is required to enter some value for this input component.
rendered	Accepts a boolean value indicating whether the component will be rendered or not.
validator	Accepts a method expression and represents the validator method to be invoked to validate the current value of the component.
value	Allows you to set the current value of the component. A value expression can be used to bind the current value with a backing bean property.
valueChangeListener	Allows you to set the method expression to define a listener to handle the value change event for this component.

The following code snippet shows the use of the `<h:selectManyCheckbox>` tag:

```
<h:selectManyCheckbox id="country" value="#{user.country}">
   <f:selectItem itemLabel="India" itemValue="ind"/>
   <f:selectItem itemLabel="Pakistan" itemValue="pak"/>
   <f:selectItem itemLabel="Sri Lanka" itemValue="srl"/>
</h:selectManyCheckbox>
```

The `<h:selectManyCheckbox>` tag displays a group of checkboxes with id (equals to country). This tag represents each item of a group using the `<f:selectItem>` tag.

The <h:selectManyListbox> Tag

The `<h:selectManyListbox>` tag corresponds to `HtmlSelectManyListbox` component, which renders to the HTML `<select>` element. All the child components of the `<f:selectItem> tag` are rendered to the HTML `<option>` element. The `<h:selectManyListbox>` tag provides a list box of choices, which allows the selection of multiple options from the list. The `size` attribute of this tag defines the total number of options that can be displayed at a time. Table 20.22 shows the most commonly used attributes of the `<h:selectManyListbox>` tag:

Table 20.22: Showing the Common Attributes of <h:selectManyListbox> Tag	
Attribute	**Description**
binding	Accepts a value expression, which binds this attribute with some backing bean property.
converter	Allows you to set the converter instance registered with a component
id	Accepts a string, which is a component identifier and must be unique within the closest parent component.
immediate	Allows you to set the process validation early in the life cycle of the JSF.
styleClass	Allows you to set the CSS style class to be applied when the component is rendered.
required	Specifies whether a value is required for input component or not, and setting it to true ensures that the user is required to enter some value for this input component.
rendered	Accepts a boolean value indicating whether the component should be rendered or not.
validator	Accepts a method expression and represents the validator method to be invoked to validate the current value of the component.
value	Allows you to set the current value of the component. A value expression can be used to bind the current value with some backing bean property.
valueChangeListener	Allows you to set a method expression to define a listener to handle value change event for this component

The following code snippet shows the use of `<h:selectManyListbox>` tag:

```
<h:selectManyListbox id="country" value="#{user.country}" size="2">
   <f:selectItem itemLabel="India" itemValue="ind"/>
```

```
    <f:selectItem itemLabel="Pakistan" itemValue="pak"/>
    <f:selectItem itemLabel="Sri Lanka" itemValue="srl"/>
</h:selectManyListbox>
```

The preceding code snippet uses the <h:selectManyListbox> tag to display a listbox. The <f:selectItem> tag is used to specify different options to be selected in this listbox. These options are rendered as the <option> element.

The <h:selectManyMenu> Tag

The <h:selectManyMenu> tag creates a multiselect menu, which corresponds to the HtmlSelectManyMenu component. The HtmlSelectManyMenu component is similar to the HtmlSelectManyListbox component, except that the number of options displayed using this component is always one. As the <h:selectManyListbox> tag, the <h:selectManyMenu> tag also renders to the HTML <select> element with all child elements rendered to its <option> elements. Table 20.23 shows the most commonly used attributes of the <h:selectManyMenu> tag:

Table 20.23: Showing the Common Attributes of the <h:selectManyMenu> Tag

Attribute	Description
binding	Accepts a value expression, which binds this attribute with some backing bean property.
converter	Allows you to set the converter instance registered with the component.
id	Accepts a string, which is a component identifier and must be unique within the closest parent component.
immediate	Allows you to set a boolean value to process validation early in the life cycle of the JSF.
styleClass	Allows you to set the CSS style class to be applied when the component is rendered.
required	Specifies whether a value is required for input component or not, and setting it to true ensures that the user is required to enter some value for the input component.
rendered	Accepts a boolean value indicating whether the component should be rendered or not.
validator	Accepts a method expression and represents the validator method to be invoked to validate the current value of the component.
value	Allows you to set the current value of a component. A value expression can be used to bind the current value with some backing bean property.
valueChangeListener	Allows you to set a method expression to define a listener to handle the value change event for the menu component.

The following code snippet shows the use of the <h:selectManyMenu> tag:

```
<h:selectManyMenu id="country" value="#{user.country}">
    <f:selectItem itemLabel="India" itemValue="ind"/>
    <f:selectItem itemLabel="Pakistan" itemValue="pak"/>
    <f:selectItem itemLabel="Shri Lanka" itemValue="srl"/>
</h:selectManyMenu>
```

In the preceding code snippet, the <h:selectManyMenu> tag is created, whose id is country and contains three items, India, Pakistan, and Srilanka. This tag can be accessed from request processing page by using its id, country. Let's now discuss the <h:selectOneListbox> tag in the next subsection.

The <h:selectOneListbox> Tag

The <h:selectOneListbox> tag corresponds to the HtmlSelectOneListbox component and is rendered similar to HtmlSelectManyListbox component. The only difference between these tags is that the <h:selectOneListbox> tag does not allow the selection of more than one option from a list box. You can set the size of a list box to set the number of options to be displayed at a time.

Table 20.24 shows the most commonly used attributes of the <h:selectOneListbox> tag:

Table 20.24: Showing the Common Attributes of the <h:selectOneListbox> Tag

Attribute	Description
binding	Accepts a value expression, which binds this attribute with some backing bean property.
converter	Allows you to set the converter instance registered with the component.
id	Accepts a string, which is a component identifier and its value should be unique within the ancestor component.
immediate	Allows you to set a boolean value that specifies the phase during which the value change event of JSF life cycle would occur.
styleClass	Allows you to set the CSS style class to be applied when a component is rendered.
required	Allows you to set a boolean value and if it is set to true the user is required to enter some value for this input component.
rendered	Accepts a boolean value indicating whether or not the component will be rendered.
validator	Accepts method expression and represents the validator method to be invoked to validate the current value of the component.
value	Allows you to set the current value of a component. A value expression can be used to bind the current value with some backing bean property.
valueChangeListener	Allows you to set a method expression to define a listener to handle the value change event for this component that is listbox.

The following code snippet shows the use of the <h:selectOneListbox> tag:

```
<h:selectOneListbox id="country" value="#{user.country}" size="3">
   <f:selectItem itemLabel="France" itemValue="frc"/>
   <f:selectItem itemLabel="America" itemValue="usa"/>
   <f:selectItem itemLabel="Germany" itemValue="grm"/>
   <f:selectItem itemLabel="England" itemValue="eng"/>
</h:selectOneListbox>
```

The preceding code snippet uses the <h:selectOneListbox> tag to display a listbox on browser. In this listbox, you can select only one option out of various options given in it.

The <h:selectOneMenu> Tag

The <h:selectOneMenu> tag represents the HtmlSelectOneMenu component, which provides a list of options and out of the list of options only one option is allowed to be selected. This tag displays a drop-down list on browser. Table 20.25 shows the most commonly used attributes of the <h:selectOneMenu> tag:

Table 20.25: Showing the Common Attributes of the <h:selectOneMenu> Tag

Attribute	Description
binding	Accepts a value expression, which binds this attribute with some backing bean property.
converter	Allows you to set the converter instance registered with a component.
id	Accepts a string, which is a component identifier and its value should be unique within the ancestor component.
immediate	Allows you to set a boolean value that specifies in which phase of the JSF life-cycle the value change event should occur.
styleClass	Allows you to set the CSS style class to be applied when the component is rendered.
required	Specifies whether a value is required for input component or not, and if the value is set to true the user is required to enter some value for this input component.
rendered	Accepts a boolean value indicating whether the component will be rendered or not.
validator	Accepts a method expression and represents the validator method to be invoked to validate the current value of the component.
value	Allows you to set the current value of the component. A value expression can be used to

Table 20.25: Showing the Common Attributes of the <h:selectOneMenu> Tag

Attribute	Description
	bind the current value with some backing bean property.
valueChangeListener	Accepts an expression for method binding. This expression represents a method of value change listener. This method is invoked when a new value is set for the menu component.

The following code snippet shows the use of the <h:selectOneMenu> tag:

```
<h:selectOneMenu id="country" value="#{user.country}">
    <f:selectItem itemLabel="France" itemValue="frc"/>
    <f:selectItem itemLabel="America" itemValue="usa"/>
    <f:selectItem itemLabel="Germany" itemValue="grm"/>
</h:selectOneMenu>
```

The preceding code snippet uses the <h:selectOneMenu> tag to display the drop-down list. You can select only one option from this drop-down list.

The <h:selectOneRadio> Tag

The <h:selectOneRadio> tag is rendered similar to the <h:selectManyCheckbox> tag. In JSF an HTML <table> element is rendered that contains input elements of radio type. The only difference is that from the HTML <table> table element when you select an option then previously selected option will be deselected automatically. The <h:selectOneRadio> tag represents the HtmlSelectOneRadio component. Table 20.26 shows the most commonly used attributes of the <h:selectOneRadio> tag:

Table 20.26: Showing the Common Attributes of the <h:selectOneRadio> Tag

Attribute	Description
binding	Accepts a value expression, which binds this attribute with some backing bean property.
converter	Allows you to set the converter instance registered with a component.
disabledClass	Specifies a CSS style class that should be applied on disabled option.
enabledClass	Specifies a CSS style class that should be applied on enabled option.
id	Accepts a string, which is a component identifier and the value should be unique within the ancestor component.
immediate	Allows you to set a boolean value that specifies the phase of the JSF life-cycle the value change event should occur.
layout	Allows you to set the orientation of the list of options on the JSF page. The allowed values are pageDirection and lineDirection. The default value is lineDirection and all options are rendered horizontally.
styleClass	Allows you to set the CSS style class to be applied when the component is rendered.
required	Allows you to set a boolean value and if this value is set to true, the user is required to enter some value for this input component.
rendered	Accepts a boolean value that specifies whether the component is rendered or not.
validator	Accepts a method expression and represents the validator method to be invoked to validate the current value of the component.
value	Allows you to set the current value of the component. A value expression can be used to bind the current value with some backing bean property.
valueChangeListener	Allows you to set a method expression to define a listener to handle the value change event for the radio button component.

The following code snippet shows the use of <h:selectOneRadio> tag:

```
<h:selectOneRadio id="sex" value="#{student.sex}">
    <f:selectItem itemValue="Male" itemLabel="Male" />
    <f:selectItem itemValue="Female" itemLabel="Female"/>
</h:selectOneRadio>
```

The preceding code snippet uses the `<h:selectOneRadio>` tag to display radio buttons labeled as Male and Female, respectively.

The <h:column> Tag

The `<h:column>` tag is used with the `<h:dataTable>` tag to define the columns provided in a data grid. You can set CSS classes for any header and footer generated for the table using the `headerClass` and `footerClass` attributes. Table 20.27 shows the most commonly used attributes of the `<h:column>` tag:

Table 20.27: Showing the Common Attributes of the <h:column> Tag

Attribute	Description
binding	Accepts a value expression, which binds this attribute with some backing bean property.
id	Accepts a string, which is a component identifier and the value should be unique within the ancestor component.
rendered	Accepts a boolean value that specifies whether the component is rendered or not.
footerClass	Allows you to set the CSS style class for the footer generated for a column in a table.
headerClass	Allows you to set the CSS style class for the header generated for a column in a table.

The following code snippet shows the use of the `<h:column>` tag:

```
<h:dataTable value="#{school.students}" var="stud">

    <h:column>

            <f:facet name="header">
                    <h:outputText value="Roll No."/>
            </f:facet>
            <h:outputText value="#{stud.roll}"/>

    </h:column>

    <h:column>
            <f:facet name="header">
                    <h:outputText value="Student Name"/>
            </f:facet>
            <h:outputText value="#{stud.name}"/>

    </h:column>

</h:dataTable>
```

The preceding code snippet uses the `<h:column>` tag inside the `<h:dataTable>` tag to define two columns named Roll no. and Student Name, respectively. The `<h:column>` tag uses the `<h:facet>` tag, (discussed later in this chapter).

Apart from the above tag there are two tags: `<h:outputStylesheet>` and `<h:outputScript>`. `<h:outputStylesheet>` is used to add external stylesheet file to JSF page and `<h:outputScript>` tag is used to add external javascript file to JSF page. `<h:outputStylesheet>` tag renders an HTML element of the type "link" with type "text/CSS". `<h:outputScript>` tag renders an HTML element of the type "script" with type "text/javascript".

JSF Core Tags

The JSF core tag library contains tags for different JSF custom actions and these tags do not depend on any particular render kit. The JSF core tags can be categorized according to their usage in an application. For example, core tags support event handling, implement standard JSF validators and converters, and create items and items in a list. Table 20.28 shows various tag types and their respective tags that the JSF core tag library contains:

Table 20.28: Showing the JSF Core Tag Types and Tags under These Types

Tag types	Tags
Event handling tags	f:actionListener
	f:valueChangeListener
Container for form tags	f:view
Component attributes Configuration tag	f:attribute
Data conversion tags	f:converter
	f:convertDateTime
	f:convertNumber
Facet tag	f:facet
Localization tag	f:loadBundle
Parameter substitution tag	f:param
Tags for representing items in a list	f:selectItem
	f:selectItems
Container tag	f:subview
Validator tags	f:validateDoubleRange
	f:validateLength
	f:validateLongRange
	f:validator
Output tag	f:verbatim

The <f:actionListener> Tag

The `<f:actionListener>` tag adds an action listener to a component. It registers an `ActionListener` instance with the closest parent component. However, you can use the `actionListener` attribute of the component tag, but this tag registers only a single action listener method with the component. The `<f:actionListener>` tag is used to register more than one action listener with a single action event generated. All action listener classes used in JSF must implement the `javax.faces.event.ActionListener` interface. Table 20.29 describes the attributes of `<f:actionListener>` tag:

Table 20.29: Describing the Attributes of the <f:actionListener> Tag

Attribute	Description
type	Accepts a fully qualified name of the class that has implemented the `ActionListener` interface and defines the `processAction()` method.
binding	Accepts a value as a binding expression, which evaluates an object. This object should implement `javax.faces.event.ActionListener` interface.

The following code snippet shows the use of the `<f:actionListener>` tag:

```
<h:commandButton value="Add Student">
        <f:actionListener type="com.dt.Listener1" />
        <f:actionListener type="com.dt.Listener2" />
  </h:commandButton>
```

The preceding code snippet uses the `<f:actionListener>` tag inside the `<h:commandButton>` tag to register `Listener1` and `Listener2` classes with the Add Student button.

The <f:valueChangeListener> Tag

The `<f:valueChangeListener>` tag is used to register a value change listener for the closest parent component. Using this tag, you can register more than one value change listeners with a single component. All listener classes registered using `<f:valueChangeListener>` tag must implement `javax.faces.event.ValueChangeListener` interface. Table 20.30 lists the most commonly used attributes of the `<f:valueChangeListener>` tag:

Table 20.30: Showing the Common Attributes of the <f:valueChangeListener> Tag

Attribute	Description
`type`	Takes a fully qualified name of the class that has implemented the ValueChangeListener interface and defines the `processValueChange()` method.
`binding`	Accepts a value as a binding expression, which evaluates an object. This object should implement `javax.faces.event.ValueChangeListener` interface.

The following code snippet shows the use of the `<f:valueChangeListener>` tag:

```
<h:inputText id="rollno" immediate="true" onchange="submit()">
   <f:valueChangeListener type="com.dt.SomeListener"/>
</h:inputText>
```

The preceding code snippet shows the use of the `<f:valueChangeListener>` tag to register the `SomeListener` class with the value change event that will occur in rollno text field.

The <f:view> Tag

The `<f:view>` tag encloses all other JSF components on a Web page. As you have learned earlier, all the components of a Web page are grouped into a component tree, also known as view. There is a `UIViewRoot` component at the root of every view; otherwise, a view cannot exist. The `<f:view>` tag is used to create the `UIViewRoot` on a Web page; therefore, all components of a JSF page should be enclosed within the `<f:view>` and `</f:view>` tags. Table 20.31 lists the important attributes of the `<f:view>` tag:

Table 20.31: Showing the Common Attributes of the <f:view> Tag

Attribute	Description
`locale`	Allows you to set a Locale, which needs to be supported by a Web page. If the expression is given, it must evaluate to `java.util.Locale` or a string convertible to `Locale`.
`renderKitId`	Allows you to set the identifier for the RenderKit to be used.
`beforePhase`	Accepts a method binding expression and binds the expression to a method that is called before every phase except the Restore View phase. The method should take `javax.faces.event.PhaseEvent` object and return void.
`afterPhase`	Accepts a method binding expression and binds the expression to a method that is called after every phase except the Restore View phase. The method should take the `javax.faces.event.PhaseEvent` object and return void.

The following code snippet shows the use of the `<f:view>` tag:

```
<f:view>
   ...........Other JSF components of the JSF page..........
</f:view>
```

The `<f:view>` tag may contain other component tags, such as `<h:form>`, `<h:commandButton>` and many more. Let's now discuss the `<f:attribute>` tag in the next subsection.

The <f:attribute> Tag

The `<f:attribute>` tag is used to add an attribute, which is a key/value pair, to the closest parent component. The name attribute takes the name for the nearest parent component and the value attribute takes the value that needs to be set for the component attribute. Table 20.32 shows the most commonly used attributes of the `<f:attribute>` tag:

Table 20.32: Showing the Common Attributes of <f:attribute> Tag

Attribute	Description
`name`	Specifies the name of the nearest parent component attribute
`value`	Specifies the value of the nearest parent component attribute

The following code snippet shows the use of the <f:attribute> tag:

```
<h:commandButton id="cmd1">
   <f:attribute name="value" value="Add New"></f:attribute>
</h:commandButton>
```

The preceding code snippet uses <f:attribute> tag to add attribute (value) to the HtmlCommandButton component.

The <f:converter> Tag

The <f:converter> tag is used to register a converter instance for a component. There are various ways to register converters for a component, such as using the <f:converter> tag. The <f:converter> tag can be nested within a component by specify the name of the class, which implements the javax faces.convert.Converter interface as a value of the converterId attribute of the <f:converter> tag. Table 20.33 shows the most commonly used attributes of the <f:converter> tag:

Table 20.33: Displaying the Common Attributes of the <f:converter> Tag

Attribute	Description
converterId	Specifies an ID for the Converter class, which is used during the custom conversion.
binding	Accepts a value expression that must evaluate to an object, which implements javax.faces.convert.Converter interface.

The following code snippet uses the <f:converter> tag:

```
<h:inputText value="#{student.rollno}" >
   <f:converter converterId="javax.faces.Integer"/>
</h:inputText>
```

In the preceding code snippet, the <f:converter> tag registers a converter instance.

The <f:convertDateTime> Tag

The <f:convertDateTime> tag is used to register datetime converter for a component. This represents a standard JSF validator that converts a string into the date object. Table 20.34 shows the most commonly used attributes of the <f:convertDateTime> tag:

Table 20.34: Showing the Common Attributes of the <f:convertDateTime> Tag

Attribute	Description
dateStyle	Allows you to set the predefined formatting style for the date string that needs to be displayed. The dateStyle style is applied only when the type attribute is set to date or both. The allowed values for the dateStyle attribute are default, short, medium, long, and full.
locale	Allows you to set the Locale whose predefined style needs to be used while formatting and parsing.
pattern	Allows you to set custom formatting style as defined in the java.text.SimpleDateFormat class. This attribute defines how the date can be formatted.
timeStyle	Allows you to set the predefined formatting style for the time component of the date string. This is applied only when the type attribute is set to time or both (date or time). The allowed values for the timeStyle attribute are default, short, medium, long, and full.
timeZone	Allows you to set the time zone in which date and time can be formatted. By default it is GMT.
type	Specifies whether only date or date and time both needs to be formatted. Its default value is date and it can take either date, time, or both.
binding	Accepts a value expression, which evaluates to an instance of the javax.faces.convert.DateTimeConverter class.

The following code snippet shows the use of the <f:convertDateTime> tag:

```
<h:inputText id="dateofbirth" value="#{student.birthDate}" required="true">
   <f:convertDateTime type="date" pattern="dd-MM-yyyy"/>
</h:inputText>
```

In the preceding code snippet, the <f:convertDateTime> tag registers the date-time converter with the dateofbirth text field component.

The <f:convertNumber> Tag

The <f:convertNumber> tag is used to register a NumberConverter instance for the closest parent component. You can customize the input component using the <f:convertNumber> tag to take the specified number in a specific format type for currency, simple number, and percentage. Table 20.35 shows the commonly used attributes of the <f:convertNumber> tag:

Table 20.35:Showing the Common Attributes of the <f:convertNumber> Tag

Attribute	Description
currencyCode	Allows you to set the currency code as defined in ISO 4217, whenever you need to convert the currency into your desired format
currencySymbol	Defines the currency symbol to be used
groupingUsed	Accepts a boolean value, which indicates whether the formatted output contains grouping separators or not
integerOnly	Accepts a boolean value, which indicates whether parsing and formatting of a value could be done on integer part
locale	Defines the Locale whose predefined styles for numbers will be used
maxFractionDigits	Allows you to set the maximum number of digits that needs to be formatted in the output's fractional portion
maxIntegerDigits	Allows you to set the maximum number of digits that needs to be formatted in the output's integer portion
minFractionDigits	Allows you to set the minimum number of digits that needs to be formatted in the output's fractional portion
minIntegerDigits	Allows you to set the minimum number of digits that needs to be formatted in the output's integer portion
pattern	Defines the custom formatting pattern
type	Specifies the formatting style of the number. The allowed values are number, currency, and percentage. The default value is number.
binding	Accepts a value expression that evaluates to an instance of javax.faces.convert.NumberConverter class.

The following code snippet uses the <f:convertNumber> tag:

```
<h:inputText value="#{book.price}" >
    <f:convertNumber type="currency" currencySymbol="$"/>
</h:inputText>
```

The preceding code snippet uses the <f:convertNumber> tag to register the NumberConverter instance with price property of the book backing bean.

The <f:facet> Tag

The <f:facet> tag adds facet to a component and identifies a nested component that has a special relationship with its enclosing tag. This tag registers a named facet on the closest parent component. Table 20.36 shows the most commonly used attributes of the <f:facet> tag:

Table 20.36: Showing the Common Attribute of the <f:facet> Tag

Attribute	Description
Name	Specifies the name of the facet to be created

The following code snippet shows the use of the <f:facet> tag:

```
<h:panelGrid id="panel" columns="2" border="1" rules="rows">
    <f:facet name="header">
            <h:outputText>Login Form</h:outputText>
```

```
    </f:facet>
    <f:facet name="footer">
        <h:outputText>Some footer Text.</h:outputText>
    </f:facet>
    <h:outputLabel for="uid">User ID</h:outputLabel>
    <h:inputText id="uid" value="#{user.userName}"/>
    <h:outputLabel for="pwd">Password</h:outputLabel>
    <h:inputText id="pwd" value="#{user.password}"/>
</h:panelGrid>
```

The preceding code snippet uses the `<f:facet>` tag inside the `<h:panelGrid>` tag to add header and footer to a panel grid, named panel.

The <f:loadBundle> Tag

The `<f:loadBundle>` tag loads the resource bundle and stores it in the request scope. The key/value pairs from the resource bundle are stored as `Map`. You can directly use the name of the variable assigned to resource bundle to access the localized messages in other component tags used in the JSF page. Table 20.37 shows the most commonly used attributes of the `<f:loadBundle>` tag:

Table 20.37: Showing the Common Attributes of the <f:loadBundle> Tag

Attribute	Description
basename	Defines the base name of the resource bundle to be loaded.
var	Specifies the reference name of a request scope attribute, and under that reference name the resource bundle will be exposed as a `Map`.

The following code snippet uses the `<f:loadBundle>` tag:

```
<f:loadBundle basename="com.dt.ApplicationMessages" var="msg"/>
.... .... ....
<h:commandLink action="addnew" value="#{msg.addnew}"/>
```

The preceding snippet uses the `<f:loadBundle>` tag to display the text messages written inside the `ApplicationMessages.properties` file on JSF UI components.

The <f:param> Tag

At times, you may need to specify additional parameters for a component. This can be done by using the `UIParameter` component, which is created by using the `<f:param>` tag. The parameters are added to enclosing component using a name/value pair created by the `<f:param>` tag. Table 20.38 shows the most commonly used attributes of the `<f:param>` tag:

Table 20.38: Showing the Common Attributes of the <f:param> Tag

Attribute	Description
binding	Accepts a value binding expression to link the specified value to the backing bean property and this value is later bound to the component of the UI component created by the current custom action.
id	Defines the component identifier
name	Defines the name of the parameter to be created
value	Allows you to set the value of a parameter

The following code snippet shows the use of the `<f:param>` tag:

```
<h:outputLink value="edit.faces">
    <h:outputText value="Edit"/>
    <f:param name="roll" value="#{student.rollno}"/>
</h:outputLink>
```

The preceding code snippet displays a hyperlink (named Edit) on browser. When the user clicks the hyperlink, roll parameter specified using `<f:param>` tag is also passed as a parameter to the URL request to edit.faces Web page.

The <f:selectItem> Tag

The `<f:selectItem>` tag is a `UISelectItem` component and provides a single option to select one or more components. The `UISelectItem` component is not displayed by default. Its rendering depends on the enclosing parent component. The `<f:selectItem>` tag element may render to checkbox, radio button, or items in the list box or the drop-down list. Table 20.39 shows the most commonly used attributes of the `<f:selectItem>` tag:

Table 20.39: Showing the Common Attributes of the <f:selectItem> Tag

Attribute	Description
binding	Accepts a value binding expression to a backing bean property bound to the component.
id	Defines the component identifier
itemDescription	Allows you to provide the description of the selectItem instance
itemDisabled	Accepts a boolean value indicating whether the option created by this tag will be disabled or not
itemLabel	Specifies the label that needs to be displayed for the selectItem instance.
itemValue	Allows you to set the value, which needs to be submitted to the server if an option is selected from the `selectItem` instance.
value	Accepts a value binding expression, which points to the `SelectItem` instance.

The following code snippet shows the use of the `<f:selectItem>` tag:

```
<h:selectOneMenu id="department" value="#{employee.department}" required="true">
   <f:selectItem itemValue="prod" itemLabel="Production"/>
   <f:selectItem itemValue="test" itemLabel="Testing"/>
   <f:selectItem itemValue="sal" itemLabel="Sales"/>
</h:selectOneMenu>
```

The preceding code snippet uses the `<f:selectItem>` tag to represent each option of the `HtmlSelectOneMenu` component.

The <f:selectItems> Tag

The `<f:selectItems>` tag works similar to the `<f:selectItem>` tag, but this tag provides a list of options to select one or more components. The `<f:selectItems>` tag corresponds to the `UISelectItems` component, which is used to configure multiple choices in one request. Table 20.40 shows the most commonly used attributes of the `<f:selectItems>` tag:

Table 20.40: Showing the Common Attributes of the <f:selectItems> Tag

Attribute	Description
binding	Accepts a value binding expression to a backing bean property bound to the component.
id	Defines the component identifier.
value	Accepts a value binding expression, which points to a list or array of `SelectItem` instances.

The following code snippet shows the use of the `<f:selectItems>` tag:

```
<h:selectOneRadio id="cities" value="#{student.city}">
   <f:selectItems value="#{citybean.options}"/>
</h:selectOneRadio>
```

In the preceding code snippet, the `<f:selectItems>` tag represents all the cities mentioned as options in the `HtmlSelectOneRadio` component.

Let's create a managed bean named citybean in the `faces-config.xml` file. Listing 20.1 shows the code to create `citybean`, which returns a list of the `SelectItem` objects:

Listing 20.1: Showing the Code to Create the CityBean.java File

```
package com.dt;
import java.util.ArrayList;
import java.util.List;
import javax.faces.model.SelectItem;
```

```
public class CityBean{
  private List cities;
  public CityBean(){
        cities = new ArrayList();
        SelectItem city = new SelectItem("del", "Delhi");
        cities.add(city);
        city = new SelectItem("fdb", "Faridabad");
        cities.add(city);
        city = new SelectItem("lck", "Lucknow");
        cities.add(city);
  }
  public void setOptions(List cities){
        this.cities =cities ;
  }
  public List getOptions(){
        return this.cities;
  }
}
```

In preceding code snippet, the CityBean class has a getter and setter method corresponding to the <f:selectItems> tag. Let's discuss the <f:subview> tag in next subsection.

The <f:subview> Tag

The <f:subview> tag creates a subview of a view. It works as a container for all JSF core and custom components that are used in a nested page included by using the <jsp:include> tag or JSTL's <c:import> tag. Table 20.41 shows the most commonly used attributes of the <f:subview> tag:

Table 20.41: Showing the Common Attributes of the <f:subview> Tag

Attribute	Description
binding	Accepts a value binding expression to a backing bean property bound to a component
id	Defines component identifier
rendered	Allows you to set a boolean value, that specifies whether a component will be rendered or not

The following code snippet shows the use of the <f:subview> tag:

```
<f:subview id="footer">
  <jsp:include page="footer.jsp">
</f:subview>
```

The <f subview> tag represents footer as a subview of a Web page on a browser. Let's discuss the <f:validateDoubleRange> tag in the next subsection.

The <f:validateDoubleRange> Tag

The <f:validateDoubleRange> tag is used to register the DoubleRangeValidator instance on the input UI component. The DoubleRangeValidator validator validates the current value of a component for the given range of specified value. Table 20.42 shows the most commonly used attributes of the <f:validateDoubleRenge> tag:

Table 20.42: Showing the Common Attributes of the <f:validateDoubleRange> Tag

Attribute	Description
maximum	Sets the maximum value allowed for this component
minimum	Sets the minimum value allowed for this component
binding	Accepts a value expression, which must evaluate to an instance of DoubleRangeValidator

The following code snippet shows the use of the <f:validateDoubleRange> tag:

```
<h:inputText id="num" value="#{bean.number}" required="true">
  <f:validateDoubleRange minimum="2.0" maximum="10.0"/>
</h:inputText>
```

Let's learn about the <f:validateLength> tag.

The <f:validateLength> Tag

The <f:validateLength> tag is used to register the LengthValidator instance on the input UI component. Using the <f:validateLength> tag with an input component specifies the length of the input string. Table 20.43 shows the commonly used attributes of the <f:validateLength> tag:

Table 20.43: Showing the Common Attributes of the <f:validateLength> Tag

Attribute	Description
maximum	Sets the maximum length specified for this component
minimum	Sets the minimum length specified for this component
binding	Accepts a value expression, which must evaluate to an instance of LengthValidator

The following code snippet shows the use of the <f:validateLength> tag:

```
<h:inputSecret id="pwd" label="Password" value="#{user.password}" required="true">
   <f:validateLength minimum="4" maximum="10"/>
</h:inputSecret>
```

Let's learn about the <f:validateLongRange> tag.

The <f:validateLongRange> Tag

The <f:validateLongRange> tag is used to register LongRangeValidator on a component. Using the <f:validateLongRange> tag with the input component specifies the range of the input value. Table 20.44 shows the commonly used attributes of the <f:validateLongRange> tag:

Table 20.44: Showing the Common Attributes of the <f:validateLongRange> Tag

Attribute	Description
maximum	Sets the maximum value specified for this component
minimum	Sets the minimum value specified for this component
binding	Accepts a value expression, which must evaluate to an instance of LongRangeValidator

The following code snippet shows the use of the <f:validateLongRange> tag:

```
<h:inputText id="num" value="#{bean.number}">
   <f:validateLongRange maximum="30" minimum="15"/>
</h:inputText>
```

Let's learn about the <f:validator> tag.

The <f:validator> Tag

The <f:validator> tag is used to register a custom validator on an input UI component. You need to create a custom validator class implementing the javax.faces.validator.Validator interface and configure it in the faces-config.xml file, so that the custom validator class can be used by the <f:validator/> tag. Table 20.45 shows the commonly used attributes of the <f:validator> tag:

Table 20.45: Showing the Common Attributes of the <f:validator> Tag

Attribute	Description
validatorId	Specifies the validator identifier of the Validator class that needs to be created and registered on the component.
binding	Accepts a value expression, which must evaluate to an object that implements javax.faces.validator.Validator interface

The following code snippet shows the use of the <f:validator> tag:

```
<h:inputText id="email" required="true" value="#{student.email}">
   <f:validator validatorId="MyEmailValidator" />
</h:inputText>
```

The preceding code snippet registers a custom validator class (MyEmailValidator) with a text field component (email). You need to manually create the MyEmailValidator class to implement the javax.faces.validator.Validator interface. The MyEmailValidator class should to be configured in the faces-config.xml file using the validator, validator-id, and validator-class elements.

The <f:verbatim> Tag

The <f:verbatim> tag is used to create as well as register the UIOutput child component on the UIComponent parent component. All the components inside the <f:view> tag should be provided in JSF component tree; therefore, the HTML and JSP tags can be nested with <f:verbatim> tag. It solves the problem occurred when a page contains both the JSF elements as well as the HTML elements and you cannot control the HTML elements programmatically. You cannot use any JSF components within the <f:verbatim> tag. Table 20.46 shows the commonly used attributes of the <f:verbatim> tag:

Table 20.46: Showing the Common Attributes of the <f:verbatim> Tag

Attribute	Description
escape	Accepts a boolean value indicating whether the generated markup should be escaped or not. The default value of the escape attribute is false.
rendered	Accepts a boolean value indicating whether the component will be rendered or not. The default value of the rendered attribute is true.

The following code snippet shows the use of the <f:verbatim> tag:

```
<f:verbatim>
    <h3>Some Heading</h3>
</f:verbatim>
```

In the preceding code snippet, the <f:verbatim> tag is used to provide the head in the HTML page. Let's now discuss the <f:phaseListener> tag.

The <f:phaseListener> Tag

The <f:phaseListener> tag is used to register a PhaseListener instance on the UIViewRoot component in which it is enclosed. It registers a phase listener for the current page or view. Table 20.47 shows the most commonly used attributes of the <f:phaseListener> tag:

Table 20.47: Showing the Important Attributes of the <f:phaseListener> Tag

Attribute	Description
type	Accepts a fully qualified name of the phase listener class that needs to be created and registered for the current Web page.
binding	Accepts a value expression that should bind to an object, which implements the javax.faces.event.PhaseListener interface.

The following code snippet shows the use of the <f:phaseListener> tag:

```
<f:view>
    <f:PhaseListener type = "com.dt.MyPhaseListener"/>
</f:view>
```

In the preceding code snippet, a phase listener class is used. This class can be created by implementing the javax.faces.event.PhaseListener interface. The structure of the MyPhaseListener class is shown in Listing 20.2:

Listing 20.2: Showing the MyPhaseListener.java File

```
package com.dt;

import javax.faces.event.PhaseEvent;
import javax.faces.event.PhaseId;
import javax.faces.event.PhaseListener;

public class MyPhaseListener implements PhaseListener
{
```

```
    public void beforePhase(PhaseEvent event){
    }
    public void afterPhase(PhaseEvent event){

    }

    public PhaseId getPhaseId(){
        return PhaseId.ANY_PHASE;
    }
}
```

In Listing 20.2, the methods, such as `beforePhase()`, `afterPhase()`, and `getPhaseId()` of the `PhaseListener` interface are implemented.

The <f:setPropertyActionListener> Tag

The `<f:setPropertyActionListener>` tag creates a special `ActionListener` instance and registers it with the associated `ActionSource`, such as `HtmlCommandButton`. The `<f:setPropertyActionListener>` tag is used to create and register the instance of `ActionListener`, when the instance of this component is created for the first time. Table 20.48 shows the commonly used attributes of the `<f:setPropertyActionListener>` tag:

Table 20.48: Showing the Common Attributes of the <f:setPropertyActionListener> Tag

Attribute	Description
`value`	Accepts a value expression that is used to store the value of target attribute
`target`	Accepts a value expression that defines the destination of value attribute

The following code snippet shows the use of the `<f:setPropertyActionListener>` tag:

```
<h:commandLink action="#{student.delete}" value="Delete">
   <f:setPropertyActionListener target="#{student.roll}" value="#{user.roll}"/>
</h:commandLink>
```

In the preceding code snippet, the roll property of the backing bean, student is set with the value of roll property of user bean before the action invoke phase, which is before the `delete()` method of student backing bean is executed.

Exploring Backing Beans

Backing beans are normal JavaBeans that contain properties and event listener methods to store and manipulate user data. The event listener methods can also manipulate the UI or execute the application logic at the backend. We can associate a UI component with a property of a backing bean through EL value binding. We can also bind the methods of backing beans with some UI action components (such as buttons) to process the logic. For example, we can enable the execution of a backing bean method to perform some action when a button is clicked. The following code snippet shows the binding of a UI component with a property of a given backing bean:

```
<h:inputText label="Name" id="name" value="#{student.name}" required="true"/>
```

We can also bind a backing bean instance directly to a UI component instance. This binding is useful when we need to manipulate the UI component by using Java. We can bind a backing bean property with the component instance directly by using the binding property of component's tag, as shown in the following code snippet:

```
<h:inputText label="Name" id="name" value="#{student.name}"
binding="#{student.inputName}" required="true"/>
```

The Model objects are not directly bound to UI components; rather a backing bean manipulates Model objects. We do not require writing code to create and instantiate backing bean objects, since JSF provides a declarative mechanism to create them. It means, we can configure the backing beans in the `faces-config.xml` file and define the name of the object, the scope of that object, and the class to be instantiated in the file. Such configured beans are also known as managed beans. Therefore, backing beans can also be called managed beans. Let's look at an example to configure a backing bean, as shown in the following code snippet:

```
<managed-bean>
  <managed-bean-name>student</managed-bean-name>
  <managed-bean-class>com.dt.Student</managed-bean-class>

  <managed-bean-scope>session</managed-bean-scope>
</managed-bean>
```

An Example of Using a Backing Bean

We learned about backing beans earlier. Let's now look at an example to develop a backing bean to be used with a given view.

In our example, we have a JSP page, named student.jsp. You can see the code of the student.jsp JSF page in Listing 20.3:

Listing 20.3: Displaying the Code of the student.jsp File

```
<%@ page language="java" pageEncoding="ISO-8859-1"%>
<%@ taglib uri="http://java.sun.com/jsf/html" prefix="h"%>
<%@ taglib uri="http://java.sun.com/jsf/core" prefix="f"%>
<html>
  <head>
        <title>Welcome</title>
        <link rel="stylesheet" href="mystyle.css" type="text/css" />
  </head>
  <body>
  <f:view>
  <h:form id="studentForm">
        <h:outputText id="message" value="Welcome, Guest!"
        binding="#{student.outputText}"/>
        <h:panelGrid id="panel" columns="2" border="1">
        <h:outputText value="Roll No." />
        <h:inputText id="rollno" value="#{student.rollno}" />
        <h:outputText value="Name" />
        <h:inputText label="Name" id="name" value="#{student.name}" />
        <h:commandButton id="button1"
        actionListener="#{student.showMessage}" value="Show Message"/>
        <h:commandButton id="button2"
              action="#{student.showDetail}" value="Show Detail"/>
        </h:panelGrid>
  </h:form>
  </f:view>
  </body>
</html>
```

In Listing 20.3, we have created an `HtmlForm` component with different child components such as `HtmlInputText` and `HtmlCommandButton`. We have bound values of two input field components (with id, `rollno` and `name`) created here with two different properties of the `Student` backing bean.

We have bound an `HtmlOutputText` component (with id message) with another property of the `Student` backing bean, i.e., `outputText`. We can bind a backing bean property with the value of a component by using the value expression for the value attribute.

The structure of the `Student` backing bean has been shown in Listing 20.4:

Listing 20.4: Displaying the Code of the `Student.java` File

```
package com.dt;

import javax.faces.component.html.HtmlOutputText;
import javax.faces.event.ActionEvent;
public class Student {
  private String rollno;
  private String name;
```

```
    private HtmlOutputText outputText;

    public String getName() {
        return name;
    }
    public void setName(String name) {
        this.name = name;
    }
    public String getRollno() {
        return rollno;
    }
    public void setRollno(String rollno) {
        this.rollno = rollno;
    }
    public HtmlOutputText getOutputText() {
        return outputText;
    }
    public void setOutputText(HtmlOutputText outputText) {
        this.outputText = outputText;
    }

    public void showMessage(ActionEvent event){
        //Some application logic..
        outputText.setValue("Welcome "+this.name);
    }

    public String showDetail(){
        //Some application logic..
        return "success";
    }
}
```

In Listing 20.4, the backing bean class is `com.dt.Student`. We refer to the backing bean class with the name `student` in the JSF page, which is the reference name for the `Student` bean when managed in the `faces-config.xml` file. All the three properties of the `Student` backing bean are automatically populated during the Apply Request Values phase. The binding of component with the backing bean property enables the logical manipulation of the backing bean.

Using a Backing Bean Method as an Event Handler

A backing bean can have various methods, which can be used event listeners. We can handle two types of events through backing bean methods, action events and value change events. Action listeners can also be of two types, one that affects navigation, and one that does not.

The backing bean method that can be used as action listener and does not affect navigation, must have a signature void `methodName (ActionEvent event)`. You can see the void `showMessage (ActionEvent event)` method that has been created in the `Student` class given in Listing 20.4. This method does not affect navigation and the current view is redisplayed. The `showMessage (ActionEvent event)` method is shown here:

```
public void showMessage(ActionEvent event){
  //Some application logic..
  outputText.setValue("Welcome "+this.name);
}
```

Such methods are commonly referred as action listener methods and are registered with the action resources, such as `HtmlCommandButton`, by using its `actionListener` attribute, as shown in the following code snippet:

```
<h:commandButton id="button"
actionListener="#{student.showMessage}" value="Submit"/>
```

Further, we can have another type of backing bean methods, which can be registered with action resources and are used by some default action listener affecting the navigation from one view to another. Such backing bean methods are known as action methods and can be associated with the action resource component using its action attribute, as shown in the following code snippet:

```
<h:commandButton id="button2"
action="#{student.showDetail}" value="Show Detail"/>
```

The signature of an action method must be `String methodName()`. The string returned by the action method, which is an outcome of some application logic execution, is further used by navigation rule defined in the `faces-config.xml` file to display the next view. You can see the action method created in the `Student` class in the following code snippet:

```
public String showDetail(){
    //Some application Logic
    return "success";
}
```

In addition, we can also register a backing bean method as a value change event listener. The signature of such method must be `void methodName(ValueChangeEvent event)`. This method is fired only when there is any change in the value of the associated component and a value change event is fired. We can register a value change listener with different input components, such as `HtmlInputText` and `HtmlInputTextarea`, by giving a method expression for their `valueChangeListener` attribute, as shown in the following code snippet:

```
<h:inputText id="rollno" value="#{student.rollno}"
valueChangeListener="#{student.rollChanged}"/>
```

In the preceding code snippet, we have registered the `rollChanged()` backing bean method as the `ValueChangeEvent` listener. This method is invoked before the invocation of any action or action listener methods. The method that can be added to the `Student` class as a `ValueChangeEvent` listener has been shown in Listing 20.5:

Listing 20.5: A Sample ValueChangeEvent Listener Method

```
public void rollChanged(ValueChangeEvent event){
    HtmlInputText component=(HtmlInputText)event.getComponent();
    if(((String)event.getNewValue()).length()!=3)
    component.setStyle("color:red");

    else
    component.setStyle("color:black");
    }
```

Working with Managed Beans

We have seen an example of backing bean, its properties and its various methods, which can be used as event listeners and validators. The backing beans need to be created and initialized automatically using the Managed Bean Creation facility, which allows declaration of different backing beans with their initialization in one central location, which is the JSF configuration file. Since backing beans are created and managed automatically by JSF, which is configured by developer in `faces-config.xml` file, these are also known as Managed beans. The point to remember here is that all backing bean should be managed and not all managed beans are supposed to be backing beans.

We can also define the scope of the bean, such as request, session, or application, where the bean must be stored. All managed beans can be accessed using Expression Language (EL). We can configure a manage bean with the `<managed-bean>` element, as shown in Listing 20.6:

Listing 20.6: Managing Bean in the `faces-config.xml` File

```
<managed-bean>
    <managed-bean-name>student</managed-bean-name>
    <managed-bean-class>com.dt.Student</managed-bean-class>
    <managed-bean-scope>request</managed-bean-scope>
</managed-bean>
```

While declaring a managed bean, we need to specify its name, class, and scope. The `<managed-bean-name>` element defines the reference name, which can be used in JSF EL to access this bean. We can also initialize simple properties when declaring a managed beans, by using the `<managed-property>` element, as shown in Listing 20.7:

Listing 20.7: Initializing Simple Properties of a Managed Bean

```
<managed-bean>
   <managed-bean-name>student</managed-bean-name>
   <managed-bean-class>com.dt.Student</managed-bean-class>
   <managed-bean-scope>request</managed-bean-scope>
   <managed-property>
         <property-name>name</property-name>
         <value>Prakash</value>
   </managed-property>
</managed-bean>
```

In addition to simple bean properties, we can also initialize the `List` or `Map` type of properties by using the `<list-entries>` and `<map-entries>` elements, respectively. For example, a bean having property cities of type `List` and property locales of type `Map` can be initialized, as shown in Listing 20.8:

Listing 20.8: Initializing `List` and `Map` Type Properties of a Managed Bean

```
<managed-bean>
   <managed-bean-name>citybean</managed-bean-name>
   <managed-bean-class>com.dt.CityBean</managed-bean-class>
   <managed-bean-scope>application</managed-bean-scope>
   <managed-property>
         <property-name>cities</property-name>
         <list-entries>
                <value>Delhi</value>
                <value>Pune</value>
                <value>Mumbai</value>
         </list-entries>
   </managed-property>
   <managed-property>
         <property-name>locales</property-name>
         <map-entries>
                <map-entry>
                       <key>en</key>
                       <value>English</value>
                </map-entry>
                <map-entry>
                       <key>fr</key>
                       <value>Frech</value>
                </map-entry>
         </map-entries>
   </managed-property>
</managed-bean>
```

We can also declare `ArrayList` and `Maps` as managed beans, which can be done by setting the `<managed-bean-class>` tag as `java.util.ArrayList` or `java.util.HashMap` in the `faces-config.xml` file, as shown in Listing 20.9:

Listing 20.9: Declaring an `ArrayList` Object as a Managed Bean

```
<managed-bean>
   <managed-bean-name>cities</managed-bean-name>
   <managed-bean-class>java.util.ArrayList</managed-bean-class>
   <managed-bean-scope>application</managed-bean-scope>
   <list-entries>
         <value>Delhi</value>
         <value>Mumbai</value>
```

```
        <value>Kolkata</value>
    </list-entries>
  </managed-bean>
```

Let's now move on to discuss JSF input validation.

JSF Input Validation

The user input validation is required before any application logic execution in all types of Web applications. This is because invalid data submitted by a user may cause some unexpected errors and may create inconsistency. JSF framework validates and uses submitted data in the Process Validation phase of the JSF life cycle, which comes before the Update Model Values and Invoke Application phases. This reduces the risk of updating model layer with some invalid data. JSF, being a UI framework, equips all input component classes and corresponding tags to validate their respective values. JSF provides the following two basic ways to apply validation on the UI components:

- Using the validator method in a backing bean
- Using validators

Using the Validator Method

We have already seen the example of creating a validator method in a backing bean and associating it with the input component using a method expression of its validator attribute. The signature of the validator method must be `void methodName(FacesContext, UIComponent, Object) throws ValidatorException`. In the following code snippet, we use a validator method, `validateEmail()`, of the student backing bean with an input component:

```
<h:inputText id="email" value="#{student.email}" size="30"
validator="#{student.validateEmail}" />
```

We can define this `validateEmail()` method in the backing bean class as shown in the following code snippet:

```
public void validateEmail(FacesContext facesContext, UIComponent uiComponent,
Object value) throws ValidatorException{
   //Logic to validate value for being a valid email id.
}
```

We can create numerous validator methods in a backing bean. The only disadvantage while using the validator method is that we can use a single validator method with a component, and it also unnecessarily makes backing bean complex.

Using Validators

Another way to validate an input component value is to associate it with Validators, which are special classes implementing the `javax.faces.validator`.Validator interfaces. JSF provides a set of validators, known as standard JSF validators. We can also create custom validator classes.

The validators can be associated with the component in the following two ways:

- Using validator's custom tag inside the component tag
- Using the `<f:validator>` tag inside the component tag

Examples of using these two ways to associate a specific validator with the input component are shown in the following code snippet:

```
// Using validator's custom tag
<h:inputText id="uid" label="User ID" value="#{user.userName}">
   <f:validateLength minimum="4" maximum="10"/>
</h:inputText>

// Using <f:validator> tag

<h:inputText id="uid" label="User ID" value="#{user.userName}" >
   <f:validator validatorId="someID"/>
</h:inputText>
```

In the preceding code snippet, the first example uses the custom tag of the `LengthValidator` validator and the second example uses the `<f:validator>` element with the validator's identifier.

We can associate single input components with multiple validators, which is not possible when the validator method is used.

Standard JSF Validators

JSF provides some standard validators to support some common validation rules, such as validating a string for length and validating the input value for a given range. We have a set of three standard JSF validators, which can be used with their custom tags. These three standard validators have been described in Table 20.49:

Table 20.49: Standard JSF Validators

Validator Class	Validator's Custom Tag	Properties
LengthValidator	<f:validateLength>	maximum, minimum
DoubleRangeValidator	<f:validateDoubleRange>	maximum, minimum
LongRangeValidator	<f:validateLongRange>	maximum, minimum

We have already described these standard validator tags while discussing JSF Core Tags earlier in this chapter. You can refer the section "**Using JSF Core Tags**" for their examples.

This concludes our discussion about the JSF input validation support provided in terms of JSF standard validators. Let's now move ahead and learn about JSF type conversion.

JSF Type Conversion

A user input, normally a text string, is entered and submitted to the server for further processing. However, when the request parameters are mapped to different backing bean properties internally, these string values need to be converted to different Java types such as Integer, Boolean, Short, Double, and so on. On the other hand, when the response is created for the user, these Java types are again changed to strings. That is where JSF converters are helpful. The JSF converters create the string presentation of an object and the object presentation of a string. If some value cannot be converted, the converters generate error messages that are displayed to the user by using the `<h:messages>` element.

JSF provides its own set of standard converters, which can be registered with intput as well as output UI components. We can register a converter with a component in the following three ways:

- Setting the converter identifier with the converter attribute of the component's tag.

```
<h:inputText id="price" value="#{book.price}" converter="javax.faces.Double"/>
```

- Using the `<f:converter>` element with the converter's identifier inside the component tag.

```
<h:inputText id="price" value="#{book.price}">
   <f:converter converterId="javax.faces.Double"/>
</h:inputText>
Or
<h:inputText id="price" value="#{book.price}">
   <f:converter converterId="myConverter"/>
</h:inputText>
```

- Using the converter's custom tag inside the component tag.

```
<h:inputText value="#{book.price}" >
   <f:convertNumber type="currency" currencySymbol="$"/>
</h:inputText>
```

There are two standard JSF converters, `DateTimeConverter` and `NumberConverter`, which come with their custom tags. These two standard converters allow us to configure the format of the component data by setting different tag attributes. These standard tag converter tags are:

- `<f:convertDateTime/>`
- `<f:convertNumber/>`

These two tags have been discussed under the heading JSF Core Tags earlier in this chapter with all their attributes and examples.

We can create our own converter too and use it after registering the converter extension in the faces-config.xml file.

Let's now learn about handling page navigation in JSF.

Handling Page Navigation in JSF

One of the elegant features provided by the JSF framework is its support for navigation from one view to another. JSF allows defining all possible navigation rules in a centralized location, that is the JSF configuration file. It reduces the need to embed navigation logic in other component. Placing all navigation logic at one location ensures easy maintenance of a Web application.

The navigation handler plays the vital role as the navigation handler is the actual code that decides the next view to be loaded as well as displayed to the user. We are discussing default navigation handlers, which operate in response to action events. Different action resources, such as HtmlCommandButton and HtmlCommandLink, cause the action events. An action resource may be associated either with a hardcoded outcome string or with an action method, which can return a logical outcome after some application logic execution. You can see both types of action resource associations in the following code snippet:

```
//An HtmlCommandButton associated with hardcode outcome string "home"
<h:commandButton id="home" action="home" value="Home"/>

//An HtmlCommandButton associated with an action method, which returns a logical
outcome.
<h:commandButton id="add" action="#{student.addNew}" value="Add New"/>
```

The navigation handler takes this resultant string and operates on a set of navigation rules, which define the possible navigation paths in an application. A navigation rule can be defined as the specification that tells which page can be navigated to or from a given page or a set of pages according to different outcomes of pages. The outcome can be any string but some common outcome strings are success, failure, error, login, and so on. You can see a simple navigation rule, defined in the faces-config.xml file, in the following code snippet:

```
<navigation-rule>
   <from-view-id>/student.jsp</from-view-id>
   <navigation-case>
         <from-outcome>success</from-outcome>
         <to-view-id>/display.jsp</to-view-id>
   </navigation-case>
</navigation-rule>
```

This navigation rule defines that if the action event is generated from the student.jsp page and the outcome string is success, the next page to be loaded is display.jsp. The <from-view-id> and <to-view-id> elements takes the view id, which is name of the JSP page. In this way, we can define different navigation cases from one view as shown here:

```
<navigation-rule>
   <from-view-id>/login.jsp</from-view-id>
   <navigation-case>
         <from-outcome>success</from-outcome>
         <to-view-id>/welcome.jsp</to-view-id>
   </navigation-case>
   <navigation-case>
         <from-outcome>failure</from-outcome>
         <to-view-id>/login_failure.jsp</to-view-id>
   </navigation-case>
</navigation-rule>
```

In the preceding code snippet, we have declared navigations from login.jsp, which can result in the navigation to welcome.jsp or login_failure.jsp page. This navigation will be according the resultant string. If the resultant string is 'success', then the login.jsp page navigates to welcome.jsp; otherwise, it navigates to login_failure.jsp page.

We can define navigation rules not only for specific page but also for all pages simultaneously. This navigation rule can be defined as global in the sense that it can work for all pages. For example, if an action method has outcome "home", the user will be forwarded to the home.jsp page, irrespective of the current page the user is navigating. This global navigation rule is shown in the following code snippet:

```
<navigation-rule>
   <from-view-id>*</from-view-id>
   <navigation-case>
         <from-outcome>home</from-outcome>
         <to-view-id>/home.jsp</to-view-id>
   </navigation-case>
</navigation-rule>
```

We can even ensure in a global navigation rule that the outcome is from a particular action method. This is helpful in case we have two action methods, which return same outcome string and are associated with action resources on the same view. We can use the `<from-action>` element to specify the action method, as shown in the following code snippet:

```
<navigation-case>
   <from-action>#{user.login}</from-action>
   <from-outcome>success</from-outcome>
   <to-view-id>/welcome.jsp</to-view-id>
</navigation-case>
```

In this way, we find that the declarative support in JSF (for navigation rules) has made development procedure more flexible and simple in terms of implementation and maintenance.

After discussing how to define navigation rules, let's see how to configure your JSF application.

Configuring JSF Applications

The configuration of a Web application includes adding different mappings to the configuration files. In a JSF application, the basic configuration starts by updating Deployment Descriptors to support the JSF framework. In addition, the JSF application has its own configuration file which helps in the implementation of various framework features in the application. Therefore, configuring a JSF application includes setting Deployment Descriptor, that is the `web.xml` file, and setting the JSF configuration file, i.e., `faces-config.xml`.

Setting the web.xml File

JSF needs to implement its own style of request processing life cycle for all requests. This is handled by an important class, which works as an engine for a JSF-based application. This is the `javax.faces.webapp.FacesServlet` class, which is a simple Servlet. We need to map JSF requests to the `javax.faces.webapp.FacesServlet` class so that they can be processed through the framework standard phases. Like any other Servlet, we need to provide Servlet mapping for JSF with a specific URL pattern. In Listing 20.10, we define the `FacesServlet` Servlet and define its mapping in the `web.xml` file:

Listing 20.10: Servlet Mapping in `web.xml` File

```
<?xml version="1.0" encoding="UTF-8"?>
<web-app          version="3.1"          xmlns="http://xmlns.jcp.org/xml/ns/javaee"
xmlns:xsi="http://www.w3.org/2001/XMLSchema-instance"
xsi:schemaLocation="http://xmlns.jcp.org/xml/ns/javaee http://xmlns.jcp.org/xml/ns/javaee/web-
app_3_1.xsd">
   <servlet>
         <servlet-name>Faces Servlet</servlet-name>
         <servlet-class>javax.faces.webapp.FacesServlet</servlet-class>
         <load-on-startup>0</load-on-startup>
   </servlet>
   <servlet-mapping>
         <servlet-name>Faces Servlet</servlet-name>
         <url-pattern>*.faces</url-pattern>
   </servlet-mapping>
   <welcome-file-list>
```

```
        <welcome-file>index.jsp</welcome-file>
    </welcome-file-list>
</web-app>
```

We can save the Servlet with any name, but the use of `javax.faces.webapp.FacesServlet` inside the `<servlet-class>` tag is mandatory. We have also mapped all requests ending with `.faces` to this Servlet. This is known as suffix mapping. It means that the JSF Servlet will process any requested page with the `.faces` extension. The JSF Servlet always looks for the resource with the default extension. The default suffix for resources to load is `.jsp`. For example, for any request ending with home.faces, the Servlet looks for the home.jsp page to process the request.

We also set some JSF Web application parameters to be used by the `FacesServlet`. These parameters are set as context parameters by using the `<context-param>` element, as shown here:

```
<context-param>
  <param-name>javax.faces.STATE_SAVING_METHOD </param-name>
  <param-value>server</param-value>
</context-param>

<context-param>
  <param-name>javax.faces.CONFIG_FILES</param-name>
  <param-value>/WEB-INF/faces-config.xml</param-value>
</context-param>
```

After configuring the Web application Deployment Descriptor, we can now move on to configure the `faces-config.xml` file.

Configuring the faces-config.xml File

Similar to other Web application frameworks, the JSF configuration file provides essential mapping for an application. The configuration details such as navigation rules, managed beans, and internationalization settings, are provided in the `faces-config.xml` file. In addition, we can configure customized validators, converters and components in this file. We have seen examples of defining navigation rules and managed beans in `faces-config.xml` earlier in the chapter. Here, we can summarize all allowed configuration details of the JSF configuration file.

We can categorize different elements, which can be provided in `faces-config.xml` file. The first category includes elements such as `<application>`, `<managed-bean>`, `<referenced-bean>`, and `<navigation-rule>`. This is most commonly used elements in the JSF application.

The `<application>` element is used to declare supported locales, to specify the location of resource bundle, and to define default render kit and other pluggable components. The `<managed-bean>` element is used to implement managed bean creation facility and helps in creating and managing different beans in given scopes. The `<navigation-rule>` element is used to define navigation rules to be followed in the application. We can see an example of using elements of this first category in the faces-config.xml file, as shown in Listing 20.11:

Listing 20.11: Configurations in the `faces-config.xml` File

```
<?xml version='1.0' encoding='UTF-8'?>
<faces-config version="2.2"
          xmlns="http://xmlns.jcp.org/xml/ns/javaee"
          xmlns:xsi="http://www.w3.org/2001/XMLSchema-instance"
          xsi:schemaLocation="http://xmlns.jcp.org/xml/ns/javaee
http://xmlns.jcp.org/xml/ns/javaee/web-facesconfig_2_2.xsd">
    <application>
        <locale-config>
            <supported-locale>en</supported-locale>
            <supported-locale>fr</supported-locale>
        </locale-config>
        <message-bundle>com.dt.ApplicationMessages</message-bundle>
    </application>

    <navigation-rule>
```

```
            <from-view-id>/login.jsp</from-view-id>
            <navigation-case>
                    <from-outcome>success</from-outcome>
                    <to-view-id>/welcome.jsp</to-view-id>
            </navigation-case>
            <navigation-case>
                    <from-outcome>failure</from-outcome>
                    <to-view-id>/login.jsp</to-view-id>
            </navigation-case>
        </navigation-rule>

        <managed-bean>
            <managed-bean-name>beanName</managed-bean-name>
            <managed-bean-class>com.kogent.BeanClassName</managed-bean-class>
            <managed-bean-scope>request</managed-bean-scope>
        </managed-bean>

    </faces-config>
```

Whenever we are extending the framework by creating our custom UI component, converter, validator or renderer, we need to register these custom components in the JSF configuration file. The elements used here are `<component>`, `<render-kit>`, `<validator>` and `<converter>`. We can see the basic structure registering these extensions in `faces-config.xml` file here:

```
    <validator>
      <validator-id>myValidator</validator-id>
      <validator-class>com.dt.validator.MyValidator</validator-class>
    </validator>

    <converter>
      <converter-id>myConverter</converter-id>
      <converter-class>com.dt.converter.MyConverter</converter-class>
    </converter>

    <component>
      <component-type>SomeType</component-type>
      <component-class>com.dt.component.MyUIComponent</component-class>
    </component>
```

JSF framework can support multiple configuration files, which can easily be defined by setting the `javax.faces.CONFIG_FILES` context parameter in the Deployment Descriptor. However, the `faces-config.xml` file need not to be configured in the web.xml file as JSF by default searches for the `WEB-INF/faces-config.xml` file and loads it automatically. The `faces-config.xml` file is the location where we place most of the application configuration details. We may need additional configuration files only when we are working on a large application divided into different modules.

We can now move on to the development of a full JSF-based Web application that implements what we have discussed in the chapter.

Creating a Simple JSF Application

Here, we are going to create an application, which demonstrates the life cycle of JSF application. The application name is **FirstJSF**, which prompts the user to enter some information and then the application displays what the user has entered. You can find the source code files for this application online in the "code/Chapter20" folder. The following files are required for creating the **FirstJSF** application:

- index.html
- index.jsp
- display.jsp
- Bean. java

- faces-config.xml
- web.xml

Let's start creating these files one by one.

Creating the views

The index.html file is a simple HTML file, which internally calls the index.jsp file. The source code for the index.html file is given in Listing 20.12:

Listing 20.12: Displaying the Code of the index.html File

```
<HTML>
   <HEAD>
          <meta http-equiv="Refresh" content= "0; URL=index.faces"/>
   </HEAD>
</HTML>
```

In this file, the content attribute of the meta tag contains the URL of the index.faces, which means it will redirect the request to index.faces.

The index.jsp file is a JSP page, which displays an HTML form built using JSF tags. The index.jsp page prompts the user to enter their Name, Department, and Roll No. The source code for this file is given in Listing 20.13:

Listing 20.13: Displaying the Code of the index.jsp File

```
<%@ page language="java" pageEncoding="ISO-8859-1"%>
<%@ taglib uri="http://java.sun.com/jsf/html" prefix="h"%>
<%@ taglib uri="http://java.sun.com/jsf/core" prefix="f"%>
<html>
<head>
<title>enter your name page</title>
</head>
<body>
<f:view>
   <h:form>
         <h:messages style="color: red;"></h:messages>
         <table>
                 <h:outputText value="Enter following information" />
                 <tr>
                         <td>
                                 <h:outputText value="Name" />
                         </td>
                         <td>
                         <h:inputText id="name" value="#{Bean.name}" required="true">
                                 <f:validateLength minimum="2"
                                  maximum="25"></f:validateLength>
                                 </h:inputText>
                         </td>
                 </tr>
                 <tr>
                         <td>
                                 <h:outputText value="Department " />
                         </td>
                         <td>
                                 <h:inputText id="dept"
                                 value="#{Bean.dept}" required="true">
                                 <f:validateLength minimum="2"
                                  maximum="25"></f:validateLength>
                                 </h:inputText>
                         </td>
                 </tr>
                 <tr>
                         <td>
```

```
                                    <h:outputText value="Roll No." />
                              </td>
                              <td>
    <h:inputText id="rollno" value="#{Bean.rollno}" />
                              </td>
                        </tr>
                        <tr>
                              <td>
    <h:commandButton id="button" action="result" value="Submit" />
                              </td>
                        </tr>
                  </table>
      </h:form>
    </f:view>
    </body>
    </html>
```

In the preceding JSP page, we include two JSP custom tag libraries, which are defined by the JSF technology. These taglib directives are as follows:

```
<%@ taglib uri="http://java.sun.com/jsf/html" prefix="h"%>
<%@ taglib uri="http://java.sun.com/jsf/core" prefix="f"%>
```

Each taglib directive has two attributes "uri" and "prefix". The uri `http://java.sun.com/jsf/html` contains the custom action elements to represent JSF objects tied for rendering them as HTML elements. The default prefix name used for this library is h, which represents HTML. The uri `http://java.sun.com/jsf/core` contains the custom action elements to represent JSF objects. These JSF objects are independent of the page markup language, which is HTML in our case.

Next, we use JSF `<f:view>` element, which is an action element. This view contains many components that make up a specific user interface. The `<h:form>` element represents a form component. It acts as a container for all input components. The input components hold values that need to be processed together. In our case, the `<h:form>` element contains the following input components:

- **<h:outputText>**—The `<h:outputText>` element represents a String value that displays a text on the page, which is given in its "value" attribute.
- **<h:inputText>**—The `<h:inputText>` element represents an input field component, which holds a value entered by the user. The value attribute informs the JSF implementation to link the object properties in the Servlet. In our case, `#{Bean.name}` informs the JSF implementation to link the text field with the name property of a Bean object in the Servlet.
- **<h:commandButton>**—It represents a command component, which renders an HTML input element with type button. The action attributes of this element specifies the action to be taken after submitting the form.

Besides these components, the page also uses validator components for validation. In our case, we use the `<f:validateLength>` component, which checks whether the value entered in the corresponding text field comes under the specified range or not. If not, the appropriate error message is displayed by the `<h:messages>` component.

The `display.jsp` page displays the information entered by the user in the `index.jsp` page. The source code for this file is shown in Listing 20.14:

Listing 20.14: Displaying the Code of the `display.jsp` File

```
<%@ taglib uri="http://java.sun.com/jsf/html" prefix="h"%>
<%@ taglib uri="http://java.sun.com/jsf/core" prefix="f"%>
<html>
  <head>
        <title>greeting page</title>
  </head>

  <body>
        <f:view>
```

```
            <table>
                  <tr>
                        <td>
                              <h:outputText value="Student Name:-
                              #{Bean.name}" />
                        </td>
                  </tr>
                  <tr>
                        <td>
                              <h:outputText value="Department Name:-
                              #{Bean.dept}" />
                        </td>
                  </tr>
                  <tr>
                        <td>
                              <h:outputText value="Roll no:-
                              #{Bean.rollno}" />
                        </td>
                  </tr>
                  <tr>
                  <td><a href="/FirstJSF/index.faces">Back</a></td>
                  </tr>
                  </table>
            </f:view>
      </body>
   </html>
```

The preceding page uses the <h:outputText> component for displaying the information entered by the user.

Creating Backing Bean

The Bean.java file is a simple Java Bean class, which holds the Name, Department, and Roll No. of the property. The class defines the get and set method for these properties. The source code for the Bean.java file is given in Listing 20.15:

Listing 20.15: Displaying the Code of the Bean.java File

```
public class Bean {
   private String name;
   private String dept;
   private int rollno;

   public String getDept() {
         return dept;
   }
   public void setDept(String dept) {
         this.dept = dept;
   }
   public String getName() {
         return name;
   }
   public void setName(String name) {
         this.name = name;
   }
   public int getRollno() {
         return rollno;
   }
   public void setRollno(int rollno) {
         this.rollno = rollno;
   }
}
```

When the index.jsp page is displayed, the `getName()` method is invoked to obtain the current property value of Name. After the submission of index.jsp page, the `setName()` method is invoked to set the value that the user entered in the Name text component. The Name property is referenced by the `<h:inputText>` element and `<h:outputText>` element in the index.jsp and display.jsp file.

Configuring the Application

A JSF application has a number of resources. These resources are validators, converters, managed beans, and navigation rules. All these resources are registered into the Application's configuration resource file. This configuration file is `faces-config.xml`. The source code for the `faces-config.xml` file is given in Listing 20.16:

Listing 20.16: Displaying the Code of the `faces-config.xml` File

```
<?xml version='1.0' encoding='UTF-8'?>
<faces-config version="2.2"
              xmlns="http://xmlns.jcp.org/xml/ns/javaee"
              xmlns:xsi="http://www.w3.org/2001/XMLSchema-instance"
              xsi:schemaLocation="http://xmlns.jcp.org/xml/ns/javaee
http://xmlns.jcp.org/xml/ns/javaee/web-facesconfig_2_2.xsd">
        <navigation-rule>
                <from-view-id>/index.jsp</from-view-id>
                <navigation-case>
                        <from-outcome>result</from-outcome>
                        <to-view-id>/display.jsp</to-view-id>
                </navigation-case>
        </navigation-rule>
        <managed-bean>
                <managed-bean-name>Bean</managed-bean-name>
                <managed-bean-class>Bean</managed-bean-class>
                <managed-bean-scope>request</managed-bean-scope>
        </managed-bean>
</faces-config>
```

Application resource files are registered in `CONFIG-FILES` setting of the application's `web.xml` file.

Some rules can be declared inside the JSF configuration file, i.e., `faces-config.xml`, for defining the navigation from one page of the application to another page. For each page, a navigation rule is defined in the JSF configuration file. All the navigation cases for each rule are defined inside the navigation rule element with the help of other child elements.

An action attribute is used for each UI component. The attribute action specifies a value or an action method that returns a value, which represents an outcome. In case of action method, one or more outcomes can be defined depending on the number of possible results of the processing. In our case, we define the navigation rule for the index.jsp page as follows:

```
<navigation-rule>

  <from-view-id>/index.jsp</from-view-id>

  <navigation-case>

        <from-outcome>result</from-outcome>
        <to-view-id>/display.jsp</to-view-id>

  </navigation-case>

</navigation-rule>
```

It defines that if the outcome of the action is "result", then the page display.jsp is displayed.

Next, we configured our Java Bean class "Bean". A simple Java Bean class is used to manage data between the various tiers of the applications. These Java Beans are configured as managed beans in the faces-config.xml file.

The bean is instantiated, populated with the default values, and placed in the specified scope. The dynamic data can be sent and displayed by binding the bean with UI components, or component tag attributes. By registering the JavaBean as managed bean, the application can instantiate the bean when accessed. The data held by the bean can be displayed and updated automatically, when the data is submitted.

In our case, we configured the Java Bean "Bean" as managed bean in our `faces-config.xml` file as follows:

```
<managed-bean>

  <managed-bean-name>Bean</managed-bean-name>

  <managed-bean-class>Bean</managed-bean-class>

  <managed-bean-scope>request</managed-bean-scope>

</managed-bean>
```

Every JSF application requires that the `FacesServlet` be specified. `FacesServlet` manages the JSF page life cycle. All requests must be mapped with the `FacesServlet`. For JSF MVC application, `FacesServlet` acts as Controller Served. Initialization and context parameters for the JSF Servlet can be provided in the Deployment Descriptor, which is `web.xml` file. Elements named `<servlet>`, `<servlet-mapping>` are used to map JSF Servlet to a symbolic name and to map this symbolic name to the URL pattern, respectively, as shown in Listing 20.17:

Listing 20.17: Displaying the Code of the `web.xml` File

```
<web-app>
    <context-param>
        <param-name>javax.faces.STATE_SAVING_METHOD</param-name>
        <param-value>server</param-value>
    </context-param>

    <context-param>
        <param-name>javax.faces.CONFIG_FILES</param-name>
        <param-value>/WEB-INF/faces-config.xml</param-value>
    </context-param>

    <listener>
        <listener-class>com.sun.faces.config.ConfigureListener</listener-class>
    </listener>
    <servlet>
        <servlet-name>Faces Servlet</servlet-name>
        <servlet-class>javax.faces.webapp.FacesServlet</servlet-class>
        <load-on-startup>1</load-on-startup>

    </servlet>

    <servlet-mapping>
        <servlet-name>Faces Servlet</servlet-name>
        <url-pattern>*.faces</url-pattern>

    </servlet-mapping>

    <welcome-file-list>
        <welcome-file>index.html</welcome-file>

    </welcome-file-list>
</web-app>
```

The URL pattern shows that the `FacesServlet` handles all the requests that ends with "faces".

After creating all the preceding files, now create a directory structure as shown in Figure 20.4 and arrange all the files accordingly:

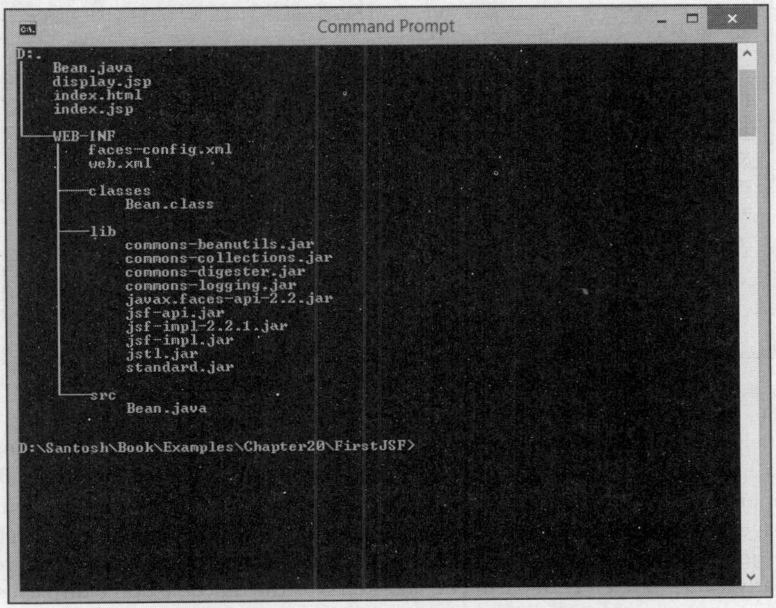

Figure 20.4: Directory Structure for the FirstJSF Application

Once you arrange all the files in the directory structure as shown in Figure 20.4, copy the FirstJSF folder into `<Tomcat home>\webapps` folder.

Now start the server, if it is already in started mode then no need to restart it. We are using port number 9090 because at our machine, Tomcat is running on this port. To run this example, use this URL `http://localhost:9090/FirstJSF/`. The first page of this application is shown in Figure 20.5:

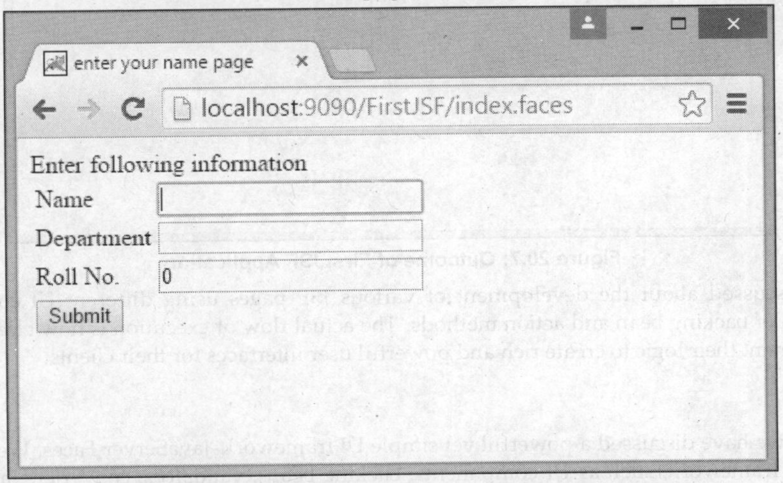

Figure 20.5: Displaying the First Page of FirstJSF Application

Now suppose that the user leave the field Name empty and entered the value 'A' for the Department field and 24 for the Roll No. field. Now when the user tries to submit the form then the appropriate validation error message in red color is displayed. The messages are displayed by using the `<h:messages>` element, which is defined in the index.jsp page, as shown in Figure 20.6:

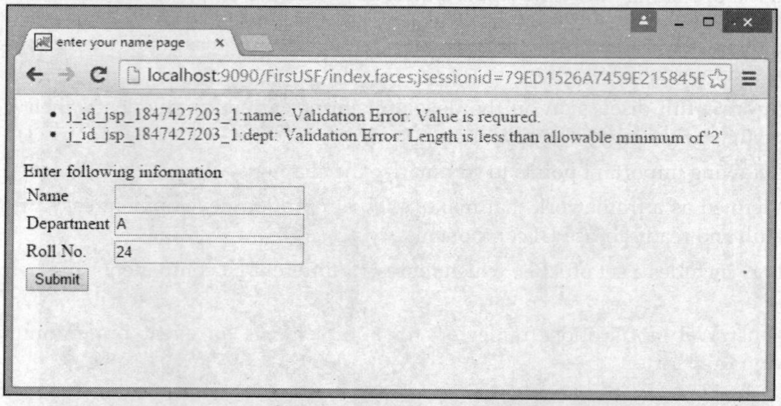

Figure 20.6: Page showing Validation Error

Now enter Name, Department, and Roll No. as "Santosh", "Computer Science", and 24, respectively, in the corresponding field and press the submit button. After submitting the information, the `setName()`, `setDept()`, and `setRollno()` method of the Bean class are invoked. At this point, the Bean class is binded with the UI component of the index.jsp page. Now the outcome of the action is "result", which is mapped with the display.jsp page. The display.jsp page is also binded with the Bean class; therefore, when the display.jsp page is displayed, the `getName()`, `getDept()`, and `getRollno()` method of the Bean class are invoked to obtain the current property value for Name, Department, and Roll No. The outcome of the display.jsp page is shown in Figure 20.7:

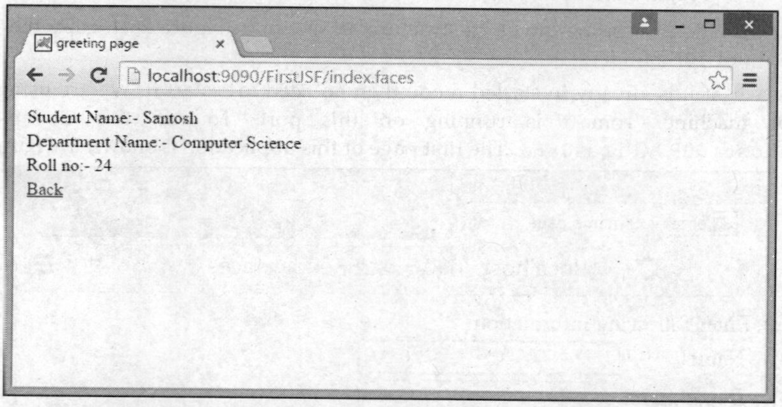

Figure 20.7: Outcome of FirstJSF Application

So, here we discussed about the development of various JSF pages using different UI components and the implementation of backing bean and action methods. The actual flow of execution is now clear to the reader and they can implement their logic to create rich and powerful user interfaces for their clients.

Summary

In this chapter, we have discussed a powerful yet simple UI framework–JavaServer Faces. We have described all elements of the framework, such as UI components, backing beans, validators, converters, and event handlers. The various phases of JSF request process life cycle have also been described in detail to make the actual flow in the framework clear to the reader.

All JSF HTML and core tags have been explained with examples and their attributes. JSF provides an elegant way to implement event handling through backing bean methods, which are most important components in the JSF based Web application, which need to be created by the developer. The backing bean concept and managed bean facility are the key features of JSF. Further, the chapter also discusses JSF's support for input validation, type conversion, and internationalization.

The chapter includes a full discussion on the development of various components, their implementation, and configuration through a running Web application.

Let's recall the following important points to summarize the chapter:

- JSF can be defined as a framework that makes Web application development easy by supporting different rich, powerful, and ready-to-use UI components.
- JSF technology includes a set of APIs, which represent different UI components and helps in managing their states.
- JSF is a robust Web application framework that implements an event programming model to handle different events and actions performed by the client on different UI components.
- Faces Flow is useful in business tasks as it can be used to encapsulate a set of steps that can guide a user through the execution of business task.
- JSF 2.2 has introduced five types of nodes. These nodes are used to define the entry and exit point of a flow.
- The Model in JSF architecture is a set of server-side JavaBeans that retrieves the values from the model components, such as the database and defines methods on the basis of these values.
- JSF technology has its own set of elements, such as, UI component, renderer, converter, and backing beans, which altogether form the JSF framework.
- UI components are the basic reusable components for developing UIs using the JSF framework.
- JSF architecture follows MVC design pattern and consequently focuses on separating business logic and data from presentation logic.
- A converter is a translator, which can convert a Java object into a string and an input string into some Java object.
- There are two types of action listeners, one that affects navigation, and the other does not.
- The data model events are associated with data-aware UI components.
- In JSF 2.0, a new tag `<h:link>` was introduced. It is used to render the HTML anchor element.
- `<h:outputStylesheet>` is used to add external stylesheet file to JSF page and `<h:outputScript>` tag is used to add external javascript file to JSF page.
- The JSF core Tag library contains tags for different JSF custom actions and these tags do not depend on any particular render kit.
- Backing beans are normal JavaBeans that contain properties and event listener methods to store and manipulate user data.
- A backing bean can have various methods, which can be used as event listeners. We can handle two types of events through backing bean methods, action events and value change events
- The user input validation is required before any application logic execution in all types of Web applications.
- JSF provides its own set of standard converters, which can be registered with intput as well as output UI components.
- The navigation handler plays the vital role as the navigation handler is the actual code that decides the next view to be loaded as well as displayed to the user.
- JSF needs to implement its own style of request processing life cycle for all requests.
- A JSF application has a number of resources. These resources are validators, converters, managed beans, and navigation rules.

In the next chapter, we will discuss about various types of Java EE Design Patterns.

Exercise

Q. 20.1 What is JSF?

Q. 20.2 What are the basic elements of JSF?

Q. 20.3 List the different types of JSF standard actions.

Q. 20.4 Write the element of the faces configuration file that describes the navigation rules of a JSF view.

Q. 20.5 List the six faces of the JSF request processing.

Q. 20.6 Which JSF UI components values are validated in the Apply Request Values phase of the JSF? request processing?

Q. 20.7 Write the URI used to refer the JSF html tag library.

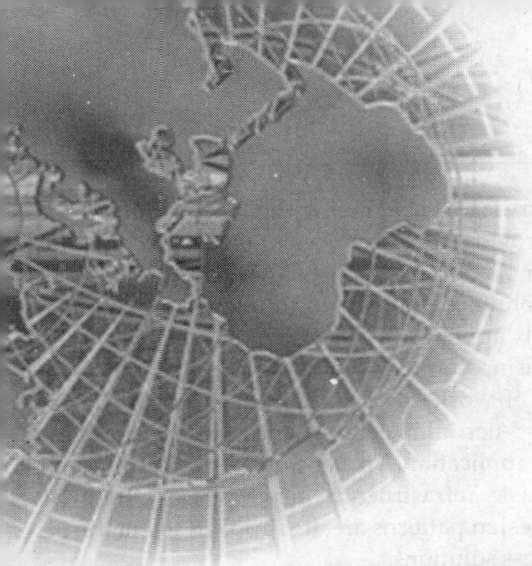

21

Java EE Design Patterns

With the advent of Web technologies, almost all the industries are trying to use the Internet. Web applications are developed to reach customers, expand business domains, and provide better services to the clients. Java EE provides a platform for the development of distributed enterprise or Web applications. However, as the size of the enterprise increases, there arises a need for more effective Web solutions; thereby, resulting in an increase in the size and complexity of Web applications. Therefore, the Web applications need to be scalable, easily expandable, and reusable to ensure effective management of increasing complexity and size. Development of such Web applications requires some standard architecture. A lot of work has been done in this domain of developing Web applications. All the Web applications follow the 3-tier architecture, which provides a clear separation between business logic and presentation logic of the Web application. This ensures a standard format to be followed in the development and maintenance of the basic infrastructure of Java EE Enterprise Applications. Along with a standard architecture, various standard design patterns are also applied to enterprise applications to ensure consistency and delivery of high quality business solutions.

In this chapter, you learn about the Java EE application architecture. Next, you learn about the design patterns. Further, you learn about the role of design patterns in Web applications. Finally, the chapter discusses the different types of design patterns.

Let's start the chapter by learning about the Java EE application architecture.

Describing the Java EE Application Architecture

A proper technical architecture is necessarily required to ensure development and management of an enterprise application, which is scalable, robust, flexible, and reusable. Java EE allows various architectures to be used for managing enterprise applications. However, the 3-tier architecture is the most commonly used architecture. Java EE employs a component-based approach for developing, managing, and deploying enterprise applications. The 3-tier architecture consists of three tiers or layers, namely presentation tier or client tier, business tier or application tier, and data tier or enterprise information service tier. The client tier or presentation tier manages the user interface of the application. This tier is responsible for handling user inputs and interactions as well as presentation of data to the user. The business tier or application tier implements the business logic for the application. This tier is responsible for processing the input data and generating response accordingly. The data tier or enterprise information service tier handles the data for the application. This tier manages a database and stores persistent data for the application. Figure 21.1 shows a representation of the 3-tier architecture:

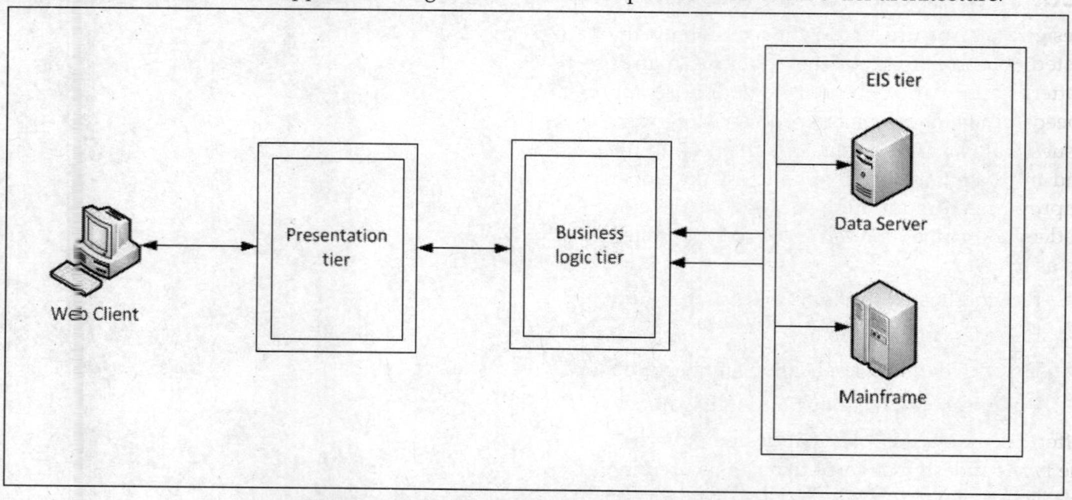

Figure 21.1: Displaying the 3-tier Architecture

Figure 21.1 shows a representation of the 3-tier architecture, where a client interacts with the presentation tier, which provides the user interface; the requests made by the client are processed at the business tier, which provides the business logic; and the client data is stored at the enterprise information service tier. For example, if a client wants to store some data on the data server, then instead of forwarding the request directly to the data server, the request is first forwarded to the presentation tier; the business tier then processes the request and validates the user before forwarding the data to the data server. In this way, the enterprise applications are designed using the 3-tier architecture.

However, designing Web applications is not an easy task. A lot of considerations need to be examined before reaching to a conclusion about how to develop a Web application or an enterprise application. To facilitate the development process for developing Web applications, a lot of design patterns have been proposed. Before discussing about the various available design patterns that are applied in Web application development and designing, let's first examine what is meant by a design pattern in context to a Web or an enterprise application.

Introducing a Design Pattern

Design patterns refer to language-independent solutions provided for solving commonly recurring design problems. A design pattern first describes the problem and then the solution that can be applied to the problem. The design patterns are implemented in the form of objects and classes that provide solutions to the problem. The concept of design patterns was first applied to object-oriented programming. Later, this concept was also applied to the development of enterprise applications.

There are various problems concerning the designing issues of Web applications that may arise while developing the application. Some of the problems occur more often and creating a solution from scratch all over again every time the problem occurs, results in wastage of time and effort involved in the process of development of the Web or enterprise application. Therefore, design patterns have been developed which provide well-examined and proven solution to recurring problems while designing applications. The design patterns can be divided into various categories on the basis of their application domains.

After understanding about a design pattern, let's learn in what ways it can be helpful in designing enterprise applications.

Discussing the Role of Design Patterns

Design patterns are used while designing the enterprise applications to provide standardized, proven, and tested solutions to recurring problems that arise during the development of enterprise applications. Design patterns offer various benefits to enterprise application development. The application of design patterns greatly speeds up the development process. Moreover, reusing design patterns help in recognizing and avoiding subtle issues that can later become a bottleneck to the development process. Design patterns provide code reusability and improve readability of code for developers who are familiar with the design patterns. They also help in improving communication between the developers by providing a vocabulary which uses well-known and well-understood names and terms for software interaction. The important benefits of design patterns can be summed up as follows:

- Provides tested solutions to frequently and repeatedly occurring problems
- Provides code reusability
- Helps in defining application architecture more efficiently and clearly
- Provides more reliability and transparency to the design of the application

After discussing the roles that design patterns play in an enterprise application, let's move forward and explore the types of design patterns that can be used in the development of such applications.

Exploring Types of Patterns

Design patterns became widely acceptable in the field of computer science after the publication of the book *Design Patterns: Elements of Reusable Object-Oriented Software* by Gamma, Erich; Richard Helm, Ralph Johnson, and John Vlissides in 1994. Java EE design patterns help in recognizing potential problems that have been observed while using various Java EE technologies and finding appropriate implementable solutions to those problems according to the application architecture. The various available patterns can be categorized on the basis of the architectural tier in which they are applied. Figure 21.2 shows some patterns as provided by Sun Java Center:

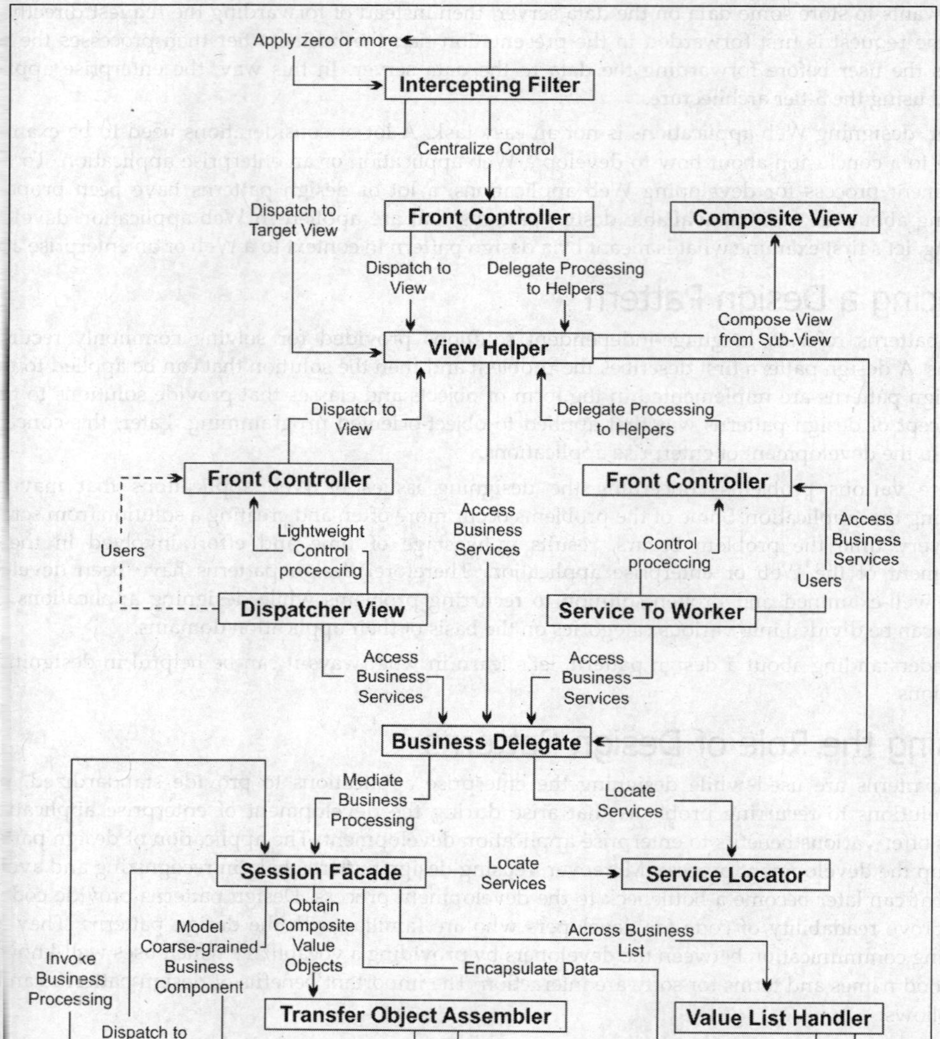

Figure 21.2: Displaying the Java EE Design Patterns from Sun Java Center

Table 21.1 lists the design patterns on the basis of the architectural tiers to which they belong:

Table 21.1: Describing the List of Design Patterns

Tier	Pattern Name	Description
Presentation Tier	Composite View	Manages the layout of a Web page and presentation of data on it. It represents a composite view, in which data is presented in the form of sections which are built by using reusable sub-views.
	Dispatcher View	Provides services for data processing, such as authentication; and request handling by offering limited amount of business processing. It solves a combination of problems handled by the Front Controller and View Helper patterns.
	Front Controller	Implements a central controller in an enterprise application to process the requests.
	Intercepting Filter	Intercepts the request reception and response transmission. It also helps in pre-processing or redirection of a request; and post-processing or content replacement of a response.
	Service to Worker	Maintains a separation between the actions, views, and controllers. The workers and views are managed by a dispatcher object.
	View Helper	Helps in maintaining a separation between the presentation logic and business logic. The business logic is implemented for a view using the view helper class.
Business Tier	Business Delegate	Manages the complexity involved in lookup and exception handling for distributed components by introducing an intermediate business delegate class which reduces coupling between presentation tier users and business tier.
	Composite Entity	Manages a network of interrelated persistent objects.
	Fast Lane Reader	Helps in accessing the tabular read-only data more efficiently. Persistent data can be accessed directly by the Fast Lane Reader component using Java Database Connectivity (JDBC).
	Service Locator	Allows the users to uniformly access business components and services. To accomplish this, the Service Locator pattern uses Java Naming and Directory Interface (JNDI).
	Session Facade	Provides a simple interface to a client by hiding all the complexities involved in the interaction between various business components by encapsulating the complex implementation details in a session bean that acts as a facade.
	Transfer Object	Provides a way to transfer bulk data from a remote server by using a serialized Java object.
	Value List Handler	Provides a handler object that enables the users to iterate over a read-only list.
Integration Tier	Data Access Object	Allows the code for accessing and manipulating data to be encapsulated in a separate layer.
	Service Activator	Allows asynchronous invocation of the business services.

Table 21.1 lists the design patterns offered by Sun Java Center. The design patterns are categorized according to their implementation in Presentation, Business, and Integration tiers. The succeeding sections discuss some of the design patterns listed in Table 21.1 in detail. For each pattern, the discussion covers the definition of the problem, forces, possible solution, strategies, and consequences of applying the pattern.

The Problem section of each pattern discusses the problem that led to the creation of that pattern. The Forces section discusses the tasks need to be done in the context of the problem. The Solution section discusses how the concerned pattern has helped to solve the discussed problem. The Strategies section discusses the various strategies that can be used to implement the pattern and the result of the pattern is discussed in the Consequences section.

Let's start exploring some of the design patterns listed in Table 21.1, starting with the Front Controller pattern, in the next section.

The Front Controller Pattern

The Front Controller pattern provides a centralized control to the application request processing. It introduces a central controller component that acts as a common entry point for all application requests. The controller component provides the logic for handling user requests, invoking security services, managing content retrieval, delegating business processing, and selecting appropriate views. The controller component may delegate some processing to a helper component or dispatcher component. The helper component takes the responsibility of helping a view or controller in completing its processing. For example, the helper component may help in gathering the data required by the view. The data can be provided as raw data, or the helper component may format that data as required by the view. The dispatcher component helps the controller in managing and selecting the next view to be presented to a user.

Problem

The Presentation tier requires a centralized control to handle multiple user requests for effectively managing the activities of content retrieval, view management, and security service invocation. However, users can access the views directly without following a centralized mechanism. This approach requires the code for processing logic and system services to be duplicated for each view. When the responsibility of view navigation and management is left to the views themselves, then this may lead to commingled view content and navigation. For example, in an online shopping Web site, multiple user requests need to be handled at the same time and the sequence of steps involved in shopping process also needs to be controlled. There may be multiple users logged in the Web site at a time. This scenario requires that consistency and security should be maintained across multiple requests. A lot of code duplication can occur if the code that controls the input is scattered across multiple objects.

Forces

The problem described in the preceding section results in the following forces:

- Replication of code in multiple views
- Similar business requests responded by multiple views
- Complex logic for view management
- Completion of common system services on a per request basis

Solution

The solution is obtained by introducing a Front Controller component that acts as a common entry point for handling multiple client requests. The Front Controller component provides a centralized control mechanism for request handling that reduces code duplication and encourages code reusability. The Front Controller pattern helps to achieve the following tasks:

- Calling up the security services, such as authentication and access control
- Managing request handling
- Managing view selection and navigation
- Managing client's state
- Handling errors

Figure 21.3 shows the representation of the Front Controller pattern:

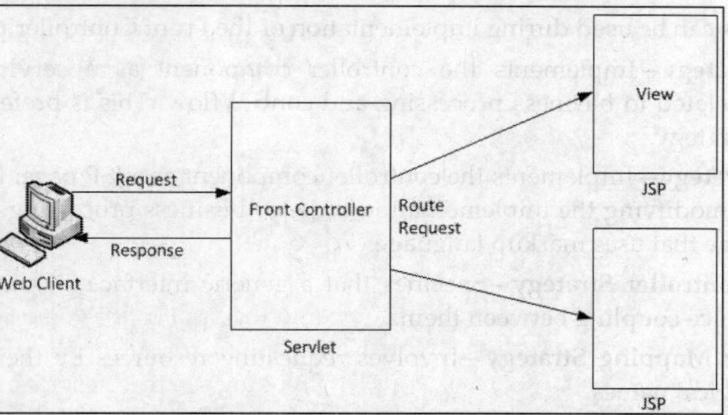

Figure 21.3: Representing the Front Controller Pattern

As shown in Figure 21.3, the central Front Controller component implemented as a servlet receives a request from a client and redirects it to respective views. It also forwards back the response to the client. Multiple controllers can also be used in an application, where each controller is mapped to a distinct set of services. Figure 21.4 shows the class diagram of Front Controller:

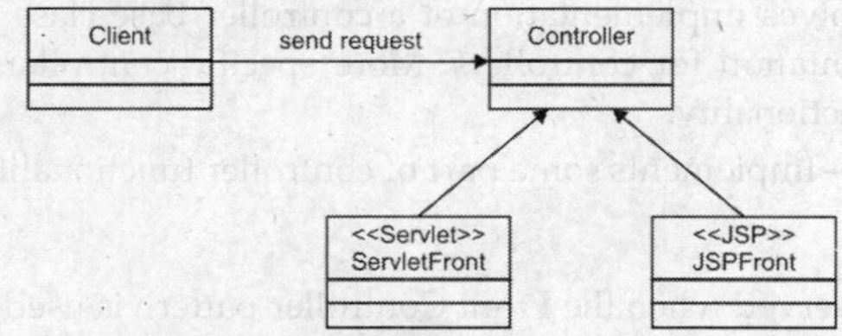

Figure 21.4: Displaying the Front Controller Class Diagram

The Front Controller component may use a separate dispatcher component for implementing the required workflow. It can also use helper components, which are implemented as JavaBean components and custom tags. Figure 21.5 shows a sequence diagram representing the interaction between the components involved in the Front Controller pattern:

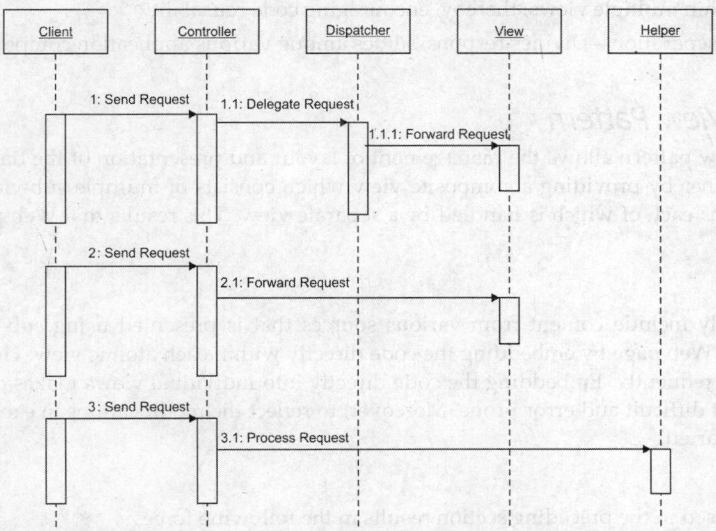

Figure 21.5: Displaying the Sequence Diagram for the Front Controller Pattern

The sequence diagram shown in Figure 21.5 depicts how a request is handled by the controller component.

Strategies

The following strategies can be used during implementation of the Front Controller pattern:

- **Servlet Front Strategy**—Implements the controller component as a servlet, which manages request handling aspects related to business processing and control flow. This is preferred over Java Server Pages (JSP) Page Front strategy.
- **JSP Page Front Strategy**—Implements the controller component as a JSP page. However, this strategy is not preferred because modifying the implementation code for business processing logic involves modifications to be made in a page that uses markup language.
- **Command and Controller Strategy**—Specifies that a generic interface should be provided to the helper components to reduce coupling between them.
- **Physical Resource Mapping Strategy**—Involves requesting resources by their specific physical resource name instead of logical names.
- **Logical Resource Mapping Strategy**—Involves requesting resources by their logical names.
- **Multiplexed Resource Mapping Strategy**—Involves requesting a single physical resource by not just one but a complete set of logical names.
- **Dispatcher in Controller Strategy**—Involves implementation of the dispatcher functionality within the controller, where the dispatcher only has a minimal functionality.
- **Base Front Strategy**—Involves implementation of a controller base class that contains common code and provides default implementation for controllers. More specific controllers can extend the controller base class to acquire default functionality.
- **Filter Controller Strategy**—Implements some part of controller functionality using a filter.

Consequences

Following consequences are observed when the Front Controller pattern is used:

- **Centralizes control**—Implements a central controller component for handling requests and implementing business logic. Therefore, requests can be easily tracked and logged.
- Improves manageability—Provides a single entry point for all requests, which requires fewer resources; thereby, improving manageability.
- Improves reusability—Moves common code to a single controller component. Therefore, the code is not duplicated within multiple views; thereby, encouraging code reusability.
- Improves role separation—Divides responsibilities among various application components for effective role separation.

The Composite View Pattern

The Composite View pattern allows the management of layout and presentation of the data on a Web page in a more effective manner by providing a composite view which consists of multiple sub-views. The Web page is divided into sections each of which is handled by a separate view. This results in a Web page that consists of a set of views.

Problem

Web pages normally include content from various sources that is presented using sub-views. The content is incorporated in the Web page by embedding the code directly within each atomic view. However, the content of the views changes frequently. Embedding the code directly into individual views makes code modification and layout management difficult and error prone. Moreover, to reflect the modifications in each sub-view; the server may need to be restarted.

Forces

The problem discussed in the preceding section results in the following forces:

- The atomic content of the view more often changes

- Multiple composite views utilize similar sub-views which are presented either by using surrounding template text, or may be displayed at different location within the Web page
- It is difficult and error-prone to maintain and manage changes in the layout and code
- The frequent embedding of code, which controls the frequently changing portions, directly into views greatly affects the availability and maintenance of the system

Solution

The solution to the problem mentioned with respect to Composite View pattern is to implement a composite view which is made up of multiple atomic sub-views. This involves dynamic inclusion of each component of the Web page template into the page. This allows you to manage the layout independent of the content of the page. The composite view pattern provides the following benefits:

- Encourages code reusability and modular design
- Allows you to create pages using components that can be incorporated dynamically by combining them in a variety of ways
- Allows layout of the page to be modified independent of the page content
- Helps in creating a prototype for examining the layout of a site

The responsibilities of various components which participate in the Composite View pattern are listed as follows:

- **Composite view**—Provides a view which is an aggregate of multiple independent atomic sub-views.
- **View Manager**—Manages page structure and layout by managing and controlling the inclusion of code fragments in the composite view. It can be implemented as a JavaBean helper or custom tag helper.
- **Included view**—Refers to a sub-view which is an atomic portion of a larger view. The sub-view can either be composite or can itself include multiple views.

Figure 21.6 shows the class diagram representing the Composite View pattern:

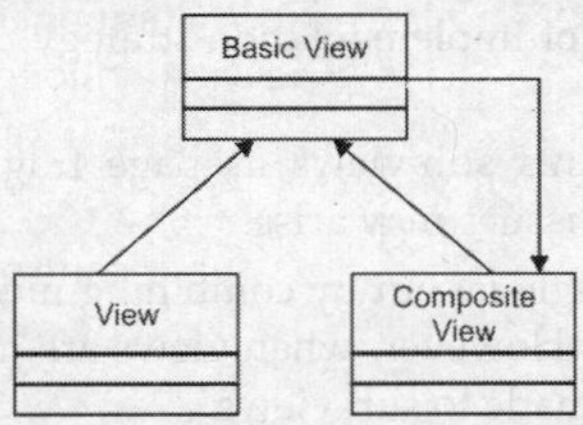

Figure 21.6: Displaying the Class Diagram Representing the Composite View Pattern

Figure 21.7 shows the sequence diagram for the Composite View pattern:

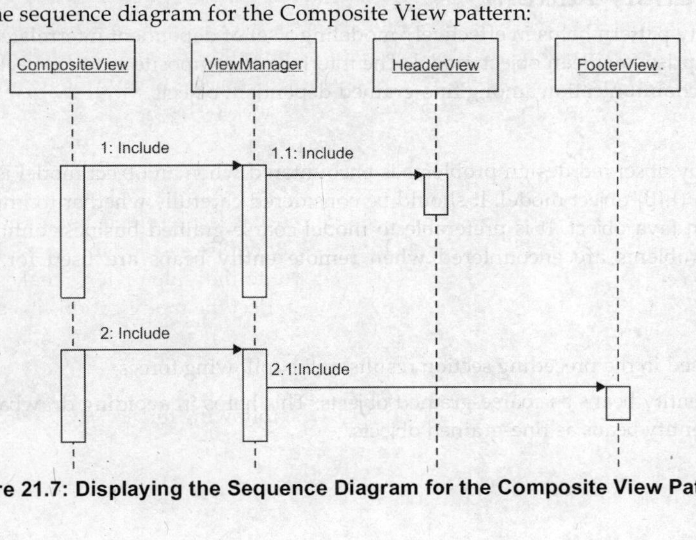

Figure 21.7: Displaying the Sequence Diagram for the Composite View Pattern

Figure 21.7 describes the sequence of interaction between the components of the Composite View pattern. The `CompositeView` component partitions the user interface into multiple views, and then, the `ViewManager` component controls the layout and structure of the Web page.

Strategies

The strategies to implement the Composite View pattern are as follows:

- **JavaBeans View Management Strategy**—Implements a JavaBean component for handling view management.
- **Standard Tag View Management Strategy**—Uses standard JSP page tags for managing views.
- **Custom Tag View Management Strategy**—Uses custom tags for implementing view management.
- **Transformer View Management Strategy**—Uses an Extensible Stylesheet Language (XSL) Transformer for handling view management.
- **Early-Binding Resource Strategy**—Refers to translation time content inclusion. As the name suggests, content is included in the page at translation time. This strategy is appropriate to be used for maintaining and updating static templates.
- **Late-Binding Resource Strategy**—Refers to runtime-content inclusion. As the name suggests, content is included in the page at runtime. This strategy is appropriate to be used for maintenance of composite pages.

Consequences

The following consequences are observed when Composite View pattern is used:

- **Promotes modular design**—Encourages modular design. The code of atomic portions of a template can be used in multiple views and at different locations of a page; thereby, improving maintainability.
- **Enhances flexibility**—Includes views conditionally at runtime on the basis of user role or security policy.
- **Enhances Maintainability**—Allows you to make changes to the content of portions of a template, without affecting its layout as the template code is not directly hard coded into a view. The changes made can be reflected immediately, on the basis of implementation strategy. The page layout can also be changed easily since modifications are centralized.
- **Reduces Manageability**—Implements sub-views as page fragments. When these atomic fragments are aggregated together, manageability issues may arise.
- **Performance Impact**—Creates a single layout by combining multiple sub-views. When views are included at runtime, some delay is observed. However, when views are included at translation time, some problems are encountered while changes are made to sub-views.

The Composite Entity Pattern

The Composite Entity pattern helps in effectively modeling a set of dependent interrelated objects when they are mapped to an Enterprise JavaBean object model. The interface of composite entity is itself coarse-grained, which internally manages communication among fine-grained dependent objects.

Problem

One of the repeatedly observed design problems is encountered when an object model is directly mapped to an Enterprise JavaBean (EJB) object model. It should be considered carefully whether to implement an object as an entity EJB or a plain Java object. It is preferable to model coarse-grained business entities using remote entity beans. However, problems are encountered when remote entity beans are used for modeling fine-grained entities.

Forces

The problem discussed in the preceding section results in the following forces:

- Implementing entity beans as coarse-grained objects. This helps in avoiding drawbacks observed in case of implementing entity beans as fine-grained objects.

- Mapping relational database schema to entity beans. This involves a large number of fine-grained entity beans to be created. It is more preferable to have coarse-grained entity beans. At the same time, it is also recommended that the overall number of entity beans should be kept less.
- Mapping object model to EJB model. This results in creation of fine-grained entity beans which map to database schema. This mapping leads to problems concerning performance security issues, manageability, and transaction processing. Moreover, it is difficult and expensive to manage inter-entity bean relationship.
- Mapping of entity beans to database schema. This result in a tight coupling between entity beans and database schema where changes made to one are reflected in the other.

Solution

The solution to the problem stated with respect to the Composite Entity pattern is to implement the set of dependent persistent objects by using a composite entity instead of implementing the dependent objects as individual fine-grained entity bean. A persistent object stores its state in a data store and is shared by multiple clients. These persistent objects can either be coarse-grained objects or dependent objects. Dependent objects are usually managed by the coarse-grained parent objects and are not directly accessible by the client. A composite entity bean represents a coarse-grained object and all its dependent objects as well. It aggregates interrelated dependent persistent objects into single entity bean; thereby, reducing the overall number of entity beans in the application. Figure 21.8 shows the class diagram representing Composite Entity pattern:

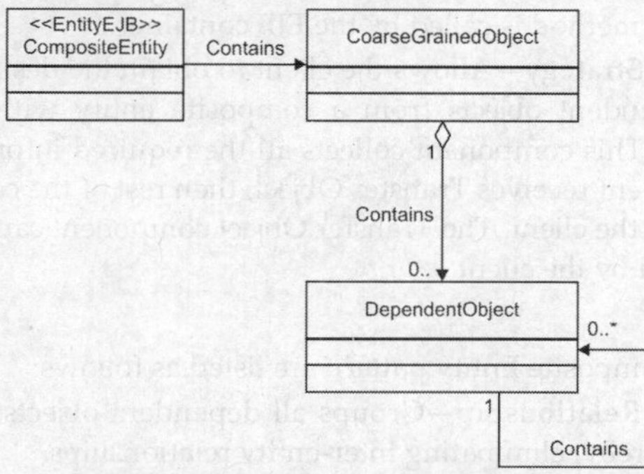

Figure 21.8: Showing the Class Diagram Representing the Composite Entity Pattern

The class diagram shown in Figure 21.8 shows that the `CompositeEntity` component contains the `CoarseGrainedObject` component, which in turn contains the `DependentObject` component. Figure 21.9 shows the sequence diagram for the Composite Entity pattern displaying the interaction among its various components:

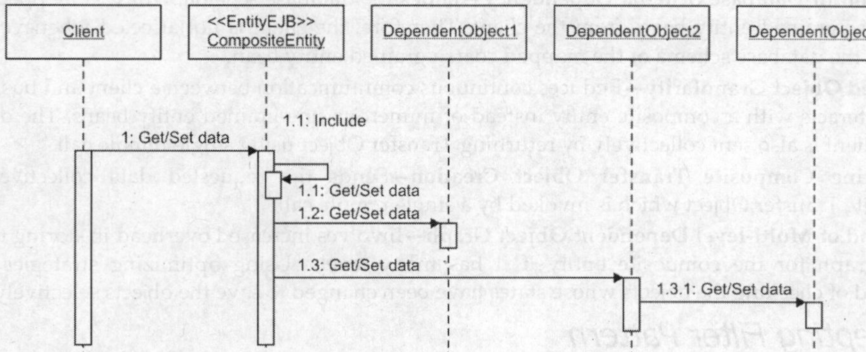

Figure 21.9: Showing the Sequence Diagram for Composite Entity Pattern

Strategies

The strategies used for implementing the Composite Entity pattern are as follows:

- **Composite Entity Contains Coarse-Grained Entity Strategy**—Specifies that the coarse-grained entity object is contained by the composite entity. The coarse-grained entity object maintains connection with the dependent objects as well.
- **Composite Entity Implements Coarse-Grained Entity Strategy**—Implies that composite entity is itself a coarse-grained entity object which implements the coarse-grained entity and thereby contains its attributes and methods. The dependent objects are represented as attributes of the composite entity which maintains and manages the relationship between the coarse-grained object and its dependent objects.
- **Lazy Loading Strategy**—Implies that all the dependent objects related to the composite entity are not loaded in an application while the composite entity bean is initialized by the EJB container. Only the most important required dependent objects are loaded during initialization. The remaining dependent objects are loaded on an on-demand basis when they are required or accessed by the client.
- **Store Optimization (Dirty Marker) Strategy**—Involves the creation, implementation, and usage of the `DirtyMarker` interface that contains methods, which can be used by the dependent objects to let the caller be aware of the changes in their state. This enables the caller of the objects to selectively save only the dependent objects that have changed since the last call to the `ejbStore()` operation while persisting the composite entity. Otherwise, the complete dependent object graph needs to be persisted to the database whenever the `ejbStore()` method is called by the EJB container.
- **Composite Transfer Object Strategy**—Allows the client to obtain the desired information about the coarse-grained object and its dependent objects from a composite entity with just one remote call using the Transfer Object component. This component collects all the required information into a single object using one remote call. When the client receives Transfer Object, then rest of the calls made by the client to Transfer Object are invoked locally to the client. The Transfer Object component can also gather data from a subset of dependent objects if required by the client.

Consequences

The consequences of using the Composite Entity pattern are listed as follows:

- **Elimination of Inter-Entity Relationship**—Groups all dependent objects into a single entity bean using a composite entity pattern; thereby, eliminating inter-entity relationships.
- **Improved Manageability**—Uses a composite entity for grouping fine-grained entities; thereby, resulting in fewer numbers of coarse-grained entities instead of more number of fine-grained entities. This, in turn, improves manageability.
- **Improved Network Performance**—Reduces inter-entity bean communication between fine-grained entity bean objects; thereby, resulting in an improved network performance.
- **Reduction in Database Schema Dependency**—Hides the database schema, which is mapped internally to the coarse-grained entity bean, from the client. Therefore, the client is not affected whenever changes are made to the database schema of the mapped coarse-grained entity bean.
- **Increased Object Granularity**—Reduces continuous communication between a client and business tier. The client interacts with a composite entity instead of numerous fine-grained entity beans. The data requested by the client is also sent collectively by returning Transfer Object using single remote call.
- **Facilitating Composite Transfer Object Creation**—Sends the requested data collectively using the composite Transfer Object which is invoked by a single remote call.
- **Overhead of Multi-level Dependent Object Graph**—Involves increased overhead in storing the dependent object graph for the composite entity if it has many levels. Using optimizing strategies involves the overhead of checking the objects whose states have been changed to save the objects selectively.

The Intercepting Filter Pattern

The Intercepting Filter pattern introduces a filter that intercepts and intermediates the request to be received and the responses to be transmitted. The filter allows pre-processing and post-processing of the request and response, respectively. Therefore, the filter can either modify or redirect the request; and post-process or replace the content in the response.

Problem

All the requests received by the presentation tier cannot be directly forwarded to a request handler. Sometimes, the request needs to be modified or pre-processed before it is handed over to the request handler. Similarly, the responses generated in response to a request cannot always be forwarded back to the client directly. Sometimes, the content of the response need to be post-processed or replaced before it is sent to the client. The Intercepting Filter pattern solves this problem by introducing an intercepting filter between incoming requests and outgoing responses; thereby, allowing requests to be pre-processed and responses to be post-processed.

Forces

Following forces are involved in the problem stated in the preceding section:

- Implementation of common processing logic, such as, logging client information, and authentication by a centralized filter. This allows the processing to be carried out on a per request basis.
- Centralization of common logic.
- Addition and removal of services without affecting existing components.

Solution

The problem stated in the preceding section can be solved by introducing intercepting filters that implement common code to process common services for pre-processing incoming requests and post-processing outgoing responses. In this approach, whenever a change is required to be introduced in the processing logic for common services, the core request processing code need not be modified. The intercepting filters implementing the code for common services are independent of the main application and can be added or removed without affecting the application. The intercepting filters can also be chained together in sequence, one after the other.

Figure 21.10 shows the class diagram depicting the Intercepting Filter pattern:

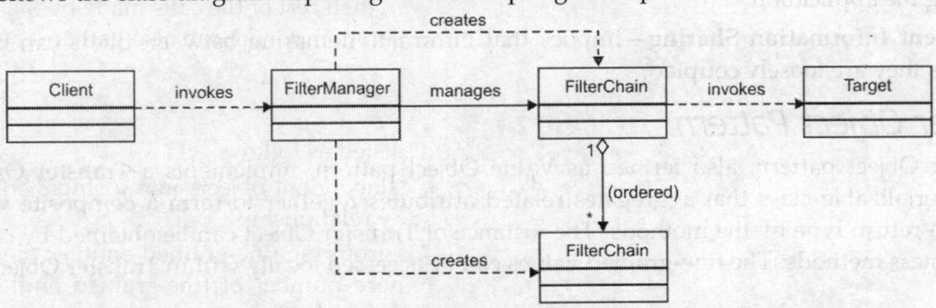

Figure 21.10: Showing the Class Diagram for the Intercepting Filter Pattern

Figure 21.11 shows the sequence diagram representing the interactions between various components of the Intercepting Filter pattern:

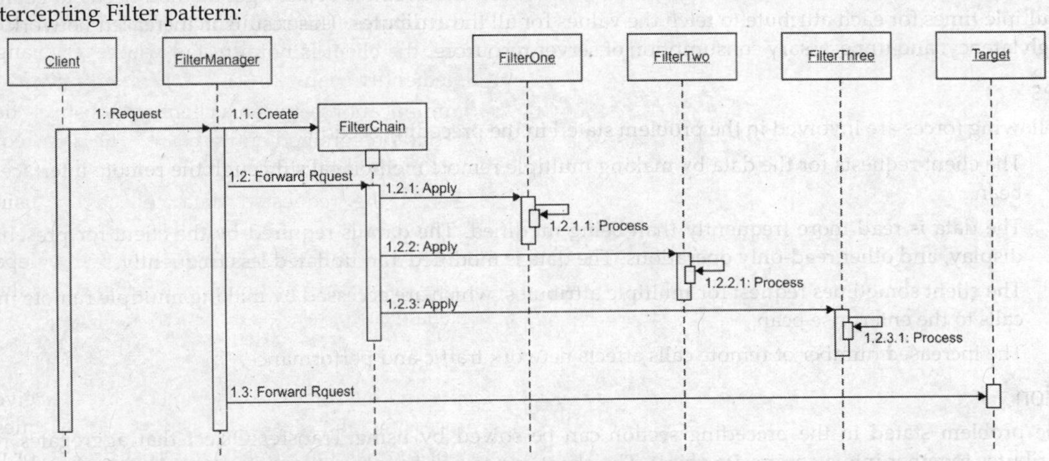

Figure 21.11: Showing the Sequence Diagram for the Intercepting Filter Pattern

Strategies

The Intercepting Filter pattern can be implemented by using the following strategies:

- **Custom Filter Strategy**—Implements the filter by using a user-defined custom strategy. However, it is less effective and less preferable because it does not request and response object in a standard manner.
- **Standard Filter Strategy**—Declares filters using the deployment descriptor. Creation of filter chains as well as addition and removal of filters to those chains follow a standard mechanism. Filters are added and removed declaratively by modifying the deployment descriptor.
- **Base Filter Strategy**—Implements a base filter that acts as a common superclass for all filters. Common features are implemented in the base filter and shared among all the other filters.
- **Template Filter Strategy**—Implements a base filter that is inherited by all other filters and provides template methods whose specific implementations are provided by the respective inheriting filters. The base filter only defines the methods indicating what is to be done. How to accomplish the process using the method is left to individual inheriting filter.

Consequences

The consequences of using Intercepting Filter pattern are as follows:

- **Centralized Control with Loosely Coupled Handlers**—Provides central control mechanism for common services.
- **Improved Reusability**—Implements filters as independent components which can be added or removed independently and reused across varying applications.
- **Declarative and Flexible Configuration**—Implements numerous services in a flexible manner without affecting the application.
- **Inefficient Information Sharing**—Implies that information sharing between filters can be inefficient and costly as they are loosely coupled.

The Transfer Object Pattern

The Transfer Object pattern, also termed as Value Object pattern, implements a Transfer Object component, which is a serializable class that aggregates related attributes together to form a composite value that can be returned as a return type by the methods. The instance of Transfer Object can be obtained by calling the coarse-grained business methods. The fine-grained values can be accessed locally within Transfer Object.

Problem

Sometimes the client requires to access bulk data from an enterprise bean. The requested data may include a set of attributes that are to be accessed together. In such a case, the business object's get method needs to be invoked multiple times for each attribute to fetch the values for all the attributes. This results in increased network traffic, high latency, and unnecessary consumption of server resources.

Forces

Following forces are involved in the problem stated in the preceding section:

- The client requests for the data by making multiple remote method calls through the remote interface to the bean.
- The data is read more frequently than being modified. The data is required by the client for presentation, display, and other read-only operations. The data is modified and updated less frequently.
- The client sometimes request for multiple attributes, which are accessed by making multiple remote method calls to the enterprise bean.
- The increased number of remote calls affects network traffic and performance.

Solution

The problem stated in the preceding section can be solved by using Transfer Object that aggregates related attributes together into a composite object. The client can access Transfer Objects by a single remote method call.

Individual attributes can then be accessed locally from Transfer Object. This significantly helps in reducing network traffic as well as latency, and also provides better resource utilization.

Figure 21.12 shows the class diagram representing the Transfer Object pattern:

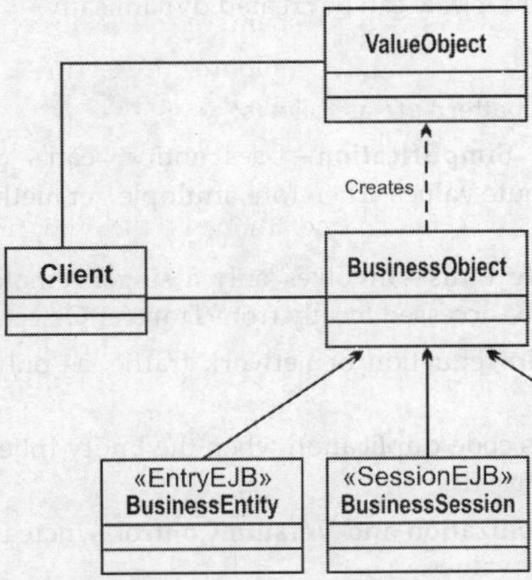

Figure 21.12: Showing the Class Diagram Representing the Transfer Object Pattern

As shown in Figure 21.12, Transfer Object is created on an on-demand basis by the enterprise bean. Figure 21.13 shows the sequence diagram depicting the interaction between various components of the Transfer Object pattern:

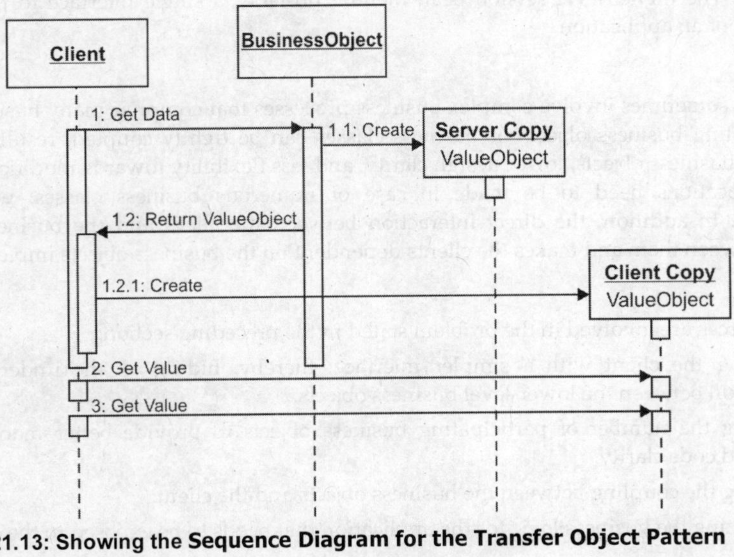

Figure 21.13: Showing the Sequence Diagram for the Transfer Object Pattern

Strategies

Following strategies can be applied to implement the Transfer Object pattern:

- **Updatable Transfer Object Strategy**—Implements Transfer Object that can make data accessible from the business object to the client, as well as from the client back to the business object.
- **Multiple Transfer Object Strategy**—Creates multiple Transfer Objects to manage a single business object.

- **Entity Inherits Transfer Object Strategy**—Specifies that the entity bean inherits the Transfer Object class. Therefore, the attributes specified in the Transfer Object class do not get duplicated in the entity bean.
- **Transfer Object Factory Strategy**—Allows on-demand creation of Transfer Objects by using the concept of reflection. Therefore, multiple Transfer Objects can be created dynamically.

Consequences

The consequences of using Transfer Object pattern are as follows:

- **Entity Bean and Remote Interface Simplification**—Uses entity bean's `getData()` method to fetch Transfer Object that contains the attribute values. Therefore, multiple get methods need not be implemented in the bean's remote interface.
- **More data Transfer in Fewer Remote Calls**—Involves only a single remote call to be made to Transfer Object. Individual attributes can then be accessed locally from Transfer Object.
- **Reduced Network Traffic**—Results in reduction of network traffic, as only one remote call to Transfer Object needs to be made.
- **Reduced Code Duplication**—Reduces code duplication when the Entity Inherit Transfer Object strategy or the Transfer Object Factory strategy is used.
- **Increased Complexity due to Synchronization and Version Control**—Increases complexity when multiple clients request for updates to the entity values.

The Session Facade Pattern

The Session Facade pattern uses a central high level component, which is implemented as a session bean and contains the functionality of the complex interactions that occur between various lower-level business components. The higher-level session bean thereby provides a single interface to the client for accessing the functionality of an application.

Problem

Applications sometimes involve complex business processes that comprise many business objects. In such cases, the participating business objects or business classes can be tightly coupled, resulting in higher dependence between the business objects, lower design clarity, and less flexibility towards modifications. Moreover, multiple method invocations need to be made in case of numerous business classes, which affects the network performance. In addition, the direct interaction between the client and the business objects results in tight coupling between them and makes the clients dependent on the business objects implementation.

Forces

Following forces are involved in the problem stated in the preceding section:

- Providing the client with a simpler interface; thereby, hiding all the underlying complexities in the interaction between the lower-level business objects.
- Reducing the number of participating business objects to provide better manageability, flexibility, and enhanced code clarity.
- Reducing the coupling between the business objects and the client.
- Centralizing the business logic for the application that needs to be exposed to the client.

Solution

The solution to the problem stated in the preceding section lies in aggregating and encapsulating the code for the complex interactions between the business objects into a centralized session bean. The session bean acts as a facade for the lower-level business processes. The session facade provides a simpler centralized higher-level interface for the application's functionality and manages the interaction between the lower-lever business processes. Figure 21.14 shows the class diagram representing the Session Facade pattern:

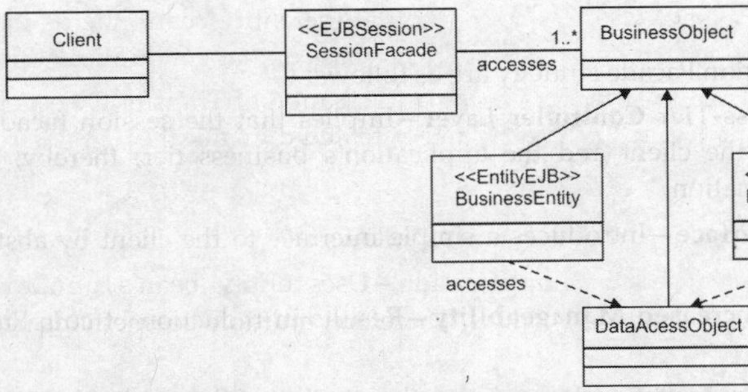

Figure 21.14: Showing the Class Diagram Representing the Session Facade Pattern

As shown in Figure 21.14, business objects are not accessed directly by the client; however, every request to the business object is made through the session bean. Figure 21.15 shows the sequence diagram depicting the interaction between various components of the Session Facade pattern:

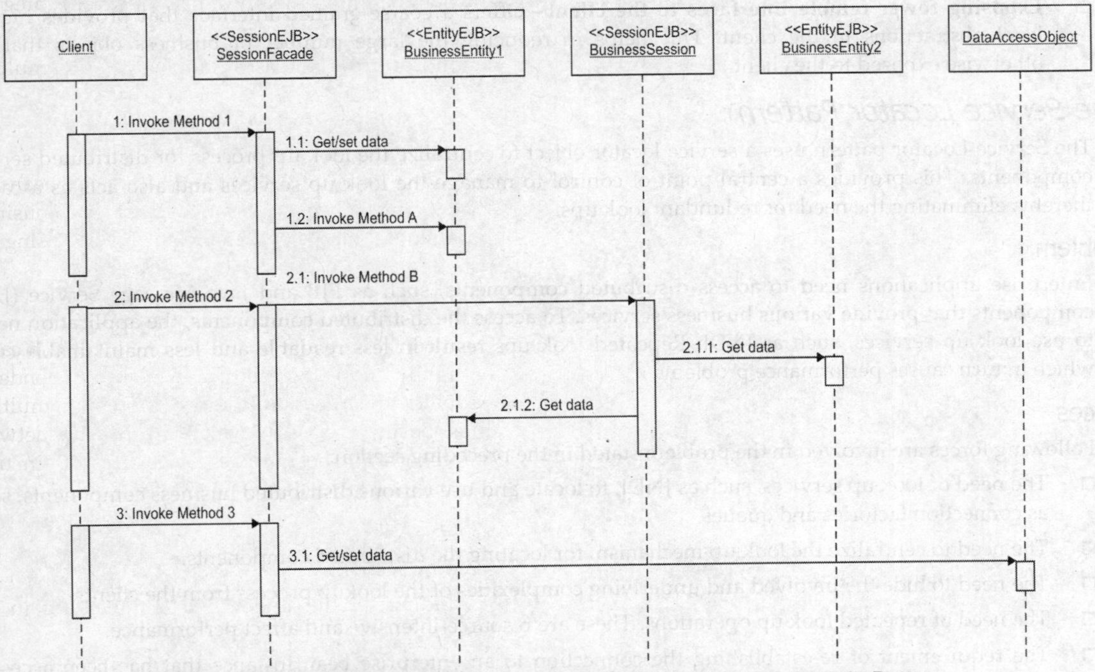

Figure 21.15: Showing the Sequence Diagram for the Session Facade Pattern

Strategies

Following strategies can be used to implement the Session Facade pattern:

- **Stateless Session Facade Strategy**—Implements a business process as a stateless session facade object by using a stateless session bean if the process is non-conversational. Being non-conversational means that the process implemented using stateless session faced strategy gets completed in a single call. The conversational state between subsequent method calls need not be saved.
- **Stateful Session Facade Strategy**—Implements the session facade as a stateful session bean object. This strategy is applied if the business process is conversational and requires multiple method invocations for completion. The conversational state between subsequent method calls need to be saved when this strategy is applied.

Consequences

The consequences of using Session Facade strategy are as follows:

- **Introduction of a Business-Tier Controller Layer**—Implies that the session facade component acts as a controller layer between the client and the application's business tier; thereby, manages all the client interactions with the application.
- **Providing a Uniform Interface**—Introduces a simple interface to the client by abstracting the underlying complex interactions.
- **Reduced Coupling and Increased Manageability**—Results in reduction of coupling between the various objects and the client.
- **Improved Performance**—Improves performance as the number of fine-grained objects is greatly reduced.
- **Providing Coarse-Grained Access**—Provides a coarse-grained abstraction of the application's functionality.
- **Centralized Security Management**—Implements security policy only at the level of the session facade.
- **Centralized Transaction Control**—Applies transaction control at the level of the session facade.
- **Exposing fewer remote interfaces to the client**—Offers a coarse-grained interface that provides higher-level abstractions to the client. This helps in reducing the large number of business objects that are otherwise exposed to the client.

The Service Locator Pattern

The Service Locator pattern uses a service locator object to centralize the look up process for distributed service components. This provides a central point of control to manage the look up services and also acts as a cache; thereby, eliminating the need for redundant look ups.

Problem

Enterprise applications need to access distributed components, such as EJB and Java Message Service (JMS) components that provide various business services. To access the distributed components, the application needs to use look up services, such as JNDI. Repeated look ups result in less readable and less maintainable code, which in turn causes performance problems.

Forces

Following forces are involved in the problem stated in the preceding section:

- The need of look up services, such as JNDI, to locate and use various distributed business components, such as connection factories and queues.
- The need to centralize the look up mechanism for locating the distributed components.
- The need to hide the involved and underlying complexities of the lookup process from the client.
- The need of repeated look up operations. These are resource-intensive and affect performance.
- The requirement of re-establishing the connection to an enterprise bean instance that has been accessed previously.

Solution

The solution to the problem stated in the previous section can be obtained by providing a service locator object that offers a centralized mechanism for the look up process to locate various requested distributed components required by the client. The service locator object abstracts the underlying complexities involved in the look up process. It also provides caching facilities; thereby, providing better management for repeated look up operations. Figure 21.16 shows the class diagram representing the Service Locator pattern:

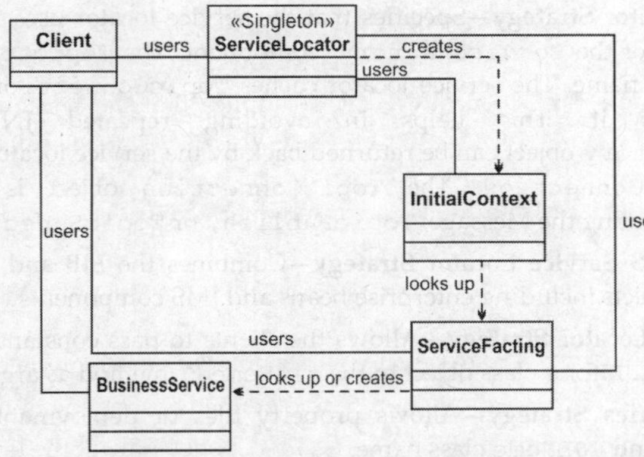

Figure 21.16: Showing the Class Diagram Representing the Service Locator Pattern

Figure 21.17 shows the sequence diagram depicting the interaction between various components of the Service Locator pattern:

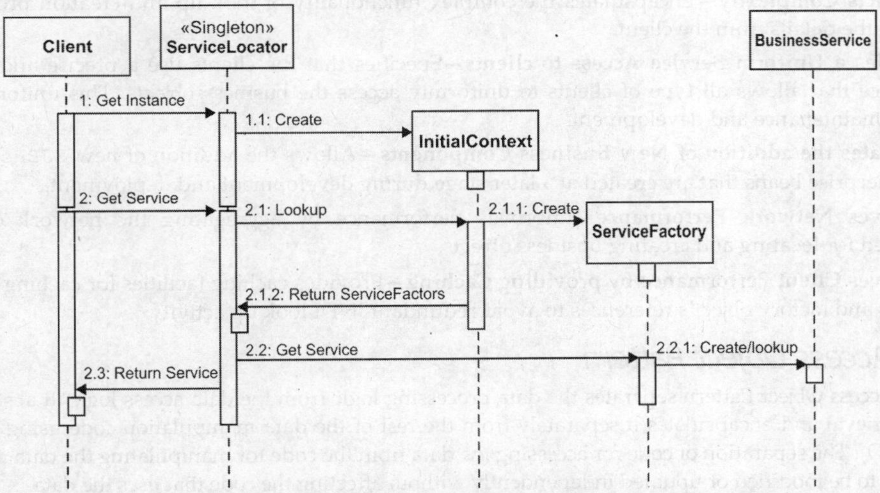

Figure 21.17: Showing the Sequence Diagram of the Service Locator Pattern

Strategies

The Service Locator pattern can be implemented using the following strategies:

- **EJB Service Locator Strategy**—Specifies that the service locator component uses an `EJBHome` object for implementing the `ServiceFactory` component. After obtaining the `EJBHome` object, the service locator component caches it for future use, so that the `EJBHome` object can be easily accessed by the client on next request; thereby, avoiding another JNDI look up. The `EJBHome` object can either be returned to the client who can use it for performing look up operations, or for creating, and removing enterprise beans. Alternatively, the `EJBHome` object can also be retained by the service locator component for later use.
- **JMS Queue Service Locator Strategy**—Specifies that the service locator uses `QueueConnectionFactory` objects to implement the `ServiceFactory` component. The `QueueConnectionFactory` object is obtained using its JNDI name. The service locator caches `QueueConnectionFactory` to use it in future, which avoids multiple look ups to be applied when `QueueConnectionFactory` is required again by the client. The `QueueConnectionFactory` object can be returned by the service locator to the client, who can use it to create a `QueueConnection`. The `QueueConnection` object is required for obtaining a `QueueSession` object, and creating Message, `QueueSender`, or `QueueReciever` objects.

- **JMS Topic Service Locator Strategy**—Specifies that the service locator uses `TopicConnectionFactory` objects to play the role of the `ServiceFactory` component. The `TopicConnectionFactory` object is obtained using its JNDI name. The service locator caches `TopicConnectionFactory` to use it in future when client requires it. This helps in avoiding repeated JNDI look up calls. The `TopicConnectionFactory` object can be returned back by the service locator to the client, who can use it for creating a `TopicConnection`. The `TopicConnection` object is required for obtaining a `TopicSession`, and creating the Message, `TopicPublish`, or `TopicSubscribe` objects.
- **Combined EJB and JMS Service Locator Strategy**—Combines the EJB and JMS strategies for providing service locator for all objects including enterprise beans and JMS components.
- **Type Checked Service Locator Strategy**—Allows the clients to pass constants instead of string names for JNDI service name and `EJBHome` class object to the `getHome()` method as arguments.
- **Service Locator Properties Strategy**—Allows property files or deployment descriptors to be used for specifying JNDI names and `EJBHome` class name.

Consequences

The consequences of using Service Locator pattern are as follows:

- **Abstracts Complexity**—Encapsulates the complex functionality of look up and creation process; thereby, hiding the details from the client.
- **Provides a Uniform Service Access to clients**—Specifies that the clients use a precise and user-friendly interface that allows all type of clients to uniformly access the business objects. This uniformity helps in better maintenance and development.
- **Facilitates the addition of New Business Components**—Allows the addition of new `EJBHome` objects for the enterprise beans that are created at a later stage during development and deployment.
- **Improves Network Performance**—Improves performance by aggregating the network calls that are required for locating and creating business objects.
- **Improves Client Performance by providing Caching**—Provides caching facilities for caching initial context objects and factory object's references to avoid redundant JNDI look up activity.

The Data Access Object Pattern

The Data Access Object Pattern separates the data processing logic from the data access logic. It abstracts the code for data retrieval and encapsulates it separately from the rest of the data manipulation code using a Data Access Object (DAO). The separation of code for accessing the data from the code for manipulating the data allows the data access logic to be modified or updated independently without affecting the code that uses the data.

Problem

In many cases, applications that provide code, which depends on a specific feature of data resources, combine the data processing logic with data access logic. Sometimes, applications need to access data from different resources. The data access code, in such cases, also varies according to the source of data. For example, the code for accessing data from a relational database will be different than the code that accesses data from a flat file. However, when the data processing code is combined with data access code, the code that accesses the data cannot be flexibly replaced or modified as and when the source of data changes.

Forces

Following forces are involved in the problem stated in the preceding section:

- Implementing the code for accessing the data into a persistent storage.
- Providing a uniform data access Application Programming Interface (API) and persistent storage APIs to various data sources.
- Separating persistent storage implementation from the rest of the code.
- Managing the data access logic by encapsulating it into a separate code block; thereby, facilitating maintainability and portability.

- Allowing the code to be flexibly modified and being adaptable when there is a change in the data source, storage type, or product vendor type.

Solution

The solution to the problem stated in the previous section lies in using a DAO that abstracts and encapsulates the logic for accessing the data from various data sources. DAO manages the establishment of a connection with the respective data source. It also fetches and stores the data that can be further used by some other processing block for manipulation and further processing. DAO hides the entire implementation details from the clients. The clients always see a uniform interface that does not change with the change in the data source. Therefore, the Data Access Object pattern allows DAO to flexibly adapt to the changes in the data sources without affecting the clients or the rest of the code. Figure 21.18 shows the class diagram for the Data Access Object pattern:

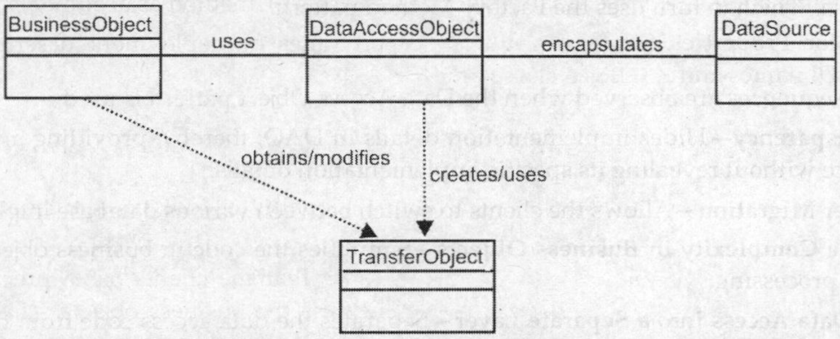

Figure 21.18: Showing the Class Diagram Representing the Data Access Object Pattern

Figure 21.19 shows the sequence diagram for the Data Access Object pattern depicting the relationship between its various participants:

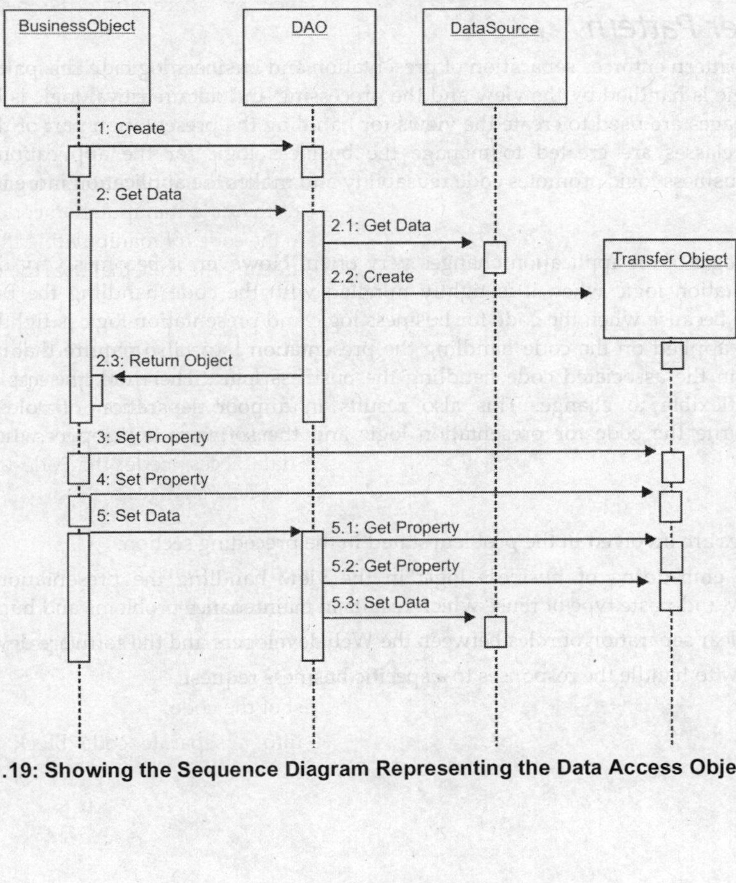

Figure 21.19: Showing the Sequence Diagram Representing the Data Access Object Pattern

Strategies

The Data Access Object pattern can be implemented by applying the following strategies:

- **Automatic DAO Code Generation Strategy**—Implements an application-specific code-generation utility to generate the code for all DAOs that the application requires. To implement this strategy, a relationship between the `BusinessObject` component, the DAO component, and the underlying implementation needs to be established.
- **Factory for Data Access Objects Strategy**—Uses Abstract Factory and Factory Method patterns to create DAO. This strategy is implemented using the Factory Method pattern to create the DAOs required by the application when the storage does not change between multiple implementations. When the storage is expected to change between various implementations, this strategy is implemented using the Abstract Factory pattern, which in turn uses the Factory Method pattern.

Consequences

The following consequences are observed when the Data Access Object pattern is used:

- **Enables Transparency**—Hides implementation details in DAO; thereby, providing a transparent access to the data source without revealing its specific implementation details.
- **Enables Easier Migration**—Allows the clients to switch between various database implementations.
- **Reduces Code Complexity in Business Objects**—Simplifies the code in business objects that use DAOs to fetch data for processing.
- **Centralizes Data Access into a Separate Layer**—Separates the data access code from the rest of the code of the application; thereby, allowing better management and maintenance of the application.
- **Adds Extra Layer**—Creates an additional layer between the data source and the data client that requires additional effort for implementation.

The View Helper Pattern

The View Helper pattern enforces separation of presentation and business logic. In this pattern, the presentation and formatting logic is handled by the view and the processing and data retrieval logic is handled by the View Helper class. JSP pages are used to create the views for handling the presentation part of the application, while JavaBeans helper classes are created to manage the business logic for the application. The separation of presentation and business logic promotes code reusability and makes the application more manageable.

Problem

The presentation logic of an application changes very often. However, it becomes very difficult to modify or change the presentation logic when it is tightly mingled with the code handling the business logic for the application. This is because when the code for business logic and presentation logic is tightly intermingled, then any changes to be applied on the code handling the presentation logic also require that considerable relevant changes be made in the associated code handling the business logic. Therefore, the application becomes less manageable and flexible to change. This also results in a poor separation of roles between the Web developers who write the code for presentation logic and the software developers who write the code for business logic.

Forces

The following forces are involved in the problem stated in the preceding section:

- Avoiding the embedding of business logic in the view handling the presentation logic because that promotes copy-and-paste type of reuse which results in maintenance problems and bugs.
- Promoting a clear separation of roles between the Web developers and the software developers.
- Using one view to handle the responses to a specific business request.

Solution

The solution to the problem stated in the previous section is to provide a clear separation between the presentation logic and the business logic. The presentation logic is provided by the views which are JSP pages in most of the cases. The views handle formatting and presentation of content, and delegate the responsibility of processing to the helper classes. The helper classes, normally implemented as JavaBeans or custom tags, handle the business logic for the application. These classes also store any intermediate data for the views. This separation of presentation logic from business logic makes the code more manageable and flexible to change as any change in the presentation logic can be made without affecting the business logic for the application. The View Helper pattern also provides a clear separation of roles between the Web developers and the software developers. Figure 21.20 shows the class diagram representing the View Helper pattern:

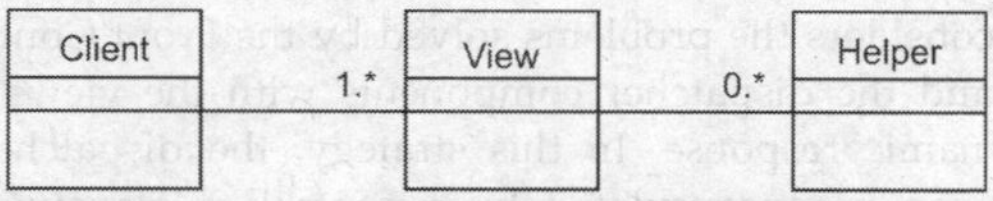

Figure 21.20: Showing the Class Diagram Representing the View Helper Pattern

Figure 21.21 shows the sequence diagram for the View Helper pattern depicting the interaction between its various participants:

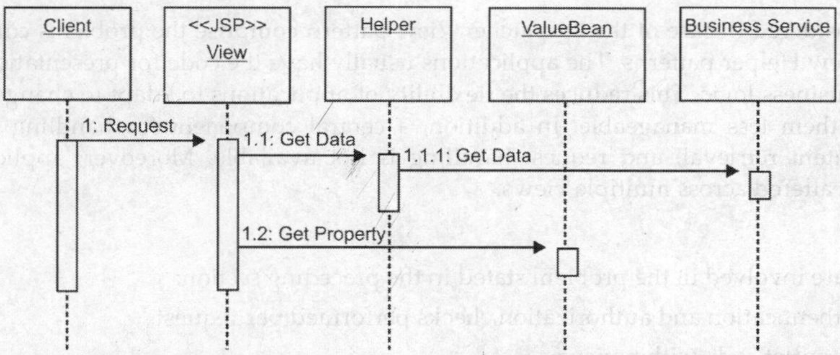

Figure 21.21: Showing the Sequence Diagram for the View Helper Pattern

Strategies

Following strategies can be applied for implementing the View Helper pattern:

- **JSP View Strategy**—Specifies that a view is implemented as JSP page. This strategy is preferred over the Servlet View strategy. JSP pages are used more commonly and provide a more elegant solution for creating the views as it is easier to code JSP pages as compared to creating servlets.
- **Servlet View Strategy**—Uses a servlet for implementing a view. However, it is more difficult to code servlets because servlets have markup tags embedded directly within Java code. This makes it very difficult to modify and update the code.
- **JavaBean Helper Strategy**—Uses a JavaBean to implement a helper. The JavaBean helper encapsulates the code for implementing the business logic. Using JavaBeans to implement helper classes makes the code more manageable. Moreover, it is easier to create JavaBeans.
- **Custom Tag Helper Strategy**—Uses a custom tag component to implement the helper that encapsulates the business logic. However, developing custom tags is a complicated task as compared to creating JavaBeans. To use the Custom Tag Helper strategy, the environment is required to be configured with various tags, tag library descriptors, and configuration files.
- **Business Delegate as Helper Strategy**—Specifies that a Business Delegate component should be introduced between the helper and the business tier. This allows the helper to directly invoke a business service without worrying about its implementation details. The business delegate can be implemented as a JavaBean and can be considered as a specialized type of helper.
- **Transformer Helper Strategy**—Implements the helper as an extensible Stylesheet Language Transformer.

Consequences

The consequences of using the View Helper pattern are as follows:

- **Improves reusability, manageability and application partitioning**—Makes the application more manageable by clearly separating business logic from presentation logic. This also improves code reusability and maintainability.
- **Improves Separation of Roles**—Provides clear role separation between the Web developers who code the presentation logic for the views and the software developers who code the business logic for the view helper classes.

The Dispatcher View Pattern

The Dispatcher View pattern considers the problems solved by the Front Controller and View Helper patterns, and combines the controller and the dispatcher components with the views and helpers for handling client requests and providing a dynamic response. In this strategy, the dispatcher handles view navigation and management. The dispatcher can be encapsulated by a controller, a view, or some other component. The controllers do not directly delegate the activity of content retrieval to the handlers. The activities are postponed until views are processed.

Problem

The problems considered in case of the Dispatcher View pattern comprise the problems considered in the Front Controller and View Helper patterns. The applications usually have the code for presentation logic intermingled with that of the business logic. This reduces the flexibility of applications to adapt to changes and modifications; thereby, making them less manageable. In addition, a central component for handling access control, view management, content retrieval, and request handling is not available. Moreover, applications usually have redundant code scattered across multiple views.

Forces

Following forces are involved in the problem stated in the preceding section:

- Complete authentication and authorization checks performed per request
- Minimized scriptlet code within views
- Encapsulation of business logic in separate components other than views
- Simplified control flow based on values supplied with request
- Limited and simpler view management logic

Solution

The solution to the problem stated in the previous section lies in combining the controller and the dispatcher with the views and helpers for handling the client requests and preparing a dynamic presentation as the response. In this strategy, the controllers do not delegate the content retrieval activities directly to the helpers. The dispatcher plays a minimized role and forwards the request to the views on the basis of input received from the controller; thereby, handling view navigation and management. On processing, the views handle the request and generate a response by accessing the helper classes. Figure 21.22 shows the class diagram for the Dispatcher View pattern:

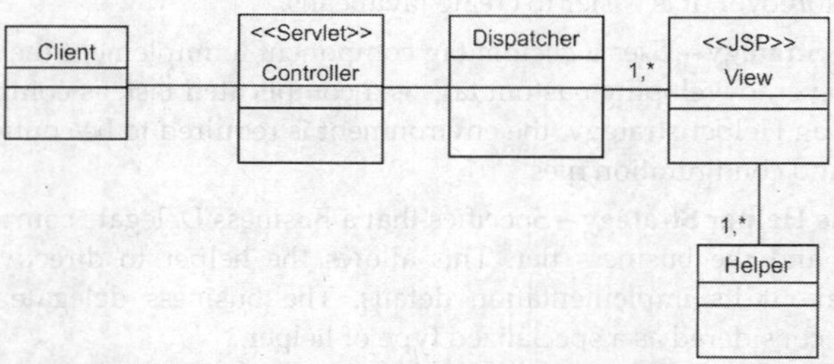

Figure 21.22: Showing the Class Diagram Representing the Dispatcher View Pattern

Figure 21.23 shows the sequence diagram for the Dispatcher View pattern depicting the interactions between its various participants:

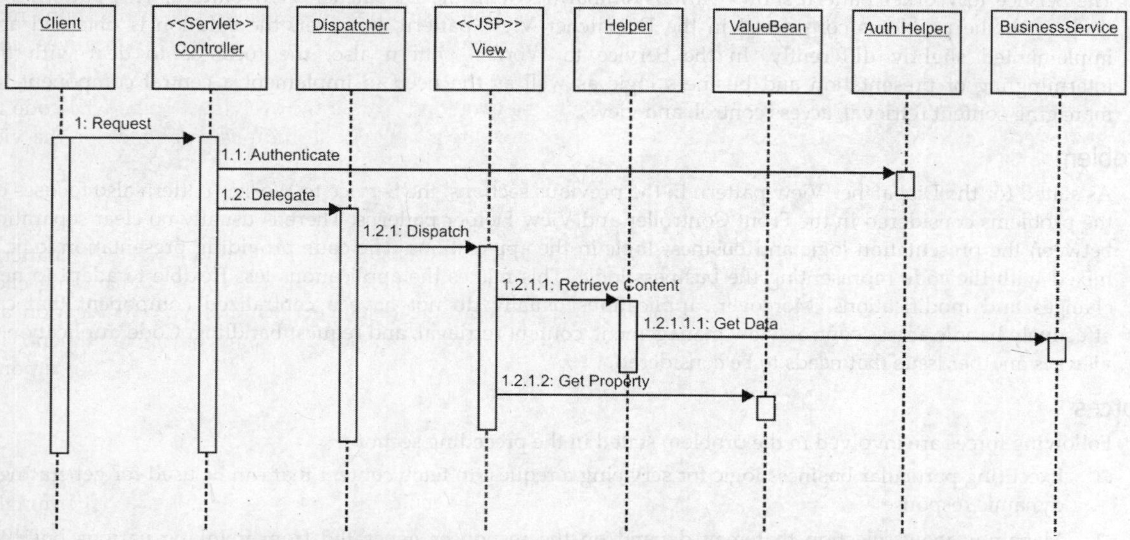

Figure 21.23: Showing the Sequence Diagram for the Dispatcher View Pattern

Strategies

The Dispatcher View pattern can be applied by using various strategies that are listed as follows:

- Servlet Front Strategy
- JSP Page Front Strategy
- JSP View Strategy
- Servlet View Strategy
- JavaBean Helper Strategy
- Custom Tag Helper Strategy
- Dispatcher in Controller Strategy
- Transformer Helper Strategy

Besides the preceding strategies, another strategy that can be used for implementing the Dispatcher View pattern is described as follows:

- **Dispatcher in View Strategy**—Specifies that in case when the controller has a limited role and therefore, is removed from the application implementation; then the dispatcher can be moved into a view. This design is found useful when there is one view that is mapped to a particular request while a secondary view can be used infrequently.

Consequences

The consequences of using Dispatcher View pattern are as follows:

- **Centralizes control thereby improving reusability and maintainability**—Provides a centralized control for the process of request handling and dispatching; thereby, enhancing code reusability and making the application more manageable.
- **Improves application partitioning**—Provides clear separation between the presentation logic coded in views and the business logic coded in helpers.
- **Improves the separation of roles**—Provides clear role separation between Web developers who code the views and the software developers who code the helper classes.

The Service to Worker Pattern

The Service to Worker pattern shows various similarities with the Dispatcher View pattern. This pattern also deals with the problems considered in the Dispatcher View pattern; however, the solution is obtained and implemented slightly differently. In the Service to Worker pattern also, the focus is to deal with the intermingling of presentation and business logic as well as the need to implement a central component for managing content retrieval, access control, and views.

Problem

As stated for the Dispatcher View pattern in the previous sections, the Service to Worker pattern also focuses on the problems considered in the Front Controller and View Helper patterns. There is usually no clear separation between the presentation logic and business logic in the applications. The code providing presentation logic is mixed with the code representing the business logic. This makes the applications less flexible to adapt to new changes and modifications. Moreover, applications usually do not have a centralized component that can effectively handle access control, view management, content retrieval, and request handling. Code duplication in views is another issue that needs to be considered.

Forces

Following forces are involved in the problem stated in the preceding section:

- Executing particular business logic for servicing a request to fetch content that can be used for generating a dynamic response
- Managing view selection that may depend on the responses generated from invoking various business services
- Minimizing scriptlet code within views
- Encapsulating business logic in separate components other than views
- Generating content dynamically
- Using multiple views for responding to similar requests

Solution

As in case of the Dispatcher View pattern, the solution in this case is also obtained by combining the controller and the dispatcher with the views and helpers for handling the client requests and preparing a dynamic presentation as the response. However, in the Service to Worker pattern, unlike the Dispatcher View pattern, the controller delegates the content retrieval activities directly to the helpers. The dispatcher, in this case, submits the request to the appropriate view; thereby, handling view navigation and management. The views then handle the request and generate a dynamic response accordingly with the help of the helper classes. In the Service to Worker pattern, the dispatcher plays a comparatively larger role as compared to the Dispatcher View pattern, and can be implemented as a separate component or within a controller. Figure 21.24 shows the class diagram for the Service to Worker pattern:

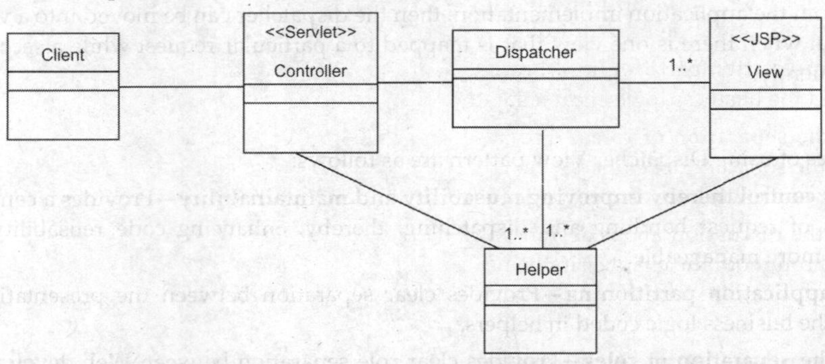

Figure 21.24: Showing the Class Diagram Representing the Service to Worker Pattern

Figure 21.25 shows the sequence diagram depicting the relationship between various participants of the Service to Worker pattern:

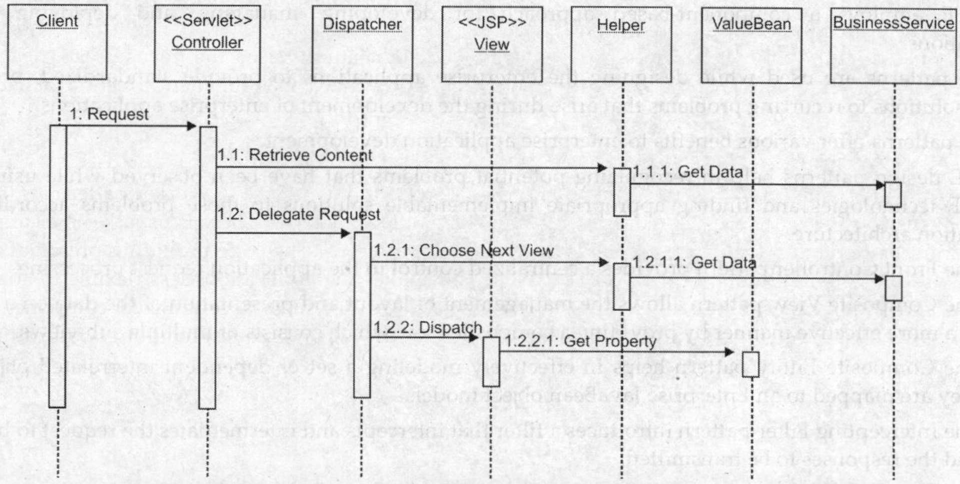

Figure 21.25: Showing the Sequence Diagram for the Service to Worker Pattern

Strategies

The Service to Worker pattern can be applied by using various strategies, which are listed as follows:

- Servlet Front Strategy
- JSP Page Front Strategy
- JSP View Strategy
- Servlet View Strategy
- JavaBean Helper Strategy
- Custom Tag Helper Strategy
- Dispatcher in Controller Strategy
- Transformer Helper Strategy

Consequences

The consequences of using the Service to Worker pattern are as follows:

- **Centralizes control thereby improving modularity and reusability**—Provides a centralized control for the process of handling business services and processing across multiple requests. The Service to Worker pattern also provides improved modularity by allowing clearer partitioning between various components and moving common code into controllers, helpers, and views.
- **Improves application partitioning**—Provides clear separation between the presentation logic encapsulated in views and the business logic encapsulated in helpers.
- **Improves the separation of roles**—Provides clear role separation between Web developers who code the views and the software developers who code the helper classes. This separation also reduces dependencies among the people working on the application.

This completes the discussion about design patterns. Before finishing the chapter, let's quickly summarize the topics covered throughout the chapter, in the next section.

Summary

In this chapter, you have learned about the Java EE application architecture. Next, the chapter introduced the concept of design patterns. Further, it discussed the role of design patterns. You have also learned the different types of design patterns, including the problems faced, forces involved, solution implemented by the pattern, strategies that can be applied to implement the pattern, and the consequences observed when the various patterns are applied. Let's recall the following important points to summarize the chapter:

Java EE employs a component-based approach for developing, managing, and deploying enterprise applications.

Design patterns are used while designing the enterprise applications to provide standardized, proven, and tested solutions to recurring problems that arise during the development of enterprise applications.

Design patterns offer various benefits to enterprise application development.

Java EE design patterns help in recognizing potential problems that have been observed while using various Java EE technologies and finding appropriate implementable solutions to those problems according to the application architecture.

- The Front Controller pattern provides a centralized control to the application request processing.
- The Composite View pattern allows the management of layout and presentation of the data on a Web page in a more effective manner by providing a composite view which consists of multiple sub-views.
- The Composite Entity pattern helps in effectively modeling a set of dependent interrelated objects when they are mapped to an Enterprise JavaBean object model.
- The Intercepting Filter pattern introduces a filter that intercepts and intermediates the request to be received and the responses to be transmitted.
- The Transfer Object pattern, also termed as Value Object pattern, implements a Transfer Object component, which is a serializable class that aggregates related attributes together to form a composite value that can be returned as a return type by the methods.
- The Session Facade pattern uses a central high level component, which is implemented as a session bean and contains the functionality of the complex interactions that occur between various lower-level business components.
- The Service Locator pattern uses a service locator object to centralize the look up process for distributed service components.
- The Data Access Object Pattern separates the data processing logic from the data access logic.
- The View Helper pattern enforces separation of presentation and business logic.
- The Dispatcher View pattern considers the problems solved by the Front Controller and View Helper patterns, and combines the controller and the dispatcher components with the views and helpers for handling client requests and providing a dynamic response.
- The Service to Worker pattern shows various similarities with the Dispatcher View pattern.

Exercise

Q. 21.1 What is a design pattern?

Q. 21.2 What are the benefits of using design patterns?

Q. 21.3 What are the benefits of using the Front Controller pattern?

Q. 21.4 What is Session Facade?

Q. 21.5 What is a Data Access Object (DAO)?

Q. 21.6 What is the use of Service Locator pattern?

22

Implementing Security in Web Applications

Web applications need to be protected and their resources secured against malicious users who can cause harm to the applications in numerous ways, such as by disclosing confidential information, modifying or destroying original information, or inappropriately using the resources. Although it is not possible to completely secure a Web application, the threats to it can be reduced to an acceptable level by using security mechanisms such as authentication and authorization. We have various security technologies in the Java platform, which include a large set of APIs, implementations for commonly used security mechanisms, and protocols. The Java security APIs provide various features including cryptography, public key infrastructure, secure communication, authentication, and access control.

This chapter describes various security mechanisms used in Web applications, such as authentication and authorization, and explains how these mechanisms are used to secure the applications. The chapter also discusses various HTTP authentication mechanisms. In addition, it explains how to implement Web security using declarative security and programmatic security. However, before we start discussing these security mechanisms, let's first look at the Java Authentication and Authorization Service (JAAS) API, which is used to implement authentication in Web applications.

Exploring JAAS

JAAS API is used to implement authentication and authorization in Java applications. JAAS was introduced as an optional package in the Java 2 Platform, Standard Edition, version 1.3; and has been integrated into the Java 2 Platform, Standard Edition, version 1.4. JAAS authentication is based on the Pluggable Authentication Module (PAM) framework or architecture, described later in the chapter. JAAS enables Java applications to remain independent from the underlying authentication technologies. The JAAS API is a set of classes that enable services to authenticate and enforce access controls on users. The JAAS API is used for three purposes:

- Authenticating users to securely determine who is executing the Java code, regardless of whether the code is a stand-alone Java application, an Applet, a Bean, or a Servlet.
- Authorizing users to ensure they have the right permissions required to perform the respective actions.
- Implementing data integrity

Let's now look at authentication, authorization, and data integrity in detail.

Implementing Authentication with JAAS

Authentication is the process of checking the validity of the security details submitted by a user. It is used by Web applications to relate a user identity to an HTTP session accessing a resource of a Web application. This resource may be protected; and authentication is used to validate the user identity and check whether the user is authorized to access the resource. To understand the concept of authentication better, take the example of Internet banking or Web-based emails. In these cases, identity of a user is related to a real person and access depends on some proof of the identity based on authentication parameters.

An application that performs authentication is known as authenticator. An authenticator requires certain security details, which vary for different applications. Therefore, different authenticators (or different authentication technologies) are required to handle different security requirements. This, in turn, has brought in third-party vendors to provide various authenticators. Apart from this, we can also develop our own authenticators using the JAAS API. The JAAS API provides a standard abstraction through which a Java application can communicate with any vendor-provided authenticators.

As already stated, JAAS authentication is based on the PAM framework, as shown in Figure 22.1.

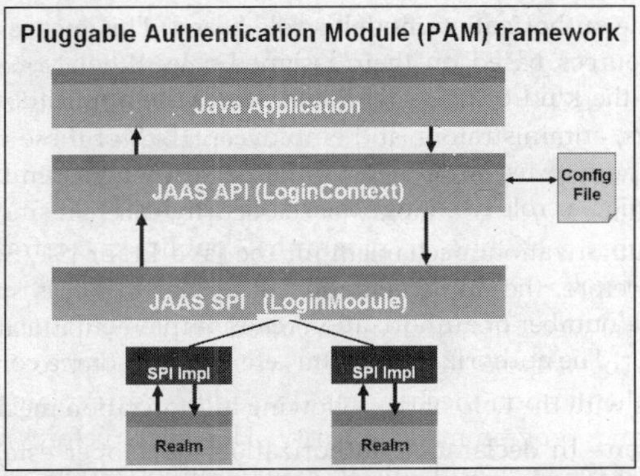

Figure 22.1: Showing the Authentication Architecture of the PAM Framework

As shown in Figure 22.1, when a Web application creates a `LoginContext` object and requests for login, the following operations are performed:

i. One or more `LoginModule` implementations are configured according to their names in the `Config` file associated with the `LoginContext` object. This is done during the creation of the `LoginContext` object.

ii. When the login method is invoked on the `LoginContext` object, the `LoginContext` object instantiates a new empty `javax.security.auth.Subject` object. The `LoginContext` object constructs the configured `LoginModule` implementation class and initializes it with the `Subject` object and the given `CallBackHandler` class, which receives all JAAS events, and then returns the results back to JAAS.

iii. The login method of the `LoginContext` object calls the methods in the `LoginModule` implementation class to perform login and authentication. The `LoginModule` implementation class utilizes the given `CallBackHandler` class to obtain the security details and checks their validity.

iv. If authentication is successful, the `LoginModule` implementation class associates the relevant Principals (authenticated identities) and credentials (authentication data such as cryptographic keys) with the `Subject` object.

The Servlet specification provides support for the Web container to perform authentication through the `<security-constraint>` element in the deployment descriptor, `web.xml`. The Servlet specification provides the following types of authentication:

- **HTTP basic authentication**—It refers to protect Web resources through specified username and password. This is the simplest authentication method supported by a Web application.
- **HTTP digest authentication**—This is similar to the HTTP basic authentication, but with a small difference — the information transmitted from the Web browser to the server in HTTP basic authentication contains a password in HTTP digest authentication. However, HTTP digest authentication is rarely used because only few Web browsers support this type of authentication.
- **Form-based authentication**—This type of authentication is more advantageous than HTTP basic authentication because of two reasons. First, form-based authentication provides a visual effect by using HTML in a Web application; and second, form-based authentication is implemented by using server-side session tracking, so the session can be invalidated when the user logs out.

We discuss HTTP authentication mechanisms later in this chapter. For now, let's take up authorization.

Describing Authorization in Web Applications

Authorization is a process of ascertaining whether an authenticated user has permission to access a requested service. The application performing this operation is known as an authorizer. Authentication is different from authorization in that authorization determines whether the user has permission to access specific resources, whereas authentication checks the identity of the user accessing the resources. The authorization process verifies whether the user has permission to access the resources by comparing the Principal role submitted by the user during the logon process with the role of the same user existing in the authorization database.

In the Servlet specification, the authorization model is role-based. This means that once a user is authenticated, he or she can access the resources based on their assigned role. When you develop a Web application, you should always keep in mind the kind of users who will access the application. For example, a `Login` module may be accessed by customers, administrators, and employees. Each of these user categories is called a security role, an abstract logical grouping of users defined by the person who assembles the application. Users can be added or removed from a particular role to change their access rights.

The implementation of the authorization mechanism for the Java EE or JSP/Servlet container is not defined by the Servlet specification. Therefore, the implementation of authorization is specific to the Web container. The Tomcat Web server supports a number of authorization realm implementations, such as an XML file, the relation database and LDAP connector. The authorization realm refers to a resource containing authorization details.

You can access Web resources with the help of the following authorization mechanisms:

- **Declarative Authorization**—In declarative authorization, developer establishes container-enforced access control rules associated with a Java EE application. This model is based on client-initiated requests.
- **Programmatic Authorization**—This model requires the implementation of rules of authorization within the Java code of a Web application, but it uses the Servlet security framework to authenticate the users.

Let's now discuss data integrity with reference to JAAS API.

Implementing Data Integrity with JAAS API

Data integrity is the property that restricts or prevents data from being modified during data transmission. A Web application developer can do little to affect data integrity since this is the responsibility of the Servlet container. Additionally, we can use the HTTP/SSL connection, which provides the data integrity feature.

Now, after understanding the concept of security in the context of authorization, authentication, and data integrity, let's learn about HTTP authentication mechanisms.

Exploring HTTP Authentication Mechanisms

When a user tries to access a protected Web resource, the Web container activates the authentication mechanism configured for that resource in the `web.xml` file. You can use the following authentication mechanisms to protect your resources:

- HTTP basic authentication
- Form-based authentication
- Client-certificate authentication
- HTTP digest authentication

NOTE

If you do not specify any of these mechanisms in the `web.xml` file, authentication will not be performed.

Let's now discuss these mechanisms in detail one by one.

Describing HTTP Basic Authentication

Figure 22.2 shows the process of HTTP basic authentication.

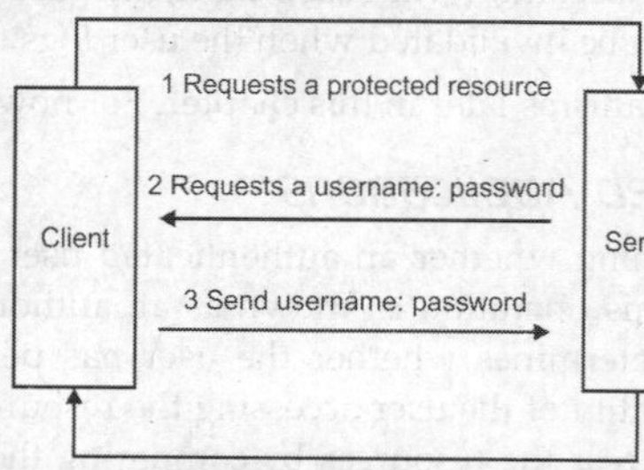

Figure 22.2: Showing HTTP Basic Authentication

As shown in Figure 22.2, the following events occur in HTTP basic authentication:

1. A client requests access to a protected resource.
2. The Web server requests the client's name and password of the client, which are entered through a dialog box.
3. The Web server validates the user credentials and, if successful, the server returns the requested resource.

Note that HTTP basic authentication is not particularly secure since it sends user names and passwords over the Internet as UU-encoded (Unix-to-Unix encoded) encrypted text, which can be easily decoded.

Describing Form-based Authentication

In form-based authentication, the user name and password of a client is sent as plain text, and the target server is not authenticated. This authentication mechanism can expose user names and passwords, which can be easily decoded, unless the connections are established over **Secure Sockets Layer (SSL)**. In form-based authentication, you can customize the login and error pages of an application, which are displayed for the user. Figure 22.3 shows the working of form-based authentication.

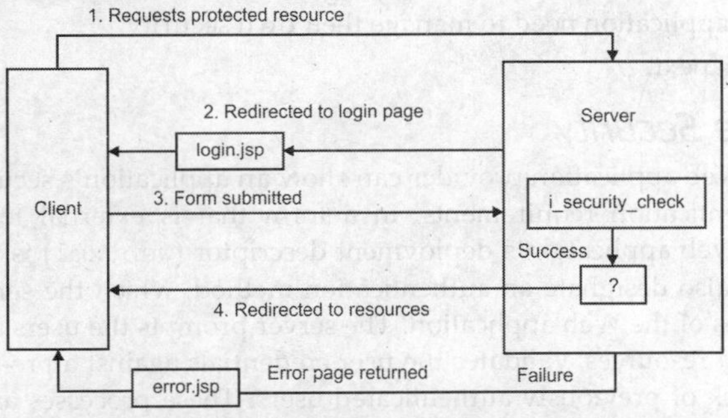

Figure 22.3: Showing Form-based Authentication

As shown in Figure 22.3, the following events occur in form-based authentication:

1. A client requests access to a protected resource.
2. If the client is authenticated, the server redirects the client to the login page.
3. The client submits the login form to the Web server.
4. If the login is successful, the server redirects the client to the requested resource. However, if the login fails, the client is redirected to an error page.

Describing Client-Certificate Authentication

Client-certificate authentication is a more secure method of authentication than either basic or form-based authentication since it uses HTTP over SSL (HTTPS). In client-certificate authentication, the server and, optionally, the client, authenticate each other using public key certificates. A public key certificate is a digitally signed document used to validate a username and authorization. It is issued by a trusted organization, called a certificate authority (CA), and provides identification for the bearer. SSL (HTTPS) provides data encryption, server authentication, message integrity, and optional client authentication for a TCP/IP connection.

If you specify client-certificate authentication, the Web server authenticates the client by using the client's X.509 certificate, which is a public key certificate that conforms to a standard defined by X.509 Public Key Infrastructure (PKI). Before running an application that uses SSL (HTTPS), you must configure SSL (HTTPS) support on the Web server and set up the public key certificate.

Describing HTTP Digest Authentication

Similar to HTTP basic authentication, HTTP digest authentication authenticates users based on their user names and passwords. However, HTTP digest authentication is performed by transmitting the password in encrypted form, which is more secure than the simple base64 encoding used by basic authentication. Digest authentication is currently not widely used since it is a new HTTP 1.1 feature and not supported by all browsers. If a non-compliant browser makes a request on a server that requires digest authentication, the server rejects the request and sends an error message.

After learning about various authentication mechanisms, let's now learn about Web security, and see how it can be implemented in Web applications by using the different authentication mechanisms.

Securing Web Applications

A Web application contains resources, which can be accessed by multiple users. These resources often traverse unprotected, open networks, such as the Internet. Consequently, a Web application needs to implement security. Web containers provide support to implement security for Web applications through the JAAS API. Web security can be implemented in the following two ways:

1. **Declarative Security**—When implementing declarative security in a Web application, the Servlets or JSP pages of the Web application do not need any security-related code. Instead, the major security aspects are handled by the Web container.
2. **Programmatic Security**—When implementing programmatic security in a Web application, Servlets and JSP pages of the Web application need to manage their own security.

Let's explore these in detail next.

Describing Declarative Security

In declarative security, a Web application provider can show an application's security structure, including roles, access control, and authentication requirements, in a form that is external to the application. To prevent unauthorized access, the Web application's deployment descriptor (`web.xml`) is used to declare the URLs that need protection. You can also designate an authentication method, which the server uses to identify the users requesting for the resources of the Web application. The server prompts the users for user names and passwords when they access restricted resources, validates the user credentials against a pre-defined set of user names and passwords, and keeps track of previously authenticated users. These processes are performed in a transparent manner in Servlets and JSP pages.

Declarative security is server-based in most cases. This means that the server's configuration is used to provide protection to a resource or a set of resources. The container's authentication and authorization schemes are used to protect the resources from unauthorized users. This security model applies to the static content of a Web application and to the dynamic code (Servlets, filters and JSP pages) requested by a client within the application.

Using Declarative Security

In this section, we create a simple application (which we call **simpledeclarativeex**) to demonstrate the implementation of declarative security through the basic authentication method. In this application, the user name and password dialog box appears when a user submits an HTML form. The server then validates the credentials and if validation is successful, the protected resource requested by the user is displayed. Otherwise, an error message is displayed.

Now, perform the following broad-level steps to create the application:

1. Create a Web Client for HTTP Basic Authentication
2. Configure the Application
3. Create the Web Resource Servlet
4. Create Roles and Users
5. Arranging Files
6. Run the Application

Creating a Web Client for HTTP Basic Authentication

In this section, we create a Web client, Hello.html, which initiates the request for a protected resource. Listing 22.1 provides the code for the Hello.html file. The Hello.html file creates two HTML submit type buttons. When a user submits this form by clicking either of these buttons, the control is forwarded to the URL path `testser`, which is mapped to `TestServlet` in Listing 22.2 (you can file this file online in the code/Chapter22 folder).

Listing 22.1: Creating the Hello.html File

```
<html>
    <body>
            <form method=post action="testser">
<input type="submit" value="Make a POST Request to access TestServlet"/>
            </form><br><br>
            <form method=get action="testser">
<input type="submit" value="Make a GET Request to access TestServlet"/>
            </form>
    </body>
</html>
```

In Listing 22.1, Hello.html is the Web client for HTTP basic authentication. Now, let's learn how to configure the **simpledeclarativeex** application and implement the HTTP basic method of authentication.

Configuring the Application

To configure this application, we use the `web.xml` file. This file maps the action URL `testser` forwarded by Home.html to the `TestServlet` class, and defines the security constraints. Listing 22.2 provides the code for the web.xml file. You can also find this file online in the code/Chapter22 folder.

Listing 22.2: Creating the `web.xml` File

```
<?xml version="1.0" encoding="UTF-8"?>
<web-app>
    <servlet>
            <servlet-name>ts</servlet-name>
            <servlet-class>com.santosh.servlets.TestServlet</servlet-class>
    </servlet>
    <servlet-mapping>
            <servlet-name>ts</servlet-name>
            <url-pattern>/testser</url-pattern>
    </servlet-mapping>
    <security-constraint>
            <web-resource-collection>
                    <web-resource-name>myres</web-resource-name>
                    <url-pattern>/testser</url-pattern>
                    <!--<http-method>POST</http-method>-->
                    <!--Uncomment the above line to perform security
                            check only for HTTP POST method request-->
            </web-resource-collection>
            <auth-constraint>
                    <role-name>myrole1</role-name>
            </auth-constraint>
    </security-constraint>
    <login-config>
            <auth-method>BASIC</auth-method>
    </login-config>
    <security-role>
            <role-name>myrole1</role-name>
    </security-role>
    <welcome-file-list>
            <welcome-file>Hello.html</welcome-file>
    </welcome-file-list>
</web-app>
```

In Listing 22.2, the <security-constraint></security-constraint> element defines the Web resource being protected. The Web resource with `testser`, url-pattern is protected for users assigned the myrole1 role. The <security-role> element defines the logical grouping of the users defined by the application developer or assembler. Note that the authentication method specified in Listing 22.2 is BASIC.

The `TestServlet` class is mapped to the URL path `testser`. Therefore, the `TestServlet` class is a protected Web resource for the users who are assigned the `myrole1` role group.

Creating the Web Resource Servlet

As discussed, `TestServlet` is the Web resource accessed by users defined under the `myrole1` role group. Listing 22.3 provides the code for the TestServlet.java file. The TestServlet.java file is created in the `com.santosh.servlets` package. You can find this file online in the code/Chapter22 folder as well.

Listing 22.3: Creating the TestServlet.java File

```
package com.santosh.servlets;

import javax.servlet.*;
import javax.servlet.http.*;
import java.security.*;
import java.io.*;
/**
 * @author Santosh
 */
public class TestServlet extends HttpServlet {

    public void service(HttpServletRequest req, HttpServletResponse res)
    throws ServletException,IOException {

        Principal p=req.getUserPrincipal();
        String principal_name="UnAuthenticated";
        if (p!=null)
                principal_name=p.getName();

        PrintWriter out=res.getWriter();
out.println("User <b>"+principal_name+"</b> has requested for TestServlet");
  }// end doGet
}// end class
```

In Listing 22.3, `TestServlet` is the `HttpServlet` class, which calls the `getUserPrincipal ()` method on the request object. The `getUserPrincipal()` method returns a `java.security.Principal` object containing the name of the current authenticated user.

Next, let's create roles and users for the application.

Creating Roles and Users

Create the role named `myrole1` and username `santosh` with password as `myrole1` in the `tomcat-users.xml` file.

Now, it is time to arrange files according to the directory structure.

Arranging Files

Arrange all the files according to the directory structure of the standard Web application, as shown in Figure 22.4:

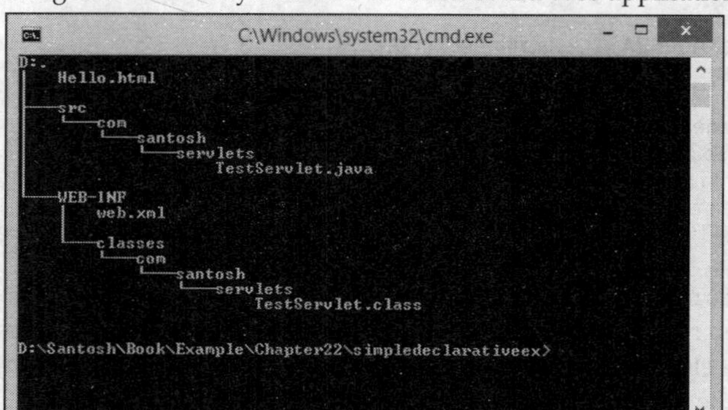

Figure 22.4: Displaying the Directory Structure of simpledeclarativeex Application

Let's now run the **simpledeclarativeex** application to see its output.

Running the Application

To run the application, copy the **simpledeclarativeex** folder into the `<Tomcat home>\webapps` folder. Start the Tomcat server, use the `http://localhost:9090/simpledeclarativeex/Hello.html` URL in Internet Explorer Web browser. The Hello.html page is displayed on the screen, as shown in Figure 22.5:

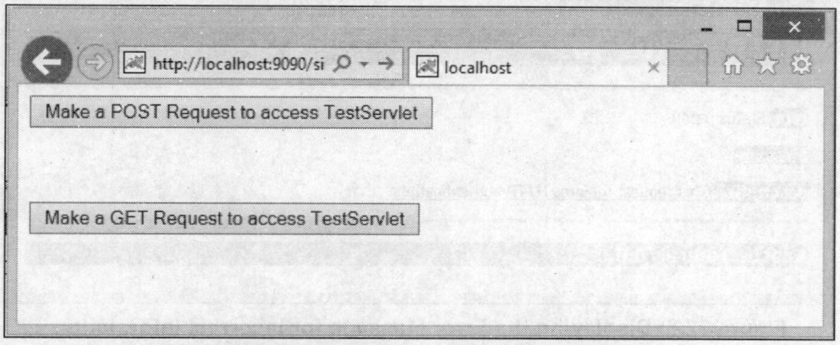

Figure 22.5: Displaying the Hello.html Page

The two buttons displayed in Figure 22.5 are used to make requests through the GET and POST methods. Clicking either of these buttons displays the Windows Security dialog box with blank user name and password fields, as shown in Figure 22.6:

Figure 22.6: Displaying the Windows Security Dialog Box

In the above dialog box, enter the user name as `santosh` and password as `myrole1`. If the given user name and password are valid, the user will be able to access `TestServlet`, as shown in Figure 22.7:

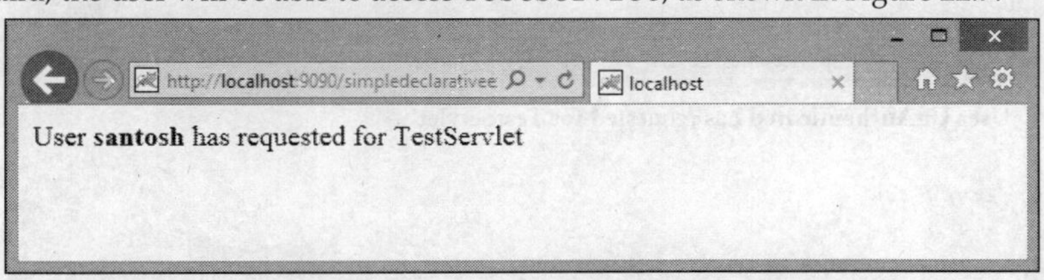

Figure 22.7: Displaying the Response after Accessing TestServlet

Figure 22.7 shows the result on entering a valid user name and password. However, if this information is incorrect, the server displays a 401 error, as shown in Figure 22.8:

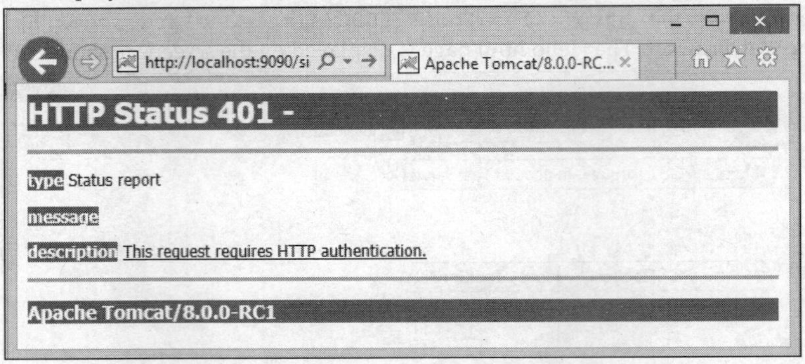

Figure 22.8: Displaying the Error Message for Incorrect Information

Alternatively, if the user name and password are correct, but the user is not associated with the `myrole1` role (for example, if we type the user name as `admin` and leave the password field blank), the server displays the 403-access denied error, as shown in Figure 22.9:

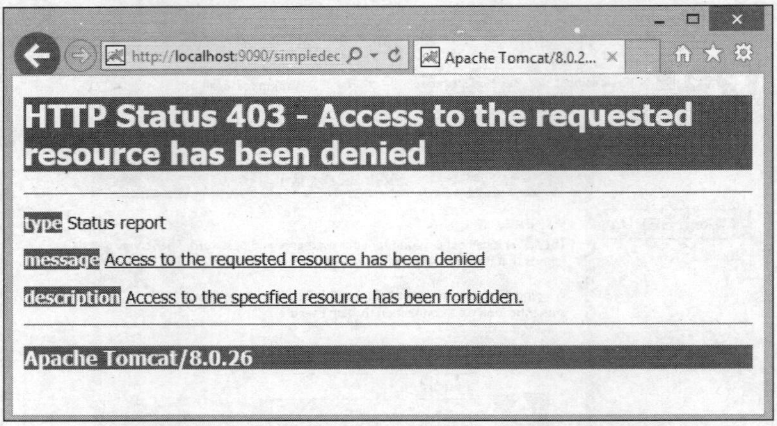

Figure 22.9: Displaying the Access Denied Error Message

NOTE

In this case, the user is authenticated but is not authorized to access the request resource.

Now, if you add `<http-method> POST</http-method>` in the `web.xml` file, as shown in Listing 22.2, and run the example, a security check is performed only in the case of the HTTP POST method and not in the default HTTP GET method request. A request made by using the HTTP GET method displays the response as shown in Figure 22.10:

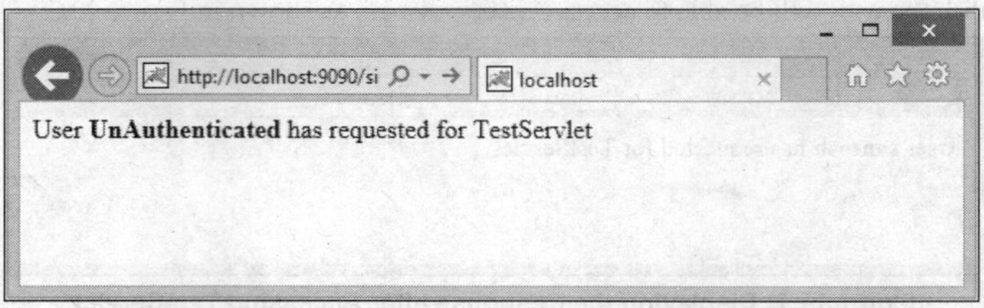

Figure 22.10: Displaying the Response for HTTP GET Method

In this application, we used the <auth-method>BASIC</auth-method> element to implement basic authentication. However, if we want to display our own login page instead of a dialog box, we can use the <auth-method>FORM</auth-method> element.

Using Form-based Authentication for Declarative Security

Next, let's convert the **simpledeclarativeex** application from HTTP basic authentication to form-based authentication. To do this, we need to perform the following broad-level steps:

1. Change the `web.xml` file for form-based authentication
2. Create the Login.jsp and MyError.jsp pages
3. Change the directory structure
4. Run the application

You can find the **simpledeclarativeex** application online in the code/Chapter22 folder as well.

Changing the web.xml File

To implement form-based authentication in the **simpledeclarativeex** application, the <login-config></login-config> element defined in Listing 22.2 must be changed as shown in Listing 22.4. The bold-faced code snippets depict the changes made in Listing 22.2.

Listing 22.4: Creating the `web.xml` File

```
<?xml version="1.0" encoding="UTF-8"?>
<web-app>
  <login-config>
        <auth-method>FORM</auth-method>
        <form-login-config>
              <form-login-page>/Login.jsp</form-login-page>
              <form-error-page>/MyError.jsp</form-error-page>
        </form-login-config>
  </login-config>
  <security-constraint>
        <web-resource-collection>
              <web-resource-name>myres</web-resource-name>
              <url-pattern>/testser/*</url-pattern>
        </web-resource-collection>
        <auth-constraint>
              <role-name>myrole1</role-name>
        </auth-constraint>
  </security-constraint>
  <servlet>
        <servlet-name>ts</servlet-name>
        <servlet-class>com.santosh.servlets.TestServlet</servlet-class>
  </servlet>
  <servlet-mapping>
        <servlet-name>ts</servlet-name>
        <url-pattern>/testser/*</url-pattern>
  </servlet-mapping>
  <security-role>
        <role-name>myrole1</role-name>
  </security-role>
  <welcome-file-list>
        <welcome-file>Home.html</welcome-file>
  </welcome-file-list>
</web-app>
```

In Listing 22.4, the authentication method has changed from `BASIC` to `FORM`. The listing also specifies the login page as Login.html and the error page as MyError.html.

Let's now create the login form and error pages for the application.

Creating the Login.jsp and MyError.jsp Pages

While discussing form-based authentication, we had seen that a login page is displayed when a user requests for a protected resource (See Figure 22.2), and when the user submits the login page, the server verifies the credentials. If the login is successful, the requested protected resource is displayed; otherwise, an error page appears. Therefore, to implement form-based authentication in the **simpledeclarativeex** application, we must create the login and error pages. Listing 22.5 provides the code for the Login.jsp page.

Listing 22.5: Creating the Login.jsp File

```
<!DOCTYPE>
<html>
  <head>
  </head>
  <body>
        <form action="j_security_check" method="POST">
                Username:<input type="text" name="j_username"><br>
                Password:<input type="password" name="j_password">
                <input type="submit" value="Login">
        </form><br>
  </body>
</html>
```

In Listing 22.5, a simple login form is designed with two textboxes, to enter the user name and password, respectively. As can be seen in Listing 22.5, the form action is `j_security_check` and the field names are `j_username` and `j_password`, which take the user name and password, respectively.

Next, we create an error page to display an error message for unauthenticated user names and passwords. Listing 22.6 provides the code for the MyError.jsp page.

Listing 22.6: Creating the MyError.jsp File

```
<!DOCTYPE>
<html>
  <head>
        <title>Login Test: Error logging in</title>
  </head>
  <body>
        <h1>User Name Password entered are not valid</h1>
        <br/>
  </body>
</html>
```

In Listing 22.6, an HTML page is created to display a simple error message for unauthenticated users.

Next, we change the directory structure of the **simpledeclarativeex** application.

Changing the Directory Structure

The directory structure for the **simpledeclarativeex** application, as shown in Figure 22.4, has to be changed; since we have added two JSP files to the application. The modified directory structure is shown in Figure 22.11.

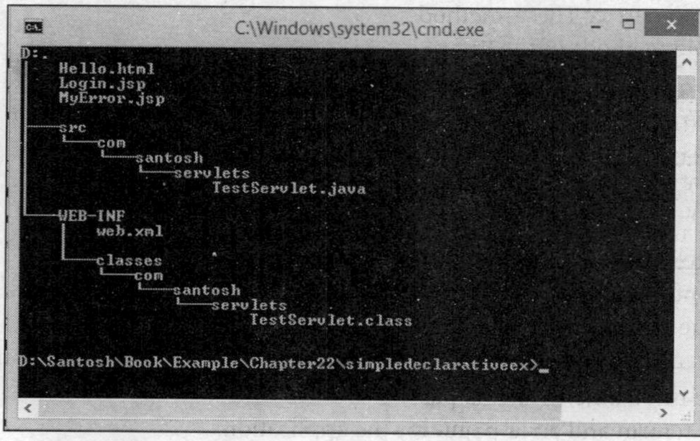

Figure 22.11: Displaying the Changed Directory Structure

In Figure 22.11, the two JSP pages—Login.jsp and MyError.jsp—have been added under the **simpledeclarativeex** folder.

Now, let's run the **simpledeclarativeex** application.

Running the Application

To run the **simpledeclarativeex** application, open the Web browser and type the http://localhost:8090/simpledeclarativeex/Hello.html URL.

This displays the Hello.html page (Figure 22.5). After clicking any of the two buttons of the Hello.html page shown in Figure 22.5, the Login.jsp page is displayed, as shown in Figure 22.12.

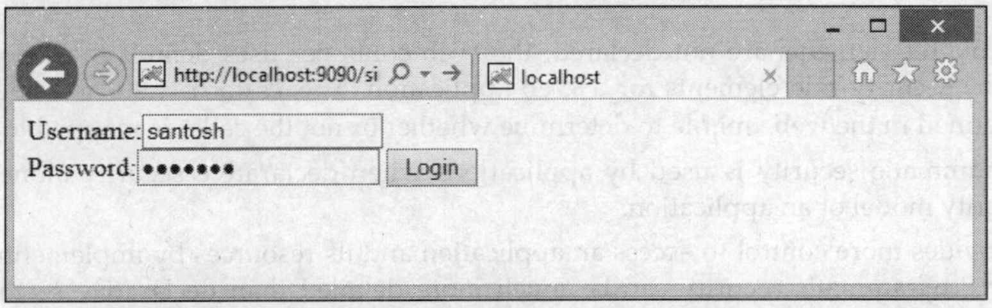

Figure 22.12: Displaying the Login Form for Form-based Authentication

Figure 22.13 is displayed when a user enters `santosh` in the Username and `myrole1`in the Password fields.

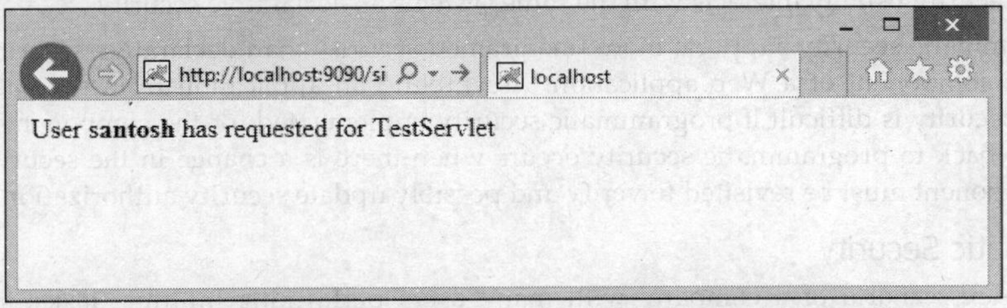

Figure 22.13: Displaying the Form-based Authentication Response

We learned that declarative security only verifies the user credentials. To implement security for accessing resources, we should implement programmatic security, which we learn next.

Describing Programmatic Security

In case of programmatic security, the Web application is responsible for authorizing a client, that is, it checks whether or not the client has permissions to access the resource(s). This mechanism is called programmatic security because the security implementation is coded into the application programmatically. In support of this requirement, the Servlet specifications include some methods in the `HttpServletRequest` interface to perform programmatic security. These methods allow Servlets to make business logic decisions based on the user's information. Some methods of the `HttpServletRequest` interface used in programmatic security are:

- **`String getRemoteUser()`** — Returns the user name used by a client for authentication. If the user is not authenticated, this method returns *null*.
- **`Principal getUserPrincipal()`** — Returns a `java.security.Principal` object. The Principal object is used to get the Principal name of the user. If the user is not authenticated, this method returns *null*.
- **`boolean isUserInRole(String)`** — Checks if a user is included in the specified security role. If the user is not authenticated, this method returns *false*. The `isUserInRole()` method takes a String, which has the same value as that of the role-name parameter.

A `<security-role-ref>` element must be declared in the deployment descriptor with a `<role-name>` sub-element containing the role name, which is passed to the `isUserInRole (String rolename)` method. The `<security-role-ref>` element must contain a `<role-link>` sub-element whose value is the name of the security role that the user is mapped into. The Web container uses the mapping of `<security-role-ref>` to the security-role to determine the return value of the call to the `HttpServletRequest.isUserInRole(String rolename)` method. The following code snippet shows how to map `myrole1ref` (role name) to `myrole1` (role link) by using the `<security-role-ref>` element:

```
<security-role-ref>
<role-name>myrole1ref</role-name>
<role-link> myrole1</role-link>
</security-role-ref>
```

According to this mapping, only a user belonging to the `myrole1` security role can call the specified Servlet. To check the role of the user, use the `isUserInRole(myrole1ref)` method, which returns the Boolean value, true.

If the security-role-ref elements are not declared, the Web container uses default role references to verify the role-names of the security-role elements for a Web application. The `isUserInRole()` method references the security roles defined in the web.xml file to determine whether or not the caller is mapped to a security role.

Note that programmatic security is used by applications when declarative security alone is not sufficient to express the security model of an application.

A developer provides more control to access an application and its resources by implementing the user-defined security model. Programmatic security can be much more detailed than declarative security. For example, a developer using the programmatic security can allow or deny a user's access to a particular component of a Web application. Although programmatic security is typically configured by the developer of the application, programmatic security usually interacts with the same systems as declarative security.

Though programmatic security supports more fine-grained security than declarative security, it can restrict the reusability of a component of a Web application. Assembling an application from several components using programmatic security is difficult if programmatic security implemented for the components is inconsistent. An additional drawback to programmatic security occurs when there is a change in the security policy. In such a case, every component must be revisited to verify and possibly update security authorization.

Using Programmatic Security

Imagine a real-life scenario of a company with many users performing multiple tasks, such as adding and modifying employee records, and maintaining transaction records. Users can perform these tasks according to the roles assigned to them. For example, a clerk working in the organization does not have the right to make additions to the employee records. This can be done only by the manager of the organization. Therefore, the manager, as a user, is assigned the admin role, authorizing him or her to make changes in the employee records.

In this section, we create an application by the name of **programmaticex**, to authenticate users based on their user name and password. An invalid user name or password displays an error message. A successful login allows users to perform the tasks based on the roles assigned to them. For example, users assigned the administrator role can modify or add the records of the employees, but if their assigned role is that of a clerk's, they will be restricted from such changes.

Before creating the **programmaticex** application, it is important to understand the directory structure of the application. You can find the code files of this application online in the code/Chapter22/programmaticex folder.

Perform the following broad-level steps to create the application:

1. Create the JSP pages for programmatic security
2. Create the Login.java and User.java files
3. Configure the application
4. Arranging Files
5. Run the application

Creating JSP Pages

In the **programmaticex** application, various JSP pages are used to validate user details, add employee details, view employee details, and display the welcome page to authenticated users. In the application, we need six JSP pages to perform different tasks, which are:

- **index.jsp**—Displays the login screen for users to enter their user names and passwords.
- **validateuser.jsp**—Redirects users to the validateuser.jsp page. The validateuser.jsp page uses the Login bean to verify the user.
- **retry.jsp**—Displays an error message if an invalid username or password is entered. The error message prompts the user to enter a valid or correct user name and password.
- **welcome.jsp**—Displays a welcome message and provides the reference for the addemployee.jsp and viewemployee.jsp pages if the login is successful.
- **addemployee.jsp**—Redirects a user to the addemployee.jsp page. If the entered user name has been assigned an administrator role, the form to add employee records is displayed; otherwise, a message of non-authorization is displayed.
- **viewemployee.jsp**—Displays a table with employee names and their designation.

Let's now create these pages.

Creating the index.jsp Page

Listing 22.7 provides the code for the index.jsp page. The index.jsp page displays the login screen for entering the user name and password.

Listing 22.7: Creating the index.jsp File

```
<%@ page language="java" session="true" pageEncoding="ISO-8859-1"%>
<html>
   <head>
         <title>Programmatic Security</title>
   </head>
   <body>
         <form action="validateuser.jsp" method="POST">
               <table align="center">
               <tr>
                     <td><font size=5> Enter the User Name </font> </td>
                     <td><input type="text" name="userName"><br>
                     </td>
               </tr>
               <tr>
                     <td><font size=5> Enter the Password </font></td>
                     <td><input type="password" name="passWord"></td><br>
               </tr>
               <tr>
                     <td>
                           <br/>
                           <input type="submit" value="Submit"/>
                           <input type="reset" value="Reset"/>
                     </td>
               </tr>
               </table>
         </form>
   </body>
</html>
```

Creating the validateuser.jsp Page

In Listing 22.7, two textboxes, userName and passWord, are used to enter the user name and password, respectively. When the user enters these details and submits the form, the validateuser.jsp page is displayed. Listing 22.8 provides the code for the validateuser.jsp page.

Listing 22.8: Creating the validateuser.jsp File

```
<%@ page language="java" session="true" pageEncoding="ISO-8859-1"%>
<jsp:useBean id="idHandler" class="com.mycompany.login.Login" scope="request">
<jsp:setProperty name="idHandler" property="*"/></jsp:useBean>
<html>
```

```
    <head>
          <title>Programmatic Security</title>
    </head>
    <body>
    <%
          String userName = request.getParameter("userName");
          ServletContext context=getServletContext();
          context.setAttribute("name",userName);
          String password = request.getParameter("password");
          if(idHandler.authenticate(userName, password))
          {
                response.sendRedirect("welcome.jsp");
          }
          else
          {
                response.sendRedirect("retry.jsp");
          }
    %>
    </body>
</html>
```

The validateuser.jsp page implements authentication by verifying the user name and password entered by the user, with the user name and password defined in the Login bean.

In Listing 22.8, `idHandler` is created to handle the Login bean, defined in the `com.mycompany.login` package. The user name and the password entered by the user in index.jsp is retrieved here, and the `authenticate()` method of the Login bean is invoked. The `authenticate()` method of the Login bean is discussed later in the chapter.

Creating the retry.jsp Page

The `authenticate()` method in Listing 22.8 returns a boolean value; if this value is true, the welcome.jsp page is called; otherwise, the retry.jsp page is invoked. The retry.jsp page displays an error message for invalid user names and passwords, and prompts the user to reenter the details. Listing 22.9 shows the code for the retry.jsp page.

Listing 22.9: Creating the retry.jsp File

```
<%@ page language="java" session="true" pageEncoding="ISO-8859-1"%>
<html>
<head>
   <body>
          <h1>
                Invalid User name and Password.
                Please Try Again!!!!!
          </h1>
          <jsp:include page="index.jsp"/>
   </body>
</html>
```

In Listing 22.9, the retry.jsp page displays an error message and includes the output of the index.jsp page.

Creating the welcome.jsp Page

The welcome.jsp page is displayed if the user name and password are correct and the login is successful. Listing 22.10 provides the code of the welcome.jsp page.

Listing 22.10: Creating the welcome.jsp File

```
<%@ page language="java" session="true" pageEncoding="ISO-8859-1" %>
<html>
   <head>
          <title>Programmatic Security</title>
   </head>
   <body>
```

```
        <br/>
        <h1>Welcome!!!! </h1>
        <h2>You have successfully Log In</h2>
        <a href="addemployee.jsp">Add Employee</a><br/>
        <a href="viewemployee.jsp">View Employee</a>
    </body>
</html>
```

Creating the addemployee.jsp Page

The welcome.jsp page in Listing 22.10 displays a welcome message and the reference link for the Add Employee and View Employee pages. Clicking the Add Employee reference displays the addemployee.jsp page. This page determines the role assigned to the user based on the user name entered by him or her. In other words, the addemeployee.jsp page implements the authorization. If the user name entered by the authenticated user has been assigned the administrator role, the employee form is displayed. However, if the user has been assigned the role of a clerk, he or she is unauthorized to add anything in the employee records. Listing 22.11 provides the code for the addemployee.jsp page.

Listing 22.11: Creating the addemployee.jsp File

```
<%@ page language="java" session="true" pageEncoding="ISO-8859-1" %>
<jsp:useBean id="idHandler" class="com.mycompany.login.Login" scope="request">
<jsp:setProperty name="idHandler" property="*"/></jsp:useBean>
<html>
   <head>
        <title>Programmatic Security</title>
   </head>
   <body>
        <br/><br/><br/>
        <%
        ServletContext context=getServletContext();
        String userName = context.getAttribute("name").toString();
        if(idHandler.authorize(userName))
        {
        %>
        <br/>
        <h1 align=center>Enter the Employee Details</h1>
        <table border=4 cellpadding=1 align=center>
                <tr>
                        <td>Enter the Employee Name</td>
                        <td><input type="text" name="empname"/></td>
                </tr>
                <tr>
                        <td>Enter the Designation</td>
                        <td><input type="text" name="empdesg"/></td>
                </tr>
                <tr>
                        <td>
                                <input type="submit" value="Add Employee"/>
                        </td>
                </tr>
        </table>
        <%
        }
        else {
 out.println("<h2>" + "you are Unauthorized to add records" + "</h2>");
 out.println("<a href=viewemployee.jsp>" + "View Employee" + "</a>");
        }
        %>
   </body>
</html>
```

In Listing 22.11, the addemployee.jsp page uses a Login bean, and invokes the `authorize()` method of the bean to check if the authenticated user name entered by the user has been assigned the administrator role. If the user has been assigned the administrator role, the `authorize()` method of the Login bean returns true; otherwise, it returns false.

If the value is true, the employee form is displayed to enter employee details. However, if the value retuned is false, an unauthorization message is displayed.

Creating the viewemployee.jsp Page

If the user clicks the View Employee reference link in the welcome.jsp page, the viewemployee.jsp page is displayed. The code for the viewemployee.jsp page is provided in Listing 22.12.

Listing 22.12: Creating the viewemployee.jsp FIle

```
<%@ page language="java" session="true" pageEncoding="ISO-8859-1" %>
<html>
  <head>
        <title>Programmatic Security</title>
  </head>
  <body>
        <h1 align=center>Employee Records<h1/>
        <table border=4 cellpadding=1 align=center>
                <tr>
                        <td>Ambika Sharma</td>
                        <td>Project Manager</td>
                </tr>
                <tr>
                        <td>Sam Malik</td>
                        <td>Technical Consultant</td>
                </tr>
                <tr>
                        <td>John Smith</td>
                        <td>Technical Writer</td>
                </tr>
        </table><br> </body>
</html>
```

The viewemployee.jsp page displays the employee names and their designation, as shown in Listing 22.12. The viewemployee.jsp page can be accessed by an authenticated user defined in the Login bean. However, only the authenticated user with the administrator role can make additions in employee records.

The `authenticate()` and `authorize()` methods of the Login bean implement the authentication and authorization respectively of the user.

Creating the Login.java and User.java Files

In this section, we create the Login.java and User.java files used in the **programmaticex** application. However, before we do this, let's understand what we are going to implement in the Login.java file and why it is required. In declarative security, the Web server manages users and their roles, as was done in the **simpledeclarativeex** application. However, in programmatic security, users and their roles are not managed by the server; instead, this is defined by the developer. Therefore, Login.java defines the users and associates the roles to these users. The Login.java file also implements the authorization and authentication modes of security based on these roles. Listing 22.13 provides the code for the Login.java file.

Listing 22.13: Creating the Login.java File

```
package com.mycompany.login;
import java.io.*;
import java.util.HashMap;
import java.util.Map;

public class Login
{
```

```
    private Map users;
    private static final String ADMIN_ROLE = "administrator";
    private static final String CLERK_ROLE = "clerk";
    public Login()
    {
          users = new HashMap();
  users.put("manager", new User("manager","manager",new String[] {ADMIN_ROLE, CLERK_ROLE}));
  users.put("clerk", new User("clerk", "clerk", new String[] {CLERK_ROLE}));
    }

  public boolean authenticate(String username, String password)throws IOException
    {
          User user = (User) users.get(username);
          boolean passwordIsValid = user.passwordMatch(password);
          if(user != null && !passwordIsValid )
          {
                return false;
          }
          else
          {
                return true;
          }
    }

    public boolean authorize(String username) throws IOException
    {
          User user = (User) users.get(username);
          boolean role = user.isAdministrator();
          if (!role)
          {
                return false;
          }
          else
          {
                return true;
          }
    }

  }
```

In Listing 22.13, we create a user's object of type `HashMap` to provide the two users namely, `manager` and `clerk`. The manager user has been assigned the administrator role and the clerk user has been assigned the clerk role. This indicates that the manager and clerk are authenticated user names; however, only the manager user is authorized to add employee records.

The manager and clerk users are defined with the help of the User class by passing three parameters (username, password, and role assigned) in the `User` class constructor. In Listing 22.13, the `authenticate()` method checks the password assigned in the `User` class for the user name based on the parameters passed by the validateuser.jsp page. If the password is correct, the true Boolean value is returned; otherwise, false is returned to the validateuser.jsp page.

Similarly, in Listing 22.13, the `authorize()` method invokes the `isAdministrator()` method of the User class. The `isAdministrator()` method returns true if the user has the administrator role assigned to him or her; otherwise, it returns false. Based on this Boolean value, the `authorize()` method also returns the Boolean value to the addemployee.jsp page. The code for the User class is provided in Listing 22.14.

Listing 22.14: Creating the User.java File

```
  package com.mycompany.login;
  import java.io.Serializable;
  public class User implements Serializable {
```

```
    private String username;
    private String password;
    private String[] roles;
    public User() {
    }
    public User(String name, String pwd, String[] assignedRoles) {
          username  = name;
          password  = pwd;
          roles=assignedRoles;
    }
    public String getUsername() {
          return username;
    }
    boolean passwordMatch(String pwd) {
          return password.equals(pwd);
    }
    public boolean hasRole(String role) {
          if (roles.length > 0) {
                for (int i=0; i<roles.length; i++) {
                      if (role.equals(roles[i]))
                      return true;
                }
          }
          return false;
    }
    public boolean isAdministrator() {
          return hasRole("administrator");
    }
}
```

In Listing 22.14, the `User` class is defined in the `com.mycompany.login` package. The user name, password, and role are assigned through the Login bean. In the `User` class, the `getUsername()` method returns the user name and the `passwordMatch()` method returns the Boolean value after verifying whether the password entered by the user is same as provided in the `User` class. The `isAdministrator()` method verifies whether the user has been assigned the administrator role; if yes, it returns true; otherwise, it returns false.

After compiling the Login.java and User.java files, the resultant package is placed in the WEB-INF/classes folder, as shown in Figure 22.14.

Configuring the Application

The `web.xml` file, placed in the WEB-INF\ folder as shown in Figure 22.14, is used to configure the **programmaticex** application. Listing 22.15 provides the code for `web.xml`.

Listing 22.15: Creating the web.xml File

```
<?xml version="1.0" encoding="UTF-8"?>
<web-app version="2.4"
  xmlns="http://java.sun.com/xml/ns/j2ee"
  xmlns:xsi="http://www.w3.org/2001/XMLSchema-instance"
  xsi:schemaLocation="http://java.sun.com/xml/ns/j2ee
  http://java.sun.com/xml/ns/j2ee/web-app_2_4.xsd">
  <welcome-file-list>
        <welcome-file>index.jsp</welcome-file>
  </welcome-file-list>
</web-app>
```

In Listing 22.15, the `<welcome-file>` element contains the index.jsp page, which is the home page of the **programmaticex** application.

Now, it is time to arrange files according to the directory structure.

Arranging Files

Arrange all the files according to the directory structure of the standard Web application, as shown in Figure 22.14:

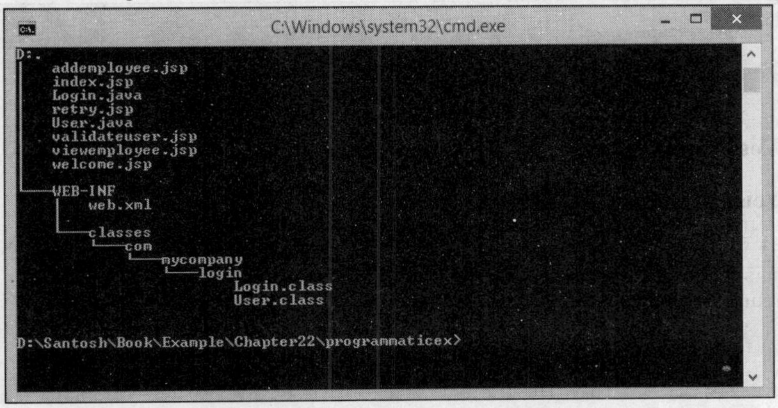

Figure 22.14: Displaying the Directory Structure of programmaticex Application

Let's now run the **programmaticex** application to see its output.

Running the Application

To run the **programmaticex** application, start the Tomcat Server and navigate to the `http://localhost:9090/programmaticex/` URL. Figure 22.15 displays the index.jsp page.

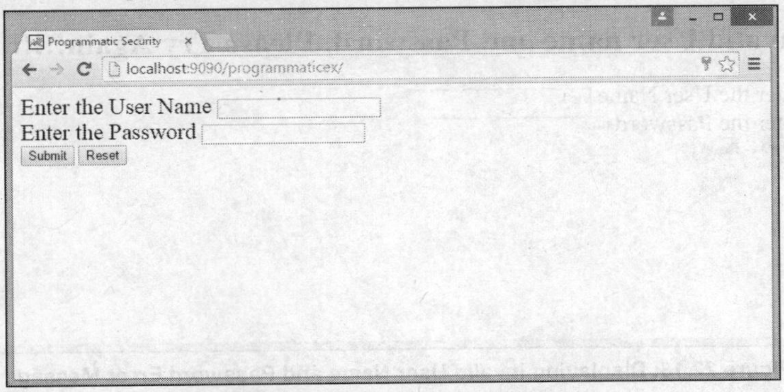

Figure 22.15: Displaying the Login Screen

When a user enters the user name and password and clicks the Submit button as shown in Figure 22.16, the validate.jsp page checks the authenticity of this information.

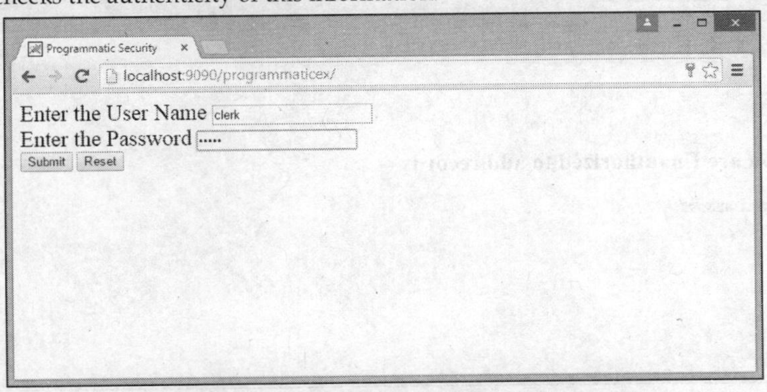

Figure 22.16: Entering a Username and Password

If the user name and password are authentic, the welcome.jsp page is displayed, as shown in Figure 22.17; however, if the information entered is incorrect, the retry.jsp page is displayed, as shown in Figure 22.18.

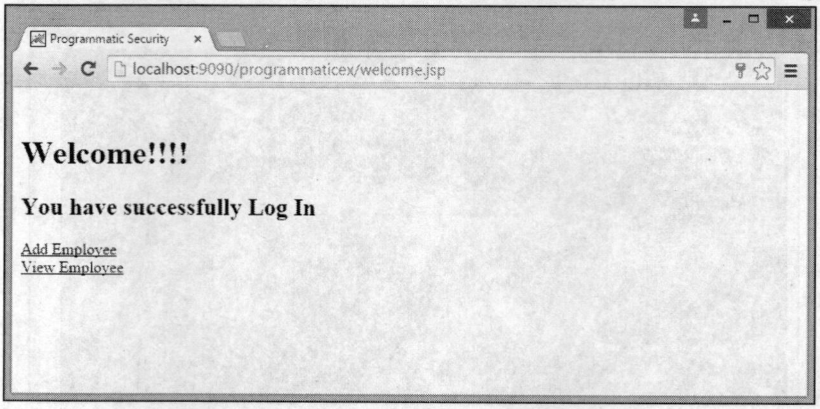

Figure 22.17: Displaying the welcome.jsp Page

Figure 22.18 displays the invalid user name and password error message. The user is directed to enter the required information again.

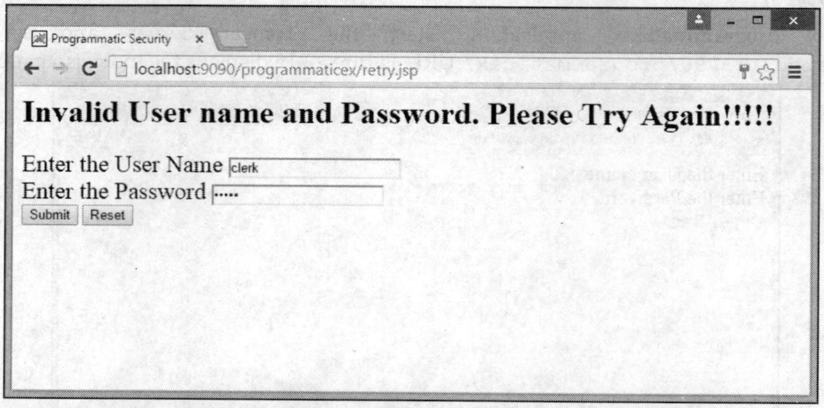

Figure 22.18: Displaying Invalid User Name and Password Error Message

If a user who entered the user name and password as a clerk clicks the Add Employee hyperlink (Figure 22.17), he or she gets the message shown in Figure 22.19.

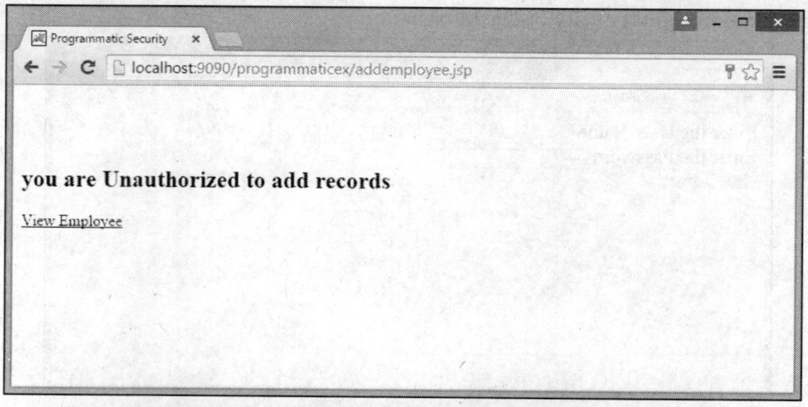

Figure 22.19: Displaying the Error Message for Unauthorized Users

However, if the clerk user clicks the **View Employee** reference link (Figure 22.19), the viewemployee.jsp page is displayed, as shown in Figure 22.20.

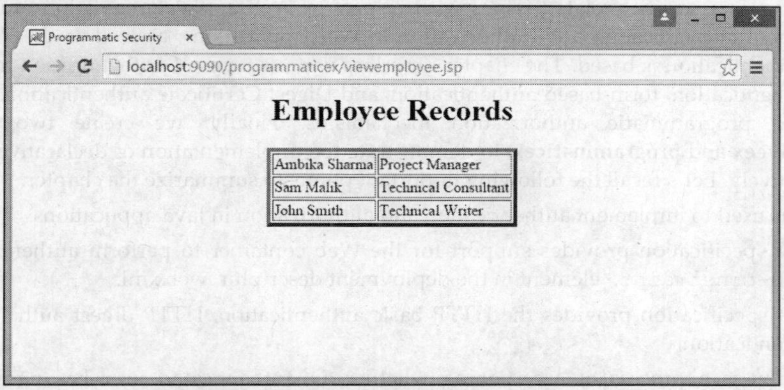

Figure 22.20: Displaying the viewemployee.jsp Page

However, if the user uses 'manager' as user name and password to login, as shown in Figure 22.21, the user is authorized to add employee records.

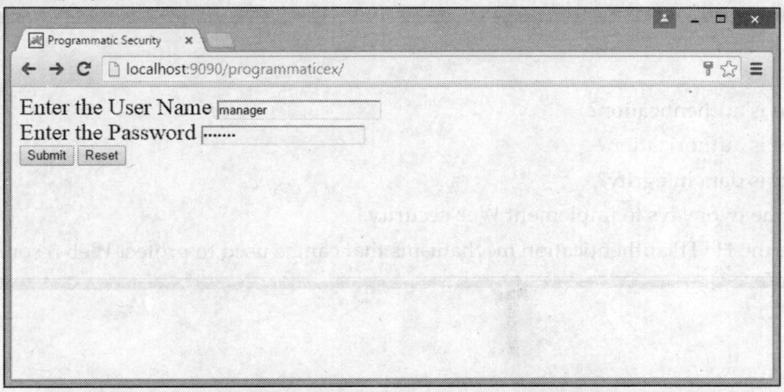

Figure 22.21: Displaying the Login Screen for the manager User

After logging with 'manager' user name and password, the welcome.jsp page is displayed. In this page, when the user clicks the Add Employee reference link (Figure 22.17), the addemployee.jsp page is displayed, as shown in Figure 22.22.

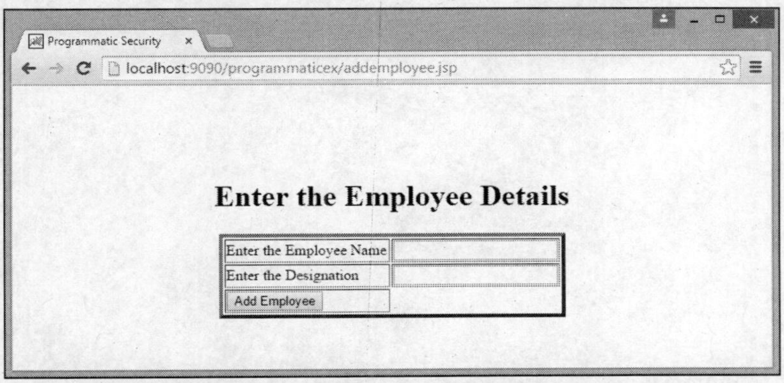

Figure 22.22: Displaying the addemployee.jsp Page for Authorized Users

This concludes the chapter. Now let's go through a brief summary.

Summary

This chapter discusses security-related issues with respect to Web applications. It introduces JAAS, which is used to implement authentication and authorization in Web applications, as well as the PAM framework, on which JAAS authentication is based. The chapter describes various types of authentication mechanisms, such as HTTP basic authentication, form-based authentication, and Digest Certificate authentication. It also explains the declarative and programmatic authorization mechanisms. Finally, we create two Web applications, **simpledeclarativeex** and **programmaticex**, to demonstrate the implementation of declarative and programmatic security, respectively. Let's recall the following important points to summarize the chapter.

- JAAS API is used to implement authentication and authorization in Java applications.
- The Servlet specification provides support for the Web container to perform authentication through the `<security-constraint>` element in the deployment descriptor, web.xml.
- The Servlet specification provides the HTTP basic authentication, HTTP digest authentication and Form-based authentication.
- Authorization is a process of ascertaining whether an authenticated user has permission to access a requested service. The application performing this operation is known as an authorizer.
- In case of programmatic security, the Web application is responsible for authorizing a client, that is, it checks whether or not the client has permissions to access the resource(s).

Exercise

Q. 22.1 What is authentication?

Q. 22.2 What is authorization?

Q. 22.3 What is data integrity?

Q. 22.4 List the two ways to implement Web security.

Q. 22.5 State the HTTP authentication mechanisms that can be used to protect Web resources.

A

Introduction to DBMS

A Database is a collection of information stored in the form of data and records. Data can be a collection of group of facts; and records are the related fields of a particular event. Therefore, a database is the collection of logically related records, also called files. A database designer decides how much data should be stored within a database; he/she also decides the auxiliary information to be initially stored in the database. The database designer is also responsible for creating and managing the database. Data management involves all the database related operations such as creating, modifying, adding, and deleting data in files, and using this data to generate reports or execute and process database queries. The system that allows the user to perform these operations is called a Database Management System (DBMS). You can use DBMS with Java applications to store and retrieve the data required in your applications. For example, you can use a DBMS to authenticate user credentials or retrieve other required data. Java applications can connect with any DBMS using JDBC drivers. Let's look at the basic concepts of DBMS and understand the SQL language, which can be used by Java applications to retrieve data from a DBMS.

What is a DBMS?

A DBMS (Database Management System) is a complex software program used to control the storage, retrieval, and over all management of data in a database. DBMS manages the requests sent by a user and ensures the integrity and security of data (ensures that only authorized users can access the data).

A DBMS includes the followings:

- **Modeling language**—Defines the database schemas. Schemas are formed according to the data models available in the DBMS. The four most commonly used data models are hierarchical, network, relational, and object models.
- **Data structures**—Provides various data structures to organize data into the DBMS. These data structures include fields, records, files, and objects in a database.
- **Database query language**—Used by the programmers to interact effectively with the database. The interaction includes accessing the database, analyzing its data, and updating the records according to user requirements.
- **Data security**—Controls the security of the database. Data security prevents unauthorized access of data from the database.
- **Transaction mechanism**—Provides Atomicity, Consistency, Isolation and Durability (ACID) properties and ensures data integrity and concurrency control. The transaction mechanism maintains data integrity by preventing multiple users from working on a single record or file simultaneously. It also prevents duplication of records based on the same index keys. This indicates that you cannot enter two records with same index numbers into the database.

- **Request processing mechanism**—Accepts user requests for programs and instructs the operating system to access the appropriate data. Database servers are designed to store the actual database and to run DBMS related software only. Database servers are multiprocessor computers, which have Redundant Array of Independent Disks (RAID) to store data. Database accelerators are also used along with the database to enhance the transaction processing environments.

Need for DBMS

Since almost all the enterprise applications in big enterprises deal with persistence data, data storage is one of the most important requirements in big enterprises. Earlier, enterprises used to store data in various formats such as flat and proprietary file systems. This approach of storing and retrieving data is a complicated process, and has the following drawbacks:

- Enhancing the data model becomes difficult and may require diverse changes in the existing system
- Integrating various systems and sharing data between them is difficult
- Increases the maintenance cost of data.

In addition to these drawbacks, convention file storage systems are incapable of effectively maintaining the following ACID properties and concurrency controls:

- Data redundancy and consistency
- Data isolation
- Integrity problems
- Atomicity problems
- Concurrent access inconsistency
- Security Problems

To solve these problems, we need a generic format to store and handle data, so that enterprise applications can efficiently interact with the data. This requirement has resulted in the release of some generic applications (data management systems), which have slowly evolved into DBMS. In DBMS, we also use RDBMS to differentiate the Relational database model. This adds to its functionality of maintaining the relationship between various database tables.

In case of RDBMS, the table data is structured in tables, fields, and records. All the tables in a relational database must be related by some common fields or records in the tables. In RDBMS, data and the relationship among the data are stored in tables. To define the RDBMS features clearly, Dr E. F Codd introduced the concept of the relational database model and the 12 rules for the relational database model. We describe the Codd's rule for RDBMS next.

Describing Codd's 12 Rule

RDBMS became more popular by using the rules proposed by Dr. E.F Codd, which have further reinforced the goal of convenient and efficient data storage and retrieval. These rules are designed to define the primary and basic functionalities a DBMS must provide, and are known as Codd's 12 Rules. Table A.1 describes Codd's Rules:

Table A.1: Codd's Rule

Rule	Description
Rule 0	A relational DBMS must manage database within itself by using the relational capabilities, without using an external language
Rule 1 Information Rule (Representation of Information)	All information in a relational database is represented at the logical level in only one way, that is, by using tables
Rule 2 Guaranteed Access	Each record in a relational database must be logically accessible by providing the table name, column name, and PRIMARY KEY.
Rule 3 Systematic Treatment of Null Values	This rule specifies that users are allowed to insert a null value for a field in a database table. Null value represents the missing information for a particular field

Table A.1: Codd's Rule

Rule	Description
Rule 4: Dynamic Online Catalog	The RDBMS must maintain data dictionary (DD) tables to keep track of current state of the database. The DD contains information on table definition, view definition, column definition, and other types of database objects. The entire schema (physical, logical, and external) is stored in the DD. The description of the database is held in the same way as ordinary data, that is, in tables and columns; and is accessible to authorized users
Rule 5: Comprehensive Data Sublanguage	The database must support any language that provides the functionality to interact with the database using the DDL, DML, and DCL statements
Rule 6: View Updating	Each distinct row of a view must correspond to a distinct and uniquely identifiable row of the base tables. Each view in a database must support the features of data manipulation and direct access of data from the tables
Rule 7: High level Insert, Update & Delete	Multiple data can be retrieved from multiple rows and columns of multiple tables. This rules states that the insert, update, and delete operations can be performed on multiple tables rather than a single row of a single table
Rule 8: Physical Data Independence	The physical method of storing data must be independent of user-interaction and must be logically consistent when changes are made to the hardware representation or disk storage methods
Rule 9: Logical Data Independence	The logical changes made to tables and views such as adding or deleting columns or changing field lengths, must not require any modification in the application programs being used to access data. That is, the database can be scaled to reflect changes without requiring changes in the application programs
Rule 10: Integrity Independence	Integrity on a database can be maintained by using integrity constraints on each record
Rule 11: Distribution Independence	Irrespective of whether or not a system supports database distribution, it must have a data sublanguage that can support distributed databases without changing the application programs
Rule 12: The Nonsubversion Rule	The low level database language cannot bypass the integrity rules and the constraints available in a relational database. So the multiple row database language is used to bypass multiple records at a time

Out of the twelve rules, an RDBMS must satisfy at least six rules and Rule 0.

Now we are familiar with RDBMS and it is time to understand how to query the database for records. In the next section, we learn about SQL, which is the most commonly used language for interacting with database.

Introducing SQL

You need a language to manipulate data in an RDBMS. IBM was the first to come up with standard language to meet this requirement in 1970s, and this language was named as Structured English Query Language (SEQUEL). SEQUEL later became SQL (Structured Query Language) and was standardized in 1980s. Now, a SQL standard published by the American National Standards Institute (ANSI) and International Organization for Standardization (ISO) is accepted as the standard RDBMS Language. Many Database vendors such as Oracle actively participate in defining these committees.

SQL is used to create and manipulate Database Management Systems. SQL statements are used to make user requests. The process of making a request to a database and receiving back the result of the request is termed as an SQL Query. Therefore, the process is named Structured Query Language. The main function of SQL is to handle all the functions provided by a Database Management System. SQL handles the following functions provided by the Database Management System:

- **Data definition**—Defines the structure and organization of the stored data and also the relationship between the stored data items.
- **Data retrieval**—Allows users to access the requested data from the database and to use them in their required application programs.

- **Data Manipulation**—Allows user to access the required data from the database and to update them according to their use. The updating procedure involves adding new records into the database, modifying existing record, and deleting existing record.
- **Access Control**—Restricts unauthorized access of data from the database.
- **Data Sharing**—Helps co-ordinate sharing of data by the multiple users.
- **Data Integrity**—Defines data integrity in the existing database to protect the database from inconsistent updates or from system failure.

SQL has proved to be a comprehensive language for controlling and interacting with a Database Management System. Although a few standard versions of SQL exists, American National Standards Institute (ANSI) language, also known as (ANSI) SQL, is the widely used SQL version.

Features of SQL

SQL provides the following features:

- Processes the set of data as groups rather than as individual units. For example, if we want to retrieve a set of rows from a table, we define a condition to filter the rows. All rows satisfying the condition are retrieved in a single step and can be passed as a unit to another SQL statement.
- Allows us to work with data at the logical level, which means we need not worry about how data are physically stored.
- Provides a simple process to manipulate data, since SQL uses simple syntax, (English words, operators and phrases), for the data manipulation commands.

SQL statements make data manipulation requests by using the set of SQL commands available in the Database Management System. These commands, along with the SQL statements, are described further in detail.

Describing SQL Statements

SQL is popular as the simple relational database language. SQL statements are simple English statements used to perform necessary operations on a database. SQL is also termed as a non-procedural database language. This implies that the user does not need to instruct where to access the required data. The user only needs to tell what data is to be retrieved in the form of query language. The DBMS, in turn, searches for the required data in the database. Users can construct database queries to access and modify the database. SQL is used in following two different ways:

- **Interactive SQL**—In this case, SQL commands are typed directly from the command line. The DBMS interprets and executes the SQL statements and displays the result to the user. This method of processing the SQL commands is termed as Interactive SQL.
- **Programmatic SQL**—In this case, SQL statements are embedded within a host language. Since SQL is not a programming language, it needs a host language to provide computational features on the database. SQL doesn't contains any flow of control commands such as IF . . . THEN . . . ELSE, GO TO, or DO . . . WHILE. The host language provides these features of looping and branching and also interfaces between the user and the SQL, which enable the command to interact with the DBMS.

Types of SQL Statements

SQL statements are generally used to build queries, which are used to communicate with the database. SQL statements are divided into three major categories:

- Data definition language (DDL)
- Data manipulation language (DML)
- Data control language (DCL)

Introducing Data Definition Language

DDL statements are SQL statements used to define the data structure as a table. Some of the most commonly used DDL statements are:

- Create table

- Alter table
- Drop table

Creating a Table

The Create Table command is used to create a table in an existing database. While creating the table, we can also insert new data into the table according to the required commands. The following rules are to be considered while creating tables in a database:

- Table name must be unique and can contain a maximum of 30 alpha numeric characters
- The Table name can contain the [A-Z], [a-z], [0-9], -, $, # characters.
- It should not start with a number.
- It cannot contain reserved words, such as select, insert, delete, update, and alter, which are used as standard keywords in databases or SQL statements.
- The user must have the required permissions to create a table.

A table must contain some specific data types for the records that are to be inserted into the table. The records must match the defined data types available in the table. Various SQL data types are given in the Table A.2.

Table A.2: SQL Data Types

Data Type	Syntax	Description
`character`	`Char(x)`	Allows the user to insert only character values into the specified column in the table. Here, x indicates the number of character to be inserted
`Character varying`	`Varchar2(x)`	Is also used to insert character data together with numeric data into the table
`Numeric`	`Numeric (p, s)`	Is used to insert numeric values into the table. Here, *p* indicates the precision and *s* indicates the scale of numeric value
`Date`	`Date`	Is used to store the year, month and day values
`Time`	`Time`	Is used to store the hour, minute and second values
`Timestamp`	`Timestamp`	Is used to store the date and time values into the database

Syntax for Creating a Table

The syntax shown in Listing A.1 is used to create a table in an existing database. The names of the columns in the table are specified along with the required data type. We can create any number of rows in a table.

Listing A.1: Syntax and example for creating a table in Oracle

```
CREATE table <table name> (
   <column_name1> <type>
   <counmn_name2> <type>,
   …
   <column_namen> <type>;
Example:
CREATE table MyCompany (
EmpID number,
Ename varchar2(20),
EmpAdd varchar2(20),
Email varchar2(20),
DOJ date,
Deptno number);
```

The listing A.1 creates a table "MyCompany" in the Oracle database. The table "MyCompany" contains 6 columns with names "EmpID", "Ename", "EmpAdd", "Email", "DOJ" and "Depno".

Altering a Table

Altering a table in a database allows the user to add, modify, or drop a column from an existing table. The syntax for altering a table by using the ADD and MODIFY commands are discussed here in Listing A.2. The syntax for the drop command is described later in the chapter. The add command is used to insert more columns into an existing database. The modify command is used in an alter statement to modify an existing column name in an existing table in the database.

Listing A.2: Syntax and example for altering a table in Oracle

```
Syntax: Using ADD ()
ALTER table <table-name>
ADD <column_name> <type>;
Using Modify ()
ALTER table <table_name>
MODIFY <column_name1><type><column_name2><type>…<column_namen><type>;
Example:
ALTER table MyCompany ADD Ph_no number(20); //
ALTER table MyCompany MODIFY EmpAdd varchar2(100);
```

Dropping a Table

The DROP table command is used to drop a table, along with the columns, from an existing database. However, if you want to drop only a single column in a table, you can use the DROP statement with the ALTER statement. The syntax shown in Listing A.3 is used to drop a table from the database. The DROP command in this Listing is used to completely delete a table and its structure from the database.

Listing A.3: Syntax and example for dropping a table in Oracle Syntax, Drop a Table.

```
DROP table <Table_name>
Example:
DROP table MyCompany;
```

Introducing Data Manipulation Language (DML)

DML stands for Data Manipulation Language. DML statements are used to manipulate data in the existing tables of a database. DML statements constitute the INSERT, UPDATE, DELETE statements. The different types of DML statements available are discussed here:

Inserting a Record

The INSERT command is used to insert a new records into an existing table in a database. The syntax to insert a table into the database is given in Listing A.4.

Listing A.4: Syntax and example for inserting data in to a table in Oracle

```
Syntax:
INSERT into <table_name> [(<column_name1>,<column_name2>…)]
values (column_value_1, column_value_2,…);
Example:
INSERT into MyCompany (EmpID, Ename, EmpAdd, Email, DOJ,deptno)
  values (1,'Santosh','New Delhi','santoshj@abc.com','02-aug-2006', 1);
INSERT into MyCompany values(2,'Rupali','New delhi','rupalis@abc.com',
'21-may-2007',1);
```

If the INSERT command is used to insert the values of records in various columns that have already been created, it is not mandatory to include column names in the query. We must; however, ensure that the sequence of values is similar to the sequence of the columns in the table. On the contrary, if we want to insert records only in selected columns, or if we do not know the sequence of the columns in the table, we need to specify the column names in the query. Listing A.5 shows the syntax to insert records in few specific columns of a table.

Listing A.5: Syntax and example for inserting data into selected columns of a table

```
INSERT into MyCompany (EmpID, Ename, EmpAdd, Email)
values (1,'Santosh','New Delhi','santoshj@abc.com');
```

Selecting a Record

The SELECT statement is used to access all the results in an existing table. When we execute the SELECT statement, we can access all the results in the specified table in the database. The simple SELECT statement can be formed by using three different clauses, as mentioned here:

- **SELECT** – This clause is used to specify the columns of the table to be retrieved.

- **FROM**—This clause specifies the tables that are to be accessed. It indicates the location of the columns in the database.
- **WHERE**—This is an optional clause used by the SELECT statement. The WHERE clause generally specifies one or more conditions. If the WHERE clause is used to specify a condition, the records matching the condition are displayed, otherwise all the records of the table are displayed.

The syntax of SELECT statement is given in Listing A.6.

Listing A.6: Syntax to use the SELECT statement.

```
SELECT * from <table_name>;
```

For example, to select the reords from the table named "MyCompany", the following SELECT statement is used.

```
SELECT * from MyCompany;
```

The preceding syntax displays the following result set, as shown in Figure A.1:

```
SQL> select * from MyCompany ;

EMPID ENAME          EMPADD          EMAIL               DOJ          DEPTNO
----- -------------- --------------- ------------------- ------------ ------
    1 Santosh        New Delhi       santoshj@abc.com    02-AUG-06    1
    2 Rupali         New delhi       rupalis@abc.com     21-MAY-07    1
    3 John           London          John@abc.com        21-JUN-07    2
    4 Michel         Mumbai          michel@abc.com      18-AUG-07    3
```

Figure A.1: Output of the SELECT Statement.

Note that Figure 3.1 displays all the data in the preceding mentioned table. We can also specify the conditions to access specific columns from a table in a database. The syntax to retrieve specific data by using the WHERE clause has been provided in Listing A.7.

Listing A.7: Syntax and example for selecting data from a table in Oracle using the WHERE clause

```
Sytnatx: Accessing Records with WHERE clause
SELECT * from <table_name> WHERE <Condition>;
SELECT * from MyCompany where deptno=1;
```

The preceding statement works on the given condition, that is, it displays the records where the value of the deptno column is 1. So, the query executes and retrieves the records having deptno as 1, as shown in Figure A.2.

```
SQL> select * from MyCompany Where Deptno=1;

EMPID ENAME          EMPADD          EMAIL               DOJ          DEPTNO
----- -------------- --------------- ------------------- ------------ ------
    1 Santosh        New Delhi       santoshj@abc.com    02-AUG-06    1
    2 Rupali         New delhi       rupalis@abc.com     21-MAY-07    1
```

Figure A.2: Output of the SELECT Statement by using the WHERE clause.

Updating a Record

The UPDATE command is used to update the contents of a record in an existing table. It only modifies the data already present in the table. This command contains the WHERE clause and an additional clause named SET. The WHERE clause is the optional clause and it is used with the UPDATE command when we want to make a conditional update. The syntax of the UPDATE command for a given statement is provided in the Listing A.8.

Listing A.8: Syntax and example for updating recorders in a table in Oracle

```
Syntax:
UPDATE <table_name> SET <column_name_1>=<column1_newvalue>,
<column_name_2>=<column2_newvalue>,… [WHERE <condition>];
Example:
UPDATE MyCompany SET EmpAdd='INDIA', DOJ='30-dec-06' WHERE Ename='john';
```

- **SET Clause**—The SET clause in the preceding statement is used to update the columns in the selected tables. The syntax for assigning new values to the existing values is as follows:

  SET column_1 = value_1, [column_2 = value_2]……[column_n = value_n]

In this case, column_n refers to the names of the columns to be updated by the UPDATE statement and value_n refers to the new values to be assigned to the corresponding columns.

Deleting a Record

The DELETE command is used to delete a row from a table. The WHERE clause can also be used as an optional clause with the DELETE command. It specifies the condition for deleting a row from an existing table. The syntax for deleting a row from a database is given in Listing A.9.

Listing A.9: Syntax and example for deleting recorders in a table

```
Syntax:
DELETE from <table_name> [WHERE <condition>];
Example:
DELETE from MyCompany WHERE EmpID=4;
```

In the preceding example, the DELETE command deletes the specific record where EmpID is 4.

Data Control Language

DCL stands for Data Control Language. DCL statements are used to allow SQL statements to be grouped together into transactions. These statements also control the security and permissions of the objects or parts of the database. The different types of DCL statements are described here:

- **COMMIT**—The COMMIT statement is used to terminate the current transaction performed by a user and make all changes under the transaction permanent. It commits all the changes to the database. This indicates that all the changes made by the user are made permanent to the database. The syntax of the COMMIT statement is shown in Listing A.10:

Listing A.10: Syntax and example of the COMMIT Statement

```
Syntax;
DELETE from MyCompany where EmpID=4;
COMMIT [work]
```

- **ROLLBACK** —This statement is used to terminate the changes made by a user in the database. It rolls back the changes to the database. The ROLLBACK statement can use WORK an optional keyword. The ROLLBACK statement has the following format, as shown in Listing A.11.

Listing A.11: Syntax and example of the ROLLBACK Statement in Oracle

```
Syntax;
DELETE from MyCompany where EmpID=4;
ROLLBACK [work]
```

- **GRANT**—The GRANT statement grants access privileges for database objects to users or database programmers. The syntax of the GRANT statement is shown in Listing A.12.

Listing A.12: Syntax and example of the GRANT Statement

```
Syntax: GRANt privilege-list ON [TABLE] object-list TO user-list
GRANT SELECT ON MyCompany TO PUBLIC
```

In the previous syntax:

- **Privilege-list**—A list of SQL statements such as SELECT, INSERT, DELETE, REFERENCES, and UPDATE, separated by commas.
- **object-list**—A list of table names or views, separated by commas
- **User-list**—A list of users, separated by commas.

- **Revoke**—The REVOKE statement is used to revoke the privileges for the data objects that were previously granted to the users. The syntax of the REVOKE statement is shown in Listing A.13.

Listing A.13: Syntax and example of the REVOKE Statement in Oracle

```
Syntax
REVOKE privilege-list ON [TABLE] object-list FROM user-list
```

Summary

In this chapter, we have introduced DBMS and RDBMS. The chapter also gives a brief introduction to Structured Query Language. Different types of commonly used SQL statements, such as DDL, DML and DCL, have been explained with their respective syntax and output. This brief explanation of RDBMS concepts and SQL statements has been provided to recall the things related to database management, which will help us while using programmatic SQL with JDBC.

B

Hospital Management System

Background

GetWellSoon hospital is multi-specialty hospital with many patients visiting the hospital every day. This hospital offers treatment for various diseases. The hospital also provides outpatient services and surgical consultations. The hospital administration wishes to have a hospital management system that is easy to navigate and can be accessed online. The hospital management system must be assessable to doctors, hospital administration, and patients. However, the information and modification rights available to these users would be different for different, depending on the type of users. For example, patients would be allowed to view the records but would not be allowed to modify them.

Problems

GetWellSoon Hospital wants to manage the information about doctors and patients. The need was to create a cost-efficient and practical system. In spite of the large volume of information, the structure and navigation of the hospital management system needs to be simple and user-friendly. With multiple departments and information running into hundreds of pages, the hospital felt it was critical for the information to be organized systematically in an uncomplicated way. Budget was obviously a major challenge.

Solution

To resolve the above problem, GetWellSoon hired a team of developers, who performed the need assessment and started with the development of the hospital management system. The team of developers decides to develop this Software in three phases:

- **Phase 1**—Administration
- **Phase 2**—Doctor
- **Phase 3**—Patients

Phase 1: Administration

In this phase, Developers need to deliver a basic system that can provide convenience for administrators to store, remove, and search for patient details, doctors, and medication. The system must be designed to easily accommodate any future enhancements.

This phase of the hospital management system enables the hospital to enter the existing patient, doctor, and medication details into a database.

The system should be accessible over the Internet through a Web browser, so that if the hospital expands its operations in other cities in future, the employees and patients can access the hospital management system.

The case study given in this book includes the code for this phase. This part of the system is designed with its own small framework for easy future enhancements, which makes the development of the remaining phases of this system very easy and fast. You can see the details of Phase 1 in Figure B.1.

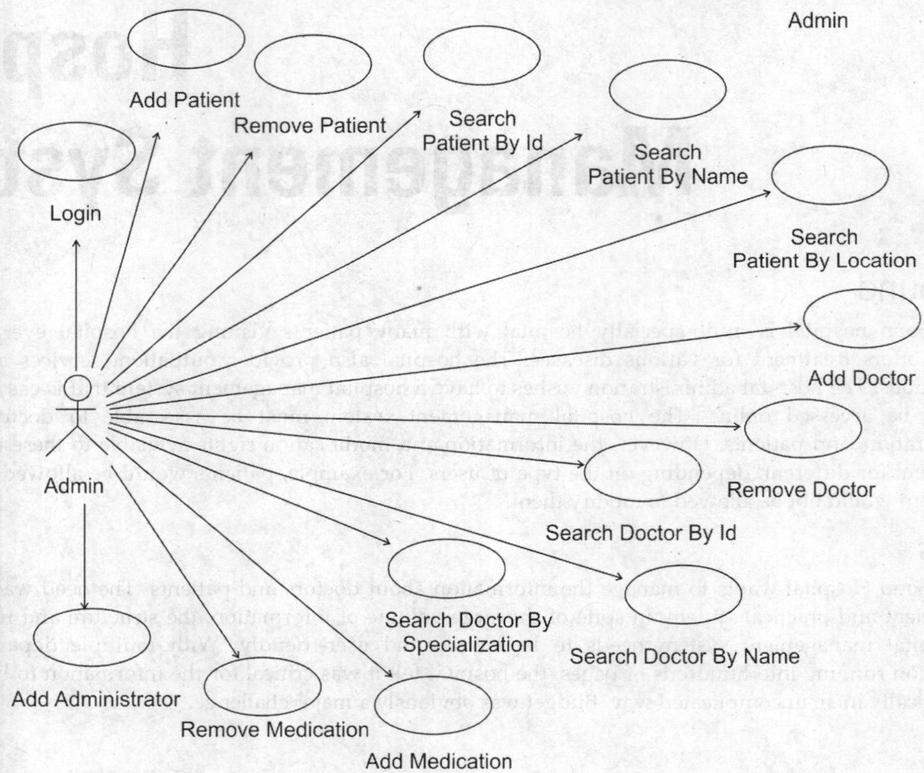

Figure B.1: Phase 1-Administration.

Phase 2: Doctor

In this phase, the developers need to enhance the system delivered in phase-1 by adding the following services:

- Ability to access the patients and medications database to prepare prescriptions, which would help the doctors to view the patients allergies, medications side effects, usage, and precautions for making an optimum diagnosis and prescription.
- Allow the doctors to take a print of the prescription prepared

- Allow the doctor to block the medication in case he finds the response to a particular medication is not as desired
- Allow the doctors to post comments on medications
- You can see the details of the Phase 2 in the Figure B.2.

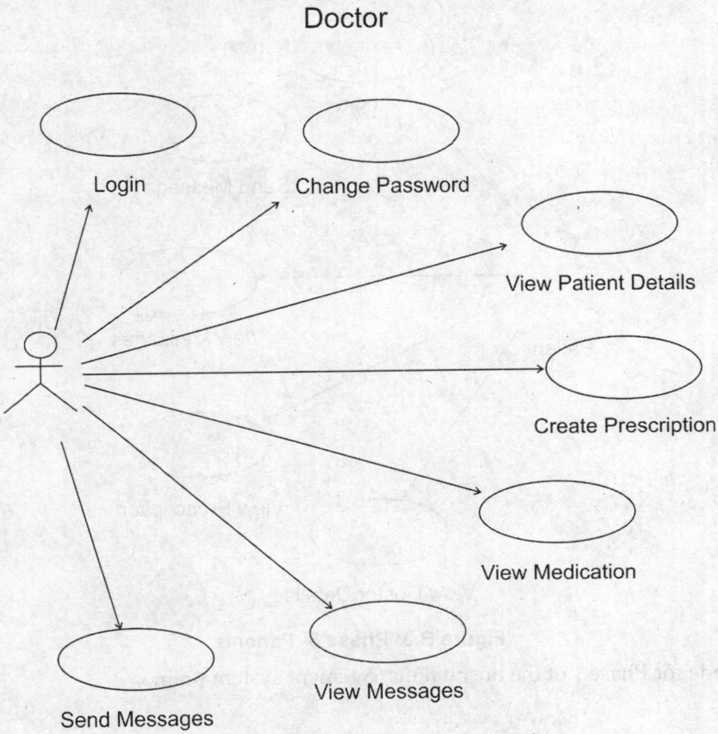

Figure B.2: Phase 2-Doctor

Phase 3: Patient

In this phase, the developers need to further enhance the system delivered in phase-2 by allowing the patients to use this system. The following services have to be implemented in this phase:

- Allow the patients to login and view their details
- Allow the patients to view the prescriptions and send some messages to the doctors in case of any clarifications
- Allow the doctors to view the queries requested by the patients and send replies
- Allow the patients to view the messages sent by the doctors
- Allow the patients to write comments on the hospital / medication

You can see the details of Phase 3 in Figure B.3.

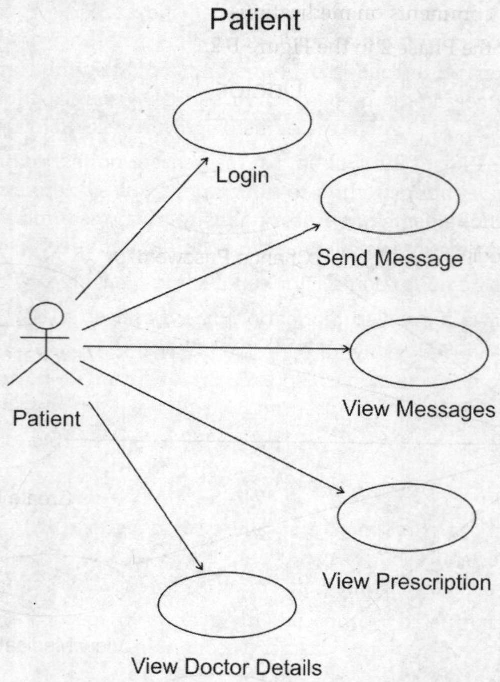

Figure B.3: Phase 3- Patients

You can find the code for Phase 1 of the hospital management system online.

That's it.

Answers

CHAPTER 1

Ans. 1.1 A Web application can be defined as an application that can be accessed through the Internet using a Web browser and Web protocols such as HTTP.

Ans. 1.2 Common Gateway Interface

Ans. 1.3 CGI is an open standard abstraction between HTTP adapter (Web server) and an external application written by using any of the programming language such as C or C++.

Ans. 1.4 CGI is not dependent on any particular Web server architecture.

Ans. 1.5 Java Servlets came as an alternative to CGI, by providing high level, component-based, platform-independent, and server-independent standards for developing Web applications in Java.

Ans. 1.6 The requirement of tag based instructions has necessitated the introduction of JSP.

Ans. 1.7 MVC stands for Model, View, Controller, and is an architectural pattern that divides the complex system in three important tiers/layers named Model, View, and Controller.

Ans. 1.8 Model-1 and Mode-2 are the development models used to develop Web applications.

CHAPTER 2

Ans. 2.1 ODBC (Open Database Connectivity) provides a uniform method to access different Database Management Systems (DBMSs).

Ans. 2.2 In general, the term JDBC implies Java Database Connectivity. JDBC provides a standard abstraction (JDBC API) for Java applications to communicate with different databases.

Ans. 2.3 There are 4 types of JDBC drivers.

Ans. 2.4 This type of driver is generally used in the development and testing phases of Java applications. However, this is used in production environment also if a database does not have any other JDBC driver implementations.

Ans. 2.5 JDBC driver implementations that convert JDBC call to DB specific native call are categorized as Type-2 driver.

Ans. 2.6 Type-3 driver is a driver that converts a JDBC call into database server independent and middleware server specific net protocol call (network call), which is then translated into database server specific call by the middleware server.

Ans. 2.7 Type-4 driver makes a direct call to DBMS over a socket and is a preferable solution for Internet access.

Ans. 2.8 The example of Type-5 driver is `DataDirect` Connect for JDBC.

CHAPTER 3

Ans. 3.1 JDBC core API and JDBC extension API

Ans. 3.2 Two new features added in JDBC 4.2 are JDBC Type `enum` and SQL Type interface.

Ans. 3.3 java.sql.Connection is an interface provided by the java.sql package. This standard interface defines an abstraction to access the session established with a database server.

Ans. 3.4	`java.sql.Statement` is an interface provided by the `java.sql` package. This interface defines a standard abstraction to execute SQL statements requested by a user and return the results by using the `ResultSet` object.
Ans. 3.5	jdbc:<sub protocol>:<info>
Ans. 3.6	jdbc:oracle:thin:@localhost:1521:sandb

CHAPTER 4

Ans. 4.1	createStatement()
Ans. 4.2	The return type of the `executeUpdate()` method is `int`. This value specifies the number of records affected by the query executed; or alternatively, returns the `Statement.SUCCESS_NO_INFO` value, which indicates that the given SQL statement has been successfully executed but the number of records affected is not known.
Ans. 4.3	executeQuery()
Ans. 4.4	`java.sql.PreparedStatement` is an interface used to represent a precompiled query, which can be executed multiple times without compiling the query again and again.
Ans. 4.5	The main disadvantage of `PreparedStatement` is that it can represent only one SQL statement. That is, we cannot execute more than one statement by using a single `PreparedStatement`.
Ans. 4.6	java.sql.CallableStatement is an interface that provides a standard abstraction for all the data stores to call stored procedures and functions in a vendor independent way.
Ans. 4.7	java.sql
Ans. 4.8	Using the column index form of the `getXXX()` methods is more efficient than the column name form, because the driver does not have to deal with the extra steps of parsing the column name, finding it in the select list, and then turning it into a number.
Ans. 4.9	wasNull()
Ans. 4.10	The `ResultSetMetaData` interface provides information about the columns in a `ResultSet`, such as the column name, column data type, and length of the columns.
Ans. 4.11	The `ResultSet` Holdability determines whether the `ResultSet` object has to be closed when a commit operation is implicitly or explicitly performed.

CHAPTER 5

Ans. 5.1	The `BLOB` type of objects store large objects, such as images, audios, or multimedia clips
Ans. 5.2	createBlob()
Ans. 5.3	The `CLOB` type of objects store large amount of textual data
Ans. 5.4	The syntax for creating an array type in a database is: create Type <type name> as VARRAY(<length>) of <type>
Ans. 5.5	Batch update allows you to submit multiple DML/DDL operations to a data source for processing simultaneously.
Ans. 5.6	Transactions are used to provide data integrity over multiple users.
Ans. 5.7	Atomicity specifies the ability to guarantee that either all or none of the tasks of a transaction have been performed. This property provides an ability to save (commit) or cancel (rollback) the transaction at any point, and controls all the statements of a transaction.
Ans. 5.8	SavePoints are points in a transaction to which the user can roll back without affecting the changes.
Ans. 5.9	setAutoCommit(boolean)

Ans. 5.10 Isolation refers to the ability of a transaction to isolate or hide the data used by it from other transactions until the current transaction ends. This is done by preparing locks on the data.

CHAPTER 6

Ans. 6.1 CGI stands for Common Gateway Interface. CGI is an open standard abstraction between Hyper Text Transfer Protocol (HTTP) adapter (Web server) and an external application written using any of the programming languages, such as C or C++.

Ans. 6.2 Servlets are the components of Java that are used to create dynamic Web applications.

Ans. 6.3 Two important changes introduced in Servlet 3.1 are Non-Blocking I/O mechanism and HTTP protocol upgrade mechanism.

Ans. 6.4 Servlet container, sometimes also known as Servlet engine, is an integrated set of objects that provides runtime environment for Servlets.

Ans. 6.5 A Servlet container can be configured within a Web server to manage Servlets in the following three ways:

a. As a standalone container

b. As an in-process container

c. As an out-process container

Ans. 6.6 javax.servlet and javax.servlet.http

Ans. 6.7 The `init()` method

Ans. 6.8 init(), service(), and destroy().

Ans. 6.9 GenericServlet is an abstract class and subtype of the Servlet and ServletConfig interfaces. It provides a simplified approach to develop Servlets by giving a simple version of the Servlet lifecycle methods.

Ans. 6.10 Wrapper/Adapter pattern

CHAPTER 7

Ans. 7.1 a. String getParameter(String paramName)

b. String[] getParameterValues(String paramName)

c. Enumeration getParameterNames()

Ans. 7.2 Servlet Context parameters are accessible to all Servlets and Jsp pages of a Web application. The servlet initialization parameters defined for a particular Servlet cannot be accessed by any other component of the Web application.

Ans. 7.3 ServletConfig

Ans. 7.4 <init-param>

<param-name>name</param-name>

<param-value>value</param-value>

</init-param>

Ans. 7.5 In case of the `getRequestDispatcher()` method of `ServletContext`, we can locate the resource relative to the context path; whereas in case of the `getRequestDispatcher()` method of `ServletRequest`, we can also locate the resource by using the path relative to current request path.

Ans. 7.6 setAttribute(String name, Object value)

Ans. 7.7 Status codes are used by the client application to know the status of a request being processed in the server.

CHAPTER 8

Ans. 8.1 A session is a collection of HTTP requests, over a period of time, between a client and a Web server.

Ans. 8.2 Session tracking, also known as session handling, is a mechanism used to maintain the state of the user within the lifetime of a session.

Ans. 8.3
a. URL rewriting
b. Hidden form fields
c. Cookies
d. HTTP Session

Ans. 8.4 Query string is a string appended after the requested uniform resource identifier (URI), with the '?' character as a separator.

Ans. 8.5 The `encodeURL()` method determines if the URL needs to be rewritten, and if necessary, includes the session ID in the URL.

Ans. 8.6 With HTTP Sessions, we cannot share the data among multiple Web applications, which can be done using cookies.

Ans. 8.7 Parameters are set by the Web container based on the request data or data configured in web.xml. The web.xml file configures the request parameters or initialization parameter used by the servlets. The parameter values can only be retrieved whereas attribute values can be retrieved and changed by using the set and get methods.

Ans. 8.8 Page, Request, Session, and Context

Ans. 8.9 The `javax.servlet.SingleThreadModel` interface is a marker interface that marks our Servlet instance to be thread safe.

CHAPTER 9

Ans. 9.1 Filters are reusable Web components that can transform the content of requests, responses, and header information from one format to another.

Ans. 9.2 Filter, FilterConfig, and FilterChain

Ans. 9.3 `FilterConfig` is an interface that defines a standard abstraction to fetch configuration information about a filter specified in the Deployment Descriptor.

Ans. 9.4 The `FilterChain` object represents a chain of filters. The `doFilter()` method of this object can be used to invoke the next filter on changed request/response pair.

Ans. 9.5 `init()`

Ans. 9.6 UnavailableException or ServletException. In the ServletException, UnavailableException is the sub type of ServletException.

Ans. 9.7

<filter>

<filter-name>myFilter1<filter-name>

<filter-class>com.santosh.servlets.TestFilter<filter-class>

</filter>

Ans. 9.8 Listeners are used to recognize application events, which help Web developers in controlling the life cycle of the `ServletContext`, `ServletRequest`, and `HttpSession` objects.

Ans. 9.9
HttpSessionListener
HttpSessionActivationListener
HttpSessionAttributeListener
HttpSessionBindingListener

Ans. 9.10 The wrappers allow a Web application developer to add additional functionalities to the request and response objects given by the Servlet container.

CHAPTER 10

Ans. 10.1 Trusted applets are those applets that operate normally like any other application and have full access to the client machine.

Ans. 10.2 JDK 1.2

Ans. 10.3 In HTTP connection with CGI programs the applet is only allowed to communicate with a safe server. It is done by utilizing the encrypted HTTPS (HTTP + SSL) protocol.

Ans. 10.4 RMI means Remote Method Invocation.

Ans. 10.5 RMI uses naming registry for communication. It also uses special stub and skeleton class for all the remote object. So RMI is bit difficult to use.

CHAPTER 11

Ans. 11.1 Interservlet communication means the communications between the servlets.

Ans. 11.2 The three types of Interservlet communication are:

- Direct servlet manipulation
- Servlet reuse
- Servlet collaboration

Ans. 11.3 Direct servlet manipulation is the method in which a servlet has the permission to access the loaded servlets on its server and perform operations on one or more servlets.

Ans. 11.4 At times servlets have to share some useful information. When this type of communication happens we call it servlet collaboration.

Ans. 11.5 The three methods through which servlet collaboration can be performed are as follows:

- Collaboration through the system properties list
- Collaboration through a shared object
- Collaboration through inheritance

CHAPTER 12

Ans. 12.1 New features introduced in Servlet 3.1 are as follows:

- Non-Blocking I/O Mechanism
- HTTP protocol upgrade mechanism
- Security enhancement

Ans. 12.2 With the help of Asynchronous support, servlet 3.0 do not need to wait for a response from a resource. Rather the thread can continue to process and thus in servlet 3.0 threads is not blocked.

Ans. 12.3 `ServletRequest.startAsync()` method can be used to get an instance of AsyncContext.

Ans. 12.4 Scalability of application means that if a program is designed for a small set of records, it cannot work well on large set of records.

Ans. 12.5 `ReadListener` interface should be implemented when it is required to perform non-blocking threads whereas `WriteListener` interface should be implemented when it is required to perform non-blocking writes.

Ans. 12.6 HttpServletRequest.changeSessionId and HttpSessionIdListener

CHAPTER 13

Ans. 13.1 JSP stands for Java Server Pages. JSP is a standard Java extension used to simplify the creation and management of dynamic Web pages.

Ans. 13.2 Major shortcomings of Java Servlet are:

- ❑ Inability to use IDEs
- ❑ Inability to use HTML Designer
- ❑ Dependence on Web configuration
- ❑ Recurring Recompilation

Ans. 13.3 Both, Servlets and JSPs are server-side components used to generate dynamic HTML pages; however, JSP is preferred over Servlet as it is developed by using a simple HTML template and is automatically handled by the JSP container.

Ans. 13.4 The stages of the JSP lifecycle are as follows:

- ❑ Page Translation
- ❑ Compilation
- ❑ Loading and Initialization
- ❑ Request Handling
- ❑ Destroying (End of service)

Ans. 13.5 In the loading and initialization stage of the JSP life cycle, the JSP container loads and instantiates the Servlet.

CHAPTER 14

Ans. 14.1 Scriptlet, Declarative, and Expression

Ans. 14.2 The various types of JSP implicit objects are as follows:

- ❑ Request
- ❑ Response
- ❑ Out
- ❑ Page
- ❑ PageContext
- ❑ Application
- ❑ Session
- ❑ Config
- ❑ Exception

Ans. 14.3 The directive tags available as per JSP specifications are:

- ❑ page
- ❑ include
- ❑ taglib

Ans. 14.4

- ❑ **`Page directive tag`**: The page directive tag holds the instructions used by the translator during the translation stage of the JSP lifecycle. These instructions affect the various properties associated with the JSP page.
- ❑ **`Include directive tag`**: The include directive tag is used to merge the contents of two or more files during the translation stage of the JSP lifecycle.

Ans. 14.5 Yes.

CHAPTER 15

Ans. 15.1 JSP 1.1

Ans. 15.2
- ❑ id
- ❑ scope
- ❑ class
- ❑ beanName
- ❑ type

Ans. 15.3 <jsp:getProperty name= " " property= " "/>

Ans. 15.4 No

Ans. 15.5 The `fallback` action tag allows us to specify a text message to be displayed if the required plug-in cannot run.

CHAPTER 16

Ans. 16.1 Tag handler is a Java class that implements one of the subtypes of JspTag interface, which defines the run time behavior of the custom tag.

Ans. 16.2 setBodyContent()

Ans. 16.3
a. SKIP_BODY
b. EVAL_BODY_INCLUDE
c. EVAL_BODY_BUFFERED

Ans. 16.4 EVAL_BODY_AGAIN

Ans. 16.5 Object findAttribute(String name)

Ans. 16.6 Javax.servlet.jsp.tagext.TryCatchFinally

Ans. 16.7 Classic tag handlers are cached and reused by container but simple tag handlers are not cached and reused by the JSP container.

Ans. 16.8 doTag()

CHAPTER 17

Ans. 17.1 EL expressions can be categorized into the following types:
- ❑ Immediate and deferred expressions
- ❑ Value expressions
- ❑ Method expressions

Ans. 17.2 Method expressions are used to call public methods, which return a value or object.

Ans. 17.3
- ❑ Arithmetic operators
- ❑ Relational and logical operators
- ❑ The empty operator

Ans. 17.4 sessionScope

Ans. 17.5 cookie

CHAPTER 18

Ans. 18.1 Internationalization, also known as I18N, is the process of designing an application that encompasses its content specific to locales based on the different languages and regions easily, cost-effectively, and in particular without doing any changes to the application.

Ans. 18.2 Locale is a relatively simple object, which defines the specific language and geographic region.

Ans. 18.3 The three important properties are:

a. Language

b. Country

c. Varient

Ans. 18.4 java.util.PropertyResourceBundle

Ans. 18.5 getBundle()

Ans. 18.6 Accepts-Languages

Ans. 18.7

- **`Locale (String language)`** : Constructs a Locale object with the given language code.
- **`Locale (String language, String country)`** : Constructs a Locale object with the given language, country code.
- Locale (String language, String country, String variant): Constructs a Locale object with the given language, country, and variant.

Ans. 18.8 <basename>[_<language>[_<country>[_<varient>].protperties

CHAPTER 19

Ans. 19.1 JSP Standard Tag Library (JSTL) is a collection of custom tag libraries, which provide core functionality used for JSP documents.

Ans. 19.2 JSTL provides 4 types of tag libraries that can be used with JSP pages.

Ans. 19.3 The JSTL core tags are used to perform iteration, conditional processing, and also provide support of expression language for the tags in JSP pages.

Ans. 19.4 `<c:out>`

Ans. 19.5 The `<c: import>` tag is used to include another resource, such as another JSP or HTML page, in a JSP page.

Ans. 19.6 The `<c: import>` tag is similar to the `<jsp: include>` tag. However, the `<c: import>` tag allows us to include the pages in another Web application. This tag also allows us to save the included page output into a variable instead of directly writing it to the output, which allows us to process the included page output before writing it to the output, if necessary.

Ans. 19.7 The SQL tags are used to access the relational database specified in JSP pages. The SQL tags are used for rapid prototyping and developing Web applications.

Ans. 19.8 6

Ans. 19.9 The format Tag library provides the support for internationalization. This tag provides the formatting of data in different domains. The data can be dates, numbers, or time specifications in different domains.

Ans. 19.10 The XML tag library is used to work with XML data used in the JSP pages. The XML tag library helps parse and transform the data used in a JSP page.

CHAPTER 20

Ans. 20.1 JavaServer Faces (JSF) can be defined as a framework, which makes Web application development easy by providing rich, powerful, and ready to use User Interface (UI) components.

Ans. 20.2 The basic elements of JSF are:

a. UI Component
b. Renderer
c. Validator
d. Backing Beans
e. Converter
f. Events and Listeners
g. Message
h. Navigation

Ans. 20.3 The different types of JSF standard actions are:

a. Action events
b. Value-change events
c. Data model events
d. Phase events

Ans. 20.4

```
<navigation-rule>
<from-view-id>/login.jsp</from-view-id>
<navigation-case>
        <from-outcome>success</from-outcome>
        <to-view-id>/welcome.jsp</to-view-id>
</navigation-case>
<navigation-case>
        <from-outcome>failure</from-outcome>
        <to-view-id>/login.jsp</to-view-id>
</navigation-case>
</navigation-rule>
```

Ans. 20.5 The six faces of the JSF request processing are:

a. Restore View
b. Apply Request Values
c. Process Validations
d. Update Model Values
e. Invoke Application
f. Render Response

Ans. 20.6 All the JSF UI components configured with immediate property set to true are validated in Apply Request Values phase of JSF request processing.

Ans. 20.7 http://java.sun.com/jsf/html

CHAPTER 21

Ans. 21.1 Design patterns refer to language-independent solutions provided for solving commonly recurring design problems. A design pattern first describes the problem and then the solution that can be applied to the problem. The design patterns are implemented in the form of objects and classes that provide solutions to the problem.

Ans. 21.2 The important benefits of design patterns are as follows:

- ❑ Provides tested solutions to frequently and repeatedly occurring problems
- ❑ Provides code reusability
- ❑ Helps in defining application architecture more efficiently and clearly
- ❑ Provides more reliability and transparency to the design of the application

Ans. 21.3 The Front Controller pattern provides following benefits:

- ❑ **Centralizes control**—Implements a central controller component for handling requests and implementing business logic. Therefore, requests can be easily tracked and logged.
- ❑ **Improves manageability**—Provides a single entry point for all requests, which requires fewer resources; thereby, improving manageability.
- ❑ **Improves reusability**—Moves common code to a single controller component. Therefore, code is not duplicated within multiple views; thereby, encouraging code reusability.
- ❑ **Improves role separation**—Divides responsibilities among various application components for effective role separation.

Ans. 21.4 Session Facade is a design pattern that is used for developing enterprise applications. The Session Facade pattern uses a central high level component, which is implemented as a session bean and contains the functionality of the complex interactions that occur between various lower-level business components. The higher-level session bean thereby provides a single interface to the client for accessing the functionality of an application.

Ans. 21.5 Data Access Object provides application components with a user-friendly and common interface to access the data from various multiple data sources. It reduces the dependency of various components on the details of the database implementations. The DAO communicates with the actual underlying database and handles the different types of data access mechanisms.

Ans. 21.6 The Service Locator pattern is useful for locating various business components and services. This pattern uses a service locator object to centralize the look up process for distributed service components. This provides a central point of control to manage the look up services and also acts as a cache; thereby, eliminating the need for redundant look ups.

CHAPTER 22

Ans. 22.1 Authentication is the process of checking the validity of the security details submitted by a user.

Ans. 22.2 Authorization is a process of ascertaining whether an authenticated user has permission to access a requested service.

Ans. 22.3 Data integrity is the property that restricts or prevents data from being modified during data transmission.

Ans. 22.4 The two ways to implement Web security are:

- ❑ Declarative Security
- ❑ Programmatic Security

Ans. 22.5 The HTTP authentication mechanisms that can be used to protect Web resources are:

- ❑ HTTP basic authentication
- ❑ Form-based authentication
- ❑ Client-certificate authentication
- ❑ HTTP digest authentication

Index

A

B

C

D

T

U

V

W